Handbook of
U.S. Labor Statistics

Employment, Earnings, Prices, Productivity, and Other Labor Data

Sixth Edition, 2003

Handbook of
U.S. Labor Statistics

Employment, Earnings, Prices, Productivity, and Other Labor Data

Sixth Edition, 2003

EDITOR
Eva E. Jacobs

ASSOCIATE EDITOR
Mary Meghan Ryan

ISBN: 0-89059-619-0

ISSN: 1526-2553

Printed by Automated Graphic Systems, Inc., White Plains, MD, on acid-free paper that meets the American National Standards Institute Z39-48 standard.

2003 2002   4 3 2 1

BERNAN
4611-F Assembly Drive
Lanham, MD 20706
email: info@bernan.com

CONTENTS

LIST OF TABLES

CONTINGENT AND ALTERNATIVE WORK ARRANGEMENTS

EMPLOYMENT BY INDUSTRY

HOURS AND EARNINGS BY INDUSTRY

EMPLOYMENT, HOURS, AND EARNINGS BY STATE

ABOUT THE EDITORS

Eva E. Jacobs, editor of *Handbook of U.S. Labor Statistics* since the first edition, served as Chief of the Division of Consumer Expenditure Surveys at the U.S. Bureau of Labor Statistics (BLS) for over twenty years. As manager of this division, Ms. Jacobs was responsible for the ongoing Consumer Expenditure Survey, which tracked the expenditure patterns of U.S. households over time. Ms. Jacobs also held positions in the Productivity Division and the Economic Growth Division. More recently, she acted as advisor on cost of living projects for both government and private consultants. Currently, Ms. Jacobs serves as chair of a panel advising the Safe Harbor Working Group on issues related to cost of living adjustments for federal employees in Alaska, Hawaii, Guam, Puerto Rico, and the Virgin Islands. Ms. Jacobs was the 1998 recipient of the Julius Shiskin Award, given by the National Association of Business Economists and the Washington Statistical Society for distinguished contributions to Economic Statistics.

Mary Meghan Ryan, a Bernan data analyst, is a former economist with the American Economics Group. Additionally, she has worked as a research assistant for FRANDATA. Ms. Ryan, an assistant editor of the eighth edition of Bernan's Business Statistics of the United States, received her Bachelor's degree in Economics from the University of Maryland.

PREFACE

To the usual questions that our changing society and dynamic economy have raised in the past, questions of health care costs, labor force changes, industry growth rates, etc. has been added the questions raised by the slowdown in growth and increase in unemployment that occurred in 2001–2002. Among which areas and parts of the population is the unemployment taking place? What is the demographic pattern of the labor force? What are the implications of these changes? Are prices remaining stable? How has the structure of employee benefits changed? Are we providing the education for occupations that the economy will require in the future? Of increasing interest is the problem of pensions. What is the pattern of pensions offered by employers?

Other policy questions continue to be debated even as the growth of the economy has slowed. As an example an important factor that has stimulated the health care policy debate has been the increase in the price of prescription drugs, and medical services. How much have these prices increased? How have medical benefits offered by employers also been affected by price increases?

Answering questions such as these for the future requires information about the present and the past. The U.S. Bureau of Labor Statistics (BLS) provides a treasure trove of historical information about the labor market, prices and productivity. Bernan Associates is pleased to present this sixth edition of its award-winning *Handbook of U.S. Labor Statistics* containing a compilation of such BLS data. The current publication maintains and updates the content of the previous edition and adds additional data and new features.

FEATURES OF THE PUBLICATION

- Over 160 tables presenting authoritative data on workers, industries, and prices.

- Introductory articles which call attention to new surveys or major restructuring of existing surveys. There are two new articles in this handbook: The American Time Use Survey (ATUS) describes the new survey, which will collect data on how households spend their time. The North American Industry Classification System (NAICS) describes the system, which is being introduced in all federal surveys. Earlier articles have described the National Compensation Survey (NCS, 5th ed.) and the new Standard Occupational Classification (SOC, 3rd ed.)

- An introduction to each chapter which highlights some salient data in the following numerous tables. Also included is a chart showing a particularly noteworthy trend.

- Each major section is preceded by a concise description of the data sources, definitions and methodology from which the tables are derived.

- The introductory notes also contain references to more comprehensive reports.

NEW IN THIS EDITION

In addition to updating the series published in earlier editions, new tables are introduced as they become available. New tables in this edition are:

- Fatal Occupational Injuries from (the) Events of September 11, 2001, by Industry and Occupational Status. (Table 8-6)

- Occupations With the Largest Job Growth, 2000–2010. (Table 3-2)

- Industries With the Largest Output Growth, 2000–2010. (Table 3-3)

- Employment and Total Job Openings, 2000–2010, and 2000 Average Annual Earnings by Education or Training Category. (Table 3-4)

- Added wholesale trade industries to existing table on productivity by industry. (Table 4-3)

- Employer Compensation Costs per Hour Worked and Percent of Total Compensation, Private Industry, by Region and Bargaining Status. (Table 5-6)

- Employer Compensation Costs per Hour Worked and Percent of Total Compensation, Private Industry, by Occupational and Industry Group, March 2002. (Table 5-8)

- Medical Care Benefits: Percent of Participants Required to Contribute and Average Employee Contribution, private industry 1999–2000. (Table 5-11)

SOURCES OF ADDITIONAL INFORMATION

BLS data for the most part are derived from surveys conducted by the federal government or through federal-state cooperative arrangements. The comparability of data over time can be affected by the changes in the surveys that are needed to keep pace with the current structure of economic institutions or to take advantage of improved survey techniques. Revisions of current data are also made periodically as a result of the availability of new information. In addition, some tables in this handbook were dropped because the data are from a one time survey that is now outdated, such as the data on training (1995) or the survey has been restructured entirely. Introductory notes to each chapter summarize the specific factors that may affect the data in that chapter. In the tables, the ellipsis character ("…") has been used to indicate data that are not available, not applicable or equal to zero.

More extensive methodological information, including sampling and estimation procedures for all BLS programs, is contained in The BLS *Handbook of Methods* (BLS Bulletin 2490, April 1997; a new edition is forthcoming). Other sources of current data and analytical articles are the *Monthly Labor Review* and *The Report on the American Workforce*, a biennial publication of BLS, and a daily Internet publication, TED, from The Editor's Desk. The Internet address for the BLS home page is <http://stats.bls.gov>.

ACKNOWLEDGEMENTS

Preparation of this book was very much a team activity. Mary Meghan Ryan ably researched the data and prepared the tables, with guidance from senior data analyst Katherine DeBrandt. (Cornelia Strawser, Ph.D., reviewed the chapter highlights and made many useful suggestions on the content.) Deirdre Gaquin prepared the special tabulations of data from the Current Population Survey. Kara Gottschlich, assisted by Christopher Jorgenson, prepared all graphics and layout. Jacalyn Houston copyedited this edition. Tamera Wells-Lee managed the overall editorial and production aspects of this volume. I extend my sincere gratitude to these individuals for their skills, professionalism, and cooperative effort—all of which made this publication possible.

Particular thanks go to the BLS staff members too numerous to mention by name who patiently answered questions and provided material.

BERNAN'S DATABOOK SERIES

The *Handbook of U.S. Labor Statistics* is one of a number of Bernan publications providing the public with statistical information from official government sources. Other titles in the Bernan U.S. databook series include *Business Statistics of the United States, Education Statistics of the United States, Health and Healthcare in the United States, Housing Statistics of the United States, Foreign Trade of the United States, State Profiles* and *Statistical Portrait of the United States.* In each of these publications, intense efforts have been made to provide a useful, accurate, and up-to-date selection of information.

We welcome you to the world of government statistics and urge you to provide us with your suggestions on how we may make future editions even more useful. Please contact us by email at bpress@bernan.com or write us at Bernan Press, 4611-F Assembly Dr., Lanham, MD 20706. Visit our Web site at <http://www.bernan.com>.

AMERICAN TIME USE SURVEY

The Bureau of Labor Statistics (BLS) has been testing and will soon begin to collect data for the American Time Use Survey (ATUS). The following is abstracted from the justification statement prepared for the Office of Management and Budget.

The ATUS will be the nation's first federally administered, continuous survey on time use in the United States. A nationally representative sample of persons from households completing their final month of interviews for the Current Population Survey (CPS) will be drawn for ATUS. BLS will contract with the Census Bureau to conduct one interview with one person over the age of 15 from each selected household. The primary focus of the interview will be on activities done "yesterday" (from 4 a.m. to 4 a.m.), though additional questions will be asked about work during the prior week and travel during the prior 1–2 months.

The new (ATUS) is scheduled to begin full production in January 2003, following a 2-month pre-fielding period from November–December 2002. The 2-month pre-fielding will be conducted to develop interviewer skills, particularly in the use of conversational interviewing, to develop coding skills, and to ensure that all data collection and processing systems are running smoothly.

According to economist William Nordhaus, "Inadequate data on time use is the single most important gap in federal statistics" (Time Use Conference, 1997). Approximately 50 other countries collect, or soon will collect, time-use data. Such data are considered important indicators of both quality of life and the contribution of non-market work to national economies. They measure, for example, time spent caring for children, volunteering, working, sleeping, or doing leisure activities. Using time-use data in conjunction with wage data will allow analysts to better compare production between nations that have different mixes of market and non-market activities. In the United States, several existing federal surveys collect income and wage data for individuals and families, and analysts often use such measures of material prosperity as proxies for quality of life. Time-use data will substantially augment these quality-of-life measures.

PURPOSE OF THE SURVEY

The major purpose of the ATUS is to develop nationally representative estimates of how people spend their time. Many ATUS users will be interested in the amount of time Americans spend doing non-market work activities. These include unpaid childcare and adult care, housework, and volunteering. The survey will also provide information on the amount of time people spend in many other activities, such as commuting, religious activities, socializing, exercising, and relaxing. To produce these estimates, data must be collected not only about what people did, but also about where and with whom each activity occurred, and whether the activities were paid work or work related. This additional contextual information enables coders to assign codes that describe each activity with consistency.

Because the ATUS sample will be drawn from a subset of households that completed interviews for the CPS, the same demographic information collected from that survey will be available for the ATUS respondents. Comparisons of activity patterns across characteristics such as sex, race, age, and educational attainment of the respondent, as well as the presence of children and the number of adults living in the respondent's household,

will be possible. Since the data will be collected on an ongoing, monthly basis, time series data eventually will be available, enabling analysts to identify changes in how people spend their time. Also, the ATUS activity coding lexicon was designed to ensure that time-use information in the United States can be compared, at broad levels, with information from other countries.

BLS expects wide interest in time-use data among economists, sociologists, journalists and reporters, business persons, government policy makers, educators, lawyers, and others, as the survey information will have numerous applications. The survey will capture not only hours worked on a typical weekday or weekend day, but will show the distribution of where work is being done—at home, at an office, or somewhere else[1]—and whether, over time, these distributions are changing.

Unpaid activities such as raising children and doing volunteer or housework are not currently counted in the National Income and Product Accounts—even though they are critical to society and to national well being. ATUS data will provide more comprehensive information on a continuous basis, which will significantly improve analysts' understanding of these issues. Analysts will be able to use measures of time spent

---

[1] Interviewers for the ATUS will assign one of 20 location codes to each activity reported by respondents.

doing such activities to estimate the contribution they make to overall economic activity.

For decades, economists have acknowledged that changes in GDP may reflect changes in institutional arrangements rather than actual changes in economic activity (Landefeld and McCulla, 2000). For example, under traditional methods used to value the nation's output, the worker who decides he will wash and iron his own dress shirts rather than send them to cleaners as he has previously done contributes to a decline in GDP, because the washing and ironing activity is no longer captured as a market transaction. However, ATUS respondents will report on the ways they use their own time. The availability of this detailed information will allow economists to more accurately value a household's final products by estimating the value of the time (labor services) used to produce final goods and services. Child and adult care, meal preparation, and home repair projects are just a few of the non-market activities that ATUS data will be used to evaluate. The survey will also help lawyers and economists evaluate compensation for lost time (or life) in wrongful injury or death cases, as calculations could incorporate a valuation of non-market activities.

Sociologists will use the data to examine social contact, such as how much time people spend with their children, or if there are shifts in with whom people are spending their time—such as more or less time spent with colleagues or family. They will also examine the degree to which people are trading off time with family and other activities to do market or non-market work. Businesses, by knowing how people spend their time, may be able to better evaluate the population that demands their products and develop new goods and services accordingly. The ATUS data will help federal, state, and local government policy makers more fully understand non-economic, as well as economic, effects of policy decisions, and to better determine when to develop new or change existing policies to address the needs of our society. For example, city planners and other public officials may—based on their knowledge of how and where people spend their time—develop or revise emergency preparedness plans.

To ensure the widest distribution of information, BLS will release the data to the public at least annually, and possibly quarterly, in the form of published tables. Microdata sets containing greater detail than the published tables will also be available, as will special analyses by BLS and outside analysts in the *Monthly Labor Review* (published by BLS) and other publications.

NORTH AMERICAN INDUSTRY CLASSIFICATION SYSTEM (NAICS)

Two major statistical series have been restructured in recent years. The first was the revision of Standard Occupational Classification (SOC) system, which was described in the third edition of this Handbook. The second is the revision of the Standard Industrial Classification (SIC), which is gradually being replaced by the North American Industry Classification System (NAICS). This article, abstracted from Bureau of Labor Statistics (BLS) publications is a summary of the background and provides a description of NAICS. (Please see page xx for a list of new NAICS industries.)

BACKGROUND

For over 60 years, the Standard Industrial Classification (SIC) system has served as the structure for the collection, aggregation, presentation, and analysis of the U.S. economy. An industry consists of a group of establishments primarily engaged in producing or handling the same product or group of products or in rendering the same services. Industry definitions used in BLS programs come from the 1987 Standard Industrial Classification (SIC) Manual. Because the SIC is used by many other federal government statistical programs, it is possible for users to assemble a comprehensive statistical picture of an industry.

The SIC system was developed in the 1930s at a time when manufacturing dominated the U.S. economic scene. Over the last 60 years, there have been numerous revisions to the SIC system, reflecting the economy's changing industrial composition. However, despite these revisions, the system has received increasing criticism about its ability to handle rapid changes in the U.S. economy. Recent developments in information services, new forms of health care provision, expansion of services, and high tech manufacturing are examples of industrial changes that cannot be studied under the current SIC system.

INTRODUCING NAICS
Developed in cooperation with Canada and Mexico, the North American Industry Classification System (NAICS) represents one of the most profound changes for statistical programs focusing on emerging economic activities. NAICS, developed using a production-oriented conceptual framework, groups establishments into industries based on the activity in which they are primarily engaged. Establishments using similar raw material inputs, similar capital equipment, and similar labor are classified in the same industry. In other words, establishments that do similar things in similar ways are classified together.

NAICS provides a new tool that ensures that economic statistics reflect our nation's changing economy. However, improved statistics will result in time series breaks. Every sector of the economy has been restructured and redefined: A new Information sector combines communications, publishing, motion picture and sound recording, and online services, recognizing our information-based economy. Manufacturing is restructured to recognize new high-tech industries. A new sub-sector is devoted to computers and electronics, including reproduction of software. Retail Trade is redefined. In addition, eating and drinking places are transferred to a new Accommodation and Food Services sector. The difference between Retail and Wholesale is now based on how each store conducts business. For example, many computer stores are reclassified from wholesale to retail. Nine new service sectors and 250 new service industries are recognized.

NAICS CODING STRUCTURE
NAICS uses a six digit hierarchical coding system to classify all economic activity into 20 industry sectors. Five sectors are mainly goods-producing sectors and 15 are entirely services-producing sectors. This six digit hierarchical structure allows greater coding flexibility than the four digit structure of the SIC. NAICS allows for the identification of 1,170 industries compared with the 1,004 found in the SIC system.

NEW NAICS INDUSTRIES

Semiconductor machinery manufacturing
Fiber optic cable manufacturing
Software reproducing
Convenience stores
Gasoline stations with convenience stores

Warehouse clubs and superstores
Food (health) supplement stores
Pet and pet supply stores
Pet care services
Cable networks

Satellite telecommunications
Paging
Cellular and other wireless telecommunications
Telecommunications resellers
Credit card issuing

Temporary help services
Telemarketing bureaus
Hazardous waste collection
HMO medical centers
Continuing care retirement communities

Casinos
Casino hotels
Bed-and-breakfast inns
Limited-service restaurants
Automotive oil change and lubrication shops
Diet and weight reducing centers

BLS IMPLEMENTATION SCHEDULE

The NAICS implementation schedule within the U.S. Statistical community is spread over a 7-year period. The Bureau of Labor Statistics schedule is as follows:

Employment and Wages Report (annual) 2001
Current Employment Statistics survey (monthly) 2003
Occupational Employment Statistics 2003
Producer Price Index/Net Output Indexes (monthly) 2004

Complete detail is available in the *Standard Occupational Classification Manual,* published the National Technical Information Service and Bernan Press and the *North American Industry Classification System (NAICS): United States, 2002,* published by Bernan Press and the U.S. Office of Management and Budget. Both publications are available from Bernan Press.

PART ONE

POPULATION, LABOR FORCE, AND EMPLOYMENT STATUS

POPULATION, LABOR FORCE, AND EMPLOYMENT STATUS

HIGHLIGHTS

This chapter presents detailed historical information on the employment status of the population collected in a survey of households, the Current Population Survey (CPS). Basic data on labor force, employment and unemployment are shown for various characteristics of the population such as age, sex, race, and marital status.

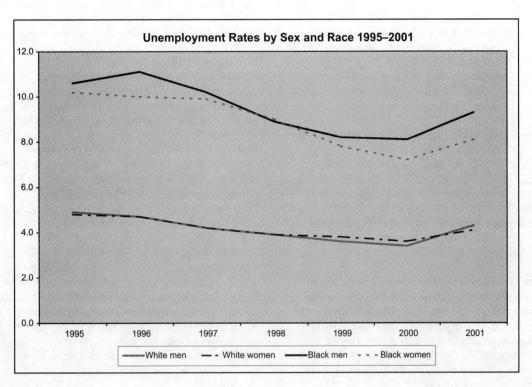

The unemployment rate for men and women rose in 2001 after more than 6 years of steady decline. The largest increase in the unemployment rate was for black men and the lowest for white women. (Table 1-27)

OTHER HIGHLIGHTS:

• The unemployment rate for all civilian workers increased from 4.0 to 4.8 in 2001. This is the largest percentage increase since 1991. (Table 1-25)
• For only the second time since 1962, the labor force participation rate for women declined slightly after years of a steady increase. (Table 1-8)
• The labor force participation rate for women with children under 3 years continued the decline begun in 1999. (Table 1-24)
• The labor force participation rate for men ages 20-54 declined from 2000–2001 but for men 55 and over the rate increased. For men 65 and over, the rate was the highest since the 1980s. The labor force participation rate for women between 20 and 54 also declined in 2001, but for women over 55 rates continued their long-term increase. (Table 1-8)
• The proportion of Hispanics (Hispanics may be black or white) in the labor force has risen from 9.5 percent to 11.1 percent in the last 5 years. (Table 1-3)
• Four states and the District of Columbia had unemployment rates equal to or exceeding 6.0 percent in 2001. The District of Columbia had the highest unemployment rate at 6.5 percent, followed by Washington State at 6.4 percent, Alaska and Oregon at 6.3 percent, and Louisiana at 6.0 percent. (Table 1-5)
• From 2000 to 2001, the number of persons unemployed 15 weeks and over increased by one-third. (Table 1-31)

NOTES AND DEFINITIONS

CURRENT POPULATION SURVEY OF HOUSEHOLDS

Collection and Coverage

Statistics on the employment status of the population and related data are compiled by the Bureau of Labor Statistics (BLS) using data from the Current Population Survey (CPS). This monthly survey of households is conducted for BLS by the Bureau of the Census using a scientifically selected sample of the civilian noninstitutional population.

The CPS sample has been increased to 60,000 households from 50,000. The new sample was introduced beginning September 2, 2000. However, the estimates of the national labor force from the additional sample were not introduced at that time in order to evaluate the impact of the change. Since the estimates from the two samples were virtually the same, BLS incorporated the additional sample into the official national estimates beginning in July 2001.

Respondents are interviewed to obtain information about the employment status of each member of the household 16 years of age and over. The inquiry relates to activity or status during the calendar week, Sunday through Saturday, which includes the 12th day of the month. This is known as the "reference week." Actual field interviewing is conducted in the following week, referred to as the "survey week."

Part of the sample is changed each month. The rotation plan provides for three-fourths of the sample to be common from one month to the next, and one-half to be common with the same month a year earlier.

Concepts and Definitions

The concepts and definitions underlying labor force data have been modified, but not substantially altered, since the inception of the survey in 1940. Current definitions of some of the major concepts used in the CPS are given below.

The civilian noninstitutional population includes persons 16 years of age and older residing in the 50 states and the District of Columbia who are not inmates of institutions (such as penal and mental facilities, homes for the aged), and who are not on active duty in the armed forces.

Employed persons are all persons who, during the reference week, (a) did any work at all (at least one hour) as paid employees, worked in their own business, profession, or on their own farm, or who worked 15 hours or more as unpaid workers in an enterprise operated by a member of the family, and (b) all those who were not working but who had jobs or businesses from which they were temporarily absent because of vacation, illness, bad weather, child-care problems, maternity or paternity leave, labor-management disputes, job training, or other family or personal reasons, whether or not they were paid for the time off or were seeking other jobs.

Each employed person is counted only once, even if he or she holds more than one job. For purposes of occupation and industry classification, multiple jobholders are counted in the job at which they worked the greatest number of hours during the reference week.

Included in the total are employed citizens of foreign countries who are temporarily in the United States but not living on the premises of an embassy. Excluded are persons whose only activity consisted of work around their own house (painting, repairing, or own home housework) or volunteer work for religious, charitable, and other organizations.

Unemployed persons are all persons who had no employment during the reference week, were available for work, except for temporary illness, and had made specific efforts to find employment some time during the four-week period ending with the reference week. Persons who were waiting to be recalled to a job from which they had been laid off need not have been looking for work to be classified as unemployed.

Duration of unemployment represents the length of time (through the current reference week) that persons classified as unemployed had been looking for work. For persons on layoff, duration of unemployment represents the number of full weeks they had been on layoff. Mean duration is the arithmetic average computed from single weeks of unemployment; median duration is the midpoint of a distribution of weeks of unemployment.

Reason for unemployment is determined by the status of individuals at the time they began to look for work. The reasons for unemployment are divided into five major groups: (1) Job losers, comprised of (a) persons on temporary layoff, who have been given a date to return to work or who expect to return within six months (persons on layoff need not be looking for work to qualify as unemployed), and (b) permanent job losers, whose employment ended involuntarily and who began looking for work; (2) Job leavers, persons who quit or otherwise terminated their employment voluntarily and immediately began looking for work; (3) Persons who completed temporary jobs and immediately began looking for work; (4) Reentrants, persons who previously worked but were out of the labor force prior to beginning their job search; and (5) New entrants, persons who have never worked. Each of these categories of the unemployed can be expressed as a proportion of the entire civilian labor force; the sum of the rates thus equals the unemployment rate for all civilian workers.

The civilian labor force comprises all civilians classified as employed or unemployed.

The unemployment rate is the number unemployed as a percent of the civilian labor force.

The participation rate represents the proportion of the civilian noninstitutional population that is in the labor force.

The employment to population ratio represents the proportion of the population that is employed.

Persons not in the labor force are all persons in the civilian noninstitutional population who are neither employed nor unemployed. Information is collected on their desire for and availability to take a job at the time of the CPS interview, job search activity in the prior year, and reason for not looking in the four-week period prior to the survey week. This group includes discouraged workers.

Discouraged workers are defined as persons not in the labor force who want and are available for a job and who have looked for work sometime in the past 12 months (or since the end of their last job if they held one within the past 12 months), but are not currently looking, because they believe there are no jobs available or there are none for which they would qualify.

Usual full- or part-time status refers to hours usually worked per week. Full-time workers are those who usually worked 35 hours or more. This group includes some individuals who worked less than 35 hours in the reference week for either economic or noneconomic reasons. Part-time workers are those who usually work less than 35 hours per week (at all jobs), regardless of the number of hours worked in the reference week. These concepts are used to differentiate a person's normal schedule from their specific activity during the reference week. Unemployed persons who are looking for full-time work or are on layoff from full-time jobs are counted as part of the full-time labor force; unemployed persons who are seeking or who are on layoff from part-time jobs are counted as part of the part-time labor force. Unemployment rates for full- and part-time workers are calculated using the concepts of the full- and part-time labor force.

Occupation, industry, and class of worker for the employed is determined by the job held in the reference week. Persons with two or more jobs are classified in the job at which they worked the greatest number of hours. The unemployed are classified according to their last job. The occupational and industrial classification of CPS

data is based on the coding systems used in the 1990 Census. The class-of-worker breakdown assigns workers to the following categories: private and government wage and salary workers; self-employed workers; and unpaid family workers. Wage and salary workers receive wages, salaries, commissions, tips, or pay in kind from a private employer or from a government unit. Self-employed persons are those who work for profit or fees in their own business, profession, trade, or farm. Only the unincorporated self-employed are included in the self-employed category in the class-of-worker typology. Self-employed persons who respond that their businesses are incorporated are included among wage and salary workers, because technically, they are paid employees of a corporation. Unpaid family workers are persons working without pay for 15 hours a week or more on a farm or in a business operated by a member of the household to whom they are related by birth or marriage.

Multiple jobholders are employed persons who, during the reference week, had two or more jobs as a wage and salary worker, were self-employed and also held a wage and salary job, or worked as an unpaid family worker and also held a wage and salary job. A person employed only in private households (cleaner, gardener, babysitter, etc.) who worked for two or more employers during the reference week is not counted as a multiple jobholder, since working for several employers is considered an inherent characteristic of private household work. Also excluded are self-employed persons with multiple businesses and persons with multiple jobs as unpaid family workers.

At work part-time for economic reasons, sometimes referred to as involuntary part-time, refers to individuals who gave an economic reason for working one to 34 hours during the reference week. Economic reasons include slack work or unfavorable business conditions, inability to find full-time work, and seasonal declines in demand. Those who usually work part-time must also indicate that they want and are available to work full-time to be classified as on part-time for economic reasons.

At work part-time for noneconomic reasons refers to persons who usually work part-time and were at work one to 34 hours during the reference week for a noneconomic reason. Non-economic reasons include, for example: illness or other medical limitations; childcare problems or other family or personal obligations; school or training; retirement or Social Security limits on earnings; and being in a job where full-time work is less than 35 hours. The group also includes those who gave an economic reason for usually working one to 34 hours but said they do not want to work full-time or were unavailable for such work.

White, Black, and Other are terms used to describe the race of persons. Included in the "Other" group are Native Americans, Alaskan Natives, and Asians and Pacific

Islanders. Because of the relatively small sample size, data for "Other" races are not published. In the enumeration process, race is determined by the household respondent.

Hispanic origin refers to persons who identified themselves in the enumeration process as Mexican, Puerto Rican, Cuban, Central or South American, or of other Hispanic origin or descent. Persons of Hispanic origin may be of any race; thus some are included in the White, some in the Black, and possibly some in the Other population groups.

Single, never married; married, spouse present; and other marital status are the terms used to define the marital status of individuals at the time of interview. Married, spouse present, applies to husband and wife if both were living in the same household, even though one may be temporarily absent on business, vacation, on a visit, in a hospital, etc. Other marital status applies to persons who are married, spouse absent; widowed; or divorced. Married, spouse absent relates to persons who are separated due to marital problems, as well as husbands and wives who are living apart because one or the other was employed elsewhere, on duty with the armed forces, or any other reasons.

A household consists of all persons—related family members and all unrelated persons—who occupy a housing unit and have no other usual address. A house, an apartment, a group of rooms, or a single room is regarded as a housing unit when occupied or intended for occupancy as separate living quarters. A householder is the person (or one of the persons) in whose name the housing unit is owned or rented. The term is not applied to either husbands or wives in married-couple families but only to persons in families maintained by either men or women without a spouse.

Family is defined as a group of two or more persons residing together who are related by birth, marriage, or adoption; all such persons are considered as members of one family. Families are classified either as married-couple families or as families maintained by women or men without spouses. A family maintained by a woman or a man is one in which the householder is single; widowed; divorced; or married, spouse absent.

The annual CPS data on the employment characteristics of families and family members begin with data for 1995. These data are not strictly comparable with family data derived from the March CPS. The annual data are derived by averaging the data for each month of the year, whereas the March data refer to that month. The annual average data provide a larger sample size, while the March family data provide a longer historical series.

Additional Concepts and Definitions: CPS Supplements

In addition to the above concepts and definitions, the definitions below apply to the special labor force data collected annually in the March supplement to the monthly CPS, and the data on tenure usually collected in a February supplement.

Persons with work experience are civilians who worked at any time during the preceding calendar year at full- or part-time jobs for pay or profit (including paid vacations and sick leave) or worked without pay on a farm or in a business that was family operated. From 1989 forward, these supplementary tables also include members of the armed forces within the United States.

Tenure refers to length of time a worker has been continuously employed by the current employer. The data were collected through a supplement to the CPS. The question asked of all employed persons was how long the person has been working continuously for their present employer and, if one or two years, the exact number of months. The follow-up question was asked for the first time in the 1998 February supplement. Prior to 1983 the question was asked differently; data prior to 1983 are not strictly comparable to data for subsequent years.

Year-round full-time workers are workers who worked primarily at full-time jobs for 50 weeks or more during the preceding calendar year. *Part-year workers* worked either full or part-time for one to 49 weeks.

Spell of unemployment is a continuous period of unemployment of at least one week's duration. A spell is terminated by employment or withdrawal from the labor force.

Extent of unemployment refers to the number and proportion of the labor force that were unemployed at some time during the year. The number of weeks unemployed is the total number of weeks accumulated during the entire year.

Children refer to "own" children of the husband, wife, or person maintaining the family, including sons and daughters, stepchildren, and adopted children. Excluded are other related children, such as grandchildren, nieces, nephews, and cousins, and unrelated children.

Earnings are all money income of $1 or more from wages and salaries and net money income of $1 or more from farm and nonfarm self-employment.

Educational attainment refers to years of school completed in regular schools, which include graded public, private, and parochial elementary and high schools, whether day or night school; also college, university, or professional school.

Minimum wages. The prevailing federal minimum wage was $5.15 per hour in 2001. Data are for wage and salary workers who are paid hourly rates. They refer to a person's earnings on their sole or principal job.

Absences are defined as instances when persons who usually work 35 or more hours a week worked less than that during the reference period for reasons of illness or family obligations. Excluded are situations in which work was missed for vacation, holidays or other reasons. The estimates are based on one-fourth of the sample only.

Historical Comparability

While current survey concepts and methods are very similar to those introduced at the inception of the survey in 1940, a number of changes have been made over the years to improve the accuracy and usefulness of the data. Only the latest changes are described here.

In 1994, major changes to the CPS were introduced, which included a complete redesign of the questionnaire and the use of computer-assisted interviewing for the entire survey. In addition, there were revisions to some of the labor force concepts and definitions, including the implementation of some changes recommended in 1979 by the National Commission on Employment and Unemployment Statistics (NCEUS, also known as the Levitan Commission). Some of the major changes to the survey were:

a) The introduction of a redesigned and automated questionnaire. The CPS questionnaire was totally redesigned in order to obtain more accurate, comprehensive, and relevant information, and to take advantage of state-of-the-art computer interviewing techniques.

b) The addition of two, more objective, criteria to the definition of discouraged workers. Beginning in 1994, persons classified as discouraged must also have looked for a job within the past year (or since their last job, if they worked during the year), and must have been available for work during the reference week (a direct question on availability was added in 1994). These changes were made because the NCEUS and others felt that the previous definition of discouraged workers was too subjective, relying mainly on an individual's stated desire for a job and not on prior testing of the labor market.

c) Similarly, the identification of persons employed part-time for economic reasons (working less than 35 hours in the reference week because of poor business conditions or because of an inability to find full-time work) was tightened by adding two new criteria for persons who usually work part-time: They must want and be available for full-time work. (Persons who usually work full-time but worked part-time for an economic reason during the reference week are assumed to meet these criteria.)

d) Specific questions were added about the expectation of recall for persons who indicate that they are on layoff. To be classified as "on temporary layoff," persons must expect to be recalled to their jobs.

e) Persons volunteering that they were waiting to start a new job within 30 days must have looked for work in the four weeks prior to the survey in order to be classified as unemployed.

Comparability of Labor Force Levels

In addition to the refinements in concepts, definitions, and methods made over the years, other changes—made to improve the accuracy of the estimates—have also affected the comparability of the labor force data. The most important of these is the adjustment of the population totals as a result of new information from the decennial censuses and to correct for estimating errors during the intercensal years. Those affecting the most recent decade are described below.

Beginning in January 1994, 1990 census-based population controls were introduced, adjusted for the undercount as measured by the Census Bureau's Post-Enumeration Survey. In February 1996, these population controls were introduced into the estimates for 1990–1993 as well. This change increased the civilian non-institutional population for 1990 by about 1.1 million, employment by about 880,000, and unemployment by about 175,000. The overall unemployment rate rose by about 0.1 percentage point.

In the case of data from the March supplement to the CPS, the 1990 controls were introduced in 1994 and have not been carried back to 1990.

Beginning in January 1997, updated information on the demographic characteristics of immigrants and emigrants was introduced. This raised the overall population by about 470,000, labor force by 320,000, and employment by 290,000, with similar upward adjustments for Hispanics. Unemployment and other percentage rates were not affected.

Beginning in January 1998, new estimating procedures were introduced, which reduced labor force by about 229,000 and employment by 256,000 but raised unemployment by 27,000. New information about immigration and emigration was also incorporated which increased the Hispanic population by about 57,000. Unemployment rates were not significantly affected.

Beginning in January 1999, new information on immigration raised the population by about 310,000, with differing impacts on different demographic groups. The population of men was lowered by about 185,000, but of women was raised by 490,000. The Hispanic population was lowered by about 165,000 while the rest of the population was raised by about 470,000. Hispanic labor force and employment estimates were each reduced by over 200,000. The impact on unemployment rates and other percentages was small.

Beginning in January 2000, the population controls used in the survey were revised to reflect newly updated information on immigration and an upward revision in the number of deaths. As a result, the civilian noninstitutional population 16 years and over was lowered by about 215,000. The labor force and employment levels were decreased by about 125,000 and 120,000, respectively. Overall and subgroup unemployment rates and other percentages of labor market participation were not significantly affected.

Changes in the Occupational and Industrial Classification System

Beginning in January 1983, the occupational and industrial classification systems used in the 1980 Census were introduced into the CPS. The 1980 Census occupational classification system was so radically different in concepts and nomenclature from the 1970 system that comparisons of historical data are not possible without major adjustments.

The industrial classification system used in the 1980 Census was based on the 1972 Standard Industrial Classification (SIC) system, as modified in 1977. The adoption of the new industrial system had much less of an adverse effect on historical comparability than did the new occupational system.

Beginning in January 1992, the occupational and industrial classification systems used in the 1990 Census were introduced into the CPS. There were a few breaks in comparability between the 1980 and 1990 census-based systems, particularly within the "technical, sales, and administrative support" categories. The most notable changes in industry classification were the shift of several industries from "business services" to "professional services" and the splitting of some industries into smaller, more detailed categories.

Future Plans

Industries: The new North American Industry Classification System (NAICS), published by the Office of Management and Budget in July 1998, will be introduced over the next several years to supplant the current SIC system. The NAICS classifications incorporate major changes. A number of new major sectors are created and a new 6-digit industry numbering system is used.

Occupations: A new system for classifying occupations will be introduced into the CPS in 2003. (The new system is already in use in the Occupational Wage Survey; see Part 5 of this book.) The Standard Occupational Classification (SOC) reflects the many changes in recent decades to the types of jobs workers perform, especially the shift towards more service-oriented and high technology jobs. (See article in the third edition of this handbook.)

Sources of Additional Information

Descriptions of sampling and estimation procedures and further information on the impact of the historical changes in the survey can be found in the *Monthly Labor Review*, September 1993; *Employment and Earnings*, February 1994, March 1996, and subsequent February issues of that publication; and the BLS *Handbook of Methods*, BLS Bulletin 2490, April 1997, Technical Paper 63 RV, *The Current Population Survey* Design and Methodology, March 2002, Expansion of the Current Population Survey Sample from *Employment and Earnings,* August 2001.

Table 1-1. Employment Status of the Civilian Noninstitutional Population, 1947–2001

(Thousands of persons, percent.)

Year	Civilian noninstitutional population	Civilian labor force								Not in labor force
		Total	Participation rate	Employed				Unemployed		
				Total	Percent of population	Agriculture	Nonagricultural industries	Number	Unemploy-ment rate	
1947	101 827	59 350	58.3	57 038	56.0	7 890	49 148	2 311	3.9	42 477
1948	103 068	60 621	58.8	58 343	56.6	7 629	50 714	2 276	3.8	42 447
1949	103 994	61 286	58.9	57 651	55.4	7 658	49 993	3 637	5.9	42 708
1950	104 995	62 208	59.2	58 918	56.1	7 160	51 758	3 288	5.3	42 787
1951	104 621	62 017	59.2	59 961	57.3	6 726	53 235	2 055	3.3	42 604
1952	105 231	62 138	59.0	60 250	57.3	6 500	53 749	1 883	3.0	43 093
1953	107 056	63 015	58.9	61 179	57.1	6 260	54 919	1 834	2.9	44 041
1954	108 321	63 643	58.8	60 109	55.5	6 205	53 904	3 532	5.5	44 678
1955	109 683	65 023	59.3	62 170	56.7	6 450	55 722	2 852	4.4	44 660
1956	110 954	66 552	60.0	63 799	57.5	6 283	57 514	2 750	4.1	44 402
1957	112 265	66 929	59.6	64 071	57.1	5 947	58 123	2 859	4.3	45 336
1958	113 727	67 639	59.5	63 036	55.4	5 586	57 450	4 602	6.8	46 088
1959	115 329	68 369	59.3	64 630	56.0	5 565	59 065	3 740	5.5	46 960
1960	117 245	69 628	59.4	65 778	56.1	5 458	60 318	3 852	5.5	47 617
1961	118 771	70 459	59.3	65 746	55.4	5 200	60 546	4 714	6.7	48 312
1962	120 153	70 614	58.8	66 702	55.5	4 944	61 759	3 911	5.5	49 539
1963	122 416	71 833	58.7	67 762	55.4	4 687	63 076	4 070	5.7	50 583
1964	124 485	73 091	58.7	69 305	55.7	4 523	64 782	3 786	5.2	51 394
1965	126 513	74 455	58.9	71 088	56.2	4 361	66 726	3 366	4.5	52 058
1966	128 058	75 770	59.2	72 895	56.9	3 979	68 915	2 875	3.8	52 288
1967	129 874	77 347	59.6	74 372	57.3	3 844	70 527	2 975	3.8	52 527
1968	132 028	78 737	59.6	75 920	57.5	3 817	72 103	2 817	3.6	53 291
1969	134 335	80 734	60.1	77 902	58.0	3 606	74 296	2 832	3.5	53 602
1970	137 085	82 771	60.4	78 678	57.4	3 463	75 215	4 093	4.9	54 315
1971	140 216	84 382	60.2	79 367	56.6	3 394	75 972	5 016	5.9	55 834
1972	144 126	87 034	60.4	82 153	57.0	3 484	78 669	4 882	5.6	57 091
1973	147 096	89 429	60.8	85 064	57.8	3 470	81 594	4 365	4.9	57 667
1974	150 120	91 949	61.3	86 794	57.8	3 515	83 279	5 156	5.6	58 171
1975	153 153	93 775	61.2	85 846	56.1	3 408	82 438	7 929	8.5	59 377
1976	156 150	96 158	61.6	88 752	56.8	3 331	85 421	7 406	7.7	59 991
1977	159 033	99 009	62.3	92 017	57.9	3 283	88 734	6 991	7.1	60 025
1978	161 910	102 251	63.2	96 048	59.3	3 387	92 661	6 202	6.1	59 659
1979	164 863	104 962	63.7	98 824	59.9	3 347	95 477	6 137	5.8	59 900
1980	167 745	106 940	63.8	99 303	59.2	3 364	95 938	7 637	7.1	60 806
1981	170 130	108 670	63.9	100 397	59.0	3 368	97 030	8 273	7.6	61 460
1982	172 271	110 204	64.0	99 526	57.8	3 401	96 125	10 678	9.7	62 067
1983	174 215	111 550	64.0	100 834	57.9	3 383	97 450	10 717	9.6	62 665
1984	176 383	113 544	64.4	105 005	59.5	3 321	101 685	8 539	7.5	62 839
1985	178 206	115 461	64.8	107 150	60.1	3 179	103 971	8 312	7.2	62 744
1986	180 587	117 834	65.3	109 597	60.7	3 163	106 434	8 237	7.0	62 752
1987	182 753	119 865	65.6	112 440	61.5	3 208	109 232	7 425	6.2	62 888
1988	184 613	121 669	65.9	114 968	62.3	3 169	111 800	6 701	5.5	62 944
1989	186 393	123 869	66.5	117 342	63.0	3 199	114 142	6 528	5.3	62 523
1990	189 164	125 840	66.5	118 793	62.8	3 223	115 570	7 047	5.6	63 324
1991	190 925	126 346	66.2	117 718	61.7	3 269	114 449	8 628	6.8	64 578
1992	192 805	128 105	66.4	118 492	61.5	3 247	115 245	9 613	7.5	64 700
1993	194 838	129 200	66.3	120 259	61.7	3 115	117 144	8 940	6.9	65 638
1994	196 814	131 056	66.6	123 060	62.5	3 409	119 651	7 996	6.1	65 758
1995	198 584	132 304	66.6	124 900	62.9	3 440	121 460	7 404	5.6	66 280
1996	200 591	133 943	66.8	126 708	63.2	3 443	123 264	7 236	5.4	66 647
1997	203 133	136 297	67.1	129 558	63.8	3 399	126 159	6 739	4.9	66 837
1998	205 220	137 673	67.1	131 463	64.1	3 378	128 085	6 210	4.5	67 547
1999	207 753	139 368	67.1	133 488	64.3	3 281	130 207	5 880	4.2	68 385
2000	209 699	140 863	67.2	135 208	64.5	3 305	131 903	5 655	4.0	68 836
2001	211 864	141 815	66.9	135 073	63.8	3 144	131 929	6 742	4.8	70 050

Note: See "Notes and Definitions" for information on historical comparability.

Table 1-2. Employment Status of the Civilian Noninstitutional Population by Sex, 1967–2001

(Thousands of persons, percent.)

Year	Civilian noninstitutional population	Civilian labor force		Employed				Unemployed		Not in labor force
		Total	Participation rate	Total	Percent of population	Agriculture	Non-agricultural industries	Number	Unemploy-ment rate	
MEN										
1967	60 905	48 987	80.4	47 479	78.0	3 164	44 315	1 508	3.1	11 919
1968	61 847	49 533	80.1	48 114	77.8	3 157	44 957	1 419	2.9	12 315
1969	62 898	50 221	79.8	48 818	77.6	2 963	45 855	1 403	2.8	12 677
1970	64 304	51 228	79.7	48 990	76.2	2 862	46 128	2 238	4.4	13 076
1971	65 942	52 180	79.1	49 390	74.9	2 795	46 595	2 789	5.3	13 762
1972	67 835	53 555	78.9	50 896	75.0	2 849	48 047	2 659	5.0	14 280
1973	69 292	54 624	78.8	52 349	75.5	2 847	49 502	2 275	4.2	14 667
1974	70 808	55 739	78.7	53 024	74.9	2 919	50 105	2 714	4.9	15 069
1975	72 291	56 299	77.9	51 857	71.7	2 824	49 032	4 442	7.9	15 993
1976	73 759	57 174	77.5	53 138	72.0	2 744	50 394	4 036	7.1	16 585
1977	75 193	58 396	77.7	54 728	72.8	2 671	52 057	3 667	6.3	16 797
1978	76 576	59 620	77.9	56 479	73.8	2 718	53 761	3 142	5.3	16 956
1979	78 020	60 726	77.8	57 607	73.8	2 686	54 921	3 120	5.1	17 293
1980	79 398	61 453	77.4	57 186	72.0	2 709	54 477	4 267	6.9	17 945
1981	80 511	61 974	77.0	57 397	71.3	2 700	54 697	4 577	7.4	18 537
1982	81 523	62 450	76.6	56 271	69.0	2 736	53 534	6 179	9.9	19 073
1983	82 531	63 047	76.4	56 787	68.8	2 704	54 083	6 260	9.9	19 484
1984	83 605	63 835	76.4	59 091	70.7	2 668	56 423	4 744	7.4	19 771
1985	84 469	64 411	76.3	59 891	70.9	2 535	57 356	4 521	7.0	20 058
1986	85 798	65 422	76.3	60 892	71.0	2 511	58 381	4 530	6.9	20 376
1987	86 899	66 207	76.2	62 107	71.5	2 543	59 564	4 101	6.2	20 692
1988	87 857	66 927	76.2	63 273	72.0	2 493	60 780	3 655	5.5	20 930
1989	88 762	67 840	76.4	64 315	72.5	2 513	61 802	3 525	5.2	20 923
1990	90 377	69 011	76.4	65 104	72.0	2 546	62 559	3 906	5.7	21 367
1991	91 278	69 168	75.8	64 223	70.4	2 589	61 634	4 946	7.2	22 110
1992	92 270	69 964	75.8	64 440	69.8	2 575	61 866	5 523	7.9	22 306
1993	93 332	70 404	75.4	65 349	70.0	2 478	62 871	5 055	7.2	22 927
1994	94 355	70 817	75.1	66 450	70.4	2 554	63 896	4 367	6.2	23 538
1995	95 178	71 360	75.0	67 377	70.8	2 559	64 818	3 983	5.6	23 818
1996	96 206	72 087	74.9	68 207	70.9	2 573	65 634	3 880	5.4	24 119
1997	97 715	73 261	75.0	69 685	71.3	2 552	67 133	3 577	4.9	24 454
1998	98 758	73 959	74.9	70 693	71.6	2 553	68 140	3 266	4.4	24 799
1999	99 722	74 512	74.7	71 446	71.6	2 432	69 014	3 066	4.1	25 210
2000	100 731	75 247	74.7	72 293	71.8	2 434	69 859	2 954	3.9	25 484
2001	101 858	75 743	74.4	72 080	70.8	2 275	69 805	3 663	4.8	26 114
WOMEN										
1967	68 968	28 360	41.1	26 893	39.0	680	26 212	1 468	5.2	40 608
1968	70 179	29 204	41.6	27 807	39.6	660	27 147	1 397	4.8	40 976
1969	71 436	30 513	42.7	29 084	40.7	643	28 441	1 429	4.7	40 924
1970	72 782	31 543	43.3	29 688	40.8	601	29 087	1 855	5.9	41 239
1971	74 274	32 202	43.4	29 976	40.4	599	29 377	2 227	6.9	42 072
1972	76 290	33 479	43.9	31 257	41.0	635	30 622	2 222	6.6	42 811
1973	77 804	34 804	44.7	32 715	42.0	622	32 093	2 089	6.0	43 000
1974	79 312	36 211	45.7	33 769	42.6	596	33 173	2 441	6.7	43 101
1975	80 860	37 475	46.3	33 989	42.0	584	33 404	3 486	9.3	43 386
1976	82 390	38 983	47.3	35 615	43.2	588	35 027	3 369	8.6	43 406
1977	83 840	40 613	48.4	37 289	44.5	612	36 677	3 324	8.2	43 227
1978	85 334	42 631	50.0	39 569	46.4	669	38 900	3 061	7.2	42 703
1979	86 843	44 235	50.9	41 217	47.5	661	40 556	3 018	6.8	42 608
1980	88 348	45 487	51.5	42 117	47.7	656	41 461	3 370	7.4	42 861
1981	89 618	46 696	52.1	43 000	48.0	667	42 333	3 696	7.9	42 922
1982	90 748	47 755	52.6	43 256	47.7	665	42 591	4 499	9.4	42 993
1983	91 684	48 503	52.9	44 047	48.0	680	43 367	4 457	9.2	43 181
1984	92 778	49 709	53.6	45 915	49.5	653	45 262	3 794	7.6	43 068
1985	93 736	51 050	54.5	47 259	50.4	644	46 615	3 791	7.4	42 686
1986	94 789	52 413	55.3	48 706	51.4	652	48 054	3 707	7.1	42 376
1987	95 853	53 658	56.0	50 334	52.5	666	49 668	3 324	6.2	42 195
1988	96 756	54 742	56.6	51 696	53.4	676	51 020	3 046	5.6	42 014
1989	97 630	56 030	57.4	53 027	54.3	687	52 341	3 003	5.4	41 601
1990	98 787	56 829	57.5	53 689	54.3	678	53 011	3 140	5.5	41 957
1991	99 646	57 178	57.4	53 496	53.7	680	52 815	3 683	6.4	42 468
1992	100 535	58 141	57.8	54 052	53.8	672	53 380	4 090	7.0	42 394
1993	101 506	58 795	57.9	54 910	54.1	637	54 273	3 885	6.6	42 711
1994	102 460	60 239	58.8	56 610	55.3	855	55 755	3 629	6.0	42 221
1995	103 406	60 944	58.9	57 523	55.6	881	56 642	3 421	5.6	42 462
1996	104 385	61 857	59.3	58 501	56.0	871	57 630	3 356	5.4	42 528
1997	105 418	63 036	59.8	59 873	56.8	847	59 026	3 162	5.0	42 382
1998	106 462	63 714	59.8	60 771	57.1	825	59 945	2 944	4.6	42 748
1999	108 031	64 855	60.0	62 042	57.4	849	61 193	2 814	4.3	43 175
2000	108 968	65 616	60.2	62 915	57.7	871	62 044	2 701	4.1	43 352
2001	110 007	66 071	60.1	62 992	57.3	869	62 124	3 079	4.7	43 935

Note: See "Notes and Definitions" for information on historical comparability.

Table 1-3. Employment Status of the Civilian Noninstitutional Population by Sex, Race, Hispanic Origin, and Age, 1982–2001

(Thousands of persons.)

Employment status, sex, and age	1982	1983	1984	1985	1986	1987	1988	1989	1990	1991	1992
TOTAL CIVILIAN NONINSTITUTIONAL POPULATION											
Civilian noninstitutional population	172 271	174 215	176 383	178 206	180 587	182 753	184 613	186 393	189 164	190 925	192 805
Civilian labor force	110 204	111 550	113 544	115 461	117 834	119 865	121 669	123 869	125 840	126 346	128 105
Employed	99 526	100 834	105 005	107 150	109 597	112 440	114 968	117 342	118 793	117 718	118 492
Agriculture	3 401	3 383	3 321	3 179	3 163	3 208	3 169	3 199	3 223	3 269	3 247
Nonagricultural industries	96 125	97 450	101 685	103 971	106 434	109 232	111 800	114 142	115 570	114 449	115 245
Unemployed	10 678	10 717	8 539	8 312	8 237	7 425	6 701	6 528	7 047	8 628	9 613
Not in labor force	62 067	62 665	62 839	62 744	62 752	62 888	62 944	62 523	63 324	64 578	64 700
MEN, 16 YEARS AND OLDER											
Civilian noninstitutional population	81 523	82 531	83 605	84 469	85 798	86 899	87 857	88 762	90 377	91 278	92 270
Civilian labor force	62 450	63 047	63 835	64 411	65 422	66 207	66 927	67 840	69 011	69 168	69 964
Employed	56 271	56 787	59 091	59 891	60 892	62 107	63 273	64 315	65 104	64 223	64 440
Agriculture	2 736	2 704	2 668	2 535	2 511	2 543	2 493	2 513	2 546	2 589	2 575
Nonagricultural industries	53 534	54 083	56 423	57 356	58 381	59 564	60 780	61 802	62 559	61 634	61 866
Unemployed	6 179	6 260	4 744	4 521	4 530	4 101	3 655	3 525	3 906	4 946	5 523
Not in labor force	19 073	19 484	19 771	20 058	20 376	20 692	20 930	20 923	21 367	22 110	22 306
MEN, 20 YEARS AND OLDER											
Civilian noninstitutional population	73 644	74 872	76 219	77 195	78 523	79 565	80 553	81 619	83 030	84 144	85 247
Civilian labor force	57 980	58 744	59 701	60 277	61 320	62 095	62 768	63 704	64 916	65 374	66 213
Employed	52 891	53 487	55 769	56 562	57 569	58 726	59 781	60 837	61 678	61 178	61 496
Agriculture	2 422	2 429	2 418	2 278	2 292	2 329	2 271	2 307	2 329	2 383	2 385
Nonagricultural industries	50 469	51 058	53 351	54 284	55 277	56 397	57 510	58 530	59 349	58 795	59 111
Unemployed	5 089	5 257	3 932	3 715	3 751	3 369	2 987	2 867	3 239	4 195	4 717
Not in labor force	15 664	16 129	16 518	16 918	17 203	17 470	17 785	17 915	18 114	18 770	19 034
WOMEN, 16 YEARS AND OLDER											
Civilian noninstitutional population	90 748	91 684	92 778	93 736	94 789	95 853	96 756	97 630	98 787	99 646	100 535
Civilian labor force	47 755	48 503	49 709	51 050	52 413	53 658	54 742	56 030	56 829	57 178	58 141
Employed	43 256	44 047	45 915	47 259	48 706	50 334	51 696	53 027	53 689	53 496	54 052
Agriculture	665	680	653	644	652	666	676	687	678	680	672
Nonagricultural industries	42 591	43 367	45 262	46 615	48 054	49 668	51 020	52 341	53 011	52 815	53 380
Unemployed	4 499	4 457	3 794	3 791	3 707	3 324	3 046	3 003	3 140	3 683	4 090
Not in labor force	42 993	43 181	43 068	42 686	42 376	42 195	42 014	41 601	41 957	42 468	42 394
WOMEN, 20 YEARS AND OLDER											
Civilian noninstitutional population	82 864	84 069	85 429	86 506	87 567	88 583	89 532	90 550	91 614	92 708	93 718
Civilian labor force	43 699	44 636	45 900	47 283	48 589	49 783	50 870	52 212	53 131	53 708	54 796
Employed	40 086	41 004	42 793	44 154	45 556	47 074	48 383	49 745	50 535	50 634	51 328
Agriculture	601	620	595	596	614	622	625	642	631	639	625
Nonagricultural industries	39 485	40 384	42 198	43 558	44 943	46 453	47 757	49 103	49 904	49 995	50 702
Unemployed	3 613	3 632	3 107	3 129	3 032	2 709	2 487	2 467	2 596	3 074	3 469
Not in labor force	39 165	39 433	39 529	39 222	38 979	38 800	38 662	38 339	38 483	39 000	38 922
BOTH SEXES, 16–19 YEARS											
Civilian noninstitutional population	15 763	15 274	14 735	14 506	14 496	14 606	14 527	14 223	14 520	14 073	13 840
Civilian labor force	8 526	8 171	7 943	7 901	7 926	7 988	8 031	7 954	7 792	7 265	7 096
Employed	6 549	6 342	6 444	6 434	6 472	6 640	6 805	6 759	6 581	5 906	5 669
Agriculture	378	334	309	305	258	258	273	250	264	247	237
Nonagricultural industries	6 171	6 008	6 135	6 129	6 215	6 382	6 532	6 510	6 317	5 659	5 432
Unemployed	1 977	1 829	1 499	1 468	1 454	1 347	1 226	1 194	1 212	1 359	1 427
Not in labor force	7 238	7 104	6 791	6 604	6 570	6 618	6 497	6 270	6 727	6 808	6 745

See *Note* at end of table.

Table 1-3. Employment Status of the Civilian Noninstitutional Population by Sex, Race, Hispanic Origin, and Age, 1982–2001—*Continued*

(Thousands of persons.)

Employment status, sex, and age	1993	1994	1995	1996	1997	1998	1999	2000	2001
TOTAL CIVILIAN NONINSTITUTIONAL POPULATION									
Civilian noninstitutional population	194 838	196 814	198 584	200 591	203 133	205 220	207 753	209 699	211 864
Civilian labor force	129 200	131 056	132 304	133 943	136 297	137 673	139 368	140 863	141 815
Employed	120 259	123 060	124 900	126 708	129 558	131 463	133 488	135 208	135 073
Agriculture	3 115	3 409	3 440	3 443	3 399	3 378	3 281	3 305	3 144
Nonagricultural industries	117 144	119 651	121 460	123 264	126 159	128 085	130 207	131 903	131 929
Unemployed	8 940	7 996	7 404	7 236	6 739	6 210	5 880	5 655	6 742
Not in labor force	65 638	65 758	66 280	66 647	66 837	67 547	68 385	68 836	70 050
MEN, 16 YEARS AND OLDER									
Civilian noninstitutional population	93 332	94 355	95 178	96 206	97 715	98 758	99 722	100 731	101 858
Civilian labor force	70 404	70 817	71 360	72 087	73 261	73 959	74 512	75 247	75 743
Employed	65 349	66 450	67 377	68 207	69 685	70 693	71 446	72 293	72 080
Agriculture	2 478	2 554	2 559	2 573	2 552	2 553	2 432	2 434	2 275
Nonagricultural industries	62 871	63 896	64 818	65 634	67 133	68 140	69 014	69 859	69 805
Unemployed	5 055	4 367	3 983	3 880	3 577	3 266	3 066	2 954	3 663
Not in labor force	22 927	23 538	23 818	24 119	24 454	24 799	25 210	25 484	26 114
MEN, 20 YEARS AND OLDER									
Civilian noninstitutional population	86 256	87 151	87 811	88 606	89 879	90 790	91 555	92 580	93 659
Civilian labor force	66 642	66 921	67 324	68 044	69 166	69 715	70 194	70 930	71 590
Employed	62 355	63 294	64 085	64 897	66 284	67 135	67 761	68 580	68 587
Agriculture	2 293	2 351	2 335	2 356	2 356	2 350	2 244	2 252	2 102
Nonagricultural industries	60 063	60 943	61 750	62 541	63 927	64 785	65 517	66 328	66 485
Unemployed	4 287	3 627	3 239	3 146	2 882	2 580	2 433	2 350	3 003
Not in labor force	19 613	20 230	20 487	20 563	20 713	21 075	21 362	21 650	22 069
WOMEN, 16 YEARS AND OLDER									
Civilian noninstitutional population	101 506	102 460	103 406	104 385	105 418	106 462	108 031	108 968	110 007
Civilian labor force	58 795	60 239	60 944	61 857	63 036	63 714	64 855	65 616	66 071
Employed	54 910	56 610	57 523	58 501	59 873	60 771	62 042	62 915	62 992
Agriculture	637	855	881	871	847	825	849	871	869
Nonagricultural industries	54 273	55 755	56 642	57 630	59 026	59 945	61 193	62 044	62 124
Unemployed	3 885	3 629	3 421	3 356	3 162	2 944	2 814	2 701	3 079
Not in labor force	42 711	42 221	42 462	42 528	42 382	42 748	43 175	43 352	43 935
WOMEN, 20 YEARS AND OLDER									
Civilian noninstitutional population	94 647	95 467	96 262	97 050	97 889	98 786	100 158	101 078	102 060
Civilian labor force	55 388	56 655	57 215	58 094	59 198	59 702	60 840	61 565	62 148
Employed	52 099	53 606	54 396	55 311	56 613	57 278	58 555	59 352	59 596
Agriculture	598	809	830	827	798	768	803	818	817
Nonagricultural industries	51 501	52 796	53 566	54 484	55 815	56 510	57 752	58 535	58 779
Unemployed	3 288	3 049	2 819	2 783	2 585	2 424	2 285	2 212	2 551
Not in labor force	39 260	38 813	39 047	38 956	38 691	39 084	39 318	39 513	39 912
BOTH SEXES, 16–19 YEARS									
Civilian noninstitutional population	13 935	14 196	14 511	14 934	15 365	15 644	16 040	16 042	16 146
Civilian labor force	7 170	7 481	7 765	7 806	7 932	8 256	8 333	8 369	8 077
Employed	5 805	6 161	6 419	6 500	6 661	7 051	7 172	7 276	6 889
Agriculture	224	249	275	261	244	261	234	235	225
Nonagricultural industries	5 580	5 912	6 144	6 239	6 417	6 790	6 938	7 041	6 664
Unemployed	1 365	1 320	1 346	1 306	1 271	1 205	1 162	1 093	1 187
Not in labor force	6 765	6 715	6 746	7 128	7 433	7 388	7 706	7 673	8 069

See *Note* at end of table.

Table 1-3. Employment Status of the Civilian Noninstitutional Population by Sex, Race, Hispanic Origin, and Age, 1982–2001—*Continued*

(Thousands of persons.)

Employment status, sex, and age	1982	1983	1984	1985	1986	1987	1988	1989	1990	1991	1992
TOTAL, WHITE											
Civilian noninstitutional population	149 441	150 805	152 347	153 679	155 432	156 958	158 194	159 338	160 625	161 759	162 972
Civilian labor force	96 143	97 021	98 492	99 926	101 801	103 290	104 756	106 355	107 447	107 743	108 837
Employed	87 903	88 893	92 120	93 736	95 660	97 789	99 812	101 584	102 261	101 182	101 669
Agriculture	3 142	3 119	3 057	2 936	2 958	2 986	2 965	2 996	2 998	3 026	3 018
Nonagricultural industries	84 761	85 774	89 063	90 799	92 703	94 803	96 846	98 588	99 263	98 157	98 650
Unemployed	8 241	8 128	6 372	6 191	6 140	5 501	4 944	4 770	5 186	6 560	7 169
Not in labor force	53 298	53 784	53 855	53 753	53 631	53 669	53 439	52 983	53 178	54 016	54 135
WHITE MEN, 16 YEARS AND OLDER											
Civilian noninstitutional population	71 211	71 922	72 723	73 373	74 390	75 189	75 855	76 468	77 369	77 977	78 651
Civilian labor force	55 133	55 480	56 062	56 472	57 217	57 779	58 317	58 988	59 638	59 656	60 168
Employed	50 287	50 621	52 462	53 046	53 785	54 647	55 550	56 352	56 703	55 797	55 959
Agriculture	2 518	2 484	2 437	2 325	2 340	2 354	2 318	2 345	2 353	2 384	2 378
Nonagricultural industries	47 770	48 138	50 025	50 720	51 444	52 293	53 232	54 007	54 350	53 413	53 580
Unemployed	4 846	4 859	3 600	3 426	3 433	3 132	2 766	2 636	2 935	3 859	4 209
Not in labor force	16 078	16 441	16 661	16 901	17 173	17 410	17 538	17 480	17 731	18 321	18 484
WHITE MEN, 20 YEARS AND OLDER											
Civilian noninstitutional population	64 655	65 581	66 610	67 386	68 413	69 175	69 887	70 654	71 457	72 274	73 040
Civilian labor force	51 200	51 716	52 453	52 895	53 675	54 232	54 734	55 441	56 116	56 387	56 976
Employed	47 209	47 618	49 461	50 061	50 818	51 649	52 466	53 292	53 685	53 103	53 357
Agriculture	2 218	2 225	2 201	2 085	2 131	2 150	2 104	2 149	2 148	2 192	2 197
Nonagricultural industries	44 990	45 393	47 260	47 976	48 687	49 499	50 362	51 143	51 537	50 912	51 160
Unemployed	3 991	4 098	2 992	2 834	2 857	2 584	2 268	2 149	2 431	3 284	3 620
Not in labor force	13 455	13 865	14 157	14 490	14 738	14 942	15 153	15 213	15 340	15 887	16 064
WHITE WOMEN, 16 YEARS AND OLDER											
Civilian noninstitutional population	78 230	78 884	79 624	80 306	81 042	81 769	82 340	82 871	83 256	83 781	84 321
Civilian labor force	41 010	41 541	42 431	43 455	44 584	45 510	46 439	47 367	47 809	48 087	48 669
Employed	37 615	38 272	39 659	40 690	41 876	43 142	44 262	45 232	45 558	45 385	45 710
Agriculture	624	635	620	611	617	632	648	651	645	641	640
Nonagricultural industries	36 991	37 636	39 038	40 079	41 259	42 509	43 614	44 581	44 913	44 744	45 070
Unemployed	3 395	3 270	2 772	2 765	2 708	2 369	2 177	2 135	2 251	2 701	2 959
Not in labor force	37 220	37 342	37 193	36 852	36 458	36 258	35 901	35 504	35 447	35 695	35 651
WHITE WOMEN, 20 YEARS AND OLDER											
Civilian noninstitutional population	71 711	72 601	73 590	74 394	75 140	75 845	76 470	77 154	77 539	78 285	78 928
Civilian labor force	37 425	38 119	39 087	40 190	41 264	42 164	43 081	44 105	44 648	45 111	45 839
Employed	34 710	35 476	36 823	37 907	39 050	40 242	41 316	42 346	42 796	42 862	43 327
Agriculture	565	580	564	566	580	590	599	608	598	601	594
Nonagricultural industries	34 144	34 896	36 259	37 341	38 471	39 652	40 717	41 738	42 198	42 261	42 733
Unemployed	2 715	2 643	2 264	2 283	2 213	1 922	1 766	1 758	1 852	2 248	2 512
Not in labor force	34 286	34 482	34 503	34 204	33 876	33 681	33 389	33 050	32 891	33 174	33 089
WHITE BOTH SEXES, 16–19 YEARS											
Civilian noninstitutional population	13 076	12 623	12 147	11 900	11 879	11 939	11 838	11 530	11 630	11 200	11 004
Civilian labor force	7 518	7 186	6 952	6 841	6 862	6 893	6 940	6 809	6 683	6 245	6 022
Employed	5 984	5 799	5 836	5 768	5 792	5 898	6 030	5 946	5 779	5 216	4 985
Agriculture	358	314	292	285	247	246	263	239	252	233	228
Nonagricultural industries	5 626	5 485	5 544	5 483	5 545	5 652	5 767	5 707	5 528	4 984	4 757
Unemployed	1 534	1 387	1 116	1 074	1 070	995	910	863	903	1 029	1 037
Not in labor force	5 557	5 436	5 195	5 058	5 017	5 045	4 897	4 721	4 947	4 955	4 982

See *Note* at end of table.

Table 1-3. Employment Status of the Civilian Noninstitutional Population by Sex, Race, Hispanic Origin, and Age, 1982–2001—*Continued*

(Thousands of persons.)

Employment status, sex, and age	1993	1994	1995	1996	1997	1998	1999	2000	2001
TOTAL, WHITE									
Civilian noninstitutional population	164 289	165 555	166 914	168 317	169 993	171 478	173 085	174 428	175 888
Civilian labor force	109 700	111 082	111 950	113 108	114 693	115 415	116 509	117 574	118 144
Employed	103 045	105 190	106 490	107 808	109 856	110 931	112 235	113 475	113 220
Agriculture	2 895	3 162	3 194	3 276	3 208	3 160	3 083	3 099	2 968
Nonagricultural industries	100 150	102 027	103 296	104 532	106 648	107 770	109 152	110 376	110 252
Unemployed	6 655	5 892	5 459	5 300	4 836	4 484	4 273	4 099	4 923
Not in labor force	54 589	54 473	54 965	55 209	55 301	56 064	56 577	56 854	57 744
WHITE MEN, 16 YEARS AND OLDER									
Civilian noninstitutional population	79 371	80 059	80 733	81 489	82 577	83 352	83 930	84 647	85 421
Civilian labor force	60 484	60 727	61 146	61 783	62 639	63 034	63 413	63 861	64 141
Employed	56 656	57 452	58 146	58 888	59 998	60 604	61 139	61 696	61 411
Agriculture	2 286	2 347	2 347	2 436	2 389	2 376	2 273	2 266	2 130
Nonagricultural industries	54 370	55 104	55 800	56 452	57 608	58 228	58 866	59 429	59 281
Unemployed	3 828	3 275	2 999	2 896	2 641	2 431	2 274	2 165	2 730
Not in labor force	18 887	19 332	19 587	19 706	19 938	20 317	20 517	20 786	21 280
WHITE MEN, 20 YEARS AND OLDER									
Civilian noninstitutional population	73 721	74 311	74 879	75 454	76 320	76 966	77 432	78 151	78 888
Civilian labor force	57 284	57 411	57 719	58 340	59 126	59 421	59 747	60 182	60 609
Employed	54 021	54 676	55 254	55 977	56 986	57 500	57 934	58 469	58 367
Agriculture	2 114	2 151	2 132	2 224	2 201	2 182	2 094	2 092	1 961
Nonagricultural industries	51 907	52 525	53 122	53 753	54 785	55 319	55 839	56 377	56 406
Unemployed	3 263	2 735	2 465	2 363	2 140	1 920	1 813	1 713	2 242
Not in labor force	16 436	16 900	17 161	17 114	17 194	17 545	17 685	17 969	18 279
WHITE WOMEN, 16 YEARS AND OLDER									
Civilian noninstitutional population	84 918	85 496	86 181	86 828	87 417	88 126	89 156	89 781	90 467
Civilian labor force	49 216	50 356	50 804	51 325	52 054	52 380	53 096	53 714	54 003
Employed	46 390	47 738	48 344	48 920	49 859	50 327	51 096	51 780	51 810
Agriculture	609	815	847	840	819	784	810	833	839
Nonagricultural industries	45 780	46 923	47 497	48 080	49 040	49 543	50 286	50 947	50 971
Unemployed	2 827	2 617	2 460	2 404	2 195	2 053	1 999	1 934	2 193
Not in labor force	35 702	35 141	35 377	35 503	35 363	35 746	36 060	36 068	36 464
WHITE WOMEN, 20 YEARS AND OLDER									
Civilian noninstitutional population	79 490	79 980	80 567	81 041	81 492	82 073	82 953	83 570	84 214
Civilian labor force	46 311	47 314	47 686	48 162	48 847	49 029	49 714	50 318	50 700
Employed	43 910	45 116	45 643	46 164	47 063	47 342	48 098	48 736	48 884
Agriculture	572	772	799	798	771	729	765	784	790
Nonagricultural industries	43 339	44 344	44 844	45 366	46 292	46 612	47 333	47 953	48 094
Unemployed	2 400	2 197	2 042	1 998	1 784	1 688	1 616	1 581	1 815
Not in labor force	33 179	32 666	32 881	32 879	32 645	33 044	33 239	33 253	33 514
WHITE BOTH SEXES, 16–19 YEARS									
Civilian noninstitutional population	11 078	11 264	11 468	11 822	12 181	12 439	12 700	12 707	12 786
Civilian labor force	6 105	6 357	6 545	6 607	6 720	6 965	7 048	7 075	6 835
Employed	5 113	5 398	5 593	5 667	5 807	6 089	6 204	6 270	5 969
Agriculture	209	239	262	254	236	250	224	224	217
Nonagricultural industries	4 904	5 158	5 331	5 413	5 571	5 839	5 980	6 046	5 752
Unemployed	992	960	952	939	912	876	844	805	866
Not in labor force	4 973	4 907	4 923	5 215	5 462	5 475	5 652	5 632	5 951

See *Note* at end of table.

Table 1-3. Employment Status of the Civilian Noninstitutional Population by Sex, Race, Hispanic Origin, and Age, 1982–2001—*Continued*

(Thousands of persons.)

Employment status, sex, and age	1982	1983	1984	1985	1986	1987	1988	1989	1990	1991	1992
TOTAL, BLACK											
Civilian noninstitutional population	18 584	18 925	19 348	19 664	19 989	20 352	20 692	21 021	21 477	21 799	22 147
Civilian labor force	11 331	11 647	12 033	12 364	12 654	12 993	13 205	13 497	13 740	13 797	14 162
Employed	9 189	9 375	10 119	10 501	10 814	11 309	11 658	11 953	12 175	12 074	12 151
Agriculture	188	193	196	189	155	164	153	150	142	160	153
Nonagricultural industries	9 001	9 182	9 923	10 312	10 659	11 145	11 505	11 803	12 034	11 914	11 997
Unemployed	2 142	2 272	1 914	1 864	1 840	1 684	1 547	1 544	1 565	1 723	2 011
Not in labor force	7 254	7 278	7 315	7 299	7 335	7 359	7 487	7 524	7 737	8 002	7 985
BLACK MEN, 16 YEARS AND OLDER											
Civilian noninstitutional population	8 283	8 447	8 654	8 790	8 956	9 128	9 289	9 439	9 573	9 725	9 896
Civilian labor force	5 804	5 966	6 126	6 220	6 373	6 486	6 596	6 701	6 802	6 851	6 997
Employed	4 637	4 753	5 124	5 270	5 428	5 661	5 824	5 928	5 995	5 961	5 930
Agriculture	163	165	174	167	133	142	133	127	124	139	138
Nonagricultural industries	4 474	4 587	4 950	5 103	5 295	5 519	5 691	5 802	5 872	5 822	5 791
Unemployed	1 167	1 213	1 003	951	946	826	771	773	806	890	1 067
Not in labor force	2 481	2 482	2 528	2 570	2 583	2 642	2 694	2 738	2 772	2 874	2 899
BLACK MEN, 20 YEARS AND OLDER											
Civilian noninstitutional population	7 186	7 360	7 599	7 731	7 907	8 063	8 215	8 364	8 479	8 652	8 840
Civilian labor force	5 368	5 533	5 686	5 749	5 915	6 023	6 127	6 221	6 357	6 451	6 568
Employed	4 414	4 531	4 871	4 992	5 150	5 357	5 509	5 602	5 692	5 706	5 681
Agriculture	150	152	161	154	125	135	129	119	117	131	131
Nonagricultural industries	4 264	4 379	4 710	4 837	5 025	5 222	5 381	5 483	5 576	5 575	5 550
Unemployed	954	1 002	815	757	765	666	617	619	664	745	886
Not in labor force	1 819	1 828	1 913	1 982	1 991	2 040	2 089	2 143	2 122	2 202	2 272
BLACK WOMEN, 16 YEARS AND OLDER											
Civilian noninstitutional population	10 300	10 477	10 694	10 873	11 033	11 224	11 402	11 582	11 904	12 074	12 251
Civilian labor force	5 527	5 681	5 907	6 144	6 281	6 507	6 609	6 796	6 938	6 946	7 166
Employed	4 552	4 622	4 995	5 231	5 386	5 648	5 834	6 025	6 180	6 113	6 221
Agriculture	25	28	22	22	22	22	20	24	18	21	15
Nonagricultural industries	4 527	4 595	4 973	5 209	5 364	5 626	5 814	6 001	6 162	6 092	6 206
Unemployed	975	1 059	911	913	894	858	776	772	758	833	944
Not in labor force	4 773	4 796	4 787	4 729	4 752	4 717	4 793	4 786	4 965	5 129	5 086
BLACK WOMEN, 20 YEARS AND OLDER											
Civilian noninstitutional population	9 146	9 340	9 588	9 773	9 945	10 126	10 298	10 482	10 760	10 959	11 152
Civilian labor force	5 140	5 306	5 520	5 727	5 855	6 071	6 190	6 352	6 517	6 572	6 778
Employed	4 347	4 428	4 773	4 977	5 128	5 365	5 548	5 727	5 884	5 874	5 978
Agriculture	21	25	21	19	22	20	18	23	18	20	15
Nonagricultural industries	4 326	4 403	4 752	4 959	5 106	5 345	5 530	5 703	5 867	5 853	5 963
Unemployed	793	878	747	750	728	706	642	625	633	698	800
Not in labor force	4 006	4 034	4 069	4 046	4 090	4 054	4 108	4 130	4 243	4 388	4 374
BLACK, BOTH SEXES, 16–19 YEARS											
Civilian noninstitutional population	2 252	2 225	2 161	2 160	2 137	2 163	2 179	2 176	2 238	2 187	2 155
Civilian labor force	824	809	827	889	883	899	889	925	866	774	816
Employed	428	416	474	532	536	587	601	625	598	494	492
Agriculture	16	16	13	16	8	9	7	8	7	8	7
Nonagricultural industries	412	400	460	516	529	578	594	617	591	486	485
Unemployed	396	392	353	357	347	312	288	300	268	280	324
Not in labor force	1 429	1 416	1 334	1 271	1 254	1 264	1 291	1 251	1 372	1 413	1 339

See *Note* at end of table.

Table 1-3. Employment Status of the Civilian Noninstitutional Population by Sex, Race, Hispanic Origin, and Age, 1982–2001—*Continued*

(Thousands of persons.)

Employment status, sex, and age	1993	1994	1995	1996	1997	1998	1999	2000	2001
TOTAL, BLACK									
Civilian noninstitutional population	22 521	22 879	23 246	23 604	24 003	24 373	24 855	25 218	25 559
Civilian labor force	14 225	14 502	14 817	15 134	15 529	15 982	16 365	16 603	16 719
Employed	12 382	12 835	13 279	13 542	13 969	14 556	15 056	15 334	15 270
Agriculture	143	136	101	98	117	138	117	138	114
Nonagricultural industries	12 239	12 699	13 178	13 444	13 852	14 417	14 939	15 196	15 156
Unemployed	1 844	1 666	1 538	1 592	1 560	1 426	1 309	1 269	1 450
Not in labor force	8 296	8 377	8 429	8 470	8 474	8 391	8 490	8 615	8 840
BLACK MEN, 16 YEARS AND OLDER									
Civilian noninstitutional population	10 083	10 258	10 411	10 575	10 763	10 927	11 143	11 320	11 468
Civilian labor force	7 019	7 089	7 183	7 264	7 354	7 542	7 652	7 816	7 858
Employed	6 047	6 241	6 422	6 456	6 607	6 871	7 027	7 180	7 127
Agriculture	128	118	93	86	103	118	99	116	101
Nonagricultural industries	5 919	6 122	6 329	6 371	6 504	6 752	6 928	7 064	7 026
Unemployed	971	848	762	808	747	671	626	636	731
Not in labor force	3 064	3 169	3 228	3 311	3 409	3 386	3 491	3 504	3 610
BLACK MEN, 20 YEARS AND OLDER									
Civilian noninstitutional population	9 008	9 171	9 280	9 414	9 575	9 727	9 926	10 107	10 250
Civilian labor force	6 594	6 646	6 730	6 806	6 910	7 053	7 182	7 343	7 395
Employed	5 793	5 964	6 137	6 167	6 325	6 530	6 702	6 832	6 805
Agriculture	120	115	89	83	101	112	96	111	99
Nonagricultural industries	5 673	5 849	6 048	6 084	6 224	6 418	6 606	6 720	6 707
Unemployed	801	682	593	639	585	524	480	511	590
Not in labor force	2 413	2 525	2 550	2 608	2 665	2 673	2 743	2 765	2 855
BLACK WOMEN, 16 YEARS AND OLDER									
Civilian noninstitutional population	12 438	12 621	12 835	13 029	13 241	13 446	13 711	13 898	14 091
Civilian labor force	7 206	7 413	7 634	7 869	8 175	8 441	8 713	8 787	8 861
Employed	6 334	6 595	6 857	7 086	7 362	7 685	8 029	8 154	8 143
Agriculture	15	18	8	13	14	20	18	21	12
Nonagricultural industries	6 320	6 577	6 849	7 073	7 348	7 665	8 011	8 133	8 130
Unemployed	872	818	777	784	813	756	684	633	719
Not in labor force	5 231	5 208	5 201	5 159	5 066	5 005	4 999	5 111	5 230
BLACK WOMEN, 20 YEARS AND OLDER									
Civilian noninstitutional population	11 332	11 496	11 682	11 833	12 016	12 203	12 451	12 643	12 830
Civilian labor force	6 824	7 004	7 175	7 405	7 686	7 912	8 224	8 293	8 390
Employed	6 095	6 320	6 556	6 762	7 013	7 290	7 663	7 774	7 801
Agriculture	14	17	7	12	13	19	17	20	11
Nonagricultural industries	6 081	6 303	6 548	6 749	7 000	7 272	7 646	7 754	7 790
Unemployed	729	685	620	643	673	622	561	519	589
Not in labor force	4 508	4 492	4 507	4 428	4 330	4 291	4 226	4 350	4 440
BLACK, BOTH SEXES, 16–19 YEARS									
Civilian noninstitutional population	2 181	2 211	2 284	2 356	2 412	2 443	2 479	2 468	2 479
Civilian labor force	807	852	911	923	933	1 017	959	967	934
Employed	494	552	586	613	631	736	691	729	663
Agriculture	9	1	5	3	3	8	4	7	4
Nonagricultural industries	485	547	581	611	628	728	687	722	660
Unemployed	313	300	325	310	302	281	268	239	271
Not in labor force	1 374	1 360	1 372	1 434	1 479	1 427	1 520	1 500	1 545

See *Note* at end of table.

Table 1-3. Employment Status of the Civilian Noninstitutional Population by Sex, Race, Hispanic Origin, and Age, 1982–2001—*Continued*

(Thousands of persons.)

Employment status, sex, and age	1982	1983	1984	1985	1986	1987	1988	1989	1990	1991	1992
TOTAL, HISPANIC											
Civilian noninstitutional population	10 580	11 029	11 478	11 915	12 344	12 867	13 325	13 791	15 904	16 425	16 961
Civilian labor force	6 734	7 033	7 451	7 698	8 076	8 541	8 982	9 323	10 720	10 920	11 338
Employed	5 805	6 072	6 651	6 888	7 219	7 790	8 250	8 573	9 845	9 828	10 027
Agriculture	285	316	341	302	329	398	407	440	517	512	524
Nonagricultural industries	5 521	5 756	6 310	6 586	6 890	7 391	7 843	8 133	9 328	9 315	9 503
Unemployed	929	961	800	811	857	751	732	750	876	1 092	1 311
Not in labor force	3 846	3 997	4 027	4 217	4 268	4 327	4 342	4 468	5 184	5 506	5 623
HISPANIC MEN, 16 YEARS AND OLDER											
Civilian noninstitutional population	5 203	5 432	5 661	5 885	6 106	6 371	6 604	6 825	8 041	8 296	8 553
Civilian labor force	4 148	4 362	4 563	4 729	4 948	5 163	5 409	5 595	6 546	6 664	6 900
Employed	3 583	3 771	4 083	4 245	4 428	4 713	4 972	5 172	6 021	5 979	6 093
Agriculture	243	271	296	264	287	351	356	393	449	453	468
Nonagricultural industries	3 340	3 499	3 787	3 981	4 140	4 361	4 616	4 779	5 572	5 526	5 625
Unemployed	565	591	480	483	520	451	437	423	524	685	807
Not in labor force	1 055	1 070	1 098	1 157	1 158	1 208	1 195	1 230	1 495	1 632	1 654
HISPANIC MEN, 20 YEARS AND OLDER											
Civilian noninstitutional population	4 539	4 771	5 005	5 232	5 451	5 700	5 921	6 114	7 126	7 392	7 655
Civilian labor force	3 815	4 014	4 218	4 395	4 612	4 818	5 031	5 195	6 034	6 198	6 432
Employed	3 354	3 523	3 825	3 994	4 174	4 444	4 680	4 853	5 609	5 623	5 757
Agriculture	222	246	271	239	263	327	327	366	415	419	437
Nonagricultural industries	3 132	3 276	3 554	3 754	3 911	4 118	4 353	4 487	5 195	5 204	5 320
Unemployed	461	491	393	401	438	374	351	342	425	575	675
Not in labor force	724	758	787	837	839	882	890	919	1 092	1 194	1 223
HISPANIC WOMEN, 16 YEARS AND OLDER											
Civilian noninstitutional population	5 377	5 597	5 816	6 029	6 238	6 496	6 721	6 965	7 863	8 130	8 408
Civilian labor force	2 586	2 671	2 888	2 970	3 128	3 377	3 573	3 728	4 174	4 256	4 439
Employed	2 222	2 301	2 568	2 642	2 791	3 077	3 278	3 401	3 823	3 848	3 934
Agriculture	42	44	46	38	42	47	51	48	68	59	57
Nonagricultural industries	2 180	2 257	2 522	2 604	2 749	3 030	3 227	3 353	3 755	3 789	3 877
Unemployed	364	369	320	327	337	300	296	327	351	407	504
Not in labor force	2 792	2 927	2 929	3 059	3 110	3 119	3 147	3 237	3 689	3 874	3 969
HISPANIC WOMEN, 20 YEARS AND OLDER											
Civilian noninstitutional population	4 734	4 954	5 173	5 385	5 591	5 835	6 050	6 278	7 041	7 301	7 569
Civilian labor force	2 333	2 429	2 615	2 725	2 893	3 112	3 281	3 448	3 857	3 941	4 110
Employed	2 040	2 127	2 357	2 456	2 615	2 872	3 047	3 172	3 567	3 603	3 693
Agriculture	35	40	37	31	39	45	49	44	62	53	51
Nonagricultural industries	2 006	2 086	2 320	2 424	2 576	2 827	2 998	3 128	3 505	3 549	3 642
Unemployed	293	302	258	269	278	241	234	276	289	339	418
Not in labor force	2 401	2 525	2 558	2 660	2 698	2 723	2 769	2 830	3 184	3 360	3 459
HISPANIC BOTH SEXES, 16–19 YEARS											
Civilian noninstitutional population	1 307	1 304	1 300	1 298	1 302	1 332	1 354	1 399	1 737	1 732	1 737
Civilian labor force	585	590	618	579	571	610	671	680	829	781	796
Employed	410	423	468	438	430	474	523	548	668	602	577
Agriculture	28	29	34	31	27	27	32	31	40	41	36
Nonagricultural industries	382	394	435	407	403	447	492	517	628	562	541
Unemployed	175	167	149	141	141	136	148	132	161	179	219
Not in labor force	722	714	682	719	730	722	683	719	907	951	941

See *Note* at end of table.

Table 1-3. Employment Status of the Civilian Noninstitutional Population by Sex, Race, Hispanic Origin, and Age, 1982–2001—*Continued*

(Thousands of persons.)

Employment status, sex, and age	1993	1994	1995	1996	1997	1998	1999	2000	2001
TOTAL, HISPANIC									
Civilian noninstitutional population	17 532	18 117	18 629	19 213	20 321	21 070	21 650	22 393	23 122
Civilian labor force	11 610	11 975	12 267	12 774	13 796	14 317	14 665	15 368	15 751
Employed	10 361	10 788	11 127	11 642	12 726	13 291	13 720	14 492	14 714
Agriculture	523	560	604	609	660	742	734	745	639
Nonagricultural industries	9 838	10 227	10 524	11 033	12 067	12 549	12 986	13 747	14 075
Unemployed	1 248	1 187	1 140	1 132	1 069	1 026	945	876	1 037
Not in labor force	5 922	6 142	6 362	6 439	6 526	6 753	6 985	7 025	7 371
HISPANIC MEN, 16 YEARS AND OLDER									
Civilian noninstitutional population	8 824	9 104	9 329	9 604	10 368	10 734	10 713	11 064	11 400
Civilian labor force	7 076	7 210	7 376	7 646	8 309	8 571	8 546	8 919	9 098
Employed	6 328	6 530	6 725	7 039	7 728	8 018	8 067	8 478	8 556
Agriculture	469	494	527	537	571	651	642	639	547
Nonagricultural industries	5 860	6 036	6 198	6 502	7 157	7 367	7 425	7 839	8 009
Unemployed	747	680	651	607	582	552	480	441	542
Not in labor force	1 749	1 894	1 952	1 957	2 059	2 164	2 167	2 145	2 302
HISPANIC MEN, 20 YEARS AND OLDER									
Civilian noninstitutional population	7 930	8 178	8 375	8 611	9 250	9 573	9 523	9 859	10 170
Civilian labor force	6 621	6 747	6 898	7 150	7 779	8 005	7 950	8 306	8 453
Employed	5 992	6 189	6 367	6 655	7 307	7 570	7 576	7 961	8 022
Agriculture	441	466	501	510	544	621	602	601	515
Nonagricultural industries	5 551	5 722	5 866	6 145	6 763	6 949	6 974	7 360	7 508
Unemployed	629	558	530	495	471	436	374	345	431
Not in labor force	1 309	1 431	1 477	1 461	1 471	1 568	1 573	1 554	1 717
HISPANIC WOMEN, 16 YEARS AND OLDER									
Civilian noninstitutional population	8 708	9 014	9 300	9 610	9 953	10 335	10 937	11 329	11 722
Civilian labor force	4 534	4 765	4 891	5 128	5 486	5 746	6 119	6 449	6 653
Employed	4 033	4 258	4 403	4 602	4 999	5 273	5 653	6 014	6 159
Agriculture	55	66	76	72	89	91	92	106	92
Nonagricultural industries	3 978	4 191	4 326	4 531	4 910	5 182	5 561	5 908	6 066
Unemployed	501	508	488	525	488	473	466	435	495
Not in labor force	4 174	4 248	4 409	4 482	4 466	4 589	4 819	4 880	5 069
HISPANIC WOMEN, 20 YEARS AND OLDER									
Civilian noninstitutional population	7 846	8 122	8 382	8 654	8 950	9 292	9 821	10 193	10 559
Civilian labor force	4 218	4 421	4 520	4 779	5 106	5 304	5 666	5 979	6 176
Employed	3 800	3 989	4 116	4 341	4 705	4 928	5 290	5 629	5 769
Agriculture	49	61	72	69	83	85	88	100	87
Nonagricultural industries	3 751	3 928	4 044	4 272	4 622	4 843	5 202	5 529	5 682
Unemployed	418	431	404	438	401	376	376	350	407
Not in labor force	3 628	3 701	3 863	3 875	3 845	3 988	4 155	4 214	4 383
HISPANIC BOTH SEXES, 16–19 YEARS									
Civilian noninstitutional population	1 756	1 818	1 872	1 948	2 121	2 204	2 307	2 341	2 393
Civilian labor force	771	807	850	845	911	1 007	1 049	1 083	1 122
Employed	570	609	645	646	714	793	854	902	923
Agriculture	33	32	31	29	33	36	45	44	38
Nonagricultural industries	537	577	614	617	682	757	809	858	886
Unemployed	201	198	205	199	197	214	196	181	199
Not in labor force	985	1 010	1 022	1 103	1 210	1 197	1 257	1 258	1 271

Note: Detail for the above race and Hispanic-origin groups will not sum to totals because data for the Other races group are not presented and Hispanics are included in both the White and Black population groups. See "Notes and Definitions" for information on historical comparability.

Table 1-4. Employment Status of the Civilian Noninstitutional Population by Marital Status, Sex, and Race, 1983–2001

(Thousands of persons.)

Year	Men				Women			
	Civilian noninstitutional population	Civilian labor force			Civilian noninstitutional population	Civilian labor force		
		Total	Employed	Unemployed		Total	Employed	Unemployed
TOTAL: SINGLE								
1983	22 965	16 657	13 783	2 874	19 479	12 659	10 996	1 663
1984	23 233	16 997	14 699	2 298	19 628	12 867	11 444	1 423
1985	23 328	17 208	15 022	2 186	19 768	13 163	11 758	1 404
1986	23 662	17 553	15 407	2 146	20 113	13 512	12 071	1 442
1987	23 947	17 772	15 794	1 978	20 596	13 885	12 561	1 323
1988	24 572	18 345	16 521	1 824	20 961	14 194	12 979	1 215
1989	24 831	18 738	16 936	1 801	21 141	14 377	13 175	1 202
1990	25 870	19 357	17 405	1 952	21 901	14 612	13 336	1 276
1991	26 197	19 411	17 011	2 400	22 173	14 681	13 198	1 482
1992	26 436	19 709	17 098	2 611	22 475	14 872	13 263	1 609
1993	26 570	19 706	17 261	2 445	22 713	15 031	13 484	1 547
1994	26 786	19 786	17 604	2 181	23 000	15 333	13 847	1 486
1995	26 918	19 841	17 833	2 007	23 151	15 467	14 053	1 413
1996	27 387	20 071	18 055	2 016	23 623	15 842	14 403	1 439
1997	28 311	20 689	18 783	1 906	24 285	16 492	15 037	1 455
1998	28 693	21 037	19 240	1 798	24 941	17 087	15 755	1 332
1999	29 104	21 351	19 686	1 665	25 576	17 575	16 267	1 308
2000	29 709	21 827	20 164	1 663	25 879	17 847	16 623	1 224
2001	30 375	22 042	20 064	1 979	26 381	17 987	16 594	1 393
TOTAL: MARRIED, SPOUSE PRESENT								
1983	51 118	40 601	37 967	2 634	51 084	26 468	24 603	1 865
1984	51 732	40 952	39 056	1 896	51 557	27 199	25 636	1 562
1985	52 128	41 014	39 248	1 767	51 832	27 894	26 336	1 558
1986	52 769	41 477	39 658	1 819	52 158	28 623	27 144	1 479
1987	53 223	41 889	40 265	1 625	52 532	29 381	28 107	1 273
1988	53 246	41 832	40 472	1 360	52 775	29 921	28 756	1 166
1989	53 530	42 036	40 760	1 276	52 885	30 548	29 404	1 145
1990	53 793	42 275	40 829	1 446	52 917	30 901	29 714	1 188
1991	54 158	42 303	40 429	1 875	53 169	31 112	29 698	1 415
1992	54 509	42 491	40 341	2 150	53 501	31 700	30 100	1 600
1993	55 178	42 834	40 935	1 899	53 838	31 980	30 499	1 482
1994	55 560	43 005	41 414	1 592	54 155	32 888	31 536	1 352
1995	56 100	43 472	42 048	1 424	54 716	33 359	32 063	1 296
1996	56 363	43 739	42 417	1 322	54 970	33 618	32 406	1 211
1997	56 396	43 808	42 642	1 167	54 915	33 802	32 755	1 047
1998	56 670	43 957	42 923	1 034	55 331	33 857	32 872	985
1999	57 089	44 244	43 254	990	56 178	34 372	33 450	921
2000	57 270	44 260	43 368	891	56 517	34 631	33 708	923
2001	57 473	44 456	43 243	1 213	56 508	34 671	33 613	1 058
TOTAL: DIVORCED, WIDOWED OR SEPARATED								
1983	8 448	5 788	5 036	752	21 121	9 376	8 447	929
1984	8 640	5 886	5 335	551	21 592	9 644	8 835	809
1985	9 013	6 190	5 621	568	22 136	9 993	9 165	828
1986	9 367	6 392	5 827	565	22 518	10 277	9 491	787
1987	9 729	6 546	6 048	498	22 726	10 393	9 665	727
1988	10 039	6 751	6 280	471	23 020	10 627	9 962	665
1989	10 401	7 066	6 618	448	23 604	11 104	10 448	656
1990	10 714	7 378	6 871	508	23 968	11 315	10 639	676
1991	10 924	7 454	6 783	671	24 304	11 385	10 600	786
1992	11 325	7 763	7 001	762	24 559	11 570	10 689	881
1993	11 584	7 864	7 153	711	24 955	11 784	10 927	856
1994	12 008	8 026	7 432	594	25 304	12 018	11 227	791
1995	12 160	8 047	7 496	551	25 539	12 118	11 407	712
1996	12 456	8 277	7 735	541	25 791	12 397	11 691	706
1997	13 009	8 764	8 260	504	26 218	12 742	12 082	660
1998	13 394	8 965	8 530	435	26 190	12 771	12 143	628
1999	13 528	8 918	8 507	411	26 276	12 909	12 324	585
2000	13 752	9 161	8 761	400	26 573	13 138	12 585	553
2001	14 010	9 245	8 774	472	27 117	13 413	12 785	628

See *Note* at end of table.

Table 1-4. Employment Status of the Civilian Noninstitutional Population by Marital Status, Sex, and Race, 1983–2001—*Continued*

(Thousands of persons.)

Year	Men				Women			
	Civilian noninstitutional population	Civilian labor force			Civilian noninstitutional population	Civilian labor force		
		Total	Employed	Unemployed		Total	Employed	Unemployed
WHITE: SINGLE								
1983	18 934	14 074	11 991	2 084	15 342	10 413	9 352	1 061
1984	19 034	14 281	12 677	1 605	15 365	10 528	9 622	906
1985	19 100	14 426	12 875	1 550	15 472	10 705	9 828	877
1986	19 316	14 672	13 162	1 510	15 686	10 965	10 060	906
1987	19 526	14 850	13 449	1 401	15 990	11 196	10 382	815
1988	19 966	15 279	13 982	1 297	16 218	11 428	10 674	754
1989	20 076	15 511	14 249	1 263	16 289	11 474	10 741	734
1990	20 746	15 993	14 617	1 376	16 555	11 522	10 729	794
1991	20 899	15 989	14 233	1 756	16 569	11 497	10 557	939
1992	21 025	16 129	14 285	1 844	16 684	11 502	10 526	976
1993	20 974	16 033	14 303	1 730	16 768	11 613	10 633	980
1994	21 071	16 074	14 539	1 535	16 936	11 805	10 885	920
1995	21 132	16 080	14 674	1 406	17 046	11 830	10 967	864
1996	21 454	16 285	14 891	1 394	17 282	11 977	11 099	878
1997	22 236	16 810	15 507	1 303	17 728	12 322	11 443	879
1998	22 513	17 007	15 746	1 261	18 247	12 742	11 945	797
1999	22 788	17 272	16 116	1 157	18 635	13 029	12 206	823
2000	23 226	17 587	16 433	1 154	18 847	13 265	12 497	767
2001	23 788	17 792	16 392	1 400	19 242	13 377	12 497	881
WHITE: MARRIED, SPOUSE PRESENT								
1983	46 099	36 631	34 416	2 215	46 226	23 585	22 018	1 567
1984	46 616	36 905	35 318	1 588	46 599	24 196	22 888	1 308
1985	46 925	36 934	35 472	1 462	46 728	24 777	23 468	1 308
1986	47 399	37 230	35 727	1 503	46 892	25 368	24 141	1 226
1987	47 690	37 486	36 127	1 359	47 180	26 014	24 969	1 045
1988	47 685	37 429	36 304	1 125	47 364	26 499	25 540	959
1989	47 883	37 589	36 545	1 044	47 382	27 030	26 083	947
1990	47 841	37 515	36 338	1 177	47 240	27 271	26 285	986
1991	48 137	37 507	35 923	1 585	47 456	27 479	26 290	1 189
1992	48 416	37 671	35 886	1 785	47 705	27 951	26 623	1 329
1993	48 937	37 953	36 396	1 557	47 944	28 221	26 993	1 228
1994	49 169	38 008	36 719	1 288	48 120	29 017	27 888	1 129
1995	49 597	38 376	37 211	1 165	48 497	29 360	28 290	1 070
1996	49 800	38 616	37 522	1 094	48 684	29 517	28 496	1 020
1997	49 719	38 593	37 636	957	48 542	29 664	28 809	855
1998	49 901	38 629	37 793	836	48 722	29 534	28 727	808
1999	50 091	38 765	37 968	797	49 296	29 806	29 056	749
2000	50 193	38 715	38 009	706	49 518	30 042	29 287	755
2001	50 133	38 683	37 713	969	49 367	30 003	29 157	846
WHITE: DIVORCED, WIDOWED OR SEPARATED								
1983	6 889	4 775	4 214	560	17 316	7 543	6 902	642
1984	7 073	4 875	4 467	407	17 660	7 706	7 148	558
1985	7 348	5 112	4 698	414	18 106	7 973	7 393	580
1986	7 675	5 315	4 896	420	18 463	8 251	7 675	576
1987	7 974	5 443	5 070	373	18 599	8 300	7 791	509
1988	8 204	5 608	5 265	344	18 758	8 512	8 047	464
1989	8 509	5 887	5 558	329	19 200	8 863	8 409	454
1990	8 782	6 131	5 748	382	19 461	9 016	8 544	471
1991	8 941	6 159	5 641	518	19 757	9 111	8 538	573
1992	9 210	6 368	5 788	580	19 931	9 216	8 561	654
1993	9 459	6 498	5 957	541	20 206	9 382	8 764	618
1994	9 819	6 644	6 193	451	20 439	9 533	8 965	569
1995	10 005	6 689	6 261	428	20 638	9 613	9 087	526
1996	10 234	6 883	6 474	408	20 862	9 831	9 325	506
1997	10 622	7 236	6 855	382	21 147	10 068	9 607	461
1998	10 937	7 398	7 064	334	21 157	10 104	9 656	449
1999	11 050	7 375	7 056	320	21 225	10 261	9 834	427
2000	11 228	7 558	7 254	304	21 417	10 407	9 996	412
2001	11 500	7 667	7 306	361	21 859	10 623	10 157	466

See *Note* at end of table.

Table 1-4. Employment Status of the Civilian Noninstitutional Population by Marital Status, Sex, and Race, 1983–2001—*Continued*

(Thousands of persons.)

Year	Men				Women			
	Civilian noninstitutional population	Civilian labor force			Civilian noninstitutional population	Civilian labor force		
		Total	Employed	Unemployed		Total	Employed	Unemployed
BLACK AND OTHER: SINGLE								
1983	4 031	2 583	1 793	790	4 138	2 246	1 644	602
1984	4 199	2 716	2 023	693	4 263	2 338	1 821	517
1985	4 228	2 782	2 147	635	4 297	2 458	1 930	528
1986	4 345	2 881	2 245	636	4 427	2 547	2 011	536
1987	4 421	2 922	2 345	577	4 606	2 688	2 179	509
1988	4 606	3 066	2 539	527	4 743	2 766	2 304	461
1989	4 755	3 227	2 687	538	4 852	2 903	2 434	468
1990	5 124	3 364	2 788	576	5 346	3 090	2 607	482
1991	5 298	3 422	2 778	644	5 604	3 184	2 641	543
1992	5 411	3 580	2 813	767	5 791	3 370	2 737	633
1993	5 596	3 673	2 958	715	5 945	3 418	2 851	567
1994	5 715	3 712	3 065	646	6 064	3 528	2 962	566
1995	5 786	3 761	3 159	601	6 105	3 637	3 086	549
1996	5 933	3 786	3 164	622	6 341	3 865	3 304	561
1997	6 075	3 879	3 276	603	6 557	4 170	3 594	576
1998	6 180	4 030	3 494	537	6 694	4 345	3 810	535
1999	6 316	4 079	3 570	508	6 941	4 546	4 061	485
2000	6 483	4 240	3 731	509	7 032	4 582	4 126	457
2001	6 587	4 250	3 672	579	7 139	4 610	4 097	512
BLACK AND OTHER: MARRIED, SPOUSE PRESENT								
1983	5 019	3 970	3 551	419	4 858	2 883	2 585	298
1984	5 116	4 046	3 739	308	4 958	3 002	2 748	254
1985	5 203	4 080	3 775	305	5 104	3 118	2 868	250
1986	5 370	4 247	3 931	316	5 266	3 255	3 003	253
1987	5 534	4 403	4 137	266	5 352	3 367	3 138	228
1988	5 560	4 403	4 168	234	5 411	3 422	3 215	207
1989	5 647	4 447	4 215	232	5 503	3 518	3 321	198
1990	5 952	4 760	4 491	269	5 677	3 630	3 429	202
1991	6 021	4 796	4 506	290	5 713	3 633	3 408	226
1992	6 093	4 820	4 455	365	5 796	3 749	3 477	271
1993	6 241	4 881	4 539	342	5 894	3 759	3 506	254
1994	6 391	4 997	4 695	304	6 035	3 871	3 648	223
1995	6 503	5 096	4 837	259	6 219	3 999	3 773	226
1996	6 563	5 123	4 895	228	6 286	4 101	3 910	191
1997	6 677	5 215	5 006	210	6 373	4 138	3 946	192
1998	6 769	5 328	5 130	198	6 609	4 323	4 145	177
1999	6 998	5 479	5 286	193	6 882	4 566	4 394	172
2000	7 077	5 545	5 359	185	6 999	4 589	4 421	168
2001	7 340	5 773	5 530	244	7 141	4 668	4 456	212
BLACK AND OTHER: DIVORCED, WIDOWED OR SEPARATED								
1983	1 559	1 014	822	192	3 805	1 833	1 546	287
1984	1 568	1 011	868	143	3 932	1 938	1 687	251
1985	1 665	1 078	923	155	4 030	2 020	1 772	248
1986	1 692	1 076	931	146	4 055	2 026	1 816	210
1987	1 755	1 103	977	125	4 127	2 093	1 875	218
1988	1 836	1 142	1 015	127	4 262	2 115	1 914	201
1989	1 892	1 179	1 060	119	4 404	2 241	2 039	202
1990	1 932	1 247	1 123	126	4 507	2 299	2 095	205
1991	1 983	1 295	1 142	153	4 547	2 274	2 062	213
1992	2 115	1 395	1 213	182	4 628	2 354	2 128	227
1993	2 125	1 366	1 196	170	4 749	2 402	2 163	238
1994	2 189	1 382	1 239	143	4 865	2 485	2 262	222
1995	2 155	1 358	1 235	123	4 901	2 505	2 320	186
1996	2 222	1 394	1 261	133	4 929	2 566	2 366	200
1997	2 387	1 528	1 405	122	5 071	2 674	2 475	199
1998	2 457	1 567	1 466	101	5 033	2 667	2 487	179
1999	2 478	1 543	1 451	91	5 051	2 648	2 490	158
2000	2 524	1 603	1 507	96	5 156	2 731	2 589	141
2001	2 510	1 578	1 468	111	5 258	2 790	2 628	162

Note: See "Notes and Definitions" for information on historical comparability.

Table 1-5. Employment Status of the Civilian Noninstitutional Population by Region, Division, and State, 2000–2001

(Thousands of persons, percent.)

Region, division, and state	2000						2001					
	Civilian noninstitutional population	Civilian labor force					Civilian noninstitutional population	Civilian labor force				
		Total	Participation rate	Employed	Unemployed	Unemployment rate		Total	Participation rate	Employed	Unemployed	Unemployment rate
UNITED STATES [1]	209 699	140 863	67.2	135 208	5 655	4.0	211 864	141 815	66.9	135 073	6 742	4.8
Northeast	40 247	26 295	65.3	25 281	1 014	3.9	40 404	26 296	65.1	25 140	1 156	4.4
New England	10 502	7 194	68.5	6 995	199	2.8	10 571	7 212	68.2	6 948	264	3.7
Connecticut	2 537	1 746	68.8	1 707	39	2.3	2 545	1 718	67.5	1 661	56	3.3
Maine	998	689	69.0	665	24	3.5	1 011	684	67.7	657	27	4.0
Massachusetts	4 804	3 237	67.4	3 151	86	2.6	4 828	3 284	68.0	3 163	121	3.7
New Hampshire	939	686	73.1	666	19	2.8	954	689	72.2	664	24	3.5
Rhode Island	753	505	67.1	484	21	4.1	757	504	66.6	480	24	4.7
Vermont	471	332	70.5	322	10	2.9	476	335	70.4	323	12	3.6
Middle Atlantic	29 745	19 101	64.2	18 286	815	4.3	29 833	19 084	64.0	18 192	892	4.7
New Jersey	6 292	4 188	66.6	4 030	157	3.8	6 322	4 179	66.1	4 004	176	4.2
New York	14 163	8 941	63.1	8 533	408	4.6	14 209	8 832	62.2	8 402	429	4.9
Pennsylvania	9 290	5 972	64.3	5 722	250	4.2	9 301	6 073	65.3	5 786	287	4.7
Midwest	48 222	33 729	69.9	32 493	1 236	3.7	48 517	33 904	69.9	32 356	1 548	4.6
East North Central	33 931	23 422	69.0	22 517	905	3.9	34 111	23 478	68.8	22 338	1 140	4.9
Illinois	9 199	6 419	69.8	6 140	279	4.4	9 244	6 349	68.7	6 006	343	5.4
Indiana	4 529	3 084	68.1	2 984	100	3.2	4 557	3 106	68.2	2 970	136	4.4
Michigan	7 548	5 201	68.9	5 016	185	3.6	7 594	5 175	68.1	4 901	274	5.3
Ohio	8 624	5 783	67.1	5 546	237	4.1	8 646	5 857	67.7	5 606	251	4.3
Wisconsin	4 031	2 935	72.8	2 831	104	3.5	4 070	2 991	73.5	2 854	136	4.6
West North Central	14 291	10 307	72.1	9 976	331	3.2	14 406	10 426	72.4	10 018	408	3.9
Iowa	2 193	1 563	71.3	1 522	41	2.6	2 199	1 588	72.2	1 535	53	3.3
Kansas	2 001	1 411	70.5	1 359	52	3.7	2 013	1 381	68.6	1 322	59	4.3
Minnesota	3 648	2 739	75.1	2 649	90	3.3	3 697	2 814	76.1	2 710	104	3.7
Missouri	4 166	2 930	70.3	2 828	101	3.5	4 200	2 970	70.7	2 830	140	4.7
Nebraska	1 254	924	73.7	897	28	3.0	1 262	928	73.5	899	29	3.1
North Dakota	477	339	71.1	329	10	3.0	477	339	71.1	329	10	2.8
South Dakota	552	401	72.6	392	9	2.3	557	405	72.7	392	13	3.3
South	74 337	49 035	66.0	47 104	1 931	3.9	75 277	49 426	65.7	47 076	2 350	4.8
South Atlantic	38 528	25 534	66.3	24 624	910	3.6	39 040	25 792	66.1	24 618	1 174	4.6
Delaware	588	409	69.6	393	16	4.0	595	419	70.4	404	15	3.5
District of Columbia	413	279	67.6	263	16	5.8	412	278	67.5	260	18	6.5
Florida	11 960	7 490	62.6	7 221	269	3.6	12 144	7 674	63.2	7 309	365	4.8
Georgia	5 967	4 173	69.9	4 019	154	3.7	6 077	4 132	68.0	3 966	165	4.0
Maryland	4 015	2 805	69.9	2 697	108	3.9	4 057	2 837	69.9	2 722	116	4.1
North Carolina	5 809	3 958	68.1	3 814	144	3.6	5 863	3 995	68.1	3 773	221	5.5
South Carolina	3 032	1 985	65.5	1 909	77	3.9	3 072	1 949	63.4	1 843	106	5.4
Virginia	5 299	3 610	68.1	3 530	80	2.2	5 374	3 675	68.4	3 548	127	3.5
West Virginia	1 445	825	57.1	779	46	5.5	1 444	833	57.7	792	41	4.9
East South Central	12 853	8 261	64.3	7 895	366	4.4	12 949	8 229	63.5	7 809	420	5.1
Alabama	3 401	2 154	63.3	2 055	99	4.6	3 418	2 148	62.8	2 033	114	5.3
Kentucky	3 082	1 982	64.3	1 900	82	4.1	3 110	1 968	63.3	1 860	108	5.5
Mississippi	2 086	1 326	63.6	1 251	75	5.7	2 100	1 296	61.7	1 225	72	5.5
Tennessee	4 284	2 798	65.3	2 688	110	3.9	4 320	2 818	65.2	2 692	126	4.5
West South Central	22 956	15 240	66.4	14 585	655	4.3	23 288	15 405	66.1	14 649	756	4.9
Arkansas	1 977	1 238	62.6	1 183	55	4.4	1 999	1 227	61.4	1 164	63	5.1
Louisiana	3 289	2 030	61.7	1 917	112	5.5	3 299	2 050	62.1	1 928	122	6.0
Oklahoma	2 558	1 648	64.4	1 598	50	3.0	2 576	1 665	64.6	1 602	64	3.8
Texas	15 132	10 325	68.2	9 887	437	4.2	15 414	10 463	67.9	9 955	507	4.9
West	46 891	31 806	67.8	30 333	1 473	4.6	47 666	32 189	67.5	30 501	1 688	5.2
Mountain	13 033	8 949	68.7	8 614	336	3.8	13 271	9 110	68.6	8 702	407	4.5
Arizona	3 626	2 347	64.7	2 256	91	3.9	3 690	2 420	65.6	2 307	113	4.7
Colorado	3 141	2 276	72.5	2 213	63	2.7	3 203	2 295	71.7	2 210	85	3.7
Idaho	951	658	69.2	626	32	4.9	969	682	70.4	648	34	5.0
Montana	691	479	69.3	456	24	4.9	698	465	66.6	444	21	4.6
Nevada	1 408	986	70.0	946	40	4.1	1 453	1 023	70.4	969	55	5.3
New Mexico	1 318	833	63.2	792	40	4.9	1 331	838	63.0	798	40	4.8
Utah	1 527	1 104	72.3	1 068	36	3.2	1 552	1 115	71.8	1 067	49	4.4
Wyoming	371	267	72.0	257	10	3.9	375	271	72.3	261	11	3.9
Pacific	33 858	22 856	67.5	21 719	1 137	5.0	34 395	23 079	67.1	21 798	1 281	5.5
Alaska	438	322	73.5	301	21	6.6	442	322	72.9	302	20	6.3
California	25 489	17 091	67.1	16 246	845	4.9	25 939	17 362	66.9	16 435	927	5.3
Hawaii	889	595	66.9	570	26	4.3	893	606	67.9	577	28	4.6
Oregon	2 608	1 803	69.1	1 715	87	4.9	2 633	1 794	68.1	1 680	114	6.3
Washington	4 434	3 045	68.7	2 888	158	5.2	4 487	2 996	66.8	2 804	192	6.4
Puerto Rico [2]	2 834	1 306	46.1	1 174	132	10.1	2 873	1 297	45.1	1 150	147	11.4

Note: Region and division data are derived from summing the component states.

1. Because of separate processing and weighing procedures, totals for the United States differ from the results obtained by aggregating data for regions, divisions, or states.
2. The source of these data is the Puerto Rico Department of Labor and Human Resources.

Table 1-6. Civilian Noninstitutional Population by Race, Hispanic Origin, Sex, and Age, 1948–2001

(Thousands of persons.)

Year, race, Hispanic origin, and sex	16 years and over	16 to 19 years			20 years and over						
		Total	16 to 17 years	18 to 19 years	Total	20 to 24 years	25 to 34 years	35 to 44 years	45 to 54 years	55 to 64 years	65 years and over
TOTAL											
1948	103 068	8 449	4 265	4 185	94 618	11 530	22 610	20 097	16 771	12 885	10 720
1949	103 994	8 215	4 139	4 079	95 778	11 312	22 822	20 401	17 002	13 201	11 035
1950	104 995	8 143	4 076	4 068	96 851	11 080	23 013	20 681	17 240	13 469	11 363
1951	104 621	7 865	4 096	3 771	96 755	10 167	22 843	20 863	17 464	13 692	11 724
1952	105 231	7 922	4 234	3 689	97 305	9 389	23 044	21 137	17 716	13 889	12 126
1953	107 056	8 014	4 241	3 773	99 041	8 960	23 266	21 922	17 991	13 830	13 075
1954	108 321	8 224	4 336	3 889	100 095	8 885	23 304	22 135	18 305	14 085	13 375
1955	109 683	8 364	4 440	3 925	101 318	9 036	23 249	22 348	18 643	14 309	13 728
1956	110 954	8 434	4 482	3 953	102 518	9 271	23 072	22 567	19 012	14 516	14 075
1957	112 265	8 612	4 587	4 026	103 653	9 486	22 849	22 786	19 424	14 727	14 376
1958	113 727	8 986	4 872	4 114	104 737	9 733	22 563	23 025	19 832	14 923	14 657
1959	115 329	9 618	5 337	4 282	105 711	9 975	22 201	23 207	20 203	15 134	14 985
1960	117 245	10 187	5 573	4 615	107 056	10 273	21 998	23 437	20 601	15 409	15 336
1961	118 771	10 513	5 462	5 052	108 255	10 583	21 829	23 585	20 893	15 675	15 685
1962	120 153	10 652	5 503	5 150	109 500	10 852	21 503	23 797	20 916	15 874	16 554
1963	122 416	11 370	6 301	5 070	111 045	11 464	21 400	23 948	21 144	16 138	16 945
1964	124 485	12 111	6 974	5 139	112 372	12 017	21 367	23 940	21 452	16 442	17 150
1965	126 513	12 930	6 936	5 995	113 582	12 442	21 417	23 832	21 728	16 727	17 432
1966	128 058	13 592	6 914	6 679	114 463	12 638	21 543	23 579	21 977	17 007	17 715
1967	129 874	13 480	7 003	6 480	116 391	13 421	22 057	23 313	22 256	17 310	18 029
1968	132 028	13 698	7 200	6 499	118 328	13 891	22 912	23 036	22 534	17 614	18 338
1969	134 335	14 095	7 422	6 673	120 238	14 488	23 645	22 709	22 806	17 930	18 657
1970	137 085	14 519	7 643	6 876	122 566	15 323	24 435	22 489	23 059	18 250	19 007
1971	140 216	15 022	7 849	7 173	125 193	16 345	25 337	22 274	23 244	18 581	19 406
1972	144 126	15 510	8 076	7 435	128 614	17 143	26 740	22 358	23 338	19 007	20 023
1973	147 096	15 840	8 227	7 613	131 253	17 692	28 172	22 287	23 431	19 281	20 389
1974	150 120	16 180	8 373	7 809	133 938	17 994	29 439	22 461	23 578	19 517	20 945
1975	153 153	16 418	8 419	7 999	136 733	18 595	30 710	22 526	23 535	19 844	21 525
1976	156 150	16 614	8 442	8 171	139 536	19 109	31 953	22 796	23 409	20 185	22 083
1977	159 033	16 688	8 482	8 206	142 345	19 582	33 117	23 296	23 197	20 557	22 597
1978	161 910	16 695	8 484	8 211	145 216	20 007	34 091	24 099	22 977	20 875	23 166
1979	164 863	16 657	8 389	8 268	148 205	20 353	35 261	24 861	22 752	21 210	23 767
1980	167 745	16 543	8 279	8 264	151 202	20 635	36 558	25 578	22 563	21 520	24 350
1981	170 130	16 214	8 068	8 145	153 916	20 820	37 777	26 291	22 422	21 756	24 850
1982	172 271	15 763	7 714	8 049	156 508	20 845	38 492	27 611	22 264	21 909	25 387
1983	174 215	15 274	7 385	7 889	158 941	20 799	39 147	28 932	22 167	22 003	25 892
1984	176 383	14 735	7 196	7 538	161 648	20 688	39 999	30 251	22 226	22 052	26 433
1985	178 206	14 506	7 232	7 274	163 700	20 097	40 670	31 379	22 418	22 140	26 997
1986	180 587	14 496	7 386	7 110	166 091	19 569	41 731	32 550	22 732	22 011	27 497
1987	182 753	14 606	7 501	7 104	168 147	18 970	42 297	33 755	23 183	21 835	28 108
1988	184 613	14 527	7 284	7 243	170 085	18 434	42 611	34 784	24 004	21 641	28 612
1989	186 393	14 223	6 886	7 338	172 169	18 025	42 845	35 977	24 744	21 406	29 173
1990	189 164	14 520	6 893	7 626	174 644	18 902	42 976	37 719	25 081	20 719	29 247
1991	190 925	14 073	6 901	7 173	176 852	18 963	42 688	39 116	25 709	20 675	29 700
1992	192 805	13 840	6 907	6 933	178 965	18 846	42 278	39 852	27 206	20 604	30 179
1993	194 838	13 935	7 010	6 925	180 903	18 642	41 771	40 733	28 549	20 574	30 634
1994	196 814	14 196	7 245	6 951	182 619	18 353	41 306	41 534	29 778	20 635	31 012
1995	198 584	14 511	7 407	7 104	184 073	17 864	40 798	42 254	30 974	20 735	31 448
1996	200 591	14 934	7 678	7 256	185 656	17 409	40 252	43 086	32 167	20 990	31 751
1997	203 133	15 365	7 861	7 504	187 769	17 442	39 559	43 883	33 391	21 505	31 989
1998	205 220	15 644	7 895	7 749	189 576	17 593	38 778	44 299	34 373	22 296	32 237
1999	207 753	16 040	8 060	7 979	191 714	17 968	37 976	44 635	35 587	23 064	32 484
2000	209 699	16 042	8 003	8 038	193 658	18 411	37 417	44 605	36 904	23 615	32 705
2001	211 864	16 146	8 044	8 101	195 719	18 879	37 055	44 390	38 341	24 203	32 849

See *Note* at end of table.

Table 1-6. Civilian Noninstitutional Population by Race, Hispanic Origin, Sex, and Age, 1948–2001—*Continued*

(Thousands of persons.)

Year, race, Hispanic origin, and sex	16 years and over	16 to 19 years			20 years and over						
		Total	16 to 17 years	18 to 19 years	Total	20 to 24 years	25 to 34 years	35 to 44 years	45 to 54 years	55 to 64 years	65 years and over
WHITE											
1954	97 705	7 180	3 786	3 394	90 524	7 794	20 818	19 915	16 569	12 993	12 438
1955	98 880	7 292	3 874	3 419	91 586	7 912	20 742	20 110	16 869	13 169	12 785
1956	99 976	7 346	3 908	3 438	92 629	8 106	20 564	20 314	17 198	13 341	13 105
1957	101 119	7 505	4 007	3 498	93 612	8 293	20 342	20 514	17 562	13 518	13 383
1958	102 392	7 843	4 271	3 573	94 547	8 498	20 063	20 734	17 924	13 681	13 645
1959	103 803	8 430	4 707	3 725	95 370	8 697	19 715	20 893	18 257	13 858	13 951
1960	105 282	8 924	4 909	4 016	96 355	8 927	19 470	21 049	18 578	14 070	14 260
1961	106 604	9 211	4 785	4 427	97 390	9 203	19 289	21 169	18 845	14 304	14 581
1962	107 715	9 343	4 818	4 526	98 371	9 484	18 974	21 293	18 872	14 450	15 297
1963	109 705	9 978	5 549	4 430	99 725	10 069	18 867	21 398	19 082	14 681	15 629
1964	111 534	10 616	6 137	4 481	100 916	10 568	18 838	21 375	19 360	14 957	15 816
1965	113 284	11 319	6 049	5 271	101 963	10 935	18 882	21 258	19 604	15 215	16 070
1966	114 566	11 862	5 993	5 870	102 702	11 094	18 989	21 005	19 822	15 469	16 322
1967	116 100	11 682	6 051	5 632	104 417	11 797	19 464	20 745	20 067	15 745	16 602
1968	117 948	11 840	6 225	5 616	106 107	12 184	20 245	20 474	20 310	16 018	16 875
1969	119 913	12 179	6 418	5 761	107 733	12 677	20 892	20 156	20 546	16 305	17 156
1970	122 174	12 521	6 591	5 931	109 652	13 359	21 546	19 929	20 760	16 591	17 469
1971	124 758	12 937	6 750	6 189	111 821	14 208	22 295	19 694	20 907	16 884	17 833
1972	127 906	13 301	6 910	6 392	114 603	14 897	23 555	19 673	20 950	17 250	18 278
1973	130 097	13 533	7 021	6 512	116 563	15 264	24 685	19 532	20 991	17 484	18 607
1974	132 417	13 784	7 114	6 671	118 632	15 502	25 711	19 628	21 061	17 645	19 085
1975	134 790	13 941	7 132	6 808	120 849	15 980	26 746	19 641	20 981	17 918	19 587
1976	137 106	14 055	7 125	6 930	123 050	16 368	27 757	19 827	20 816	18 220	20 064
1977	139 380	14 095	7 150	6 944	125 285	16 728	28 703	20 231	20 575	18 540	20 508
1978	141 612	14 060	7 132	6 928	127 552	17 038	29 453	20 932	20 322	18 799	21 007
1979	143 894	13 994	7 029	6 964	129 900	17 284	30 371	21 579	20 058	19 071	21 538
1980	146 122	13 854	6 912	6 943	132 268	17 484	31 407	22 174	19 837	19 316	22 050
1981	147 908	13 516	6 704	6 813	134 392	17 609	32 367	22 778	19 666	19 485	22 487
1982	149 441	13 076	6 383	6 693	136 366	17 579	32 863	23 910	19 478	19 591	22 945
1983	150 805	12 623	6 089	6 534	138 183	17 492	33 286	25 027	19 349	19 625	23 403
1984	152 347	12 147	5 918	6 228	140 200	17 304	33 889	26 124	19 348	19 629	23 906
1985	153 679	11 900	5 922	5 978	141 780	16 853	34 450	27 100	19 405	19 620	24 352
1986	155 432	11 879	6 036	5 843	143 553	16 353	35 293	28 062	19 587	19 477	24 780
1987	156 958	11 939	6 110	5 829	145 020	15 808	35 667	29 036	19 965	19 242	25 301
1988	158 194	11 838	5 893	5 945	146 357	15 276	35 876	29 818	20 652	18 996	25 739
1989	159 338	11 530	5 506	6 023	147 809	14 879	35 951	30 774	21 287	18 743	26 175
1990	160 625	11 630	5 464	6 166	148 996	15 538	35 661	31 739	21 535	18 204	26 319
1991	161 759	11 200	5 451	5 749	150 558	15 516	35 342	32 854	22 052	18 074	26 721
1992	162 972	11 004	5 478	5 526	151 968	15 354	34 885	33 305	23 364	17 951	27 108
1993	164 289	11 078	5 562	5 516	153 210	15 087	34 365	33 919	24 456	17 892	27 493
1994	165 555	11 264	5 710	5 554	154 291	14 708	33 865	34 582	25 435	17 924	27 776
1995	166 914	11 468	5 822	5 646	155 446	14 313	33 355	35 222	26 418	17 986	28 153
1996	168 317	11 822	6 026	5 796	156 495	13 907	32 852	35 810	27 403	18 136	28 387
1997	169 993	12 181	6 213	5 968	157 812	13 983	32 091	36 325	28 388	18 511	28 514
1998	171 478	12 439	6 264	6 176	159 039	14 138	31 286	36 610	29 132	19 231	28 642
1999	173 085	12 700	6 342	6 358	160 386	14 394	30 516	36 755	30 048	19 855	28 818
2000	174 428	12 707	6 312	6 395	161 721	14 721	29 951	36 688	31 091	20 324	28 947
2001	175 888	12 786	6 335	6 452	163 102	15 081	29 553	36 402	32 188	20 826	29 051

See *Note* at end of table.

Table 1-6. Civilian Noninstitutional Population by Race, Hispanic Origin, Sex, and Age, 1948–2001—Continued

(Thousands of persons.)

Year, race, Hispanic origin, and sex	16 years and over	16 to 19 years			20 years and over						
		Total	16 to 17 years	18 to 19 years	Total	20 to 24 years	25 to 34 years	35 to 44 years	45 to 54 years	55 to 64 years	65 years and over
BLACK											
1972	14 526	2 018	1 061	956	12 508	2 027	2 809	2 329	2 139	1 601	1 605
1973	14 917	2 095	1 095	1 000	12 823	2 132	2 957	2 333	2 156	1 616	1 628
1974	15 329	2 137	1 122	1 014	13 192	2 137	3 103	2 382	2 202	1 679	1 689
1975	15 751	2 191	1 146	1 046	13 560	2 228	3 258	2 395	2 211	1 717	1 755
1976	16 196	2 264	1 165	1 098	13 932	2 303	3 412	2 435	2 220	1 736	1 826
1977	16 605	2 273	1 175	1 097	14 332	2 400	3 566	2 493	2 225	1 765	1 883
1978	16 970	2 270	1 169	1 101	14 701	2 483	3 717	2 547	2 226	1 794	1 932
1979	17 397	2 276	1 167	1 109	15 121	2 556	3 899	2 615	2 240	1 831	1 980
1980	17 824	2 289	1 171	1 119	15 535	2 606	4 095	2 687	2 249	1 870	2 030
1981	18 219	2 288	1 161	1 127	15 931	2 642	4 290	2 758	2 260	1 913	2 069
1982	18 584	2 252	1 119	1 134	16 332	2 697	4 438	2 887	2 263	1 935	2 113
1983	18 925	2 225	1 092	1 133	16 700	2 734	4 607	2 999	2 260	1 964	2 135
1984	19 348	2 161	1 056	1 105	17 187	2 783	4 789	3 167	2 288	1 977	2 183
1985	19 664	2 160	1 083	1 077	17 504	2 649	4 873	3 290	2 372	2 060	2 259
1986	19 989	2 137	1 090	1 048	17 852	2 625	5 026	3 410	2 413	2 079	2 298
1987	20 352	2 163	1 123	1 040	18 189	2 578	5 139	3 563	2 460	2 097	2 352
1988	20 692	2 179	1 130	1 049	18 513	2 527	5 234	3 716	2 524	2 110	2 402
1989	21 021	2 176	1 116	1 060	18 846	2 479	5 308	3 900	2 587	2 118	2 454
1990	21 477	2 238	1 101	1 138	19 239	2 554	5 407	4 328	2 618	1 970	2 362
1991	21 799	2 187	1 085	1 102	19 612	2 585	5 419	4 538	2 682	1 985	2 403
1992	22 147	2 155	1 086	1 069	19 992	2 615	5 404	4 722	2 809	1 996	2 446
1993	22 521	2 181	1 113	1 069	20 339	2 600	5 409	4 886	2 941	2 016	2 487
1994	22 879	2 211	1 168	1 044	20 668	2 616	5 362	5 038	3 084	2 045	2 524
1995	23 246	2 284	1 198	1 086	20 962	2 554	5 337	5 178	3 244	2 079	2 571
1996	23 604	2 356	1 238	1 118	21 248	2 519	5 311	5 290	3 408	2 110	2 609
1997	24 003	2 412	1 255	1 158	21 591	2 515	5 279	5 410	3 571	2 164	2 653
1998	24 373	2 443	1 241	1 202	21 930	2 546	5 221	5 510	3 735	2 224	2 695
1999	24 855	2 479	1 250	1 229	22 376	2 615	5 197	5 609	3 919	2 295	2 741
2000	25 218	2 468	1 246	1 222	22 750	2 690	5 145	5 669	4 117	2 351	2 778
2001	25 559	2 479	1 251	1 228	23 080	2 747	5 097	5 683	4 332	2 423	2 798
HISPANIC											
1973	6 104	867	...	...	5 238	...	...	...	...	...	...
1974	6 564	926	...	...	5 645	...	...	...	...	...	...
1975	6 862	962	...	...	5 900	...	...	...	...	...	...
1976	6 910	953	494	480	6 075	1 053	1 775	1 261	936	570	479
1977	7 362	1 024	513	508	6 376	1 163	1 869	1 283	989	587	485
1978	7 912	1 076	561	515	6 836	1 265	2 004	1 378	1 033	627	529
1979	8 207	1 095	544	551	7 113	1 296	2 117	1 458	1 015	659	566
1980	9 598	1 281	638	643	8 317	1 564	2 508	1 575	1 190	782	698
1981	10 120	1 301	641	660	8 819	1 650	2 698	1 680	1 231	832	728
1982	10 580	1 307	639	668	9 273	1 724	2 871	1 779	1 264	880	755
1983	11 029	1 304	635	670	9 725	1 790	3 045	1 883	1 298	928	781
1984	11 478	1 300	633	667	10 178	1 839	3 224	1 996	1 336	973	810
1985	11 915	1 298	638	661	10 617	1 864	3 401	2 117	1 377	1 015	843
1986	12 344	1 302	658	644	11 042	1 899	3 510	2 239	1 496	1 023	875
1987	12 867	1 332	651	681	11 536	1 910	3 714	2 464	1 492	1 061	895
1988	13 325	1 354	662	692	11 970	1 948	3 807	2 565	1 571	1 159	920
1989	13 791	1 399	672	727	12 392	1 950	3 953	2 658	1 649	1 182	1 001
1990	15 904	1 737	821	915	14 167	2 428	4 589	3 001	1 817	1 247	1 084
1991	16 425	1 732	819	913	14 693	2 481	4 674	3 243	1 879	1 283	1 134
1992	16 961	1 737	836	901	15 224	2 444	4 806	3 458	1 980	1 321	1 216
1993	17 532	1 756	855	901	15 776	2 487	4 887	3 632	2 094	1 324	1 353
1994	18 117	1 818	902	916	16 300	2 518	5 000	3 756	2 223	1 401	1 401
1995	18 629	1 872	903	969	16 757	2 528	5 050	3 965	2 294	1 483	1 437
1996	19 213	1 948	962	986	17 265	2 524	5 181	4 227	2 275	1 546	1 512
1997	20 321	2 121	1 088	1 033	18 200	2 623	5 405	4 453	2 581	1 580	1 558
1998	21 070	2 204	1 070	1 135	18 865	2 731	5 447	4 636	2 775	1 615	1 662
1999	21 650	2 307	1 113	1 194	19 344	2 700	5 512	4 833	2 868	1 713	1 718
2000	22 393	2 341	1 120	1 221	20 052	2 775	5 627	5 007	3 033	1 819	1 791
2001	23 122	2 393	1 106	1 287	20 729	2 880	5 747	5 047	3 287	1 886	1 883

See *Note* at end of table.

Table 1-6. Civilian Noninstitutional Population by Race, Hispanic Origin, Sex, and Age, 1948–2001—*Continued*

(Thousands of persons.)

Year, race, Hispanic origin, and sex	16 years and over	16 to 19 years			20 years and over						
		Total	16 to 17 years	18 to 19 years	Total	20 to 24 years	25 to 34 years	35 to 44 years	45 to 54 years	55 to 64 years	65 years and over
MEN											
1948	49 996	4 078	2 128	1 951	45 918	5 527	10 767	9 798	8 290	6 441	5 093
1949	50 321	3 946	2 062	1 884	46 378	5 405	10 871	9 926	8 379	6 568	5 226
1950	50 725	3 962	2 043	1 920	46 763	5 270	10 963	10 034	8 472	6 664	5 357
1951	49 727	3 725	2 039	1 687	46 001	4 451	10 709	10 049	8 551	6 737	5 503
1952	49 700	3 767	2 121	1 647	45 932	3 788	10 855	10 164	8 655	6 798	5 670
1953	50 750	3 823	2 122	1 701	46 927	3 482	11 020	10 632	8 878	6 798	6 119
1954	51 395	3 953	2 174	1 780	47 441	3 509	11 067	10 718	9 018	6 885	6 241
1955	52 109	4 022	2 225	1 798	48 086	3 708	11 068	10 804	9 164	6 960	6 380
1956	52 723	4 020	2 238	1 783	48 704	3 970	10 983	10 889	9 322	7 032	6 505
1957	53 315	4 083	2 284	1 800	49 231	4 166	10 889	10 965	9 499	7 109	6 602
1958	54 033	4 293	2 435	1 858	49 740	4 339	10 787	11 076	9 675	7 179	6 683
1959	54 793	4 652	2 681	1 971	50 140	4 488	10 625	11 149	9 832	7 259	6 785
1960	55 662	4 963	2 805	2 159	50 698	4 679	10 514	11 230	10 000	7 373	6 901
1961	56 286	5 112	2 742	2 371	51 173	4 844	10 440	11 286	10 112	7 483	7 006
1962	56 831	5 150	2 764	2 386	51 681	4 925	10 207	11 389	10 162	7 610	7 386
1963	57 921	5 496	3 162	2 334	52 425	5 240	10 165	11 476	10 274	7 740	7 526
1964	58 847	5 866	3 503	2 364	52 981	5 520	10 144	11 466	10 402	7 873	7 574
1965	59 782	6 318	3 488	2 831	53 463	5 701	10 182	11 427	10 512	7 990	7 649
1966	60 262	6 658	3 478	3 180	53 603	5 663	10 224	11 294	10 598	8 099	7 723
1967	60 905	6 537	3 528	3 010	54 367	5 977	10 495	11 161	10 705	8 218	7 809
1968	61 847	6 683	3 634	3 049	55 165	6 127	10 944	11 040	10 819	8 336	7 897
1969	62 898	6 928	3 741	3 187	55 969	6 379	11 309	10 890	10 935	8 464	7 990
1970	64 304	7 145	3 848	3 299	57 157	6 861	11 750	10 810	11 052	8 590	8 093
1971	65 942	7 430	3 954	3 477	58 511	7 511	12 227	10 721	11 129	8 711	8 208
1972	67 835	7 705	4 081	3 624	60 130	8 061	12 911	10 762	11 167	8 895	8 330
1973	69 292	7 855	4 152	3 703	61 436	8 429	13 641	10 746	11 202	8 990	8 426
1974	70 808	8 012	4 231	3 781	62 796	8 600	14 262	10 834	11 315	9 140	8 641
1975	72 291	8 134	4 252	3 882	64 158	8 950	14 899	10 874	11 298	9 286	8 852
1976	73 759	8 244	4 266	3 978	65 515	9 237	15 528	11 010	11 243	9 444	9 053
1977	75 193	8 288	4 290	4 000	66 904	9 477	16 108	11 260	11 144	9 616	9 297
1978	76 576	8 309	4 295	4 014	68 268	9 693	16 598	11 665	11 045	9 758	9 509
1979	78 020	8 310	4 251	4 060	69 709	9 873	17 193	12 046	10 944	9 907	9 746
1980	79 398	8 260	4 195	4 064	71 138	10 023	17 833	12 400	10 861	10 042	9 979
1981	80 511	8 092	4 087	4 005	72 419	10 116	18 427	12 758	10 797	10 151	10 170
1982	81 523	7 879	3 911	3 968	73 644	10 136	18 787	13 410	10 726	10 215	10 371
1983	82 531	7 659	3 750	3 908	74 872	10 140	19 143	14 067	10 689	10 261	10 573
1984	83 605	7 386	3 655	3 731	76 219	10 108	19 596	14 719	10 724	10 285	10 788
1985	84 469	7 275	3 689	3 586	77 195	9 746	19 864	15 265	10 844	10 392	11 084
1986	85 798	7 275	3 768	3 507	78 523	9 498	20 498	15 858	10 986	10 336	11 347
1987	86 899	7 335	3 824	3 510	79 565	9 195	20 781	16 475	11 215	10 267	11 632
1988	87 857	7 304	3 715	3 588	80 553	8 931	20 937	17 008	11 625	10 193	11 859
1989	88 762	7 143	3 524	3 619	81 619	8 743	21 080	17 590	11 981	10 092	12 134
1990	90 377	7 347	3 534	3 813	83 030	9 320	21 117	18 529	12 238	9 778	12 049
1991	91 278	7 134	3 548	3 586	84 144	9 367	20 977	19 213	12 554	9 780	12 254
1992	92 270	7 023	3 542	3 481	85 247	9 326	20 792	19 585	13 271	9 776	12 496
1993	93 332	7 076	3 595	3 481	86 256	9 216	20 569	20 037	13 944	9 773	12 717
1994	94 355	7 203	3 718	3 486	87 151	9 074	20 361	20 443	14 545	9 810	12 918
1995	95 178	7 367	3 794	3 573	87 811	8 835	20 079	20 800	15 111	9 856	13 130
1996	96 206	7 600	3 955	3 645	88 606	8 611	19 775	21 222	15 674	9 997	13 327
1997	97 715	7 836	4 053	3 783	89 879	8 706	19 478	21 669	16 276	10 282	13 469
1998	98 758	7 968	4 059	3 909	90 790	8 804	19 094	21 857	16 773	10 649	13 613
1999	99 722	8 167	4 143	4 024	91 555	8 899	18 565	21 969	17 335	11 008	13 779
2000	100 731	8 151	4 108	4 043	92 580	9 154	18 289	21 951	18 004	11 257	13 925
2001	101 858	8 199	4 125	4 074	93 659	9 366	18 147	21 864	18 718	11 544	14 022

See *Note* at end of table.

Table 1-6. Civilian Noninstitutional Population by Race, Hispanic Origin, Sex, and Age, 1948–2001—Continued

(Thousands of persons.)

Year, race, Hispanic origin, and sex	16 years and over	16 to 19 years			20 years and over						
		Total	16 to 17 years	18 to 19 years	Total	20 to 24 years	25 to 34 years	35 to 44 years	45 to 54 years	55 to 64 years	65 years and over
WOMEN											
1948	53 071	4 371	2 137	2 234	48 700	6 003	11 843	10 299	8 481	6 444	5 627
1949	53 670	4 269	2 077	2 195	49 400	5 907	11 951	10 475	8 623	6 633	5 809
1950	54 270	4 181	2 033	2 148	50 088	5 810	12 050	10 647	8 768	6 805	6 006
1951	54 895	4 140	2 057	2 084	50 754	5 716	12 134	10 814	8 913	6 955	6 221
1952	55 529	4 155	2 113	2 042	51 373	5 601	12 189	10 973	9 061	7 091	6 456
1953	56 305	4 191	2 119	2 072	52 114	5 478	12 246	11 290	9 113	7 032	6 956
1954	56 925	4 271	2 162	2 109	52 654	5 376	12 237	11 417	9 287	7 200	7 134
1955	57 574	4 342	2 215	2 127	53 232	5 328	12 181	11 544	9 479	7 349	7 348
1956	58 228	4 414	2 244	2 170	53 814	5 301	12 089	11 678	9 690	7 484	7 570
1957	58 951	4 529	2 303	2 226	54 421	5 320	11 960	11 821	9 925	7 618	7 774
1958	59 690	4 693	2 437	2 256	54 997	5 394	11 776	11 949	10 157	7 744	7 974
1959	60 534	4 966	2 656	2 311	55 570	5 487	11 576	12 058	10 371	7 875	8 200
1960	61 582	5 224	2 768	2 456	56 358	5 594	11 484	12 207	10 601	8 036	8 435
1961	62 484	5 401	2 720	2 681	57 082	5 739	11 389	12 299	10 781	8 192	8 679
1962	63 321	5 502	2 739	2 764	57 819	5 927	11 296	12 408	10 754	8 264	9 168
1963	64 494	5 874	3 139	2 736	58 620	6 224	11 235	12 472	10 870	8 398	9 419
1964	65 637	6 245	3 471	2 775	59 391	6 497	11 223	12 474	11 050	8 569	9 576
1965	66 731	6 612	3 448	3 164	60 119	6 741	11 235	12 405	11 216	8 737	9 783
1966	67 795	6 934	3 436	3 499	60 860	6 975	11 319	12 285	11 379	8 908	9 992
1967	68 968	6 943	3 475	3 470	62 026	7 445	11 562	12 152	11 551	9 092	10 220
1968	70 179	7 015	3 566	3 450	63 164	7 764	11 968	11 996	11 715	9 278	10 441
1969	71 436	7 167	3 681	3 486	64 269	8 109	12 336	11 819	11 871	9 466	10 667
1970	72 782	7 373	3 796	3 578	65 408	8 462	12 684	11 679	12 008	9 659	10 914
1971	74 274	7 591	3 895	3 697	66 682	8 834	13 110	11 553	12 115	9 870	11 198
1972	76 290	7 805	3 994	3 811	68 484	9 082	13 829	11 597	12 171	10 113	11 693
1973	77 804	7 985	4 076	3 909	69 819	9 263	14 531	11 541	12 229	10 290	11 963
1974	79 312	8 168	4 142	4 028	71 144	9 393	15 177	11 627	12 263	10 377	12 304
1975	80 860	8 285	4 168	4 117	72 576	9 645	15 811	11 652	12 237	10 558	12 673
1976	82 390	8 370	4 176	4 194	74 020	9 872	16 425	11 786	12 166	10 742	13 030
1977	83 840	8 400	4 193	4 206	75 441	10 103	17 008	12 036	12 053	10 940	13 300
1978	85 334	8 386	4 189	4 197	76 948	10 315	17 493	12 435	11 932	11 118	13 658
1979	86 843	8 347	4 139	4 208	78 496	10 480	18 070	12 815	11 808	11 303	14 021
1980	88 348	8 283	4 083	4 200	80 065	10 612	18 725	13 177	11 701	11 478	14 372
1981	89 618	8 121	3 981	4 140	81 497	10 705	19 350	13 533	11 625	11 605	14 680
1982	90 748	7 884	3 804	4 081	82 864	10 709	19 705	14 201	11 538	11 694	15 017
1983	91 684	7 616	3 635	3 981	84 069	10 660	20 004	14 865	11 478	11 742	15 319
1984	92 778	7 349	3 542	3 807	85 429	10 580	20 403	15 532	11 501	11 768	15 645
1985	93 736	7 231	3 543	3 688	86 506	10 351	20 805	16 114	11 574	11 748	15 913
1986	94 789	7 221	3 618	3 603	87 567	10 072	21 233	16 692	11 746	11 675	16 150
1987	95 853	7 271	3 677	3 594	88 583	9 776	21 516	17 279	11 968	11 567	16 476
1988	96 756	7 224	3 569	3 655	89 532	9 503	21 674	17 776	12 378	11 448	16 753
1989	97 630	7 080	3 361	3 719	90 550	9 282	21 765	18 387	12 763	11 314	17 039
1990	98 787	7 173	3 359	3 813	91 614	9 582	21 859	19 190	12 843	10 941	17 198
1991	99 646	6 939	3 353	3 586	92 708	9 597	21 711	19 903	13 155	10 895	17 446
1992	100 535	6 818	3 366	3 452	93 718	9 520	21 486	20 267	13 935	10 828	17 682
1993	101 506	6 859	3 415	3 444	94 647	9 426	21 202	20 696	14 605	10 801	17 917
1994	102 460	6 993	3 528	3 465	95 467	9 279	20 945	21 091	15 233	10 825	18 094
1995	103 406	7 144	3 613	3 531	96 262	9 029	20 719	21 454	15 862	10 879	18 318
1996	104 385	7 335	3 723	3 612	97 050	8 798	20 477	21 865	16 493	10 993	18 424
1997	105 418	7 528	3 808	3 721	97 889	8 736	20 081	22 214	17 115	11 224	18 520
1998	106 462	7 676	3 835	3 840	98 786	8 790	19 683	22 442	17 600	11 646	18 625
1999	108 031	7 873	3 917	3 955	100 158	9 069	19 411	22 666	18 251	12 056	18 705
2000	108 968	7 890	3 895	3 995	101 078	9 257	19 128	22 655	18 901	12 358	18 780
2001	110 007	7 947	3 919	4 027	102 060	9 514	18 908	22 527	19 624	12 660	18 828

See *Note* at end of table.

Table 1-6. Civilian Noninstitutional Population by Race, Hispanic Origin, Sex, and Age, 1948–2001—*Continued*

(Thousands of persons.)

Year, race, Hispanic origin, and sex	16 years and over	16 to 19 years			20 years and over						
		Total	16 to 17 years	18 to 19 years	Total	20 to 24 years	25 to 34 years	35 to 44 years	45 to 54 years	55 to 64 years	65 years and over
WHITE MEN											
1954	46 462	3 455	1 902	1 553	43 007	3 074	9 948	9 688	8 172	6 341	5 787
1955	47 076	3 507	1 945	1 563	43 569	3 241	9 936	9 768	8 303	6 398	5 923
1956	47 602	3 500	1 955	1 546	44 102	3 464	9 851	9 848	8 446	6 455	6 038
1957	48 119	3 556	2 000	1 557	44 563	3 638	9 758	9 917	8 605	6 518	6 127
1958	48 745	3 747	2 140	1 607	44 998	3 783	9 656	10 018	8 765	6 574	6 203
1959	49 408	4 079	2 370	1 710	45 329	3 903	9 499	10 081	8 909	6 639	6 298
1960	50 065	4 349	2 476	1 874	45 716	4 054	9 373	10 131	9 042	6 721	6 395
1961	50 608	4 479	2 407	2 073	46 129	4 204	9 290	10 178	9 148	6 819	6 490
1962	51 054	4 520	2 426	2 094	46 534	4 306	9 080	10 239	9 191	6 917	6 801
1963	52 031	4 827	2 792	2 036	47 204	4 610	9 039	10 309	9 297	7 031	6 919
1964	52 869	5 148	3 090	2 059	47 721	4 862	9 024	10 301	9 417	7 153	6 963
1965	53 681	5 541	3 050	2 492	48 140	5 017	9 056	10 262	9 516	7 261	7 028
1966	54 061	5 820	3 023	2 798	48 241	4 974	9 085	10 136	9 592	7 362	7 092
1967	54 608	5 671	3 058	2 613	48 937	5 257	9 339	10 013	9 688	7 474	7 167
1968	55 434	5 787	3 153	2 635	49 647	5 376	9 752	9 902	9 790	7 585	7 242
1969	56 348	6 005	3 246	2 759	50 343	5 589	10 074	9 760	9 895	7 705	7 320
1970	57 516	6 179	3 329	2 851	51 336	5 988	10 441	9 678	9 999	7 822	7 409
1971	58 900	6 420	3 412	3 008	52 481	6 546	10 841	9 578	10 066	7 933	7 517
1972	60 473	6 627	3 503	3 125	53 845	7 042	11 495	9 568	10 078	8 089	7 573
1973	61 577	6 737	3 555	3 182	54 842	7 312	12 075	9 514	10 099	8 178	7 664
1974	62 791	6 851	3 604	3 247	55 942	7 476	12 599	9 564	10 165	8 288	7 849
1975	63 981	6 929	3 609	3 320	57 052	7 766	13 131	9 578	10 134	8 413	8 031
1976	65 132	6 993	3 609	3 384	58 138	7 987	13 655	9 674	10 063	8 556	8 203
1977	66 301	7 024	3 625	3 399	59 278	8 175	14 139	9 880	9 957	8 708	8 420
1978	67 401	7 022	3 619	3 404	60 378	8 335	14 528	10 236	9 845	8 826	8 608
1979	68 547	7 007	3 568	3 439	61 540	8 470	15 008	10 563	9 730	8 949	8 820
1980	69 634	6 941	3 508	3 433	62 694	8 581	15 529	10 863	9 636	9 059	9 027
1981	70 480	6 764	3 401	3 363	63 715	8 644	16 005	11 171	9 560	9 139	9 195
1982	71 211	6 556	3 249	3 307	64 655	8 621	16 260	11 756	9 463	9 188	9 367
1983	71 922	6 340	3 098	3 242	65 581	8 597	16 499	12 314	9 408	9 208	9 556
1984	72 723	6 113	3 019	3 094	66 610	8 522	16 816	12 853	9 434	9 217	9 768
1985	73 373	5 987	3 026	2 961	67 386	8 246	17 042	13 337	9 488	9 262	10 010
1986	74 390	5 977	3 084	2 894	68 413	8 002	17 564	13 840	9 578	9 201	10 229
1987	75 189	6 015	3 125	2 890	69 175	7 729	17 754	14 338	9 771	9 101	10 481
1988	75 855	5 968	3 015	2 953	69 887	7 473	17 867	14 743	10 114	9 001	10 688
1989	76 468	5 813	2 817	2 996	70 654	7 279	17 908	15 237	10 434	8 900	10 897
1990	77 369	5 913	2 809	3 103	71 457	7 764	17 766	15 770	10 598	8 680	10 879
1991	77 977	5 704	2 805	2 899	72 274	7 748	17 615	16 340	10 856	8 640	11 074
1992	78 651	5 611	2 819	2 792	73 040	7 676	17 403	16 579	11 513	8 602	11 268
1993	79 371	5 650	2 862	2 788	73 721	7 545	17 158	16 900	12 058	8 590	11 470
1994	80 059	5 748	2 938	2 810	74 311	7 357	16 915	17 247	12 545	8 618	11 629
1995	80 733	5 854	2 995	2 859	74 879	7 163	16 653	17 567	13 028	8 653	11 815
1996	81 489	6 035	3 099	2 936	75 454	6 971	16 395	17 868	13 518	8 734	11 968
1997	82 577	6 257	3 209	3 048	76 320	7 087	16 043	18 163	14 030	8 929	12 067
1998	83 352	6 386	3 233	3 153	76 966	7 170	15 644	18 310	14 400	9 286	12 155
1999	83 930	6 498	3 266	3 232	77 432	7 244	15 150	18 340	14 834	9 581	12 283
2000	84 647	6 496	3 250	3 246	78 151	7 420	14 870	18 304	15 356	9 811	12 390
2001	85 421	6 533	3 260	3 273	78 888	7 595	14 679	18 171	15 906	10 060	12 476

See *Note* at end of table.

Table 1-6. Civilian Noninstitutional Population by Race, Hispanic Origin, Sex, and Age, 1948–2001—*Continued*

(Thousands of persons.)

Year, race, Hispanic origin, and sex	16 years and over	16 to 19 years			20 years and over						
		Total	16 to 17 years	18 to 19 years	Total	20 to 24 years	25 to 34 years	35 to 44 years	45 to 54 years	55 to 64 years	65 years and over
WHITE WOMEN											
1954	51 242	3 725	1 884	1 841	47 517	4 720	10 870	10 227	8 397	6 652	6 651
1955	51 802	3 785	1 929	1 856	48 017	4 671	10 806	10 342	8 566	6 771	6 862
1956	52 373	3 846	1 953	1 892	48 527	4 642	10 713	10 466	8 752	6 886	7 067
1957	52 998	3 949	2 007	1 941	49 049	4 655	10 584	10 597	8 957	7 000	7 256
1958	53 645	4 096	2 131	1 966	49 549	4 715	10 407	10 716	9 159	7 107	7 442
1959	54 392	4 351	2 337	2 015	50 041	4 794	10 216	10 812	9 348	7 219	7 653
1960	55 214	4 575	2 433	2 142	50 639	4 873	10 097	10 918	9 536	7 349	7 865
1961	55 993	4 732	2 378	2 354	51 261	4 999	9 999	10 991	9 697	7 485	8 091
1962	56 660	4 823	2 392	2 432	51 837	5 178	9 894	11 054	9 681	7 533	8 496
1963	57 672	5 151	2 757	2 394	52 521	5 459	9 828	11 089	9 785	7 650	8 710
1964	58 663	5 468	3 047	2 422	53 195	5 706	9 814	11 074	9 943	7 804	8 853
1965	59 601	5 778	2 999	2 779	53 823	5 918	9 826	10 996	10 088	7 954	9 042
1966	60 503	6 042	2 970	3 072	54 461	6 120	9 904	10 869	10 230	8 107	9 230
1967	61 491	6 011	2 993	3 019	55 480	6 540	10 125	10 732	10 379	8 271	9 435
1968	62 512	6 053	3 072	2 981	56 460	6 809	10 493	10 572	10 520	8 433	9 633
1969	63 563	6 174	3 172	3 002	57 390	7 089	10 818	10 396	10 651	8 600	9 836
1970	64 656	6 342	3 262	3 080	58 315	7 370	11 105	10 251	10 761	8 769	10 060
1971	65 857	6 518	3 338	3 180	59 340	7 662	11 454	10 117	10 841	8 951	10 315
1972	67 431	6 673	3 407	3 267	60 758	7 855	12 000	10 105	10 872	9 161	10 705
1973	68 517	6 796	3 466	3 331	61 721	7 951	12 610	10 018	10 891	9 306	10 943
1974	69 623	6 933	3 510	3 424	62 690	8 026	13 112	10 064	10 896	9 356	11 236
1975	70 810	7 011	3 523	3 488	63 798	8 214	13 615	10 063	10 847	9 505	11 556
1976	71 974	7 062	3 516	3 546	64 912	8 381	14 102	10 153	10 752	9 664	11 860
1977	73 077	7 071	3 525	3 545	66 007	8 553	14 564	10 351	10 618	9 832	12 088
1978	74 213	7 038	3 513	3 524	67 174	8 704	14 926	10 696	10 476	9 974	12 399
1979	75 347	6 987	3 460	3 527	68 360	8 815	15 363	11 017	10 327	10 122	12 717
1980	76 489	6 914	3 403	3 511	69 575	8 904	15 878	11 313	10 201	10 256	13 022
1981	77 428	6 752	3 303	3 449	70 677	8 965	16 362	11 606	10 106	10 346	13 292
1982	78 230	6 519	3 134	3 385	71 711	8 959	16 603	12 154	10 015	10 402	13 579
1983	78 884	6 282	2 991	3 292	72 601	8 895	16 788	12 714	9 941	10 418	13 847
1984	79 624	6 034	2 899	3 135	73 590	8 782	17 073	13 271	9 914	10 412	14 138
1985	80 306	5 912	2 895	3 017	74 394	8 607	17 409	13 762	9 917	10 358	14 342
1986	81 042	5 902	2 953	2 949	75 140	8 351	17 728	14 223	10 009	10 277	14 551
1987	81 769	5 924	2 985	2 939	75 845	8 079	17 913	14 698	10 194	10 141	14 820
1988	82 340	5 869	2 878	2 991	76 470	7 804	18 009	15 074	10 537	9 994	15 052
1989	82 871	5 716	2 690	3 027	77 154	7 600	18 043	15 537	10 853	9 843	15 278
1990	83 256	5 717	2 654	3 063	77 539	7 774	17 895	15 969	10 937	9 524	15 440
1991	83 781	5 497	2 646	2 850	78 285	7 768	17 726	16 514	11 196	9 435	15 647
1992	84 321	5 393	2 659	2 734	78 928	7 678	17 482	16 727	11 851	9 350	15 841
1993	84 918	5 428	2 700	2 728	79 490	7 542	17 206	17 019	12 398	9 302	16 023
1994	85 496	5 516	2 772	2 744	79 980	7 351	16 950	17 335	12 890	9 306	16 148
1995	86 181	5 614	2 827	2 787	80 567	7 150	16 702	17 654	13 390	9 333	16 337
1996	86 828	5 787	2 927	2 860	81 041	6 936	16 457	17 943	13 884	9 402	16 419
1997	87 417	5 924	3 004	2 920	81 492	6 896	16 047	18 162	14 357	9 582	16 447
1998	88 126	6 053	3 031	3 023	82 073	6 969	15 642	18 300	14 732	9 944	16 486
1999	89 156	6 202	3 076	3 127	82 953	7 150	15 366	18 415	15 214	10 274	16 536
2000	89 781	6 211	3 062	3 149	83 570	7 300	15 081	18 384	15 736	10 513	16 557
2001	90 467	6 253	3 074	3 178	84 214	7 486	14 874	18 231	16 281	10 766	16 575

See *Note* at end of table.

Table 1-6. Civilian Noninstitutional Population by Race, Hispanic Origin, Sex, and Age, 1948–2001—*Continued*

(Thousands of persons.)

Year, race, Hispanic origin, and sex	16 years and over	16 to 19 years			20 years and over						
		Total	16 to 17 years	18 to 19 years	Total	20 to 24 years	25 to 34 years	35 to 44 years	45 to 54 years	55 to 64 years	65 years and over
BLACK MEN											
1972	6 538	978	525	453	5 559	921	1 251	1 027	963	720	680
1973	6 704	1 007	539	468	5 697	979	1 326	1 027	962	718	684
1974	6 875	1 027	555	472	5 848	956	1 380	1 055	996	753	708
1975	7 060	1 051	565	486	6 009	1 002	1 452	1 061	998	769	730
1976	7 265	1 099	580	518	6 167	1 037	1 522	1 078	1 000	774	756
1977	7 431	1 102	585	516	6 329	1 080	1 588	1 103	997	786	775
1978	7 577	1 093	580	513	6 484	1 120	1 656	1 128	995	795	789
1979	7 761	1 100	581	520	6 661	1 151	1 739	1 160	998	809	804
1980	7 944	1 110	584	526	6 834	1 171	1 828	1 191	999	825	822
1981	8 117	1 110	577	534	7 007	1 189	1 914	1 224	1 003	844	835
1982	8 283	1 097	556	542	7 186	1 225	1 983	1 282	1 003	848	846
1983	8 447	1 087	542	545	7 360	1 254	2 068	1 333	1 000	857	847
1984	8 654	1 055	524	531	7 599	1 292	2 164	1 411	1 012	858	861
1985	8 790	1 059	543	517	7 731	1 202	2 180	1 462	1 060	924	902
1986	8 956	1 049	548	503	7 907	1 195	2 264	1 517	1 072	934	924
1987	9 128	1 065	566	499	8 063	1 173	2 320	1 587	1 092	944	947
1988	9 289	1 074	569	505	8 215	1 151	2 367	1 656	1 121	951	970
1989	9 439	1 075	575	501	8 364	1 128	2 403	1 741	1 146	956	990
1990	9 573	1 094	555	540	8 479	1 144	2 412	1 968	1 183	856	916
1991	9 725	1 072	546	526	8 652	1 168	2 416	2 060	1 211	864	933
1992	9 896	1 056	544	512	8 840	1 194	2 409	2 149	1 267	869	951
1993	10 083	1 075	559	517	9 008	1 181	2 426	2 227	1 330	874	969
1994	10 258	1 087	586	501	9 171	1 206	2 399	2 300	1 392	889	986
1995	10 411	1 131	601	530	9 280	1 162	2 389	2 362	1 462	901	1 006
1996	10 575	1 161	623	538	9 414	1 155	2 373	2 413	1 534	914	1 025
1997	10 763	1 188	635	554	9 575	1 153	2 363	2 471	1 607	936	1 045
1998	10 927	1 201	623	578	9 727	1 166	2 335	2 519	1 682	956	1 069
1999	11 143	1 218	628	589	9 926	1 197	2 321	2 566	1 765	986	1 091
2000	11 320	1 213	626	587	10 107	1 235	2 300	2 597	1 856	1 015	1 105
2001	11 468	1 218	627	591	10 250	1 258	2 275	2 604	1 955	1 045	1 114
BLACK WOMEN											
1972	7 988	1 040	536	503	6 948	1 106	1 558	1 302	1 176	881	925
1973	8 214	1 088	556	532	7 126	1 153	1 631	1 306	1 194	898	944
1974	8 454	1 110	567	542	7 344	1 181	1 723	1 327	1 206	926	981
1975	8 691	1 141	581	560	7 550	1 226	1 806	1 334	1 213	948	1 025
1976	8 931	1 165	585	580	7 765	1 266	1 890	1 357	1 220	962	1 070
1977	9 174	1 171	590	581	8 003	1 320	1 978	1 390	1 228	979	1 108
1978	9 394	1 177	589	588	8 217	1 363	2 061	1 419	1 231	999	1 143
1979	9 636	1 176	586	589	8 460	1 405	2 160	1 455	1 242	1 022	1 176
1980	9 880	1 180	587	593	8 700	1 435	2 267	1 496	1 250	1 045	1 208
1981	10 102	1 178	584	593	8 924	1 453	2 376	1 534	1 257	1 069	1 234
1982	10 300	1 155	563	592	9 146	1 472	2 455	1 605	1 260	1 087	1 267
1983	10 477	1 138	550	588	9 340	1 480	2 539	1 666	1 260	1 107	1 288
1984	10 694	1 106	532	574	9 588	1 491	2 625	1 756	1 276	1 119	1 322
1985	10 873	1 101	540	560	9 773	1 447	2 693	1 828	1 312	1 136	1 357
1986	11 033	1 088	542	545	9 945	1 430	2 762	1 893	1 341	1 145	1 374
1987	11 224	1 098	557	541	10 126	1 405	2 819	1 976	1 368	1 153	1 405
1988	11 402	1 105	561	544	10 298	1 376	2 867	2 060	1 403	1 159	1 432
1989	11 582	1 100	541	559	10 482	1 351	2 905	2 159	1 441	1 162	1 464
1990	11 904	1 144	546	598	10 760	1 410	2 995	2 360	1 435	1 114	1 446
1991	12 074	1 115	539	576	10 959	1 417	3 003	2 478	1 471	1 121	1 470
1992	12 251	1 099	542	557	11 152	1 421	2 995	2 573	1 542	1 127	1 495
1993	12 438	1 106	554	552	11 332	1 419	2 983	2 659	1 611	1 142	1 518
1994	12 621	1 125	582	543	11 496	1 410	2 963	2 738	1 692	1 156	1 538
1995	12 835	1 153	597	556	11 682	1 392	2 948	2 816	1 782	1 178	1 565
1996	13 029	1 195	615	580	11 833	1 364	2 938	2 877	1 874	1 196	1 584
1997	13 241	1 225	620	604	12 016	1 362	2 916	2 939	1 964	1 228	1 608
1998	13 446	1 243	618	624	12 203	1 380	2 886	2 991	2 053	1 268	1 626
1999	13 711	1 261	621	640	12 451	1 418	2 876	3 043	2 153	1 310	1 650
2000	13 898	1 255	620	634	12 643	1 455	2 844	3 072	2 262	1 336	1 673
2001	14 091	1 261	624	637	12 830	1 490	2 822	3 080	2 377	1 378	1 684

See *Note* at end of table.

Table 1-6. Civilian Noninstitutional Population by Race, Hispanic Origin, Sex, and Age, 1948–2001—*Continued*

(Thousands of persons.)

Year, race, Hispanic origin, and sex	16 years and over	16 to 19 years			20 years and over						
		Total	16 to 17 years	18 to 19 years	Total	20 to 24 years	25 to 34 years	35 to 44 years	45 to 54 years	55 to 64 years	65 years and over
HISPANIC MEN											
1973	2 891	...	...	...	2 472	...	...	...	...	...	...
1974	3 130	...	...	...	2 680	...	...	...	...	...	...
1975	3 219	...	...	...	2 741	...	...	...	...	...	...
1976	3 241	485	251	234	2 764	494	824	579	444	260	211
1977	3 483	495	247	248	2 982	561	884	601	465	271	216
1978	3 750	525	287	238	3 228	621	934	655	484	293	240
1979	3 917	555	285	271	3 362	623	1 001	690	495	299	253
1980	4 689	653	326	327	4 036	792	1 245	760	570	367	301
1981	4 968	663	327	336	4 306	842	1 354	816	591	392	312
1982	5 203	664	324	340	4 539	882	1 450	865	607	414	321
1983	5 432	661	321	340	4 771	918	1 548	916	623	436	330
1984	5 661	656	319	337	5 005	944	1 649	973	641	457	341
1985	5 885	654	322	332	5 232	956	1 750	1 036	660	476	354
1986	6 106	655	330	325	5 451	1 006	1 787	1 088	735	466	368
1987	6 371	671	336	335	5 700	985	1 925	1 205	741	463	383
1988	6 604	683	319	364	5 921	1 003	1 963	1 268	775	516	397
1989	6 825	711	343	368	6 114	1 005	2 017	1 311	810	538	434
1990	8 041	915	431	484	7 126	1 319	2 369	1 512	890	573	463
1991	8 296	904	425	479	7 392	1 358	2 441	1 632	890	594	477
1992	8 553	899	436	463	7 655	1 306	2 547	1 728	972	603	499
1993	8 824	894	437	457	7 930	1 306	2 602	1 812	1 032	600	579
1994	9 104	926	472	454	8 178	1 346	2 627	1 871	1 076	644	614
1995	9 329	954	481	473	8 375	1 337	2 657	1 966	1 127	668	619
1996	9 604	992	485	507	8 611	1 321	2 692	2 144	1 111	712	630
1997	10 368	1 119	585	534	9 250	1 439	2 872	2 275	1 266	747	651
1998	10 734	1 161	586	575	9 573	1 462	2 907	2 377	1 342	771	714
1999	10 713	1 190	571	619	9 523	1 398	2 805	2 407	1 397	767	749
2000	11 064	1 205	575	631	9 859	1 457	2 820	2 506	1 491	826	759
2001	11 400	1 230	574	656	10 170	1 468	2 870	2 573	1 603	869	787
HISPANIC WOMEN											
1973	3 213	...	...	...	2 766	...	...	...	...	...	...
1974	3 434	...	...	...	2 959	...	...	...	...	...	...
1975	3 644	...	...	...	3 161	...	...	...	...	...	...
1976	3 669	490	244	246	3 263	559	952	682	493	310	268
1977	3 879	526	266	259	3 377	602	984	682	524	317	269
1978	4 159	551	274	277	3 608	642	1 069	723	548	335	289
1979	4 291	540	259	281	3 751	674	1 117	767	520	361	313
1980	4 909	628	312	316	4 281	771	1 263	815	619	415	398
1981	5 151	638	314	324	4 513	808	1 344	864	640	441	417
1982	5 377	643	314	329	4 734	842	1 421	914	657	466	434
1983	5 597	644	313	330	4 954	872	1 497	967	675	492	451
1984	5 816	644	313	330	5 173	895	1 575	1 022	695	516	469
1985	6 029	644	316	328	5 385	908	1 652	1 081	716	539	489
1986	6 238	647	328	319	5 591	893	1 723	1 151	760	557	507
1987	6 496	661	316	345	5 835	925	1 789	1 259	751	598	513
1988	6 721	671	343	328	6 050	945	1 844	1 297	796	643	524
1989	6 965	687	329	359	6 278	945	1 936	1 347	839	644	567
1990	7 863	822	391	431	7 041	1 109	2 220	1 489	927	675	621
1991	8 130	828	394	435	7 301	1 122	2 233	1 611	989	689	657
1992	8 408	839	400	439	7 569	1 138	2 259	1 729	1 008	718	716
1993	8 708	862	418	444	7 846	1 182	2 285	1 820	1 062	724	774
1994	9 014	892	430	462	8 122	1 173	2 373	1 885	1 147	757	787
1995	9 300	918	422	496	8 382	1 191	2 393	1 999	1 167	815	818
1996	9 610	956	477	479	8 654	1 203	2 489	2 082	1 164	834	882
1997	9 953	1 003	503	500	8 950	1 184	2 533	2 178	1 315	833	907
1998	10 335	1 044	483	560	9 292	1 269	2 539	2 259	1 433	844	948
1999	10 937	1 116	542	575	9 821	1 302	2 707	2 425	1 470	947	969
2000	11 329	1 136	545	590	10 193	1 319	2 806	2 501	1 542	993	1 032
2001	11 722	1 163	532	631	10 559	1 411	2 876	2 475	1 685	1 017	1 096

Note: Detail for the above race and Hispanic-origin groups will not sum to totals because data for the Other races group are not presented and Hispanics are included in both the White and Black population groups. See "Notes and Definitions" for information on historical comparability.

Table 1-7. Civilian Labor Force by Race, Hispanic Origin, Sex, and Age, 1948–2001

(Thousands of persons.)

Year, race, Hispanic origin, and sex	16 years and over	16 to 19 years			20 years and over						
		Total	16 to 17 years	18 to 19 years	Total	20 to 24 years	25 to 34 years	35 to 44 years	45 to 54 years	55 to 64 years	65 years and over
TOTAL											
1948	60 621	4 435	1 780	2 654	56 187	7 392	14 258	13 397	10 914	7 329	2 897
1949	61 286	4 288	1 704	2 583	57 000	7 340	14 415	13 711	11 107	7 426	3 010
1950	62 208	4 216	1 659	2 557	57 994	7 307	14 619	13 954	11 444	7 633	3 036
1951	62 017	4 103	1 743	2 360	57 914	6 594	14 668	14 100	11 739	7 796	3 020
1952	62 138	4 064	1 806	2 257	58 075	5 840	14 904	14 383	11 961	7 980	3 005
1953	63 015	4 027	1 727	2 299	58 989	5 481	14 898	15 099	12 249	8 024	3 236
1954	63 643	3 976	1 643	2 300	59 666	5 475	14 983	15 221	12 524	8 269	3 192
1955	65 023	4 092	1 711	2 382	60 931	5 666	15 058	15 400	12 992	8 513	3 305
1956	66 552	4 296	1 878	2 418	62 257	5 940	14 961	15 694	13 407	8 830	3 423
1957	66 929	4 275	1 843	2 433	62 653	6 071	14 826	15 847	13 768	8 853	3 290
1958	67 639	4 260	1 818	2 442	63 377	6 272	14 668	16 028	14 179	9 031	3 199
1959	68 369	4 492	1 971	2 522	63 876	6 413	14 435	16 127	14 518	9 227	3 158
1960	69 628	4 841	2 095	2 747	64 788	6 702	14 382	16 269	14 852	9 385	3 195
1961	70 459	4 936	1 984	2 951	65 524	6 950	14 319	16 402	15 071	9 636	3 146
1962	70 614	4 916	1 919	2 997	65 699	7 082	14 023	16 589	15 096	9 757	3 154
1963	71 833	5 139	2 171	2 966	66 695	7 473	14 050	16 788	15 338	10 006	3 041
1964	73 091	5 388	2 449	2 940	67 702	7 963	14 056	16 771	15 637	10 182	3 090
1965	74 455	5 910	2 486	3 425	68 543	8 259	14 233	16 840	15 756	10 350	3 108
1966	75 770	6 558	2 664	3 893	69 219	8 410	14 458	16 738	15 984	10 575	3 053
1967	77 347	6 521	2 734	3 786	70 825	9 010	15 055	16 703	16 172	10 792	3 097
1968	78 737	6 619	2 817	3 803	72 118	9 305	15 708	16 591	16 397	10 964	3 153
1969	80 734	6 970	3 009	3 959	73 763	9 879	16 336	16 458	16 730	11 135	3 227
1970	82 771	7 249	3 135	4 115	75 521	10 597	17 036	16 437	16 949	11 283	3 222
1971	84 382	7 470	3 192	4 278	76 913	11 331	17 714	16 305	17 024	11 390	3 149
1972	87 034	8 054	3 420	4 636	78 980	12 130	18 960	16 398	16 967	11 412	3 114
1973	89 429	8 507	3 665	4 839	80 924	12 846	20 376	16 492	16 983	11 256	2 974
1974	91 949	8 871	3 810	5 059	83 080	13 314	21 654	16 763	17 131	11 284	2 934
1975	93 775	8 870	3 740	5 131	84 904	13 750	22 864	16 903	17 084	11 346	2 956
1976	96 158	9 056	3 767	5 288	87 103	14 284	24 203	17 317	16 982	11 422	2 895
1977	99 009	9 351	3 919	5 431	89 658	14 825	25 500	17 943	16 878	11 577	2 934
1978	102 251	9 652	4 127	5 526	92 598	15 370	26 703	18 821	16 891	11 744	3 070
1979	104 962	9 638	4 079	5 559	95 325	15 769	27 938	19 685	16 897	11 931	3 104
1980	106 940	9 378	3 883	5 496	97 561	15 922	29 227	20 463	16 910	11 985	3 054
1981	108 670	8 988	3 647	5 340	99 682	16 099	30 392	21 211	16 970	11 969	3 042
1982	110 204	8 526	3 336	5 189	101 679	16 082	31 186	22 431	16 889	12 062	3 030
1983	111 550	8 171	3 073	5 098	103 379	16 052	31 834	23 611	16 851	11 992	3 040
1984	113 544	7 943	3 050	4 894	105 601	16 046	32 723	24 933	17 006	11 961	2 933
1985	115 461	7 901	3 154	4 747	107 560	15 718	33 550	26 073	17 322	11 991	2 907
1986	117 834	7 926	3 287	4 639	109 908	15 441	34 591	27 232	17 739	11 894	3 010
1987	119 865	7 988	3 384	4 604	111 878	14 977	35 233	28 460	18 210	11 877	3 119
1988	121 669	8 031	3 286	4 745	113 638	14 505	35 503	29 435	19 104	11 808	3 284
1989	123 869	7 954	3 125	4 828	115 916	14 180	35 896	30 601	19 916	11 877	3 446
1990	125 840	7 792	2 937	4 856	118 047	14 700	35 929	32 145	20 248	11 575	3 451
1991	126 346	7 265	2 789	4 476	119 082	14 548	35 507	33 312	20 828	11 473	3 413
1992	128 105	7 096	2 769	4 327	121 009	14 521	35 369	33 899	22 160	11 587	3 473
1993	129 200	7 170	2 831	4 338	122 030	14 354	34 780	34 562	23 296	11 599	3 439
1994	131 056	7 481	3 134	4 347	123 576	14 131	34 353	35 226	24 318	11 713	3 834
1995	132 304	7 765	3 225	4 540	124 539	13 688	34 198	35 751	25 223	11 860	3 819
1996	133 943	7 806	3 263	4 543	126 137	13 377	33 833	36 556	26 397	12 146	3 828
1997	136 297	7 932	3 237	4 695	128 365	13 532	33 380	37 326	27 574	12 665	3 887
1998	137 673	8 256	3 335	4 921	129 417	13 638	32 813	37 536	28 368	13 215	3 847
1999	139 368	8 333	3 337	4 996	131 033	13 933	32 143	37 882	29 388	13 682	4 005
2000	140 863	8 369	3 284	5 085	132 495	14 346	31 669	37 838	30 467	13 974	4 200
2001	141 815	8 077	3 105	4 972	133 738	14 565	31 144	37 585	31 563	14 579	4 303

See *Note* at end of table.

Table 1-7. Civilian Labor Force by Race, Hispanic Origin, Sex, and Age, 1948–2001—*Continued*

(Thousands of persons.)

Year, race, Hispanic origin, and sex	16 years and over	16 to 19 years			20 years and over						
		Total	16 to 17 years	18 to 19 years	Total	20 to 24 years	25 to 34 years	35 to 44 years	45 to 54 years	55 to 64 years	65 years and over
WHITE											
1954	56 816	3 501	1 448	2 054	53 315	4 752	13 226	13 540	11 258	7 591	2 946
1955	58 085	3 598	1 511	2 087	54 487	4 941	13 267	13 729	11 680	7 810	3 062
1956	59 428	3 771	1 656	2 113	55 657	5 194	13 154	14 000	12 061	8 080	3 166
1957	59 754	3 775	1 637	2 135	55 979	5 283	13 044	14 117	12 382	8 091	3 049
1958	60 293	3 757	1 615	2 144	56 536	5 449	12 884	14 257	12 727	8 254	2 964
1959	60 952	4 000	1 775	2 225	56 952	5 544	12 670	14 355	13 048	8 411	2 925
1960	61 915	4 275	1 871	2 405	57 640	5 787	12 594	14 450	13 322	8 522	2 964
1961	62 656	4 362	1 767	2 594	58 294	6 026	12 503	14 557	13 517	8 773	2 917
1962	62 750	4 354	1 709	2 645	58 396	6 164	12 218	14 695	13 551	8 856	2 912
1963	63 830	4 559	1 950	2 608	59 271	6 537	12 229	14 859	13 789	9 067	2 790
1964	64 921	4 784	2 211	2 572	60 137	6 952	12 235	14 852	14 043	9 239	2 817
1965	66 137	5 267	2 221	3 044	60 870	7 189	12 391	14 900	14 162	9 392	2 839
1966	67 276	5 827	2 367	3 460	61 449	7 324	12 591	14 785	14 370	9 583	2 793
1967	68 699	5 749	2 432	3 318	62 950	7 886	13 123	14 765	14 545	9 817	2 821
1968	69 976	5 839	2 519	3 320	64 137	8 109	13 740	14 683	14 756	9 968	2 884
1969	71 778	6 168	2 698	3 470	65 611	8 614	14 289	14 564	15 057	10 132	2 954
1970	73 556	6 442	2 824	3 617	67 113	9 238	14 896	14 525	15 269	10 255	2 930
1971	74 963	6 681	2 894	3 787	68 282	9 889	15 445	14 374	15 343	10 351	2 880
1972	77 275	7 193	3 096	4 098	70 082	10 605	16 584	14 399	15 283	10 402	2 809
1973	79 151	7 579	3 320	4 260	71 572	11 182	17 764	14 440	15 256	10 240	2 687
1974	81 281	7 899	3 441	4 459	73 381	11 600	18 862	14 644	15 375	10 241	2 656
1975	82 831	7 899	3 375	4 525	74 932	12 019	19 897	14 753	15 308	10 287	2 668
1976	84 767	8 088	3 410	4 679	76 678	12 444	20 990	15 088	15 187	10 371	2 599
1977	87 141	8 352	3 562	4 790	78 789	12 892	22 099	15 604	15 053	10 495	2 647
1978	89 634	8 555	3 715	4 839	81 079	13 309	23 067	16 353	15 004	10 602	2 745
1979	91 923	8 548	3 668	4 881	83 375	13 632	24 101	17 123	14 965	10 767	2 787
1980	93 600	8 312	3 485	4 827	85 286	13 769	25 181	17 811	14 956	10 812	2 759
1981	95 052	7 962	3 274	4 688	87 089	13 926	26 208	18 445	14 993	10 764	2 753
1982	96 143	7 518	3 001	4 518	88 625	13 866	26 814	19 491	14 879	10 832	2 742
1983	97 021	7 186	2 765	4 421	89 835	13 816	27 237	20 488	14 798	10 732	2 766
1984	98 492	6 952	2 720	4 232	91 540	13 733	27 958	21 588	14 899	10 701	2 660
1985	99 926	6 841	2 777	4 065	93 085	13 469	28 640	22 591	15 101	10 679	2 605
1986	101 801	6 862	2 895	3 967	94 939	13 176	29 497	23 571	15 379	10 583	2 732
1987	103 290	6 893	2 963	3 931	96 396	12 764	29 956	24 581	15 792	10 497	2 806
1988	104 756	6 940	2 861	4 079	97 815	12 311	30 167	25 358	16 573	10 462	2 943
1989	106 355	6 809	2 685	4 124	99 546	11 940	30 388	26 312	17 278	10 533	3 094
1990	107 447	6 683	2 543	4 140	100 764	12 397	30 174	27 265	17 515	10 290	3 123
1991	107 743	6 245	2 432	3 813	101 498	12 248	29 794	28 213	18 028	10 129	3 086
1992	108 837	6 022	2 388	3 633	102 815	12 187	29 518	28 580	19 200	10 196	3 135
1993	109 700	6 105	2 458	3 647	103 595	11 987	29 027	29 056	20 181	10 215	3 129
1994	111 082	6 357	2 681	3 677	104 725	11 688	28 580	29 626	21 026	10 319	3 486
1995	111 950	6 545	2 749	3 796	105 404	11 266	28 325	30 112	21 804	10 432	3 466
1996	113 108	6 607	2 780	3 826	106 502	11 003	27 901	30 683	22 781	10 648	3 485
1997	114 693	6 720	2 779	3 941	107 973	11 127	27 362	31 171	23 709	11 086	3 517
1998	115 415	6 965	2 860	4 105	108 450	11 244	26 707	31 221	24 282	11 548	3 448
1999	116 509	7 048	2 849	4 199	109 462	11 436	25 978	31 391	25 102	11 960	3 595
2000	117 574	7 075	2 800	4 275	110 499	11 762	25 482	31 346	25 968	12 192	3 749
2001	118 144	6 835	2 650	4 185	111 309	11 942	24 978	31 031	26 822	12 718	3 818

See *Note* at end of table.

Table 1-7. Civilian Labor Force by Race, Hispanic Origin, Sex, and Age, 1948–2001—*Continued*

(Thousands of persons.)

Year, race, Hispanic origin, and sex	16 years and over	16 to 19 years			20 years and over						
		Total	16 to 17 years	18 to 19 years	Total	20 to 24 years	25 to 34 years	35 to 44 years	45 to 54 years	55 to 64 years	65 years and over
BLACK											
1972	8 707	788	293	496	7 919	1 393	2 107	1 735	1 496	909	281
1973	8 976	833	307	525	8 143	1 489	2 242	1 741	1 513	901	258
1974	9 167	851	317	534	8 317	1 492	2 358	1 777	1 517	917	253
1975	9 263	838	312	524	8 426	1 477	2 466	1 775	1 519	929	258
1976	9 561	837	304	532	8 724	1 544	2 646	1 824	1 518	925	268
1977	9 932	861	304	557	9 072	1 641	2 798	1 894	1 530	943	267
1978	10 432	930	341	589	9 501	1 739	2 961	1 975	1 560	978	289
1979	10 678	912	340	572	9 766	1 793	3 094	2 039	1 584	974	281
1980	10 865	891	326	565	9 975	1 802	3 259	2 081	1 596	978	257
1981	11 086	862	308	554	10 224	1 828	3 365	2 164	1 608	1 009	249
1982	11 331	824	268	556	10 507	1 849	3 492	2 303	1 610	1 012	243
1983	11 647	809	248	561	10 838	1 871	3 675	2 406	1 630	1 032	224
1984	12 033	827	268	558	11 206	1 926	3 800	2 565	1 671	1 020	224
1985	12 364	889	311	578	11 476	1 854	3 888	2 681	1 742	1 059	252
1986	12 654	883	322	562	11 770	1 881	4 028	2 793	1 793	1 051	224
1987	12 993	899	336	563	12 094	1 818	4 147	2 942	1 838	1 098	251
1988	13 205	889	344	545	12 316	1 782	4 226	3 069	1 894	1 069	276
1989	13 497	925	353	572	12 573	1 789	4 295	3 227	1 954	1 023	285
1990	13 740	866	306	560	12 874	1 758	4 307	3 566	2 003	977	262
1991	13 797	774	266	508	13 023	1 750	4 254	3 719	2 042	1 001	256
1992	14 162	816	285	532	13 346	1 763	4 309	3 843	2 142	1 029	259
1993	14 225	807	283	524	13 418	1 764	4 232	3 960	2 212	1 013	237
1994	14 502	852	351	501	13 650	1 800	4 199	4 068	2 308	1 007	267
1995	14 817	911	366	545	13 906	1 754	4 267	4 165	2 404	1 046	271
1996	15 134	923	366	556	14 211	1 738	4 305	4 287	2 553	1 073	255
1997	15 529	933	352	580	14 596	1 783	4 329	4 401	2 724	1 093	265
1998	15 982	1 017	370	646	14 966	1 797	4 332	4 531	2 863	1 163	278
1999	16 365	959	352	607	15 406	1 866	4 430	4 653	2 992	1 180	285
2000	16 603	967	366	602	15 635	1 932	4 328	4 665	3 161	1 227	322
2001	16 719	934	341	593	15 785	1 922	4 263	4 656	3 289	1 299	356
HISPANIC											
1973	3 673	407	...	...	...	...	...	...	...	...	...
1974	4 012	442	...	...	...	...	...	...	...	...	...
1975	4 171	444	...	...	...	...	...	...	...	...	...
1976	4 205	447	176	285	3 820	729	1 248	875	625	294	48
1977	4 536	493	184	305	4 059	813	1 325	916	656	293	55
1978	4 979	533	221	312	4 446	901	1 446	1 008	701	323	67
1979	5 219	551	207	343	4 668	960	1 532	1 062	704	339	72
1980	6 146	645	241	404	5 502	1 136	1 843	1 163	860	414	85
1981	6 492	603	215	388	5 888	1 231	2 015	1 239	886	430	87
1982	6 734	585	192	393	6 148	1 251	2 163	1 313	891	444	85
1983	7 033	590	189	401	6 442	1 282	2 267	1 380	931	495	86
1984	7 451	618	209	409	6 833	1 325	2 436	1 509	954	524	84
1985	7 698	579	199	379	7 119	1 358	2 571	1 595	985	527	82
1986	8 076	571	203	368	7 505	1 414	2 685	1 713	1 097	511	84
1987	8 541	610	206	404	7 931	1 425	2 890	1 904	1 086	545	81
1988	8 982	671	234	437	8 311	1 486	2 957	1 996	1 147	621	103
1989	9 323	680	224	456	8 643	1 483	3 118	2 092	1 205	625	120
1990	10 720	829	276	554	9 891	1 839	3 590	2 386	1 320	647	110
1991	10 920	781	249	532	10 139	1 835	3 596	2 539	1 376	681	111
1992	11 338	796	263	533	10 542	1 815	3 740	2 735	1 442	687	122
1993	11 610	771	246	525	10 839	1 811	3 800	2 865	1 534	684	145
1994	11 975	807	285	522	11 168	1 863	3 865	2 965	1 626	698	151
1995	12 267	850	291	559	11 417	1 818	3 943	3 113	1 671	720	152
1996	12 774	845	284	561	11 929	1 845	4 054	3 361	1 697	806	166
1997	13 796	911	315	596	12 884	2 004	4 298	3 601	1 945	850	186
1998	14 317	1 007	320	688	13 310	2 077	4 372	3 707	2 090	894	169
1999	14 665	1 049	333	717	13 615	2 052	4 330	3 929	2 178	927	199
2000	15 368	1 083	338	745	14 285	2 155	4 485	4 086	2 357	983	218
2001	15 751	1 122	327	795	14 629	2 183	4 556	4 119	2 532	1 031	208

See *Note* at end of table.

Table 1-7. Civilian Labor Force by Race, Hispanic Origin, Sex, and Age, 1948–2001—*Continued*

(Thousands of persons.)

Year, race, Hispanic origin, and sex	16 years and over	16 to 19 years			20 years and over						
		Total	16 to 17 years	18 to 19 years	Total	20 to 24 years	25 to 34 years	35 to 44 years	45 to 54 years	55 to 64 years	65 years and over
MEN											
1948	43 286	2 600	1 109	1 490	40 687	4 673	10 327	9 596	7 943	5 764	2 384
1949	43 498	2 477	1 056	1 420	41 022	4 682	10 418	9 722	8 008	5 748	2 454
1950	43 819	2 504	1 048	1 456	41 316	4 632	10 527	9 793	8 117	5 794	2 453
1951	43 001	2 347	1 081	1 266	40 655	3 935	10 375	9 799	8 205	5 873	2 469
1952	42 869	2 312	1 101	1 210	40 558	3 338	10 585	9 945	8 326	5 949	2 416
1953	43 633	2 320	1 070	1 249	41 315	3 053	10 736	10 437	8 570	5 975	2 543
1954	43 965	2 295	1 023	1 272	41 669	3 051	10 771	10 513	8 702	6 105	2 526
1955	44 475	2 369	1 070	1 299	42 106	3 221	10 806	10 595	8 838	6 122	2 526
1956	45 091	2 433	1 142	1 291	42 658	3 485	10 685	10 663	9 002	6 220	2 602
1957	45 197	2 415	1 127	1 289	42 780	3 629	10 571	10 731	9 153	6 222	2 477
1958	45 521	2 428	1 133	1 295	43 092	3 771	10 475	10 843	9 320	6 304	2 378
1959	45 886	2 596	1 206	1 390	43 289	3 940	10 346	10 899	9 438	6 345	2 322
1960	46 388	2 787	1 290	1 496	43 603	4 123	10 251	10 967	9 574	6 399	2 287
1961	46 653	2 794	1 210	1 583	43 860	4 253	10 176	11 012	9 668	6 530	2 220
1962	46 600	2 770	1 178	1 592	43 831	4 279	9 920	11 115	9 715	6 560	2 241
1963	47 129	2 907	1 321	1 586	44 222	4 514	9 876	11 187	9 836	6 675	2 135
1964	47 679	3 074	1 499	1 575	44 604	4 754	9 876	11 156	9 956	6 741	2 124
1965	48 255	3 397	1 532	1 866	44 857	4 894	9 903	11 120	10 045	6 763	2 132
1966	48 471	3 685	1 609	2 075	44 788	4 820	9 948	10 983	10 100	6 847	2 089
1967	48 987	3 634	1 658	1 976	45 354	5 043	10 207	10 859	10 189	6 937	2 118
1968	49 533	3 681	1 687	1 995	45 852	5 070	10 610	10 725	10 267	7 025	2 154
1969	50 221	3 870	1 770	2 100	46 351	5 282	10 941	10 556	10 344	7 058	2 170
1970	51 228	4 008	1 810	2 199	47 220	5 717	11 327	10 469	10 417	7 126	2 165
1971	52 180	4 172	1 856	2 315	48 009	6 233	11 731	10 347	10 451	7 155	2 090
1972	53 555	4 476	1 955	2 522	49 079	6 766	12 350	10 372	10 412	7 155	2 026
1973	54 624	4 693	2 073	2 618	49 932	7 183	13 056	10 338	10 416	7 028	1 913
1974	55 739	4 861	2 138	2 721	50 879	7 387	13 665	10 401	10 431	7 063	1 932
1975	56 299	4 805	2 065	2 740	51 494	7 565	14 192	10 398	10 401	7 023	1 914
1976	57 174	4 886	2 069	2 817	52 288	7 866	14 784	10 500	10 293	7 020	1 826
1977	58 396	5 048	2 155	2 893	53 348	8 109	15 353	10 771	10 158	7 100	1 857
1978	59 620	5 149	2 227	2 923	54 471	8 327	15 814	11 159	10 083	7 151	1 936
1979	60 726	5 111	2 192	2 919	55 615	8 535	16 387	11 531	10 008	7 212	1 943
1980	61 453	4 999	2 102	2 897	56 455	8 607	16 971	11 836	9 905	7 242	1 893
1981	61 974	4 777	1 957	2 820	57 197	8 648	17 479	12 166	9 868	7 170	1 866
1982	62 450	4 470	1 776	2 694	57 980	8 604	17 793	12 781	9 784	7 174	1 845
1983	63 047	4 303	1 621	2 682	58 744	8 601	18 038	13 398	9 746	7 119	1 842
1984	63 835	4 134	1 591	2 542	59 701	8 594	18 488	14 037	9 776	7 050	1 755
1985	64 411	4 134	1 663	2 471	60 277	8 283	18 808	14 506	9 870	7 060	1 750
1986	65 422	4 102	1 707	2 395	61 320	8 148	19 383	15 029	9 994	6 954	1 811
1987	66 207	4 112	1 745	2 367	62 095	7 837	19 656	15 587	10 176	6 940	1 899
1988	66 927	4 159	1 714	2 445	62 768	7 594	19 742	16 074	10 566	6 831	1 960
1989	67 840	4 136	1 630	2 505	63 704	7 458	19 905	16 622	10 919	6 783	2 017
1990	69 011	4 094	1 537	2 557	64 916	7 866	19 872	17 481	11 103	6 627	1 967
1991	69 168	3 795	1 452	2 343	65 374	7 820	19 641	18 077	11 362	6 550	1 924
1992	69 964	3 751	1 453	2 297	66 213	7 770	19 495	18 347	12 040	6 551	2 010
1993	70 404	3 762	1 497	2 265	66 642	7 671	19 214	18 713	12 562	6 502	1 980
1994	70 817	3 896	1 630	2 266	66 921	7 540	18 854	18 966	12 962	6 423	2 176
1995	71 360	4 036	1 668	2 368	67 324	7 338	18 670	19 189	13 421	6 504	2 201
1996	72 087	4 043	1 665	2 378	68 044	7 104	18 430	19 602	13 967	6 693	2 247
1997	73 261	4 095	1 676	2 419	69 166	7 184	18 110	20 058	14 564	6 952	2 298
1998	73 959	4 244	1 728	2 516	69 715	7 221	17 796	20 242	14 963	7 253	2 240
1999	74 512	4 318	1 732	2 587	70 195	7 291	17 318	20 382	15 394	7 477	2 333
2000	75 247	4 317	1 688	2 629	70 930	7 558	17 073	20 334	15 951	7 574	2 439
2001	75 743	4 153	1 581	2 572	71 590	7 629	16 817	20 222	16 574	7 866	2 482

See *Note* at end of table.

Table 1-7. Civilian Labor Force by Race, Hispanic Origin, Sex, and Age, 1948–2001—*Continued*

(Thousands of persons.)

Year, race, Hispanic origin, and sex	16 years and over	16 to 19 years			20 years and over						
		Total	16 to 17 years	18 to 19 years	Total	20 to 24 years	25 to 34 years	35 to 44 years	45 to 54 years	55 to 64 years	65 years and over
WOMEN											
1948	17 335	1 835	671	1 164	15 500	2 719	3 931	3 801	2 971	1 565	513
1949	17 788	1 811	648	1 163	15 978	2 658	3 997	3 989	3 099	1 678	556
1950	18 389	1 712	611	1 101	16 678	2 675	4 092	4 161	3 327	1 839	583
1951	19 016	1 756	662	1 094	17 259	2 659	4 293	4 301	3 534	1 923	551
1952	19 269	1 752	705	1 047	17 517	2 502	4 319	4 438	3 635	2 031	589
1953	19 382	1 707	657	1 050	17 674	2 428	4 162	4 662	3 679	2 049	693
1954	19 678	1 681	620	1 028	17 997	2 424	4 212	4 708	3 822	2 164	666
1955	20 548	1 723	641	1 083	18 825	2 445	4 252	4 805	4 154	2 391	779
1956	21 461	1 863	736	1 127	19 599	2 455	4 276	5 031	4 405	2 610	821
1957	21 732	1 860	716	1 144	19 873	2 442	4 255	5 116	4 615	2 631	813
1958	22 118	1 832	685	1 147	20 285	2 501	4 193	5 185	4 859	2 727	821
1959	22 483	1 896	765	1 132	20 587	2 473	4 089	5 228	5 080	2 882	836
1960	23 240	2 054	805	1 251	21 185	2 579	4 131	5 302	5 278	2 986	908
1961	23 806	2 142	774	1 368	21 664	2 697	4 143	5 390	5 403	3 106	926
1962	24 014	2 146	741	1 405	21 868	2 803	4 103	5 474	5 381	3 197	913
1963	24 704	2 232	850	1 380	22 473	2 959	4 174	5 601	5 502	3 331	906
1964	25 412	2 314	950	1 365	23 098	3 209	4 180	5 615	5 681	3 441	966
1965	26 200	2 513	954	1 559	23 686	3 365	4 330	5 720	5 711	3 587	976
1966	27 299	2 873	1 055	1 818	24 431	3 590	4 510	5 755	5 884	3 728	964
1967	28 360	2 887	1 076	1 810	25 475	3 966	4 848	5 844	5 983	3 855	979
1968	29 204	2 938	1 130	1 808	26 266	4 235	5 098	5 866	6 130	3 939	999
1969	30 513	3 100	1 239	1 859	27 413	4 597	5 395	5 902	6 386	4 077	1 057
1970	31 543	3 241	1 325	1 916	28 301	4 880	5 708	5 968	6 532	4 157	1 056
1971	32 202	3 298	1 336	1 963	28 904	5 098	5 983	5 957	6 573	4 234	1 059
1972	33 479	3 578	1 464	2 114	29 901	5 364	6 610	6 027	6 555	4 257	1 089
1973	34 804	3 814	1 592	2 221	30 991	5 663	7 320	6 154	6 567	4 228	1 061
1974	36 211	4 010	1 672	2 338	32 201	5 926	7 989	6 362	6 699	4 221	1 002
1975	37 475	4 065	1 674	2 391	33 410	6 185	8 673	6 505	6 683	4 323	1 042
1976	38 983	4 170	1 698	2 470	34 814	6 418	9 419	6 817	6 689	4 402	1 069
1977	40 613	4 303	1 765	2 538	36 310	6 717	10 149	7 171	6 720	4 477	1 078
1978	42 631	4 503	1 900	2 603	38 128	7 043	10 888	7 662	6 807	4 593	1 134
1979	44 235	4 527	1 887	2 639	39 708	7 234	11 551	8 154	6 889	4 719	1 161
1980	45 487	4 381	1 781	2 599	41 106	7 315	12 257	8 627	7 004	4 742	1 161
1981	46 696	4 211	1 691	2 520	42 485	7 451	12 912	9 045	7 101	4 799	1 176
1982	47 755	4 056	1 561	2 495	43 699	7 477	13 393	9 651	7 105	4 888	1 185
1983	48 503	3 868	1 452	2 416	44 636	7 451	13 796	10 213	7 105	4 873	1 198
1984	49 709	3 810	1 458	2 351	45 900	7 451	14 234	10 896	7 230	4 911	1 177
1985	51 050	3 767	1 491	2 276	47 283	7 434	14 742	11 567	7 452	4 932	1 156
1986	52 413	3 824	1 580	2 244	48 589	7 293	15 208	12 204	7 746	4 940	1 199
1987	53 658	3 875	1 638	2 237	49 783	7 140	15 577	12 873	8 034	4 937	1 221
1988	54 742	3 872	1 572	2 300	50 870	6 910	15 761	13 361	8 537	4 977	1 324
1989	56 030	3 818	1 495	2 323	52 212	6 721	15 990	13 980	8 997	5 095	1 429
1990	56 829	3 698	1 400	2 298	53 131	6 834	16 058	14 663	9 145	4 948	1 483
1991	57 178	3 470	1 337	2 133	53 708	6 728	15 867	15 235	9 465	4 924	1 489
1992	58 141	3 345	1 316	2 030	54 796	6 750	15 875	15 552	10 120	5 035	1 464
1993	58 795	3 408	1 335	2 073	55 388	6 683	15 566	15 849	10 733	5 097	1 459
1994	60 239	3 585	1 504	2 081	56 655	6 592	15 499	16 259	11 357	5 289	1 658
1995	60 944	3 729	1 557	2 172	57 215	6 349	15 528	16 562	11 801	5 356	1 618
1996	61 857	3 763	1 599	2 164	58 094	6 273	15 403	16 954	12 430	5 452	1 581
1997	63 036	3 837	1 561	2 277	59 198	6 348	15 271	17 268	13 010	5 713	1 590
1998	63 714	4 012	1 607	2 405	59 702	6 418	15 017	17 294	13 405	5 962	1 607
1999	64 855	4 015	1 606	2 410	60 841	6 643	14 826	17 501	13 994	6 204	1 673
2000	65 616	4 051	1 596	2 456	61 565	6 788	14 596	17 504	14 515	6 400	1 762
2001	66 071	3 924	1 524	2 399	62 148	6 936	14 326	17 362	14 990	6 713	1 821

See *Note* at end of table.

Table 1-7. Civilian Labor Force by Race, Hispanic Origin, Sex, and Age, 1948–2001—*Continued*

(Thousands of persons.)

Year, race, Hispanic origin, and sex	16 years and over	16 to 19 years			20 years and over						
		Total	16 to 17 years	18 to 19 years	Total	20 to 24 years	25 to 34 years	35 to 44 years	45 to 54 years	55 to 64 years	65 years and over
WHITE MEN											
1954	39 759	1 989	896	1 095	37 770	2 654	9 695	9 516	7 913	5 653	2 339
1955	40 197	2 056	935	1 121	38 141	2 803	9 721	9 597	8 025	5 654	2 343
1956	40 734	2 114	1 002	1 110	38 620	3 036	9 595	9 661	8 175	5 736	2 417
1957	40 826	2 108	992	1 114	38 718	3 152	9 483	9 719	8 317	5 735	2 307
1958	41 080	2 116	1 001	1 116	38 964	3 278	9 386	9 822	8 465	5 800	2 213
1959	41 397	2 279	1 077	1 202	39 118	3 409	9 261	9 876	8 581	5 833	2 158
1960	41 743	2 433	1 140	1 293	39 310	3 559	9 153	9 919	8 689	5 861	2 129
1961	41 986	2 439	1 067	1 372	39 547	3 681	9 072	9 961	8 776	5 988	2 068
1962	41 931	2 432	1 041	1 391	39 499	3 726	8 846	10 029	8 820	5 995	2 082
1963	42 404	2 563	1 183	1 380	39 841	3 955	8 805	10 079	8 944	6 090	1 967
1964	42 894	2 716	1 345	1 371	40 178	4 166	8 800	10 055	9 053	6 161	1 942
1965	43 400	2 999	1 359	1 639	40 401	4 279	8 824	10 023	9 130	6 188	1 959
1966	43 572	3 253	1 423	1 830	40 319	4 200	8 859	9 892	9 189	6 250	1 928
1967	44 041	3 191	1 464	1 727	40 851	4 416	9 102	9 785	9 260	6 348	1 944
1968	44 553	3 236	1 504	1 732	41 318	4 432	9 477	9 662	9 340	6 427	1 981
1969	45 185	3 413	1 583	1 830	41 772	4 615	9 773	9 509	9 413	6 467	1 996
1970	46 035	3 551	1 629	1 922	42 483	4 988	10 099	9 414	9 487	6 517	1 978
1971	46 904	3 719	1 681	2 039	43 185	5 448	10 444	9 294	9 528	6 550	1 922
1972	48 118	3 980	1 758	2 223	44 138	5 937	11 039	9 278	9 473	6 562	1 846
1973	48 920	4 174	1 875	2 300	44 747	6 274	11 621	9 212	9 445	6 452	1 740
1974	49 843	4 312	1 922	2 391	45 532	6 470	12 135	9 246	9 455	6 464	1 759
1975	50 324	4 290	1 871	2 418	46 034	6 642	12 579	9 231	9 415	6 425	1 742
1976	51 033	4 357	1 869	2 489	46 675	6 890	13 092	9 289	9 310	6 437	1 657
1977	52 033	4 496	1 949	2 548	47 537	7 097	13 575	9 509	9 175	6 492	1 688
1978	52 955	4 565	2 002	2 563	48 390	7 274	13 939	9 858	9 068	6 508	1 744
1979	53 856	4 537	1 974	2 563	49 320	7 421	14 415	10 183	8 968	6 571	1 761
1980	54 473	4 424	1 881	2 543	50 049	7 479	14 893	10 455	8 877	6 618	1 727
1981	54 895	4 224	1 751	2 473	50 671	7 521	15 340	10 740	8 836	6 530	1 704
1982	55 133	3 933	1 602	2 331	51 200	7 438	15 549	11 289	8 727	6 520	1 677
1983	55 480	3 764	1 452	2 312	51 716	7 406	15 707	11 817	8 649	6 446	1 691
1984	56 062	3 609	1 420	2 189	52 453	7 370	16 037	12 348	8 683	6 410	1 606
1985	56 472	3 576	1 467	2 109	52 895	7 122	16 306	12 767	8 730	6 376	1 595
1986	57 217	3 542	1 502	2 040	53 675	6 986	16 769	13 207	8 791	6 260	1 663
1987	57 779	3 547	1 524	2 023	54 232	6 717	16 963	13 674	8 945	6 200	1 733
1988	58 317	3 583	1 487	2 095	54 734	6 468	17 018	14 068	9 285	6 108	1 787
1989	58 988	3 546	1 401	2 146	55 441	6 316	17 077	14 516	9 615	6 082	1 835
1990	59 638	3 522	1 333	2 189	56 116	6 688	16 920	15 026	9 713	5 957	1 811
1991	59 656	3 269	1 266	2 003	56 387	6 619	16 709	15 523	9 926	5 847	1 763
1992	60 168	3 192	1 260	1 932	56 976	6 542	16 512	15 701	10 570	5 821	1 830
1993	60 484	3 200	1 292	1 908	57 284	6 449	16 244	15 971	11 010	5 784	1 825
1994	60 727	3 315	1 403	1 912	57 411	6 294	15 879	16 188	11 327	5 726	1 998
1995	61 146	3 427	1 429	1 998	57 719	6 096	15 669	16 414	11 730	5 809	2 000
1996	61 783	3 444	1 421	2 023	58 340	5 922	15 475	16 728	12 217	5 943	2 054
1997	62 639	3 513	1 440	2 073	59 126	6 029	15 120	17 019	12 710	6 154	2 094
1998	63 034	3 614	1 487	2 127	59 421	6 063	14 770	17 157	13 003	6 415	2 013
1999	63 413	3 666	1 478	2 188	59 747	6 151	14 292	17 201	13 368	6 618	2 117
2000	63 861	3 679	1 439	2 240	60 182	6 308	14 043	17 158	13 783	6 692	2 198
2001	64 141	3 532	1 351	2 181	60 609	6 377	13 779	17 012	14 282	6 942	2 217

See *Note* at end of table.

Table 1-7. Civilian Labor Force by Race, Hispanic Origin, Sex, and Age, 1948–2001—*Continued*

(Thousands of persons.)

Year, race, Hispanic origin, and sex	16 years and over	16 to 19 years			20 years and over						
		Total	16 to 17 years	18 to 19 years	Total	20 to 24 years	25 to 34 years	35 to 44 years	45 to 54 years	55 to 64 years	65 years and over
WHITE WOMEN											
1954	17 057	1 512	552	959	15 545	2 098	3 531	4 024	3 345	1 938	607
1955	17 888	1 542	576	966	16 346	2 138	3 546	4 132	3 655	2 156	719
1956	18 694	1 657	654	1 003	17 037	2 158	3 559	4 339	3 886	2 344	749
1957	18 928	1 667	645	1 021	17 261	2 131	3 561	4 398	4 065	2 356	742
1958	19 213	1 641	614	1 028	17 572	2 171	3 498	4 435	4 262	2 454	751
1959	19 555	1 721	698	1 023	17 834	2 135	3 409	4 479	4 467	2 578	767
1960	20 172	1 842	731	1 112	18 330	2 228	3 441	4 531	4 633	2 661	835
1961	20 670	1 923	700	1 222	18 747	2 345	3 431	4 596	4 741	2 785	849
1962	20 819	1 922	668	1 254	18 897	2 438	3 372	4 666	4 731	2 861	830
1963	21 426	1 996	767	1 228	19 430	2 582	3 424	4 780	4 845	2 977	823
1964	22 027	2 068	866	1 201	19 959	2 786	3 435	4 797	4 990	3 078	875
1965	22 737	2 268	862	1 405	20 469	2 910	3 567	4 877	5 032	3 204	880
1966	23 704	2 574	944	1 630	21 130	3 124	3 732	4 893	5 181	3 333	865
1967	24 658	2 558	968	1 591	22 100	3 471	4 021	4 980	5 285	3 469	877
1968	25 423	2 603	1 015	1 588	22 821	3 677	4 263	5 021	5 416	3 541	903
1969	26 593	2 755	1 115	1 640	23 839	3 999	4 516	5 055	5 644	3 665	958
1970	27 521	2 891	1 195	1 695	24 630	4 250	4 797	5 111	5 781	3 738	952
1971	28 060	2 962	1 213	1 748	25 097	4 441	5 001	5 080	5 816	3 801	958
1972	29 157	3 213	1 338	1 875	25 945	4 668	5 544	5 121	5 810	3 839	963
1973	30 231	3 405	1 445	1 960	26 825	4 908	6 143	5 228	5 811	3 788	947
1974	31 437	3 588	1 520	2 068	27 850	5 131	6 727	5 399	5 920	3 777	897
1975	32 508	3 610	1 504	2 107	28 898	5 378	7 318	5 522	5 892	3 862	926
1976	33 735	3 731	1 541	2 189	30 004	5 554	7 898	5 799	5 877	3 935	940
1977	35 108	3 856	1 614	2 243	31 253	5 795	8 523	6 095	5 877	4 003	959
1978	36 679	3 990	1 713	2 276	32 689	6 035	9 128	6 495	5 936	4 094	1 001
1979	38 067	4 011	1 694	2 318	34 056	6 211	9 687	6 940	5 997	4 196	1 024
1980	39 127	3 888	1 605	2 284	35 239	6 290	10 289	7 356	6 079	4 194	1 032
1981	40 157	3 739	1 523	2 216	36 418	6 406	10 868	7 704	6 157	4 235	1 049
1982	41 010	3 585	1 399	2 186	37 425	6 428	11 264	8 202	6 152	4 313	1 065
1983	41 541	3 422	1 314	2 109	38 119	6 410	11 530	8 670	6 149	4 285	1 074
1984	42 431	3 343	1 300	2 043	39 087	6 363	11 922	9 240	6 217	4 292	1 054
1985	43 455	3 265	1 310	1 955	40 190	6 348	12 334	9 824	6 371	4 303	1 010
1986	44 584	3 320	1 393	1 927	41 264	6 191	12 729	10 364	6 588	4 323	1 069
1987	45 510	3 347	1 439	1 908	42 164	6 047	12 993	10 907	6 847	4 297	1 073
1988	46 439	3 358	1 374	1 984	43 081	5 844	13 149	11 291	7 288	4 354	1 156
1989	47 367	3 262	1 284	1 978	44 105	5 625	13 311	11 796	7 663	4 451	1 259
1990	47 809	3 161	1 210	1 951	44 648	5 709	13 254	12 239	7 802	4 333	1 312
1991	48 087	2 976	1 166	1 810	45 111	5 629	13 085	12 689	8 101	4 282	1 324
1992	48 669	2 830	1 128	1 702	45 839	5 645	13 006	12 879	8 630	4 375	1 305
1993	49 216	2 905	1 167	1 739	46 311	5 539	12 783	13 085	9 171	4 430	1 304
1994	50 356	3 042	1 278	1 764	47 314	5 394	12 702	13 439	9 699	4 593	1 487
1995	50 804	3 118	1 320	1 798	47 686	5 170	12 656	13 697	10 074	4 622	1 466
1996	51 325	3 163	1 360	1 803	48 162	5 081	12 426	13 955	10 563	4 706	1 431
1997	52 054	3 207	1 339	1 867	48 847	5 099	12 242	14 153	10 999	4 932	1 422
1998	52 380	3 351	1 373	1 977	49 029	5 180	11 937	14 064	11 279	5 133	1 435
1999	53 096	3 382	1 371	2 010	49 714	5 285	11 685	14 190	11 734	5 342	1 478
2000	53 714	3 396	1 360	2 035	50 318	5 455	11 439	14 188	12 186	5 500	1 550
2001	54 003	3 303	1 298	2 005	50 700	5 565	11 199	14 019	12 540	5 777	1 601

See *Note* at end of table.

Table 1-7. Civilian Labor Force by Race, Hispanic Origin, Sex, and Age, 1948–2001—*Continued*

(Thousands of persons.)

Year, race, Hispanic origin, and sex	16 years and over	16 to 19 years			20 years and over						
		Total	16 to 17 years	18 to 19 years	Total	20 to 24 years	25 to 34 years	35 to 44 years	45 to 54 years	55 to 64 years	65 years and over
BLACK MEN											
1972	4 816	453	180	272	4 364	761	1 158	935	824	522	165
1973	4 924	460	175	286	4 464	819	1 217	935	842	499	153
1974	5 020	480	189	291	4 540	798	1 279	953	838	519	152
1975	5 016	447	168	279	4 569	790	1 328	948	833	520	150
1976	5 101	454	168	285	4 648	820	1 383	969	824	504	149
1977	5 263	476	178	299	4 787	856	1 441	1 003	818	515	154
1978	5 435	491	186	306	4 943	883	1 504	1 022	829	540	166
1979	5 559	480	179	301	5 079	928	1 577	1 049	844	524	156
1980	5 612	479	181	298	5 134	935	1 659	1 061	830	509	138
1981	5 685	462	169	293	5 223	940	1 702	1 093	829	524	134
1982	5 804	436	137	300	5 368	964	1 769	1 152	824	525	135
1983	5 966	433	134	300	5 533	997	1 840	1 196	845	536	119
1984	6 126	440	141	299	5 686	1 022	1 924	1 270	847	505	118
1985	6 220	471	162	310	5 749	950	1 937	1 313	879	544	125
1986	6 373	458	164	294	5 915	957	2 029	1 359	901	552	116
1987	6 486	463	179	284	6 023	914	2 074	1 406	915	586	130
1988	6 596	469	186	283	6 127	913	2 114	1 459	936	565	139
1989	6 701	480	190	291	6 221	904	2 157	1 544	945	530	141
1990	6 802	445	161	284	6 357	879	2 142	1 733	988	496	119
1991	6 851	400	140	260	6 451	896	2 111	1 806	1 010	507	122
1992	6 997	429	149	280	6 568	900	2 121	1 859	1 037	521	130
1993	7 019	425	154	270	6 594	875	2 118	1 918	1 065	506	112
1994	7 089	443	176	266	6 646	891	2 068	1 975	1 102	484	125
1995	7 183	453	184	269	6 730	866	2 089	1 987	1 148	490	150
1996	7 264	458	182	276	6 806	848	2 077	2 036	1 204	509	132
1997	7 354	444	178	266	6 910	832	2 052	2 096	1 287	508	134
1998	7 542	488	181	307	7 053	837	2 034	2 142	1 343	548	150
1999	7 652	470	180	291	7 182	835	2 069	2 206	1 387	547	138
2000	7 816	473	187	286	7 343	906	2 019	2 214	1 467	580	157
2001	7 858	463	169	294	7 395	877	1 971	2 208	1 536	617	186
BLACK WOMEN											
1972	3 890	335	113	224	3 555	632	949	800	672	387	116
1973	4 052	373	133	240	3 678	670	1 026	806	670	402	105
1974	4 148	371	128	243	3 777	694	1 079	824	679	398	100
1975	4 247	391	144	245	3 857	687	1 138	827	686	409	108
1976	4 460	384	136	247	4 076	723	1 264	855	694	421	119
1977	4 670	385	127	258	4 286	785	1 357	891	712	429	113
1978	4 997	439	155	283	4 558	856	1 456	953	731	439	124
1979	5 119	432	161	271	4 687	865	1 517	990	740	451	124
1980	5 253	412	144	267	4 841	867	1 600	1 020	767	469	119
1981	5 401	400	139	261	5 001	888	1 663	1 071	779	485	115
1982	5 527	387	131	256	5 140	885	1 723	1 151	786	487	108
1983	5 681	375	114	261	5 306	874	1 835	1 210	785	496	105
1984	5 907	387	127	260	5 520	904	1 876	1 294	823	515	106
1985	6 144	417	149	268	5 727	904	1 951	1 368	862	515	127
1986	6 281	425	157	268	5 855	924	1 999	1 434	892	499	107
1987	6 507	435	157	278	6 071	904	2 073	1 537	924	512	121
1988	6 609	419	158	262	6 190	869	2 112	1 610	958	504	137
1989	6 796	445	163	281	6 352	885	2 138	1 683	1 009	493	144
1990	6 938	421	145	276	6 517	879	2 165	1 833	1 015	481	143
1991	6 946	374	126	248	6 572	854	2 143	1 913	1 032	494	135
1992	7 166	387	135	252	6 778	863	2 188	1 985	1 105	508	129
1993	7 206	383	129	254	6 824	889	2 115	2 042	1 147	506	125
1994	7 413	409	174	235	7 004	909	2 131	2 093	1 206	523	142
1995	7 634	458	182	276	7 175	887	2 177	2 178	1 256	556	121
1996	7 869	464	184	280	7 405	890	2 228	2 251	1 349	565	122
1997	8 175	489	175	314	7 686	951	2 277	2 305	1 437	585	131
1998	8 441	528	189	339	7 912	960	2 298	2 390	1 520	615	128
1999	8 713	489	172	316	8 224	1 031	2 360	2 447	1 606	633	147
2000	8 787	494	179	315	8 293	1 026	2 310	2 451	1 694	647	165
2001	8 861	471	171	300	8 390	1 045	2 292	2 448	1 753	682	170

See *Note* at end of table.

Table 1-7. Civilian Labor Force by Race, Hispanic Origin, Sex, and Age, 1948–2001—*Continued*

(Thousands of persons.)

Year, race, Hispanic origin, and sex	16 years and over	16 to 19 years			20 years and over						
		Total	16 to 17 years	18 to 19 years	Total	20 to 24 years	25 to 34 years	35 to 44 years	45 to 54 years	55 to 64 years	65 years and over
HISPANIC MEN											
1973	2 356	...	...	...	2 124	...	...	...	...	...	...
1974	2 556	...	...	...	2 306	...	...	...	...	...	...
1975	2 597	...	...	...	2 343	...	...	...	...	...	...
1976	2 580	260	104	155	2 326	433	771	541	398	189	34
1977	2 817	285	105	179	2 530	485	828	567	416	197	42
1978	3 041	299	129	171	2 742	546	882	620	425	217	52
1979	3 184	315	121	194	2 869	562	941	648	445	216	56
1980	3 818	392	147	245	3 426	697	1 161	713	522	270	62
1981	4 005	359	130	229	3 647	747	1 269	756	535	278	61
1982	4 148	333	111	221	3 815	759	1 361	808	539	290	58
1983	4 362	348	109	239	4 014	789	1 447	852	557	311	58
1984	4 563	345	113	232	4 218	822	1 540	910	570	325	51
1985	4 729	334	116	218	4 395	835	1 629	957	591	331	53
1986	4 948	336	114	222	4 612	888	1 669	1 015	661	323	56
1987	5 163	345	112	233	4 818	865	1 801	1 121	652	325	55
1988	5 409	378	123	255	5 031	897	1 834	1 189	686	355	69
1989	5 595	400	129	271	5 195	909	1 899	1 221	719	375	71
1990	6 546	512	165	346	6 034	1 182	2 230	1 403	775	380	65
1991	6 664	466	141	325	6 198	1 202	2 260	1 487	780	401	67
1992	6 900	468	154	314	6 432	1 141	2 366	1 593	844	414	74
1993	7 076	455	145	310	6 621	1 147	2 417	1 675	900	394	88
1994	7 210	463	163	300	6 747	1 184	2 430	1 713	922	410	89
1995	7 376	479	168	311	6 898	1 153	2 469	1 795	965	417	98
1996	7 646	496	156	340	7 150	1 132	2 510	1 966	967	469	105
1997	8 309	531	177	354	7 779	1 267	2 684	2 091	1 112	511	113
1998	8 571	565	188	377	8 005	1 288	2 733	2 173	1 164	541	106
1999	8 546	596	181	415	7 950	1 231	2 633	2 219	1 205	526	136
2000	8 919	613	183	431	8 306	1 299	2 652	2 338	1 305	573	138
2001	9 098	645	183	461	8 453	1 277	2 682	2 382	1 388	591	133
HISPANIC WOMEN											
1973	1 317	...	...	...	1 142	...	...	...	...	...	...
1974	1 456	...	...	...	1 264	...	...	...	...	...	...
1975	1 574	...	...	...	1 384	...	...	...	...	...	...
1976	1 625	201	71	130	1 454	295	479	334	227	105	13
1977	1 720	204	80	125	1 523	327	497	349	240	96	13
1978	1 938	233	93	142	1 704	354	564	388	275	106	16
1979	2 035	235	86	149	1 800	397	590	413	258	124	15
1980	2 328	252	93	159	2 076	439	682	450	337	144	22
1981	2 486	244	85	159	2 242	484	745	483	351	152	27
1982	2 586	252	81	172	2 333	492	802	504	352	155	28
1983	2 671	242	80	162	2 429	493	820	529	374	184	29
1984	2 888	273	96	177	2 615	503	896	599	384	199	34
1985	2 970	245	84	161	2 725	524	943	639	394	196	29
1986	3 128	236	89	147	2 893	526	1 016	698	436	189	28
1987	3 377	265	94	171	3 112	559	1 090	783	434	220	27
1988	3 573	293	111	182	3 281	589	1 123	806	461	267	34
1989	3 728	280	95	185	3 448	574	1 219	871	486	251	49
1990	4 174	318	110	207	3 857	657	1 360	983	545	268	45
1991	4 256	315	107	207	3 941	633	1 336	1 052	596	279	44
1992	4 439	328	110	219	4 110	674	1 374	1 142	599	273	48
1993	4 534	316	101	215	4 218	664	1 383	1 190	633	290	57
1994	4 765	345	122	222	4 421	679	1 435	1 252	704	288	62
1995	4 891	371	123	249	4 520	666	1 473	1 318	706	303	54
1996	5 128	349	128	221	4 779	713	1 544	1 395	729	338	61
1997	5 486	381	138	242	5 106	737	1 614	1 510	833	338	73
1998	5 746	442	132	310	5 304	789	1 639	1 533	927	353	62
1999	6 119	453	151	302	5 666	821	1 698	1 710	973	401	63
2000	6 449	470	155	315	5 979	856	1 833	1 748	1 053	410	80
2001	6 653	477	144	333	6 176	907	1 874	1 737	1 144	441	74

Note: Detail for the above race and Hispanic-origin groups will not sum to totals because data for the Other races group are not presented and Hispanics are included in both the White and Black population groups. See "Notes and Definitions" for information on historical comparability.

Table 1-8. Civilian Labor Force Participation Rates by Race, Hispanic Origin, Sex, and Age, 1948–2001

(Percent.)

Year, race, Hispanic origin, and sex	16 years and over	16 to 19 years	20 years and over						
			Total	20 to 24 years	25 to 34 years	35 to 44 years	45 to 54 years	55 to 64 years	65 years and over
TOTAL									
1948	58.8	52.5	59.4	64.1	63.1	66.7	65.1	56.9	27.0
1949	58.9	52.2	59.5	64.9	63.2	67.2	65.3	56.2	27.3
1950	59.2	51.8	59.9	65.9	63.5	67.5	66.4	56.7	26.7
1951	59.2	52.2	59.8	64.8	64.2	67.6	67.2	56.9	25.8
1952	59.0	51.3	59.7	62.2	64.7	68.0	67.5	57.5	24.8
1953	58.9	50.2	59.6	61.2	64.0	68.9	68.1	58.0	24.8
1954	58.8	48.3	59.6	61.6	64.3	68.8	68.4	58.7	23.9
1955	59.3	48.9	60.1	62.7	64.8	68.9	69.7	59.5	24.1
1956	60.0	50.9	60.7	64.1	64.8	69.5	70.5	60.8	24.3
1957	59.6	49.6	60.4	64.0	64.9	69.5	70.9	60.1	22.9
1958	59.5	47.4	60.5	64.4	65.0	69.6	71.5	60.5	21.8
1959	59.3	46.7	60.4	64.3	65.0	69.5	71.9	61.0	21.1
1960	59.4	47.5	60.5	65.2	65.4	69.4	72.2	60.9	20.8
1961	59.3	46.9	60.5	65.7	65.6	69.5	72.1	61.5	20.1
1962	58.8	46.1	60.0	65.3	65.2	69.7	72.2	61.5	19.1
1963	58.7	45.2	60.1	65.1	65.6	70.1	72.5	62.0	17.9
1964	58.7	44.5	60.2	66.3	65.8	70.0	72.9	61.9	18.0
1965	58.9	45.7	60.3	66.4	66.4	70.7	72.5	61.9	17.8
1966	59.2	48.2	60.5	66.5	67.1	71.0	72.7	62.2	17.2
1967	59.6	48.4	60.9	67.1	68.2	71.6	72.7	62.3	17.2
1968	59.6	48.3	60.9	67.0	68.6	72.0	72.8	62.2	17.2
1969	60.1	49.4	61.3	68.2	69.1	72.5	73.4	62.1	17.3
1970	60.4	49.9	61.6	69.2	69.7	73.1	73.5	61.8	17.0
1971	60.2	49.7	61.4	69.3	69.9	73.2	73.2	61.3	16.2
1972	60.4	51.9	61.4	70.8	70.9	73.3	72.7	60.0	15.6
1973	60.8	53.7	61.7	72.6	72.3	74.0	72.5	58.4	14.6
1974	61.3	54.8	62.0	74.0	73.6	74.6	72.7	57.8	14.0
1975	61.2	54.0	62.1	73.9	74.4	75.0	72.6	57.2	13.7
1976	61.6	54.5	62.4	74.7	75.7	76.0	72.5	56.6	13.1
1977	62.3	56.0	63.0	75.7	77.0	77.0	72.8	56.3	13.0
1978	63.2	57.8	63.8	76.8	78.3	78.1	73.5	56.3	13.3
1979	63.7	57.9	64.3	77.5	79.2	79.2	74.3	56.2	13.1
1980	63.8	56.7	64.5	77.2	79.9	80.0	74.9	55.7	12.5
1981	63.9	55.4	64.8	77.3	80.5	80.7	75.7	55.0	12.2
1982	64.0	54.1	65.0	77.1	81.0	81.2	75.9	55.1	11.9
1983	64.0	53.5	65.0	77.2	81.3	81.6	76.0	54.5	11.7
1984	64.4	53.9	65.3	77.6	81.8	82.4	76.5	54.2	11.1
1985	64.8	54.5	65.7	78.2	82.5	83.1	77.3	54.2	10.8
1986	65.3	54.7	66.2	78.9	82.9	83.7	78.0	54.0	10.9
1987	65.6	54.7	66.5	78.9	83.3	84.3	78.6	54.4	11.1
1988	65.9	55.3	66.8	78.7	83.3	84.6	79.6	54.6	11.5
1989	66.5	55.9	67.3	78.7	83.8	85.1	80.5	55.5	11.8
1990	66.5	53.7	67.6	77.8	83.6	85.2	80.7	55.9	11.8
1991	66.2	51.6	67.3	76.7	83.2	85.2	81.0	55.5	11.5
1992	66.4	51.3	67.6	77.0	83.7	85.1	81.5	56.2	11.5
1993	66.3	51.5	67.5	77.0	83.3	84.9	81.6	56.4	11.2
1994	66.6	52.7	67.7	77.0	83.2	84.8	81.7	56.8	12.4
1995	66.6	53.5	67.7	76.6	83.8	84.6	81.4	57.2	12.1
1996	66.8	52.3	67.9	76.8	84.1	84.8	82.1	57.9	12.1
1997	67.1	51.6	68.4	77.6	84.4	85.1	82.6	58.9	12.2
1998	67.1	52.8	68.3	77.5	84.6	84.7	82.5	59.3	11.9
1999	67.1	52.0	68.3	77.5	84.6	84.9	82.6	59.3	12.3
2000	67.2	52.2	68.4	77.9	84.6	84.8	82.6	59.2	12.8
2001	66.9	50.0	68.3	77.1	84.0	84.7	82.3	60.2	13.1

See *Note* at end of table.

Table 1-8. Civilian Labor Force Participation Rates by Race, Hispanic Origin, Sex, and Age, 1948–2001—*Continued*

(Percent.)

Year, race, Hispanic origin, and sex	16 years and over	16 to 19 years	20 years and over						
			Total	20 to 24 years	25 to 34 years	35 to 44 years	45 to 54 years	55 to 64 years	65 years and over
WHITE									
1954	58.2	48.8	58.9	61.0	63.5	68.0	67.9	58.4	23.7
1955	58.7	49.3	59.5	62.4	64.0	68.3	69.2	59.3	23.9
1956	59.4	51.3	60.1	64.1	64.0	68.9	70.1	60.6	24.2
1957	59.1	50.3	59.8	63.7	64.1	68.8	70.5	59.9	22.8
1958	58.9	47.9	59.8	64.1	64.2	68.8	71.0	60.3	21.7
1959	58.7	47.4	59.7	63.7	64.3	68.7	71.5	60.7	21.0
1960	58.8	47.9	59.8	64.8	64.7	68.6	71.7	60.6	20.8
1961	58.8	47.4	59.9	65.5	64.8	68.8	71.7	61.3	20.0
1962	58.3	46.6	59.4	65.0	64.4	69.0	71.8	61.3	19.0
1963	58.2	45.7	59.4	64.9	64.8	69.4	72.3	61.8	17.9
1964	58.2	45.1	59.6	65.8	64.9	69.5	72.5	61.8	17.8
1965	58.4	46.5	59.7	65.7	65.6	70.1	72.2	61.7	17.7
1966	58.7	49.1	59.8	66.0	66.3	70.4	72.5	61.9	17.1
1967	59.2	49.2	60.3	66.8	67.4	71.2	72.5	62.3	17.0
1968	59.3	49.3	60.4	66.6	67.9	71.7	72.7	62.2	17.1
1969	59.9	50.6	60.9	67.9	68.4	72.3	73.3	62.1	17.2
1970	60.2	51.4	61.2	69.2	69.1	72.9	73.5	61.8	16.8
1971	60.1	51.6	61.1	69.6	69.3	73.0	73.4	61.3	16.1
1972	60.4	54.1	61.2	71.2	70.4	73.2	72.9	60.3	15.4
1973	60.8	56.0	61.4	73.3	72.0	73.9	72.7	58.6	14.4
1974	61.4	57.3	61.9	74.8	73.4	74.6	73.0	58.0	13.9
1975	61.5	56.7	62.0	75.2	74.4	75.1	73.0	57.4	13.6
1976	61.8	57.5	62.3	76.0	75.6	76.1	73.0	56.9	13.0
1977	62.5	59.3	62.9	77.1	77.0	77.1	73.2	56.6	12.9
1978	63.3	60.8	63.6	78.1	78.3	78.1	73.8	56.4	13.1
1979	63.9	61.1	64.2	78.9	79.4	79.3	74.6	56.5	12.9
1980	64.1	60.0	64.5	78.7	80.2	80.3	75.4	56.0	12.5
1981	64.3	58.9	64.8	79.1	81.0	81.0	76.2	55.2	12.2
1982	64.3	57.5	65.0	78.9	81.6	81.5	76.4	55.3	12.0
1983	64.3	56.9	65.0	79.0	81.8	81.9	76.5	54.7	11.8
1984	64.6	57.2	65.3	79.4	82.5	82.6	77.0	54.5	11.1
1985	65.0	57.5	65.7	79.9	83.1	83.4	77.8	54.4	10.7
1986	65.5	57.8	66.1	80.6	83.6	84.0	78.5	54.3	11.0
1987	65.8	57.7	66.5	80.7	84.0	84.7	79.1	54.6	11.1
1988	66.2	58.6	66.8	80.6	84.1	85.0	80.3	55.1	11.4
1989	66.7	59.1	67.3	80.2	84.5	85.5	81.2	56.2	11.8
1990	66.9	57.5	67.6	79.8	84.6	85.9	81.3	56.5	11.9
1991	66.6	55.8	67.4	78.9	84.3	85.9	81.8	56.0	11.6
1992	66.8	54.7	67.7	79.4	84.6	85.8	82.2	56.8	11.6
1993	66.8	55.1	67.6	79.5	84.5	85.7	82.5	57.1	11.4
1994	67.1	56.4	67.9	79.5	84.4	85.7	82.7	57.6	12.5
1995	67.1	57.1	67.8	78.7	84.9	85.5	82.5	58.0	12.3
1996	67.2	55.9	68.1	79.1	84.9	85.7	83.1	58.7	12.3
1997	67.5	55.2	68.4	79.6	85.3	85.8	83.5	59.9	12.3
1998	67.3	56.0	68.2	79.5	85.4	85.3	83.4	60.1	12.0
1999	67.3	55.5	68.2	79.5	85.1	85.4	83.5	60.2	12.5
2000	67.4	55.7	68.3	79.9	85.1	85.4	83.5	60.0	13.0
2001	67.2	53.5	68.2	79.2	84.5	85.2	83.3	61.1	13.1

See *Note* at end of table.

Table 1-8. Civilian Labor Force Participation Rates by Race, Hispanic Origin, Sex, and Age, 1948–2001—*Continued*

(Percent.)

Year, race, Hispanic origin, and sex	16 years and over	16 to 19 years	20 years and over						
			Total	20 to 24 years	25 to 34 years	35 to 44 years	45 to 54 years	55 to 64 years	65 years and over
BLACK									
1972	59.9	39.0	63.3	68.7	75.0	74.5	69.9	56.8	17.5
1973	60.2	39.8	63.5	69.8	75.8	74.6	70.2	55.8	15.8
1974	59.8	39.8	63.0	69.8	76.0	74.6	68.9	54.6	15.0
1975	58.8	38.2	62.1	66.3	75.7	74.1	68.7	54.1	14.7
1976	59.0	37.0	62.6	67.0	77.5	74.9	68.4	53.3	14.7
1977	59.8	37.9	63.3	68.4	78.5	76.0	68.8	53.4	14.2
1978	61.5	41.0	64.6	70.0	79.7	77.5	70.1	54.5	15.0
1979	61.4	40.1	64.6	70.1	79.4	78.0	70.7	53.2	14.2
1980	61.0	38.9	64.2	69.1	79.6	77.4	71.0	52.3	12.7
1981	60.8	37.7	64.2	69.2	78.4	78.5	71.2	52.7	12.0
1982	61.0	36.6	64.3	68.6	78.7	79.8	71.1	52.3	11.5
1983	61.5	36.4	64.9	68.4	79.8	80.2	72.1	52.5	10.5
1984	62.2	38.3	65.2	69.2	79.3	81.0	73.0	51.6	10.3
1985	62.9	41.2	65.6	70.0	79.8	81.5	73.4	51.4	11.2
1986	63.3	41.3	65.9	71.7	80.1	81.9	74.3	50.6	9.7
1987	63.8	41.6	66.5	70.5	80.7	82.6	74.7	52.4	10.7
1988	63.8	40.8	66.5	70.5	80.7	82.6	75.0	50.7	11.5
1989	64.2	42.5	66.7	72.2	80.9	82.7	75.5	48.3	11.6
1990	64.0	38.7	66.9	68.8	79.7	82.4	76.5	49.6	11.1
1991	63.3	35.4	66.4	67.7	78.5	82.0	76.1	50.4	10.7
1992	63.9	37.9	66.8	67.4	79.7	81.4	76.3	51.6	10.6
1993	63.2	37.0	66.0	67.8	78.2	81.0	75.2	50.2	9.5
1994	63.4	38.5	66.0	68.8	78.3	80.7	74.8	49.2	10.6
1995	63.7	39.9	66.3	68.7	80.0	80.4	74.1	50.3	10.5
1996	64.1	39.2	66.9	69.0	81.1	81.0	74.9	50.9	9.8
1997	64.7	38.7	67.6	70.9	82.0	81.3	76.3	50.5	10.0
1998	65.6	41.6	68.2	70.6	83.0	82.2	76.7	52.3	10.3
1999	65.8	38.7	68.9	71.4	85.2	83.0	76.4	51.4	10.4
2000	65.8	39.2	68.7	71.8	84.1	82.3	76.8	52.2	11.6
2001	65.4	37.7	68.4	70.0	83.6	81.9	75.9	53.6	12.7
HISPANIC									
1980	64.0	50.3	66.2	72.6	73.5	73.8	72.3	52.9	12.2
1981	64.2	46.4	66.8	74.6	74.7	73.8	72.0	51.7	12.0
1982	63.6	44.8	66.3	72.6	75.3	73.8	70.5	50.5	11.3
1983	63.8	45.3	66.2	71.6	74.4	73.3	71.7	53.3	11.0
1984	64.9	47.5	67.1	72.1	75.6	75.6	71.4	53.9	10.4
1985	64.6	44.6	67.1	72.9	75.6	75.3	71.5	51.9	9.7
1986	65.4	43.9	68.0	74.5	76.5	76.5	73.3	50.0	9.6
1987	66.4	45.8	68.8	74.6	77.8	77.3	72.8	51.4	9.1
1988	67.4	49.6	69.4	76.3	77.7	77.8	73.0	53.6	11.2
1989	67.6	48.6	69.7	76.1	78.9	78.7	73.1	52.9	12.0
1990	67.4	47.8	69.8	75.7	78.2	79.5	72.6	51.9	10.1
1991	66.5	45.1	69.0	74.0	76.9	78.3	73.2	53.1	9.8
1992	66.8	45.8	69.2	74.3	77.8	79.1	72.8	52.0	10.0
1993	66.2	43.9	68.7	72.8	77.8	78.9	73.3	51.7	10.7
1994	66.1	44.4	68.5	74.0	77.3	78.9	73.1	49.8	10.8
1995	65.8	45.4	68.1	71.9	78.1	78.5	72.8	48.6	10.6
1996	66.5	43.4	69.1	73.1	78.2	79.5	74.6	52.1	11.0
1997	67.9	43.0	70.8	76.4	79.5	80.9	75.4	53.8	11.9
1998	67.9	45.7	70.6	76.1	80.3	80.0	75.3	55.4	10.2
1999	67.7	45.5	70.4	76.0	78.6	81.3	75.9	54.1	11.6
2000	68.6	46.3	71.2	77.7	79.7	81.6	77.7	54.1	12.2
2001	68.1	46.9	70.6	75.8	79.3	81.6	77.0	54.7	11.0

See *Note* at end of table.

Table 1-8. Civilian Labor Force Participation Rates by Race, Hispanic Origin, Sex, and Age, 1948–2001—*Continued*

(Percent.)

Year, race, Hispanic origin, and sex	16 years and over	16 to 19 years	20 years and over						
			Total	20 to 24 years	25 to 34 years	35 to 44 years	45 to 54 years	55 to 64 years	65 years and over
MEN									
1948	86.6	63.7	88.6	84.6	95.9	97.9	95.8	89.5	46.8
1949	86.4	62.8	88.5	86.6	95.8	97.9	95.6	87.5	47.0
1950	86.4	63.2	88.4	87.9	96.0	97.6	95.8	86.9	45.8
1951	86.3	63.0	88.2	88.4	96.9	97.5	95.9	87.2	44.9
1952	86.3	61.3	88.3	88.1	97.5	97.8	96.2	87.5	42.6
1953	86.0	60.7	88.0	87.7	97.4	98.2	96.5	87.9	41.6
1954	85.5	58.0	87.8	86.9	97.3	98.1	96.5	88.7	40.5
1955	85.4	58.9	87.6	86.9	97.6	98.1	96.4	87.9	39.6
1956	85.5	60.5	87.6	87.8	97.3	97.9	96.6	88.5	40.0
1957	84.8	59.1	86.9	87.1	97.1	97.9	96.3	87.5	37.5
1958	84.2	56.6	86.6	86.9	97.1	97.9	96.3	87.8	35.6
1959	83.7	55.8	86.3	87.8	97.4	97.8	96.0	87.4	34.2
1960	83.3	56.1	86.0	88.1	97.5	97.7	95.7	86.8	33.1
1961	82.9	54.6	85.7	87.8	97.5	97.6	95.6	87.3	31.7
1962	82.0	53.8	84.8	86.9	97.2	97.6	95.6	86.2	30.3
1963	81.4	52.9	84.4	86.1	97.1	97.5	95.7	86.2	28.4
1964	81.0	52.4	84.2	86.1	97.3	97.3	95.7	85.6	28.0
1965	80.7	53.8	83.9	85.8	97.2	97.3	95.6	84.6	27.9
1966	80.4	55.3	83.6	85.1	97.3	97.2	95.3	84.5	27.1
1967	80.4	55.6	83.4	84.4	97.2	97.3	95.2	84.4	27.1
1968	80.1	55.1	83.1	82.8	96.9	97.1	94.9	84.3	27.3
1969	79.8	55.9	82.8	82.8	96.7	96.9	94.6	83.4	27.2
1970	79.7	56.1	82.6	83.3	96.4	96.9	94.3	83.0	26.8
1971	79.1	56.1	82.1	83.0	95.9	96.5	93.9	82.1	25.5
1972	78.9	58.1	81.6	83.9	95.7	96.4	93.2	80.4	24.3
1973	78.8	59.7	81.3	85.2	95.7	96.2	93.0	78.2	22.7
1974	78.7	60.7	81.0	85.9	95.8	96.0	92.2	77.3	22.4
1975	77.9	59.1	80.3	84.5	95.2	95.6	92.1	75.6	21.6
1976	77.5	59.3	79.8	85.2	95.2	95.4	91.6	74.3	20.2
1977	77.7	60.9	79.7	85.6	95.3	95.7	91.1	73.8	20.0
1978	77.9	62.0	79.8	85.9	95.3	95.7	91.3	73.3	20.4
1979	77.8	61.5	79.8	86.4	95.3	95.7	91.4	72.8	19.9
1980	77.4	60.5	79.4	85.9	95.2	95.5	91.2	72.1	19.0
1981	77.0	59.0	79.0	85.5	94.9	95.4	91.4	70.6	18.4
1982	76.6	56.7	78.7	84.9	94.7	95.3	91.2	70.2	17.8
1983	76.4	56.2	78.5	84.8	94.2	95.2	91.2	69.4	17.4
1984	76.4	56.0	78.3	85.0	94.4	95.4	91.2	68.5	16.3
1985	76.3	56.8	78.1	85.0	94.7	95.0	91.0	67.9	15.8
1986	76.3	56.4	78.1	85.8	94.6	94.8	91.0	67.3	16.0
1987	76.2	56.1	78.0	85.2	94.6	94.6	90.7	67.6	16.3
1988	76.2	56.9	77.9	85.0	94.3	94.5	90.9	67.0	16.5
1989	76.4	57.9	78.1	85.3	94.4	94.5	91.1	67.2	16.6
1990	76.4	55.7	78.2	84.4	94.1	94.3	90.7	67.8	16.3
1991	75.8	53.2	77.7	83.5	93.6	94.1	90.5	67.0	15.7
1992	75.8	53.4	77.7	83.3	93.8	93.7	90.7	67.0	16.1
1993	75.4	53.2	77.3	83.2	93.4	93.4	90.1	66.5	15.6
1994	75.1	54.1	76.8	83.1	92.6	92.8	89.1	65.5	16.8
1995	75.0	54.8	76.7	83.1	93.0	92.3	88.8	66.0	16.8
1996	74.9	53.2	76.8	82.5	93.2	92.4	89.1	67.0	16.9
1997	75.0	52.3	77.0	82.5	93.0	92.6	89.5	67.6	17.1
1998	74.9	53.3	76.8	82.0	93.2	92.6	89.2	68.1	16.5
1999	74.7	52.9	76.7	81.9	93.3	92.8	88.8	67.9	16.9
2000	74.7	53.0	76.6	82.6	93.4	92.6	88.6	67.3	17.5
2001	74.4	50.7	76.4	81.5	92.7	92.5	88.5	68.1	17.7

See *Note* at end of table.

Table 1-8. Civilian Labor Force Participation Rates by Race, Hispanic Origin, Sex, and Age, 1948–2001—*Continued*

(Percent.)

Year, race, Hispanic origin, and sex	16 years and over	16 to 19 years	20 years and over						
			Total	20 to 24 years	25 to 34 years	35 to 44 years	45 to 54 years	55 to 64 years	65 years and over
WOMEN									
1948	32.7	42.0	31.8	45.3	33.2	36.9	35.0	24.3	9.1
1949	33.1	42.4	32.3	45.0	33.4	38.1	35.9	25.3	9.6
1950	33.9	41.0	33.3	46.0	34.0	39.1	37.9	27.0	9.7
1951	34.6	42.4	34.0	46.5	35.4	39.8	39.7	27.6	8.9
1952	34.7	42.2	34.1	44.7	35.4	40.4	40.1	28.7	9.1
1953	34.4	40.7	33.9	44.3	34.0	41.3	40.4	29.1	10.0
1954	34.6	39.4	34.2	45.1	34.4	41.2	41.2	30.0	9.3
1955	35.7	39.7	35.4	45.9	34.9	41.6	43.8	32.5	10.6
1956	36.9	42.2	36.4	46.3	35.4	43.1	45.5	34.9	10.8
1957	36.9	41.1	36.5	45.9	35.6	43.3	46.5	34.5	10.5
1958	37.1	39.0	36.9	46.3	35.6	43.4	47.8	35.2	10.3
1959	37.1	38.2	37.1	45.1	35.3	43.4	49.0	36.6	10.2
1960	37.7	39.3	37.6	46.1	36.0	43.4	49.9	37.2	10.8
1961	38.1	39.7	38.0	47.0	36.4	43.8	50.1	37.9	10.7
1962	37.9	39.0	37.8	47.3	36.3	44.1	50.0	38.7	10.0
1963	38.3	38.0	38.3	47.5	37.2	44.9	50.6	39.7	9.6
1964	38.7	37.0	38.9	49.4	37.2	45.0	51.4	40.2	10.1
1965	39.3	38.0	39.4	49.9	38.5	46.1	50.9	41.1	10.0
1966	40.3	41.4	40.1	51.5	39.8	46.8	51.7	41.8	9.6
1967	41.1	41.6	41.1	53.3	41.9	48.1	51.8	42.4	9.6
1968	41.6	41.9	41.6	54.5	42.6	48.9	52.3	42.4	9.6
1969	42.7	43.2	42.7	56.7	43.7	49.9	53.8	43.1	9.9
1970	43.3	44.0	43.3	57.7	45.0	51.1	54.4	43.0	9.7
1971	43.4	43.4	43.3	57.7	45.6	51.6	54.3	42.9	9.5
1972	43.9	45.8	43.7	59.1	47.8	52.0	53.9	42.1	9.3
1973	44.7	47.8	44.4	61.1	50.4	53.3	53.7	41.1	8.9
1974	45.7	49.1	45.3	63.1	52.6	54.7	54.6	40.7	8.1
1975	46.3	49.1	46.0	64.1	54.9	55.8	54.6	40.9	8.2
1976	47.3	49.8	47.0	65.0	57.3	57.8	55.0	41.0	8.2
1977	48.4	51.2	48.1	66.5	59.7	59.6	55.8	40.9	8.1
1978	50.0	53.7	49.6	68.3	62.2	61.6	57.1	41.3	8.3
1979	50.9	54.2	50.6	69.0	63.9	63.6	58.3	41.7	8.3
1980	51.5	52.9	51.3	68.9	65.5	65.5	59.9	41.3	8.1
1981	52.1	51.8	52.1	69.6	66.7	66.8	61.1	41.4	8.0
1982	52.6	51.4	52.7	69.8	68.0	68.0	61.6	41.8	7.9
1983	52.9	50.8	53.1	69.9	69.0	68.7	61.9	41.5	7.8
1984	53.6	51.8	53.7	70.4	69.8	70.1	62.9	41.7	7.5
1985	54.5	52.1	54.7	71.8	70.9	71.8	64.4	42.0	7.3
1986	55.3	53.0	55.5	72.4	71.6	73.1	65.9	42.3	7.4
1987	56.0	53.3	56.2	73.0	72.4	74.5	67.1	42.7	7.4
1988	56.6	53.6	56.8	72.7	72.7	75.2	69.0	43.5	7.9
1989	57.4	53.9	57.7	72.4	73.5	76.0	70.5	45.0	8.4
1990	57.5	51.6	58.0	71.3	73.5	76.4	71.2	45.2	8.6
1991	57.4	50.0	57.9	70.1	73.1	76.5	72.0	45.2	8.5
1992	57.8	49.1	58.5	70.9	73.9	76.7	72.6	46.5	8.3
1993	57.9	49.7	58.5	70.9	73.4	76.6	73.5	47.2	8.1
1994	58.8	51.3	59.3	71.0	74.0	77.1	74.6	48.9	9.2
1995	58.9	52.2	59.4	70.3	74.9	77.2	74.4	49.2	8.8
1996	59.3	51.3	59.9	71.3	75.2	77.5	75.4	49.6	8.6
1997	59.8	51.0	60.5	72.7	76.0	77.7	76.0	50.9	8.6
1998	59.8	52.3	60.4	73.0	76.3	77.1	76.2	51.2	8.6
1999	60.0	51.0	60.7	73.2	76.4	77.2	76.7	51.5	8.9
2000	60.2	51.3	60.9	73.3	76.3	77.3	76.8	51.8	9.4
2001	60.1	49.4	60.9	72.9	75.8	77.1	76.4	53.0	9.7

See *Note* at end of table.

Table 1-8. Civilian Labor Force Participation Rates by Race, Hispanic Origin, Sex, and Age, 1948–2001—*Continued*

(Percent.)

Year, race, Hispanic origin, and sex	16 years and over	16 to 19 years	20 years and over						
			Total	20 to 24 years	25 to 34 years	35 to 44 years	45 to 54 years	55 to 64 years	65 years and over
WHITE MEN									
1954	85.6	57.6	87.8	86.3	97.5	98.2	96.8	89.1	40.4
1955	85.4	58.6	87.5	86.5	97.8	98.2	96.7	88.4	39.6
1956	85.6	60.4	87.6	87.6	97.4	98.1	96.8	88.9	40.0
1957	84.8	59.2	86.9	86.6	97.2	98.0	96.7	88.0	37.7
1958	84.3	56.5	86.6	86.7	97.2	98.0	96.6	88.2	35.7
1959	83.8	55.9	86.3	87.3	97.5	98.0	96.3	87.9	34.3
1960	83.4	55.9	86.0	87.8	97.7	97.9	96.1	87.2	33.3
1961	83.0	54.5	85.7	87.6	97.7	97.9	95.9	87.8	31.9
1962	82.1	53.8	84.9	86.5	97.4	97.9	96.0	86.7	30.6
1963	81.5	53.1	84.4	85.8	97.4	97.8	96.2	86.6	28.4
1964	81.1	52.7	84.2	85.7	97.5	97.6	96.1	86.1	27.9
1965	80.8	54.1	83.9	85.3	97.4	97.7	95.9	85.2	27.9
1966	80.6	55.9	83.6	84.4	97.5	97.6	95.8	84.9	27.2
1967	80.6	56.3	83.5	84.0	97.5	97.7	95.6	84.9	27.1
1968	80.4	55.9	83.2	82.4	97.2	97.6	95.4	84.7	27.4
1969	80.2	56.8	83.0	82.6	97.0	97.4	95.1	83.9	27.3
1970	80.0	57.5	82.8	83.3	96.7	97.3	94.9	83.3	26.7
1971	79.6	57.9	82.3	83.2	96.3	97.0	94.7	82.6	25.6
1972	79.6	60.1	82.0	84.3	96.0	97.0	94.0	81.1	24.4
1973	79.4	62.0	81.6	85.8	96.2	96.8	93.5	78.9	22.7
1974	79.4	62.9	81.4	86.6	96.3	96.7	93.0	78.0	22.4
1975	78.7	61.9	80.7	85.5	95.8	96.4	92.9	76.4	21.7
1976	78.4	62.3	80.3	86.3	95.9	96.0	92.5	75.2	20.2
1977	78.5	64.0	80.2	86.8	96.0	96.2	92.1	74.6	20.0
1978	78.6	65.0	80.1	87.3	95.9	96.3	92.1	73.7	20.3
1979	78.6	64.8	80.1	87.6	96.0	96.4	92.2	73.4	20.0
1980	78.2	63.7	79.8	87.2	95.9	96.2	92.1	73.1	19.1
1981	77.9	62.4	79.5	87.0	95.8	96.1	92.4	71.5	18.5
1982	77.4	60.0	79.2	86.3	95.6	96.0	92.2	71.0	17.9
1983	77.1	59.4	78.9	86.1	95.2	96.0	91.9	70.0	17.7
1984	77.1	59.0	78.7	86.5	95.4	96.1	92.0	69.5	16.4
1985	77.0	59.7	78.5	86.4	95.7	95.7	92.0	68.8	15.9
1986	76.9	59.3	78.5	87.3	95.5	95.4	91.8	68.0	16.3
1987	76.8	59.0	78.4	86.9	95.5	95.4	91.6	68.1	16.5
1988	76.9	60.0	78.3	86.6	95.2	95.4	91.8	67.9	16.7
1989	77.1	61.0	78.5	86.8	95.4	95.3	92.2	68.3	16.8
1990	77.1	59.6	78.5	86.2	95.2	95.3	91.7	68.6	16.6
1991	76.5	57.3	78.0	85.4	94.9	95.0	91.4	67.7	15.9
1992	76.5	56.9	78.0	85.2	94.9	94.7	91.8	67.7	16.2
1993	76.2	56.6	77.7	85.5	94.7	94.5	91.3	67.3	15.9
1994	75.9	57.7	77.3	85.5	93.9	93.9	90.3	66.4	17.2
1995	75.7	58.5	77.1	85.1	94.1	93.4	90.0	67.1	16.9
1996	75.8	57.1	77.3	85.0	94.4	93.6	90.4	68.0	17.2
1997	75.9	56.1	77.5	85.1	94.2	93.7	90.6	68.9	17.4
1998	75.6	56.6	77.2	84.6	94.4	93.7	90.3	69.1	16.6
1999	75.6	56.4	77.2	84.9	94.3	93.8	90.1	69.1	17.2
2000	75.4	56.6	77.0	85.0	94.4	93.7	89.8	68.2	17.7
2001	75.1	54.1	76.8	84.0	93.9	93.6	89.8	69.0	17.8

See *Note* at end of table.

Table 1-8. Civilian Labor Force Participation Rates by Race, Hispanic Origin, Sex, and Age, 1948–2001—*Continued*

(Percent.)

Year, race, Hispanic origin, and sex	16 years and over	16 to 19 years	20 years and over						
			Total	20 to 24 years	25 to 34 years	35 to 44 years	45 to 54 years	55 to 64 years	65 years and over
WHITE WOMEN									
1954	33.3	40.6	32.7	44.4	32.5	39.3	39.8	29.1	9.1
1955	34.5	40.7	34.0	45.8	32.8	40.0	42.7	31.8	10.5
1956	35.7	43.1	35.1	46.5	33.2	41.5	44.4	34.0	10.6
1957	35.7	42.2	35.2	45.8	33.6	41.5	45.4	33.7	10.2
1958	35.8	40.1	35.5	46.0	33.6	41.4	46.5	34.5	10.1
1959	36.0	39.6	35.6	44.5	33.4	41.4	47.8	35.7	10.0
1960	36.5	40.3	36.2	45.7	34.1	41.5	48.6	36.2	10.6
1961	36.9	40.6	36.6	46.9	34.3	41.8	48.9	37.2	10.5
1962	36.7	39.8	36.5	47.1	34.1	42.2	48.9	38.0	9.8
1963	37.2	38.7	37.0	47.3	34.8	43.1	49.5	38.9	9.4
1964	37.5	37.8	37.5	48.8	35.0	43.3	50.2	39.4	9.9
1965	38.1	39.2	38.0	49.2	36.3	44.4	49.9	40.3	9.7
1966	39.2	42.6	38.8	51.0	37.7	45.0	50.6	41.1	9.4
1967	40.1	42.5	39.8	53.1	39.7	46.4	50.9	41.9	9.3
1968	40.7	43.0	40.4	54.0	40.6	47.5	51.5	42.0	9.4
1969	41.8	44.6	41.5	56.4	41.7	48.6	53.0	42.6	9.7
1970	42.6	45.6	42.2	57.7	43.2	49.9	53.7	42.6	9.5
1971	42.6	45.4	42.3	58.0	43.7	50.2	53.6	42.5	9.3
1972	43.2	48.1	42.7	59.4	46.0	50.7	53.4	41.9	9.0
1973	44.1	50.1	43.5	61.7	48.7	52.2	53.4	40.7	8.7
1974	45.2	51.7	44.4	63.9	51.3	53.6	54.3	40.4	8.0
1975	45.9	51.5	45.3	65.5	53.8	54.9	54.3	40.6	8.0
1976	46.9	52.8	46.2	66.3	56.0	57.1	54.7	40.7	7.9
1977	48.0	54.5	47.3	67.8	58.5	58.9	55.3	40.7	7.9
1978	49.4	56.7	48.7	69.3	61.2	60.7	56.7	41.1	8.1
1979	50.5	57.4	49.8	70.5	63.1	63.0	58.1	41.5	8.1
1980	51.2	56.2	50.6	70.6	64.8	65.0	59.6	40.9	7.9
1981	51.9	55.4	51.5	71.5	66.4	66.4	60.9	40.9	7.9
1982	52.4	55.0	52.2	71.8	67.8	67.5	61.4	41.5	7.8
1983	52.7	54.5	52.5	72.1	68.7	68.2	61.9	41.1	7.8
1984	53.3	55.4	53.1	72.5	69.8	69.6	62.7	41.2	7.5
1985	54.1	55.2	54.0	73.8	70.9	71.4	64.2	41.5	7.0
1986	55.0	56.3	54.9	74.1	71.8	72.9	65.8	42.1	7.3
1987	55.7	56.5	55.6	74.8	72.5	74.2	67.2	42.4	7.2
1988	56.4	57.2	56.3	74.9	73.0	74.9	69.2	43.6	7.7
1989	57.2	57.1	57.2	74.0	73.8	75.9	70.6	45.2	8.2
1990	57.4	55.3	57.6	73.4	74.1	76.6	71.3	45.5	8.5
1991	57.4	54.1	57.6	72.5	73.8	76.8	72.4	45.4	8.5
1992	57.7	52.5	58.1	73.5	74.4	77.0	72.8	46.8	8.2
1993	58.0	53.5	58.3	73.4	74.3	76.9	74.0	47.6	8.1
1994	58.9	55.1	59.2	73.4	74.9	77.5	75.2	49.4	9.2
1995	59.0	55.5	59.2	72.3	75.8	77.6	75.2	49.5	9.0
1996	59.1	54.7	59.4	73.3	75.5	77.8	76.1	50.1	8.7
1997	59.5	54.1	59.9	73.9	76.3	77.9	76.6	51.5	8.6
1998	59.4	55.4	59.7	74.3	76.3	76.9	76.6	51.6	8.7
1999	59.6	54.5	59.9	73.9	76.0	77.1	77.1	52.0	8.9
2000	59.8	54.7	60.2	74.7	75.9	77.2	77.4	52.3	9.4
2001	59.7	52.8	60.2	74.3	75.3	76.9	77.0	53.7	9.7

See *Note* at end of table.

Table 1-8. Civilian Labor Force Participation Rates by Race, Hispanic Origin, Sex, and Age, 1948–2001—*Continued*

(Percent.)

Year, race, Hispanic origin, and sex	16 years and over	16 to 19 years	20 years and over						
			Total	20 to 24 years	25 to 34 years	35 to 44 years	45 to 54 years	55 to 64 years	65 years and over
BLACK MEN									
1972	73.7	46.3	78.5	82.6	92.6	91.0	85.6	72.5	24.3
1973	73.4	45.7	78.4	83.7	91.8	91.0	87.5	69.5	22.4
1974	73.0	46.7	77.6	83.5	92.7	90.3	84.1	68.9	21.5
1975	71.0	42.5	76.0	78.8	91.5	89.3	83.5	67.6	20.5
1976	70.2	41.3	75.4	79.1	90.9	89.9	82.4	65.1	19.7
1977	70.8	43.2	75.6	79.3	90.7	90.9	82.0	65.5	19.9
1978	71.7	44.9	76.2	78.8	90.8	90.6	83.3	67.9	21.0
1979	71.6	43.6	76.2	80.6	90.7	90.4	84.6	64.8	19.4
1980	70.6	43.2	75.1	79.8	90.8	89.1	83.1	61.7	16.8
1981	70.0	41.6	74.5	79.1	88.9	89.3	82.7	62.1	16.0
1982	70.1	39.7	74.7	78.7	89.2	89.9	82.2	61.9	16.0
1983	70.6	39.8	75.2	79.5	89.0	89.7	84.5	62.5	14.0
1984	70.8	41.7	74.8	79.1	88.9	90.0	83.7	58.9	13.7
1985	70.8	44.5	74.4	79.0	88.9	89.8	82.9	58.9	13.9
1986	71.2	43.7	74.8	80.1	89.6	89.6	84.0	59.1	12.6
1987	71.1	43.5	74.7	77.9	89.4	88.6	83.8	62.1	13.7
1988	71.0	43.7	74.6	79.3	89.3	88.1	83.5	59.4	14.3
1989	71.0	44.7	74.4	80.1	89.8	88.7	82.5	55.4	14.2
1990	71.1	40.7	75.0	76.8	88.8	88.1	83.5	57.9	13.0
1991	70.4	37.3	74.6	76.7	87.4	87.7	83.4	58.7	13.1
1992	70.7	40.6	74.3	75.4	88.0	86.5	81.8	60.0	13.7
1993	69.6	39.5	73.2	74.1	87.3	86.1	80.1	57.9	11.6
1994	69.1	40.8	72.5	73.9	86.2	85.9	79.2	54.4	12.7
1995	69.0	40.1	72.5	74.5	87.4	84.1	78.5	54.4	14.9
1996	68.7	39.4	72.3	73.4	87.5	84.4	78.5	55.7	12.9
1997	68.3	37.4	72.2	72.2	86.8	84.8	80.1	54.3	12.8
1998	69.0	40.6	72.5	71.8	87.1	85.0	79.8	57.3	14.0
1999	68.7	38.6	72.4	69.8	89.2	86.0	78.5	55.5	12.7
2000	69.0	39.0	72.6	73.4	87.7	85.3	79.1	57.1	14.2
2001	68.5	38.0	72.1	69.7	86.7	84.8	78.6	59.1	16.7
BLACK WOMEN									
1972	48.7	32.2	51.2	57.1	60.9	61.4	57.1	43.9	12.5
1973	49.3	34.3	51.6	58.1	62.9	61.7	56.1	44.8	11.1
1974	49.1	33.4	51.4	58.8	62.6	62.1	56.3	43.0	10.2
1975	48.9	34.3	51.1	56.0	63.0	62.0	56.6	43.1	10.5
1976	49.9	33.0	52.5	57.1	66.9	63.0	56.9	43.8	11.1
1977	50.9	32.9	53.6	59.5	68.6	64.1	58.0	43.8	10.2
1978	53.2	37.3	55.5	62.8	70.6	67.2	59.4	43.9	10.8
1979	53.1	36.7	55.4	61.6	70.2	68.0	59.6	44.1	10.5
1980	53.2	34.9	55.6	60.4	70.6	68.2	61.4	44.9	9.9
1981	53.5	34.0	56.0	61.1	70.0	69.8	62.0	45.4	9.3
1982	53.7	33.5	56.2	60.1	70.2	71.7	62.4	44.8	8.5
1983	54.2	33.0	56.8	59.1	72.3	72.6	62.3	44.8	8.2
1984	55.2	35.0	57.6	60.6	71.5	73.7	64.5	46.0	8.0
1985	56.5	37.9	58.6	62.5	72.4	74.8	65.7	45.3	9.4
1986	56.9	39.1	58.9	64.6	72.4	75.8	66.5	43.6	7.8
1987	58.0	39.6	60.0	64.3	73.5	77.8	67.5	44.4	8.6
1988	58.0	37.9	60.1	63.2	73.7	78.2	68.3	43.5	9.6
1989	58.7	40.5	60.6	65.5	73.6	78.0	70.0	42.4	9.8
1990	58.3	36.8	60.6	62.3	72.3	77.7	70.7	43.2	9.9
1991	57.5	33.5	60.0	60.3	71.4	77.2	70.2	44.1	9.2
1992	58.5	35.2	60.8	60.7	73.1	77.1	71.7	45.1	8.6
1993	57.9	34.6	60.2	62.6	70.9	76.8	71.2	44.3	8.2
1994	58.7	36.4	60.9	64.5	71.9	76.4	71.3	45.2	9.2
1995	59.5	39.7	61.4	63.7	73.8	77.3	70.5	47.2	7.7
1996	60.4	38.8	62.6	65.2	75.8	78.2	72.0	47.2	7.7
1997	61.7	39.9	64.0	69.8	78.1	78.4	73.2	47.6	8.1
1998	62.8	42.5	64.8	69.6	79.6	79.9	74.0	48.5	7.9
1999	63.5	38.8	66.1	72.7	82.1	80.4	74.6	48.4	8.9
2000	63.2	39.4	65.6	70.5	81.2	79.8	74.9	48.4	9.9
2001	62.9	37.4	65.4	70.2	81.2	79.5	73.7	49.5	10.1

See *Note* at end of table.

Table 1-8. Civilian Labor Force Participation Rates by Race, Hispanic Origin, Sex, and Age, 1948–2001—*Continued*

(Percent.)

Year, race, Hispanic origin, and sex	16 years and over	16 to 19 years	20 years and over						
			Total	20 to 24 years	25 to 34 years	35 to 44 years	45 to 54 years	55 to 64 years	65 years and over
HISPANIC MEN									
1980	81.4	60.0	84.9	88.0	93.3	93.8	91.6	73.6	20.6
1981	80.6	54.1	84.7	88.7	93.7	92.6	90.5	70.9	19.6
1982	79.7	50.2	84.0	86.1	93.9	93.4	88.8	70.0	18.1
1983	80.3	52.6	84.1	85.9	93.5	93.0	89.4	71.3	17.6
1984	80.6	52.6	84.3	87.1	93.4	93.5	88.9	71.1	15.0
1985	80.4	51.1	84.0	87.3	93.1	92.4	89.5	69.5	15.0
1986	81.0	51.3	84.6	88.3	93.4	93.3	89.9	69.3	15.2
1987	81.0	51.4	84.5	87.8	93.6	93.0	88.0	70.2	14.4
1988	81.9	55.3	85.0	89.4	93.4	93.8	88.5	68.8	17.4
1989	82.0	56.3	85.0	90.4	94.1	93.1	88.8	69.7	16.4
1990	81.4	56.0	84.7	89.6	94.1	92.8	87.1	66.3	14.0
1991	80.3	51.5	83.8	88.5	92.6	91.1	87.6	67.5	14.0
1992	80.7	52.1	84.0	87.4	92.9	92.2	86.8	68.7	14.8
1993	80.2	50.9	83.5	87.8	92.9	92.4	87.2	65.7	15.2
1994	79.2	50.0	82.5	88.0	92.5	91.6	85.7	63.7	14.5
1995	79.1	50.2	82.4	86.2	92.9	91.3	85.6	62.4	15.8
1996	79.6	50.0	83.0	85.7	93.2	91.7	87.0	65.9	16.7
1997	80.1	47.5	84.1	88.0	93.5	91.9	87.8	68.4	17.4
1998	79.8	48.7	83.6	88.1	94.0	91.4	86.7	70.2	14.8
1999	79.8	50.1	83.5	88.1	93.9	92.2	86.2	68.6	18.2
2000	80.6	50.9	84.2	89.2	94.0	93.3	87.5	69.4	18.2
2001	79.8	52.4	83.1	86.9	93.4	92.6	86.6	67.9	16.9
HISPANIC WOMEN									
1980	47.4	40.1	48.5	56.9	54.0	55.2	54.4	34.7	5.5
1981	48.3	38.2	49.7	59.9	55.4	55.9	54.8	34.5	6.5
1982	48.1	39.2	49.3	58.4	56.4	55.1	53.6	33.3	6.5
1983	47.7	37.6	49.0	56.5	54.8	54.7	55.4	37.4	6.4
1984	49.7	42.4	50.6	56.2	56.9	58.6	55.3	38.6	7.2
1985	49.3	38.0	50.6	57.7	57.1	59.1	55.0	36.4	5.9
1986	50.1	36.5	51.7	58.9	59.0	60.6	57.4	33.9	5.5
1987	52.0	40.1	53.3	60.4	60.9	62.2	57.8	36.8	5.3
1988	53.2	43.7	54.2	62.3	60.9	62.1	57.9	41.5	6.5
1989	53.5	40.8	54.9	60.7	63.0	64.7	57.9	39.0	8.6
1990	53.1	38.7	54.8	59.2	61.3	66.0	58.8	39.7	7.2
1991	52.3	38.0	54.0	56.4	59.8	65.3	60.3	40.5	6.7
1992	52.8	39.1	54.3	59.2	60.8	66.0	59.4	38.0	6.7
1993	52.1	36.7	53.8	56.2	60.5	65.4	59.6	40.1	7.4
1994	52.9	38.7	54.4	57.9	60.5	66.4	61.4	38.0	7.9
1995	52.6	40.4	53.9	55.9	61.6	65.9	60.5	37.2	6.6
1996	53.4	36.5	55.2	59.3	62.0	67.0	62.6	40.5	6.9
1997	55.1	38.0	57.1	62.2	63.7	69.3	63.3	40.6	8.0
1998	55.6	42.3	57.1	62.2	64.6	67.9	64.7	41.8	6.5
1999	55.9	40.6	57.7	63.0	62.7	70.5	66.2	42.4	6.5
2000	56.9	41.4	58.7	64.9	65.3	69.9	68.3	41.3	7.7
2001	56.8	41.0	58.5	64.3	65.2	70.2	67.9	43.3	6.8

Note: Detail for the above race and Hispanic-origin groups will not sum to totals because data for the Other races group are not presented and Hispanics are included in both the White and Black population groups. See "Notes and Definitions" for information on historical comparability.

Table 1-9. Employed and Unemployed Full- and Part-Time Workers by Age, Sex, and Race, 1994–2001

(Thousands of persons.)

Year, age, sex, and race	Employed [1]								Unemployed	
	Full-time workers				Part-time workers					
		At work				At work [2]				
	Total	35 hours or more	1 to 34 hours for economic or noneconomic reasons	Not at work	Total	Part-time for economic reasons	Part-time for noneconomic reasons	Not at work	Looking for full-time work	Looking for part-time work
TOTAL, 16 YEARS AND OVER										
1994	99 772	85 686	9 980	4 106	23 288	3 453	18 321	1 513	6 513	1 483
1995	101 679	87 736	9 924	4 020	23 220	3 215	18 443	1 562	5 909	1 495
1996	103 537	89 020	10 381	4 137	23 170	3 080	18 459	1 631	5 803	1 433
1997	106 334	92 399	9 922	4 013	23 224	2 826	18 856	1 542	5 395	1 344
1998	108 202	91 880	12 260	4 062	23 261	2 497	19 239	1 524	4 916	1 293
1999	110 302	96 276	10 079	3 947	23 186	2 216	19 509	1 461	4 669	1 211
2000	112 291	99 136	9 020	4 135	22 917	1 985	19 451	1 481	4 502	1 153
2001	111 832	97 517	10 312	4 003	23 241	2 280	19 408	1 552	5 493	1 249
TOTAL, 20 YEARS AND OVER										
1994	97 890	84 126	9 711	4 052	19 010	3 094	14 580	1 337	5 865	811
1995	99 651	86 043	9 643	3 965	18 830	2 853	14 613	1 365	5 253	806
1996	101 496	87 344	10 070	4 083	18 712	2 733	14 556	1 423	5 157	773
1997	104 168	90 613	9 601	3 954	18 729	2 500	14 872	1 357	4 748	719
1998	105 882	89 966	11 915	4 001	18 530	2 197	15 007	1 326	4 332	672
1999	107 917	94 270	9 754	3 893	18 399	1 939	15 187	1 273	4 094	624
2000	109 769	97 019	8 678	4 073	18 163	1 726	15 148	1 290	3 936	626
2001	109 531	95 585	9 998	3 948	18 652	1 985	15 315	1 351	4 887	668
MEN, 16 YEARS AND OVER										
1994	58 832	51 615	5 144	2 073	7 617	1 524	5 691	403	3 745	622
1995	59 936	52 833	5 120	1 984	7 441	1 401	5 626	414	3 374	609
1996	60 762	53 425	5 290	2 047	7 445	1 322	5 692	431	3 276	604
1997	62 258	55 216	5 040	2 001	7 427	1 187	5 821	418	3 012	564
1998	63 189	55 080	6 136	1 973	7 504	1 063	6 026	416	2 707	559
1999	63 930	57 034	4 971	1 924	7 516	946	6 178	392	2 548	518
2000	64 938	58 440	4 495	2 003	7 355	845	6 099	412	2 465	489
2001	64 524	57 394	5 164	1 966	7 557	1 011	6 123	422	3 122	541
MEN, 20 YEARS AND OVER										
1994	57 707	50 678	4 989	2 040	5 587	1 351	3 908	329	3 359	269
1995	58 707	51 793	4 960	1 955	5 377	1 228	3 828	322	2 988	251
1996	59 543	52 411	5 117	2 015	5 354	1 155	3 859	341	2 899	248
1997	60 974	54 148	4 857	1 969	5 310	1 023	3 944	343	2 644	239
1998	61 837	53 947	5 950	1 940	5 297	925	4 050	322	2 366	214
1999	62 514	55 827	4 790	1 897	5 247	809	4 127	311	2 222	211
2000	63 458	57 179	4 307	1 972	5 122	721	4 076	325	2 138	212
2001	63 188	56 262	4 991	1 936	5 399	864	4 204	330	2 771	232
WOMEN, 16 YEARS AND OVER										
1994	40 940	34 071	4 836	2 033	15 670	1 929	12 631	1 111	2 768	861
1995	41 743	34 903	4 805	2 036	15 779	1 814	12 817	1 148	2 535	886
1996	42 776	35 594	5 091	2 090	15 725	1 758	12 767	1 200	2 527	829
1997	44 076	37 183	4 882	2 011	15 797	1 638	13 035	1 124	2 383	779
1998	45 014	36 800	6 124	2 090	15 757	1 435	13 214	1 108	2 210	734
1999	46 372	39 242	5 108	2 022	15 670	1 270	13 330	1 069	2 121	693
2000	47 353	40 696	4 526	2 131	15 562	1 140	13 352	1 069	2 037	663
2001	47 308	40 122	5 149	2 037	15 684	1 269	13 285	1 130	2 371	708
WOMEN, 20 YEARS AND OVER										
1994	40 183	33 449	4 722	2 012	13 423	1 743	10 672	1 008	2 506	543
1995	40 943	34 250	4 683	2 010	13 453	1 623	10 785	1 043	2 265	554
1996	41 953	34 933	4 953	2 068	13 357	1 579	10 697	1 082	2 258	525
1997	43 194	36 465	4 744	1 985	13 419	1 477	10 927	1 015	2 105	480
1998	44 045	36 019	5 965	2 061	13 233	1 272	10 957	1 004	1 966	458
1999	45 403	38 443	4 964	1 996	13 152	1 131	11 059	962	1 872	413
2000	46 312	39 840	4 371	2 101	13 041	1 005	11 072	964	1 798	414
2001	46 343	39 323	5 007	2 012	13 253	1 121	11 111	1 022	2 116	436

See footnotes and *Note* at end of table.

Table 1-9. Employed and Unemployed Full- and Part-Time Workers by Age, Sex, and Race, 1994–2001—*Continued*

(Thousands of persons.)

Year, age, sex, and race	Employed [1]								Unemployed	
	Full-time workers				Part-time workers					
		At work				At work [2]			Looking for full-time work	Looking for part-time work
	Total	35 hours or more	1 to 34 hours for economic or noneconomic reasons	Not at work	Total	Part-time for economic reasons	Part-time for noneconomic reasons	Not at work		
WHITE MEN, 16 YEARS AND OVER										
1994	50 964	44 750	4 431	1 783	6 487	1 192	4 946	350	2 800	475
1995	51 768	45 634	4 406	1 728	6 378	1 100	4 921	357	2 525	475
1996	52 527	46 208	4 547	1 772	6 361	1 046	4 941	374	2 426	470
1997	53 640	47 563	4 358	1 719	6 358	909	5 084	365	2 202	440
1998	54 206	47 239	5 257	1 709	6 398	829	5 209	360	1 999	432
1999	54 756	48 834	4 274	1 647	6 383	730	5 314	339	1 883	391
2000	55 455	49 877	3 859	1 720	6 241	650	5 240	351	1 783	382
2001	55 023	48 897	4 447	1 678	6 388	782	5 242	364	2 302	428
WHITE MEN, 20 YEARS AND OVER										
1994	49 959	43 912	4 291	1 756	4 717	1 048	3 382	287	2 533	203
1995	50 691	44 726	4 263	1 702	4 563	958	3 330	275	2 260	204
1996	51 442	45 300	4 397	1 745	4 534	907	3 330	297	2 167	197
1997	52 498	46 609	4 199	1 691	4 488	771	3 419	298	1 946	194
1998	53 017	46 240	5 095	1 682	4 483	716	3 487	280	1 756	164
1999	53 513	47 764	4 124	1 626	4 420	618	3 534	268	1 651	162
2000	54 146	48 762	3 692	1 691	4 323	550	3 496	277	1 547	165
2001	53 836	47 891	4 292	1 653	4 531	660	3 587	284	2 051	190
WHITE WOMEN, 16 YEARS AND OVER										
1994	33 906	28 170	4 031	1 705	13 832	1 517	11 316	1 000	1 935	682
1995	34 422	28 685	4 039	1 697	13 922	1 431	11 448	1 043	1 755	705
1996	35 057	29 124	4 196	1 737	13 863	1 388	11 398	1 077	1 749	656
1997	35 965	30 286	4 036	1 643	13 894	1 260	11 623	1 011	1 587	608
1998	36 553	29 792	5 039	1 722	13 774	1 089	11 695	990	1 481	572
1999	37 417	31 577	4 157	1 684	13 679	947	11 768	964	1 469	530
2000	38 126	32 674	3 703	1 750	13 653	865	11 833	955	1 413	521
2001	38 075	32 186	4 205	1 683	13 735	973	11 757	1 006	1 642	551
WHITE WOMEN, 20 YEARS AND OVER										
1994	33 250	27 628	3 936	1 686	11 866	1 359	9 596	912	1 754	443
1995	33 728	28 116	3 938	1 674	11 916	1 277	9 690	949	1 579	463
1996	34 350	28 553	4 078	1 719	11 814	1 243	9 598	973	1 570	427
1997	35 216	29 677	3 919	1 620	11 847	1 136	9 788	923	1 396	388
1998	35 738	29 130	4 910	1 698	11 604	953	9 749	902	1 318	370
1999	36 602	30 905	4 036	1 662	11 496	839	9 789	867	1 297	319
2000	37 258	31 960	3 572	1 726	11 479	750	9 865	864	1 245	337
2001	37 259	31 509	4 088	1 661	11 625	852	9 861	913	1 464	352

See footnotes and *Note* at end of table.

Table 1-9. Employed and Unemployed Full- and Part-Time Workers by Age, Sex, and Race, 1994–2001—*Continued*

(Thousands of persons.)

Year, age, sex, and race	Employed [1]								Unemployed	
	Full-time workers				Part-time workers				Looking for full-time work	Looking for part-time work
		At work		Not at work		At work [2]		Not at work		
	Total	35 hours or more	1 to 34 hours for economic or noneconomic reasons		Total	Part-time for economic reasons	Part-time for noneconomic reasons			
BLACK MEN, 16 YEARS AND OVER										
1994	5 452	4 723	520	209	788	247	504	38	738	111
1995	5 685	4 995	513	177	737	216	479	43	660	101
1996	5 723	4 971	547	206	733	199	494	40	705	103
1997	5 894	5 193	490	211	713	203	474	36	648	98
1998	6 148	5 322	637	189	723	168	520	34	572	99
1999	6 263	5 574	494	196	764	163	568	33	528	97
2000	6 434	5 780	450	204	746	146	559	41	555	80
2001	6 342	5 654	483	205	785	174	570	41	646	85
BLACK MEN, 20 YEARS AND OVER										
1994	5 369	4 655	509	205	595	223	343	29	634	47
1995	5 582	4 906	502	175	554	193	326	36	558	35
1996	5 622	4 892	528	201	545	177	338	30	602	37
1997	5 790	5 111	471	208	535	179	326	30	549	35
1998	6 023	5 218	620	185	507	147	334	25	487	37
1999	6 140	5 477	471	192	561	142	392	27	446	35
2000	6 303	5 668	434	201	529	126	369	33	479	32
2001	6 228	5 556	471	201	577	153	392	33	559	31
BLACK WOMEN, 16 YEARS AND OVER										
1994	5 289	4 408	627	253	1 306	319	906	79	678	140
1995	5 542	4 679	594	268	1 315	290	952	74	637	140
1996	5 776	4 785	710	280	1 310	289	933	88	652	132
1997	6 026	5 085	652	289	1 336	305	952	79	677	136
1998	6 281	5 166	828	288	1 404	278	1 045	81	624	131
1999	6 641	5 651	734	256	1 388	257	1 059	72	554	130
2000	6 845	5 918	638	289	1 309	214	1 017	78	524	109
2001	6 820	5 827	720	273	1 322	226	1 013	83	594	124
BLACK WOMEN, 20 YEARS AND OVER										
1994	5 211	4 346	612	251	1 108	300	740	69	608	76
1995	5 469	4 623	580	266	1 087	263	757	66	553	66
1996	5 684	4 714	693	277	1 078	263	737	79	570	73
1997	5 921	5 001	634	286	1 092	273	755	64	603	70
1998	6 159	5 073	803	283	1 131	256	807	68	555	66
1999	6 519	5 549	717	252	1 145	230	850	65	486	75
2000	6 711	5 805	621	285	1 062	199	796	68	462	57
2001	6 702	5 730	701	271	1 099	204	822	73	528	61

Note: See "Notes and Definitions" for information on historical comparability.

1. Employed persons are classified as full- or part-time workers based on their usual weekly hours at all jobs regardless of the number of hours they are at work during the reference week. Persons absent from work also are classified according to their usual status.
2. Includes some persons at work 35 hours or more classified by their reason for working part time.

Table 1-10. Persons Not in the Labor Force by Desire and Availability for Work, Age, and Sex, 1996–2001

(Thousands of persons.)

Category	Total		Age						Sex			
			16 to 24 years		25 to 54 years		55 and over		Men		Women	
	1996	1997	1996	1997	1996	1997	1996	1997	1996	1997	1996	1997
TOTAL, NOT IN THE LABOR FORCE	66647	66837	11160	11343	18720	18552	36768	36942	24119	24454	42528	42382
Do Not Want A Job Now [1]	61197	61895	9110	9434	16205	16311	35882	36151	21929	22420	39267	39475
Want A Job [1]	5451	4941	2050	1909	2514	2241	886	791	2190	2034	3261	2907
Did not search for work in the previous year	3161	2857	1100	1034	1407	1245	654	579	1185	1118	1976	1739
Searched for work in the previous year [2]	2290	2084	950	875	1108	997	232	212	1005	917	1285	1168
Not available to work now	732	669	365	346	328	289	40	34	277	257	455	412
Available to work now	1558	1416	585	529	780	708	192	178	728	659	830	756
Reason not currently looking:												
Discouragement over job prospects [3]	397	343	115	107	225	184	58	52	233	200	164	143
Reasons other than discouragement	1160	1073	471	423	555	524	135	126	495	460	666	613
Family responsibilities	177	139	35	26	125	97	17	16	31	21	146	117
In school or training	257	235	211	188	43	45	3	2	138	113	119	121
Ill health or disability	121	116	22	17	73	71	27	28	49	52	72	64
Other [4]	605	583	203	191	314	311	88	81	277	273	328	311

Category	Total		Age						Sex			
			16 to 24 years		25 to 54 years		55 and over		Men		Women	
	1998	1999	1998	1999	1998	1999	1998	1999	1998	1999	1998	1999
TOTAL, NOT IN THE LABOR FORCE	67547	68385	11343	11740	18732	18785	37472	37861	24799	25210	42748	43175
Do Not Want A Job Now [1]	62735	63818	9491	9938	16580	16814	36664	37066	22790	23307	39945	40511
Want A Job [1]	4812	4568	1852	1802	2152	1971	807	795	2008	1903	2803	2665
Did not search for work in the previous year	2859	2723	1011	981	1240	1144	608	599	1134	1083	1725	1640
Searched for work in the previous year [2]	1953	1844	841	822	912	827	200	196	875	820	1078	1024
Not available to work now	643	644	332	345	275	258	36	41	250	249	392	395
Available to work now	1310	1201	509	477	637	569	164	155	624	571	686	629
Reason not currently looking:												
Discouragement over job prospects [3]	331	273	108	86	170	146	53	41	198	161	133	113
Reasons other than discouragement	979	927	401	391	467	423	111	114	427	411	552	517
Family responsibilities	143	132	37	29	93	92	13	11	23	29	120	103
In school or training	206	214	173	176	32	34	1	4	105	110	102	104
Ill health or disability	104	97	14	13	69	57	21	26	52	39	52	58
Other [4]	525	485	177	173	273	239	75	73	247	234	278	251

Category	Total		Age						Sex			
			16 to 24 years		25 to 54 years		55 and over		Men		Women	
	2000	2001	2000	2001	2000	2001	2000	2001	2000	2001	2000	2001
TOTAL, NOT IN THE LABOR FORCE	68836	70050	11738	12384	18953	19495	38146	38171	25484	26114	43352	43935
Do Not Want A Job Now [1]	64459	65483	10107	10629	17007	17509	37345	37345	23627	24119	40832	41363
Want A Job [1]	4377	4567	1631	1755	1945	1986	801	826	1856	1995	2521	2572
Did not search for work in the previous year	2675	2705	903	946	1143	1130	629	629	1068	1130	1607	1575
Searched for work in the previous year [2]	1703	1862	728	809	802	856	172	197	788	865	914	997
Not available to work now	550	591	280	306	237	248	33	36	217	227	334	364
Available to work now	1152	1271	448	503	565	608	139	161	572	638	581	634
Reason not currently looking:												
Discouragement over job prospects [3]	260	319	79	105	143	165	39	49	160	191	100	128
Reasons other than discouragement	892	952	369	398	422	443	101	112	412	447	481	505
Family responsibilities	118	131	26	31	83	87	10	13	23	30	96	101
In school or training	185	208	158	174	26	32	1	2	97	112	88	96
Ill health or disability	95	95	15	16	58	55	22	24	49	45	46	50
Other [4]	493	518	171	177	255	268	68	74	243	260	250	258

Note: See "Notes and Definitions" for information on historical comparability.

1. Includes some persons who are not asked if they want a job.
2. Persons who had a job in the prior 12 months must have searched since the end of that job .
3. Includes believes no work available, could not find work, lacks necessary schooling or training, employer thinks too young or old, and other types of discrimination.
4. Includes those who did not actively look for work in the prior 4 weeks for such reasons as child-care and transportation problems, as well as a small number for which reason for nonparticipation was not ascertained.

Table 1-11. Employed Civilians by Race, Hispanic Origin, Sex, and Age, 1948–2001

(Thousands of persons.)

Year, race, Hispanic origin, and sex	16 years and over	16 to 19 years			20 years and over						
		Total	16 to 17 years	18 to 19 years	Total	20 to 24 years	25 to 34 years	35 to 44 years	45 to 54 years	55 to 64 years	65 years and over
TOTAL											
1948	58343	4026	1600	2426	54318	6937	13801	13050	10624	7103	2804
1949	57651	3712	1466	2246	53940	6660	13639	13108	10636	7042	2864
1950	58918	3703	1433	2270	55218	6746	13917	13424	10966	7265	2899
1951	59961	3767	1575	2192	56196	6321	14233	13746	11421	7558	2917
1952	60250	3719	1626	2092	56536	5572	14515	14058	11687	7785	2919
1953	61179	3720	1577	2142	57460	5225	14519	14774	11969	7806	3166
1954	60109	3475	1422	2053	56634	4971	14190	14541	11976	7895	3060
1955	62170	3642	1500	2143	58528	5270	14481	14879	12556	8158	3185
1956	63799	3818	1647	2171	59983	5545	14407	15218	12978	8519	3314
1957	64071	3778	1613	2167	60291	5641	14253	15348	13320	8553	3179
1958	63036	3582	1519	2063	59454	5571	13675	15157	13448	8559	3045
1959	64630	3838	1670	2168	60791	5870	13709	15454	13915	8822	3023
1960	65778	4129	1770	2360	61648	6119	13630	15598	14238	8989	3073
1961	65746	4108	1621	2486	61638	6227	13429	15552	14320	9120	2987
1962	66702	4195	1607	2588	62508	6446	13311	15901	14491	9346	3013
1963	67762	4255	1751	2504	63508	6815	13318	16114	14749	9596	2915
1964	69305	4516	2013	2503	64789	7303	13449	16166	15094	9804	2973
1965	71088	5036	2075	2962	66052	7702	13704	16294	15320	10028	3005
1966	72895	5721	2269	3452	67178	7964	14017	16312	15615	10310	2961
1967	74372	5682	2334	3348	68690	8499	14575	16281	15789	10536	3011
1968	75920	5781	2403	3377	70141	8762	15265	16220	16083	10745	3065
1969	77902	6117	2573	3543	71785	9319	15883	16100	16410	10919	3155
1970	78678	6144	2598	3546	72534	9731	16318	15922	16473	10974	3118
1971	79367	6208	2596	3613	73158	10201	16781	15675	16451	11009	3040
1972	82153	6746	2787	3959	75407	10999	18082	15822	16457	11044	3003
1973	85064	7271	3032	4239	77793	11839	19509	16041	16553	10966	2886
1974	86794	7448	3111	4338	79347	12101	20610	16203	16633	10964	2835
1975	85846	7104	2941	4162	78744	11885	21087	15953	16190	10827	2801
1976	88752	7336	2972	4363	81416	12570	22493	16468	16224	10912	2747
1977	92017	7688	3138	4550	84329	13196	23850	17157	16212	11126	2787
1978	96048	8070	3330	4739	87979	13887	25281	18128	16338	11400	2946
1979	98824	8083	3340	4743	90741	14327	26492	18981	16357	11585	2999
1980	99303	7710	3106	4605	91593	14087	27204	19523	16234	11586	2960
1981	100397	7225	2866	4359	93172	14122	28180	20145	16255	11525	2945
1982	99526	6549	2505	4044	92978	13690	28149	20879	15923	11414	2923
1983	100834	6342	2320	4022	94491	13722	28756	21960	15812	11315	2927
1984	105005	6444	2404	4040	98562	14207	30348	23598	16178	11395	2835
1985	107150	6434	2492	3941	100716	13980	31208	24732	16509	11474	2813
1986	109597	6472	2622	3850	103125	13790	32201	25861	16949	11405	2919
1987	112440	6640	2736	3905	105800	13524	33105	27179	17487	11465	3041
1988	114968	6805	2713	4092	108164	13244	33574	28269	18447	11433	3197
1989	117342	6759	2588	4172	110582	12962	34045	29443	19279	11499	3355
1990	118793	6581	2410	4171	112213	13401	33935	30817	19525	11189	3346
1991	117718	5906	2202	3704	111812	12975	33061	31593	19882	11001	3300
1992	118492	5669	2128	3540	112824	12872	32667	31923	21022	10998	3341
1993	120259	5805	2226	3579	114455	12840	32385	32666	22175	11058	3331
1994	123060	6161	2510	3651	116899	12758	32286	33599	23348	11228	3681
1995	124900	6419	2573	3846	118481	12443	32356	34202	24378	11435	3666
1996	126708	6500	2646	3853	120208	12138	32077	35051	25514	11739	3690
1997	129558	6661	2648	4012	122897	12380	31809	35908	26744	12296	3761
1998	131463	7051	2762	4289	124413	12557	31394	36278	27587	12872	3725
1999	133488	7172	2793	4379	126316	12891	30865	36728	28635	13315	3882
2000	135208	7276	2778	4498	127933	13321	30501	36697	29717	13627	4070
2001	135073	6889	2573	4316	128183	13361	29697	36226	30592	14133	4174

See *Note* at end of table.

Table 1-11. Employed Civilians by Race, Hispanic Origin, Sex, and Age, 1948–2001—*Continued*

(Thousands of persons.)

Year, race, Hispanic origin, and sex	16 years and over	16 to 19 years			20 years and over						
		Total	16 to 17 years	18 to 19 years	Total	20 to 24 years	25 to 34 years	35 to 44 years	45 to 54 years	55 to 64 years	65 years and over
WHITE											
1954	53957	3078	1257	1822	50879	4358	12616	13000	10811	7262	2831
1955	55833	3225	1330	1896	52608	4637	12855	13327	11322	7510	2957
1956	57269	3389	1465	1922	53880	4897	12748	13637	11706	7822	3068
1957	57465	3374	1442	1931	54091	4952	12619	13716	12009	7829	2951
1958	56613	3216	1370	1847	53397	4908	12128	13571	12113	7849	2828
1959	58006	3475	1520	1955	54531	5138	12144	13830	12552	8063	2805
1960	58850	3700	1598	2103	55150	5331	12021	13930	12820	8192	2855
1961	58913	3693	1472	2220	55220	5460	11835	13905	12906	8335	2778
1962	59698	3774	1447	2327	55924	5676	11703	14173	13066	8511	2795
1963	60622	3851	1600	2250	56771	6036	11689	14341	13304	8718	2683
1964	61922	4076	1846	2230	57846	6444	11794	14380	13596	8916	2717
1965	63446	4562	1892	2670	58884	6752	11992	14473	13804	9116	2748
1966	65021	5176	2052	3124	59845	6986	12268	14449	14072	9356	2713
1967	66361	5114	2121	2993	61247	7493	12763	14429	14224	9596	2746
1968	67750	5195	2193	3002	62555	7687	13410	14386	14487	9781	2804
1969	69518	5508	2347	3161	64010	8182	13935	14270	14788	9947	2888
1970	70217	5571	2386	3185	64645	8559	14326	14092	14854	9979	2835
1971	70878	5670	2404	3266	65208	9000	14713	13858	14843	10014	2780
1972	73370	6173	2581	3592	67197	9718	15904	13940	14845	10077	2714
1973	75708	6623	2806	3816	69086	10424	17099	14083	14886	9983	2610
1974	77184	6796	2881	3916	70388	10676	18040	14196	14948	9958	2568
1975	76411	6487	2721	3770	69924	10546	18485	13979	14555	9827	2533
1976	78853	6724	2762	3962	72129	11119	19662	14407	14549	9923	2470
1977	81700	7068	2926	4142	74632	11696	20844	14984	14483	10107	2518
1978	84936	7367	3085	4282	77569	12251	22008	15809	14550	10311	2642
1979	87259	7356	3079	4278	79904	12594	23033	16578	14522	10477	2699
1980	87715	7021	2861	4161	80694	12405	23653	17071	14405	10475	2684
1981	88709	6588	2645	3943	82121	12477	24551	17617	14414	10386	2676
1982	87903	5984	2317	3667	81918	12097	24531	18268	14083	10283	2656
1983	88893	5799	2156	3643	83094	12138	24955	19194	13961	10169	2678
1984	92120	5836	2209	3627	86284	12451	26235	20552	14239	10227	2580
1985	93736	5768	2270	3498	87968	12235	26945	21552	14459	10247	2530
1986	95660	5792	2386	3406	89869	12027	27746	22515	14750	10176	2654
1987	97789	5898	2468	3431	91890	11748	28429	23596	15216	10164	2738
1988	99812	6030	2424	3606	93782	11438	28796	24468	16054	10153	2874
1989	101584	5946	2278	3668	95638	11084	29091	25442	16775	10223	3024
1990	102261	5779	2141	3638	96481	11498	28773	26282	16933	9960	3035
1991	101182	5216	1971	3246	95966	11116	27989	26883	17269	9719	2990
1992	101669	4985	1904	3081	96684	11031	27552	27097	18285	9701	3019
1993	103045	5113	1990	3123	97932	10931	27274	27645	19273	9772	3037
1994	105190	5398	2210	3188	99792	10736	27101	28442	20247	9912	3354
1995	106490	5593	2273	3320	100897	10400	27014	28951	21127	10070	3335
1996	107808	5667	2325	3343	102141	10149	26678	29566	22071	10313	3364
1997	109856	5807	2341	3466	104049	10362	26294	30137	23061	10785	3411
1998	110931	6089	2436	3653	104842	10512	25729	30320	23662	11272	3347
1999	112235	6204	2435	3769	106032	10716	25113	30548	24507	11657	3491
2000	113475	6270	2411	3859	107205	11078	24678	30522	25384	11901	3643
2001	113220	5969	2246	3723	107252	11114	23965	30047	26068	12348	3709

See *Note* at end of table.

Table 1-11. Employed Civilians by Race, Hispanic Origin, Sex, and Age, 1948–2001—*Continued*

(Thousands of persons.)

Year, race, Hispanic origin, and sex	16 years and over	16 to 19 years			20 years and over						
		Total	16 to 17 years	18 to 19 years	Total	20 to 24 years	25 to 34 years	35 to 44 years	45 to 54 years	55 to 64 years	65 years and over
BLACK											
1972	7802	509	180	329	7292	1166	1924	1629	1434	872	269
1973	8128	570	194	378	7559	1258	2062	1659	1460	872	249
1974	8203	554	190	364	7649	1231	2157	1682	1452	884	243
1975	7894	507	183	325	7386	1115	2145	1617	1393	874	241
1976	8227	508	170	338	7719	1193	2309	1679	1416	870	252
1977	8540	508	169	339	8031	1244	2443	1754	1448	892	251
1978	9102	571	191	380	8531	1359	2641	1848	1479	932	273
1979	9359	579	204	376	8780	1424	2759	1902	1502	927	266
1980	9313	547	192	356	8765	1376	2827	1910	1487	925	239
1981	9355	505	170	335	8849	1346	2872	1957	1489	954	231
1982	9189	428	138	290	8761	1283	2830	2025	1469	928	225
1983	9375	416	123	294	8959	1280	2976	2107	1456	937	204
1984	10119	474	146	328	9645	1423	3223	2311	1533	945	209
1985	10501	532	175	356	9969	1399	3325	2427	1598	985	235
1986	10814	536	183	353	10278	1429	3464	2524	1666	982	214
1987	11309	587	203	385	10722	1421	3614	2695	1714	1036	241
1988	11658	601	223	378	11057	1433	3725	2839	1783	1018	261
1989	11953	625	237	388	11328	1467	3801	2981	1844	970	265
1990	12175	598	194	404	11577	1409	3803	3287	1897	933	248
1991	12074	494	161	334	11580	1373	3714	3401	1892	957	243
1992	12151	492	157	335	11659	1343	3699	3441	1964	965	246
1993	12382	494	171	323	11888	1377	3700	3584	2059	941	226
1994	12835	552	224	328	12284	1449	3732	3722	2178	953	251
1995	13279	586	223	363	12693	1443	3844	3861	2288	1004	253
1996	13542	613	233	380	12929	1411	3851	3974	2426	1025	241
1997	13969	631	229	401	13339	1456	3903	4094	2588	1048	249
1998	14556	736	246	490	13820	1496	3967	4238	2739	1118	262
1999	15056	691	243	448	14365	1594	4091	4404	2872	1134	271
2000	15334	729	266	462	14606	1642	4036	4404	3031	1190	302
2001	15270	663	235	429	14606	1610	3917	4359	3130	1248	341
HISPANIC											
1973	3396	325	...	...	...	...	...	...	...	...	...
1974	3687	355	...	...	...	...	...	...	...	...	...
1975	3663	322	...	...	...	...	...	...	...	...	...
1976	3720	341	124	230	3436	614	1135	803	573	269	42
1977	4079	381	135	245	3715	715	1212	860	608	269	50
1978	4527	423	159	264	4104	803	1330	942	661	307	62
1979	4785	445	152	292	4340	860	1430	996	666	319	69
1980	5527	500	174	325	5028	998	1675	1074	811	389	80
1981	5813	459	155	304	5354	1060	1837	1147	829	399	82
1982	5805	410	119	291	5394	1030	1896	1173	816	399	80
1983	6072	423	125	297	5649	1068	1997	1224	837	441	81
1984	6651	468	148	320	6182	1160	2201	1385	883	474	79
1985	6888	438	144	294	6449	1187	2316	1473	913	486	75
1986	7219	430	146	284	6789	1231	2427	1570	1011	474	76
1987	7790	474	149	325	7316	1273	2668	1775	1010	512	76
1988	8250	523	171	353	7727	1341	2749	1876	1078	585	97
1989	8573	548	165	383	8025	1325	2900	1968	1129	589	114
1990	9845	668	208	460	9177	1672	3327	2229	1235	611	103
1991	9828	602	169	433	9225	1622	3264	2333	1266	637	103
1992	10027	577	169	408	9450	1575	3350	2468	1316	628	112
1993	10361	570	160	410	9792	1574	3446	2605	1402	630	135
1994	10788	609	195	415	10178	1643	3517	2737	1495	647	139
1995	11127	645	194	450	10483	1609	3618	2889	1565	666	135
1996	11642	646	199	447	10996	1628	3758	3115	1595	748	152
1997	12726	714	228	487	12012	1798	4029	3371	1846	794	173
1998	13291	793	230	563	12498	1883	4113	3504	1994	846	158
1999	13720	854	254	600	12866	1881	4097	3738	2074	886	190
2000	14492	902	261	641	13590	1994	4270	3903	2278	939	206
2001	14714	923	248	675	13791	2004	4290	3903	2423	972	198

See *Note* at end of table.

Table 1-11. Employed Civilians by Race, Hispanic Origin, Sex, and Age, 1948–2001—*Continued*

(Thousands of persons.)

Year, race, Hispanic origin, and sex	16 years and over	16 to 19 years			20 years and over						
		Total	16 to 17 years	18 to 19 years	Total	20 to 24 years	25 to 34 years	35 to 44 years	45 to 54 years	55 to 64 years	65 years and over
MEN											
1948	41725	2344	996	1348	39382	4349	10038	9363	7742	5587	2303
1949	40925	2124	911	1213	38803	4197	9879	9308	7661	5438	2329
1950	41578	2186	909	1277	39394	4255	10060	9445	7790	5508	2336
1951	41780	2156	979	1177	39626	3780	10134	9607	8012	5711	2382
1952	41682	2107	985	1121	39578	3183	10352	9753	8144	5804	2343
1953	42430	2136	976	1159	40296	2901	10500	10229	8374	5808	2483
1954	41619	1985	881	1104	39634	2724	10254	10082	8330	5830	2414
1955	42621	2095	936	1159	40526	2973	10453	10267	8553	5857	2424
1956	43379	2164	1008	1156	41216	3245	10337	10385	8732	6004	2512
1957	43357	2115	987	1130	41239	3346	10222	10427	8851	6002	2394
1958	42423	2012	948	1064	40411	3293	9790	10291	8828	5955	2254
1959	43466	2198	1015	1183	41267	3597	9862	10492	9048	6058	2210
1960	43904	2361	1090	1271	41543	3754	9759	10552	9182	6105	2191
1961	43656	2315	989	1325	41342	3795	9591	10505	9195	6155	2098
1962	44177	2362	990	1372	41815	3898	9475	10711	9333	6260	2138
1963	44657	2406	1073	1334	42251	4118	9431	10801	9478	6385	2038
1964	45474	2587	1242	1345	42886	4370	9531	10832	9637	6478	2039
1965	46340	2918	1285	1634	43422	4583	9611	10837	9792	6542	2057
1966	46919	3253	1389	1863	43668	4599	9709	10764	9904	6668	2024
1967	47479	3186	1417	1769	44294	4809	9988	10674	9990	6774	2058
1968	48114	3255	1453	1802	44859	4812	10405	10554	10102	6893	2093
1969	48818	3430	1526	1904	45388	5012	10736	10401	10187	6931	2122
1970	48990	3409	1504	1905	45581	5237	10936	10216	10170	6928	2094
1971	49390	3478	1510	1968	45912	5593	11218	10028	10139	6916	2019
1972	50896	3765	1598	2167	47130	6138	11884	10088	10139	6929	1953
1973	52349	4039	1721	2318	48310	6655	12617	10126	10197	6857	1856
1974	53024	4103	1744	2359	48922	6739	13119	10135	10181	6880	1869
1975	51857	3839	1621	2219	48018	6484	13205	9891	9902	6722	1811
1976	53138	3947	1626	2321	49190	6915	13869	10069	9881	6724	1732
1977	54728	4174	1733	2441	50555	7232	14483	10399	9832	6848	1761
1978	56479	4336	1800	2535	52143	7559	15124	10845	9806	6954	1855
1979	57607	4300	1799	2501	53308	7791	15688	11202	9735	7015	1876
1980	57186	4085	1672	2412	53101	7532	15832	11355	9548	6999	1835
1981	57397	3815	1526	2289	53582	7504	16266	11613	9478	6909	1812
1982	56271	3379	1307	2072	52891	7197	16002	11902	9234	6781	1776
1983	56787	3300	1213	2087	53487	7232	16216	12450	9133	6686	1770
1984	59091	3322	1244	2078	55769	7571	17166	13309	9326	6694	1703
1985	59891	3328	1300	2029	56562	7339	17564	13800	9411	6753	1695
1986	60892	3323	1352	1971	57569	7250	18092	14266	9554	6654	1753
1987	62107	3381	1393	1988	58726	7058	18487	14898	9750	6682	1850
1988	63273	3492	1403	2089	59781	6918	18702	15457	10201	6591	1911
1989	64315	3477	1327	2150	60837	6799	18952	16002	10569	6548	1968
1990	65104	3427	1254	2173	61678	7151	18779	16771	10690	6378	1909
1991	64223	3044	1135	1909	61178	6909	18265	17086	10813	6245	1860
1992	64440	2944	1096	1848	61496	6819	17966	17230	11365	6173	1943
1993	65349	2994	1155	1839	62355	6805	17877	17665	11927	6166	1916
1994	66450	3156	1288	1868	63294	6771	17741	18111	12439	6142	2089
1995	67377	3292	1316	1977	64085	6665	17709	18374	12958	6272	2108
1996	68207	3310	1318	1992	64897	6429	17527	18816	13483	6470	2172
1997	69685	3401	1355	2045	66284	6548	17338	19327	14107	6735	2229
1998	70693	3558	1398	2161	67135	6638	17097	19634	14544	7052	2171
1999	71446	3685	1437	2249	67762	6729	16694	19811	14991	7274	2263
2000	72293	3713	1405	2308	68580	7009	16494	19770	15561	7389	2357
2001	72080	3493	1283	2210	68587	6949	16086	19500	16043	7601	2407

See *Note* at end of table.

Table 1-11. Employed Civilians by Race, Hispanic Origin, Sex, and Age, 1948–2001—*Continued*

(Thousands of persons.)

Year, race, Hispanic origin, and sex	16 years and over	16 to 19 years			20 years and over						
		Total	16 to 17 years	18 to 19 years	Total	20 to 24 years	25 to 34 years	35 to 44 years	45 to 54 years	55 to 64 years	65 years and over
WOMEN											
1948	16617	1682	604	1078	14936	2588	3763	3687	2882	1516	501
1949	16723	1588	555	1033	15137	2463	3760	3800	2975	1604	535
1950	17340	1517	524	993	15824	2491	3857	3979	3176	1757	563
1951	18181	1611	596	1015	16570	2541	4099	4139	3409	1847	535
1952	18568	1612	641	971	16958	2389	4163	4305	3543	1981	576
1953	18749	1584	601	983	17164	2324	4019	4545	3595	1998	683
1954	18490	1490	541	949	17000	2247	3936	4459	3646	2065	646
1955	19551	1547	564	984	18002	2297	4028	4612	4003	2301	761
1956	20419	1654	639	1015	18767	2300	4070	4833	4246	2515	802
1957	20714	1663	626	1037	19052	2295	4031	4921	4469	2551	785
1958	20613	1570	571	999	19043	2278	3885	4866	4620	2604	791
1959	21164	1640	655	985	19524	2273	3847	4962	4867	2764	813
1960	21874	1768	680	1089	20105	2365	3871	5046	5056	2884	882
1961	22090	1793	632	1161	20296	2432	3838	5047	5125	2965	889
1962	22525	1833	617	1216	20693	2548	3836	5190	5158	3086	875
1963	23105	1849	678	1170	21257	2697	3887	5313	5271	3211	877
1964	23831	1929	771	1158	21903	2933	3918	5334	5457	3326	934
1965	24748	2118	790	1328	22630	3119	4093	5457	5528	3486	948
1966	25976	2468	880	1589	23510	3365	4308	5548	5711	3642	937
1967	26893	2496	917	1579	24397	3690	4587	5607	5799	3762	953
1968	27807	2526	950	1575	25281	3950	4860	5666	5981	3852	972
1969	29084	2687	1047	1639	26397	4307	5147	5699	6223	3988	1033
1970	29688	2735	1094	1641	26952	4494	5382	5706	6303	4046	1023
1971	29976	2730	1086	1645	27246	4609	5563	5647	6313	4093	1021
1972	31257	2980	1188	1792	28276	4861	6197	5734	6318	4115	1051
1973	32715	3231	1310	1920	29484	5184	6893	5915	6356	4109	1029
1974	33769	3345	1367	1978	30424	5363	7492	6068	6451	4084	966
1975	33989	3263	1320	1943	30726	5401	7882	6061	6288	4105	989
1976	35615	3389	1346	2043	32226	5655	8624	6400	6343	4188	1017
1977	37289	3514	1403	2110	33775	5965	9367	6758	6380	4279	1027
1978	39569	3734	1530	2204	35836	6328	10157	7282	6532	4446	1091
1979	41217	3783	1541	2242	37434	6538	10802	7779	6622	4569	1124
1980	42117	3625	1433	2192	38492	6555	11370	8168	6686	4587	1125
1981	43000	3411	1340	2070	39590	6618	11914	8532	6777	4616	1133
1982	43256	3170	1198	1972	40086	6492	12147	8977	6689	4634	1147
1983	44047	3043	1107	1935	41004	6490	12540	9510	6678	4629	1157
1984	45915	3122	1161	1962	42793	6636	13182	10289	6852	4700	1133
1985	47259	3105	1193	1913	44154	6640	13644	10933	7097	4721	1118
1986	48706	3149	1270	1879	45556	6540	14109	11595	7395	4751	1165
1987	50334	3260	1343	1917	47074	6466	14617	12281	7737	4783	1191
1988	51696	3313	1310	2003	48383	6326	14872	12811	8246	4841	1286
1989	53027	3282	1261	2021	49745	6163	15093	13440	8711	4950	1388
1990	53689	3154	1156	1998	50535	6250	15155	14046	8835	4811	1437
1991	53496	2862	1067	1794	50634	6066	14796	14507	9069	4756	1440
1992	54052	2724	1032	1692	51328	6053	14701	14693	9657	4825	1398
1993	54910	2811	1071	1740	52099	6035	14508	15002	10248	4892	1414
1994	56610	3005	1222	1783	53606	5987	14545	15488	10908	5085	1592
1995	57523	3127	1258	1869	54396	5779	14647	15828	11421	5163	1558
1996	58501	3190	1328	1862	55311	5709	14549	16235	12031	5269	1518
1997	59873	3260	1293	1967	56613	5831	14471	16581	12637	5561	1532
1998	60771	3493	1364	2128	57278	5919	14298	16644	13043	5820	1554
1999	62042	3487	1357	2130	58555	6163	14171	16917	13644	6041	1619
2000	62915	3563	1373	2190	59352	6312	14006	16927	14156	6238	1713
2001	62992	3396	1290	2106	59596	6412	13611	16726	14549	6532	1768

See *Note* at end of table.

Table 1-11. Employed Civilians by Race, Hispanic Origin, Sex, and Age, 1948–2001—*Continued*

(Thousands of persons.)

Year, race, Hispanic origin, and sex	16 years and over	16 to 19 years			20 years and over						
		Total	16 to 17 years	18 to 19 years	Total	20 to 24 years	25 to 34 years	35 to 44 years	45 to 54 years	55 to 64 years	65 years and over
WHITE MEN											
1954	37846	1723	771	953	36123	2394	9287	9175	7614	5412	2241
1955	38719	1824	821	1004	36895	2607	9461	9351	7792	5431	2254
1956	39368	1893	890	1002	37475	2850	9330	9449	7950	5559	2336
1957	39349	1865	874	990	37484	2930	9226	9480	8067	5542	2234
1958	38591	1783	852	932	36808	2896	8861	9386	8061	5501	2103
1959	39494	1961	915	1046	37533	3153	8911	9560	8261	5588	2060
1960	39755	2092	973	1119	37663	3264	8777	9589	8372	5618	2043
1961	39588	2055	891	1164	37533	3311	8630	9566	8394	5670	1961
1962	40016	2098	883	1215	37918	3426	8514	9718	8512	5749	1998
1963	40428	2156	972	1184	38272	3646	8463	9782	8650	5844	1887
1964	41115	2316	1128	1188	38799	3856	8538	9800	8787	5945	1872
1965	41844	2612	1159	1453	39232	4025	8598	9795	8924	5998	1892
1966	42331	2913	1245	1668	39418	4028	8674	9719	9029	6096	1871
1967	42833	2849	1278	1571	39985	4231	8931	9632	9093	6208	1892
1968	43411	2908	1319	1589	40503	4226	9315	9522	9198	6316	1926
1969	44048	3070	1385	1685	40978	4401	9608	9379	9279	6359	1953
1970	44178	3066	1374	1692	41112	4601	9784	9202	9271	6340	1914
1971	44595	3157	1393	1764	41438	4935	10026	9026	9256	6339	1856
1972	45944	3416	1470	1947	42528	5431	10664	9047	9236	6363	1786
1973	47085	3660	1590	2071	43424	5863	11268	9046	9257	6299	1689
1974	47674	3728	1611	2117	43946	5965	11701	9027	9242	6304	1706
1975	46697	3505	1502	2002	43192	5770	11783	8818	9005	6160	1656
1976	47775	3604	1501	2103	44171	6140	12362	8944	8968	6176	1579
1977	49150	3824	1607	2217	45326	6437	12893	9212	8898	6279	1605
1978	50544	3950	1664	2286	46594	6717	13413	9608	8840	6339	1677
1979	51452	3904	1654	2250	47546	6868	13888	9930	8748	6406	1707
1980	51127	3708	1534	2174	47419	6652	14009	10077	8586	6412	1684
1981	51315	3469	1402	2066	47846	6652	14398	10307	8518	6309	1662
1982	50287	3079	1214	1865	47209	6372	14164	10593	8267	6188	1624
1983	50621	3003	1124	1879	47618	6386	14297	11062	8152	6084	1637
1984	52462	3001	1140	1861	49461	6647	15045	11776	8320	6108	1564
1985	53046	2985	1185	1800	50061	6428	15374	12214	8374	6118	1552
1986	53785	2966	1225	1741	50818	6340	15790	12620	8442	6012	1612
1987	54647	2999	1252	1747	51649	6150	16084	13138	8596	5991	1690
1988	55550	3084	1248	1836	52466	5987	16241	13590	8992	5909	1748
1989	56352	3060	1171	1889	53292	5839	16383	14046	9335	5891	1797
1990	56703	3018	1119	1899	53685	6179	16124	14496	9383	5744	1760
1991	55797	2694	1017	1677	53103	5942	15644	14743	9488	5578	1707
1992	55959	2602	990	1612	53357	5855	15357	14842	10027	5503	1772
1993	56656	2634	1031	1603	54021	5830	15230	15178	10497	5514	1772
1994	57452	2776	1144	1632	54676	5738	15052	15562	10910	5490	1925
1995	58146	2892	1169	1723	55254	5613	14958	15793	11359	5609	1921
1996	58888	2911	1161	1750	55977	5444	14820	16136	11834	5755	1987
1997	59998	3011	1206	1806	56986	5590	14567	16470	12352	5972	2037
1998	60604	3103	1233	1870	57500	5659	14259	16715	12661	6251	1955
1999	61139	3205	1254	1951	57934	5753	13851	16781	13046	6447	2056
2000	61696	3227	1220	2007	58469	5939	13634	16749	13484	6532	2130
2001	61411	3043	1121	1922	58367	5888	13257	16481	13871	6717	2152

See *Note* at end of table.

Table 1-11. Employed Civilians by Race, Hispanic Origin, Sex, and Age, 1948–2001—Continued

(Thousands of persons.)

Year, race, Hispanic origin, and sex	16 years and over	16 to 19 years			20 years and over						
		Total	16 to 17 years	18 to 19 years	Total	20 to 24 years	25 to 34 years	35 to 44 years	45 to 54 years	55 to 64 years	65 years and over
WHITE WOMEN											
1954	16111	1355	486	869	14756	1964	3329	3825	3197	1850	590
1955	17114	1401	509	892	15713	2030	3394	3976	3530	2079	703
1956	17901	1496	575	920	16405	2047	3418	4188	3756	2263	732
1957	18116	1509	568	941	16607	2022	3393	4236	3942	2287	717
1958	18022	1433	518	915	16589	2012	3267	4185	4052	2348	725
1959	18512	1514	605	909	16998	1985	3233	4270	4291	2475	745
1960	19095	1608	625	984	17487	2067	3244	4341	4448	2574	812
1961	19325	1638	581	1056	17687	2149	3205	4339	4512	2665	817
1962	19682	1676	564	1112	18006	2250	3189	4455	4554	2762	797
1963	20194	1695	628	1066	18499	2390	3226	4559	4654	2874	796
1964	20807	1760	718	1042	19047	2588	3256	4580	4809	2971	845
1965	21602	1950	733	1217	19652	2727	3394	4678	4880	3118	856
1966	22690	2263	807	1456	20427	2958	3594	4730	5043	3260	842
1967	23528	2265	843	1422	21263	3262	3832	4797	5131	3388	854
1968	24339	2287	874	1413	22052	3461	4095	4864	5289	3465	878
1969	25470	2438	962	1476	23032	3781	4327	4891	5509	3588	935
1970	26039	2505	1012	1493	23534	3959	4542	4890	5582	3640	921
1971	26283	2513	1011	1502	23770	4065	4687	4831	5588	3675	924
1972	27426	2755	1111	1645	24669	4286	5240	4893	5608	3714	928
1973	28623	2962	1217	1746	25661	4562	5831	5036	5628	3684	920
1974	29511	3069	1269	1799	26442	4711	6340	5169	5706	3654	862
1975	29714	2983	1215	1767	26731	4775	6701	5161	5550	3667	877
1976	31078	3120	1260	1860	27958	4978	7300	5462	5580	3746	891
1977	32550	3244	1319	1923	29306	5259	7950	5772	5585	3829	912
1978	34392	3416	1420	1996	30975	5535	8595	6201	5710	3972	964
1979	35807	3451	1423	2027	32357	5726	9145	6648	5773	4071	993
1980	36587	3314	1327	1986	33275	5753	9644	6994	5818	4064	1001
1981	37394	3119	1242	1877	34275	5826	10153	7311	5896	4077	1013
1982	37615	2905	1103	1802	34710	5724	10367	7675	5816	4095	1032
1983	38272	2796	1032	1764	35476	5751	10659	8132	5809	4084	1041
1984	39659	2835	1069	1766	36823	5804	11190	8776	5920	4118	1015
1985	40690	2783	1085	1698	37907	5807	11571	9338	6084	4128	978
1986	41876	2825	1160	1665	39050	5687	11956	9895	6307	4164	1042
1987	43142	2900	1216	1684	40242	5598	12345	10459	6620	4172	1047
1988	44262	2946	1176	1770	41316	5450	12555	10878	7062	4244	1126
1989	45232	2886	1107	1779	42346	5245	12708	11395	7440	4332	1227
1990	45558	2762	1023	1739	42796	5319	12649	11785	7551	4217	1275
1991	45385	2523	954	1569	42862	5174	12344	12139	7781	4141	1283
1992	45710	2383	915	1468	43327	5176	12195	12254	8258	4198	1246
1993	46390	2479	959	1520	43910	5101	12044	12467	8776	4258	1265
1994	47738	2622	1066	1556	45116	4997	12049	12880	9338	4423	1429
1995	48344	2701	1104	1597	45643	4787	12056	13157	9768	4461	1415
1996	48920	2756	1164	1592	46164	4705	11858	13430	10237	4558	1376
1997	49859	2796	1136	1660	47063	4773	11727	13667	10709	4813	1374
1998	50327	2986	1203	1783	47342	4853	11470	13604	11001	5021	1392
1999	51096	2999	1181	1817	48099	4963	11262	13767	11461	5211	1435
2000	51780	3043	1191	1852	48736	5140	11043	13772	11899	5369	1512
2001	51810	2925	1125	1801	48884	5226	10707	13566	12197	5631	1557

See *Note* at end of table.

Table 1-11. Employed Civilians by Race, Hispanic Origin, Sex, and Age, 1948–2001—*Continued*

(Thousands of persons.)

Year, race, Hispanic origin, and sex	16 years and over	16 to 19 years			20 years and over						
		Total	16 to 17 years	18 to 19 years	Total	20 to 24 years	25 to 34 years	35 to 44 years	45 to 54 years	55 to 64 years	65 years and over
BLACK MEN											
1972	4368	309	114	195	4058	648	1074	890	793	499	156
1973	4527	330	112	220	4197	711	1142	898	816	483	148
1974	4527	322	114	209	4204	668	1176	912	803	500	145
1975	4275	276	98	179	3998	595	1159	865	755	487	137
1976	4404	283	100	184	4120	635	1217	897	763	472	137
1977	4565	291	105	186	4273	659	1271	940	777	484	143
1978	4796	312	106	206	4483	697	1357	969	788	516	155
1979	4923	316	111	205	4606	754	1425	983	801	498	147
1980	4798	299	109	191	4498	713	1438	975	770	478	126
1981	4794	273	95	178	4520	693	1457	991	764	492	123
1982	4637	223	65	158	4414	660	1414	997	750	471	122
1983	4753	222	64	158	4531	684	1483	1034	749	477	105
1984	5124	252	79	173	4871	750	1635	1138	780	460	108
1985	5270	278	92	186	4992	726	1669	1187	795	501	114
1986	5428	278	96	182	5150	732	1756	1211	831	507	112
1987	5661	304	109	195	5357	728	1821	1283	853	547	124
1988	5824	316	122	193	5509	736	1881	1348	878	536	131
1989	5928	327	124	202	5602	742	1931	1415	886	498	131
1990	5995	303	99	204	5692	702	1895	1586	926	469	114
1991	5961	255	85	170	5706	695	1859	1634	923	481	114
1992	5930	249	78	170	5681	679	1819	1650	930	478	124
1993	6047	254	88	166	5793	674	1858	1717	978	461	106
1994	6241	276	107	169	5964	718	1850	1795	1030	455	115
1995	6422	285	111	174	6137	714	1895	1836	1085	468	138
1996	6456	289	109	180	6167	685	1867	1878	1129	482	126
1997	6607	282	108	174	6325	668	1874	1955	1215	487	127
1998	6871	341	120	221	6530	686	1886	2008	1284	524	142
1999	7027	325	120	205	6701	700	1926	2092	1327	525	131
2000	7180	348	133	215	6832	755	1882	2087	1396	564	147
2001	7127	322	116	206	6805	724	1808	2056	1450	588	178
BLACK WOMEN											
1972	3433	200	65	134	3233	519	850	739	641	373	113
1973	3601	239	81	158	3362	546	920	761	644	389	101
1974	3677	232	77	155	3445	562	981	770	649	383	98
1975	3618	231	85	146	3388	520	985	752	638	387	104
1976	3823	224	70	154	3599	558	1092	782	653	398	115
1977	3975	217	64	153	3758	585	1172	814	671	408	109
1978	4307	260	85	175	4047	662	1283	879	691	416	118
1979	4436	263	92	171	4174	670	1333	919	702	428	119
1980	4515	248	82	165	4267	663	1389	936	717	448	113
1981	4561	232	75	157	4329	653	1415	966	725	462	108
1982	4552	205	73	132	4347	623	1416	1028	719	457	103
1983	4622	194	59	136	4428	596	1493	1073	707	460	99
1984	4995	222	67	155	4773	673	1588	1173	753	485	101
1985	5231	254	83	171	4977	673	1656	1240	804	484	121
1986	5386	259	87	171	5128	696	1708	1313	835	475	102
1987	5648	283	93	190	5365	693	1793	1412	860	489	117
1988	5834	285	101	184	5548	697	1844	1491	905	482	129
1989	6025	298	113	185	5727	725	1870	1566	959	472	134
1990	6180	296	96	200	5884	707	1907	1701	971	464	135
1991	6113	239	76	164	5874	677	1855	1768	969	476	129
1992	6221	243	79	164	5978	664	1880	1791	1034	487	123
1993	6334	239	82	157	6095	703	1842	1867	1081	480	121
1994	6595	275	117	158	6320	731	1882	1926	1147	497	136
1995	6857	301	112	189	6556	729	1949	2025	1202	536	114
1996	7086	324	124	200	6762	726	1984	2096	1297	543	115
1997	7362	349	122	227	7013	789	2029	2139	1373	561	122
1998	7685	395	126	268	7290	810	2081	2230	1455	594	120
1999	8029	366	123	243	7663	893	2165	2312	1545	609	139
2000	8154	380	133	247	7774	887	2154	2317	1635	626	155
2001	8143	342	119	223	7801	886	2109	2303	1680	660	163

See *Note* at end of table.

Table 1-11. Employed Civilians by Race, Hispanic Origin, Sex, and Age, 1948–2001—*Continued*

(Thousands of persons.)

Year, race, Hispanic origin, and sex	16 years and over	16 to 19 years			20 years and over						
		Total	16 to 17 years	18 to 19 years	Total	20 to 24 years	25 to 34 years	35 to 44 years	45 to 54 years	55 to 64 years	65 years and over
HISPANIC MEN											
1973	2198	...	...	...	2010	...	...	...	...	...	...
1974	2369	...	...	...	2165	...	...	...	...	...	...
1975	2301	...	...	...	2117	...	...	...	...	...	...
1976	2303	199	74	125	2109	364	708	504	369	173	30
1977	2564	225	78	147	2335	427	763	540	394	184	37
1978	2808	241	93	147	2568	494	824	590	405	207	47
1979	2962	260	93	168	2701	511	891	615	427	205	53
1980	3448	306	109	198	3142	611	1065	662	491	254	58
1981	3597	272	90	182	3325	642	1157	707	504	259	56
1982	3583	229	66	162	3354	621	1192	729	498	261	53
1983	3771	248	71	177	3523	655	1280	760	499	275	53
1984	4083	258	78	180	3825	718	1398	841	530	292	46
1985	4245	251	82	169	3994	727	1473	888	550	308	48
1986	4428	254	82	172	4174	773	1510	929	614	297	51
1987	4713	268	81	188	4444	777	1664	1044	606	303	50
1988	4972	292	87	205	4680	815	1706	1120	645	331	64
1989	5172	319	94	225	4853	821	1787	1152	676	350	67
1990	6021	412	126	286	5609	1083	2076	1312	722	355	61
1991	5979	356	94	263	5623	1063	2050	1360	719	369	62
1992	6093	336	97	238	5757	985	2127	1437	768	372	69
1993	6328	337	95	242	5992	1003	2200	1527	822	360	80
1994	6530	341	109	233	6189	1056	2227	1600	847	379	80
1995	6725	358	110	248	6367	1030	2284	1675	908	384	86
1996	7039	384	107	277	6655	1015	2345	1842	918	438	97
1997	7728	420	130	290	7307	1142	2547	1978	1059	477	104
1998	8018	449	133	315	7570	1173	2592	2077	1115	512	101
1999	8067	491	139	352	7577	1135	2524	2135	1151	502	130
2000	8478	517	142	375	7961	1214	2554	2249	1264	550	130
2001	8556	534	135	398	8022	1173	2559	2275	1335	553	127
HISPANIC WOMEN											
1973	1198	...	...	...	1060	...	...	...	...	...	...
1974	1319	...	...	...	1166	...	...	...	...	...	...
1975	1362	...	...	...	1224	...	...	...	...	...	...
1976	1417	155	50	106	1288	249	427	300	204	96	12
1977	1516	155	57	98	1370	288	449	320	214	86	13
1978	1719	182	65	117	1537	308	506	352	256	99	15
1979	1824	185	60	125	1638	349	539	381	241	115	15
1980	2079	193	65	128	1886	387	610	412	320	136	22
1981	2216	187	65	122	2029	418	680	440	326	139	26
1982	2222	181	52	129	2040	409	704	444	318	139	26
1983	2301	175	54	120	2127	413	717	464	338	166	28
1984	2568	211	71	140	2357	442	804	544	354	181	33
1985	2642	187	62	125	2456	460	843	585	362	178	27
1986	2791	176	64	112	2615	458	917	641	397	177	25
1987	3077	206	69	137	2872	496	1004	732	405	209	26
1988	3278	231	84	147	3047	526	1042	756	434	254	33
1989	3401	229	71	158	3172	504	1114	816	453	239	46
1990	3823	256	82	174	3567	588	1251	917	513	256	42
1991	3848	246	76	170	3603	559	1214	972	548	268	41
1992	3934	242	72	170	3693	591	1223	1031	548	256	43
1993	4033	233	65	168	3800	571	1246	1077	581	269	55
1994	4258	268	86	182	3989	587	1290	1137	648	268	59
1995	4403	287	85	202	4116	579	1334	1213	657	282	50
1996	4602	261	92	169	4341	612	1412	1273	677	310	56
1997	4999	294	98	196	4705	656	1482	1393	787	318	69
1998	5273	345	97	247	4928	710	1521	1428	879	334	57
1999	5653	363	115	248	5290	746	1574	1603	923	384	60
2000	6014	385	120	265	5629	780	1716	1654	1015	389	76
2001	6159	390	113	277	5769	831	1730	1628	1089	419	71

Note: Detail for the above race and Hispanic-origin groups will not sum to totals because data for the Other races group are not presented and Hispanics are included in both the White and Black population groups. See "Notes and Definitions" for information on historical comparability.

Table 1-12. Civilian Employment to Population Ratios by Sex, Race, Hispanic Origin, and Age, 1948–2001

(Percent.)

Year, race, and Hispanic origin	Total			Men			Women		
	16 years and over	16 to 19 years	20 years and over	16 years and over	16 to 19 years	20 years and over	16 years and over	16 to 19 years	20 years and over
TOTAL									
1948	56.6	47.7	57.4	83.5	57.5	85.8	31.3	38.5	30.7
1949	55.4	45.2	56.3	81.3	53.8	83.7	31.2	37.2	30.6
1950	56.1	45.5	57.0	82.0	55.2	84.2	32.0	36.3	31.6
1951	57.3	47.9	58.1	84.0	57.9	86.1	33.1	38.9	32.6
1952	57.3	46.9	58.1	83.9	55.9	86.2	33.4	38.8	33.0
1953	57.1	46.4	58.0	83.6	55.9	85.9	33.3	37.8	32.9
1954	55.5	42.3	56.6	81.0	50.2	83.5	32.5	34.9	32.3
1955	56.7	43.5	57.8	81.8	52.1	84.3	34.0	35.6	33.8
1956	57.5	45.3	58.5	82.3	53.8	84.6	35.1	37.5	34.9
1957	57.1	43.9	58.2	81.3	51.8	83.8	35.1	36.7	35.0
1958	55.4	39.9	56.8	78.5	46.9	81.2	34.5	33.5	34.6
1959	56.0	39.9	57.5	79.3	47.2	82.3	35.0	33.0	35.1
1960	56.1	40.5	57.6	78.9	47.6	81.9	35.5	33.8	35.7
1961	55.4	39.1	56.9	77.6	45.3	80.8	35.4	33.2	35.6
1962	55.5	39.4	57.1	77.7	45.9	80.9	35.6	33.3	35.8
1963	55.4	37.4	57.2	77.1	43.8	80.6	35.8	31.5	36.3
1964	55.7	37.3	57.7	77.3	44.1	80.9	36.3	30.9	36.9
1965	56.2	38.9	58.2	77.5	46.2	81.2	37.1	32.0	37.6
1966	56.9	42.1	58.7	77.9	48.9	81.5	38.3	35.6	38.6
1967	57.3	42.2	59.0	78.0	48.7	81.5	39.0	35.9	39.3
1968	57.5	42.2	59.3	77.8	48.7	81.3	39.6	36.0	40.0
1969	58.0	43.4	59.7	77.6	49.5	81.1	40.7	37.5	41.1
1970	57.4	42.3	59.2	76.2	47.7	79.7	40.8	37.1	41.2
1971	56.6	41.3	58.4	74.9	46.8	78.5	40.4	36.0	40.9
1972	57.0	43.5	58.6	75.0	48.9	78.4	41.0	38.2	41.3
1973	57.8	45.9	59.3	75.5	51.4	78.6	42.0	40.5	42.2
1974	57.8	46.0	59.2	74.9	51.2	77.9	42.6	41.0	42.8
1975	56.1	43.3	57.6	71.7	47.2	74.8	42.0	39.4	42.3
1976	56.8	44.2	58.3	72.0	47.9	75.1	43.2	40.5	43.5
1977	57.9	46.1	59.2	72.8	50.4	75.6	44.5	41.8	44.8
1978	59.3	48.3	60.6	73.8	52.2	76.4	46.4	44.5	46.6
1979	59.9	48.5	61.2	73.8	51.7	76.5	47.5	45.3	47.7
1980	59.2	46.6	60.6	72.0	49.5	74.6	47.7	43.8	48.1
1981	59.0	44.6	60.5	71.3	47.1	74.0	48.0	42.0	48.6
1982	57.8	41.5	59.4	69.0	42.9	71.8	47.7	40.2	48.4
1983	57.9	41.5	59.5	68.8	43.1	71.4	48.0	40.0	48.8
1984	59.5	43.7	61.0	70.7	45.0	73.2	49.5	42.5	50.1
1985	60.1	44.4	61.5	70.9	45.7	73.3	50.4	42.9	51.0
1986	60.7	44.6	62.1	71.0	45.7	73.3	51.4	43.6	52.0
1987	61.5	45.5	62.9	71.5	46.1	73.8	52.5	44.8	53.1
1988	62.3	46.8	63.6	72.0	47.8	74.2	53.4	45.9	54.0
1989	63.0	47.5	64.2	72.5	48.7	74.5	54.3	46.4	54.9
1990	62.8	45.3	64.3	72.0	46.6	74.3	54.3	44.0	55.2
1991	61.7	42.0	63.2	70.4	42.7	72.7	53.7	41.2	54.6
1992	61.5	41.0	63.0	69.8	41.9	72.1	53.8	40.0	54.8
1993	61.7	41.7	63.3	70.0	42.3	72.3	54.1	41.0	55.0
1994	62.5	43.4	64.0	70.4	43.8	72.6	55.3	43.0	56.2
1995	62.9	44.2	64.4	70.8	44.7	73.0	55.6	43.8	56.5
1996	63.2	43.5	64.7	70.9	43.6	73.2	56.0	43.5	57.0
1997	63.8	43.4	65.5	71.3	43.4	73.7	56.8	43.3	57.8
1998	64.1	45.1	65.6	71.6	44.7	73.9	57.1	45.5	58.0
1999	64.3	44.7	65.9	71.6	45.1	74.0	57.4	44.3	58.5
2000	64.5	45.4	66.1	71.8	45.6	74.1	57.7	45.2	58.7
2001	63.8	42.7	65.5	70.8	42.6	73.2	57.3	42.7	58.4

See *Note* at end of table.

Table 1-12. Civilian Employment to Population Ratios by Sex, Race, Hispanic Origin, and Age, 1948–2001—*Continued*

(Percent.)

Year, race, and Hispanic origin	Total			Men			Women		
	16 years and over	16 to 19 years	20 years and over	16 years and over	16 to 19 years	20 years and over	16 years and over	16 to 19 years	20 years and over
WHITE									
1954	55.2	42.9	56.2	81.5	49.9	84.0	31.4	36.4	31.1
1955	56.5	44.2	57.4	82.2	52.0	84.7	33.0	37.0	32.7
1956	57.3	46.1	58.2	82.7	54.1	85.0	34.2	38.9	33.8
1957	56.8	45.0	57.8	81.8	52.4	84.1	34.2	38.2	33.9
1958	55.3	41.0	56.5	79.2	47.6	81.8	33.6	35.0	33.5
1959	55.9	41.2	57.2	79.9	48.1	82.8	34.0	34.8	34.0
1960	55.9	41.5	57.2	79.4	48.1	82.4	34.6	35.1	34.5
1961	55.3	40.1	56.7	78.2	45.9	81.4	34.5	34.6	34.5
1962	55.4	40.4	56.9	78.4	46.4	81.5	34.7	34.8	34.7
1963	55.3	38.6	56.9	77.7	44.7	81.1	35.0	32.9	35.2
1964	55.5	38.4	57.3	77.8	45.0	81.3	35.5	32.2	35.8
1965	56.0	40.3	57.8	77.9	47.1	81.5	36.2	33.7	36.5
1966	56.8	43.6	58.3	78.3	50.1	81.7	37.5	37.5	37.5
1967	57.2	43.8	58.7	78.4	50.2	81.7	38.3	37.7	38.3
1968	57.4	43.9	59.0	78.3	50.3	81.6	38.9	37.8	39.1
1969	58.0	45.2	59.4	78.2	51.1	81.4	40.1	39.5	40.1
1970	57.5	44.5	59.0	76.8	49.6	80.1	40.3	39.5	40.4
1971	56.8	43.8	58.3	75.7	49.2	79.0	39.9	38.6	40.1
1972	57.4	46.4	58.6	76.0	51.5	79.0	40.7	41.3	40.6
1973	58.2	48.9	59.3	76.5	54.3	79.2	41.8	43.6	41.6
1974	58.3	49.3	59.3	75.9	54.4	78.6	42.4	44.3	42.2
1975	56.7	46.5	57.9	73.0	50.6	75.7	42.0	42.5	41.9
1976	57.5	47.8	58.6	73.4	51.5	76.0	43.2	44.2	43.1
1977	58.6	50.1	59.6	74.1	54.4	76.5	44.5	45.9	44.4
1978	60.0	52.4	60.8	75.0	56.3	77.2	46.3	48.5	46.1
1979	60.6	52.6	61.5	75.1	55.7	77.3	47.5	49.4	47.3
1980	60.0	50.7	61.0	73.4	53.4	75.6	47.8	47.9	47.8
1981	60.0	48.7	61.1	72.8	51.3	75.1	48.3	46.2	48.5
1982	58.8	45.8	60.1	70.6	47.0	73.0	48.1	44.6	48.4
1983	58.9	45.9	60.1	70.4	47.4	72.6	48.5	44.5	48.9
1984	60.5	48.0	61.5	72.1	49.1	74.3	49.8	47.0	50.0
1985	61.0	48.5	62.0	72.3	49.9	74.3	50.7	47.1	51.0
1986	61.5	48.8	62.6	72.3	49.6	74.3	51.7	47.9	52.0
1987	62.3	49.4	63.4	72.7	49.9	74.7	52.8	49.0	53.1
1988	63.1	50.9	64.1	73.2	51.7	75.1	53.8	50.2	54.0
1989	63.8	51.6	64.7	73.7	52.6	75.4	54.6	50.5	54.9
1990	63.7	49.7	64.8	73.3	51.0	75.1	54.7	48.3	55.2
1991	62.6	46.6	63.7	71.6	47.2	73.5	54.2	45.9	54.8
1992	62.4	45.3	63.6	71.1	46.4	73.1	54.2	44.2	54.9
1993	62.7	46.2	63.9	71.4	46.6	73.3	54.6	45.7	55.2
1994	63.5	47.9	64.7	71.8	48.3	73.6	55.8	47.5	56.4
1995	63.8	48.8	64.9	72.0	49.4	73.8	56.1	48.1	56.7
1996	64.1	47.9	65.3	72.3	48.2	74.2	56.3	47.6	57.0
1997	64.6	47.7	65.9	72.7	48.1	74.7	57.0	47.2	57.8
1998	64.7	48.9	65.9	72.7	48.6	74.7	57.1	49.3	57.7
1999	64.8	48.8	66.1	72.8	49.3	74.8	57.3	48.3	58.0
2000	65.1	49.3	66.3	72.9	49.7	74.8	57.7	49.0	58.3
2001	64.4	46.7	65.8	71.9	46.6	74.0	57.3	46.8	58.0

See *Note* at end of table.

Table 1-12. Civilian Employment to Population Ratios by Sex, Race, Hispanic Origin, and Age, 1948–2001—*Continued*

(Percent.)

Year, race, and Hispanic origin	Total			Men			Women		
	16 years and over	16 to 19 years	20 years and over	16 years and over	16 to 19 years	20 years and over	16 years and over	16 to 19 years	20 years and over
BLACK									
1972	53.7	25.2	58.3	66.8	31.6	73.0	43.0	19.2	46.5
1973	54.5	27.2	58.9	67.5	32.8	73.7	43.8	22.0	47.2
1974	53.5	25.9	58.0	65.8	31.4	71.9	43.5	20.9	46.9
1975	50.1	23.1	54.5	60.6	26.3	66.5	41.6	20.2	44.9
1976	50.8	22.4	55.4	60.6	25.8	66.8	42.8	19.2	46.4
1977	51.4	22.3	56.0	61.4	26.4	67.5	43.3	18.5	47.0
1978	53.6	25.2	58.0	63.3	28.5	69.1	45.8	22.1	49.3
1979	53.8	25.4	58.1	63.4	28.7	69.1	46.0	22.4	49.3
1980	52.3	23.9	56.4	60.4	27.0	65.8	45.7	21.0	49.1
1981	51.3	22.1	55.5	59.1	24.6	64.5	45.1	19.7	48.5
1982	49.4	19.0	53.6	56.0	20.3	61.4	44.2	17.7	47.5
1983	49.5	18.7	53.6	56.3	20.4	61.6	44.1	17.0	47.4
1984	52.3	21.9	56.1	59.2	23.9	64.1	46.7	20.1	49.8
1985	53.4	24.6	57.0	60.0	26.3	64.6	48.1	23.1	50.9
1986	54.1	25.1	57.6	60.6	26.5	65.1	48.8	23.8	51.6
1987	55.6	27.1	58.9	62.0	28.5	66.4	50.3	25.8	53.0
1988	56.3	27.6	59.7	62.7	29.4	67.1	51.2	25.8	53.9
1989	56.9	28.7	60.1	62.8	30.4	67.0	52.0	27.1	54.6
1990	56.7	26.7	60.2	62.6	27.7	67.1	51.9	25.8	54.7
1991	55.4	22.6	59.0	61.3	23.8	65.9	50.6	21.5	53.6
1992	54.9	22.8	58.3	59.9	23.6	64.3	50.8	22.1	53.6
1993	55.0	22.6	58.4	60.0	23.6	64.3	50.9	21.6	53.8
1994	56.1	24.9	59.4	60.8	25.4	65.0	52.3	24.5	55.0
1995	57.1	25.7	60.5	61.7	25.2	66.1	53.4	26.1	56.1
1996	57.4	26.0	60.8	61.1	24.9	65.5	54.4	27.1	57.1
1997	58.2	26.1	61.8	61.4	23.7	66.1	55.6	28.5	58.4
1998	59.7	30.1	63.0	62.9	28.4	67.1	57.2	31.8	59.7
1999	60.6	27.9	64.2	63.1	26.7	67.5	58.6	29.0	61.6
2000	60.8	29.5	64.2	63.4	28.7	67.6	58.7	30.3	61.5
2001	59.7	26.8	63.3	62.1	26.4	66.4	57.8	27.1	60.8
HISPANIC									
1973	55.6	37.5	...	76.0	...	81.3	37.3	...	38.3
1974	56.2	38.3	...	75.7	...	80.8	38.4	...	39.4
1975	53.4	33.5	...	71.5	...	77.2	37.4	...	38.7
1976	53.8	35.8	56.6	71.1	41.0	76.3	38.6	31.6	39.5
1977	55.4	37.2	58.3	73.6	45.5	78.3	39.1	29.5	40.6
1978	57.2	39.3	60.0	74.9	45.9	79.6	41.3	33.0	42.6
1979	58.3	40.6	61.0	75.6	46.8	80.3	42.5	34.3	43.7
1980	57.6	39.0	60.5	73.5	46.9	77.8	42.4	30.7	44.1
1981	57.4	35.3	60.7	72.4	41.0	77.2	43.0	29.3	45.0
1982	54.9	31.4	58.2	68.9	34.5	73.9	41.3	28.1	43.1
1983	55.1	32.4	58.1	69.4	37.5	73.8	41.1	27.2	42.9
1984	57.9	36.0	60.7	72.1	39.3	76.4	44.2	32.8	45.6
1985	57.8	33.7	60.7	72.1	38.4	76.3	43.8	29.0	45.6
1986	58.5	33.0	61.5	72.5	38.8	76.6	44.7	27.2	46.8
1987	60.5	35.6	63.4	74.0	39.9	78.0	47.4	31.2	49.2
1988	61.9	38.6	64.6	75.3	42.8	79.0	48.8	34.4	50.4
1989	62.2	39.2	64.8	75.8	44.9	79.4	48.8	33.3	50.5
1990	61.9	38.5	64.8	74.9	45.0	78.7	48.6	31.1	50.7
1991	59.8	34.8	62.8	72.1	39.4	76.1	47.3	29.7	49.3
1992	59.1	33.2	62.1	71.2	37.4	75.2	46.8	28.8	48.8
1993	59.1	32.5	62.1	71.7	37.7	75.6	46.3	27.0	48.4
1994	59.5	33.5	62.4	71.7	36.8	75.7	47.2	30.0	49.1
1995	59.7	34.5	62.6	72.1	37.5	76.0	47.3	31.3	49.1
1996	60.6	33.2	63.7	73.3	38.7	77.3	47.9	27.0	50.2
1997	62.6	33.7	66.0	74.5	37.5	79.0	50.2	29.3	52.6
1998	63.1	36.0	66.2	74.7	38.7	79.1	51.0	33.0	53.0
1999	63.4	37.0	66.5	75.3	41.2	79.6	51.7	32.5	53.9
2000	64.7	38.5	67.8	76.6	42.9	80.7	53.1	33.9	55.2
2001	63.6	38.6	66.5	75.0	43.4	78.9	52.5	33.5	54.6

Note: Detail for the above race and Hispanic-origin groups will not sum to totals because data for the Other races group are not presented and Hispanics are included in both the White and Black population groups. See "Notes and Definitions" for information on historical comparability.

Table 1-13. Employed Civilians by Occupation, Sex, Race, and Hispanic Origin, 1984–2001

(Thousands of persons.)

Occupation	1984						1985					
	Total	Men	Women	White	Black	Hispanic	Total	Men	Women	White	Black	Hispanic
TOTAL	105005	59091	45915	92120	10119	6651	107150	59891	47259	93736	10501	6888
Managerial and professional specialty	24858	14529	10329	22702	1422	797	25851	14802	11049	23561	1514	871
Executive, administrative, and managerial	11571	7683	3889	10704	582	417	12221	7871	4351	11256	649	442
Professional specialty	13286	6846	6440	11998	840	379	13630	6932	6699	12305	865	429
Technical, sales, and administrative support	32476	11556	20920	29082	2592	1677	33231	11725	21507	29553	2785	1705
Technicians and related support	3172	1646	1527	2783	262	142	3255	1719	1537	2823	291	134
Sales occupations	12582	6550	6032	11673	627	584	12667	6579	6088	11669	696	575
Administrative support, including clerical	16722	3361	13361	14626	1703	951	17309	3427	13882	15061	1798	995
Service occupations	14151	5545	8607	11214	2478	1174	14441	5695	8747	11432	2522	1211
Private household	993	38	955	667	301	107	1006	38	968	692	291	101
Protective service	1678	1461	217	1395	252	85	1718	1491	227	1428	259	103
Service, except private household and protective	11481	4046	7435	9152	1925	982	11718	4166	7552	9312	1972	1006
Precision production, craft, and repair	13057	11945	1112	11844	939	967	13340	12213	1127	12107	946	1025
Operators, fabricators, and laborers	16864	12479	4385	14036	2411	1655	16816	12539	4277	13951	2465	1737
Machine operators, assemblers, and inspectors	7984	4702	3282	6600	1132	888	7840	4681	3159	6483	1120	944
Transportation and material moving occupations	4467	4098	369	3782	625	304	4535	4160	375	3849	620	328
Handlers, equipment cleaners, helpers, and laborers	4413	3679	734	3655	654	463	4441	3697	744	3618	725	466
Farming, forestry, and fishing	3600	3037	562	3242	277	381	3470	2917	552	3132	269	337

Occupation	1986						1987					
	Total	Men	Women	White	Black	Hispanic	Total	Men	Women	White	Black	Hispanic
TOTAL	109597	60892	48706	95660	10814	7219	112440	62107	50334	97789	11309	7790
Managerial and professional specialty	26554	15029	11525	24134	1594	923	27742	15457	12286	25107	1712	1018
Executive, administrative, and managerial	12642	7990	4653	11649	658	466	13316	8263	5053	12200	741	509
Professional specialty	13911	7039	6872	12485	936	457	14426	7194	7232	12907	972	509
Technical, sales, and administrative support	34354	12130	22223	30497	2923	1812	35082	12378	22704	30949	3099	1969
Technicians and related support	3364	1783	1581	2953	277	134	3346	1721	1624	2914	283	130
Sales occupations	13245	6862	6383	12168	750	646	13480	7015	6465	12295	806	713
Administrative support, including clerical	17745	3485	14260	15377	1896	1032	18256	3642	14614	15740	2010	1126
Service occupations	14680	5775	8905	11685	2480	1298	15054	5924	9130	11916	2614	1369
Private household	981	39	942	721	235	127	934	34	900	703	211	120
Protective service	1787	1566	221	1487	268	99	1907	1637	271	1558	316	111
Service, except private household and protective	11913	4170	7742	9478	1977	1071	12213	4253	7960	9655	2087	1139
Precision production, craft, and repair	13405	12256	1150	12083	1009	1031	13568	12416	1153	12262	996	1083
Operators, fabricators, and laborers	17160	12805	4355	14107	2583	1795	17486	12978	4508	14340	2659	1890
Machine operators, assemblers, and inspectors	7911	4725	3187	6462	1167	956	7994	4699	3295	6498	1195	1001
Transportation and material moving occupations	4564	4158	406	3847	641	344	4712	4317	395	3934	699	360
Handlers, equipment cleaners, helpers, and laborers	4685	3923	762	3798	776	494	4779	3962	817	3909	765	528
Farming, forestry, and fishing	3444	2896	548	3154	224	360	3507	2954	554	3214	229	461

Occupation	1988						1989					
	Total	Men	Women	White	Black	Hispanic	Total	Men	Women	White	Black	Hispanic
TOTAL	114968	63273	51696	99812	11658	8250	117342	64315	53027	101584	11953	8573
Managerial and professional specialty	29190	16139	13050	26408	1794	1086	30398	16652	13746	27459	1862	1126
Executive, administrative, and managerial	14216	8626	5590	13022	789	570	14848	8944	5904	13555	840	599
Professional specialty	14974	7513	7460	13386	1005	516	15550	7708	7842	13903	1022	527
Technical, sales, and administrative support	35532	12494	23038	31178	3239	2064	36127	12687	23440	31619	3346	2057
Technicians and related support	3521	1833	1688	3019	329	152	3645	1887	1759	3125	347	157
Sales occupations	13747	7025	6722	12495	839	730	14065	7124	6941	12741	906	730
Administrative support, including clerical	18264	3636	14628	15664	2071	1182	18416	3676	14741	15752	2094	1169
Service occupations	15332	6056	9275	12105	2698	1560	15556	6164	9391	12237	2731	1684
Private household	909	34	875	687	205	152	872	36	836	628	219	138
Protective service	1944	1664	279	1584	324	122	1960	1654	305	1594	329	113
Service, except private household and protective	12479	4358	8121	9834	2169	1286	12724	4474	8250	10016	2184	1433
Precision production, craft, and repair	13664	12474	1190	12305	1029	1116	13818	12627	1190	12369	1089	1173
Operators, fabricators, and laborers	17814	13234	4580	14665	2672	1975	18022	13327	4695	14752	2714	2059
Machine operators, assemblers, and inspectors	8117	4806	3311	6642	1197	1079	8248	4878	3370	6721	1202	1121
Transportation and material moving occupations	4831	4397	434	4027	719	343	4886	4436	450	4080	712	371
Handlers, equipment cleaners, helpers, and laborers	4866	4031	835	3997	755	552	4888	4013	875	3950	800	567
Farming, forestry, and fishing	3437	2875	562	3150	226	448	3421	2857	565	3149	210	474

See *Note* at end of table.

Table 1-13. Employed Civilians by Occupation, Sex, Race, and Hispanic Origin, 1984–2001—*Continued*

(Thousands of persons.)

Occupation	1990						1991					
	Total	Men	Women	White	Black	Hispanic	Total	Men	Women	White	Black	Hispanic
TOTAL	118793	65104	53689	102261	12175	9845	117718	64223	53496	101182	12074	9828
Managerial and professional specialty	30602	16601	14001	27416	1945	1208	30934	16623	14311	27706	1972	1259
Executive, administrative, and managerial	14802	8872	5931	13432	869	630	14904	8858	6046	13513	875	653
Professional specialty	15800	7729	8071	13984	1076	578	16030	7765	8265	14193	1097	606
Technical, sales, and administrative support	36913	13054	23859	32136	3465	2366	36318	12852	23466	31524	3443	2413
Technicians and related support	3866	1973	1893	3298	357	182	3814	1937	1877	3257	344	196
Sales occupations	14285	7247	7038	12871	937	848	14052	7180	6872	12590	955	867
Administrative support, including clerical	18762	3834	14928	15967	2170	1336	18452	3735	14717	15677	2145	1349
Service occupations	16012	6470	9543	12565	2757	1984	16254	6610	9644	12739	2783	2005
Private household	792	29	763	571	191	168	799	33	766	608	162	179
Protective service	2000	1708	293	1618	334	131	2083	1765	318	1682	351	144
Service, except private household and protective	13220	4732	8488	10376	2233	1685	13372	4812	8560	10449	2270	1682
Precision production, craft, and repair	13745	12580	1166	12255	1083	1301	13250	12112	1138	11824	1039	1269
Operators, fabricators, and laborers	18071	13494	4577	14732	2715	2436	17456	13075	4380	14205	2613	2311
Machine operators, assemblers, and inspectors	8200	4931	3269	6668	1184	1249	7820	4693	3127	6284	1159	1142
Transportation and material moving occupations	4886	4449	436	4010	757	466	4913	4476	437	4022	774	462
Handlers, equipment cleaners, helpers, and laborers	4985	4114	871	4054	775	721	4723	3906	816	3899	680	707
Farming, forestry, and fishing	3450	2907	544	3157	209	550	3506	2951	556	3184	224	570

Occupation	1992						1993					
	Total	Men	Women	White	Black	Hispanic	Total	Men	Women	White	Black	Hispanic
TOTAL	118492	64440	54052	101669	12151	10027	120259	65349	54910	103045	12382	10361
Managerial and professional specialty	31085	16387	14698	27719	2044	1322	32231	16811	15419	28647	2181	1437
Executive, administrative, and managerial	14722	8612	6110	13327	872	683	15338	8897	6441	13783	977	762
Professional specialty	16363	7775	8588	14393	1172	639	16893	7915	8978	14863	1204	675
Technical, sales, and administrative support	37048	13379	23669	32167	3423	2492	37058	13417	23641	32096	3501	2578
Technicians and related support	4277	2185	2092	3620	418	216	4039	2000	2039	3433	395	223
Sales occupations	14014	7286	6728	12576	891	882	14342	7418	6924	12824	974	940
Administrative support, including clerical	18757	3908	14849	15971	2114	1395	18677	3999	14679	15839	2132	1415
Service occupations	16377	6676	9701	12778	2843	2037	16821	6867	9953	13145	2901	2069
Private household	891	37	854	695	162	187	928	45	883	735	154	214
Protective service	2114	1760	354	1669	383	168	2165	1792	373	1729	380	160
Service, except private household and protective	13373	4879	8493	10414	2298	1682	13727	5030	8697	10681	2367	1695
Precision production, craft, and repair	13225	12087	1137	11798	1016	1345	13429	12279	1150	11990	1006	1372
Operators, fabricators, and laborers	17247	12954	4294	14018	2599	2243	17341	13109	4232	14090	2580	2310
Machine operators, assemblers, and inspectors	7658	4623	3035	6141	1153	1130	7553	4642	2911	6066	1117	1140
Transportation and material moving occupations	4908	4482	426	4069	730	460	5036	4570	465	4195	706	481
Handlers, equipment cleaners, helpers, and laborers	4682	3850	832	3808	716	653	4753	3897	856	3829	757	689
Farming, forestry, and fishing	3510	2957	553	3188	226	588	3379	2864	515	3078	212	596

Occupation	1994						1995					
	Total	Men	Women	White	Black	Hispanic	Total	Men	Women	White	Black	Hispanic
TOTAL	123060	66450	56610	105190	12835	10788	124900	67377	57523	106490	13279	11127
Managerial and professional specialty	33847	17583	16264	30045	2405	1517	35318	18378	16940	31323	2651	1548
Executive, administrative, and managerial	16312	9298	7014	14605	1103	807	17186	9840	7346	15398	1233	821
Professional specialty	17536	8285	9250	15439	1302	709	18132	8539	9593	15924	1418	727
Technical, sales, and administrative support	37306	13322	23984	32232	3637	2639	37417	13310	24107	32184	3808	2719
Technicians and related support	3869	1856	2013	3301	376	205	3909	1900	2009	3361	378	240
Sales occupations	14817	7543	7273	13235	1056	1010	15119	7634	7485	13366	1183	1048
Administrative support, including clerical	18620	3923	14697	15696	2205	1424	18389	3776	14613	15457	2248	1431
Service occupations	16912	6840	10072	13207	2890	2131	16930	6774	10155	13208	2880	2195
Private household	817	30	787	643	136	223	821	37	784	638	137	204
Protective service	2249	1873	376	1778	407	167	2237	1881	356	1772	406	166
Service, except private household and protective	13847	4938	8909	10787	2346	1741	13872	4857	9015	10799	2337	1825
Precision production, craft, and repair	13489	12241	1248	11974	1040	1407	13524	12323	1201	11949	1073	1430
Operators, fabricators, and laborers	17876	13535	4341	14416	2677	2474	18068	13675	4393	14496	2712	2577
Machine operators, assemblers, and inspectors	7754	4800	2954	6166	1167	1151	7907	4958	2949	6221	1218	1250
Transportation and material moving occupations	5136	4654	483	4227	749	511	5171	4682	490	4254	760	512
Handlers, equipment cleaners, helpers, and laborers	4986	4081	904	4023	760	811	4990	4035	955	4022	734	816
Farming, forestry, and fishing	3629	2928	701	3315	187	620	3642	2916	726	3330	154	658

See *Note* at end of table.

Table 1-13. Employed Civilians by Occupation, Sex, Race, and Hispanic Origin, 1984–2001—Continued

(Thousands of persons.)

Occupation	1996						1997					
	Total	Men	Women	White	Black	Hispanic	Total	Men	Women	White	Black	Hispanic
TOTAL	126708	68207	58501	107808	13542	11642	129558	69685	59873	109856	13969	12726
Managerial and professional specialty	36497	18744	17754	32116	2706	1654	37686	19249	18437	33089	2764	1867
Executive, administrative, and managerial	17746	9979	7767	15807	1218	854	18440	10271	8170	16420	1267	1001
Professional specialty	18752	8764	9987	16309	1488	799	19245	8978	10267	16669	1497	866
Technical, sales, and administrative support	37683	13489	24194	32177	3877	2849	38309	13760	24549	32624	4032	3026
Technicians and related support	3926	1865	2061	3334	368	248	4214	2028	2186	3571	410	256
Sales occupations	15404	7782	7622	13519	1218	1085	15734	7840	7894	13730	1271	1198
Administrative support, including clerical	18353	3842	14511	15323	2291	1516	18361	3892	14469	15323	2352	1572
Service occupations	17177	6967	10210	13447	2962	2349	17537	7122	10416	13604	3092	2560
Private household	804	41	764	637	139	211	795	37	758	642	129	212
Protective service	2187	1811	375	1748	389	175	2300	1890	411	1800	430	202
Service, except private household and protective	14186	5115	9071	11062	2435	1963	14442	5195	9247	11162	2533	2146
Precision production, craft, and repair	13587	12368	1219	12020	1069	1498	14124	12868	1256	12472	1144	1714
Operators, fabricators, and laborers	18197	13750	4447	14697	2789	2607	18399	13858	4540	14813	2781	2839
Machine operators, assemblers, and inspectors	7874	4902	2972	6270	1193	1295	7962	4962	3000	6322	1178	1426
Transportation and material moving occupations	5302	4799	504	4412	772	548	5389	4872	518	4435	819	592
Handlers, equipment cleaners, helpers, and laborers	5021	4049	971	4016	824	764	5048	4025	1023	4057	784	821
Farming, forestry, and fishing	3566	2889	677	3350	139	685	3503	2828	675	3254	156	721

Occupation	1998						1999					
	Total	Men	Women	White	Black	Hispanic	Total	Men	Women	White	Black	Hispanic
TOTAL	131463	70693	60771	110931	14556	13291	133488	71446	62042	112235	15056	13720
Managerial and professional specialty	38937	19867	19070	34063	2947	1933	40467	20446	20021	35125	3233	2040
Executive, administrative, and managerial	19054	10585	8469	16903	1368	1028	19584	10744	8840	17235	1484	1097
Professional specialty	19883	9282	10602	17160	1579	905	20883	9702	11181	17890	1749	943
Technical, sales, and administrative support	38521	13792	24728	32490	4264	3186	38921	14079	24842	32779	4356	3286
Technicians and related support	4261	1976	2285	3557	441	283	4355	2094	2261	3622	467	279
Sales occupations	15850	7875	7975	13704	1415	1245	16118	8049	8069	13956	1405	1267
Administrative support, including clerical	18410	3941	14469	15229	2408	1657	18448	3936	14512	15201	2484	1740
Service occupations	17836	7222	10614	13807	3148	2670	17915	7093	10822	13725	3275	2716
Private household	847	46	801	704	116	262	831	40	791	670	126	244
Protective service	2417	1986	431	1892	463	204	2440	1980	460	1886	484	200
Service, except private household and protective	14572	5190	9382	11211	2569	2204	14644	5074	9570	11168	2666	2271
Precision production, craft, and repair	14411	13208	1203	12729	1158	1793	14593	13286	1307	12908	1174	1871
Operators, fabricators, and laborers	18256	13769	4487	14609	2866	2917	18167	13793	4374	14535	2847	3014
Machine operators, assemblers, and inspectors	7791	4882	2909	6146	1200	1340	7386	4637	2749	5824	1143	1364
Transportation and material moving occupations	5363	4818	545	4351	872	640	5516	4968	548	4488	879	659
Handlers, equipment cleaners, helpers, and laborers	5102	4069	1033	4112	795	938	5265	4188	1077	4223	825	992
Farming, forestry, and fishing	3502	2835	668	3233	172	792	3426	2749	676	3165	172	793

Occupation	2000						2001					
	Total	Men	Women	White	Black	Hispanic	Total	Men	Women	White	Black	Hispanic
TOTAL	135208	72293	62915	113475	15334	14492	135073	72080	62992	113220	15270	14714
Managerial and professional specialty	40887	20543	20345	35304	3349	2036	41894	20966	20928	36125	3457	2150
Executive, administrative, and managerial	19774	10814	8960	17372	1512	1072	20338	10990	9348	17803	1603	1148
Professional specialty	21113	9728	11385	17932	1836	964	21556	9976	11580	18323	1854	1002
Technical, sales, and administrative support	39442	14288	25154	33146	4497	3504	39044	14167	24877	32718	4461	3556
Technicians and related support	4385	2118	2267	3611	492	303	4497	2097	2400	3731	463	338
Sales occupations	16340	8231	8110	14169	1436	1385	16044	8120	7924	13807	1464	1402
Administrative support, including clerical	18717	3939	14778	15366	2570	1816	18503	3950	14553	15180	2533	1816
Service occupations	18278	7245	11034	14066	3301	2867	18359	7263	11096	14083	3281	3000
Private household	792	35	757	631	118	251	715	27	688	593	87	234
Protective service	2399	1944	455	1860	471	208	2478	1972	507	1908	492	244
Service, except private household and protective	15087	5265	9822	11575	2712	2408	15166	5264	9902	11582	2702	2521
Precision production, craft, and repair	14882	13532	1351	13133	1191	2075	14833	13545	1287	13128	1152	2176
Operators, fabricators, and laborers	18319	13988	4331	14680	2830	3202	17698	13569	4129	14167	2758	3134
Machine operators, assemblers, and inspectors	7319	4622	2697	5802	1080	1416	6734	4286	2448	5336	997	1320
Transportation and material moving occupations	5557	5003	554	4476	915	662	5638	5049	589	4553	922	697
Handlers, equipment cleaners, helpers, and laborers	5443	4363	1080	4402	835	1125	5326	4234	1092	4278	838	1118
Farming, forestry, and fishing	3399	2698	701	3146	166	807	3245	2570	675	3000	161	698

Note: Detail for the above race and Hispanic-origin groups will not sum to totals because data for the Other races group are not presented and Hispanics are included in both the White and Black population groups. See "Notes and Definitions" for information on historical comparability.

Table 1-14. Employed Civilians by Industry and Occupation, 1990–2001

(Thousands of persons.)

Industry	Total employed	Managerial and professional specialty		Technical, sales, and administrative support			Service occupations		Precision production, craft, and repair	Operators, fabricators, and laborers			Farming, forestry, and fishing
		Executive, administrative, and managerial	Professional specialty	Technicians and related support	Sales	Administrative support, including clerical	Private household	Other services, including protective		Machine operators, assemblers, and inspectors	Transportation and material moving	Handlers, equipment cleaners, helpers, and laborers	
1990													
Agriculture	3 223	95	85	30	23	108	...	17	42	13	49	21	2 740
Mining	724	110	63	32	9	72	...	9	243	26	123	36	2
Construction	7 764	1 034	133	64	75	426	...	35	4 445	114	524	890	23
Manufacturing	21 346	2 530	1 794	765	779	2 363	...	374	3 964	6 696	805	1 173	102
Durable goods	12 630	1 521	1 225	533	326	1 363	...	197	2 721	3 685	416	552	91
Nondurable goods	8 717	1 010	569	232	453	1 000	...	178	1 243	3 011	389	621	11
Transportation and public utilities	8 168	915	459	306	340	2 166	...	293	1 259	122	1 812	481	14
Wholesale trade	4 669	528	88	50	1 862	788	...	39	323	138	464	380	10
Retail trade	19 953	1 557	379	89	8 295	1 633	...	4 584	1 181	197	512	1 498	27
Finance, insurance, and real estate	8 051	2 087	225	155	1 904	3 097	...	296	155	19	17	25	71
Services	39 267	4 745	11 786	2 125	971	6 561	792	8 194	1 898	831	521	436	408
Services, except private households	38 231	4 742	11 773	2 121	969	6 552	...	8 098	1 881	829	514	417	336
Professional services	25 351	2 642	10 425	1 719	162	4 763	...	4 545	400	228	276	101	91
Public administration	5 627	1 199	788	251	26	1 549	...	1 380	235	43	60	44	53
1991													
Agriculture	3 269	91	78	31	22	102	...	18	41	12	54	16	2 803
Mining	732	112	65	37	8	81	...	12	244	24	115	34	1
Construction	7 140	969	137	53	71	386	...	29	4 077	100	497	797	24
Manufacturing	20 580	2 499	1 777	749	729	2 283	...	355	3 837	6 402	780	1 076	92
Durable goods	12 015	1 489	1 178	512	292	1 260	...	185	2 630	3 459	404	525	80
Nondurable goods	8 565	1 010	599	237	437	1 023	...	170	1 207	2 943	376	551	13
Transportation and public utilities	8 234	973	474	301	331	2 170	...	262	1 285	125	1 833	465	16
Wholesale trade	4 660	537	77	37	1 868	776	...	36	319	135	490	374	11
Retail trade	19 758	1 591	372	103	8 181	1 589	...	4 605	1 142	173	530	1 450	23
Finance, insurance, and real estate	7 806	2 027	216	133	1 849	3 022	...	270	167	18	14	20	69
Services	39 884	4 873	12 035	2 148	967	6 534	799	8 455	1 884	792	537	444	416
Services, except private households	38 868	4 871	12 029	2 144	966	6 522	...	8 375	1 870	791	531	422	346
Professional services	25 853	2 706	10 629	1 742	162	4 788	...	4 749	393	211	295	87	92
Public administration	5 655	1 231	798	223	27	1 508	...	1 414	253	41	62	46	51
1992													
Agriculture	3 247	91	74	44	21	118	...	17	45	10	44	19	2 764
Mining	666	100	58	31	7	79	...	12	214	28	106	31	1
Construction	7 063	892	147	67	73	410	...	34	4 073	99	480	762	28
Manufacturing	20 124	2 401	1 640	758	768	2 268	...	330	3 808	6 244	749	1 074	84
Durable goods	11 561	1 405	1 069	525	306	1 251	...	158	2 569	3 344	374	485	75
Nondurable goods	8 563	996	571	234	462	1 017	...	172	1 239	2 901	375	589	8
Transportation and public utilities	8 284	946	461	375	250	2 281	...	274	1 227	114	1 874	464	18
Wholesale trade	4 783	556	85	46	1 883	820	...	42	302	118	490	405	38
Retail trade	19 938	1 603	374	146	8 229	1 591	...	4 717	1 117	180	530	1 428	25
Finance, insurance, and real estate	7 780	1 966	224	162	1 851	2 991	...	290	171	19	13	22	73
Services	40 967	4 937	12 473	2 379	908	6 728	891	9 259	2 022	810	563	440	449
Services, except private households	39 821	4 933	12 463	2 373	906	6 714	...	8 368	2 007	807	555	421	372
Professional services	27 713	3 150	11 168	2 040	175	5 032	...	5 017	411	208	314	102	95
Public administration	5 640	1 231	829	268	25	1 472	...	1 404	246	37	59	38	31
1993													
Agriculture	3 115	99	87	39	14	114	...	15	45	8	53	20	2 621
Mining	672	102	75	24	4	73	...	8	233	25	103	25	...
Construction	7 276	928	137	46	74	390	...	35	4 292	79	517	753	25
Manufacturing	19 711	2 432	1 688	693	739	2 161	...	312	3 744	6 124	710	1 012	95
Durable goods	11 385	1 415	1 085	463	282	1 181	...	161	2 553	3 352	361	446	87
Nondurable goods	8 326	1 017	603	231	457	981	...	151	1 191	2 772	349	566	9
Transportation and public utilities	8 526	975	500	329	241	2 318	...	266	1 271	131	2 000	479	18
Wholesale trade	4 622	533	85	49	1 819	771	...	40	296	115	492	378	44
Retail trade	20 521	1 652	351	129	8 543	1 571	...	4 873	1 095	179	543	1 563	23
Finance, insurance, and real estate	7 975	2 089	244	161	1 918	2 967	...	290	183	21	13	19	70
Services	42 059	5 234	12 864	2 300	963	6 841	928	8 579	2 047	831	551	467	453
Services, except private households	40 924	5 231	12 857	2 298	961	6 830	...	8 497	2 035	831	547	446	392
Professional services	28 365	3 299	11 476	1 969	176	5 111	...	5 163	419	223	314	108	105
Public administration	5 782	1 294	862	270	26	1 469	...	1 475	224	39	54	39	31

See *Note* at end of table.

Table 1-14. Employed Civilians by Industry and Occupation, 1990–2001—*Continued*

(Thousands of persons.)

Industry	Total employed	Managerial and professional specialty		Technical, sales, and administrative support			Service occupations		Precision production, craft, and repair	Operators, fabricators, and laborers			Farming, forestry, and fishing
		Executive, administrative, and managerial	Professional specialty	Technicians and related support	Sales	Administrative support, including clerical	Private household	Other services, including protective		Machine operators, assemblers, and inspectors	Transportation and material moving	Handlers, equipment cleaners, helpers, and laborers	
1994													
Agriculture	3 409	97	88	38	14	145	...	18	42	5	45	19	2 897
Mining	669	110	76	22	10	67	...	9	222	21	109	21	1
Construction	7 493	1 055	138	60	59	429	...	34	4 263	86	529	818	22
Manufacturing	20 157	2 588	1 814	611	745	2 093	...	290	3 803	6 298	744	1 082	89
Durable goods	11 792	1 555	1 170	412	310	1 146	...	152	2 622	3 415	416	514	80
Nondurable goods	8 365	1 033	644	200	435	946	...	138	1 181	2 883	328	569	9
Transportation and public utilities	8 692	1 065	486	329	248	2 337	...	246	1 270	120	2 049	528	15
Wholesale trade	4 713	531	89	37	1 880	775	...	34	296	150	464	398	60
Retail trade	20 986	1 704	402	119	8 772	1 555	...	4 948	1 145	197	548	1 569	27
Finance, insurance, and real estate	8 141	2 198	272	160	2 029	2 915	...	282	167	18	17	18	66
Services	42 986	5 649	13 319	2 274	1 032	6 864	817	8 654	2 071	825	567	493	421
Services, except private households	42 009	5 645	13 311	2 272	1 031	6 855	...	8 584	2 063	825	564	480	380
Professional services	29 030	3 559	11 888	1 968	193	5 083	...	5 134	470	222	314	94	105
Public administration	5 814	1 315	853	221	28	1 440	...	1 579	211	32	64	39	30
1995													
Agriculture	3 440	105	92	45	15	145	...	16	35	17	45	19	2 907
Mining	627	100	60	22	4	53	...	5	228	28	101	25	2
Construction	7 668	1 117	145	43	63	431	...	33	4 362	85	513	858	18
Manufacturing	20 493	2 804	1 787	615	756	2 108	...	294	3 837	6 386	728	1 067	111
Durable goods	12 015	1 683	1 160	404	311	1 117	...	156	2 660	3 498	390	535	100
Nondurable goods	8 478	1 121	627	211	445	991	...	138	1 177	2 888	338	532	11
Transportation and public utilities	8 709	1 124	510	310	259	2 337	...	247	1 223	121	2 079	487	12
Wholesale trade	4 986	554	108	48	1 979	792	...	37	308	187	488	423	62
Retail trade	21 086	1 740	425	141	8 949	1 501	...	4 844	1 111	214	578	1 548	34
Finance, insurance, and real estate	7 983	2 258	268	148	1 985	2 757	...	269	183	14	14	19	68
Services	43 953	6 029	13 755	2 307	1 086	6 848	821	8 788	2 008	824	572	510	405
Services, except private households	42 982	6 023	13 746	2 305	1 086	6 838	...	8 719	2 002	822	569	497	374
Professional services	29 661	3 721	12 233	1 974	199	5 114	...	5 284	465	178	312	87	94
Public administration	5 957	1 356	981	230	24	1 417	...	1 577	229	32	52	35	25
1996													
Agriculture	3 443	108	88	40	19	174	...	28	41	11	34	13	2 888
Mining	569	90	44	21	10	47	...	7	208	21	105	17	1
Construction	7 943	1 221	165	45	65	452	...	32	4 442	96	513	890	21
Manufacturing	20 518	2 840	1 882	631	766	2 033	...	264	3 814	6 350	767	1 069	101
Durable goods	12 202	1 690	1 204	425	337	1 131	...	144	2 677	3 561	425	518	90
Nondurable goods	8 316	1 150	678	206	429	903	...	120	1 137	2 789	342	551	11
Transportation and public utilities	8 817	1 159	529	332	288	2 319	...	251	1 185	132	2 126	489	7
Wholesale trade	4 956	563	100	52	2 005	749	...	48	320	142	515	400	62
Retail trade	21 541	1 818	410	123	9 055	1 577	...	4 983	1 137	204	614	1 583	39
Finance, insurance, and real estate	8 076	2 274	271	162	2 052	2 744	...	298	165	15	13	28	54
Services	45 043	6 347	14 312	2 312	1 120	6 905	804	8 876	2 055	875	573	496	367
Services, except private households	44 107	6 343	14 302	2 310	1 119	6 900	...	8 821	2 048	875	572	484	335
Professional services	30 085	3 853	12 592	1 941	204	5 090	...	5 340	417	190	301	88	69
Public administration	5 802	1 325	951	208	25	1 353	...	1 585	221	28	43	37	25
1997													
Agriculture	3 399	124	83	48	19	160	...	24	34	10	51	26	2 821
Mining	634	92	51	25	10	66	...	4	236	24	101	24	1
Construction	8 302	1 274	158	45	72	425	...	35	4 731	97	558	884	22
Manufacturing	20 835	2 882	1 938	689	785	2 029	...	268	3 887	6 471	762	1 027	96
Durable goods	12 437	1 699	1 261	441	316	1 133	...	145	2 753	3 685	406	512	87
Nondurable goods	8 399	1 183	677	249	469	896	...	123	1 134	2 786	356	515	9
Transportation and public utilities	9 182	1 230	562	342	283	2 297	...	301	1 257	133	2 230	531	16
Wholesale trade	4 907	589	110	47	1 928	740	...	56	326	133	520	393	66
Retail trade	21 869	1 893	427	155	9 303	1 480	...	5 048	1 173	202	572	1 580	36
Finance, insurance, and real estate	8 297	2 428	308	151	2 092	2 749	...	307	175	12	11	28	38
Services	46 393	6 642	14 677	2 490	1 210	7 113	795	9 055	2 115	854	537	521	384
Services, except private households	45 472	6 638	14 671	2 485	1 210	7 107	...	8 988	2 109	853	537	514	359
Professional services	30 935	4 057	12 846	2 110	225	5 177	...	5 432	420	207	279	89	93
Public administration	5 738	1 287	932	221	32	1 303	...	1 644	191	27	46	33	23

See *Note* at end of table.

Table 1-14. Employed Civilians by Industry and Occupation, 1990–2001—*Continued*

(Thousands of persons.)

Industry	Total employed	Managerial and professional specialty		Technical, sales, and administrative support			Service occupations		Precision production, craft, and repair	Operators, fabricators, and laborers			Farming, forestry, and fishing
		Executive, administrative, and managerial	Professional specialty	Technicians and related support	Sales	Administrative support, including clerical	Private household	Other services, including protective		Machine operators, assemblers, and inspectors	Transportation and material moving	Handlers, equipment cleaners, helpers, and laborers	
1998													
Agriculture	3 378	110	105	51	23	136	...	21	39	20	42	19	2 814
Mining	620	101	63	19	11	53	...	8	208	31	105	18	1
Construction	8 518	1 380	144	47	56	415	...	28	4 889	94	535	910	21
Manufacturing	20 733	3 008	2 007	646	764	1 982	...	291	3 956	6 219	765	1 019	76
Durable goods	12 566	1 796	1 351	430	318	1 127	...	150	2 807	3 594	415	509	71
Nondurable goods	8 168	1 212	656	217	446	856	...	141	1 150	2 625	350	510	5
Transportation and public utilities	9 307	1 307	561	324	273	2 349	...	296	1 285	135	2 243	522	13
Wholesale trade	5 090	622	131	43	2 054	756	...	57	346	137	493	380	71
Retail trade	22 113	1 916	459	188	9 306	1 438	...	5 125	1 177	230	575	1 670	30
Finance, insurance, and real estate	8 605	2 489	356	166	2 143	2 860	...	323	177	12	13	17	49
Services	47 212	6 793	15 090	2 541	1 197	7 118	847	9 117	2 154	887	551	516	399
Services, except private households	46 244	6 787	15 084	2 540	1 196	7 109	...	9 061	2 151	887	548	509	374
Professional services	31 392	4 164	13 122	2 132	213	5 132	...	5 485	473	195	294	99	85
Public administration	5 887	1 329	968	234	25	1 302	...	1 722	182	27	40	30	27
1999													
Agriculture	3 281	118	97	53	15	149	...	15	36	10	48	18	2 722
Mining	565	83	69	19	7	35	...	6	198	24	102	21	1
Construction	8 987	1 379	159	60	67	406	...	33	5 224	108	543	984	22
Manufacturing	20 070	2 955	1 981	645	736	1 883	...	242	3 883	5 896	726	1 035	88
Durable goods	12 283	1 799	1 286	440	351	1 067	...	125	2 715	3 504	394	520	82
Nondurable goods	7 787	1 156	694	205	385	816	...	117	1 168	2 391	332	515	7
Transportation and public utilities	9 554	1 340	557	359	275	2 386	...	304	1 335	123	2 318	546	14
Wholesale trade	5 189	630	158	50	2 047	819	...	52	324	118	523	406	62
Retail trade	22 383	1 967	461	207	9 489	1 495	...	5 122	1 108	229	625	1 643	38
Finance, insurance, and real estate	8 815	2 664	380	200	2 224	2 780	...	294	177	10	12	23	50
Services	48 687	7 061	16 031	2 533	1 230	7 242	831	9 275	2 119	847	575	547	395
Services, except private households	47 747	7 056	16 026	2 530	1 230	7 234	...	9 219	2 116	847	573	535	382
Professional services	32 370	4 307	13 796	2 074	210	5 333	...	5 536	463	167	301	91	90
Public administration	5 958	1 386	992	229	28	1 253	...	1 741	189	22	42	42	34
2000													
Agriculture	3 305	106	105	60	13	145	...	15	54	17	55	18	2 718
Mining	521	79	52	15	5	41	...	7	194	19	87	22	...
Construction	9 433	1 302	182	60	94	435	...	30	5 555	120	546	1 093	17
Manufacturing	19 940	3 016	1 920	621	749	1 917	...	271	3 785	5 850	681	1 045	85
Durable goods	12 168	1 834	1 282	438	319	1 059	...	148	2 659	3 450	380	525	74
Nondurable goods	7 772	1 182	639	182	430	858	...	123	1 126	2 399	301	520	12
Transportation and public utilities	9 740	1 356	614	339	286	2 445	...	318	1 327	99	2 355	584	16
Wholesale trade	5 421	642	165	66	2 184	800	...	63	354	148	526	415	58
Retail trade	22 411	1 925	496	211	9 378	1 479	...	5 316	1 117	205	613	1 643	27
Finance, insurance, and real estate	8 727	2 571	380	194	2 288	2 751	...	298	157	10	12	20	45
Services	49 695	7 413	16 178	2 602	1 313	7 367	792	9 459	2 144	822	635	564	406
Services, except private households	48 801	7 410	16 172	2 600	1 312	7 361	...	9 410	2 142	822	633	559	380
Professional services	32 784	4 450	13 812	2 113	230	5 390	...	5 658	449	165	335	93	89
Public administration	6 015	1 364	1 021	219	29	1 336	...	1 709	196	29	47	38	27
2001													
Agriculture	3 144	96	107	57	24	162	...	9	41	8	54	15	2 571
Mining	567	93	60	14	11	54	...	5	196	22	94	18	...
Construction	9 581	1 376	176	74	77	433	...	34	5 648	104	541	1 100	19
Manufacturing	18 970	2 938	1 977	613	704	1 733	...	256	3 603	5 365	697	1 010	73
Durable goods	11 588	1 737	1 305	414	305	975	...	133	2 567	3 195	371	521	65
Nondurable goods	7 381	1 202	672	199	400	758	...	123	1 036	2 169	325	489	8
Transportation and public utilities	9 738	1 343	635	384	326	2 376	...	314	1 280	104	2 392	576	10
Wholesale and retail trade	27 672	2 652	654	277	11 410	2 282	...	5 311	1 501	322	1 167	2 003	92
wholesale trade	5 102	658	142	64	2 047	745	...	57	327	113	511	388	50
retail trade	22 571	1 994	511	213	9 363	1 538	...	5 254	1 174	209	656	1 615	42
Finance, insurance and real estate	8 797	2 668	346	187	2 274	2 756	...	309	163	13	8	23	50
Services	50 478	7 739	16 583	2 650	1 193	7 415	715	9 647	2 173	774	647	552	391
Services, except private households	49 662	7 734	16 577	2 648	1 193	7 407	...	9 599	2 171	773	643	541	376
Professional services	33 445	4 641	14 131	2 168	192	5 417	...	5 748	444	160	355	102	89
Public administration	6 126	1 433	1 018	241	26	1 292	...	1 758	228	21	39	31	40

Note: See "Notes and Definitions" for information on historical comparability.

Table 1-15. Employed Civilians in Agriculture and Nonagricultural Industries by Class of Worker and Sex, 1978–2001

(Thousands of persons.)

Year and sex	Total employed	Agriculture				Nonagricultural industries						
		Total	Wage and salary workers	Self employed workers	Unpaid family workers	Total	Wage and salary workers				Self-employed workers	Unpaid family workers
							Total	Government	Private household	Other private		
TOTAL												
1978	96 048	3 387	1 452	1 618	316	92 661	85 753	15 525	1 384	68 844	6 429	479
1979	98 824	3 347	1 451	1 593	304	95 477	88 222	15 635	1 264	71 323	6 791	463
1980	99 302	3 364	1 425	1 642	297	95 938	88 525	15 912	1 192	71 421	7 000	413
1981	100 398	3 368	1 464	1 638	266	97 030	89 543	15 689	1 208	72 646	7 097	390
1982	99 526	3 401	1 505	1 636	261	96 125	88 462	15 516	1 207	71 739	7 262	401
1983	100 833	3 383	1 579	1 565	240	97 450	89 500	15 537	1 244	72 719	7 575	376
1984	105 006	3 321	1 555	1 553	213	101 685	93 565	15 770	1 238	76 557	7 785	335
1985	107 150	3 179	1 535	1 458	185	103 971	95 871	16 031	1 249	78 591	7 811	289
1986	109 597	3 163	1 547	1 447	169	106 434	98 299	16 342	1 235	80 722	7 881	255
1987	112 440	3 208	1 632	1 423	153	109 232	100 771	16 800	1 208	82 763	8 201	260
1988	114 969	3 169	1 621	1 398	150	111 800	103 021	17 114	1 153	84 754	8 519	260
1989	117 341	3 199	1 665	1 403	131	114 142	105 259	17 469	1 101	86 689	8 605	279
1990	118 793	3 223	1 740	1 378	105	115 570	106 598	17 769	1 027	87 802	8 719	253
1991	117 718	3 269	1 729	1 423	118	114 449	105 373	17 934	1 010	86 429	8 851	226
1992	118 492	3 247	1 750	1 385	112	115 245	106 437	18 136	1 135	87 166	8 575	233
1993	120 259	3 115	1 689	1 320	106	117 144	107 966	18 579	1 126	88 261	8 959	218
1994	123 060	3 409	1 715	1 645	49	119 651	110 517	18 293	966	91 258	9 003	131
1995	124 900	3 440	1 814	1 580	45	121 460	112 448	18 362	963	93 123	8 902	110
1996	126 707	3 443	1 869	1 518	56	123 264	114 171	18 217	928	95 026	8 971	122
1997	129 558	3 399	1 890	1 457	51	126 159	116 983	18 131	915	97 937	9 056	120
1998	131 463	3 378	2 000	1 341	38	128 085	119 019	18 383	962	99 674	8 962	103
1999	133 488	3 281	1 944	1 297	40	130 207	121 323	18 903	933	101 487	8 790	95
2000	135 208	3 305	2 034	1 233	38	131 903	123 128	19 053	890	103 186	8 674	101
2001	135 074	3 144	1 884	1 233	27	131 930	123 235	19 127	803	103 305	8 594	101
MEN												
1978	56 479	2 718	1 162	1 465	91	53 761	49 103	7 836	181	41 086	4 614	44
1979	57 607	2 686	1 160	1 429	98	54 921	50 068	7 790	159	42 119	4 810	43
1980	57 186	2 709	1 149	1 458	101	54 477	49 517	7 822	149	41 546	4 904	56
1981	57 397	2 700	1 168	1 442	91	54 697	49 745	7 676	192	41 877	4 905	47
1982	56 270	2 736	1 208	1 433	95	53 534	48 529	7 598	188	40 743	4 954	52
1983	56 787	2 704	1 265	1 355	84	54 083	48 896	7 623	208	41 065	5 136	51
1984	59 091	2 668	1 254	1 350	65	56 423	51 151	7 720	178	43 253	5 219	52
1985	59 891	2 535	1 230	1 244	60	57 356	52 111	7 757	170	44 184	5 207	38
1986	60 892	2 511	1 230	1 227	54	58 381	53 075	7 805	180	45 090	5 271	35
1987	62 107	2 543	1 290	1 194	58	59 564	54 102	8 013	180	45 909	5 423	39
1988	63 273	2 493	1 268	1 174	50	60 780	55 177	8 074	157	46 946	5 564	39
1989	64 315	2 513	1 302	1 167	44	61 802	56 202	8 116	156	47 930	5 562	38
1990	65 105	2 546	1 355	1 151	39	62 559	56 913	8 245	149	48 519	5 597	48
1991	64 223	2 589	1 359	1 185	45	61 634	55 899	8 300	143	47 456	5 700	35
1992	64 441	2 575	1 371	1 164	40	61 866	56 212	8 348	156	47 708	5 613	41
1993	65 349	2 478	1 323	1 117	39	62 871	56 926	8 435	146	48 345	5 894	50
1994	66 450	2 554	1 330	1 197	27	63 896	58 300	8 327	99	49 874	5 560	37
1995	67 377	2 559	1 395	1 138	26	64 818	59 332	8 267	96	50 969	5 461	25
1996	68 207	2 573	1 418	1 124	31	65 634	60 133	8 110	99	51 924	5 465	36
1997	69 685	2 552	1 439	1 084	29	67 133	61 595	8 015	81	53 499	5 506	31
1998	70 693	2 553	1 526	1 005	23	68 140	62 630	8 178	86	54 366	5 480	29
1999	71 446	2 432	1 450	962	20	69 014	63 624	8 278	74	55 272	5 366	25
2000	72 293	2 434	1 512	898	24	69 859	64 574	8 215	67	56 292	5 256	29
2001	72 080	2 275	1 362	897	16	69 806	64 589	8 240	58	56 291	5 189	28
WOMEN												
1978	39 569	669	290	155	225	38 900	36 651	7 689	1 204	27 758	1 814	435
1979	41 217	661	290	165	206	40 556	38 154	7 845	1 105	29 204	1 982	419
1980	42 117	656	275	184	197	41 461	39 007	8 090	1 044	29 873	2 097	357
1981	43 000	667	296	196	176	42 333	39 798	8 013	1 016	30 769	2 192	343
1982	43 256	665	296	203	166	42 591	39 934	7 918	1 019	30 997	2 309	348
1983	44 047	680	314	210	156	43 367	40 603	7 913	1 036	31 654	2 439	325
1984	45 915	653	301	203	148	45 262	42 413	8 050	1 061	33 302	2 566	283
1985	47 259	644	305	214	125	46 615	43 761	8 274	1 078	34 409	2 603	251
1986	48 706	652	317	220	115	48 054	45 225	8 537	1 055	35 633	2 610	219
1987	50 334	666	342	229	95	49 668	46 669	8 788	1 029	36 852	2 778	221
1988	51 696	676	353	224	99	51 020	47 844	9 039	996	37 809	2 955	220
1989	53 028	687	363	236	87	52 341	49 057	9 353	945	38 759	3 043	240
1990	53 689	678	385	227	66	53 011	49 685	9 524	879	39 282	3 122	205
1991	53 495	680	369	237	73	52 815	49 474	9 635	867	38 972	3 150	191
1992	54 052	672	379	221	73	53 380	50 225	9 788	979	39 458	2 963	192
1993	54 910	637	367	204	67	54 273	51 040	10 144	980	39 916	3 065	168
1994	56 610	855	384	448	23	55 755	52 217	9 965	867	41 385	3 443	95
1995	57 523	881	419	442	20	56 642	53 115	10 095	867	42 153	3 440	86
1996	58 501	871	452	394	25	57 630	54 037	10 107	830	43 100	3 506	87
1997	59 873	847	451	373	23	59 026	55 388	10 116	834	44 438	3 550	89
1998	60 770	825	474	336	15	59 945	56 389	10 205	876	45 308	3 482	74
1999	62 042	849	494	335	20	61 193	57 699	10 625	859	46 215	3 424	70
2000	62 915	871	521	336	14	62 044	58 544	10 838	823	46 894	3 417	72
2001	62 992	869	522	336	11	62 123	58 646	10 887	745	47 014	3 404	73

Note: See "Notes and Definitions" for information on historical comparabilty.

Table 1-16. Number of Employed Persons 25 Years and Over by Educational Attainment, Race, Hispanic Origin, and Sex, 1992–2001

(Thousands of persons.)

Year, race, Hispanic origin, and sex	Total	Less than a high school diploma	High school graduates, no college	Some college, no degree	Associate degree	College graduates Total	College graduates Bachelor's degree only
TOTAL							
1992	99 947	11 843	35 305	7 519	18 007	27 273	17 662
1993	101 615	11 201	35 395	8 174	18 729	28 115	18 300
1994	104 141	11 053	35 135	8 834	19 861	29 257	19 225
1995	106 037	10 945	34 999	9 245	20 436	30 412	19 924
1996	108 070	11 317	36 300	9 404	20 590	31 459	20 742
1997	110 518	11 546	36 163	9 643	20 678	32 488	21 524
1998	111 855	11 673	35 976	9 850	20 626	33 730	22 260
1999	113 425	11 294	36 017	10 079	21 129	34 905	22 973
2000	114 612	11 283	35 886	10 591	21 374	35 478	23 382
2001	114 822	11 229	35 412	11 004	21 182	35 995	23 623
WHITE							
1992	85 649	9 531	30 282	6 502	15 420	23 914	15 441
1993	87 001	9 109	30 242	7 052	15 987	24 613	15 962
1994	89 057	8 879	30 004	7 622	16 893	25 658	16 719
1995	90 498	8 690	29 776	7 970	17 265	26 796	17 434
1996	91 992	9 258	30 042	8 072	17 249	27 371	17 978
1997	93 687	9 414	30 552	8 271	17 302	28 148	18 801
1998	94 330	9 510	30 249	8 426	17 101	29 044	19 107
1999	95 316	9 235	30 211	8 556	17 388	29 925	19 668
2000	96 127	9 232	30 015	8 995	17 615	30 270	19 943
2001	96 137	9 194	29 602	9 297	17 432	30 614	20 035
BLACK							
1992	10 313	1 781	4 011	744	2 017	1 760	1 219
1993	10 511	1 580	4 075	815	2 180	1 862	1 315
1994	10 834	1 543	4 016	902	2 340	2 034	1 483
1995	11 249	1 482	4 142	960	2 517	2 149	1 538
1996	11 518	1 534	4 192	969	2 640	2 183	1 539
1997	11 882	1 578	4 409	984	2 681	2 230	1 591
1998	12 324	1 579	4 504	1 020	2 776	2 446	1 741
1999	12 771	1 488	4 631	1 108	2 924	2 621	1 814
2000	12 964	1 490	4 609	1 176	2 949	2 741	1 889
2001	12 996	1 494	4 542	1 245	2 936	2 779	1 958
HISPANIC							
1992	7 875	2 964	2 349	458	1 153	952	644
1993	8 218	2 996	2 422	514	1 276	1 009	697
1994	8 535	3 078	2 503	530	1 353	1 071	740
1995	8 873	3 204	2 624	534	1 427	1 084	759
1996	9 368	3 450	2 746	568	1 453	1 151	813
1997	10 214	3 738	2 945	611	1 603	1 316	926
1998	10 615	3 889	3 018	660	1 622	1 427	1 007
1999	10 985	3 926	3 213	660	1 696	1 491	1 034
2000	11 596	4 190	3 410	706	1 706	1 585	1 111
2001	11 787	4 249	3 471	717	1 761	1 588	1 119
MEN							
1992	54 672	7 299	18 422	3 652	9 549	15 751	9 864
1993	55 550	6 977	18 575	4 012	9 878	16 109	10 170
1994	56 523	6 851	18 418	4 184	10 402	16 668	10 672
1995	57 420	6 691	18 426	4 394	10 653	17 255	10 983
1996	58 468	7 058	18 639	4 416	10 759	17 596	11 266
1997	59 736	7 210	19 124	4 517	10 876	18 010	11 587
1998	60 497	7 238	19 188	4 731	10 684	18 656	12 028
1999	61 032	6 921	19 125	4 838	10 941	19 208	12 343
2000	61 571	6 889	19 086	4 960	11 133	19 503	12 576
2001	61 638	6 858	18 912	5 170	10 892	19 806	12 750
WOMEN							
1992	45 275	4 544	16 883	3 868	8 458	11 522	7 798
1993	46 064	4 224	16 820	4 163	8 851	12 006	8 130
1994	47 618	4 202	16 717	4 650	9 459	12 589	8 553
1995	48 617	4 254	16 573	4 851	9 783	13 157	8 941
1996	49 602	4 259	16 661	4 988	9 831	13 863	9 475
1997	50 782	4 336	17 039	5 126	9 802	14 478	9 937
1998	51 359	4 435	16 788	5 119	9 943	15 074	10 231
1999	52 392	4 372	16 893	5 242	10 189	15 697	10 630
2000	53 041	4 394	16 799	5 631	10 240	15 975	10 806
2001	53 184	4 372	16 500	5 835	10 289	16 189	10 873

See *Note* at end of table.

Table 1-16. Number of Employed Persons 25 Years and Over by Educational Attainment, Race, Hispanic Origin, and Sex, 1992–2001—*Continued*

(Thousands of persons.)

Year, race, Hispanic origin, and sex	Total	Less than a high school diploma	High school graduates, no college	Some college, no degree	Associate degree	College graduates	
						Total	Bachelor's degree only
WHITE MEN							
1992	47 497	6 030	15 962	3 200	8 303	14 002	8 778
1993	48 191	5 807	16 002	3 514	8 581	14 288	9 020
1994	48 938	5 633	15 833	3 667	8 990	14 814	9 435
1995	49 641	5 444	15 760	3 856	9 155	15 426	9 780
1996	50 533	5 920	15 995	3 861	9 197	15 559	9 965
1997	51 397	6 049	16 330	3 941	9 245	15 832	10 191
1998	51 842	6 123	16 308	4 118	9 009	16 284	10 490
1999	52 180	5 883	16 193	4 160	9 182	16 763	10 806
2000	52 530	5 833	16 145	4 284	9 350	16 919	10 962
2001	52 479	5 794	15 985	4 456	9 174	17 070	11 025
WHITE WOMEN							
1992	38 152	3 500	14 321	3 302	7 117	9 912	6 663
1993	38 810	3 301	14 240	3 538	7 406	10 325	6 941
1994	40 119	3 246	14 171	3 955	7 902	10 844	7 285
1995	40 857	3 246	14 016	4 115	8 110	11 370	7 655
1996	41 459	3 337	14 046	4 211	8 052	11 812	8 012
1997	42 290	3 365	14 222	4 330	8 058	12 316	8 410
1998	42 488	3 387	13 941	4 308	8 092	12 760	8 618
1999	43 135	3 352	14 018	4 396	8 207	13 162	8 862
2000	43 597	3 399	13 870	4 711	8 265	13 351	8 981
2001	43 658	3 400	13 617	4 841	8 257	13 543	9 011
BLACK MEN							
1992	5 002	976	1 955	320	940	809	554
1993	5 119	875	2 014	353	998	879	617
1994	5 246	844	2 001	373	1 057	970	712
1995	5 423	778	2 101	393	1 142	1 010	717
1996	5 483	861	2 104	382	1 177	960	666
1997	5 658	868	2 181	385	1 241	983	710
1998	5 844	811	2 248	413	1 267	1 104	802
1999	6 001	741	2 339	469	1 313	1 140	789
2000	6 077	749	2 280	475	1 348	1 226	841
2001	6 081	768	2 279	501	1 299	1 234	868
BLACK WOMEN							
1992	5 312	805	2 056	424	1 077	951	665
1993	5 392	705	2 060	462	1 182	983	698
1994	5 589	699	2 015	529	1 283	1 064	771
1995	5 826	704	2 042	566	1 375	1 139	822
1996	6 035	673	2 088	587	1 463	1 224	873
1997	6 225	710	2 229	600	1 439	1 247	882
1998	6 480	768	2 256	607	1 509	1 341	939
1999	6 770	746	2 292	639	1 612	1 481	1 025
2000	6 887	741	2 329	701	1 601	1 515	1 048
2001	6 915	726	2 263	744	1 637	1 545	1 090
HISPANIC MEN							
1992	4 773	1 982	1 337	245	660	549	364
1993	4 989	2 019	1 365	281	742	582	401
1994	5 133	2 059	1 416	287	761	610	413
1995	5 337	2 125	1 501	279	818	615	408
1996	5 640	2 320	1 588	271	790	671	456
1997	6 165	2 502	1 714	302	899	747	502
1998	6 397	2 594	1 764	336	913	790	547
1999	6 441	2 554	1 839	334	917	797	540
2000	6 747	2 695	1 939	364	907	841	577
2001	6 849	2 745	1 934	345	967	858	601
HISPANIC WOMEN							
1992	3 102	982	1 012	214	493	402	279
1993	3 229	977	1 057	233	535	428	296
1994	3 402	1 019	1 087	242	592	461	327
1995	3 536	1 079	1 123	255	609	470	351
1996	3 729	1 131	1 159	297	663	480	357
1997	4 049	1 236	1 231	309	704	569	425
1998	4 219	1 295	1 254	325	708	637	459
1999	4 544	1 372	1 373	327	778	694	494
2000	4 850	1 495	1 470	342	798	744	534
2001	4 938	1 504	1 537	372	794	730	517

Note: Detail for the above race and Hispanic-origin groups will not sum to totals because data for the Other races group are not presented and Hispanics are included in both the White and Black population groups. See "Notes and Definitions" for information on historical comparability.

Table 1-17. Multiple Jobholders and Multiple Jobholding Rates by Selected Characteristics, May of Selected Years, 1970–2001

(Thousands of persons, percent, not seasonally adjusted.)

| Year | Multiple jobholders | | | | Multiple jobholding rate [1] | | | | |
| | Total | Men | Women | | Total | Men | Women | White | Black [2] |
			Number	Percent of all multiple jobholders					
1970	4 048	3 412	636	15.7	5.2	7.0	2.2	5.3	4.4
1971	4 035	3 270	765	19.0	5.1	6.7	2.6	5.3	3.8
1972	3 770	3 035	735	19.5	4.6	6.0	2.4	4.8	3.7
1973	4 262	3 393	869	20.4	5.1	6.6	2.7	5.1	4.7
1974	3 889	3 022	867	22.3	4.5	5.8	2.6	4.6	3.8
1975	3 918	2 962	956	24.4	4.7	5.8	2.9	4.8	3.7
1976	3 948	3 037	911	23.1	4.5	5.8	2.6	4.7	2.8
1977	4 558	3 317	1 241	27.2	5.0	6.2	3.4	5.3	2.6
1978	4 493	3 212	1 281	28.5	4.8	5.8	3.3	5.0	3.1
1979	4 724	3 317	1 407	29.8	4.9	5.9	3.5	5.1	3.0
1980	4 759	3 210	1 549	32.5	4.9	5.8	3.8	5.1	3.2
1985	5 730	3 537	2 192	38.3	5.4	5.9	4.7	5.7	3.2
1989	7 225	4 115	3 109	43.0	6.2	6.4	5.9	6.5	4.3
1991	7 183	4 054	3 129	43.6	6.2	6.4	5.9	6.4	4.9
1994	7 316	3 973	3 343	45.7	6.0	6.0	5.9	6.1	4.9
1995	7 952	4 225	3 727	46.9	6.4	6.3	6.5	6.6	5.2
1996	7 846	4 352	3 494	44.5	6.2	6.4	6.0	6.4	5.1
1997	8 197	4 398	3 800	46.4	6.3	6.3	6.4	6.5	5.7
1998	8 126	4 438	3 688	45.4	6.2	6.3	6.1	6.3	5.5
1999	7 895	4 117	3 778	47.9	5.9	5.8	6.1	6.0	5.5
2000	7 710	4 059	3 650	47.3	5.7	5.6	5.8	5.9	4.9
2001	7 482	3 880	3 602	48.1	5.5	5.4	5.7	5.6	5.3

Note: Comprehensive surveys of multiple jobholders were not conducted in 1981–1984, 1986–88, and 1990. See "Notes and Definitions" for information on historical comparability.

1. Multiple jobholders as a percent of all employed persons in specified group.
2. Data for years prior to 1977 refer to the Black-and-Other population group.

Table 1-18. Multiple Jobholders by Sex, Age, Marital Status, Race, Hispanic Origin, and Job Status, 1998–2001

(Thousands of persons, percent.)

Characteristic	Both sexes				Men				Women			
	Number		Rate [1]		Number		Rate [1]		Number		Rate [1]	
	1998	1999	1998	1999	1998	1999	1998	1999	1998	1999	1998	1999
AGE												
Total, 16 years and over [2]	7926	7802	6.0	5.8	4178	4104	5.9	5.7	3748	3698	6.2	6.0
16 to 19 years	335	343	4.8	4.8	138	153	3.9	4.1	198	190	5.7	5.5
20 to 24 years	788	751	6.3	5.8	363	341	5.5	5.1	425	410	7.2	6.7
25 to 34 years	1939	1843	6.2	6.0	1082	1013	6.3	6.1	857	830	6.0	5.9
35 to 44 years	2285	2268	6.3	6.2	1238	1238	6.3	6.3	1048	1029	6.3	6.1
45 to 54 years	1787	1775	6.5	6.2	908	895	6.2	6.0	878	880	6.7	6.5
55 to 64 years	682	701	5.3	5.3	378	387	5.4	5.3	303	314	5.2	5.2
65 years and over	109	122	2.9	3.1	71	77	3.3	3.4	39	45	2.5	2.7
MARITAL STATUS												
Single	2127	2137	6.1	5.9	1016	1048	5.3	5.3	1110	1089	7.0	6.7
Married, spouse present	4414	4309	5.8	5.6	2664	2566	6.2	5.9	1750	1744	5.3	5.2
Widowed, divorced or separated	1385	1356	6.7	6.5	498	490	5.8	5.8	887	866	7.3	7.0
RACE AND HISPANIC ORIGIN												
White	6832	6674	6.2	5.9	3622	3514	6.0	5.7	3210	3159	6.4	6.2
Black	802	831	5.5	5.5	406	442	5.9	6.3	396	389	5.2	4.8
Hispanic origin	503	490	3.8	3.6	299	280	3.7	3.5	204	210	3.9	3.7
FULL– OR PART–TIME STATUS												
Primary job full-time, secondary job part-time	4478	4293	...	...	2608	2497	...	...	1870	1796	...	...
Primary and secondary jobs both part-time	1635	1657	...	...	512	519	...	...	1124	1138	...	...
Primary and secondary jobs both full-time	266	298	...	...	188	204	...	...	78	94	...	...
Hours vary on primary or secondary job	1504	1513	...	...	848	861	...	...	656	652	...	...

Characteristic	Both sexes				Men				Women			
	Number		Rate [1]		Number		Rate [1]		Number		Rate [1]	
	2000	2001	2000	2001	2000	2001	2000	2001	2000	2001	2000	2001
AGE												
Total, 16 years and over [2]	7556	7319	5.6	5.4	3968	3808	5.5	5.3	3588	3511	5.7	5.6
16 to 19 years	346	318	4.8	4.6	145	130	3.9	3.7	201	188	5.6	5.5
20 to 24 years	752	756	5.6	5.7	337	345	4.8	5.0	415	411	6.6	6.4
25 to 34 years	1715	1598	5.6	5.4	929	858	5.6	5.3	786	741	5.6	5.4
35 to 44 years	2130	2064	5.8	5.7	1170	1116	5.9	5.7	960	947	5.7	5.7
45 to 54 years	1770	1750	6.0	5.7	912	894	5.9	5.6	858	856	6.1	5.9
55 to 64 years	695	686	5.1	4.9	379	372	5.1	4.9	317	314	5.1	4.8
65 years and over	148	146	3.6	3.5	95	92	4.1	3.8	52	54	3.1	3.0
MARITAL STATUS												
Single	2101	1994	5.7	5.4	1000	956	5.0	4.8	1102	1038	6.6	6.3
Married, spouse present	4156	4028	5.4	5.2	2499	2380	5.8	5.5	1656	1648	4.9	4.9
Widowed, divorced or separated	1299	1297	6.1	6.0	469	472	5.3	5.4	830	824	6.6	6.4
RACE AND HISPANIC ORIGIN												
White	6462	6281	5.7	5.5	3433	3275	5.6	5.3	3029	3006	5.8	5.8
Black	818	759	5.3	5.0	396	390	5.5	5.5	422	369	5.2	4.5
Hispanic origin	490	504	3.4	3.4	298	290	3.5	3.4	192	214	3.2	3.5
FULL– OR PART–TIME STATUS												
Primary job full-time, secondary job part-time	4173	3992	...	...	2409	2311	...	...	1764	1681	...	...
Primary and secondary jobs both part-time	1595	1581	...	...	518	507	...	...	1077	1073	...	...
Primary and secondary jobs both full-time	317	280	...	...	210	181	...	...	106	100	...	...
Hours vary on primary or secondary job	1429	1425	...	...	811	787	...	...	618	639	...	...

Note: Detail for the above race and Hispanic-origin groups will not sum to totals because data for the Other races group are not presented and Hispanics are included in both the White and Black population groups. See "Notes and Definitions" for information on historical comparability.

1. Multiple jobholders as a percent of all employed persons in specified group.
2. Includes a small number of persons who work part time on their primary job and full time on their secondary job(s), not shown separately.

Table 1-19. Multiple Jobholders by Industry of Principal Secondary Job, and Sex, 2000–2001, Annual Averages

(Thousands of persons.)

Industry of secondary job	Total	Men	Women
2000			
Nonagricultural wage and salary workers	5 284	2 538	2 746
Mining	7	5	2
Construction	134	98	36
Manufacturing	226	154	72
Durable goods	95	66	29
Nondurable goods	131	88	43
Transportation, communications, and other public utilities	245	170	75
Transportation	189	131	58
Communications and other public utilities	56	39	17
Wholesale and retail trade	1 576	689	886
Wholesale trade	106	72	34
Retail trade	1 470	618	853
Finance, insurance, and real estate	240	127	113
Services	2 630	1 138	1 491
Private household	92	9	84
Miscellaneous services	2 538	1 130	1 408
Business, auto, and repair services	392	244	148
Personal services, except private households	170	70	99
Entertainment and recreation services	344	186	158
Professional and related services	1 631	628	1 002
Hospitals	184	66	118
Health services, except hospitals	344	75	268
Educational services	595	270	325
Social services	167	53	114
Other professional services	341	164	177
Forestry and fisheries	2	2	0
Public administration	226	156	70
2001			
Nonagricultural wage and salary workers	5 144	2 471	2 673
Mining	6	6	0
Construction	134	100	34
Manufacturing	205	131	73
Durable goods	80	54	26
Nondurable goods	125	77	48
Transportation and other public utilities	250	183	67
Transportation	200	147	53
Communications and other public utilities	50	36	15
Wholesale and retail trade	1 528	695	832
Wholesale trade	89	60	30
Retail trade	1 438	636	803
Finance, insurance, and real estate	213	108	106
Services	2 601	1 100	1 501
Private household	76	11	64
Miscellaneous services	2 526	1 089	1 437
Business, auto, and repair services	365	217	147
Personal services, except private households	184	67	117
Entertainment and recreation services	359	174	185
Professional and related services	1 610	626	984
Hospitals	202	71	131
Health services, except hospitals	315	67	248
Educational services	586	268	318
Social services	172	49	123
Other professional services	336	172	164
Forestry and fisheries	8	5	3
Public administration	206	147	59

Table 1-20. Employment and Unemployment in Families by Race and Hispanic Origin, 1995–2001, Annual Averages

(Thousands of persons, percent.)

Characteristic	1995	1996	1997	1998	1999	2000	2001
TOTAL							
Total Families	68 552	69 203	69 714	70 218	71 250	71 680	71 980
With employed member(s)	55 633	56 342	57 289	57 986	59 185	59 626	59 699
As percent of total families	81.2	81.4	82.2	82.6	83.1	83.2	82.9
Some usually work full time [1]	51 473	52 249	53 226	53 945	55 123	55 683	55 599
With no employed member	12 919	12 860	12 425	12 232	12 065	12 054	12 281
As percent of total families	18.8	18.6	17.8	17.4	16.9	16.8	17.1
With unemployed member(s)	5 404	5 270	4 913	4 503	4 260	4 110	4 775
As percent of total families	7.9	7.6	7.0	6.4	6.0	5.7	6.6
Some member(s) employed	3 795	3 678	3 445	3 177	3 091	2 973	3 441
As percent of families with unemployed member(s)	70.2	69.8	70.1	70.6	72.6	72.3	72.1
Some usually work full time [1]	3 334	3 265	3 070	2 830	2 771	2 675	3 076
As percent of families with unemployed member(s)	61.7	62.0	62.5	62.8	65.0	65.1	64.4
WHITE							
Total Families	57 650	58 315	58 514	58 930	59 661	59 918	59 943
With employed member(s)	47 216	47 882	48 378	48 850	49 632	49 877	49 804
As percent of total families	81.9	82.1	82.7	82.9	83.2	83.2	83.1
Some usually work full time [1]	43 804	44 522	45 069	45 567	46 333	46 639	46 429
With no employed member	10 433	10 434	10 135	10 080	10 029	10 042	10 140
As percent of total families	18.1	17.9	17.3	17.1	16.8	16.8	16.9
With unemployed member(s)	4 002	3 896	3 566	3 299	3 134	3 010	3 506
As percent of total families	6.9	6.7	6.1	5.6	5.3	5.0	5.8
Some member(s) employed	2 934	2 875	2 632	2 463	2 374	2 276	2 629
As percent of families with unemployed member(s)	73.3	73.8	73.8	74.7	75.8	75.6	75.0
Some usually work full time [1]	2 579	2 557	2 353	2 204	2 132	2 052	2 351
As percent of families with unemployed member(s)	64.4	65.6	66.0	66.8	68.0	68.2	67.1
BLACK							
Total Families	8 015	8 149	8 308	8 317	8 498	8 600	8 737
With employed member(s)	5 991	6 137	6 409	6 554	6 847	6 964	6 988
As percent of total families	74.7	75.3	77.1	78.8	80.6	81.0	80.0
Some usually work full time [1]	5 419	5 563	5 810	5 953	6 249	6 401	6 425
With no employed member	2 024	2 012	1 899	1 763	1 652	1 636	1 749
As percent of total families	25.3	24.7	22.9	21.2	19.4	19.0	20.0
With unemployed member(s)	1 080	1 121	1 104	984	905	881	1 000
As percent of total families	13.5	13.8	13.3	11.8	10.6	10.2	11.4
Some member(s) employed	631	627	631	555	551	535	601
As percent of families with unemployed member(s)	58.4	55.9	57.2	56.4	60.9	60.8	60.1
Some usually work full time [1]	556	553	553	485	486	476	538
As percent of families with unemployed member(s)	51.5	49.3	50.1	49.3	53.7	54.1	53.8
HISPANIC							
Total Families	6 233	6 465	6 779	7 025	7 403	7 581	7 766
With employed member(s)	5 086	5 312	5 701	5 947	6 405	6 633	6 746
As percent of total families	81.6	82.2	84.1	84.7	86.5	87.5	86.9
Some usually work full time [1]	4 673	4 917	5 285	5 545	6 017	6 255	6 355
With no employed member	1 147	1 153	1 078	1 078	998	947	1 020
As percent of total families	18.4	17.8	15.9	15.3	13.5	12.5	13.1
With unemployed member(s)	841	841	789	744	715	679	771
As percent of total families	13.5	13.0	11.6	10.6	9.7	9.0	9.9
Some member(s) employed	568	563	532	522	518	493	567
As percent of families with unemployed member(s)	67.5	66.9	67.4	70.2	72.5	72.7	73.5
Some usually work full time [1]	490	497	473	467	467	446	514
As percent of families with unemployed member(s)	58.3	59.1	59.9	62.8	65.3	65.8	66.7

Note: Detail for the above race and Hispanic-origin groups will not sum to totals because data for the Other races group are not presented and Hispanics are included in both the White and Black population groups. See "Notes and Definitions" for information on historical comparability.

1. Usually work 35 hours or more a week at all jobs.

Table 1-21. Families by Presence and Relationship of Employed Members and Family Type, 1996–2001, Annual Averages

(Thousands of persons, percent.)

Characteristic	Number						Percent distribution					
	1996	1997	1998	1999	2000	2001	1996	1997	1998	1999	2000	2001
MARRIED-COUPLE FAMILIES												
Total	53 214	53 248	53 689	54 468	54 704	54 665	100.0	100.0	100.0	100.0	100.0	100.0
Member(s) employed, total	44 448	44 641	45 061	45 800	45 967	45 868	83.5	83.8	83.9	84.1	84.0	83.9
Husband only	10 103	9 959	10 285	10 533	10 500	10 598	19.0	18.7	19.2	19.3	19.2	19.4
Wife only	2 846	2 839	2 843	2 980	2 946	3 183	5.3	5.3	5.3	5.5	5.4	5.8
Husband and wife	28 077	28 422	28 531	28 882	29 128	28 801	52.8	53.4	53.1	53.0	53.2	52.7
Other employment combinations	3 422	3 421	3 402	3 404	3 394	3 287	6.4	6.4	6.3	6.2	6.2	6.0
No member(s) employed	8 766	8 607	8 628	8 668	8 737	8 796	16.5	16.2	16.1	15.9	16.0	16.1
FAMILIES MAINTAINED BY WOMEN [1]												
Total	12 264	12 524	12 447	12 625	12 775	12 880	100.0	100.0	100.0	100.0	100.0	100.0
Member(s) employed, total	8 788	9 263	9 417	9 797	10 026	10 014	71.7	74.0	75.7	77.6	78.5	77.7
Householder only	4 964	5 282	5 322	5 566	5 581	5 623	40.5	42.2	42.8	44.1	43.7	43.7
Householder and other member(s)	2 385	2 484	2 582	2 663	2 806	2 741	19.4	19.8	20.7	21.1	22.0	21.3
Other member(s), not householder	1 438	1 497	1 513	1 568	1 639	1 650	11.7	12.0	12.2	12.4	12.8	12.8
No member(s) employed	3 477	3 261	3 029	2 827	2 749	2 865	28.4	26.0	24.3	22.4	21.5	22.2
FAMILIES MAINTAINED BY MEN [1]												
Total	3 724	3 942	4 083	4 158	4 200	4 435	100.0	100.0	100.0	100.0	100.0	100.0
Member(s) employed, total	3 106	3 385	3 509	3 588	3 632	3 816	83.4	85.9	85.9	86.3	86.5	86.0
Householder only	1 614	1 703	1 746	1 718	1 761	1 854	43.3	43.2	42.8	41.3	41.9	41.8
Householder and other member(s)	1 076	1 228	1 283	1 353	1 358	1 400	28.9	31.2	31.4	32.5	32.3	31.6
Other member(s), not householder	416	455	480	517	514	563	11.2	11.5	11.8	12.4	12.2	12.7
No member(s) employed	618	557	574	569	567	619	16.6	14.1	14.1	13.7	13.5	14.0

Note: See "Notes and Definitions" for information on historical comparability.

1. No spouse present.

Table 1-22. Unemployment in Families by Presence and Relationship of Employed Members and Family Type, 1996–2001, Annual Averages

(Thousands of persons, percent.)

Characteristic	Number						Percent distribution					
	1996	1997	1998	1999	2000	2001	1996	1997	1998	1999	2000	2001
MARRIED-COUPLE FAMILIES												
With Unemployed Member(s),Total	3 378	3 056	2 815	2 705	2 584	3 028	100.0	100.0	100.0	100.0	100.0	100.0
No member employed	601	530	471	440	411	520	17.8	17.3	16.7	16.3	15.9	17.2
Some member(s) employed	2 777	2 526	2 343	2 265	2 174	2 507	82.2	82.7	83.2	83.7	84.1	82.8
Husband unemployed	1 207	1 048	948	924	836	1 137	35.7	34.3	33.7	34.2	32.3	37.5
Wife employed	746	651	594	589	531	722	22.1	21.3	21.1	21.8	20.5	23.8
Wife unemployed	1 016	906	844	790	789	899	30.1	29.6	30.0	29.2	30.5	29.7
Husband employed	891	787	745	696	694	792	26.4	25.8	26.5	25.8	26.8	26.2
Other family member unemployed	1 155	1 102	1 023	991	959	992	34.2	36.1	36.3	36.6	37.1	32.8
FAMILIES MAINTAINED BY WOMEN [1]												
With Unemployed Member(s), Total	1 485	1 456	1 301	1 222	1 194	1 315	100.0	100.0	100.0	100.0	100.0	100.0
No member employed	809	782	696	613	587	638	54.5	53.7	53.5	50.2	49.1	48.5
Some member(s) employed	676	674	605	609	607	676	45.5	46.3	46.5	49.8	50.9	51.4
Householder unemployed	670	694	612	560	522	590	45.1	47.7	47.0	45.8	43.7	44.9
Other member(s) employed	102	122	99	110	102	127	6.9	8.4	7.6	9.0	8.5	9.7
Other member(s) unemployed	569	572	689	662	672	725	38.3	39.3	53.0	54.2	56.3	55.1
FAMILIES MAINTAINED BY MEN [1]												
With Unemployed Member(s), Total	407	400	388	333	331	433	100.0	100.0	100.0	100.0	100.0	100.0
No member employed	182	156	158	115	139	175	44.7	39.0	40.7	34.6	42.0	40.4
Some member(s) employed	224	244	229	218	192	258	55.0	61.0	59.0	65.4	58.0	59.6
Householder unemployed	200	197	186	154	173	229	49.1	49.2	47.9	46.4	52.2	52.9
Other member(s) employed	67	77	69	71	67	93	16.5	19.2	17.8	21.4	20.4	21.5
Other member(s) unemployed	206	204	202	178	158	204	50.6	51.0	52.1	53.6	47.8	47.1

Note: Detail may not sum to totals due to rounding. See "Notes and Definitions" for information on historical comparability.

1. No spouse present.

Table 1-23. Employment Status of the Population by Sex, Marital Status, and Presence and Age of Own Children Under 18, 1996–2001, Annual Averages

(Thousands of persons, percent.)

Characteristic	1996			1997			1998		
	Total	Men	Women	Total	Men	Women	Total	Men	Women
WITH OWN CHILDREN UNDER 18 YEARS, TOTAL									
Civilian noninstitutional population	62 733	27 319	35 415	62 787	27 349	35 438	62 912	27 489	35 423
Civilian labor force	50 866	25 803	25 063	51 343	25 877	25 466	51 462	26 018	25 443
Participation rate	81.1	94.5	70.8	81.8	94.6	71.9	81.8	94.6	71.8
Employed	48 521	24 933	23 588	49 178	25 111	24 067	49 480	25 333	24 147
Employment-population ratio	77.3	91.3	66.6	78.3	91.8	67.9	78.6	92.2	68.2
Full-time workers [1]	41 164	24 085	17 080	41 934	24 306	17 628	42 372	24 562	17 811
Part-time workers [2]	7 356	848	6 508	7 244	806	6 439	7 108	771	6 337
Unemployed	2 345	870	1 475	2 165	766	1 399	1 981	686	1 296
Unemployment rate	4.6	3.4	5.9	4.2	3.0	5.5	3.8	2.6	5.1
MARRIED, SPOUSE PRESENT									
Civilian noninstitutional population	51 128	25 349	25 779	50 995	25 292	25 704	51 061	25 325	25 737
Civilian labor force	42 185	24 043	18 141	42 192	24 027	18 165	42 088	24 080	18 009
Participation rate	82.5	94.8	70.4	82.7	95.0	70.7	82.4	95.1	70.0
Employed	40 743	23 305	17 438	40 918	23 383	17 535	40 914	23 506	17 408
Employment-population ratio	79.7	91.9	67.6	80.2	92.5	68.2	80.1	92.8	67.6
Full-time workers [1]	34 732	22 559	12 173	35 042	22 685	12 357	35 197	22 839	12 357
Part-time workers [2]	6 011	747	5 265	5 877	698	5 179	5 718	667	5 051
Unemployed	1 441	738	703	1 273	644	630	1 174	573	601
Unemployment rate	3.4	3.1	3.9	3.0	2.7	3.5	2.8	2.4	3.3
OTHER MARITAL STATUS [3]									
Civilian noninstitutional population	11 606	1 970	9 636	11 791	2 057	9 734	11 851	2 166	9 686
Civilian labor force	8 680	1 759	6 921	9 151	1 850	7 301	9 374	1 939	7 434
Participation rate	74.8	89.3	71.8	77.6	89.9	75.0	79.1	89.5	76.7
Employed	7 777	1 628	6 149	8 259	1 728	6 531	8 565	1 826	6 739
Employment-population ratio	67.0	82.6	63.8	70.0	84.0	67.1	72.3	84.3	69.6
Full-time workers [1]	6 432	1 526	4 907	6 893	1 621	5 272	7 177	1 724	5 453
Part-time workers [2]	1 344	101	1 244	1 367	107	1 261	1 391	104	1 286
Unemployed	903	132	772	891	123	770	807	113	695
Unemployment rate	10.4	7.5	11.2	9.7	6.6	10.5	8.6	5.8	9.3
WITH OWN CHILDREN 6 TO 17 YEARS, NONE YOUNGER									
Civilian noninstitutional population	33 411	14 601	18 809	33 997	14 822	19 175	34 329	14 947	19 383
Civilian labor force	28 221	13 645	14 576	28 812	13 877	14 935	29 003	13 969	15 033
Participation rate	84.5	93.5	77.5	84.7	93.6	77.9	84.5	93.5	77.6
Employed	27 123	13 229	13 894	27 752	13 480	14 273	28 046	13 629	14 417
Employment-population ratio	81.2	90.6	73.9	81.6	90.9	74.4	81.7	91.2	74.4
Full-time workers [1]	23 267	12 810	10 456	23 885	13 071	10 814	24 286	13 238	11 048
Part-time workers [2]	3 857	418	3 438	3 868	409	3 459	3 760	391	3 369
Unemployed	1 097	416	681	1 060	397	662	957	340	617
Unemployment rate	3.9	3.0	4.7	3.7	2.9	4.4	3.3	2.4	4.1
WITH OWN CHILDREN UNDER 6 YEARS									
Civilian noninstitutional population	29 323	12 718	16 605	28 789	12 526	16 263	28 583	12 543	16 040
Civilian labor force	22 645	12 158	10 487	22 530	12 000	10 531	22 459	12 049	10 410
Participation rate	77.2	95.6	63.2	78.3	95.8	64.8	78.6	96.1	64.9
Employed	21 398	11 704	9 694	21 426	11 632	9 794	21 434	11 703	9 731
Employment-population ratio	73.0	92.0	58.4	74.4	92.9	60.2	75.0	93.3	60.7
Full-time workers [1]	17 898	11 274	6 623	18 049	11 235	6 814	18 086	11 323	6 763
Part-time workers [2]	3 500	430	3 070	3 376	397	2 980	3 348	380	2 968
Unemployed	1 247	454	794	1 105	368	737	1 025	346	679
Unemployment rate	5.5	3.7	7.6	4.9	3.1	7.0	4.6	2.9	6.5
WITH NO OWN CHILDREN UNDER 18 YEARS									
Civilian noninstitutional population	135 902	66 931	68 970	138 365	68 385	69 980	140 436	69 396	71 040
Civilian labor force	81 618	44 736	36 882	83 524	45 847	37 677	84 735	46 464	38 271
Participation rate	60.1	66.8	53.5	60.4	67.0	53.8	60.3	67.0	53.9
Employed	76 717	41 748	34 969	78 917	43 045	35 873	80 545	43 922	36 623
Employment-population ratio	56.5	62.4	50.7	57.0	62.9	51.3	57.4	63.3	51.6
Full-time workers [1]	60 920	35 200	25 719	62 902	36 452	26 449	64 429	37 226	27 203
Part-time workers [2]	15 797	6 548	9 250	16 016	6 592	9 424	16 116	6 696	9 420
Unemployed	4 901	2 988	1 913	4 606	2 802	1 804	4 190	2 542	1 648
Unemployment rate	6.0	6.7	5.2	5.5	6.1	4.8	4.9	5.5	4.3

See footnotes and *Note* at end of table.

Table 1-23. Employment Status of the Population by Sex, Marital Status, and Presence and Age of Own Children Under 18, 1996–2001, Annual Averages—*Continued*

(Thousands of persons, percent.)

Characteristic	1999			2000			2001		
	Total	Men	Women	Total	Men	Women	Total	Men	Women
WITH OWN CHILDREN UNDER 18 YEARS, TOTAL									
Civilian noninstitutional population	63 158	27 573	35 585	63 267	27 673	35 595	63 185	27 641	35 543
Civilian labor force	51 778	26 092	25 686	51 944	26 202	25 742	51 775	26 142	25 633
Participation rate	82.0	94.6	72.2	82.1	94.7	72.3	81.9	94.6	72.1
Employed	50 010	25 472	24 538	50 259	25 622	24 637	49 773	25 358	24 415
Employment-population ratio	79.2	92.4	69.0	79.4	92.6	69.2	78.8	91.7	68.7
Full-time workers [1]	43 033	24 712	18 321	43 365	24 922	18 443	42 815	24 586	18 229
Part-time workers [2]	6 977	761	6 216	6 894	699	6 195	6 958	773	6 186
Unemployed	1 768	620	1 149	1 685	581	1 104	2 002	784	1 218
Unemployment rate	3.4	2.4	4.5	3.2	2.2	4.3	3.9	3.0	4.8
MARRIED, SPOUSE PRESENT									
Civilian noninstitutional population	51 302	25 462	25 840	51 415	25 540	25 874	51 175	25 390	25 785
Civilian labor force	42 260	24 222	18 038	42 361	24 290	18 072	42 083	24 129	17 954
Participation rate	82.4	95.1	69.8	82.4	95.1	69.8	82.2	95.0	69.6
Employed	41 193	23 688	17 505	41 357	23 816	17 541	40 828	23 481	17 347
Employment-population ratio	80.3	93.0	67.7	80.4	93.2	67.8	79.8	92.5	67.3
Full-time workers [1]	35 568	23 024	12 544	35 793	23 212	12 581	35 232	22 813	12 419
Part-time workers [2]	5 625	664	4 961	5 564	604	4 960	5 597	668	4 928
Unemployed	1 067	534	533	1 004	474	531	1 255	648	607
Unemployment rate	2.5	2.2	3.0	2.4	2.0	2.9	3.0	2.7	3.4
OTHER MARITAL STATUS [3]									
Civilian noninstitutional population	11 856	2 110	9 746	11 853	2 132	9 720	12 010	2 252	9 758
Civilian labor force	9 518	1 870	7 648	9 583	1 913	7 670	9 693	2 013	7 679
Participation rate	80.3	88.6	78.5	80.8	89.7	78.9	80.7	89.4	78.7
Employed	8 817	1 784	7 032	8 902	1 806	7 096	8 945	1 877	7 068
Employment-population ratio	74.4	84.6	72.2	75.1	84.7	73.0	74.5	83.3	72.4
Full-time workers [1]	7 465	1 687	5 777	7 572	1 710	5 862	7 584	1 773	5 811
Part-time workers [2]	1 352	97	1 255	1 330	96	1 234	1 361	105	1 257
Unemployed	702	86	616	681	107	574	747	136	611
Unemployment rate	7.4	4.6	8.1	7.1	5.6	7.5	7.7	6.8	8.0
WITH OWN CHILDREN 6 TO 17 YEARS, NONE YOUNGER									
Civilian noninstitutional population	34 662	15 090	19 572	34 737	15 165	19 572	35 191	15 341	19 850
Civilian labor force	29 403	14 092	15 311	29 576	14 178	15 398	29 908	14 358	15 550
Participation rate	84.8	93.4	78.2	85.1	93.5	78.7	85.0	93.6	78.3
Employed	28 528	13 782	14 747	28 744	13 877	14 868	28 912	13 970	14 942
Employment-population ratio	82.3	91.3	75.3	82.7	91.5	76.0	82.2	91.1	75.3
Full-time workers [1]	24 807	13 385	11 422	25 042	13 513	11 529	25 148	13 568	11 580
Part-time workers [2]	3 722	397	3 325	3 703	364	3 339	3 764	402	3 362
Unemployed	875	310	564	832	302	530	995	387	608
Unemployment rate	3.0	2.2	3.7	2.8	2.1	3.4	3.3	2.7	3.9
WITH OWN CHILDREN UNDER 6 YEARS									
Civilian noninstitutional population	28 496	12 482	16 014	28 530	12 508	16 022	27 993	12 301	15 693
Civilian labor force	22 375	12 000	10 375	22 368	12 024	10 344	21 867	11 784	10 083
Participation rate	78.5	96.1	64.8	78.4	96.1	64.6	78.1	95.8	64.3
Employed	21 482	11 691	9 791	21 515	11 745	9 770	20 861	11 388	9 473
Employment-population ratio	75.4	93.7	61.1	75.4	93.9	61.0	74.5	92.6	60.4
Full-time workers [1]	18 227	11 327	6 900	18 323	11 410	6 914	17 667	11 017	6 649
Part-time workers [2]	3 255	364	2 891	3 191	335	2 856	3 194	370	2 824
Unemployed	894	310	584	853	279	574	1 006	396	610
Unemployment rate	4.0	2.6	5.6	3.8	2.3	5.6	4.6	3.4	6.0
WITH NO OWN CHILDREN UNDER 18 YEARS									
Civilian noninstitutional population	143 160	70 714	72 446	145 199	71 825	73 374	147 196	72 733	74 464
Civilian labor force	86 424	47 255	39 169	88 014	48 140	39 874	88 948	48 510	40 438
Participation rate	60.4	66.8	54.1	60.6	67.0	54.3	60.4	66.7	54.3
Employed	82 333	44 828	37 504	84 058	45 781	38 278	84 227	45 650	38 577
Employment-population ratio	57.5	63.4	51.8	57.9	63.7	52.2	57.2	62.8	51.8
Full-time workers [1]	66 136	38 086	28 051	68 046	39 136	28 910	67 977	38 898	29 079
Part-time workers [2]	16 196	6 743	9 454	16 012	6 645	9 367	16 250	6 752	9 498
Unemployed	4 091	2 426	1 665	3 956	2 359	1 596	4 721	2 860	1 861
Unemployment rate	4.7	5.1	4.3	4.5	4.9	4.0	5.3	5.9	4.6

Note: Own children include sons, daughters, step-children, and adopted children. Not included are nieces, nephews, grandchildren, and other related and unrelated children. Detail may not sum to totals due to rounding. See "Notes and Definitions" for information on historical comparability.

1. Usually work 35 hours or more a week at all jobs.
2. Usually work less than 35 hours a week at all jobs.
3. Includes never-married, divorced, separated, and widowed persons.

Table 1-24. Employment Status of Mothers with Own Children Under 3 Years Old by Age of Youngest Child, and Marital Status, 1997–2001, Annual Averages

(Thousands of persons, percent.)

Year and characteristic	Civilian noninsti- tutional population	Civilian labor force		Employed				Unemployed	
		Total	Percent of population	Total	Percent of population	Full-time workers [1]	Part-time workers [2]	Number	Percent of labor force
1997									
Total Mothers With Own Children Under 3 Years	9 347	5 738	61.4	5 306	56.8	3 560	1 746	432	7.5
2 years	2 871	1 890	65.8	1 763	61.4	1 208	555	127	6.7
1 year	3 306	2 012	60.9	1 851	56.0	1 205	646	161	8.0
Under 1 year	3 170	1 836	57.9	1 692	53.4	1 147	545	144	7.8
Married, Spouse Present With Own Children Under 3 years	7 049	4 296	60.9	4 105	58.2	2 718	1 387	191	4.4
2 years	2 142	1 380	64.4	1 327	62.0	883	444	53	3.8
1 year	2 459	1 468	59.7	1 399	56.9	890	509	69	4.7
Under 1 year	2 448	1 448	59.2	1 379	56.3	945	434	69	4.8
Other Marital Status With Own Children Under 3 Years [3]	2 297	1 445	62.9	1 201	52.3	842	361	241	16.7
2 years	729	511	70.1	436	59.8	325	112	74	14.5
1 year	847	545	64.3	452	53.4	315	138	92	16.9
Under 1 year	721	389	54.0	313	43.4	202	111	75	19.3
1998									
Total Mothers With Own Children Under 3 Years	9 333	5 779	61.9	5 384	57.7	3 626	1 758	395	6.8
2 years	2 772	1 786	64.4	1 673	60.4	1 149	524	113	6.3
1 year	3 213	2 055	64.0	1 917	59.7	1 281	636	138	6.7
Under 1 year	3 348	1 938	57.9	1 794	53.6	1 196	598	144	7.4
Married, Spouse Present With Own Children Under 3 years	7 110	4 316	60.7	4 145	58.3	2 765	1 380	171	4.0
2 years	2 073	1 291	62.3	1 244	60.0	831	413	47	3.6
1 year	2 493	1 560	62.6	1 497	60.0	989	508	63	4.0
Under 1 year	2 544	1 465	57.6	1 404	55.2	945	459	61	4.2
Other Marital Status With Own Children Under 3 Years [3]	2 225	1 463	65.8	1 238	55.6	860	379	223	15.2
2 years	700	495	70.7	429	61.3	318	111	65	13.1
1 year	721	495	68.7	420	58.3	292	129	75	15.2
Under 1 year	804	473	58.8	389	48.4	250	139	83	17.5
1999									
Total Mothers With Own Children Under 3 Years	9 339	5 742	61.5	5 389	57.7	3 692	1 697	353	6.1
2 years	2 890	1 888	65.3	1 788	61.9	1 257	530	101	5.3
1 year	3 283	2 062	62.8	1 934	58.9	1 298	635	128	6.2
Under 1 year	3 166	1 792	56.6	1 668	52.7	1 137	531	124	6.9
Married, Spouse Present With Own Children Under 3 years	7 089	4 224	59.6	4 078	57.5	2 744	1 334	147	3.5
2 years	2 175	1 356	62.4	1 316	60.5	898	419	40	2.9
1 year	2 522	1 532	60.8	1 477	58.6	964	513	56	3.6
Under 1 year	2 392	1 336	55.8	1 285	53.7	882	403	51	3.8
Other Marital Status With Own Children Under 3 Years [3]	2 251	1 517	67.4	1 311	58.3	949	362	206	13.6
2 years	715	532	74.4	472	65.9	360	112	61	11.4
1 year	761	529	69.5	457	60.0	334	123	72	13.7
Under 1 year	774	456	58.8	383	49.5	255	128	73	16.0
2000									
Total Mothers With Own Children Under 3 Years	9 356	5 653	60.4	5 311	56.8	3 614	1 697	342	6.0
2 years	2 803	1 807	64.5	1 712	61.1	1 193	519	95	5.3
1 year	3 300	2 069	62.7	1 939	58.8	1 310	629	130	6.3
Under 1 year	3 253	1 777	54.6	1 660	51.0	1 112	548	117	6.6
Married, Spouse Present With Own Children Under 3 years	7 056	4 090	58.0	3 940	55.8	2 613	1 327	150	3.7
2 years	2 096	1 276	60.9	1 233	58.9	823	411	42	3.3
1 year	2 499	1 503	60.1	1 448	57.9	953	495	55	3.6
Under 1 year	2 461	1 312	53.3	1 259	51.1	837	421	53	4.1
Other Marital Status With Own Children Under 3 Years [3]	2 300	1 563	67.9	1 371	59.6	1 002	370	191	12.2
2 years	707	531	75.1	478	67.6	370	108	53	9.9
1 year	801	566	70.7	491	61.3	357	134	75	13.2
Under 1 year	792	465	58.8	402	50.7	275	127	64	13.7
2001									
Total Mothers With Own Children Under 3 Years	9 177	5 526	60.2	5 142	56.0	3 527	1 616	383	6.9
2 years	2 787	1 834	65.8	1 719	61.7	1 194	525	115	6.3
1 year	3 344	2 020	60.4	1 881	56.2	1 285	597	139	6.9
Under 1 year	3 046	1 672	54.9	1 542	50.6	1 048	494	129	7.7
Married, Spouse Present With Own Children Under 3 years	6 921	3 979	57.5	3 808	5.5	2 546	1 263	171	4.3
2 years	2 069	1 280	61.9	1 229	59.4	818	411	51	4.0
1 year	2 533	1 450	57.2	1 389	54.8	920	469	62	4.3
Under 1 year	2 319	1 249	53.9	1 190	51.3	808	383	58	4.6
Other Marital Status With Own Children Under 3 Years [3]	2 256	1 546	68.5	1 335	59.2	982	354	213	13.8
2 years	718	553	77.0	490	68.2	378	114	65	11.8
1 year	812	570	70.2	493	60.7	365	129	77	13.5
Under 1 year	726	423	58.3	352	48.5	239	111	71	16.8

Note: Own children include sons, daughters, step-children, and adopted children. Not included are nieces, nephews, grandchildren, and other related and unrelated children. Detail may not sum to totals due to rounding. See "Notes and Definitions" for information on historical comparability.

1. Usually work 35 hours or more a week at all jobs.
2. Usually work less than 35 hours a week at all jobs.
3. Includes never-married, divorced, separated, and widowed persons.

Table 1-25. Major Unemployment Indicators, 1948–2001

(Unemployment as a percent of civilian labor force.)

Year	All civilian workers	Men 20 years and over	Women 20 years and over	Both sexes 16 to 19 years	Both sexes 25 years and over	White	Black	Hispanic	Full-time workers	Part-time workers	Women who maintain families	Married men, spouse present
1948	3.8	3.2	3.6	9.2	2.9	...	...	...	...	...	...	...
1949	5.9	5.4	5.3	13.4	4.8	...	...	...	...	...	...	...
1950	5.3	4.7	5.1	12.2	4.4	...	...	...	...	...	...	...
1951	3.3	2.5	4.0	8.2	2.8	...	...	...	...	...	...	...
1952	3.0	2.4	3.2	8.5	2.4	...	...	...	...	...	...	...
1953	2.9	2.5	2.9	7.6	2.4	...	...	...	...	...	...	...
1954	5.5	4.9	5.5	12.6	4.7	5.0	...	...	...	...	...	...
1955	4.4	3.8	4.4	11.0	3.6	3.9	...	...	...	...	...	2.6
1956	4.1	3.4	4.2	11.1	3.3	3.6	...	...	...	...	...	2.3
1957	4.3	3.6	4.1	11.6	3.4	3.8	...	...	...	...	...	2.8
1958	6.8	6.2	6.1	15.9	5.6	6.1	...	...	...	...	...	5.1
1959	5.5	4.7	5.2	14.6	4.4	4.8	...	...	...	...	...	3.6
1960	5.5	4.7	5.1	14.7	4.4	5.0	...	...	...	...	...	3.7
1961	6.7	5.7	6.3	16.8	5.4	6.0	...	...	...	...	...	4.6
1962	5.5	4.6	5.4	14.7	4.4	4.9	...	...	...	...	...	3.6
1963	5.7	4.5	5.4	17.2	4.3	5.0	...	...	5.5	7.3	...	3.4
1964	5.2	3.9	5.2	16.2	3.8	4.6	...	...	4.9	7.2	...	2.8
1965	4.5	3.2	4.5	14.8	3.2	4.1	...	...	4.2	6.7	...	2.4
1966	3.8	2.5	3.8	12.8	2.6	3.4	...	...	3.5	6.2	...	1.9
1967	3.8	2.3	4.2	12.9	2.6	3.4	...	...	3.4	6.9	4.9	1.8
1968	3.6	2.2	3.8	12.7	2.3	3.2	...	...	3.2	6.0	4.4	1.6
1969	3.5	2.1	3.7	12.2	2.2	3.1	...	...	3.1	5.7	4.4	1.5
1970	4.9	3.5	4.8	15.3	3.3	4.5	...	...	4.6	6.9	5.4	2.6
1971	5.9	4.4	5.7	16.9	4.0	5.4	...	...	5.6	7.8	7.3	3.2
1972	5.6	4.0	5.4	16.2	3.6	5.1	10.4	...	5.2	7.7	7.2	2.8
1973	4.9	3.3	4.9	14.5	3.1	4.3	9.4	7.5	4.4	7.2	7.1	2.3
1974	5.6	3.8	5.5	16.0	3.6	5.0	10.5	8.1	5.2	7.7	7.0	2.7
1975	8.5	6.8	8.0	19.9	6.0	7.8	14.8	12.2	8.4	9.0	10.0	5.1
1976	7.7	5.9	7.4	19.0	5.5	7.0	14.0	11.5	7.5	8.8	10.1	4.2
1977	7.1	5.2	7.0	17.8	4.9	6.2	14.0	10.1	6.8	8.6	9.4	3.6
1978	6.1	4.3	6.0	16.4	4.1	5.2	12.8	9.1	5.7	7.9	8.5	2.8
1979	5.8	4.2	5.7	16.1	3.9	5.1	12.3	8.3	5.5	7.7	8.3	2.8
1980	7.1	5.9	6.4	17.8	5.1	6.3	14.3	10.1	7.1	7.6	9.2	4.2
1981	7.6	6.3	6.8	19.6	5.4	6.7	15.6	10.4	7.5	7.9	10.4	4.3
1982	9.7	8.8	8.3	23.2	7.4	8.6	18.9	13.8	10.0	8.5	11.7	6.5
1983	9.6	8.9	8.1	22.4	7.5	8.4	19.5	13.7	9.9	8.1	12.2	6.5
1984	7.5	6.6	6.8	18.9	5.8	6.5	15.9	10.7	7.5	7.4	10.3	4.6
1985	7.2	6.2	6.6	18.6	5.6	6.2	15.1	10.5	7.1	7.5	10.4	4.3
1986	7.0	6.1	6.2	18.3	5.4	6.0	14.5	10.6	6.9	7.4	9.8	4.4
1987	6.2	5.4	5.4	16.9	4.8	5.3	13.0	8.8	6.0	6.9	9.2	3.9
1988	5.5	4.8	4.9	15.3	4.3	4.7	11.7	8.2	5.3	6.4	8.1	3.3
1989	5.3	4.5	4.7	15.0	4.0	4.5	11.4	8.0	5.1	6.2	8.1	3.0
1990	5.6	5.0	4.9	15.5	4.4	4.8	11.4	8.2	5.4	6.4	8.3	3.4
1991	6.8	6.4	5.7	18.7	5.4	6.1	12.5	10.0	6.8	7.0	9.3	4.4
1992	7.5	7.1	6.3	20.1	6.1	6.6	14.2	11.6	7.5	7.5	10.0	5.1
1993	6.9	6.4	5.9	19.0	5.6	6.1	13.0	10.8	6.9	7.2	9.7	4.4
1994	6.1	5.4	5.4	17.6	4.8	5.3	11.5	9.9	6.1	6.0	8.9	3.7
1995	5.6	4.8	4.9	17.3	4.3	4.9	10.4	9.3	5.5	6.0	8.0	3.3
1996	5.4	4.6	4.8	16.7	4.2	4.7	10.5	8.9	5.3	5.8	8.2	3.0
1997	4.9	4.2	4.4	16.0	3.8	4.2	10.0	7.7	4.8	5.5	8.1	2.7
1998	4.5	3.7	4.1	14.6	3.4	3.9	8.9	7.2	4.3	5.3	7.2	2.4
1999	4.2	3.5	3.8	13.9	3.1	3.7	8.0	6.4	4.1	5.0	6.4	2.2
2000	4.0	3.3	3.6	13.1	3.0	3.5	7.6	5.7	3.9	4.8	5.9	2.0
2001	4.8	4.2	4.1	14.7	3.7	4.2	8.7	6.6	4.7	5.1	6.6	2.7

Note: Data for the Other races group are not presented and Hispanics are included in both the White and Black population groups. See "Notes and Definitions" for information on historical comparability.

Table 1-26. Unemployed Persons by Race, Hispanic Origin, Sex, and Age, 1948–2001

(Thousands of persons.)

Year, race, Hispanic origin, and sex	16 years and over	16 to 19 years			20 years and over						
		Total	16 to 17 years	18 to 19 years	Total	20 to 24 years	25 to 34 years	35 to 44 years	45 to 54 years	55 to 64 years	65 years and over
TOTAL											
1948	2 276	409	180	228	1 869	455	457	347	290	226	93
1949	3 637	576	238	337	3 060	680	776	603	471	384	146
1950	3 288	513	226	287	2 776	561	702	530	478	368	137
1951	2 055	336	168	168	1 718	273	435	354	318	238	103
1952	1 883	345	180	165	1 539	268	389	325	274	195	86
1953	1 834	307	150	157	1 529	256	379	325	280	218	70
1954	3 532	501	221	247	3 032	504	793	680	548	374	132
1955	2 852	450	211	239	2 403	396	577	521	436	355	120
1956	2 750	478	231	247	2 274	395	554	476	429	311	109
1957	2 859	497	230	266	2 362	430	573	499	448	300	111
1958	4 602	678	299	379	3 923	701	993	871	731	472	154
1959	3 740	654	301	354	3 085	543	726	673	603	405	135
1960	3 852	712	325	387	3 140	583	752	671	614	396	122
1961	4 714	828	363	465	3 886	723	890	850	751	516	159
1962	3 911	721	312	409	3 191	636	712	688	605	411	141
1963	4 070	884	420	462	3 187	658	732	674	589	410	126
1964	3 786	872	436	437	2 913	660	607	605	543	378	117
1965	3 366	874	411	463	2 491	557	529	546	436	322	103
1966	2 875	837	395	441	2 041	446	441	426	369	265	92
1967	2 975	839	400	438	2 140	511	480	422	383	256	86
1968	2 817	838	414	426	1 978	543	443	371	314	219	88
1969	2 832	853	436	416	1 978	560	453	358	320	216	72
1970	4 093	1 106	537	569	2 987	866	718	515	476	309	104
1971	5 016	1 262	596	665	3 755	1 130	933	630	573	381	109
1972	4 882	1 308	633	676	3 573	1 132	878	576	510	368	111
1973	4 365	1 235	634	600	3 130	1 008	866	451	430	290	88
1974	5 156	1 422	699	722	3 733	1 212	1 044	559	498	321	99
1975	7 929	1 767	799	968	6 161	1 865	1 776	951	893	520	155
1976	7 406	1 719	796	924	5 687	1 714	1 710	849	758	510	147
1977	6 991	1 663	781	881	5 330	1 629	1 650	785	666	450	147
1978	6 202	1 583	796	787	4 620	1 483	1 422	694	552	345	123
1979	6 137	1 555	739	816	4 583	1 442	1 446	705	540	346	104
1980	7 637	1 669	778	890	5 969	1 835	2 024	940	676	399	94
1981	8 273	1 763	781	981	6 510	1 976	2 211	1 065	715	444	98
1982	10 678	1 977	831	1 145	8 701	2 392	3 037	1 552	966	647	107
1983	10 717	1 829	753	1 076	8 888	2 330	3 078	1 650	1 039	677	114
1984	8 539	1 499	646	854	7 039	1 838	2 374	1 335	828	566	97
1985	8 312	1 468	662	806	6 844	1 738	2 341	1 340	813	518	93
1986	8 237	1 454	665	789	6 783	1 651	2 390	1 371	790	489	91
1987	7 425	1 347	648	700	6 077	1 453	2 129	1 281	723	412	78
1988	6 701	1 226	573	653	5 475	1 261	1 929	1 166	657	375	87
1989	6 528	1 194	537	657	5 333	1 218	1 851	1 159	637	379	91
1990	7 047	1 212	527	685	5 835	1 299	1 995	1 328	723	386	105
1991	8 628	1 359	587	772	7 269	1 573	2 447	1 719	946	473	113
1992	9 613	1 427	641	787	8 186	1 649	2 702	1 976	1 138	589	132
1993	8 940	1 365	606	759	7 575	1 514	2 395	1 896	1 121	541	108
1994	7 996	1 320	624	696	6 676	1 373	2 067	1 627	971	485	153
1995	7 404	1 346	652	695	6 058	1 244	1 841	1 549	844	425	153
1996	7 236	1 306	617	689	5 929	1 239	1 757	1 505	883	406	139
1997	6 739	1 271	589	683	5 467	1 152	1 571	1 418	830	369	127
1998	6 210	1 205	573	632	5 005	1 081	1 419	1 258	782	343	122
1999	5 880	1 162	544	618	4 718	1 042	1 278	1 154	753	367	124
2000	5 655	1 093	506	587	4 562	1 025	1 168	1 141	749	347	131
2001	6 742	1 187	532	655	5 555	1 203	1 447	1 359	972	446	129

See *Note* at end of table.

Table 1-26. Unemployed Persons by Race, Hispanic Origin, Sex, and Age, 1948–2001—*Continued*

(Thousands of persons.)

Year, race, Hispanic origin, and sex	16 years and over	16 to 19 years			20 years and over						
		Total	16 to 17 years	18 to 19 years	Total	20 to 24 years	25 to 34 years	35 to 44 years	45 to 54 years	55 to 64 years	65 years and over
WHITE											
1954	2 859	423	191	232	2 436	394	610	540	447	329	115
1955	2 252	373	181	191	1 879	304	412	402	358	300	105
1956	2 159	382	191	191	1 777	297	406	363	355	258	98
1957	2 289	401	195	204	1 888	331	425	401	373	262	98
1958	3 680	541	245	297	3 139	541	756	686	614	405	136
1959	2 946	525	255	270	2 421	406	526	525	496	348	120
1960	3 065	575	273	302	2 490	456	573	520	502	330	109
1961	3 743	669	295	374	3 074	566	668	652	611	438	139
1962	3 052	580	262	318	2 472	488	515	522	485	345	117
1963	3 208	708	350	358	2 500	501	540	518	485	349	107
1964	2 999	708	365	342	2 291	508	441	472	447	323	100
1965	2 691	705	329	374	1 986	437	399	427	358	276	91
1966	2 255	651	315	336	1 604	338	323	336	298	227	80
1967	2 338	635	311	325	1 703	393	360	336	321	221	75
1968	2 226	644	326	318	1 582	422	330	297	269	187	80
1969	2 260	660	351	309	1 601	432	354	294	269	185	66
1970	3 339	871	438	432	2 468	679	570	433	415	275	95
1971	4 085	1 011	491	521	3 074	887	732	517	500	338	100
1972	3 906	1 021	515	506	2 885	887	679	459	439	324	95
1973	3 442	955	513	443	2 486	758	664	358	371	257	77
1974	4 097	1 104	561	544	2 993	925	821	448	427	283	88
1975	6 421	1 413	657	755	5 007	1 474	1 413	774	753	460	136
1976	5 914	1 364	649	715	4 550	1 326	1 329	682	637	448	128
1977	5 441	1 284	636	648	4 157	1 195	1 255	621	569	388	129
1978	4 698	1 189	631	558	3 509	1 059	1 059	543	453	290	104
1979	4 664	1 193	589	603	3 472	1 038	1 068	545	443	290	87
1980	5 884	1 291	625	666	4 593	1 364	1 528	740	550	335	74
1981	6 343	1 374	629	745	4 968	1 449	1 658	827	578	379	77
1982	8 241	1 534	683	851	6 707	1 770	2 283	1 223	796	549	86
1983	8 128	1 387	609	778	6 741	1 678	2 282	1 294	837	563	88
1984	6 372	1 116	510	605	5 256	1 282	1 723	1 036	660	475	81
1985	6 191	1 074	507	567	5 117	1 235	1 695	1 039	642	432	75
1986	6 140	1 070	509	561	5 070	1 149	1 751	1 056	629	407	78
1987	5 501	995	495	500	4 506	1 017	1 527	984	576	333	68
1988	4 944	910	437	473	4 033	874	1 371	890	520	309	69
1989	4 770	863	407	456	3 908	856	1 297	871	503	311	70
1990	5 186	903	401	502	4 283	899	1 401	983	582	330	88
1991	6 560	1 029	461	568	5 532	1 132	1 805	1 330	759	410	96
1992	7 169	1 037	484	553	6 132	1 156	1 967	1 483	915	495	116
1993	6 655	992	468	523	5 663	1 057	1 754	1 411	907	442	92
1994	5 892	960	471	489	4 933	952	1 479	1 184	779	407	132
1995	5 459	952	476	476	4 507	866	1 311	1 161	676	362	131
1996	5 300	939	456	484	4 361	854	1 223	1 117	709	336	122
1997	4 836	912	438	475	3 924	765	1 068	1 035	648	302	106
1998	4 484	876	424	451	3 608	731	978	901	620	276	101
1999	4 273	844	414	430	3 429	720	865	843	595	303	104
2000	4 099	805	389	416	3 294	684	804	825	585	290	106
2001	4 923	866	404	463	4 057	827	1 013	984	754	370	109

See *Note* at end of table.

Table 1-26. Unemployed Persons by Race, Hispanic Origin, Sex, and Age, 1948–2001—*Continued*

(Thousands of persons.)

Year, race, Hispanic origin, and sex	16 years and over	16 to 19 years			20 years and over						
		Total	16 to 17 years	18 to 19 years	Total	20 to 24 years	25 to 34 years	35 to 44 years	45 to 54 years	55 to 64 years	65 years and over
BLACK											
1972	906	279	113	167	627	226	183	106	62	37	12
1973	846	262	114	148	584	231	181	82	53	29	9
1974	965	297	127	170	666	261	201	95	65	33	10
1975	1 369	330	130	200	1 040	362	321	157	126	54	17
1976	1 334	330	134	195	1 005	350	338	145	101	54	16
1977	1 393	354	135	218	1 040	397	355	140	81	51	16
1978	1 330	360	150	210	972	379	320	127	82	47	17
1979	1 319	333	137	197	986	369	335	137	82	48	15
1980	1 553	343	134	210	1 209	426	433	171	109	53	18
1981	1 731	357	138	219	1 374	483	493	207	119	55	17
1982	2 142	396	130	266	1 747	565	662	278	141	84	17
1983	2 272	392	125	267	1 879	591	700	299	174	95	21
1984	1 914	353	122	230	1 561	504	577	253	138	75	15
1985	1 864	357	135	221	1 507	455	562	254	143	74	18
1986	1 840	347	138	209	1 493	453	564	269	127	69	10
1987	1 684	312	134	178	1 373	397	533	247	124	62	10
1988	1 547	288	121	167	1 259	349	502	230	111	51	15
1989	1 544	300	116	184	1 245	322	494	246	109	53	20
1990	1 565	268	112	156	1 297	349	505	278	106	44	14
1991	1 723	280	105	175	1 443	378	539	318	151	44	13
1992	2 011	324	127	197	1 687	421	610	402	178	64	13
1993	1 844	313	112	201	1 530	387	532	376	153	72	11
1994	1 666	300	127	173	1 366	351	468	346	130	55	16
1995	1 538	325	143	182	1 213	311	423	303	116	42	18
1996	1 592	310	133	177	1 282	327	454	313	127	48	13
1997	1 560	302	123	179	1 258	327	426	307	136	45	16
1998	1 426	281	124	156	1 146	301	366	294	125	45	16
1999	1 309	268	109	159	1 041	273	339	249	121	46	14
2000	1 269	239	100	139	1 030	290	292	261	130	37	20
2001	1 450	271	106	165	1 179	312	346	297	158	51	15
HISPANIC											
1976	485	106	51	55	385	116	113	72	53	26	6
1977	456	113	50	60	344	98	114	56	48	24	5
1978	452	110	63	47	342	98	116	65	41	16	5
1979	434	106	54	51	329	100	102	65	37	20	4
1980	620	145	66	79	474	138	168	90	49	24	5
1981	678	144	60	84	533	171	178	92	57	31	5
1982	929	175	73	102	754	221	267	140	75	45	5
1983	961	167	64	104	793	214	270	156	93	54	5
1984	800	149	60	88	651	164	235	124	71	51	5
1985	811	141	55	85	670	171	256	123	73	41	7
1986	857	141	57	84	716	183	258	143	85	38	9
1987	751	136	57	79	615	152	222	128	75	33	5
1988	732	148	63	84	585	145	209	120	69	36	6
1989	750	132	59	73	618	158	218	124	76	36	6
1990	876	161	68	94	714	167	263	156	85	36	7
1991	1 092	179	79	99	913	214	332	206	110	44	8
1992	1 311	219	94	124	1 093	240	390	267	126	59	10
1993	1 248	201	86	115	1 047	237	354	261	132	54	10
1994	1 187	198	90	108	989	220	348	227	132	51	12
1995	1 140	205	96	109	934	209	325	224	106	54	16
1996	1 132	199	85	114	933	217	296	246	101	59	14
1997	1 069	197	87	110	872	206	269	229	99	56	13
1998	1 026	214	89	125	812	194	260	203	96	48	11
1999	945	196	79	117	750	171	233	190	104	42	10
2000	876	181	77	105	695	162	215	183	79	44	12
2001	1 037	199	79	120	839	179	267	216	109	59	9

See *Note* at end of table.

Table 1-26. Unemployed Persons by Race, Hispanic Origin, Sex, and Age, 1948–2001—*Continued*

(Thousands of persons.)

Year, race, Hispanic origin, and sex	16 years and over	16 to 19 years			20 years and over						
		Total	16 to 17 years	18 to 19 years	Total	20 to 24 years	25 to 34 years	35 to 44 years	45 to 54 years	55 to 64 years	65 years and over
MEN											
1948	1 559	256	113	142	1 305	324	289	233	201	177	81
1949	2 572	353	145	207	2 219	485	539	414	347	310	125
1950	2 239	318	139	179	1 922	377	467	348	327	286	117
1951	1 221	191	102	89	1 029	155	241	192	193	162	87
1952	1 185	205	116	89	980	155	233	192	182	145	73
1953	1 202	184	94	90	1 019	152	236	208	196	167	60
1954	2 344	310	142	168	2 035	327	517	431	372	275	112
1955	1 854	274	134	140	1 580	248	353	328	285	265	102
1956	1 711	269	134	135	1 442	240	348	278	270	216	90
1957	1 841	300	140	159	1 541	283	349	304	302	220	83
1958	3 098	416	185	231	2 681	478	685	552	492	349	124
1959	2 420	398	191	207	2 022	343	484	407	390	287	112
1960	2 486	426	200	225	2 060	369	492	415	392	294	96
1961	2 997	479	221	258	2 518	458	585	507	473	375	122
1962	2 423	408	188	220	2 016	381	445	404	382	300	103
1963	2 472	501	248	252	1 971	396	445	386	358	290	97
1964	2 205	487	257	230	1 718	384	345	324	319	263	85
1965	1 914	479	247	232	1 435	311	292	283	253	221	75
1966	1 551	432	220	212	1 120	221	239	219	196	179	65
1967	1 508	448	241	207	1 060	235	219	185	199	163	60
1968	1 419	426	234	193	993	258	205	171	165	132	61
1969	1 403	440	244	196	963	270	205	155	157	127	48
1970	2 238	599	306	294	1 638	479	391	253	247	198	71
1971	2 789	693	346	347	2 097	640	513	320	313	239	71
1972	2 659	711	357	355	1 948	628	466	284	272	227	73
1973	2 275	653	352	300	1 624	528	439	211	219	171	57
1974	2 714	757	394	362	1 957	649	546	266	250	183	63
1975	4 442	966	445	521	3 476	1 081	986	507	499	302	103
1976	4 036	939	443	496	3 098	951	914	431	411	296	94
1977	3 667	874	421	453	2 794	877	869	373	326	252	97
1978	3 142	813	426	388	2 328	768	691	314	277	198	81
1979	3 120	811	393	418	2 308	744	699	329	272	196	67
1980	4 267	913	429	485	3 353	1 076	1 137	482	357	243	58
1981	4 577	962	431	531	3 615	1 144	1 213	552	390	261	55
1982	6 179	1 090	469	621	5 089	1 407	1 791	879	550	393	69
1983	6 260	1 003	408	595	5 257	1 369	1 822	947	613	433	73
1984	4 744	812	348	464	3 932	1 023	1 322	728	450	356	53
1985	4 521	806	363	443	3 715	944	1 244	706	459	307	55
1986	4 530	779	355	424	3 751	899	1 291	763	440	301	58
1987	4 101	732	353	379	3 369	779	1 169	689	426	258	49
1988	3 655	667	311	356	2 987	676	1 040	617	366	240	49
1989	3 525	658	303	355	2 867	660	953	619	351	234	49
1990	3 906	667	283	384	3 239	715	1 092	711	413	249	59
1991	4 946	751	317	433	4 195	911	1 375	990	550	305	64
1992	5 523	806	357	449	4 717	951	1 529	1 118	675	378	67
1993	5 055	768	342	426	4 287	865	1 338	1 049	636	336	64
1994	4 367	740	342	398	3 627	768	1 113	855	522	281	88
1995	3 983	744	352	391	3 239	673	961	815	464	233	94
1996	3 880	733	347	387	3 146	675	903	786	484	223	76
1997	3 577	694	321	373	2 882	636	772	732	457	217	69
1998	3 266	686	330	355	2 580	583	699	609	420	201	69
1999	3 066	633	295	338	2 433	562	624	571	403	203	70
2000	2 954	604	283	321	2 350	549	579	564	391	185	82
2001	3 663	660	298	362	3 003	680	731	722	531	265	76

See *Note* at end of table.

Table 1-26. Unemployed Persons by Race, Hispanic Origin, Sex, and Age, 1948–2001—*Continued*

(Thousands of persons.)

Year, race, Hispanic origin, and sex	16 years and over	16 to 19 years			20 years and over						
		Total	16 to 17 years	18 to 19 years	Total	20 to 24 years	25 to 34 years	35 to 44 years	45 to 54 years	55 to 64 years	65 years and over
WOMEN											
1948	717	153	67	86	564	131	168	114	89	49	12
1949	1 065	223	93	130	841	195	237	189	124	74	21
1950	1 049	195	87	108	854	184	235	182	151	82	20
1951	834	145	66	79	689	118	194	162	125	76	16
1952	698	140	64	76	559	113	156	133	92	50	13
1953	632	123	56	67	510	104	143	117	84	51	10
1954	1 188	191	79	79	997	177	276	249	176	99	20
1955	998	176	77	99	823	148	224	193	151	90	18
1956	1 039	209	97	112	832	155	206	198	159	95	19
1957	1 018	197	90	107	821	147	224	195	146	80	28
1958	1 504	262	114	148	1 242	223	308	319	239	123	30
1959	1 320	256	110	147	1 063	200	242	266	213	118	23
1960	1 366	286	125	162	1 080	214	260	256	222	102	26
1961	1 717	349	142	207	1 368	265	305	343	278	141	37
1962	1 488	313	124	189	1 175	255	267	284	223	111	38
1963	1 598	383	172	210	1 216	262	287	288	231	120	29
1964	1 581	385	179	207	1 195	276	262	281	224	115	32
1965	1 452	395	164	231	1 056	246	237	263	183	101	28
1966	1 324	405	175	229	921	225	202	207	173	86	27
1967	1 468	391	159	231	1 078	277	261	237	184	93	26
1968	1 397	412	180	233	985	285	238	200	149	87	27
1969	1 429	413	192	220	1 015	290	248	203	163	89	24
1970	1 855	506	231	275	1 349	387	327	262	229	111	33
1971	2 227	568	250	318	1 658	489	420	310	260	142	38
1972	2 222	598	276	322	1 625	503	413	293	237	141	38
1973	2 089	583	282	301	1 507	480	427	240	212	119	31
1974	2 441	665	305	360	1 777	564	497	294	248	137	36
1975	3 486	802	355	447	2 684	783	791	444	395	219	52
1976	3 369	780	352	429	2 588	763	795	417	346	214	53
1977	3 324	789	361	428	2 535	752	782	412	340	198	50
1978	3 061	769	370	399	2 292	714	731	381	275	148	43
1979	3 018	743	346	396	2 276	697	748	375	268	150	38
1980	3 370	755	349	407	2 615	760	886	459	318	155	36
1981	3 696	800	350	450	2 895	833	998	513	325	184	43
1982	4 499	886	362	524	3 613	985	1 246	673	416	254	38
1983	4 457	825	344	481	3 632	961	1 255	703	427	244	41
1984	3 794	687	298	390	3 107	815	1 052	607	378	211	45
1985	3 791	661	298	363	3 129	794	1 098	634	355	211	39
1986	3 707	675	310	365	3 032	752	1 099	609	350	189	33
1987	3 324	616	295	321	2 709	674	960	592	298	155	30
1988	3 046	558	262	297	2 487	585	889	550	291	136	38
1989	3 003	536	234	302	2 467	558	897	540	286	144	41
1990	3 140	544	243	301	2 596	584	902	617	310	137	46
1991	3 683	608	270	338	3 074	662	1 071	728	396	168	49
1992	4 090	621	283	338	3 469	698	1 173	858	463	210	66
1993	3 885	597	264	333	3 288	648	1 058	847	485	205	45
1994	3 629	580	282	298	3 049	605	954	772	449	204	66
1995	3 421	602	299	303	2 819	571	880	735	381	193	60
1996	3 356	573	270	303	2 783	564	854	720	399	183	63
1997	3 162	577	268	310	2 585	516	800	686	373	152	58
1998	2 944	519	242	277	2 424	498	720	650	362	141	53
1999	2 814	529	249	280	2 285	480	654	584	350	163	54
2000	2 701	489	223	266	2 212	476	590	577	359	162	49
2001	3 079	527	234	294	2 551	523	716	637	441	181	53

See *Note* at end of table.

Table 1-26. Unemployed Persons by Race, Hispanic Origin, Sex, and Age, 1948–2001—*Continued*

(Thousands of persons.)

Year, race, Hispanic origin, and sex	16 years and over	16 to 19 years			20 years and over						
		Total	16 to 17 years	18 to 19 years	Total	20 to 24 years	25 to 34 years	35 to 44 years	45 to 54 years	55 to 64 years	65 years and over
WHITE MEN											
1954	1 913	266	125	142	1 647	260	408	341	299	241	98
1955	1 478	232	114	117	1 246	196	260	246	233	223	89
1956	1 366	221	112	108	1 145	186	265	212	225	177	81
1957	1 477	243	118	124	1 234	222	257	239	250	193	73
1958	2 489	333	149	184	2 156	382	525	436	404	299	110
1959	1 903	318	162	156	1 585	256	350	316	320	245	98
1960	1 988	341	167	174	1 647	295	376	330	317	243	86
1961	2 398	384	176	208	2 014	370	442	395	382	318	107
1962	1 915	334	158	176	1 581	300	332	311	308	246	84
1963	1 976	407	211	196	1 569	309	342	297	294	246	80
1964	1 779	400	217	183	1 379	310	262	255	266	216	70
1965	1 556	387	200	186	1 169	254	226	228	206	190	67
1966	1 241	340	178	162	901	172	185	173	160	154	57
1967	1 208	342	186	156	866	185	171	153	167	140	52
1968	1 142	328	185	143	814	206	162	140	142	111	55
1969	1 137	343	198	145	794	214	165	130	134	108	43
1970	1 857	485	255	230	1 372	388	316	212	216	177	64
1971	2 309	562	288	275	1 747	513	418	268	272	211	66
1972	2 173	564	288	276	1 610	506	375	231	237	199	60
1973	1 836	513	284	229	1 323	411	353	166	188	153	51
1974	2 169	584	311	274	1 585	505	434	218	213	161	53
1975	3 627	785	369	416	2 841	871	796	412	411	265	86
1976	3 258	754	368	385	2 504	750	730	346	341	259	78
1977	2 883	672	342	330	2 211	660	682	297	276	213	82
1978	2 411	615	338	277	1 797	558	525	250	227	169	68
1979	2 405	633	319	313	1 773	553	526	253	220	165	56
1980	3 345	716	347	369	2 629	827	884	378	291	206	44
1981	3 580	755	349	406	2 825	869	943	433	317	221	42
1982	4 846	854	387	467	3 991	1 066	1 385	696	460	331	53
1983	4 859	761	328	433	4 098	1 019	1 410	755	497	362	54
1984	3 600	608	280	328	2 992	722	991	572	363	302	42
1985	3 426	592	282	310	2 834	694	931	553	356	257	43
1986	3 433	576	276	299	2 857	645	978	586	349	248	51
1987	3 132	548	272	276	2 584	568	879	536	350	209	43
1988	2 766	499	239	260	2 268	480	777	477	293	200	40
1989	2 636	487	230	257	2 149	476	694	470	280	191	38
1990	2 935	504	214	290	2 431	510	796	530	330	214	51
1991	3 859	575	249	327	3 284	677	1 064	780	438	269	55
1992	4 209	590	270	319	3 620	686	1 155	858	543	318	58
1993	3 828	565	261	305	3 263	619	1 015	793	512	270	53
1994	3 275	540	259	280	2 735	555	827	626	417	236	74
1995	2 999	535	260	275	2 465	483	711	621	371	200	79
1996	2 896	532	260	273	2 363	478	655	592	383	188	67
1997	2 641	502	234	268	2 140	439	553	549	358	182	58
1998	2 431	510	254	257	1 920	405	512	441	342	164	58
1999	2 274	461	223	237	1 813	398	441	419	322	172	61
2000	2 165	452	219	233	1 713	369	409	409	298	159	68
2001	2 730	489	230	259	2 242	489	522	531	411	225	65

See *Note* at end of table.

Table 1-26. Unemployed Persons by Race, Hispanic Origin, Sex, and Age, 1948–2001—*Continued*

(Thousands of persons.)

Year, race, Hispanic origin, and sex	16 years and over	16 to 19 years			20 years and over						
		Total	16 to 17 years	18 to 19 years	Total	20 to 24 years	25 to 34 years	35 to 44 years	45 to 54 years	55 to 64 years	65 years and over
WOMEN											
1954	946	157	66	90	789	134	202	199	148	88	17
1955	774	141	67	74	633	108	152	156	125	77	16
1956	793	161	79	83	632	111	141	151	130	81	17
1957	812	158	77	80	654	109	168	162	123	69	25
1958	1 191	208	96	113	983	159	231	250	210	106	26
1959	1 043	207	93	114	836	150	176	209	176	103	22
1960	1 077	234	106	128	843	161	197	190	185	87	23
1961	1 345	285	119	166	1 060	196	226	257	229	120	32
1962	1 137	246	104	142	891	188	183	211	177	99	33
1963	1 232	301	139	162	931	192	198	221	191	103	27
1964	1 220	308	148	159	912	198	179	217	181	107	30
1965	1 135	318	129	188	817	183	173	199	152	86	24
1966	1 014	311	137	174	703	166	138	163	138	73	23
1967	1 130	293	125	169	837	209	189	183	154	81	23
1968	1 084	316	141	175	768	216	168	157	127	76	25
1969	1 123	317	153	164	806	218	189	164	135	77	23
1970	1 482	386	183	202	1 096	291	254	221	199	98	31
1971	1 777	449	203	246	1 328	376	314	249	228	126	34
1972	1 733	457	227	230	1 275	381	304	227	202	125	35
1973	1 606	442	228	214	1 164	347	311	192	183	104	26
1974	1 927	519	250	270	1 408	420	387	230	214	122	35
1975	2 794	628	288	340	2 166	602	617	362	342	195	49
1976	2 656	611	280	330	2 045	577	598	336	296	188	49
1977	2 558	612	294	318	1 946	536	573	323	293	175	47
1978	2 287	574	292	281	1 713	500	533	294	226	122	37
1979	2 260	560	270	290	1 699	485	542	293	223	125	32
1980	2 540	576	278	298	1 964	537	645	362	259	129	31
1981	2 762	620	281	339	2 143	580	715	394	261	158	36
1982	3 395	680	296	384	2 715	704	898	527	337	217	33
1983	3 270	626	282	345	2 643	659	872	539	340	201	33
1984	2 772	508	231	277	2 264	559	731	464	297	173	39
1985	2 765	482	225	257	2 283	541	763	486	286	175	32
1986	2 708	495	233	262	2 213	504	773	470	281	159	27
1987	2 369	447	223	224	1 922	449	648	448	227	124	25
1988	2 177	412	198	214	1 766	393	594	413	227	110	30
1989	2 135	376	177	199	1 758	380	603	401	223	120	32
1990	2 251	399	187	212	1 852	389	605	453	251	116	37
1991	2 701	453	212	241	2 248	455	741	550	320	141	41
1992	2 959	447	214	233	2 512	469	811	625	372	177	58
1993	2 827	426	208	219	2 400	438	739	618	395	172	39
1994	2 617	420	211	208	2 197	397	652	558	361	170	58
1995	2 460	418	216	201	2 042	384	600	540	306	162	52
1996	2 404	407	196	211	1 998	376	568	525	326	148	55
1997	2 195	411	204	207	1 784	326	515	486	290	119	49
1998	2 053	365	171	195	1 688	327	467	460	279	112	43
1999	1 999	383	190	193	1 616	322	423	423	273	131	43
2000	1 934	353	170	183	1 581	315	396	415	286	131	38
2001	2 193	378	174	204	1 815	338	491	453	343	145	44

See *Note* at end of table.

Table 1-26. Unemployed Persons by Race, Hispanic Origin, Sex, and Age, 1948–2001—*Continued*

(Thousands of persons.)

Year, race, Hispanic origin, and sex	16 years and over	16 to 19 years			20 years and over						
		Total	16 to 17 years	18 to 19 years	Total	20 to 24 years	25 to 34 years	35 to 44 years	45 to 54 years	55 to 64 years	65 years and over
BLACK MEN											
1972	448	143	66	77	305	113	84	45	31	23	9
1973	395	128	62	66	267	108	75	37	27	16	5
1974	494	159	75	82	336	129	103	41	35	19	8
1975	741	170	71	100	571	195	169	83	78	33	13
1976	698	170	69	103	528	185	166	73	60	32	13
1977	698	187	73	114	512	197	170	63	40	31	12
1978	641	180	80	101	462	185	148	53	40	24	11
1979	636	164	68	97	473	174	152	66	44	27	10
1980	815	179	72	108	636	222	222	88	60	32	12
1981	891	188	73	115	703	248	245	102	65	32	10
1982	1 167	213	72	141	954	304	355	154	74	54	12
1983	1 213	211	70	142	1 002	313	358	162	96	59	14
1984	1 003	188	62	126	815	272	289	132	67	45	9
1985	951	193	69	124	757	224	268	127	85	43	11
1986	946	180	68	112	765	225	273	148	70	44	5
1987	826	160	70	90	666	186	253	122	61	39	6
1988	771	154	64	90	617	177	233	111	58	30	8
1989	773	153	65	88	619	162	226	129	59	33	10
1990	806	142	62	80	664	177	247	146	62	27	6
1991	890	145	54	91	745	201	252	172	87	25	7
1992	1 067	180	71	109	886	221	301	208	107	42	6
1993	971	170	66	104	801	201	260	201	87	46	7
1994	848	167	69	97	682	173	218	180	72	29	10
1995	762	168	73	95	593	153	195	150	63	21	11
1996	808	169	73	96	639	163	210	158	75	26	7
1997	747	162	70	92	585	165	178	141	72	22	7
1998	671	147	61	86	524	151	148	133	60	24	8
1999	626	145	60	85	480	135	143	114	60	22	7
2000	636	125	54	71	511	151	136	127	71	16	10
2001	731	141	53	88	590	152	163	152	85	29	8
BLACK WOMEN											
1972	458	136	47	90	322	113	99	61	31	14	3
1973	451	134	51	82	317	123	105	45	26	13	4
1974	470	139	51	87	331	132	98	55	30	14	2
1975	629	160	60	100	469	167	153	75	48	22	4
1976	637	160	66	93	477	165	172	73	41	23	3
1977	695	167	63	104	528	200	185	77	41	21	4
1978	690	179	70	110	510	194	173	74	41	23	6
1979	683	169	69	100	513	195	183	71	38	21	5
1980	738	164	62	102	574	204	211	83	49	21	6
1981	840	169	65	104	671	235	248	105	54	23	7
1982	975	182	58	124	793	261	307	123	67	29	5
1983	1 059	181	56	125	878	278	342	137	77	36	7
1984	911	165	60	104	747	231	288	121	71	30	5
1985	913	164	66	98	750	231	295	127	58	31	7
1986	894	167	70	97	728	228	291	121	57	25	5
1987	858	152	64	88	706	211	280	125	63	23	4
1988	776	134	57	78	642	172	269	118	53	22	7
1989	772	147	51	96	625	160	267	118	50	21	9
1990	758	126	49	76	633	172	258	132	44	17	8
1991	833	135	51	84	698	177	288	145	64	19	6
1992	944	144	56	88	800	200	308	194	71	22	6
1993	872	143	46	97	729	186	272	175	66	26	5
1994	818	133	57	76	685	178	249	166	59	26	6
1995	777	157	. . .	87	620	158	228	153	53	20	. . .
1996	784	141	60	80	643	164	244	155	52	21	7
1997	813	140	53	87	673	163	248	166	64	24	9
1998	756	134	63	71	622	150	218	160	65	21	8
1999	684	123	49	74	561	138	196	135	61	25	7
2000	633	114	46	68	519	139	156	134	59	21	10
2001	719	130	53	77	589	159	183	145	73	22	7

See *Note* at end of table.

Table 1-26. Unemployed Persons by Race, Hispanic Origin, Sex, and Age, 1948–2001—*Continued*

(Thousands of persons.)

Year, race, Hispanic origin, and sex	16 years and over	16 to 19 years			20 years and over						
		Total	16 to 17 years	18 to 19 years	Total	20 to 24 years	25 to 34 years	35 to 44 years	45 to 54 years	55 to 64 years	65 years and over
HISPANIC MEN											
1976	278	60	30	31	217	69	63	38	29	16	4
1977	253	60	27	33	195	57	65	28	22	15	4
1978	234	59	35	24	175	51	59	30	20	10	4
1979	223	55	29	27	168	52	50	33	19	11	3
1980	370	86	39	47	284	85	96	51	31	16	5
1981	408	87	40	47	321	105	113	49	31	19	4
1982	565	104	45	59	461	138	169	80	40	29	4
1983	591	100	38	62	491	134	168	92	57	36	4
1984	480	87	36	51	393	103	142	69	41	33	4
1985	483	82	34	49	401	108	156	69	40	23	5
1986	520	82	33	50	438	115	159	86	46	26	5
1987	451	77	32	45	374	88	137	77	46	22	4
1988	437	86	36	50	351	83	128	70	42	24	5
1989	423	81	36	45	342	88	113	69	43	25	4
1990	524	100	40	60	425	99	154	91	53	25	4
1991	685	110	47	62	575	139	210	126	62	33	5
1992	807	132	56	75	675	156	239	156	75	42	6
1993	747	118	50	68	629	144	217	148	79	33	8
1994	680	121	54	67	558	128	203	113	75	30	9
1995	651	121	59	63	530	123	185	120	57	33	13
1996	607	112	49	63	495	117	165	124	49	31	9
1997	582	110	47	63	471	125	137	113	54	35	8
1998	552	117	54	62	436	115	142	97	49	29	5
1999	480	106	42	63	374	96	109	83	54	24	7
2000	441	96	41	55	345	85	98	89	41	23	9
2001	542	111	48	63	431	104	123	107	53	38	6
HISPANIC WOMEN											
1976	207	45	22	24	166	47	52	33	22	10	2
1977	204	50	23	27	153	40	49	28	25	11	1
1978	219	51	28	23	168	46	58	36	20	8	1
1979	211	50	26	24	160	48	52	32	18	10	1
1980	249	59	28	31	190	53	72	39	18	8	0
1981	269	57	20	37	212	65	65	43	25	13	1
1982	364	71	28	43	293	83	98	60	35	16	1
1983	369	68	26	42	302	80	102	65	36	18	1
1984	320	62	25	37	258	61	93	55	30	17	1
1985	327	58	22	37	269	63	100	54	32	18	2
1986	337	59	25	35	278	68	99	57	39	12	3
1987	300	59	25	34	241	64	85	51	29	11	1
1988	296	62	27	34	234	63	81	50	27	12	1
1989	327	51	23	28	276	70	105	55	33	11	2
1990	351	62	28	34	289	68	109	65	32	11	3
1991	407	69	32	37	339	74	122	80	48	12	3
1992	504	87	38	49	418	84	151	111	51	17	4
1993	501	83	36	47	418	93	136	113	53	21	1
1994	508	77	36	40	431	92	145	115	57	21	2
1995	488	84	38	46	404	86	140	104	50	21	3
1996	525	88	36	52	438	100	131	122	52	27	5
1997	488	87	40	46	401	81	132	117	46	21	4
1998	473	98	35	63	376	80	118	106	48	19	5
1999	466	90	36	54	376	75	124	107	50	17	3
2000	435	85	36	49	350	77	117	94	38	21	4
2001	495	87	31	56	407	76	144	109	55	21	3

Note: Detail for the above race and Hispanic-origin groups will not sum to totals because data for the Other races group are not presented and Hispanics are included in both the White and Black population groups. See "Notes and Definitions" for information on historical comparability.

Table 1-27. Unemployment Rates of Civilian Workers by Race, Hispanic Origin, Sex, and Age, 1948–2001

(Percent of labor force.)

Year, race, Hispanic origin, and sex	16 years and over	16 to 19 years			20 years and over						
		Total	16 to 17 years	18 to 19 years	Total	20 to 24 years	25 to 34 years	35 to 44 years	45 to 54 years	55 to 64 years	65 years and over
TOTAL											
1948	3.8	9.2	10.1	8.6	3.3	6.2	3.2	2.6	2.7	3.1	3.2
1949	5.9	13.4	14.0	13.0	5.4	9.3	5.4	4.4	4.2	5.2	4.9
1950	5.3	12.2	13.6	11.2	4.8	7.7	4.8	3.8	4.2	4.8	4.5
1951	3.3	8.2	9.6	7.1	3.0	4.1	3.0	2.5	2.7	3.1	3.4
1952	3.0	8.5	10.0	7.3	2.7	4.6	2.6	2.3	2.3	2.4	2.9
1953	2.9	7.6	8.7	6.8	2.6	4.7	2.5	2.2	2.3	2.7	2.2
1954	5.5	12.6	13.5	10.7	5.1	9.2	5.3	4.5	4.4	4.5	4.1
1955	4.4	11.0	12.3	10.0	3.9	7.0	3.8	3.4	3.4	4.2	3.6
1956	4.1	11.1	12.3	10.2	3.7	6.6	3.7	3.0	3.2	3.5	3.2
1957	4.3	11.6	12.5	10.9	3.8	7.1	3.9	3.1	3.3	3.4	3.4
1958	6.8	15.9	16.4	15.5	6.2	11.2	6.8	5.4	5.2	5.2	4.8
1959	5.5	14.6	15.3	14.0	4.8	8.5	5.0	4.2	4.2	4.4	4.3
1960	5.5	14.7	15.5	14.1	4.8	8.7	5.2	4.1	4.1	4.2	3.8
1961	6.7	16.8	18.3	15.8	5.9	10.4	6.2	5.2	5.0	5.4	5.1
1962	5.5	14.7	16.3	13.6	4.9	9.0	5.1	4.1	4.0	4.2	4.5
1963	5.7	17.2	19.3	15.6	4.8	8.8	5.2	4.0	3.8	4.1	4.1
1964	5.2	16.2	17.8	14.9	4.3	8.3	4.3	3.6	3.5	3.7	3.8
1965	4.5	14.8	16.5	13.5	3.6	6.7	3.7	3.2	2.8	3.1	3.3
1966	3.8	12.8	14.8	11.3	2.9	5.3	3.1	2.5	2.3	2.5	3.0
1967	3.8	12.9	14.6	11.6	3.0	5.7	3.2	2.5	2.4	2.4	2.8
1968	3.6	12.7	14.7	11.2	2.7	5.8	2.8	2.2	1.9	2.0	2.8
1969	3.5	12.2	14.5	10.5	2.7	5.7	2.8	2.2	1.9	1.9	2.2
1970	4.9	15.3	17.1	13.8	4.0	8.2	4.2	3.1	2.8	2.7	3.2
1971	5.9	16.9	18.7	15.5	4.9	10.0	5.3	3.9	3.4	3.3	3.5
1972	5.6	16.2	18.5	14.6	4.5	9.3	4.6	3.5	3.0	3.2	3.6
1973	4.9	14.5	17.3	12.4	3.9	7.8	4.2	2.7	2.5	2.6	3.0
1974	5.6	16.0	18.3	14.3	4.5	9.1	4.8	3.3	2.9	2.8	3.4
1975	8.5	19.9	21.4	18.9	7.3	13.6	7.8	5.6	5.2	4.6	5.2
1976	7.7	19.0	21.1	17.5	6.5	12.0	7.1	4.9	4.5	4.5	5.1
1977	7.1	17.8	19.9	16.2	5.9	11.0	6.5	4.4	3.9	3.9	5.0
1978	6.1	16.4	19.3	14.2	5.0	9.6	5.3	3.7	3.3	2.9	4.0
1979	5.8	16.1	18.1	14.7	4.8	9.1	5.2	3.6	3.2	2.9	3.4
1980	7.1	17.8	20.0	16.2	6.1	11.5	6.9	4.6	4.0	3.3	3.1
1981	7.6	19.6	21.4	18.4	6.5	12.3	7.3	5.0	4.2	3.7	3.2
1982	9.7	23.2	24.9	22.1	8.6	14.9	9.7	6.9	5.7	5.4	3.5
1983	9.6	22.4	24.5	21.1	8.6	14.5	9.7	7.0	6.2	5.6	3.7
1984	7.5	18.9	21.2	17.4	6.7	11.5	7.3	5.4	4.9	4.7	3.3
1985	7.2	18.6	21.0	17.0	6.4	11.1	7.0	5.1	4.7	4.3	3.2
1986	7.0	18.3	20.2	17.0	6.2	10.7	6.9	5.0	4.5	4.1	3.0
1987	6.2	16.9	19.1	15.2	5.4	9.7	6.0	4.5	4.0	3.5	2.5
1988	5.5	15.3	17.4	13.8	4.8	8.7	5.4	4.0	3.4	3.2	2.7
1989	5.3	15.0	17.2	13.6	4.6	8.6	5.2	3.8	3.2	3.2	2.6
1990	5.6	15.5	17.9	14.1	4.9	8.8	5.6	4.1	3.6	3.3	3.0
1991	6.8	18.7	21.0	17.2	6.1	10.8	6.9	5.2	4.5	4.1	3.3
1992	7.5	20.1	23.1	18.2	6.8	11.4	7.6	5.8	5.1	5.1	3.8
1993	6.9	19.0	21.4	17.5	6.2	10.5	6.9	5.5	4.8	4.7	3.2
1994	6.1	17.6	19.9	16.0	5.4	9.7	6.0	4.6	4.0	4.1	4.0
1995	5.6	17.3	20.2	15.3	4.9	9.1	5.4	4.3	3.3	3.6	4.0
1996	5.4	16.7	18.9	15.2	4.7	9.3	5.2	4.1	3.3	3.3	3.6
1997	4.9	16.0	18.2	14.5	4.3	8.5	4.7	3.8	3.0	2.9	3.3
1998	4.5	14.6	17.2	12.8	3.9	7.9	4.3	3.4	2.8	2.6	3.2
1999	4.2	13.9	16.3	12.4	3.6	7.5	4.0	3.0	2.6	2.7	3.1
2000	4.0	13.1	15.4	11.5	3.4	7.1	3.7	3.0	2.5	2.5	3.1
2001	4.8	14.7	17.1	13.2	4.2	8.3	4.6	3.6	3.1	3.1	3.0

See *Note* at end of table.

Table 1-27. Unemployment Rates of Civilian Workers by Race, Hispanic Origin, Sex, and Age, 1948–2001—*Continued*

(Percent of labor force.)

Year, race, Hispanic origin, and sex	16 years and over	16 to 19 years			20 years and over						
		Total	16 to 17 years	18 to 19 years	Total	20 to 24 years	25 to 34 years	35 to 44 years	45 to 54 years	55 to 64 years	65 years and over
WHITE											
1954	5.0	12.1	13.2	11.3	4.6	8.3	4.6	4.0	4.0	4.3	3.9
1955	3.9	10.4	12.0	9.2	3.4	6.2	3.1	2.9	3.1	3.8	3.4
1956	3.6	10.1	11.5	9.0	3.2	5.7	3.1	2.6	2.9	3.2	3.1
1957	3.8	10.6	11.9	9.6	3.4	6.3	3.3	2.8	3.0	3.2	3.2
1958	6.1	14.4	15.2	13.9	5.6	9.9	5.9	4.8	4.8	4.9	4.6
1959	4.8	13.1	14.4	12.1	4.3	7.3	4.2	3.7	3.8	4.1	4.1
1960	5.0	13.5	14.6	12.6	4.3	7.9	4.5	3.6	3.8	3.9	3.7
1961	6.0	15.3	16.7	14.4	5.3	9.4	5.3	4.5	4.5	5.0	4.8
1962	4.9	13.3	15.3	12.0	4.2	7.9	4.2	3.6	3.6	3.9	4.0
1963	5.0	15.5	17.9	13.7	4.2	7.7	4.4	3.5	3.5	3.8	3.8
1964	4.6	14.8	16.5	13.3	3.8	7.3	3.6	3.2	3.2	3.5	3.5
1965	4.1	13.4	14.8	12.3	3.3	6.1	3.2	2.9	2.5	2.9	3.2
1966	3.4	11.2	13.3	9.7	2.6	4.6	2.6	2.3	2.1	2.4	2.9
1967	3.4	11.0	12.8	9.8	2.7	5.0	2.7	2.3	2.2	2.3	2.7
1968	3.2	11.0	12.9	9.6	2.5	5.2	2.4	2.0	1.8	1.9	2.8
1969	3.1	10.7	13.0	8.9	2.4	5.0	2.5	2.0	1.8	1.8	2.2
1970	4.5	13.5	15.5	11.9	3.7	7.3	3.8	3.0	2.7	2.7	3.2
1971	5.4	15.1	17.0	13.8	4.5	9.0	4.7	3.6	3.3	3.3	3.5
1972	5.1	14.2	16.6	12.3	4.1	8.4	4.1	3.2	2.9	3.1	3.4
1973	4.3	12.6	15.4	10.4	3.5	6.8	3.7	2.5	2.4	2.5	2.9
1974	5.0	14.0	16.3	12.2	4.1	8.0	4.4	3.1	2.8	2.8	3.3
1975	7.8	17.9	19.5	16.7	6.7	12.3	7.1	5.2	4.9	4.5	5.1
1976	7.0	16.9	19.0	15.3	5.9	10.7	6.3	4.5	4.2	4.3	4.9
1977	6.2	15.4	17.9	13.5	5.3	9.3	5.7	4.0	3.8	3.7	4.9
1978	5.2	13.9	17.0	11.5	4.3	8.0	4.6	3.3	3.0	2.7	3.8
1979	5.1	14.0	16.1	12.4	4.2	7.6	4.4	3.2	3.0	2.7	3.1
1980	6.3	15.5	17.9	13.8	5.4	9.9	6.1	4.2	3.7	3.1	2.7
1981	6.7	17.3	19.2	15.9	5.7	10.4	6.3	4.5	3.9	3.5	2.8
1982	8.6	20.4	22.8	18.8	7.6	12.8	8.5	6.3	5.4	5.1	3.1
1983	8.4	19.3	22.0	17.6	7.5	12.1	8.4	6.3	5.7	5.2	3.2
1984	6.5	16.0	18.8	14.3	5.7	9.3	6.2	4.8	4.4	4.4	3.0
1985	6.2	15.7	18.3	13.9	5.5	9.2	5.9	4.6	4.3	4.0	2.9
1986	6.0	15.6	17.6	14.1	5.3	8.7	5.9	4.5	4.1	3.8	2.9
1987	5.3	14.4	16.7	12.7	4.7	8.0	5.1	4.0	3.7	3.2	2.4
1988	4.7	13.1	15.3	11.6	4.1	7.1	4.5	3.5	3.1	3.0	2.4
1989	4.5	12.7	15.2	11.1	3.9	7.2	4.3	3.3	2.9	3.0	2.3
1990	4.8	13.5	15.8	12.1	4.3	7.3	4.6	3.6	3.3	3.2	2.8
1991	6.1	16.5	19.0	14.9	5.5	9.2	6.1	4.7	4.2	4.0	3.1
1992	6.6	17.2	20.3	15.2	6.0	9.5	6.7	5.2	4.8	4.9	3.7
1993	6.1	16.2	19.0	14.4	5.5	8.8	6.0	4.9	4.5	4.3	3.0
1994	5.3	15.1	17.6	13.3	4.7	8.1	5.2	4.0	3.7	3.9	3.8
1995	4.9	14.5	17.3	12.5	4.3	7.7	4.6	3.9	3.1	3.5	3.8
1996	4.7	14.2	16.4	12.6	4.1	7.8	4.4	3.6	3.1	3.2	3.5
1997	4.2	13.6	15.8	12.0	3.6	6.9	3.9	3.3	2.7	2.7	3.0
1998	3.9	12.6	14.8	11.0	3.3	6.5	3.7	2.9	2.6	2.4	2.9
1999	3.7	12.0	14.5	10.2	3.1	6.3	3.3	2.7	2.4	2.5	2.9
2000	3.5	11.4	13.9	9.7	3.0	5.8	3.2	2.6	2.3	2.4	2.8
2001	4.2	12.7	15.2	11.1	3.6	6.9	4.1	3.2	2.8	2.9	2.8

See *Note* at end of table.

Table 1-27. Unemployment Rates of Civilian Workers by Race, Hispanic Origin, Sex, and Age, 1948–2001—*Continued*

(Percent of labor force.)

Year, race, Hispanic origin, and sex	16 years and over	16 to 19 years			20 years and over						
		Total	16 to 17 years	18 to 19 years	Total	20 to 24 years	25 to 34 years	35 to 44 years	45 to 54 years	55 to 64 years	65 years and over
BLACK											
1972	10.4	35.4	38.7	33.6	7.9	16.3	8.7	6.1	4.2	4.1	4.3
1973	9.4	31.5	37.0	28.1	7.2	15.5	8.1	4.7	3.5	3.2	3.5
1974	10.5	35.0	40.0	31.8	8.0	17.5	8.5	5.4	4.3	3.6	3.9
1975	14.8	39.5	41.6	38.1	12.3	24.5	13.0	8.9	8.3	5.9	6.6
1976	14.0	39.3	44.2	36.7	11.5	22.7	12.8	8.0	6.7	5.9	5.9
1977	14.0	41.1	44.5	39.2	11.5	24.2	12.7	7.4	5.3	5.5	5.9
1978	12.8	38.7	43.9	35.7	10.2	21.8	10.8	6.4	5.2	4.8	5.8
1979	12.3	36.5	40.2	34.4	10.1	20.6	10.8	6.7	5.2	4.9	5.3
1980	14.3	38.5	41.1	37.1	12.1	23.6	13.3	8.2	6.8	5.4	6.9
1981	15.6	41.4	44.8	39.5	13.4	26.4	14.7	9.5	7.4	5.5	7.0
1982	18.9	48.0	48.6	47.8	16.6	30.6	19.0	12.1	8.7	8.3	7.1
1983	19.5	48.5	50.5	47.6	17.3	31.6	19.0	12.4	10.7	9.2	9.2
1984	15.9	42.7	45.7	41.2	13.9	26.1	15.2	9.9	8.2	7.4	6.5
1985	15.1	40.2	43.6	38.3	13.1	24.5	14.5	9.5	8.2	7.0	7.0
1986	14.5	39.3	43.0	37.2	12.7	24.1	14.0	9.6	7.1	6.6	4.5
1987	13.0	34.7	39.7	31.6	11.3	21.8	12.8	8.4	6.8	5.6	3.9
1988	11.7	32.4	35.1	30.7	10.2	19.6	11.9	7.5	5.9	4.8	5.5
1989	11.4	32.4	32.9	32.2	9.9	18.0	11.5	7.6	5.6	5.2	6.9
1990	11.4	30.9	36.5	27.8	10.1	19.9	11.7	7.8	5.3	4.6	5.3
1991	12.5	36.1	39.5	34.4	11.1	21.6	12.7	8.5	7.4	4.4	5.2
1992	14.2	39.7	44.7	37.1	12.6	23.8	14.2	10.5	8.3	6.2	4.9
1993	13.0	38.8	39.7	38.4	11.4	21.9	12.6	9.5	6.9	7.1	4.7
1994	11.5	35.2	36.1	34.6	10.0	19.5	11.1	8.5	5.6	5.4	6.2
1995	10.4	35.7	39.1	33.4	8.7	17.7	9.9	7.3	4.8	4.0	6.7
1996	10.5	33.6	36.3	31.7	9.0	18.8	10.5	7.3	5.0	4.4	5.3
1997	10.0	32.4	35.0	30.8	8.6	18.3	9.9	7.0	5.0	4.2	6.1
1998	8.9	27.6	33.6	24.2	7.7	16.8	8.4	6.5	4.4	3.9	5.6
1999	8.0	27.9	31.0	26.2	6.8	14.6	7.6	5.3	4.0	3.9	5.0
2000	7.6	24.7	27.2	23.2	6.6	15.0	6.8	5.6	4.1	3.0	6.1
2001	8.7	29.0	31.1	27.8	7.5	16.2	8.1	6.4	4.8	3.9	4.2
HISPANIC											
1973	7.5	19.7	23.4	17.3	6.0	8.5	5.7	5.6	4.7	5.5	3.9
1974	8.1	19.8	23.5	17.2	6.6	9.8	6.3	5.9	4.6	6.1	6.3
1975	12.2	27.7	30.0	26.5	10.3	16.7	9.9	8.6	8.1	7.7	9.9
1976	11.5	23.8	29.2	19.2	10.1	15.9	9.1	8.2	8.4	8.8	12.6
1977	10.1	22.9	27.0	19.6	8.5	12.0	8.6	6.1	7.3	8.2	9.2
1978	9.1	20.7	28.3	15.1	7.7	10.9	8.0	6.5	5.8	5.0	7.5
1979	8.3	19.2	26.0	14.9	7.0	10.4	6.7	6.2	5.2	6.0	5.7
1980	10.1	22.5	27.6	19.5	8.6	12.1	9.1	7.7	5.7	5.9	6.0
1981	10.4	23.9	28.0	21.7	9.1	13.9	8.8	7.4	6.4	7.3	5.4
1982	13.8	29.9	38.1	25.9	12.3	17.7	12.3	10.7	8.4	10.1	6.5
1983	13.7	28.4	33.8	25.8	12.3	16.7	11.9	11.3	10.0	10.9	5.8
1984	10.7	24.1	28.9	21.6	9.5	12.4	9.7	8.2	7.5	9.7	6.1
1985	10.5	24.3	27.8	22.5	9.4	12.6	9.9	7.7	7.4	7.8	8.1
1986	10.6	24.7	28.1	22.9	9.5	12.9	9.6	8.4	7.8	7.3	10.1
1987	8.8	22.3	27.7	19.5	7.8	10.6	7.7	6.7	6.9	6.0	6.5
1988	8.2	22.0	27.1	19.3	7.0	9.8	7.1	6.0	6.0	5.8	5.6
1989	8.0	19.4	26.4	16.0	7.2	10.7	7.0	5.9	6.3	5.8	5.3
1990	8.2	19.5	24.5	16.9	7.2	9.1	7.3	6.6	6.4	5.6	6.0
1991	10.0	22.9	31.9	18.7	9.0	11.6	9.2	8.1	8.0	6.5	7.0
1992	11.6	27.5	35.7	23.4	10.4	13.2	10.4	9.8	8.8	8.6	8.1
1993	10.8	26.1	35.1	21.8	9.7	13.1	9.3	9.1	8.6	8.0	6.6
1994	9.9	24.5	31.7	20.6	8.9	11.8	9.0	7.7	8.1	7.3	7.9
1995	9.3	24.1	33.1	19.5	8.2	11.5	8.2	7.2	6.4	7.5	10.6
1996	8.9	23.6	30.0	20.3	7.8	11.8	7.3	7.3	6.0	7.3	8.2
1997	7.7	21.6	27.7	18.4	6.8	10.3	6.3	6.4	5.1	6.5	6.8
1998	7.2	21.3	28.0	18.1	6.1	9.4	5.9	5.5	4.6	5.3	6.4
1999	6.4	18.6	23.7	16.3	5.5	8.3	5.4	4.8	4.8	4.5	5.0
2000	5.7	16.7	22.7	14.0	4.9	7.5	4.8	4.5	3.3	4.5	5.7
2001	6.6	17.7	24.1	15.0	5.7	8.2	5.9	5.2	4.3	5.7	4.4

See *Note* at end of table.

Table 1-27. Unemployment Rates of Civilian Workers by Race, Hispanic Origin, Sex, and Age, 1948–2001—*Continued*

(Percent of labor force.)

Year, race, Hispanic origin, and sex	16 years and over	16 to 19 years			20 years and over						
		Total	16 to 17 years	18 to 19 years	Total	20 to 24 years	25 to 34 years	35 to 44 years	45 to 54 years	55 to 64 years	65 years and over
MEN											
1948	3.6	9.8	10.2	9.5	3.2	6.9	2.8	2.4	2.5	3.1	3.4
1949	5.9	14.3	13.7	14.6	5.4	10.4	5.2	4.3	4.3	5.4	5.1
1950	5.1	12.7	13.3	12.3	4.7	8.1	4.4	3.6	4.0	4.9	4.8
1951	2.8	8.1	9.4	7.0	2.5	3.9	2.3	2.0	2.4	2.8	3.5
1952	2.8	8.9	10.5	7.4	2.4	4.6	2.2	1.9	2.2	2.4	3.0
1953	2.8	7.9	8.8	7.2	2.5	5.0	2.2	2.0	2.3	2.8	2.4
1954	5.3	13.5	13.9	13.2	4.9	10.7	4.8	4.1	4.3	4.5	4.4
1955	4.2	11.6	12.5	10.8	3.8	7.7	3.3	3.1	3.2	4.3	4.0
1956	3.8	11.1	11.7	10.5	3.4	6.9	3.3	2.6	3.0	3.5	3.5
1957	4.1	12.4	12.4	12.3	3.6	7.8	3.3	2.8	3.3	3.5	3.4
1958	6.8	17.1	16.3	17.8	6.2	12.7	6.5	5.1	5.3	5.5	5.2
1959	5.2	15.3	15.8	14.9	4.7	8.7	4.7	3.7	4.1	4.5	4.8
1960	5.4	15.3	15.5	15.0	4.7	8.9	4.8	3.8	4.1	4.6	4.2
1961	6.4	17.1	18.3	16.3	5.7	10.8	5.7	4.6	4.9	5.7	5.5
1962	5.2	14.7	16.0	13.8	4.6	8.9	4.5	3.6	3.9	4.6	4.6
1963	5.2	17.2	18.8	15.9	4.5	8.8	4.5	3.5	3.6	4.3	4.5
1964	4.6	15.8	17.1	14.6	3.9	8.1	3.5	2.9	3.2	3.9	4.0
1965	4.0	14.1	16.1	12.4	3.2	6.4	2.9	2.5	2.5	3.3	3.5
1966	3.2	11.7	13.7	10.2	2.5	4.6	2.4	2.0	1.9	2.6	3.1
1967	3.1	12.3	14.5	10.5	2.3	4.7	2.1	1.7	2.0	2.3	2.8
1968	2.9	11.6	13.9	9.7	2.2	5.1	1.9	1.6	1.6	1.9	2.8
1969	2.8	11.4	13.8	9.3	2.1	5.1	1.9	1.5	1.5	1.8	2.2
1970	4.4	15.0	16.9	13.4	3.5	8.4	3.5	2.4	2.4	2.8	3.3
1971	5.3	16.6	18.7	15.0	4.4	10.3	4.4	3.1	3.0	3.3	3.4
1972	5.0	15.9	18.3	14.1	4.0	9.3	3.8	2.7	2.6	3.2	3.6
1973	4.2	13.9	17.0	11.4	3.3	7.3	3.4	2.0	2.1	2.4	3.0
1974	4.9	15.6	18.4	13.3	3.8	8.8	4.0	2.6	2.4	2.6	3.3
1975	7.9	20.1	21.6	19.0	6.8	14.3	6.9	4.9	4.8	4.3	5.4
1976	7.1	19.2	21.4	17.6	5.9	12.1	6.2	4.1	4.0	4.2	5.1
1977	6.3	17.3	19.5	15.6	5.2	10.8	5.7	3.5	3.2	3.6	5.2
1978	5.3	15.8	19.1	13.3	4.3	9.2	4.4	2.8	2.7	2.8	4.2
1979	5.1	15.9	17.9	14.3	4.2	8.7	4.3	2.9	2.7	2.7	3.4
1980	6.9	18.3	20.4	16.7	5.9	12.5	6.7	4.1	3.6	3.4	3.1
1981	7.4	20.1	22.0	18.8	6.3	13.2	6.9	4.5	4.0	3.6	2.9
1982	9.9	24.4	26.4	23.1	8.8	16.4	10.1	6.9	5.6	5.5	3.7
1983	9.9	23.3	25.2	22.2	8.9	15.9	10.1	7.1	6.3	6.1	3.9
1984	7.4	19.6	21.9	18.3	6.6	11.9	7.2	5.2	4.6	5.0	3.0
1985	7.0	19.5	21.9	17.9	6.2	11.4	6.6	4.9	4.6	4.3	3.1
1986	6.9	19.0	20.8	17.7	6.1	11.0	6.7	5.1	4.4	4.3	3.2
1987	6.2	17.8	20.2	16.0	5.4	9.9	5.9	4.4	4.2	3.7	2.6
1988	5.5	16.0	18.2	14.6	4.8	8.9	5.3	3.8	3.5	3.5	2.5
1989	5.2	15.9	18.6	14.2	4.5	8.8	4.8	3.7	3.2	3.5	2.4
1990	5.7	16.3	18.4	15.0	5.0	9.1	5.5	4.1	3.7	3.8	3.0
1991	7.2	19.8	21.8	18.5	6.4	11.6	7.0	5.5	4.8	4.6	3.3
1992	7.9	21.5	24.6	19.5	7.1	12.2	7.8	6.1	5.6	5.8	3.3
1993	7.2	20.4	22.9	18.8	6.4	11.3	7.0	5.6	5.1	5.2	3.2
1994	6.2	19.0	21.0	17.6	5.4	10.2	5.9	4.5	4.0	4.4	4.0
1995	5.6	18.4	21.1	16.5	4.8	9.2	5.1	4.2	3.5	3.6	4.3
1996	5.4	18.1	20.8	16.3	4.6	9.5	4.9	4.0	3.5	3.3	3.4
1997	4.9	16.9	19.1	15.4	4.2	8.9	4.3	3.6	3.1	3.1	3.0
1998	4.4	16.2	19.1	14.1	3.7	8.1	3.9	3.0	2.8	2.8	3.1
1999	4.1	14.7	17.0	13.1	3.5	7.7	3.6	2.8	2.6	2.7	3.0
2000	3.9	14.0	16.8	12.2	3.3	7.3	3.4	2.8	2.4	2.4	3.4
2001	4.8	15.9	18.8	14.1	4.2	8.9	4.3	3.6	3.2	3.4	3.0

See *Note* at end of table.

Table 1-27. Unemployment Rates of Civilian Workers by Race, Hispanic Origin, Sex, and Age, 1948–2001—*Continued*

(Percent of labor force.)

Year, race, Hispanic origin, and sex	16 years and over	16 to 19 years			20 years and over						
		Total	16 to 17 years	18 to 19 years	Total	20 to 24 years	25 to 34 years	35 to 44 years	45 to 54 years	55 to 64 years	65 years and over
WOMEN											
1948	4.1	8.3	10.0	7.4	3.6	4.8	4.3	3.0	3.0	3.1	2.3
1949	6.0	12.3	14.4	11.2	5.3	7.3	5.9	4.7	4.0	4.4	3.8
1950	5.7	11.4	14.2	9.8	5.1	6.9	5.7	4.4	4.5	4.5	3.4
1951	4.4	8.3	10.0	7.2	4.0	4.4	4.5	3.8	3.5	4.0	2.9
1952	3.6	8.0	9.1	7.3	3.2	4.5	3.6	3.0	2.5	2.5	2.2
1953	3.3	7.2	8.5	6.4	2.9	4.3	3.4	2.5	2.3	2.5	1.4
1954	6.0	11.4	12.7	7.7	5.5	7.3	6.6	5.3	4.6	4.6	3.0
1955	4.9	10.2	12.0	9.1	4.4	6.1	5.3	4.0	3.6	3.8	2.3
1956	4.8	11.2	13.2	9.9	4.2	6.3	4.8	3.9	3.6	3.6	2.3
1957	4.7	10.6	12.6	9.4	4.1	6.0	5.3	3.8	3.2	3.0	3.4
1958	6.8	14.3	16.6	12.9	6.1	8.9	7.3	6.2	4.9	4.5	3.7
1959	5.9	13.5	14.4	13.0	5.2	8.1	5.9	5.1	4.2	4.1	2.8
1960	5.9	13.9	15.5	12.9	5.1	8.3	6.3	4.8	4.2	3.4	2.9
1961	7.2	16.3	18.3	15.1	6.3	9.8	7.4	6.4	5.1	4.5	4.0
1962	6.2	14.6	16.7	13.5	5.4	9.1	6.5	5.2	4.1	3.5	4.2
1963	6.5	17.2	20.2	15.2	5.4	8.9	6.9	5.1	4.2	3.6	3.2
1964	6.2	16.6	18.8	15.2	5.2	8.6	6.3	5.0	3.9	3.3	3.3
1965	5.5	15.7	17.2	14.8	4.5	7.3	5.5	4.6	3.2	2.8	2.9
1966	4.8	14.1	16.6	12.6	3.8	6.3	4.5	3.6	2.9	2.3	2.8
1967	5.2	13.5	14.8	12.8	4.2	7.0	5.4	4.1	3.1	2.4	2.7
1968	4.8	14.0	15.9	12.9	3.8	6.7	4.7	3.4	2.4	2.2	2.7
1969	4.7	13.3	15.5	11.8	3.7	6.3	4.6	3.4	2.6	2.2	2.3
1970	5.9	15.6	17.4	14.4	4.8	7.9	5.7	4.4	3.5	2.7	3.1
1971	6.9	17.2	18.7	16.2	5.7	9.6	7.0	5.2	4.0	3.3	3.6
1972	6.6	16.7	18.8	15.2	5.4	9.4	6.2	4.9	3.6	3.3	3.5
1973	6.0	15.3	17.7	13.5	4.9	8.5	5.8	3.9	3.2	2.8	2.9
1974	6.7	16.6	18.2	15.4	5.5	9.5	6.2	4.6	3.7	3.2	3.6
1975	9.3	19.7	21.2	18.7	8.0	12.7	9.1	6.8	5.9	5.1	5.0
1976	8.6	18.7	20.8	17.4	7.4	11.9	8.4	6.1	5.2	4.9	5.0
1977	8.2	18.3	20.5	16.9	7.0	11.2	7.7	5.7	5.1	4.4	4.7
1978	7.2	17.1	19.5	15.3	6.0	10.1	6.7	5.0	4.0	3.2	3.8
1979	6.8	16.4	18.3	15.0	5.7	9.6	6.5	4.6	3.9	3.2	3.3
1980	7.4	17.2	19.6	15.6	6.4	10.4	7.2	5.3	4.5	3.3	3.1
1981	7.9	19.0	20.7	17.9	6.8	11.2	7.7	5.7	4.6	3.8	3.6
1982	9.4	21.9	23.2	21.0	8.3	13.2	9.3	7.0	5.9	5.2	3.2
1983	9.2	21.3	23.7	19.9	8.1	12.9	9.1	6.9	6.0	5.0	3.4
1984	7.6	18.0	20.4	16.6	6.8	10.9	7.4	5.6	5.2	4.3	3.8
1985	7.4	17.6	20.0	16.0	6.6	10.7	7.4	5.5	4.8	4.3	3.3
1986	7.1	17.6	19.6	16.3	6.2	10.3	7.2	5.0	4.5	3.8	2.8
1987	6.2	15.9	18.0	14.3	5.4	9.4	6.2	4.6	3.7	3.1	2.4
1988	5.6	14.4	16.6	12.9	4.9	8.5	5.6	4.1	3.4	2.7	2.9
1989	5.4	14.0	15.7	13.0	4.7	8.3	5.6	3.9	3.2	2.8	2.9
1990	5.5	14.7	17.4	13.1	4.9	8.5	5.6	4.2	3.4	2.8	3.1
1991	6.4	17.5	20.2	15.9	5.7	9.8	6.8	4.8	4.2	3.4	3.3
1992	7.0	18.6	21.5	16.6	6.3	10.3	7.4	5.5	4.6	4.2	4.5
1993	6.6	17.5	19.8	16.1	5.9	9.7	6.8	5.3	4.5	4.0	3.1
1994	6.0	16.2	18.7	14.3	5.4	9.2	6.2	4.7	4.0	3.9	4.0
1995	5.6	16.1	19.2	14.0	4.9	9.0	5.7	4.4	3.2	3.6	3.7
1996	5.4	15.2	15.4	14.0	4.8	9.0	5.5	4.2	3.2	3.4	4.0
1997	5.0	15.0	17.2	13.6	4.4	8.1	5.2	4.0	2.9	2.7	3.6
1998	4.6	12.9	15.1	11.5	4.1	7.8	4.8	3.8	2.7	2.4	3.3
1999	4.3	13.2	15.5	11.6	3.8	7.2	4.4	3.3	2.5	2.6	3.2
2000	4.1	12.1	14.0	10.8	3.6	7.0	4.0	3.3	2.5	2.5	2.8
2001	4.7	13.4	15.3	12.2	4.1	7.5	5.0	3.7	2.9	2.7	2.9

See *Note* at end of table.

Table 1-27. Unemployment Rates of Civilian Workers by Race, Hispanic Origin, Sex, and Age, 1948–2001—*Continued*

(Percent of labor force.)

Year, race, Hispanic origin, and sex	16 years and over	16 to 19 years			20 years and over						
		Total	16 to 17 years	18 to 19 years	Total	20 to 24 years	25 to 34 years	35 to 44 years	45 to 54 years	55 to 64 years	65 years and over
WHITE MEN											
1954	4.8	13.4	14.0	13.0	4.4	9.8	4.2	3.6	3.8	4.3	4.2
1955	3.7	11.3	12.2	10.4	3.3	7.0	2.7	2.6	2.9	3.9	3.8
1956	3.4	10.5	11.2	9.7	3.0	6.1	2.8	2.2	2.8	3.1	3.4
1957	3.6	11.5	11.9	11.1	3.2	7.0	2.7	2.5	3.0	3.4	3.2
1958	6.1	15.7	14.9	16.5	5.5	11.7	5.6	4.4	4.8	5.2	5.0
1959	4.6	14.0	15.0	13.0	4.1	7.5	3.8	3.2	3.7	4.2	4.5
1960	4.8	14.0	14.6	13.5	4.2	8.3	4.1	3.3	3.6	4.1	4.0
1961	5.7	15.7	16.5	15.2	5.1	10.1	4.9	4.0	4.4	5.3	5.2
1962	4.6	13.7	15.2	12.7	4.0	8.1	3.8	3.1	3.5	4.1	4.0
1963	4.7	15.9	17.8	14.2	3.9	7.8	3.9	2.9	3.3	4.0	4.1
1964	4.1	14.7	16.1	13.3	3.4	7.4	3.0	2.5	2.9	3.5	3.6
1965	3.6	12.9	14.7	11.3	2.9	5.9	2.6	2.3	2.3	3.1	3.4
1966	2.8	10.5	12.5	8.9	2.2	4.1	2.1	1.7	1.7	2.5	3.0
1967	2.7	10.7	12.7	9.0	2.1	4.2	1.9	1.6	1.8	2.2	2.7
1968	2.6	10.1	12.3	8.3	2.0	4.6	1.7	1.4	1.5	1.7	2.8
1969	2.5	10.0	12.5	7.9	1.9	4.6	1.7	1.4	1.4	1.7	2.2
1970	4.0	13.7	15.7	12.0	3.2	7.8	3.1	2.3	2.3	2.7	3.2
1971	4.9	15.1	17.1	13.5	4.0	9.4	4.0	2.9	2.9	3.2	3.4
1972	4.5	14.2	16.4	12.4	3.6	8.5	3.4	2.5	2.5	3.0	3.3
1973	3.8	12.3	15.2	10.0	3.0	6.6	3.0	1.8	2.0	2.4	2.9
1974	4.4	13.5	16.2	11.5	3.5	7.8	3.6	2.4	2.2	2.5	3.0
1975	7.2	18.3	19.7	17.2	6.2	13.1	6.3	4.5	4.4	4.1	5.0
1976	6.4	17.3	19.7	15.5	5.4	10.9	5.6	3.7	3.7	4.0	4.7
1977	5.5	15.0	17.6	13.0	4.7	9.3	5.0	3.1	3.0	3.3	4.9
1978	4.6	13.5	16.9	10.8	3.7	7.7	3.8	2.5	2.5	2.6	3.9
1979	4.5	13.9	16.1	12.2	3.6	7.5	3.7	2.5	2.5	2.5	3.2
1980	6.1	16.2	18.5	14.5	5.3	11.1	5.9	3.6	3.3	3.1	2.5
1981	6.5	17.9	19.9	16.4	5.6	11.6	6.1	4.0	3.6	3.4	2.4
1982	8.8	21.7	24.2	20.0	7.8	14.3	8.9	6.2	5.3	5.1	3.2
1983	8.8	20.2	22.6	18.7	7.9	13.8	9.0	6.4	5.7	5.6	3.2
1984	6.4	16.8	19.7	15.0	5.7	9.8	6.2	4.6	4.2	4.7	2.6
1985	6.1	16.5	19.2	14.7	5.4	9.7	5.7	4.3	4.1	4.0	2.7
1986	6.0	16.3	18.4	14.7	5.3	9.2	5.8	4.4	4.0	4.0	3.0
1987	5.4	15.5	17.9	13.7	4.8	8.4	5.2	3.9	3.9	3.4	2.5
1988	4.7	13.9	16.1	12.4	4.1	7.4	4.6	3.4	3.2	3.3	2.2
1989	4.5	13.7	16.4	12.0	3.9	7.5	4.1	3.2	2.9	3.1	2.1
1990	4.9	14.3	16.1	13.2	4.3	7.6	4.7	3.5	3.4	3.6	2.8
1991	6.5	17.6	19.7	16.3	5.8	10.2	6.4	5.0	4.4	4.6	3.1
1992	7.0	18.5	21.5	16.5	6.4	10.5	7.0	5.5	5.1	5.5	3.2
1993	6.3	17.7	20.2	16.0	5.7	9.6	6.2	5.0	4.7	4.7	2.9
1994	5.4	16.3	18.5	14.7	4.8	8.8	5.2	3.9	3.7	4.1	3.7
1995	4.9	15.6	18.2	13.8	4.3	7.9	4.5	3.8	3.2	3.4	4.0
1996	4.7	15.5	18.3	13.5	4.1	8.1	4.2	3.5	3.1	3.2	3.2
1997	4.2	14.3	16.3	12.9	3.6	7.3	3.7	3.2	2.8	3.0	2.7
1998	3.9	14.1	17.1	12.1	3.2	6.7	3.5	2.6	2.6	2.6	2.9
1999	3.6	12.6	15.1	10.8	3.0	6.5	3.1	2.4	2.4	2.6	2.9
2000	3.4	12.3	15.2	10.4	2.8	5.9	2.9	2.4	2.2	2.4	3.1
2001	4.3	13.8	17.0	11.9	3.7	7.7	3.8	3.1	2.9	3.2	2.9

See *Note* at end of table.

Table 1-27. Unemployment Rates of Civilian Workers by Race, Hispanic Origin, Sex, and Age, 1948–2001—*Continued*

(Percent of labor force.)

Year, race, Hispanic origin, and sex	16 years and over	16 to 19 years			20 years and over						
		Total	16 to 17 years	18 to 19 years	Total	20 to 24 years	25 to 34 years	35 to 44 years	45 to 54 years	55 to 64 years	65 years and over
WHITE WOMEN											
1954	5.5	10.4	12.0	9.4	5.1	6.4	5.7	4.9	4.4	4.5	2.8
1955	4.3	9.1	11.6	7.7	3.9	5.1	4.3	3.8	3.4	3.6	2.2
1956	4.2	9.7	12.1	8.3	3.7	5.1	4.0	3.5	3.3	3.5	2.3
1957	4.3	9.5	11.9	7.8	3.8	5.1	4.7	3.7	3.0	2.9	3.4
1958	6.2	12.7	15.6	11.0	5.6	7.3	6.6	5.6	4.9	4.3	3.5
1959	5.3	12.0	13.3	11.1	4.7	7.0	5.2	4.7	3.9	4.0	2.9
1960	5.3	12.7	14.5	11.5	4.6	7.2	5.7	4.2	4.0	3.3	2.8
1961	6.5	14.8	17.0	13.6	5.7	8.4	6.6	5.6	4.8	4.3	3.8
1962	5.5	12.8	15.6	11.3	4.7	7.7	5.4	4.5	3.7	3.5	4.0
1963	5.8	15.1	18.1	13.2	4.8	7.4	5.8	4.6	3.9	3.5	3.3
1964	5.5	14.9	17.1	13.2	4.6	7.1	5.2	4.5	3.6	3.5	3.4
1965	5.0	14.0	15.0	13.4	4.0	6.3	4.9	4.1	3.0	2.7	2.7
1966	4.3	12.1	14.5	10.7	3.3	5.3	3.7	3.3	2.7	2.2	2.7
1967	4.6	11.5	12.9	10.6	3.8	6.0	4.7	3.7	2.9	2.3	2.6
1968	4.3	12.1	13.9	11.0	3.4	5.9	3.9	3.1	2.3	2.1	2.8
1969	4.2	11.5	13.7	10.0	3.4	5.5	4.2	3.2	2.4	2.1	2.4
1970	5.4	13.4	15.3	11.9	4.4	6.9	5.3	4.3	3.4	2.6	3.3
1971	6.3	15.1	16.7	14.1	5.3	8.5	6.3	4.9	3.9	3.3	3.6
1972	5.9	14.2	17.0	12.3	4.9	8.2	5.5	4.4	3.5	3.3	3.7
1973	5.3	13.0	15.8	10.9	4.3	7.1	5.1	3.7	3.2	2.7	2.8
1974	6.1	14.5	16.4	13.0	5.1	8.2	5.8	4.3	3.6	3.2	3.9
1975	8.6	17.4	19.2	16.1	7.5	11.2	8.4	6.5	5.8	5.0	5.3
1976	7.9	16.4	18.2	15.1	6.8	10.4	7.6	5.8	5.0	4.8	5.3
1977	7.3	15.9	18.2	14.2	6.2	9.3	6.7	5.3	5.0	4.4	4.9
1978	6.2	14.4	17.1	12.4	5.2	8.3	5.8	4.5	3.8	3.0	3.7
1979	5.9	14.0	15.9	12.5	5.0	7.8	5.6	4.2	3.7	3.0	3.1
1980	6.5	14.8	17.3	13.1	5.6	8.5	6.3	4.9	4.3	3.1	3.0
1981	6.9	16.6	18.4	15.3	5.9	9.1	6.6	5.1	4.2	3.7	3.4
1982	8.3	19.0	21.2	17.6	7.3	10.9	8.0	6.4	5.5	5.0	3.1
1983	7.9	18.3	21.4	16.4	6.9	10.3	7.6	6.2	5.5	4.7	3.1
1984	6.5	15.2	17.8	13.6	5.8	8.8	6.1	5.0	4.8	4.0	3.7
1985	6.4	14.8	17.2	13.1	5.7	8.5	6.2	4.9	4.5	4.1	3.1
1986	6.1	14.9	16.7	13.6	5.4	8.1	6.1	4.5	4.3	3.7	2.6
1987	5.2	13.4	15.5	11.7	4.6	7.4	5.0	4.1	3.3	2.9	2.4
1988	4.7	12.3	14.4	10.8	4.1	6.7	4.5	3.7	3.1	2.5	2.6
1989	4.5	11.5	13.8	10.1	4.0	6.8	4.5	3.4	2.9	2.7	2.5
1990	4.7	12.6	15.5	10.9	4.1	6.8	4.6	3.7	3.2	2.7	2.8
1991	5.6	15.2	18.2	13.3	5.0	8.1	5.7	4.3	4.0	3.3	3.1
1992	6.1	15.8	18.9	13.7	5.5	8.3	6.2	4.9	4.3	4.0	4.5
1993	5.7	14.7	17.8	12.6	5.2	7.9	5.8	4.7	4.3	3.9	3.0
1994	5.2	13.8	16.6	11.8	4.6	7.4	5.1	4.2	3.7	3.7	3.9
1995	4.8	13.4	16.4	11.2	4.3	7.4	4.7	3.9	3.0	3.5	3.5
1996	4.7	12.9	14.4	11.7	4.1	7.4	4.6	3.8	3.1	3.1	3.8
1997	4.2	12.8	15.2	11.1	3.7	6.4	4.2	3.4	2.6	2.4	3.4
1998	3.9	10.9	12.4	9.8	3.4	6.3	3.9	3.3	2.5	2.2	3.0
1999	3.8	11.3	13.9	9.6	3.3	6.1	3.6	3.0	2.3	2.5	2.9
2000	3.6	10.4	12.5	9.0	3.1	5.8	3.5	2.9	2.3	2.4	2.4
2001	4.1	11.4	13.4	10.2	3.6	6.1	4.4	3.2	2.7	2.5	2.8

See *Note* at end of table.

Table 1-27. Unemployment Rates of Civilian Workers by Race, Hispanic Origin, Sex, and Age, 1948–2001—*Continued*

(Percent of labor force.)

Year, race, Hispanic origin, and sex	16 years and over	16 to 19 years			20 years and over						
		Total	16 to 17 years	18 to 19 years	Total	20 to 24 years	25 to 34 years	35 to 44 years	45 to 54 years	55 to 64 years	65 years and over
BLACK MEN											
1972	9.3	31.7	36.7	28.4	7.0	14.9	7.2	4.8	3.8	4.4	5.4
1973	8.0	27.8	35.7	23.0	6.0	13.2	6.2	3.9	3.2	3.2	3.3
1974	9.8	33.1	39.9	28.3	7.4	16.2	8.1	4.3	4.2	3.6	5.3
1975	14.8	38.1	41.9	35.9	12.5	24.7	12.7	8.7	9.3	6.3	8.7
1976	13.7	37.5	40.8	36.0	11.4	22.6	12.0	7.5	7.3	6.3	8.7
1977	13.3	39.2	41.0	38.2	10.7	23.0	11.8	6.2	4.9	6.0	7.8
1978	11.8	36.7	43.0	32.9	9.3	21.0	9.8	5.1	4.9	4.4	6.6
1979	11.4	34.2	37.9	32.2	9.3	18.7	9.6	6.3	5.2	5.1	6.4
1980	14.5	37.5	39.7	36.2	12.4	23.7	13.4	8.2	7.2	6.2	8.7
1981	15.7	40.7	43.2	39.2	13.5	26.4	14.4	9.3	7.8	6.1	7.5
1982	20.1	48.9	52.7	47.1	17.8	31.5	20.1	13.4	9.0	10.3	9.3
1983	20.3	48.8	52.2	47.3	18.1	31.4	19.4	13.5	11.4	11.0	11.8
1984	16.4	42.7	44.0	42.2	14.3	26.6	15.0	10.4	7.9	8.9	7.9
1985	15.3	41.0	42.9	40.0	13.2	23.5	13.8	9.6	9.7	7.9	8.9
1986	14.8	39.3	41.4	38.2	12.9	23.5	13.5	10.9	7.8	8.0	4.3
1987	12.7	34.4	39.0	31.6	11.1	20.3	12.2	8.7	6.7	6.6	4.3
1988	11.7	32.7	34.4	31.7	10.1	19.4	11.0	7.6	6.2	5.2	5.6
1989	11.5	31.9	34.4	30.3	10.0	17.9	10.5	8.4	6.2	6.2	7.4
1990	11.9	31.9	38.8	28.0	10.4	20.1	11.5	8.4	6.3	5.4	4.6
1991	13.0	36.3	39.0	34.8	11.5	22.4	11.9	9.5	8.6	5.0	6.1
1992	15.2	42.0	47.5	39.1	13.5	24.6	14.2	11.2	10.3	8.1	4.9
1993	13.8	40.1	42.7	38.6	12.1	23.0	12.3	10.5	8.1	9.0	5.8
1994	12.0	37.6	39.3	36.5	10.3	19.4	10.6	9.1	6.5	6.0	8.2
1995	10.6	37.1	39.7	35.4	8.8	17.6	9.3	7.6	5.5	4.4	7.6
1996	11.1	36.9	39.9	34.9	9.4	19.2	10.1	7.8	6.3	5.2	5.0
1997	10.2	36.5	39.5	34.4	8.5	19.8	8.7	6.7	5.6	4.2	5.5
1998	8.9	30.1	33.9	27.9	7.4	18.0	7.3	6.2	4.4	4.5	5.2
1999	8.2	30.9	33.3	29.4	6.7	16.2	6.9	5.2	4.3	3.9	5.0
2000	8.1	26.4	28.6	25.0	7.0	16.7	6.8	5.7	4.8	2.7	6.3
2001	9.3	30.5	31.3	30.0	8.0	17.4	8.3	6.9	5.6	4.7	4.1
BLACK WOMEN											
1972	11.8	40.5	42.0	40.1	9.0	17.9	10.5	7.6	4.6	3.7	2.6
1973	11.1	36.1	38.6	34.2	8.6	18.4	10.3	5.6	3.9	3.3	3.7
1974	11.3	37.4	40.2	36.0	8.8	19.0	9.0	6.6	4.4	3.6	1.9
1975	14.8	41.0	41.2	40.6	12.2	24.3	13.4	9.0	7.0	5.3	3.6
1976	14.3	41.6	48.4	37.6	11.7	22.8	13.6	8.5	5.9	5.4	2.4
1977	14.9	43.4	49.5	40.4	12.3	25.5	13.6	8.7	5.8	4.8	3.4
1978	13.8	40.8	45.0	38.7	11.2	22.7	11.9	7.8	5.6	5.2	4.7
1979	13.3	39.1	42.7	36.9	10.9	22.6	12.1	7.2	5.2	4.7	3.9
1980	14.0	39.8	42.9	38.2	11.9	23.5	13.2	8.2	6.4	4.5	4.9
1981	15.6	42.2	46.5	39.8	13.4	26.4	14.9	9.8	6.9	4.7	6.0
1982	17.6	47.1	44.2	48.6	15.4	29.6	17.8	10.7	8.5	6.1	4.5
1983	18.6	48.2	48.6	48.0	16.5	31.8	18.6	11.4	9.9	7.3	6.3
1984	15.4	42.6	47.5	40.2	13.5	25.6	15.4	9.4	8.6	5.9	4.9
1985	14.9	39.2	44.3	36.4	13.1	25.6	15.1	9.3	6.8	6.0	5.2
1986	14.2	39.2	44.6	36.1	12.4	24.7	14.6	8.5	6.4	5.0	4.9
1987	13.2	34.9	40.5	31.7	11.6	23.3	13.5	8.1	6.9	4.5	3.4
1988	11.7	32.0	35.9	29.6	10.4	19.8	12.7	7.4	5.6	4.3	5.4
1989	11.4	33.0	31.1	34.0	9.8	18.1	12.5	7.0	5.0	4.2	6.4
1990	10.9	29.9	34.1	27.6	9.7	19.6	11.9	7.2	4.3	3.6	5.9
1991	12.0	36.0	40.1	33.9	10.6	20.7	13.4	7.6	6.2	3.8	4.4
1992	13.2	37.2	41.7	34.8	11.8	23.1	14.1	9.8	6.4	4.2	5.0
1993	12.1	37.4	36.1	38.1	10.7	20.9	12.9	8.6	5.8	5.1	3.6
1994	11.0	32.6	32.9	32.5	9.8	19.6	11.7	8.0	4.9	4.9	4.4
1995	10.2	34.3	0.0	31.5	8.6	17.8	10.5	7.0	4.2	3.6	0.0
1996	10.0	30.3	32.8	28.6	8.7	18.4	11.0	6.9	3.8	3.8	5.6
1997	9.9	28.7	30.3	27.8	8.8	17.1	10.9	7.2	4.4	4.1	6.6
1998	9.0	25.3	33.2	20.9	7.9	15.7	9.5	6.7	4.3	3.4	6.1
1999	7.8	25.1	28.5	23.3	6.8	13.4	8.3	5.5	3.8	3.9	5.0
2000	7.2	23.0	25.7	21.5	6.3	13.5	6.8	5.5	3.5	3.3	6.0
2001	8.1	27.5	30.8	25.6	7.0	15.2	8.0	5.9	4.2	3.2	4.2

See *Note* at end of table.

Table 1-27. Unemployment Rates of Civilian Workers by Race, Hispanic Origin, Sex, and Age, 1948–2001—*Continued*

(Percent of labor force.)

Year, race, Hispanic origin, and sex	16 years and over	16 to 19 years			20 years and over						
		Total	16 to 17 years	18 to 19 years	Total	20 to 24 years	25 to 34 years	35 to 44 years	45 to 54 years	55 to 64 years	65 years and over
HISPANIC MEN											
1973	6.7	19.0	20.9	17.7	5.4	8.2	5.0	4.2	4.5	5.4	5.5
1974	7.3	19.0	22.0	17.1	6.0	9.9	5.5	5.0	4.3	5.4	5.3
1975	11.4	27.6	29.3	26.5	9.6	16.3	9.6	7.9	7.0	6.8	11.0
1976	10.8	23.3	28.7	19.7	9.4	16.0	8.1	7.0	7.4	8.7	12.1
1977	9.0	20.9	25.9	18.2	7.7	11.7	7.9	4.9	5.4	7.4	9.7
1978	7.7	19.7	27.5	13.9	6.4	9.4	6.6	4.8	4.8	4.4	7.8
1979	7.0	17.5	23.5	13.8	5.8	9.2	5.3	5.1	4.4	5.0	5.5
1980	9.7	21.9	26.2	19.3	8.3	12.2	8.3	7.1	6.0	5.9	7.6
1981	10.2	24.3	30.9	20.3	8.8	14.1	8.9	6.5	5.9	6.7	6.7
1982	13.6	31.3	40.2	26.8	12.1	18.2	12.4	9.9	7.5	10.0	7.4
1983	13.6	28.7	34.7	25.9	12.2	17.0	11.6	10.8	10.3	11.7	6.8
1984	10.5	25.2	31.5	22.2	9.3	12.5	9.2	7.6	7.2	10.2	8.2
1985	10.2	24.7	29.1	22.4	9.1	12.9	9.6	7.2	6.8	7.0	9.4
1986	10.5	24.5	28.5	22.4	9.5	13.0	9.5	8.5	7.0	8.0	9.6
1987	8.7	22.2	28.2	19.3	7.8	10.2	7.6	6.9	7.1	6.7	7.9
1988	8.1	22.7	29.5	19.5	7.0	9.2	7.0	5.9	6.1	6.7	6.9
1989	7.6	20.2	27.6	16.8	6.6	9.7	5.9	5.7	6.0	6.6	5.6
1990	8.0	19.5	24.0	17.4	7.0	8.4	6.9	6.5	6.8	6.5	5.8
1991	10.3	23.5	33.6	19.2	9.3	11.6	9.3	8.5	7.9	8.1	7.0
1992	11.7	28.2	36.6	24.0	10.5	13.7	10.1	9.8	8.9	10.2	7.7
1993	10.6	25.9	34.5	21.9	9.5	12.6	9.0	8.8	8.8	8.5	9.5
1994	9.4	26.3	33.3	22.5	8.3	10.8	8.4	6.6	8.1	7.4	10.5
1995	8.8	25.3	34.8	20.2	7.7	10.6	7.5	6.7	5.9	7.9	12.9
1996	7.9	22.5	31.5	18.4	6.9	10.3	6.6	6.3	5.1	6.7	8.3
1997	7.0	20.8	26.5	17.9	6.1	9.8	5.1	5.4	4.8	6.8	7.2
1998	6.4	20.6	29.0	16.4	5.4	8.9	5.2	4.5	4.2	5.3	5.0
1999	5.6	17.8	23.4	15.3	4.7	7.8	4.1	3.8	4.5	4.6	5.0
2000	4.9	15.7	22.5	12.8	4.2	6.5	3.7	3.8	3.1	4.1	6.3
2001	6.0	17.2	26.1	13.7	5.1	8.1	4.6	4.5	3.8	6.4	4.7
HISPANIC WOMEN											
1973	9.0	20.7	26.8	16.7	7.3	9.0	6.9	8.3	5.1	5.6	0.0
1974	9.4	20.8	25.3	17.4	7.7	9.7	7.7	7.5	5.3	7.5	9.5
1975	13.5	27.9	31.0	26.4	11.5	17.2	10.5	9.9	10.0	9.3	6.5
1976	12.7	22.2	30.3	18.7	11.4	15.8	10.8	10.0	9.8	9.0	14.7
1977	11.9	24.4	28.5	21.9	10.1	12.1	9.8	8.2	10.6	11.0	7.1
1978	11.3	21.8	29.9	16.6	9.8	13.0	10.3	9.2	7.4	7.2	5.7
1979	10.3	21.2	30.0	15.8	8.9	12.1	8.9	7.7	7.1	7.9	6.0
1980	10.7	23.4	29.7	19.8	9.2	12.0	10.6	8.6	5.3	5.8	1.1
1981	10.8	23.4	23.5	23.4	9.5	13.5	8.7	8.9	7.2	8.4	2.5
1982	14.1	28.2	35.1	25.0	12.5	16.8	12.2	11.9	9.9	10.4	4.8
1983	13.8	28.0	32.5	25.7	12.4	16.2	12.5	12.2	9.7	9.6	3.5
1984	11.1	22.8	26.1	21.0	9.9	12.2	10.3	9.1	7.9	8.8	3.4
1985	11.0	23.8	26.2	22.6	9.9	12.1	10.6	8.5	8.1	9.2	5.5
1986	10.8	25.1	27.6	23.6	9.6	12.9	9.8	8.2	8.9	6.2	11.2
1987	8.9	22.4	27.1	19.9	7.7	11.4	7.8	6.5	6.7	5.0	3.7
1988	8.3	21.0	24.5	18.9	7.1	10.7	7.2	6.2	5.9	4.6	3.0
1989	8.8	18.2	24.7	14.9	8.0	12.2	8.6	6.3	6.7	4.5	4.7
1990	8.4	19.4	25.4	16.2	7.5	10.4	8.0	6.7	6.0	4.3	6.4
1991	9.6	21.9	29.6	17.9	8.6	11.7	9.1	7.6	8.1	4.1	6.9
1992	11.4	26.4	34.5	22.4	10.2	12.4	11.0	9.7	8.5	6.2	8.7
1993	11.0	26.3	36.0	21.7	9.9	14.0	9.9	9.5	8.3	7.2	2.2
1994	10.7	22.2	29.7	18.1	9.8	13.5	10.1	9.2	8.0	7.1	3.6
1995	10.0	22.6	30.7	18.7	8.9	13.0	9.5	7.9	7.0	6.8	6.4
1996	10.2	25.1	28.2	23.3	9.2	14.1	8.5	8.7	7.2	8.1	8.0
1997	8.9	22.7	29.2	19.1	7.9	11.0	8.2	7.7	5.5	6.1	6.0
1998	8.2	22.1	26.4	20.2	7.1	10.1	7.2	6.9	5.1	5.4	8.8
1999	7.6	19.8	24.0	17.7	6.6	9.1	7.3	6.3	5.1	4.3	4.8
2000	6.7	18.1	22.9	15.7	5.9	8.9	6.4	5.4	3.6	5.1	4.8
2001	7.4	18.3	21.6	16.9	6.6	8.3	7.7	6.3	4.8	4.8	3.9

Note: Detail for the above race and Hispanic-origin groups will not sum to totals because data for the Other races group are not presented and Hispanics are included in both the White and Black population groups. See "Notes and Definitions" for information on historical comparability.

Table 1-28. Unemployed Persons and Unemployment Rates by Occupation, 1987–2001

(Thousands of persons, percent of civilian labor force.)

Occupation	1987	1988	1989	1990	1991	1992	1993	1994	1995	1996	1997	1998	1999	2000	2001
UNEMPLOYED PERSONS, TOTAL, 16 YEARS AND OVER [1]	7 425	6 701	6 528	7 047	8 628	9 613	8 940	7 996	7 404	7 236	6 739	6 210	5 880	5 655	6 742
Managerial and professional specialty	650	577	614	666	889	1 009	984	907	880	869	761	722	770	725	973
Executive, administrative, and managerial	350	311	348	350	494	576	527	454	420	431	359	343	376	356	491
Professional specialty	300	266	265	316	395	433	457	453	460	438	403	380	394	369	482
Technical, sales, and administrative support	1 595	1 479	1 470	1 641	1 977	2 308	2 111	1 962	1 744	1 766	1 646	1 550	1 477	1 464	1 699
Technicians and related support	104	95	90	116	133	176	165	127	113	114	104	96	101	97	133
Sales occupations	691	652	643	720	857	985	927	907	795	843	814	745	714	684	794
Administrative support, including clerical	799	732	738	804	988	1 147	1 020	928	836	810	728	710	662	684	772
Service occupations	1 259	1 136	1 088	1 139	1 330	1 461	1 401	1 471	1 378	1 334	1 255	1 216	1 081	1 023	1 150
Private household	55	54	55	47	56	66	65	91	99	79	73	74	67	58	53
Protective service	94	81	74	74	101	108	108	96	86	84	89	85	72	65	74
Service, except private household and protective	1 110	1 000	960	1 018	1 172	1 287	1 228	1 285	1 193	1 170	1 093	1 057	943	900	1 023
Precision production, craft, and repair	875	773	762	861	1 149	1 294	1 155	910	860	795	719	630	607	554	711
Mechanics and repairers	191	166	161	175	246	281	258	201	182	174	167	149	136	129	153
Construction trades	470	405	428	483	655	730	631	518	501	456	406	338	330	312	391
Other precision production, craft, and repair	214	202	173	202	248	284	266	191	177	165	145	143	142	113	167
Operators, fabricators, and laborers	1 820	1 620	1 578	1 714	2 062	2 151	1 926	1 761	1 618	1 570	1 490	1 304	1 207	1 228	1 481
Machine operators, assemblers, and inspectors	777	673	678	727	903	922	816	672	629	654	551	494	440	455	573
Transportation and material moving occupations	366	317	306	329	398	428	404	364	329	292	306	279	235	253	298
Handlers, equipment cleaners, helpers, and laborers	677	630	594	657	761	802	706	725	660	625	633	531	532	520	610
Construction laborers	189	192	152	177	204	200	172	172	179	158	167	136	140	133	155
Other handlers, equipment cleaners, helpers, and laborers	488	439	442	481	556	601	534	552	481	467	467	395	392	387	455
Farming, forestry, and fishing	268	260	234	237	299	320	310	333	311	293	267	244	249	215	259
UNEMPLOYED PERSONS, TOTAL, 16 YEARS AND OVER [1]	6.2	5.5	5.3	5.6	6.8	7.5	6.9	6.1	5.6	5.4	4.9	4.5	4.2	4.0	4.8
Managerial and professional specialty	2.3	1.9	2.0	2.1	2.8	3.1	3.0	2.6	2.4	2.3	2.0	1.8	1.9	1.7	2.3
Executive, administrative, and managerial	2.6	2.1	2.3	2.3	3.2	3.8	3.3	2.7	2.4	2.4	1.9	1.8	1.9	1.8	2.4
Professional specialty	2.0	1.7	1.7	2.0	2.4	2.6	2.6	2.5	2.5	2.3	2.1	1.9	1.9	1.7	2.2
Technical, sales, and administrative support	4.3	4.0	3.9	4.3	5.2	5.9	5.4	5.0	4.5	4.5	4.1	3.9	3.7	3.6	4.2
Technicians and related support	3.0	2.6	2.4	2.9	3.4	4.0	3.9	3.2	2.8	2.8	2.4	2.2	2.3	2.2	2.9
Sales occupations	4.9	4.5	4.4	4.8	5.7	6.6	6.1	5.8	5.0	5.2	4.9	4.5	4.2	4.0	4.7
Administrative support, including clerical	4.2	3.9	3.9	4.1	5.1	5.8	5.2	4.7	4.3	4.2	3.8	3.7	3.5	3.5	4.0
Service occupations	7.7	6.9	6.5	6.6	7.6	8.2	7.7	8.0	7.5	7.2	6.7	6.4	5.7	5.3	5.9
Private household	5.6	5.7	5.9	5.6	6.5	6.9	6.5	10.0	10.7	9.0	8.4	8.0	7.4	6.9	6.9
Protective service	4.7	4.0	3.6	3.6	4.6	4.9	4.7	4.1	3.7	3.7	3.7	3.4	2.9	2.6	2.9
Service, except private household and protective	8.3	7.4	7.0	7.1	8.1	8.8	8.2	8.5	7.9	7.6	7.0	6.8	6.0	5.6	6.3
Precision production, craft, and repair	6.1	5.4	5.2	5.9	8.0	8.9	7.9	6.3	6.0	5.5	4.8	4.2	4.0	3.6	4.6
Mechanics and repairers	4.1	3.6	3.4	3.8	5.2	5.9	5.5	4.3	4.0	3.7	3.5	3.0	2.7	2.6	3.1
Construction trades	8.6	7.4	7.7	8.5	11.9	13.1	11.1	9.4	9.0	8.2	7.0	5.7	5.4	4.9	5.9
Other precision production, craft, and repair	5.0	4.7	4.0	4.7	5.9	6.7	6.3	4.5	4.2	4.0	3.4	3.4	3.5	2.8	4.2
Operators, fabricators, and laborers	9.4	8.3	8.0	8.7	10.6	11.1	10.0	9.0	8.2	7.9	7.5	6.7	6.2	6.3	7.7
Machine operators, assemblers, and inspectors	8.9	7.7	7.6	8.1	10.4	10.7	9.7	8.0	7.4	7.7	6.5	6.0	5.6	5.9	7.8
Transportation and material moving occupations	7.2	6.2	5.9	6.3	7.5	8.0	7.4	6.6	6.0	5.2	5.4	4.9	4.1	4.4	5.0
Handlers, equipment cleaners, helpers, and laborers	12.4	11.5	10.8	11.6	13.9	14.6	12.9	12.7	11.7	11.1	11.1	9.4	9.2	8.7	10.3
Construction laborers	19.8	19.4	16.8	18.1	22.1	22.9	20.3	18.9	18.7	16.3	17.1	14.2	13.2	11.6	13.1
Other handlers, equipment cleaners, helpers, and laborers	10.8	9.7	9.7	10.3	12.2	13.0	11.6	11.5	10.3	10.0	9.9	8.4	8.3	8.0	9.6
Farming, forestry, and fishing	7.1	7.0	6.4	6.4	7.9	8.3	8.4	8.4	7.9	7.6	7.1	6.5	6.8	6.0	7.4

Note: See "Notes and Definitions" for information on historical comparability.

1. Includes a small number of persons whose last job was in the Armed Forces.

Table 1-29. Unemployed Persons by Industry and Class of Worker, 1948–2001

(Thousands of persons.)

Year			Experienced wage and salary workers									
			Wage and salary workers in private nonagricultural industries, except private households									
	Total [1]	Agriculture	Total	Mining	Construction	Manufacturing			Transportation and public utilities	Wholesale and retail trade	Finance, insurance, and real estate	Services, except private households
						Total	Durable goods	Nondurable goods				
1948	2 046	96	1 756	28	232	678	339	339	149	415	30	224
1949	3 310	132	2 871	73	380	1 242	652	590	252	578	36	310
1950	2 990	162	2 512	61	348	981	466	515	189	580	40	313
1951	1 857	71	1 578	36	218	637	271	366	95	373	27	192
1952	1 707	73	1 453	35	218	573	266	307	95	326	33	173
1953	1 671	81	1 419	45	227	536	253	283	90	315	34	172
1954	3 230	133	2 827	106	386	1 232	720	512	231	549	46	277
1955	2 568	124	2 188	69	337	821	436	385	163	464	49	285
1956	2 443	126	2 081	50	313	832	448	384	127	459	39	261
1957	2 542	118	2 181	41	349	901	502	399	139	461	42	248
1958	4 096	180	3 584	72	523	1 605	1 036	569	246	705	68	365
1959	3 252	158	2 782	59	466	1 055	611	444	178	617	63	344
1960	3 337	159	2 847	59	463	1 103	626	477	193	637	63	329
1961	4 061	173	3 516	67	544	1 376	835	541	218	783	91	437
1962	3 342	127	2 889	46	466	1 045	575	470	166	678	82	406
1963	3 415	158	2 916	41	456	1 061	573	488	170	689	75	424
1964	3 134	158	2 643	37	390	941	498	443	143	649	75	408
1965	2 732	114	2 320	29	364	775	382	393	118	585	70	379
1966	2 331	89	1 957	20	286	651	325	326	88	528	62	322
1967	2 489	96	2 098	19	257	775	418	357	100	521	80	346
1968	2 356	86	1 971	16	247	691	368	323	87	513	74	343
1969	2 372	76	1 997	15	225	705	382	323	99	530	73	350
1970	3 526	94	3 070	16	380	1 195	719	475	150	732	102	495
1971	4 300	100	3 731	23	428	1 401	841	559	178	948	128	625
1972	4 122	103	3 537	19	450	1 154	653	501	168	994	138	613
1973	3 646	95	3 091	19	407	939	500	439	143	896	117	570
1974	4 391	110	3 769	20	486	1 257	703	554	162	1 058	139	648
1975	6 970	151	6 110	31	807	2 333	1 431	902	278	1 493	217	952
1976	6 387	180	5 421	37	694	1 700	987	714	246	1 527	200	1 017
1977	5 915	171	4 987	33	593	1 474	805	669	242	1 473	186	986
1978	5 220	142	4 359	37	530	1 244	661	583	201	1 295	161	891
1979	5 217	148	4 391	45	541	1 306	702	603	206	1 250	165	879
1980	6 634	175	5 710	65	740	1 991	1 254	736	280	1 443	188	1 004
1981	7 129	201	6 089	70	809	1 915	1 139	777	304	1 609	199	1 182
1982	9 275	260	8 128	154	1 031	2 771	1 788	983	397	2 066	276	1 433
1983	9 276	300	7 985	182	1 005	2 454	1 562	892	424	2 109	272	1 539
1984	7 236	243	6 145	103	817	1 654	955	699	330	1 710	232	1 299
1985	7 074	233	6 088	96	778	1 694	1 004	690	316	1 679	228	1 297
1986	7 019	222	6 097	134	809	1 559	910	650	313	1 706	239	1 336
1987	6 313	191	5 434	87	724	1 305	749	556	277	1 582	225	1 234
1988	5 718	192	4 943	62	669	1 161	653	508	246	1 433	221	1 151
1989	5 616	176	4 866	42	634	1 140	634	506	251	1 412	230	1 157
1990	6 104	190	5 354	36	718	1 289	762	527	252	1 551	221	1 287
1991	7 512	231	6 593	60	946	1 572	950	621	353	1 851	290	1 522
1992	8 361	251	7 344	56	1 020	1 663	979	685	373	2 097	332	1 802
1993	7 708	224	6 751	52	874	1 487	842	645	352	1 964	303	1 719
1994	7 092	218	6 113	37	724	1 154	630	524	340	1 899	271	1 688
1995	6 533	225	5 636	34	737	1 030	534	496	314	1 682	240	1 599
1996	6 389	213	5 532	30	666	1 013	563	450	291	1 679	201	1 653
1997	5 900	190	5 131	24	623	885	445	440	260	1 645	229	1 465
1998	5 477	180	4 781	20	532	816	426	390	254	1 493	197	1 470
1999	5 202	189	4 511	33	520	739	434	305	235	1 422	191	1 371
2000	5 022	165	4 610	21	499	733	413	320	243	1 381	185	1 314
2001	6 091	202	5 666	27	598	1 024	632	391	329	1 554	226	1 650

Note: See "Notes and Definitions" for information on historical comparability.

1. Includes private household members, not shown separately.

Table 1-30. Unemployment Rates by Industry and Class of Worker, 1948–2001

(Percent of civilian labor force.)

Year	Total [1]	Agriculture	Experienced wage and salary workers									
			Wage and salary workers in private nonagricultural industries, except private households									
			Total	Mining	Construction	Manufacturing			Transportation and public utilities	Wholesale and retail trade	Finance, insurance, and real estate	Services, except private households
						Total	Durable goods	Nondurable goods				
1948	4.3	5.5	4.5	3.1	8.7	4.2	4.0	4.4	3.5	4.7	1.8	5.0
1949	6.8	7.1	7.3	8.9	14.0	8.0	8.1	7.8	5.9	6.2	2.1	6.5
1950	6.0	9.0	6.2	6.9	12.2	6.2	5.7	6.7	4.6	6.0	2.2	6.2
1951	3.7	4.4	3.9	4.0	7.2	3.9	3.1	4.7	2.3	3.9	1.5	4.0
1952	3.4	4.8	3.6	3.8	6.7	3.5	3.0	4.1	2.3	3.5	1.8	3.4
1953	3.2	5.6	3.4	4.6	7.2	3.1	2.6	3.8	2.2	3.4	1.8	3.3
1954	6.2	9.0	6.7	14.4	12.9	7.1	7.3	6.9	5.6	5.7	2.3	5.2
1955	4.8	7.2	5.1	9.1	10.9	4.7	4.4	5.2	4.0	4.7	2.4	5.1
1956	4.4	7.4	4.7	6.8	10.0	4.7	4.4	5.2	3.0	4.5	1.8	4.4
1957	4.6	6.9	4.9	5.9	10.9	5.1	4.9	5.3	3.3	4.5	1.8	4.0
1958	7.3	10.3	8.0	11.0	15.3	9.3	10.6	7.7	6.1	6.8	2.9	5.6
1959	5.7	9.1	6.2	9.7	13.4	6.1	6.2	6.0	4.4	5.8	2.5	5.1
1960	5.7	8.3	6.2	9.7	13.5	6.2	6.4	6.1	4.6	5.9	2.4	4.8
1961	6.8	9.6	7.5	11.1	15.7	7.8	8.5	6.8	5.3	7.3	3.3	6.0
1962	5.6	7.5	6.2	7.8	13.5	5.8	5.7	6.0	4.1	6.3	3.0	5.4
1963	5.6	9.2	6.1	7.2	13.3	5.7	5.5	6.0	4.2	6.2	2.7	5.6
1964	5.0	9.7	5.4	6.7	11.2	5.0	4.7	5.4	3.5	5.7	2.6	5.2
1965	4.3	7.6	4.6	5.4	10.1	4.0	3.5	4.7	2.9	5.0	2.3	4.6
1966	3.5	6.6	3.8	3.7	8.0	3.2	2.8	3.8	2.1	4.4	2.1	3.8
1967	3.6	6.9	3.9	3.4	7.4	3.7	3.4	4.1	2.4	4.2	2.5	3.9
1968	3.4	6.3	3.6	3.1	6.9	3.3	3.0	3.7	2.0	4.0	2.2	3.7
1969	3.3	6.1	3.5	2.9	6.0	3.3	3.0	3.7	2.2	4.1	2.1	3.5
1970	4.8	7.5	5.3	3.1	9.7	5.6	5.7	5.4	3.2	5.3	2.8	4.7
1971	5.7	7.9	6.3	4.0	10.4	6.8	7.0	6.5	3.8	6.4	3.3	5.8
1972	5.3	7.7	5.8	3.2	10.3	5.6	5.5	5.8	3.5	6.4	3.4	5.4
1973	4.5	7.0	4.9	2.9	8.9	4.4	3.9	5.0	3.0	5.7	2.7	4.8
1974	5.3	7.5	5.8	3.0	10.7	5.8	5.4	6.3	3.3	6.5	3.1	5.2
1975	8.2	10.4	9.2	4.1	18.0	10.9	11.3	10.4	5.6	8.7	4.9	7.2
1976	7.3	11.8	8.0	4.6	15.5	7.9	7.7	8.2	5.0	8.6	4.3	7.3
1977	6.6	11.2	7.1	3.8	12.7	6.7	6.2	7.4	4.7	8.0	3.8	6.8
1978	5.6	8.9	6.0	4.2	10.6	5.5	5.0	6.3	3.7	6.9	3.1	5.8
1979	5.5	9.3	5.8	4.9	10.3	5.6	5.0	6.5	3.7	6.5	3.0	5.5
1980	6.9	11.0	7.4	6.4	14.1	8.5	8.9	7.9	4.9	7.4	3.4	6.0
1981	7.3	12.1	7.7	6.0	15.6	8.3	8.2	8.4	5.2	8.1	3.5	6.7
1982	9.3	14.7	10.2	13.4	20.0	12.3	13.3	10.8	6.8	10.0	4.7	7.7
1983	9.2	16.0	9.9	17.0	18.4	11.2	12.1	10.0	7.4	10.0	4.5	7.9
1984	7.1	13.5	7.4	10.0	14.3	7.5	7.2	7.8	5.5	8.0	3.7	6.5
1985	6.8	13.2	7.2	9.5	13.1	7.7	7.6	7.8	5.1	7.6	3.5	6.2
1986	6.6	12.5	7.0	13.5	13.1	7.1	6.9	7.4	5.1	7.6	3.5	6.1
1987	5.8	10.5	6.2	10.0	11.6	6.0	5.8	6.3	4.5	6.9	3.1	5.4
1988	5.2	10.6	5.5	7.9	10.6	5.3	5.0	5.7	3.9	6.2	3.0	4.8
1989	5.0	9.6	5.3	5.8	10.0	5.1	4.8	5.5	3.9	6.0	3.1	4.7
1990	5.3	9.8	5.7	4.8	11.1	5.8	5.8	5.8	3.9	6.4	3.0	5.0
1991	6.6	11.8	7.1	7.8	15.5	7.3	7.5	6.9	5.3	7.6	4.0	5.8
1992	7.2	12.5	7.8	8.0	16.8	7.8	8.0	7.6	5.5	8.4	4.6	6.5
1993	6.6	11.7	7.1	7.4	14.4	7.2	7.1	7.4	5.1	7.8	4.1	6.1
1994	5.9	11.3	6.3	5.4	11.8	5.6	5.2	6.0	4.8	7.4	3.6	5.7
1995	5.4	11.1	5.7	5.2	11.5	4.9	4.4	5.7	4.5	6.5	3.3	5.2
1996	5.2	10.2	5.5	5.1	10.1	4.8	4.5	5.2	4.1	6.4	2.7	5.2
1997	4.7	9.1	5.0	3.8	9.0	4.2	3.5	5.1	3.5	6.2	3.0	4.5
1998	4.3	8.3	4.6	3.2	7.5	3.9	3.4	4.7	3.4	5.5	2.5	4.4
1999	4.0	8.9	4.3	5.7	7.0	3.6	3.5	3.9	3.0	5.2	2.3	4.0
2000	3.9	7.5	4.2	3.9	6.4	3.6	3.4	4.0	3.1	5.0	2.3	3.7
2001	4.6	9.7	5.1	4.7	7.3	5.2	5.3	5.1	4.1	5.6	2.8	4.5

Note: See "Notes and Definitions" for information on historical comparability.

1. Includes private household members, not shown separately.

Table 1-31. Unemployed Persons by Duration of Unemployment, 1948–2001

(Thousands of persons.)

Year	Total	Less than 5 weeks	5 to 14 weeks	15 weeks and over			Average duration, in weeks	Median duration, in weeks
				Total	15 to 26 weeks	27 weeks and over		
1948	2 276	1 300	669	309	193	116	8.6	...
1949	3 637	1 756	1 194	684	428	256	10.0	...
1950	3 288	1 450	1 055	782	425	357	12.1	...
1951	2 055	1 177	574	303	166	137	9.7	...
1952	1 883	1 135	516	232	148	84	8.4	...
1953	1 834	1 142	482	210	132	78	8.0	...
1954	3 532	1 605	1 116	812	495	317	11.8	...
1955	2 852	1 335	815	702	366	336	13.0	...
1956	2 750	1 412	805	533	301	232	11.3	...
1957	2 859	1 408	891	560	321	239	10.5	...
1958	4 602	1 753	1 396	1 452	785	667	13.9	...
1959	3 740	1 585	1 114	1 040	469	571	14.4	...
1960	3 852	1 719	1 176	957	503	454	12.8	...
1961	4 714	1 806	1 376	1 532	728	804	15.6	...
1962	3 911	1 663	1 134	1 119	534	585	14.7	...
1963	4 070	1 751	1 231	1 088	535	553	14.0	...
1964	3 786	1 697	1 117	973	491	482	13.3	...
1965	3 366	1 628	983	755	404	351	11.8	...
1966	2 875	1 573	779	526	287	239	10.4	...
1967	2 975	1 634	893	448	271	177	8.7	2.3
1968	2 817	1 594	810	412	256	156	8.4	4.5
1969	2 832	1 629	827	375	242	133	7.8	4.4
1970	4 093	2 139	1 290	663	428	235	8.6	4.9
1971	5 016	2 245	1 585	1 187	668	519	11.3	6.3
1972	4 882	2 242	1 472	1 167	601	566	12.0	6.2
1973	4 365	2 224	1 314	826	483	343	10.0	5.2
1974	5 156	2 604	1 597	955	574	381	9.8	5.2
1975	7 929	2 940	2 484	2 505	1 303	1 203	14.2	8.4
1976	7 406	2 844	2 196	2 366	1 018	1 348	15.8	8.2
1977	6 991	2 919	2 132	1 942	913	1 028	14.3	7.0
1978	6 202	2 865	1 923	1 414	766	648	11.9	5.9
1979	6 137	2 950	1 946	1 241	706	535	10.8	5.4
1980	7 637	3 295	2 470	1 871	1 052	820	11.9	6.5
1981	8 273	3 449	2 539	2 285	1 122	1 162	13.7	6.9
1982	10 678	3 883	3 311	3 485	1 708	1 776	15.6	8.7
1983	10 717	3 570	2 937	4 210	1 652	2 559	20.0	10.1
1984	8 539	3 350	2 451	2 737	1 104	1 634	18.2	7.9
1985	8 312	3 498	2 509	2 305	1 025	1 280	15.6	6.8
1986	8 237	3 448	2 557	2 232	1 045	1 187	15.0	6.9
1987	7 425	3 246	2 196	1 983	943	1 040	14.5	6.5
1988	6 701	3 084	2 007	1 610	801	809	13.5	5.9
1989	6 528	3 174	1 978	1 375	730	646	11.9	4.8
1990	7 047	3 265	2 257	1 525	822	703	12.0	5.3
1991	8 628	3 480	2 791	2 357	1 246	1 111	13.7	6.8
1992	9 613	3 376	2 830	3 408	1 453	1 954	17.7	8.7
1993	8 940	3 262	2 584	3 094	1 297	1 798	18.0	8.3
1994	7 996	2 728	2 408	2 860	1 237	1 623	18.8	9.2
1995	7 404	2 700	2 342	2 363	1 085	1 278	16.6	8.3
1996	7 236	2 633	2 287	2 316	1 053	1 262	16.7	8.3
1997	6 739	2 538	2 138	2 062	995	1 067	15.8	8.0
1998	6 210	2 622	1 950	1 637	763	875	14.5	6.7
1999	5 880	2 568	1 832	1 480	755	725	13.4	6.4
2000	5 655	2 543	1 803	1 309	665	644	12.6	5.9
2001	6 742	2 833	2 163	1 746	949	797	13.2	6.8

Note: See "Notes and Definitions" for information on historical comparability.

Table 1-32. Long-Term Unemployment by Industry and Occupation, 1987–2001

(Thousands of persons.)

Industry and occupation	1987	1988	1989	1990	1991	1992	1993	1994	1995	1996	1997	1998	1999	2000	2001
UNEMPLOYED 15 WEEKS AND OVER															
Total	1 983	1 610	1 375	1 525	2 357	3 408	3 094	2 860	2363	2 316	2 062	1 637	1 480	1 309	1 746
WAGE AND SALARY WORKERS BY INDUSTRY [1]															
Agriculture	42	39	32	31	47	57	56	72	58	65	50	44	41	35	49
Mining	42	28	15	11	23	25	27	21	13	11	9	3	...	...	...
Construction	209	169	153	162	285	402	330	238	233	208	171	134	127	102	132
Manufacturing	449	361	299	353	525	725	655	482	371	374	309	230	221	203	313
Durable goods	273	228	177	221	334	457	394	283	198	207	155	115	137	102	189
Nondurable goods	176	133	123	132	192	268	262	199	172	168	154	115	84	101	124
Transportation and public utilities	99	86	74	75	130	190	171	171	135	118	103	80	74	73	95
Wholesale and retail trade	387	295	268	303	448	699	630	628	493	486	456	359	318	287	379
Finance and services	457	405	350	403	615	921	840	825	711	729	645	533	460	419	...
Finance, insurance, and real estate	...	...	...	...	...	...	...	...	...	...	...	...	...	55	68
Services	...	...	...	...	...	...	...	...	...	...	...	...	...	364	491
Public administration	79	55	42	36	66	71	85	79	57	63	50	44	45	39	42
EXPERIENCED WORKERS BY OCCUPATION															
Managerial and professional specialty	202	164	156	184	310	473	429	371	320	316	258	211	214	191	276
Technical, sales, and administrative support	403	338	281	352	543	858	773	699	553	558	487	393	347	337	429
Service occupations	293	232	209	215	308	427	404	470	407	396	376	320	271	225	278
Precision production, craft, and repair	266	215	193	211	363	533	460	335	287	262	222	161	147	123	163
Operators, fabricators, and laborers	1 040	462	376	413	1 111	1 954	1 798	1 623	1 278	1 262	1 067	341	322	290	409
Farming, forestry, and fishing	65	63	48	43	62	75	82	113	81	91	75	63	57	48	70
UNEMPLOYED 27 WEEKS AND OVER															
Total	1,040	809	646	703	1,111	1,954	1,798	1,623	1,278	1,262	1,067	875	725	644	797
WAGE AND SALARY WORKERS BY INDUSTRY [1]															
Agriculture	19	16	13	13	17	26	26	36	27	29	25	20	17	15	17
Mining	28	17	8	5	13	19	16	14	9	7	4	2	...	...	...
Construction	101	78	66	69	125	219	188	125	125	105	78	66	55	43	60
Manufacturing	249	194	146	168	255	455	392	282	203	207	167	113	108	109	132
Durable goods	159	128	85	102	160	294	237	170	108	116	84	58	67	49	76
Nondurable goods	90	66	62	65	95	162	155	113	95	90	83	56	41	60	55
Transportation and public utilities	52	46	39	34	67	120	102	107	77	62	53	49	38	36	41
Wholesale and retail trade	189	154	120	139	203	378	368	350	259	251	218	191	151	130	176
Finance and services	239	191	160	179	293	527	492	452	380	409	333	282	228	205	...
Finance, insurance, and real estate	...	...	...	...	...	...	...	...	...	...	...	...	...	31	32
Services	...	...	...	...	...	...	...	...	...	...	...	...	...	174	230
Public administration	43	28	22	20	32	45	53	50	32	37	30	27	24	23	18
EXPERIENCED WORKERS BY OCCUPATION															
Managerial and professional specialty	107	73	73	86	153	290	266	214	181	177	143	112	107	91	117
Technical, sales, and administrative support	198	162	119	152	247	498	460	389	289	295	232	206	157	158	191
Service occupations	157	125	97	104	146	231	234	268	228	220	209	177	148	118	145
Precision production, craft, and repair	143	108	98	95	169	308	270	184	156	144	108	84	66	59	67
Operators, fabricators, and laborers	312	247	183	197	302	480	416	373	276	280	234	177	156	140	187
Farming, forestry, and fishing	33	29	22	17	25	33	39	57	41	42	39	27	26	24	25

Note: See "Notes and Definitions" for information on historical comparability.

1. Includes wage and salary workers only.

Table 1-33. Unemployed Persons and Unemployment Rates by Sex, Age, and Reason for Unemployment, 1968–2001

(Thousands of persons, percent.)

Year and sex	Number of unemployed					Unemployed as a percent of the total civilian labor force			
	Total	Job losers	Job leavers	Entrants		Job losers	Job leavers	Entrants	
				Reentrants	New entrants			Reentrants	New entrants
TOTAL									
1968	2 817	1 070	431	909	407	1.4	0.5	1.2	0.5
1969	2 832	1 017	436	965	413	1.3	0.5	1.2	0.5
1970	4 093	1 811	550	1 228	504	2.2	0.7	1.5	0.6
1971	5 016	2 323	590	1 472	630	2.8	0.7	1.7	0.7
1972	4 882	2 108	641	1 456	677	2.4	0.7	1.7	0.8
1973	4 365	1 694	683	1 340	649	1.9	0.8	1.5	0.7
1974	5 156	2 242	768	1 463	681	2.4	0.8	1.6	0.7
1975	7 929	4 386	827	1 892	823	4.7	0.9	2.0	0.9
1976	7 406	3 679	903	1 928	895	3.8	0.9	2.0	0.9
1977	6 991	3 166	909	1 963	953	3.2	0.9	2.0	1.0
1978	6 202	2 585	874	1 857	885	2.5	0.9	1.8	0.9
1979	6 137	2 635	880	1 806	817	2.5	0.8	1.7	0.8
1980	7 637	3 947	891	1 927	872	3.7	0.8	1.8	0.8
1981	8 273	4 267	923	2 102	981	3.9	0.8	1.9	0.9
1982	10 678	6 268	840	2 384	1 185	5.7	0.8	2.2	1.1
1983	10 717	6 258	830	2 412	1 216	5.6	0.7	2.2	1.1
1984	8 539	4 421	823	2 184	1 110	3.9	0.7	1.9	1.0
1985	8 312	4 139	877	2 256	1 039	3.6	0.8	2.0	0.9
1986	8 237	4 033	1 015	2 160	1 029	3.4	0.9	1.8	0.9
1987	7 425	3 566	965	1 974	920	3.0	0.8	1.6	0.8
1988	6 701	3 092	983	1 809	816	2.5	0.8	1.5	0.7
1989	6 528	2 983	1 024	1 843	677	2.4	0.8	1.5	0.5
1990	7 047	3 387	1 041	1 930	688	2.7	0.8	1.5	0.5
1991	8 628	4 694	1 004	2 139	792	3.7	0.8	1.7	0.6
1992	9 613	5 389	1 002	2 285	937	4.2	0.8	1.8	0.7
1993	8 940	4 848	976	2 198	919	3.8	0.8	1.7	0.7
1994	7 996	3 815	791	2 786	604	2.9	0.6	2.1	0.5
1995	7 404	3 476	824	2 525	579	2.6	0.6	1.9	0.4
1996	7 236	3 370	774	2 512	580	2.5	0.6	1.9	0.4
1997	6 739	3 037	795	2 338	569	2.2	0.6	1.7	0.4
1998	6 210	2 822	734	2 132	520	2.1	0.5	1.5	0.4
1999	5 880	2 622	783	2 005	469	1.9	0.6	1.4	0.3
2000	5 655	2 492	775	1 957	431	1.8	0.6	1.4	0.3
2001	6 742	3 428	832	2 029	453	2.4	0.6	1.4	0.3
MEN, 20 YEARS AND OVER									
1968	993	599	167	205	22	1.3	0.4	0.4	0.1
1969	963	556	164	216	27	1.2	0.4	0.5	0.1
1970	1 638	1 066	209	318	44	2.2	0.4	0.7	0.1
1971	2 097	1 391	239	411	57	2.9	0.5	0.9	0.1
1972	1 948	1 219	248	420	60	2.5	0.5	0.9	0.1
1973	1 624	959	258	350	56	1.9	0.5	0.7	0.1
1974	1 957	1 276	276	356	48	2.5	0.5	0.7	0.1
1975	3 476	2 598	298	506	76	5.0	0.6	1.0	0.1
1976	3 098	2 167	323	521	86	4.1	0.6	1.0	0.2
1977	2 794	1 816	335	540	103	3.4	0.6	1.0	0.2
1978	2 328	1 433	337	471	86	2.6	0.6	0.9	0.2
1979	2 308	1 464	325	446	73	2.6	0.6	0.8	0.1
1980	3 353	2 389	359	516	90	4.2	0.6	0.9	0.2
1981	3 615	2 565	356	592	102	4.5	0.6	1.0	0.2
1982	5 089	3 965	327	678	119	6.8	0.6	1.2	0.2
1983	5 257	4 088	336	695	138	6.9	0.6	1.2	0.2
1984	3 932	2 800	324	663	146	4.7	0.5	1.1	0.2
1985	3 715	2 568	352	671	124	4.3	0.6	1.1	0.2
1986	3 751	2 568	444	611	128	4.1	0.7	1.0	0.2
1987	3 369	2 289	413	558	108	3.7	0.7	0.9	0.2
1988	2 987	1 939	416	534	98	3.1	0.7	0.9	0.2
1989	2 867	1 843	394	541	88	2.9	0.6	0.8	0.1
1990	3 239	2 100	431	626	82	3.2	0.7	1.0	0.1
1991	4 195	2 982	411	698	105	4.6	0.6	1.1	0.2
1992	4 717	3 420	421	765	111	5.2	0.6	1.2	0.2
1993	4 287	2 996	429	747	114	4.5	0.6	1.1	0.2
1994	3 627	2 296	367	898	65	3.4	0.5	1.3	0.1
1995	3 239	2 051	356	775	57	3.0	0.5	1.2	0.1
1996	3 146	2 043	322	731	51	3.0	0.5	1.1	0.1
1997	2 882	1 795	358	675	55	2.6	0.5	1.0	0.1
1998	2 580	1 588	318	611	63	2.3	0.5	0.9	0.1
1999	2 433	1 459	336	592	46	2.1	0.5	0.8	0.1
2000	2 350	1 398	324	574	54	2.0	0.5	0.8	0.1
2001	3 003	1 977	369	606	52	2.8	0.5	0.8	0.1

See *Note* at end of table.

Table 1-33. Unemployed Persons and Unemployment Rates by Sex, Age, and Reason for Unemployment, 1968–2001— *Continued*

(Thousands of persons, percent.)

Year and sex	Number of unemployed					Unemployed as a percent of the total civilian labor force			
	Total	Job losers	Job leavers	Entrants		Job losers	Job leavers	Entrants	
				Reentrants	New entrants			Reentrants	New entrants
WOMEN, 20 YEARS AND OVER									
1968	985	341	167	422	55	1.3	0.6	1.6	0.2
1969	1 015	335	171	455	55	1.2	0.6	1.7	0.2
1970	1 349	546	214	531	58	1.9	0.8	1.9	0.2
1971	1 658	700	235	651	72	2.5	0.8	2.3	0.2
1972	1 625	641	264	641	80	2.2	0.9	2.1	0.2
1973	1 507	522	280	625	80	1.6	0.9	2.0	0.3
1974	1 777	685	319	673	100	2.1	1.0	2.1	0.3
1975	2 684	1 339	375	858	114	4.0	1.1	2.6	0.3
1976	2 588	1 124	427	912	126	3.2	1.2	2.6	0.4
1977	2 535	1 031	419	945	140	2.8	1.2	2.6	0.4
1978	2 292	852	371	930	138	2.2	1.2	2.4	0.4
1979	2 276	851	370	908	145	2.1	1.0	2.3	0.4
1980	2 615	1 170	376	930	139	2.8	0.9	2.3	0.3
1981	2 895	1 317	404	1 023	151	3.1	1.0	2.4	0.3
1982	3 613	1 844	379	1 197	192	4.2	0.9	2.7	0.4
1983	3 632	1 801	384	1 235	212	4.0	0.9	2.8	0.4
1984	3 107	1 350	386	1 151	220	2.9	0.8	2.5	0.5
1985	3 129	1 296	412	1 195	227	2.7	0.9	2.5	0.5
1986	3 032	1 225	426	1 175	206	2.5	0.9	2.4	0.4
1987	2 709	1 067	406	1 041	194	2.2	0.8	2.1	0.4
1988	2 487	946	408	965	168	1.9	0.8	1.9	0.3
1989	2 467	942	430	958	137	1.8	0.8	1.8	0.3
1990	2 596	1 054	429	966	146	2.0	0.8	1.8	0.3
1991	3 074	1 423	413	1 075	163	2.6	0.8	2.0	0.3
1992	3 469	1 710	433	1 142	183	3.1	0.8	2.1	0.3
1993	3 288	1 619	395	1 098	176	2.9	0.7	2.0	0.3
1994	3 049	1 334	339	1 253	122	2.4	0.6	2.2	0.2
1995	2 819	1 211	366	1 135	107	2.1	0.6	2.0	0.2
1996	2 783	1 145	361	1 156	120	2.0	0.6	2.0	0.2
1997	2 585	1 069	333	1 057	126	1.8	0.6	1.8	0.2
1998	2 424	1 053	330	944	97	1.8	0.6	1.6	0.2
1999	2 285	990	333	866	96	1.6	0.5	1.4	0.2
2000	2 212	934	340	860	78	1.5	0.6	1.4	0.1
2001	2 551	1 265	362	835	90	2.0	0.6	1.3	0.1
BOTH SEXES, 16 TO 19 YEARS									
1968	838	130	97	281	330	2.0	1.5	4.2	5.0
1969	853	127	101	295	331	1.8	1.5	4.2	4.8
1970	1 106	200	126	378	401	2.8	1.7	5.2	5.5
1971	1 262	233	117	410	501	3.1	1.6	5.5	6.7
1972	1 308	248	129	395	536	3.1	1.6	4.9	6.6
1973	1 235	212	146	364	513	2.4	1.7	4.3	6.0
1974	1 422	280	173	436	533	3.1	2.0	4.9	6.0
1975	1 767	450	155	529	634	5.1	1.7	6.0	7.1
1976	1 719	387	153	496	683	4.3	1.7	5.5	7.5
1977	1 663	318	156	477	711	3.4	1.7	5.1	7.6
1978	1 583	300	167	455	660	3.1	1.7	4.7	6.8
1979	1 555	319	184	452	599	3.3	1.9	4.7	6.2
1980	1 669	388	156	481	643	4.1	1.7	5.1	6.9
1981	1 763	385	162	487	728	4.3	1.8	5.4	8.1
1982	1 977	460	134	509	874	5.4	1.6	6.0	10.2
1983	1 829	370	110	482	867	4.6	1.3	5.9	10.6
1984	1 499	271	114	370	745	3.4	1.4	4.7	9.4
1985	1 468	275	113	390	689	3.5	1.4	4.9	8.7
1986	1 454	240	145	374	695	3.0	1.8	4.7	8.8
1987	1 347	210	146	375	617	2.7	1.8	4.7	7.7
1988	1 226	207	159	310	550	2.6	2.0	3.9	6.8
1989	1 194	198	200	345	452	2.5	2.5	4.3	5.7
1990	1 212	233	181	338	460	3.0	2.3	4.3	5.9
1991	1 359	289	180	365	524	4.0	2.5	5.0	7.2
1992	1 427	259	149	377	643	3.6	2.1	5.3	9.1
1993	1 365	233	151	353	628	3.3	2.1	4.9	8.8
1994	1 320	185	84	634	416	2.5	1.1	8.5	5.6
1995	1 346	214	102	615	415	2.8	1.3	7.9	5.3
1996	1 306	182	91	625	409	2.3	1.2	8.0	5.2
1997	1 271	174	104	606	388	2.2	1.3	7.6	4.9
1998	1 205	181	86	577	361	2.2	1.0	7.0	4.4
1999	1 162	173	114	547	328	2.1	1.4	6.6	3.9
2000	1 093	160	111	522	300	1.9	1.3	6.2	3.6
2001	1 187	186	101	589	311	2.3	1.3	7.3	3.9

Note: See "Notes and Definitions" for information on historical comparability.

Table 1-34. Percent of the Population with Work Experience During the Year by Sex and Age, 1987–2000

Year	Total	16 to 17 years	18 to 19 years	20 to 24 years	25 to 34 years	35 to 44 years	45 to 54 years	55 to 59 years	60 to 64 years	65 to 69 years	70 years and over
TOTAL											
1987	69.7	51.8	76.6	85.5	85.7	86.1	81.6	69.4	51.3	26.2	10.2
1988	70.2	50.6	75.5	85.7	86.0	86.8	82.2	70.5	52.2	27.9	10.3
1989	70.5	51.9	75.4	84.9	86.6	86.9	82.8	70.4	52.5	28.4	10.0
1990	70.2	48.6	74.2	84.1	86.2	87.0	82.8	70.9	53.4	28.3	10.2
1991	69.5	43.4	70.8	83.4	85.9	86.6	83.0	70.3	52.9	27.2	9.8
1992	69.1	43.8	69.9	82.7	85.2	85.9	82.8	70.8	53.5	25.5	9.8
1993	69.2	42.1	70.4	82.0	85.0	85.3	82.8	71.6	51.6	27.5	10.7
1994	69.6	44.1	71.5	82.5	85.5	85.6	83.8	72.2	52.8	27.5	10.0
1995	69.6	44.4	71.2	82.0	85.6	85.9	83.4	72.2	53.3	28.0	10.2
1996	69.9	43.3	70.5	83.1	86.1	85.7	84.3	73.3	54.3	27.8	10.4
1997	70.1	43.6	70.5	83.0	87.1	85.9	84.4	73.8	53.8	28.5	10.0
1998	70.1	42.1	69.9	82.9	86.7	86.3	84.2	73.7	54.5	29.2	10.6
1999	70.7	43.7	71.2	82.7	87.3	86.9	85.0	72.3	55.8	30.5	11.6
2000	70.5	42.2	69.6	82.6	87.1	87.0	84.6	72.9	55.1	30.8	11.4
MEN											
1987	78.9	52.4	77.4	90.4	94.3	94.1	91.9	83.3	63.2	34.2	15.4
1988	79.1	51.8	78.9	90.7	94.3	94.6	91.6	82.1	63.1	35.6	15.6
1989	79.4	53.2	77.7	89.9	94.7	94.7	91.9	82.0	64.2	35.4	15.1
1990	78.9	50.3	76.7	88.7	94.4	94.7	91.3	82.0	65.8	35.8	14.0
1991	77.9	45.4	72.2	87.9	93.5	93.6	91.3	81.5	63.6	35.0	14.4
1992	77.4	46.6	73.7	87.1	93.3	92.8	89.9	80.9	63.2	32.4	14.3
1993	76.8	43.9	71.4	86.6	92.5	92.0	89.3	79.8	59.1	34.3	15.3
1994	77.2	44.4	74.7	87.2	92.9	92.0	90.0	81.3	61.4	33.9	14.8
1995	77.0	43.7	73.6	86.4	92.6	92.2	89.7	81.5	62.1	34.5	14.9
1996	77.2	44.1	71.8	86.7	93.4	92.1	90.4	81.8	62.5	33.6	15.2
1997	77.1	43.4	70.3	86.6	94.1	92.3	90.7	81.4	62.9	33.8	13.9
1998	76.9	40.4	71.6	86.4	93.5	92.7	90.1	81.7	63.5	35.5	14.7
1999	77.3	44.7	72.3	85.5	93.9	93.2	89.9	79.2	65.1	37.4	16.5
2000	77.1	42.1	70.2	85.1	93.4	93.6	89.8	80.6	64.4	38.4	16.0
WOMEN											
1987	61.3	51.1	75.8	81.0	77.3	78.5	71.9	56.7	41.0	19.6	6.8
1988	62.1	49.3	72.2	81.0	78.1	79.4	73.5	60.0	42.5	21.4	6.8
1989	62.3	50.6	73.1	80.2	78.6	79.3	74.2	59.9	42.4	22.5	6.7
1990	62.2	46.8	71.7	79.6	78.0	79.6	74.9	60.4	42.5	22.1	7.7
1991	61.8	41.4	69.4	79.0	78.3	79.9	75.3	59.9	43.6	20.6	6.7
1992	61.5	40.9	66.1	78.4	77.2	79.1	76.1	61.5	44.4	20.0	6.7
1993	62.1	40.3	69.4	77.5	77.6	78.7	76.5	63.9	44.7	22.1	7.7
1994	62.5	43.7	68.4	77.8	78.1	79.4	78.0	63.9	45.0	22.2	6.8
1995	62.8	45.2	68.7	77.7	78.8	79.8	77.6	63.2	45.6	22.4	7.1
1996	63.2	42.5	69.2	79.5	78.9	79.5	78.4	65.4	46.9	23.0	7.1
1997	63.6	43.9	70.7	79.5	80.1	79.6	78.4	66.7	45.6	24.0	7.3
1998	63.7	44.1	68.2	79.4	80.1	80.0	78.6	66.3	46.2	23.8	7.8
1999	64.5	42.6	70.1	79.9	80.9	80.7	80.3	66.2	47.3	24.4	8.2
2000	64.3	42.3	69.0	80.2	80.9	80.5	79.5	65.7	47.0	23.9	8.2

Note: See "Notes and Definitions" for information on historical comparability.

Table 1-35. Persons with Work Experience During the Year by Industry and Class of Worker of Job Held the Longest, 1988–2000

(Thousands of persons.)

Industry and class of worker	1988	1989	1990	1991	1992	1993	1994	1995	1996	1997	1998	1999	2000
TOTAL	130 450	132 817	133 534	133 410	133 912	136 354	138 469	139 723	142 200	143 967	145 566	148 295	149 361
Agriculture	3 754	3 770	3 743	3 555	3 793	3 844	3 924	3 918	3 624	3 422	3 608	3 679	3 563
Wage and salary workers	2 262	2 197	2 149	2 150	2 286	2 186	2 364	2 448	2 262	2 344	2 308	2 430	2 348
Self-employed workers	1 359	1 453	1 458	1 313	1 398	1 591	1 502	1 419	1 333	1 057	1 269	1 215	1 171
Unpaid family workers	133	120	136	92	109	67	58	51	29	20	32	34	44
Nonagricultural industries	126 696	129 047	129 791	129 856	130 118	132 510	134 544	135 805	138 575	140 545	141 958	148 295	145 798
Wage and salary workers	117 757	120 019	120 416	120 734	120 924	123 314	125 567	126 916	129 232	132 140	133 039	138 315	137 024
Mining	807	735	858	775	718	709	683	612	643	703	606	558	544
Construction	7 235	7 491	7 236	6 888	6 607	6 690	7 134	7 226	7 720	7 996	8 103	8 211	8 534
Manufacturing	22 957	22 764	22 435	21 624	21 174	21 198	. . .	21 475	22 130	21 652	21 268	21 737	21 143
Durable goods	13 196	13 379	13 155	12 353	11 983	12 309	12 082	12 552	12 988	12 943	13 056	13 172	12 781
Lumber and wood products	789	840	797	639	632	653	752	891	860	800	767	822	760
Furniture and fixtures	727	683	621	600	694	757	651	647	684	694	632	667	609
Stone, clay, and glass products	628	721	691	594	549	629	656	664	637	521	649	651	638
Primary metal industries	768	892	852	830	823	784	733	845	801	706	802	809	852
Fabricated metal products	1 367	1 386	1 348	1 375	1 293	1 325	1 339	1 265	1 469	1 443	1 419	1 310	1 417
Machinery, except electrical	2 778	2 601	2 631	2 442	2 264	2 445	2 557	2 502	2 603	2 659	2 707	2 739	2 720
Electrical equipment	2 231	2 280	2 281	2 142	1 925	1 857	1 945	1 966	1 996	2 047	2 149	2 068	2 138
Transportation equipment	2 693	2 669	2 661	2 483	2 460	2 476	2 124	2 262	2 399	2 520	2 432	2 546	2 160
Automobiles	1 284	1 273	1 206	1 157	1 214	1 205	1 102	1 258	1 361	1 446	1 342	1 447	1 259
Other transportation equipment	1 409	1 396	1 455	1 326	1 246	1 271	1 022	1 004	1 038	1 074	1 090	1 099	901
Other durable goods	1 215	1 307	1 274	1 248	1 344	1 383	1 324	1 510	1 539	1 552	1 499	1 562	1 487
Nondurable goods	9 761	9 385	9 280	9 271	9 191	8 889	9 406	8 923	9 142	8 709	8 212	8 565	8 362
Food and kindred products	2 083	2 048	2 000	1 920	2 028	1 879	1 906	1 952	1 952	1 846	1 808	1 863	1 848
Textile mill products	785	747	800	716	639	694	807	695	716	624	642	568	533
Apparel and related products	1 343	1 214	1 174	1 172	1 290	1 189	1 235	1 138	1 066	973	857	800	734
Printing and publishing	1 951	2 018	1 880	2 013	1 933	1 905	2 053	1 882	1 883	1 862	1 840	2 041	1 945
Chemicals and allied products	1 533	1 404	1 356	1 405	1 276	1 396	1 402	1 373	1 496	1 306	1 160	1 431	1 304
Other nondurable goods	2 066	1 953	2 069	2 046	2 025	1 827	2 002	1 881	2 029	2 098	1 904	1 863	1 998
Transportation and public utilities	8 195	8 267	8 364	8 490	8 495	8 639	8 567	8 586	9 114	9 487	9 536	9 786	9 826
Transportation	4 856	4 952	5 021	5 066	5 219	5 411	5 373	5 430	5 888	6 079	6 087	6 125	6 209
Communications and utilities	3 339	3 315	3 343	3 425	3 276	3 227	3 194	3 155	3 226	3 408	3 449	3 661	3 617
Wholesale and retail trade	26 078	26 387	26 879	26 846	26 943	27 328	27 837	28 563	28 852	29 193	29 593	30 155	29 779
Wholesale trade	4 454	4 642	4 809	4 822	4 583	4 509	4 933	4 954	4 841	4 906	5 224	5 466	5 365
Retail trade	21 624	21 745	22 070	22 025	22 360	22 819	22 904	23 609	24 011	24 287	24 370	24 689	24 413
Finance and services	46 321	47 370	47 587	49 117	49 786	51 659	52 360	53 402	54 141	56 263	56 704	58 323	59 707
Finance, insurance, and real estate	7 980	8 091	7 760	7 730	7 629	7 971	7 869	7 911	8 000	8 508	8 619	8 535	8 797
Business and repair services	6 646	6 985	7 040	6 135	6 308	6 849	7 002	7 547	8 035	8 282	8 547	8 856	9 558
Private households	1 535	1 238	1 161	1 266	1 395	1 254	1 241	1 171	1 038	1 131	1 067	1 213	1 045
Personal services, except private households	3 019	3 196	3 177	3 110	2 999	3 272	3 181	3 219	3 099	3 209	3 227	3 186	3 429
Entertainment and recreation	1 568	1 673	1 752	2 235	2 294	2 371	2 407	2 571	2 705	2 904	2 908	2 947	2 852
Medical and other health services	9 247	9 389	9 904	10 457	10 573	10 979	11 029	11 412	11 788	11 756	11 680	11 842	12 066
Social services	2 092	2 264	2 335	2 479	2 606	2 752	2 632	3 038	3 016	3 068	3 198	3 292	3 390
Educational services	9 895	10 094	9 976	10 328	10 705	10 882	11 454	11 064	11 076	11 539	11 627	12 167	12 387
Other professional services	4 181	4 270	4 296	5 251	5 079	5 144	5 398	5 326	5 241	5 729	5 692	6 119	6 063
Forestry and fisheries	160	169	186	125	198	184	148	144	145	137	139	165	122
Public administration	6 163	7 005	7 057	6 917	7 097	7 088	7 498	7 053	6 630	6 846	7 229	7 115	7 492
Self-employed workers	8 580	8 717	9 120	8 855	8 965	8 992	8 843	8 753	9 235	8 257	8 806	9 833	8 607
Unpaid family workers	359	312	255	267	229	204	135	137	109	147	114	146	167

Note: See "Notes and Definitions" for information on historical comparability.

Table 1-36. Number of Persons with Work Experience During the Year by Sex and Extent of Employment, 1987–2000

(Thousands of persons.)

Year and sex	Total	Full-time				Part-time			
		Total	50 to 52 weeks	27 to 49 weeks	1 to 26 weeks	Total	50 to 52 weeks	27 to 49 weeks	1 to 26 weeks
TOTAL									
1987	128 315	100 288	77 015	13 361	9 912	28 027	10 973	6 594	10 460
1988	130 451	102 131	79 627	12 875	9 629	28 320	11 384	6 624	10 312
1989	132 817	104 876	81 117	14 271	9 488	27 941	11 275	6 987	9 679
1990	133 535	105 323	80 932	14 758	9 633	28 212	11 507	7 012	9 693
1991	133 410	104 472	80 385	14 491	9 596	28 938	11 946	7 003	9 989
1992	133 912	104 813	81 523	13 587	9 703	29 099	12 326	6 841	9 932
1993	136 354	106 299	83 384	13 054	9 861	30 055	12 818	6 777	10 460
1994	138 468	108 141	85 764	13 051	9 326	30 327	12 936	6 956	10 435
1995	139 724	110 063	88 173	12 970	8 920	29 661	12 725	6 831	10 105
1996	142 201	112 313	90 252	12 997	9 064	29 888	13 382	6 643	9 863
1997	143 968	113 879	92 631	12 508	8 740	30 089	13 810	6 565	9 714
1998	145 566	116 412	95 772	12 156	8 484	29 155	13 538	6 480	9 137
1999	148 295	119 096	97 941	12 294	8 861	29 199	13 680	6 317	9 202
2000	149 361	120 591	100 349	12 071	8 171	28 770	13 865	6 161	8 744
MEN									
1987	69 144	59 736	47 040	7 503	5 193	9 408	3 260	2 191	3 957
1988	70 021	60 504	48 299	7 329	4 876	9 517	3 468	2 199	3 850
1989	71 640	62 108	49 693	7 642	4 773	9 532	3 619	2 254	3 659
1990	71 953	62 319	49 175	8 188	4 956	9 634	3 650	2 322	3 662
1991	71 700	61 636	47 895	8 324	5 417	10 064	3 820	2 342	3 902
1992	72 007	61 722	48 300	7 965	5 457	10 285	3 864	2 354	4 067
1993	72 872	62 513	49 832	7 317	5 364	10 359	4 005	2 144	4 210
1994	73 958	63 634	51 582	7 094	4 958	10 324	3 948	2 358	4 018
1995	74 381	64 145	52 671	6 973	4 501	10 236	4 034	2 257	3 945
1996	75 760	65 356	53 795	6 891	4 670	10 404	4 321	2 136	3 947
1997	76 408	66 089	54 918	6 638	4 533	10 319	4 246	2 274	3 799
1998	76 918	67 250	56 953	6 208	4 089	9 669	4 197	2 090	3 382
1999	78 145	68 347	57 520	6 401	4 426	9 797	4 297	2 062	3 438
2000	78 804	68 925	58 756	6 094	4 075	9 879	4 485	1 957	3 437
WOMEN									
1987	59 171	40 552	29 975	5 858	4 719	18 619	7 713	4 403	6 503
1988	60 430	41 627	31 328	5 546	4 753	18 803	7 916	4 425	6 462
1989	61 178	42 768	31 424	6 629	4 715	18 410	7 656	4 733	6 021
1990	61 582	43 004	31 757	6 570	4 677	18 578	7 857	4 690	6 031
1991	61 712	42 837	32 491	6 167	4 179	18 875	8 126	4 662	6 087
1992	61 904	43 090	33 223	5 621	4 246	18 814	8 462	4 487	5 865
1993	63 481	43 785	33 552	5 736	4 497	19 696	8 813	4 633	6 250
1994	64 511	44 508	34 182	5 957	4 369	20 003	8 988	4 598	6 417
1995	65 342	45 917	35 502	5 997	4 418	19 425	8 691	4 574	6 160
1996	66 439	46 955	36 457	6 105	4 393	19 484	9 061	4 507	5 916
1997	67 559	47 790	37 713	5 870	4 207	19 769	9 564	4 291	5 914
1998	68 648	49 162	38 819	5 948	4 395	19 486	9 341	4 390	5 755
1999	70 150	50 748	40 421	5 892	4 435	19 402	9 383	4 255	5 764
2000	70 556	51 665	41 593	5 977	4 095	18 891	9 380	4 204	5 307

Note: See "Notes and Definitions" for information on historical comparability.

Table 1-37. Percent Distribution of the Population with Work Experience During the Year by Sex and Extent of Employment, 1987–2000

(Percent of total persons with work experience.)

Year and sex	Total	Full-time				Part-time			
		Total	50 to 52 weeks	27 to 49 weeks	1 to 26 weeks	Total	50 to 52 weeks	27 to 49 weeks	1 to 26 weeks
TOTAL									
1987	100.0	78.1	60.0	10.4	7.7	21.9	8.6	5.1	8.2
1988	100.0	78.3	61.0	9.9	7.4	21.7	8.7	5.1	7.9
1989	100.0	78.9	61.1	10.7	7.1	21.1	8.5	5.3	7.3
1990	100.0	78.9	60.6	11.1	7.2	21.2	8.6	5.3	7.3
1991	100.0	78.4	60.3	10.9	7.2	21.7	9.0	5.2	7.5
1992	100.0	78.2	60.9	10.1	7.2	21.7	9.2	5.1	7.4
1993	100.0	78.0	61.2	9.6	7.2	22.1	9.4	5.0	7.7
1994	100.0	78.0	61.9	9.4	6.7	21.8	9.3	5.0	7.5
1995	100.0	78.8	63.1	9.3	6.4	21.2	9.1	4.9	7.2
1996	100.0	79.0	63.5	9.1	6.4	21.0	9.4	4.7	6.9
1997	100.0	79.1	64.3	8.7	6.1	20.9	9.6	4.6	6.7
1998	100.0	80.0	65.8	8.4	5.8	20.1	9.3	4.5	6.3
1999	100.0	80.3	66.0	8.3	6.0	19.7	9.2	4.3	6.2
2000	100.0	80.8	67.2	8.1	5.5	19.3	9.3	4.1	5.9
MEN									
1987	100.0	86.4	68.0	10.9	7.5	13.6	4.7	3.2	5.7
1988	100.0	86.5	69.0	10.5	7.0	13.6	5.0	3.1	5.5
1989	100.0	86.8	69.4	10.7	6.7	13.3	5.1	3.1	5.1
1990	100.0	86.6	68.3	11.4	6.9	13.4	5.1	3.2	5.1
1991	100.0	86.0	66.8	11.6	7.6	14.0	5.3	3.3	5.4
1992	100.0	85.8	67.1	11.1	7.6	14.3	5.4	3.3	5.6
1993	100.0	85.8	68.4	10.0	7.4	14.2	5.5	2.9	5.8
1994	100.0	86.0	69.7	9.6	6.7	13.9	5.3	3.2	5.4
1995	100.0	86.3	70.8	9.4	6.1	13.7	5.4	3.0	5.3
1996	100.0	86.3	71.0	9.1	6.2	13.7	5.7	2.8	5.2
1997	100.0	86.5	71.9	8.7	5.9	13.6	5.6	3.0	5.0
1998	100.0	87.4	74.0	8.1	5.3	12.6	5.5	2.7	4.4
1999	100.0	87.5	73.6	8.2	5.7	12.5	5.5	2.6	4.4
2000	100.0	87.5	74.6	7.7	5.2	12.6	5.7	2.5	4.4
WOMEN									
1987	100.0	68.6	50.7	9.9	8.0	31.4	13.0	7.4	11.0
1988	100.0	68.9	51.8	9.2	7.9	31.1	13.1	7.3	10.7
1989	100.0	69.9	51.4	10.8	7.7	30.0	12.5	7.7	9.8
1990	100.0	69.9	51.6	10.7	7.6	30.2	12.8	7.6	9.8
1991	100.0	69.4	52.6	10.0	6.8	30.7	13.2	7.6	9.9
1992	100.0	69.7	53.7	9.1	6.9	30.4	13.7	7.2	9.5
1993	100.0	69.0	52.9	9.0	7.1	31.0	13.9	7.3	9.8
1994	100.0	69.0	53.0	9.2	6.8	30.9	13.9	7.1	9.9
1995	100.0	70.3	54.3	9.2	6.8	29.7	13.3	7.0	9.4
1996	100.0	70.7	54.9	9.2	6.6	29.3	13.6	6.8	8.9
1997	100.0	70.7	55.8	8.7	6.2	29.4	14.2	6.4	8.8
1998	100.0	71.6	56.5	8.7	6.4	28.4	13.6	6.4	8.4
1999	100.0	72.3	57.6	8.4	6.3	27.7	13.4	6.1	8.2
2000	100.0	73.2	58.9	8.5	5.8	26.8	13.3	6.0	7.5

Note: See "Notes and Definitions" for information on historical comparability.

Table 1-38. Extent of Unemployment During the Year by Sex, 1988–2000

(Thousands of persons, percent.)

Sex and extent of unemployment	1988	1989	1990	1991	1992	1993	1994	1995	1996	1997	1998	1999	2000
TOTAL													
Total Who Worked Or Looked For Work	132 185	134 394	135 408	135 826	136 654	139 786	141 325	142 413	144 528	146 096	147 295	149 798	150 786
Percent with unemployment	12.9	12.9	14.6	15.7	15.7	14.7	13.4	12.7	11.6	10.7	9.5	8.7	8.1
Total With Unemployment	17 096	17 273	19 809	21 276	21 455	20 527	18 966	18 067	16 789	15 637	14 044	13 068	12 269
Did not work but looked for work	1 735	1 577	1 874	2 415	2 742	3 432	2 857	2 690	2 329	2 129	1 729	1 503	1 425
Worked during the year	15 362	15 697	17 936	18 861	18 714	17 094	16 109	15 377	14 460	13 508	12 316	11 566	10 845
Year-round workers with 1 or 2 weeks of unemployment	830	833	1 056	966	871	688	746	715	589	611	630	562	573
Part-year workers with unemployment	14 532	14 864	16 880	17 895	17 843	16 406	15 363	14 662	13 871	12 897	11 686	11 004	10 272
1 to 4 weeks	3 256	3 489	3 645	3 224	2 944	2 626	2 788	2 812	2 550	2 582	2 323	2 361	2 233
5 to 10 weeks	3 148	3 359	3 669	3 655	3 496	2 898	2 983	2 725	2 671	2 601	2 495	2 218	2 014
11 to 14 weeks	2 128	2 235	2 501	2 587	2 574	2 300	2 265	2 147	2 020	1 822	1 701	1 594	1 505
15 to 26 weeks	3 479	3 600	4 316	4 927	4 877	4 549	4 158	4 013	3 662	3 378	3 019	2 803	2 641
27 weeks or more	2 521	2 181	2 749	3 502	3 952	4 033	3 169	2 965	2 968	2 514	2 148	2 028	1 879
With 2 spells or more of unemployment	5 136	5 073	5 811	5 864	5 734	5 338	4 783	4 468	4 237	4 044	3 628	3 225	3 079
2 spells	2 460	2 460	2 855	2 738	2 698	2 572	2 207	1 963	1 982	1 853	1 650	1 449	1 397
3 spells or more	2 676	2 613	2 956	3 126	3 036	2 766	2 576	2 505	2 255	2 191	1 978	1 776	1 682
MEN													
Total Who Worked Or Looked For Work	70 738	72 362	72 844	72 909	73 387	74 516	75 244	75 698	76 786	77 385	77 704	78 905	79 546
Percent with unemployment	13.7	13.5	15.5	17.3	17.5	15.7	14.1	13.2	11.9	11.1	9.4	9.0	8.6
Total With Unemployment	9 696	9 792	11 307	12 642	12 844	11 723	10 582	9 996	9 157	8 604	7 284	7 091	6 806
Did not work but looked for work	717	723	891	1 210	1 379	1 641	1 286	1 317	1 026	978	787	760	742
Worked during the year	8 978	9 071	10 415	11 432	11 466	10 082	9 296	8 679	8 130	7 626	6 497	6 332	6 064
Year-round workers with 1 or 2 weeks of unemployment	585	568	711	612	567	449	527	462	395	382	386	373	379
Part-year workers with unemployment	8 393	8 503	9 704	10 820	10 899	9 633	8 769	8 217	7 735	7 244	6 111	5 959	5 685
1 to 4 weeks	1 633	1 742	1 819	1 591	1 563	1 343	1 365	1 398	1 272	1 275	1 085	1 166	1 070
5 to 10 weeks	1 808	1 890	2 041	2 111	2 039	1 647	1 666	1 434	1 478	1 474	1 363	1 168	1 135
11 to 14 weeks	1 279	1 365	1 462	1 659	1 615	1 354	1 370	1 253	1 258	1 068	980	937	880
15 to 26 weeks	2 124	2 188	2 645	3 206	3 165	2 862	2 449	2 439	2 076	1 949	1 585	1 655	1 595
27 weeks or more	1 549	1 318	1 737	2 253	2 517	2 427	1 919	1 693	1 651	1 478	1 098	1 033	1 005
With 2 spells or more of unemployment	3 366	3 178	3 689	3 886	3 889	3 451	2 940	2 793	2 554	2 437	2 014	1 845	1 809
2 spells	1 560	1 517	1 676	1 742	1 781	1 580	1 266	1 110	1 109	1 078	880	787	804
3 spells or more	1 806	1 661	2 013	2 144	2 108	1 871	1 674	1 683	1 445	1 359	1 134	1 058	1 005
WOMEN													
Total Who Worked Or Looked For Work	61 447	62 032	62 564	62 917	63 267	65 270	66 081	66 716	67 742	68 710	69 591	70 893	71 240
Percent with unemployment	12.0	12.1	13.6	13.7	13.6	13.5	12.7	12.1	11.3	10.2	9.7	8.4	7.7
Total With Unemployment	7 400	7 481	8 502	8 634	8 611	8 804	8 383	8 070	7 632	7 033	6 760	5 976	5 463
Did not work but looked for work	1 017	854	982	1 205	1 363	1 791	1 570	1 373	1 303	1 151	942	743	683
Worked during the year	6 382	6 628	7 520	7 427	7 247	7 014	6 813	6 696	6 330	5 882	5 816	5 234	4 779
Year-round workers with 1 or 2 weeks of unemployment	244	265	344	354	304	239	219	253	194	229	243	189	193
Part-year workers with unemployment	6 138	6 363	7 176	7 073	6 943	6 775	6 594	6 443	6 136	5 653	5 573	5 045	4 586
1 to 4 weeks	1 623	1 747	1 827	1 633	1 380	1 284	1 422	1 413	1 279	1 307	1 237	1 194	1 164
5 to 10 weeks	1 340	1 469	1 627	1 544	1 457	1 252	1 317	1 291	1 192	1 127	1 131	1 050	878
11 to 14 weeks	849	870	1 038	927	959	946	896	893	762	754	721	657	625
15 to 26 weeks	1 354	1 413	1 671	1 720	1 712	1 687	1 708	1 574	1 586	1 429	1 434	1 148	1 045
27 weeks or more	972	864	1 013	1 249	1 435	1 606	1 251	1 272	1 317	1 036	1 050	996	874
With 2 spells or more of unemployment	1 769	1 895	2 122	1 979	1 844	1 887	1 843	1 675	1 682	1 607	1 614	1 379	1 270
2 spells	899	943	1 179	997	916	992	941	853	872	775	770	662	593
3 spells or more	870	952	943	982	928	895	902	822	810	832	844	717	677

Note: See "Notes and Definitions" for information on historical comparability.

Table 1-39. Percent Distribution of Persons with Unemployment During the Year by Sex and Extent of Unemployment, 1988–2000

Sex and extent of unemployment	1988	1989	1990	1991	1992	1993	1994	1995	1996	1997	1998	1999	2000
TOTAL													
Total With Unemployment Who Worked During The Year	100.0	100.0	100.0	100.0	100.0	100.0	100.0	100.0	100.0	100.0	100.0	100.0	100.0
Year-round workers with 1 or 2 weeks of unemployment	5.4	5.3	5.9	5.1	4.7	4.0	4.6	4.6	4.1	4.5	5.1	4.9	5.3
Part-year workers with unemployment	94.5	94.6	94.1	94.8	95.4	96.1	95.4	95.4	96.0	95.5	95.0	95.1	94.8
1 to 4 weeks	21.2	22.2	20.3	17.1	15.7	15.4	17.3	18.3	17.6	19.1	18.9	20.4	20.6
5 to 10 weeks	20.5	21.4	20.5	19.4	18.7	17.0	18.5	17.7	18.5	19.3	20.3	19.2	18.6
11 to 14 weeks	13.8	14.2	13.9	13.7	13.8	13.5	14.1	14.0	14.0	13.5	13.8	13.8	13.9
15 to 26 weeks	22.6	22.9	24.1	26.1	26.1	26.6	25.8	26.1	25.3	25.0	24.5	24.2	24.4
27 weeks or more	16.4	13.9	15.3	18.5	21.1	23.6	19.7	19.3	20.6	18.6	17.5	17.5	17.3
With 2 spells or more of unemployment	33.4	32.3	32.4	31.1	30.6	31.2	29.7	29.1	29.3	29.9	29.5	27.9	28.4
2 spells	16.0	15.7	15.9	14.5	14.4	15.0	13.7	12.8	13.7	13.7	13.4	12.5	12.9
3 spells or more	17.4	16.6	16.5	16.6	16.2	16.2	16.0	16.3	15.6	16.2	16.1	15.4	15.5
MEN													
Total With Unemployment Who Worked During The Year	100.0	100.0	100.0	100.0	100.0	100.0	100.0	100.0	100.0	100.0	100.0	100.0	100.0
Year-round workers with 1 or 2 weeks of unemployment	6.5	6.3	6.8	5.4	4.9	4.4	5.7	5.3	4.9	5.0	5.9	5.9	6.3
Part-year workers with unemployment	93.4	93.7	93.2	94.6	95.0	95.5	94.3	94.7	95.1	95.1	94.1	94.0	93.6
1 to 4 weeks	18.2	19.2	17.5	13.9	13.6	13.3	14.7	16.1	15.6	16.7	16.7	18.4	17.6
5 to 10 weeks	20.1	20.8	19.6	18.5	17.8	16.3	17.9	16.5	18.2	19.3	21.0	18.4	18.7
11 to 14 weeks	14.2	15.1	14.0	14.5	14.1	13.4	14.7	14.4	15.5	14.0	15.1	14.8	14.5
15 to 26 weeks	23.7	24.1	25.4	28.0	27.6	28.4	26.4	28.1	25.5	25.6	24.4	26.1	26.3
27 weeks or more	17.2	14.5	16.7	19.7	21.9	24.1	20.6	19.5	20.3	19.4	16.9	16.3	16.5
With 2 spells or more of unemployment	37.5	35.0	35.4	34.0	33.9	34.3	31.6	32.2	31.4	31.9	31.0	29.1	29.9
2 spells	17.4	16.7	16.1	15.2	15.5	15.7	13.6	12.8	13.6	14.1	13.5	12.4	13.3
3 spells or more	20.1	18.3	19.3	18.8	18.4	18.6	18.0	19.4	17.8	17.8	17.5	16.7	16.6
WOMEN													
Total With Unemployment Who Worked During The Year	100.0	100.0	100.0	100.0	100.0	100.0	100.0	100.0	100.0	100.0	100.0	100.0	100.0
Year-round workers with 1or 2 weeks of unemployment	3.8	4.0	4.6	4.8	4.2	3.4	3.2	3.8	3.1	3.9	4.2	3.6	4.0
Part-year workers with unemployment	96.1	96.0	95.3	95.3	95.7	96.6	96.7	96.2	96.9	96.1	95.8	96.4	96.0
1 to 4 weeks	25.4	26.4	24.3	22.0	19.0	18.3	20.9	21.1	20.2	22.2	21.3	22.8	24.3
5 to 10 weeks	21.0	22.2	21.6	20.8	20.1	17.8	19.3	19.3	18.8	19.2	19.4	20.1	18.4
11 to 14 weeks	13.3	13.1	13.8	12.5	13.2	13.5	13.1	13.3	12.0	12.8	12.4	12.6	13.1
15 to 26 weeks	21.2	21.3	22.2	23.2	23.6	24.1	25.1	23.5	25.1	24.3	24.7	21.9	21.9
27 weeks or more	15.2	13.0	13.4	16.8	19.8	22.9	18.3	19.0	20.8	17.6	18.0	19.0	18.3
With 2 spells or more of unemployment	27.7	28.6	28.2	26.6	25.4	26.9	27.0	25.0	26.6	27.3	27.7	26.3	26.6
2 spells	14.1	14.2	15.7	13.4	12.6	14.1	13.8	12.7	13.8	13.2	13.2	12.6	12.4
3 spells or more	13.6	14.4	12.5	13.2	12.8	12.8	13.2	12.3	12.8	14.1	14.5	13.7	14.2

Note: See "Notes and Definitions" for information on historical comparability.

Table 1-40. Number and Median Annual Earnings of Year-Round Full-Time Wage and Salary Workers by Age, Sex, and Race, 1987–2000

(Thousands of persons, dollars.)

Age, sex and race	1987	1988	1989	1990	1991	1992	1993	1994	1995	1996	1997	1998	1999	2000
NUMBER														
Total, 16 Years And Over	71 069	73 598	74 898	74 728	74 449	75 517	77 427	79 875	83 407	85 611	86 905	89 748	91 722	94 359
16 to 24 years	7 563	7 400	7 471	6 978	6 571	6 224	6 685	6 684	6 892	6 809	7 063	7 618	7 631	8 384
25 to 44 years	42 211	44 036	45 082	45 086	44 811	45 022	45 951	47 150	48 695	49 225	49 513	50 264	50 532	51 159
25 to 34 years	22 884	23 727	23 721	23 201	22 541	22 469	22 637	23 193	23 310	23 071	23 186	23 048	22 952	23 044
35 to 44 years	19 327	20 309	21 361	21 885	22 270	22 553	23 314	23 957	25 385	26 154	26 327	27 216	27 580	28 115
45 to 54 years	12 764	13 506	13 848	14 070	14 718	15 652	16 424	17 366	18 436	19 714	20 109	21 274	22 375	23 307
55 to 64 years	7 406	7 529	7 321	7 458	7 219	7 590	7 208	7 500	8 122	8 455	8 901	9 273	9 594	9 870
65 years and over	1 125	1 127	1 177	1 137	1 130	1 029	1 159	1 174	1 263	1 408	1 318	1 318	1 590	1 639
Men, 16 Years And Over	42 490	43 785	45 107	44 574	43 523	43 894	45 494	47 255	49 334	50 407	50 772	52 509	53 132	54 477
16 to 24 years	4 145	4 165	4 223	3 982	3 596	3 457	3 853	3 918	4 094	3 942	4 021	4 479	4 347	4 602
25 to 44 years	25 293	26 246	27 321	27 069	26 353	26 335	27 161	28 000	28 940	29 282	29 453	29 763	29 738	30 080
25 to 34 years	13 659	14 163	14 439	13 941	13 146	13 146	13 400	13 749	13 844	13 817	13 612	13 471	13 497	13 496
35 to 44 years	11 634	12 083	12 882	13 128	13 050	13 189	13 761	14 251	15 096	15 465	15 718	16 151	16 267	16 583
45 to 54 years	7 726	8 086	8 276	8 168	8 479	8 908	9 522	10 120	10 589	11 372	11 388	12 030	12 546	13 045
55 to 64 years	4 654	4 616	4 562	4 650	4 403	4 588	4 238	4 460	4 884	4 908	5 133	5 438	5 498	5 693
65 years and over	672	672	725	705	694	606	719	757	827	903	775	801	1 003	1 057
Women, 16 Years And Over	28 579	29 812	29 791	30 155	30 925	31 622	31 933	32 619	34 073	35 203	36 133	37 239	38 591	39 887
16 to 24 years	3 418	3 235	3 249	2 995	2 976	2 767	2 832	2 767	2 798	2 867	3 041	3 140	3 285	3 782
25 to 44 years	16 918	17 790	17 760	18 017	18 458	18 688	18 790	19 150	19 755	19 942	20 060	20 503	20 794	21 081
25 to 34 years	9 225	9 564	9 282	9 260	9 238	9 323	9 237	9 444	9 467	9 254	9 437	9 437	9 594	9 548
35 to 44 years	7 693	8 226	8 478	8 757	9 220	9 365	9 553	9 706	10 288	10 688	10 609	11 066	11 313	11 533
45 to 54 years	5 037	5 420	5 572	5 902	6 239	6 744	6 902	7 246	7 847	8 343	8 721	9 244	9 829	10 263
55 to 64 years	2 752	2 913	2 758	2 808	2 816	3 002	2 970	3 040	3 238	3 547	3 767	3 836	4 096	4 178
65 years and over	453	455	451	433	436	423	439	417	436	505	543	517	586	583
White, 16 Years And Over	61 546	63 357	64 246	64 128	63 926	64 706	65 656	67 370	70 430	72 068	72 650	75 046	76 203	77 790
Men	37 461	38 449	39 430	38 915	38 018	38 267	39 347	40 589	42 608	43 554	43 429	44 901	45 211	46 105
Women	24 085	24 908	24 815	25 213	25 908	26 439	26 309	26 782	27 822	28 514	29 221	30 145	30 992	31 685
Black, 16 Years And Over	7 440	7 907	8 140	8 027	7 941	7 995	8 478	9 074	9 446	9 706	10 248	10 532	11 145	11 899
Men	3 838	3 976	4 219	4 162	4 001	4 011	4 259	4 598	4 686	4 682	5 026	5 202	5 411	5 636
Women	3 602	3 931	3 920	3 865	3 940	3 984	4 219	4 476	4 759	5 024	5 222	5 329	5 734	6 264
MEDIAN ANNUAL EARNINGS														
Total, 16 Years And Over	21 000	22 000	23 000	24 000	25 000	25 871	26 000	26 620	27 000	28 000	30 000	30 000	31 000	32 000
16 to 24 years	13 000	13 500	14 000	14 400	14 100	15 000	15 000	15 000	15 500	15 600	16 000	18 000	18 000	19 000
25 to 34 years	20 000	21 000	22 000	22 000	23 000	24 000	24 000	24 480	25 000	25 300	27 000	28 500	30 000	30 000
35 to 44 years	25 000	26 000	27 000	27 970	28 000	29 483	30 000	30 000	30 000	31 000	32 000	33 000	34 992	35 000
45 to 54 years	25 000	26 000	27 000	28 000	29 000	30 000	30 500	32 343	32 000	33 000	35 000	35 000	36 000	38 000
55 to 64 years	23 000	24 000	26 000	26 000	27 000	27 430	28 000	30 000	30 000	30 000	32 000	34 000	35 000	35 000
65 years and over	18 000	19 500	23 000	23 841	22 000	24 000	24 000	24 377	29 600	26 496	28 200	26 000	30 000	32 000
Men, 16 Years And Over	25 900	26 570	27 300	28 000	29 120	30 000	30 000	30 000	31 000	32 000	34 000	35 000	36 000	37 600
16 to 24 years	14 000	14 200	15 000	15 000	15 000	15 000	15 000	15 000	16 000	17 000	17 000	18 720	19 000	20 000
25 to 34 years	23 000	24 000	24 000	25 000	25 000	26 000	25 000	26 000	27 000	28 000	29 852	30 000	32 000	33 500
35 to 44 years	30 000	31 000	32 000	32 000	33 000	34 000	35 000	35 000	35 000	36 000	37 000	38 000	40 000	40 000
45 to 54 years	31 200	32 000	34 000	35 000	36 000	37 000	38 000	40 000	40 000	40 000	41 000	42 000	44 616	45 000
55 to 64 years	29 181	30 000	32 000	31 875	33 000	33 000	34 000	36 000	36 000	36 000	36 000	39 000	40 000	44 000
65 years and over	24 000	25 000	30 000	29 000	28 000	30 000	28 000	30 000	36 000	33 000	36 400	35 000	36 000	35 999
Women, 16 Years And Over	17 000	18 000	18 574	20 000	20 000	21 500	22 000	22 150	23 000	24 000	25 000	25 000	26 000	27 500
16 to 24 years	12 000	13 000	13 167	13 392	13 800	14 000	14 872	14 560	15 000	15 000	15 000	17 000	17 000	18 000
25 to 34 years	17 000	18 000	19 000	19 500	20 000	21 000	21 000	22 000	22 000	23 000	24 000	25 000	26 000	27 000
35 to 44 years	19 000	20 000	20 200	22 000	22 510	23 397	24 000	25 000	25 000	25 000	26 000	27 200	28 000	29 000
45 to 54 years	18 148	19 000	20 000	21 000	22 000	24 000	24 000	25 000	25 000	26 000	27 040	28 132	30 000	30 000
55 to 64 years	17 000	17 000	18 000	19 000	20 000	22 000	21 500	22 000	22 500	24 000	24 800	25 775	27 000	28 000
65 years and over	16 000	15 600	17 566	18 586	17 000	18 500	20 000	19 000	23 290	20 800	24 000	22 000	20 800	24 000
White, 16 Years And Over	22 000	23 000	24 000	25 000	25 000	26 200	27 000	28 000	28 000	29 000	30 000	31 000	32 000	34 000
Men	26 500	27 489	28 500	29 000	30 000	31 000	30 700	32 000	32 000	33 000	35 000	36 000	37 200	39 000
Women	17 000	18 000	19 000	20 000	20 500	22 000	22 000	23 000	23 000	24 000	25 000	26 000	27 000	28 000
Black, 16 Years And Over	17 000	18 000	19 000	19 350	20 000	21 000	20 800	21 000	22 000	23 784	24 000	25 000	25 760	26 000
Men	18 850	20 000	20 000	20 800	22 000	22 312	23 000	23 500	24 500	26 000	26 000	27 000	30 000	30 000
Women	15 500	16 200	17 115	18 000	18 500	20 000	19 843	20 000	20 000	21 000	22 000	23 000	24 000	25 000

Note: Detail for the above race groups will not sum to totals because data for the Other races group are not presented. See "Notes and Definitions" for information on historical comparability.

Table 1-41. Number and Median Annual Earnings of Year-Round Full-Time Wage and Salary Workers by Sex and Occupation of Job Held the Longest, 1988–2000

(Thousands of persons, dollars.)

Occupation	1988	1989	1990	1991	1992	1993	1994	1995	1996	1997	1998	1999	2000
TOTAL, NUMBER OF WORKERS													
Managerial and professional specialty	22 213	21 972	21 996	22 037	23 479	23 682	24 816	26 215	27 377	27 943	29 250	30 033	31 428
Executive, administrative, and managerial	11 715	11 735	11 662	11 644	12 167	12 361	12 954	13 839	14 693	14 592	15 367	15 937	16 793
Professional specialty	10 498	10 237	10 334	10 393	11 312	11 321	11 862	12 376	12 684	13 351	13 883	14 096	14 635
Technical, sales, and administrative support	22 280	23 119	22 889	23 749	23 193	23 353	23 525	24 380	24 575	25 182	25 418	26 108	26 597
Technicians and related support	2 716	2 893	2 842	3 163	2 963	2 972	2 962	2 984	3 179	3 281	3 302	3 478	3 631
Sales occupations	7 565	7 856	7 605	7 665	7 826	8 120	8 484	8 989	9 170	9 186	9 537	9 802	9 955
Administrative support, including clerical	11 999	12 370	12 442	12 921	12 404	12 261	12 079	12 407	12 226	12 715	12 579	12 828	13 011
Service occupations	6 857	7 118	7 264	7 392	7 721	7 823	8 257	8 432	8 874	8 921	9 591	9 858	9 902
Private household	236	215	192	165	227	206	218	252	266	232	254	339	285
Protective service	1 551	1 637	1 639	1 674	1 761	1 748	1 776	1 756	1 746	1 886	2 078	2 002	2 008
Service, except private household and protective	5 070	5 266	5 433	5 553	5 733	5 869	6 263	6 424	6 862	6 803	7 259	7 517	7 609
Precision production, craft, and repair	9 640	9 542	9 373	8 710	8 570	9 226	9 420	9 655	10 225	10 465	10 904	10 785	11 249
Mechanics and repairers	3 550	3 395	3 519	3 345	3 168	3 449	3 420	3 590	3 799	3 751	4 045	3 939	4 036
Construction trades	2 877	2 880	2 850	2 412	2 431	2 540	2 940	3 054	3 270	3 496	3 779	3 724	4 047
Other precision production, craft, and repair	3 213	3 267	3 004	2 953	2 971	3 237	3 060	3 011	3 156	3 218	3 080	3 122	3 166
Operators, fabricators, and laborers	11 584	11 278	11 343	10 790	10 717	11 471	11 887	12 556	12 497	12 425	12 642	13 021	13 210
Machine operators, assemblers, and inspectors	5 989	5 664	5 733	5 341	5 231	5 534	5 821	6 084	6 123	6 022	5 818	5 905	5 772
Transportation and material moving occupations	3 187	3 168	3 165	3 025	3 129	3 364	3 370	3 630	3 711	3 658	3 690	3 933	4 160
Handlers, equipment cleaners, helpers, and laborers	2 408	2 446	2 445	2 424	2 357	2 573	2 696	2 842	2 663	2 745	3 134	3 183	3 278
Farming, forestry, and fishing	916	993	995	926	1 067	1 059	1 145	1 481	1 373	1 217	1 221	1 238	1 329
Armed forces	106	876	869	845	769	813	824	690	691	751	724	679	648
TOTAL, MEDIAN ANNUAL EARNINGS													
Managerial and professional specialty	$30 000	$33 000	$34 000	$35 000	$35 624	$37 000	$38 300	$39 000	$40 000	$40 000	$43 000	$45 000	$46 500
Executive, administrative, and managerial	30 000	33 000	33 372	35 000	35 200	36 000	38 000	39 000	39 000	41 000	43 275	45 000	47 500
Professional specialty	30 200	32 645	34 000	35 000	36 000	37 953	38 500	40 000	40 000	40 000	42 000	45 000	46 000
Technical, sales, and administrative support	19 800	20 000	21 000	22 000	23 200	24 000	24 000	24 500	25 000	26 000	27 000	28 000	29 500
Technicians and related support	25 000	25 400	27 000	27 000	28 000	30 000	30 000	30 000	31 000	31 200	34 000	35 000	35 000
Sales occupations	22 000	23 400	24 000	25 000	26 000	26 000	27 000	27 000	28 000	30 000	30 000	31 200	33 000
Administrative support, including clerical	17 500	18 200	19 500	20 000	21 000	21 000	21 700	22 000	23 000	24 000	25 000	25 000	25 142
Service occupations	14 000	15 000	15 000	15 000	16 000	16 000	16 400	17 000	17 616	18 000	18 000	19 600	20 000
Private household	7 600	7 200	7 280	9 100	10 000	8 000	10 000	10 000	10 400	13 000	12 000	11 960	20 000
Protective service	26 000	27 000	26 000	27 000	30 000	30 000	30 000	30 700	30 000	33 000	35 800	33 000	36 000	35 000
Service, except private household and protective	12 000	13 000	13 000	13 800	14 000	14 847	15 000	15 000	15 600	16 000	16 000	17 400	18 000
Precision production, craft, and repair	25 000	25 600	26 000	27 000	28 000	27 387	29 000	30 000	30 000	30 000	31 000	33 280	34 000
Mechanics and repairers	25 432	26 000	27 000	28 000	30 000	28 000	30 000	31 000	30 000	32 000	34 000	35 000	35 000
Construction trades	24 000	25 000	25 000	27 000	27 200	26 000	28 343	28 500	29 000	30 000	29 440	32 711	33 500
Other precision production, craft, and repair	25 000	26 000	25 000	27 000	28 000	27 000	28 542	29 000	30 000	30 000	30 000	31 000	32 000
Operators, fabricators, and laborers	18 045	19 500	20 000	20 000	20 770	20 000	21 000	21 000	23 000	24 000	25 000	25 000	25 000
Machine operators, assemblers, and inspectors	17 100	19 000	18 458	19 200	20 000	20 000	20 658	21 000	22 000	23 000	24 960	25 000	25 000
Transportation and material moving occupations	22 700	23 000	24 000	24 000	25 000	25 000	25 000	25 968	27 000	27 395	30 000	30 000	30 000
Handlers, equipment cleaners, helpers, and laborers	16 000	17 200	17 000	17 000	18 000	17 000	17 000	18 000	20 000	20 000	20 000	20 000	20 800
Farming, forestry, and fishing	13 000	13 600	14 000	14 400	15 000	15 600	15 028	17 000	18 000	17 000	19 000	18 200	19 500
Armed forces	13 000	19 700	19 751	20 000	22 000	24 000	25 000	24 103	26 000	27 574	30 000	29 000	30 271
MEN, NUMBER OF WORKERS													
Managerial and professional specialty	12 846	12 860	12 597	12 301	12 860	13 168	13 898	14 464	15 028	15 173	15 774	16 260	16 773
Executive, administrative, and managerial	7 070	7 187	7 061	6 887	7 100	7 166	7 554	8 031	8 406	8 240	8 552	8 978	9 267
Professional specialty	5 776	5 673	5 536	5 414	5 760	6 002	6 344	6 433	6 622	6 933	7 222	7 282	7 506
Technical, sales, and administrative support	8 856	9 320	9 048	9 322	9 306	9 312	9 562	9 965	9 884	9 977	10 281	10 306	10 482
Technicians and related support	1 524	1 561	1 567	1 666	1 585	1 454	1 540	1 454	1 620	1 561	1 698	1 712	1 789
Sales occupations	4 652	4 876	4 671	4 784	4 798	4 950	5 202	5 467	5 409	5 397	5 621	5 720	5 729
Administrative support, including clerical	2 680	2 883	2 810	2 872	2 923	2 908	2 820	3 044	2 855	3 019	2 962	2 874	2 964
Service occupations	3 540	3 804	3 947	3 938	3 933	4 066	4 210	4 310	4 554	4 581	4 762	4 879	4 857
Private household	13	17	9	22	25	16	13	10	9	7	9	14	18
Protective service	1 373	1 459	1 442	1 416	1 528	1 508	1 560	1 526	1 483	1 596	1 728	1 715	1 695
Service, except private household and protective	2 154	2 328	2 496	2 500	2 380	2 542	2 637	2 774	3 062	2 978	3 025	3 150	3 144
Precision production, craft, and repair	8 887	8 749	8 610	8 021	7 891	8 316	8 651	8 882	9 411	9 645	10 008	9 766	10 369
Mechanics and repairers	3 416	3 271	3 385	3 227	3 057	3 280	3 272	3 451	3 638	3 598	3 851	3 722	3 879
Construction trades	2 806	2 825	2 815	2 391	2 410	2 491	2 890	3 018	3 230	3 456	3 715	3 652	3 975
Other precision production, craft, and repair	2 665	2 653	2 410	2 403	2 424	2 545	2 489	2 413	2 543	2 591	2 442	2 392	2 515
Operators, fabricators, and laborers	8 747	8 653	8 699	8 295	8 197	8 940	9 149	9 761	9 700	9 656	9 929	10 213	10 262
Machine operators, assemblers, and inspectors	3 681	3 554	3 657	3 443	3 295	3 608	3 787	4 010	4 002	3 961	3 893	3 966	3 763
Transportation and material moving occupations	3 029	2 990	3 002	2 872	2 935	3 150	3 141	3 403	3 483	3 412	3 440	3 659	3 853
Handlers, equipment cleaners, helpers, and laborers	2 037	2 109	2 040	1 980	1 967	2 182	2 221	2 348	2 215	2 283	2 596	2 588	2 646
Farming, forestry, and fishing	817	891	887	847	979	948	1 022	1 295	1 207	1 082	1 088	1 095	1 146
Armed forces	91	830	787	801	728	745	762	658	625	657	667	612	587

See *Note* at end of table.

Table 1-41. Number and Median Annual Earnings of Year-Round Full-Time Wage and Salary Workers by Sex and Occupation of Job Held the Longest, 1988–2000—Continued

(Thousands of persons, dollars.)

Occupation	1988	1989	1990	1991	1992	1993	1994	1995	1996	1997	1998	1999	2000
MEN, MEDIAN ANNUAL EARNINGS													
Managerial and professional specialty	$37 000	$39 500	$40 000	$42 000	$43 000	$44 000	$45 613	$47 000	$48 000	$50 000	$50 700	$55 000	$58 000
Executive, administrative, and managerial	37 299	40 000	41 000	42 000	44 000	45 000	46 000	47 500	47 100	50 000	52 000	55 000	58 000
Professional specialty	36 500	38 000	40 000	42 000	42 270	43 995	45 000	47 000	48 000	50 000	50 000	53 250	57 741
Technical, sales, and administrative support	26 050	28 000	29 000	30 000	30 000	31 000	31 197	32 000	33 600	34 000	35 000	37 000	39 000
Technicians and related support	30 000	31 000	30 300	31 100	33 000	34 000	35 000	35 000	36 000	38 000	40 000	41 000	44 000
Sales occupations	27 000	29 000	30 000	30 000	32 000	33 000	34 000	35 000	35 000	35 000	37 800	38 027	40 000
Administrative support, including clerical	24 000	25 000	25 220	27 000	27 000	26 632	27 000	27 286	30 000	29 000	30 000	31 400	32 800
Service occupations	18 000	18 400	18 000	19 315	20 000	20 000	20 500	21 000	20 400	22 000	23 000	24 000	25 000
Private household	11 200	11 000	14 000	9 600	10 800	18 000	5 000	12 318	9 000	10 000	13 000	13 000	24 000
Protective service	27 000	28 000	27 000	28 500	30 000	30 000	32 800	32 400	34 000	37 000	35 000	38 000	37 000
Service, except private household and protective	15 000	15 000	15 000	16 000	15 600	16 000	17 000	17 000	18 000	18 000	18 000	20 000	20 560
Precision production, craft, and repair	25 434	26 000	27 000	28 000	29 000	28 000	30 000	30 000	30 000	31 200	32 000	35 000	35 000
Mechanics and repairers	25 000	26 000	27 000	28 000	30 000	28 000	30 000	31 000	30 000	32 000	34 000	35 000	35 439
Construction trades	24 500	25 000	25 000	27 000	27 116	26 000	28 600	28 500	29 000	30 000	29 097	32 760	34 000
Other precision production, craft, and repair	27 000	29 000	28 000	30 000	30 000	30 000	30 000	31 200	33 000	33 800	35 000	35 000	35 000
Operators, fabricators, and laborers	20 500	21 000	22 000	22 000	23 000	23 000	23 000	23 500	25 000	26 000	26 500	26 400	28 000
Machine operators, assemblers, and inspectors	21 000	22 000	22 000	23 500	24 000	23 400	24 000	24 000	25 000	27 000	27 935	28 600	29 000
Transportation and material moving occupations	23 800	23 200	24 000	24 960	25 000	26 000	25 500	26 000	27 250	28 000	30 000	30 000	30 000
Handlers, equipment cleaners, helpers, and laborers	16 858	18 000	18 000	17 053	18 144	17 623	18 000	18 824	20 000	21 000	21 000	20 800	21 900
Farming, forestry, and fishing	13 400	14 000	14 000	14 000	15 000	15 600	16 000	17 350	18 000	17 000	19 500	19 084	19 916
Armed forces	12 725	20 000	19 200	20 700	22 202	24 748	25 000	24 103	26 000	28 000	30 000	30 000	31 684
WOMEN, NUMBER OF WORKERS													
Managerial and professional specialty	9 367	9 113	9 398	9 736	10 618	10 515	10 918	11 751	12 349	12 769	13 476	13 773	14 655
Executive, administrative, and managerial	4 645	4 548	4 600	4 757	5 067	5 195	5 400	5 808	6 287	6 352	6 815	6 959	7 526
Professional specialty	4 722	4 565	4 798	4 979	5 551	5 320	5 518	5 943	6 062	6 417	6 661	6 814	7 129
Technical, sales, and administrative support	13 425	13 800	13 842	14 427	13 888	14 041	13 962	14 415	14 691	15 206	15 135	15 801	16 113
Technicians and related support	1 192	1 332	1 275	1 497	1 379	1 518	1 422	1 530	1 559	1 721	1 604	1 765	1 841
Sales occupations	2 913	2 981	2 934	2 882	3 028	3 170	3 281	3 522	3 761	3 789	3 915	4 082	4 225
Administrative support, including clerical	9 320	9 487	9 633	10 048	9 481	9 353	9 259	9 363	9 371	9 696	9 616	9 954	10 047
Service occupations	3 318	3 313	3 318	3 455	3 787	3 758	4 048	4 120	4 320	4 340	4 829	4 979	5 046
Private household	224	197	183	144	202	190	206	241	257	225	245	325	267
Protective service	179	178	197	258	232	241	216	229	263	290	350	287	314
Service, except private household and protective	2 915	2 938	2 938	3 053	3 353	3 327	3 626	3 650	3 800	3 825	4 234	4 367	4 465
Precision production, craft, and repair	753	793	764	689	679	910	770	773	813	821	897	1 019	880
Mechanics and repairers	134	124	134	118	111	169	148	139	160	154	194	217	157
Construction trades	71	55	36	21	21	49	50	36	40	40	64	72	72
Other precision production, craft, and repair	548	614	594	550	547	692	572	598	613	627	639	730	651
Operators, fabricators, and laborers	2 836	2 625	2 644	2 495	2 521	2 531	2 738	2 795	2 796	2 769	2 713	2 810	2 948
Machine operators, assemblers, and inspectors	2 308	2 110	2 076	1 898	1 936	1 926	2 034	2 074	2 121	2 061	1 925	1 940	2 009
Transportation and material moving occupations	157	178	163	153	195	214	229	227	227	246	250	274	307
Handlers, equipment cleaners, helpers, and laborers	371	337	405	444	390	391	475	494	448	462	538	596	632
Farming, forestry, and fishing	99	102	108	79	88	111	123	187	166	135	133	143	182
Armed forces	15	45	83	45	41	68	62	32	67	94	57	67	61
WOMEN, MEDIAN ANNUAL EARNINGS													
Managerial and professional specialty	$25 000	$26 000	$27 500	$29 000	$29 863	$30 000	$31 000	$32 000	$32 000	$34 500	$35 000	$37 000	$38 000
Executive, administrative, and managerial	23 500	24 755	25 400	27 000	28 000	29 000	30 000	30 000	31 000	33 600	35 000	36 000	37 000
Professional specialty	25 000	28 000	29 000	30 000	30 000	30 000	32 000	32 000	33 000	34 000	35 000	35 500	38 000	38 800
Technical, sales, and administrative support	16 600	17 594	18 500	19 111	20 000	20 000	21 000	21 000	22 000	23 000	24 000	24 960	25 000
Technicians and related support	20 500	21 800	24 000	22 270	24 353	26 000	27 000	26 000	27 000	27 300	28 000	29 161	30 000
Sales occupations	15 000	15 500	17 000	18 000	18 000	18 720	19 000	20 000	21 000	21 000	23 000	23 000	25 000
Administrative support, including clerical	16 376	17 500	18 000	19 000	20 000	20 000	20 260	20 800	21 840	22 500	24 000	24 000	25 000
Service occupations	11 000	12 000	12 444	12 000	13 000	13 513	13 500	14 749	15 000	15 400	15 000	16 000	17 000
Private household	7 000	7 000	7 280	7 800	9 200	8 000	10 000	10 000	10 400	13 000	12 000	11 960	12 000
Protective service	22 000	21 267	22 314	23 000	23 570	26 000	23 550	24 000	28 000	28 496	26 000	26 052	26 000
Service, except private household and protective	11 000	12 000	12 050	12 000	13 000	13 000	13 200	14 539	15 000	15 000	15 000	16 000	16 640
Precision production, craft, and repair	17 000	17 836	18 852	18 707	20 000	21 000	22 000	21 000	21 000	21 000	24 000	25 000	25 000
Mechanics and repairers	28 000	26 000	26 500	30 000	29 000	30 000	33 000	33 000	22 000	33 000	31 601	32 000	27 000
Construction trades	20 000	29 000	20 000	20 000	42 000	26 000	24 000	29 000	20 000	25 700	35 000	29 000	25 000
Other precision production, craft, and repair	15 000	16 000	17 900	17 000	18 000	20 000	20 000	19 000	20 500	19 000	21 000	22 000	25 000
Operators, fabricators, and laborers	13 000	14 000	14 300	15 000	15 000	15 000	16 000	16 000	17 000	17 200	18 500	18 200	19 872
Machine operators, assemblers, and inspectors	13 000	14 000	14 374	15 000	15 000	15 000	16 000	16 000	17 576	17 839	18 867	18 200	20 000
Transportation and material moving occupations	13 000	15 000	16 100	19 000	20 000	19 000	24 000	18 000	17 500	20 000	21 000	20 000	20 200
Handlers, equipment cleaners, helpers, and laborers	13 500	13 500	13 441	16 000	14 200	14 520	14 600	14 800	16 640	15 800	16 000	18 000	17 280
Farming, forestry, and fishing	10 400	12 000	11 799	12 200	13 000	15 600	10 700	16 000	18 000	17 000	15 600	15 000	18 000
Armed forces	15 000	14 000	22 000	14 000	18 500	18 300	24 000	25 000	22 000	25 000	28 000	26 000	28 000

Note: See "Notes and Definitions" for information on historical comparability.

Table 1-42. Wage and Salary Workers Paid Hourly Rates with Earnings at or below the Prevailing Federal Minimum Wage by Selected Characteristics, 2000–2001

(Thousands of persons, percent.)

Characteristic	Workers paid hourly rates				
	Total	Below prevailing federal minimum wage	At prevailing federal minimum wage	Total at or below prevailing federal minimum wage	
				Number	Percent of hourly-paid workers
2000					
Sex And Age					
Total, 16 years and over	72 744	1 844	866	2 710	3.7
16 to 24 years	16 938	938	510	1 447	8.5
25 years and over	55 806	906	357	1 263	2.3
Men, 16 years and over	36 228	632	322	954	2.6
16 to 24 years	8 743	346	202	548	6.3
25 years and over	27 485	286	120	406	1.5
Women, 16 years and over	36 516	1 212	544	1 757	4.8
16 to 24 years	8 194	592	308	899	11.0
25 years and over	28 321	621	237	857	3.0
Race, Hispanic Origin, And Sex					
White, 16 years and over	59 374	1 555	687	2 242	3.8
Men	29 970	506	246	752	2.5
Women	29 404	1 049	441	1 490	5.1
Black, 16 years and over	10 105	213	148	361	3.6
Men	4 648	94	63	157	3.4
Women	5 457	119	85	204	3.7
Hispanic origin, 16 years and over	9 847	189	129	318	3.2
Men	5 787	91	50	141	2.4
Women	4 060	99	78	177	4.4
Full-And Part-Time Status And Sex[1]					
Full-time workers	55 701	736	289	1 025	1.8
Men	30 856	286	113	400	1.3
Women	24 845	450	176	626	2.5
Part-time workers	16 909	1 096	577	1 673	9.9
Men	5 308	342	208	550	10.4
Women	11 601	754	369	1 123	9.7
2001					
Sex And Age					
Total, 16 years and over	72 486	1 602	636	2 238	3.1
16 to 24 years	16 602	830	376	1 206	7.3
25 years and over	55 884	771	260	1 032	1.8
Men, 16 years and over	36 029	529	255	784	2.2
16 to 24 years	8 491	296	177	473	5.6
25 years and over	27 538	233	78	311	1.1
Women, 16 years and over	36 457	1 073	381	1 454	4.0
16 to 24 years	8 111	534	199	733	9.0
25 years and over	28 346	539	182	721	2.5
Race, Hispanic Origin, And Sex					
White, 16 years and over	59 152	1 359	502	1 861	3.1
Men	29 792	444	198	641	2.2
Women	29 360	915	304	1 219	4.2
Black, 16 years and over	10 014	183	114	297	3.0
Men	4 583	64	50	114	2.5
Women	5 431	119	64	183	3.4
Hispanic origin, 16 years and over	10 030	187	114	302	3.0
Men	5 772	83	55	138	2.4
Women	4 258	104	59	164	3.8
Full-And Part-Time Status And Sex[1]					
Full-time workers	55 232	662	191	853	1.5
Men	30 452	249	79	328	1.1
Women	24 780	413	112	525	2.1
Part-time workers	17 124	937	441	1 378	8.0
Men	5 511	279	176	455	8.3
Women	11 613	657	266	923	7.9

Note: Detail for the above race and Hispanic origin groups will not sum to totals because data for the Other races groups are not presented and Hispanics are included in both the White and Black population groups.

1. The distinction between full- and part-time workers is based on the hours usually worked. These data will not sum to totals because full- or part-time status on the principal job is not identifiable for a small number of multiple jobholders.

Table 1-43. Absences from Work of Employed Full-Time Wage and Salary Workers by Age and Sex, 2000–2001

(Thousands of persons, percent.)

Age and sex	Total employed	Absence rate			Lost worktime rate [1]		
		Total	Illness or injury	Other reasons	Total	Illness or injury	Other reasons
2000							
Total, 16 Years And Over	99 846	3.8	2.7	1.0	2.0	1.4	0.6
16 to 19 years	2 382	4.2	3.1	1.1	1.9	1.3	0.6
20 to 24 years	9 608	4.0	2.7	1.3	1.9	1.2	0.7
25 years and over	87 856	3.8	2.7	1.0	2.0	1.5	0.5
25 to 54 years	77 120	3.7	2.7	1.1	2.0	1.4	0.6
55 years and over	10 736	3.9	3.2	0.7	2.3	2.0	0.3
Men, 16 Years And Over	56 228	2.8	2.2	0.6	1.5	1.2	0.3
16 to 19 years	1 414	3.2	2.5	0.7	1.5	1.1	0.4
20 to 24 years	5 420	2.8	2.1	0.7	1.3	1.0	0.3
25 years and over	49 394	2.7	2.2	0.6	1.5	1.2	0.3
25 to 54 years	43 353	2.7	2.1	0.6	1.4	1.2	0.3
55 years and over	6 041	3.3	2.7	0.6	2.0	1.7	0.3
Women, 16 Years And Over	43 618	5.1	3.5	1.6	2.7	1.8	1.0
16 to 19 years	968	5.6	3.9	1.7	2.6	1.5	1.1
20 to 24 years	4 188	5.5	3.5	2.0	2.7	1.5	1.2
25 years and over	38 461	5.1	3.5	1.6	2.7	1.8	0.9
25 to 54 years	33 767	5.1	3.4	1.7	2.7	1.7	1.0
55 years and over	4 694	4.8	3.9	0.9	2.6	2.3	0.4
2001							
Total, 16 Years And Over	99 508	3.6	2.5	1.0	1.9	1.3	0.5
16 to 19 years	2 179	3.4	2.5	0.9	1.5	1.1	0.4
20 to 24 years	9 429	3.5	2.3	1.2	1.7	1.0	0.7
25 years and over	87 899	3.6	2.6	1.0	1.9	1.4	0.5
25 to 54 years	76 680	3.5	2.5	1.1	1.9	1.3	0.6
55 years and over	11 220	3.8	3.1	0.8	2.2	1.8	0.4
Men, 16 Years And Over	55 931	2.6	2.0	0.6	1.4	1.1	0.3
16 to 19 years	1 274	2.6	2.0	0.6	1.2	0.9	0.3
20 to 24 years	5 279	2.5	1.8	0.6	1.1	0.9	0.2
25 years and over	49 378	2.6	2.0	0.6	1.4	1.2	0.3
25 to 54 years	43 121	2.5	1.9	0.6	1.4	1.1	0.3
55 years and over	6 257	3.2	2.6	0.6	1.9	1.6	0.2
Women, 16 Years And Over	43 576	4.8	3.2	1.6	2.6	1.7	0.9
16 to 19 years	905	4.4	3.2	1.2	2.1	1.3	0.7
20 to 24 years	4 150	4.9	2.9	2.0	2.6	1.3	1.3
25 years and over	38 521	4.8	3.2	1.6	2.6	1.7	0.9
25 to 54 years	33 559	4.8	3.2	1.6	2.6	1.6	0.9
55 years and over	4 963	4.7	3.6	1.0	2.5	2.0	0.5

1. Hours absent as a percentage of the hours usually worked.

Table 1-44. Median Years of Tenure with Current Employer for Employed Wage and Salary Workers by Age and Sex, Selected Years, 1983–2000

Age and sex	January 1983	January 1987	January 1991	February 1996	February 1998	February 2000
TOTAL						
16 Years And Over	3.5	3.4	3.6	3.8	3.6	3.5
16 to 17 years	0.7	0.6	0.7	0.7	0.6	0.6
18 to 19 years	0.8	0.7	0.8	0.7	0.7	0.7
20 to 24 years	1.5	1.3	1.3	1.2	1.1	1.1
25 years and over	5.0	5.0	4.8	5.0	4.7	4.7
25 to 34 years	3.0	2.9	2.9	2.8	2.7	2.6
35 to 44 years	5.2	5.5	5.4	5.3	5.0	4.8
45 to 54 years	9.5	8.8	8.9	8.3	8.1	8.2
55 to 64 years	12.2	11.6	11.1	10.2	10.1	10.0
65 years and over	9.6	9.5	8.1	8.4	7.8	9.5
MEN						
16 Years And Over	4.1	4.0	4.1	4.0	3.8	3.8
16 to 17 years	0.7	0.6	0.7	0.6	0.6	0.6
18 to 19 years	0.8	0.7	0.8	0.7	0.7	0.7
20 to 24 years	1.5	1.3	1.4	1.2	1.2	1.2
25 years and over	5.9	5.7	5.4	5.3	4.9	5.0
25 to 34 years	3.2	3.1	3.1	3.0	2.8	2.7
35 to 44 years	7.3	7.0	6.5	6.1	5.5	5.4
45 to 54 years	12.8	11.8	11.2	10.1	9.4	9.5
55 to 64 years	15.3	14.5	13.4	10.5	11.2	10.2
65 years and over	8.3	8.3	7.0	8.3	7.1	9.1
WOMEN						
16 Years And Over	3.1	3.0	3.2	3.5	3.4	3.3
16 to 17 years	0.7	0.6	0.7	0.7	0.7	0.6
18 to 19 years	0.8	0.7	0.8	0.7	0.7	0.7
20 to 24 years	1.5	1.3	1.3	1.2	1.1	1.0
25 years and over	4.2	4.3	4.3	4.7	4.4	4.4
25 to 34 years	2.8	2.6	2.7	2.7	2.5	2.5
35 to 44 years	4.1	4.4	4.5	4.8	4.5	4.3
45 to 54 years	6.3	6.8	6.7	7.0	7.2	7.3
55 to 64 years	9.8	9.7	9.9	10.0	9.6	9.9
65 years and over	10.1	9.9	9.5	8.4	8.7	9.7

Note: Data exclude the incorporated and unincorporated self-employed. See "Notes and Definitions" for information on historical comparability.

Table 1-45. Median Years of Tenure with Current Employer for Employed Wage and Salary Workers by Industry, Selected Years, 1983–2000

Industry	January 1983	January 1987	January 1991	February 1996	February 1998	February 2000
TOTAL, 16 YEARS AND OVER	3.5	3.4	3.6	3.8	3.6	3.5
Agriculture	2.2	2.4	2.6	3.4	2.9	3.1
Nonagricultural Industries	3.6	3.4	3.6	3.8	3.6	3.5
Government	5.8	6.5	6.5	6.9	7.3	7.2
Private industries	3.2	3.0	3.2	3.3	3.2	3.2
Mining	3.4	6.1	5.8	6.1	5.6	6.5
Construction	2.0	2.0	2.6	2.9	2.7	2.8
Manufacturing	5.4	5.5	5.2	5.4	4.9	5.0
Durable goods[1]	5.6	6.0	5.8	5.3	4.9	4.9
Lumber and wood products	4.0	3.2	3.6	3.3	3.8	4.0
Furniture and fixtures	4.2	3.2	4.0	4.2	3.9	4.1
Stone, clay, and glass products	7.0	6.8	6.3	5.1	6.1	5.4
Primary metal industries	10.0	10.2	9.7	8.1	8.0	7.0
Fabricated metal products	5.7	5.5	5.5	5.1	4.0	4.7
Machinery and computing equipment	5.8	6.7	5.9	5.2	4.4	4.5
Electrical machinery, equipment, and supplies	4.7	4.8	5.5	4.9	5.0	4.7
Transportation equipment[1]	8.8	8.0	7.6	8.3	7.8	6.4
Motor vehicles and equipment	13.0	11.2	11.7	7.8	6.4	5.8
Aircraft and parts	6.4	6.8	6.3	9.8	9.6	9.7
Professional and photographic equipment and watches	4.7	5.9	5.1	5.1	5.5	5.2
Toys, amusements, and sporting goods	3.6	5.8	3.2	2.7	3.6	3.7
Nondurable goods[1]	5.1	4.9	4.7	5.4	4.9	5.1
Food and kindred products	5.2	4.4	4.2	5.1	5.1	5.0
Textile mill products	7.0	7.0	5.6	5.4	6.7	7.4
Apparel and other finished textile products	3.8	3.2	3.8	3.8	3.8	3.3
Paper and allied products	7.6	8.6	7.6	8.4	7.5	6.1
Printing and publishing	3.2	3.2	3.5	4.3	4.0	4.4
Chemicals and allied products	7.0	7.2	5.7	6.9	5.4	5.8
Petroleum and coal products	6.0	11.7	8.4	10.3	9.4	7.5
Rubber and miscellaneous plastic products	5.4	4.4	4.7	4.7	4.6	4.9
Transportation and public utilities	5.8	5.7	5.8	5.2	4.8	4.4
Transportation	4.6	3.9	4.2	4.1	3.8	3.9
Communications and other public utilities	8.3	8.4	9.9	8.2	8.2	5.2
Wholesale trade	3.8	3.7	3.4	3.9	4.1	3.9
Retail trade	1.9	1.8	1.9	1.9	1.8	2.0
Finance, insurance, and real estate	3.2	3.0	3.4	4.1	3.5	3.6
Banking and other finance	3.3	3.1	3.6	3.9	3.7	3.3
Insurance and real estate	3.0	2.9	3.2	4.2	3.4	3.9
Services[1]	2.5	2.5	2.7	3.0	2.9	2.9
Private households	1.8	1.7	1.9	2.3	2.3	2.9
Services, except private households	2.5	2.5	2.7	3.0	2.9	2.9
Business services	1.5	1.6	1.8	2.0	1.9	1.8
Automobile and repair services	2.3	2.0	2.2	2.9	2.4	2.7
Personal services, except private households	2.0	2.0	2.1	2.3	2.3	2.7
Entertainment and recreation services	1.8	1.8	2.3	1.9	1.9	2.3
Hospitals	3.5	4.6	4.2	5.2	5.2	5.2
Health services, except hospitals	2.5	2.4	2.7	2.9	2.9	3.2
Educational services	2.7	3.1	3.5	3.8	3.5	3.3
Social services	2.2	2.3	2.3	2.8	2.7	2.6
Other professional services	2.9	2.8	3.3	3.5	3.3	3.2

Note: Data exclude the incorporated and unincorporated self-employed. See "Notes and Definitions" for information on historical comparability.

1. Includes other industries, not shown separately.

Table 1-46. Employment Status of the Population by Marital Status and Sex, March 1989–2001

(Thousands of persons, percent.)

Marital status and year	Men						Women					
	Popula-tion	Labor force					Popula-tion	Labor force				
		Total		Employed	Unemployed			Total		Employed	Unemployed	
		Number	Percent of popula-tion		Number	Percent of labor force		Number	Percent of popula-tion		Number	Percent of labor force
SINGLE												
1989	25 714	18 867	73.4	16 999	1 868	9.9	21 153	13 969	66.0	12 843	1 126	8.1
1990	25 757	18 829	73.1	16 893	1 936	10.3	21 088	14 003	66.4	12 856	1 147	8.2
1991	26 220	19 014	72.5	16 418	2 596	13.7	21 688	14 125	65.1	12 887	1 238	8.8
1992	26 529	19 229	72.5	16 401	2 828	14.7	21 738	14 072	64.7	12 793	1 279	9.1
1993	26 951	19 625	72.8	16 858	2 767	14.1	21 848	14 091	64.5	12 711	1 380	9.8
1994	28 350	20 365	71.8	17 826	2 539	12.5	22 885	14 903	65.1	13 419	1 484	10.0
1995	28 318	20 449	72.2	18 286	2 163	10.6	22 853	14 974	65.5	13 673	1 301	8.7
1996	28 695	20 561	71.7	18 097	2 464	12.0	23 632	15 417	65.2	14 084	1 333	8.6
1997	29 294	20 942	71.5	18 683	2 259	10.8	24 215	16 178	66.8	14 747	1 431	8.8
1998	29 558	21 255	71.9	19 124	2 131	10.0	24 808	16 885	68.1	15 626	1 259	7.5
1999	29 883	21 329	71.4	19 465	1 864	8.7	25 674	17 486	68.1	16 185	1 301	7.4
2000	30 232	21 641	71.6	19 823	1 818	8.4	25 863	17 749	68.6	16 446	1 303	7.3
2001	30 968	22 232	71.8	20 239	1 993	9.0	26 180	17 900	68.4	16 631	1 269	7.1
MARRIED, SPOUSE PRESENT												
1989	52 155	40 912	78.4	39 516	1 396	3.4	52 889	30 489	57.6	29 446	1 043	3.4
1990	52 464	41 020	78.2	39 562	1 458	3.6	53 207	30 967	58.2	29 870	1 097	3.5
1991	52 460	40 883	77.9	38 843	2 040	5.0	53 176	31 103	58.5	29 668	1 435	4.6
1992	52 780	40 930	77.5	38 650	2 280	5.6	53 464	31 686	59.3	30 130	1 556	4.9
1993	53 488	41 255	77.1	39 069	2 186	5.3	54 146	32 158	59.4	30 757	1 401	4.4
1994	53 436	40 993	76.7	39 085	1 908	4.7	54 198	32 863	60.6	31 397	1 466	4.5
1995	54 166	41 806	77.2	40 262	1 544	3.7	54 902	33 563	61.1	32 267	1 296	3.9
1996	53 996	41 837	77.5	40 356	1 481	3.5	54 640	33 382	61.1	32 258	1 124	3.4
1997	53 981	41 967	77.7	40 628	1 339	3.2	54 611	33 907	62.1	32 836	1 071	3.2
1998	54 685	42 288	77.3	41 039	1 249	3.0	55 241	34 136	61.8	33 028	1 108	3.2
1999	55 256	42 557	77.0	41 476	1 081	2.5	55 801	34 349	61.6	33 403	946	2.8
2000	55 897	43 254	77.4	42 261	993	2.3	56 432	34 959	61.9	33 998	961	2.7
2001	56 152	43 463	77.4	42 245	1 218	2.8	56 740	35 234	62.1	34 273	961	2.7
WIDOWED, DIVORCED, OR SEPARATED												
1989	10 641	7 108	66.8	6 552	556	7.8	23 346	10 733	46.0	10 119	614	5.7
1990	11 152	7 513	67.4	6 959	554	7.4	23 857	11 168	46.8	10 530	638	5.7
1991	11 588	7 804	67.3	6 985	819	10.5	24 105	11 145	46.2	10 386	759	6.8
1992	11 927	8 049	67.5	7 140	909	11.3	24 582	11 486	46.7	10 610	876	7.6
1993	11 861	7 956	67.1	7 055	901	11.3	24 661	11 308	45.9	10 528	780	6.9
1994	12 239	8 156	66.6	7 382	774	9.5	25 098	11 879	47.3	10 995	884	7.4
1995	12 410	8 315	67.0	7 632	683	8.2	25 373	12 001	47.3	11 308	693	5.8
1996	13 176	8 697	66.0	7 976	721	8.3	25 786	12 430	48.2	11 742	688	5.5
1997	14 113	9 420	66.7	8 715	705	7.5	26 301	12 814	48.7	12 071	743	5.8
1998	14 166	9 482	66.9	8 954	528	5.6	26 092	12 880	49.4	12 235	645	5.0
1999	14 225	9 449	66.4	8 971	478	5.1	26 199	12 951	49.4	12 307	644	5.0
2000	14 289	9 623	67.3	9 152	471	4.9	26 354	13 228	50.2	12 657	571	4.3
2001	14 392	9 421	65.5	8 927	494	5.2	26 747	13 454	50.3	12 887	567	4.2

See *Note* at end of table.

Table 1-46. Employment Status of the Population by Marital Status and Sex, March 1989–2001—*Continued*

(Thousands of persons, percent.)

Marital status and year	Men						Women					
	Popula-tion	Labor force					Popula-tion	Labor force				
		Total		Employed	Unemployed			Total		Employed	Unemployed	
		Number	Percent of popula-tion		Number	Percent of labor force		Number	Percent of popula-tion		Number	Percent of labor force
WIDOWED												
1989	2 279	536	23.5	521	15	2.8	11 493	2 309	20.1	2 231	78	3.4
1990	2 331	519	22.3	490	29	5.6	11 477	2 243	19.5	2 149	94	4.2
1991	2 385	486	20.4	448	38	7.8	11 288	2 150	19.0	2 044	106	4.9
1992	2 529	566	22.4	501	65	11.5	11 325	2 131	18.8	2 029	102	4.8
1993	2 468	596	24.1	535	61	10.2	11 214	1 961	17.5	1 856	105	5.4
1994	2 220	474	21.4	440	34	7.2	11 073	1 945	17.6	1 825	120	6.2
1995	2 282	496	21.7	469	27	5.4	11 080	1 941	17.5	1 844	97	5.0
1996	2 476	487	19.7	466	21	4.3	11 070	1 916	17.3	1 820	96	5.0
1997	2 686	559	20.8	529	30	5.4	11 058	2 018	18.2	1 926	92	4.6
1998	2 567	563	21.9	551	12	2.1	11 027	2 157	19.6	2 071	86	4.0
1999	2 540	562	22.1	532	30	5.3	10 943	2 039	18.6	1 942	97	4.8
2000	2 601	583	22.4	547	36	6.2	11 061	2 011	18.2	1 911	100	5.0
2001	2 638	568	21.5	546	22	3.9	11 182	2 137	19.1	2 045	92	4.3
DIVORCED												
1989	6 023	4 819	80.0	4 433	386	8.0	8 521	6 396	75.1	6 035	361	5.6
1990	6 256	5 004	80.0	4 639	365	7.3	8 845	6 678	75.5	6 333	345	5.2
1991	6 586	5 262	79.9	4 722	540	10.3	9 152	6 779	74.1	6 365	414	6.1
1992	6 743	5 418	80.3	4 823	595	11.0	9 569	7 076	73.9	6 578	498	7.0
1993	6 770	5 330	78.7	4 736	594	11.1	9 879	7 183	72.7	6 736	447	6.2
1994	7 222	5 548	76.8	5 028	520	9.4	10 113	7 473	73.9	6 962	511	6.8
1995	7 343	5 739	78.2	5 266	473	8.2	10 262	7 559	73.7	7 206	353	4.7
1996	7 734	5 954	77.0	5 468	486	8.2	10 508	7 829	74.5	7 468	361	4.6
1997	8 191	6 298	76.9	5 851	447	7.1	11 102	8 092	72.9	7 666	426	5.3
1998	8 307	6 378	76.8	6 045	333	5.2	11 065	8 038	72.6	7 687	351	4.4
1999	8 529	6 481	76.0	6 151	330	5.1	11 130	8 171	73.4	7 841	330	4.0
2000	8 532	6 583	77.2	6 279	304	4.6	11 061	8 505	76.9	8 217	288	3.4
2001	8 580	6 403	74.6	6 074	329	5.1	11 719	8 662	73.9	8 335	327	3.8
SEPARATED												
1989	2 339	1 753	74.9	1 598	155	8.8	3 332	2 028	60.9	1 853	175	8.6
1990	2 565	1 990	77.6	1 830	160	8.0	3 535	2 247	63.6	2 048	199	8.9
1991	2 616	2 057	78.6	1 816	241	11.7	3 665	2 216	60.5	1 977	239	10.8
1992	2 655	2 065	77.8	1 816	249	12.1	3 688	2 279	61.8	2 003	276	12.1
1993	2 623	2 030	77.4	1 784	246	12.1	3 568	2 165	60.7	1 937	228	10.5
1994	2 797	2 134	76.3	1 914	220	10.3	3 911	2 461	62.9	2 208	253	10.3
1995	2 784	2 081	74.7	1 898	183	8.8	4 031	2 501	62.0	2 258	243	9.7
1996	2 966	2 255	76.0	2 041	214	9.5	4 209	2 684	63.8	2 453	231	8.6
1997	3 236	2 563	79.2	2 335	228	8.9	4 141	2 705	65.3	2 480	225	8.3
1998	3 293	2 542	77.2	2 358	184	7.2	4 000	2 683	67.1	2 476	207	7.7
1999	3 156	2 405	76.2	2 287	118	4.9	4 126	2 740	66.4	2 523	217	7.9
2000	3 157	2 456	77.8	2 326	130	5.3	4 012	2 711	67.6	2 528	183	6.8
2001	3 174	2 450	77.2	2 307	143	5.8	3 846	2 654	69.0	2 507	147	5.5

Note: See "Notes and Definitions" for information on historical comparability.

Table 1-47. Employment Status of All Women and Single Women by Presence and Age of Children, March 1988–2001

(Thousands of persons, percent.)

Age of children and year	All women							Single women						
	Civilian labor force	Civilian labor force as percent of population	Employed		Unemployed			Civilian labor force	Civilian labor force as percent of population	Employed		Unemployed		
			Number	Percent full-time	Percent part-time	Number	Percent of labor force			Number	Percent full-time	Percent part-time	Number	Percent of labor force
WOMEN WITH NO CHILDREN UNDER 18														
1988	32 490	51.2	30 911	73.6	26.4	1 580	4.9	12 417	67.3	11 538	66.7	33.3	880	7.1
1989	33 255	51.9	31 761	73.7	26.3	1 495	4.5	12 445	67.8	11 643	66.1	33.9	803	6.5
1990	33 942	52.3	32 391	74.4	25.6	1 551	4.6	12 478	68.1	11 611	65.9	34.1	866	6.9
1991	34 047	52.0	32 167	74.0	26.0	1 880	5.5	12 472	67.0	11 529	66.2	33.8	943	7.6
1992	34 487	52.3	32 481	74.3	25.7	2 006	5.8	12 355	66.9	11 374	66.6	33.4	982	7.9
1993	34 495	52.1	32 476	74.6	25.4	2 020	5.9	12 223	66.4	11 201	66.1	33.9	1 022	8.4
1994	35 454	53.1	33 343	72.7	27.3	2 110	6.0	12 737	66.8	11 674	64.5	35.5	1 063	8.3
1995	35 843	52.9	34 054	72.9	27.1	1 789	5.0	12 870	67.1	11 919	64.5	35.5	951	7.4
1996	36 509	53.0	34 698	73.3	26.7	1 811	5.0	13 172	66.1	12 255	64.6	35.4	918	7.0
1997	37 295	53.6	35 572	73.7	26.3	1 723	4.6	13 405	66.5	12 442	64.0	36.0	964	7.2
1998	38 253	54.1	36 680	74.1	25.9	1 573	4.1	13 888	67.2	13 082	64.8	35.2	806	5.8
1999	39 316	54.3	37 589	74.6	25.4	1 727	4.4	14 435	67.1	13 491	65.6	34.4	944	6.5
2000	40 142	54.8	38 408	75.4	24.6	1 733	4.3	14 677	67.6	13 713	66.6	33.4	964	6.6
2001	40 836	54.9	39 219	75.7	24.3	1 617	4.0	14 877	67.4	13 993	67.3	32.7	884	5.9
WOMEN WITH CHILDREN UNDER 18														
1988	21 545	65.1	20 141	73.0	27.0	1 404	6.5	1 375	51.6	1 068	79.8	20.2	308	22.4
1989	20 936	65.7	20 647	72.8	27.2	1 289	6.2	1 524	54.7	1 200	79.0	21.0	324	21.3
1990	22 196	66.7	20 865	73.0	27.0	1 331	6.0	1 525	55.2	1 244	79.1	20.9	280	18.4
1991	22 327	66.6	20 774	73.0	27.0	1 552	7.0	1 654	53.6	1 358	76.4	23.6	296	17.9
1992	22 756	67.2	21 052	73.8	26.2	1 704	7.5	1 716	52.5	1 420	75.9	24.1	297	17.3
1993	23 063	66.9	21 521	73.9	26.1	1 541	6.7	1 869	54.4	1 510	74.8	25.2	359	19.2
1994	24 191	68.4	22 467	70.8	29.2	1 724	7.1	2 166	56.9	1 745	73.9	26.1	421	19.4
1995	24 695	69.7	23 195	71.7	28.3	1 500	6.1	2 104	57.5	1 754	73.6	26.4	350	16.6
1996	24 720	70.2	23 386	72.6	27.4	1 334	5.4	2 245	60.5	1 829	73.5	26.5	416	18.5
1997	25 604	72.1	24 082	74.1	25.9	1 522	5.9	2 772	68.1	2 305	76.6	23.4	467	16.8
1998	25 647	72.3	24 209	74.0	26.0	1 438	5.6	2 997	72.5	2 544	75.6	24.4	453	15.1
1999	25 469	72.1	24 305	74.1	25.9	1 165	4.6	3 051	73.4	2 694	75.8	24.2	357	11.7
2000	25 795	72.9	24 693	74.6	25.4	1 102	4.3	3 073	73.9	2 734	79.7	20.3	339	11.0
2001	25 751	73.1	24 572	75.6	24.4	1 179	4.6	3 022	73.8	2 638	81.8	18.2	385	12.7
WOMEN WITH CHILDREN UNDER 6														
1988	8 862	56.1	8 099	69.5	30.5	763	8.6	831	44.9	621	78.8	21.2	211	25.4
1989	9 136	56.7	8 478	68.8	31.2	657	7.2	966	48.9	722	79.2	20.8	244	25.3
1990	9 397	58.2	8 732	69.6	30.4	664	7.1	929	48.7	736	75.0	25.0	194	20.9
1991	9 636	58.4	8 758	69.5	30.5	878	9.1	1 050	48.8	819	72.2	27.8	231	22.0
1992	9 573	58.0	8 662	70.2	29.8	911	9.5	1 029	45.8	829	73.2	26.8	200	19.4
1993	9 621	57.9	8 764	70.1	29.9	857	8.9	1 125	47.4	869	70.0	30.0	257	22.8
1994	10 328	60.3	9 394	67.1	32.9	935	9.1	1 379	52.2	1 062	70.0	30.0	317	23.0
1995	10 395	62.3	9 587	67.5	32.5	809	7.8	1 328	53.0	1 069	68.6	31.4	259	19.5
1996	10 293	62.3	9 592	68.4	31.6	701	6.8	1 378	55.1	1 099	67.3	32.7	279	20.2
1997	10 610	65.0	9 800	70.5	29.5	810	7.6	1 755	65.1	1 424	71.6	28.4	330	18.8
1998	10 619	65.2	9 839	69.8	30.2	780	7.3	1 755	67.3	1 448	71.7	28.3	307	17.5
1999	10 322	64.4	9 674	69.0	31.0	648	6.3	1 811	68.1	1 565	71.0	29.0	246	13.6
2000	10 316	65.3	9 763	70.5	29.5	553	5.4	1 835	70.5	1 603	75.3	24.7	232	12.6
2001	10 200	64.9	9 618	71.2	28.8	582	5.7	1 783	69.7	1 542	79.1	20.9	242	13.6

Note: See "Notes and Definitions" for information on historical comparability.

Table 1-48. Employment Status of Ever-Married Women and Married Women, Spouse Present, by Presence and Age of Children, March 1988–2001

(Thousands of persons, percent.)

Age of children and year	Ever-married women [1]							Married women, spouse present						
	Civilian labor force	Civilian labor force as percent of population	Employed			Unemployed		Civilian labor force	Civilian labor force as percent of population	Employed			Unemployed	
			Number	Percent full-time	Percent part-time	Number	Percent of labor force			Number	Percent full-time	Percent part-time	Number	Percent of labor force
WOMEN WITH NO CHILDREN UNDER 18														
1988	20 073	44.6	19 373	77.7	22.3	700	3.5	13 460	48.9	13 058	76.3	23.7	401	3.0
1989	20 810	45.6	20 118	78.1	21.9	692	3.3	14 044	50.5	13 633	77.2	22.8	411	2.9
1990	21 464	46.1	20 779	79.1	20.9	685	3.2	14 467	51.1	14 068	77.3	22.7	399	2.8
1991	21 575	46.1	20 637	78.4	21.6	937	4.3	14 529	51.2	13 976	77.6	22.4	552	3.8
1992	22 132	46.6	21 108	78.5	21.5	1 024	4.6	14 851	51.9	14 247	77.8	22.2	604	4.1
1993	22 273	46.6	21 275	79.0	21.0	998	4.5	15 211	52.4	14 630	77.6	22.4	581	3.8
1994	22 716	47.6	21 669	77.1	22.9	1 047	4.6	15 234	53.2	14 641	75.6	24.4	593	3.9
1995	22 973	47.3	22 134	77.4	22.6	839	3.7	15 594	53.2	15 072	76.3	23.7	522	3.3
1996	23 337	47.7	22 444	78.1	21.9	893	3.8	15 628	53.4	15 123	76.8	23.2	506	3.2
1997	23 890	48.3	23 130	78.9	21.1	760	3.2	15 750	54.2	15 315	77.7	22.3	435	2.8
1998	24 366	48.7	23 598	79.3	20.7	767	3.1	16 007	54.1	15 581	78.3	21.7	426	2.7
1999	24 881	48.9	24 098	79.7	20.3	783	3.1	16 484	54.4	16 061	78.2	21.8	423	2.6
2000	25 465	49.4	24 695	80.3	19.7	769	3.0	16 786	54.7	16 357	79.1	20.9	429	2.6
2001	25 959	49.6	25 226	80.4	19.6	733	2.8	16 909	54.8	16 528	78.7	21.3	381	2.3
WOMEN WITH CHILDREN UNDER 18														
1988	20 170	66.3	19 074	72.6	27.4	1 096	5.4	16 218	65.0	15 441	69.6	30.4	776	4.8
1989	20 411	66.7	19 446	72.5	27.5	965	4.7	16 445	65.6	15 813	69.6	30.4	632	3.8
1990	20 671	67.8	19 621	72.6	27.4	1 051	5.1	16 500	66.3	15 803	69.8	30.2	698	4.2
1991	20 673	67.9	19 416	72.8	27.2	1 257	6.1	16 575	66.8	15 692	70.1	29.9	883	5.3
1992	21 040	68.8	19 633	73.6	26.4	1 407	6.7	16 835	67.8	15 884	71.3	28.7	952	5.7
1993	21 194	68.3	20 011	73.9	26.1	1 183	5.6	16 947	67.5	16 127	71.4	28.6	820	4.8
1994	22 025	69.8	20 722	70.5	29.5	1 303	5.9	17 628	69.0	16 755	68.0	32.0	873	5.0
1995	22 591	71.1	21 441	71.5	28.5	1 150	5.1	17 969	70.2	17 195	68.8	31.2	774	4.3
1996	22 475	71.4	21 556	72.5	27.5	919	4.1	17 754	70.0	17 136	69.6	30.4	618	3.5
1997	22 831	72.6	21 777	73.9	26.1	1 054	4.6	18 157	71.1	17 521	71.6	28.4	636	3.5
1998	22 650	72.3	21 665	73.8	26.2	985	4.3	18 129	70.6	17 447	71.5	28.5	682	3.8
1999	22 419	71.9	21 611	73.9	26.1	808	3.6	17 865	70.1	17 342	71.5	28.5	523	2.9
2000	22 722	72.7	21 960	74.0	26.0	763	3.4	18 174	70.6	17 641	71.7	28.3	533	2.9
2001	22 729	73.0	21 934	74.9	25.1	795	3.5	18 325	70.8	17 745	72.6	27.4	580	3.2
WOMEN WITH CHILDREN UNDER 6														
1988	8 031	57.6	7 478	68.7	31.3	552	6.9	6 950	57.1	6 527	66.4	33.6	422	6.1
1989	8 169	57.8	7 756	67.8	32.2	413	5.1	7 034	57.4	6 749	66.0	34.0	285	4.1
1990	8 467	59.5	7 996	69.1	30.9	471	5.6	7 247	58.9	6 901	67.4	32.6	346	4.8
1991	8 585	59.9	7 938	69.2	30.8	647	7.5	7 434	59.9	6 933	67.5	32.5	501	6.7
1992	8 544	60.0	7 832	69.9	30.1	711	8.3	7 333	59.9	6 819	68.5	31.5	514	7.0
1993	8 496	59.6	7 895	70.2	29.8	600	7.1	7 289	59.6	6 840	68.8	31.2	450	6.2
1994	8 949	61.8	8 332	66.7	33.3	617	6.9	7 723	61.7	7 291	65.4	34.6	432	5.6
1995	9 067	63.9	8 517	67.4	32.6	550	6.1	7 759	63.5	7 349	66.1	33.9	409	5.3
1996	8 915	63.6	8 493	68.6	31.4	422	4.7	7 590	62.7	7 297	66.5	33.5	293	3.9
1997	8 856	64.9	8 376	70.3	29.7	480	5.4	7 582	63.6	7 252	69.1	30.9	330	4.4
1998	8 864	64.8	8 391	69.5	30.5	473	5.3	7 655	63.7	7 309	68.1	31.9	346	4.5
1999	8 511	63.7	8 109	68.6	31.4	402	4.7	7 246	61.8	6 979	67.1	32.9	267	3.7
2000	8 481	64.3	8 159	69.5	30.5	321	3.8	7 341	62.8	7 087	68.1	31.9	254	3.5
2001	8 417	64.0	8 077	69.7	30.3	340	4.0	7 319	62.5	7 062	68.5	31.5	257	3.5

Note: See "Notes and Definitions" for information on historical comparability.

1. Ever-married women are women who are, or have been married.

Table 1-49. Employment Status of Women Who Maintain Families by Marital Status and Presence and Age of Children, March 1988–2001

(Thousands of persons, percent.)

Family status, age of children, and year	Civilian noninstitutional population	Civilian labor force					Not in the labor force
		Number	Percent of the population	Employed	Unemployed		
					Number	Percent of the labor force	
WOMEN WHO MAINTAIN FAMILIES, TOTAL							
1988	11 074	6 851	61.9	6 296	555	8.1	4 222
1989	11 280	6 999	62.0	6 420	579	8.3	4 281
1990	11 309	7 088	62.7	6 471	617	8.7	4 221
1991	11 765	7 329	62.3	6 657	672	9.2	4 436
1992	12 214	7 517	61.5	6 798	719	9.6	4 697
1993	12 489	7 777	62.3	7 093	684	8.8	4 712
1994	12 963	8 214	63.4	7 413	801	9.8	4 750
1995	12 762	8 192	64.2	7 527	665	8.1	4 570
1996	12 993	8 460	65.1	7 832	628	7.4	4 532
1997	13 258	8 998	67.9	8 192	806	9.0	4 260
1998	13 102	8 976	68.5	8 309	667	7.4	4 127
1999	13 191	9 213	69.8	8 596	617	6.7	3 978
2000	13 145	9 226	70.2	8 592	634	6.9	3 918
2001	12 930	9 034	69.9	8 453	581	6.4	3 897
WOMEN WITH NO CHILDREN UNDER 18							
1988	4 315	2 299	53.3	2 213	86	3.7	2 015
1989	4 375	2 291	52.4	2 213	78	3.4	2 084
1990	4 290	2 227	51.9	2 132	95	4.3	2 062
1991	4 447	2 364	53.2	2 231	133	5.6	2 083
1992	4 651	2 427	52.2	2 307	120	4.9	2 223
1993	4 708	2 466	52.4	2 339	127	5.2	2 242
1994	4 758	2 609	54.8	2 489	120	4.6	2 149
1995	4 610	2 471	53.6	2 394	77	3.1	2 139
1996	4 847	2 552	52.7	2 462	90	3.5	2 295
1997	4 909	2 663	54.2	2 571	92	3.5	2 246
1998	4 952	2 649	53.5	2 578	71	2.7	2 303
1999	4 942	2 667	54.0	2 556	111	4.2	2 275
2000	5 097	2 707	53.1	2 546	161	5.9	2 390
2001	5 185	2 772	53.5	2 668	104	3.8	2 413
SINGLE WOMEN WITH NO CHILDREN UNDER 18							
1988	6 759	4 552	67.3	4 083	469	10.3	2 207
1989	6 905	4 707	68.2	4 206	501	10.6	2 197
1990	7 018	4 860	69.3	4 338	522	10.7	2 159
1991	7 318	4 965	67.8	4 426	539	10.9	2 353
1992	7 564	5 090	67.3	4 491	599	11.8	2 473
1993	7 781	5 311	68.3	4 755	556	10.5	2 470
1994	8 205	5 604	68.3	4 924	680	12.1	2 601
1995	8 152	5 720	70.2	5 132	588	10.3	2 431
1996	8 146	5 908	72.5	5 370	538	9.1	2 237
1997	8 348	6 335	75.9	5 621	714	11.3	2 014
1998	8 151	6 327	77.6	5 731	596	9.4	1 823
1999	8 248	6 546	79.4	6 040	506	7.7	1 702
2000	8 048	6 520	81.0	6 046	474	7.3	1 528
2001	7 746	6 261	80.8	5 785	476	7.6	1 484
WIDOWED, DIVORCED OR SEPARATED WOMEN WITH NO CHILDREN							
1988	609	427	70.1	415	12	2.8	183
1989	665	466	70.1	452	14	3.0	198
1990	642	450	70.1	425	25	5.6	192
1991	682	469	68.8	441	28	6.0	214
1992	745	505	67.8	475	30	5.9	241
1993	752	531	70.6	494	37	7.0	221
1994	704	490	69.6	451	39	8.0	213
1995	779	534	68.5	508	26	4.9	245
1996	895	588	65.7	572	16	2.7	308
1997	860	585	68.0	563	22	3.8	275
1998	893	637	71.3	613	24	3.8	256
1999	969	674	69.6	638	36	5.3	295
2000	1 004	720	71.7	642	78	10.8	284
2001	1 096	787	71.8	756	31	3.9	309

See *Note* at end of table.

Table 1-49. Employment Status of Women Who Maintain Families by Marital Status and Presence and Age of Children, March 1988–2001—*Continued*

(Thousands of persons, percent.)

Family status, age of children, and year	Civilian noninstitutional population	Civilian labor force					Not in the labor force
		Number	Percent of the population	Employed	Unemployed		
					Number	Percent of the labor force	
WOMEN WITH CHILDREN UNDER 18							
1988	1 778	950	53.4	754	196	20.6	829
1989	1 921	1 116	58.1	905	211	18.9	805
1990	1 953	1 095	56.1	874	221	20.2	858
1991	2 208	1 187	53.8	985	202	17.0	1 021
1992	2 376	1 256	52.9	1 067	189	15.0	1 120
1993	2 445	1 414	57.8	1 161	253	17.9	1 031
1994	2 790	1 625	58.2	1 328	297	18.3	1 165
1995	2 613	1 510	57.8	1 261	249	16.5	1 102
1996	2 639	1 633	61.9	1 346	287	17.6	1 006
1997	3 012	2 087	69.3	1 749	338	16.2	925
1998	3 083	2 280	74.0	1 960	320	14.0	803
1999	3 163	2 415	76.4	2 146	269	11.1	748
2000	3 167	2 413	76.2	2 151	262	10.9	754
2001	3 097	2 351	75.9	2 055	296	12.6	745
SINGLE WOMEN WITH CHILDREN UNDER 18							
1988	3 705	1 872	50.5	1 798	74	4.0	1 833
1989	3 711	1 825	49.2	1 761	64	3.5	1 886
1990	3 648	1 778	48.7	1 708	70	3.9	1 870
1991	3 765	1 896	50.4	1 791	105	5.5	1 869
1992	3 905	1 923	49.2	1 832	91	4.7	1 982
1993	3 956	1 935	48.9	1 845	90	4.7	2 021
1994	4 054	2 118	52.2	2 037	81	3.8	1 936
1995	3 831	1 938	50.6	1 887	51	2.6	1 894
1996	3 952	1 964	49.7	1 890	74	3.8	1 988
1997	4 049	2 077	51.3	2 008	69	3.3	1 971
1998	4 058	2 011	49.6	1 965	46	2.3	2 047
1999	3 974	1 993	50.2	1 918	75	3.8	1 980
2000	4 093	1 987	48.5	1 904	83	4.2	2 106
2001	4 088	1 985	48.6	1 912	73	3.7	2 104
WIDOWED, DIVORCED OR SEPARATED WOMEN WITH CHILDREN UNDER 18							
1988	4 981	3 602	72.3	3 329	273	7.6	1 379
1989	4 983	3 591	72.1	3 302	289	8.0	1 392
1990	5 065	3 765	74.3	3 464	301	8.0	1 301
1991	5 109	3 778	73.9	3 441	337	8.9	1 331
1992	5 187	3 834	73.9	3 424	410	10.7	1 353
1993	5 336	3 897	73.0	3 594	303	7.8	1 439
1994	5 415	3 979	73.5	3 596	383	9.6	1 436
1995	5 539	4 210	76.0	3 871	339	8.1	1 329
1996	5 507	4 275	77.6	4 024	251	5.9	1 231
1997	5 337	4 248	79.6	3 872	376	8.9	1 089
1998	5 068	4 047	79.9	3 771	276	6.8	1 020
1999	5 086	4 131	81.2	3 894	237	5.7	955
2000	4 881	4 107	84.1	3 895	212	5.2	774
2001	4 649	3 910	84.1	3 730	180	4.6	739

Note: See "Notes and Definitions" for information on historical comparability.

Table 1-50. Number and Age of Children in Families by Type of Family and Labor Force Status of Mother, March 1988–2001

(Thousands of children.)

Age of children and year	Total children	Mother in labor force	Mother not in labor force	Married-couple families			Families maintained by women			Families maintained by men
				Total	Mother in labor force	Mother not in labor force	Total	Mother in labor force	Mother not in labor force	
CHILDREN UNDER 16 YEARS										
1988	58 716	35 279	21 799	45 474	28 091	17 384	11 603	7 188	4 415	1 638
1989	59 483	36 050	21 757	45 988	28 673	17 315	11 819	7 377	4 442	1 676
1990	59 596	36 712	21 110	45 898	29 077	16 820	11 925	7 635	4 290	1 774
1991	60 330	36 968	21 526	45 912	29 056	16 856	12 582	7 912	4 670	1 836
1992	61 262	38 081	21 176	45 966	29 882	16 084	13 291	8 199	5 093	2 005
1993	62 020	38 542	21 444	46 499	30 054	16 445	13 487	8 488	4 999	2 034
1994	63 407	40 186	21 188	47 247	31 279	15 968	14 127	8 907	5 220	2 033
1995	63 989	41 365	20 421	47 675	32 190	15 486	14 111	9 176	4 935	2 202
1996	64 506	41 573	20 449	47 484	31 764	15 720	14 538	9 809	4 729	2 484
1997	64 710	42 747	19 223	47 529	32 263	15 265	14 441	10 483	3 958	2 740
1998	65 043	43 156	19 069	47 909	32 533	15 376	14 317	10 623	3 694	2 818
1999	65 191	43 419	19 074	47 945	32 193	15 752	14 547	11 226	3 322	2 699
2000	65 601	44 188	18 674	48 902	33 149	15 753	13 960	11 039	2 921	2 739
2001	65 777	44 051	18 864	49 352	33 436	15 916	13 563	10 615	2 948	2 862
CHILDREN FROM 6 TO 17 YEARS										
1988	38 744	24 957	12 614	29 304	19 394	9 910	8 268	5 563	2 705	1 172
1989	39 084	25 421	12 451	29 637	19 861	9 777	8 235	5 561	2 674	1 212
1990	39 095	25 805	12 079	29 726	20 067	9 659	8 157	5 737	2 420	1 211
1991	39 470	25 806	12 392	29 598	19 907	9 691	8 599	5 899	2 701	1 272
1992	40 064	26 666	12 067	29 673	20 586	9 087	9 060	6 079	2 980	1 331
1993	40 622	27 046	12 291	30 233	20 796	9 437	9 104	6 249	2 854	1 285
1994	41 795	28 179	12 287	30 895	21 663	9 233	9 570	6 516	3 054	1 329
1995	42 423	28 931	12 000	31 298	22 239	9 059	9 633	6 692	2 941	1 492
1996	42 964	29 381	11 897	31 231	22 092	9 139	10 047	7 289	2 758	1 685
1997	43 488	30 308	11 400	31 509	22 602	8 906	10 199	7 705	2 493	1 781
1998	43 771	30 579	11 367	31 707	22 706	9 001	10 238	7 873	2 365	1 826
1999	44 110	30 885	11 370	31 975	22 706	9 269	10 281	8 179	2 101	1 855
2000	44 562	31 531	11 198	32 732	23 393	9 339	9 997	8 138	1 859	1 833
2001	44 458	31 411	11 153	32 957	23 599	9 358	9 608	7 813	1 795	1 894
CHILDREN UNDER 6 YEARS										
1988	19 972	10 321	9 185	16 171	8 696	7 474	3 335	1 625	1 711	466
1989	20 399	10 628	9 306	16 351	8 812	7 539	3 584	1 816	1 767	465
1990	20 502	10 907	9 031	16 171	9 010	7 161	3 767	1 897	1 870	563
1991	20 860	11 162	9 134	16 313	9 148	7 165	3 983	2 013	1 969	563
1992	21 198	11 415	9 109	16 293	9 296	6 997	4 232	2 119	2 112	674
1993	21 398	11 496	9 153	16 266	9 258	7 008	4 383	2 239	2 145	749
1994	21 612	12 007	8 901	16 352	9 617	6 735	4 556	2 391	2 166	704
1995	21 566	12 435	8 421	16 377	9 951	6 427	4 478	2 484	1 995	710
1996	21 542	12 192	8 552	16 253	9 672	6 581	4 491	2 520	1 971	799
1997	21 222	12 439	7 823	16 020	9 661	6 359	4 243	2 778	1 464	959
1998	21 272	12 577	7 703	16 201	9 827	6 375	4 079	2 751	1 328	992
1999	21 081	12 533	7 704	15 971	9 487	6 484	4 267	3 046	1 220	844
2000	21 039	12 657	7 476	16 170	9 757	6 413	3 963	2 901	1 062	906
2001	21 318	12 640	7 711	16 395	9 837	6 558	3 956	2 802	1 153	968

Note: See "Notes and Definitions" for information on historical comparability.

Table 1-51. Number of Families and Median Family Income by Type of Family and Earner Status of Members, 1988–2000

(Thousands of families, dollars.)

Number of families and median family income	1988	1989	1990	1991	1992	1993	1994	1995	1996	1997	1998	1999	2000
NUMBER OF FAMILIES													
Married-Couple Families, Total	52 149	52 385	52 241	52 549	53 254	53 248	53 929	53 621	53 654	54 362	54 829	55 352	55 650
No earners	6 751	6 812	6 765	7 101	7 250	7 281	7 225	7 276	7 145	7 286	7 257	7 160	7 297
One earner	11 938	11 737	11 630	11 553	12 053	11 806	11 715	11 708	11 493	11 700	12 246	12 290	12 450
Husband	9 508	9 196	9 110	8 907	9 182	8 715	8 673	8 792	8 611	8 770	9 173	9 062	9 319
Wife	1 782	1 844	1 816	1 987	2 145	2 405	2 364	2 251	2 207	2 298	2 411	2 585	2 545
Other family member	648	697	703	659	726	686	678	666	674	632	662	643	586
Two earners	25 397	25 681	25 896	26 037	26 344	26 742	27 263	27 180	27 260	27 712	27 593	28 010	28 329
Husband and wife	23 237	23 534	23 697	23 880	24 255	24 543	25 123	25 274	25 274	25 731	25 696	26 134	26 447
Husband and other family member	1 652	1 718	1 711	1 633	1 447	1 582	1 565	1 393	1 483	1 406	1 306	1 325	1 277
Husband not an earner	509	429	487	524	642	617	574	513	502	575	590	552	605
Three earners or more	8 062	8 155	7 950	7 858	7 606	7 419	7 727	7 456	7 756	7 664	7 733	7 892	7 575
Husband and wife	7 140	7 245	7 029	7 052	6 882	6 723	6 987	6 770	7 126	7 023	7 102	7 220	6 917
Husband, not wife	744	761	756	595	550	535	543	531	479	478	456	528	537
husband not an earner	178	150	165	211	175	162	196	155	150	163	176	144	120
Families Maintained By Women, Total	11 288	11 310	11 771	12 214	12 504	12 982	12 771	13 007	13 277	13 115	13 206	13 164	12 950
No earners	2 547	2 496	2 623	2 925	2 968	3 100	2 848	2 664	2 574	2 332	2 143	1 883	1 786
One earner	5 390	5 467	5 672	5 926	6 184	6 407	6 506	6 815	7 027	7 091	7 351	7 441	7 462
Householder	4 300	4 396	4 585	4 812	5 042	5 278	5 415	5 590	5 817	5 841	6 167	6 127	6 132
Other family member	1 090	1 071	1 087	1 114	1 142	1 129	1 091	1 225	1 211	1 251	1 183	1 314	1 331
Two earners or more	3 350	3 347	3 476	3 363	3 352	3 476	3 417	3 527	3 675	3 692	3 712	3 840	3 702
Householder and other family member(s)	3 022	2 975	3 146	3 058	2 998	3 139	3 126	3 225	3 431	3 398	3 399	3 508	3 376
Householder not an earner	328	372	330	305	354	337	291	302	245	294	313	332	325
Families Maintained By Men, Total	2 874	2 929	2 948	3 079	3 094	2 992	3 287	3 557	3 924	3 982	4 041	4 086	4 316
No earners	296	281	296	310	345	329	383	357	359	344	381	376	380
One earner	1 263	1 350	1 396	1 541	1 544	1 593	1 705	1 800	1 972	2 104	2 027	2 044	2 223
Householder	992	1 103	1 133	1 289	1 305	1 352	1 428	1 548	1 667	1 791	1 725	1 721	1 879
Other family member	271	247	263	253	239	241	277	253	305	313	302	323	344
Two earners or more	1 315	1 298	1 257	1 228	1 204	1 070	1 198	1 400	1 593	1 534	1 634	1 666	1 713
Householder and other family member(s)	1 242	1 225	1 180	1 157	1 117	1 002	1 128	1 302	1 469	1 427	1 532	1 522	1 585
Householder not an earner	73	73	76	71	88	67	71	98	124	107	102	143	128
MEDIAN FAMILY INCOME													
Married-Couple Families, Total	36 267	38 415	39 802	40 746	42 000	43 000	44 893	47 000	49 614	51 475	54 043	56 792	59 200
No earners	17 000	17 820	19 221	20 415	20 023	19 983	20 604	21 888	22 622	23 782	24 525	25 262	25 356
One earner	28 701	30 700	31 020	31 671	32 500	32 084	33 393	35 100	36 468	39 140	40 519	41 261	44 424
Husband	30 030	32 236	32 422	33 208	34 714	34 401	35 000	36 052	38 150	40 300	42 000	44 200	47 010
Wife	23 771	24 000	25 228	26 500	27 343	27 502	28 661	32 098	30 301	34 050	35 625	35 546	36 458
Other family member	27 840	29 992	33 262	33 042	33 622	30 254	32 578	37 784	39 644	40 317	42 414	41 120	45 492
Two earners	40 030	42 208	44 000	45 359	47 737	49 650	51 190	53 500	56 000	58 020	61 300	64 007	67 500
Husband and wife	40 050	42 285	44 031	45 516	48 050	49 980	51 500	53 626	56 392	58 564	61 900	64 950	68 132
Husband and other family member	41 388	43 000	42 602	45 000	45 694	48 862	49 610	52 530	53 854	57 680	53 541	56 503	56 503
Husband not an earner	33 333	35 201	39 494	40 495	40 124	38 800	42 800	47 121	46 990	47 979	50 955	52 466	53 430
Three earners or more	54 556	56 500	59 336	61 120	61 640	63 535	66 172	68 996	70 400	75 593	78 973	81 940	83 990
Husband and wife	54 672	56 980	59 646	61 448	62 674	64 099	66 674	69 371	71 148	76 105	79 907	83 000	84 634
Husband, not wife	56 600	53 928	59 675	60 592	57 015	60 712	63 633	60 360	61 824	68 890	71 001	69 561	79 050
Husband not earner	40 900	47 656	49 107	44 874	47 551	54 805	54 655	61 196	55 495	62 684	63 205	69 275	68 050
Families Maintained By Women, Total	14 935	15 800	16 351	16 054	16 431	16 800	17 600	19 306	19 416	20 470	21 875	23 100	25 000
No earners	5 396	5 618	5 880	6 060	5 964	6 492	6 805	7 440	7 092	7 476	7 737	8 010	8 988
One earner	14 235	15 187	15 987	16 284	16 468	16 745	17 226	18 824	18 500	19 000	20 000	20 092	22 306
Householder	13 754	14 700	15 001	15 542	15 905	15 700	16 603	17 890	18 000	18 000	18 840	19 000	20 148
Other family member	16 580	18 628	20 173	20 220	19 709	20 800	21 300	23 166	21 000	22 870	25 981	26 800	27 524
Two earners or more	28 302	30 038	30 500	31 508	32 705	33 300	33 820	35 000	36 400	39 275	40 000	41 144	43 035
Householder and other family member(s)	28 000	30 000	30 367	31 550	33 280	33 165	33 357	34 674	36 400	39 000	39 713	40 855	43 000
Householder not an earner	33 590	33 524	32 800	29 477	30 460	35 394	37 531	39 444	38 249	47 471	43 725	48 004	45 600
Families Maintained By Men, Total	26 610	27 600	28 493	28 000	27 400	25 856	27 486	30 000	31 500	32 984	35 000	37 000	37 040
No earners	10 200	9 800	11 386	11 196	9 416	10 900	11 293	12 240	12 030	14 252	15 468	13 752	14 946
One earner	22 357	22 732	25 000	23 715	23 020	22 300	24 011	25 337	26 100	26 897	29 125	31 038	30 160
Householder	23 053	23 000	24 159	23 309	23 309	22 079	24 000	25 069	25 874	27 000	29 125	30 483	30 816
Other family member	19 869	21 196	27 620	25 720	24 359	26 916	26 253	27 291	28 584	25 486	28 241	34 756	29 118
Two earners or more	36 500	37 601	40 000	37 700	39 000	38 000	41 439	43 100	44 275	49 900	51 288	51 040	55 010
Householder and other family member(s)	36 525	37 859	40 256	37 550	39 300	38 363	41 534	43 000	43 065	50 000	50 954	50 960	55 400
Householder not an earner	34 335	35 390	34 064	40 000	36 445	33 700	37 386	55 133	47 001	44 786	68 257	57 407	51 945

Note: See "Notes and Definitions" for information on historical comparability.

Table 1-52. Employment Status of the Civilian Noninstitutional Population by Citizenship Status and Sex, March 1996–2000

(Thousands of persons, percent.)

Year, employment status, and sex	Total		Citizenship status					
			Native		Naturalized citizen		Not a citizen	
	Number	Percent	Number	Percent	Number	Percent	Number	Percent
1996								
Total, 16 Years And Over								
Civilian labor force	132 324	100.0	118 026	100.0	4 883	100.0	9 416	100.0
Employed	124 513	94.1	111 309	94.3	4 674	95.7	8 530	90.6
Unemployed	7 811	5.9	6 716	5.7	209	4.3	886	9.4
Men, 16 Years And Over								
Civilian labor force	71 095	100.0	62 709	100.0	2 641	100.0	5 745	100.0
Employed	66 429	93.4	58 695	93.6	2 532	95.9	5 203	90.6
Unemployed	4 666	6.6	4 014	6.4	110	4.1	542	9.4
Women, 16 Years And Over								
Civilian labor force	61 229	100.0	55 317	100.0	2 241	100.0	3 671	100.0
Employed	58 084	94.9	52 615	95.1	2 142	95.6	3 327	90.6
Unemployed	3 145	5.1	2 702	4.9	99	4.4	344	9.4
1997								
Total, 16 Years And Over								
Civilian labor force	135 227	100.0	119 635	100.0	5 792	100.0	9 800	100.0
Employed	127 680	94.4	113 156	94.6	5 542	95.7	8 981	91.6
Unemployed	7 547	5.6	6 479	5.4	250	4.3	819	8.4
Men, 16 Years And Over								
Civilian labor force	72 329	100.0	63 069	100.0	3 198	100.0	6 061	100.0
Employed	68 026	94.1	59 367	94.1	3 072	96.1	5 587	92.2
Unemployed	4 302	5.9	3 702	5.9	126	3.9	474	7.8
Women, 16 Years And Over								
Civilian labor force	62 899	100.0	56 565	100.0	2 594	100.0	3 739	100.0
Employed	59 654	94.8	53 789	95.1	2 470	95.2	3 395	90.8
Unemployed	3 245	5.2	2 776	4.9	124	4.8	344	9.2
1998								
Total, 16 Years And Over								
Civilian labor force	136 926	100.0	120 725	100.0	6 160	100.0	10 041	100.0
Employed	130 007	94.9	114 746	95.0	5 927	96.2	9 333	92.9
Unemployed	6 919	5.1	5 979	5.0	232	3.8	708	7.1
Men, 16 Years And Over								
Civilian labor force	73 026	100.0	63 386	100.0	3 424	100.0	6 215	100.0
Employed	69 117	94.6	60 018	94.7	3 315	96.8	5 784	93.1
Unemployed	3 908	5.4	3 368	5.3	110	3.2	431	6.9
Women, 16 Years And Over								
Civilian labor force	63 900	100.0	57 339	100.0	2 735	100.0	3 826	100.0
Employed	60 889	95.3	54 728	95.4	2 613	95.5	3 549	92.8
Unemployed	3 011	4.7	2 611	4.6	123	4.5	277	7.2
1999								
Total, 16 Years And Over								
Civilian labor force	138 120	100.0	122 006	100.0	6 171	100.0	9 943	100.0
Employed	131 806	95.4	116 569	95.5	5 915	95.9	9 322	93.8
Unemployed	6 314	4.6	5 437	4.5	256	4.1	621	6.2
Men, 16 Years And Over								
Civilian labor force	73 334	100.0	63 844	100.0	3 306	100.0	6 183	100.0
Employed	69 912	95.3	60 890	95.4	3 184	96.3	5 838	94.4
Unemployed	3 422	4.7	2 955	4.6	122	3.7	345	5.6
Women, 16 Years And Over								
Civilian labor force	64 786	100.0	58 161	100.0	2 864	100.0	3 760	100.0
Employed	61 894	95.5	55 679	95.7	2 731	95.3	3 485	92.7
Unemployed	2 891	4.5	2 482	4.3	134	4.7	275	7.3
2000								
Total, 16 Years And Over								
Civilian labor force	140 454	100.0	123 070	100.0	6 720	100.0	10 664	100.0
Employed	134 338	95.6	117 806	95.7	6 499	96.7	10 033	94.1
Unemployed	6 116	4.4	5 264	4.3	221	3.3	631	5.9
Men, 16 Years And Over								
Civilian labor force	74 517	100.0	64 183	100.0	3 623	100.0	6 712	100.0
Employed	71 237	95.6	61 364	95.6	3 520	97.2	6 353	94.7
Unemployed	3 281	4.4	2 820	4.4	102	2.8	359	5.3
Women, 16 Years And Over								
Civilian labor force	65 937	100.0	58 886	100.0	3 098	100.0	3 953	100.0
Employed	63 102	95.7	56 442	95.8	2 979	96.2	3 680	93.1
Unemployed	2 835	4.3	2 444	4.2	119	3.8	273	6.9

Table 1-53. Employed Civilians by Occupation, Citizenship Status, and Sex, March 2000

(Thousands of persons, percent.)

Occupation and sex	Total		Citizenship status					
			Native		Naturalized citizen		Not a citizen	
	Number	Percent	Number	Percent	Number	Percent	Number	Percent
TOTAL	134 338	100.0	117 806	100.0	6 499	100.0	10 033	100.0
Managerial and professional specialty	40 493	30.1	36 408	30.9	2 183	33.6	1 902	19.0
Executive, administrative, and managerial	19 764	14.7	18 004	15.3	1 000	15.4	759	7.6
Professional specialty	20 729	15.4	18 404	15.6	1 182	18.2	1 143	11.4
Technical, sales, and administrative support	39 541	29.4	36 093	30.6	1 677	25.8	1 771	17.7
Technicians and related support	4 384	3.3	3 889	3.3	236	3.6	258	2.6
Sales occupations	16 138	12.0	14 580	12.4	714	11.0	843	8.4
Administrative support, including clerical	19 020	14.2	17 624	15.0	727	11.2	669	6.7
Service occupations	18 671	13.9	15 497	13.2	1 002	15.4	2 171	21.6
Private household	884	0.7	572	0.5	75	1.2	237	2.4
Protective service	2 364	1.8	2 233	1.9	65	1.0	66	0.7
Other service occupations	15 423	11.5	12 692	10.8	862	13.3	1 868	18.6
Precision production, craft, and repair	14 386	10.7	12 389	10.5	648	10.0	1 348	13.4
Mechanics and repairers	4 798	3.6	4 335	3.7	192	3.0	272	2.7
Construction trades	5 716	4.3	4 791	4.1	215	3.3	710	7.1
Other precision production, craft, and repair	3 871	2.9	3 263	2.8	242	3.7	366	3.6
Operators, fabricators, and laborers	18 002	13.4	14 914	12.7	867	13.3	2 221	22.1
Operators, assemblers, and inspectors	7 352	5.5	5 844	5.0	440	6.8	1 067	10.6
Transportation and material moving occupations	5 340	4.0	4 712	4.0	205	3.2	423	4.2
Other laborers	5 310	4.0	4 358	3.7	222	3.4	731	7.3
Farming, forestry, and fishing	3 245	2.4	2 503	2.1	122	1.9	620	6.2
Farm operators and managers	1 089	0.8	1 066	0.9	15	0.2	8	0.1
Other farming, forestry, and fishing occupations	2 155	1.6	1 437	1.2	106	1.6	612	6.1
MEN	71 237	53.0	61 364	52.1	3 520	54.2	6 353	63.3
Managerial and professional specialty	20 297	15.1	17 912	15.2	1 206	18.6	1 179	11.8
Executive, administrative, and managerial	10 877	8.1	9 841	8.4	544	8.4	492	4.9
Professional specialty	9 420	7.0	8 071	6.9	662	10.2	687	6.8
Technical, sales, and administrative support	14 174	10.6	12 611	10.7	712	11.0	851	8.5
Technicians and related support	2 060	1.5	1 788	1.5	133	2.0	139	1.4
Sales occupations	8 207	6.1	7 333	6.2	397	6.1	477	4.8
Administrative support, including clerical	3 908	2.9	3 491	3.0	182	2.8	235	2.3
Service occupations	7 459	5.6	6 118	5.2	354	5.4	987	9.8
Private household	40	(1)	34	(1)	5	0.1	2	(1)
Protective service	1 934	1.4	1 822	1.5	53	0.8	59	0.6
Other service occupations	5 485	4.1	4 263	3.6	296	4.6	926	9.2
Precision production, craft, and repair	12 975	9.7	11 239	9.5	531	8.2	1 205	12.0
Mechanics and repairers	4 541	3.4	4 119	3.5	161	2.5	261	2.6
Construction trades	5 557	4.1	4 640	3.9	210	3.2	707	7.0
Other precision production, craft, and repair	2 877	2.1	2 479	2.1	160	2.5	237	2.4
Operators, fabricators, and laborers	13 816	10.3	11 604	9.9	609	9.4	1 603	16.0
Operators, assemblers, and inspectors	4 775	3.6	3 930	3.3	253	3.9	592	5.9
Transportation and material moving occupations	4 786	3.6	4 191	3.6	195	3.0	399	4.0
Other laborers	4 254	3.2	3 483	3.0	161	2.5	611	6.1
Farming, forestry, and fishing	2 515	1.9	1 878	1.6	109	1.7	528	5.3
Farm operators and managers	800	0.6	781	0.7	13	0.2	7	0.1
Other farming, forestry, and fishing occupations	1 715	1.3	1 098	0.9	96	1.5	521	5.2
WOMEN	63 102	47.0	56 442	47.9	2 979	45.8	3 680	36.7
Managerial and professional specialty	20 196	15.0	18 496	15.7	977	15.0	723	7.2
Executive, administrative, and managerial	8 888	6.6	8 163	6.9	457	7.0	268	2.7
Professional specialty	11 309	8.4	10 333	8.8	520	8.0	455	4.5
Technical, sales, and administrative support	25 367	18.9	23 482	19.9	965	14.8	920	9.2
Technicians and related support	2 324	1.7	2 101	1.8	103	1.6	119	1.2
Sales occupations	7 931	5.9	7 248	6.2	317	4.9	367	3.7
Administrative support, including clerical	15 112	11.2	14 133	12.0	545	8.4	434	4.3
Service occupations	11 212	8.3	9 379	8.0	649	10.0	1 185	11.8
Private household	843	0.6	538	0.5	70	1.1	235	2.3
Protective service	431	0.3	411	0.3	12	0.2	7	0.1
Other service occupations	9 938	7.4	8 430	7.2	566	8.7	942	9.4
Precision production, craft, and repair	1 410	1.0	1 151	1.0	117	1.8	143	1.4
Mechanics and repairers	257	0.2	216	0.2	30	0.5	11	0.1
Construction trades	159	0.1	151	0.1	4	0.1	3	(1)
Other precision production, craft, and repair	995	0.7	784	0.7	82	1.3	129	1.3
Operators, fabricators, and laborers	4 187	3.1	3 310	2.8	258	4.0	618	6.2
Operators, assemblers, and inspectors	2 576	1.9	1 914	1.6	187	2.9	475	4.7
Transportation and material moving occupations	554	0.4	521	0.4	10	0.2	24	0.2
Other laborers	1 056	0.8	875	0.7	62	1.0	119	1.2
Farming, forestry, and fishing	729	0.5	624	0.5	13	0.2	92	0.9
Farm operators and managers	289	0.2	285	0.2	2	(1)	1	(1)
Other farming, forestry, and fishing occupations	440	0.3	339	0.3	10	0.2	91	0.9

1. Value less than 0.05.

Table 1-54. Total Money Earnings[1] of Year-Round Full-Time Workers by Citizenship Status and Sex, March 2000

(Thousands of persons, percent.)

Sex and money earnings	Total		Citizenship status					
			Native		Naturalized citizen		Not a citizen	
	Number	Percent	Number	Percent	Number	Percent	Number	Percent
TOTAL	97 914	100.0	85 677	100.0	5 109	100.0	7 128	100.0
$1 to $2,499	1 107	1.1	950	1.1	49	1.0	107	1.5
$2,500 to $4,999	477	0.5	401	0.5	27	0.5	49	0.7
$5,000 to $9,999	2 695	2.8	2 226	2.6	104	2.0	365	5.1
$10,000 to $14,999	7 923	8.1	6 073	7.1	448	8.8	1 402	19.7
$15,000 to $19,999	10 487	10.7	8 588	10.0	559	10.9	1 341	18.8
$20,000 to $24,999	11 409	11.7	9 877	11.5	607	11.9	925	13.0
$25,000 to $34,999	20 403	20.8	18 264	21.3	981	19.2	1 158	16.2
$35,000 to $49,999	19 984	20.4	18 203	21.2	997	19.5	783	11.0
$50,000 to $74,999	14 424	14.7	13 034	15.2	800	15.7	589	8.3
$75,000 and over	9 007	9.2	8 062	9.4	536	10.5	409	5.7
MEN	57 511	100.0	49 659	100.0	3 014	100.0	4 838	100.0
$1 to $2,499	641	1.1	534	1.1	32	1.1	74	1.5
$2,500 to $4,999	181	0.3	149	0.3	14	0.5	19	0.4
$5,000 to $9,999	1 159	2.0	917	1.8	33	1.1	210	4.3
$10,000 to $14,999	3 385	5.9	2 378	4.8	187	6.2	820	16.9
$15,000 to $19,999	4 849	8.4	3 673	7.4	289	9.6	887	18.3
$20,000 to $24,999	5 511	9.6	4 531	9.1	328	10.9	652	13.5
$25,000 to $34,999	10 993	19.1	9 639	19.4	556	18.5	797	16.5
$35,000 to $49,999	12 631	22.0	11 488	23.1	586	19.4	557	11.5
$50,000 to $74,999	10 667	18.5	9 642	19.4	553	18.3	472	9.7
$75,000 and over	7 494	13.0	6 708	13.5	437	14.5	350	7.2
WOMEN	40 404	100.0	36 018	100.0	2 095	100.0	2 290	100.0
$1 to $2,499	466	1.2	416	1.2	17	0.8	33	1.4
$2,500 to $4,999	296	0.7	252	0.7	13	0.6	30	1.3
$5,000 to $9,999	1 536	3.8	1 310	3.6	72	3.4	155	6.7
$10,000 to $14,999	4 537	11.2	3 695	10.3	261	12.4	582	25.4
$15,000 to $19,999	5 639	14.0	4 915	13.6	270	12.9	454	19.8
$20,000 to $24,999	5 898	14.6	5 346	14.8	279	13.3	272	11.9
$25,000 to $34,999	9 410	23.3	8 625	23.9	425	20.3	361	15.8
$35,000 to $49,999	7 353	18.2	6 715	18.6	412	19.7	226	9.9
$50,000 to $74,999	3 757	9.3	3 392	9.4	247	11.8	117	5.1
$75,000 and over	1 512	3.7	1 353	3.8	99	4.7	60	2.6

Note: Age 15 years and over.

1. Income for previous calendar year. Total money income is the algebraic sum of money wages and salaries, net income from self-employment, and income other than earnings.

Table 1-55. Percent Distribution of the Civilian Labor Force 25 to 64 Years of Age by Educational Attainment, Sex, and Race, March 1989–2001

Sex, race, and year	Civilian labor force (thousands)	Percent distribution				
		Total	Less than a high school diploma	4 years of high school only	1 to 3 years of college	4 or more years of college
TOTAL						
1989	97 318	100.0	14.0	39.6	20.0	26.4
1990	99 175	100.0	13.4	39.5	20.7	26.4
1991	100 480	100.0	13.0	39.4	21.1	26.5
1992	102 387	100.0	12.2	36.2	25.2	26.4
1993	103 504	100.0	11.5	35.2	26.3	27.0
1994	104 868	100.0	11.0	34.0	27.7	27.3
1995	106 519	100.0	10.8	33.1	27.8	28.3
1996	108 037	100.0	10.9	32.9	27.7	28.5
1997	110 514	100.0	10.9	33.0	27.4	28.6
1998	111 857	100.0	10.7	32.8	27.4	29.1
1999	112 542	100.0	10.3	32.3	27.4	30.0
2000	114 052	100.0	9.8	31.8	27.9	30.4
2001	115 073	100.0	9.8	31.4	28.1	30.7
MEN						
1989	53 668	100.0	15.7	36.9	19.2	28.2
1990	54 476	100.0	15.1	37.2	19.7	28.0
1991	55 165	100.0	14.7	37.5	20.2	27.6
1992	55 917	100.0	13.9	34.7	23.8	27.5
1993	56 544	100.0	13.2	33.9	24.7	28.1
1994	56 633	100.0	12.7	32.9	25.8	28.6
1995	57 454	100.0	12.2	32.3	25.7	29.7
1996	58 121	100.0	12.7	32.2	26.0	29.1
1997	59 268	100.0	12.8	32.2	25.8	29.2
1998	59 905	100.0	12.3	32.3	25.8	29.6
1999	60 030	100.0	11.7	32.0	25.8	30.5
2000	60 510	100.0	11.1	31.8	26.1	30.9
2001	61 091	100.0	11.0	31.6	26.3	31.1
WOMEN						
1989	43 650	100.0	11.9	42.9	20.9	24.3
1990	44 699	100.0	11.3	42.4	21.9	24.5
1991	45 315	100.0	10.9	41.6	22.2	25.2
1992	46 469	100.0	10.2	37.9	26.9	25.0
1993	46 961	100.0	9.3	36.7	28.2	25.8
1994	48 235	100.0	9.1	35.3	29.8	25.8
1995	49 065	100.0	9.1	34.1	30.2	26.6
1996	49 916	100.0	8.8	33.7	29.7	27.8
1997	51 246	100.0	8.7	34.0	29.3	28.0
1998	51 953	100.0	8.8	33.3	29.3	28.6
1999	52 512	100.0	8.7	32.7	29.2	29.5
2000	53 541	100.0	8.4	31.8	30.0	29.8
2001	53 982	100.0	8.5	31.1	30.1	30.2
WHITE						
1989	83 694	100.0	13.0	39.7	20.0	27.2
1990	85 238	100.0	12.6	39.6	20.6	27.1
1991	86 344	100.0	12.2	39.3	21.1	27.4
1992	87 656	100.0	11.3	36.1	25.5	27.1
1993	88 457	100.0	10.7	35.0	26.4	27.9
1994	89 009	100.0	10.5	33.7	27.7	28.1
1995	90 192	100.0	10.0	32.8	27.8	29.3
1996	91 506	100.0	10.4	32.8	27.5	29.3
1997	93 179	100.0	10.4	32.8	27.3	29.5
1998	93 527	100.0	10.2	32.7	27.4	29.8
1999	94 216	100.0	9.8	32.2	27.2	30.8
2000	95 073	100.0	9.5	31.8	27.7	31.0
2001	95 562	100.0	9.5	31.0	28.0	31.4
BLACK						
1989	10 358	100.0	21.7	42.3	20.5	15.6
1990	10 537	100.0	19.9	42.5	22.1	15.5
1991	10 650	100.0	19.5	42.9	22.1	15.4
1992	10 936	100.0	19.2	40.3	24.9	15.6
1993	11 051	100.0	16.8	39.5	27.6	16.1
1994	11 368	100.0	14.5	39.3	29.2	17.0
1995	11 695	100.0	14.1	38.6	29.6	17.7
1996	11 891	100.0	14.2	37.2	31.2	17.4
1997	12 253	100.0	14.3	37.8	31.3	16.6
1998	12 893	100.0	14.3	37.3	30.1	18.2
1999	12 945	100.0	13.0	37.2	30.4	19.5
2000	13 383	100.0	11.8	36.1	31.5	20.7
2001	13 617	100.0	12.0	37.1	31.1	19.8

Note: Data for the above race groups will not sum to totals because data for the Other races group are not presented. See "Notes and Definitions" for information on historical comparability.

Table 1-56. Labor Force Participation Rates of Persons 25 to 64 Years of Age by Educational Attainment, Sex, and Race, March 1989–2001

(Civilian labor force as a percent of the civilian noninstitutional population.)

Sex, race, and year	Participation rates				
	Total	Less than a high school diploma	4 years of high school only	1 to 3 years of college	4 or more years of college
TOTAL					
1989	78.2	60.5	77.9	83.3	88.4
1990	78.6	60.7	78.2	83.3	88.4
1991	78.6	60.7	78.1	83.2	88.4
1992	79.0	60.3	78.3	83.5	88.4
1993	78.9	59.6	77.7	82.9	88.3
1994	78.9	58.3	77.8	83.2	88.2
1995	79.3	59.8	77.3	83.2	88.7
1996	79.4	60.2	77.9	83.7	87.8
1997	80.1	61.7	78.5	83.7	88.5
1998	80.2	63.0	78.4	83.5	88.0
1999	80.0	62.7	78.1	83.0	87.6
2000	80.3	62.7	78.4	83.2	87.8
2001	80.2	63.5	78.4	83.0	87.0
MEN					
1989	88.8	75.9	89.6	91.8	94.5
1990	88.8	75.1	89.9	91.5	94.5
1991	88.6	75.1	89.3	92.0	94.2
1992	88.6	75.1	89.0	91.8	93.7
1993	88.1	74.9	88.1	90.6	93.7
1994	87.0	71.5	86.8	90.3	93.2
1995	87.4	72.0	86.9	90.1	93.8
1996	87.5	74.3	86.9	90.0	92.9
1997	87.7	75.2	86.4	90.6	93.5
1998	87.8	75.3	86.7	90.0	93.4
1999	87.5	74.4	86.6	89.4	93.0
2000	87.5	74.9	86.2	88.9	93.3
2001	87.4	75.4	85.8	89.1	92.9
WOMEN					
1989	68.3	45.5	68.5	75.4	81.1
1990	68.9	46.2	68.7	75.9	81.1
1991	69.1	46.2	68.6	75.2	81.8
1992	70.0	45.6	69.1	76.2	82.2
1993	70.0	44.2	68.8	76.1	82.2
1994	71.1	44.7	70.0	77.0	82.5
1995	71.5	47.2	68.9	77.3	82.8
1996	71.8	45.7	69.8	78.1	82.3
1997	72.8	47.1	71.4	77.6	83.2
1998	73.0	49.8	70.9	77.8	82.3
1999	72.8	50.5	70.4	77.4	81.9
2000	73.5	50.4	71.2	78.3	82.0
2001	73.4	51.7	71.3	77.7	80.9
WHITE					
1989	78.7	61.6	77.8	83.2	88.5
1990	79.2	62.5	78.4	83.3	88.3
1991	79.4	62.5	78.3	83.1	88.6
1992	79.8	61.5	78.7	83.8	88.7
1993	79.7	61.1	78.2	83.1	88.8
1994	79.8	60.3	78.3	83.5	88.5
1995	80.1	61.6	77.9	83.4	88.8
1996	80.4	62.5	78.6	83.9	88.2
1997	81.0	63.8	79.2	83.9	89.0
1998	80.6	63.8	78.6	83.5	88.3
1999	80.6	64.2	78.5	83.3	87.9
2000	80.8	64.2	78.7	83.1	87.9
2001	80.7	64.5	78.7	83.1	87.2
BLACK					
1989	74.9	56.7	78.9	83.9	90.4
1990	74.6	54.5	78.2	84.2	92.0
1991	73.9	53.9	77.1	84.1	90.2
1992	74.4	55.4	76.9	83.4	89.1
1993	73.8	53.4	74.7	83.0	89.6
1994	73.5	49.4	75.2	82.4	89.5
1995	74.2	51.0	74.5	82.8	90.9
1996	73.7	50.1	74.3	83.0	87.9
1997	74.9	52.9	75.0	83.8	89.0
1998	77.7	59.3	77.0	85.0	88.8
1999	76.5	55.1	76.5	82.9	88.6
2000	77.9	55.5	77.0	84.2	90.3
2001	78.1	58.7	76.8	83.0	90.5

Note: Data for the above race groups will not sum to totals because data for the Other races group are not presented. See "Notes and Definitions" for information on historical comparability.

Table 1-57. Unemployment Rates of Persons 25 to 64 Years of Age by Educational Attainment, Sex, and Race, March 1989–2001

(Unemployment as a percent of the civilian labor force.)

Sex, race, and year	Unemployment rates				
	Total	Less than a high school diploma	4 years of high school only	1 to 3 years of college	4 or more years of college
TOTAL					
1989	4.4	8.9	4.8	3.4	2.2
1990	4.5	9.6	4.9	3.7	1.9
1991	6.1	12.3	6.7	5.0	2.9
1992	6.7	13.5	7.7	5.9	2.9
1993	6.4	13.0	7.3	5.5	3.2
1994	5.8	12.6	6.7	5.0	2.9
1995	4.8	10.0	5.2	4.5	2.5
1996	4.8	10.9	5.5	4.1	2.2
1997	4.4	10.4	5.1	3.8	2.0
1998	4.0	8.5	4.8	3.6	1.8
1999	3.5	7.7	4.0	3.1	1.9
2000	3.3	7.9	3.8	3.0	1.5
2001	3.5	8.1	4.2	2.9	2.0
MEN					
1989	4.7	9.4	5.4	3.2	2.3
1990	4.8	9.6	5.3	3.9	2.1
1991	6.8	13.4	7.7	5.2	3.2
1992	7.5	14.8	8.8	6.4	3.2
1993	7.3	14.1	8.7	6.3	3.4
1994	6.2	12.8	7.2	5.3	2.9
1995	5.1	10.9	5.7	4.4	2.6
1996	5.3	11.0	6.4	4.5	2.3
1997	4.7	9.9	5.6	4.0	2.1
1998	4.1	8.0	5.1	3.7	1.7
1999	3.5	7.0	4.1	3.2	1.9
2000	3.3	7.1	3.9	3.1	1.6
2001	3.7	7.5	4.6	3.2	1.9
WOMEN					
1989	4.0	8.1	4.2	3.7	2.0
1990	4.2	9.5	4.6	3.5	1.7
1991	5.2	10.7	5.5	4.8	2.5
1992	5.7	11.4	6.5	5.3	2.5
1993	5.2	11.2	5.8	4.6	2.9
1994	5.4	12.4	6.2	4.7	2.9
1995	4.4	8.6	4.6	4.5	2.4
1996	4.1	10.7	4.4	3.8	2.1
1997	4.1	11.3	4.5	3.6	2.0
1998	3.9	9.3	4.4	3.5	1.9
1999	3.5	8.8	3.9	3.0	1.9
2000	3.2	9.1	3.6	2.9	1.4
2001	3.3	8.9	3.8	2.6	2.0
WHITE					
1989	3.8	7.7	4.2	3.0	2.0
1990	4.0	8.3	4.4	3.3	1.8
1991	5.6	11.6	6.2	4.6	2.7
1992	6.0	12.9	6.8	5.3	2.7
1993	5.8	12.4	6.5	5.0	3.1
1994	5.2	11.7	5.8	4.5	2.6
1995	4.3	9.2	4.6	4.2	2.3
1996	4.2	10.2	4.6	3.7	2.1
1997	3.9	9.4	4.6	3.4	1.8
1998	3.5	7.5	4.2	3.2	1.7
1999	3.1	7.0	3.4	2.8	1.7
2000	3.0	7.5	3.3	2.7	1.4
2001	3.1	7.2	3.6	2.7	1.8
BLACK					
1989	9.2	14.6	9.2	6.9	4.7
1990	8.6	15.9	8.6	6.5	1.9
1991	10.1	15.9	10.3	8.0	5.2
1992	12.4	17.2	14.1	10.7	4.8
1993	10.9	17.3	12.4	8.7	4.1
1994	10.6	17.4	12.2	8.3	4.9
1995	7.7	13.7	8.4	6.3	4.1
1996	8.9	15.3	10.8	6.9	3.3
1997	8.1	16.6	8.2	6.1	4.4
1998	7.3	13.4	8.4	6.4	2.1
1999	6.3	12.0	6.7	5.2	3.3
2000	5.4	10.4	6.3	4.3	2.5
2001	6.5	14.0	7.7	4.3	3.3

Note: Data for the above race groups will not sum to totals because data for the Other races group are not presented. See "Notes and Definitions" for information on historical comparability.

Table 1-58. Workers Age 25 to 64 by Educational Attainment, Occupation of Longest Held Job, and Sex, 2000

(Thousands of persons with work experience during the year.)

Sex and occupation	Total	Less than a high school diploma	4 years of high school only	1 to 3 years of college	4 or more years of college
TOTAL	119 186	11 705	37 360	33 702	36 419
Managerial and professional specialty	39 238	536	4 765	8 866	25 071
Executive, administrative, and managerial	19 414	410	3 734	5 590	9 680
Professional specialty	19 824	126	1 031	3 276	15 391
Technical, sales, and administrative support	33 020	1 581	11 073	12 518	7 849
Technicians and related support	4 222	56	826	2 022	1 317
Sales occupations	12 710	844	3 866	4 003	3 998
Administrative support, including clerical	16 089	681	6 381	6 493	2 534
Service occupations	14 253	2 852	6 109	4 045	1 247
Private household	608	223	262	92	31
Protective service	2 181	84	768	950	380
Service, except private household and protective	11 464	2 545	5 080	3 003	836
Precision production, craft, and repair	13 653	2 218	6 262	4 168	1 006
Mechanics and repairers	4 455	542	1 991	1 580	341
Construction trades	5 680	1 196	2 539	1 588	357
Other precision production, craft, and repair	3 519	480	1 731	999	308
Operators, fabricators, and laborers	15 763	3 659	7 950	3 353	800
Machine operators, assemblers, and inspectors	6 644	1 665	3 376	1 313	290
Transportation and material moving occupations	5 216	947	2 658	1 296	316
Handlers, equipment cleaners, helpers, and laborers	3 903	1 047	1 916	745	194
Farming, forestry, and fishing	2 698	859	1 071	485	282
Armed forces	561	...	130	267	164
MEN	62 957	6 913	19 858	16 709	19 475
Managerial and professional specialty	19 370	312	2 251	3 903	12 904
Executive, administrative, and managerial	10 353	251	1 764	2 645	5 693
Professional specialty	9 017	61	487	1 259	7 210
Technical, sales, and administrative support	11 612	450	3 000	4 145	4 017
Technicians and related support	1 902	23	325	823	731
Sales occupations	6 579	261	1 684	2 061	2 572
Administrative support, including clerical	3 131	166	991	1 261	714
Service occupations	5 292	908	2 118	1 643	623
Private household	32	16	4	12	...
Protective service	1 759	56	598	779	325
Service, except private household and protective	3 501	836	1 515	852	298
Precision production, craft, and repair	12 446	1 980	5 717	3 839	910
Mechanics and repairers	4 245	512	1 919	1 488	325
Construction trades	5 547	1 165	2 479	1 550	352
Other precision production, craft, and repair	2 654	303	1 319	800	233
Operators, fabricators, and laborers	11 629	2 603	5 787	2 586	653
Machine operators, assemblers, and inspectors	4 009	938	1 960	906	205
Transportation and material moving occupations	4 596	844	2 345	1 118	289
Handlers, equipment cleaners, helpers, and laborers	3 024	821	1 482	561	160
Farming, forestry, and fishing	2 094	660	865	358	211
Armed forces	514	...	121	236	157
WOMEN	56 229	4 791	17 500	16 991	16 942
Managerial and professional specialty	19 869	224	2 514	4 963	12 167
Executive, administrative, and managerial	9 061	159	1 970	2 945	3 987
Professional specialty	10 807	65	545	2 017	8 180
Technical, sales, and administrative support	21 408	1 132	8 072	8 373	3 831
Technicians and related support	2 320	33	501	1 200	586
Sales occupations	6 131	583	2 181	1 942	1 425
Administrative support, including clerical	12 957	515	5 390	5 231	1 820
Service occupations	8 960	1 943	3 991	2 402	624
Private household	576	207	258	80	31
Protective service	422	28	169	170	54
Service, except private household and protective	7 962	1 708	3 564	2 151	539
Precision production, craft, and repair	1 207	238	544	329	96
Mechanics and repairers	210	30	72	92	15
Construction trades	133	30	59	38	5
Other precision production, craft, and repair	865	178	413	199	75
Operators, fabricators, and laborers	4 134	1 056	2 164	768	147
Machine operators, assemblers, and inspectors	2 635	726	1 416	406	86
Transportation and material moving occupations	620	103	313	178	27
Handlers, equipment cleaners, helpers, and laborers	879	227	434	184	34
Farming, forestry, and fishing	604	199	206	127	71
Armed forces	47	...	9	31	7

Table 1-59. Percent Distribution of Workers Age 25 to 64 by Educational Attainment, Occupation of Longest Held Job, and Sex, 2000

(Percent of total workers in occupation.)

Sex and occupation	Total	Less than a high school diploma	4 years of high school only	1 to 3 years of college	4 or more years of college
TOTAL	100.0	9.8	31.3	28.3	30.6
Managerial and professional specialty	100.0	1.4	12.1	22.6	63.9
Executive, administrative, and managerial	100.0	2.1	19.2	28.8	49.9
Professional specialty	100.0	0.6	5.2	16.5	77.6
Technical, sales, and administrative support	100.0	4.8	33.5	37.9	23.8
Technicians and related support	100.0	1.3	19.6	47.9	31.2
Sales occupations	100.0	6.6	30.4	31.5	31.5
Administrative support, including clerical	100.0	4.2	39.7	40.4	15.7
Service occupations	100.0	20.0	42.9	28.4	8.7
Private household	100.0	36.7	43.1	15.1	5.1
Protective service	100.0	3.8	35.2	43.6	17.4
Service, except private household and protective	100.0	22.2	44.3	26.2	7.3
Precision production, craft, and repair	100.0	16.2	45.9	30.5	7.4
Mechanics and repairers	100.0	12.2	44.7	35.5	7.7
Construction trades	100.0	21.0	44.7	28.0	6.3
Other precision production, craft, and repair	100.0	13.7	49.2	28.4	8.7
Operators, fabricators, and laborers	100.0	23.2	50.4	21.3	5.1
Machine operators, assemblers, and inspectors	100.0	25.1	50.8	19.8	4.4
Transportation and material moving occupations	100.0	18.2	51.0	24.8	6.1
Handlers, equipment cleaners, helpers, and laborers	100.0	26.8	49.1	19.1	5.0
Farming, forestry, and fishing	100.0	31.9	39.7	18.0	10.5
Armed forces	100.0	...	23.2	47.6	29.3
MEN	100.0	11.0	31.5	26.5	30.9
Managerial and professional specialty	100.0	1.6	11.6	20.2	66.6
Executive, administrative, and managerial	100.0	2.4	17.0	25.5	55.0
Professional specialty	100.0	0.7	5.4	14.0	80.0
Technical, sales, and administrative support	100.0	3.9	25.8	35.7	34.6
Technicians and related support	100.0	1.2	17.1	43.2	38.5
Sales occupations	100.0	4.0	25.6	31.3	39.1
Administrative support, including clerical	100.0	5.3	31.6	40.3	22.8
Service occupations	100.0	17.2	40.0	31.1	11.8
Private household	100.0	50.8	11.8	37.4	...
Protective service	100.0	3.2	34.0	44.3	18.5
Service, except private household and protective	100.0	23.9	43.3	24.3	8.5
Precision production, craft, and repair	100.0	15.9	45.9	30.8	7.3
Mechanics and repairers	100.0	12.1	45.2	35.1	7.7
Construction trades	100.0	21.0	44.7	27.9	6.3
Other precision production, craft, and repair	100.0	11.4	49.7	30.1	8.8
Operators, fabricators, and laborers	100.0	22.4	49.8	22.2	5.6
Machine operators, assemblers, and inspectors	100.0	23.4	48.9	22.6	5.1
Transportation and material moving occupations	100.0	18.4	51.0	24.3	6.3
Handlers, equipment cleaners, helpers, and laborers	100.0	27.1	49.0	18.6	5.3
Farming, forestry, and fishing	100.0	31.5	41.3	17.1	10.1
Armed forces	100.0	...	23.6	45.9	30.5
WOMEN	100.0	8.5	31.1	30.2	30.1
Managerial and professional specialty	100.0	1.1	12.7	25.0	61.2
Executive, administrative, and managerial	100.0	1.8	21.7	32.5	44.0
Professional specialty	100.0	0.6	5.0	18.7	75.7
Technical, sales, and administrative support	100.0	5.3	37.7	39.1	17.9
Technicians and related support	100.0	1.4	21.6	51.7	25.3
Sales occupations	100.0	9.5	35.6	31.7	23.2
Administrative support, including clerical	100.0	4.0	41.6	40.4	14.0
Service occupations	100.0	21.7	44.5	26.8	7.0
Private household	100.0	35.9	44.8	13.9	5.3
Protective service	100.0	6.6	40.1	40.4	12.9
Service, except private household and protective	100.0	21.5	44.8	27.0	6.8
Precision production, craft, and repair	100.0	19.7	45.1	27.3	7.9
Mechanics and repairers	100.0	14.3	34.5	43.9	7.4
Construction trades	100.0	22.8	44.7	28.6	3.8
Other precision production, craft, and repair	100.0	20.6	47.7	23.0	8.7
Operators, fabricators, and laborers	100.0	25.5	52.3	18.6	3.6
Machine operators, assemblers, and inspectors	100.0	27.6	53.8	15.4	3.3
Transportation and material moving occupations	100.0	16.6	50.4	28.6	4.4
Handlers, equipment cleaners, helpers, and laborers	100.0	25.8	49.4	20.9	3.8
Farming, forestry, and fishing	100.0	33.0	34.1	21.1	11.8
Armed forces	100.0	...	19.1	66.0	14.9

Table 1-60. Median Annual Earnings by Educational Attainment and Sex, Year-Round Full-Time Wage and Salary Workers, Age 25 to 64, 1997–2000

(Thousands of workers, dollars.)

Year and sex	Total	Less than a high school diploma	4 years of high school only	1 to 3 years of college	4 or more years of college
1997					
Total					
Number of workers (thousands)	78 524	7 218	25 432	21 742	24 131
Median annual earnings	30 000	19 000	25 740	30 000	44 000
Men					
Number of workers (thousands)	45 976	4 873	14 686	12 126	14 291
Median annual earnings	35 000	21 840	30 000	35 000	50 000
Women					
Number of workers (thousands)	32 548	2 345	10 746	9 617	9 840
Median annual earnings	25 000	15 000	21 000	25 000	36 000
1998					
Total					
Number of workers (thousands)	80 812	7 353	25 595	22 526	25 338
Median annual earnings	32 000	19 000	26 300	31 619	45 000
Men					
Number of workers (thousands)	47 230	4 872	14 744	12 473	15 142
Median annual earnings	36 400	22 000	30 000	36 000	52 000
Women					
Number of workers (thousands)	33 582	2 482	10 851	10 053	10 197
Median annual earnings	27 000	15 000	22 000	26 500	38 000
1999					
Total					
Number of workers (thousands)	82 501	7 208	25 792	23 380	26 120
Median annual earnings	33 000	20 000	27 000	33 000	48 000
Men					
Number of workers (thousands)	47 781	4 693	14 806	12 824	15 459
Median annual earnings	38 500	22 000	32 000	39 000	55 600
Women					
Number of workers (thousands)	34 720	2 516	10 986	10 556	10 662
Median annual earnings	27 040	15 000	22 000	27 280	40 000
2000					
Total					
Number of workers (thousands)	84 337	7 354	26 144	24 064	26 775
Median annual earnings	35 000	20 000	28 600	34 000	50 000
Men					
Number of workers (thousands)	48 816	4 738	15 057	13 242	15 780
Median annual earnings	40 000	22 500	33 000	40 000	60 000
Women					
Number of workers (thousands)	35 521	2 616	11 087	10 822	10 995
Median annual earnings	29 000	16 000	24 000	28 000	40 000

Table 1–61. Employed Workers with Alternative and Traditional Work Arrangements by Selected Characteristics, February 2001

(Thousands of persons.)

Characteristic	Total employed	Workers with alternative arrangements				Workers with traditional arrangements
		Independent contractors	On-call workers	Temporary help agency workers	Workers provided by contract firms	
AGE AND SEX						
Total, 16 years and over	134 605	8 585	2 089	1 169	633	121 917
16 to 19 years	6 597	104	202	41	7	6 217
20 to 24 years	13 259	235	309	220	69	12 356
25 to 34 years	30 079	1 314	355	310	148	27 905
35 to 44 years	36 740	2 486	538	291	183	33 194
45 to 54 years	29 946	2 410	374	165	151	26 824
55 to 64 years	13 955	1 357	191	124	48	12 227
65 years and over	4 029	679	119	18	28	3 193
Men, 16 years and over	71 376	5 537	1 109	480	447	63 656
16 to 19 years	3 320	61	82	15	7	3 139
20 to 24 years	6 778	120	178	82	57	6 289
25 to 34 years	16 235	776	245	130	115	14 935
35 to 44 years	19 668	1 632	251	154	138	17 461
45 to 54 years	15 567	1 545	180	51	76	13 704
55 to 64 years	7 449	911	98	42	39	6 353
65 years and over	2 358	491	76	7	15	1 775
Women, 16 years and over	63 229	3 048	981	689	187	58 261
16 to 19 years	3 277	43	121	26	...	3 079
20 to 24 years	6 481	115	131	138	12	6 067
25 to 34 years	13 844	538	111	180	32	12 971
35 to 44 years	17 071	854	287	138	45	15 733
45 to 54 years	14 379	864	194	114	75	13 120
55 to 64 years	6 506	446	93	82	9	5 873
65 years and over	1 671	188	43	11	13	1 418
RACE AND HISPANIC ORIGIN						
White	112 976	7 580	1 747	800	487	102 170
Black	15 182	600	277	297	94	13 897
Hispanic origin	14 638	616	232	205	66	13 424
FULL- OR PART-TIME STATUS						
Full-time workers	110 570	6 452	1 100	925	568	101 386
Part-time workers	24 035	2 133	989	244	65	20 530

Note: Detail may not add to totals because the total employed includes day laborers, an alternative arrangement not shown separately, and a small number of workers were both on call and provided by contract firms. Detail for the above race and Hispanic origin groups will not sum to totals because data for the Other races group are not presented and Hispanics are included in both the White and Black population groups. Detail for other characteristics may not sum to totals due to rounding.

Table 1-62. Employed Contingent and Noncontingent Workers by Occupation and Industry, February 2001

(Thousands of persons, percent.)

Characteristic	Contingent workers			Noncontingent workers
	Estimate 1	Estimate 2	Estimate 3	
OCCUPATION				
Total, 16 years and over (thousands)	2 295	2 963	5 369	129 236
Total, 16 years and over (percent distribution)	100.0	100.0	100.0	100.0
Executive, administrative and managerial	6.2	8.2	9.1	15.4
Professional specialty	15.2	14.2	20.0	16.0
Technicians and related support	2.3	2.5	2.4	3.4
Sales occupations	8.7	8.7	6.5	12.3
Administrative support, including clerical	19.4	17.8	17.2	14.0
Services occupations	17.9	18.0	16.5	13.0
Precision production, craft, and repair	12.2	12.8	11.4	10.9
Operators, fabricators and laborers	15.1	14.1	13.0	13.0
Farming, forestry, and fishing	3.0	3.6	4.0	1.9
INDUSTRY				
Total, 16 years and over (thousands)	2 295.0	2 963.0	5 369.0	129 236.0
Total, 16 years and over (percent distribution)	100.0	100.0	100.0	100.0
Agriculture	2.5	3.2	3.6	2.0
Mining	0.1	0.2	0.1	0.4
Construction	12.4	12.1	9.9	6.3
Manufacturing	6.9	6.8	7.5	15.0
Transportation and public utilities	2.9	4.1	3.7	7.3
Wholesale trade	1.9	1.6	1.9	4.0
Retail trade	14.1	13.7	11.6	16.6
Finance, insurance, and real estate	3.6	3.2	2.8	7.1
Services	51.7	52.1	55.4	36.7
Public administration	3.8	3.0	3.6	4.6

Note: See "Notes and Definitions" for explanation of Estimate 1, 2, and 3. Detail may not sum to totals due to rounding.

Table 1-63. Employed Contingent Workers by Their Preference for Contingent or Noncontingent Work Arrangements, February 2001

(Thousands of persons, percent.)

Preference	Estimate 1	Estimate 2	Estimate 3
TOTAL, 16 YEARS AND OVER	2 295	2 963	5 369
Percent	100.0	100.0	100.0
Prefer noncontingent employment	57.8	52.0	52.1
Prefer contingent employment	35.2	40.1	40.3
It depends	5.8	6.0	5.3
Not available	1.2	1.9	2.2

Note: See "Notes and Definitions" for explanation of Estimate 1, 2, and 3. Detail may not sum to totals due to rounding.

Table 1-64. Employed Contingent and Noncontingent Workers with Alternative and Traditional Work Arrangements by Health Insurance Coverage and Eligibility for Employer-Provided Pension Plans, February 2001

(Thousands of persons, percent.)

Characteristic	Total employed	Percent with heath insurance coverage		Percent eligible for employer-provided pension plan [2]	
		Total	Provided by employer [1]	Total	Included in employer-provided pension plan
BY CONTINGENCY					
Contingent Workers					
Estimate 1	2 295	55.8	10.2	10.8	6.9
Estimate 2	2 963	57.9	9.1	10.4	6.8
Estimate 3	5 369	63.6	20.4	21.7	16.0
Noncontingent Workers	129 236	82.5	55.0	51.8	47.0
BY TYPE OF ARRANGEMENT					
With Alternative Arrangements					
Independent contractors	8 585	72.5	...	3.5	2.3
On-call workers	2 089	70.0	29.8	36.9	31.3
Temporary help agency workers	1 169	48.1	10.7	13.3	7.6
Workers provided by contract firms	633	80.1	52.1	55.7	47.7
With Traditional Arrangements	121 917	83.1	58.3	54.5	49.5

Note: See "Notes and Definitions" for explanation of Estimate 1, 2, and 3. Detail may not sum to totals due to rounding.

1. Excludes the self-employed (incorporated and unincorporated) and independent contractors.
2. Excludes the self-employed (incorporated and unincorporated); includes independent contractors who were self-employed.

Table 1-65. Median Usual Weekly Earnings of Workers with Contingent and Alternative Work Arrangements by Selected Characteristics, February 2001

(Dollars.)

Characteristic	By contingency			By type of arrangement			
	Contingent workers			Workers with alternative arrangements			
	Estimate 1	Estimate 2	Estimate 3	Independent contractors	On-call workers	Temporary help agency workers	Workers provided by contract firms
FULL-TIME WORKERS							
Total, 16 years and over	$388	$397	$432	$644	$517	$396	$790
Men	418	436	488	732	596	435	880
Women	341	347	364	489	380	367	530
White	392	398	429	659	536	416	801
Black	366	374	422	519	477	351	(1)
Hispanic origin	308	310	302	473	332	310	(1)
PART-TIME WORKERS							
Total, 16 years and over	117	120	121	243	139	186	(1)
Men	135	137	134	326	130	(1)	(1)
Women	107	110	115	205	145	178	(1)
White	111	113	116	255	132	189	(1)
Black	134	140	137	131	164	(1)	(1)
Hispanic origin	104	104	93	221	136	(1)	(1)

Note: See "Notes and Definitions" for definitions of Estimate 1, 2, and 3. Data for independent contractors include the incorporated and unincorporated self-employed; these groups, however, are excluded from the data for workers with other arrangements. Data for the Other races group are not presented and Hispanics are included in both the White and Black population groups.

1. Data not shown where base number of workers is less than 75,000.

PART TWO

EMPLOYMENT, HOURS, AND EARNINGS

EMPLOYMENT, HOURS, AND EARNINGS

HIGHLIGHTS

The employment, hours and earnings data by industry and state in this chapter are derived from a survey of over 300,000 nonfarm establishments. The employment numbers differ from chapter 1 because of differences in methodology, concepts, definitions and coverage. Since the data are obtained from payroll records, the data are consistent for industry classifications and the data on hours and earnings are likely to be accurate.

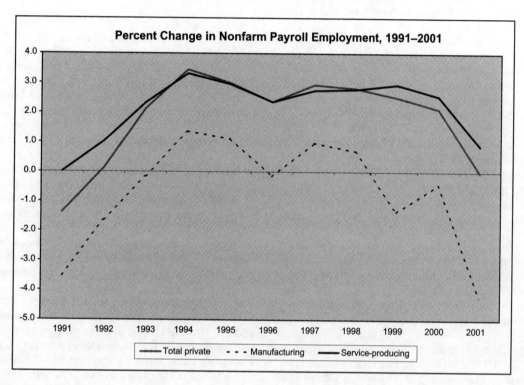

For the first time since 1991 employment in the private nonfarm sector declined in 2001, driven by the continued decline in manufacturing employment. The service producing sector increased slightly as did the services part of that sector.

OTHER HIGHLIGHTS:

- Manufacturing employment continued to decline as a share of total private employment in 2001. Services continued to increase but at a slower rate in 2001. (Table 2-1)
- Almost all of the jobs added to U.S. payrolls in the last 10 years were in the service-producing sector, which includes wholesale and retail trade and finance, insurance and real estate. Almost half of that increase was in the services part, which includes business services and health care. Employment in construction reached a peak in 2001. (Table 2-1)
- Business services provided a substantial part of the total payroll job increase in the past 10 years. However in 2001 that industry showed a steep loss driven by a decline in employment in personnel supply services. (Table 2-1)
- Health care services also contributed to the growth in the services sector. (Table 2-1)
- Employment in state and local government continued to increase in 2001, while employment in the federal government, excluding the Postal Service, declined to its lowest level since the mid-60s. (Table 2-1)
- Average weekly hours of production workers declined in the private sector, largely as a result of the decline in manufacturing hours, where overtime hours declined to its lowest level since 1992. (Table 2-6 and Table 2-8)
- Average hourly earnings of production workers on private nonfarm payrolls increased 4.1 percent in 2001 but most of the increase was reduced by price increases. Earnings in constant dollars rose less than 1 percent. (Table 2-11 and Table 2-13)
- Women employees increased slightly in 2001. (Table 2-2)

NOTES AND DEFINITIONS

Collection and Coverage

Statistics on employment, hours, and earnings are compiled from payroll records reported monthly on a voluntary basis to the Bureau of Labor Statistics (BLS) and its cooperating state agencies by about 390,000 establishments representing all industries except agriculture. This Current Employment Statistics, or CES, program also is referred to as the "establishment" or "payroll" survey. In most industries, the sampling probabilities are based on the size of the establishment; most large establishments are therefore in the sample. An establishment is not necessarily a firm; it may be a branch plant, for example, or a warehouse. Self-employed persons and others not on a regular civilian payroll are outside the scope of the survey. Persons are considered employed if they receive pay for any part of the specified pay period.

The exclusion from the payroll survey of farm employment, self-employment, and domestic service employment accounts in part for the differences in employment figures between the household and payroll surveys. The payroll survey also excludes persons on leave without pay, who are counted as employed in the household survey. Persons who worked in more than one establishment during the reporting period are counted each time their names appear on payrolls, whereas such persons are only counted once in the household survey.

Industries are classified in accordance with the 1987 Standard Industrial Classification. For an establishment making more than one product or engaging in more than one activity, the entire employment of the establishment is included under the industry indicated by the principal product or activity.

Establishment survey data are adjusted annually to accord with comprehensive counts of employment in March of the preceding year, called "benchmarks." The adjustments are published with the release of May data each year. The benchmarks are derived mainly from employment reports from all employers subject to unemployment insurance. Each year's benchmarking results in recalculation of employment data for the current and 2 previous years. The related series on production and non-supervisory workers, hours, and earnings are recalculated consistent with the employment benchmarks.

For employment, the sum of the state figures will differ from the official U.S. national totals because of the effects of differing industrial and geographic stratifications used in the process of expanding sample totals to universe estimates, as well as differences in the timing of benchmark adjustments. The national estimation procedures used by BLS are designed to produce accurate national data by detailed industry; the state estimation procedures are designed to produce accurate data for each individual state. State estimates are not forced to sum to national totals, nor vice versa. Because each state series is subject to larger sampling and nonsampling errors than the national series, summing them cumulates individual state level errors and can cause distortions at an aggregate level, particularly at turning points for the economy.

The data include Alaska and Hawaii beginning in 1959. This inclusion resulted in an increase of 212,000 (0.4 percent) in total nonfarm employment for the March 1959 benchmark month. In 1996, BLS completed implementation of computer assisted reporting through telephone interviews, touch-tone self-reporting, and voice recognition systems and introduced electronic data interchange.

CES Sample Redesign

In June of 1995, the Bureau of Labor Statistics (BLS) announced plans for a comprehensive sample redesign of its monthly payroll survey. The original CES survey was based on a quota sample. The redesign introduces a probability-based sample. In addition, procedures have been developed for regular sample updates of employment from new business births, lack of which was the main source of systemic bias in the old procedure.

The initial research phase for the Current Employment Statistics (CES) sample redesign was completed in 1997, and the Bureau launched a production test of the new sample design at that time. The production test for the wholesale trade industry was concluded in June 2000, when the first estimates from the new design for that industry were published with the 1999 benchmark revisions. With the 2000 benchmark revisions, estimates for the mining, construction and manufacturing industries were published under the new design for the first time, and transportation, public utilities, retail trade, and finance, insurance and real estate were brought in with the 2001 benchmark revision. The services industries will have its first published estimates in June 2003. The conversion of the CES series from industry coding based on the 1987 Standard Industrial Classification (SIC) system to industry coding based on the North American Industrial Classification System (NAICS) will also take place in 2003.

Concepts and Definitions

An *establishment* is an economic unit that produces goods or services (such as a factory or store) at a single location and is engaged in one type of economic activity.

Employed persons are all persons who received pay (including holiday and sick pay) for any part of the payroll period including the 12th day of the month. Persons holding more than one job (about 5 percent of all persons in the labor force) are counted in each establishment that reports them. The data exclude proprietors, the self-employed, unpaid volunteer or family workers, farm workers, and domestic workers. Salaried officers of corporations are included. Government employment covers only civilian employees and excludes military personnel. Employees of the Central Intelligence Agency and the National Security Agency are also excluded.

Production or nonsupervisory workers are a subgroup of employment accounting for about four-fifths of total employment on private nonagricultural payrolls. They comprise production workers in manufacturing and mining, construction workers in construction, and nonsupervisory employees elsewhere. Separate employment figures are tabulated for this group and the data on hours and earnings refer to this group only.

Manufacturing and mining production workers are working supervisors and nonsupervisory workers closely associated with production operations, including those engaged in fabricating, processing, assembling, inspecting, receiving, storing, handling, packing, warehousing, shipping, trucking, hauling, maintenance, repair, janitorial and guard services, product development, and record keeping. Construction workers are working supervisors and others engaged in new work, alterations, demolition, repair, maintenance, etc., whether working at the site or in shops or yards at jobs ordinarily performed by members of the construction trades.

Nonsupervisory workers are enumerated in the following industries: transportation and public utilities; wholesale and retail trade; finance, insurance, and real estate; and services. The category includes employees not above the working supervisory level, such as office and clerical workers, repairers, salespersons, operators, drivers, physicians, lawyers, accountants, nurses, social workers, research aides, teachers, drafters, photographers, beauticians, musicians, restaurant workers, custodial workers, attendants, line installers and repairers, laborers, janitors, guards, and other employees at similar occupational levels whose services are closely associated with those of the employees listed.

Earnings of production or nonsupervisory workers are the payments they receive during the survey period, including premium pay for overtime or late-shift work and holiday, vacation, and sick pay paid directly by the firm. Earnings exclude irregular bonuses, retroactive pay, tips, and payments in kind. Earnings also exclude employee benefits such as health or other insurance and contributions to Social Security and other retirement. Payroll earnings are reported before deductions of any kind, e.g., the employee share of Social Security contributions, group insurance, withholding tax, bonds, or union dues. Real earnings are earnings adjusted to reflect the effects of changes in consumer prices using the Consumer Price Index for Urban Wage Earners and Clerical Workers (CPI-W). Real earnings are expressed in 1982 dollars.

Hours are hours paid for during the pay period including the 12th of the month for production or nonsupervisory workers, including hours paid for holidays, vacations, and sick leave.

Average weekly hours for any industry grouping are total production or nonsupervisory hours paid for divided by total reported production or nonsupervisory employment. These are not the same as standard or scheduled weekly hours because hours paid reflect such factors as unpaid absenteeism, labor turnover, part-time work, and work stoppages. Averages for industries and for all production and nonsupervisory workers reflect changes in the workweeks of component industries and shifts in the composition of employment among industries with shorter and longer workweeks. Because the survey reports multiple jobholders separately at each job, average hours refer to jobs and not to individuals. Thus, if a worker with a full-time job takes a part-time job and nothing changes for any other worker, the average workweek will decline, even though every person is working the same or longer hours.

Aggregate weekly hours for individual industries are the products of average hours and production worker or nonsupervisory worker employment. At all higher levels of industry aggregation, hours aggregates are the sum of the component aggregates. They are published in the form of indexes, 1982=100. The indexes are calculated by dividing each year's aggregate by the 1982 average and expressing the result in percentage form. Thus, these indexes measure changes in the labor inputs of production or nonsupervisory workers.

Average overtime hours are the portion of average weekly hours that exceed regular hours and for which overtime premiums were paid.

Average hourly earnings reflect not only changes in basic hourly and incentive wage rates, but also such variable factors as premium pay for overtime and late-shift work and changes in output of workers paid on an incentive plan. They also reflect shifts in the number of employees between relatively high-paid and low-paid work, as well as changes in workers' earnings in individual establishments. Averages for groups and divisions (such as total private industry, total goods-producing, and total service-producing) further reflect shifts among component industries, as well as changes in average hourly earnings for individual industries. Earnings do not measure the level of total labor costs to the employers since many items are not included (see above) nor are the earnings for those employees not covered under production worker, construction worker, or non-supervisory employee definitions.

Average weekly earnings are derived by multiplying average weekly hours estimates by average hourly earnings estimates. Therefore, weekly earnings are affected not only by changes in average hourly earnings but also by changes in the length of the workweek. Average weekly earnings are per job and will not necessarily reflect trends in income per worker (because of multiple job-holders) or per family (because of families with more than one earner).

Sources of Additional Information

For further details on estimation methods and relation to household data, see Bureau of Labor Statistics,

Employment and Earnings, June 1996 and subsequent issues of that monthly publication, as well as the BLS *Handbook of Methods*, BLS Bulletin 2490, April 1997 and occasional articles in the *Monthly Labor Review*. For a complete description of the CES sample redesign see BLS, *Employment and Earnings*, June 2002.

Table 2-1. Employees on Nonfarm Payrolls by Major Industry and Selected Component Groups, 1946–2001

(Thousands of persons.)

Industry	1946	1947	1948	1949	1950	1951	1952	1953	1954	1955	1956	1957	1958	1959
TOTAL	41 652	43 857	44 866	43 754	45 197	47 819	48 793	50 202	48 990	50 641	52 369	52 855	51 322	53 270
TOTAL PRIVATE	36 056	38 382	39 216	37 897	39 170	41 430	42 185	43 556	42 238	43 727	45 091	45 239	43 483	45 186
GOODS–PRODUCING	17 248	18 509	18 774	17 565	18 506	19 959	20 198	21 074	19 751	20 513	21 104	20 967	19 513	20 411
Mining	862	955	994	930	901	929	898	866	791	792	822	828	751	732
Metal mining	87.8	103.0	104.2	97.7	96.9	101.0	99.8	106.0	99.3	101.5	108.8	111.4	93.2	83.7
Coal mining	...	...	...	...	...	...	...	...	...	...	...	...	215	198
Oil and gas extraction	230.6	248.5	274.0	266.3	266.1	284.4	303.4	311.4	318.1	331.9	340.1	344.0	327.5	329.5
Nonmetallic minerals, except fuels	89.5	97.8	99.6	95.0	95.1	102.4	103.8	105.9	105.1	108.3	115.2	114.3	114.9	120.4
Construction	1 683	2 009	2 198	2 194	2 364	2 637	2 668	2 659	2 646	2 839	3 039	2 962	2 817	3 004
General building contractors	...	...	...	...	...	...	...	...	...	...	...	...	861	928
Heavy construction, except building	...	...	...	...	...	...	...	...	...	...	...	...	...	...
Special trade contractors	...	...	...	...	...	...	...	...	...	...	...	...	...	...
Manufacturing	14 703	15 545	15 582	14 441	15 241	16 393	16 632	17 549	16 314	16 882	17 243	17 176	15 945	16 675
Durable goods	7 785	8 358	8 298	7 462	8 066	9 059	9 320	10 080	9 101	9 511	9 802	9 825	8 801	9 342
Lumber and wood products	...	881.6	854.6	775.3	845.9	879.4	830.4	813.4	747.0	780.9	772.8	697.2	655.3	703.4
Furniture and fixtures	...	319.8	329.2	301.1	346.3	340.1	340.0	352.1	325.6	346.5	357.7	356.5	343.4	366.5
Stone, clay, and glass products	471.8	508.4	519.7	486.0	518.1	555.6	533.9	550.3	523.2	557.0	573.1	563.6	532.5	571.9
Primary metal industries	...	1 224.8	1 236.2	1 086.5	1 194.0	1 307.0	1 228.3	1 325.1	1 168.1	1 266.9	1 298.4	1 298.4	1 106.5	1 133.2
Fabricated metal products	...	1 049.2	1 040.8	935.2	1 042.3	1 158.1	1 173.0	1 286.5	1 171.3	1 221.5	1 239.9	1 267.3	1 169.9	1 218.9
Industrial machinery and equipment	...	1 386.1	1 381.9	1 191.5	1 221.0	1 469.6	1 532.5	1 572.7	1 433.7	1 465.4	1 588.5	1 603.3	1 378.2	1 469.1
Computer and office equipment	...	...	...	...	...	...	...	...	...	...	...	...	130	135
Electronic and other electrical equipment	768.7	855.1	819.1	712.6	819.0	926.7	999.0	1 127.7	1 000.9	1 039.3	1 106.1	1 123.3	1 045.1	1 165.6
Electronic components and accessories	...	...	...	...	...	...	...	...	...	...	...	...	174.0	207.5
Transportation equipment	1 234.7	1 260.9	1 256.0	1 196.4	1 252.6	1 515.5	1 738.9	2 021.5	1 783.7	1 874.1	1 871.1	1 927.8	1 634.5	1 714.5
Motor vehicles and equipment	655.2	767.8	780.7	751.3	816.2	833.3	777.5	917.3	765.7	891.2	792.5	769.3	606.5	692.3
Aircraft and parts	228.6	230.5	228.9	254.5	272.7	450.7	645.9	766.3	754.2	733.3	806.5	862.9	742.6	694.2
Instruments and related products	...	451.0	438.6	392.9	426.5	500.9	549.9	610.0	556.7	563.4	591.7	599.8	562.8	611.3
Miscellaneous manufacturing industries	...	420.8	421.6	384.9	400.2	406.0	393.7	420.9	390.7	396.2	403.0	387.2	373.0	387.7
Nondurable goods	6 918	7 187	7 285	6 979	7 175	7 334	7 313	7 468	7 213	7 370	7 442	7 351	7 144	7 333
Food and kindred products	1 767.0	1 799.0	1 801.0	1 778.0	1 790.0	1 823.2	1 827.8	1 838.9	1 818.3	1 824.7	1 841.9	1 805.4	1 772.8	1 789.6
Tobacco products	...	118.0	114.0	109.0	103.0	104.1	105.6	103.6	103.3	102.5	99.6	97.0	94.5	94.5
Textile mill products	1 264.0	1 298.0	1 332.0	1 187.0	1 256.0	1 237.7	1 163.4	1 154.8	1 042.3	1 050.2	1 032.0	981.1	918.8	945.7
Apparel and other textile products	1 146.0	1 154.0	1 190.0	1 173.0	1 202.0	1 207.2	1 216.4	1 248.0	1 183.6	1 219.2	1 223.4	1 210.1	1 171.8	1 225.9
Paper and allied products	444.0	462.0	469.0	452.0	482.0	507.8	500.4	527.0	527.7	546.4	564.1	566.8	560.4	583.3
Printing and publishing	669.0	721.0	739.0	740.0	748.0	767.6	779.9	802.8	813.9	834.7	862.0	870.0	872.6	888.5
Chemicals and allied products	633.0	649.0	655.0	618.0	640.0	707.0	730.1	768.2	752.7	773.1	796.5	810.0	794.1	809.2
Petroleum and coal products	208.0	221.0	228.0	221.0	218.0	231.3	234.6	241.4	238.1	237.1	235.5	232.2	223.8	215.5
Rubber and miscellaneous plastics products	345.0	353.0	344.0	312.0	342.0	367.9	370.6	394.3	360.0	396.7	403.8	406.0	376.2	407.0
Leather and leather products	408.0	412.0	412.0	389.0	395.0	380.0	384.2	389.2	373.0	385.9	382.7	372.7	359.2	374.0
SERVICE–PRODUCING	24 404	25 348	26 092	26 189	26 691	27 860	28 595	29 128	29 239	30 128	31 264	31 889	31 811	32 857
Transportation and Public Utilities	4 061	4 166	4 189	4 001	4 034	4 226	4 248	4 290	4 084	4 141	4 244	4 241	3 976	4 011
Transportation	...	...	...	...	...	...	...	...	...	...	...	...	...	...
Railroad transportation	...	1 557.0	1 517.0	1 367.0	1 391.0	1 449.3	1 399.8	1 376.9	1 215.4	1 205.4	1 190.4	1 121.4	957.4	924.8
Local and interurban passenger transit	...	...	...	...	...	...	...	...	...	...	...	...	284.8	281.3
Trucking and warehousing	...	...	...	...	...	...	...	...	...	...	...	...	...	...
Water transportation	...	...	...	...	...	...	...	...	...	...	...	...	...	...
Transportation by air	...	...	...	...	...	...	...	...	...	...	...	...	...	...
Pipelines, except natural gas	...	...	...	...	...	...	...	...	...	...	25.9	26.5	25.7	24.3
Transportation services	...	...	...	...	...	...	...	...	...	...	...	...	...	...
Communications and public utilities	...	...	...	...	...	...	...	...	...	...	...	...	860.0	836.8
Communications	...	...	...	...	...	...	...	...	...	...	...	...	...	...
Electric, gas, and sanitary services	...	...	...	...	...	...	...	...	...	...	...	...	...	...
Wholesale Trade	2 298	2 478	2 612	2 610	2 643	2 735	2 821	2 862	2 875	2 934	3 027	3 037	2 989	3 092
Durable goods	...	...	...	...	...	...	...	...	...	...	...	...	...	...
Nondurable goods	...	...	...	...	...	...	...	...	...	...	...	...	...	...

See *Note* at end of table.

Table 2-1. Employees on Nonfarm Payrolls by Major Industry and Selected Component Groups, 1946–2001—Continued

(Thousands of persons.)

	1960	1961	1962	1963	1964	1965	1966	1967	1968	1969	1970	1971	1972	1973
TOTAL	54 189	53 999	55 549	56 653	58 283	60 763	63 901	65 803	67 897	70 384	70 880	71 211	73 675	76 790
TOTAL PRIVATE	45 836	45 404	46 660	47 429	48 686	50 689	53 116	54 413	56 058	58 189	58 325	58 331	60 341	63 058
GOODS–PRODUCING	20 434	19 857	20 451	20 640	21 005	21 926	23 158	23 308	23 737	24 361	23 578	22 935	23 668	24 893
Mining	712	672	650	635	634	632	627	613	606	619	623	609	628	642
Metal mining	93.8	87.4	82.3	79.7	79.5	83.8	86.5	79.2	82.0	89.2	93.3	86.6	82.7	87.4
Coal mining	186.1	161.3	151.9	149.0	147.3	141.4	137.3	138.8	132.3	135.3	145.1	145.6	160.9	161.8
Oil and gas extraction	309.2	303.1	298.0	289.2	291.1	287.1	281.8	275.8	275.6	279.9	270.1	264.2	267.9	273.9
Nonmetallic minerals, except fuels	123.0	119.8	118.1	117.0	116.2	119.6	121.2	119.6	116.2	114.9	114.7	114.8	116.2	118.6
Construction	2 926	2 859	2 948	3 010	3 097	3 232	3 317	3 248	3 350	3 575	3 588	3 704	3 889	4 097
General building contractors	877.1	848.2	857.9	888.5	919.9	961.1	991.7	946.5	975.9	1 071.0	1 065.6	1 102.0	1 164.6	1 221.1
Heavy construction, except building	...	...	...	...	...	...	...	...	...	...	...	...	773.5	789.6
Special trade contractors	...	...	...	...	...	...	...	...	...	...	...	...	1 950.6	2 086.7
Manufacturing	16 796	16 326	16 853	16 995	17 274	18 062	19 214	19 447	19 781	20 167	19 367	18 623	19 151	20 154
Durable goods	9 429	9 041	9 450	9 586	9 785	10 374	11 250	11 408	11 594	11 862	11 176	10 604	11 022	11 863
Lumber and wood products	670.1	624.3	634.3	641.4	657.8	665.1	677.4	661.5	674.0	690.8	658.1	680.9	740.2	774.1
Furniture and fixtures	364.9	350.0	366.8	371.3	386.5	410.2	439.6	434.1	449.5	461.3	439.9	443.6	483.3	506.8
Stone, clay, and glass products	572.0	551.1	561.0	569.0	581.2	595.1	610.3	595.4	602.1	622.0	609.8	610.6	644.6	680.4
Primary metal industries	1 184.8	1 100.1	1 120.9	1 127.3	1 187.8	1 252.8	1 296.5	1 267.0	1 261.0	1 305.0	1 260.4	1 171.0	1 173.3	1 259.1
Fabricated metal products	1 230.0	1 180.9	1 237.7	1 263.8	1 295.0	1 372.1	1 489.0	1 556.1	1 609.2	1 665.0	1 559.1	1 479.4	1 540.9	1 644.9
Industrial machinery and equipment	1 496.1	1 435.4	1 511.2	1 547.5	1 627.0	1 753.9	1 931.1	1 991.1	1 988.2	2 054.7	2 003.0	1 833.7	1 908.8	2 110.8
Computer and office equipment	143.5	148.9	155.5	159.6	169.1	186.3	213.4	233.8	244.3	269.2	281.0	256.6	252.3	276.1
Electronic and other electrical equipment	1 220.9	1 221.6	1 295.9	1 282.4	1 273.1	1 367.6	1 571.3	1 614.6	1 629.1	1 664.3	1 583.6	1 476.7	1 535.0	1 667.2
Electronic components and accessories	227.1	236.3	258.8	255.4	257.6	298.7	378.1	374.4	371.0	383.3	356.8	320.4	345.1	399.5
Transportation equipment	1 668.1	1 574.4	1 682.8	1 748.6	1 732.1	1 853.1	2 031.0	2 058.4	2 132.8	2 120.0	1 832.9	1 743.0	1 776.7	1 914.5
Motor vehicles and equipment	724.1	632.3	691.7	741.3	752.9	842.7	861.6	815.8	873.7	911.4	799.0	848.5	874.8	976.5
Aircraft and parts	604.8	587.3	615.0	615.7	583.1	601.3	725.6	803.0	820.7	774.8	644.1	509.0	481.3	510.1
Instruments and related products	632.2	624.6	650.3	647.7	646.7	684.3	770.0	801.1	814.4	838.3	803.6	753.1	786.2	850.8
Miscellaneous manufacturing industries	389.9	378.2	389.6	386.8	397.6	419.5	433.7	428.4	433.4	441.0	425.7	411.7	433.3	454.4
Nondurable goods	7 367	7 285	7 403	7 410	7 489	7 688	7 963	8 039	8 187	8 304	8 190	8 019	8 129	8 291
Food and kindred products	1 790.0	1 775.2	1 763.0	1 752.0	1 750.4	1 756.7	1 777.2	1 786.3	1 781.5	1 790.8	1 786.2	1 765.6	1 745.2	1 714.8
Tobacco products	94.0	90.7	90.5	88.6	90.2	86.8	84.3	86.5	84.6	82.9	82.9	77.1	74.9	77.5
Textile mill products	924.4	893.4	902.3	885.4	892.0	925.6	963.5	958.5	993.9	1 002.5	974.8	954.7	985.7	1 009.8
Apparel and other textile products	1 233.2	1 214.5	1 263.7	1 282.8	1 302.5	1 354.2	1 401.9	1 397.5	1 405.8	1 409.1	1 363.8	1 342.6	1 382.7	1 438.1
Paper and allied products	597.2	597.4	610.4	614.5	621.4	634.9	662.5	674.6	686.7	706.4	700.9	677.4	678.8	694.4
Printing and publishing	911.3	917.3	926.4	930.6	951.5	979.4	1 016.9	1 047.8	1 065.1	1 093.6	1 104.3	1 080.5	1 094.0	1 110.7
Chemicals and allied products	828.2	828.2	848.5	865.3	878.6	907.8	961.4	1 001.4	1 029.9	1 059.9	1 049.3	1 010.7	1 009.2	1 037.6
Petroleum and coal products	211.9	201.9	195.3	188.7	183.9	182.9	184.2	183.2	186.8	182.3	191.2	194.2	195.4	192.9
Rubber and miscellaneous plastics products	413.3	408.3	442.0	452.6	470.8	506.5	547.4	552.4	597.5	633.6	616.7	616.9	666.9	731.1
Leather and leather products	363.4	358.2	360.7	349.2	347.6	352.9	363.6	350.9	355.2	343.2	319.5	299.1	296.0	284.0
SERVICE–PRODUCING	33 755	34 142	35 098	36 013	37 278	38 839	40 743	42 495	44 158	46 023	47 302	48 276	50 007	51 897
Transportation and Public Utilities	4 004	3 903	3 906	3 903	3 951	4 036	4 158	4 268	4 318	4 442	4 515	4 476	4 541	4 656
Transportation	...	...	...	...	2 487	2 530	2 598	2 655	2 680	2 722	2 694	2 639	2 676	2 746
Railroad transportation	885.3	816.8	796.4	771.6	756.1	735.3	725.2	698.1	667.9	649.2	633.8	605.7	581.5	579.1
Local and interurban passenger transit	284.4	276.9	270.7	269.2	266.9	268.8	270.5	279.4	281.5	280.6	280.5	278.9	276.1	277.5
Trucking and warehousing	...	...	...	...	...	...	...	...	...	...	...	...	...	...
Water transportation	...	...	...	...	229.0	228.4	237.8	240.9	238.9	229.0	212.3	194.1	210.7	199.1
Transportation by air	...	...	...	...	...	...	...	...	...	...	...	...	...	...
Pipelines, except natural gas	23.1	22.2	21.6	20.7	20.0	19.5	18.9	18.7	18.5	17.9	17.6	17.3	16.7	16.8
Transportation services	...	...	...	...	...	...	...	...	...	...	...	...	...	...
Communications and public utilities	...	...	...	...	1 464.0	1 506.0	1 560.0	1 614.0	1 638.0	1 721.0	1 822.0	1 841.0	1 865.0	1 910.0
Communications	839.7	828.9	824.1	823.8	847.9	880.8	928.3	969.6	982.3	1 049.3	1 129.4	1 143.4	1 152.0	1 179.5
Electric, gas, and sanitary services	...	...	...	...	616.5	625.2	631.3	644.0	655.7	671.7	692.3	698.1	713.2	730.9
Wholesale Trade	3 153	3 142	3 207	3 258	3 347	3 477	3 608	3 700	3 791	3 919	4 006	4 014	4 127	4 291
Durable goods	...	...	...	...	...	...	...	...	...	...	...	...	2 336	2 457
Nondurable goods	...	...	...	...	...	...	...	...	...	...	...	...	1 791	1 835

See *Note* at end of table.

Table 2-1. Employees on Nonfarm Payrolls by Major Industry and Selected Component Groups, 1946–2001—Continued

(Thousands of persons.)

	1974	1975	1976	1977	1978	1979	1980	1981	1982	1983	1984	1985	1986	1987
TOTAL	78 265	76 945	79 382	82 471	86 697	89 823	90 406	91 152	89 544	90 152	94 408	97 387	99 344	101 958
TOTAL PRIVATE	64 095	62 259	64 511	67 344	71 026	73 876	74 166	75 121	73 707	74 282	78 384	80 992	82 651	84 948
GOODS–PRODUCING	24 794	22 600	23 352	24 346	25 585	26 461	25 658	25 497	23 812	23 330	24 718	24 842	24 533	24 674
Mining	697	752	779	813	851	958	1 027	1 139	1 128	952	966	927	777	717
Metal mining	95.4	93.5	94.1	90.3	93.7	101.0	98.2	103.7	72.9	56.4	55.1	46.4	41.1	43.8
Coal mining	179.5	212.7	225.0	225.3	209.6	258.8	246.3	224.5	236.6	193.5	195.5	187.3	175.9	161.8
Oil and gas extraction	300.2	328.8	345.7	381.4	429.3	474.2	559.7	692.1	708.3	597.8	606.4	582.7	450.3	401.5
Nonmetallic minerals, except fuels	121.8	116.7	114.6	115.9	118.5	123.8	122.7	118.6	109.7	104.3	108.5	110.1	109.6	110.0
Construction	4 020	3 525	3 576	3 851	4 229	4 463	4 346	4 188	3 904	3 946	4 380	4 668	4 810	4 958
General building contractors	1 191.7	1 011.9	1 022.4	1 108.4	1 228.5	1 272.0	1 173.0	1 094.2	990.3	1 019.2	1 160.5	1 251.4	1 289.2	1 317.8
Heavy construction, except building	799.0	733.9	747.3	759.8	827.6	898.1	894.6	865.1	794.7	753.4	757.8	764.6	749.5	738.6
Special trade contractors	2 029.0	1 778.8	1 805.8	1 982.7	2 172.6	2 292.6	2 278.3	2 228.6	2 119.2	2 173.6	2 461.7	2 652.2	2 770.6	2 901.4
Manufacturing	20 077	18 323	18 997	19 682	20 505	21 040	20 285	20 170	18 780	18 432	19 372	19 248	18 947	18 999
Durable goods	11 897	10 662	11 051	11 570	12 245	12 730	12 159	12 082	11 014	10 707	11 476	11 458	11 195	11 154
Lumber and wood products	726.6	626.9	692.5	736.0	769.8	781.8	704.2	679.8	610.3	670.5	717.9	711.1	724.0	753.8
Furniture and fixtures	489.3	416.9	444.3	464.3	494.1	497.8	465.8	464.7	432.0	448.0	486.4	492.9	497.5	514.8
Stone, clay, and glass products	672.8	597.8	612.7	635.7	663.7	673.5	628.9	606.1	547.5	540.7	561.6	557.1	553.9	554.3
Primary metal industries	1 288.8	1 139.0	1 154.9	1 181.6	1 214.9	1 253.9	1 142.2	1 122.4	921.9	831.8	857.4	807.9	751.4	746.2
Fabricated metal products	1 632.2	1 452.9	1 505.2	1 576.9	1 666.7	1 712.6	1 609.0	1 586.3	1 424.4	1 368.4	1 461.6	1 463.9	1 422.4	1 399.4
Industrial machinery and equipment	2 230.0	2 076.2	2 084.6	2 194.7	2 346.9	2 507.7	2 517.0	2 520.7	2 264.3	2 052.6	2 217.9	2 194.7	2 073.7	2 027.8
Computer and office equipment	296.2	278.0	278.3	302.5	339.8	385.5	420.1	446.8	460.0	473.8	514.8	500.2	469.1	461.2
Electronic and other electrical equipment	1 666.4	1 441.5	1 502.7	1 590.5	1 699.0	1 793.1	1 770.9	1 773.6	1 700.5	1 703.8	1 868.5	1 859.0	1 790.1	1 749.6
Electronic components and accessories	409.6	329.0	356.1	393.6	444.8	510.4	538.5	542.2	543.0	562.9	657.4	645.1	610.1	602.3
Transportation equipment	1 853.0	1 700.4	1 784.8	1 857.1	1 986.6	2 058.9	1 880.5	1 878.9	1 717.6	1 730.4	1 882.8	1 959.6	2 002.6	2 027.5
Motor vehicles and equipment	907.7	792.4	881.0	947.3	1 004.9	990.4	788.8	788.7	699.3	753.6	861.5	883.1	871.8	865.9
Aircraft and parts	524.1	499.4	473.2	467.3	511.1	592.5	633.1	626.4	584.0	561.6	574.9	616.2	655.8	678.0
Instruments and related products	885.4	803.7	839.8	894.9	951.9	1 006.3	1 021.9	1 041.3	1 013.3	990.2	1 040.4	1 047.7	1 018.4	1 011.1
Miscellaneous manufacturing industries	452.0	406.8	429.1	438.4	451.5	444.8	418.0	408.3	382.1	370.3	381.6	366.5	360.7	369.5
Nondurable goods	8 181	7 661	7 946	8 112	8 259	8 310	8 127	8 089	7 766	7 725	7 896	7 790	7 752	7 845
Food and kindred products	1 706.7	1 657.5	1 688.9	1 711.0	1 724.1	1 732.5	1 708.0	1 671.1	1 635.8	1 614.4	1 611.4	1 600.9	1 606.7	1 616.8
Tobacco products	77.1	75.5	76.6	70.7	70.6	70.0	68.9	70.4	68.7	67.9	64.2	63.9	58.5	55.0
Textile mill products	965.0	867.9	918.8	910.2	899.1	885.1	847.7	823.0	749.4	741.3	746.1	702.2	702.9	725.3
Apparel and other textile products	1 362.6	1 243.3	1 318.1	1 316.3	1 332.3	1 304.3	1 263.5	1 244.4	1 161.1	1 163.2	1 184.8	1 120.4	1 099.6	1 096.9
Paper and allied products	696.1	633.4	666.4	682.1	688.8	697.3	684.6	680.5	655.4	653.9	673.8	670.9	667.1	674.0
Printing and publishing	1 111.3	1 083.4	1 099.2	1 141.4	1 192.0	1 235.1	1 252.1	1 266.3	1 271.8	1 298.2	1 375.2	1 426.1	1 456.0	1 502.7
Chemicals and allied products	1 060.5	1 014.7	1 042.5	1 073.7	1 095.5	1 109.3	1 107.4	1 109.0	1 075.1	1 042.8	1 049.0	1 043.5	1 021.0	1 024.6
Petroleum and coal products	197.0	194.4	198.5	202.3	207.7	209.8	197.9	214.0	200.8	195.6	188.9	179.3	168.8	163.9
Rubber and miscellaneous plastics products	733.4	642.7	674.7	749.9	792.6	820.6	763.8	772.3	729.3	742.8	813.2	818.2	822.5	842.1
Leather and leather products	271.1	248.2	262.7	254.8	256.8	245.7	232.9	237.7	218.9	204.9	189.4	164.9	149.0	143.3
SERVICE–PRODUCING	53 471	54 345	56 030	58 125	61 113	63 363	64 748	65 655	65 732	66 821	69 690	72 544	74 811	77 284
Transportation and Public Utilities	4 725	4 542	4 582	4 713	4 923	5 136	5 146	5 165	5 081	4 952	5 156	5 233	5 247	5 362
Transportation	2 779	2 634	2 678	2 781	2 905	3 019	2 960	2 920	2 787	2 742	2 914	2 997	3 051	3 156
Railroad transportation	590.4	548.2	537.9	544.9	539.2	556.3	532.1	494.9	429.4	375.9	375.7	359.0	331.5	308.7
Local and interurban passenger transit	278.6	270.3	264.3	261.5	258.2	262.6	264.6	265.1	263.2	256.5	270.3	277.1	286.0	294.2
Trucking and warehousing	...	...	...	...	...	...	...	...	...	...	...	...	...	...
Water transportation	202.9	193.8	194.0	194.5	207.8	214.2	211.2	217.6	200.3	189.0	190.0	184.5	174.0	172.2
Transportation by air	...	...	...	...	...	...	...	...	...	...	...	...	...	...
Pipelines, except natural gas	17.3	17.5	17.7	18.5	19.6	20.1	21.3	21.8	21.3	20.1	19.1	18.7	18.2	18.8
Transportation services	...	...	...	...	...	...	...	...	...	...	...	...	...	...
Communications and public utilities	1 947.0	1 908.0	1 904.0	1 932.0	2 018.0	2 116.0	2 186.0	2 245.0	2 294.0	2 210.0	2 242.0	2 235.0	2 196.0	2 206.0
Communications	1 202.5	1 175.6	1 169.4	1 185.2	1 239.8	1 309.0	1 357.0	1 390.5	1 417.1	1 323.9	1 340.3	1 318.8	1 274.8	1 281.5
Electric, gas, and sanitary services	744.2	732.6	734.5	747.2	778.4	807.4	829.1	854.2	877.3	886.3	901.6	916.3	921.4	924.7
Wholesale Trade	4 447	4 430	4 562	4 723	4 985	5 221	5 292	5 375	5 295	5 283	5 568	5 727	5 761	5 848
Durable goods	2 578	2 539	2 615	2 732	2 917	3 098	3 139	3 182	3 107	3 087	3 291	3 402	3 395	3 437
Nondurable goods	1 869	1 891	1 946	1 991	2 068	2 123	2 153	2 193	2 188	2 197	2 277	2 325	2 365	2 411

See *Note* at end of table.

Table 2-1. Employees on Nonfarm Payrolls by Major Industry and Selected Component Groups, 1946–2001—*Continued*

(Thousands of persons.)

	1988	1989	1990	1991	1992	1993	1994	1995	1996	1997	1998	1999	2000	2001
TOTAL	105 209	107 884	109 403	108 249	108 601	110 713	114 163	117 191	119 608	122 690	125 865	128 916	131 720	131 922
TOTAL PRIVATE	87 823	90 105	91 098	89 847	89 956	91 872	95 036	97 885	100 189	103 133	106 042	108 709	111 018	110 989
GOODS–PRODUCING	25 125	25 254	24 905	23 745	23 231	23 352	23 908	24 265	24 493	24 962	25 414	25 507	25 669	24 944
Mining	713	692	709	689	635	610	601	581	580	596	590	539	543	565
Metal mining	49.8	55.7	57.8	55.9	53.2	49.8	48.6	51.3	53.8	53.6	49.3	44.3	40.5	35.6
Coal mining	150.8	143.7	146.5	135.5	126.8	108.6	111.8	104.4	97.7	96.0	91.8	84.6	77.8	79.9
Oil and gas extraction	400.3	381.0	394.7	392.9	352.6	349.8	336.5	320.1	322.0	339.0	339.1	297.4	311.6	338.0
Nonmetallic minerals, except fuels	111.8	111.2	110.3	104.5	101.8	101.5	103.6	105.3	106.2	107.8	109.8	112.8	113.3	111.0
Construction	5 098	5 171	5 120	4 650	4 492	4 668	4 986	5 160	5 418	5 691	6 020	6 415	6 653	6 685
General building contractors	1 349.8	1 331.8	1 298.0	1 140.4	1 076.8	1 119.5	1 188.2	1 207.0	1 257.2	1 309.6	1 376.7	1 457.6	1 502.4	1 462.5
Heavy construction, except building	742.7	767.0	770.4	726.6	711.2	712.6	739.6	752.2	776.8	798.9	839.6	874.0	899.3	922.0
Special trade contractors	3 005.2	3 072.1	3 051.0	2 783.3	2 704.1	2 835.6	3 058.4	3 201.1	3 383.6	3 582.3	3 803.6	4 083.7	4 251.2	4 300.5
Manufacturing	19 314	19 391	19 076	18 406	18 104	18 075	18 321	18 524	18 495	18 675	18 805	18 552	18 473	17 695
Durable goods	11 363	11 394	11 109	10 569	10 277	10 221	10 448	10 683	10 789	11 010	11 205	11 111	11 141	10 636
Lumber and wood products	767.3	756.2	733.3	675.2	679.9	709.1	754.3	769.2	778.4	796.0	813.5	834.3	830.4	786.1
Furniture and fixtures	526.7	524.3	505.8	474.7	477.7	486.9	504.6	509.7	504.3	512.2	532.9	548.2	556.3	519.9
Stone, clay, and glass products	567.4	568.4	556.2	521.5	513.3	517.0	531.6	539.6	543.8	552.4	561.5	566.4	579.4	570.7
Primary metal industries	770.3	771.8	756.2	722.6	694.5	683.1	697.7	712.0	710.5	710.7	714.6	699.1	699.4	656.2
Fabricated metal products	1 428.4	1 445.4	1 419.0	1 355.1	1 329.1	1 338.5	1 388.1	1 437.0	1 448.7	1 478.5	1 509.2	1 521.0	1 539.0	1 482.5
Industrial machinery and equipment	2 088.6	2 124.9	2 094.6	1 999.6	1 928.6	1 930.6	1 989.5	2 067.1	2 114.6	2 167.8	2 205.8	2 136.3	2 120.8	2 010.6
Computer and office equipment	459.1	458.7	437.6	415.3	391.0	363.4	354.2	352.2	361.6	375.9	381.7	367.5	358.0	343.3
Electronic and other electrical equipment	1 764.1	1 744.3	1 673.4	1 591.1	1 528.1	1 525.7	1 570.6	1 625.0	1 660.6	1 689.3	1 707.1	1 671.5	1 726.2	1 630.9
Electronic components and accessories	622.0	611.4	582.3	554.8	527.4	527.7	544.2	580.8	616.6	650.3	659.7	640.8	687.1	661.0
Transportation equipment	2 036.1	2 051.5	1 988.9	1 890.0	1 829.6	1 756.2	1 761.1	1 790.2	1 784.9	1 845.2	1 892.5	1 887.6	1 851.9	1 759.9
Motor vehicles and equipment	856.4	858.5	812.1	788.8	812.5	836.6	909.3	970.9	966.8	985.6	995.3	1 018.3	1 016.5	947.0
Aircraft and parts	683.5	711.0	712.3	669.2	611.7	542.0	481.5	450.5	458.1	500.6	525.1	496.3	464.1	460.6
Instruments and related products	1 031.0	1 025.9	1 005.9	974.0	928.5	895.5	861.1	843.4	855.4	866.0	873.1	855.4	845.2	839.3
Miscellaneous manufacturing industries	382.8	381.2	375.3	365.5	367.6	378.3	389.0	389.7	387.8	391.5	394.7	391.3	392.3	379.9
Nondurable goods	7 951	7 997	7 968	7 837	7 827	7 854	7 873	7 841	7 706	7 665	7 600	7 441	7 332	7 059
Food and kindred products	1 626.1	1 644.4	1 660.5	1 666.9	1 662.5	1 679.6	1 678.0	1 691.9	1 691.9	1 685.3	1 683.2	1 682.3	1 687.0	1 690.9
Tobacco products	54.4	49.9	49.1	49.0	47.5	43.7	42.9	42.1	41.4	41.4	40.5	37.4	34.3	33.8
Textile mill products	728.3	719.8	691.4	670.0	674.1	675.1	676.4	663.2	626.5	616.1	597.6	558.9	530.5	477.5
Apparel and other textile products	1 085.1	1 075.7	1 036.2	1 006.0	1 007.2	989.1	974.0	935.8	867.7	823.6	765.8	690.1	633.6	566.0
Paper and allied products	688.8	695.7	696.7	687.9	690.3	691.7	692.3	692.8	683.6	683.1	677.2	667.9	656.2	634.4
Printing and publishing	1 542.9	1 555.9	1 569.4	1 535.6	1 506.5	1 516.7	1 537.2	1 545.9	1 540.3	1 552.4	1 564.6	1 552.3	1 547.5	1 490.8
Chemicals and allied products	1 057.3	1 073.9	1 086.1	1 075.9	1 084.1	1 080.5	1 057.0	1 038.1	1 033.8	1 035.8	1 042.9	1 035.2	1 034.0	1 021.9
Petroleum and coal products	160.1	156.0	157.4	160.0	157.6	151.5	149.1	145.2	142.1	141.0	139.1	132.1	127.0	125.8
Rubber and miscellaneous plastics products	865.6	888.0	887.6	861.9	877.6	909.0	953.1	979.9	982.7	996.1	1 004.9	1 008.6	1 011.4	958.0
Leather and leather products	142.6	137.6	133.1	123.7	119.9	117.2	112.9	105.6	95.7	90.5	84.1	76.6	70.2	59.8
SERVICE–PRODUCING	80 084	82 630	84 497	84 504	85 370	87 361	90 256	92 925	95 115	97 727	100 451	103 409	106 051	106 978
Transportation and Public Utilities	5 512	5 614	5 777	5 755	5 718	5 811	5 984	6 132	6 253	6 408	6 611	6 834	7 031	7 065
Transportation	3 301	3 404	3 511	3 495	3 495	3 598	3 761	3 904	4 019	4 123	4 273	4 411	4 518	4 497
Railroad transportation	298.0	292.5	278.6	262.0	254.3	248.3	240.5	238.4	230.9	226.5	230.5	234.5	237.2	233.5
Local and interurban passenger transit	309.3	325.7	337.8	354.1	361.4	379.4	404.0	419.2	436.9	452.4	468.5	477.7	476.2	479.2
Trucking and warehousing	1 351.1	1 379.0	1 395.2	1 377.8	1 384.6	1 443.6	1 526.1	1 587.1	1 636.8	1 676.7	1 744.0	1 809.9	1 846.7	1 847.8
Water transportation	171.3	171.6	176.6	183.6	173.3	168.2	172.4	174.5	174.1	178.7	181.3	185.5	193.9	192.4
Transportation by air	850.2	897.2	967.6	961.8	964.0	988.2	1 023.0	1 068.3	1 107.4	1 133.9	1 180.6	1 226.7	1 279.9	1 266.0
Pipelines, except natural gas	18.5	18.5	18.5	19.0	19.2	18.4	17.1	15.1	14.5	14.2	13.8	13.4	14.0	15.0
Transportation services	302.4	319.0	336.1	336.3	338.4	351.7	377.9	401.2	418.2	440.5	454.0	463.3	469.8	462.8
Communications and public utilities	2 211.0	2 210.0	2 266.0	2 260.0	2 223.0	2 214.0	2 223.0	2 229.0	2 234.0	2 285.0	2 338.0	2 423.0	2 513.0	2 569.0
Communications	1 279.9	1 272.1	1 308.9	1 298.8	1 268.9	1 269.1	1 294.8	1 317.6	1 350.6	1 419.3	1 477.2	1 560.1	1 659.5	1 716.5
Electric, gas, and sanitary services	931.0	938.1	957.1	961.2	954.0	944.4	928.3	910.9	883.7	865.8	860.7	862.8	853.9	852.2
Wholesale Trade	6 030	6 187	6 173	6 081	5 997	5 981	6 162	6 378	6 482	6 648	6 800	6 911	6 947	6 776
Durable goods	3 564	3 653	3 614	3 531	3 446	3 433	3 559	3 715	3 805	3 927	4 043	4 117	4 152	4 024
Nondurable goods	2 466	2 534	2 559	2 550	2 552	2 549	2 604	2 663	2 677	2 721	2 757	2 793	2 795	2 752

See *Note* at end of table.

Table 2-1. Employees on Nonfarm Payrolls by Major Industry and Selected Component Groups, 1946–2001—*Continued*

(Thousands of persons.)

	1946	1947	1948	1949	1950	1951	1952	1953	1954	1955	1956	1957	1958	1959
Retail Trade	6 077	6 477	6 659	6 654	6 743	7 007	7 184	7 385	7 360	7 601	7 831	7 848	7 761	8 035
Building materials and garden supplies	...	...	...	...	...	...	...	...	...	...	...	...	...	...
General merchandise stores	...	...	...	...	...	...	...	...	...	...	...	...	...	...
Department stores	...	...	...	...	...	...	...	...	...	...	...	...	867.3	899.7
Food stores	...	...	...	...	...	...	...	...	...	...	...	...	1 264.5	1 305.4
Automotive dealers and service stations	...	...	...	...	...	...	...	...	...	...	...	...	1 207.7	1 243.6
New and used car dealers	...	...	...	...	...	...	...	...	...	...	...	...	...	...
Apparel and accessory stores	...	585.2	600.1	585.8	573.4	594.8	608.1	617.9	609.4	616.1	629.9	625.0	610.8	624.0
Furniture and home furnishing stores	...	...	...	...	...	381.2	383.5	388.4	383.0	396.1	405.9	398.6	388.4	395.9
Eating and drinking places	...	...	...	...	...	...	...	...	...	...	...	...	1 528.9	1 602.9
Miscellaneous retail establishments	...	...	...	...	...	...	...	...	...	...	...	...	...	...
Finance, Insurance, and Real Estate	1 675	1 728	1 800	1 828	1 888	1 956	2 035	2 111	2 200	2 298	2 389	2 438	2 481	2 549
Finance	...	...	...	...	...	...	...	...	...	...	...	...	...	...
Depository institutions	...	...	...	...	...	...	...	...	...	...	...	...	...	...
Commercial banks	...	...	...	...	...	...	...	...	...	...	...	...	...	...
Savings banks	...	...	...	...	...	...	...	...	...	...	...	...	...	...
Nondepository institutions	...	...	...	...	...	...	...	...	...	...	...	...	...	...
Mortgage bankers and brokers	...	...	...	...	...	...	...	...	...	...	...	...	...	...
Security and commodity bankers	...	62.8	60.7	58.3	62.4	66.7	68.2	68.9	70.7	81.3	86.9	90.3	93.8	106.7
Holding and other investment offices	...	...	...	...	...	...	...	...	...	...	...	...	...	...
Insurance	...	...	...	...	...	...	...	...	...	...	...	...	...	...
Insurance carriers	...	...	...	...	...	...	...	...	...	...	...	...	813.6	816.9
Insurance agents, brokers, and service	...	...	...	...	...	...	...	...	...	...	...	...	...	...
Real estate	...	...	...	...	...	...	...	...	...	...	...	...	...	...
Services	4 697	5 025	5 181	5 239	5 356	5 547	5 699	5 835	5 969	6 240	6 497	6 708	6 765	7 087
Agricultural services	...	...	...	...	...	...	...	...	...	...	...	...	...	...
Hotels and other lodging places	...	...	...	...	...	...	...	...	...	...	...	...	...	...
Personal services	...	...	...	...	...	...	...	...	...	...	...	...	796.2	808.7
Business services	...	...	...	...	...	...	...	...	...	...	...	...	...	607.6
Services to buildings	...	...	...	...	...	...	...	...	...	...	...	...	...	...
Personnel supply services	...	...	...	...	...	...	...	...	...	...	...	...	...	...
Help supply services	...	...	...	...	...	...	...	...	...	...	...	...	...	...
Computer and data processing services	...	...	...	...	...	...	...	...	...	...	...	...	...	...
Auto repair, services, and parking	...	...	...	...	...	...	...	...	...	...	...	...	...	...
Miscellaneous repair services	...	...	...	...	...	...	...	...	...	...	...	...	...	...
Motion pictures	...	...	...	...	...	...	...	...	...	...	...	...	...	...
Amusement and recreation services	...	...	...	...	...	...	...	...	...	...	...	...	...	...
Health services	...	...	...	...	...	...	...	...	...	...	...	...	1 365.2	1 453.7
Offices and clinics of medical doctors	...	...	...	...	...	...	...	...	...	...	...	...	...	...
Nursing and personal care facilities	...	...	...	...	...	...	...	...	...	...	...	...	...	...
Hospitals	...	...	...	...	...	...	...	...	...	...	...	...	908.3	967.3
Home health care services	...	...	...	...	...	...	...	...	...	...	...	...	...	...
Legal services	...	...	...	...	...	...	...	...	...	...	...	...	...	...
Educational services	...	...	...	...	...	...	...	...	...	...	...	...	572.1	598.1
Social services	...	...	...	...	...	...	...	...	...	...	...	...	...	...
Child day care services	...	...	...	...	...	...	...	...	...	...	...	...	...	...
Residental care	...	...	...	...	...	...	...	...	...	...	...	...	...	...
Museums and botanical and zoological gardens	...	...	...	...	...	...	...	...	...	...	...	...	...	...
Membership organizations	...	...	...	...	...	...	...	...	...	...	...	...	...	...
Engineering and management services	...	...	...	...	...	...	...	...	...	...	...	...	...	...
Engineering and architectural services	...	...	...	...	...	...	...	...	...	...	...	...	173.1	183.7
Management and public relations	...	...	...	...	...	...	...	...	...	...	...	...	...	...
Government	5 595	5 474	5 650	5 856	6 026	6 389	6 609	6 645	6 751	6 914	7 278	7 616	7 839	8 083
Federal	2 254	1 892	1 863	1 908	1 928	2 302	2 420	2 305	2 188	2 187	2 209	2 217	2 191	2 233
Federal, except Postal Service	1 785.4	1 425.0	1 369.2	1 385.4	1 415.5	1 784.4	1 882.0	1 778.4	1 658.3	1 657.4	1 674.0	1 665.5	1 628.2	1 658.0
State	...	...	...	...	...	...	...	...	...	1 168	1 250	1 328	1 415	1 484
Education	...	...	...	...	...	...	...	...	...	308.3	333.8	362.5	388.8	419.8
Other state government	...	...	...	...	...	...	...	...	...	859.8	915.6	965.8	1 026.6	1 064.7
Local	...	...	...	...	...	...	...	...	...	3 558	3 819	4 071	4 232	4 366
Education	...	...	...	...	...	...	...	...	...	1 792.2	1 928.4	2 073.3	2 164.7	2 249.9
Other local government	...	...	...	...	...	...	...	...	...	1 766.3	1 890.6	1 997.3	2 065.0	2 116.0

See *Note* at end of table.

Table 2-1. Employees on Nonfarm Payrolls by Major Industry and Selected Component Groups, 1946–2001—Continued

(Thousands of persons.)

	1960	1961	1962	1963	1964	1965	1966	1967	1968	1969	1970	1971	1972	1973
Retail Trade	8 238	8 195	8 359	8 520	8 812	9 239	9 637	9 906	10 308	10 785	11 034	11 338	11 822	12 315
Building materials and garden supplies	...	...	...	...	...	...	...	...	...	...	...	...	508.4	534.5
General merchandise stores	...	...	...	...	...	...	...	...	...	...	...	...	2 149.4	2 229.3
Department stores	920.2	927.6	974.6	1 024.5	1 091.3	1 176.8	1 259.0	1 328.6	1 410.8	1 488.0	1 519.4	1 563.1	1 660.5	1 721.5
Food stores	1 355.8	1 354.6	1 363.6	1 383.8	1 419.4	1 468.6	1 535.5	1 571.6	1 619.9	1 682.8	1 730.6	1 752.4	1 805.1	1 855.5
Automotive dealers and service stations	1 267.2	1 239.8	1 272.6	1 324.4	1 366.8	1 424.2	1 462.3	1 491.7	1 549.0	1 610.9	1 617.4	1 642.3	1 722.6	1 777.8
New and used car dealers	...	...	...	...	...	...	...	...	...	...	...	...	775.3	802.6
Apparel and accessory stores	639.3	631.5	636.5	632.0	636.2	660.8	681.1	694.4	725.1	752.8	760.6	778.6	783.8	794.7
Furniture and home furnishing stores	400.1	389.0	388.5	389.0	394.5	409.6	419.9	425.9	440.0	464.2	471.6	487.2	513.2	532.5
Eating and drinking places	1 654.3	1 664.8	1 720.5	1 747.9	1 848.1	1 987.9	2 117.9	2 191.4	2 308.8	2 465.7	2 574.6	2 700.4	2 860.2	3 053.8
Miscellaneous retail establishments	...	...	...	...	...	...	...	...	...	...	...	...	1 479.7	1 537.4
Finance, Insurance, and Real Estate	2 628	2 688	2 754	2 830	2 911	2 977	3 058	3 185	3 337	3 512	3 645	3 772	3 908	4 046
Finance	...	...	...	...	...	...	...	...	...	...	...	...	1 778	1 866
Depository institutions	...	...	...	...	...	...	...	...	...	...	...	...	...	...
Commercial banks	...	...	...	...	...	...	...	...	...	...	...	...	1 012.7	1 068.0
Savings banks	...	...	...	...	...	...	...	...	...	...	...	...	...	...
Nondepository institutions	...	...	...	...	...	...	...	...	...	...	...	...	...	...
Mortgage bankers and brokers	...	...	...	...	...	...	...	...	...	...	...	...	...	...
Security and commodity bankers	114.4	128.5	131.8	123.9	125.8	129.0	140.8	156.0	192.1	225.5	204.5	197.7	202.7	192.0
Holding and other investment offices	...	...	...	...	...	...	...	...	...	...	...	...	72.7	77.1
Insurance	...	...	...	...	...	...	...	...	...	...	...	...	1 373	1 401
Insurance carriers	831.7	843.7	852.4	871.9	889.5	893.4	908.2	946.8	980.6	998.8	1 029.7	1 046.9	1 054.3	1 071.0
Insurance agents, brokers, and service	...	...	...	...	...	...	...	...	...	...	...	...	319.1	329.6
Real estate	...	...	...	...	...	...	...	...	...	...	...	...	756	778
Services	7 378	7 619	7 982	8 277	8 660	9 036	9 498	10 045	10 567	11 169	11 548	11 797	12 276	12 857
Agricultural services	...	...	...	...	...	...	...	...	...	...	...	...	813.1	854.2
Hotels and other lodging places	...	...	...	...	...	...	...	...	...	...	...	...	828.4	823.0
Personal services	812.0	816.4	830.9	845.4	866.1	894.7	923.8	933.2	936.5	930.5	898.0	847.9	...	...
Business services	655.7	693.2	753.7	813.7	880.8	954.9	1 051.5	1 146.6	1 210.0	1 328.5	1 397.3	1 401.7	1 490.5	1 609.5
Services to buildings	...	...	...	...	167.5	182.5	199.7	224.9	241.3	267.9	294.7	308.3	336.2	363.9
Personnel supply services	...	...	...	...	...	...	...	...	...	...	...	...	213.5	246.6
Help supply services	...	...	...	...	...	...	...	...	...	...	...	...	...	...
Computer and data processing services	...	...	...	...	...	...	...	...	...	...	...	...	106.7	119.5
Auto repair, services, and parking	...	...	...	...	...	...	...	...	...	...	...	...	398.6	422.0
Miscellaneous repair services	...	...	...	...	148.8	155.0	161.4	167.9	174.1	183.5	188.7	193.1	198.9	205.1
Motion pictures	...	...	...	...	...	...	...	...	...	...	...	...	...	...
Amusement and recreation services	...	...	...	...	...	...	...	...	...	...	...	...	...	...
Health services	1 547.6	1 640.1	1 739.3	1 837.0	1 963.0	2 079.5	2 204.2	2 434.3	2 638.6	2 862.1	3 052.5	3 238.5	3 411.9	3 640.8
Offices and clinics of medical doctors	...	...	...	...	...	...	...	...	...	...	...	...	467.1	518.7
Nursing and personal care facilities	...	...	...	...	...	...	...	...	...	...	...	...	591.2	659.0
Hospitals	1 030.0	1 087.1	1 144.7	1 217.4	1 295.1	1 356.5	1 419.7	1 554.2	1 653.9	1 769.6	1 863.2	1 934.9	1 980.2	2 051.3
Home health care services	...	...	...	...	...	...	...	...	...	...	...	...	...	...
Legal services	...	...	...	...	...	...	...	...	...	...	...	...	271.1	295.5
Educational services	616.1	636.8	678.7	707.5	743.4	772.1	803.9	842.1	891.2	929.7	939.6	947.8	958.4	974.8
Social services	...	...	...	...	...	...	...	...	...	...	...	...	552.9	552.1
Child day care services	...	...	...	...	...	...	...	...	...	...	...	...	...	151.0
Residental care	...	...	...	...	...	...	...	...	...	...	...	...	...	...
Museums and botanical and zoological gardens	...	...	...	...	...	...	...	...	...	...	...	...	...	...
Membership organizations	...	...	...	...	...	...	...	...	...	...	...	...	1 402.7	1 410.3
Engineering and management services	...	...	...	...	...	...	...	...	...	...	...	...	...	...
Engineering and architectural services	190.0	193.3	205.4	216.1	225.9	242.4	266.3	281.2	289.3	306.2	304.0	310.1	339.3	372.3
Management and public relations	...	...	...	...	...	...	...	...	...	...	...	...	...	...
Government	8 353	8 594	8 890	9 225	9 596	10 074	10 784	11 391	11 839	12 195	12 554	12 881	13 334	13 732
Federal	2 270	2 279	2 340	2 358	2 348	2 378	2 564	2 719	2 737	2 758	2 731	2 696	2 684	2 663
Federal, except Postal Service	1 683.4	1 682.5	1 742.7	1 759.5	1 747.9	1 763.7	1 882.9	2 005.2	2 013.2	2 025.2	1 994.7	1 969.3	1 985.6	1 970.2
State	1 536	1 607	1 668	1 747	1 856	1 996	2 141	2 302	2 442	2 533	2 664	2 747	2 859	2 923
Education	447.5	474.2	510.5	557.1	608.8	679.1	775.1	873.4	958.0	1 042.1	1 104.4	1 148.7	1 187.7	1 205.2
Other state government	1 088.3	1 133.1	1 158.0	1 189.6	1 247.3	1 316.8	1 365.8	1 428.5	1 483.6	1 491.1	1 560.1	1 598.6	1 671.6	1 717.3
Local	4 547	4 708	4 881	5 121	5 392	5 700	6 080	6 371	6 660	6 904	7 158	7 437	7 790	8 146
Education	2 368.9	2 467.6	2 581.2	2 737.5	2 905.7	3 102.4	3 374.6	3 572.0	3 735.6	3 874.4	4 004.1	4 187.8	4 362.6	4 537.4
Other local government	2 178.3	2 240.3	2 300.0	2 383.4	2 486.3	2 597.8	2 705.1	2 798.6	2 924.2	3 030.0	3 154.4	3 249.6	3 427.4	3 608.4

See *Note* at end of table.

Table 2-1. Employees on Nonfarm Payrolls by Major Industry and Selected Component Groups, 1946–2001—Continued

(Thousands of persons.)

	1974	1975	1976	1977	1978	1979	1980	1981	1982	1983	1984	1985	1986	1987
Retail Trade	12 539	12 630	13 193	13 792	14 556	14 972	15 018	15 171	15 158	15 587	16 512	17 315	17 880	18 422
Building materials and garden supplies	542.2	520.9	546.4	575.8	608.1	629.2	617.4	606.8	588.3	615.1	658.8	689.5	703.9	743.0
General merchandise stores	2 209.5	2 113.0	2 155.3	2 204.3	2 307.8	2 287.4	2 244.6	2 230.0	2 183.7	2 165.2	2 267.0	2 323.2	2 364.9	2 410.7
Department stores	1 711.3	1 649.0	1 685.5	1 738.4	1 839.5	1 828.4	1 821.6	1 822.3	1 790.1	1 782.3	1 866.4	1 897.0	1 928.7	1 959.7
Food stores	1 947.6	2 007.2	2 038.6	2 106.3	2 198.9	2 296.8	2 383.6	2 448.4	2 477.3	2 555.5	2 635.9	2 773.5	2 896.3	2 958.3
Automotive dealers and service stations	1 665.8	1 677.1	1 743.6	1 800.8	1 860.6	1 812.3	1 688.5	1 653.0	1 631.5	1 673.6	1 797.6	1 888.5	1 941.4	2 000.8
New and used car dealers	753.3	730.6	769.9	801.9	839.9	835.3	745.2	707.4	694.3	722.1	794.3	856.1	895.7	924.6
Apparel and accessory stores	810.8	805.7	841.7	869.9	909.2	949.4	956.7	968.3	942.4	962.5	1 007.5	1 039.1	1 075.3	1 122.8
Furniture and home furnishing stores	538.0	516.5	539.8	562.5	594.7	614.9	606.4	595.4	583.4	607.8	677.4	733.2	766.5	789.3
Eating and drinking places	3 231.2	3 379.5	3 656.2	3 948.6	4 277.2	4 513.1	4 625.8	4 749.0	4 829.4	5 038.0	5 380.9	5 698.6	5 901.5	6 085.7
Miscellaneous retail establishments	1 594.1	1 609.8	1 671.8	1 724.0	1 799.8	1 868.7	1 894.9	1 920.3	1 922.1	1 969.7	2 087.0	2 169.7	2 230.5	2 311.1
Finance, Insurance, and Real Estate	4 148	4 165	4 271	4 467	4 724	4 975	5 160	5 298	5 340	5 466	5 684	5 948	6 273	6 533
Finance	1 936	1 964	2 026	2 113	2 233	2 369	2 483	2 593	2 647	2 741	2 852	2 974	3 145	3 264
Depository institutions	...	...	...	...	...	...	...	...	...	...	...	...	...	...
Commercial banks	1 130.2	1 150.4	1 182.0	1 220.6	1 280.8	1 349.7	1 412.5	1 461.1	1 485.0	1 484.1	1 496.0	1 521.8	1 542.2	1 539.0
Savings banks	...	...	...	...	...	...	...	...	...	...	...	...	...	...
Nondepository institutions	...	...	...	...	...	...	...	...	...	...	...	...	...	...
Mortgage bankers and brokers	...	...	...	...	...	...	...	...	61.5	81.3	100.8	116.0	151.2	174.2
Security and commodity bankers	173.5	169.5	176.4	181.8	188.8	204.2	227.4	259.0	273.8	308.4	338.7	354.5	393.2	442.2
Holding and other investment offices	81.9	86.6	90.6	95.4	103.4	111.2	114.6	122.5	134.0	136.3	144.2	165.8	189.5	201.0
Insurance	1 434	1 442	1 468	1 528	1 591	1 643	1 688	1 713	1 723	1 728	1 765	1 840	1 944	2 027
Insurance carriers	1 087.2	1 085.3	1 101.3	1 140.9	1 173.6	1 199.8	1 224.1	1 236.9	1 237.3	1 228.9	1 239.7	1 291.6	1 364.8	1 415.0
Insurance agents, brokers, and service	346.4	356.6	366.9	387.5	417.7	442.8	463.8	475.8	485.9	498.9	525.0	548.2	579.4	611.8
Real estate	778	760	776	826	900	963	989	992	970	997	1 067	1 135	1 184	1 242
Services	13 441	13 892	14 551	15 302	16 252	17 112	17 890	18 615	19 021	19 664	20 746	21 927	22 957	24 110
Agricultural services	...	...	184.3	197.3	216.7	234.2	246.2	257.7	266.7	286.6	328.2	361.2	388.6	410.9
Hotels and other lodging places	877.7	898.4	929.4	956.1	988.0	1 059.8	1 075.8	1 118.7	1 132.9	1 171.5	1 262.8	1 331.3	1 377.8	1 464.2
Personal services	806.6	781.7	790.4	806.4	826.7	820.8	817.8	827.6	844.2	869.1	918.3	956.6	990.7	1 027.1
Business services	1 685.8	1 697.2	1 805.9	1 957.6	2 180.5	2 410.1	2 563.5	2 699.6	2 722.2	2 948.0	3 352.7	3 679.4	3 957.4	4 278.3
Services to buildings	393.8	390.6	405.1	422.3	451.7	487.0	495.0	511.0	523.5	558.8	608.5	649.8	684.9	724.3
Personnel supply services	256.7	242.0	292.7	357.2	438.1	507.8	543.3	585.3	541.0	618.6	796.7	890.7	990.2	1 176.8
Help supply services	...	...	...	...	...	...	...	...	417.0	488.1	642.5	732.0	836.5	988.9
Computer and data processing services	134.6	143.0	159.4	186.6	223.8	270.8	304.3	336.6	364.6	415.6	474.4	541.5	588.1	628.6
Auto repair, services, and parking	429.6	438.8	465.6	497.7	549.2	575.1	570.9	573.6	589.1	618.5	682.3	729.7	761.5	793.6
Miscellaneous repair services	217.1	217.5	227.4	240.7	261.4	281.8	288.8	292.8	286.6	287.4	310.4	318.9	321.8	321.4
Motion pictures	...	...	...	...	...	...	...	...	...	...	...	...	...	...
Amusement and recreation services	...	...	...	...	...	...	...	...	...	...	...	...	...	...
Health services	3 886.7	4 133.8	4 350.4	4 583.9	4 791.6	4 992.8	5 278.0	5 562.1	5 810.8	5 986.2	6 118.3	6 292.8	6 527.6	6 794.2
Offices and clinics of medical doctors	567.1	607.9	644.4	680.5	719.7	760.8	801.7	844.9	887.2	933.5	977.2	1 028.2	1 081.4	1 139.1
Nursing and personal care facilities	708.1	759.3	809.1	860.0	910.6	950.8	996.6	1 028.8	1 066.9	1 106.0	1 147.2	1 197.5	1 244.6	1 282.6
Hospitals	2 160.1	2 273.7	2 363.2	2 465.2	2 538.2	2 608.4	2 750.2	2 904.2	3 014.4	3 036.6	3 003.6	2 996.8	3 037.4	3 142.1
Home health care services	...	...	...	...	...	...	...	...	...	...	...	...	...	...
Legal services	325.5	340.9	363.8	394.4	427.1	460.3	498.1	532.3	565.3	601.6	645.1	692.0	746.6	800.9
Educational services	990.1	1 000.9	1 012.5	1 031.0	1 062.4	1 089.7	1 138.2	1 178.5	1 198.5	1 225.2	1 270.4	1 358.9	1 421.3	1 449.2
Social services	624.9	689.9	763.0	854.6	990.6	1 081.3	1 134.3	1 149.0	1 149.4	1 188.4	1 222.4	1 324.6	1 405.7	1 453.8
Child day care services	172.0	198.9	214.6	245.2	284.8	303.1	298.9	289.8	282.4	283.8	291.7	310.0	321.9	333.4
Residental care	...	...	...	...	...	...	...	...	236.0	250.7	269.1	294.0	320.8	351.6
Museums and botanical and zoological gardens	...	...	...	...	...	...	...	...	...	...	...	...	...	...
Membership organizations	1 437.9	1 452.3	1 486.8	1 495.4	1 501.6	1 516.2	1 539.3	1 527.2	1 525.5	1 509.8	1 504.0	1 517.1	1 536.4	1 613.6
Engineering and management services	...	...	...	...	...	...	...	...	...	...	...	...	...	...
Engineering and architectural services	394.7	382.3	386.9	424.0	472.6	515.0	544.9	571.9	572.2	575.6	625.0	656.4	681.4	705.7
Management and public relations	...	...	...	...	...	...	...	...	...	...	...	...	...	...
Government	14 170	14 686	14 871	15 127	15 672	15 947	16 241	16 031	15 837	15 869	16 024	16 394	16 693	17 010
Federal	2 724	2 748	2 733	2 727	2 753	2 773	2 866	2 772	2 739	2 774	2 807	2 875	2 899	2 943
Federal, except Postal Service	2 019.2	2 051.1	2 062.5	2 073.2	2 103.8	2 111.8	2 205.0	2 110.9	2 076.2	2 088.2	2 104.5	2 132.6	2 109.8	2 132.8
State	3 039	3 179	3 273	3 377	3 474	3 541	3 610	3 640	3 640	3 662	3 734	3 832	3 893	3 967
Education	1 266.8	1 322.7	1 371.3	1 385.2	1 367.2	1 378.3	1 397.9	1 420.2	1 432.6	1 450.1	1 488.0	1 539.9	1 560.9	1 586.2
Other state government	1 771.7	1 856.5	1 901.6	1 991.8	2 106.3	2 162.4	2 211.9	2 220.1	2 207.2	2 212.2	2 246.4	2 291.8	2 331.9	2 380.6
Local	8 407	8 758	8 865	9 023	9 446	9 633	9 765	9 619	9 458	9 434	9 482	9 687	9 901	10 100
Education	4 691.9	4 833.8	4 898.8	4 974.2	5 075.2	5 107.3	5 210.4	5 215.7	5 168.7	5 138.7	5 195.8	5 343.9	5 484.3	5 598.1
Other local government	3 715.1	3 924.1	3 965.9	4 048.3	4 370.3	4 526.1	4 554.6	4 402.8	4 289.7	4 294.7	4 286.0	4 343.4	4 417.0	4 502.1

See *Note* at end of table.

Table 2-1. Employees on Nonfarm Payrolls by Major Industry and Selected Component Groups, 1946–2001—Continued

(Thousands of persons.)

	1988	1989	1990	1991	1992	1993	1994	1995	1996	1997	1998	1999	2000	2001
Retail Trade	19 023	19 475	19 601	19 284	19 356	19 773	20 507	21 187	21 597	21 966	22 295	22 848	23 337	23 522
Building materials and garden supplies	779.1	783.4	771.2	746.5	757.7	779.0	833.4	867.5	893.7	929.2	947.7	988.0	1 023.9	1 043.9
General merchandise stores	2 471.6	2 544.3	2 540.0	2 452.8	2 451.0	2 488.3	2 582.8	2 680.5	2 701.8	2 700.8	2 730.1	2 798.0	2 867.8	2 897.3
Department stores	2 010.3	2 116.3	2 149.8	2 073.7	2 080.0	2 140.1	2 246.1	2 345.6	2 367.4	2 379.5	2 415.4	2 458.5	2 522.4	2 559.7
Food stores	3 073.9	3 163.5	3 215.0	3 203.7	3 179.8	3 224.1	3 291.2	3 366.0	3 435.5	3 478.1	3 483.5	3 496.8	3 497.5	3 450.8
Automotive dealers and service stations	2 071.4	2 092.4	2 063.1	1 983.8	1 966.3	2 013.8	2 116.2	2 189.6	2 266.7	2 310.8	2 332.3	2 368.1	2 409.6	2 424.8
New and used car dealers	958.1	953.7	924.3	879.3	875.4	908.3	962.5	996.0	1 030.5	1 046.1	1 047.4	1 080.1	1 111.5	1 120.5
Apparel and accessory stores	1 164.7	1 196.7	1 183.4	1 150.6	1 130.9	1 143.6	1 144.0	1 125.4	1 098.4	1 108.5	1 140.6	1 171.4	1 183.6	1 189.0
Furniture and home furnishing stores	802.0	826.4	820.4	801.4	799.8	827.5	889.1	945.5	975.2	998.8	1 025.2	1 086.8	1 133.9	1 141.4
Eating and drinking places	6 258.2	6 401.9	6 509.1	6 476.3	6 609.3	6 821.4	7 077.8	7 354.2	7 516.6	7 645.7	7 767.8	7 960.6	8 144.0	8 256.9
Miscellaneous retail establishments	2 401.9	2 466.8	2 498.6	2 468.4	2 461.4	2 475.5	2 572.5	2 658.3	2 708.5	2 793.9	2 867.9	2 977.9	3 076.5	3 117.5
Finance, Insurance, and Real Estate	6 630	6 668	6 709	6 646	6 602	6 757	6 896	6 806	6 911	7 109	7 389	7 555	7 578	7 712
Finance	3 274	3 283	3 268	3 187	3 160	3 238	3 299	3 231	3 303	3 424	3 588	3 688	3 719	3 800
Depository institutions	2 255.0	2 273.4	2 250.5	2 164.2	2 095.7	2 088.8	2 065.7	2 025.1	2 018.6	2 027.2	2 046.0	2 055.6	2 030.8	2 053.4
Commercial banks	1 533.8	1 555.0	1 563.8	1 529.0	1 489.5	1 497.2	1 484.3	1 465.5	1 458.3	1 462.5	1 471.8	1 467.8	1 432.1	1 433.6
Savings banks	497.2	481.5	438.0	382.4	345.9	324.1	305.1	275.8	265.8	259.8	256.3	254.2	250.3	255.8
Nondepository institutions	363.3	361.2	372.8	379.4	405.5	454.9	490.6	462.9	522.0	577.3	657.6	709.3	687.6	720.2
Mortgage bankers and brokers	157.2	149.1	152.1	152.4	180.2	224.8	248.9	204.9	233.0	262.7	326.2	352.7	312.3	326.9
Security and commodity bankers	446.5	430.2	424.2	419.6	440.1	471.6	515.5	525.4	553.0	596.0	646.5	688.8	752.0	768.9
Holding and other investment offices	209.3	217.7	220.7	223.6	219.0	222.6	226.5	217.2	209.9	223.2	238.2	234.1	248.7	257.4
Insurance	2 075	2 090	2 126	2 161	2 152	2 197	2 236	2 225	2 226	2 264	2 335	2 368	2 352	2 369
Insurance carriers	1 435.4	1 438.4	1 462.2	1 494.6	1 495.6	1 529.0	1 551.9	1 528.8	1 517.1	1 538.8	1 591.1	1 610.0	1 591.9	1 595.3
Insurance agents, brokers, and service	639.6	651.8	663.3	666.3	656.6	668.0	683.6	695.5	708.6	725.2	744.2	757.8	760.0	773.3
Real estate	1 280	1 296	1 315	1 299	1 290	1 322	1 361	1 351	1 382	1 421	1 465	1 500	1 507	1 544
Services	25 504	26 907	27 934	28 336	29 052	30 197	31 579	33 117	34 454	36 040	37 533	39 055	40 457	40 970
Agricultural services	447.3	464.9	490.1	486.5	489.6	519.0	564.1	581.8	627.2	678.2	707.9	766.0	805.7	849.0
Hotels and other lodging places	1 540.1	1 595.8	1 631.1	1 589.4	1 576.4	1 595.7	1 630.9	1 668.1	1 715.0	1 745.7	1 789.4	1 848.1	1 899.7	1 870.0
Personal services	1 055.8	1 085.7	1 103.5	1 111.5	1 116.2	1 137.1	1 140.4	1 162.9	1 180.2	1 185.9	1 201.2	1 225.6	1 250.3	1 269.4
Business services	4 638.3	4 940.6	5 139.3	5 086.2	5 315.3	5 734.7	6 280.7	6 812.4	7 293.0	7 987.5	8 618.0	9 299.9	9 852.3	9 572.3
Services to buildings	780.2	797.5	806.5	796.0	805.4	823.0	857.3	882.2	906.8	930.2	949.7	983.1	993.9	1 016.4
Personnel supply services	1 350.4	1 454.5	1 534.5	1 484.5	1 629.3	1 906.1	2 271.7	2 475.5	2 653.5	2 985.0	3 278.1	3 615.8	3 883.4	3 446.0
Help supply services	1 125.9	1 215.8	1 288.2	1 268.4	1 410.6	1 669.2	2 017.1	2 188.8	2 352.4	2 656.3	2 925.8	3 247.8	3 489.6	3 084.0
Computer and data processing services	673.3	736.3	771.9	797.0	835.5	892.8	958.6	1 089.9	1 227.7	1 409.4	1 615.0	1 875.4	2 104.7	2 225.0
Auto repair, services, and parking	833.6	884.1	913.7	881.8	881.3	924.7	968.3	1 020.1	1 080.0	1 119.6	1 145.2	1 196.4	1 234.2	1 257.2
Miscellaneous repair services	350.0	374.3	374.4	341.0	347.0	348.5	338.2	359.1	371.8	374.1	376.1	371.6	368.8	373.9
Motion pictures	340.9	374.7	407.7	410.9	400.9	412.0	441.2	487.6	524.7	550.4	576.0	598.8	590.3	583.0
Amusement and recreation services	976.8	1 033.3	1 076.0	1 122.2	1 188.1	1 258.2	1 334.1	1 417.4	1 476.1	1 552.3	1 594.4	1 651.4	1 722.4	1 721.8
Health services	7 105.4	7 462.8	7 814.3	8 182.9	8 490.0	8 755.9	8 991.9	9 230.4	9 477.9	9 702.7	9 852.5	9 976.6	10 103.4	10 380.7
Offices and clinics of medical doctors	1 199.5	1 267.9	1 338.2	1 404.5	1 463.1	1 506.0	1 544.9	1 608.9	1 678.3	1 739.0	1 805.7	1 875.0	1 930.6	2 002.1
Nursing and personal care facilities	1 310.6	1 355.7	1 415.4	1 492.6	1 532.8	1 585.0	1 648.6	1 691.4	1 730.4	1 756.2	1 771.6	1 786.1	1 802.0	1 846.6
Hospitals	3 293.8	3 438.5	3 548.7	3 655.1	3 749.9	3 779.1	3 763.0	3 772.1	3 811.5	3 860.4	3 930.2	3 973.5	3 989.2	4 095.8
Home health care services	216.1	243.7	290.6	344.5	397.8	469.0	559.4	628.7	674.6	710.4	666.4	636.1	639.4	636.2
Legal services	844.5	880.4	907.7	911.9	913.5	920.0	924.0	921.4	927.5	944.4	971.4	996.2	1 010.7	1 037.1
Educational services	1 567.3	1 647.0	1 660.7	1 709.7	1 677.6	1 711.3	1 850.0	1 965.2	2 029.9	2 103.6	2 178.3	2 266.6	2 333.7	2 433.9
Social services	1 551.7	1 643.6	1 734.2	1 844.8	1 958.6	2 070.3	2 199.7	2 335.6	2 412.6	2 517.7	2 646.3	2 783.3	2 899.1	3 056.9
Child day care services	356.3	378.4	391.4	417.2	450.8	473.4	515.1	562.6	564.7	575.9	620.8	680.0	701.7	716.2
Residental care	389.4	422.7	461.1	501.3	533.5	567.2	603.8	642.6	676.8	715.5	743.7	771.3	808.8	864.0
Museums and botanical and zoological gardens	58.0	62.0	66.2	69.1	72.7	75.5	78.6	80.4	85.4	90.1	93.5	99.2	106.5	110.3
Membership organizations	1 740.4	1 835.7	1 945.5	1 981.9	1 973.0	2 034.6	2 081.5	2 145.9	2 201.4	2 276.6	2 372.1	2 436.0	2 466.0	2 468.0
Engineering and management services	2 230.4	2 389.2	2 477.6	2 433.4	2 470.8	2 520.9	2 578.5	2 731.1	2 844.3	2 987.8	3 139.1	3 255.6	3 437.4	3 593.1
Engineering and architectural services	730.4	770.3	786.3	750.1	742.4	757.1	778.3	814.8	836.2	865.2	908.0	956.6	1 017.3	1 053.6
Management and public relations	508.1	570.0	610.4	617.1	655.1	688.4	718.7	805.2	869.5	938.8	1 000.2	1 031.1	1 099.7	1 166.2
Government	17 386	17 779	18 304	18 402	18 645	18 841	19 128	19 305	19 419	19 557	19 823	20 206	20 702	20 933
Federal	2 971	2 988	3 085	2 966	2 969	2 915	2 870	2 822	2 757	2 699	2 686	2 669	2 777	2 616
Federal, except Postal Service	2 140.1	2 155.4	2 266.6	2 158.8	2 177.0	2 127.5	2 052.8	1 978.3	1 900.9	1 841.5	1 819.3	1 796.1	1 917.4	1 766.9
State	4 076	4 182	4 305	4 355	4 408	4 488	4 576	4 635	4 606	4 582	4 612	4 709	4 786	4 885
Education	1 620.5	1 668.1	1 729.9	1 767.6	1 798.6	1 834.1	1 881.9	1 919.0	1 910.7	1 904.0	1 922.2	1 983.2	2 035.0	2 096.2
Other state government	2 455.7	2 513.8	2 574.4	2 587.2	2 609.6	2 653.7	2 693.5	2 715.4	2 695.0	2 677.9	2 690.1	2 725.5	2 751.4	2 788.0
Local	10 339	10 609	10 914	11 081	11 267	11 438	11 682	11 849	12 056	12 276	12 525	12 829	13 139	13 432
Education	5 722.1	5 875.4	6 041.5	6 135.7	6 219.5	6 352.9	6 479.0	6 605.6	6 748.1	6 918.3	7 084.5	7 288.7	7 466.3	7 646.1
Other local government	4 616.8	4 733.8	4 873.0	4 945.1	5 048.0	5 085.1	5 202.5	5 243.4	5 308.1	5 357.2	5 440.2	5 540.2	5 672.2	5 785.7

Note: Data include Alaska and Hawaii beginning in 1959.

Table 2-2. Women Employees on Nonfarm Payrolls by Major Industry, 1959–2001

(Thousands of persons.)

Year	Total	Mining	Construc-tion	Manufacturing			Transpor-tation and public utilities	Whole-sale trade	Retail trade	Finance, insur-ance, and real estate	Services	Government			
				Total	Durable goods	Nondura-ble goods						Total	Federal	State	Local
1959	...	...	...	4 358	1 692	2 667	...	...	...	...	...	...	...	...	...
1960	...	36	...	4 371	1 702	2 670	...	717	3 579	...	...	...	...	...	...
1961	...	35	...	4 292	1 662	2 630	...	703	3 564	...	...	...	...	...	...
1962	...	35	...	4 474	1 770	2 705	...	712	3 643	...	...	...	...	...	...
1963	...	35	...	4 482	1 767	2 715	...	720	3 708	...	...	...	...	...	...
1964	19 662	34	152	4 537	1 777	2 760	723	741	3 878	1 464	4 415	3 718	530	708	2 480
1965	20 660	34	152	4 768	1 911	2 857	748	768	4 113	1 496	4 611	3 970	542	768	2 660
1966	22 168	34	156	5 213	2 204	3 009	786	809	4 315	1 549	4 931	4 375	610	841	2 924
1967	23 272	35	158	5 353	2 300	3 053	835	832	4 465	1 624	5 267	4 703	674	931	3 099
1968	24 395	36	164	5 490	2 361	3 129	860	857	4 669	1 709	5 632	4 979	710	1 013	3 256
1969	25 595	37	174	5 667	2 469	3 197	911	904	4 937	1 819	5 994	5 153	723	1 087	3 343
1970	26 132	37	186	5 448	2 307	3 141	957	924	5 083	1 907	6 224	5 365	723	1 126	3 517
1971	26 466	37	199	5 229	2 152	3 078	955	917	5 211	1 978	6 438	5 502	715	1 118	3 669
1972	27 541	40	219	5 470	2 280	3 190	953	939	5 410	2 032	6 718	5 759	747	1 162	3 849
1973	28 988	43	241	5 865	2 567	3 298	987	996	5 686	2 138	7 023	6 010	780	1 216	4 014
1974	30 124	49	262	5 849	2 618	3 230	1 018	1 050	5 928	2 245	7 454	6 270	798	1 287	4 185
1975	30 178	55	256	5 257	2 271	2 985	996	1 053	5 998	2 287	7 822	6 454	805	1 373	4 276
1976	31 570	60	281	5 607	2 444	3 163	1 010	1 100	6 301	2 371	8 256	6 586	808	1 448	4 329
1977	33 252	65	304	5 880	2 645	3 235	1 051	1 153	6 611	2 511	8 771	6 907	856	1 510	4 540
1978	35 349	76	331	6 237	2 894	3 343	1 133	1 243	7 036	2 708	9 368	7 216	866	1 537	4 813
1979	37 096	91	355	6 466	3 085	3 380	1 237	1 328	7 369	2 882	9 919	7 450	860	1 572	5 018
1980	38 186	105	372	6 317	3 003	3 314	1 292	1 371	7 480	3 039	10 452	7 759	908	1 632	5 219
1981	39 035	129	380	6 341	3 029	3 312	1 340	1 404	7 585	3 158	10 969	7 730	878	1 659	5 193
1982	39 041	134	377	5 990	2 822	3 168	1 339	1 424	7 653	3 198	11 330	7 595	883	1 637	5 075
1983	39 826	117	388	5 964	2 788	3 176	1 313	1 463	7 912	3 277	11 755	7 637	939	1 584	5 114
1984	42 022	118	427	6 295	3 031	3 265	1 386	1 557	8 519	3 430	12 413	7 878	975	1 678	5 224
1985	43 851	120	463	6 230	3 022	3 208	1 448	1 632	9 037	3 634	13 129	8 159	1 009	1 776	5 374
1986	45 476	106	495	6 181	2 974	3 207	1 480	1 684	9 404	3 886	13 819	8 420	1 031	1 848	5 541
1987	47 188	95	523	6 242	2 987	3 255	1 532	1 736	9 764	4 076	14 549	8 672	1 048	1 919	5 705
1988	49 053	96	539	6 352	3 032	3 320	1 619	1 815	10 113	4 134	15 454	8 931	1 060	2 000	5 870
1989	50 690	94	547	6 399	3 048	3 351	1 643	1 891	10 384	4 188	16 296	9 248	1 105	2 070	6 073
1990	51 894	95	552	6 285	2 969	3 316	1 714	1 892	10 445	4 239	16 958	9 714	1 258	2 141	6 315
1991	52 016	97	532	6 067	2 824	3 243	1 722	1 864	10 304	4 215	17 352	9 862	1 226	2 177	6 460
1992	52 483	93	511	5 964	2 736	3 228	1 711	1 838	10 312	4 192	17 830	10 033	1 226	2 202	6 606
1993	53 560	88	521	5 933	2 710	3 222	1 740	1 826	10 471	4 279	18 507	10 197	1 211	2 245	6 742
1994	55 164	85	546	5 987	2 761	3 226	1 799	1 890	10 834	4 354	19 271	10 397	1 197	2 289	6 911
1995	56 643	81	573	6 010	2 814	3 195	1 857	1 959	11 169	4 295	20 131	10 568	1 184	2 335	7 049
1996	57 855	80	605	5 950	2 845	3 105	1 908	2 000	11 372	4 359	20 883	10 699	1 164	2 326	7 209
1997	59 388	82	632	5 992	2 920	3 073	1 940	2 057	11 567	4 478	21 787	10 853	1 146	2 335	7 372
1998	60 846	84	666	6 001	2 983	3 018	1 989	2 095	11 750	4 639	22 559	11 064	1 139	2 366	7 558
1999	62 383	80	711	5 896	2 963	2 933	2 091	2 132	12 030	4 727	23 370	11 347	1 132	2 425	7 790
2000	63 834	76	736	5 860	2 990	2 870	2 188	2 151	12 251	4 754	24 150	11 668	1 199	2 477	7 993
2001	64 229	77	728	5 563	2 839	2 723	2 217	2 099	12 348	4 851	24 519	11 828	1 094	2 529	8 205

Note: Data include Alaska and Hawaii beginning in 1959.

Table 2-3. Production or Nonsupervisory Workers on Private Nonfarm Payrolls by Major Industry, 1947–2001

(Thousands of persons.)

Year	Total private	Mining	Construction	Manufacturing			Transportation and public utilities	Wholesale trade	Retail trade	Finance, insurance, and real estate	Services
				Total	Durable goods	Nondurable goods					
1947	33 747	871	1 786	12 990	7 064	5 926	...	2 248	6 000	1 436	...
1948	34 489	906	1 954	12 910	6 962	5 950	...	2 361	6 275	1 496	...
1949	33 159	839	1 949	11 790	6 158	5 633	...	2 354	6 248	1 517	...
1950	34 349	816	2 101	12 523	6 741	5 781	...	2 382	6 368	1 565	...
1951	36 225	840	2 343	13 368	7 514	5 854	...	2 456	6 642	1 622	...
1952	36 643	801	2 360	13 359	7 583	5 777	...	2 533	6 807	1 683	...
1953	37 694	765	2 341	14 055	8 186	5 869	...	2 554	6 964	1 742	...
1954	36 276	686	2 316	12 817	7 226	5 591	...	2 536	6 928	1 807	...
1955	37 500	680	2 477	13 288	7 580	5 708	...	2 574	7 109	1 889	...
1956	38 495	702	2 653	13 436	7 701	5 735	...	2 645	7 296	1 961	...
1957	38 384	695	2 577	13 189	7 581	5 607	...	2 639	7 292	1 998	...
1958	36 608	611	2 420	11 997	6 611	5 387	...	2 572	7 174	2 029	...
1959	38 080	590	2 577	12 603	7 065	5 538	...	2 661	7 434	2 086	...
1960	38 516	570	2 497	12 586	7 060	5 526	...	2 705	7 618	2 145	...
1961	37 989	532	2 426	12 083	6 650	5 433	...	2 684	7 558	2 189	...
1962	38 979	512	2 500	12 488	6 967	5 521	...	2 726	7 682	2 237	...
1963	39 553	498	2 562	12 555	7 059	5 495	...	2 758	7 811	2 291	...
1964	40 560	497	2 637	12 781	7 245	5 537	3 490	2 832	8 037	2 346	7 939
1965	42 278	494	2 749	13 434	7 746	5 688	3 561	2 932	8 426	2 388	8 295
1966	44 249	487	2 818	14 296	8 400	5 895	3 638	3 033	8 787	2 441	8 749
1967	45 137	469	2 741	14 308	8 396	5 912	3 718	3 095	9 026	2 533	9 246
1968	46 473	461	2 822	14 514	8 489	6 024	3 757	3 164	9 378	2 651	9 727
1969	48 208	472	3 012	14 767	8 683	6 084	3 863	3 271	9 822	2 797	10 205
1970	48 156	473	2 990	14 044	8 088	5 956	3 914	3 340	10 034	2 879	10 481
1971	48 148	455	3 071	13 544	7 697	5 847	3 872	3 327	10 288	2 936	10 655
1972	49 939	475	3 257	14 045	8 025	6 022	3 943	3 418	10 717	3 024	11 059
1973	52 201	486	3 405	14 838	8 699	6 138	4 034	3 560	11 152	3 121	11 606
1974	52 809	530	3 294	14 638	8 634	6 004	4 079	3 683	11 316	3 169	12 100
1975	50 991	571	2 808	13 043	7 532	5 510	3 894	3 650	11 373	3 173	12 479
1976	52 897	592	2 814	13 638	7 888	5 750	3 918	3 759	11 890	3 243	13 043
1977	55 179	618	3 021	14 135	8 280	5 855	4 008	3 892	12 424	3 397	13 683
1978	58 156	638	3 354	14 734	8 777	5 956	4 142	4 109	13 110	3 593	14 476
1979	60 367	719	3 565	15 068	9 082	5 986	4 299	4 290	13 458	3 776	15 193
1980	60 331	762	3 421	14 214	8 416	5 798	4 293	4 328	13 484	3 907	15 921
1981	60 923	841	3 261	14 020	8 270	5 751	4 283	4 375	13 582	3 999	16 562
1982	59 468	821	2 998	12 742	7 290	5 451	4 190	4 261	13 594	3 996	16 867
1983	60 028	673	3 031	12 528	7 095	5 433	4 072	4 239	13 989	4 066	17 429
1984	63 339	686	3 404	13 280	7 715	5 565	4 258	4 466	14 736	4 226	18 284
1985	65 475	658	3 655	13 084	7 618	5 466	4 335	4 607	15 421	4 410	19 305
1986	66 866	545	3 770	12 864	7 399	5 465	4 339	4 623	15 925	4 637	20 163
1987	68 771	511	3 870	12 952	7 409	5 543	4 446	4 685	16 378	4 797	21 132
1988	71 099	512	3 980	13 193	7 582	5 611	4 555	4 858	16 869	4 811	22 323
1989	73 017	493	4 035	13 230	7 594	5 636	4 655	4 981	17 262	4 829	23 532
1990	73 774	509	3 974	12 947	7 363	5 584	4 781	4 959	17 358	4 860	24 387
1991	72 631	489	3 549	12 434	6 967	5 467	4 774	4 872	17 006	4 795	24 712
1992	72 918	448	3 431	12 287	6 822	5 466	4 768	4 817	17 048	4 772	25 347
1993	74 761	431	3 589	12 341	6 849	5 492	4 862	4 823	17 428	4 908	26 380
1994	77 607	427	3 858	12 632	7 104	5 528	5 012	4 972	18 056	5 018	27 632
1995	80 125	424	3 993	12 826	7 317	5 508	5 140	5 163	18 639	4 961	28 979
1996	82 092	430	4 199	12 776	7 386	5 390	5 260	5 238	19 002	5 043	30 144
1997	84 541	450	4 415	12 907	7 553	5 354	5 366	5 355	19 337	5 193	31 518
1998	86 805	447	4 669	12 952	7 666	5 287	5 481	5 449	19 592	5 429	32 786
1999	88 997	406	4 963	12 747	7 596	5 150	5 666	5 527	20 103	5 536	34 049
2000	90 994	418	5 148	12 636	7 595	5 041	5 873	5 538	20 552	5 520	35 310
2001	90 921	442	5 175	11 933	7 126	4 808	5 961	5 393	20 681	5 604	35 733

Note: Data include Alaska and Hawaii beginning in 1959.

Table 2-4. Production Workers on Durable Goods Manufacturing Payrolls by Industry, Selected Years, 1939–2001

(Thousands of persons.)

Year	Total	Lumber and wood products	Furniture and fixtures	Stone, clay, and glass products	Primary metal industries Total	Blast furnaces and basic steel products	Fabricated metal products	Industrial machinery and equipment	Electronic and other electrical equipment	Transportation equipment Total	Motor vehicles and equipment	Instruments and related products	Miscellaneous manufacturing
1939	3 926	...	...	297.0	...	452.6	...	...	...	539.5	388.3	...	...
1940	4 506	...	...	310.7	...	519.6	...	...	...	710.7	448.6	...	...
1945	7 571	...	...	334.4	...	527.3	...	...	...	2 057.4	519.7	...	...
1950	6 741	777.2	301.8	447.6	1 030.5	586.8	861.5	938.6	...	1 016.4	677.1	...	343.7
1955	7 580	706.3	292.6	469.1	1 069.4	604.5	974.5	1 082.1	...	1 418.1	718.3	...	330.4
1956	7 701	696.0	300.6	479.9	1 084.6	595.4	977.0	1 170.9	...	1 366.2	619.5	...	333.1
1957	7 581	622.0	298.2	466.5	1 071.4	600.1	989.1	1 155.6	...	1 394.5	601.7	...	315.3
1958	6 611	581.8	284.4	433.5	890.8	486.5	892.2	956.3	...	1 128.8	452.5	...	299.5
1959	7 065	628.5	305.7	469.7	914.2	470.9	939.5	1 038.9	...	1 183.8	537.5	...	312.9
1960	7 060	595.8	303.5	465.5	956.9	528.4	943.4	1 047.4	...	1 134.6	563.3	...	314.3
1961	6 650	551.4	289.5	444.4	880.8	478.4	896.5	987.3	...	1 029.2	479.1	...	303.5
1962	6 967	562.7	304.5	452.3	901.5	476.3	944.8	1 049.4	...	1 096.5	534.0	...	313.2
1963	7 059	565.8	308.7	458.1	911.7	479.1	965.4	1 070.9	...	1 142.9	573.6	...	310.4
1964	7 245	574.8	320.9	467.4	967.1	515.6	992.2	1 131.8	...	1 144.7	579.2	...	317.9
1965	7 746	579.3	340.3	477.8	1 022.7	538.4	1 059.5	1 227.4	...	1 259.2	658.9	...	335.5
1966	8 400	587.4	364.4	489.9	1 055.5	530.9	1 158.9	1 358.1	...	1 385.3	670.3	...	346.1
1967	8 396	570.6	357.6	473.5	1 015.7	509.5	1 204.8	1 383.2	...	1 390.9	626.9	...	338.3
1968	8 489	581.0	371.5	482.0	1 002.6	506.2	1 243.5	1 357.5	...	1 449.9	680.8	...	340.4
1969	8 683	594.3	382.9	498.5	1 042.2	513.6	1 283.6	1 397.1	...	1 443.3	708.0	...	344.6
1970	8 088	563.5	362.4	484.9	999.7	499.7	1 188.3	1 335.8	...	1 222.7	605.3	...	328.7
1971	7 697	588.4	364.5	485.5	923.3	454.6	1 128.0	1 195.1	...	1 196.1	655.4	...	317.6
1972	8 025	636.7	400.4	515.5	932.9	452.6	1 189.1	1 258.4	...	1 225.7	676.0	...	339.9
1973	8 699	664.9	420.0	545.8	1 010.5	484.8	1 276.7	1 415.9	...	1 324.1	754.9	...	356.4
1974	8 634	618.1	401.9	539.1	1 029.5	487.3	1 255.9	1 494.3	...	1 256.3	687.5	...	353.8
1975	7 532	525.6	337.3	472.7	886.6	428.1	1 089.6	1 350.2	...	1 141.7	602.4	...	310.6
1976	7 888	585.4	364.0	486.2	904.4	430.5	1 138.2	1 352.0	...	1 222.5	682.4	...	328.7
1977	8 280	625.8	381.8	504.6	922.1	432.6	1 197.5	1 434.7	...	1 277.0	734.7	...	334.2
1978	8 777	656.5	406.3	524.9	954.3	441.7	1 269.3	1 540.0	...	1 369.5	781.7	...	344.5
1979	9 082	663.7	405.9	529.1	986.4	451.3	1 298.3	1 648.2	...	1 408.5	764.4	...	338.8
1980	8 416	587.2	375.8	486.0	877.6	395.7	1 194.3	1 614.4	...	1 220.3	575.4	...	313.1
1981	8 270	562.5	373.8	464.8	861.9	391.6	1 170.6	1 592.4	...	1 206.8	586.0	...	302.1
1982	7 290	496.7	341.8	412.7	683.4	293.9	1 027.5	1 367.1	...	1 067.7	511.9	...	276.4
1983	7 095	555.3	356.1	411.6	619.8	256.3	993.6	1 206.9	...	1 084.8	568.3	...	266.7
1984	7 715	598.2	389.9	431.0	651.4	256.8	1 078.4	1 342.3	...	1 202.5	663.9	...	277.5
1985	7 618	592.2	393.6	426.7	611.4	231.5	1 082.9	1 319.8	...	1 243.6	684.5	...	264.0
1986	7 399	605.0	397.4	426.2	565.3	208.7	1 051.0	1 233.7	...	1 258.0	670.2	...	261.6
1987	7 409	627.8	412.0	428.7	562.2	202.8	1 037.6	1 203.4	...	1 278.2	673.1	...	269.4
1988	7 582	638.9	420.2	442.7	589.0	215.4	1 061.5	1 256.1	1 112.3	1 272.8	667.4	508.0	280.3
1989	7 594	625.7	417.7	443.6	588.9	215.2	1 070.4	1 281.5	1 101.7	1 277.7	663.8	509.4	277.6
1990	7 363	603.2	399.5	432.1	573.9	211.9	1 044.5	1 260.1	1 054.6	1 223.6	617.1	499.1	272.3
1991	6 967	552.5	372.6	402.5	544.8	199.6	991.0	1 193.2	999.0	1 169.2	601.5	479.4	262.9
1992	6 822	558.0	376.6	396.2	525.1	188.8	975.2	1 151.9	970.8	1 146.6	621.9	456.5	264.7
1993	6 849	583.8	384.7	398.6	520.3	183.2	988.1	1 169.5	974.5	1 120.0	642.0	438.2	270.9
1994	7 104	622.9	399.6	410.7	536.9	182.1	1 037.2	1 233.0	1 010.4	1 154.3	703.9	422.1	276.8
1995	7 317	632.1	403.1	417.9	552.8	184.5	1 079.8	1 294.6	1 044.9	1 200.3	761.4	416.5	275.5
1996	7 386	639.6	398.4	423.1	553.4	184.5	1 088.3	1 320.9	1 056.0	1 209.6	763.6	423.1	273.3
1997	7 553	655.0	406.8	430.9	555.4	180.9	1 114.8	1 364.1	1 068.6	1 255.8	779.1	427.0	274.8
1998	7 666	668.6	424.6	438.5	559.8	180.4	1 137.3	1 392.2	1 070.8	1 264.1	764.4	434.4	275.6
1999	7 596	683.8	437.4	443.4	546.9	176.5	1 143.7	1 345.3	1 044.3	1 250.7	774.0	429.0	271.9
2000	7 595	677.1	443.6	456.5	547.5	174.8	1 158.8	1 323.3	1 072.4	1 221.8	768.5	423.5	270.2
2001	7 126	634.4	410.2	446.2	508.2	161.8	1 102.4	1 227.4	982.6	1 144.5	706.1	413.9	255.6

Note: Data include Alaska and Hawaii beginning in 1959.

Table 2-5. Production Workers on Nondurable Goods Manufacturing Payrolls by Industry, Selected Years, 1939–2001

(Thousands of persons.)

Year	Total	Food and kindred products	Tobacco products	Textile mill products	Apparel and other textile products	Paper and allied products	Printing and publishing	Chemicals and allied products	Petroleum and coal products	Rubber and miscella- neous plastics products	Leather and leather products
1939	4 392	989.0	...	1 108.0	814.0	264.6	320.0	252.0	100.0	149.0	349.0
1940	4 434	1 003.0	...	1 090.0	819.0	276.8	321.0	274.0	105.0	161.0	337.0
1945	5 438	1 380.0	...	1 074.0	973.0	342.8	381.0	518.0	148.0	255.0	325.0
1950	5 781	1 331.0	95.0	1 169.0	1 080.0	413.0	494.0	461.0	165.0	279.0	355.0
1955	5 708	1 291.7	94.4	961.6	1 086.4	450.6	539.0	518.1	163.2	316.3	344.0
1956	5 735	1 302.1	90.1	944.3	1 088.1	461.5	559.6	525.7	161.2	319.5	340.9
1957	5 607	1 263.2	85.3	893.3	1 072.0	460.3	563.7	519.7	156.6	318.1	331.0
1958	5 387	1 222.0	84.1	832.5	1 039.5	451.2	563.2	493.7	146.9	290.2	318.2
1959	5 538	1 222.1	83.9	857.4	1 091.4	468.7	575.1	505.6	139.9	317.7	332.9
1960	5 526	1 211.8	83.3	835.1	1 098.2	476.5	588.9	509.9	137.9	320.5	320.9
1961	5 433	1 191.1	79.6	805.0	1 079.6	474.9	591.7	505.0	129.9	314.7	316.4
1962	5 521	1 178.4	78.7	812.1	1 122.9	482.8	594.5	519.3	125.5	343.3	318.9
1963	5 495	1 167.1	76.6	793.4	1 138.0	483.2	590.3	525.3	119.9	349.8	307.8
1964	5 537	1 157.3	78.4	798.2	1 158.3	485.6	602.1	529.4	114.2	364.1	305.5
1965	5 688	1 159.1	74.8	826.7	1 205.6	494.4	620.6	546.1	112.9	394.3	310.0
1966	5 895	1 180.0	71.8	858.8	1 245.7	514.9	646.4	574.3	114.7	427.1	318.5
1967	5 912	1 187.3	73.9	850.2	1 237.2	522.9	661.6	592.3	114.7	425.3	303.7
1968	6 024	1 191.6	71.9	880.7	1 240.1	532.7	667.0	609.9	118.0	463.2	306.3
1969	6 084	1 201.8	69.6	884.0	1 237.9	547.0	681.7	621.9	112.2	491.3	294.4
1970	5 956	1 206.9	69.0	855.0	1 196.4	539.6	679.0	604.0	118.2	472.7	273.4
1971	5 847	1 203.2	63.4	837.2	1 177.5	518.4	658.0	587.8	124.1	478.5	257.1
1972	6 022	1 191.8	62.2	866.6	1 208.0	528.1	665.7	592.8	125.1	524.8	256.4
1973	6 138	1 166.8	64.8	886.2	1 249.7	539.6	672.9	610.5	123.9	579.1	245.0
1974	6 004	1 163.6	63.8	842.2	1 174.9	540.8	660.4	623.0	126.1	576.5	232.3
1975	5 510	1 120.3	62.4	752.4	1 066.6	476.6	624.0	579.6	123.0	492.7	212.6
1976	5 750	1 145.1	63.6	800.4	1 134.3	505.0	624.7	600.1	127.8	521.6	227.0
1977	5 855	1 161.0	57.0	792.3	1 129.4	514.8	646.5	616.0	131.3	587.7	218.4
1978	5 956	1 173.9	56.2	783.1	1 144.6	521.3	671.9	627.6	135.5	622.1	220.4
1979	5 986	1 190.8	55.5	770.9	1 116.8	532.1	697.2	633.3	137.1	643.0	209.1
1980	5 798	1 174.6	53.6	736.9	1 079.4	519.3	698.9	625.8	124.7	588.2	196.6
1981	5 751	1 149.5	54.7	712.5	1 059.5	515.0	699.3	628.3	133.9	596.8	201.1
1982	5 451	1 125.5	53.4	642.1	981.2	490.7	699.1	598.6	119.9	557.8	182.9
1983	5 433	1 113.5	52.0	639.2	983.5	491.2	711.5	578.6	118.0	574.2	171.1
1984	5 565	1 118.9	48.6	645.6	1 002.1	508.1	757.7	582.8	111.3	632.2	158.0
1985	5 466	1 117.0	48.0	606.3	943.9	508.4	787.9	577.4	108.5	631.7	136.6
1986	5 465	1 129.4	44.1	608.1	926.0	507.2	815.7	567.6	105.9	638.5	122.7
1987	5 543	1 145.1	41.5	629.5	921.7	512.3	839.4	574.6	106.8	652.6	119.7
1988	5 611	1 154.8	40.7	631.8	912.4	516.3	863.6	596.0	104.3	673.5	117.8
1989	5 636	1 176.2	37.0	621.9	906.8	520.5	863.2	603.1	101.8	691.5	114.1
1990	5 584	1 193.8	36.3	592.9	868.5	522.3	871.2	599.6	102.9	686.9	109.4
1991	5 467	1 205.2	36.3	574.1	841.1	517.4	847.0	579.7	103.4	662.0	100.2
1992	5 466	1 211.9	35.7	577.1	843.9	519.8	833.1	567.1	103.3	677.1	96.9
1993	5 492	1 227.8	32.8	574.5	828.6	521.6	838.5	572.6	98.9	703.3	93.7
1994	5 528	1 230.9	33.0	574.5	814.7	524.2	845.5	577.5	96.6	741.8	89.6
1995	5 508	1 247.5	32.0	560.2	776.1	525.4	847.6	580.2	93.8	762.7	82.7
1996	5 390	1 253.7	32.0	529.4	711.2	519.0	841.3	575.4	92.0	762.0	73.9
1997	5 354	1 251.7	31.9	522.3	672.6	520.9	847.3	572.7	93.0	772.5	68.8
1998	5 287	1 251.1	31.5	506.2	615.9	516.0	844.6	586.7	91.8	779.4	63.3
1999	5 150	1 254.9	27.9	471.6	548.1	505.4	827.9	582.8	88.9	785.7	57.0
2000	5 041	1 252.4	25.4	443.7	496.2	497.8	818.4	575.2	86.9	792.1	52.6
2001	4 808	1 248.5	24.8	399.5	436.7	481.3	782.7	560.3	87.1	741.8	45.0

Note: Data include Alaska and Hawaii beginning in 1959.

Table 2-6. Average Weekly Hours of Production or Nonsupervisory Workers on Private Nonfarm Payrolls by Major Industry, 1947–2001

| Year | Total private | Mining | Construction | Manufacturing | | | Transportation and public utilities | Wholesale trade | Retail trade | Finance, insurance, and real estate | Services |
				Total	Durable goods	Nondurable goods					
1947	40.3	40.8	38.2	40.4	40.5	40.2	...	41.1	40.3	37.9	...
1948	40.0	39.4	38.1	40.0	40.4	39.6	...	41.0	40.2	37.9	...
1949	39.4	36.3	37.7	39.1	39.4	38.9	...	40.8	40.4	37.8	...
1950	39.8	37.9	37.4	40.5	41.1	39.7	...	40.7	40.4	37.7	...
1951	39.9	38.4	38.1	40.6	41.5	39.6	...	40.8	40.4	37.7	...
1952	39.9	38.6	38.9	40.7	41.4	39.7	...	40.7	39.8	37.8	...
1953	39.6	38.8	37.9	40.5	41.2	39.6	...	40.6	39.1	37.7	...
1954	39.1	38.6	37.2	39.6	40.1	39.0	...	40.5	39.2	37.6	...
1955	39.6	40.7	37.1	40.7	41.3	39.9	...	40.7	39.0	37.6	...
1956	39.3	40.8	37.5	40.4	41.0	39.6	...	40.5	38.6	36.9	...
1957	38.8	40.1	37.0	39.8	40.3	39.2	...	40.3	38.1	36.7	...
1958	38.5	38.9	36.8	39.2	39.5	38.8	...	40.2	38.1	37.1	...
1959	39.0	40.5	37.0	40.3	40.7	39.7	...	40.6	38.2	37.3	...
1960	38.6	40.4	36.7	39.7	40.1	39.2	...	40.5	38.0	37.2	...
1961	38.6	40.5	36.9	39.8	40.2	39.3	...	40.5	37.6	36.9	...
1962	38.7	41.0	37.0	40.4	40.9	39.7	...	40.6	37.4	37.3	...
1963	38.8	41.6	37.3	40.5	41.1	39.6	...	40.6	37.3	37.5	...
1964	38.7	41.9	37.2	40.7	41.5	39.7	41.1	40.7	37.0	37.3	36.1
1965	38.8	42.3	37.4	41.2	42.0	40.1	41.3	40.8	36.6	37.2	35.9
1966	38.6	42.7	37.6	41.4	42.1	40.2	41.2	40.7	35.9	37.3	35.5
1967	38.0	42.6	37.7	40.6	41.2	39.7	40.5	40.3	35.3	37.1	35.1
1968	37.8	42.6	37.3	40.7	41.4	39.8	40.6	40.1	34.7	37.0	34.7
1969	37.7	43.0	37.9	40.6	41.3	39.7	40.7	40.2	34.2	37.1	34.7
1970	37.1	42.7	37.3	39.8	40.3	39.1	40.5	39.9	33.8	36.7	34.4
1971	36.9	42.4	37.2	39.9	40.3	39.3	40.1	39.4	33.7	36.6	33.9
1972	37.0	42.6	36.5	40.5	41.2	39.7	40.4	39.4	33.4	36.6	33.9
1973	36.9	42.4	36.8	40.7	41.4	39.6	40.5	39.2	33.1	36.6	33.8
1974	36.5	41.9	36.6	40.0	40.6	39.1	40.2	38.8	32.7	36.5	33.6
1975	36.1	41.9	36.4	39.5	39.9	38.8	39.7	38.6	32.4	36.5	33.5
1976	36.1	42.4	36.8	40.1	40.6	39.4	39.8	38.7	32.1	36.4	33.3
1977	36.0	43.4	36.5	40.3	41.0	39.4	39.9	38.8	31.6	36.4	33.0
1978	35.8	43.4	36.8	40.4	41.1	39.4	40.0	38.8	31.0	36.4	32.8
1979	35.7	43.0	37.0	40.2	40.8	39.3	39.9	38.8	30.6	36.2	32.7
1980	35.3	43.3	37.0	39.7	40.1	39.0	39.6	38.4	30.2	36.2	32.6
1981	35.2	43.7	36.9	39.8	40.2	39.2	39.4	38.5	30.1	36.3	32.6
1982	34.8	42.7	36.7	38.9	39.3	38.4	39.0	38.3	29.9	36.2	32.6
1983	35.0	42.5	37.1	40.1	40.7	39.4	39.0	38.5	29.8	36.2	32.7
1984	35.2	43.3	37.8	40.7	41.4	39.7	39.4	38.5	29.8	36.5	32.6
1985	34.9	43.4	37.7	40.5	41.2	39.6	39.5	38.4	29.4	36.4	32.5
1986	34.8	42.2	37.4	40.7	41.3	39.9	39.2	38.3	29.2	36.4	32.5
1987	34.8	42.4	37.8	41.0	41.5	40.2	39.2	38.1	29.2	36.3	32.5
1988	34.7	42.3	37.9	41.1	41.8	40.2	38.2	38.1	29.1	35.9	32.6
1989	34.6	43.0	37.9	41.0	41.6	40.2	38.3	38.0	28.9	35.8	32.6
1990	34.5	44.1	38.2	40.8	41.3	40.0	38.4	38.1	28.8	35.8	32.5
1991	34.3	44.4	38.1	40.7	41.1	40.2	38.1	38.1	28.6	35.7	32.4
1992	34.4	43.9	38.0	41.0	41.5	40.4	38.3	38.2	28.8	35.8	32.5
1993	34.5	44.3	38.5	41.4	42.1	40.6	39.3	38.2	28.8	35.8	32.5
1994	34.7	44.8	38.9	42.0	42.9	40.9	39.7	38.4	28.9	35.8	32.5
1995	34.5	44.7	38.9	41.6	42.4	40.5	39.4	38.3	28.8	35.9	32.4
1996	34.4	45.3	39.0	41.6	42.4	40.5	39.6	38.3	28.8	35.9	32.4
1997	34.6	45.4	39.0	42.0	42.8	40.9	39.7	38.4	28.9	36.1	32.6
1998	34.6	43.9	38.9	41.7	42.3	40.9	39.5	38.3	29.0	36.4	32.6
1999	34.5	43.2	39.1	41.7	42.2	40.9	38.7	38.3	29.0	36.2	32.6
2000	34.5	43.1	39.3	41.6	42.1	40.8	38.4	38.5	28.9	36.4	32.7
2001	34.2	43.5	39.3	40.7	41.0	40.3	38.2	38.2	28.9	36.1	32.7

Note: Data include Alaska and Hawaii beginning in 1959.

Table 2-7. Average Weekly Hours of Production Workers on Manufacturing Payrolls by Industry, 1947–2001

Year	Durable goods												
	Total	Lumber and wood products	Furniture and fixtures	Stone, clay, and glass products	Primary metal industries		Fabricated metal products	Industrial machinery and equipment	Electronic and other electrical equipment	Transportation equipment		Instruments and related products	Miscellaneous manufacturing
					Total	Blast furnaces and basic steel products				Total	Motor vehicles and equipment		
1947	40.5	40.3	41.5	41.0	39.9	39.0	40.9	41.5	...	39.7	39.8	...	40.5
1948	40.4	40.0	41.0	40.7	40.2	39.5	40.7	41.3	...	39.4	39.2	...	40.6
1949	39.4	39.2	40.0	39.7	38.4	38.2	39.7	39.6	...	39.6	39.7	...	39.6
1950	41.1	39.5	41.8	41.1	40.9	39.9	41.5	41.9	...	41.4	42.1	...	40.8
1951	41.5	39.3	41.1	41.4	41.6	40.9	41.8	43.5	...	41.2	40.4	...	40.5
1952	41.4	39.7	41.4	41.1	40.8	40.0	41.7	43.0	...	41.8	41.4	...	40.7
1953	41.2	39.3	40.9	40.8	41.0	40.5	41.8	42.4	...	41.6	42.0	...	40.5
1954	40.1	39.1	40.0	40.5	38.8	37.8	40.8	40.7	...	40.9	41.5	...	39.6
1955	41.3	39.5	41.4	41.4	41.3	40.5	41.7	41.9	...	42.3	43.6	...	40.3
1956	41.0	38.9	40.7	41.1	41.0	40.5	41.3	42.3	...	41.4	41.2	...	40.0
1957	40.3	38.4	39.9	40.4	39.6	39.1	40.9	41.1	...	40.8	40.9	...	39.7
1958	39.5	38.6	39.3	40.0	38.3	37.5	39.9	39.8	...	40.0	39.7	...	39.2
1959	40.7	39.7	40.7	41.2	40.5	40.1	40.9	41.5	...	40.7	41.1	...	39.9
1960	40.1	39.1	40.0	40.6	39.0	38.2	40.5	41.0	...	40.7	41.0	...	39.3
1961	40.2	39.5	40.0	40.7	39.5	38.9	40.5	40.9	...	40.5	40.1	...	39.5
1962	40.9	39.8	40.7	41.0	40.2	39.2	41.1	41.7	...	42.0	42.7	...	39.7
1963	41.1	40.2	40.9	41.4	41.0	40.2	41.3	41.8	...	42.0	42.8	...	39.6
1964	41.5	40.4	41.2	41.7	41.7	41.2	41.7	42.4	...	42.1	43.0	...	39.6
1965	42.0	40.9	41.5	42.0	42.1	41.2	42.1	43.1	...	42.9	44.2	...	39.9
1966	42.1	40.8	41.5	42.0	42.1	41.0	42.4	43.8	...	42.6	42.8	...	40.0
1967	41.2	40.3	40.4	41.6	41.1	40.2	41.5	42.5	...	41.4	40.8	...	39.4
1968	41.4	40.6	40.6	41.8	41.6	41.0	41.7	42.0	...	42.2	43.1	...	39.4
1969	41.3	40.2	40.4	41.9	41.8	41.3	41.6	42.5	...	41.5	41.7	...	39.0
1970	40.3	39.6	39.2	41.2	40.4	40.0	40.7	41.1	...	40.3	40.3	...	38.7
1971	40.3	39.8	39.8	41.6	40.1	39.6	40.4	40.6	...	40.7	41.2	...	38.9
1972	41.2	40.4	40.2	42.0	41.4	40.6	41.2	42.1	...	41.7	43.0	...	39.5
1973	41.4	40.0	40.0	41.9	42.3	41.7	41.6	42.8	...	42.1	43.5	...	39.0
1974	40.6	39.2	39.1	41.3	41.6	41.3	40.8	42.1	...	40.5	40.6	...	38.7
1975	39.9	38.8	38.0	40.4	40.0	39.5	40.1	40.8	...	40.4	40.3	...	38.5
1976	40.6	39.9	38.8	41.1	40.8	40.3	40.8	41.2	...	41.7	42.9	...	38.8
1977	41.0	39.9	39.0	41.3	41.3	40.5	41.0	41.5	...	42.5	44.0	...	38.8
1978	41.1	39.8	39.3	41.6	41.8	41.5	41.0	42.0	...	42.2	43.3	...	38.8
1979	40.8	39.5	38.7	41.5	41.4	41.2	40.7	41.7	...	41.1	41.1	...	38.8
1980	40.1	38.6	38.1	40.8	40.1	39.4	40.4	41.0	...	40.6	40.0	...	38.7
1981	40.2	38.7	38.4	40.6	40.5	40.4	40.3	40.9	...	40.9	40.9	...	38.8
1982	39.3	38.1	37.2	40.1	38.6	37.9	39.2	39.7	...	40.5	40.5	...	38.4
1983	40.7	40.1	39.4	41.5	40.5	39.5	40.6	40.5	...	42.1	43.3	...	39.1
1984	41.4	39.9	39.7	42.0	41.7	40.7	41.4	41.9	...	42.7	43.8	...	39.4
1985	41.2	39.9	39.4	41.9	41.5	41.1	41.3	41.5	...	42.6	43.5	...	39.4
1986	41.3	40.4	39.8	42.2	41.9	41.7	41.3	41.6	...	42.3	42.6	...	39.6
1987	41.5	40.6	40.0	42.3	43.1	43.4	41.6	42.2	...	42.0	42.2	...	39.4
1988	41.8	40.1	39.4	42.3	43.5	44.0	41.9	42.7	41.0	42.7	43.5	41.4	39.2
1989	41.6	40.1	39.5	42.3	43.0	43.4	41.6	42.4	40.8	42.4	43.1	41.1	39.4
1990	41.3	40.2	39.1	42.0	42.7	43.4	41.3	41.9	40.8	42.0	42.4	41.1	39.5
1991	41.1	40.0	38.9	41.7	42.2	42.7	41.2	41.7	40.7	41.9	42.3	41.0	39.7
1992	41.5	40.6	39.7	42.2	43.0	43.5	41.6	42.2	41.2	41.8	42.4	41.1	39.9
1993	42.1	40.8	40.1	42.7	43.7	44.1	42.1	43.0	41.8	43.0	44.3	41.1	39.8
1994	42.9	41.2	40.4	43.4	44.7	44.9	42.9	43.7	42.2	44.3	46.0	41.7	40.0
1995	42.4	40.6	39.6	43.0	44.0	44.4	42.4	43.4	41.6	43.8	44.9	41.4	39.9
1996	42.4	40.8	39.4	43.3	44.2	44.5	42.4	43.1	41.5	44.0	44.9	41.7	39.7
1997	42.8	41.0	40.2	43.2	44.9	44.9	42.6	43.6	42.0	44.5	45.0	42.0	40.4
1998	42.3	41.1	40.5	43.5	44.2	44.6	42.3	42.8	41.4	43.4	43.5	41.3	39.9
1999	42.2	41.1	40.3	43.4	44.5	45.2	42.4	42.1	41.2	43.8	45.0	41.3	39.8
2000	42.1	41.0	40.1	43.1	44.9	46.0	42.6	42.2	41.1	43.4	44.4	41.3	39.0
2001	41.0	40.6	39.0	43.6	43.6	44.6	41.4	40.6	39.4	41.9	42.7	40.9	37.9

See *Note* at end of table.

Table 2-7. Average Weekly Hours of Production Workers on Manufacturing Payrolls by Industry, 1947–2001—*Continued*

Year	Nondurable goods										
	Total	Food and kindred products	Tobacco products	Textile mill products	Apparel and other textile products	Paper and allied products	Printing and publishing	Chemicals and allied products	Petroleum and coal products	Rubber and miscellaneous plastics products	Leather and leather products
1947	40.2	43.2	38.9	39.6	36.0	43.1	40.2	41.2	40.6	40.0	38.6
1948	39.6	42.4	38.3	39.2	35.8	42.8	39.4	41.2	40.6	39.3	37.2
1949	38.9	41.9	37.3	37.7	35.4	41.7	38.8	40.7	40.3	38.5	36.6
1950	39.7	41.9	38.1	39.6	36.0	43.3	38.9	41.2	40.8	41.0	37.6
1951	39.6	42.1	38.5	38.8	35.6	43.1	38.9	41.3	40.8	40.8	36.9
1952	39.7	41.9	38.4	39.1	36.3	42.8	38.9	40.9	40.5	40.9	38.4
1953	39.6	41.5	38.1	39.1	36.1	43.0	39.0	41.0	40.7	40.4	37.7
1954	39.0	41.3	37.6	38.3	35.3	42.3	38.5	40.8	40.7	39.8	36.9
1955	39.9	41.5	38.7	40.1	36.3	43.1	38.9	41.1	40.9	41.7	37.9
1956	39.6	41.3	38.8	39.7	36.0	42.8	38.9	41.1	41.0	40.4	37.6
1957	39.2	40.8	38.4	38.9	35.7	42.3	38.6	40.9	40.8	40.6	37.4
1958	38.8	40.8	39.1	38.6	35.1	41.9	38.0	40.7	40.9	39.3	36.7
1959	39.7	41.0	39.1	40.4	36.3	42.8	38.5	41.4	41.2	41.3	37.9
1960	39.2	40.8	38.2	39.5	35.5	42.1	38.4	41.3	41.1	40.0	36.9
1961	39.3	40.9	39.0	39.9	35.4	42.5	38.2	41.4	41.2	40.4	37.4
1962	39.7	41.0	38.6	40.6	36.2	42.6	38.3	41.6	41.6	41.0	37.6
1963	39.6	41.0	38.7	40.6	36.1	42.7	38.3	41.6	41.7	40.9	37.5
1964	39.7	41.0	38.8	41.0	35.9	42.8	38.5	41.6	41.8	41.3	37.9
1965	40.1	41.1	37.9	41.7	36.4	43.1	38.6	41.9	42.2	42.0	38.2
1966	40.2	41.2	38.9	41.9	36.4	43.4	38.8	42.0	42.4	42.0	38.6
1967	39.7	40.9	38.6	40.9	36.0	42.8	38.4	41.6	42.7	41.4	38.2
1968	39.8	40.8	37.9	41.2	36.1	42.9	38.3	41.8	42.5	41.5	38.3
1969	39.7	40.8	37.4	40.8	35.9	43.0	38.3	41.8	42.6	41.2	37.2
1970	39.1	40.5	37.8	39.9	35.3	41.9	37.7	41.6	42.8	40.3	37.2
1971	39.3	40.3	37.8	40.6	35.6	42.1	37.5	41.6	42.8	40.4	37.7
1972	39.7	40.5	37.6	41.3	36.0	42.8	37.7	41.7	42.7	41.2	38.3
1973	39.6	40.4	38.6	40.9	35.9	42.9	37.7	41.8	42.4	41.2	37.8
1974	39.1	40.4	38.3	39.5	35.2	42.2	37.5	41.5	42.1	40.6	36.9
1975	38.8	40.3	38.2	39.3	35.2	41.6	36.9	41.0	41.2	39.9	37.1
1976	39.4	40.5	37.5	40.1	35.8	42.5	37.5	41.6	42.1	40.7	37.4
1977	39.4	40.0	37.8	40.4	35.6	42.9	37.7	41.7	42.7	41.1	36.9
1978	39.4	39.7	38.1	40.4	35.6	42.9	37.6	41.9	43.6	40.9	37.1
1979	39.3	39.9	38.0	40.4	35.3	42.6	37.5	41.9	43.8	40.6	36.5
1980	39.0	39.7	38.1	40.1	35.4	42.2	37.1	41.5	41.8	40.0	36.7
1981	39.2	39.7	38.8	39.6	35.7	42.5	37.3	41.6	43.2	40.3	36.7
1982	38.4	39.4	37.8	37.5	34.7	41.8	37.1	40.9	43.9	39.6	35.6
1983	39.4	39.5	37.4	40.4	36.2	42.6	37.6	41.6	43.9	41.2	36.8
1984	39.7	39.8	38.9	39.9	36.4	43.1	37.9	41.9	43.7	41.7	36.8
1985	39.6	40.0	37.2	39.7	36.4	43.1	37.8	41.9	43.0	41.1	37.2
1986	39.9	40.0	37.4	41.1	36.7	43.2	38.0	41.9	43.8	41.4	36.9
1987	40.2	40.2	39.0	41.8	37.0	43.4	38.0	42.3	44.0	41.6	38.2
1988	40.2	40.3	39.8	41.0	37.0	43.3	38.0	42.2	44.4	41.7	37.5
1989	40.2	40.7	38.6	40.9	36.9	43.3	37.9	42.4	44.3	41.4	37.9
1990	40.0	40.8	39.2	39.9	36.4	43.3	37.9	42.6	44.6	41.1	37.4
1991	40.2	40.6	39.1	40.6	37.0	43.3	37.7	42.9	44.1	41.1	37.5
1992	40.4	40.6	38.6	41.1	37.2	43.6	38.1	43.1	43.8	41.7	38.0
1993	40.6	40.7	37.4	41.4	37.2	43.6	38.3	43.1	44.2	41.8	38.6
1994	40.9	41.3	39.3	41.6	37.5	43.9	38.6	43.2	44.4	42.2	38.5
1995	40.5	41.1	39.6	40.8	37.0	43.1	38.2	43.2	43.7	41.5	38.0
1996	40.5	41.0	40.0	40.6	37.0	43.3	38.2	43.2	43.6	41.5	38.1
1997	40.9	41.3	38.9	41.4	37.3	43.7	38.5	43.2	43.1	41.8	38.4
1998	40.9	41.7	38.3	41.0	37.3	43.4	38.3	43.2	43.6	41.7	37.6
1999	40.9	41.8	38.4	40.9	37.5	43.4	38.1	43.0	42.4	41.7	37.4
2000	40.8	41.7	40.5	41.2	37.8	42.5	38.3	42.5	42.4	41.4	37.5
2001	40.3	41.1	39.6	39.9	37.3	41.6	38.1	42.3	42.8	40.7	36.3

Note: Data include Alaska and Hawaii beginning in 1959.

Table 2-8. Average Weekly Overtime Hours of Production Workers on Manufacturing Payrolls by Industry, 1956–2001

Year	Total manufac-turing	Durable goods												
		Total	Lumber and wood products	Furniture and fixtures	Stone, clay, and glass products	Primary metal industries		Fabricat-ed metal products	Indus-trial machin-ery and equip-ment	Elec-tronic and other electrical equip-ment	Transportation equipment		Instru-ments and related products	Miscella-neous manufac-turing indus-tries
						Total	Blast furnaces and basic steel products				Total	Motor vehicles and equip-ment		
1956	2.8	3.0	2.6	2.3	3.3	2.8	...	3.1	3.9	...	3.1	...	...	2.8
1957	2.3	2.4	2.2	1.9	2.8	2.0	...	2.8	2.8	...	2.5	...	...	2.4
1958	2.0	1.9	2.3	2.0	2.8	1.4	0.9	2.1	1.8	...	2.1	2.3	...	1.9
1959	2.7	2.7	3.2	2.8	3.6	2.6	2.2	2.8	2.9	...	2.6	3.1	...	2.4
1960	2.5	2.4	2.9	2.5	3.1	1.8	1.3	2.6	2.7	...	2.7	3.2	...	2.1
1961	2.4	2.4	2.9	2.4	3.2	1.9	1.3	2.4	2.5	...	2.5	2.6	...	2.2
1962	2.8	2.8	3.2	2.9	3.4	2.2	1.4	2.9	3.1	...	3.5	4.1	...	2.3
1963	2.8	3.0	3.3	3.0	3.7	2.7	1.9	3.0	3.2	...	3.6	4.4	...	2.2
1964	3.1	3.3	3.4	3.2	3.9	3.2	2.4	3.4	3.9	...	3.9	5.0	...	2.4
1965	3.6	3.9	3.8	3.6	4.2	3.8	2.8	4.0	4.6	...	4.8	6.2	...	2.7
1966	3.9	4.3	4.0	3.8	4.5	4.0	2.7	4.5	5.5	...	4.7	4.9	...	3.0
1967	3.4	3.5	3.6	3.0	4.2	3.2	2.1	3.8	4.4	...	3.7	3.4	...	2.6
1968	3.6	3.8	3.9	3.4	4.5	3.8	2.9	4.1	4.0	...	4.6	5.8	...	2.5
1969	3.6	3.8	3.8	3.3	4.8	4.1	3.2	4.2	4.5	...	3.8	4.2	...	2.6
1970	3.0	3.0	3.3	2.3	4.2	3.0	2.3	3.3	3.2	...	2.9	3.2	...	2.2
1971	2.9	2.9	3.6	2.6	4.5	3.0	2.3	2.8	2.6	...	3.1	3.6	...	2.2
1972	3.5	3.6	4.0	3.1	4.8	3.6	2.6	3.5	3.8	...	4.3	5.3	...	2.7
1973	3.8	4.1	3.9	3.1	5.0	4.5	3.5	4.1	4.8	...	4.9	6.1	...	2.6
1974	3.3	3.4	3.3	2.4	4.4	3.9	3.1	3.5	4.2	...	3.4	3.5	...	2.2
1975	2.6	2.6	2.9	1.8	3.7	2.6	1.9	2.6	2.9	...	2.8	2.6	...	1.9
1976	3.1	3.2	3.5	2.0	4.1	3.3	2.5	3.2	3.3	...	4.2	5.4	...	2.2
1977	3.5	3.7	3.7	2.4	4.6	3.7	2.8	3.6	4.0	...	5.0	6.4	...	2.2
1978	3.6	3.8	3.7	2.7	4.8	4.2	3.5	3.8	4.3	...	5.0	6.1	...	2.4
1979	3.3	3.5	3.5	2.2	4.5	3.9	3.4	3.4	4.0	...	4.2	4.4	...	2.2
1980	2.8	2.8	2.8	1.7	3.8	2.8	2.2	2.8	3.4	...	3.2	2.6	...	1.9
1981	2.8	2.8	2.6	1.8	3.8	3.0	2.7	2.7	3.2	...	3.2	3.0	...	1.9
1982	2.3	2.2	2.3	1.5	3.5	2.0	1.5	2.0	2.2	...	2.7	2.5	...	1.6
1983	3.0	3.0	3.1	2.3	4.1	3.0	2.3	2.9	2.7	...	3.9	4.8	...	2.0
1984	3.4	3.6	3.2	2.5	4.8	3.9	3.1	3.6	3.7	...	4.7	5.6	...	2.2
1985	3.3	3.5	3.2	2.4	4.8	3.8	3.2	3.5	3.4	...	4.8	5.4	...	2.2
1986	3.4	3.5	3.5	2.6	4.9	4.1	3.8	3.5	3.4	...	4.3	4.4	...	2.4
1987	3.7	3.8	3.8	2.8	5.1	4.9	5.0	3.8	4.0	...	4.2	4.3	...	2.6
1988	3.9	4.1	3.6	2.7	5.2	5.5	5.8	4.1	4.4	3.4	4.7	5.2	3.0	2.5
1989	3.8	3.9	3.5	2.7	5.1	5.2	5.5	3.9	4.3	3.2	4.6	4.7	2.8	2.5
1990	3.6	3.7	3.5	2.4	4.9	5.0	5.6	3.6	3.9	3.1	4.0	4.1	2.8	2.5
1991	3.6	3.5	3.3	2.4	4.6	4.6	4.8	3.5	3.7	3.2	3.8	4.0	2.9	2.6
1992	3.8	3.7	3.8	2.8	4.9	5.0	5.3	3.8	4.0	3.4	3.8	4.1	2.8	2.8
1993	4.1	4.3	4.1	3.1	5.2	5.6	5.8	4.3	4.7	3.9	4.8	5.8	2.8	2.8
1994	4.7	5.0	4.5	3.4	5.8	6.6	6.5	5.1	5.4	4.3	6.2	7.6	3.3	3.1
1995	4.4	4.7	4.1	3.0	5.5	6.1	6.4	4.7	5.1	4.0	5.8	6.6	3.4	3.0
1996	4.5	4.8	4.2	3.1	5.9	6.3	6.4	4.8	5.0	4.0	5.9	6.5	3.7	3.1
1997	4.8	5.1	4.3	3.5	5.9	6.7	6.5	5.1	5.5	4.2	6.4	6.8	3.9	3.3
1998	4.6	4.8	4.4	3.6	6.3	6.3	6.1	4.8	5.0	3.8	5.5	5.6	3.3	3.0
1999	4.6	4.8	4.8	3.8	6.1	6.7	6.4	4.8	4.9	3.8	5.3	5.9	3.3	3.0
2000	4.6	4.7	4.8	3.5	6.1	7.0	7.4	4.8	4.9	3.9	4.9	5.4	3.4	2.3
2001	3.9	3.9	4.7	2.7	6.0	6.0	6.4	3.7	3.7	2.6	4.3	4.4	2.9	1.8

See *Note* at end of table.

Table 2-8. Average Weekly Overtime Hours of Production Workers on Manufacturing Payrolls by Industry, 1956–2001—*Continued*

Year	Nondurable goods										
	Total	Food and kindred products	Tobacco products	Textile mill products	Apparel and other textile products	Paper and allied products	Printing and publishing	Chemicals and allied products	Petroleum and coal products	Rubber and miscellaneous plastics products	Leather and leather products
1956	2.4	3.1	1.3	2.6	1.0	4.5	3.1	2.1	2.2	2.2	1.4
1957	2.3	2.9	1.4	2.2	1.0	4.2	2.9	2.0	2.0	2.2	1.3
1958	2.2	3.1	1.3	2.1	1.0	3.9	2.5	1.9	1.8	2.0	1.1
1959	2.7	3.3	1.2	3.1	1.3	4.5	2.8	2.5	2.0	3.5	1.4
1960	2.5	3.3	1.0	2.6	1.2	4.1	2.9	2.3	2.0	2.4	1.2
1961	2.5	3.3	1.1	2.7	1.1	4.2	2.7	2.3	2.0	2.7	1.4
1962	2.7	3.4	1.0	3.2	1.3	4.4	2.8	2.5	2.3	3.1	1.4
1963	2.7	3.4	1.1	3.2	1.3	4.5	2.7	2.5	2.3	3.0	1.4
1964	2.9	3.6	1.6	3.6	1.3	4.7	2.9	2.7	2.5	3.5	1.7
1965	3.2	3.8	1.1	4.2	1.4	5.0	3.1	3.0	2.8	4.1	1.8
1966	3.4	4.0	1.4	4.4	1.5	5.5	3.5	3.3	3.2	4.4	2.1
1967	3.1	4.0	1.8	3.7	1.3	5.0	3.2	3.0	3.5	4.0	1.9
1968	3.3	4.1	1.8	4.1	1.4	5.3	3.1	3.3	3.6	4.2	2.1
1969	3.4	4.2	1.4	3.9	1.3	5.5	3.4	3.4	3.9	4.2	1.8
1970	3.0	4.0	1.7	3.3	1.1	4.6	2.8	3.1	3.8	3.4	1.7
1971	3.0	3.8	1.7	3.8	1.2	4.6	2.6	3.1	3.7	3.3	1.9
1972	3.3	4.0	1.6	4.5	1.5	4.9	2.9	3.2	3.8	4.0	2.3
1973	3.4	4.1	2.4	4.4	1.5	5.2	3.0	3.5	3.9	4.3	2.1
1974	3.0	4.1	2.1	3.3	1.2	4.6	2.7	3.3	3.9	3.5	1.8
1975	2.7	3.9	2.0	3.1	1.2	4.0	2.2	2.7	3.0	2.9	1.9
1976	3.0	4.1	1.3	3.4	1.3	4.8	2.5	3.2	3.5	3.6	1.9
1977	3.2	4.1	1.9	3.5	1.3	4.8	2.8	3.4	4.0	3.7	1.8
1978	3.2	4.0	2.1	3.6	1.3	5.1	3.0	3.5	4.3	3.7	1.8
1979	3.1	4.0	1.3	3.5	1.0	4.8	2.8	3.5	4.3	3.1	1.4
1980	2.8	3.8	1.7	3.2	1.0	4.3	2.5	3.1	3.7	2.7	1.5
1981	2.8	3.7	2.0	3.0	1.1	4.5	2.4	3.3	3.8	3.1	1.4
1982	2.5	3.6	1.4	2.2	1.0	4.1	2.3	2.8	3.9	2.7	1.2
1983	3.0	3.6	1.2	3.5	1.3	4.6	2.6	3.1	4.0	3.5	1.4
1984	3.1	3.8	1.4	3.2	1.4	4.9	2.8	3.4	4.2	3.9	1.4
1985	3.1	3.8	1.1	3.2	1.4	4.7	2.7	3.3	4.2	3.6	1.5
1986	3.3	3.9	1.4	4.0	1.6	4.8	2.9	3.6	4.5	3.8	1.5
1987	3.6	4.1	2.8	4.4	1.8	5.2	3.1	4.0	5.0	4.1	2.2
1988	3.6	4.2	2.6	4.0	1.8	5.0	3.1	4.1	5.5	4.1	2.0
1989	3.6	4.4	2.1	4.0	1.9	4.5	3.0	4.2	5.8	3.8	2.0
1990	3.6	4.5	2.3	3.6	1.6	4.8	3.0	4.4	6.1	3.6	1.8
1991	3.7	4.5	2.0	4.1	1.8	4.9	2.7	4.5	6.2	3.6	1.9
1992	3.8	4.5	2.1	4.3	1.8	5.3	2.9	4.8	6.2	4.1	2.1
1993	4.0	4.6	1.9	4.4	1.8	5.4	3.1	4.8	6.0	4.4	2.3
1994	4.3	4.9	3.7	4.7	2.1	5.6	3.4	5.0	6.4	4.7	2.5
1995	4.0	4.8	4.7	4.2	1.8	5.2	3.1	4.9	6.1	4.1	2.0
1996	4.1	4.8	4.9	4.3	2.0	5.5	3.1	5.0	6.1	4.3	2.0
1997	4.4	5.0	3.1	4.6	2.2	5.7	3.4	5.2	6.2	4.6	2.2
1998	4.3	5.2	2.6	4.5	2.1	5.6	3.2	5.1	6.6	4.4	2.2
1999	4.4	5.5	2.9	4.3	2.4	5.7	3.1	5.0	6.3	4.5	2.0
2000	4.4	5.4	4.0	4.2	2.3	5.6	3.4	4.9	6.1	4.1	2.3
2001	4.0	5.2	3.1	3.4	1.8	4.9	3.1	4.7	6.3	3.5	1.3

Note: Data include Alaska and Hawaii beginning in 1959.

Table 2-9. Indexes of Aggregate Weekly Hours of Production or Nonsupervisory Workers on Private Nonfarm Payrolls by Industry, 1947–2001

(1982=100.)

| Year | Total private | Goods–producing | | | | | | Service–producing | | | | | |
| | | Total | Mining | Construc-tion | Manufacturing | | | Total | Transpor-tation and public utilities | Wholesale trade | Retail trade | Finance, insurance, and real estate | Services |
					Total	Durable goods	Nondura-ble goods						
1947	...	98.0	101.4	62.0	105.8	99.2	114.9	...	...	56.8	...	...	...
1948	...	97.8	101.9	67.6	104.2	97.4	113.8	...	...	59.5	...	...	...
1949	...	88.2	86.8	66.7	93.0	84.0	105.6	...	...	59.0	...	...	...
1950	...	96.1	88.3	71.3	102.2	96.0	110.8	...	...	59.7	...	...	...
1951	...	103.7	91.9	81.0	109.6	108.0	111.7	...	...	61.7	...	...	...
1952	...	103.9	88.2	83.3	109.6	108.9	110.6	...	...	63.3	...	...	...
1953	...	107.3	84.8	80.5	114.8	116.9	112.0	...	...	63.7	...	...	...
1954	...	96.8	75.5	78.2	102.4	100.5	105.3	...	...	63.1	...	...	...
1955	...	103.0	78.9	83.4	109.0	108.5	109.8	...	...	64.4	...	...	...
1956	...	104.7	81.5	90.2	109.5	109.5	109.5	...	...	65.9	...	...	...
1957	...	101.1	79.6	86.6	105.9	105.8	106.0	...	...	65.4	...	...	...
1958	...	90.9	67.9	80.8	94.8	90.4	100.9	...	...	63.6	...	...	...
1959	...	97.8	68.1	86.7	102.3	99.6	106.1	...	...	66.4	...	...	...
1960	...	95.8	65.7	83.2	100.7	98.1	104.4	...	...	67.3	...	...	...
1961	...	92.4	61.5	81.4	97.0	92.8	103.0	...	...	66.8	...	...	...
1962	...	96.3	59.8	83.9	101.6	98.8	105.6	...	...	68.1	...	...	...
1963	...	97.4	59.1	86.8	102.4	100.6	105.0	...	...	68.8	...	...	...
1964	75.8	99.7	59.4	89.1	104.9	104.1	106.1	65.1	87.7	70.6	73.2	60.4	51.9
1965	79.1	105.6	59.6	93.4	111.5	112.7	109.9	67.3	89.9	73.3	75.9	61.4	54.0
1966	82.5	112.0	59.3	96.3	119.2	122.7	114.4	69.3	91.7	75.7	77.6	62.8	56.4
1967	82.9	109.8	57.0	93.8	117.1	119.8	113.3	70.8	92.1	76.5	78.3	64.8	58.9
1968	84.9	111.7	56.0	95.6	119.2	121.7	115.7	72.8	93.4	77.7	80.1	67.8	61.3
1969	87.7	114.5	57.9	103.6	121.0	124.2	116.5	75.7	96.3	80.6	82.6	71.6	64.2
1970	86.3	107.8	57.6	101.3	112.8	113.0	112.4	76.7	96.9	81.7	83.4	73.0	65.3
1971	85.8	105.0	54.9	103.6	108.8	107.4	110.8	77.2	95.1	80.4	85.3	74.3	65.6
1972	89.2	110.5	57.8	107.9	114.8	115.4	114.1	79.6	97.3	82.5	88.2	76.5	68.0
1973	93.2	116.9	58.8	113.7	121.7	125.8	116.0	82.5	99.9	85.6	90.9	78.9	71.3
1974	93.2	113.7	63.4	109.5	118.1	122.4	112.1	84.0	100.4	87.6	91.0	79.8	73.9
1975	88.8	99.9	68.3	92.7	103.8	104.9	102.1	83.9	94.6	86.4	90.6	79.9	76.0
1976	92.3	105.4	71.5	94.0	110.3	111.9	108.1	86.4	95.5	89.1	93.9	81.5	78.8
1977	96.0	110.3	76.5	100.2	115.0	118.4	110.2	89.5	97.9	92.5	96.5	85.4	82.0
1978	100.7	116.5	79.0	112.2	120.1	125.9	112.0	93.6	101.3	97.7	100.0	90.3	86.3
1979	104.0	119.9	88.2	119.9	122.1	129.1	112.3	96.9	104.9	102.0	101.5	94.4	90.2
1980	102.8	112.9	94.1	115.1	113.8	117.8	108.1	98.3	104.1	101.9	100.1	97.8	94.3
1981	104.1	111.6	104.8	109.3	112.5	116.1	107.6	100.8	103.3	103.3	100.6	105.5	98.2
1982	100.0	100.0	100.0	100.0	100.0	100.0	100.0	100.0	100.0	100.0	100.0	100.0	100.0
1983	101.5	100.5	81.5	102.2	101.4	100.7	102.4	102.0	97.3	99.9	102.7	101.6	103.6
1984	107.7	109.0	84.9	116.8	109.0	111.5	105.5	107.1	102.8	105.3	108.2	106.4	108.2
1985	110.5	108.7	81.4	125.3	106.9	109.5	103.4	111.3	104.6	108.4	111.7	110.9	114.0
1986	112.3	107.3	65.7	128.2	105.7	106.8	104.2	114.6	104.0	108.5	114.3	116.7	119.2
1987	115.6	109.0	61.8	132.7	107.0	107.4	106.6	118.5	106.5	109.4	117.9	120.1	124.9
1988	119.3	111.4	61.7	136.9	109.3	110.5	107.7	122.8	108.2	113.3	121.0	119.2	132.2
1989	122.1	111.7	60.5	138.9	109.3	110.1	108.2	126.8	111.1	116.1	122.9	119.5	139.3
1990	123.0	109.5	63.9	138.0	106.4	106.1	106.8	129.1	114.5	115.7	123.0	120.2	144.2
1991	120.4	103.4	62.0	122.8	102.1	99.3	105.9	128.0	113.4	113.7	119.5	118.3	145.3
1992	121.2	102.1	56.2	118.4	101.7	98.2	106.6	129.7	113.6	112.8	120.6	118.1	149.3
1993	124.6	104.2	54.3	125.4	103.1	100.0	107.4	133.7	118.2	112.8	123.4	121.2	155.4
1994	130.0	109.2	54.6	136.4	107.0	106.2	108.1	139.4	121.8	116.9	128.6	124.0	163.1
1995	133.5	110.3	54.1	140.9	107.5	108.2	106.6	143.9	123.9	121.1	132.2	122.9	170.7
1996	136.7	111.5	55.6	148.7	107.2	109.2	104.3	148.0	127.5	122.9	134.6	125.0	177.4
1997	141.5	114.6	58.3	156.2	109.4	112.9	104.6	153.6	130.5	126.1	137.7	129.6	186.6
1998	145.1	115.6	56.0	164.7	109.0	112.4	104.2	158.3	132.3	127.9	140.0	136.3	194.2
1999	148.2	115.9	50.1	176.1	107.2	111.2	101.6	162.7	134.3	129.6	143.5	138.4	201.5
2000	151.5	116.4	51.4	183.8	106.0	111.6	98.3	167.3	138.1	130.6	146.4	138.6	209.9
2001	150.3	110.5	54.8	184.6	97.9	101.9	92.5	168.1	139.2	126.4	146.8	139.8	212.3

Note: Data include Alaska and Hawaii beginning in 1959.

Table 2-10. Indexes of Aggregate Weekly Hours of Production Workers on Manufacturing Payrolls by Industry, 1947–2001

(1982=100.)

Year	Durable goods												
	Total	Lumber and wood products	Furniture and fixtures	Stone, clay, and glass products	Primary metal industries		Fabricated metal products	Industrial machinery and equipment	Electronic and other electrical equipment	Transportation equipment		Instruments and related products	Miscellaneous manufacturing industries
					Total	Blast furnaces and basic steel products				Total	Motor vehicles and equipment		
1947	99.2	173.6	92.0	110.4	161.7	201.2	89.1	83.9	...	94.3	120.4	...	140.1
1948	97.4	167.0	93.3	111.7	163.5	210.8	87.0	82.4	...	92.6	119.5	...	139.1
1949	84.0	146.9	82.0	100.4	135.0	180.8	74.9	66.3	...	88.3	117.7	...	121.9
1950	96.0	162.4	99.2	111.1	159.7	210.1	88.8	72.5	...	97.4	137.5	...	131.8
1951	108.0	167.4	94.5	120.2	177.4	227.4	98.4	91.4	...	115.6	132.9	...	132.1
1952	108.9	158.2	94.7	112.7	160.7	194.4	97.7	93.1	...	130.8	123.8	...	127.3
1953	116.9	152.8	96.7	115.3	174.6	225.7	107.8	93.6	...	151.5	149.9	...	136.0
1954	100.5	139.1	86.3	107.6	143.5	185.5	94.1	79.5	...	127.4	120.5	...	121.6
1955	108.5	147.5	95.1	117.5	167.3	219.8	100.9	83.7	...	138.7	151.2	...	125.2
1956	109.5	143.1	96.1	119.2	168.7	216.3	100.2	91.4	...	130.8	123.1	...	125.4
1957	105.8	126.3	93.5	113.9	161.0	210.7	100.6	87.5	...	131.7	118.7	...	117.6
1958	90.4	118.9	87.9	104.8	129.1	163.7	88.5	70.2	...	104.4	86.8	...	110.5
1959	99.6	132.0	97.7	117.0	140.2	169.3	95.6	79.4	...	111.4	106.5	...	117.6
1960	98.1	123.1	95.4	114.1	141.4	181.1	95.0	79.2	...	106.8	111.4	...	116.4
1961	92.8	115.2	90.9	109.3	132.0	166.9	90.2	74.5	...	96.4	92.8	...	113.0
1962	98.8	118.5	97.5	112.0	137.4	167.5	96.5	80.7	...	106.6	110.0	...	117.1
1963	100.6	120.2	99.2	114.6	141.7	172.7	99.2	82.5	...	111.2	118.5	...	115.7
1964	104.1	122.8	103.8	117.9	153.0	190.6	102.8	88.5	...	111.5	120.3	...	118.3
1965	112.7	125.3	111.1	121.2	163.2	199.1	110.8	97.6	...	125.0	140.5	...	126.0
1966	122.7	126.9	118.8	124.4	168.4	195.2	122.1	109.6	...	136.7	138.4	...	130.3
1967	119.8	121.5	113.5	119.1	158.1	184.0	124.2	108.5	...	133.2	123.4	...	125.6
1968	121.7	124.8	118.6	121.9	158.1	186.1	128.8	105.2	...	141.7	141.6	...	126.1
1969	124.2	126.5	121.5	126.4	165.1	190.5	132.6	109.4	...	138.5	142.4	...	126.5
1970	113.0	117.9	111.6	120.9	152.9	179.5	120.3	101.2	...	114.1	117.7	...	119.8
1971	107.4	123.8	114.0	122.2	140.5	161.5	113.2	89.5	...	112.6	130.3	...	116.2
1972	115.4	136.1	126.6	131.1	146.3	165.1	121.9	97.8	...	118.4	140.5	...	126.2
1973	125.8	140.6	132.0	138.4	161.8	181.5	131.8	111.8	...	129.1	158.5	...	130.9
1974	122.4	128.2	123.4	134.5	162.4	180.7	127.4	116.1	...	117.9	134.9	...	128.8
1975	104.9	107.8	100.7	115.6	134.3	151.8	108.4	101.6	...	106.8	117.3	...	112.5
1976	111.9	123.5	111.0	120.8	140.0	155.6	115.3	102.6	...	117.9	141.2	...	120.1
1977	118.4	132.0	117.2	125.9	144.2	157.2	121.9	109.8	...	125.6	156.0	...	122.2
1978	125.9	138.3	125.6	132.1	151.3	164.6	129.3	119.4	...	133.6	163.3	...	125.9
1979	129.1	138.6	123.5	132.8	154.8	167.0	131.4	126.9	...	134.1	151.8	...	123.8
1980	117.8	119.9	112.4	119.8	133.4	139.8	119.8	122.1	...	114.6	111.0	...	113.9
1981	116.1	115.1	112.7	114.1	132.5	141.9	117.1	120.2	...	114.2	115.7	...	110.5
1982	100.0	100.0	100.0	100.0	100.0	100.0	100.0	100.0	...	100.0	100.0	...	100.0
1983	100.7	117.7	110.3	103.2	95.2	90.8	100.3	90.1	...	105.7	118.9	...	98.1
1984	111.5	126.3	121.6	109.5	102.9	93.7	111.0	103.8	...	118.9	140.2	...	102.9
1985	109.5	124.9	121.9	108.1	96.1	85.3	111.2	101.0	...	122.7	143.6	...	97.8
1986	106.8	129.2	124.2	108.7	89.8	78.2	107.8	94.7	...	123.3	137.7	...	97.5
1987	107.4	134.9	129.5	109.7	91.8	79.0	107.1	93.8	...	124.3	137.2	...	99.9
1988	110.5	135.6	130.1	113.3	97.2	85.1	110.5	98.8	113.1	125.8	140.0	89.9	103.5
1989	110.1	132.6	129.6	113.5	96.0	83.9	110.6	100.3	111.5	125.3	138.0	89.6	103.0
1990	106.1	128.2	122.8	109.7	93.0	82.6	107.1	97.5	106.5	119.1	126.2	87.6	101.1
1991	99.3	116.9	113.9	101.4	87.2	76.4	101.4	91.8	100.7	113.3	122.9	84.0	98.1
1992	98.2	119.9	117.6	101.2	85.6	73.7	100.7	89.6	99.1	110.9	127.3	80.2	99.4
1993	100.0	126.1	121.3	102.9	86.2	72.6	103.3	92.7	100.9	111.4	137.4	77.0	101.6
1994	106.2	135.8	127.0	107.9	91.0	73.4	110.4	99.3	105.6	118.5	156.2	75.2	104.2
1995	108.2	135.7	125.6	108.7	92.1	73.6	113.6	103.5	107.8	121.6	164.9	73.7	103.4
1996	109.2	138.0	123.4	110.8	92.6	73.6	114.5	105.0	108.5	123.1	165.5	75.4	102.1
1997	112.9	142.1	128.6	112.4	94.5	72.9	118.1	109.6	111.1	129.2	169.2	76.7	104.4
1998	112.4	145.4	135.3	115.4	93.7	72.1	119.5	110.9	109.9	127.0	160.5	76.7	103.5
1999	111.2	148.7	138.6	116.4	92.2	71.6	120.4	104.5	106.7	126.9	168.2	75.8	101.8
2000	111.6	146.7	139.7	118.8	93.2	72.2	122.5	102.9	109.2	122.7	164.7	74.9	99.1
2001	101.9	136.1	125.7	117.5	84.0	64.8	113.3	92.0	96.0	110.9	145.5	72.3	91.3

See *Note* at end of table.

Table 2-10. Indexes of Aggregate Weekly Hours of Production Workers on Manufacturing Payrolls by Industry, 1947–2001—*Continued*

(1982=100.)

Year	Nondurable goods										
	Total	Food and kindred products	Tobacco products	Textile mill products	Apparel and other textile products	Paper and allied products	Printing and publishing	Chemicals and allied products	Petroleum and coal products	Rubber and miscellaneous plastics products	Leather and leather products
1947	114.9	136.0	212.3	200.9	110.6	84.8	75.6	82.2	131.0	52.6	221.8
1948	113.8	131.3	202.2	203.3	112.7	84.6	75.0	81.6	135.3	50.0	211.2
1949	105.6	126.6	186.4	172.6	109.4	78.6	73.1	74.7	129.7	43.8	195.8
1950	110.8	125.7	178.9	192.5	114.0	87.1	74.2	77.6	127.7	51.7	205.0
1951	111.7	127.1	182.8	184.8	113.0	90.9	75.8	84.7	133.9	55.2	193.1
1952	110.6	125.7	184.8	174.5	115.8	87.5	76.6	84.6	130.0	55.0	203.0
1953	112.0	124.5	180.5	172.9	118.2	92.3	78.5	87.6	134.0	57.8	202.2
1954	105.3	120.7	177.2	151.7	109.1	90.4	78.0	83.9	129.1	51.1	188.4
1955	109.8	120.8	180.7	160.3	115.9	94.6	81.0	87.0	127.0	59.8	200.0
1956	109.5	121.2	173.0	155.6	114.9	96.3	84.0	88.2	125.6	58.5	196.9
1957	106.0	116.3	162.2	144.3	112.4	94.9	83.9	86.7	121.6	58.4	190.4
1958	100.9	112.3	162.7	133.7	107.2	92.1	82.6	82.1	114.3	51.6	179.3
1959	106.1	112.8	162.2	144.1	116.3	97.7	85.4	85.6	109.5	59.4	193.6
1960	104.4	111.5	157.6	137.1	114.3	97.9	87.4	86.0	107.7	58.0	181.9
1961	103.0	109.8	153.7	133.4	112.1	98.4	87.3	85.3	101.9	57.5	181.6
1962	105.6	108.8	150.4	137.0	119.4	100.2	87.9	88.1	99.2	63.7	184.4
1963	105.0	107.8	146.5	133.8	120.7	100.7	87.2	89.2	94.9	64.8	177.2
1964	106.1	107.0	150.8	136.1	122.1	101.3	89.4	89.9	90.9	68.2	177.7
1965	109.9	107.4	140.3	143.4	128.7	104.0	92.4	93.5	90.6	75.0	182.0
1966	114.4	109.5	138.2	149.5	133.2	109.0	96.8	98.6	92.4	81.3	188.8
1967	113.3	109.4	141.0	144.4	130.8	109.1	97.9	100.6	93.0	79.7	178.0
1968	115.7	109.5	134.8	150.6	131.3	111.4	98.5	104.1	95.4	87.0	180.0
1969	116.5	110.5	128.8	150.0	130.5	114.6	100.9	106.2	90.9	91.6	168.1
1970	112.4	110.2	129.2	141.8	123.9	110.2	98.9	102.5	96.2	86.3	156.4
1971	110.8	109.3	118.7	141.3	122.9	106.4	95.3	99.8	100.9	87.5	148.7
1972	114.1	108.7	115.9	148.9	127.8	110.3	96.5	100.9	101.5	97.8	150.7
1973	116.0	106.3	124.0	150.7	131.7	112.7	97.4	104.2	99.9	107.9	142.3
1974	112.1	106.0	120.9	138.5	121.3	111.2	95.5	105.7	100.9	105.8	131.8
1975	102.1	101.8	118.1	122.9	110.2	96.8	88.9	97.1	96.3	89.0	121.3
1976	108.1	104.4	118.2	133.3	119.3	104.7	90.3	102.0	102.3	96.1	130.6
1977	110.2	104.6	106.8	132.9	117.9	107.6	94.1	105.0	106.6	109.2	123.9
1978	112.0	105.1	106.1	131.6	119.5	109.0	97.5	107.4	112.2	115.3	125.5
1979	112.3	107.0	104.4	129.3	115.6	110.5	101.0	108.3	114.0	118.2	117.1
1980	108.1	105.1	101.2	122.7	112.2	106.9	100.1	106.0	99.1	106.7	110.7
1981	107.6	102.8	105.1	117.3	111.0	106.8	100.6	106.8	110.0	109.0	113.6
1982	100.0	100.0	100.0	100.0	100.0	100.0	100.0	100.0	100.0	100.0	100.0
1983	102.4	99.1	96.3	107.4	104.5	102.1	103.3	98.3	98.4	107.2	96.8
1984	105.5	100.3	93.5	107.0	107.2	106.8	110.9	99.8	92.5	119.6	89.3
1985	103.4	100.6	88.4	100.1	100.7	106.8	114.9	98.9	88.7	117.6	78.1
1986	104.2	101.7	81.6	103.8	99.7	106.9	119.6	97.3	88.1	119.6	69.5
1987	106.6	103.7	80.1	109.4	100.1	108.5	123.2	99.3	89.4	123.1	70.3
1988	107.7	105.0	80.1	107.7	99.0	108.9	126.7	102.9	88.1	127.3	67.9
1989	108.2	107.8	70.6	105.6	98.3	109.9	126.2	104.5	85.7	129.6	66.4
1990	106.8	109.7	70.6	98.4	92.9	110.4	127.5	104.3	87.2	127.9	62.8
1991	105.9	110.2	70.2	97.0	91.3	109.3	123.3	101.6	86.7	123.2	57.7
1992	106.6	110.9	68.2	98.6	92.2	110.5	122.3	100.0	86.0	127.8	56.6
1993	107.4	112.6	60.7	98.9	90.4	110.9	123.9	100.9	83.1	133.2	55.6
1994	108.1	114.6	64.1	99.3	89.7	112.3	126.0	102.0	81.5	142.0	53.0
1995	106.6	115.5	62.8	94.9	84.2	110.5	125.0	102.5	77.9	143.5	48.3
1996	104.3	115.9	63.3	89.2	77.2	109.5	124.0	101.5	76.3	143.2	43.3
1997	104.6	116.6	61.4	89.8	73.7	111.0	126.0	101.2	76.1	146.4	40.6
1998	104.2	117.5	59.7	86.3	67.4	109.3	124.8	103.4	76.0	147.3	36.5
1999	101.6	118.2	53.2	80.1	60.3	106.9	121.7	102.3	71.6	148.5	32.7
2000	98.3	117.8	51.1	75.9	55.1	103.2	120.9	99.9	70.1	148.4	30.3
2001	92.5	115.6	48.7	66.3	47.7	97.7	115.2	96.7	71.0	136.7	25.1

Note: Data include Alaska and Hawaii beginning in 1959.

Table 2-11. Average Hourly Earnings of Production or Nonsupervisory Workers on Private Nonfarm Payrolls by Industry, 1947–2001

(Dollars.)

Year	Total private	Mining	Construction	Manufacturing Total	Durable goods	Nondurable goods	Transportation and public utilities	Wholesale trade	Retail trade	Finance, insurance, and real estate	Services
1947	1.13	1.47	1.54	1.22	1.28	1.15	...	1.22	0.84	1.14	...
1948	1.23	1.66	1.71	1.33	1.39	1.25	...	1.31	0.90	1.20	...
1949	1.28	1.72	1.79	1.38	1.45	1.30	...	1.36	0.95	1.26	...
1950	1.34	1.77	1.86	1.44	1.45	1.30	...	1.36	0.98	1.26	...
1951	1.45	1.93	2.02	1.56	1.65	1.45	...	1.52	1.06	1.45	...
1952	1.52	2.01	2.13	1.64	1.74	1.51	...	1.61	1.09	1.51	...
1953	1.61	2.14	2.28	1.74	1.85	1.58	...	1.69	1.16	1.58	...
1954	1.65	2.14	2.38	1.78	1.89	1.62	...	1.76	1.20	1.65	...
1955	1.71	2.20	2.45	1.85	1.98	1.68	...	1.83	1.25	1.70	...
1956	1.80	2.33	2.57	1.95	2.08	1.77	...	1.93	1.30	1.78	...
1957	1.89	2.45	2.71	2.04	2.18	1.85	...	2.02	1.37	1.84	...
1958	1.95	2.47	2.82	2.10	2.25	1.92	...	2.09	1.42	1.89	...
1959	2.02	2.56	2.93	2.19	2.35	1.98	...	2.18	1.47	1.95	...
1960	2.09	2.60	3.07	2.26	2.42	2.05	...	2.24	1.52	2.02	...
1961	2.14	2.64	3.20	2.32	2.48	2.11	...	2.31	1.56	2.09	...
1962	2.22	2.70	3.31	2.39	2.55	2.17	...	2.37	1.63	2.17	...
1963	2.28	2.75	3.41	2.45	2.63	2.22	...	2.45	1.68	2.25	...
1964	2.36	2.81	3.55	2.53	2.70	2.29	2.89	2.52	1.75	2.30	1.94
1965	2.46	2.92	3.70	2.61	2.78	2.36	3.03	2.60	1.82	2.39	2.05
1966	2.56	3.05	3.89	2.71	2.89	2.45	3.11	2.73	1.91	2.47	2.17
1967	2.68	3.19	4.11	2.82	2.99	2.57	3.23	2.87	2.01	2.58	2.29
1968	2.85	3.35	4.41	3.01	3.18	2.74	3.42	3.04	2.16	2.75	2.42
1969	3.04	3.60	4.79	3.19	3.38	2.91	3.63	3.23	2.30	2.93	2.61
1970	3.23	3.85	5.24	3.35	3.55	3.08	3.85	3.43	2.44	3.07	2.81
1971	3.45	4.06	5.69	3.57	3.79	3.27	4.21	3.64	2.60	3.22	3.04
1972	3.70	4.44	6.06	3.82	4.07	3.48	4.65	3.85	2.75	3.36	3.27
1973	3.94	4.75	6.41	4.09	4.35	3.70	5.02	4.07	2.91	3.53	3.47
1974	4.24	5.23	6.81	4.42	4.70	4.01	5.41	4.38	3.14	3.77	3.75
1975	4.53	5.95	7.31	4.83	5.15	4.37	5.88	4.72	3.36	4.06	4.02
1976	4.86	6.46	7.71	5.22	5.57	4.71	6.45	5.02	3.57	4.27	4.31
1977	5.25	6.94	8.10	5.68	6.06	5.11	6.99	5.39	3.85	4.54	4.65
1978	5.69	7.67	8.66	6.17	6.58	5.54	7.57	5.88	4.20	4.89	4.99
1979	6.16	8.49	9.27	6.70	7.12	6.01	8.16	6.39	4.53	5.27	5.36
1980	6.66	9.17	9.94	7.27	7.75	6.56	8.87	6.95	4.88	5.79	5.85
1981	7.25	10.04	10.82	7.99	8.53	7.19	9.70	7.55	5.25	6.31	6.41
1982	7.68	10.77	11.63	8.49	9.03	7.75	10.32	8.08	5.48	6.78	6.92
1983	8.02	11.28	11.94	8.83	9.38	8.09	10.79	8.54	5.74	7.29	7.31
1984	8.32	11.63	12.13	9.19	9.73	8.39	11.12	8.88	5.85	7.63	7.59
1985	8.57	11.98	12.32	9.54	10.09	8.72	11.40	9.15	5.94	7.94	7.90
1986	8.76	12.46	12.48	9.73	10.28	8.95	11.70	9.34	6.03	8.36	8.18
1987	8.98	12.54	12.71	9.91	10.43	9.19	12.03	9.59	6.12	8.73	8.49
1988	9.28	12.80	13.08	10.19	10.71	9.45	12.24	9.98	6.31	9.06	8.88
1989	9.66	13.26	13.54	10.48	11.01	9.75	12.57	10.39	6.53	9.53	9.38
1990	10.01	13.68	13.77	10.83	11.35	10.12	12.92	10.79	6.75	9.97	9.83
1991	10.32	14.19	14.00	11.18	11.75	10.44	13.20	11.15	6.94	10.39	10.23
1992	10.57	14.54	14.15	11.46	12.02	10.73	13.43	11.39	7.12	10.82	10.54
1993	10.83	14.60	14.38	11.74	12.33	10.98	13.55	11.74	7.29	11.35	10.78
1994	11.12	14.88	14.73	12.07	12.68	11.24	13.78	12.06	7.49	11.83	11.04
1995	11.43	15.30	15.09	12.37	12.94	11.58	14.13	12.43	7.69	12.32	11.39
1996	11.82	15.62	15.47	12.77	13.33	11.97	14.45	12.87	7.99	12.80	11.79
1997	12.28	16.15	16.04	13.17	13.73	12.34	14.92	13.45	8.33	13.34	12.28
1998	12.78	16.91	16.61	13.49	13.98	12.76	15.31	14.07	8.74	14.07	12.84
1999	13.24	17.05	17.19	13.90	14.36	13.21	15.69	14.59	9.09	14.62	13.37
2000	13.76	17.22	17.88	14.37	14.82	13.68	16.21	15.22	9.46	15.14	13.93
2001	14.32	17.56	18.34	14.83	15.28	14.16	16.79	15.86	9.77	15.80	14.67

Note: Data include Alaska and Hawaii beginning in 1959.

Table 2-12. Average Hourly Earnings of Production Workers on Manufacturing Payrolls by Industry, 1947–2001

(Dollars.)

Year	Durable goods												
	Total	Lumber and wood products	Furniture and fixtures	Stone, clay, and glass products	Primary metal industries		Fabricated metal products	Industrial machinery and equipment	Electronic and other electrical equipment	Transportation equipment		Instruments and related products	Miscellaneous manufacturing
					Total	Blast furnaces and basic steel products				Total	Motor vehicles and equipment		
1947	1.28	1.09	1.10	1.19	1.39	1.44	1.27	1.34	...	1.44	1.47	...	1.11
1948	1.39	1.19	1.19	1.31	1.52	1.59	1.39	1.46	...	1.57	1.61	...	1.18
1949	1.45	1.23	1.23	1.37	1.59	1.65	1.45	1.52	...	1.64	1.70	...	1.22
1950	1.45	1.30	1.28	1.44	1.65	1.70	1.52	1.60	...	1.72	1.78	...	1.28
1951	1.65	1.41	1.39	1.54	1.81	1.90	1.64	1.75	...	1.84	1.91	...	1.36
1952	1.74	1.49	1.47	1.61	1.90	2.00	1.72	1.85	...	1.95	2.05	...	1.45
1953	1.85	1.56	1.54	1.72	2.06	2.18	1.83	1.95	...	2.05	2.14	...	1.52
1954	1.89	1.57	1.57	1.77	2.10	2.22	1.88	2.00	...	2.11	2.20	...	1.56
1955	1.98	1.62	1.62	1.86	2.24	2.39	1.96	2.08	...	2.21	2.29	...	1.61
1956	2.08	1.69	1.69	1.96	2.37	2.54	2.05	2.20	...	2.29	2.35	...	1.69
1957	2.18	1.74	1.75	2.05	2.50	2.70	2.16	2.29	...	2.39	2.46	...	1.75
1958	2.25	1.80	1.78	2.12	2.64	2.88	2.26	2.37	...	2.51	2.55	...	1.79
1959	2.35	1.87	1.83	2.22	2.77	3.06	2.35	2.48	...	2.64	2.71	...	1.84
1960	2.42	1.90	1.88	2.28	2.81	3.04	2.43	2.55	...	2.74	2.81	...	1.89
1961	2.48	1.95	1.91	2.34	2.90	3.16	2.49	2.62	...	2.80	2.86	...	1.92
1962	2.55	1.99	1.95	2.41	2.98	3.25	2.55	2.71	...	2.91	2.99	...	1.98
1963	2.63	2.05	2.00	2.48	3.04	3.31	2.61	2.78	...	3.01	3.10	...	2.03
1964	2.70	2.12	2.05	2.53	3.11	3.36	2.68	2.87	...	3.09	3.21	...	2.08
1965	2.78	2.18	2.12	2.62	3.18	3.42	2.76	2.95	...	3.21	3.34	...	2.14
1966	2.89	2.26	2.21	2.72	3.28	3.53	2.88	3.08	...	3.33	3.44	...	2.22
1967	2.99	2.38	2.33	2.82	3.34	3.57	2.98	3.19	...	3.44	3.55	...	2.35
1968	3.18	2.58	2.47	2.99	3.55	3.76	3.16	3.36	...	3.69	3.89	...	2.50
1969	3.38	2.75	2.62	3.19	3.79	4.02	3.34	3.58	...	3.89	4.10	...	2.66
1970	3.55	2.97	2.77	3.40	3.93	4.16	3.53	3.77	...	4.06	4.22	...	2.83
1971	3.79	3.18	2.90	3.67	4.23	4.49	3.77	4.02	...	4.45	4.72	...	2.97
1972	4.07	3.34	3.08	3.94	4.66	5.08	4.05	4.32	...	4.81	5.13	...	3.11
1973	4.35	3.62	3.29	4.22	5.04	5.51	4.29	4.60	...	5.15	5.46	...	3.29
1974	4.70	3.90	3.53	4.54	5.60	6.27	4.61	4.94	...	5.54	5.87	...	3.53
1975	5.15	4.28	3.78	4.92	6.18	6.94	5.05	5.37	...	6.07	6.44	...	3.81
1976	5.57	4.74	3.99	5.33	6.77	7.59	5.50	5.79	...	6.62	7.09	...	4.04
1977	6.06	5.11	4.34	5.81	7.40	8.36	5.91	6.26	...	7.29	7.85	...	4.36
1978	6.58	5.62	4.68	6.32	8.20	9.39	6.35	6.78	...	7.91	8.50	...	4.69
1979	7.12	6.08	5.06	6.85	8.98	10.41	6.85	7.32	...	8.53	9.06	...	5.03
1980	7.75	6.57	5.49	7.50	9.77	11.39	7.45	8.00	...	9.35	9.85	...	5.46
1981	8.53	7.02	5.91	8.27	10.81	12.60	8.20	8.81	...	10.39	11.02	...	5.97
1982	9.03	7.46	6.31	8.87	11.33	13.35	8.77	9.26	...	11.11	11.62	...	6.42
1983	9.38	7.82	6.62	9.27	11.35	12.89	9.12	9.56	...	11.67	12.14	...	6.81
1984	9.73	8.05	6.84	9.57	11.47	12.98	9.40	9.97	...	12.20	12.73	...	7.05
1985	10.09	8.25	7.17	9.84	11.67	13.33	9.71	10.30	...	12.71	13.39	...	7.30
1986	10.28	8.37	7.46	10.04	11.86	13.73	9.89	10.58	...	12.81	13.45	...	7.55
1987	10.43	8.43	7.67	10.25	11.94	13.77	10.01	10.73	...	12.94	13.53	...	7.76
1988	10.71	8.59	7.95	10.56	12.16	13.98	10.29	11.08	9.79	13.29	13.99	10.60	8.00
1989	11.01	8.84	8.25	10.82	12.43	14.25	10.57	11.40	10.05	13.67	14.25	10.83	8.29
1990	11.35	9.08	8.52	11.12	12.92	14.82	10.83	11.77	10.30	14.08	14.56	11.29	8.61
1991	11.75	9.24	8.76	11.36	13.33	15.36	11.19	12.15	10.70	14.75	15.23	11.64	8.85
1992	12.02	9.44	9.01	11.60	13.66	15.87	11.42	12.41	11.00	15.20	15.45	11.89	9.15
1993	12.33	9.61	9.27	11.85	13.99	16.36	11.69	12.73	11.24	15.80	16.10	12.23	9.39
1994	12.68	9.84	9.55	12.13	14.34	16.85	11.93	13.00	11.50	16.51	17.02	12.47	9.67
1995	12.94	10.12	9.82	12.41	14.62	17.33	12.13	13.24	11.69	16.74	17.34	12.71	10.05
1996	13.33	10.44	10.15	12.82	14.97	17.80	12.50	13.59	12.18	17.19	17.74	13.13	10.38
1997	13.73	10.76	10.55	13.18	15.22	18.03	12.78	14.07	12.70	17.55	18.04	13.52	10.60
1998	13.98	11.10	10.90	13.59	15.48	18.42	13.07	14.47	13.10	17.51	17.84	13.81	10.88
1999	14.36	11.51	11.29	13.97	15.80	18.84	13.50	15.03	13.43	17.79	18.10	14.08	11.26
2000	14.82	11.94	11.74	14.53	16.41	19.82	13.87	15.55	13.79	18.46	18.80	14.41	11.63
2001	15.28	12.26	12.24	15.00	16.92	20.41	14.25	15.89	14.51	19.06	19.40	14.81	12.16

See *Note* at end of table.

Table 2-12. Average Hourly Earnings of Production Workers on Manufacturing Payrolls by Industry, 1947–2001—*Continued*

(Dollars.)

Year	Nondurable goods										
	Total	Food and kindred products	Tobacco products	Textile mill products	Apparel and other textile products	Paper and allied products	Printing and publishing	Chemicals and allied products	Petroleum and coal products	Rubber and miscellane-ous plastics products	Leather and leather products
1947	1.15	1.06	0.90	1.04	1.16	1.15	1.48	1.22	1.50	1.29	1.04
1948	1.25	1.15	0.96	1.16	1.22	1.28	1.65	1.34	1.71	1.36	1.11
1949	1.30	1.21	1.00	1.18	1.21	1.33	1.77	1.42	1.80	1.41	1.12
1950	1.30	1.26	1.08	1.23	1.24	1.40	1.83	1.50	1.84	1.47	1.17
1951	1.45	1.35	1.14	1.32	1.31	1.51	1.91	1.62	1.99	1.58	1.25
1952	1.51	1.44	1.18	1.34	1.32	1.59	2.02	1.69	2.10	1.70	1.30
1953	1.58	1.53	1.25	1.36	1.35	1.67	2.11	1.81	2.22	1.79	1.35
1954	1.62	1.59	1.30	1.36	1.37	1.73	2.18	1.89	2.29	1.83	1.36
1955	1.68	1.66	1.34	1.38	1.37	1.81	2.26	1.97	2.37	1.95	1.39
1956	1.77	1.76	1.45	1.44	1.47	1.92	2.33	2.09	2.54	2.02	1.48
1957	1.85	1.85	1.53	1.49	1.51	2.02	2.40	2.20	2.66	2.11	1.52
1958	1.92	1.94	1.59	1.49	1.54	2.10	2.49	2.29	2.73	2.18	1.56
1959	1.98	2.02	1.65	1.56	1.56	2.18	2.59	2.40	2.85	2.27	1.59
1960	2.05	2.11	1.70	1.61	1.59	2.26	2.68	2.50	2.89	2.32	1.64
1961	2.11	2.17	1.78	1.63	1.64	2.34	2.75	2.58	3.01	2.38	1.68
1962	2.17	2.24	1.85	1.68	1.69	2.40	2.82	2.65	3.05	2.44	1.72
1963	2.22	2.30	1.91	1.71	1.73	2.48	2.89	2.72	3.16	2.47	1.76
1964	2.29	2.37	1.95	1.79	1.79	2.56	2.97	2.80	3.20	2.54	1.83
1965	2.36	2.44	2.09	1.87	1.83	2.65	3.06	2.89	3.28	2.61	1.88
1966	2.45	2.52	2.19	1.96	1.89	2.75	3.16	2.98	3.41	2.68	1.94
1967	2.57	2.64	2.27	2.06	2.03	2.87	3.28	3.10	3.58	2.75	2.07
1968	2.74	2.80	2.48	2.21	2.21	3.05	3.48	3.26	3.75	2.93	2.23
1969	2.91	2.96	2.62	2.35	2.31	3.24	3.69	3.47	4.00	3.08	2.36
1970	3.08	3.16	2.91	2.45	2.39	3.44	3.92	3.69	4.28	3.21	2.49
1971	3.27	3.38	3.16	2.57	2.49	3.67	4.20	3.97	4.57	3.41	2.59
1972	3.48	3.60	3.47	2.75	2.60	3.95	4.51	4.26	4.96	3.63	2.68
1973	3.70	3.85	3.76	2.95	2.76	4.20	4.75	4.51	5.28	3.84	2.79
1974	4.01	4.19	4.12	3.20	2.97	4.53	5.03	4.88	5.68	4.09	2.99
1975	4.37	4.61	4.55	3.42	3.17	5.01	5.38	5.39	6.48	4.42	3.21
1976	4.71	4.98	4.98	3.69	3.40	5.47	5.71	5.91	7.21	4.71	3.40
1977	5.11	5.37	5.54	3.99	3.62	5.96	6.12	6.43	7.83	5.21	3.61
1978	5.54	5.80	6.13	4.30	3.94	6.52	6.51	7.02	8.63	5.57	3.89
1979	6.01	6.27	6.67	4.66	4.23	7.13	6.94	7.60	9.36	6.02	4.22
1980	6.56	6.85	7.74	5.07	4.56	7.84	7.53	8.30	10.10	6.58	4.58
1981	7.19	7.44	8.88	5.52	4.97	8.60	8.19	9.12	11.38	7.22	4.99
1982	7.75	7.92	9.79	5.83	5.20	9.32	8.74	9.96	12.46	7.70	5.33
1983	8.09	8.19	10.38	6.18	5.38	9.93	9.11	10.58	13.28	8.06	5.54
1984	8.39	8.39	11.22	6.46	5.55	10.41	9.41	11.07	13.44	8.35	5.71
1985	8.72	8.57	11.96	6.70	5.73	10.83	9.71	11.56	14.06	8.60	5.83
1986	8.95	8.75	12.88	6.93	5.84	11.18	9.99	11.98	14.19	8.79	5.92
1987	9.19	8.93	14.07	7.17	5.94	11.43	10.28	12.37	14.58	8.98	6.08
1988	9.45	9.12	14.67	7.38	6.12	11.69	10.53	12.71	14.97	9.19	6.28
1989	9.75	9.38	15.31	7.67	6.35	11.96	10.88	13.09	15.41	9.46	6.59
1990	10.12	9.62	16.23	8.02	6.57	12.31	11.24	13.54	16.24	9.76	6.91
1991	10.44	9.90	16.77	8.30	6.77	12.72	11.48	14.04	17.04	10.07	7.18
1992	10.73	10.20	16.92	8.60	6.95	13.07	11.74	14.51	17.90	10.36	7.42
1993	10.98	10.45	16.89	8.88	7.09	13.42	11.93	14.82	18.53	10.57	7.63
1994	11.24	10.66	19.07	9.13	7.34	13.77	12.14	15.13	19.07	10.70	7.97
1995	11.58	10.93	19.41	9.41	7.64	14.23	12.33	15.62	19.36	10.91	8.17
1996	11.97	11.20	19.35	9.69	7.96	14.67	12.65	16.17	19.32	11.24	8.57
1997	12.34	11.48	19.24	10.03	8.25	15.05	13.06	16.57	20.20	11.57	8.97
1998	12.76	11.80	18.56	10.39	8.52	15.50	13.46	17.09	20.91	11.89	9.35
1999	13.21	12.11	19.87	10.81	8.92	15.88	13.96	17.42	21.43	12.40	9.71
2000	13.68	12.51	21.34	11.16	9.29	16.25	14.40	18.15	21.99	12.85	10.17
2001	14.16	12.89	21.50	11.35	9.43	16.87	14.82	18.61	22.08	13.39	10.31

Note: Data include Alaska and Hawaii beginning in 1959.

Table 2-13. Average Weekly Earnings of Production or Nonsupervisory Workers on Nonfarm Payrolls by Industry in Current and Constant Dollars, 1947–2001

Year	Total private		Mining		Construction		Manufacturing		Transportation and public utilities	
	Current dollars	1982 dollars	Current dollars	1982 dollars	Current dollars	1982 dollars	Current dollars	1982 dollars	Current dollars	1982 dollars
1947	45.58	196.47	59.89	258.15	58.83	253.58	49.13	211.77	...	...
1948	49.00	196.00	65.52	262.08	65.23	260.92	53.08	212.32	...	...
1949	50.24	202.58	62.33	251.33	67.56	272.42	53.80	216.94	...	...
1950	53.13	212.52	67.16	268.64	69.68	278.72	58.28	233.12	...	...
1951	57.86	215.09	74.11	275.50	76.96	286.10	63.34	235.46	...	...
1952	60.65	219.75	77.59	281.12	82.86	300.22	66.75	241.85	...	...
1953	63.76	229.35	83.03	298.67	86.41	310.83	70.47	253.49	...	...
1954	64.52	231.25	82.60	296.06	88.54	317.35	70.49	252.65	...	...
1955	67.72	243.60	89.54	322.09	90.90	326.98	75.30	270.86	...	...
1956	70.74	250.85	95.06	337.09	96.38	341.77	78.78	279.36	...	...
1957	73.33	251.13	98.25	336.47	100.27	343.39	81.19	278.05	...	...
1958	75.08	250.27	96.08	320.27	103.78	345.93	82.32	274.40	...	...
1959	78.78	260.86	103.68	343.31	108.41	358.97	88.26	292.25	...	...
1960	80.67	261.92	105.04	341.04	112.67	365.81	89.72	291.30	...	...
1961	82.60	265.59	106.92	343.79	118.08	379.68	92.34	296.91	...	...
1962	85.91	273.60	110.70	352.55	122.47	390.03	96.56	307.52	...	...
1963	88.46	278.18	114.40	359.75	127.19	399.97	99.23	312.04	...	...
1964	91.33	283.63	117.74	365.65	132.06	410.12	102.97	319.78	118.78	368.88
1965	95.45	291.90	123.52	377.74	138.38	423.18	107.53	328.84	125.14	382.69
1966	98.82	294.11	130.24	387.62	146.26	435.30	112.19	333.90	128.13	381.34
1967	101.84	293.49	135.89	391.61	154.95	446.54	114.49	329.94	130.82	377.00
1968	107.73	298.42	142.71	395.32	164.49	455.65	122.51	339.36	138.85	384.63
1969	114.61	300.81	154.80	406.30	181.54	476.48	129.51	339.92	147.74	387.77
1970	119.83	298.08	164.40	408.96	195.45	486.19	133.33	331.67	155.93	387.89
1971	127.31	303.12	172.14	409.86	211.67	503.98	142.44	339.14	168.82	401.95
1972	136.90	315.44	189.14	435.81	221.19	509.65	154.71	356.47	187.86	432.86
1973	145.39	315.38	201.40	436.88	235.89	511.69	166.46	361.08	203.31	441.02
1974	154.76	302.27	219.14	428.01	249.25	486.82	176.80	345.31	217.48	424.77
1975	163.53	293.06	249.31	446.79	266.08	476.85	190.79	341.92	233.44	418.35
1976	175.45	297.37	273.90	464.24	283.73	480.90	209.32	354.78	256.71	435.10
1977	189.00	300.96	301.20	479.62	295.65	470.78	228.90	364.49	278.90	444.11
1978	203.70	300.89	332.88	491.70	318.69	470.74	249.27	368.20	302.80	447.27
1979	219.91	291.66	365.07	484.18	342.99	454.89	269.34	357.21	325.58	431.80
1980	235.10	274.65	397.06	463.86	367.78	429.65	288.62	337.17	351.25	410.34
1981	255.20	270.63	438.75	465.27	399.26	423.39	318.00	337.22	382.18	405.28
1982	267.26	267.26	459.88	459.88	426.82	426.82	330.26	330.26	402.48	402.48
1983	280.70	272.52	479.40	465.44	442.97	430.07	354.08	343.77	420.81	408.55
1984	292.86	274.73	503.58	472.40	458.51	430.12	374.03	350.87	438.13	411.00
1985	299.09	271.16	519.93	471.38	464.46	421.09	386.37	350.29	450.30	408.25
1986	304.85	271.94	525.81	469.05	466.75	416.37	396.01	353.26	458.64	409.13
1987	312.50	269.16	531.70	457.97	480.44	413.82	406.31	349.97	471.58	406.18
1988	322.02	266.79	541.44	448.58	495.73	410.71	418.81	346.98	467.57	387.38
1989	334.24	264.22	570.18	450.74	513.17	405.67	429.68	339.67	481.43	380.58
1990	345.35	259.47	603.29	453.26	526.01	395.20	441.86	331.98	496.13	372.75
1991	353.98	255.40	630.04	454.57	533.40	384.85	455.03	328.30	502.92	362.86
1992	363.61	254.99	638.31	447.62	537.70	377.07	469.86	329.50	514.37	360.71
1993	373.64	254.87	646.78	441.19	553.63	377.65	486.04	331.54	532.52	363.25
1994	385.86	256.73	666.62	443.53	573.00	381.24	506.94	337.29	547.07	363.99
1995	394.34	255.07	683.91	442.37	587.00	379.69	514.59	332.85	556.72	360.10
1996	406.61	255.73	707.59	445.03	603.33	379.45	531.23	334.11	572.22	359.89
1997	424.89	261.31	733.21	450.93	625.56	384.72	553.14	340.18	592.32	364.28
1998	442.19	268.32	742.35	450.46	646.13	392.07	562.53	341.34	604.75	366.96
1999	456.78	271.25	736.56	437.39	672.13	399.13	579.63	344.20	607.20	360.57
2000	474.72	272.36	742.18	425.81	702.68	403.14	597.79	342.97	622.46	357.12
2001	489.74	273.45	763.86	426.50	720.76	402.43	603.58	337.01	641.38	358.11

See *Note* at end of table.

Table 2-13. Average Weekly Earnings of Production or Nonsupervisory Workers on Nonfarm Payrolls by Industry in Current and Constant Dollars, 1947–2001—*Continued*

Year	Wholesale trade		Retail trade		Finance, insurance, and real estate		Services	
	Current dollars	1982 dollars	Current dollars	1982 dollars	Current dollars	1982 dollars	Current dollars	1982 dollars
1947	50.06	215.95	33.77	145.56	43.21	186.25	...	...
1948	53.59	214.12	36.22	144.88	45.48	181.92	...	...
1949	55.45	223.59	38.42	154.92	47.63	192.06	...	...
1950	55.31	232.40	39.71	158.84	47.50	202.08	...	...
1951	62.02	230.93	42.82	159.18	54.67	203.20	...	...
1952	65.53	237.17	43.38	157.17	57.08	206.81	...	...
1953	68.61	246.94	45.36	163.17	59.57	214.28	...	...
1954	71.28	255.02	47.04	168.60	62.04	222.37	...	...
1955	74.48	268.02	48.75	175.36	63.92	229.93	...	...
1956	78.17	277.77	50.18	177.94	65.68	232.91	...	...
1957	81.41	278.73	52.20	178.77	67.53	231.27	...	...
1958	84.02	280.47	54.10	180.33	70.12	233.73	...	...
1959	88.51	292.78	56.15	185.93	72.74	240.83	...	...
1960	90.72	293.93	57.76	187.53	75.14	243.96	...	...
1961	93.56	299.87	58.66	188.62	77.12	247.97	...	...
1962	96.22	306.43	60.96	194.14	80.94	257.77	...	...
1963	99.47	312.61	62.66	197.04	84.38	265.35	...	...
1964	102.56	317.89	64.75	201.27	85.79	266.37	70.03	217.55
1965	106.08	324.98	66.61	203.82	88.91	271.71	73.60	225.08
1966	111.11	330.60	68.57	203.87	92.13	274.43	77.04	228.93
1967	115.66	333.86	70.95	204.21	95.72	275.79	80.38	231.41
1968	121.90	337.65	74.95	207.56	101.75	281.72	83.97	232.91
1969	129.85	340.52	78.66	206.48	108.70	284.93	90.57	237.85
1970	136.86	340.57	82.47	204.75	112.67	280.57	96.66	240.10
1971	143.42	342.10	87.62	208.36	117.85	281.00	103.06	245.33
1972	151.69	348.89	91.85	212.05	122.98	283.27	110.85	254.88
1973	159.54	346.51	96.32	209.22	129.20	280.56	117.29	254.86
1974	169.94	332.25	102.68	200.29	137.61	268.91	126.00	246.52
1975	182.19	326.92	108.86	194.68	148.19	265.04	134.67	241.45
1976	194.27	329.07	114.60	194.17	155.43	263.58	143.52	243.27
1977	209.13	332.42	121.66	193.54	165.26	263.41	153.45	244.57
1978	228.14	336.59	130.20	192.23	178.00	262.97	163.67	242.08
1979	247.93	328.45	138.62	184.12	190.77	253.21	175.27	232.57
1980	266.88	312.07	147.38	172.01	209.60	244.95	190.71	223.11
1981	290.68	308.25	158.03	167.58	229.05	242.90	208.97	221.60
1982	309.46	309.46	163.85	163.85	245.44	245.44	225.59	225.59
1983	328.79	319.21	171.05	166.07	263.90	256.21	239.04	232.08
1984	341.88	320.71	174.33	163.54	278.50	261.26	247.43	232.11
1985	351.36	318.55	174.64	158.33	289.02	262.03	256.75	232.77
1986	357.72	319.11	176.08	157.07	304.30	271.45	265.85	237.15
1987	365.38	314.71	178.70	153.92	316.90	272.95	275.93	237.67
1988	380.24	315.03	183.62	152.13	325.25	269.47	289.49	239.84
1989	394.82	312.11	188.72	149.19	341.17	269.70	305.79	241.73
1990	411.10	308.87	194.40	146.06	356.93	268.17	319.48	240.03
1991	424.82	306.51	198.48	143.20	370.92	267.62	331.45	239.14
1992	435.10	305.12	205.06	143.80	387.36	271.64	342.55	240.22
1993	448.47	305.91	209.95	143.21	406.33	277.17	350.35	238.98
1994	463.10	308.12	216.46	144.02	423.51	281.78	358.80	238.72
1995	476.07	307.94	221.47	143.25	442.29	286.09	369.04	238.71
1996	492.92	310.01	230.11	144.72	459.52	289.01	382.00	240.25
1997	516.48	317.64	240.74	148.06	481.57	296.17	400.33	246.21
1998	538.88	326.99	253.46	153.80	512.15	310.77	418.58	253.99
1999	558.80	331.83	263.61	156.54	529.24	314.28	435.86	258.82
2000	585.97	336.18	273.39	156.85	551.10	316.18	455.51	261.34
2001	605.85	338.27	282.35	157.65	570.38	318.47	479.71	267.84

Note: Data include Alaska and Hawaii beginning in 1959.

Table 2-14. Average Weekly Earnings of Production Workers on Manufacturing Payrolls by Industry, 1947–2001

(Dollars.)

Year	Total manufac- turing	Durable goods													
		Total	Lumber and wood products	Furniture and fixtures	Stone, clay, and glass products	Primary metal industries		Blast furnaces and basic steel products	Fabri- cated metal products	Industrial machin- ery and equip- ment	Elec- tronic and other electrical equip- ment	Transportation equipment		Instrum- ents and related products	Miscel- laneous manufac- turing indus- tries
						Total	Blast furnaces and basic steel products					Total	Motor vehicles and equip- ment		
1947	49.13	51.64	43.93	45.53	48.95	55.38	56.51	56.51	51.74	55.78	...	56.97	58.63	...	44.75
1948	53.08	56.24	47.64	48.83	53.20	61.14	62.84	62.84	56.37	60.38	...	61.70	63.15	...	48.03
1949	53.80	57.13	48.10	49.36	54.27	60.90	63.34	63.34	57.45	60.27	...	65.01	67.33	...	48.23
1950	58.28	59.60	51.31	53.55	59.06	67.36	67.95	67.95	63.04	67.04	...	71.29	74.85	...	52.02
1951	63.34	68.48	55.41	57.13	63.76	75.30	77.71	77.71	68.55	76.13	...	75.81	77.16	...	55.08
1952	66.75	72.04	59.15	60.86	66.17	77.52	80.00	80.00	71.72	79.55	...	81.51	84.87	...	59.02
1953	70.47	76.22	61.31	62.99	70.18	84.46	88.29	88.29	76.49	82.68	...	85.28	89.88	...	61.56
1954	70.49	75.79	61.39	62.80	71.69	81.48	83.92	83.92	76.70	81.40	...	86.30	91.30	...	61.78
1955	75.30	81.77	63.99	67.07	77.00	92.51	96.80	96.80	81.73	87.15	...	93.48	99.84	...	64.88
1956	78.78	85.28	65.74	68.78	80.56	97.17	102.87	102.87	84.67	93.06	...	94.81	96.82	...	67.60
1957	81.19	87.85	66.82	69.83	82.82	99.00	105.57	105.57	88.34	94.12	...	97.51	100.61	...	69.48
1958	82.32	88.88	69.48	69.95	84.80	101.11	108.00	108.00	90.17	94.33	...	100.40	101.24	...	70.17
1959	88.26	95.65	74.24	74.48	91.46	112.19	122.71	122.71	96.12	102.92	...	107.45	111.38	...	73.42
1960	89.72	97.04	74.29	75.20	92.57	109.59	116.13	116.13	98.42	104.55	...	111.52	115.21	...	74.28
1961	92.34	99.70	77.03	76.40	95.24	114.55	122.92	122.92	100.85	107.16	...	113.40	114.69	...	75.84
1962	96.56	104.30	79.20	79.37	98.81	119.80	127.40	127.40	104.81	113.01	...	122.22	127.67	...	78.61
1963	99.23	108.09	82.41	81.80	102.67	124.64	133.06	133.06	107.79	116.20	...	126.42	132.68	...	80.39
1964	102.97	112.05	85.65	84.46	105.50	129.69	138.43	138.43	111.76	121.69	...	130.09	138.03	...	82.37
1965	107.53	116.76	89.16	87.98	110.04	133.88	140.90	140.90	116.20	127.15	...	137.71	147.63	...	85.39
1966	112.19	121.67	92.21	91.72	114.24	138.09	144.73	144.73	122.11	134.90	...	141.86	147.23	...	88.80
1967	114.49	123.19	95.91	94.13	117.31	137.27	143.51	143.51	123.67	135.58	...	142.42	144.84	...	92.59
1968	122.51	131.65	104.75	100.28	124.98	147.68	154.16	154.16	131.77	141.12	...	155.72	167.66	...	98.50
1969	129.51	139.59	110.55	105.85	133.66	158.42	166.03	166.03	138.94	152.15	...	161.44	170.97	...	103.74
1970	133.33	143.07	117.61	108.58	140.08	158.77	166.40	166.40	143.67	154.95	...	163.62	170.07	...	109.52
1971	142.44	152.74	126.56	115.42	152.67	169.62	177.80	177.80	152.31	163.21	...	181.12	194.46	...	115.53
1972	154.71	167.68	134.94	123.82	165.48	192.92	206.25	206.25	166.86	181.87	...	200.58	220.59	...	122.85
1973	166.46	180.09	144.80	131.60	176.82	213.19	229.77	229.77	178.46	196.88	...	216.82	237.51	...	128.31
1974	176.80	190.82	152.88	138.02	187.50	232.96	258.95	258.95	188.09	207.97	...	224.37	238.32	...	136.61
1975	190.79	205.49	166.06	143.64	198.77	247.20	274.13	274.13	202.51	219.10	...	245.23	259.53	...	146.69
1976	209.32	226.14	189.13	154.81	219.06	276.22	305.88	305.88	224.40	238.55	...	276.05	304.16	...	156.75
1977	228.90	248.46	203.89	169.26	239.95	305.62	338.58	338.58	242.31	259.79	...	309.83	345.40	...	169.17
1978	249.27	270.44	223.68	183.92	262.91	342.76	389.69	389.69	260.35	284.76	...	333.80	368.05	...	181.97
1979	269.34	290.50	240.16	195.82	284.28	371.77	428.89	428.89	278.80	305.24	...	350.58	372.37	...	195.16
1980	288.62	310.78	253.60	209.17	306.00	391.78	448.77	448.77	300.98	328.00	...	379.61	394.00	...	211.30
1981	318.00	342.91	271.67	226.94	335.76	437.81	509.04	509.04	330.46	360.33	...	424.95	450.72	...	231.64
1982	330.26	354.88	284.23	234.73	355.69	437.34	505.97	505.97	343.78	367.62	...	449.96	470.61	...	246.53
1983	354.08	381.77	313.58	260.83	384.71	459.68	509.16	509.16	370.27	387.18	...	491.31	525.66	...	266.27
1984	374.03	402.82	321.20	271.55	401.94	478.30	528.29	528.29	389.16	417.74	...	520.94	557.57	...	277.77
1985	386.37	415.71	329.18	282.50	412.30	484.31	547.86	547.86	401.02	427.45	...	541.45	582.47	...	287.62
1986	396.01	424.56	338.15	296.91	423.69	496.93	572.54	572.54	408.46	440.13	...	541.86	572.97	...	298.98
1987	406.31	432.85	342.26	306.80	433.58	514.61	597.62	597.62	416.42	452.81	...	543.48	570.97	...	305.74
1988	418.81	447.68	344.46	313.23	446.69	528.96	615.12	615.12	439.71	473.12	401.39	567.48	608.57	438.84	313.60
1989	429.68	458.02	354.48	325.88	457.69	534.49	618.45	618.45	439.71	483.36	410.04	579.61	614.18	445.11	326.63
1990	441.86	468.76	365.02	333.13	467.04	551.68	643.19	643.19	447.28	493.16	420.24	591.36	617.34	464.02	340.10
1991	455.03	482.93	369.60	340.79	473.71	562.53	655.87	655.87	461.03	506.66	435.49	618.03	644.23	477.24	351.35
1992	469.86	498.83	383.26	357.70	489.52	587.38	690.35	690.35	475.07	523.70	453.20	635.36	655.08	488.68	365.09
1993	486.04	519.09	392.09	371.73	506.00	611.36	721.48	721.48	492.15	547.39	469.83	679.40	713.23	502.65	373.72
1994	506.94	543.97	405.41	385.82	526.44	641.00	756.57	756.57	511.80	568.10	485.30	731.39	782.92	520.00	386.80
1995	514.59	548.66	410.87	388.87	533.63	643.28	769.45	769.45	514.31	574.62	486.30	733.21	778.57	526.19	401.00
1996	531.23	565.19	425.95	399.91	555.11	661.67	792.10	792.10	530.00	585.73	505.47	756.36	796.53	547.52	412.09
1997	553.14	587.64	441.16	424.11	569.38	683.38	809.55	809.55	544.43	613.45	533.40	780.98	811.80	567.84	428.24
1998	562.53	591.35	456.21	441.45	591.17	684.22	821.53	821.53	552.86	619.32	542.34	759.93	776.04	570.35	434.11
1999	579.63	605.99	473.06	454.99	606.30	703.10	851.57	851.57	572.40	632.76	553.32	779.20	814.50	581.50	448.15
2000	597.79	623.92	489.54	470.77	626.24	736.81	911.72	911.72	590.86	656.21	566.77	801.16	834.72	595.13	453.57
2001	603.58	626.48	497.76	477.36	654.00	737.71	910.29	910.29	589.95	645.13	571.69	798.61	828.38	605.73	460.86

See *Note* at end of table.

Table 2-14. Average Weekly Earnings of Production Workers on Manufacturing Payrolls by Industry, 1947–2001—Continued

(Dollars.)

Year	Nondurable goods										
	Total	Food and kindred products	Tobacco products	Textile mill products	Apparel and other textile products	Paper and allied products	Printing and publishing	Chemicals and allied products	Petroleum and coal products	Rubber and miscellaneous plastics products	Leather and leather products
1947	46.03	45.92	35.17	40.99	41.80	49.69	59.30	50.26	60.94	51.60	40.07
1948	49.54	48.84	36.58	45.28	43.68	54.70	65.13	55.29	69.30	53.29	41.11
1949	50.41	50.49	37.26	44.52	42.76	55.42	68.60	57.67	72.42	54.13	41.03
1950	51.45	52.88	41.00	48.59	44.60	60.53	71.23	61.64	75.11	60.27	43.95
1951	57.42	56.84	43.89	51.22	46.64	65.08	74.30	66.91	81.19	64.46	46.13
1952	59.95	60.34	45.31	52.39	47.92	68.05	78.58	69.12	85.05	69.53	49.92
1953	62.57	63.50	47.63	53.18	48.74	71.81	82.29	74.21	90.35	72.32	50.90
1954	63.18	65.67	48.88	52.09	48.36	73.18	83.93	77.11	93.20	72.83	50.18
1955	67.03	68.89	51.86	55.34	49.73	78.01	87.91	80.97	96.93	81.32	52.68
1956	70.09	72.69	56.26	57.17	52.92	82.18	90.64	85.90	104.14	81.61	55.65
1957	72.52	75.48	58.75	57.96	53.91	85.45	92.64	89.98	108.53	85.67	56.85
1958	74.50	79.15	62.17	57.51	54.05	87.99	94.62	93.20	111.66	85.67	57.25
1959	78.61	82.82	64.52	63.02	56.63	93.30	99.72	99.36	117.42	93.75	60.26
1960	80.36	86.09	64.94	63.60	56.45	95.15	102.91	103.25	118.78	92.80	60.52
1961	82.92	88.75	69.42	65.04	58.06	99.45	105.05	106.81	124.01	96.15	62.83
1962	86.15	91.84	71.41	68.21	61.18	102.24	108.01	110.24	126.88	100.04	64.67
1963	87.91	94.30	73.92	69.43	62.45	105.90	110.69	113.15	131.77	101.02	66.00
1964	90.91	97.17	75.66	73.39	64.26	109.57	114.35	116.48	133.76	104.90	69.36
1965	94.64	100.28	79.21	77.98	66.61	114.22	118.12	121.09	138.42	109.62	71.82
1966	98.49	103.82	85.19	82.12	68.80	119.35	122.61	125.16	144.58	112.56	74.88
1967	102.03	107.98	87.62	84.25	73.08	122.84	125.95	128.96	152.87	113.85	79.07
1968	109.05	114.24	93.99	91.05	79.78	130.85	133.28	136.27	159.38	121.60	85.41
1969	115.53	120.77	97.99	95.88	82.93	139.32	141.33	145.05	170.40	126.90	87.79
1970	120.43	127.98	110.00	97.76	84.37	144.14	147.78	153.50	183.18	129.36	92.63
1971	128.51	136.21	119.45	104.34	88.64	154.51	157.50	165.15	195.60	137.76	97.64
1972	138.16	145.80	130.47	113.58	93.60	169.06	170.03	177.64	211.79	149.56	102.64
1973	146.52	155.54	145.14	120.66	99.08	180.18	179.08	188.52	223.87	158.21	105.46
1974	156.79	169.28	157.80	126.40	104.54	191.17	188.63	202.52	239.13	166.05	110.33
1975	169.56	185.78	173.81	134.41	111.58	208.42	198.52	220.99	266.98	176.36	119.09
1976	185.57	201.69	186.75	147.97	121.72	232.48	214.13	245.86	303.54	191.70	127.16
1977	201.33	214.80	209.41	161.20	128.87	255.68	230.72	268.13	334.34	214.13	133.21
1978	218.28	230.26	233.55	173.72	140.26	279.71	244.78	294.14	376.27	227.81	144.32
1979	236.19	250.17	253.46	188.26	149.32	303.74	260.25	318.44	409.97	244.41	154.03
1980	255.84	271.95	294.89	203.31	161.42	330.85	279.36	344.45	422.18	263.20	168.09
1981	281.85	295.37	344.54	218.59	177.43	365.50	305.49	379.39	491.62	290.97	183.13
1982	297.60	312.05	370.06	218.63	180.44	389.58	324.25	407.36	546.99	304.92	189.75
1983	318.75	323.51	388.21	249.67	194.76	423.02	342.54	440.13	582.99	332.07	203.87
1984	333.08	333.92	436.46	257.75	202.02	448.67	356.64	463.83	587.33	348.20	210.13
1985	345.31	342.80	444.91	265.99	208.57	466.77	367.04	484.36	604.58	353.46	216.88
1986	357.11	350.00	481.71	284.82	214.33	482.98	379.62	501.96	621.52	363.91	218.45
1987	369.44	358.99	548.73	299.71	219.78	496.06	390.64	523.25	641.52	373.57	232.26
1988	379.89	367.54	583.87	302.58	226.44	506.18	400.14	536.36	664.67	383.22	235.50
1989	391.95	381.77	590.97	313.70	234.32	517.87	412.35	555.02	682.66	391.64	249.76
1990	404.80	392.50	636.22	320.00	239.15	533.02	426.00	576.80	724.30	401.14	258.43
1991	419.69	401.94	655.71	336.98	250.49	550.78	432.80	602.32	751.46	413.88	269.25
1992	433.49	414.12	653.11	353.46	258.54	569.85	447.29	625.38	784.02	432.01	281.96
1993	445.79	425.32	631.69	367.63	263.75	585.11	456.92	638.74	819.03	441.83	294.52
1994	459.72	440.26	749.45	379.81	275.25	604.50	468.60	653.62	846.71	451.54	306.85
1995	468.99	449.22	768.64	383.93	282.68	613.31	471.01	674.78	846.03	452.77	310.46
1996	484.79	459.20	774.00	393.41	294.52	635.21	483.23	698.54	842.35	466.46	326.52
1997	504.71	474.12	748.44	415.24	307.73	657.69	502.81	715.82	870.62	483.63	344.45
1998	521.88	492.06	710.85	425.99	317.80	672.70	515.52	738.29	911.68	495.81	351.56
1999	540.29	506.20	763.01	442.13	334.50	689.19	531.88	749.06	908.63	517.08	363.15
2000	558.14	521.67	864.27	459.79	351.16	690.63	551.52	771.38	932.38	531.99	381.38
2001	570.65	529.78	851.40	452.87	351.74	701.79	564.64	787.20	945.02	544.97	374.25

Note: Data include Alaska and Hawaii beginning in 1959.

Table 2-15. Employees on Total Nonfarm Payrolls by State, 1963–2001

(Thousands of persons.)

State	1963	1964	1965	1966	1967	1968	1969	1970	1971	1972	1973	1974	1975
Alabama	812.5	843.8	886.5	935.6	951.8	970.1	1 000.2	1 010.5	1 021.9	1 072.3	1 135.5	1 169.8	1 155.4
Alaska	62.1	65.4	70.5	73.1	76.9	79.9	86.8	93.1	97.8	103.5	110.0	127.9	161.8
Arizona	377.2	389.1	403.7	434.8	445.6	473.4	517.2	547.4	581.4	646.3	714.5	746.0	729.1
Arkansas	416.3	431.8	458.8	489.8	501.0	514.6	533.8	536.2	551.0	581.5	614.5	640.7	623.8
California	5 412.3	5 606.5	5 800.3	6 145.2	6 367.6	6 642.1	6 931.5	6 946.2	6 917.0	7 209.9	7 621.9	7 834.3	7 847.2
Colorado	571.7	583.2	598.9	631.2	655.8	686.6	720.7	750.2	787.0	869.4	936.0	959.7	963.5
Connecticut	969.3	991.2	1 032.9	1 095.4	1 130.1	1 158.0	1 194.1	1 197.5	1 164.3	1 190.4	1 238.7	1 264.0	1 223.4
Delaware	163.6	170.8	184.1	193.2	197.4	202.9	211.9	216.8	224.9	232.4	239.4	233.1	229.9
DC	542.5	551.5	572.5	587.0	594.7	582.8	575.0	566.7	566.6	572.0	573.7	580.1	576.5
Florida	1 447.4	1 526.5	1 619.1	1 726.8	1 816.4	1 932.3	2 069.9	2 152.1	2 276.4	2 513.1	2 778.6	2 863.8	2 746.4
Georgia	1 139.7	1 186.7	1 257.1	1 337.9	1 394.7	1 455.6	1 531.7	1 557.5	1 602.9	1 695.2	1 802.5	1 827.5	1 755.7
Hawaii	199.6	207.8	219.4	232.1	241.7	255.3	275.9	293.7	301.5	312.7	327.5	335.9	342.8
Idaho	164.7	168.6	177.6	184.8	187.7	192.9	201.4	207.8	217.1	236.5	251.7	266.8	273.0
Illinois	3 614.4	3 712.2	3 880.4	4 095.3	4 209.7	4 284.9	4 376.1	4 345.6	4 296.4	4 314.8	4 466.9	4 545.7	4 418.9
Indiana	1 498.7	1 545.7	1 631.1	1 737.2	1 777.0	1 817.4	1 880.3	1 849.0	1 841.1	1 921.9	2 028.1	2 031.4	1 941.7
Iowa	699.8	718.3	752.2	803.8	832.8	852.1	873.4	876.9	882.7	912.3	961.3	999.0	998.7
Kansas	574.2	587.2	600.4	634.3	652.8	672.1	686.4	678.8	677.8	717.5	763.3	790.0	801.2
Kentucky	702.9	721.7	758.9	803.8	836.5	868.6	895.5	910.1	931.5	988.3	1 038.6	1 065.9	1 057.6
Louisiana	810.3	849.4	898.4	957.9	997.3	1 020.5	1 032.7	1 033.6	1 055.9	1 128.6	1 176.1	1 220.8	1 249.5
Maine	279.6	285.1	295.4	309.2	316.9	323.2	330.0	332.2	332.3	343.7	354.8	361.5	356.9
Maryland	978.6	1 009.7	1 057.6	1 132.0	1 178.6	1 223.9	1 272.4	1 349.2	1 371.5	1 415.0	1 471.5	1 493.6	1 479.3
Massachusetts	1 943.2	1 958.1	2 015.8	2 097.4	2 147.9	2 187.9	2 249.4	2 243.5	2 211.4	2 251.7	2 333.5	2 353.7	2 273.1
Michigan	2 410.4	2 512.9	2 685.3	2 861.0	2 900.5	2 959.7	3 081.1	2 999.0	2 995.0	3 118.9	3 284.3	3 277.6	3 136.6
Minnesota	1 001.7	1 028.0	1 080.6	1 148.3	1 199.8	1 243.5	1 299.8	1 315.3	1 310.2	1 357.1	1 436.1	1 481.0	1 474.4
Mississippi	443.7	460.2	486.6	521.6	535.1	551.9	573.0	583.9	602.2	649.3	693.2	710.8	692.3
Missouri	1 383.5	1 418.3	1 478.3	1 554.1	1 595.5	1 631.3	1 672.1	1 668.0	1 660.8	1 700.1	1 770.6	1 789.5	1 740.6
Montana	172.6	174.2	179.2	184.6	188.0	192.5	195.5	199.1	204.8	215.3	224.2	234.0	238.1
Nebraska	401.9	408.9	418.7	434.1	449.3	458.8	474.4	484.3	490.8	517.0	541.3	562.1	557.8
Nevada	142.8	149.3	157.4	162.0	166.1	177.3	193.5	203.3	210.5	223.4	244.6	256.1	263.1
New Hampshire	208.8	212.8	220.8	235.2	244.0	251.8	259.2	258.5	259.9	278.5	297.8	300.3	292.8
New Jersey	2 129.4	2 168.7	2 259.0	2 359.1	2 421.5	2 485.2	2 569.6	2 606.2	2 607.6	2 672.5	2 759.7	2 783.0	2 699.9
New Mexico	248.6	255.7	262.5	271.7	272.6	276.6	287.5	292.6	305.7	327.5	346.0	360.2	370.2
New York	6 273.7	6 370.7	6 518.7	6 709.5	6 858.3	7 001.7	7 182.0	7 156.4	7 011.4	7 038.5	7 132.2	7 077.1	6 829.9
North Carolina	1 298.6	1 353.7	1 431.2	1 534.2	1 600.9	1 678.5	1 747.0	1 782.7	1 813.8	1 911.9	2 018.1	2 048.2	1 979.9
North Dakota	136.7	142.6	146.1	148.3	151.5	155.6	157.8	163.6	167.0	176.1	183.9	193.8	203.6
Ohio	3 145.2	3 216.3	3 364.3	3 537.3	3 619.8	3 750.8	3 887.3	3 880.7	3 839.6	3 938.4	4 112.9	4 169.4	4 016.2
Oklahoma	606.7	619.3	642.5	676.0	699.7	720.4	748.3	762.6	774.4	811.9	851.9	886.9	899.7
Oregon	549.5	573.9	608.4	640.4	652.1	679.2	708.5	710.5	729.1	774.7	816.2	838.2	837.4
Pennsylvania	3 694.8	3 777.1	3 917.5	4 077.1	4 171.3	4 263.5	4 374.9	4 351.6	4 291.3	4 400.0	4 506.5	4 514.6	4 435.8
Rhode Island	298.1	303.9	316.3	330.0	338.3	343.0	346.4	344.1	342.8	358.1	365.9	367.0	349.2
South Carolina	630.6	651.4	686.0	734.9	754.4	782.9	819.8	842.0	862.6	920.3	984.0	1 015.8	982.6
South Dakota	152.6	152.2	155.5	160.1	163.9	167.8	172.9	175.4	179.0	189.9	199.1	206.6	209.3
Tennessee	1 002.5	1 045.5	1 108.5	1 184.4	1 218.8	1 264.0	1 309.8	1 327.6	1 356.8	1 450.1	1 531.1	1 558.2	1 505.7
Texas	2 706.5	2 808.0	2 932.4	3 108.7	3 259.4	3 424.3	3 597.1	3 624.9	3 683.5	3 884.4	4 141.7	4 360.2	4 462.9
Utah	293.7	293.2	299.8	317.4	326.6	335.1	348.2	357.0	369.3	393.0	414.8	434.1	440.3
Vermont	111.5	113.7	121.3	130.8	136.3	140.3	145.5	147.9	148.1	153.6	161.3	162.8	162.1
Virginia	1 123.8	1 163.0	1 218.9	1 285.3	1 330.2	1 385.1	1 436.4	1 518.9	1 567.2	1 655.2	1 753.4	1 804.3	1 778.7
Washington	850.6	854.7	896.4	988.4	1 045.3	1 099.4	1 120.1	1 079.4	1 064.5	1 100.1	1 152.3	1 199.1	1 225.7
West Virginia	449.9	460.9	476.6	495.1	503.6	508.4	512.3	516.5	520.0	540.5	561.6	572.4	574.7
Wisconsin	1 233.5	1 270.9	1 331.7	1 394.1	1 430.5	1 472.1	1 525.1	1 530.4	1 525.4	1 580.8	1 660.5	1 703.4	1 676.8
Wyoming	96.2	97.2	96.6	97.2	99.0	102.9	106.9	108.3	111.0	117.3	126.1	136.5	146.0
Puerto Rico	...	...	...	...	...	...	...	...	...	...	...	...	...
Virgin Islands	...	...	...	...	...	...	...	...	...	...	...	...	33.1

See footnote at end of table.

Table 2-15. Employees on Total Nonfarm Payrolls by State, 1963–2001— *Continued*

(Thousands of persons.)

State	1976	1977	1978	1979	1980	1981	1982	1983	1984	1985	1986	1987	1988
Alabama	1 207.0	1 269.2	1 336.5	1 362.0	1 356.1	1 347.6	1 312.5	1 328.8	1 387.7	1 427.1	1 463.3	1 507.7	1 558.7
Alaska	171.7	163.3	163.5	166.9	169.4	186.1	200.4	214.3	225.7	230.7	220.7	210.1	213.7
Arizona	758.7	809.3	895.4	979.9	1 014.0	1 040.8	1 029.8	1 077.8	1 181.9	1 278.6	1 337.8	1 385.8	1 419.3
Arkansas	660.0	695.6	732.7	749.4	742.3	740.1	720.1	741.3	780.2	797.1	813.8	836.6	865.4
California	8 154.2	8 599.7	9 199.8	9 664.6	9 848.8	9 985.3	9 810.3	9 917.8	10 390.0	10 769.8	11 085.5	11 472.6	11 911.5
Colorado	1 003.4	1 058.1	1 150.0	1 218.0	1 251.1	1 295.2	1 316.6	1 327.2	1 402.3	1 418.7	1 408.3	1 412.6	1 436.1
Connecticut	1 239.7	1 282.3	1 346.1	1 398.0	1 426.8	1 438.3	1 428.5	1 444.2	1 517.3	1 558.2	1 598.4	1 638.2	1 667.4
Delaware	236.7	238.8	247.8	256.7	259.2	259.2	259.2	266.1	280.0	293.4	303.2	320.7	334.2
DC	575.8	578.7	596.3	612.5	616.1	611.0	597.9	596.6	613.8	629.0	640.0	655.6	673.6
Florida	2 784.3	2 933.2	3 180.6	3 381.2	3 576.2	3 736.0	3 761.9	3 905.4	4 204.2	4 410.0	4 599.4	4 848.1	5 066.6
Georgia	1 839.1	1 926.4	2 050.1	2 127.5	2 159.4	2 198.6	2 201.5	2 279.5	2 448.7	2 569.8	2 672.4	2 782.0	2 875.9
Hawaii	349.2	359.4	377.3	394.0	404.1	404.8	399.4	406.2	412.7	425.7	438.6	460.0	478.1
Idaho	291.0	307.4	331.3	338.0	330.0	327.8	312.2	317.9	330.5	336.0	328.2	333.4	348.5
Illinois	4 565.7	4 655.5	4 788.8	4 880.0	4 850.3	4 732.3	4 593.3	4 530.6	4 672.3	4 755.3	4 790.7	4 928.3	5 097.5
Indiana	2 023.8	2 114.0	2 205.5	2 236.3	2 129.5	2 114.4	2 028.0	2 029.5	2 122.3	2 168.6	2 221.8	2 304.9	2 395.6
Iowa	1 036.9	1 079.2	1 119.2	1 131.7	1 109.9	1 088.6	1 041.9	1 040.4	1 074.7	1 074.2	1 073.8	1 109.1	1 156.2
Kansas	834.8	871.0	912.5	946.8	944.7	949.7	921.4	921.6	960.8	967.9	984.8	1 005.1	1 035.4
Kentucky	1 103.1	1 148.3	1 209.9	1 245.4	1 210.0	1 196.0	1 160.7	1 152.3	1 213.8	1 250.3	1 274.1	1 328.2	1 381.8
Louisiana	1 314.4	1 364.6	1 463.5	1 517.4	1 578.9	1 630.5	1 607.0	1 565.2	1 601.5	1 591.2	1 518.5	1 483.6	1 511.6
Maine	375.3	387.8	405.6	415.9	418.3	419.2	415.5	425.0	445.7	458.4	477.4	501.1	527.1
Maryland	1 498.3	1 545.6	1 625.8	1 691.3	1 711.8	1 715.8	1 675.8	1 724.1	1 814.0	1 887.8	1 952.0	2 028.0	2 102.3
Massachusetts	2 323.5	2 416.0	2 526.3	2 603.5	2 654.3	2 671.8	2 642.0	2 696.5	2 855.8	2 930.0	2 988.8	3 065.8	3 130.8
Michigan	3 283.0	3 442.3	3 609.4	3 637.1	3 442.8	3 364.4	3 193.3	3 223.1	3 381.0	3 561.5	3 657.3	3 735.8	3 819.2
Minnesota	1 520.9	1 597.3	1 689.3	1 767.0	1 770.2	1 761.3	1 707.3	1 718.4	1 819.8	1 865.5	1 892.5	1 962.5	2 028.1
Mississippi	727.5	765.9	813.7	838.1	829.3	819.1	790.9	792.8	820.8	838.9	848.2	864.4	896.2
Missouri	1 797.8	1 861.8	1 953.1	2 011.1	1 969.8	1 956.3	1 922.4	1 937.0	2 032.7	2 094.7	2 142.6	2 197.8	2 258.9
Montana	251.1	264.8	280.4	283.8	280.4	281.8	273.7	276.0	281.1	279.1	275.4	274.1	282.9
Nebraska	572.1	593.7	609.9	631.2	627.6	623.2	609.8	610.8	635.4	650.5	652.5	667.2	688.1
Nevada	279.8	308.2	350.3	383.7	399.9	411.2	401.1	402.8	426.0	446.4	468.1	500.2	537.6
New Hampshire	313.4	337.1	359.6	¹378.5	385.4	394.6	394.4	409.5	441.5	466.0	490.1	512.8	529.0
New Jersey	2 753.7	2 836.9	2 961.9	3 027.2	3 060.4	3 098.9	3 092.7	3 165.1	3 329.2	3 414.1	3 488.1	3 576.3	3 651.0
New Mexico	390.0	415.4	444.3	461.0	465.4	475.5	473.6	479.5	502.8	520.2	525.9	529.3	547.5
New York	6 789.5	6 857.6	7 044.5	7 179.4	7 207.1	7 287.3	7 254.6	7 313.3	7 570.4	7 751.3	7 907.9	8 059.4	8 186.9
North Carolina	2 082.7	2 170.4	2 277.4	2 373.0	2 380.0	2 391.6	2 347.0	2 419.2	2 565.2	2 651.2	2 744.1	2 862.6	2 986.6
North Dakota	215.0	221.1	234.0	244.2	245.2	249.4	249.7	250.6	252.5	252.0	249.9	252.8	256.7
Ohio	4 094.6	4 230.1	4 394.9	4 484.8	4 367.4	4 317.7	4 124.3	4 092.5	4 260.2	4 372.9	4 471.4	4 582.6	4 700.6
Oklahoma	931.1	971.5	1 035.7	1 087.9	1 138.1	1 201.2	1 216.9	1 170.6	1 180.3	1 165.3	1 124.4	1 108.5	1 131.5
Oregon	878.5	936.9	1 009.2	1 056.0	1 044.6	1 018.7	961.1	966.7	1 006.9	1 030.0	1 058.5	1 100.1	1 152.8
Pennsylvania	4 512.8	4 565.2	4 716.2	4 806.1	4 753.1	4 728.9	4 580.1	4 524.3	4 654.8	4 730.3	4 790.9	4 915.1	5 041.7
Rhode Island	366.7	381.7	395.8	400.0	398.3	401.4	390.5	396.3	416.4	429.2	442.5	451.9	459.4
South Carolina	1 038.1	1 081.7	1 137.5	1 176.0	1 188.8	1 196.4	1 162.3	1 189.0	1 262.5	1 296.2	1 338.0	1 392.2	1 449.0
South Dakota	218.6	226.6	236.6	241.4	238.0	236.0	230.2	235.3	247.0	249.4	251.9	256.9	266.1
Tennessee	1 575.4	1 648.1	1 737.0	1 777.3	1 746.6	1 755.4	1 703.0	1 719.0	1 812.0	1 867.8	1 929.8	2 011.6	2 092.1
Texas	4 683.7	4 906.8	5 271.6	5 601.8	5 851.2	6 180.0	6 263.4	6 193.6	6 492.4	6 663.1	6 564.2	6 516.9	6 677.8
Utah	462.8	488.7	525.4	548.4	550.8	558.0	560.9	566.9	601.2	624.3	634.1	640.0	660.0
Vermont	168.4	178.4	190.6	197.9	200.1	204.3	202.9	206.4	214.9	224.7	234.4	245.6	256.1
Virginia	1 848.1	1 930.4	2 033.5	2 115.0	2 157.2	2 160.8	2 146.4	2 206.9	2 333.3	2 454.7	2 557.7	2 680.4	2 772.5
Washington	1 282.9	1 367.0	1 485.4	1 581.2	1 608.0	1 612.0	1 568.6	1 586.1	1 659.6	1 710.4	1 769.9	1 851.8	1 941.4
West Virginia	596.3	611.6	633.1	658.6	645.9	628.5	607.8	582.3	596.6	597.2	597.5	599.0	609.8
Wisconsin	1 725.9	1 798.9	1 887.0	1 960.2	1 938.1	1 923.2	1 866.7	1 867.3	1 949.2	1 983.1	2 023.9	2 089.6	2 168.5
Wyoming	156.5	170.5	187.4	200.7	210.2	223.5	217.7	202.5	204.3	206.9	196.3	182.6	189.0
Puerto Rico	...	...	...	...	693.1	679.7	641.6	645.6	684.2	692.5	728.0	763.8	817.8
Virgin Islands	31.3	32.2	33.8	36.1	37.3	37.7	36.5	36.4	36.6	36.9	37.7	39.6	41.5

See footnote at end of table.

Table 2-15. Employees on Total Nonfarm Payrolls by State, 1963–2001—*Continued*

(Thousands of persons.)

State	1989	1990	1991	1992	1993	1994	1995	1996	1997	1998	1999	2000	2001
Alabama	1 601.2	1 635.7	1 642.0	1 674.5	1 716.8	1 758.5	1 803.6	1 828.6	1 866.3	1 898.1	1 919.5	1 931.2	1 913.5
Alaska	227.0	238.1	242.8	247.2	252.9	259.3	262.0	263.6	268.7	275.0	277.8	283.9	290.0
Arizona	1 454.5	1 483.0	1 491.4	1 517.0	1 584.4	1 692.1	1 795.7	1 892.3	1 984.6	2 074.7	2 163.1	2 242.8	2 265.7
Arkansas	893.4	923.5	936.4	963.1	994.0	1 034.1	1 069.4	1 086.0	1 104.0	1 122.2	1 141.7	1 158.6	1 156.2
California	12 238.5	12 499.9	12 359.0	12 153.5	12 045.3	12 159.5	12 422.2	12 743.4	13 129.7	13 596.1	13 991.8	14 488.1	14 696.6
Colorado	1 482.3	1 520.9	1 545.0	1 596.9	1 670.7	1 755.9	1 834.4	1 900.4	1 979.5	2 057.0	2 131.8	2 212.9	2 231.9
Connecticut	1 665.6	1 623.5	1 555.2	1 526.2	1 531.1	1 543.7	1 561.5	1 583.6	1 612.6	1 643.4	1 669.1	1 693.1	1 682.3
Delaware	344.5	347.6	341.8	341.3	348.6	356.0	366.4	376.4	387.9	400.2	412.9	420.0	419.3
DC	680.6	686.1	677.3	673.6	670.3	658.8	642.6	623.1	618.4	613.6	627.4	650.3	650.9
Florida	5 260.9	5 387.4	5 294.3	5 358.7	5 571.4	5 799.4	[1]5 996.1	6 183.3	6 414.4	6 636.5	6 827.0	7 080.6	7 197.8
Georgia	2 941.1	2 991.8	2 937.5	2 987.2	3 109.2	3 265.9	3 402.3	3 527.4	3 614.4	3 740.8	3 854.6	3 949.3	3 953.6
Hawaii	505.5	528.4	539.1	542.8	538.8	536.2	532.8	530.7	531.6	531.3	535.0	551.4	553.6
Idaho	365.8	384.9	398.1	416.4	436.5	460.9	477.3	492.9	509.9	521.8	538.9	559.6	569.4
Illinois	5 213.9	5 288.3	5 231.5	5 234.9	5 330.5	5 462.9	5 593.1	5 684.7	5 772.1	5 898.5	5 958.3	6 044.9	6 004.6
Indiana	2 479.3	2 521.9	2 507.3	2 554.2	2 626.9	2 712.7	2 786.5	2 814.4	2 858.6	2 917.3	2 969.9	3 000.1	2 938.3
Iowa	1 200.1	1 226.3	1 238.1	1 252.6	1 278.6	1 319.9	1 358.1	1 383.4	1 407.0	1 442.8	1 468.6	1 478.4	1 468.8
Kansas	1 064.2	1 088.5	1 095.4	1 115.0	1 133.3	1 165.8	1 198.0	1 226.7	1 268.2	1 312.2	1 327.0	1 344.6	1 356.5
Kentucky	1 433.0	1 470.5	1 474.7	1 508.5	1 547.9	1 597.2	1 642.8	1 671.7	1 711.2	1 752.8	1 795.5	1 824.6	1 816.9
Louisiana	1 538.5	1 589.9	1 613.0	1 626.9	1 658.6	1 722.1	1 772.4	1 809.7	1 849.9	1 889.5	1 896.2	1 919.9	1 931.3
Maine	541.8	534.9	513.4	511.9	519.4	531.6	538.2	542.5	553.7	569.2	586.3	603.5	609.4
Maryland	2 155.2	2 171.2	2 099.8	2 081.3	2 102.4	2 145.8	2 182.7	2 211.2	2 267.1	2 324.4	2 386.5	2 450.0	2 469.7
Massachusetts	3 108.6	2 984.8	2 821.2	2 795.1	2 840.2	2 903.8	2 976.6	3 035.4	3 109.2	3 178.6	3 236.8	3 323.3	3 334.9
Michigan	3 922.3	3 969.6	3 891.1	3 927.4	4 005.8	4 146.8	4 273.9	4 360.7	4 448.2	4 510.1	4 582.0	4 673.9	4 586.5
Minnesota	2 086.8	2 126.7	2 136.8	2 184.9	2 242.7	2 310.4	2 378.6	2 433.3	2 490.8	2 555.1	2 613.0	2 675.8	2 674.2
Mississippi	919.3	936.6	937.5	960.3	1 002.3	1 055.5	1 074.5	1 088.9	1 107.1	1 133.7	1 153.2	1 153.5	1 134.1
Missouri	2 315.0	2 345.0	2 309.1	2 333.7	2 394.5	2 470.5	2 520.9	2 567.4	2 639.4	2 684.0	2 726.6	2 748.8	2 732.0
Montana	291.0	297.3	303.7	316.6	325.6	340.2	350.8	360.3	364.9	373.0	380.4	387.5	391.7
Nebraska	708.0	730.1	739.2	750.1	767.2	796.1	816.4	834.8	854.3	876.3	892.7	908.8	909.4
Nevada	581.2	620.9	628.7	638.7	671.4	738.0	786.1	843.0	890.7	925.9	982.9	1 026.9	1 053.9
New Hampshire	529.1	508.0	482.1	487.0	502.4	523.1	539.7	553.6	570.2	589.0	605.8	622.1	627.0
New Jersey	3 689.8	3 635.1	3 498.7	3 457.9	3 493.1	3 552.8	3 600.7	3 638.9	3 724.6	3 801.3	3 901.1	3 994.5	4 024.3
New Mexico	562.2	580.4	585.4	601.5	626.2	657.2	682.4	694.6	708.5	720.0	729.6	744.9	756.8
New York	8 246.8	8 212.4	7 886.7	7 730.3	7 759.8	7 831.4	7 892.2	7 938.7	8 067.1	8 236.7	8 435.3	8 635.3	8 632.6
North Carolina	3 073.9	3 117.7	3 072.2	3 125.5	3 244.7	3 358.9	3 459.5	3 546.5	3 663.2	3 773.8	3 870.4	3 933.8	3 900.7
North Dakota	260.4	265.9	270.6	277.2	284.8	294.9	301.8	308.7	314.1	319.5	323.9	327.7	329.8
Ohio	4 817.4	4 882.3	4 818.6	4 847.7	4 918.3	5 076.0	5 221.0	5 296.4	5 392.4	5 482.2	5 563.5	5 624.7	5 566.0
Oklahoma	1 163.8	1 195.9	1 211.0	1 221.7	1 247.0	1 279.5	1 316.1	1 353.5	1 392.5	1 441.2	1 461.9	1 489.7	1 509.2
Oregon	1 205.8	1 247.1	1 244.7	1 267.6	1 308.4	1 362.9	1 418.4	1 474.6	1 526.4	1 551.8	1 575.0	1 606.8	1 596.1
Pennsylvania	5 138.5	5 170.1	5 083.7	5 075.5	5 122.8	5 192.4	5 253.1	5 306.2	5 406.5	5 494.9	5 586.1	5 691.2	5 701.1
Rhode Island	461.9	451.2	421.5	424.8	430.0	434.2	440.1	441.6	450.0	458.0	465.5	476.6	478.9
South Carolina	1 499.7	1 545.0	1 513.4	1 527.7	1 570.1	1 607.2	1 646.1	1 675.2	1 720.2	1 783.3	1 830.6	1 859.5	1 835.3
South Dakota	276.0	288.7	296.4	308.7	318.7	332.0	343.5	348.7	354.9	363.2	373.2	377.7	379.2
Tennessee	2 167.2	2 193.2	2 183.6	2 245.0	2 328.5	2 423.0	2 499.0	2 533.4	2 584.0	2 638.5	2 685.4	2 728.9	2 711.5
Texas	6 840.0	7 095.4	7 174.7	7 269.1	7 481.5	7 750.9	8 022.5	8 256.1	8 608.0	8 940.1	9 159.2	9 433.0	9 513.1
Utah	691.1	723.6	745.2	768.7	809.8	859.7	907.7	954.5	993.8	1 023.3	1 048.6	1 075.4	1 082.1
Vermont	261.8	257.5	248.9	251.0	257.2	263.8	270.0	274.9	279.2	284.8	291.3	298.5	298.8
Virginia	2 861.9	2 896.3	2 828.9	2 848.4	2 918.9	3 003.6	3 069.7	3 136.0	3 231.8	3 320.0	3 412.4	3 516.6	3 528.4
Washington	2 046.8	2 143.0	2 177.4	2 222.4	2 253.0	2 304.3	2 346.9	2 415.6	2 514.2	2 594.9	2 648.7	2 711.3	2 697.8
West Virginia	614.7	630.1	629.1	640.0	652.6	674.6	687.8	698.6	707.8	719.2	726.0	735.8	735.4
Wisconsin	2 236.4	2 291.5	2 302.0	2 357.9	2 412.7	2 490.8	2 558.5	2 600.5	2 655.7	2 718.0	2 783.9	2 833.2	2 825.7
Wyoming	192.8	198.5	203.1	205.6	210.3	216.8	219.4	221.1	224.5	228.3	233.0	239.4	245.6
Puerto Rico	837.4	843.8	835.6	855.8	869.4	895.8	927.3	970.6	986.8	994.4	1 009.0	1 022.8	1 005.1
Virgin Islands	42.0	43.1	43.8	44.8	48.6	44.6	42.1	41.3	41.5	41.7	41.1	42.5	44.4

1. Data not continuous.

Table 2-16. Employees on Manufacturing Payrolls by State, 1963–2001

(Thousands of persons.)

State	1963	1964	1965	1966	1967	1968	1969	1970	1971	1972	1973	1974	1975
Alabama	249.4	259.2	279.2	296.9	300.6	310.0	327.3	327.2	322.7	333.4	350.9	353.7	321.9
Alaska	5.7	5.6	6.3	6.6	6.6	6.9	7.3	8.6	7.8	8.1	9.5	9.7	9.6
Arizona	58.0	59.5	64.9	77.7	79.1	84.9	94.2	91.2	89.2	98.7	110.2	112.9	99.8
Arkansas	119.4	126.7	135.9	149.7	153.4	159.0	169.1	168.6	172.5	185.2	200.4	203.9	179.2
California	1 394.3	1 389.4	1 411.2	1 531.3	1 594.0	1 639.7	1 661.3	1 558.0	1 473.2	1 542.7	1 660.7	1 701.3	1 593.7
Colorado	96.4	93.5	92.6	102.7	106.1	110.5	118.3	120.8	123.5	131.5	143.3	146.6	137.2
Connecticut	420.8	421.0	436.1	471.4	479.5	474.3	471.7	441.9	399.0	400.1	420.2	430.9	389.8
Delaware	59.1	61.9	67.8	71.0	71.7	72.9	73.6	71.1	68.8	69.4	73.7	70.8	65.7
DC	20.6	20.7	21.1	21.7	22.0	21.4	20.8	19.3	18.5	17.8	17.4	17.0	15.5
Florida	229.3	237.9	252.6	276.1	293.8	311.4	329.2	322.5	322.7	351.3	380.6	375.9	339.4
Georgia	363.8	378.9	403.9	431.5	438.9	452.9	477.6	467.1	461.7	476.6	494.5	483.7	439.3
Hawaii	25.0	25.2	24.5	24.2	24.7	23.8	25.2	25.6	25.2	24.9	23.8	22.7	23.7
Idaho	30.4	31.8	33.3	35.6	35.3	37.9	39.9	40.3	41.2	43.6	46.9	48.0	47.8
Illinois	1 218.6	1 253.3	1 318.4	1 410.5	1 409.6	1 404.0	1 417.4	1 358.6	1 282.4	1 284.2	1 353.5	1 345.1	1 199.8
Indiana	614.5	630.9	673.6	719.7	716.0	722.9	752.3	710.2	683.4	709.4	758.2	737.2	647.2
Iowa	179.0	183.5	192.9	212.1	219.3	223.1	225.4	216.0	209.8	222.9	241.3	249.9	230.4
Kansas	117.9	123.1	124.7	142.3	149.3	151.0	150.6	137.2	132.5	145.7	164.5	169.2	164.2
Kentucky	184.7	194.0	207.8	228.6	234.2	242.9	250.4	255.4	253.3	268.3	288.3	290.9	259.7
Louisiana	148.9	155.4	161.1	168.3	176.7	181.9	184.6	179.0	177.7	183.2	190.5	192.5	186.2
Maine	102.8	104.0	108.0	115.0	116.3	118.0	115.7	110.4	102.7	102.4	104.5	105.1	96.3
Maryland	260.4	258.2	264.8	279.8	283.3	280.6	281.7	271.4	252.4	248.8	257.0	254.5	230.0
Massachusetts	663.5	649.9	668.2	699.1	700.8	689.5	681.5	648.2	605.7	610.2	634.7	639.3	577.8
Michigan	989.6	1 032.0	1 112.4	1 179.6	1 148.8	1 172.5	1 203.8	1 081.0	1 059.2	1 097.4	1 178.8	1 114.0	983.7
Minnesota	242.1	246.4	261.6	287.4	302.2	314.7	331.4	318.7	298.8	310.2	331.2	340.7	313.0
Mississippi	134.5	140.4	153.0	166.6	167.4	175.5	182.5	182.1	189.5	207.7	221.0	220.0	201.8
Missouri	396.8	405.7	420.1	448.7	457.4	462.7	465.7	449.4	430.3	441.5	459.7	451.6	405.3
Montana	22.3	21.4	22.1	22.9	22.4	23.2	24.1	23.9	23.9	24.5	24.8	24.5	22.1
Nebraska	66.2	67.2	68.7	74.7	79.7	82.8	86.2	84.5	82.6	85.0	90.5	93.4	85.4
Nevada	6.8	6.9	7.1	7.1	6.8	7.1	8.2	8.6	8.8	9.8	11.8	12.3	12.2
New Hampshire	85.9	85.6	89.8	96.0	97.6	99.7	97.9	91.6	86.3	90.8	96.0	94.2	85.1
New Jersey	809.4	806.7	837.5	879.3	882.8	893.7	892.5	860.7	818.3	823.3	842.6	825.9	747.9
New Mexico	17.2	17.9	17.6	18.6	18.3	18.5	20.7	21.4	22.6	26.1	28.9	29.6	28.6
New York	1 804.1	1 794.8	1 838.1	1 894.5	1 885.7	1 879.0	1 870.8	1 760.6	1 633.5	1 602.2	1 619.1	1 574.6	1 421.9
North Carolina	537.0	557.1	590.6	638.1	657.5	686.1	714.0	713.0	716.2	756.8	796.9	789.6	715.5
North Dakota	7.8	8.4	8.7	8.9	8.6	8.9	9.0	9.9	10.2	10.8	12.6	14.7	16.2
Ohio	1 236.6	1 259.1	1 326.0	1 404.4	1 401.4	1 433.5	1 471.0	1 409.9	1 333.8	1 346.8	1 426.3	1 416.6	1 267.5
Oklahoma	90.9	96.6	103.0	113.3	116.4	121.7	129.9	134.1	132.7	141.1	151.9	156.7	150.7
Oregon	145.1	151.7	158.2	167.2	165.4	173.7	180.5	172.3	174.3	184.2	196.9	197.1	182.3
Pennsylvania	1 401.0	1 434.8	1 494.1	1 565.3	1 562.4	1 570.0	1 588.9	1 528.8	1 438.1	1 444.0	1 480.1	1 464.5	1 334.8
Rhode Island	115.5	116.0	121.0	127.6	127.4	127.4	127.9	120.9	115.2	121.0	125.6	126.0	112.7
South Carolina	269.6	277.7	293.0	313.7	319.0	327.3	341.5	340.3	337.2	354.3	374.9	375.9	339.9
South Dakota	14.8	13.3	13.5	14.3	15.4	15.9	15.9	15.8	16.5	18.4	19.8	20.9	19.8
Tennessee	344.7	361.5	386.6	424.2	434.8	454.3	469.0	463.8	459.5	489.2	519.4	513.3	459.0
Texas	516.5	540.5	572.1	622.1	661.9	709.4	750.2	734.3	710.5	738.7	790.2	831.3	815.9
Utah	55.5	52.5	50.0	51.2	50.9	51.9	54.8	56.0	56.5	60.5	65.1	70.4	67.5
Vermont	34.9	34.7	38.6	43.4	44.2	43.7	43.4	40.5	37.9	38.5	41.6	42.8	39.5
Virginia	297.5	308.6	322.5	340.0	346.0	362.7	371.0	366.0	366.2	387.8	401.8	401.9	371.5
Washington	224.0	219.3	227.0	265.2	277.1	286.9	278.5	239.5	214.7	224.1	244.2	253.6	244.0
West Virginia	124.2	126.2	129.2	133.0	133.2	132.4	131.0	126.5	122.9	123.3	129.0	132.1	121.1
Wisconsin	461.4	469.6	491.9	508.6	508.7	510.3	520.9	500.9	479.6	495.4	531.7	546.1	507.0
Wyoming	7.2	7.7	7.1	6.8	7.1	6.8	7.4	7.4	7.5	7.9	8.4	8.4	8.3
Puerto Rico	...	...	...	...	...	...	...	...	...	...	...	...	...
Virgin Islands	...	...	...	...	...	...	...	...	...	...	...	...	3.1

See footnote at end of table.

Table 2-16. Employees on Manufacturing Payrolls by State, 1963–2001—*Continued*

(Thousands of persons.)

State	1976	1977	1978	1979	1980	1981	1982	1983	1984	1985	1986	1987	1988
Alabama	340.2	354.3	368.9	374.9	363.1	362.0	337.8	340.9	359.8	358.1	358.6	368.8	380.6
Alaska	10.3	10.9	11.6	12.7	13.4	14.0	12.6	11.9	11.3	12.1	12.6	12.9	15.0
Arizona	105.6	113.9	126.9	144.1	154.4	160.6	154.5	155.8	172.8	181.6	184.6	187.4	189.0
Arkansas	195.1	209.3	217.5	217.8	209.1	209.7	195.2	200.3	213.0	209.6	211.8	219.6	226.3
California	1 659.8	1 737.8	1 884.6	2 012.7	2 018.2	2 032.3	1 957.7	1 927.0	2 004.1	2 024.2	2 039.1	2 060.1	2 096.7
Colorado	144.5	152.8	168.2	180.6	180.4	186.2	183.3	180.7	195.3	192.2	185.3	184.5	189.6
Connecticut	397.0	406.7	419.6	436.5	440.8	439.0	418.7	403.2	415.1	408.0	394.0	384.2	372.3
Delaware	68.2	67.6	69.0	70.2	70.9	71.0	67.9	68.2	70.6	72.2	68.7	70.5	70.3
DC	15.3	14.8	15.0	15.3	15.4	14.5	13.7	14.2	14.5	14.8	15.7	16.1	16.3
Florida	354.0	380.9	415.5	443.6	456.4	472.2	456.7	464.3	501.9	514.4	517.2	531.0	539.6
Georgia	476.3	494.1	515.8	528.5	519.2	524.6	500.3	511.1	546.5	557.1	564.6	571.2	574.3
Hawaii	23.4	23.2	23.7	24.0	23.3	23.0	22.4	22.4	21.9	21.9	22.0	21.9	22.0
Idaho	52.0	54.1	58.1	58.3	53.3	52.7	47.8	51.4	54.8	54.7	52.1	54.3	57.9
Illinois	1 215.2	1 241.3	1 276.0	1 271.6	1 208.2	1 131.4	1 013.4	955.8	997.0	970.7	925.8	940.2	975.2
Indiana	685.1	713.2	741.5	733.2	657.0	652.6	589.0	581.6	620.5	609.8	604.0	616.6	636.7
Iowa	234.0	245.6	252.5	259.8	244.8	236.5	209.8	202.3	211.9	204.7	201.7	213.5	226.4
Kansas	166.6	172.9	185.9	198.9	190.5	188.6	168.8	164.7	176.4	174.4	175.7	176.2	181.6
Kentucky	273.3	284.9	292.2	297.2	276.2	270.5	244.8	242.5	257.4	255.3	253.8	262.5	274.1
Louisiana	195.4	203.3	209.5	213.6	214.2	222.1	202.6	180.1	182.4	178.0	166.0	164.5	171.5
Maine	102.5	105.9	111.3	114.6	113.2	113.5	108.6	109.2	110.6	105.9	103.6	104.1	108.0
Maryland	232.4	235.1	241.5	246.9	236.7	231.7	215.3	214.1	219.4	217.2	210.2	208.4	210.2
Massachusetts	593.6	621.0	652.1	672.8	673.3	668.0	636.5	629.0	667.6	649.7	614.4	599.1	584.7
Michigan	1 061.7	1 128.4	1 179.6	1 160.2	998.9	979.0	876.9	880.5	962.8	1 002.4	1 000.4	972.5	955.4
Minnesota	321.7	339.3	360.4	381.6	371.2	364.0	346.8	346.4	373.8	375.4	369.1	376.4	394.1
Mississippi	218.9	230.1	235.3	235.2	221.8	220.3	203.2	204.7	218.7	221.6	223.7	228.6	238.8
Missouri	424.9	439.6	456.8	464.4	437.0	427.5	406.8	405.4	433.8	430.3	424.7	424.0	433.9
Montana	23.7	25.1	26.3	27.0	24.2	23.2	20.6	22.1	22.5	21.8	21.1	20.8	21.3
Nebraska	87.9	90.6	94.1	99.6	96.4	94.9	87.9	84.7	90.5	88.4	86.0	88.6	93.6
Nevada	13.0	15.1	17.8	19.4	19.2	20.1	18.8	19.1	21.0	21.9	22.3	23.3	24.9
New Hampshire	94.5	101.4	109.8	116.5	116.6	116.6	111.7	113.3	123.4	122.5	118.1	117.5	117.9
New Jersey	756.2	767.4	786.8	799.1	781.0	771.1	729.6	715.1	726.7	712.8	689.7	672.2	662.1
New Mexico	30.3	32.2	33.4	34.8	34.4	34.3	34.1	34.4	36.5	37.3	37.4	38.3	40.4
New York	1 438.9	1 459.6	1 481.2	1 492.8	1 445.1	1 433.3	1 352.5	1 302.4	1 326.3	1 293.1	1 251.6	1 217.9	1 212.5
North Carolina	756.3	780.9	807.2	826.8	820.0	820.7	782.2	796.1	835.6	828.6	832.8	856.0	867.5
North Dakota	16.2	15.3	15.7	16.7	15.6	15.3	14.9	14.8	15.5	15.4	15.3	15.8	16.4
Ohio	1 295.3	1 344.1	1 377.2	1 382.3	1 264.3	1 232.6	1 099.9	1 066.0	1 127.0	1 124.2	1 109.8	1 098.9	1 110.6
Oklahoma	156.1	163.2	172.7	184.4	191.3	200.0	180.6	166.2	175.0	172.0	160.4	158.6	161.4
Oregon	193.7	206.1	219.1	228.3	215.1	202.7	185.7	188.8	201.1	199.3	198.4	206.2	214.2
Pennsylvania	1 335.2	1 341.9	1 367.8	1 386.8	1 328.2	1 299.0	1 170.5	1 095.8	1 121.9	1 089.5	1 048.9	1 044.0	1 055.2
Rhode Island	122.9	128.8	134.4	132.6	128.2	127.7	116.6	116.2	121.7	119.2	118.9	116.3	112.4
South Carolina	371.0	380.2	391.1	399.5	391.9	390.2	364.3	362.4	377.6	365.4	365.2	374.0	385.0
South Dakota	22.2	23.4	24.9	27.5	26.1	25.9	24.8	25.9	29.2	27.5	28.2	29.3	31.6
Tennessee	486.1	507.5	526.0	524.7	502.1	506.9	466.7	468.6	497.1	492.4	490.5	497.4	511.9
Texas	862.3	893.5	962.8	1 021.9	1 056.9	1 115.3	1 045.2	963.7	1 004.3	998.6	951.1	932.0	962.6
Utah	70.7	74.5	80.3	86.8	87.7	89.6	85.7	85.5	94.0	94.0	92.0	92.1	99.0
Vermont	41.0	43.4	47.7	50.8	50.9	51.3	48.6	47.6	49.0	49.8	49.5	49.6	49.7
Virginia	387.7	400.8	409.4	413.8	413.8	414.0	397.2	403.6	421.3	423.4	424.7	428.9	427.4
Washington	247.4	260.0	284.7	309.6	308.7	305.2	289.0	278.4	288.1	295.6	305.0	318.4	341.6
West Virginia	124.4	123.8	126.6	126.1	117.2	111.5	98.1	89.8	91.5	89.5	86.8	86.2	87.0
Wisconsin	519.4	540.4	569.7	591.3	558.0	543.5	498.2	486.7	518.9	513.9	514.5	528.7	551.5
Wyoming	8.4	9.0	9.6	10.1	9.6	9.9	9.1	8.2	8.0	8.0	7.9	8.2	8.7
Puerto Rico	...	...	...	...	154.6	153.1	142.7	143.7	150.1	147.5	148.8	151.3	154.5
Virgin Islands	3.1	3.1	2.9	3.2	3.2	3.1	2.7	2.5	2.3	2.2	1.8	2.1	2.4

See footnote at end of table.

Table 2-16. Employees on Manufacturing Payrolls by State, 1963–2001—*Continued*

(Thousands of persons.)

State	1989	1990	1991	1992	1993	1994	1995	1996	1997	1998	1999	2000	2001
Alabama	385.6	384.5	379.3	380.7	384.2	386.4	391.8	382.6	380.5	377.8	367.6	360.2	339.8
Alaska	15.7	17.2	18.0	18.0	17.1	16.6	16.9	15.9	15.2	14.4	14.4	14.1	13.7
Arizona	188.2	185.3	176.1	173.2	176.5	186.4	194.0	199.9	207.4	216.0	211.7	215.4	209.6
Arkansas	231.0	232.8	233.7	237.0	244.3	254.0	259.3	253.8	252.9	253.5	252.1	251.7	240.5
California	2 107.0	2 068.8	1 970.9	1 890.5	1 805.1	1 777.3	1 794.2	1 851.8	1 914.0	1 951.0	1 923.0	1 947.8	1 904.4
Colorado	193.4	193.2	185.6	185.9	188.1	190.9	192.4	197.1	204.0	207.4	204.6	205.9	199.2
Connecticut	359.3	341.0	322.5	305.7	294.1	285.1	279.0	274.8	276.1	276.9	268.4	263.2	253.8
Delaware	73.1	71.8	70.1	67.4	65.6	63.5	61.5	57.9	57.8	59.7	59.8	58.4	55.8
DC	15.8	15.7	14.6	14.0	13.8	13.0	13.0	13.0	12.7	12.2	11.6	11.4	11.3
Florida	537.9	522.1	492.8	482.9	485.2	484.0	486.5	489.7	492.0	493.5	487.7	488.1	468.9
Georgia	568.3	561.1	541.0	545.2	558.2	577.3	586.9	585.4	588.6	594.6	594.9	583.3	549.8
Hawaii	21.5	21.1	20.5	19.7	19.2	17.8	17.0	16.7	16.6	16.4	16.5	17.5	17.9
Idaho	60.5	62.9	63.3	65.7	69.2	71.9	71.0	72.9	74.6	76.1	76.3	77.2	75.5
Illinois	986.6	982.7	940.8	919.3	933.1	952.1	962.2	969.7	973.1	974.8	954.9	945.7	907.8
Indiana	646.3	638.0	618.7	628.6	642.9	664.4	683.8	676.0	676.7	684.9	690.2	686.5	642.4
Iowa	234.8	236.4	232.5	230.2	236.1	244.9	250.3	248.7	253.3	261.3	261.0	260.9	251.6
Kansas	184.4	186.0	183.9	182.7	183.5	187.9	191.4	196.7	206.6	214.1	213.1	209.8	205.6
Kentucky	284.2	287.5	281.4	286.9	294.6	305.1	313.8	311.7	316.8	320.3	320.7	322.4	307.2
Louisiana	176.3	184.4	186.4	185.0	185.4	186.5	188.0	188.6	191.1	191.0	187.1	183.9	181.8
Maine	105.5	101.9	95.2	92.2	90.9	91.4	91.1	88.3	87.8	87.1	86.2	85.2	81.2
Maryland	209.8	205.9	191.7	183.7	180.2	178.2	176.0	175.0	176.9	178.2	177.9	181.1	178.2
Massachusetts	561.1	521.3	485.0	465.7	454.8	447.2	446.1	444.7	447.9	448.2	433.6	437.3	423.5
Michigan	971.3	943.6	896.7	900.6	908.3	951.5	979.7	971.7	966.3	969.7	981.8	981.0	926.4
Minnesota	399.8	400.8	395.2	397.1	406.5	414.7	425.8	429.6	435.0	441.2	439.0	441.1	423.4
Mississippi	243.6	246.5	246.9	251.9	255.7	261.0	257.8	245.6	241.8	245.5	243.9	233.2	213.8
Missouri	440.6	438.1	415.6	412.0	411.1	414.1	420.8	416.6	418.0	418.4	411.8	401.0	379.1
Montana	22.3	22.3	21.7	22.5	23.0	23.0	23.4	23.9	24.1	24.2	24.5	24.8	23.9
Nebraska	94.7	97.8	99.6	100.7	103.8	108.8	112.2	113.6	116.4	118.9	118.2	119.8	117.3
Nevada	25.4	26.2	25.9	26.1	29.5	33.7	36.6	38.7	40.7	41.9	42.6	44.7	46.3
New Hampshire	113.6	105.6	98.2	97.4	97.6	100.3	102.6	104.4	107.2	108.6	106.6	106.7	103.9
New Jersey	639.6	596.6	558.4	530.3	516.6	509.3	499.2	483.5	481.9	476.6	466.7	464.0	450.1
New Mexico	42.6	43.4	41.8	41.0	42.7	44.7	45.1	46.0	46.2	44.7	42.4	43.2	43.1
New York	1 189.0	1 131.4	1 059.6	1 014.4	980.5	956.1	941.7	924.4	920.8	911.7	89.1	877.5	842.8
North Carolina	871.1	861.5	826.1	834.4	847.8	859.9	864.2	844.9	833.7	824.2	801.9	784.1	733.6
North Dakota	16.5	17.4	17.9	18.3	19.5	21.4	21.3	21.6	23.4	24.0	24.1	25.1	25.4
Ohio	1 122.6	1 112.3	1 066.9	1 050.6	1 049.7	1 070.2	1 102.3	1 093.9	1 091.8	1 096.6	1 090.4	1 083.3	1 027.1
Oklahoma	164.4	168.8	168.8	163.8	168.6	169.8	170.7	174.1	180.9	185.9	183.8	182.4	178.5
Oregon	218.4	220.3	211.7	209.0	211.7	221.3	229.3	235.8	243.6	246.1	242.2	243.6	236.2
Pennsylvania	1 047.0	1 019.0	973.0	953.0	943.1	942.0	940.7	929.6	938.1	943.2	930.4	927.7	892.5
Rhode Island	108.3	99.7	91.7	89.5	88.1	86.8	84.9	82.1	79.8	78.0	74.8	73.1	70.0
South Carolina	389.6	383.3	369.2	371.0	374.8	377.4	377.2	366.0	362.7	362.1	344.6	347.2	332.1
South Dakota	32.3	34.4	35.0	37.0	39.6	43.5	46.6	47.8	49.4	49.7	50.1	49.6	46.2
Tennessee	524.5	520.3	502.7	514.5	528.4	538.9	538.9	519.3	517.6	514.7	511.0	506.8	478.5
Texas	979.1	997.4	981.0	969.6	987.6	1 009.0	1 032.8	1 056.2	1 083.9	1 107.2	1 084.4	1 088.1	1 057.6
Utah	103.1	107.3	105.8	106.9	110.7	116.7	124.2	129.5	133.0	132.5	132.0	131.1	127.0
Vermont	48.6	46.4	44.2	43.7	43.6	43.9	45.1	45.9	46.6	47.9	47.9	49.0	47.7
Virginia	429.6	426.4	412.0	407.4	405.1	404.3	402.9	400.0	405.2	403.4	395.7	390.1	371.7
Washington	361.6	369.4	351.9	347.7	340.8	336.9	332.4	344.7	370.0	379.5	364.2	353.1	338.4
West Virginia	87.8	87.5	83.2	82.2	82.9	81.6	82.4	81.9	81.6	82.4	81.6	80.9	77.4
Wisconsin	558.5	558.6	546.2	549.6	561.8	583.9	601.6	601.1	608.8	618.6	617.6	615.7	587.7
Wyoming	8.9	9.5	9.3	9.3	9.6	9.9	9.7	[1]10.8	10.8	11.0	11.1	11.4	11.2
Puerto Rico	157.3	154.9	151.6	151.7	150.2	151.0	153.7	153.3	152.3	147.6	143.4	140.9	134.8
Virgin Islands	2.3	2.4	2.7	2.8	2.8	2.9	2.5	2.3	2.2	2.4	2.4	2.5	2.2

1. Data not continuous.

Table 2-17. Employees on Government Payrolls by State, 1963–2001

(Thousands of persons.)

State	1963	1964	1965	1966	1967	1968	1969	1970	1971	1972	1973	1974	1975
Alabama	170.0	173.3	179.1	191.6	197.7	201.4	204.7	209.5	213.6	220.9	225.7	235.1	247.5
Alaska	27.1	28.1	29.7	30.8	31.8	32.2	33.3	35.6	37.9	40.5	41.5	43.8	47.7
Arizona	81.6	85.3	92.2	98.9	104.7	110.0	113.4	119.5	129.5	139.2	147.6	161.0	169.7
Arkansas	74.6	76.5	84.9	91.6	93.4	97.0	100.9	102.7	104.9	108.5	110.1	115.6	120.9
California	1 001.6	1 043.5	1 105.4	1 196.7	1 274.3	1 335.8	1 391.7	1 424.7	1 446.3	1 492.7	1 524.8	1 586.0	1 670.6
Colorado	128.6	132.0	137.7	148.2	157.7	162.4	166.9	177.2	184.7	190.8	197.2	204.0	216.6
Connecticut	103.3	109.0	115.9	122.5	131.5	140.0	150.9	157.9	160.9	165.2	167.7	171.0	178.7
Delaware	22.6	23.9	25.0	26.3	27.9	29.3	31.9	35.0	36.8	39.0	39.2	39.1	40.3
DC	249.5	251.3	262.7	274.6	278.0	264.6	254.4	249.7	256.7	260.2	259.6	265.3	269.7
Florida	262.5	278.7	301.2	326.2	342.3	361.8	377.9	397.8	419.1	437.9	469.9	510.5	546.0
Georgia	204.0	210.8	222.8	243.9	263.0	275.3	286.1	297.5	309.6	320.9	328.2	340.5	354.8
Hawaii	45.9	47.2	50.5	54.9	58.3	60.9	62.5	64.3	68.4	69.3	68.0	68.7	70.8
Idaho	37.8	38.1	39.6	41.9	44.3	45.2	46.8	49.1	51.3	54.5	56.2	59.7	62.3
Illinois	459.3	475.0	502.4	536.5	572.0	593.4	615.6	638.9	648.6	654.3	666.5	680.9	714.5
Indiana	209.7	219.2	232.2	254.1	271.4	285.3	280.9	286.4	296.3	301.4	303.8	308.0	323.3
Iowa	129.5	133.1	138.8	148.8	157.1	163.8	171.7	176.0	178.3	180.2	182.8	186.7	192.0
Kansas	120.6	126.2	130.2	137.0	143.2	146.0	149.6	153.3	155.1	162.8	166.5	164.0	168.7
Kentucky	125.2	128.4	135.2	145.2	155.5	163.3	166.1	172.1	180.5	188.5	194.3	198.5	208.3
Louisiana	158.3	163.4	171.7	185.4	197.4	201.8	208.2	213.2	216.0	227.9	233.2	241.6	248.7
Maine	51.5	52.9	54.3	57.4	59.5	61.6	64.3	66.4	68.7	69.4	70.7	72.9	74.8
Maryland	166.0	174.1	183.8	201.9	218.2	232.3	243.2	301.0	314.9	327.0	338.1	349.1	366.1
Massachusetts	267.5	272.7	278.5	286.2	297.1	302.5	310.7	319.9	330.6	343.1	351.6	354.3	365.1
Michigan	359.8	373.3	395.4	433.0	455.0	471.3	494.5	506.6	509.4	526.8	534.4	562.5	583.1
Minnesota	171.8	179.3	189.9	201.6	214.1	215.4	224.1	234.9	239.7	246.2	256.6	263.8	271.5
Mississippi	97.2	99.5	105.2	114.3	120.6	125.1	128.0	131.2	133.7	139.4	145.0	150.4	153.5
Missouri	202.9	210.6	225.4	244.7	260.3	269.1	276.1	284.1	292.9	297.5	306.9	312.9	316.0
Montana	43.0	44.7	45.9	48.1	51.8	53.3	52.1	52.6	54.3	55.4	55.4	58.2	64.9
Nebraska	87.7	89.1	92.5	93.3	97.6	97.4	100.9	104.7	109.1	114.3	116.9	121.4	124.7
Nevada	24.2	26.4	28.6	30.3	32.3	34.1	35.8	36.9	38.1	39.7	41.4	43.0	45.6
New Hampshire	28.0	29.0	30.1	31.4	33.4	34.4	35.5	37.3	38.8	41.2	43.4	45.6	48.0
New Jersey	272.1	280.0	295.4	312.0	329.2	344.4	360.1	374.8	388.0	405.3	417.1	439.9	470.2
New Mexico	70.3	71.8	75.4	81.0	83.4	85.0	86.3	89.2	92.3	96.0	99.5	102.5	104.8
New York	897.2	924.1	958.6	1 012.4	1 073.1	1 123.8	1 176.0	1 218.1	1 239.8	1 243.9	1 268.6	1 301.9	1 328.7
North Carolina	185.6	192.7	201.6	217.4	231.6	244.4	254.3	264.2	268.4	275.3	281.8	303.2	328.3
North Dakota	36.4	38.8	40.3	42.1	44.4	47.2	48.4	49.3	49.3	51.3	52.2	53.3	54.5
Ohio	431.7	440.3	458.6	483.0	509.5	528.3	544.8	565.5	577.2	589.1	597.8	613.1	626.4
Oklahoma	134.9	136.9	145.8	158.8	168.2	171.9	175.5	176.7	179.0	184.9	192.2	199.0	206.3
Oregon	107.9	111.3	118.2	125.3	132.4	136.1	140.8	146.7	152.0	157.5	160.3	168.5	177.1
Pennsylvania	474.8	488.6	508.4	536.1	567.2	588.1	609.4	618.7	629.2	651.9	658.7	682.0	721.4
Rhode Island	42.4	43.4	46.1	48.7	51.2	52.3	52.8	53.6	55.9	56.8	55.5	55.1	56.6
South Carolina	103.1	106.8	111.1	121.0	128.4	134.0	140.8	149.9	156.7	165.6	170.7	182.2	199.8
South Dakota	43.0	44.4	46.6	48.2	49.3	50.3	53.0	53.1	52.6	53.7	53.8	54.9	55.7
Tennessee	163.5	173.3	185.1	195.3	201.8	208.2	214.2	225.9	231.9	240.6	246.2	256.4	271.3
Texas	480.7	500.0	525.6	567.1	607.1	630.1	651.4	662.3	684.2	714.8	745.3	776.0	815.8
Utah	71.6	73.7	79.4	90.7	98.0	98.8	99.6	100.1	103.2	105.5	105.7	108.2	110.3
Vermont	18.9	19.5	20.3	21.2	22.3	23.4	24.4	26.2	27.2	28.2	28.7	29.3	30.5
Virginia	215.7	221.2	232.2	251.2	270.5	283.6	292.4	355.1	371.9	380.0	391.2	405.9	422.8
Washington	179.9	184.6	193.1	206.2	218.5	230.1	237.4	244.5	252.4	258.7	259.0	269.3	280.5
West Virginia	72.1	75.3	81.7	88.5	92.1	94.9	95.0	95.9	98.0	99.4	104.2	106.4	108.1
Wisconsin	181.7	190.4	201.0	215.2	230.3	244.6	255.3	265.5	270.2	275.8	276.3	276.9	285.4
Wyoming	23.8	24.6	25.6	26.9	28.4	28.1	28.1	28.4	29.4	30.5	31.3	32.4	34.5
Puerto Rico	...	...	...	...	...	...	...	...	...	...	...	...	...
Virgin Islands	...	...	...	...	...	...	...	...	...	...	...	...	11.7

See footnote at end of table.

Table 2-17. Employees on Government Payrolls by State, 1963–2001—*Continued*

(Thousands of persons.)

State	1976	1977	1978	1979	1980	1981	1982	1983	1984	1985	1986	1987	1988
Alabama	252.9	266.3	285.9	291.6	297.4	291.3	290.1	292.7	293.4	295.9	298.0	300.6	309.5
Alaska	48.2	50.1	51.6	54.4	55.0	57.1	59.6	63.0	66.5	68.3	68.0	65.8	66.5
Arizona	177.3	181.9	194.8	196.2	201.8	199.5	199.9	203.1	207.5	218.1	225.0	232.0	237.2
Arkansas	125.3	128.6	135.9	139.1	141.1	138.1	136.0	137.3	139.5	143.0	145.1	146.1	150.0
California	1 695.6	1 740.7	1 753.1	1 735.0	1 763.9	1 756.4	1 735.2	1 724.3	1 747.4	1 792.8	1 838.8	1 883.7	1 934.1
Colorado	219.5	221.1	234.0	238.8	243.6	241.7	238.6	240.7	244.4	248.9	256.0	262.2	266.7
Connecticut	175.1	175.6	179.2	181.3	[1]185.2	182.4	179.6	181.9	185.2	188.8	195.3	201.2	206.3
Delaware	40.6	41.4	42.8	44.4	45.2	44.5	43.8	43.4	43.7	44.8	46.1	46.6	47.5
DC	275.9	275.6	281.6	284.5	282.2	273.2	260.8	258.8	260.6	265.0	266.9	270.6	276.1
Florida	542.8	565.7	601.8	600.5	618.8	620.1	632.5	639.3	649.5	674.4	701.9	731.8	773.0
Georgia	366.1	384.0	407.9	418.7	429.2	431.1	434.0	437.6	442.0	448.7	462.2	476.6	494.1
Hawaii	72.6	73.0	73.8	73.4	75.5	75.4	76.5	77.4	77.8	79.0	79.2	80.8	83.5
Idaho	64.5	67.3	69.8	69.6	70.5	69.2	67.8	67.8	68.9	70.2	70.9	73.3	76.0
Illinois	717.2	717.8	728.0	739.8	749.4	734.5	717.9	701.6	687.9	697.8	714.8	724.5	738.8
Indiana	332.5	342.0	349.1	347.6	346.6	339.7	328.7	327.0	328.1	332.9	339.7	347.2	354.5
Iowa	197.0	202.5	208.2	204.5	207.4	203.1	202.0	203.4	204.5	206.8	207.3	210.2	212.1
Kansas	171.6	176.9	180.0	183.3	187.4	185.9	183.8	182.9	185.2	188.7	194.1	199.0	204.4
Kentucky	213.0	212.0	220.3	230.4	230.9	224.3	218.9	216.6	223.0	230.0	236.0	240.2	246.1
Louisiana	253.0	257.4	280.3	289.7	300.8	303.8	307.3	315.0	318.6	322.4	319.3	313.1	312.6
Maine	75.2	77.7	81.5	82.6	83.3	82.6	82.1	83.1	83.9	84.9	86.7	88.4	91.6
Maryland	372.1	378.1	401.9	418.7	434.8	415.9	393.2	379.6	387.9	393.6	391.6	392.9	399.1
Massachusetts	375.8	407.9	429.2	416.7	412.3	394.6	374.7	375.4	375.4	385.3	393.0	401.2	411.3
Michigan	594.5	596.7	611.4	621.0	627.8	598.4	577.8	569.8	567.2	580.7	598.6	611.6	623.5
Minnesota	276.0	286.3	292.8	295.6	300.6	299.0	289.6	286.6	293.7	301.2	307.9	313.8	320.8
Mississippi	156.2	163.9	181.8	192.2	194.5	185.9	180.0	181.1	183.2	188.5	189.5	191.1	196.0
Missouri	316.5	321.5	335.6	338.5	339.2	326.6	328.2	323.2	321.8	334.1	338.5	344.0	351.8
Montana	65.7	70.0	71.7	70.1	70.2	69.3	67.4	68.4	68.7	69.9	70.2	69.4	70.7
Nebraska	124.3	129.2	130.3	130.6	130.8	129.7	129.3	130.2	131.1	133.8	134.9	135.3	137.8
Nevada	46.8	49.2	52.2	54.7	57.0	57.1	58.2	58.0	58.9	60.5	61.6	64.1	67.0
New Hampshire	49.9	[1]53.8	54.3	[1]55.1	57.3	56.7	55.9	56.1	57.5	60.0	62.0	65.4	68.7
New Jersey	480.5	504.0	523.0	517.8	529.7	529.0	528.6	525.9	526.6	536.0	540.8	547.1	556.2
New Mexico	108.0	111.0	116.6	120.5	125.0	125.8	126.6	127.2	129.7	132.8	135.9	137.6	141.6
New York	1 273.6	1 270.8	1 315.1	1 311.3	1 314.4	1 300.3	1 293.7	1 299.6	1 318.2	1 353.6	1 382.3	1 402.1	1 433.2
North Carolina	347.9	367.6	386.4	397.2	409.9	403.7	400.3	407.1	413.7	420.5	430.9	442.3	458.7
North Dakota	56.2	57.5	60.0	60.6	60.9	60.5	60.3	61.3	62.2	63.6	64.4	64.6	64.8
Ohio	632.2	642.3	667.5	674.0	689.9	676.0	659.6	656.1	655.2	665.2	678.9	687.3	693.8
Oklahoma	207.0	212.4	218.4	224.0	228.5	235.7	237.2	245.2	241.4	245.7	246.8	245.4	248.5
Oregon	181.6	186.8	197.1	200.7	203.2	202.6	195.5	192.3	194.1	197.7	200.2	205.6	211.2
Pennsylvania	722.1	710.9	720.7	720.7	723.3	703.4	682.5	673.7	672.9	680.2	679.8	688.7	694.6
Rhode Island	57.0	58.2	59.8	59.3	59.2	58.5	57.8	56.9	57.4	57.7	58.0	58.2	58.9
South Carolina	203.3	213.7	223.8	228.8	236.4	233.0	228.1	230.3	237.3	244.8	251.4	258.0	261.5
South Dakota	55.9	56.6	58.1	58.3	58.6	57.8	56.6	56.9	57.2	57.9	58.8	58.9	60.1
Tennessee	283.1	291.2	305.6	313.9	317.2	311.7	297.5	294.1	296.1	304.2	312.4	321.2	328.4
Texas	847.0	875.5	923.7	953.2	978.1	1 000.8	1 023.6	1 042.0	1 063.5	1 088.9	1 118.8	1 142.7	1 175.5
Utah	112.2	115.8	121.0	123.2	125.0	125.1	126.4	128.8	131.5	137.8	141.2	141.5	142.7
Vermont	30.9	[1]34.3	35.1	35.8	37.0	36.2	36.0	36.3	36.5	37.4	38.2	39.0	40.9
Virginia	436.6	453.6	482.7	493.5	511.2	506.6	500.1	500.9	505.0	515.6	519.9	530.3	544.4
Washington	284.8	294.9	308.0	315.5	330.8	326.4	318.5	[1]324.0	334.5	342.8	348.9	357.2	368.8
West Virginia	109.6	111.0	120.3	130.1	133.1	130.2	126.8	127.8	130.7	127.5	128.9	128.2	129.3
Wisconsin	288.6	287.1	298.2	310.1	321.1	318.0	314.1	312.5	314.7	320.6	325.6	325.0	327.8
Wyoming	36.1	38.0	39.1	40.8	43.0	44.5	46.0	48.9	50.9	52.2	53.1	50.5	[1]54.1
Puerto Rico	. . .	. . .	. . .	246.0	254.4	244.6	236.7	240.1	253.2	255.4	267.7	281.2	298.5
Virgin Islands	11.3	11.9	12.8	13.5	13.4	13.9	13.5	14.0	13.8	13.5	13.1	12.8	13.2

See footnotes at end of table.

Table 2-17. Employees on Government Payrolls by State, 1963–2001—*Continued*

(Thousands of persons.)

State	1989	1990	1991	1992	1993	1994	1995	1996	1997	1998	1999	2000	2001
Alabama	317.9	326.7	332.6	337.9	340.7	346.0	343.2	342.9	346.2	347.1	350.7	351.7	352.2
Alaska	68.7	71.0	71.6	73.3	74.6	73.9	72.8	73.1	73.2	73.7	73.6	74.5	[2]78.5
Arizona	246.4	258.9	271.1	276.7	[1]286.6	294.3	[1]310.5	317.9	328.2	341.5	354.1	366.7	376.6
Arkansas	154.2	159.3	163.2	167.1	169.8	173.0	177.1	180.3	183.4	185.2	187.4	190.7	193.5
California	1 998.7	2 074.8	2 090.6	2 095.6	2 080.6	2 093.2	2 107.0	2 113.3	2 140.7	2 166.1	2 239.3	2 318.1	2 383.0
Colorado	271.4	276.8	283.3	291.1	296.7	299.3	303.7	308.7	315.6	322.3	328.3	337.0	344.9
Connecticut	207.7	210.4	207.6	207.4	210.7	217.2	220.9	222.8	225.7	227.8	235.1	241.8	244.1
Delaware	47.1	47.9	48.0	48.6	49.7	50.4	50.8	52.4	53.2	54.4	55.1	56.6	56.9
DC	276.8	277.3	281.2	285.8	285.3	270.5	254.9	240.5	233.2	225.8	222.5	224.0	222.4
Florida	800.1	846.7	859.3	870.1	881.6	910.6	918.4	928.4	942.2	954.8	965.6	1 001.7	1 028.5
Georgia	512.2	531.9	536.6	537.1	548.1	564.0	570.3	569.5	577.3	586.0	587.7	597.2	604.6
Hawaii	85.0	88.1	89.9	90.9	90.4	90.2	89.8	89.0	89.7	90.1	90.5	91.7	91.8
Idaho	77.9	81.3	84.3	88.1	90.4	92.9	95.7	97.0	100.0	102.6	105.2	108.8	110.4
Illinois	744.4	766.0	770.6	773.9	774.4	786.0	798.7	809.4	808.3	816.1	825.6	839.6	843.9
Indiana	366.6	378.6	379.9	387.6	391.3	390.7	391.7	391.0	392.0	399.2	402.6	410.3	409.1
Iowa	216.7	219.0	220.6	221.0	222.5	226.9	230.3	232.9	234.6	236.2	239.4	243.3	245.6
Kansas	209.1	214.4	219.0	225.7	229.5	233.4	236.7	233.5	235.5	239.8	239.6	244.9	248.5
Kentucky	253.3	260.2	267.3	273.3	276.6	280.6	286.9	288.8	290.9	294.7	301.1	305.1	310.4
Louisiana	315.7	326.2	332.3	339.5	342.0	351.5	358.3	361.8	364.2	367.3	370.3	373.5	377.6
Maine	94.1	95.8	95.9	95.7	95.4	94.1	93.2	92.8	93.0	94.6	96.7	99.6	101.8
Maryland	411.3	419.3	416.3	414.8	417.4	420.1	421.8	420.6	420.8	431.8	439.0	445.0	452.3
Massachusetts	408.8	402.2	389.9	382.6	387.5	390.0	395.1	400.0	404.6	411.6	417.4	424.5	428.7
Michigan	623.2	633.9	635.8	639.0	639.4	638.9	640.9	643.8	647.4	656.0	667.6	681.6	686.8
Minnesota	328.7	337.7	341.8	346.1	352.1	359.5	377.9	379.5	379.6	381.3	387.4	398.4	400.6
Mississippi	199.8	203.4	203.9	207.9	210.1	213.7	214.7	216.8	219.0	223.4	227.0	233.8	239.1
Missouri	359.3	369.7	370.7	370.7	376.8	384.9	390.0	400.8	412.8	414.1	421.3	426.2	428.0
Montana	70.3	71.4	71.9	74.2	74.1	76.3	76.9	77.0	77.4	78.6	78.8	80.3	84.0
Nebraska	139.7	143.4	145.6	147.6	149.0	151.6	150.8	151.4	152.2	150.9	151.4	154.4	156.0
Nevada	70.8	75.6	81.3	86.0	88.6	92.3	96.5	101.2	106.5	111.8	117.4	121.7	126.8
New Hampshire	71.2	72.7	72.4	73.1	74.4	76.2	76.2	77.9	78.8	79.8	81.5	83.5	84.2
New Jersey	564.2	576.7	571.6	571.9	570.7	573.4	573.4	570.6	570.3	571.7	577.6	588.9	600.7
New Mexico	144.9	149.7	152.3	156.1	159.1	163.1	166.5	171.5	177.0	178.5	180.2	183.1	185.8
New York	1 447.6	1 473.4	1 445.1	1 428.0	1 433.3	1 436.0	1 416.4	1 400.6	1 406.9	1 424.0	1 445.3	1 467.7	1 472.5
North Carolina	477.2	492.0	501.7	502.5	527.1	538.6	550.6	561.4	576.3	593.6	604.2	622.2	623.5
North Dakota	65.6	65.4	65.7	66.8	67.1	67.2	71.1	70.8	70.8	71.1	71.8	73.1	73.6
Ohio	706.4	722.2	727.9	735.1	735.6	741.0	748.7	752.3	757.9	763.4	772.2	785.1	793.8
Oklahoma	257.2	261.9	264.9	270.1	269.8	270.2	269.7	271.4	276.2	278.2	282.6	287.7	295.6
Oregon	215.6	223.5	226.4	231.0	232.6	234.7	240.2	246.6	249.5	255.3	261.3	267.3	269.2
Pennsylvania	697.9	706.3	701.9	699.9	709.0	713.6	719.2	719.8	711.8	706.0	710.1	725.1	729.8
Rhode Island	59.1	62.5	60.9	61.2	61.4	61.7	61.3	61.3	63.2	62.9	63.3	64.4	64.5
South Carolina	273.1	282.2	285.7	291.9	295.8	295.3	294.2	294.6	298.9	309.5	315.3	322.9	320.2
South Dakota	61.6	62.7	63.4	65.4	66.6	67.1	71.0	70.4	70.5	71.0	71.8	70.3	[1]73.2
Tennessee	344.3	351.4	353.2	356.9	362.0	370.7	373.1	381.6	380.3	385.5	390.1	399.0	402.2
Texas	1 206.6	1 263.4	1 287.5	1 334.3	1 376.0	1 413.7	1 445.7	1 457.7	1 483.3	1 504.2	1 534.8	1 561.9	1 584.0
Utah	146.3	150.5	153.9	156.9	159.5	161.4	163.6	166.8	172.3	176.7	179.5	185.4	190.0
Vermont	42.0	43.5	43.8	43.7	44.0	44.7	45.1	45.4	45.7	46.2	47.6	49.4	50.0
Virginia	562.6	578.4	580.5	589.4	597.8	603.2	597.6	596.2	596.6	602.0	611.3	624.7	630.5
Washington	379.9	397.6	411.6	423.6	430.0	437.2	444.4	450.6	458.0	465.9	474.3	483.3	505.7
West Virginia	125.9	127.4	127.7	132.3	132.8	136.5	136.4	138.7	139.1	140.8	140.9	143.1	141.0
Wisconsin	335.0	342.9	346.4	356.9	361.5	367.1	378.7	383.5	386.7	393.2	398.8	405.6	413.8
Wyoming	54.3	55.3	55.8	56.8	57.2	58.2	57.8	58.1	58.1	58.5	59.4	60.8	61.8
Puerto Rico	298.1	294.6	290.6	295.8	289.9	300.1	304.6	316.5	310.1	307.5	291.3	286.2	276.4
Virgin Islands	13.6	13.6	13.4	13.9	13.9	13.8	13.6	14.1	13.7	13.8	13.4	13.1	12.3

1. Data not continuous.
2. Industry coding redefinition.

Table 2-18. Average Weekly Hours of Production Workers on Manufacturing Payrolls by State, 1973–2001

(Thousands of persons.)

State	1973	1974	1975	1976	1977	1978	1979	1980	1981	1982	1983	1984	1985	1986
Alabama	41.0	40.5	39.5	40.6	40.5	40.6	40.7	40.1	39.9	38.5	40.7	41.0	40.8	41.1
Alaska	36.6	40.5	36.6	40.5	43.3	42.4	43.9	42.7	40.0	38.6	36.2	39.3	[1]40.7	41.1
Arizona	39.8	39.2	39.0	39.5	40.1	40.3	40.6	40.1	39.6	38.9	40.5	40.8	[1]40.9	41.0
Arkansas	39.9	39.2	38.8	39.6	39.7	39.3	39.6	39.3	39.4	38.6	40.1	40.5	40.2	40.4
California	40.3	39.7	39.4	39.7	40.1	40.1	39.9	39.5	39.6	39.2	40.0	40.3	40.2	40.3
Colorado	...	...	...	...	39.4	39.3	39.5	39.8	39.8	39.2	[1]39.9	40.9	40.2	39.9
Connecticut	42.1	41.4	40.5	40.8	41.5	42.0	42.0	41.8	41.6	40.5	41.3	42.5	41.9	41.8
Delaware	40.3	39.4	39.3	40.0	39.6	40.0	39.5	40.5	40.3	39.2	40.6	41.5	41.1	41.3
Florida	41.0	40.2	40.0	40.4	40.7	40.9	40.5	40.8	40.6	39.9	40.7	41.2	41.3	40.8
Georgia	40.5	39.8	39.5	40.1	40.5	40.1	40.4	40.2	40.1	38.6	41.1	41.0	40.6	40.9
Hawaii	39.9	39.4	39.1	39.0	38.0	38.6	38.3	37.8	38.5	37.9	38.6	38.1	37.4	38.9
Idaho	38.8	39.0	38.8	38.7	39.3	38.8	38.3	37.1	37.8	36.7	37.4	37.6	37.8	38.2
Illinois	41.2	40.4	39.7	40.4	40.6	40.1	40.7	39.8	40.0	39.2	40.6	40.6	40.6	40.9
Indiana	...	...	...	...	...	...	...	...	...	...	...	...	...	...
Iowa	...	...	...	39.9	40.1	40.1	40.5	39.6	39.5	38.7	39.8	40.2	40.2	40.6
Kansas	...	...	...	...	...	...	40.7	40.4	40.4	39.2	39.1	40.1	39.5	40.3
Kentucky	40.3	39.6	38.7	39.4	39.5	39.6	39.4	39.1	39.3	38.4	39.2	39.2	38.9	39.2
Louisiana	41.4	40.1	42.8	41.3	41.8	41.6	41.3	41.2	42.2	41.0	40.0	41.6	41.7	41.8
Maine	40.8	40.3	39.9	39.9	39.8	40.2	40.1	40.0	40.4	40.0	39.9	39.9	40.0	40.6
Maryland	40.5	39.9	39.1	39.6	39.9	39.9	40.0	39.6	39.9	39.2	40.0	41.0	40.3	40.5
Massachusetts	40.5	39.9	39.1	39.7	39.9	40.2	40.1	39.6	40.0	39.2	39.9	40.1	40.7	41.3
Michigan	...	...	...	42.7	43.3	43.0	41.2	40.1	40.5	40.2	42.5	43.2	43.1	42.6
Minnesota	41.0	39.9	39.2	39.8	40.0	40.2	40.0	39.4	39.4	39.1	39.7	40.3	40.3	40.6
Mississippi	40.3	39.3	39.3	40.0	40.1	39.9	39.6	39.3	39.3	38.1	40.1	40.6	40.6	40.2
Missouri	39.8	39.3	39.0	39.8	40.2	40.0	39.5	39.2	39.2	38.6	39.9	40.5	40.2	40.5
Montana	39.3	38.8	38.0	39.8	41.8	42.7	42.9	43.2	41.0	39.3	39.7	39.2	39.1	39.4
Nebraska	41.8	41.2	40.5	41.1	40.8	41.1	41.3	40.6	40.3	39.9	40.3	40.5	40.3	40.4
Nevada	40.0	38.8	38.2	38.9	38.8	38.5	38.5	38.2	38.6	37.3	38.8	39.8	40.4	40.2
New Hampshire	39.8	39.3	39.1	39.6	40.0	40.3	40.1	[1]39.8	39.9	39.6	40.5	41.0	40.7	41.2
New Jersey	41.4	40.7	39.9	40.4	41.1	40.8	41.2	40.7	40.6	39.9	40.6	41.1	40.8	41.2
New Mexico	39.4	38.4	39.0	39.5	38.8	39.2	39.5	39.8	39.5	39.2	39.7	39.9	39.8	39.5
New York	39.9	39.4	38.9	39.4	39.6	39.8	39.6	39.4	39.4	38.8	39.3	39.8	39.8	39.9
North Carolina	40.1	39.1	38.4	39.4	39.6	39.8	39.6	39.3	39.1	37.3	40.0	39.9	39.6	40.7
North Dakota	40.4	40.2	39.9	39.1	38.6	39.7	39.1	37.5	38.1	37.6	38.0	38.4	38.6	38.2
Ohio	42.3	41.2	40.3	41.4	42.0	42.1	41.5	40.6	40.9	40.1	41.4	42.3	42.0	42.1
Oklahoma	40.6	40.5	40.0	40.3	40.4	40.2	40.5	40.1	40.1	39.5	40.5	41.6	41.3	41.3
Oregon	39.3	38.8	38.4	38.9	38.6	39.0	38.5	38.1	37.5	37.9	38.9	39.2	38.7	39.0
Pennsylvania	40.2	39.6	38.8	39.2	[1]39.5	40.0	39.9	38.8	39.2	38.4	39.2	40.2	39.9	40.2
Rhode Island	39.3	39.2	38.9	39.5	39.1	38.9	39.1	39.3	39.3	38.6	39.0	40.6	40.2	40.4
South Carolina	40.5	39.8	39.4	40.4	40.6	40.8	40.8	40.3	40.4	38.2	40.6	40.8	40.4	41.1
South Dakota	42.6	41.7	40.7	39.9	39.3	41.7	41.9	40.9	41.6	41.1	41.6	42.1	41.8	42.1
Tennessee	40.4	39.9	39.8	40.3	40.2	39.6	39.7	39.7	39.9	38.6	40.5	40.9	41.0	41.2
Texas	...	...	...	40.9	41.1	41.3	41.1	41.2	41.3	40.0	40.9	41.7	41.2	41.4
Utah	38.8	38.7	38.1	39.2	40.0	39.5	39.0	39.1	39.7	38.5	39.4	39.9	40.1	40.0
Vermont	41.5	41.1	40.4	41.0	40.8	41.0	40.8	40.6	40.0	39.0	40.0	40.6	40.7	40.7
Virginia	40.6	39.8	39.2	39.9	39.9	39.8	39.7	39.3	39.7	38.4	39.7	40.3	40.1	40.4
Washington	39.2	38.9	38.7	39.1	39.2	39.3	38.6	38.4	38.8	38.5	38.9	38.8	39.0	39.4
West Virginia	40.0	39.6	39.0	39.2	39.5	39.6	39.6	39.2	39.4	38.8	39.6	40.3	39.9	40.3
Wisconsin	41.4	41.1	40.4	40.6	40.6	41.0	40.9	40.2	40.1	39.6	40.7	41.1	41.1	41.3
Wyoming	38.6	38.0	38.6	40.2	39.8	38.6	37.6	38.9	40.0	38.2	36.9	39.5	40.9	39.0
Puerto Rico	...	...	...	...	...	...	...	38.0	38.2	37.5	38.7	38.7	38.5	39.0
Virgin Islands	...	...	...	...	...	40.9	40.9	41.1	42.3	42.3	41.4	42.7	41.7	41.9

See footnote at end of table.

Table 2-18. Average Weekly Hours of Production Workers on Manufacturing Payrolls by State, 1973–2001—*Continued*

(Thousands of persons.)

State	1987	1988	1989	1990	1991	1992	1993	1994	1995	1996	1997	1998	1999	2000	2001
Alabama	41.4	41.4	41.2	41.0	40.8	41.2	41.2	41.9	41.6	41.7	41.9	42.2	42.1	41.9	40.9
Alaska	42.7	[1]42.1	44.4	44.9	46.4	45.5	45.0	47.4	47.8	46.5	46.7	49.9	45.3	44.5	42.1
Arizona	40.6	41.1	41.2	40.7	40.7	40.8	40.7	42.3	42.5	42.8	41.4	40.4	40.4	40.4	40.0
Arkansas	41.0	40.9	40.8	41.0	41.2	41.4	41.4	41.8	41.0	41.5	41.4	41.7	41.7	41.7	39.7
California	40.3	40.7	40.7	40.6	40.6	40.6	40.9	41.4	41.2	41.5	41.9	41.8	41.7	41.7	41.0
Colorado	40.2	40.4	40.2	41.2	40.4	40.5	41.2	41.3	41.0	41.2	41.8	41.5	41.5	39.8	38.7
Connecticut	42.1	42.2	42.2	42.0	41.8	41.7	42.1	42.8	42.8	42.5	42.6	42.7	42.4	42.6	42.5
Delaware	40.7	40.0	41.5	41.3	40.8	40.8	42.1	42.8	41.0	40.5	41.9	42.3	43.0	43.3	42.1
Florida	40.8	40.7	40.9	40.7	40.7	40.9	41.2	41.4	41.4	41.5	41.8	41.7	41.8	41.9	41.8
Georgia	41.6	41.4	41.1	40.9	41.0	41.4	41.7	42.4	42.3	42.3	42.4	41.8	41.9	41.4	40.5
Hawaii	39.4	40.0	40.0	40.3	39.8	40.0	39.8	38.3	37.5	38.1	37.9	37.3	39.3	38.3	37.2
Idaho	38.1	38.1	38.9	38.9	39.1	39.2	40.1	40.0	39.3	39.5	40.1	38.3	39.4	39.2	38.0
Illinois	41.6	42.3	41.9	41.4	41.2	41.0	41.5	41.9	41.7	41.7	42.2	41.8	41.9	41.2	40.4
Indiana	...	...	41.6	41.3	41.2	42.0	42.7	43.3	42.2	42.8	43.2	42.9	42.9	42.1	40.8
Iowa	41.3	41.4	40.8	40.5	40.5	41.3	41.6	42.4	41.9	42.0	42.6	41.9	41.4	41.6	41.5
Kansas	40.8	40.7	40.2	40.3	40.3	40.9	41.6	41.6	41.1	42.4	42.3	41.9	41.1	40.6	39.8
Kentucky	40.5	40.5	40.0	40.1	40.3	40.3	40.5	41.3	41.3	41.1	41.8	41.5	41.7	42.1	41.3
Louisiana	41.8	42.5	42.6	42.9	42.7	42.6	42.5	43.4	43.2	44.2	44.1	44.0	43.3	42.8	42.2
Maine	41.5	41.0	40.2	40.1	40.0	40.2	40.8	40.6	39.8	39.9	40.6	40.6	40.8	41.3	40.7
Maryland	40.8	41.5	41.1	40.8	40.6	40.8	41.1	41.5	41.5	41.0	41.4	41.6	41.4	40.7	40.4
Massachusetts	41.0	40.7	40.7	40.7	41.0	41.0	41.3	41.6	41.7	41.8	42.3	42.0	42.0	41.9	40.9
Michigan	42.2	43.3	42.9	41.8	41.5	41.8	43.1	44.9	44.3	43.9	44.1	43.3	44.2	43.7	41.5
Minnesota	40.9	40.8	40.5	40.3	40.4	40.8	41.1	41.6	41.5	41.4	41.5	41.3	41.2	40.8	39.8
Mississippi	40.3	40.3	40.0	39.4	39.7	40.3	41.0	41.7	41.0	41.3	41.5	41.4	41.3	40.7	39.6
Missouri	40.6	40.8	40.7	40.7	40.4	40.6	41.4	42.0	41.3	41.5	41.6	41.5	41.5	41.3	40.6
Montana	38.6	38.7	39.2	39.0	39.1	38.9	38.6	39.3	39.4	39.1	39.9	39.3	39.0	38.5	38.9
Nebraska	40.5	41.1	40.7	40.8	40.4	41.1	41.5	42.1	41.5	41.6	41.3	41.9	41.9	41.4	40.3
Nevada	40.3	39.7	40.9	40.7	40.6	40.7	41.4	41.1	41.4	41.6	42.9	42.0	41.3	42.4	42.5
New Hampshire	41.2	40.7	41.2	40.8	41.2	41.6	42.1	42.3	41.6	41.8	42.0	41.3	40.6	41.1	41.1
New Jersey	41.2	41.0	41.0	41.4	41.4	41.5	41.5	41.8	41.8	41.8	42.0	41.8	41.7	42.0	41.3
New Mexico	39.7	40.5	40.0	40.7	40.1	40.0	40.9	40.9	39.9	40.2	39.8	38.6	39.0	38.0	38.7
New York	39.9	39.9	40.0	39.6	39.8	40.0	40.4	41.0	40.9	40.8	41.2	41.1	41.2	41.1	40.2
North Carolina	41.2	40.5	40.3	39.9	40.1	40.7	40.8	41.1	40.6	40.4	41.2	41.1	41.0	41.4	39.6
North Dakota	38.7	38.7	39.8	39.8	39.8	40.4	41.2	42.3	40.7	42.2	40.5	39.9	40.0	40.1	39.4
Ohio	42.6	43.0	42.7	42.4	42.2	42.2	43.0	43.9	43.4	43.3	43.6	42.9	42.9	42.9	41.7
Oklahoma	41.2	41.1	41.6	41.1	41.0	41.2	41.9	43.1	41.9	42.0	42.4	41.5	41.3	40.9	38.3
Oregon	39.2	39.3	39.4	39.3	39.4	39.5	39.5	40.4	40.1	40.2	40.9	40.7	40.4	40.0	39.8
Pennsylvania	40.9	41.1	41.0	40.7	40.4	40.8	41.2	41.6	41.3	[1]41.2	42.0	41.9	41.8	42.2	41.3
Rhode Island	40.0	39.7	39.3	39.7	40.0	40.1	39.8	40.3	40.5	40.0	40.9	40.6	39.9	40.4	40.2
South Carolina	41.7	41.1	41.3	41.0	41.3	41.7	41.6	41.8	41.9	41.8	42.2	42.6	42.6	42.5	41.8
South Dakota	41.7	42.5	41.8	40.6	41.2	41.2	41.3	42.0	41.8	41.5	41.9	42.6	42.9	43.1	41.6
Tennessee	41.6	41.6	40.8	38.6	39.6	40.3	40.8	40.9	40.4	40.6	41.2	40.5	40.6	40.2	39.2
Texas	41.6	41.7	41.8	41.8	42.1	42.5	42.8	43.1	42.8	43.0	43.5	43.7	43.5	43.3	42.7
Utah	39.5	40.3	40.0	39.8	39.9	40.3	39.6	40.6	39.8	40.3	40.2	40.4	40.0	39.8	39.2
Vermont	40.6	40.4	40.9	40.8	40.8	41.0	41.5	40.9	40.5	40.5	40.7	39.6	39.5	40.3	39.6
Virginia	41.1	40.8	40.9	40.4	40.5	41.0	41.0	41.7	41.6	41.5	42.2	42.3	42.4	42.3	41.6
Washington	39.9	40.1	39.4	40.6	39.9	40.0	40.2	40.5	40.8	40.8	40.6	40.8	40.9	40.7	40.1
West Virginia	40.6	40.6	40.7	40.7	40.6	40.6	40.9	41.3	41.8	41.2	41.7	41.6	41.6	41.5	40.7
Wisconsin	41.4	41.8	41.5	41.4	41.4	41.8	42.0	42.7	42.1	42.2	42.4	41.8	41.9	41.5	40.7
Wyoming	38.8	[1]38.5	39.8	39.9	38.6	38.6	38.9	40.0	39.4	40.1	40.3	40.4	39.3	38.6	38.4
Puerto Rico	38.9	39.1	39.5	39.1	39.0	39.6	39.5	39.9	39.6	38.6	39.6	40.0	41.0	40.6	40.4
Virgin Islands	42.2	40.4	41.7	42.4	41.4	42.0	43.5	42.7	41.7	41.5	42.7	40.1	43.8	44.0	42.0

1. Data not continuous.

Table 2-19. Average Hourly Earnings of Production Workers on Manufacturing Payrolls by State, 1973–2001

(Dollars.)

State	1973	1974	1975	1976	1977	1978	1979	1980	1981	1982	1983	1984	1985	1986
Alabama	3.42	3.73	4.10	4.46	4.89	5.40	5.95	6.49	7.01	7.33	7.58	7.97	8.48	8.64
Alaska	5.97	7.10	8.09	7.82	9.12	8.86	9.14	10.22	11.42	11.74	12.33	12.25	[1]12.19	11.62
Arizona	4.03	4.40	4.85	5.19	5.55	6.03	6.62	7.29	8.02	8.73	8.99	9.09	[1]9.48	9.88
Arkansas	2.99	3.30	3.69	3.91	4.30	4.72	5.19	5.71	6.26	6.69	7.05	7.31	7.57	7.76
California	4.44	4.76	5.22	5.59	6.00	6.43	7.03	7.70	8.56	9.24	9.52	9.77	10.12	10.36
Colorado	...	...	...	...	5.80	6.21	6.93	7.63	8.28	8.63	[1]8.97	9.24	9.52	9.82
Connecticut	4.14	4.42	4.78	5.12	5.56	5.96	6.43	7.08	7.67	8.23	8.76	9.22	9.57	10.07
Delaware	4.29	4.62	5.02	5.51	5.94	6.58	7.04	7.58	8.28	8.64	9.19	9.28	9.86	10.05
Florida	3.45	3.76	4.11	4.36	4.63	5.07	5.48	5.98	6.53	7.02	7.33	7.62	7.86	8.02
Georgia	3.25	3.50	3.80	4.10	4.46	4.88	5.30	5.77	6.37	6.75	7.13	7.58	8.10	8.35
Hawaii	3.93	4.24	4.68	5.14	5.51	5.90	6.38	6.83	7.53	7.97	8.23	8.35	8.65	8.86
Idaho	4.05	4.41	4.77	5.29	5.82	6.53	6.92	7.55	8.23	8.62	8.98	9.34	9.41	9.66
Illinois	4.57	4.97	5.53	5.85	6.28	6.76	7.30	8.02	8.91	9.31	9.70	10.08	10.37	10.67
Indiana	...	...	...	...	...	...	...	...	...	...	...	...	...	...
Iowa	...	...	...	5.85	6.43	7.02	7.75	8.67	9.60	10.01	10.09	10.24	10.32	10.35
Kansas	...	...	...	...	...	...	6.71	7.37	8.05	8.80	9.23	9.38	9.45	9.76
Kentucky	4.00	4.36	4.77	5.15	5.69	6.26	6.77	7.34	7.86	8.38	8.79	9.28	9.53	9.86
Louisiana	3.98	4.40	4.88	5.33	5.75	6.42	6.97	7.74	8.58	9.38	9.79	10.06	10.43	10.60
Maine	3.23	3.51	3.81	4.16	4.52	4.91	5.42	6.00	6.66	7.22	7.61	8.05	8.40	8.65
Maryland	4.22	4.62	5.04	5.52	6.05	6.46	7.09	7.61	8.39	8.78	9.02	9.45	9.73	9.91
Massachusetts	3.89	4.16	4.48	4.79	5.13	5.54	5.98	6.51	7.01	7.58	8.01	8.50	9.00	9.24
Michigan	...	...	...	6.81	7.54	8.13	8.73	9.52	10.53	11.18	11.62	12.18	12.64	12.80
Minnesota	4.22	4.67	5.10	5.53	5.97	6.44	6.93	7.61	8.40	9.11	9.56	9.75	10.05	10.20
Mississippi	2.95	3.19	3.58	3.83	4.15	4.56	4.95	5.44	6.01	6.41	6.70	6.95	7.22	7.46
Missouri	4.05	4.39	4.80	5.20	5.75	6.21	6.70	7.26	7.90	8.46	8.89	9.31	9.57	9.83
Montana	4.53	5.05	5.53	5.93	6.53	7.81	8.44	8.78	9.09	9.86	10.44	10.76	10.95	10.94
Nebraska	3.75	4.15	4.63	4.93	5.39	5.83	6.53	7.38	8.01	8.47	8.76	8.93	9.02	9.26
Nevada	4.71	4.89	5.26	5.61	6.10	6.54	6.95	7.72	8.42	8.80	9.02	9.12	9.15	9.36
New Hampshire	3.39	3.65	3.97	4.26	4.56	4.94	5.37	[1]5.87	6.41	6.94	7.42	7.86	8.39	8.77
New Jersey	4.26	4.57	4.99	5.33	5.82	6.28	6.71	7.31	8.05	8.66	9.11	9.50	9.86	10.12
New Mexico	3.08	3.31	3.63	4.07	4.43	4.79	5.36	5.79	6.54	7.22	7.60	7.97	8.41	8.75
New York	4.20	4.53	4.91	5.27	5.67	6.08	6.57	7.18	7.84	8.35	8.84	9.22	9.67	9.92
North Carolina	2.99	3.28	3.52	3.79	4.10	4.47	4.87	5.37	5.94	6.35	6.68	7.01	7.29	7.54
North Dakota	3.55	3.83	4.31	4.75	5.19	5.55	5.98	6.56	7.12	7.50	7.73	7.86	8.05	8.19
Ohio	4.76	5.13	5.57	6.10	6.74	7.29	7.84	8.57	9.53	10.07	10.56	10.96	11.38	11.56
Oklahoma	3.69	4.01	4.45	4.83	5.31	5.81	6.53	7.36	8.20	8.69	9.21	9.64	9.86	9.80
Oregon	4.60	5.01	5.53	6.07	6.67	7.23	7.92	8.65	9.47	10.02	10.25	10.44	10.50	10.57
Pennsylvania	4.16	4.57	4.98	5.36	[1]5.85	6.37	6.97	7.59	8.30	8.63	8.95	9.28	9.57	9.74
Rhode Island	3.37	3.62	3.84	4.15	4.39	4.71	5.10	5.59	6.10	6.61	6.92	7.33	7.59	7.90
South Carolina	3.03	3.32	3.59	3.91	4.28	4.66	5.10	5.59	6.18	6.68	7.03	7.28	7.61	7.92
South Dakota	3.37	3.77	4.21	4.51	4.84	5.19	5.70	6.50	7.12	7.36	7.31	7.14	7.43	7.75
Tennessee	3.29	3.62	3.93	4.24	4.68	5.13	5.56	6.08	6.72	7.16	7.49	7.93	8.29	8.58
Texas	5.42	5.88	6.46	7.15	7.95	8.60	8.88	9.04	9.41	9.65	9.85	9.97	10.25	10.47
Utah	3.83	4.19	4.61	4.89	5.18	5.68	6.29	7.02	7.74	8.40	8.69	8.92	9.64	9.98
Vermont	3.50	3.78	4.07	4.40	4.70	5.10	5.53	6.14	6.79	7.35	7.66	8.03	8.41	8.83
Virginia	3.34	3.65	3.99	4.30	4.69	5.11	5.58	6.22	6.84	7.37	7.79	8.10	8.51	8.83
Washington	4.83	5.24	5.82	6.36	6.83	7.56	8.39	9.41	10.44	11.23	11.42	11.57	11.63	11.65
West Virginia	4.14	4.53	4.93	5.42	6.06	6.68	7.41	8.08	8.80	9.40	9.74	9.93	10.24	10.38
Wisconsin	4.45	4.81	5.26	5.69	6.16	6.69	7.27	8.03	8.80	9.37	9.78	10.03	10.26	10.35
Wyoming	4.03	4.52	4.92	5.43	5.70	6.18	6.68	7.01	7.89	8.62	8.73	9.14	9.64	9.68
Puerto Rico	...	...	...	...	...	...	...	4.02	4.39	4.64	4.83	5.02	5.19	5.31
Virgin Islands	...	...	...	...	...	6.12	6.70	7.18	8.50	9.76	10.03	9.51	9.44	9.60

See footnote at end of table.

Table 2-19. Average Hourly Earnings of Production Workers on Manufacturing Payrolls by State, 1973–2001—*Continued*

(Dollars.)

State	1987	1988	1989	1990	1991	1992	1993	1994	1995	1996	1997	1998	1999	2000	2001
Alabama	8.76	8.95	9.10	9.39	9.72	9.99	10.35	10.75	11.14	11.55	11.86	12.11	12.54	12.96	13.30
Alaska	11.79	[1]11.98	12.01	12.46	11.40	10.75	11.14	10.96	11.00	11.14	11.78	11.09	12.16	12.46	13.27
Arizona	9.97	9.85	9.92	10.21	10.70	10.96	11.06	11.17	11.16	11.49	11.67	12.17	12.70	12.78	13.18
Arkansas	7.88	8.07	8.26	8.51	8.81	9.05	9.36	9.65	10.05	10.41	10.78	11.12	11.55	11.97	12.39
California	10.75	10.80	11.16	11.48	11.87	12.19	12.38	12.44	12.55	12.84	13.24	13.66	13.95	14.26	14.72
Colorado	10.05	10.38	10.44	10.94	11.33	11.32	12.01	12.26	12.51	12.83	13.31	13.74	14.19	14.82	15.37
Connecticut	10.46	10.78	11.21	11.53	11.99	12.46	13.01	13.53	13.71	14.01	14.46	14.83	15.33	15.70	16.07
Delaware	10.67	[1]11.49	12.36	12.39	12.20	12.35	13.29	13.92	14.20	14.02	14.81	15.36	15.91	16.53	16.63
Florida	8.16	8.39	8.67	8.98	9.30	9.59	9.76	9.97	10.18	10.55	10.95	11.43	11.83	12.28	12.78
Georgia	8.49	8.65	8.87	9.17	9.56	9.86	10.09	10.34	10.71	11.19	11.64	12.03	12.48	12.99	13.05
Hawaii	9.30	9.84	10.37	10.99	11.39	11.61	11.98	12.22	12.82	12.79	13.11	13.16	13.49	13.59	14.19
Idaho	9.75	10.00	10.21	10.11	11.42	11.88	11.88	11.46	12.15	12.46	12.80	13.42	14.17	15.28
Illinois	10.85	10.98	11.21	11.44	11.68	11.84	12.04	12.25	12.64	13.03	13.35	13.75	14.05	14.36	14.55
Indiana	...	...	11.70	12.03	12.43	12.79	13.17	13.55	13.91	14.33	14.79	14.97	15.26	15.83	16.20
Iowa	10.62	10.56	10.82	11.27	11.62	11.92	12.22	12.45	12.73	13.13	13.57	13.91	14.20	14.66	14.92
Kansas	9.97	10.24	10.68	10.94	11.24	11.60	11.99	12.15	12.39	12.88	13.45	13.84	14.44	14.98	15.30
Kentucky	10.02	10.16	10.37	10.70	11.00	11.28	11.47	11.81	12.22	12.70	13.17	13.82	14.27	14.83	15.34
Louisiana	10.90	10.94	11.13	11.61	11.86	12.19	12.66	13.11	13.43	13.65	14.14	14.63	15.18	15.56	15.90
Maine	8.77	9.31	9.92	10.59	11.08	11.40	11.63	11.91	12.39	12.71	13.12	13.49	13.94	14.28	15.17
Maryland	10.11	10.71	11.19	11.57	11.92	12.50	12.83	13.15	13.49	13.73	14.14	14.31	14.62	14.98	15.35
Massachusetts	9.77	10.40	10.87	11.39	11.81	12.15	12.36	12.59	12.79	13.05	13.42	13.80	14.24	14.66	15.31
Michigan	12.97	13.31	13.51	13.86	14.52	14.81	15.36	16.13	16.31	16.67	17.18	17.61	18.38	19.26	19.71
Minnesota	10.37	10.59	10.95	11.21	11.52	11.92	12.23	12.58	12.79	13.16	13.63	13.92	14.34	14.99	15.36
Mississippi	7.59	7.83	8.03	8.37	8.67	8.91	9.16	9.41	9.76	10.18	10.41	10.73	11.17	11.64	12.14
Missouri	10.00	10.24	10.49	10.74	10.86	11.24	11.55	11.77	12.17	12.57	12.98	13.38	13.93	14.34	14.81
Montana	10.61	10.68	11.15	11.51	11.57	12.18	12.40	12.49	12.94	13.00	13.29	13.76	14.17	14.34	14.68
Nebraska	9.33	9.38	9.53	9.66	9.84	10.22	10.46	10.94	11.19	11.51	12.10	12.32	12.77	12.94	13.39
Nevada	9.76	10.08	10.33	11.05	11.04	11.55	11.65	11.83	12.62	13.59	14.17	14.42	13.92	13.85	14.11
New Hampshire	9.29	9.97	10.37	10.83	10.84	11.22	11.62	11.74	11.94	12.23	12.55	12.79	13.17	13.39	13.77
New Jersey	10.40	10.86	11.17	11.76	12.17	12.57	12.98	13.36	13.56	13.85	14.24	14.58	15.11	15.47	15.88
New Mexico	8.74	8.87	8.74	9.04	9.40	9.68	9.74	10.13	10.68	10.99	11.74	12.47	12.53	13.26	14.09
New York	10.09	10.43	10.67	11.11	11.43	11.72	11.97	12.19	12.50	12.78	13.19	13.47	13.87	14.24	14.76
North Carolina	7.84	8.12	8.42	8.79	9.19	9.49	9.81	10.19	10.56	10.97	11.41	11.84	12.32	12.80	13.29
North Dakota	8.43	8.36	8.80	9.27	9.25	9.60	9.86	10.19	10.75	10.95	11.29	11.40	11.94	12.64	12.69
Ohio	11.73	12.00	12.26	12.64	13.12	13.49	14.05	14.40	14.42	14.70	15.30	15.79	16.26	16.71	17.13
Oklahoma	10.14	10.35	10.48	10.73	11.09	11.38	11.42	11.42	11.52	11.78	12.36	12.61	12.70	13.17	12.95
Oregon	10.56	10.60	10.81	11.15	11.53	11.97	12.18	12.31	12.75	13.01	13.39	14.07	14.61	15.08	15.72
Pennsylvania	9.98	10.33	10.66	11.04	11.46	11.78	12.11	12.49	12.81	[1]13.40	13.78	14.06	14.19	14.60	14.85
Rhode Island	8.20	8.64	9.06	9.45	9.73	9.92	10.20	10.35	10.62	10.95	11.31	11.61	11.98	12.17	12.20
South Carolina	8.10	8.30	8.54	8.84	9.17	9.48	9.80	10.00	10.16	10.25	10.35	10.52	10.67	10.97	11.19
South Dakota	7.92	8.09	8.30	8.48	8.79	8.84	8.89	9.19	9.36	9.59	9.96	10.22	10.58	10.70	11.45
Tennessee	8.78	8.96	9.22	9.55	9.92	10.13	10.33	10.50	10.78	11.30	11.71	12.06	12.50	12.92	13.37
Texas	10.84	10.92	11.02	11.13	11.47	11.81	12.03	12.14	12.25	12.38	12.57	...	...	...	...
Utah	9.96	10.11	10.14	10.32	10.77	11.09	11.10	11.28	11.62	12.21	12.85	13.07	13.39	13.68	13.88
Vermont	9.12	9.47	9.99	10.52	11.00	11.52	12.09	11.96	12.21	12.42	12.70	13.03	13.65	14.23	14.32
Virginia	9.14	9.37	9.69	10.07	10.43	10.62	10.85	11.24	11.72	12.19	12.51	12.90	13.37	13.82	14.28
Washington	11.73	11.90	12.12	12.61	13.13	13.59	14.01	14.86	14.73	15.16	15.76	16.14	16.75	17.59
West Virginia	10.55	10.81	11.17	11.53	11.77	12.11	12.27	12.60	12.64	12.96	13.17	13.72	14.09	14.61	14.95
Wisconsin	10.55	10.61	10.77	11.11	11.47	11.85	12.17	12.41	12.76	13.14	13.66	14.02	14.50	14.85	15.25
Wyoming	9.75	[1]10.27	10.58	10.83	10.98	11.10	11.53	11.79	11.96	13.17	14.54	14.93	15.40	16.18	16.70
Puerto Rico	5.43	5.56	5.77	6.04	6.32	6.63	6.98	7.22	7.41	7.70	7.99	8.41	8.93	9.39	9.91
Virgin Islands	9.40	9.86	10.87	11.85	12.52	13.68	14.97	15.16	15.82	17.00	18.09	18.60	18.89	21.88	20.59

1. Data not continuous.

Table 2-20. Average Weekly Earnings of Production Workers on Manufacturing Payrolls by State, 1973–2001

(Dollars.)

State	1973	1974	1975	1976	1977	1978	1979	1980	1981	1982	1983	1984	1985	1986
Alabama	140.22	151.06	161.95	181.08	198.04	219.24	242.16	260.25	279.70	282.20	308.51	326.77	345.98	355.10
Alaska	239.40	287.55	296.09	316.71	394.90	375.66	401.25	436.49	456.80	453.16	446.35	481.42	[1]496.13	477.58
Arizona	160.39	172.48	189.15	205.00	222.56	243.01	268.77	292.33	317.59	339.60	364.10	370.87	[1]387.73	405.08
Arkansas	119.30	129.36	143.17	154.84	170.71	185.50	205.52	224.40	246.64	258.23	282.71	296.06	304.31	313.50
California	178.93	188.97	205.67	221.92	240.60	257.84	280.50	304.15	338.98	362.21	380.80	393.73	406.82	417.51
Colorado	...	...	...	...	228.52	244.05	273.74	303.67	329.54	338.30	[1]357.90	377.92	382.70	391.82
Connecticut	174.29	182.99	193.59	208.90	230.74	250.32	270.06	295.94	319.07	333.32	361.79	391.85	400.98	420.93
Delaware	172.89	182.03	197.29	220.40	235.22	263.20	278.08	306.99	333.68	338.69	373.11	385.12	405.25	415.07
Florida	141.45	151.15	164.40	176.14	188.44	207.36	221.94	243.98	265.12	280.10	298.33	313.94	324.62	327.22
Georgia	131.63	139.30	150.10	164.41	180.63	195.69	214.12	231.95	255.44	260.55	293.04	310.78	328.86	341.52
Hawaii	156.81	167.06	182.99	200.46	209.38	227.74	244.35	258.17	289.90	302.06	317.68	318.14	323.51	344.65
Idaho	157.14	171.99	185.08	204.72	228.73	253.36	265.04	280.11	311.09	316.35	335.85	351.18	355.70	369.01
Illinois	187.85	200.69	219.13	236.11	254.91	271.42	296.66	319.20	356.23	364.86	393.59	409.35	421.02	436.40
Indiana	...	...	...	...	...	...	...	...	...	...	...	...	...	...
Iowa	...	...	...	233.42	257.84	281.50	313.88	343.33	379.20	387.39	401.58	411.65	414.86	420.21
Kansas	...	...	...	...	...	...	273.10	297.75	325.22	344.96	360.89	376.14	373.28	393.33
Kentucky	161.20	172.66	184.60	202.91	224.75	247.90	266.74	286.99	308.90	321.79	344.57	363.78	370.72	386.51
Louisiana	164.77	176.44	208.86	220.13	240.35	267.07	287.86	318.89	362.08	384.58	391.60	418.50	434.93	443.08
Maine	131.78	141.45	152.02	165.98	179.90	197.38	217.34	240.00	269.06	288.80	303.64	321.20	336.00	351.19
Maryland	170.91	184.34	197.06	218.59	241.40	257.75	283.60	301.36	334.76	344.18	360.80	387.45	392.12	401.36
Massachusetts	157.55	165.98	175.17	190.16	204.69	222.71	239.80	257.80	280.40	297.14	319.60	340.85	366.30	381.61
Michigan	...	...	...	290.97	326.27	349.50	359.72	381.87	426.27	449.33	494.02	526.18	544.78	545.28
Minnesota	173.02	186.33	199.92	220.09	238.80	258.89	277.20	299.83	330.96	356.20	379.53	392.93	405.02	414.12
Mississippi	118.89	125.37	140.69	153.20	166.42	181.94	196.02	213.79	236.19	244.22	268.67	282.17	293.13	299.89
Missouri	161.19	172.53	187.20	206.96	231.15	248.40	264.65	284.59	318.37	326.56	354.71	377.06	384.71	398.12
Montana	178.03	195.94	210.14	236.01	272.95	333.49	362.08	379.30	372.69	387.50	414.47	421.79	428.15	431.04
Nebraska	156.78	170.98	187.66	202.57	219.91	239.61	269.69	299.63	322.80	337.95	353.03	361.67	363.51	374.10
Nevada	188.40	189.73	200.93	218.23	236.68	251.79	267.58	294.90	325.01	328.24	349.98	362.98	369.66	376.27
New Hampshire	134.92	143.44	155.23	168.70	182.40	199.08	215.34	[1]233.63	255.76	274.82	300.51	322.26	341.47	361.32
New Jersey	176.41	186.11	199.68	215.71	239.20	256.22	276.45	297.07	327.16	345.53	369.87	390.45	402.29	416.94
New Mexico	121.35	127.10	141.57	160.77	171.88	187.77	211.72	230.44	258.33	283.02	301.72	318.00	334.72	345.63
New York	167.58	178.48	191.00	207.64	224.53	241.98	260.17	282.89	308.90	323.98	347.41	366.96	384.87	395.81
North Carolina	119.90	128.25	135.17	149.33	162.36	177.91	192.85	211.04	232.25	236.86	267.20	279.70	288.68	306.88
North Dakota	143.42	153.97	171.97	185.73	200.33	220.34	233.82	246.00	271.27	282.00	293.74	301.82	310.73	312.86
Ohio	201.35	211.36	224.47	252.54	283.08	306.91	325.36	347.94	389.78	403.81	437.18	463.61	477.96	486.68
Oklahoma	149.81	162.40	178.00	194.65	214.52	233.56	264.46	295.14	328.82	343.26	373.01	401.02	407.22	404.74
Oregon	180.78	194.39	212.35	236.12	257.46	281.97	304.92	329.57	355.13	379.76	398.73	409.25	406.35	412.23
Pennsylvania	167.23	180.97	193.22	210.11	[1]231.08	254.80	278.10	294.49	325.36	331.39	350.84	373.06	381.84	391.55
Rhode Island	132.44	141.90	149.04	163.93	171.65	183.22	199.41	219.69	239.73	255.16	269.88	299.80	305.11	319.16
South Carolina	122.72	132.14	141.45	157.96	173.77	190.13	208.08	225.28	249.67	255.18	285.30	297.07	307.44	325.51
South Dakota	143.56	157.21	171.35	179.95	190.21	216.42	238.83	265.85	296.19	302.50	304.10	300.59	310.57	326.28
Tennessee	132.92	144.44	156.41	170.87	188.14	203.15	220.73	241.38	268.13	276.38	303.34	324.34	339.72	353.50
Texas	...	...	...	203.68	222.76	242.84	265.51	294.58	328.34	344.00	363.19	376.97	387.69	399.51
Utah	148.62	162.02	175.77	191.69	207.15	224.36	245.31	274.48	307.28	323.40	342.39	355.91	386.56	399.20
Vermont	145.25	155.36	164.43	180.40	191.76	209.10	225.62	249.28	271.60	286.65	306.40	326.02	342.29	359.38
Virginia	135.60	145.27	156.41	171.57	187.13	203.38	221.53	244.45	271.55	283.01	309.26	326.43	341.25	356.73
Washington	189.34	203.84	225.23	248.68	267.74	297.11	323.85	361.34	405.07	432.36	444.24	448.92	453.57	459.01
West Virginia	165.60	179.39	192.27	212.46	239.37	264.53	293.44	316.74	346.72	364.72	385.70	400.18	408.58	418.31
Wisconsin	183.99	197.43	212.25	230.91	250.06	274.21	297.00	323.10	352.55	370.87	398.05	412.13	421.69	427.46
Wyoming	155.58	171.71	190.36	218.11	226.82	238.55	251.17	272.69	315.60	329.28	322.21	361.03	394.28	377.52
Puerto Rico	...	...	...	...	...	...	...	152.76	167.77	174.00	186.92	194.27	199.82	207.09
Virgin Islands	...	...	...	...	...	250.31	274.03	295.10	359.55	412.85	415.24	405.41	393.65	402.24

See footnote at end of table.

Table 2-20. Average Weekly Earnings of Production Workers on Manufacturing Payrolls by State, 1973–2001—*Continued*

(Dollars.)

State	1987	1988	1989	1990	1991	1992	1993	1994	1995	1996	1997	1998	1999	2000	2001
Alabama	362.66	370.53	374.92	384.99	396.58	411.59	426.42	450.43	463.42	481.64	496.93	511.04	527.93	543.02	543.97
Alaska	503.43	¹504.36	533.24	559.45	528.96	489.13	501.30	519.50	525.80	518.01	550.13	553.39	550.85	554.47	558.67
Arizona	404.78	404.84	408.70	415.55	435.49	447.17	450.14	472.49	474.30	491.77	483.14	491.67	513.08	516.31	527.20
Arkansas	323.08	330.06	337.01	348.91	362.97	374.67	387.50	403.37	412.05	432.02	446.29	463.70	481.64	490.77	491.88
California	433.23	439.56	454.21	466.09	481.92	494.91	506.34	515.02	517.06	532.86	554.76	570.99	581.72	594.64	603.52
Colorado	404.01	419.35	419.69	450.73	457.73	458.46	494.81	506.34	512.91	528.60	556.36	570.21	588.89	589.84	594.82
Connecticut	440.37	454.92	473.06	484.26	501.18	519.58	547.72	579.08	586.79	595.43	616.00	633.24	649.99	668.82	682.98
Delaware	434.27	459.60	512.94	511.71	497.76	503.88	559.50	595.78	582.20	567.81	620.54	649.73	684.13	715.75	700.12
Florida	332.93	341.47	354.60	365.49	378.51	392.23	402.11	412.76	421.45	437.83	457.71	476.63	494.49	514.53	534.20
Georgia	353.18	358.11	364.56	375.05	391.96	408.20	420.75	438.42	453.03	473.34	493.54	502.85	522.91	537.79	528.53
Hawaii	366.42	393.60	414.80	442.90	453.32	464.40	476.80	468.03	480.75	487.30	496.87	490.87	530.16	520.50	527.87
Idaho	371.48	381.00	397.16	412.34	434.40	447.66	476.39	475.20	450.38	479.93	499.65	490.24	528.75	555.46	580.64
Illinois	451.36	464.45	469.70	473.62	481.22	485.44	499.66	513.28	527.09	543.35	563.37	574.75	588.70	591.63	587.82
Indiana	...	...	486.72	496.84	512.12	537.18	562.36	586.72	587.00	613.32	638.93	642.21	654.65	666.44	660.96
Iowa	438.61	437.18	441.46	456.44	470.61	492.30	508.35	527.88	533.39	551.46	578.08	582.83	587.88	609.86	619.18
Kansas	406.78	416.77	429.34	440.88	452.97	474.44	498.78	505.44	509.23	546.11	568.94	579.90	593.48	608.19	608.94
Kentucky	405.81	411.48	414.80	429.07	443.30	454.58	464.54	487.75	504.69	521.97	550.51	573.53	595.06	624.34	633.54
Louisiana	455.62	464.95	474.14	498.07	506.42	519.29	538.05	568.97	580.18	603.33	623.57	643.72	657.29	665.97	670.98
Maine	363.96	381.71	398.78	424.66	443.20	458.28	474.50	483.55	493.12	507.13	532.67	547.69	568.75	589.76	617.42
Maryland	412.49	444.47	459.91	472.06	483.95	510.00	527.31	545.73	559.84	562.93	585.40	595.30	605.27	609.69	620.14
Massachusetts	400.57	423.28	442.41	463.57	484.21	498.15	510.47	523.74	533.34	545.49	567.67	579.60	598.08	614.25	626.18
Michigan	547.33	576.32	579.58	579.35	602.58	619.06	662.02	724.24	722.53	731.81	757.64	762.51	812.40	841.66	817.97
Minnesota	424.13	432.07	443.48	452.57	465.41	486.34	502.65	523.33	530.79	544.82	565.65	574.90	590.81	611.59	611.33
Mississippi	305.88	315.55	321.20	329.78	344.20	359.07	375.56	392.40	400.16	420.43	432.02	444.22	461.32	473.75	480.74
Missouri	406.00	417.79	426.94	437.12	438.74	456.34	478.17	494.34	502.62	521.66	539.97	555.27	578.10	592.24	601.29
Montana	409.55	413.32	437.08	448.89	452.39	473.80	478.64	490.86	509.84	508.30	530.27	540.77	552.63	552.09	571.05
Nebraska	377.87	385.52	387.87	394.13	397.54	420.04	434.09	460.57	464.39	478.82	499.73	516.21	535.06	535.72	539.62
Nevada	393.33	400.18	422.50	449.74	448.22	470.09	482.31	486.21	522.47	565.34	607.89	605.64	574.90	587.24	599.68
New Hampshire	382.75	405.78	427.24	441.86	446.61	466.75	489.20	496.60	496.70	511.21	527.10	528.23	534.70	550.33	565.95
New Jersey	428.48	445.26	457.97	486.86	503.84	521.66	538.67	558.45	566.81	578.93	598.08	609.44	630.09	649.74	655.84
New Mexico	346.98	359.24	349.60	367.93	376.94	387.20	398.37	414.32	426.13	441.80	467.25	481.34	488.67	503.88	545.28
New York	402.59	416.16	426.80	439.96	454.91	468.80	483.59	499.79	511.25	521.42	543.43	553.62	571.44	585.26	593.35
North Carolina	323.01	328.86	339.33	350.72	368.52	386.24	400.25	418.81	428.74	443.19	470.09	486.62	505.12	529.92	526.28
North Dakota	326.24	323.53	350.24	368.95	387.44	387.84	406.23	431.04	437.53	462.09	457.25	454.86	477.60	506.86	499.99
Ohio	499.70	516.00	523.50	535.94	553.66	569.28	604.15	632.16	625.83	636.51	667.00	677.39	697.55	716.86	714.32
Oklahoma	417.77	425.39	435.97	441.00	454.69	468.86	478.50	492.20	482.69	494.76	524.06	523.32	524.51	538.65	495.99
Oregon	413.95	416.58	425.91	438.20	454.28	472.82	481.11	497.32	511.28	523.00	547.65	572.65	590.24	603.20	625.66
Pennsylvania	408.18	424.56	437.06	449.33	462.98	480.62	498.93	519.58	529.05	¹552.08	578.76	589.11	593.14	616.12	613.31
Rhode Island	328.00	343.01	356.06	375.17	389.20	397.79	405.96	417.11	430.11	438.00	462.58	471.37	478.00	491.67	490.44
South Carolina	337.77	341.13	352.70	362.44	378.72	395.32	407.68	418.00	425.70	428.45	436.77	448.15	454.54	466.23	467.74
South Dakota	330.26	343.83	346.94	344.29	362.15	364.21	367.16	385.98	391.25	397.94	417.32	435.37	453.88	461.17	476.32
Tennessee	365.25	372.74	376.18	368.63	392.83	408.24	421.46	429.45	435.51	458.78	482.45	488.43	507.50	519.38	524.10
Texas	409.76	415.75	428.45	437.65	456.36	464.10	471.66	479.70	490.92	507.83	523.31	530.52	532.88	536.05	536.74
Utah	393.42	407.43	405.60	410.74	429.72	446.93	439.56	457.97	462.48	492.06	516.57	528.03	535.60	544.46	544.10
Vermont	370.27	382.59	408.59	429.22	448.80	472.32	501.74	489.16	494.51	503.01	516.89	515.99	539.18	573.47	567.07
Virginia	375.65	382.30	396.32	406.83	422.42	435.42	444.85	468.71	487.55	505.89	527.92	545.67	566.89	584.59	594.05
Washington	468.03	477.19	477.53	511.97	523.89	543.60	563.20	601.83	600.98	600.98	615.50	643.01	660.13	681.73	705.36
West Virginia	428.33	438.89	454.62	469.27	477.86	491.67	501.84	520.38	528.35	533.95	549.19	570.75	586.14	603.39	608.47
Wisconsin	436.77	443.50	446.96	459.95	474.86	495.33	511.14	529.91	537.20	554.51	579.18	586.04	607.55	616.28	620.68
Wyoming	378.30	¹395.40	421.08	432.12	423.83	428.46	448.52	471.60	471.22	528.12	585.96	603.17	605.22	624.55	641.28
Puerto Rico	211.23	217.40	227.92	236.16	246.48	262.55	275.71	288.08	293.44	297.22	316.40	336.40	366.13	381.23	400.36
Virgin Islands	396.68	398.34	453.28	502.44	518.33	574.56	651.20	647.33	659.69	705.50	772.44	745.86	827.38	962.72	864.78

1. Data not continuous.

PART THREE

PROJECTIONS OF LABOR FORCE AND EMPLOYMENT BY INDUSTRY AND OCCUPATION

PROJECTIONS OF LABOR FORCE AND EMPLOYMENT BY INDUSTRY AND OCCUPATION

HIGHLIGHTS

The BLS projections presented in this issue were completed prior to the tragic events of September 11. While there have been numerous immediate economic impacts, the nature and severity of longer-term impacts remain unclear. At this time, it is impossible to know how individual industries or occupations may be affected over the next decade. The bureau will continue to review its projections and, as the long-term consequences of September 11 become clearer, will incorporate these effects into subsequent releases of the labor force, industrial, and occupational outlook.

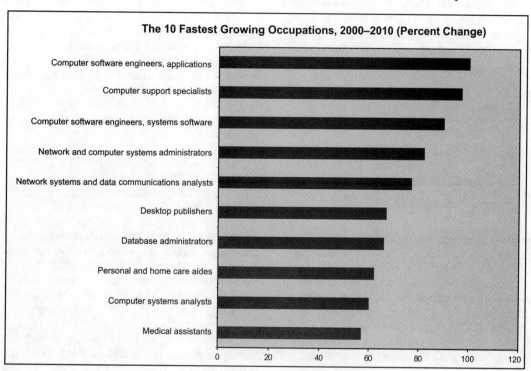

The 10 Fastest Growing Occupations, 2000–2010 (Percent Change)

Eight of the 10 projected fastest growing occupations involve computers. The other two are connected with health care.

OTHER HIGHLIGHTS:

- Only one of the 10 fastest growing industries, computer and data processing, is directly associated with computers. The others involve other business related and health services. (Table 3-5)
- The fastest growing industries do not necessarily provide the largest number of future jobs. For example, retail trade and state and local government education are expected to increase in large numbers although their rate of growth is only around 1 percent. (Table 3-5)
- The fastest labor force growth is expected to occur in the 55-64 age group, which contains the aging baby boomers. (Table 3-1)
- While the education and training requirements of the work force continues to increase, only 21 percent of the jobs in 2000 were in occupations requiring a bachelor's degree or more. However, these jobs will account for 29 percent of total job growth from 2000 to 2010. (Table 3-4)
- Total job openings occur as a result of growth and replacement needs. The relative importance of the two factors varies by occupational group. "Professional and related occupations", which includes teachers and computer occupations, is the only group where growth is expected to exceed replacement. Replacement equals projected total job openings less projected change in employment. (Table 3-3)

NOTES AND DEFINITIONS

Concepts, Definitions, and Procedures

Long-term projections of likely employment conditions in the U.S. economy have been developed by the Bureau of Labor Statistics since 1957. These projections cover the future size and composition of the labor force, the aggregate economy, detailed estimates of industrial production, and industrial and occupational employment. The resulting data serve many users who need information on likely patterns of economic growth and their effects on employment. Beginning with the projections for 1996–2006, projections have been developed for a 10-year period and published every 2 years.

To carry out the projection process, the BLS makes many underlying assumptions concerning general economic and social conditions and sets ranges of acceptability for the key results of the various stages of the projection process.

Projecting employment in industry and occupational detail requires an integrated projection of the total economy and its various sectors. BLS projections are developed in a series of six steps, each of which is based on separate projections procedures and models and various related assumptions. The six steps or analytical phases are: (1) labor force, (2) aggregate economy, (3) final demand (GDP) by sector and product, (4) inter-industry relationships (input-output), (5) industry output and employment, and (6) occupational employment. Each phase is solved separately, with the results of each used as input for the next phase, and with some results feeding back to earlier steps. In each phase, many iterations are made to ensure internal consistency as assumptions and results are reviewed and revised.

Labor force projections are determined by projections of the future age, sex and racial composition of the population and by trends in labor force participation rates—the percent of the specified group in the population who will be working or seeking work. The population projections, prepared by the U.S. Bureau of the Census, are based on trends in birth rates, death rates, and net migration. With the population projections in hand, BLS analyzes and projects changes in labor force participation rates for more than 130 age, sex, and race or Hispanic origin groups.

Projections of labor force participation rates for each group are developed by first estimating a trend rate of change based on participation rate behavior during the prior 8-year period. Second, the rate is modified when the time-series projections for the specific group appear inconsistent with the results of cross-sectional and cohort analyses. This second step ensures consistency in the projections across various groups. Finally, the size of the

labor force is derived by applying the participation rates to the population projections. The results are again reviewed for consistency.

Aggregate economic performance—the second phase of the BLS projections process—develops projections of the gross domestic product (GDP) and major categories of demand and income. These results provide control totals that are consistent with each other and with the various assumptions and conditions of the projection scenario. The values generated for each demand sector and subsector are then used in the next phase in developing detailed projections for personal consumption, business investment, foreign trade, and government.

These projections are accomplished using a macroeconomic model. The model basically consists of sets of equations that correlate various aspects of the economy with each other. It provides internally consistent, moderately detailed projections for each set of given assumptions and goals. The 2000–2010 projections were based upon a long-term macro model developed by DRI-WEFA, Inc. This model has approximately 1,300 equations, which determine those factors affecting growth in the U.S. economy. This model is driven by a set of about 300 exogenous variables, which are specified by BLS.

Final demand. The BLS projection then proceeds from the aggregate to the industrial level. For the industry output projections, the economy is disaggregated into about 190 producing sectors that cover the U.S. industrial structure, both public and private. The framework for this procedure is an input-output model. The initial input-output data used by BLS are prepared by the Bureau of Economic Analysis, U.S. Department of Commerce.

The development of projections of industry output begins with aggregate demand projections from the DRI-WEFA model. In this model, projections are made for 27 major categories of consumption, 15 categories of investment, 19 end-use categories of foreign trade, and 13 categories of government spending. A further disaggregation of the values from the model is then undertaken. For example, personal consumption expenditures are estimated for 158 detailed categories.

Provision is made to allow for shifts in the commodity makeup of a given demand category. This is accomplished by projecting "bridge tables" relating individual types of demand to the actual industries supplying the goods. The bridge table is a percent distribution for each given demand category, such as the personal consumption or investment category, among each of the sectors in the BLS input-output model. In projecting changes in these bridge tables, expected changes in technology, consumer tastes or buying patterns, the commodity pattern of exports and imports, the future composition of business investment, and other structural factors are considered.

Input-output. The next stage in the projections process is the estimation of the intermediate flow of goods and services required to produce the projected GDP. Only final sales are counted in the GDP to avoid repeated counting of intermediate inputs. An industry's total employment, however, depends on its total output, whether sold to another industry, or used as a final good. The total output of each industry is projected using an inter-industry or input-output model. This model mathematically solves for all levels of intermediate inputs given industry relationships and final demand.

The BLS input-output model consists of two basic matrices for each year, a "use" and a "make" table. The principal table is the "use" table. This table shows the purchase of commodities by each industry as inputs into its production process. Projecting this table must take into account changes in the input pattern or the way in which goods or services are produced by each industry. In general, two types of changes in these input patterns are made in developing a future input-output table: (a) Those made to the inputs of a specific industry (as, for example, the changes in inputs in the publishing industry); and, (b) those made to the inputs of a specific commodity in all or most industries (as for example increased use of business services across a wide spectrum of industries). The "make" table shows the commodity output of each industry. It allocates commodity output to the industry to which it is primary and to all other industries where the commodity is produced as a secondary product. The "use" table is the basis for the direct requirements table of coefficients showing the inputs required to produce one dollar of that industry's output. The "make" table is used to create a "market shares" table, which shows the values of the "make" table as coefficients. The coefficient tables are used to calculate the total requirements tables, which show the direct and indirect requirements to produce a dollar's worth of final demand. Projection tables are based on historical tables and on studies of specific industries.

Industry Employment. The projected level of industry employment is based on the projected levels of industry output as well as other factors such as expected technological changes and their impact on labor productivity. After the initial industry output is calculated, employment is derived from a model of the industry-level employment requirements. The employment projections by industry are constrained by the requirement that they sum to the aggregate employment level as determined by the aggregate projections. Employment for wage and salary workers is based on the Current Employment Statistics (payroll) survey, which counts jobs, whereas self-employed, unpaid family worker, agricultural, and private household data are based on the Current Population Survey (household survey), which counts

workers. Employment totals for historical periods, therefore, differ from the official employment estimates of the Bureau of Labor Statistics.

Employment by Occupation. The model used to develop the occupational employment projections is an industry-occupation matrix showing the distribution of 2000-2010 employment for 262 industries and for 695 detailed occupations. Occupational staffing patterns for the industries are based on data collected by state employment security agencies and analyzed by the BLS and reflect the 2000 standard occupational classification system. The titles and content of major occupational groups and many detailed occupations are substantially different from those used in previous projections.

Staffing patterns of industries in the base-year industry-occupation matrix are projected to the target year to account for changes expected to occur in technology, shifts in production mix, and other factors. For example, one would expect greater employment of computer specialists as computer technology spreads across industries. In projecting the staffing patterns, the changes introduced into the input-output model for expected change are also analyzed to account for the impact of that technological change on future occupational staffing patterns of industries. The projected industry total employment data are applied to the projected industry staffing patterns, yielding employment by occupation for each industry. These data are aggregated across all industries to yield total occupational employment for the projected year.

Final Review. An important element of the projection system is its comprehensive structure. To ensure the internal consistency of this large structure, the BLS procedure encompasses detailed review and analysis of the results at each stage for reasonableness and for consistency with the results from other stages of the BLS projections. The final results reflect innumerable interactions among staff members who focus on particular variables in the model. Because of this review, the projection process at BLS converges to an internally consistent set of employment projections across a substantial number of industries and occupations.

Sources of Additional Information

A complete presentation of the projections including analysis of results and additional tables and a comprehensive description of the methodology is found in the *Monthly Labor Review*, November 2001. A more detailed description of methods is contained in the BLS *Handbook of Methods,* BLS Bulletin 2490, April 1997, chapter 13 and BLS Bulletin 2521, *Occupational Projections and Training Data*, May 2000. Once the target year is reached, BLS evaluates the projections and these evaluations generally appear in articles in the *Monthly Labor Review.*

Table 3-1. Civilian Labor Force by Sex, Age, Race, and Hispanic Origin, 1980, 1990, 2000, and Projected 2010

Sex, age, race, and Hispanic origin	Level (thousands)				Change (thousands)			Percent change			Percent distribution				Annual growth rate (percent)		
	1980	1990	2000	2010	1980-1990	1990-2000	2000-2010	1980-1990	1990-2000	2000-2010	1980	1990	2000	2010	1980-1990	1990-2000	2000-2010
TOTAL, 16 YEARS AND OVER	106 940	125 840	140 863	157 721	18 900	15 023	16 858	17.7	11.9	12.0	100.0	100.0	100.0	100.0	1.8	1.1	1.1
16 to 24	25 300	22 492	22 715	26 081	-2 808	223	3 366	-11.1	1.0	14.8	23.7	17.9	16.1	16.5	-1.0	0.1	1.4
16 to 19	9 378	7 792	8 369	9 329	-1 586	577	960	-16.9	7.4	11.5	8.8	6.2	5.9	5.9	-1.8	0.7	1.1
20 to 24	15 922	14 700	14 346	16 752	-1 222	-354	2 406	-7.7	-2.4	16.8	14.9	11.7	10.2	10.6	-0.6	-0.2	1.6
25 to 54	66 600	88 322	99 974	104 994	21 722	11 652	5 020	32.6	13.2	5.0	62.3	70.2	71.0	66.6	3.0	1.2	0.5
25 to 34	29 227	35 929	31 669	34 222	6 702	-4 260	2 553	22.9	-11.9	8.1	27.3	28.6	22.5	21.7	2.9	-1.3	0.8
35 to 44	20 463	32 145	37 838	33 990	11 682	5 693	-3 849	57.1	17.7	-10.2	19.1	25.5	26.9	21.6	4.6	1.6	-1.1
45 to 54	16 910	20 248	30 467	36 783	3 338	10 219	6 316	19.7	50.5	20.7	15.8	16.1	21.6	23.3	1.2	4.2	1.9
55 and over	15 039	15 026	18 175	26 646	-13	3 149	8 471	-0.1	21.0	46.6	14.1	11.9	12.9	16.9	0.2	1.9	3.9
55 to 64	11 985	11 575	13 974	21 204	-410	2 399	7 230	-3.4	20.7	51.7	11.2	9.2	9.9	13.4	0.1	1.9	4.3
65 and over	3 054	3 451	4 200	5 442	397	749	1 242	13.0	21.7	29.6	2.9	2.7	3.0	3.5	0.7	2.0	2.6
65 to 74	2 619	2 952	3 410	4 543	333	458	1 133	12.7	15.5	33.2	2.4	2.3	2.4	2.9	0.7	1.5	2.9
75 and over	435	498	790	899	63	292	109	14.5	58.6	13.8	0.4	0.4	0.6	0.6	0.6	4.7	1.3
Men, 16 Years And Over	61 453	69 011	75 247	82 221	7 558	6 236	6 974	12.3	9.0	9.3	57.5	54.8	53.4	52.1	1.2	0.9	0.9
16 to 24	13 606	11 960	11 876	13 391	-1 646	-84	1 516	-12.1	-0.7	12.8	12.7	9.5	8.4	8.5	-1.4	-0.1	1.2
16 to 19	4 999	4 094	4 317	4 741	-905	223	424	-18.1	5.5	9.8	4.7	3.3	3.1	3.0	-2.1	0.5	0.9
20 to 24	8 607	7 866	7 558	8 650	-741	-308	1 092	-8.6	-3.9	14.4	8.0	6.3	5.4	5.5	-0.9	-0.4	1.4
25 to 54	38 712	48 456	53 359	54 566	9 744	4 903	1 208	25.2	10.1	2.3	36.2	38.5	37.9	34.6	2.3	1.0	0.2
25 to 34	16 971	19 872	17 073	17 902	2 901	-2 799	829	17.1	-14.1	4.9	15.9	15.8	12.1	11.4	2.2	-1.5	0.5
35 to 44	11 836	17 481	20 334	17 809	5 645	2 853	-2 524	47.7	16.3	-12.4	11.1	13.9	14.4	11.3	3.7	1.5	-1.3
45 to 54	9 905	11 103	15 951	18 855	1 198	4 848	2 903	12.1	43.7	18.2	9.3	8.8	11.3	12.0	0.5	3.7	1.7
55 and over	9 135	8 594	10 013	14 263	-541	1 419	4 251	-5.9	16.5	42.5	8.5	6.8	7.1	9.0	-0.3	1.5	3.6
55 to 64	7 242	6 627	7 574	11 148	-615	947	3 574	-8.5	14.3	47.2	6.8	5.3	5.4	7.1	-0.5	1.3	3.9
65 and over	1 893	1 967	2 439	3 115	74	472	677	3.9	24.0	27.8	1.8	1.6	1.7	2.0	0.1	2.2	2.5
65 to 74	1 601	1 664	1 970	2 610	63	306	640	3.9	18.4	32.5	1.5	1.3	1.4	1.7	0.1	1.7	2.9
75 and over	293	303	469	506	10	166	37	3.4	54.7	7.9	0.3	0.2	0.3	0.3	0.1	4.5	0.8
Women, 16 Years And Over	45 487	56 829	65 616	75 500	11 342	8 787	9 884	24.9	15.5	15.1	42.5	45.2	46.6	47.9	2.5	1.4	1.4
16 to 24	11 696	10 532	10 839	12 690	-1 164	307	1 851	-10.0	2.9	17.1	10.9	8.4	7.7	8.0	-0.7	0.3	1.6
16 to 19	4 381	3 698	4 051	4 588	-683	353	537	-15.6	9.6	13.2	4.1	2.9	2.9	2.9	-1.5	0.9	1.3
20 to 24	7 315	6 834	6 788	8 102	-481	-46	1 314	-6.6	-0.7	19.4	6.8	5.4	4.8	5.1	-0.2	-0.1	1.8
25 to 54	27 888	39 866	46 615	50 428	11 978	6 749	3 813	43.0	16.9	8.2	26.1	31.7	33.1	32.0	4.0	1.6	0.8
25 to 34	12 257	16 058	14 596	16 320	3 801	-1 462	1 724	31.0	-9.1	11.8	11.5	12.8	10.4	10.3	3.8	-1.0	1.1
35 to 44	8 627	14 663	17 504	16 180	6 036	2 841	-1 324	70.0	19.4	-7.6	8.1	11.7	12.4	10.3	5.7	1.8	-0.8
45 to 54	7 004	9 145	14 515	17 928	2 141	5 370	3 413	30.6	58.7	23.5	6.5	7.3	10.3	11.4	2.3	4.7	2.1
55 and over	5 904	6 431	8 162	12 383	527	1 731	4 221	8.9	26.9	51.7	5.5	5.1	5.8	7.9	1.0	2.4	4.3
55 to 64	4 742	4 948	6 400	10 056	206	1 452	3 656	4.3	29.3	57.1	4.4	3.9	4.5	6.4	0.8	2.6	4.6
65 and over	1 161	1 483	1 762	2 327	322	279	565	27.7	18.8	32.1	1.1	1.2	1.3	1.5	1.6	1.7	2.8
65 to 74	1 019	1 288	1 441	1 933	269	153	493	26.4	11.8	34.2	1.0	1.0	1.0	1.2	1.5	1.1	3.0
75 and over	142	195	321	393	53	126	72	37.3	64.7	22.4	0.1	0.2	0.2	0.2	1.7	5.1	2.0
White, 16 Years And Over	93 600	107 447	117 574	128 043	13 847	10 127	10 470	14.8	9.4	8.9	87.5	85.4	83.5	81.2	1.6	0.9	0.9
Men	54 473	59 638	63 861	68 159	5 165	4 223	4 298	9.5	7.1	6.7	50.9	47.4	45.3	43.2	1.0	0.7	0.7
Women	39 127	47 809	53 714	59 884	8 682	5 905	6 171	22.2	12.4	11.5	36.6	38.0	38.1	38.0	2.4	1.2	1.1
Black, 16 Years And Over	10 865	13 740	16 603	20 041	2 875	2 863	3 439	26.5	20.8	20.7	10.2	10.9	11.8	12.7	2.4	1.9	1.9
Men	5 612	6 802	7 816	8 991	1 190	1 014	1 175	21.2	14.9	15.0	5.2	5.4	5.5	5.7	2.0	1.4	1.4
Women	5 253	6 938	8 787	11 050	1 685	1 849	2 263	32.1	26.7	25.8	4.9	5.5	6.2	7.0	2.8	2.4	2.3
Asian And Other, 16 Years And Over[1]	2 476	4 653	6 687	9 636	2 177	2 034	2 950	87.9	43.7	44.1	2.3	3.7	4.7	6.1	5.4	3.7	3.7
Men	1 371	2 572	3 570	5 070	1 201	999	1 500	87.1	38.9	42.0	1.3	2.0	2.5	3.2	5.0	3.3	3.6
Women	1 105	2 081	3 116	4 566	971	1 033	1 449	88.3	49.3	46.5	1.0	1.7	2.2	2.9	6.0	4.1	3.9
Hispanic Origin, 16 Years And Over[2]	6 146	10 720	15 368	20 947	4 574	4 648	5 579	74.4	43.4	36.3	5.7	8.5	10.9	13.3	5.7	3.7	3.1
Men	3 817	6 546	8 919	11 723	2 729	2 373	2 804	71.5	36.3	31.4	3.6	5.2	6.3	7.4	5.5	3.1	2.8
Women	2 326	4 174	6 449	9 224	1 848	2 275	2 775	79.4	54.5	43.0	2.2	3.3	4.6	5.8	6.0	4.4	3.6
Other Than Hispanic Origin, 16 Years And Over[2]	100 794	115 120	125 495	136 774	14 326	10 375	11 279	14.2	9.0	9.0	94.3	91.5	89.1	86.7	1.3	0.9	0.9
Men	57 636	62 465	66 328	70 498	4 829	3 863	4 170	8.4	6.2	6.3	53.9	49.6	47.1	44.7	0.8	0.6	0.6
Women	43 161	52 655	59 167	66 276	9 494	6 512	7 109	22.0	12.4	12.0	40.4	41.8	42.0	42.0	2.0	1.2	1.1
White Non-Hispanic, 16 Years And Over[2]	87 633	97 818	102 963	109 118	10 185	5 144	6 155	11.6	5.3	6.0	81.9	77.7	73.1	69.2	1.1	0.5	0.6
Men	50 762	53 731	55 359	57 538	2 969	1 627	2 179	5.8	3.0	3.9	47.5	42.7	39.3	36.5	0.6	0.3	0.4
Women	36 871	44 087	47 604	51 580	7 216	3 517	3 976	19.6	8.0	8.4	34.5	35.0	33.8	32.7	1.8	0.8	0.8

1. The "Asian and Other" group includes Asians and Pacific Islanders and American Indians and Alaska Natives. The historical data are derived by subtracting "Black" from the "Black and Other" group; projections are made directly, not by subtraction.
2. Data by Hispanic origin are not available before 1980.

Table 3-2. Occupations with the Largest Job Growth, 2000–2010

(Thousands of jobs.)

Occupation	Employment		Change		Quartile rank by 200 median annual earnings [1]
	2000	2010	Number	Percent	
Combined food preparation and serving workers, including fast food	2 206	2 879	673	30	4
Customer service representatives	1 946	2 577	631	32	3
Registered nurses	2 194	2 755	561	26	1
Retail salespersons	4 109	4 619	510	12	4
Computer support specialists	506	996	490	97	2
Cashiers, except gaming	3 325	3 799	474	14	4
Office clerks, general	2 705	3 135	430	16	3
Security guards	1 106	1 497	391	35	4
Computer software engineers, applications	380	760	380	100	1
Waiters and waitresses	1 983	2 347	364	18	4
General and operations managers	2 398	2 761	363	15	1
Truck drivers, heavy and tractor-trailer	1 749	2 095	346	20	2
Nursing aides, orderlies, and attendants	1 373	1 697	323	24	3
Janitors and cleaners, except maids and housekeeping cleaners	2 348	2 665	317	13	4
Postsecondary teachers	1 344	1 659	315	23	1
Teacher assistants	1 262	1 562	301	24	4
Home health aides	615	907	291	47	4
Laborers and freight, stock, and material movers, hand	2 084	2 373	289	14	3
Computer software engineers, systems software	317	601	284	90	1
Landscaping and groundskeeping workers	894	1 154	260	29	4
Personal and home care aides	414	672	258	62	4
Computer systems analysts	431	689	258	60	1
Receptionists and information clerks	1 078	1 334	256	24	3
Truck drivers, light or delivery services	1 117	1 331	215	19	3
Packers and packagers, hand	1 091	1 300	210	19	4
Elementary school teachers, except special education	1 532	1 734	202	13	1
Medical assistants	329	516	187	57	3
Network and computer systems administrators	229	416	187	82	1
Secondary school teachers, except special and vocational education	1 004	1 190	187	19	1
Accountants and auditors	976	1 157	181	19	1

1. The quartile rankings of Occupational Employment Statistics annual earnings data are presented in the following categories: 1 = very high ($39,700 and over), 2 = high ($25,760 to $39,660), 3 = low ($18,500 to $25,760), and 4 = very low (up to $18,490.) The rankings were based on quartiles using one–fourth of total employment to define each quartile. Earnings are for wage and salary workers.

Table 3-3. Industries with the Largest Output Growth, 2000–2010

(Dollars, percent.)

Industry description	Billions of chained 1996 dollars	Change	Average annual change	Average annual rate of change
	2000	2010	2000-2010	
Computer and office equipment	386	1 531.1	1 145.4	14.8
Wholesale trade	920	1 409.6	489.3	4.4
Electronic components and accessories	386	759.9	373.6	7.0
Computer and data processing services	278	600.8	322.6	8.0
Owner-occupied dwellings	631	943.4	312.2	4.1
Retail trade exc. eating and drinking places	926	1 236.6	310.6	2.9
Telephone communications and services	341	637.9	297.1	6.5
Construction	910	1 182.1	272.1	2.6
Security and commodity brokers	292	540.4	248.7	6.4
Motor vehicles and equipment	433	664.9	231.8	4.4
Real estate	653	822.4	169.4	2.3
Depository institutions	446	596.3	150.0	2.9
Trucking and courier services except air	237	358.6	121.3	4.2
Miscellaneous business services	198	312.7	115.0	4.7
Eating and drinking places	298	393.3	95.2	2.8
Royalties	96	191.2	95.0	7.1
Automotive rentals, without drivers	63	150.8	87.7	9.1
Engineering and architectural services	133	210.7	78.1	4.7
Drugs	99	170.5	72.0	5.6
Communications equipment	107	174.8	67.5	5.0

Table 3-4. Employment and Total Job Openings, 2000–2010, and 2000 Average Annual Earnings by Education or Training Category

(Thousands of jobs.)

Occupation	Employment				Change			Total job openings due to growth and net replacements, 2000-2001 [1]		2000 mean annual earnings
	Number		Percent distribution		Number	Percent distribution	Percent	Number	Percent distribution	
	2000	2010	2000	2010						
Total, all occupations	145 594	167 754	100.0	100.0	22 160	100.0	15.2	57 932	100.0	$33 089
Bachelor's or higher degree	30 072	36 556	20.7	21.8	6 484	29.3	21.6	12 130	20.9	56 553
First professional degree	2 034	2 404	1.4	1.4	370	1.7	18.2	691	1.2	91 424
Doctoral degree	1 492	1 845	1.0	1.1	353	1.6	23.7	760	1.3	52 146
Master's degree	1 426	1 759	1.0	1.0	333	1.5	23.4	634	1.1	43 842
Bachelor's or higher degree, plus work experience	7 319	8 741	5.0	5.2	1 422	6.4	19.4	2 741	4.7	69 967
Bachelor's degree	17 801	21 807	12.2	13.0	4 006	18.1	22.5	7 304	12.6	48 440
Associate degree or postsecondary vocational award	11 761	14 600	8.1	8.7	2 839	12.8	24.1	5 383	9.3	35 701
Associate degree	5 083	6 710	3.5	4.0	1 626	7.3	32.0	2 608	4.5	41 488
Postsecondary vocational award	6 678	7 891	4.6	4.7	1 213	5.5	18.2	2 775	4.8	31 296
Work-related training	103 760	116 597	71.3	69.5	12 837	57.9	12.4	40 419	69.8	25 993
Work experience in a related occupation	10 456	11 559	7.2	6.9	1 102	5.0	10.5	3 180	5.5	40 881
Long-term on-the-job training	12 435	13 373	8.5	8.0	938	4.2	7.5	3 737	6.5	33 125
Moderate-term on-the-job training	27 671	30 794	19.0	18.4	3 123	14.1	11.3	8 767	15.1	29 069
Short-term on-the-job training	53 198	60 871	36.5	36.3	7 673	34.6	14.4	24 735	42.7	19 799

Note: Detail may not equal total or 100 percent due to rounding.

1. Total job opening represent the sum of employment increases and net replacements. If employment change is negative, job openings due to growth are zero and total job openings equal net replacements.
2. Earnings are for wage and salary workers.

Table 3-5. Employment and Output by Industry, 1990, 2000, and Projected 2010

| Industry | Employment | | | | | | | Output | | | | |
| | Thousands of jobs | | | Change | | Average annual rate of change (percent) | | Billions of chained (1996) dollars | | | Average annual rate of change (percent) | |
	1990	2000	2010	1990-2000	2000-2010	1990-2000	2000-2010	1990	2000	2010	1990-2000	2000-2010
TOTAL [1,2]	124 324	145 594	167 754	21 269	22 160	1.6	1.4	11 472	16 180	22 286	3.5	3.3
NONFARM WAGE AND SALARY [3]	108 760	130 639	152 447	21 879	21 808	1.8	1.6	10 672	15 128	20 761	3.6	3.2
Mining	709	543	487	-167	-55	-2.6	-1.1	205	212	230	0.3	0.8
Metal mining	58	41	35	-17	-6	-3.5	-1.5	11	13	16	1.2	2.6
Coal mining	147	77	54	-69	-23	-6.2	-3.5	25	26	33	0.4	2.4
Crude petroleum, natural gas, and gas liquids	196	129	100	-67	-29	-4.1	-2.5	133	122	130	-0.8	0.6
Oil and gas field services	198	182	188	-17	7	-0.9	0.4	22	31	28	3.3	-1.0
Nonmetallic minerals, except fuels	110	114	110	3	-4	0.3	-0.3	15	19	24	2.1	2.3
Construction	5 120	6 698	7 522	1 578	825	2.7	1.2	730	910	1 182	2.2	2.6
Manufacturing	19 077	18 469	19 047	-607	577	-0.3	0.3	3 022	4 601	6 279	4.3	3.2
Durable manufacturing	11 109	11 138	11 780	29	642	(4)	0.6	1 481	2 785	4 136	6.5	4.0
Lumber and wood products	733	832	905	99	73	1.3	0.8	106	115	146	0.8	2.4
Logging	85	80	80	-5	1	-0.6	0.1	23	15	18	-3.9	1.7
Sawmills and planing mills	198	185	185	-13	(4)	-0.7	(4)	27	34	44	2.2	2.6
Millwork, plywood, and structural members	262	335	361	74	25	2.5	0.7	31	36	44	1.6	2.1
Wood containers and miscellaneous wood products	130	142	152	12	10	0.9	0.7	17	19	23	1.6	1.9
Wood buildings and mobile homes	59	91	127	31	36	4.3	3.4	8	10	16	2.0	5.1
Furniture and fixtures	506	558	630	52	72	1.0	1.2	50	84	111	5.3	2.9
Household furniture	289	293	283	4	-11	0.1	-0.4	24	32	38	3.0	1.8
Partitions and fixtures	78	91	116	12	25	1.5	2.5	7	14	16	6.8	1.2
Office and miscellaneous furniture and fixtures	138	174	231	36	57	2.3	2.9	19	37	57	7.2	4.3
Glass and glass products	160	148	140	-12	-8	-0.8	-0.6	19	25	34	2.9	2.9
Hydraulic cement	18	18	16	(4)	-2	-0.2	-1.0	6	7	11	2.8	3.7
Stone, clay, and miscellaneous mineral products	172	165	152	-7	-13	-0.4	-0.8	20	29	32	3.7	1.0
Concrete, gypsum, and plaster products	206	248	263	42	14	1.9	0.6	29	42	53	3.7	2.4
Primary metal industries	756	698	650	-58	-47	-0.8	-0.7	152	200	239	2.8	1.8
Blast furnaces and basic steel products	276	225	176	-52	-49	-2.1	-2.4	65	79	73	1.8	-0.7
Iron and steel foundries	132	123	125	-10	2	-0.7	0.2	13	18	26	2.7	4.0
Primary nonferrous smelting and refining	46	36	34	-10	-2	-2.5	-0.4	14	18	21	2.5	1.3
All other primary metals	46	45	43	-2	-1	-0.3	-0.3	10	11	17	1.6	4.4
Nonferrous rolling and drawing	172	176	173	4	-3	0.2	-0.2	42	60	81	3.7	3.1
Nonferrous foundries	84	94	99	11	5	1.2	0.5	7	14	19	6.6	2.9
Fabricated metal products	1 419	1 537	1 661	118	124	0.8	0.8	176	273	387	4.5	3.6
Metal cans and shipping containers	50	36	26	-14	-10	-3.3	-3.3	14	13	18	-0.5	3.7
Cutlery, hand tools, and hardware	131	121	110	-11	-11	-0.9	-0.9	16	21	30	2.5	3.6
Plumbing and nonelectric heating equipment	60	60	55	(4)	-5	(4)	-0.8	7	11	12	4.6	0.9
Fabricated structural metal products	427	498	540	72	42	1.6	0.8	49	76	102	4.5	2.9
Screw machine products, bolts, rivets, etc.	96	107	123	11	16	1.1	1.4	9	26	42	10.6	5.0
Metal forgings and stampings	225	255	254	30	-1	1.3	(4)	31	53	70	5.5	2.9
Metal coating, engraving, and allied services	120	146	191	27	45	2.0	2.7	10	17	32	4.9	6.8
Ordanance and ammunition	75	38	35	-37	-3	-6.5	-0.9	8	6	7	-3.3	2.1
Miscellaneous fabricated metal products	237	277	327	40	51	1.6	1.7	32	51	74	4.9	3.7
Industrial machinery and equipment	2 095	2 120	2 222	26	102	0.1	0.5	214	618	1 117	11.2	6.1
Engines and turbines	89	85	83	-4	-2	-0.5	-0.2	19	30	42	4.6	3.6
Farm and garden machinery	106	96	105	-9	9	-0.9	0.9	18	24	40	3.0	5.3
Construction and related machinery	229	240	284	11	44	0.5	1.7	33	53	78	4.9	3.9
Metalworking machinery and equipment	330	330	330	(4)	(4)	(4)	(4)	29	38	51	2.8	3.0
Special industry machinery	159	172	158	13	-14	0.8	-0.8	23	44	40	6.5	-0.9
General industrial machinery and equipment	247	251	260	4	9	0.2	0.3	34	41	55	2.0	2.9
Computer and office equipment	438	361	350	-76	-11	-1.9	-0.3	28	386	1 531	30.1	14.8
Refrigeration and service industry machinery	177	212	242	35	30	1.8	1.3	29	47	65	5.1	3.2
Industrial machinery, n.e.c.	320	373	410	53	37	1.5	1.0	26	36	72	3.5	7.0
Electronic and other electronic equipment	1 674	1 719	1 820	45	102	0.3	0.6	154	587	984	14.3	5.3
Electric distribution equipment	97	85	77	-12	-8	-1.3	-1.0	11	15	19	3.3	2.0
Electrical industrial apparatus	169	150	127	-19	-23	-1.2	-1.7	20	31	51	4.2	5.2
Household appliances	124	116	97	-8	-19	-0.7	-1.8	17	24	26	3.9	0.5
Electric lighting and wiring equipment	189	183	194	-5	11	-0.3	0.6	21	32	42	4.4	2.6
Household audio and video equipment	85	80	77	-5	-3	-0.6	-0.3	9	12	18	2.5	4.0
Communications equipment	264	276	290	13	14	0.5	0.5	41	107	175	10.2	5.0
Electronic components and accessories	582	682	800	100	118	1.6	1.6	29	386	760	29.3	7.0
Miscellaneous electrical equipment	165	146	158	-19	13	-1.2	0.8	22	32	47	4.0	3.8
Transportation equipment	1 989	1 849	2 063	-140	214	-0.7	1.1	411	613	881	4.1	3.7
Motor vehicles and equipment	812	1 013	1 100	201	87	2.2	0.8	236	433	665	6.3	4.4
Aerospace	897	551	655	-346	104	-4.8	1.7	142	136	162	-0.4	1.7
Ship and boat building and repairing	188	166	170	-22	4	-1.2	0.2	20	18	17	-1.0	-0.4
Railroad equipment	33	36	38	3	2	0.8	0.7	5	10	16	5.9	5.0
Miscellaneous transportation equipment	59	83	99	24	16	3.5	1.8	8	16	22	7.7	3.1

See footnotes and *Note* at end of table.

Table 3-5. Employment and Output by Industry, 1990, 2000, and Projected 2010—*Continued*

Industry	Employment							Output				
	Thousands of jobs			Change		Average annual rate of change (percent)		Billions of chained (1996) dollars			Average annual rate of change (percent)	
	1990	2000	2010	1990-2000	2000-2010	1990-2000	2000-2010	1990	2000	2010	1990-2000	2000-2010
Instruments and related products	1 006	853	869	-153	17	-1.6	0.2	130	177	238	3.2	3.0
Search and navigation equipment	284	154	140	-130	-14	-5.9	-1.0	40	37	56	-0.6	4.2
Measuring and controlling devices	323	302	300	-21	-2	-0.7	-0.1	33	46	74	3.2	4.9
Medical equipment, instruments, and supplies	246	288	338	42	50	1.6	1.6	33	63	87	6.5	3.4
Opthalmic goods	43	33	34	-10	1	-2.5	0.2	2	4	5	7.3	2.1
Photographic equipment and supplies	100	70	55	-29	-15	-3.4	-2.4	20	27	15	3.2	-5.6
Watches, clocks and parts	11	5	2	-6	-3	-7.0	-7.2	2	1	0	-8.1	-14.7
Miscellaneous manufacturing industries	375	394	390	19	-4	0.5	-0.1	41	52	79	2.5	4.3
Jewelry, silverware, and plated ware	52	49	47	-3	-2	-0.6	-0.4	6	8	9	2.6	1.3
Toys and sporting goods	104	104	109	(4)	5	(4)	0.5	11	16	36	3.6	8.4
Manufactured products, n.e.c.	220	242	234	22	-8	1.0	-0.3	23	28	34	1.9	2.1
Nondurable manufacturing	7 968	7 331	7 267	-637	-64	-0.8	-0.1	1 553	1 835	2 220	1.7	1.9
Food and kindred products	1 661	1 684	1 634	23	-50	0.1	-0.3	411	499	542	2.0	0.8
Meat products	422	504	542	82	38	1.8	0.7	87	113	140	2.7	2.1
Dairy products	155	146	121	-10	-24	-0.6	-1.8	53	59	67	1.1	1.2
Preserved fruits and vegetables	247	220	195	-27	-25	-1.2	-1.2	49	57	45	1.6	-2.3
Grain mill products and fats and oils	159	152	150	-7	-2	-0.5	-0.1	70	87	96	2.2	1.0
Bakery products	213	204	191	-9	-13	-0.4	-0.7	29	32	35	1.0	1.0
Sugar and confectionery products	99	92	85	-7	-7	-0.7	-0.8	24	28	32	1.7	1.3
Beverages	184	187	165	3	-22	0.2	-1.3	66	85	89	2.6	0.4
Miscellaneous food and kindred products	182	180	185	-2	5	-0.1	0.3	35	39	42	1.0	0.7
Tobacco products	49	34	29	-15	-5	-3.6	-1.6	36	36	39	0.2	0.8
Textile mill products	692	529	500	-163	-29	-2.7	-0.6	69	78	86	1.3	1.0
Weaving, finishing, yarn, and thread mills	374	284	250	-90	-34	-2.7	-1.3	34	39	41	1.4	0.4
Knitting mills	205	126	120	-80	-6	-4.8	-0.5	15	15	18	0.0	1.7
Carpets and rugs	61	66	73	5	7	0.7	1.1	11	14	15	1.6	1.2
Miscellaneous textile goods	51	54	57	2	3	0.5	0.6	8	10	12	2.4	2.0
Apparel and other textile products	1 036	633	530	-403	-103	-4.8	-1.8	65	68	87	0.3	2.6
Apparel	832	418	315	-414	-103	-6.7	-2.8	47	44	51	-0.6	1.3
Miscellaneous fabricated textile products	204	215	215	11	(4)	0.5	(4)	18	23	36	2.6	4.7
Paper and allied products	697	657	626	-40	-31	-0.6	-0.5	149	168	195	1.2	1.5
Pulp, paper, and paperboard mills	246	199	176	-48	-23	-2.1	-1.2	64	59	65	-0.8	0.9
Paperboard containers and boxes	209	218	210	9	-8	0.4	-0.4	36	45	50	2.2	1.2
Converted paper products except containers	241	240	240	-1	(4)	-0.1	(4)	49	64	79	2.7	2.2
Printing and publishing	1 570	1 547	1 545	-22	-3	-0.1	(4)	195	214	240	1.0	1.1
Newspapers	474	442	432	-33	-10	-0.7	-0.2	48	44	43	-1.0	-0.2
Periodicals	129	149	165	20	16	1.5	1.0	25	38	44	4.0	1.5
Books	121	126	136	5	10	0.4	0.7	24	23	31	-0.5	2.9
Miscellaneous publishing	82	95	105	13	10	1.5	1.0	11	18	27	4.5	4.3
Commercial printing and business forms	602	603	585	1	-18	(4)	-0.3	71	76	79	0.6	0.4
Greeting cards	25	25	27	(4)	1	(4)	0.6	4	4	4	0.1	-0.3
Blankbooks and bookbinding	72	60	55	-13	-4	-1.9	-0.8	6	6	7	1.5	0.3
Service industries for the printing trade	64	47	40	-16	-7	-2.9	-1.6	5	5	5	0.1	-0.9
Chemicals and allied products	1 086	1 038	1 081	-48	43	-0.5	0.4	337	403	560	1.8	3.3
Industrial chemicals	293	218	190	-75	-28	-2.9	-1.4	116	100	94	-1.4	-0.7
Plastic materials and synthetics	180	154	130	-26	-24	-1.5	-1.7	52	69	101	2.8	4.0
Drugs	237	315	390	78	75	2.9	2.2	63	99	171	4.7	5.6
Soap, cleaners, and toilet goods	159	155	164	-4	9	-0.3	0.6	47	63	89	2.9	3.6
Paints and allied products	61	52	56	-9	4	-1.7	0.7	16	20	28	1.8	3.8
Agricultural chemicals	56	51	56	-5	5	-0.9	0.9	22	25	36	1.2	3.7
Miscellaneous chemical products	100	93	95	-7	2	-0.7	0.2	23	27	38	1.7	3.5
Petroleum and coal products	157	128	113	-30	-15	-2.1	-1.2	171	189	208	1.0	0.9
Petroleum refining	118	85	65	-33	-20	-3.3	-2.6	157	169	181	0.7	0.7
Miscellaneous petroleum and coal products	40	43	48	3	5	0.8	1.0	14	21	27	3.6	2.5
Rubber and miscellaneous plastic products	888	1 011	1 166	123	156	1.3	1.4	110	170	253	4.5	4.0
Tires and inner tubes	84	79	82	-5	2	-0.6	0.3	12	15	23	2.5	4.4
Rubber products and plastic hose and footwear	177	187	184	10	-2	0.6	-0.1	18	26	34	3.4	2.8
Miscellaneous plastic products, n.e.c.	626	744	900	118	156	1.7	1.9	79	129	196	5.0	4.2
Leather and leather products	133	72	44	-62	-27	-6.0	4.7	10	10	5	-0.2	-6.3
Footwear, except rubber and plastic	80	30	14	-50	-16	-9.3	-7.2	5	3	2	-6.3	-1.5
Luggage, handbags, and leather products, n.e.c.	53	41	30	-12	-11	-2.5	-3.2	6	8	4	3.2	-6.4
Transportation, Communications, And Utilities	5 776	7 019	8 274	1 243	1 255	2.0	1.7	931	1 278	1 962	3.2	4.4
Transportation	3 510	4 529	5 466	1 019	937	2.6	1.9	387	531	798	3.2	4.2
Railroad transportation	279	236	175	-43	-60	-1.7	-2.9	35	37	48	0.5	2.7
Local and interurban passenger transit	338	476	624	138	148	3.5	2.7	21	24	31	1.4	2.5
Trucking and warehousing	1 395	1 856	2 262	460	407	2.9	2.0	163	255	394	4.6	4.4
Trucking and courier services, except air transportation	1 278	1 649	1 962	371	313	2.6	1.8	154	237	359	4.4	4.2
Warehousing and storage	117	206	300	89	94	5.8	3.8	10	17	35	6.2	7.2
Water transportation	177	196	208	19	13	1.0	0.6	37	40	50	0.9	2.3
Air transportation	968	1 281	1 600	314	319	2.8	2.2	96	125	192	2.6	4.4
Pipelines, except natural gas	19	14	11	-5	-2	-3.0	-1.7	8	7	9	-2.2	3.3
Transportation services	336	471	585	135	114	3.4	2.2	26	43	73	5.1	5.5
Passenger transportation arrangement	188	219	235	30	17	1.5	0.7	10	19	34	6.7	6.0
Miscellaneous transportation services	148	253	350	105	97	5.5	3.3	16	24	40	4.0	5.2

See footnotes and *Note* at end of table.

Table 3-5. Employment and Output by Industry, 1990, 2000, and Projected 2010—*Continued*

Industry	Employment							Output				
	Thousands of jobs			Change		Average annual rate of change (percent)		Billions of chained (1996) dollars			Average annual rate of change (percent)	
	1990	2000	2010	1990-2000	2000-2010	1990-2000	2000-2010	1990	2000	2010	1990-2000	2000-2010
Communications	1 309	1 639	1 916	330	277	2.3	1.6	245	419	750	5.5	6.0
Telephone and telegraph communications and communication service	950	1 168	1 310	218	143	2.1	1.2	185	341	638	6.3	6.5
Cable and pay television services	126	216	325	90	109	5.5	4.2	26	35	60	2.8	5.7
Radio and television broadcasting	234	255	280	22	25	0.9	0.9	35	45	59	2.6	2.7
Utilities	957	851	893	-106	42	-1.2	0.5	299	326	417	0.9	2.5
Electric utilities	454	357	324	-98	-33	-2.4	-1.0	176	212	275	1.9	2.6
Gas utilities	165	128	120	-37	-8	-2.5	-0.6	66	49	63	-3.0	2.6
Combined utilities	193	152	138	-41	-14	-2.4	-1.0	32	38	46	1.5	2.1
Water and sanitation	145	214	310	69	96	4.0	3.8	24	29	34	1.8	1.8
Wholesale Trade	6 173	7 024	7 800	851	776	1.3	1.1	608	920	1 410	4.2	4.4
Retail Trade	19 601	23 307	26 400	3 706	3 093	1.7	1.3	897	1 222	1 628	3.1	2.9
Retail trade, excluding eating and drinking places	13 092	15 194	16 800	2 102	1 606	1.5	1.0	652	926	1 237	3.6	2.9
Eating and drinking places	6 509	8 114	9 600	1 605	1 486	2.2	1.7	245	298	393	2.0	2.8
Finance, Insurance And Real Estate	6 709	7 560	8 247	851	687	1.2	0.9	1 198	1 806	2 429	4.2	3.0
Depository institutions	2 251	2 029	1 999	-221	-31	-1.0	-0.2	266	446	596	5.3	2.9
Nondepository institutions; holding and investment offices	593	932	1 075	339	143	4.6	1.4	70	122	152	5.8	2.2
Security and commodity brokers	424	748	900	324	152	5.8	1.9	57	292	540	17.7	6.4
Insurance carriers	1 462	1 589	1 632	127	43	0.8	0.3	211	228	259	0.8	1.3
Insurance agents, brokers and service	663	757	865	93	109	1.3	1.3	68	81	103	1.8	2.4
Real estate	1 315	1 504	1 776	189	272	1.4	1.7	535	653	822	2.0	2.3
Royalties	...	...	...	...	...	...	...	55	96	191	5.8	7.1
Owner-occupied dwellings	...	...	...	...	...	...	...	493	631	943	2.5	4.1
Services [3]	27 291	39 340	52 233	12 049	12 893	3.7	2.9	2 057	3 032	4 378	4.0	3.7
Hotels	1 578	1 845	2 100	267	255	1.6	1.3	85	108	136	2.5	2.3
Other lodging places	53	67	67	14	(4)	2.3	(4)	5	7	10	2.8	4.7
Personal services	1 104	1 251	1 354	147	103	1.3	0.8	76	101	147	2.9	3.8
Laundry, cleaning, and shoe repair	433	451	470	18	19	0.4	0.4	22	25	28	1.6	0.8
Personal services, n.e.c.	200	266	287	66	21	2.9	0.8	26	40	64	4.6	4.9
Beauty and barber shops	389	433	490	44	57	1.1	1.2	20	26	40	2.6	4.5
Funeral service and crematories	83	101	107	18	6	2.0	0.6	9	10	14	1.0	4.1
Business services	5 139	9 858	14 923	4 719	5 064	6.7	4.2	342	713	1 278	7.6	6.0
Advertising	235	302	400	68	98	2.6	2.9	27	47	67	5.8	3.5
Service to buildings	807	994	1 120	188	126	2.1	1.2	31	50	71	5.0	3.6
Miscellaneous equipment rental and leasing	208	279	397	71	118	3.0	3.6	28	39	60	3.2	4.4
Personnel supply services	1 535	3 887	5 800	2 353	1 913	9.7	4.1	38	101	167	10.2	5.1
Computer and data processing services	772	2 095	3 900	1 323	1 805	10.5	6.4	99	278	601	10.8	8.0
Miscellaneous business services	1 584	2 301	3 305	717	1 004	3.8	3.7	119	198	313	5.2	4.7
Auto repair, services and garages	914	1 248	1 527	335	278	3.2	2.0	104	166	286	4.8	5.6
Automotive rentals, without drivers	173	225	265	52	41	2.7	1.7	17	63	151	14.0	9.1
Automobile parking, repair, and services	741	1 024	1 262	283	238	3.3	2.1	87	103	136	1.7	2.8
Miscellaneous repair shops	374	366	405	-9	39	-0.2	1.0	44	51	62	1.5	2.1
Electrical repair shops	112	104	103	-8	-1	-0.7	-0.1	15	15	14	-0.3	-0.2
Watch, jewelry, and furniture repair	30	29	27	(4)	-2	-0.1	-0.8	2	3	5	3.5	3.2
Miscellaneous repair shops and related services	233	233	275	-1	42	(4)	1.7	26	33	43	2.3	2.8
Motion pictures	408	594	672	186	78	3.8	1.2	45	77	86	5.7	1.1
Motion pictures	274	426	499	152	73	4.5	1.6	40	69	77	5.6	1.1
Video tape rental	134	168	173	34	5	2.3	0.3	5	9	9	5.8	0.6
Amusement and recreation services	1 076	1 728	2 325	652	597	4.9	3.0	75	137	212	6.2	4.4
Producers, orchestras, and entertainers	136	181	225	45	44	2.9	2.2	18	28	35	4.6	2.3
Bowling centers	91	81	70	-10	-11	-1.2	-1.5	4	3	3	-2.4	-2.0
Commercial sports	101	153	180	52	28	4.2	1.7	13	15	19	1.4	1.9
Amusement and recreation services, n.e.c.	748	1 314	1 850	566	536	5.8	3.5	40	91	156	8.4	5.6
Health services	7 814	10 095	12 934	2 281	2 839	2.6	2.5	595	762	882	2.5	1.5
Offices of health practitioners	2 166	3 099	4 344	933	1 245	3.6	3.4	254	317	374	2.3	1.7
Nursing and personal care facilities	1 415	1 796	2 190	381	394	2.4	2.0	55	69	85	2.4	2.1
Hospitals, private	3 549	3 990	4 500	442	510	1.2	1.2	236	292	315	2.1	0.8
Health services, n.e.c.	685	1 210	1 900	525	690	5.9	4.6	52	84	108	5.0	2.5
Legal services	908	1 010	1 350	102	340	1.1	2.9	134	143	195	0.7	3.2
Educational services	1 661	2 325	2 852	664	527	3.4	2.1	91	113	142	2.1	2.3
Social services	1 734	2 903	4 128	1 169	1 225	5.3	3.6	76	103	171	3.1	5.2
Individual and miscellaneous social services	634	1 005	1 300	372	295	4.7	2.6	31	47	77	4.1	5.1
Job training and related services	248	380	500	131	120	4.3	2.8	9	9	14	0.2	4.8
Child day care services	391	712	1 010	321	298	6.2	3.6	20	24	40	2.0	5.2
Residential care	461	806	1 318	345	512	5.7	5.0	16	24	41	4.2	5.5
Museums, botanical, and zoological gardens	66	106	135	40	29	4.9	2.4	3	6	9	5.0	4.6
Membership organizations	1 945	2 475	2 734	529	259	2.4	1.0	79	96	122	2.0	2.4
Engineering, management, and other services	2 516	3 469	4 729	953	1 260	3.3	3.1	290	434	640	4.1	3.9
Engineering and architectural services	786	1 017	1 330	231	313	2.6	2.7	103	133	211	2.6	4.7
Research and testing services	549	642	886	94	244	1.6	3.3	39	67	108	5.6	4.9
Management and public relations	610	1 090	1 550	479	460	6.0	3.6	79	147	195	6.5	2.8
Accounting, auditing, and other services	571	720	963	149	243	2.3	3.0	70	87	127	2.3	3.8

See footnotes and *Note* at end of table.

Table 3-5. Employment and Output by Industry, 1990, 2000, and Projected 2010—*Continued*

Industry	Employment							Output				
	Thousands of jobs			Change		Average annual rate of change (percent)		Billions of chained (1996) dollars			Average annual rate of change (percent)	
	1990	2000	2010	1990-2000	2000-2010	1990-2000	2000-2010	1990	2000	2010	1990-2000	2000-2010
Government	18 304	20 680	22 436	2 376	1 757	1.2	0.8	1 043	1 162	1 287	1.1	1.0
Federal Government	3 085	2 777	2 622	-308	-154	-1.0	-0.6	389	353	360	-1.0	0.2
Federal enterprises	1 026	975	952	-51	-23	-0.5	-0.2	69	85	94	2.1	0.9
U.S. Postal Service	819	860	850	41	-10	0.5	-0.1	55	65	74	1.7	1.4
Federal electric utilities	31	27	22	-4	-5	-1.3	-2.2	6	11	10	5.8	-1.4
Federal government enterprises, n.e.c.	177	88	80	-89	-8	-6.7	-0.9	9	10	10	0.9	0.5
Federal general government	2 059	1 802	1 671	-257	-131	-1.3	-0.8	256	200	190	-2.4	-0.5
Federal government capital services	...	...	...	...	...	...	...	65	68	78	0.5	1.3
State and local government	15 219	17 903	19 814	2 684	1 911	1.6	1.0	655	808	928	2.1	1.4
State and local enterprises	913	869	918	-44	49	0.5	0.5	103	139	189	3.1	3.2
Local government passenger transit	207	223	225	16	2	0.7	0.1	6	7	8	1.9	0.6
State and local electric utilities	82	89	95	7	6	0.8	0.7	19	24	28	2.4	1.3
State and local government enterprises, n.e.c.	624	557	598	-67	41	-1.1	0.7	77	107	154	3.3	3.7
State and local general government	14 306	17 034	18 896	2 728	1 862	1.8	1.0	552	670	738	2.0	1.0
State and local government hospitals	1 072	970	948	-102	-22	-1.0	-0.2	42	45	51	0.8	1.2
State and local government education	7 771	9 472	10 548	1 700	1 076	2.0	1.1	265	303	302	1.3	0.0
State and local general government, n.e.c.	5 462	6 592	7 400	1 130	808	1.9	1.2	199	227	255	1.3	1.2
State and local government capital services	...	...	...	...	...	...	...	46	96	135	7.5	3.5
AGRICULTURE [5]	3 340	3 526	3 849	186	323	0.5	0.9	257	334	405	2.6	1.9
Agricultural production	2 174	1 979	1 824	-196	-155	-1.1	-0.7	210	260	315	2.2	1.9
Agricultural services	1 166	1 548	2 025	382	477	2.9	2.7	36	58	70	4.8	1.9
Veterinary services	143	240	336	97	96	5.3	3.4	8	16	20	6.7	2.5
Landscape and horticultural services	576	808	1 093	233	285	3.5	3.1	18	27	36	4.4	2.7
Agricultural services, n.e.c.	339	403	501	63	99	1.7	2.2	10	15	14	3.9	-0.6
Forestry, fishing, hunting and trapping	108	97	95	-11	-2	-1.1	-0.2	12	15	19	2.5	2.3
PRIVATE HOUSEHOLD WAGE AND SALARY	1 014	890	664	-124	-226	-1.3	-2.9	13	15	13	1.5	-1.0
NONAGRICULTURAL SELF-EMPLOYED AND UNPAID FAMILY [6,7]	8 921	8 731	9 062	-190	331	-0.2	0.4	...	...	...	...	...
SECONDARY WAGE AND SALARY JOBS IN AGRICULTURE (EXCEPT AGRICULTURAL SERVICES); FORESTRY, FISHING, HUNTING, AND TRAPPING; PRIVATE HOUSEHOLDS[7,8]	205	155	150	-50	-5	-2.8	-0.3	...	...	...	...	...
SECONDARY JOB AS A SELF-EMPLOYED WORKER OR UNPAID FAMILY WORKER[7,9]	2 084	1 652	1 582	-432	-70	-2.3	-0.4	...	...	...	...	...

Note: n.e.c. = not elsewhere classified.

1. Differs from historical employment totals. See "Notes and Definitions."
2. Output subcategories do not necessarily add to higher categories as a by-product of chain-weighting.
3. Excludes SIC 074, 075, 078 (agricultural services) and 99 (nonclassifiable establishments). The data therefore are not exactly comparable with data published in 'Employment and Earnings'.
4. Positive value less than 0.05.
5. Excludes government wage and salary workers, and includes private sector for SIC 08 and 09 (forestry, fishing, hunting, and trapping).
6. Excludes SIC 08, 09 (forestry, fishing, hunting, and trapping).
7. Comparable estimate of output growth is not available.
8. Workers who hold a secondary wage and salary job in agriculture (except agricultural services); forestry, fishing, hunting, and trapping; and private households.
9. Wage and salary workers who hold a secondary wage and salary job as a self-employed or unpaid family worker.

Table 3-6. Employment by Occupation, 2000 and Projected 2010

(Thousands of jobs, percent.)

Occupation	Employment				Change 2000–2010		Total job openings due to growth and replacement 2000-2010
	Number		Percent distribution		Number	Percent	
	2000	2010	2000	2010			
TOTAL, ALL OCCUPATIONS	145 594	167 754	100.0	100.0	22 160	15.2	57 932
Management, business, and financial occupations	15 519	17 635	10.7	10.5	2 115	13.6	5 109
Management occupations	10 564	11 834	7.3	7.1	1 270	12.0	3 330
Administrative services managers	362	436	0.2	0.3	74	20.4	133
Advertising, marketing, promotions, public relations, and sales managers	707	936	0.5	0.6	229	32.4	331
Advertising and promotions managers	100	135	0.1	0.1	34	34.3	49
Marketing and sales managers	533	701	0.4	0.4	168	31.5	244
Marketing managers	190	246	0.1	0.1	55	29.1	83
Sales managers	343	455	0.2	0.3	112	32.8	162
Public relations managers	74	101	0.1	0.1	27	36.3	38
Agricultural managers	1 462	1 144	1.0	0.7	-318	-21.7	103
Farm, ranch, and other agricultural managers	169	179	0.1	0.1	10	6.0	30
Farmers and ranchers	1 294	965	0.9	0.6	-328	-25.4	74
Chief executives	547	641	0.4	0.4	94	17.2	266
Computer and information systems managers	313	463	0.2	0.3	150	47.9	203
Construction managers	308	358	0.2	0.2	50	16.3	100
Education administrators	453	513	0.3	0.3	61	13.4	178
Engineering managers	282	305	0.2	0.2	23	8.0	69
Financial managers	658	780	0.5	0.5	122	18.5	223
Food service managers	465	535	0.3	0.3	70	15.0	125
Funeral directors	32	32	(2)	(2)	1	3.0	6
Gaming managers	4	5	(2)	(2)	1	30.0	2
General and operations managers	2 398	2 761	1.6	1.6	363	15.2	767
Human resources managers	219	246	0.2	0.1	28	12.7	66
Industrial production managers	255	271	0.2	0.2	16	6.2	57
Legislators	54	61	(2)	(2)	7	12.7	24
Lodging managers	68	75	(2)	(2)	6	9.3	14
Medical and health services managers	250	330	0.2	0.2	81	32.3	123
Natural sciences managers	42	45	(2)	(2)	3	7.6	11
Postmasters and mail superintendents	25	26	(2)	(2)	1	2.5	5
Property, real estate, and community association managers	270	331	0.2	0.2	61	22.7	105
Purchasing managers	132	125	0.1	0.1	-7	-5.5	41
Social and community service managers	128	160	0.1	0.1	32	24.8	56
Transportation, storage, and distribution managers	149	179	0.1	0.1	30	20.2	55
All other managers	981	1 074	0.7	0.6	93	9.5	267
Business and financial operations occupations	4 956	5 801	3.4	3.5	845	17.1	1 779
Business operations specialists	2 841	3 320	2.0	2.0	479	16.8	1 053
Agents and business managers of artists, performers, and athletes	17	22	(2)	(2)	5	27.9	8
Buyers and purchasing agents	404	424	0.3	0.3	20	4.8	128
Purchasing agents and buyers, farm products	20	23	(2)	(2)	3	16.8	7
Purchasing agents, except wholesale, retail, and farm products	237	266	0.2	0.2	29	12.3	76
Wholesale and retail buyers, except farm products	148	135	0.1	0.1	-13	-8.7	45
Claims adjusters, appraisers, examiners, and investigators	207	238	0.1	0.1	31	15.0	54
Claims adjusters, examiners, and investigators	194	223	0.1	0.1	29	15.1	51
Insurance appraisers, auto damage	13	15	(2)	(2)	2	14.3	3
Compliance officers, except agriculture, construction, health and safety and transportation	140	152	0.1	0.1	12	8.9	48
Cost estimators	211	246	0.1	0.1	35	16.5	81
Emergency management specialists	10	12	(2)	(2)	2	18.1	5
Human resources, training, and labor relations specialists	490	578	0.3	0.3	88	18.0	183
Compensation, benefits, and job analysis specialists	87	100	0.1	0.1	14	15.7	30
Employment, recruitment, and placement specialists	199	234	0.1	0.1	35	17.6	73
Training and development specialists	204	244	0.1	0.1	40	19.4	79
Management analysts	501	646	0.3	0.4	145	28.9	189
Meeting and convention planners	34	42	(2)	(2)	8	23.3	14
All other business operations specialists	827	960	0.6	0.6	133	16.1	343
Financial specialists	2 115	2 481	1.5	1.5	367	17.3	726
Accountants and auditors	976	1 157	0.7	0.7	181	18.5	326
Appraisers and assessors of real estate	57	67	(2)	(2)	10	18.0	26
Budget analysts	70	80	(2)	(2)	10	14.6	24
Credit analysts	60	70	(2)	(2)	10	16.0	22
Financial analysts	145	182	0.1	0.1	37	25.5	57
Financial examiners	25	27	(2)	(2)	3	10.2	7
Insurance underwriters	107	109	0.1	0.1	2	2.0	18
Loan counselors and officers	265	281	0.2	0.2	16	6.1	69
Loan counselors	29	33	0.0	(2)	5	16.0	10
Loan officers	236	248	0.2	0.1	12	4.9	59
Personal financial advisors	94	126	0.1	0.1	32	34.0	43
Tax examiners, collectors, and revenue	79	86	0.1	0.1	7	8.3	28
Tax preparers	69	81	(2)	(2)	12	17.4	26
All other financial specialists	169	216	0.1	0.1	47	28.0	81
Professional and related occupations	26 758	33 709	18.4	20.1	6 952	26.0	12 160
Computer and mathematical occupations	2 993	4 988	2.1	3.0	1 996	66.7	2 285
Computer specialists	2 903	4 894	2.0	2.9	1 991	68.6	2 259
Computer programmers	585	680	0.4	0.4	95	16.2	217
Computer scientists and systems	459	729	0.3	0.4	269	58.6	309
Computer and information scientists, research	28	39	(2)	(2)	11	40.3	14
Computer systems analysts	431	689	0.3	0.4	258	59.7	296
Computer software engineers	697	1 361	0.5	0.8	664	95.4	711
Computer software engineers, applications	380	760	0.3	0.5	380	100.0	406
Computer software engineers, systems	317	601	0.2	0.4	284	89.7	306

See footnotes and *Note* at end of table.

Table 3-6. Employment by Occupation, 2000 and Projected 2010—*Continued*

(Thousands of jobs, percent.)

Occupation	Employment				Change 2000–2010		Total job openings due to growth and replacement 2000-2010
	Number		Percent distribution		Number	Percent	
	2000	2010	2000	2010			
Computer support specialists	506	996	0.3	0.6	490	97.0	512
Database administrators	106	176	0.1	0.1	70	65.9	74
Network and computer systems administrators	229	416	0.2	0.2	187	81.9	197
Network systems and data communications	119	211	0.1	0.1	92	77.5	97
All other computer specialists	203	326	0.1	0.2	123	60.7	141
Mathematical science occupations	89	95	0.1	0.1	5	5.7	26
Mathematical scientists and technicians	85	90	0.1	0.1	5	5.9	25
Actuaries	14	15	(2)	(2)	1	5.4	3
Mathematicians	4	4	(2)	(2)	(2)	-1.9	(2)
Operations research analysts	47	51	(2)	(2)	4	8.0	19
Statisticians	19	20	(2)	(2)	(2)	2.3	3
Miscellaneous mathematical science	5	5	(2)	(2)	(2)	2.7	1
Architecture and engineering occupations	2 605	2 930	1.8	1.7	325	12.5	868
Architects, surveyors, and cartographers	196	229	0.1	0.1	33	17.1	61
Architects, except naval	124	150	0.1	0.1	26	20.7	33
Architects, except landscape and naval	102	121	0.1	0.1	19	18.5	25
Landscape architects	22	29	(2)	(2)	7	31.1	8
Surveyors, cartographers, and photogrammetrists	65	71	(2)	(2)	6	9.2	26
Cartographers and photogrammetrists	7	8	(2)	(2)	1	18.5	3
Surveyors	58	63	(2)	(2)	5	8.1	22
All other architects, surveyors, and cartographers	6	8	(2)	(2)	2	28.5	2
Engineers	1 465	1 603	1.0	1.0	138	9.4	432
Aerospace engineers	50	57	(2)	(2)	7	13.9	22
Agricultural engineers	2	3	(2)	(2)	(2)	14.8	1
Biomedical engineers	7	9	(2)	(2)	2	31.4	4
Chemical engineers	33	34	(2)	(2)	1	4.1	7
Civil engineers	232	256	0.2	0.2	24	10.2	60
Computer hardware engineers	60	75	(2)	(2)	15	24.9	23
Electrical and electronics engineers	288	319	0.2	0.2	31	10.9	84
Electrical engineers	157	175	0.1	0.1	18	11.3	47
Electronics engineers, except computer	130	144	0.1	0.1	14	10.4	37
Environmental engineers	52	66	(2)	(2)	14	26.0	24
Industrial engineers, including health	198	210	0.1	0.1	12	5.9	45
Health and safety engineers, except mining safety engineers and inspectors	44	49	(2)	(2)	5	10.9	12
Industrial engineers	154	161	0.1	0.1	7	4.5	33
Marine engineers and naval architects	5	5	(2)	(2)	(2)	2.1	1
Materials engineers	33	35	(2)	(2)	2	5.3	9
Mechanical engineers	221	251	0.2	0.1	29	13.1	94
Mining and geological engineers, including mining safety engineers	6	6	(2)	(2)	(2)	-1.3	1
Nuclear engineers	14	14	(2)	(2)	(2)	1.8	3
Petroleum engineers	9	8	(2)	(2)	-1	-7.2	2
All other engineers	253	254	0.2	0.2	1	0.4	51
Drafters, engineering, and mapping	944	1 098	0.6	0.7	154	16.3	375
Drafters	213	255	0.1	0.2	42	19.5	106
Architectural and civil drafters	102	123	0.1	0.1	21	20.8	52
Electrical and electronics drafters	41	51	(2)	(2)	10	23.3	22
Mechanical drafters	70	81	(2)	(2)	11	15.4	32
Engineering technicians, except drafters	519	582	0.4	0.3	62	12.0	167
Aerospace engineering and operations	21	22	(2)	(2)	1	5.6	5
Civil engineering technicians	94	105	0.1	0.1	11	11.9	30
Electrical and electronic engineering	233	258	0.2	0.2	25	10.8	72
Electro-mechanical technicians	43	50	(2)	(2)	6	14.5	15
Environmental engineering technicians	18	24	(2)	(2)	5	29.1	9
Industrial engineering technicians	52	57	(2)	(2)	5	10.1	16
Mechanical engineering technicians	58	66	(2)	(2)	8	13.9	20
Surveying and mapping technicians	55	70	(2)	(2)	14	25.3	32
All other drafters, engineering, and mapping technicians	156	192	0.1	0.1	36	23.2	70
Life, physical, and social science occupations	1 164	1 386	0.8	0.8	223	19.1	559
Life scientists	184	218	0.1	0.1	33	18.1	93
Agricultural and food scientists	17	19	(2)	(2)	2	8.8	7
Biological scientists	73	88	0.1	0.1	15	21.0	42
Conservation scientists and foresters	29	31	(2)	(2)	2	7.7	12
Conservation scientists	16	18	(2)	(2)	1	8.3	7
Foresters	12	13	(2)	(2)	1	7.0	5
Medical scientists	37	47	(2)	(2)	10	26.5	18
All other life scientists	28	33	(2)	(2)	4	15.9	15
Physical scientists	239	283	0.2	0.2	44	18.3	124
Astronomers and physicists	10	11	(2)	(2)	1	10.5	4
Atmospheric and space scientists	7	8	(2)	(2)	1	17.1	3
Chemists and materials scientists	92	110	0.1	0.1	18	19.2	47
Chemists	84	100	0.1	0.1	16	19.1	43
Materials scientists	8	9	(2)	(2)	2	19.8	4
Environmental scientists and geoscientists	97	118	0.1	0.1	21	21.5	52
Environmental scientists and specialists, including health	64	78	(2)	(2)	14	22.3	35
Geoscientists, except hydrologists and geographers	25	30	(2)	(2)	5	18.1	13
Hydrologists	8	10	(2)	(2)	2	25.7	5
All other physical scientists	33	36	(2)	(2)	3	9.4	17
Social scientists and related occupations	410	492	0.3	0.3	82	20.1	178
Economists	22	26	(2)	(2)	4	18.5	9
Market and survey researchers	113	142	0.1	0.1	30	26.4	55
Market research analysts	90	112	0.1	0.1	22	24.4	42
Survey researchers	23	30	(2)	(2)	8	34.5	13
Psychologists	182	214	0.1	0.1	33	18.1	75
Social scientists, other	15	17	(2)	(2)	3	17.2	6

See footnotes and *Note* at end of table.

Table 3-6. Employment by Occupation, 2000 and Projected 2010—*Continued*

(Thousands of jobs, percent.)

Occupation	Employment				Change 2000–2010		Total job openings due to growth and replacement 2000-2010
	Number		Percent distribution		Number	Percent	
	2000	2010	2000	2010			
Urban and regional planners	30	35	(2)	(2)	5	16.4	12
All other social scientists and related workers	49	58	(2)	(2)	8	17.1	20
Life, physical, and social science technicians	330	393	0.2	0.2	63	19.0	164
Agricultural and food science technicians	18	20	(2)	(2)	3	15.2	7
Biological technicians	41	52	(2)	(2)	11	26.4	21
Chemical technicians	73	84	0.1	0.1	11	15.0	28
Geological and petroleum technicians	10	11	(2)	(2)	1	6.5	3
Nuclear technicians	3	4	(2)	(2)	1	20.7	2
Other life, physical, and social science technicians	184	221	0.1	0.1	37	20.0	104
Environmental science and protection technicians, including health	27	34	(2)	(2)	7	24.5	17
Forensic science technicians	6	7	(2)	(2)	1	13.0	3
Forest and conservation technicians	18	19	(2)	(2)	1	3.2	7
All other life, physical, and social science technicians	133	161	(2)	(2)	29	21.7	77
Community and social services occupations	1 869	2 398	(2)	(2)	529	28.3	846
Counselors	465	585	0.3	0.3	120	25.8	215
Educational, vocational, and school counselors	205	257	0.1	0.2	52	25.3	94
Marriage and family therapists	21	27	(2)	(2)	6	29.9	11
Mental health counselors	67	82	(2)	(2)	15	21.7	28
Rehabilitation counselors	110	136	0.1	0.1	26	23.6	49
Substance abuse and behavioral disorder counselors	61	82	(2)	(2)	21	35.0	34
Miscellaneous community and social service specialists	398	575	0.3	0.3	177	44.5	236
Health educators	43	53	(2)	(2)	10	23.5	17
Probation officers and correctional treatment specialists	84	105	0.1	0.1	20	23.8	33
Social and human service assistants	271	418	0.2	0.2	(2)	54.2	187
Religious workers	293	338	0.2	0.2	45	15.4	112
Clergy	171	197	0.1	0.1	26	15.0	73
Directors, religious activities and education	121	141	0.1	0.1	19	15.9	40
Social workers	468	609	0.3	0.4	141	30.1	193
Child, family, and school social workers	281	357	0.2	0.2	76	26.9	107
Medical and public health social workers	104	136	0.1	0.1	33	31.6	44
Mental health and substance abuse social workers	83	116	0.1	0.1	33	39.1	42
All other counselors, social, and religious workers	244	290	0.2	0.2	46	18.8	89
Legal occupations	1 119	1 335	0.8	0.8	216	19.3	304
Judges, magistrates, and other judicial workers	43	44	(2)	(2)	2	3.8	14
Administrative law judges, adjudicators, and hearing officers	14	14	(2)	(2)	(2)	1.1	4
Arbitrators, mediators, and conciliators	4	6	(2)	(2)	1	27.2	2
Judges, magistrate judges, and magistrates	24	24	(2)	(2)	(2)	1.1	7
Lawyers	681	803	0.5	0.5	123	18.0	168
Paralegals and legal assistants	188	251	0.1	0.1	62	33.2	74
Miscellaneous legal support workers	98	106	0.1	0.1	8	7.7	17
Court reporters	18	21	(2)	(2)	3	16.2	5
Law clerks	31	35	(2)	(2)	4	13.2	7
Title examiners, abstractors, and searchers	48	49	(2)	(2)	(2)	1.0	5
All other legal and related workers	109	131	0.1	0.1	22	20.2	32
Education, training, and library occupations	8 260	9 831	5.7	5.9	1 571	19.0	3 356
Postsecondary teachers	1 344	1 659	0.9	1.0	315	23.5	682
Primary, secondary, and special education teachers	4 284	4 995	2.9	3.0	711	16.6	1 663
Preschool and kindergarten teachers	597	707	0.4	0.4	110	18.4	184
Preschool teachers, except special education	423	507	0.3	0.3	85	20.0	137
Kindergarten teachers, except special education	175	200	0.1	0.1	25	14.5	47
Elementary and middle school teachers	2 122	2 381	1.5	1.4	260	12.2	742
Elementary school teachers, except special education	1 532	1 734	1.1	1.0	202	13.2	551
Middle school teachers, except special and vocational education	570	625	0.4	0.4	55	9.6	184
Vocational education teachers, middle school	20	22	(2)	(2)	3	13.1	7
Secondary school teachers	1 113	1 314	0.8	0.8	201	18.1	540
Secondary school teachers, except special and vocational education	1 004	1 190	0.7	0.7	187	18.6	492
Vocational education teachers, secondary school	109	123	0.1	0.1	15	13.4	48
Special education teachers	453	592	0.3	0.4	140	30.9	197
Special education teachers, preschool, kindergarten, and elementary school	234	320	0.2	0.2	86	36.8	116
Special education teachers, middle school	96	119	0.1	0.1	23	24.4	35
Special education teachers, secondary school	123	153	0.1	0.1	30	24.6	46
Other teachers and instructors	901	1 076	0.6	0.6	175	19.4	266
Adult literacy, remedial education, and GED teachers and instructors	67	80	(2)	(2)	13	19.4	20
Self-enrichment education teachers	186	220	0.1	0.1	34	18.5	53
All other teachers, primary, secondary, and adult	648	776	0.4	0.5	128	19.7	193
Library, museum, training, and other education occupations	1 731	2 101	1.2	1.3	370	21.4	745
Archivists, curators, and museum technicians	21	24	(2)	(2)	3	11.9	7
Librarians	149	160	0.1	0.1	10	7.0	41
Library technicians	109	130	0.1	0.1	21	19.5	70
Teacher assistants	1 262	1 562	0.9	0.9	301	23.9	565
Other education, training, library, and museum workers	190	225	0.1	0.1	35	18.2	62
Audio-visual collections specialists	11	13	(2)	(2)	2	13.6	3
Farm and home management advisors	11	11	(2)	(2)	1	6.1	2
Instructional coordinators	81	101	0.1	0.1	20	25.0	32
All other library, museum, training, and other education workers	87	99	0.1	0.1	12	14.0	25
Arts, design, entertainment, sports, and media occupations	2 371	2 864	1.6	1.7	493	20.8	947
Art and design occupations	750	903	0.5	0.5	153	20.3	251
Artists and related workers	147	176	0.1	0.1	29	20.0	60
Art directors	47	56	(2)	(2)	10	21.1	19
Fine artists, including painters, sculptors, and illustrators	31	35	(2)	(2)	4	13.4	10
Multi-media artists and animators	69	85	(2)	0.1	15	22.2	30
Designers	492	596	0.3	0.4	104	21.2	154
Commercial and industrial designers	50	62	(2)	(2)	12	23.8	17

See footnotes and *Note* at end of table.

Table 3-6. Employment by Occupation, 2000 and Projected 2010—*Continued*

(Thousands of jobs, percent.)

Occupation	Employment				Change 2000–2010		Total job openings due to growth and replacement 2000-2010
	Number		Percent distribution		Number	Percent	
	2000	2010	2000	2010			
Fashion designers	16	19	(2)	(2)	3	20.3	5
Floral designers	102	118	0.1	0.1	15	14.9	26
Graphic designers	190	241	0.1	0.1	51	26.7	70
Interior designers	46	54	(2)	(2)	8	17.4	13
Merchandise displayers and window trimmers	76	88	0.1	0.1	12	15.9	20
Set and exhibit designers	12	15	(2)	(2)	3	27.0	4
All other art and design workers	112	130	0.1	0.1	19	16.8	37
Entertainers and performers, sports and related occupations	626	763	0.4	0.5	136	21.8	257
Actors, producers, and directors	158	200	0.1	0.1	42	26.9	73
Actors	99	126	0.1	0.1	26	26.7	46
Producers and directors	58	74	(2)	(2)	16	27.1	27
Athletes, coaches, umpires, and related workers	129	153	0.1	0.1	24	18.7	50
Athletes and sports competitors	18	22	(2)	(2)	4	22.5	7
Coaches and scouts	99	117	0.1	0.1	17	17.6	37
Umpires, referees, and other sports officials	11	14	(2)	(2)	3	22.7	5
Dancers and choreographers	26	30	(2)	(2)	4	16.3	9
Dancers	15	18	(2)	(2)	3	17.3	6
Choreographers	11	12	(2)	(2)	2	14.9	4
Musicians, singers, and related workers	240	285	0.2	0.2	45	18.7	90
Music directors and composers	50	56	(2)	(2)	6	13.1	16
Musicians and singers	191	229	0.1	0.1	38	20.1	74
All other entertainers and performers, sports and related workers	74	95	0.1	0.1	21	28.3	35
Media and communication occupations	703	856	0.5	0.5	153	21.8	315
Announcers	71	68	(2)	(2)	-4	-5.5	11
News analysts, reporters and correspondents	78	80	0.1	(2)	2	2.8	27
Public relations specialists	137	186	0.1	0.1	49	36.1	73
Writers and editors	305	385	0.2	0.2	80	26.3	158
Editors	122	149	0.1	0.1	27	22.6	67
Technical writers	57	74	(2)	(2)	17	29.6	34
Writers and authors	126	162	0.1	0.1	36	28.4	57
Miscellaneous media and communications workers	112	137	0.1	0.1	25	22.4	47
Interpreters and translators	22	27	(2)	(2)	5	23.8	9
All other media and communication workers	90	110	0.1	0.1	20	22.1	37
Media and communication equipment occupations	291	342	0.2	0.2	51	17.5	124
Broadcast and sound engineering technicians and radio operators	87	99	0.1	0.1	12	14.0	38
Audio and video equipment technicians	37	43	(2)	(2)	6	16.8	17
Broadcast technicians	36	40	(2)	(2)	4	10.2	14
Radio operators	3	3	(2)	(2)	(2)	6.2	1
Sound engineering technicians	11	13	(2)	(2)	2	19.0	5
Photographers	131	153	0.1	0.1	22	17.0	48
Television, video, and motion picture camera operators and editors	43	53	(2)	(2)	11	25.8	19
Camera operators, television, video, and motion picture	27	33	(2)	(2)	7	25.8	12
Film and video editors	16	20	(2)	(2)	4	25.8	7
All other media and communication equipment workers	31	36	(2)	(2)	6	18.1	19
Healthcare practitioners and technical occupations	6 379	7 978	4.4	4.8	1 599	25.1	2 995
Health diagnosing and treating practitioners	3 921	4 888	2.7	2.9	966	24.6	1 773
Chiropractors	50	62	(2)	(2)	12	23.4	21
Dentists	152	161	0.1	0.1	9	5.7	43
Dietitians and nutritionists	49	56	(2)	(2)	7	15.2	21
Optometrists	31	37	(2)	(2)	6	18.7	12
Pharmacists	217	270	0.1	0.2	53	24.3	118
Physicians and surgeons	598	705	0.4	0.4	107	17.9	196
Physician assistants	58	89	(2)	0.1	31	53.5	43
Podiatrists	18	20	(2)	(2)	3	14.2	6
Registered nurses	2 194	2 755	1.5	1.6	561	25.6	1 004
Therapists	439	584	0.3	0.3	145	33.2	255
Audiologists	13	19	(2)	(2)	6	44.7	9
Occupational therapists	78	105	0.1	0.1	27	33.9	46
Physical therapists	132	176	0.1	0.1	44	33.3	77
Radiation therapists	16	19	(2)	(2)	4	22.8	7
Recreational therapists	29	32	(2)	(2)	2	8.6	10
Respiratory therapists	83	112	0.1	0.1	29	34.8	50
Speech-language pathologists	88	122	0.1	0.1	34	39.2	57
Veterinarians	59	77	(2)	(2)	19	31.8	29
All other health diagnosing and treating practitioners	57	71	(2)	(2)	14	24.8	26
Other health professionals and technicians	2 457	3 090	1.7	1.8	633	25.7	1 222
Clinical laboratory technologists and technicians	295	348	0.2	0.2	53	18.0	122
Medical and clinical laboratory technologists	148	174	0.1	0.1	25	17.0	60
Medical and clinical laboratory technicians	147	175	0.1	0.1	28	19.0	62
Dental hygienists	147	201	0.1	0.1	54	37.1	76
Diagnostic related technologists and technicians	257	322	0.2	0.2	65	25.2	121
Cardiovascular technologists and technicians	39	52	(2)	(2)	14	34.9	22
Diagnostic medical sonographers	33	41	(2)	(2)	9	26.1	16
Nuclear medicine technologists	18	22	(2)	(2)	4	22.4	8
Radiologic technologists and technicians	167	206	0.1	0.1	39	23.1	75
Emergency medical technicians and paramedics	172	226	0.1	0.1	54	31.3	97
Health diagnosing and treating practitioner support technicians	417	551	0.3	0.3	134	32.2	242
Dietetic technicians	26	33	(2)	(2)	7	27.6	14
Pharmacy technicians	190	259	0.1	0.2	69	36.4	118
Psychiatric technicians	54	59	(2)	(2)	5	8.5	19
Respiratory therapy technicians	27	36	(2)	(2)	9	34.6	16
Surgical technologists	71	96	(2)	0.1	25	34.7	43
Veterinary technologists and technicians	49	69	(2)	(2)	19	39.3	32
Licensed practical and licensed vocational nurses	700	842	0.5	0.5	142	20.3	322

See footnotes and *Note* at end of table.

Table 3-6. Employment by Occupation, 2000 and Projected 2010—*Continued*

(Thousands of jobs, percent.)

Occupation	Employment				Change 2000–2010		Total job openings due to growth and replacement 2000-2010
	Number		Percent distribution		Number	Percent	
	2000	2010	2000	2010			
Medical records and health information technicians	136	202	0.1	0.1	66	49.0	97
Opticians, dispensing	68	81	(2)	(2)	13	19.0	25
Other health practitioners and technical workers	266	317	0.2	0.2	50	19.0	119
Athletic trainers	15	17	(2)	(2)	3	18.5	6
Occupational health and safety specialists and technicians	35	40	(2)	(2)	5	15.0	14
Orthotists and prosthetists	5	6	(2)	(2)	1	17.3	2
All other health practitioners and technical workers	212	253	0.1	0.2	42	19.7	96
Service occupations	26 075	31 163	17.9	18.6	5 088	19.5	13 505
Healthcare support occupations	3 196	4 264	2.2	2.5	1 067	33.4	1 612
Dental assistants	247	339	0.2	0.2	92	37.2	136
Massage therapists	34	45	(2)	(2)	10	30.4	18
Nursing, psychiatric, and home health aides	2 053	2 676	1.4	1.6	623	30.4	885
Home health aides	615	907	0.4	0.5	291	47.3	370
Nursing aides, orderlies, and attendants	1 373	1 697	0.9	1.0	323	23.5	498
Psychiatric aides	65	73	(2)	(2)	9	13.2	17
Occupational therapist assistants and aides	25	35	(2)	(2)	10	41.5	18
Occupational therapist assistants	17	23	(2)	(2)	7	39.7	11
Occupational therapist aides	9	12	(2)	(2)	4	45.2	6
Physical therapist assistants and aides	80	116	0.1	0.1	36	45.5	60
Physical therapist assistants	44	64	(2)	(2)	20	44.8	33
Physical therapist aides	36	53	(2)	(2)	17	46.3	27
Medical assistants and other healthcare support occupations	757	1 052	0.5	0.6	295	39.0	496
Medical assistants	329	516	0.2	0.3	187	57.0	274
Medical equipment preparers	33	39	(2)	(2)	6	18.2	15
Medical transcriptionists	102	132	0.1	0.1	30	29.8	57
Pharmacy aides	57	68	(2)	(2)	11	19.5	26
Veterinary assistants and laboratory animal caretakers	55	77	(2)	(2)	22	39.8	37
All other healthcare support workers	181	219	0.1	0.1	38	21.1	86
Protective service occupations	3 087	3 896	2.1	2.3	809	26.2	1 677
First-line supervisors/managers, protective service workers	273	319	0.2	0.2	46	16.7	122
First-line supervisors/managers of correctional officers	30	38	(2)	(2)	9	29.6	14
First-line supervisors/managers of fire fighting and prevention workers	62	66	(2)	(2)	4	7.2	24
First-line supervisors/managers of police and detectives	121	136	0.1	0.1	16	13.1	48
First-line supervisors/managers of protective service workers, except police, fire, and corrections	61	78	(2)	(2)	17	27.1	35
Fire fighters	258	280	0.2	0.2	23	8.9	90
Fire inspectors	13	15	(2)	(2)	2	15.1	5
Law enforcement workers	1 150	1 445	0.8	0.9	295	25.6	551
Bailiffs, correctional officers, and jailers	427	563	0.3	0.3	136	31.8	240
Bailiffs	14	15	(2)	(2)	2	12.5	5
Correctional officers and jailers	414	548	0.3	0.3	134	32.4	235
Detectives and criminal investigators	93	108	0.1	0.1	15	16.4	36
Fish and game wardens	8	9	(2)	(2)	1	11.4	2
Parking enforcement workers	9	10	(2)	(2)	1	13.2	2
Police and sheriff's patrol officers	607	748	0.4	0.4	141	23.2	269
Transit and railroad police	6	7	(2)	(2)	1	16.5	2
Other protective service workers	1 394	1 837	1.0	1.1	443	31.8	910
Animal control workers	9	10	(2)	(2)	1	12.8	8
Crossing guards	74	81	0.1	(2)	6	8.7	32
Private detectives and investigators	39	48	(2)	(2)	9	23.5	20
Security guards and gaming surveillance officers	1 117	1 509	0.8	0.9	393	35.2	698
Gaming surveillance officers and gaming investigators	11	13	(2)	(2)	2	16.8	5
Security guards	1 106	1 497	0.8	0.9	391	35.4	693
All other protective service workers	156	190	0.1	0.1	34	21.7	153
Food preparation and serving related occupations	10 140	11 717	7.0	7.0	1 577	15.6	6 256
Supervisors, food preparation and serving workers	788	882	0.5	0.5	95	12.1	301
Chefs and head cooks	139	151	0.1	0.1	12	9.0	55
First-line supervisors/managers of food preparation and workers	649	731	0.4	0.4	83	12.7	246
Cooks and food preparation workers	2 709	3 041	1.9	1.8	333	12.3	1 193
Cooks	1 864	2 054	1.3	1.2	190	10.2	725
Cooks, fast food	522	518	0.4	0.3	-4	-0.7	148
Cooks, institution and cafeteria	465	500	0.3	0.3	35	7.6	167
Cooks, private household	5	4	(2)	(2)	-1	-18.0	1
Cooks, restaurant	668	813	0.5	0.5	145	21.7	335
Cooks, short order	205	219	0.1	0.1	14	6.8	72
Food preparation workers	844	988	0.6	0.6	143	16.9	469
Food and beverage serving workers	5 201	6 384	3.6	3.8	1 182	22.7	4 218
Bartenders	387	439	0.3	0.3	52	13.4	204
Combined food preparation and serving workers, including food	2 206	2 879	1.5	1.7	673	30.5	2 023
Counter attendants, cafeteria, food concession, and coffee	421	482	0.3	0.3	61	14.4	387
Food servers, nonrestaurant	205	238	0.1	0.1	34	16.4	124
Waiters and waitresses	1 983	2 347	1.4	1.4	364	18.3	1 479
Other food preparation and serving related workers	1 442	1 410	1.0	0.8	-33	-2.3	543
Dining room and cafeteria attendants and bartender helpers	431	402	0.3	0.2	-29	-6.7	145
Dishwashers	525	483	0.4	0.3	-42	-8.0	197
Hosts and hostesses, restaurant, lounge, and coffee shop	343	388	0.2	0.2	45	13.0	147
All other food preparation and serving related workers	143	137	0.1	0.1	-7	-4.6	54
Building and grounds cleaning and maintenance occupations	5 549	6 328	3.8	3.8	779	14.0	1 912
Supervisors, building and grounds cleaning and maintenance workers	378	441	0.3	0.3	63	16.7	131
First-line supervisors/managers of housekeeping and janitorial workers	219	250	0.2	0.1	31	14.2	91
First-line supervisors/managers of landscaping, lawn service, and groundskeeping workers	159	191	0.1	0.1	32	20.1	41
Building cleaning workers	3 981	4 381	2.7	2.6	400	10.1	1 179
Janitors and cleaners, except maids and housekeeping cleaners	2 348	2 665	1.6	1.6	317	13.5	741
Maids and housekeeping cleaners	1 633	1 716	1.1	1.0	83	5.1	438
Grounds maintenance workers	973	1 245	0.7	0.7	272	27.9	516

See footnotes and *Note* at end of table.

Table 3-6. Employment by Occupation, 2000 and Projected 2010—*Continued*

(Thousands of jobs, percent.)

Occupation	Employment				Change 2000–2010		Total job openings due to growth and replacement 2000-2010
	Number		Percent distribution		Number	Percent	
	2000	2010	2000	2010			
Landscaping and groundskeeping workers	894	1 154	0.6	0.7	260	29.0	484
Pesticide handlers, sprayers, and applicators, vegetation	27	30	(2)	(2)	4	13.6	10
Tree trimmers and pruners	52	61	(2)	(2)	8	16.3	22
Pest control workers	58	71	(2)	(2)	13	22.1	24
All other building and grounds cleaning and maintenance workers	159	190	0.1	0.1	31	19.6	63
Personal care and service occupations	4 103	4 959	2.8	3.0	856	20.9	2 047
First-line supervisors/managers of personal service workers	125	144	0.1	0.1	19	15.1	53
Animal care and service workers	145	176	0.1	0.1	31	21.2	61
Animal trainers	15	17	(2)	(2)	3	18.4	5
Nonfarm animal caretakers	131	159	0.1	0.1	28	21.6	56
Child care workers	1 193	1 319	0.8	0.8	127	10.6	531
Entertainment attendants and related workers	344	421	0.2	0.3	77	22.5	247
Motion picture projectionists	11	8	(2)	(2)	-3	-27.0	3
Ushers, lobby attendants, and ticket takers	112	124	0.1	0.1	12	11.0	102
Miscellaneous entertainment attendants and related workers	221	289	0.2	0.2	68	30.9	142
Amusement and recreation attendants	197	260	0.1	0.2	64	32.4	130
Costume, locker room and other attendants	24	28	(2)	(2)	5	19.1	13
Funeral service workers	33	38	(2)	(2)	5	13.8	12
Embalmers	7	7	(2)	(2)	(2)	-0.6	2
Funeral attendants	26	31	(2)	(2)	5	17.8	11
Gaming occupations	167	211	0.1	0.1	44	26.5	98
First-line supervisors/managers, gaming workers	46	55	(2)	(2)	9	20.0	22
Gaming supervisors	31	37	(2)	(2)	6	18.4	15
Slot key persons	14	18	(2)	(2)	3	23.3	7
Gaming services workers	100	131	0.1	0.1	31	31.1	65
Gaming and sports book writers and runners	12	15	(2)	(2)	3	21.6	7
Gaming dealers	88	116	0.1	0.1	28	32.4	59
All other gaming service workers	21	25	(2)	(2)	4	18.7	11
Personal appearance workers	790	880	0.5	0.5	90	11.4	294
Barbers	73	64	(2)	(2)	-8	-11.5	21
Hairdressers, hairstylists, and cosmetologists	636	718	0.4	0.4	82	13.0	238
Miscellaneous personal appearance workers	81	97	0.1	0.1	16	19.8	36
Manicurists and pedicurists	40	51	(2)	(2)	11	26.5	21
Shampooers	20	22	(2)	(2)	3	13.2	7
Skin care specialists	21	24	(2)	(2)	3	13.3	8
Personal and home care aides	414	672	0.3	0.4	258	62.5	322
Recreation and fitness workers	427	545	0.3	0.3	118	27.6	206
Fitness trainers and aerobics instructors	158	222	0.1	0.1	64	40.3	97
Recreation workers	269	323	0.2	0.2	54	20.1	110
Residential advisors	44	55	(2)	(2)	11	24.0	21
Transportation, tourism, and lodging attendants	259	300	0.2	0.2	41	15.7	128
Baggage porters, bellhops, and concierges	68	78	(2)	(2)	9	13.4	33
Baggage porters and bellhops	51	57	(2)	(2)	6	12.6	24
Concierges	18	20	(2)	(2)	3	15.7	9
Tour and travel guides	44	48	(2)	(2)	4	9.5	18
Transportation attendants	147	174	0.1	0.1	27	18.6	78
Flight attendants	124	147	0.1	0.1	23	18.4	65
Transportation attendants, except flight attendants and baggage porters	23	27	(2)	(2)	5	20.0	12
All other personal care and service workers	163	198	0.1	0.1	35	21.7	72
Sales and related occupations	15 513	17 365	10.7	10.4	1 852	11.9	6 712
Advertising sales agents	155	196	0.1	0.1	41	26.3	72
Cashiers	3 363	3 851	2.3	2.3	488	14.5	2 013
Cashiers, except gaming	3 325	3 799	2.3	2.3	474	14.2	1 982
Gaming change persons and booth cashiers	38	52	(2)	(2)	14	36.1	31
Counter and rental clerks	423	506	0.3	0.3	82	19.4	274
Door-to-door sales workers, news and street vendors, and related workers	166	156	0.1	0.1	-10	-6.2	42
Insurance sales agents	378	390	0.3	0.2	13	3.3	109
Models, demonstrators, and product promoters	121	152	0.1	0.1	30	24.9	70
Demonstrators and product promoters	118	147	0.1	0.1	29	24.9	68
Models	4	5	(2)	(2)	1	26.0	2
Parts salespersons	260	248	0.2	0.1	-12	-4.4	77
Real estate brokers and sales agents	432	473	0.3	0.3	41	9.5	116
Real estate brokers	93	102	0.1	0.1	9	9.6	25
Real estate sales agents	339	371	0.2	0.2	32	9.5	91
Retail salespersons	4 109	4 619	2.8	2.8	510	12.4	2 073
Sales engineers	85	100	0.1	0.1	15	17.7	37
Sales representatives, wholesale and manufacturing	1 821	1 932	1.3	1.2	111	6.1	606
Sales representatives, wholesale and manufacturing, technical and scientific products	396	426	0.3	0.3	30	7.5	137
Sales representatives, wholesale and manufacturing, except technical and scientific products	1 425	1 507	1.0	0.9	82	5.7	469
Securities, commodities, and financial services sales agents	367	449	0.3	0.3	82	22.3	112
Supervisors, sales workers	2 504	2 697	1.7	1.6	193	7.7	556
First-line supervisors/managers of retail sales workers	2 072	2 240	1.4	1.3	168	8.1	467
First-line supervisors/managers of non-retail sales workers	432	457	0.3	0.3	25	5.8	89
Telemarketers	572	699	0.4	0.4	127	22.2	244
Travel agents	135	139	0.1	0.1	4	3.2	37
All other sales and related workers	621	758	0.4	0.5	137	22.0	273
Office and administrative support occupations	23 882	26 053	16.4	15.5	2 171	9.1	7 667
First-line supervisors/managers of office and administrative support workers	1 392	1 522	1.0	0.9	130	9.4	399
Communications equipment operators	339	273	0.2	0.2	-65	-19.3	101
Switchboard operators, including answering service	259	218	0.2	0.1	-41	-15.7	77
Telephone operators	54	35	(2)	(2)	-19	-35.3	16
All other communications equipment operators	26	20	(2)	(2)	-6	-21.8	9
Financial, information, and record clerks	9 006	10 178	6.2	6.1	1 172	13.0	3 237
Financial clerks	3 696	3 821	2.5	2.3	126	3.4	1 121

See footnotes and *Note* at end of table.

Table 3-6. Employment by Occupation, 2000 and Projected 2010—*Continued*

(Thousands of jobs, percent.)

Occupation	Employment				Change 2000–2010		Total job openings due to growth and replacement 2000-2010
	Number		Percent distribution		Number	Percent	
	2000	2010	2000	2010			
Bill and account collectors	400	502	0.3	0.3	101	25.3	201
Billing and posting clerks and machine operators	506	549	0.3	0.3	43	8.5	167
Bookkeeping, accounting, and auditing clerks	1 991	2 030	1.4	1.2	39	2.0	417
Gaming cage workers	22	27	(2)	(2)	6	25.2	15
Payroll and timekeeping clerks	201	206	0.1	0.1	5	2.3	63
Procurement clerks	76	67	0.1	(2)	-9	-12.2	17
Tellers	499	440	0.3	0.3	-59	-11.8	240
Information and record clerks	5 099	6 105	3.5	3.6	1 006	19.7	2 047
Brokerage clerks	70	69	(2)	(2)	-1	-1.4	9
Correspondence clerks	38	42	(2)	(2)	3	9.1	15
Court, municipal, and license clerks	105	117	0.1	0.1	13	12.0	29
Credit authorizers, checkers, and clerks	86	90	0.1	0.1	4	4.1	11
Customer service representatives	1 946	2 577	1.3	1.5	631	32.4	796
Eligibility interviewers, government programs	117	106	0.1	0.1	-11	-9.3	34
File clerks	288	314	0.2	0.2	26	9.1	118
Hotel, motel, and resort desk clerks	177	236	0.1	0.1	59	33.4	136
Human resources assistants, except payroll and timekeeping	177	211	0.1	0.1	34	19.3	74
Interviewers, except eligibility and loan	154	205	0.1	0.1	51	33.4	84
Library assistants, clerical	98	118	0.1	0.1	19	19.7	63
Loan interviewers and clerks	139	101	0.1	0.1	-38	-27.6	9
New accounts clerks	87	89	0.1	0.1	2	2.7	21
Order clerks	348	277	0.2	0.2	-71	-20.4	74
Receptionists and information clerks	1 078	1 334	0.7	0.8	256	23.7	493
Reservation and transportation ticket agents and travel clerks	191	219	0.1	0.1	28	14.5	79
All other financial, information, and record clerks	211	252	0.1	0.2	41	19.3	69
Material recording, scheduling, dispatching, and distributing occupations	4 238	4 579	2.9	2.7	341	8.1	1 530
Cargo and freight agents	60	65	(2)	(2)	5	8.3	17
Couriers and Messengers	141	135	0.1	0.1	-5	-3.9	38
Dispatchers	254	304	0.2	0.2	50	19.6	92
Dispatchers, except police, fire, and ambulance	168	206	0.1	0.1	37	22.2	65
Police, fire, and ambulance dispatchers	86	98	0.1	0.1	12	14.5	27
Meter readers, utilities	49	36	(2)	(2)	-13	-26.0	12
Postal service workers	688	683	0.5	0.4	-5	-0.7	187
Postal service clerks	74	76	0.1	(2)	2	2.4	18
Postal service mail carriers	324	332	0.2	0.2	8	2.4	106
Postal service mail sorters, processors, and processing machine operators	289	275	0.2	0.2	-14	-4.9	63
Production, planning, and expediting clerks	332	391	0.2	0.2	60	17.9	115
Shipping, receiving, and traffic clerks	890	973	0.6	0.6	83	9.3	262
Stock clerks and order fillers	1 679	1 821	1.2	1.1	142	8.5	740
Weighers, measurers, checkers, and samplers, recordkeeping	83	98	0.1	0.1	15	17.9	35
All other material recording, scheduling, dispatching, and distributing workers	63	73	(2)	(2)	10	15.5	32
Secretaries, administrative assistants, and other office support occupations	8 908	9 500	6.1	5.7	592	6.6	2 400
Computer operators	194	161	0.1	0.1	-33	-17.1	35
Data entry and information processing workers	806	774	0.6	0.5	-32	-3.9	165
Data entry keyers	509	534	0.3	0.3	25	4.9	106
Word processors and typists	297	240	0.2	0.1	-57	-19.1	60
Desktop publishers	38	63	(2)	(2)	25	66.7	32
Insurance claims and policy processing clerks	289	231	0.2	0.1	-58	-20.2	50
Mail clerks and mail machine operators, except postal service	188	207	0.1	0.1	19	9.9	74
Office clerks, general	2 705	3 135	1.9	1.9	430	15.9	949
Office machine operators, except computer	84	68	0.1	(2)	-16	-18.8	29
Proofreaders and copy markers	35	33	(2)	(2)	-2	-5.5	13
Secretaries and administrative assistants	3 902	4 167	2.7	2.5	265	6.8	946
Executive secretaries and administrative assistants	1 445	1 612	1.0	1.0	167	11.5	412
Legal secretaries	279	336	0.2	0.2	57	20.3	104
Medical secretaries	314	373	0.2	0.2	60	19.0	113
Secretaries, except legal, medical, and executive	1 864	1 846	1.3	1.1	-18	-1.0	317
Statistical assistants	21	22	(2)	(2)	(2)	2.1	2
All other secretaries, administrative assistants, and other office support workers	645	639	0.4	0.4	-6	-0.9	104
Farming, fishing, and forestry occupations	1 429	1 480	1.0	0.9	51	3.6	485
First-line supervisors/managers/contractors of farming, fishing, and forestry workers	100	113	0.1	0.1	13	13.0	21
Agricultural workers	987	1 024	0.7	0.6	37	3.7	359
Agricultural inspectors	15	16	(2)	(2)	1	6.6	5
Farmworkers	909	939	0.6	0.6	30	3.3	334
Graders and sorters, agricultural products	63	69	(2)	(2)	6	9.1	20
Fishers and fishing vessel operators	53	46	(2)	(2)	-6	-12.2	17
Forest, conservation, and logging workers	90	88	0.1	0.1	-2	-1.8	19
Forest and conservation workers	21	22	(2)	(2)	1	3.9	6
Logging workers	69	66	(2)	(2)	-2	-3.5	13
Fallers	13	12	(2)	(2)	-1	-8.7	3
Logging equipment operators	47	46	(2)	(2)	-1	-2.0	9
Log graders and scalers	8	8	(2)	(2)	(2)	-4.0	2
All other farming, fishing, and forestry workers	199	209	0.1	0.1	10	4.9	70
Construction and extraction occupations	7 451	8 439	5.1	5.0	989	13.3	2 469
First-line supervisors/managers of construction trades and extraction workers	792	923	0.5	0.6	131	16.5	311
Construction trades and related workers	6 466	7 328	4.4	4.4	862	13.3	2 086
Boilermakers	27	28	(2)	(2)	1	2.1	8
Brickmasons, blockmasons, and stonemasons	158	179	0.1	0.1	21	13.2	50
Brickmasons and blockmasons	144	162	0.1	0.1	18	12.5	45
Stonemasons	14	17	(2)	(2)	3	20.8	5
Carpenters	1 204	1 302	0.8	0.8	98	8.2	302
Carpet, floor, and tile installers and finishers	167	189	0.1	0.1	22	13.2	50
Carpet installers	76	84	0.1	0.1	8	10.5	21
Floor layers, except carpet, wood, and hard tiles	23	27	(2)	(2)	4	15.8	8

See footnotes and *Note* at end of table.

Table 3-6. Employment by Occupation, 2000 and Projected 2010—*Continued*

(Thousands of jobs, percent.)

Occupation	Employment				Change 2000–2010		Total job openings due to growth and replacement 2000-2010
	Number		Percent distribution		Number	Percent	
	2000	2010	2000	2010			
Floor sanders and finishers	14	16	(2)	(2)	2	14.7	4
Tile and marble setters	54	62	(2)	(2)	8	15.6	17
Cement masons, concrete finishers, and terrazzo workers	166	171	0.1	0.1	5	3.0	19
Cement masons and concrete finishers	162	167	0.1	0.1	5	3.0	19
Terrazzo workers and finishers	3	4	(2)	(2)	(2)	2.0	(2)
Construction laborers	791	926	0.5	0.6	135	17.0	207
Construction equipment operators	416	450	0.3	0.3	34	8.1	123
Operating engineers and other construction equipment operators	357	382	0.2	0.2	25	6.9	103
Paving, surfacing, and tamping equipment operators	55	63	(2)	(2)	8	15.5	19
Pile-driver operators	4	5	(2)	(2)	1	14.0	1
Drywall installers, ceiling tile installers, and tapers	188	205	0.1	0.1	17	9.1	35
Drywall and ceiling tile installers	143	157	0.1	0.1	13	9.4	27
Tapers	44	48	(2)	(2)	4	8.3	8
Electricians	698	819	0.5	0.5	120	17.3	251
Glaziers	49	56	(2)	(2)	7	14.8	16
Insulation workers	53	60	(2)	(2)	7	13.6	23
Painters, construction and maintenance	491	585	0.3	0.3	94	19.1	180
Paperhangers	27	32	(2)	(2)	5	20.2	10
Pipelayers, plumbers, pipefitters, and steamfitters	568	627	0.4	0.4	59	10.4	153
Pipelayers	65	73	(2)	(2)	8	11.9	19
Plumbers, pipefitters, and steamfitters	503	554	0.3	0.3	51	10.2	134
Plasterers and stucco masons	54	61	(2)	(2)	6	11.9	16
Reinforcing iron and rebar workers	27	32	(2)	(2)	5	17.5	8
Roofers	158	188	0.1	0.1	31	19.4	67
Sheet metal workers	224	275	0.2	0.2	51	23.0	98
Structural iron and steel workers	84	99	0.1	0.1	15	18.4	24
Helpers, construction trades	450	510	0.3	0.3	60	13.3	283
Helpers-Brickmasons, blockmasons, stonemasons, and tile marble setters	58	66	(2)	(2)	8	14.1	37
Helpers-Carpenters	101	108	0.1	0.1	7	6.6	57
Helpers-Electricians	114	129	0.1	0.1	15	13.3	72
Helpers-Painters, paperhangers, plasterers, and stucco masons	27	30	(2)	(2)	3	12.9	17
Helpers-Pipelayers, plumbers, pipefitters, and steamfitters	86	96	0.1	0.1	10	11.5	53
Helpers-Roofers	23	28	(2)	(2)	5	19.3	16
All other helpers, construction trades	41	53	(2)	(2)	12	29.1	32
Other construction and related workers	465	534	0.3	0.3	69	14.8	162
Construction and building inspectors	75	86	0.1	0.1	11	15.0	28
Elevator installers and repairers	23	27	(2)	(2)	4	17.2	11
Fence erectors	29	30	(2)	(2)	1	4.6	6
Hazardous materials removal workers	37	49	(2)	(2)	12	32.8	23
Highway maintenance workers	151	159	0.1	0.1	8	5.2	31
Rail-track laying and maintenance equipment operators	12	9	(2)	(2)	-3	-26.1	3
Septic tank servicers and sewer pipe cleaners	15	18	(2)	(2)	3	16.5	6
All other construction and related workers	123	156	0.1	0.1	33	26.7	54
Extraction workers	193	189	0.1	0.1	-4	-2.1	72
Derrick, rotary drill, and service unit operators, oil, gas, and mining	45	44	(2)	(2)	-2	-3.5	16
Derrick operators, oil and gas	16	16	(2)	(2)	(2)	0.1	6
Rotary drill operators, oil and gas	18	17	(2)	(2)	-1	-8.0	6
Service unit operators, oil, gas, and mining	11	11	(2)	(2)	(2)	-1.2	4
Earth drillers, except oil and gas	24	27	(2)	(2)	3	12.6	8
Explosives workers, ordnance handling experts, and blasters	5	5	(2)	(2)	(2)	1.9	2
Helpers-Extraction workers	37	38	(2)	(2)	1	2.4	18
Mining machine operators	22	19	(2)	(2)	-3	-12.9	8
Continuous mining machine operators	10	8	(2)	(2)	-1	-13.4	3
Miscellaneous mining machine operators	12	11	(2)	(2)	-2	-12.5	4
Roustabouts, oil and gas	41	40	(2)	(2)	-2	-4.2	14
All other extraction workers	19	17	(2)	(2)	-2	-10.7	7
Installation, maintenance, and repair occupations	5 820	6 482	4.0	3.9	662	11.4	1 944
First-line supervisors/managers of mechanics, installers, and repairers	442	513	0.3	0.3	71	16.0	186
Electrical and electronic equipment mechanics, installers, and repairers	683	726	0.5	0.4	43	6.3	178
Avionics technicians	16	17	(2)	(2)	2	9.8	5
Computer, automated teller, and office machine repairers	172	197	0.1	0.1	24	14.2	43
Electric motor, power tool, and related repairers	37	40	(2)	(2)	3	7.9	11
Electrical and electronics installers and repairers, transportation equipment	14	15	(2)	(2)	2	13.6	4
Electrical and electronics repairers, industrial and utility	108	116	0.1	0.1	8	7.3	30
Electrical and electronics repairers, commercial and industrial equipment	90	98	0.1	0.1	8	9.2	26
Electrical and electronics repairers, powerhouse, substation, and relay	18	18	(2)	(2)	(2)	-2.3	4
Electronic equipment installers and repairers, motor vehicles	13	15	(2)	(2)	2	15.6	5
Electronic home entertainment equipment installers and repairers	37	30	(2)	(2)	-7	-17.9	7
Radio and telecommunications equipment installers and repairers	196	188	0.1	0.1	-7	-3.8	37
Radio mechanics	7	5	(2)	(2)	-2	-24.2	1
Telecommunications equipment installers and repairers, line installers	189	183	0.1	0.1	-6	-3.1	36
Security and fire alarm systems installers	44	54	(2)	(2)	10	23.4	18
All other electrical and electronic equipment mechanics, installers, and repairers	48	54	(2)	(2)	6	13.4	17
Vehicle and mobile equipment mechanics, installers, and repairers	1 931	2 218	1.3	1.3	286	14.8	778
Aircraft mechanics and service technicians	158	184	0.1	0.1	26	16.7	60
Automotive body and related repairers	199	219	0.1	0.1	20	10.2	69
Automotive glass installers and repairers	22	24	(2)	(2)	2	10.5	8
Automotive service technicians and mechanics	840	991	0.6	0.6	151	18.0	349
Bus and truck mechanics and diesel engine specialists	285	326	0.2	0.2	40	14.2	114
Heavy vehicle and mobile equipment service technicians and mechanics	185	203	0.1	0.1	17	9.4	66
Farm equipment mechanics	41	42	(2)	(2)	(2)	0.9	11
Mobile heavy equipment mechanics, except engines	130	148	0.1	0.1	18	14.0	52
Rail car repairers	14	13	(2)	(2)	-1	-7.6	4
Small engine mechanics	73	79	(2)	(2)	6	8.6	24
Motorboat mechanics	25	27	(2)	(2)	2	9.0	9
Motorcycle mechanics	14	16	(2)	(2)	1	8.6	5

See footnotes and *Note* at end of table.

Table 3-6. Employment by Occupation, 2000 and Projected 2010—*Continued*

(Thousands of jobs, percent.)

Occupation	Employment				Change 2000–2010		Total job openings due to growth and replacement 2000-2010
	Number		Percent distribution		Number	Percent	
	2000	2010	2000	2010			
Outdoor power equipment and other small engine mechanics	33	36	(2)	(2)	3	8.2	11
Miscellaneous vehicle and mobile equipment mechanics, installers, and repairers	170	192	0.1	0.1	22	13.2	87
Bicycle repairers	9	10	(2)	(2)	2	17.7	5
Recreational vehicle service technicians	12	15	(2)	(2)	3	25.4	8
Tire repairers and changers	89	95	0.1	0.1	6	6.8	40
All other vehicle and mobile equipment mechanics, installers, and repairers	60	72	(2)	(2)	12	19.6	35
Other installation, maintenance, and repair occupations	2 764	3 026	1.9	1.8	262	9.5	802
Coin, vending, and amusement machine servicers and repairers	37	44	(2)	(2)	7	18.5	15
Control and valve installers and repairers	46	48	(2)	(2)	2	5.2	17
Control and valve installers and repairers, except mechanical door	34	35	(2)	(2)	1	2.7	12
Mechanical door repairers	11	13	(2)	(2)	1	12.7	5
Heating, air conditioning, and refrigeration mechanics and installers	243	297	0.2	0.2	54	22.3	79
Helpers-Installation, maintenance, and repair workers	145	172	0.1	0.1	27	18.5	101
Home appliance repairers	43	46	(2)	(2)	3	6.2	11
Industrial machinery mechanics	198	205	0.1	0.1	7	3.4	60
Line installers and repairers	263	317	0.2	0.2	54	20.7	118
Electrical power-line installers and repairers	99	108	0.1	0.1	9	9.3	41
Telecommunications line installers and repairers	164	209	0.1	0.1	45	27.6	76
Locksmiths and safe repairers	23	25	(2)	(2)	2	8.7	10
Maintenance and repair workers, general	1 251	1 310	0.9	0.8	59	4.7	221
Maintenance workers, machinery	114	120	0.1	0.1	7	5.8	37
Manufactured building and mobile home installers	17	20	(2)	(2)	3	19.1	7
Millwrights	72	75	(2)	(2)	3	3.9	25
Precision instrument and equipment repairers	63	69	(2)	(2)	6	9.7	22
Camera and photographic equipment repairers	7	7	(2)	(2)	(2)	-2.1	2
Medical equipment repairers	28	33	(2)	(2)	4	14.9	11
Musical instrument repairers and tuners	7	8	(2)	(2)	1	9.4	2
Watch repairers	5	6	(2)	(2)	(2)	6.2	2
All other precision instrument and equipment repairers	15	16	(2)	(2)	1	6.8	5
Riggers	20	22	(2)	(2)	2	10.1	6
All other installation, maintenance, and repair workers	228	254	0.2	0.2	26	11.5	73
Production occupations	13 060	13 811	9.0	8.2	750	5.7	3 932
First-line supervisors/managers of production and operating workers	819	827	0.6	0.5	9	1.0	224
Assemblers and fabricators	2 653	2 824	1.8	1.7	171	6.5	702
Aircraft structure, surfaces, rigging, and systems assemblers	20	23	(2)	(2)	3	14.2	8
Electrical, electronics, and electromechanical assemblers	508	492	0.3	0.3	-16	-3.1	138
Coil winders, tapers, and finishers	56	61	(2)	(2)	5	8.2	19
Electrical and electronic equipment assemblers	379	355	0.3	0.2	-24	-6.3	97
Electromechanical equipment assemblers	73	76	0.1	(2)	3	4.5	22
Engine and other machine assemblers	67	72	(2)	(2)	5	7.1	18
Structural metal fabricators and fitters	101	120	0.1	0.1	20	19.5	35
Miscellaneous assemblers and fabricators	1 957	2 117	1.3	1.3	160	8.2	503
Fiberglass laminators and fabricators	48	53	(2)	(2)	5	11.4	14
Team assemblers	1 458	1 545	1.0	0.9	87	5.9	342
Timing device assemblers, adjusters, and calibrators	12	12	(2)	(2)	(2)	2.5	2
All other assemblers and fabricators	439	507	0.3	0.3	68	15.4	144
Food processing occupations	760	783	0.5	0.5	23	3.0	214
Bakers	160	187	0.1	0.1	27	16.8	52
Butchers and other meat, poultry, and fish processing workers	411	415	0.3	0.2	5	1.2	117
Butchers and meat cutters	141	128	0.1	0.1	-13	-8.9	34
Meat, poultry, and fish cutters and trimmers	148	162	0.1	0.1	14	9.5	50
Slaughterers and meat packers	122	125	0.1	0.1	3	2.6	33
Food and tobacco roasting, baking, and drying machine operators and tenders	18	17	(2)	(2)	-2	-9.0	4
Food batchmakers	66	67	(2)	(2)	1	1.4	17
Food cooking machine operators and tenders	37	37	(2)	(2)	(2)	0.6	7
All other food processing workers	69	61	(2)	(2)	-8	-11.6	17
Metal workers and plastic workers	2 907	3 156	2.0	1.9	249	8.6	994
Computer control programmers and operators	186	222	0.1	0.1	36	19.3	102
Computer-controlled machine tool operators, metal and plastic	162	194	0.1	0.1	32	19.7	89
Numerical tool and process control programmers	24	28	(2)	(2)	4	16.6	12
Cutting, punching, and press machine setters, operators, and tenders, metal and plastic	372	357	0.3	0.2	-15	-4.0	73
Drilling and boring machine tool setters, operators, and tenders, metal and plastic	71	68	(2)	0.0	-3	-4.5	23
Extruding and drawing machine setters, operators, and tenders, metal and plastic	126	143	0.1	0.1	17	13.5	45
Forging machine setters, operators, and tenders, metal and plastic	54	59	(2)	(2)	5	9.1	22
Grinding, lapping, polishing, and buffing machine tool setters, operators, and tenders, metal and plastic	145	156	0.1	0.1	11	7.3	46
Heat treating equipment setters, operators, and tenders, metal and plastic	43	49	(2)	(2)	6	13.4	14
Lathe and turning machine tool setters, operators, and tenders, metal and plastic	84	78	0.1	(2)	-6	-7.4	33
Lay-out workers, metal and plastic	18	17	(2)	(2)	-1	-6.0	5
Machinists	430	469	0.3	0.3	39	9.1	127
Metal furnace and kiln operators and tenders	40	43	(2)	(2)	3	7.2	14
Metal-refining furnace operators and tenders	24	26	(2)	(2)	2	7.4	8
Pourers and casters, metal	16	18	(2)	(2)	1	6.9	6
Milling and planing machine setters, operators, and tenders, metal and plastic	34	32	(2)	(2)	-2	-6.7	11
Model makers and patternmakers, metal and plastic	19	18	(2)	(2)	-1	-5.6	5
Model makers, metal and plastic	11	10	(2)	(2)	(2)	-3.2	3
Patternmakers, metal and plastic	9	8	(2)	(2)	-1	-8.4	2
Molders and molding machine setters, operators, and tenders, metal and plastic	235	252	0.2	0.2	17	7.0	65
Foundry mold and coremakers	59	59	(2)	(2)	-1	-1.2	12
Molding, coremaking, and casting machine setters, operators, and tenders, metal and plastic	176	193	0.1	0.1	17	9.8	53
Multiple machine tool setters, operators, and tenders, metal and plastic	105	121	0.1	0.1	15	14.7	32
Plating and coating machine setters, operators, and tenders, metal and plastic	65	72	(2)	(2)	7	10.2	20
Rolling machine setters, operators, and tenders, metal and plastic	49	50	(2)	(2)	1	1.4	17
Tool and die makers	130	132	0.1	0.1	3	2.2	35
Tool grinders, filers, and sharpeners	29	27	(2)	(2)	-2	-7.7	8

See footnotes and *Note* at end of table.

Table 3-6. Employment by Occupation, 2000 and Projected 2010—*Continued*

(Thousands of jobs, percent.)

Occupation	Employment				Change 2000–2010		Total job openings due to growth and replacement 2000-2010
	Number		Percent distribution		Number	Percent	
	2000	2010	2000	2010			
Welding, soldering, and brazing workers	521	618	0.4	0.4	97	18.7	244
Welders, cutters, solderers, and brazers	446	532	0.3	0.3	86	19.3	211
Welding, soldering, and brazing machine setters, operators, and tenders	74	86	0.1	0.1	11	15.1	32
All other metal workers and plastic workers	150	174	0.1	0.1	25	16.4	54
Plant and system operators	368	384	0.3	0.2	16	4.4	133
Power plant operators, distributors, and dispatchers	55	55	(2)	(2)	(2)	-0.4	17
Nuclear power reactor operators	4	4	(2)	(2)	(2)	-3.4	1
Power distributors and dispatchers	15	14	(2)	(2)	-1	-5.1	4
Power plant operators	36	37	(2)	(2)	1	1.8	11
Stationary engineers and boiler operators	57	56	(2)	(2)	-1	-1.3	16
Water and liquid waste treatment plant and system operators	88	104	0.1	0.1	16	18.1	44
Miscellaneous plant and system operators	167	168	0.1	0.1	1	0.6	56
Chemical plant and system operators	71	69	(2)	(2)	-2	-3.3	22
Gas plant operators	12	11	(2)	(2)	-1	-6.3	4
Petroleum pump system operators, refinery operators, and gaugers	35	34	(2)	(2)	-1	-4.1	11
All other plant and system operators	49	54	(2)	(2)	6	11.4	20
Printing occupations	534	543	0.4	0.3	8	1.6	160
Bookbinders and bindery workers	115	124	0.1	0.1	9	7.4	39
Bindery workers	105	113	0.1	0.1	8	7.3	36
Bookbinders	10	10	(2)	(2)	1	8.2	3
Job printers	56	59	(2)	(2)	4	6.4	18
Prepress technicians and workers	107	90	0.1	0.1	-17	-15.6	26
Printing machine operators	222	234	0.2	0.1	12	5.5	68
All other printing workers	34	35	(2)	(2)	1	2.0	9
Textile, apparel, and furnishings occupations	1 317	1 285	0.9	0.8	-32	-2.4	301
Extruding and forming machine setters, operators, and tenders, synthetic and glass fibers	41	44	(2)	(2)	2	5.7	13
Fabric and apparel patternmakers	15	14	(2)	(2)	-1	-5.4	5
Laundry and dry-cleaning workers	236	263	0.2	0.2	27	11.4	89
Pressers, textile, garment, and related materials	110	112	0.1	0.1	2	1.7	17
Sewing machine operators	399	348	0.3	0.2	-51	-12.9	42
Shoe and leather workers and repairers	19	15	(2)	(2)	-4	-21.4	7
Shoe machine operators and tenders	9	4	(2)	(2)	-5	-53.6	1
Tailors, dressmakers, and sewers	101	91	0.1	0.1	-9	-9.3	22
Sewers, hand	43	40	(2)	(2)	-3	-6.6	9
Tailors, dressmakers, and custom sewers	58	51	(2)	(2)	-7	-11.4	13
Textile bleaching and dyeing machine operators and tenders	37	41	(2)	(2)	4	10.8	11
Textile cutting machine setters, operators, and tenders	38	35	(2)	(2)	-2	-6.5	6
Textile knitting and weaving machine setters, operators, and tenders	70	68	(2)	(2)	-2	-2.4	11
Textile winding, twisting, and drawing out machine setters, operators, and tenders	90	86	0.1	0.1	-4	-4.4	19
Upholsterers	58	53	(2)	(2)	-6	-9.5	19
All other textile, apparel, and furnishings workers	95	112	0.1	0.1	17	18.0	36
Woodworkers	409	446	0.3	0.3	37	9.0	187
Cabinetmakers and bench carpenters	159	175	0.1	0.1	16	9.8	66
Furniture finishers	45	49	(2)	(2)	4	8.4	22
Model makers and patternmakers, wood	10	12	(2)	(2)	2	16.0	6
Sawing machine setters, operators, and tenders, wood	57	64	(2)	(2)	7	11.7	29
Woodworking machine setters, operators, and tenders, except sawing	103	108	0.1	0.1	5	5.3	47
All other woodworkers	35	38	(2)	(2)	4	10.6	18
Other production occupations	3 293	3 563	2.3	2.1	269	8.2	1 017
Cementing and gluing machine operators and tenders	36	38	(2)	(2)	2	6.7	11
Chemical processing machine setters, operators, and tenders	100	110	0.1	0.1	10	9.9	33
Chemical equipment operators and tenders	61	70	(2)	(2)	9	14.9	23
Separating, filtering, clarifying, precipitating, and still machine setters, operators, and tenders	39	40	(2)	(2)	1	2.2	10
Cleaning, washing, and metal pickling equipment operators and tenders	20	17	(2)	(2)	-3	-14.2	5
Cooling and freezing equipment operators and tenders	7	7	(2)	(2)	(2)	-1.3	1
Crushing, grinding, polishing, mixing, and blending workers	202	222	0.1	0.1	21	10.3	65
Crushing, grinding, and polishing machine setters, operators, and tenders	44	49	(2)	(2)	4	9.8	14
Grinding and polishing workers, hand	49	55	(2)	(2)	7	13.7	17
Mixing and blending machine setters, operators, and tenders	109	118	0.1	0.1	10	9.0	33
Cutting workers	115	117	0.1	0.1	2	1.8	23
Cutters and trimmers, hand	32	33	(2)	(2)	1	2.2	6
Cutting and slicing machine setters, operators, and tenders	83	84	0.1	0.1	1	1.7	16
Etchers and engravers	15	16	(2)	(2)	2	11.1	5
Extruding, forming, pressing, and compacting machine setters, operators, and tenders	73	80	0.1	(2)	7	9.0	24
Furnace, kiln, oven, drier, and kettle operators and tenders	33	34	(2)	(2)	1	3.2	10
Helpers-Production workers	525	587	0.4	0.3	62	11.9	194
Inspectors, testers, sorters, samplers, and weighers	602	591	0.4	0.4	-11	-1.9	133
Jewelers and precious stone and metal workers	43	44	(2)	(2)	1	1.3	12
Medical, dental, and ophthalmic laboratory workers	88	95	0.1	0.1	7	7.9	31
Dental laboratory technicians	43	46	(2)	(2)	3	6.3	14
Medical appliance technicians	13	15	(2)	(2)	2	19.0	6
Ophthalmic laboratory technicians	32	34	(2)	(2)	2	5.7	11
Molders, shapers, and casters, except metal and plastic	42	45	(2)	(2)	3	7.4	14
Packaging and filling machine operators and tenders	379	433	0.3	0.3	54	14.4	138
Painting workers	195	223	0.1	0.1	28	14.5	72
Coating, painting, and spraying machine setters, operators, and tenders	108	121	0.1	0.1	13	11.9	37
Painters, transportation equipment	49	57	(2)	(2)	9	17.5	19
Painting, coating, and decorating workers	38	45	(2)	(2)	7	17.9	15
Paper goods machine setters, operators, and tenders	123	116	0.1	0.1	-7	-5.4	24
Photographic process workers and processing machine operators	76	77	0.1	(2)	2	2.2	23
Photographic process workers	26	24	(2)	(2)	-2	-8.2	7
Photographic processing machine operators	50	53	(2)	(2)	4	7.6	17
Semiconductor processors	52	69	(2)	(2)	17	32.4	26
Tire builders	18	20	(2)	(2)	2	8.6	5
All other production workers	549	619	0.4	0.4	70	12.7	168

See footnotes and *Note* at end of table.

Table 3-6. Employment by Occupation, 2000 and Projected 2010—*Continued*

(Thousands of jobs, percent.)

Occupation	Employment				Change 2000–2010		Total job openings due to growth and replacement 2000-2010
	Number		Percent distribution		Number	Percent	
	2000	2010	2000	2010			
Transportation and material moving occupations	10 088	11 618	6.9	6.9	1 530	15.2	3 949
Supervisors, transportation and material moving workers	357	427	0.2	0.3	70	19.7	147
Aircraft cargo handling supervisors	10	13	(2)	(2)	3	27.7	5
First-line supervisors/managers of helpers, laborers, movers, hand	153	182	0.1	0.1	29	18.9	62
First-line supervisors/managers of transportation and material moving machine	194	233	0.1	0.1	39	19.9	80
Air transportation occupations	166	186	0.1	0.1	20	12.2	68
Aircraft pilots and flight engineers	117	129	0.1	0.1	11	9.8	38
Airline pilots, copilots, and flight engineers	98	104	0.1	0.1	6	6.4	29
Commercial pilots	19	24	(2)	(2)	5	26.9	10
Air traffic controllers and airfield operations specialists	31	35	(2)	(2)	3	10.2	17
Air traffic controllers	27	29	(2)	(2)	2	7.2	13
Airfield operations specialists	5	6	(2)	(2)	1	27.1	3
All other air transportation workers	17	22	(2)	(2)	5	32.2	13
Motor vehicle operators	4 237	4 982	2.9	3.0	745	17.6	1 398
Ambulance drivers and attendants, except emergency medical technicians	15	20	(2)	(2)	5	33.7	6
Bus drivers	666	754	0.5	0.4	88	13.2	257
Bus drivers, school	481	537	0.3	0.3	56	11.6	178
Bus drivers, transit and intercity	185	217	0.1	0.1	32	17.4	79
Driver/sales workers and truck drivers	3 268	3 857	2.2	2.3	589	18.0	1 038
Driver/sales workers	402	430	0.3	0.3	29	7.1	84
Truck drivers, heavy and tractor-trailer	1 749	2 095	1.2	1.2	346	19.8	586
Truck drivers, light or delivery services	1 117	1 331	0.8	0.8	215	19.2	368
Taxi drivers and chauffeurs	176	219	0.1	0.1	43	24.4	57
All other motor vehicle operators	112	132	0.1	0.1	20	18.2	39
Rail transportation occupations	115	94	0.1	0.1	-21	-18.5	52
Locomotive engineers and firers	37	38	(2)	(2)	1	2.3	18
Railroad brake, signal, and switch operators	22	9	(2)	(2)	-13	-60.8	10
Railroad conductors and yardmasters	45	36	(2)	(2)	-8	-18.9	20
Rail yard engineers, dinkey operators, and hostlers	4	4	(2)	(2)	(2)	-4.5	2
All other rail transportation workers	7	7	(2)	(2)	(2)	-4.1	3
Water transportation occupations	70	74	(2)	(2)	3	4.4	27
Sailors and marine oilers	32	33	(2)	(2)	2	4.9	12
Ship and boat captains and operators	25	26	(2)	(2)	1	3.4	9
Ship engineers	9	9	(2)	(2)	(2)	5.8	3
All other water transportation workers	5	5	(2)	(2)	(2)	4.2	2
Related transportation occupations	309	341	0.2	0.2	32	10.4	139
Bridge and lock tenders	4	4	(2)	(2)	-1	-19.1	2
Parking lot attendants	117	140	0.1	0.1	23	19.8	43
Service station attendants	112	110	0.1	0.1	-2	-1.7	57
Traffic technicians	4	5	(2)	(2)	1	14.1	2
Transportation inspectors	25	28	(2)	(2)	3	11.3	9
All other related transportation workers	46	54	(2)	(2)	8	17.9	26
Material moving occupations	4 833	5 514	3.3	3.3	681	14.1	2 118
Cleaners of vehicles and equipment	322	382	0.2	0.2	60	18.8	183
Conveyor operators and tenders	63	71	(2)	(2)	8	13.3	26
Crane and tower operators	55	59	(2)	(2)	5	8.6	21
Excavating and loading machine and dragline operators	76	88	0.1	0.1	11	14.8	34
Hoist and winch operators	9	10	(2)	(2)	1	8.3	3
Industrial truck and tractor operators	635	707	0.4	0.4	72	11.3	160
Laborers and freight, stock, and material movers, hand	2 084	2 373	1.4	1.4	289	13.9	985
Machine feeders and offbearers	182	159	0.1	0.1	-22	-12.3	63
Packers and packagers, hand	1 091	1 300	0.7	0.8	210	19.3	488
Pumping station operators	32	32	(2)	(2)	(2)	(2)	10
Gas compressor and gas pumping station operators	7	7	(2)	(2)	(2)	4.8	2
Pump operators, except wellhead pumpers	14	15	(2)	(2)	1	4.8	5
Wellhead pumpers	12	11	(2)	(2)	-1	-8.5	3
Refuse and recyclable material collectors	124	145	0.1	0.1	21	16.6	75
Tank car, truck, and ship loaders	19	21	(2)	(2)	3	13.5	8
All other material moving workers	142	165	0.1	0.1	23	16.4	62

Note: Detail may not equal total or 100 percent due to rounding.

1. Total job openings represent the sum of employment increases and net replacements. If employment change is negative, job openings due to growth are zero and total job openings equal net replacements.
2. Value less than 0.05.

PART FOUR

PRODUCTIVITY AND COSTS

PRODUCTIVITY AND COSTS

HIGHLIGHTS

This chapter covers the two kinds of productivity measures produced by BLS, output per hour, or labor productivity and multifactor productivity. Multifactor productivity is designed to measure the joint influence on economic growth of technological change, efficiency improvements, returns to scale and other factors. For some measures there is a lag in available data.

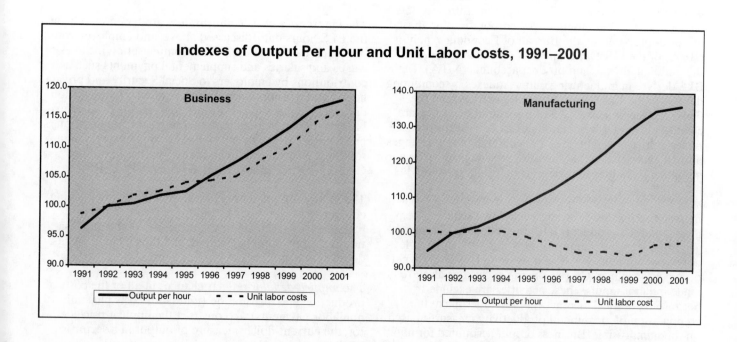

In 2001, the increase in output per hour in the business sector exceed that in the manufacturing sector by a small margin, 1.1 percent and 1.0 percent. However, this reverses the long-term trend in the relationship between the two. Unit labor costs in manufacturing increased at a much slower rate in 2001 than in the previous year. (Table 4-1)

OTHER HIGHLIGHTS:

* Both output and hours in manufacturing dropped in 2001 but hours dropped somewhat more than output, -5.5 percent and -4.8 percent, resulting in the small increase in output per man-hour. (Table 4-1)
* The changes in output and hours in the business sector were small, .14 percent decrease in output and a 1.3 percent decline in hours. (Table 4-1)
* The computer and office equipment and electronic components and accessories industries registered the largest increases in output per hour in the last decade. (Table 4-2)
* Wholesale trade was added to the industry labor productivity series in 2001. Within that sector, the largest increase in productivity in the last 10 years was in the professional and commercial equipment and supplies industry. (Table 4-3)
* A change in multifactor productivity reflects the change in output that cannot be accounted for by the change in hours. This measure in private business rose 1.8 percent in 2000 reflecting a 4.6 percent increase in output and 2.7 percent increase in combined inputs of capital and labor. Output per hour rose 3.4 percent. (Table 4-4)
* For manufacturing, multifactor productivity rose 1.9 percent in 2000, the smallest increase since 1996. The durables sector increased 3.3 percent and there was no change in the non-durables sectors. (Different sources and methods are used for deriving manufacturing multi-factor measure than used in the preceding highlights.) (Table 4-5)

NOTES AND DEFINITIONS

Concepts and Definitions

The measures of output per hour for the business, non-farm business, and manufacturing sectors describe the relationship between real output and the labor time involved in its production. The output measures for the business sectors and nonfinancial corporations are based on series prepared by the Bureau of Economic Analysis (BEA) of the U.S. Department of Commerce as part of the national income and product accounts (NIPA). The BLS derives manufacturing output indexes by combining data from the U.S. Census Bureau, the BEA, and the Federal Reserve Board. All of the output measures are chain-type annual-weighted indexes. This means that the relative prices (weights) used to combine output changes into an aggregate output measure are changed each year, minimizing the bias that arises from using fixed weights over long periods of time.

Business sector output is constructed by excluding from gross domestic product (GDP) the following outputs: general government, nonprofit institutions, paid employees of private households, and the rental value of owner-occupied dwellings. Corresponding exclusions also are made in labor inputs. These activities are excluded because theoretical or practical difficulties make the computation of meaningful productivity measures based on them impossible. Business output accounted for about 77 percent of GDP in 1996 and nonfinancial corporations about 53 percent. Manufacturing indexes are constructed by deflating current-dollar industry value of production data with deflators from the BEA. These deflators are based on data from the BLS producer price program and other sources. To avoid duplication, intrasector transactions are removed when industry shipments are aggregated.

Productivity measures show the changes from period to period in the amount of goods and services produced per hour. Although these measures relate output to hours of persons engaged in a sector, they do not measure only the specific contributions of labor, capital, or any other factor of production. Rather, they reflect the joint effects of many influences, including changes in technology; capital investment; level of output; utilization of capacity, energy, and materials; the organization of production; managerial skill; and the characteristics and effort of the work force.

Measures of labor input are based mainly on the monthly BLS survey of nonagricultural establishments. From this are drawn measures of employment and average weekly hours paid for employees of these establishments. Weekly hours paid are adjusted to hours at work using the BLS Hours at Work survey, conducted for this purpose. Supplementary information for farm workers, the self-employed, and unpaid family workers is obtained from the monthly survey of households, the Current Population Survey. Without these supplementary data, labor input would be seriously understated in the business sectors.

The indexes of hourly compensation are based mainly on the BLS hours data, discussed above, and employee compensation data from the NIPA. Compensation includes wages and salaries and supplemental payments such as contributions by employers to Social Security and private health and pension funds. The all persons' compensation data include measures of proprietors' salaries and contributions for supplementary benefits. Real compensation per hour is derived by adjusting the compensation data to reflect changes in purchasing power, based on the Consumer Price Index research series (CPI-U-RS).

The *indexes of unit labor costs* are computed by dividing compensation per hour by output per hour. Nonlabor payments are calculated by subtracting total compensation from current dollar output, and thus include profits, depreciation, interest, and indirect taxes.

The *implicit deflator* reflects changes in all of the costs of production and distribution (unit labor costs plus unit nonlabor payments). To construct the implicit price deflator, the current-dollar measure of output in a sector is divided by the real output series.

Multifactor Productivity

The *measures of output per unit of combined labor and capital input* (multifactor productivity) and related measures are produced for the private business and private nonfarm business sectors. The *private business and private nonfarm business* sectors for which multifactor productivity indexes are prepared *exclude* government enterprises, and thus differ from the business and nonfarm business sectors described above.

Multifactor productivity measures refer to the ratio of an output index to an index of combined labor and capital services inputs. *Multifactor productivity growth* reflects the amount of output growth that cannot be accounted for by the growth of weighted labor and capital inputs as they have been measured. The weights are associated cost shares; *labor's* share is the ratio of compensation to current-dollar output. *Capital's* share is equal to the ratio of capital cost to current-dollar output. As is the case with the output measures, the weights are updated annually.

Capital services measure the services derived from the stock of physical assets and software. Physical assets included are fixed business equipment, structures, inventories, and land. Structures include nonresidential structures and residential capital that is rented out by profit-making firms or persons. Software includes pre-packaged, custom and own-account software. Financial assets are excluded, as are owner-occupied residential structures. The aggregate capital measures are obtained by weighting the capital stocks for each asset type within each of 53 industries using estimated rental prices for each asset type. Data on investments in physical assets and gross product originating by industry, used in measuring the rental prices, are obtained from BEA.

Labor input in private business and private nonfarm business is obtained by weighting the hours worked by all persons, classified by education, work experience, and gender, by their shares of labor compensation. Additional information concerning data sources and methods of measuring labor composition can be found in BLS Bulletin 2426 (December 1993), "Labor Composition and U.S. Productivity Growth, 1948–90."

The *manufacturing multifactor productivity index* is derived by dividing an output index by a weighted index of combined hours, capital services, energy, materials and purchased business services. Weights (shares of total costs) are updated annually. The labor hours for the manufacturing measure are directly added and thus do not include the effect of changing labor composition, unlike those used for business multifactor productivity. The manufacturing sector coverage is the same in the multifactor and labor productivity series.

Output per Hour and Related Series in Selected Industries

The BLS industry productivity program produces annual indexes of labor productivity, labor compensation, and unit labor costs for selected 2-, 3- and 4-digit industries. These data series cover 54 percent of employment in the private, non-farm business sector, and 100 percent of manufacturing and retail trade. The data sources used in the industry measures differ from those used in the productivity and cost measures for the major sectors.

Output per hour and related indexes for manufacturing and nonmanufacturing industries are updated annually and published in a news release and on the BLS World Wide Web site at http://stats.bls.gov.

Output per hour indexes are obtained by dividing an output index by an index of aggregate hours. Although the measures relate output to one input—labor time—they do not measure the specific contribution of labor or any other factor of production. Rather, they reflect the joint effect of a number of interrelated influences, such as changes in technology, capital investment per worker, and capacity utilization. Caution is necessary when analyzing year-to-year changes in output per hour; the annual changes can be irregular and therefore not necessarily

indicative of long-term trends. Conversely, long-term trends are not necessarily applicable to any 1-year or period in the future.

An *output index* for an industry is calculated with a Tornqvist index formula that aggregates the growth rates of the industry products between two periods with weights based on the products' shares in industry value of production. The weight for each product equals its average value share in the two periods. The formula yields the ratio of output in a given period to that in the previous period. The ratios for successive years must be chained together to form a time series. The quantities of products used in the output index are measured either with deflated values of production or with actual quantities. For most industries, output indexes are developed in two stages. First, comprehensive data from the economic censuses conducted by the Bureau of the Census every 5 years are used to develop benchmark indexes for the census years. Second, less comprehensive data are used to prepare annual indexes. The latter indexes are adjusted to the benchmark indexes by means of linear interpolation. For the period following the last census year, annual indexes are linked to the most recent benchmark index.

Indexes of labor input are employee hours indexes or all person hours indexes. In manufacturing industries, employee hours are used. In nonmanufacturing industries where self-employed workers play a significant role, all person hours are used. For most industries, the hours series are based on hours paid. Total hours are calculated by multiplying the number of workers by average weekly hours. Employee hours are treated as homogenous and additive with no distinction made between hours of different groups. Annual indexes are developed by dividing the aggregate hours for each year by the base period aggregate.

Indexes of unit labor costs are calculated as the ratio of total labor compensation to real output, or equivalently, as the ratio of hourly compensation to labor productivity (output per hour). Unit labor costs measure the cost of labor input required to produce one unit of output.

Indexes of total compensation measure the change in the total costs to the employer of securing the services of labor. Compensation is defined as payroll plus supplemental payments. Payroll includes salaries, wages, commissions, dismissal pay, bonuses, vacation and sick leave pay, and compensation in kind. Supplemental payments are divided into legally required expenditures and payments for voluntary programs. The legally required expenditures include employers' contributions to Social Security, unemployment insurance taxes, and workers' compensation. Payments for voluntary programs include all programs not specifically required by legislation, such as the employer portion of private health insurance and pension plans.

Sources of Additional Information

Productivity concepts and methodology are described in the BLS *Handbook of Methods*, BLS Bulletin 2490, April 1997. Additional information on productivity is found in BLS news release USDL 02-123 for output per hour, 02-499 for multifactor productivity and 02-347 for the new wholesale trade industry.

Table 4-1. Indexes of Productivity and Related Data, 1947–2001

(1992=100.)

Year	Output per hour	Output	Hours	Compensation per hour	Real compensation per hour	Unit labor costs	Unit nonlabor payments	Implicit price deflator	Employment	Output per person	Compensation in current dollars	Nonlabor payments in current dollars
1947	31.8	20.7	65.0	6.8	39.5	21.4	18.9	20.5	54.7	37.8	4.4	3.9
1948	33.3	21.8	65.5	7.4	39.7	22.2	21.0	21.7	55.4	39.3	4.8	4.6
1949	34.0	21.6	63.3	7.5	40.8	22.0	20.8	21.5	54.1	39.8	4.7	4.5
1950	36.9	23.7	64.1	8.0	43.2	21.8	21.8	21.8	54.7	43.2	5.2	5.2
1951	38.0	25.2	66.1	8.8	43.9	23.2	24.0	23.5	56.4	44.6	5.8	6.0
1952	39.2	26.0	66.2	9.4	45.8	23.9	23.4	23.7	56.7	45.8	6.2	6.1
1953	40.7	27.2	67.0	10.0	48.4	24.5	22.9	23.9	57.6	47.3	6.7	6.2
1954	41.6	26.9	64.6	10.3	49.6	24.8	22.8	24.1	56.1	47.9	6.7	6.1
1955	43.3	29.0	67.0	10.6	51.1	24.4	24.3	24.4	57.8	50.2	7.1	7.0
1956	43.4	29.5	68.0	11.3	53.7	26.0	23.7	25.2	59.0	49.9	7.7	7.0
1957	44.7	30.0	67.0	12.0	55.4	26.9	24.4	26.0	59.0	50.8	8.1	7.3
1958	46.0	29.4	63.9	12.6	56.3	27.3	25.0	26.5	56.7	51.9	8.0	7.4
1959	47.9	31.9	66.6	13.1	58.3	27.4	25.5	26.7	58.5	54.5	8.7	8.1
1960	48.8	32.5	66.6	13.7	59.8	28.0	25.2	27.0	58.8	55.2	9.1	8.2
1961	50.6	33.1	65.5	14.2	61.6	28.1	25.5	27.2	58.1	57.0	9.3	8.5
1962	52.9	35.2	66.6	14.9	63.7	28.1	26.3	27.4	58.9	59.8	9.9	9.3
1963	55.0	36.8	67.0	15.4	65.2	28.0	26.9	27.6	59.3	62.2	10.3	9.9
1964	57.5	39.2	68.1	16.2	67.7	28.2	27.5	27.9	60.4	64.9	11.0	10.8
1965	59.6	41.9	70.4	16.8	69.1	28.2	28.6	28.4	62.1	67.5	11.8	12.0
1966	62.0	44.8	72.3	17.9	71.7	28.9	29.3	29.1	64.0	70.0	13.0	13.1
1967	63.4	45.6	72.1	19.0	73.5	29.9	29.7	29.9	64.9	70.3	13.7	13.6
1968	65.3	47.9	73.4	20.4	76.0	31.3	30.6	31.0	66.5	72.1	15.0	14.7
1969	65.7	49.4	75.2	21.9	77.1	33.3	30.9	32.4	68.6	71.9	16.4	15.3
1970	67.0	49.4	73.7	23.5	78.6	35.1	31.6	33.9	68.4	72.1	17.3	15.6
1971	69.9	51.3	73.4	25.0	80.1	35.8	34.4	35.3	68.4	75.0	18.4	17.6
1972	72.2	54.7	75.7	26.6	82.4	36.8	35.8	36.5	70.7	77.4	20.1	19.6
1973	74.5	58.5	78.5	28.9	84.2	38.8	37.7	38.4	73.6	79.5	22.7	22.0
1974	73.2	57.6	78.6	31.7	83.2	43.2	40.0	42.1	74.8	77.0	24.9	23.1
1975	75.8	57.0	75.2	34.9	84.1	46.1	46.1	46.1	72.5	78.6	26.3	26.3
1976	78.5	60.9	77.6	38.0	86.5	48.4	48.6	48.5	74.7	81.5	29.5	29.6
1977	79.8	64.3	80.6	41.0	87.6	51.4	51.5	51.4	77.9	82.6	33.1	33.2
1978	80.7	68.3	84.7	44.6	89.2	55.3	54.8	55.1	82.1	83.2	37.8	37.5
1979	80.7	70.6	87.5	48.9	89.4	60.7	58.3	59.8	85.3	82.8	42.8	41.2
1980	80.4	69.8	86.8	54.2	89.2	67.4	61.5	65.2	85.5	81.6	47.0	42.9
1981	82.0	71.7	87.4	59.4	89.3	72.4	69.2	71.2	86.4	82.9	51.9	49.6
1982	81.6	69.6	85.2	63.8	90.7	78.2	70.3	75.3	85.0	81.9	54.4	48.9
1983	84.6	73.3	86.6	66.5	90.7	78.6	76.4	77.8	85.7	85.5	57.6	56.0
1984	87.0	79.7	91.6	69.4	91.1	79.8	80.4	80.0	90.0	88.6	63.6	64.1
1985	88.7	83.1	93.6	72.9	92.5	82.1	82.2	82.2	92.3	90.0	68.2	68.3
1986	91.4	86.1	94.2	76.7	95.5	83.9	82.8	83.5	93.8	91.8	72.2	71.3
1987	91.9	89.2	97.0	79.7	96.0	86.7	83.6	85.6	96.2	92.7	77.3	74.5
1988	93.0	92.9	100.0	83.5	97.1	89.8	85.7	88.3	99.1	93.8	83.4	79.6
1989	93.9	96.2	102.4	85.8	95.7	91.3	91.8	91.5	101.2	95.1	87.9	88.4
1990	95.2	97.6	102.6	90.7	96.3	95.3	93.9	94.8	102.0	95.7	93.0	91.7
1991	96.3	96.5	100.2	95.0	97.3	98.7	97.0	98.1	100.5	96.0	95.2	93.6
1992	100.0	100.0	100.0	100.0	100.0	100.0	100.0	100.0	100.0	100.0	100.0	100.0
1993	100.5	103.1	102.6	102.5	100.0	101.9	102.5	102.2	102.0	101.1	105.1	105.7
1994	101.9	108.1	106.2	104.5	99.9	102.6	106.4	104.0	105.1	102.8	111.0	115.1
1995	102.6	111.5	108.7	106.7	99.6	104.1	109.4	106.0	107.7	103.5	116.0	122.0
1996	105.4	116.4	110.4	110.1	100.1	104.5	113.3	107.7	109.9	105.9	121.6	131.8
1997	107.8	122.5	113.6	113.5	101.0	105.3	117.1	109.7	112.4	109.0	129.0	143.4
1998	110.6	128.5	116.2	119.7	105.0	108.2	114.5	110.6	115.0	111.8	139.1	147.1
1999	113.5	134.5	118.5	125.2	107.6	110.3	113.9	111.6	117.1	114.8	148.4	153.2
2000	116.9	140.0	119.7	133.8	111.2	114.4	112.0	113.5	119.1	117.5	160.2	156.8
2001	118.2	139.8	118.2	137.7	111.4	116.5	114.7	115.8	118.6	117.8	162.8	160.2

Table 4-1. Indexes of Productivity and Related Data, 1947–2001—*Continued*

(1992=100.)

Year	Nonfarm Business											
	Output per hour	Output	Hours	Compen-sation per hour	Real compen-sation per hour	Unit labor costs	Unit nonlabor payments	Implicit price deflator	Employ-ment	Output per person	Compen-sation in current dollars	Nonlabor payments in current dollars
1947	36.7	20.3	55.3	7.3	42.4	19.9	18.0	19.2	47.3	42.9	4.0	3.7
1948	37.7	21.2	56.2	7.9	42.6	21.0	19.6	20.5	48.3	43.9	4.5	4.1
1949	39.0	21.0	53.9	8.2	44.5	21.0	20.2	20.7	46.9	44.8	4.4	4.2
1950	41.7	23.1	55.6	8.7	46.6	20.8	21.1	20.9	48.0	48.2	4.8	4.9
1951	42.7	24.9	58.2	9.4	46.9	22.1	22.7	22.3	50.2	49.5	5.5	5.6
1952	43.6	25.6	58.8	10.0	48.6	22.8	22.4	22.7	50.9	50.4	5.9	5.8
1953	44.6	26.9	60.2	10.5	51.0	23.6	22.4	23.2	52.4	51.3	6.3	6.0
1954	45.5	26.4	58.1	10.9	52.3	23.9	22.5	23.4	50.9	51.9	6.3	5.9
1955	47.4	28.6	60.4	11.3	54.5	23.8	23.9	23.8	52.5	54.5	6.8	6.8
1956	47.0	29.1	61.9	12.0	57.0	25.5	23.3	24.7	54.0	53.9	7.4	6.8
1957	48.2	29.7	61.6	12.7	58.3	26.3	24.0	25.4	54.3	54.7	7.8	7.1
1958	49.3	29.1	58.9	13.2	59.0	26.7	24.4	25.9	52.3	55.6	7.8	7.1
1959	51.3	31.6	61.6	13.7	60.9	26.7	25.2	26.2	54.2	58.3	8.4	8.0
1960	51.9	32.1	61.9	14.3	62.6	27.5	24.6	26.5	54.7	58.7	8.9	7.9
1961	53.7	32.8	61.1	14.8	64.2	27.6	25.0	26.7	54.2	60.5	9.1	8.2
1962	56.1	35.0	62.4	15.4	66.1	27.5	26.0	26.9	55.2	63.4	9.6	9.1
1963	58.1	36.6	63.1	16.0	67.5	27.5	26.5	27.1	55.9	65.6	10.1	9.7
1964	60.5	39.1	64.6	16.7	69.7	27.6	27.3	27.5	57.2	68.4	10.8	10.7
1965	62.4	41.9	67.1	17.2	70.9	27.6	28.2	27.8	59.2	70.7	11.6	11.8
1966	64.6	44.9	69.5	18.2	72.9	28.2	28.9	28.5	61.6	72.9	12.7	13.0
1967	65.8	45.7	69.4	19.3	74.9	29.4	29.4	29.4	62.6	73.0	13.4	13.4
1968	67.8	48.1	70.9	20.7	77.2	30.6	30.4	30.5	64.3	74.8	14.7	14.6
1969	67.9	49.5	73.0	22.2	78.2	32.6	30.5	31.9	66.7	74.3	16.2	15.1
1970	68.9	49.5	71.8	23.7	79.2	34.4	31.3	33.3	66.7	74.2	17.0	15.5
1971	71.8	51.4	71.5	25.3	80.8	35.2	33.9	34.7	66.8	76.9	18.1	17.4
1972	74.2	54.9	74.0	26.9	83.3	36.2	34.9	35.8	69.0	79.6	19.9	19.2
1973	76.5	58.9	76.9	29.1	84.8	38.0	35.3	37.0	72.1	81.7	22.4	20.8
1974	75.3	58.0	77.0	31.9	83.9	42.4	38.0	40.8	73.2	79.2	24.6	22.1
1975	77.4	57.0	73.7	35.2	84.7	45.5	44.6	45.1	71.0	80.2	25.9	25.4
1976	80.3	61.1	76.1	38.2	87.0	47.6	47.5	47.6	73.4	83.3	29.1	29.0
1977	81.5	64.6	79.2	41.3	88.2	50.7	50.6	50.6	76.6	84.2	32.7	32.7
1978	82.6	68.8	83.3	45.0	89.9	54.5	53.4	54.1	80.9	85.0	37.5	36.7
1979	82.2	70.9	86.3	49.3	90.0	59.9	56.5	58.7	84.3	84.2	42.5	40.1
1980	82.0	70.2	85.6	54.6	89.8	66.5	60.5	64.3	84.6	83.0	46.7	42.5
1981	83.0	71.6	86.2	59.9	90.0	72.1	67.7	70.5	85.5	83.8	51.6	48.5
1982	82.5	69.4	84.1	64.3	91.3	77.9	69.4	74.8	84.0	82.6	54.1	48.1
1983	86.2	73.8	85.6	67.1	91.5	77.8	76.2	77.2	84.8	87.1	57.4	56.2
1984	88.1	80.0	90.8	69.9	91.7	79.4	79.3	79.4	89.3	89.5	63.5	63.4
1985	89.3	83.0	93.0	73.2	92.9	82.0	81.6	81.9	91.8	90.4	68.1	67.8
1986	92.0	86.2	93.8	77.0	96.0	83.7	82.4	83.2	93.4	92.3	72.2	71.1
1987	92.3	89.3	96.7	80.0	96.4	86.6	83.2	85.4	96.0	93.0	77.3	74.2
1988	93.5	93.3	99.8	83.6	97.2	89.4	85.4	87.9	99.0	94.3	83.4	79.7
1989	94.2	96.5	102.4	85.8	95.7	91.1	91.3	91.2	101.2	95.4	87.9	88.1
1990	95.3	97.8	102.7	90.5	96.2	95.0	93.6	94.5	102.1	95.8	92.9	91.5
1991	96.4	96.6	100.2	95.0	97.3	98.5	97.1	98.0	100.5	96.1	95.1	93.8
1992	100.0	100.0	100.0	100.0	100.0	100.0	100.0	100.0	100.0	100.0	100.0	100.0
1993	100.5	103.3	102.9	102.2	99.7	101.7	103.0	102.2	102.2	101.2	105.1	106.4
1994	101.8	108.2	106.2	104.3	99.7	102.5	106.9	104.1	105.2	102.8	110.9	115.7
1995	102.8	111.8	108.8	106.6	99.4	103.7	110.4	106.1	107.8	103.7	116.0	123.5
1996	105.4	116.7	110.7	109.8	99.8	104.2	113.5	107.6	110.2	105.9	121.6	132.5
1997	107.5	122.7	114.1	113.1	100.6	105.2	118.0	109.8	112.8	108.7	129.0	144.7
1998	110.3	128.8	116.8	119.1	104.5	108.0	115.7	110.8	115.6	111.5	139.2	149.0
1999	112.9	134.8	119.4	124.3	106.8	110.1	115.5	112.1	118.0	114.3	148.5	155.7
2000	116.2	140.2	120.6	133.0	110.6	114.4	113.5	114.1	120.0	116.8	160.4	159.1
2001	117.5	140.1	119.2	136.6	110.5	116.3	116.4	116.3	119.6	117.1	162.9	163.0

Table 4-1. Indexes of Productivity and Related Data, 1947–2001—*Continued*

(1992=100.)

Year	Nonfinancial corporations												
	Output per hour	Output	Hours	Compensation per hour	Real compensation per hour	Unit labor costs	Unit nonlabor costs	Unit nonlabor payments	Implicit price deflator	Employment	Output per person	Compensation in current dollars	Nonlabor payments in current dollars
1947	...	...	...	...	...	...	...	...	...	...	...	...	...
1948	...	...	...	...	...	...	...	...	...	...	...	...	...
1949	...	...	...	...	...	...	...	...	...	...	...	...	...
1950	...	...	...	...	...	...	...	...	...	...	...	...	...
1951	...	...	...	...	...	...	...	...	...	...	...	...	...
1952	...	...	...	...	...	...	...	...	...	...	...	...	...
1953	...	...	...	...	...	...	...	...	...	...	...	...	...
1954	...	...	...	...	...	...	...	...	...	...	...	...	...
1955	...	...	...	...	...	...	...	...	...	...	...	...	...
1956	...	...	...	...	...	...	...	...	...	...	...	...	...
1957	...	...	...	...	...	...	...	...	...	...	...	...	...
1958	51.8	25.5	49.3	14.4	64.5	27.8	23.5	47.3	28.4	44.1	57.9	7.1	7.5
1959	54.4	28.4	52.3	14.9	66.5	27.5	22.6	55.1	28.6	46.2	61.6	7.8	8.8
1960	55.4	29.4	53.0	15.6	68.1	28.1	23.3	50.2	28.8	47.2	62.3	8.2	8.9
1961	57.3	30.0	52.4	16.1	69.7	28.1	23.8	50.3	28.9	46.7	64.3	8.4	9.2
1962	59.7	32.5	54.5	16.7	71.7	28.0	23.4	54.6	29.1	48.3	67.3	9.1	10.2
1963	61.7	34.4	55.8	17.2	72.9	27.9	23.3	57.8	29.3	49.4	69.7	9.6	11.1
1964	64.1	36.9	57.5	18.0	75.0	28.0	23.3	60.2	29.6	50.8	72.5	10.3	12.0
1965	65.8	39.9	60.7	18.5	76.0	28.1	23.1	64.8	30.0	53.4	74.7	11.2	13.5
1966	66.7	42.7	64.0	19.5	77.9	29.2	23.2	64.7	30.7	56.5	75.6	12.5	14.4
1967	67.7	43.8	64.7	20.6	79.7	30.4	24.6	60.5	31.5	58.1	75.4	13.3	14.8
1968	70.0	46.6	66.6	22.1	82.3	31.6	26.2	60.3	32.7	60.1	77.5	14.7	16.3
1969	70.0	48.4	69.2	23.6	83.4	33.7	28.3	54.4	34.1	62.9	77.0	16.3	16.9
1970	70.4	48.0	68.2	25.3	84.4	35.9	31.9	44.4	35.6	63.1	76.0	17.2	16.8
1971	73.3	49.9	68.0	26.9	85.9	36.7	33.4	50.2	37.0	63.3	78.8	18.3	18.8
1972	75.3	53.8	71.5	28.4	88.1	37.8	33.5	54.1	38.1	66.3	81.2	20.3	20.8
1973	76.0	57.0	74.9	30.7	89.6	40.4	35.1	55.5	40.3	69.7	81.7	23.0	23.0
1974	74.4	56.0	75.2	33.6	88.4	45.2	40.5	49.2	44.4	71.1	78.7	25.3	23.9
1975	77.2	55.1	71.3	37.0	89.0	47.9	45.9	64.1	48.8	68.4	80.5	26.4	27.8
1976	79.7	59.5	74.6	40.0	91.1	50.2	45.9	72.3	51.0	71.5	83.2	29.8	31.3
1977	81.6	63.8	78.2	43.1	92.2	52.9	47.4	79.4	53.8	75.2	84.8	33.7	35.5
1978	82.1	68.1	82.9	46.8	93.5	57.0	50.0	82.5	57.4	80.2	84.8	38.8	39.7
1979	81.5	70.2	86.1	51.1	93.4	62.7	55.1	76.7	62.0	83.8	83.7	44.0	42.5
1980	81.1	69.2	85.4	56.4	92.9	69.6	65.1	68.8	68.4	84.1	82.3	48.2	45.7
1981	82.6	71.5	86.5	61.6	92.7	74.6	74.8	82.4	75.3	85.4	83.7	53.3	54.9
1982	83.4	70.0	83.9	66.0	93.8	79.2	82.3	75.0	79.6	83.5	83.8	55.4	56.2
1983	85.9	73.3	85.3	68.4	93.2	79.6	81.5	91.2	81.1	84.1	87.1	58.3	61.6
1984	88.2	80.2	91.0	71.2	93.4	80.7	81.1	108.6	83.2	89.3	89.9	64.8	70.7
1985	89.9	83.8	93.2	74.4	94.4	82.7	82.4	104.2	84.5	92.1	91.1	69.4	73.8
1986	91.7	85.9	93.7	78.0	97.2	85.1	85.7	88.0	85.5	93.6	91.7	73.1	74.1
1987	94.7	90.7	95.8	81.6	98.4	86.2	85.3	98.1	87.0	95.2	95.3	78.2	80.4
1988	95.9	95.8	99.8	84.2	97.9	87.7	87.4	108.0	89.4	99.0	96.7	84.0	88.7
1989	94.7	97.4	102.8	86.3	96.2	91.1	94.6	97.3	92.5	101.6	95.9	88.7	92.8
1990	95.4	98.3	103.0	90.8	96.5	95.2	98.0	94.3	95.8	102.5	95.9	93.5	95.4
1991	97.7	97.5	99.8	95.3	97.6	97.5	102.1	93.0	98.3	100.3	97.2	95.1	97.3
1992	100.0	100.0	100.0	100.0	100.0	100.0	100.0	100.0	100.0	100.0	100.0	100.0	100.0
1993	100.7	103.0	102.3	102.0	99.6	101.3	100.2	113.2	102.1	101.8	101.2	104.4	106.7
1994	103.1	109.6	106.3	104.2	99.6	101.0	101.3	131.7	103.7	105.3	104.1	110.8	119.5
1995	104.2	114.2	109.6	106.2	99.0	101.9	102.2	139.0	105.1	108.6	105.1	116.3	127.4
1996	107.5	119.9	111.5	109.0	99.0	101.4	100.6	152.2	105.5	111.2	107.9	121.5	136.4
1997	108.4	127.0	117.1	110.3	98.1	101.8	100.9	156.9	106.2	116.1	109.4	129.2	146.3
1998	111.7	134.3	120.2	116.0	101.7	103.8	102.2	141.7	106.6	119.3	112.6	139.4	150.8
1999	114.7	141.2	123.1	121.1	104.1	105.6	104.1	131.7	107.3	122.0	115.7	149.1	156.3
2000	117.1	146.3	125.0	129.2	107.4	110.3	106.9	113.2	110.0	124.7	117.3	161.4	160.3
2001	118.3	145.6	123.0	132.4	107.0	111.9	111.6	100.3	111.9	123.8	117.6	162.9	162.8

Table 4-1. Indexes of Productivity and Related Data, 1947–2001—*Continued*

(1992=100.)

Year	Output per hour	Output	Hours	Compensation per hour	Real compensation per hour	Unit labor costs	Unit nonlabor payments	Implicit price deflator	Employment	Output per person	Compensation in current dollars	Nonlabor payments in current dollars
							Manufacturing					
1947	...	...	...	...	...	...	...	...	...	...	...	...
1948	...	...	...	...	...	...	...	...	...	...	...	...
1949	33.5	26.5	79.1	8.3	44.9	24.6	23.5	24.0	80.1	33.1	6.5	6.2
1950	34.0	29.1	85.5	8.7	46.6	25.5	23.9	24.5	84.3	34.5	7.4	7.0
1951	33.8	31.1	92.1	9.5	47.6	28.2	25.8	26.8	90.6	34.4	8.8	8.0
1952	35.2	32.9	93.3	10.2	49.8	28.9	25.2	26.7	91.8	35.8	9.5	8.3
1953	36.4	35.7	98.1	10.7	52.1	29.5	24.7	26.6	96.8	36.8	10.5	8.8
1954	37.3	33.4	89.6	11.2	54.1	30.1	25.0	27.0	90.1	37.1	10.1	8.3
1955	38.8	36.7	94.6	11.7	56.4	30.1	25.4	27.2	93.1	39.4	11.0	9.3
1956	38.6	37.1	96.0	12.4	59.1	32.1	25.6	28.1	95.0	39.0	11.9	9.5
1957	39.4	37.2	94.5	13.2	60.6	33.4	26.5	29.1	94.7	39.3	12.4	9.9
1958	40.0	34.7	86.6	13.8	61.7	34.4	27.0	29.9	87.9	39.4	11.9	9.4
1959	40.9	37.8	92.5	14.3	63.5	34.9	27.4	30.3	91.9	41.2	13.2	10.3
1960	41.8	38.5	92.1	14.9	65.0	35.6	26.8	30.2	92.6	41.6	13.7	10.3
1961	42.8	38.4	89.7	15.3	66.3	35.7	26.8	30.3	90.0	42.6	13.7	10.3
1962	44.2	41.3	93.4	15.9	68.1	36.0	26.7	30.3	92.8	44.4	14.8	11.0
1963	45.7	43.1	94.4	16.4	69.2	35.8	26.8	30.3	93.5	46.1	15.4	11.6
1964	47.4	45.7	96.4	17.0	71.2	36.0	26.8	30.3	94.9	48.2	16.4	12.2
1965	48.5	49.5	102.0	17.4	71.6	35.9	27.4	30.7	99.3	49.8	17.8	13.6
1966	49.1	53.3	108.6	18.2	72.8	37.1	28.0	31.5	105.4	50.6	19.8	14.9
1967	50.9	54.9	108.0	19.2	74.4	37.7	28.4	32.0	106.7	51.5	20.7	15.6
1968	52.7	57.7	109.6	20.7	76.9	39.2	28.6	32.7	108.5	53.2	22.6	16.5
1969	53.5	59.4	110.9	22.2	78.2	41.4	29.0	33.8	110.6	53.7	24.6	17.2
1970	54.2	56.5	104.4	23.7	79.2	43.8	29.3	35.0	106.3	53.2	24.8	16.6
1971	57.8	58.1	100.5	25.2	80.5	43.5	31.6	36.2	102.2	56.9	25.3	18.4
1972	60.3	63.3	105.1	26.5	82.0	43.9	33.4	37.4	105.0	60.3	27.8	21.1
1973	61.4	67.8	110.4	28.5	83.1	46.4	36.5	40.3	110.5	61.4	31.5	24.8
1974	61.2	66.1	107.9	31.6	83.1	51.7	44.6	47.3	110.1	60.0	34.2	29.5
1975	64.3	62.5	97.2	35.5	85.4	55.2	51.6	53.0	100.6	62.1	34.5	32.2
1976	67.0	68.2	101.9	38.4	87.5	57.4	53.9	55.3	104.2	65.4	39.2	36.8
1977	69.7	73.9	106.1	41.8	89.3	60.0	57.8	58.7	108.2	68.4	44.4	42.8
1978	70.4	77.8	110.6	45.2	90.3	64.2	61.7	62.7	112.7	69.0	50.0	48.0
1979	69.8	78.7	112.7	49.6	90.6	71.1	69.1	69.8	115.6	68.1	55.9	54.3
1980	70.1	75.3	107.5	55.6	91.4	79.3	80.2	79.9	111.6	67.5	59.7	60.4
1981	70.7	75.6	107.0	61.1	91.9	86.3	87.7	87.2	111.0	68.1	65.3	66.3
1982	74.2	72.7	97.9	67.0	95.1	90.2	89.3	89.6	103.5	70.2	65.6	64.9
1983	76.7	75.9	98.9	68.8	93.8	89.7	90.2	90.0	101.8	74.6	68.1	68.5
1984	79.5	83.7	105.3	71.2	93.4	89.6	92.7	91.5	106.8	78.4	75.0	77.6
1985	82.3	86.0	104.6	75.1	95.3	91.3	90.8	91.0	106.0	81.2	78.5	78.1
1986	85.9	88.5	103.0	78.5	97.8	91.3	85.0	87.5	104.5	84.7	80.8	75.2
1987	88.3	91.6	103.8	80.7	97.3	91.4	87.8	89.2	104.7	87.5	83.8	80.5
1988	90.2	96.1	106.6	84.0	97.7	93.1	90.9	91.8	106.6	90.2	89.5	87.4
1989	90.3	96.6	107.1	86.6	96.6	96.0	95.3	95.6	107.0	90.3	92.8	92.1
1990	92.9	97.3	104.8	90.8	96.4	97.8	99.8	99.0	105.4	92.3	95.1	97.1
1991	95.0	95.4	100.4	95.6	98.0	100.6	99.0	99.6	101.8	93.7	96.0	94.4
1992	100.0	100.0	100.0	100.0	100.0	100.0	100.0	100.0	100.0	100.0	100.0	100.0
1993	101.9	103.3	101.4	102.7	100.2	100.8	100.9	100.9	100.1	103.2	104.2	104.2
1994	105.0	108.7	103.6	105.6	101.0	100.7	102.8	102.0	101.3	107.3	109.4	111.8
1995	109.0	113.4	104.0	107.9	100.6	99.0	106.9	103.9	102.5	110.7	112.2	121.2
1996	112.8	117.0	103.6	109.4	99.4	96.9	109.9	104.8	102.2	114.5	113.4	128.5
1997	117.6	124.0	105.4	111.5	99.1	94.8	110.0	104.1	103.2	120.1	117.5	136.3
1998	123.3	129.8	105.2	117.4	103.0	95.2	103.7	100.4	104.0	124.8	123.5	134.5
1999	129.7	135.3	104.4	122.1	104.9	94.1	104.9	100.7	102.4	132.2	127.4	141.9
2000	134.9	138.7	102.8	131.1	109.0	97.2	107.0	103.2	101.8	136.3	134.8	148.5
2001	136.2	132.1	97.1	133.1	107.7	97.8	...	...	97.6	135.4	129.2	...

Table 4-2. Average Annual Percent Change in Output per Hour and Related Series: Manufacturing Industries, 1990–2000

Industry	SIC Code	2000 Employment (thousands)	Average annual percent change 1990–2000				
			Output per hour	Output	Employee hours	Total compensation	Unit labor costs
Meat products	201	504	0.6	2.7	2.1	5.1	2.3
Dairy products	202	146	0.6	0.2	-0.4	2.7	2.5
Preserved fruits and vegetables	203	220	2.6	1.6	-1.0	2.7	1.1
Grain mill products	204	124	1.9	1.7	-0.2	2.6	0.9
Bakery products	205	204	1.5	1.2	-0.3	3.8	2.6
Sugar and confectionery products	206	92	2.4	1.9	-0.5	2.5	0.6
Fats and oils	207	28	2.5	0.8	-1.7	1.9	1.1
Beverages	208	187	0.9	1.5	0.6	2.8	1.2
Miscellaneous food and kindred products	209	180	1.6	1.2	-0.4	3.0	1.8
Cigarettes	211	23	2.1	-1.2	-3.3	-0.4	0.9
Broadwoven fabric mills, cotton	221	62	3.1	-0.4	-3.4	-0.9	-0.5
Broadwoven fabric mills, manmade	222	55	4.2	0.8	-3.2	0.6	-0.3
Narrow fabric mills	224	20	2.0	0.2	-1.7	3.3	3.1
Knitting mills	225	126	3.8	-1.1	-4.7	-0.9	0.2
Textile finishing, except wool	226	58	1.5	0.9	-0.7	2.5	1.7
Carpets and rugs	227	66	1.0	1.9	0.9	2.7	0.8
Yarn and thread mills	228	81	3.5	1.6	-1.8	0.7	-0.9
Miscellaneous textile goods	229	54	2.1	2.6	0.4	4.1	1.5
Men's and boys' furnishings	232	131	7.0	-0.4	-6.9	-2.6	-2.2
Women's and misses' outerwear	233	185	6.2	0.7	-5.1	-2.1	-2.8
Women's and children's undergarments	234	21	13.2	0.8	-11.0	-6.3	-7.0
Hats, caps, and millinery	235	15	1.7	1.1	-0.6	3.2	2.0
Miscellaneous apparel and accessories	238	30	2.1	-2.0	-4.0	-1.3	0.7
Miscellaneous fabricated textile products	239	215	2.9	3.6	0.7	5.2	1.6
Sawmills and planing mills	242	185	2.2	1.7	-0.5	3.5	1.8
Millwork, plywood, and structural members	243	335	-0.7	2.3	3.0	5.5	3.1
Wood containers	244	59	-0.6	2.2	2.9	5.6	3.3
Wood buildings and mobile homes	245	91	-0.9	2.8	3.6	7.1	4.3
Miscellaneous wood products	249	83	3.1	3.0	-0.2	4.0	1.0
Household furniture	251	293	2.1	2.4	0.4	3.6	1.1
Office furniture	252	79	1.6	3.6	1.9	3.6	0.0
Public building and related furniture	253	59	5.4	11.3	5.7	9.4	-1.7
Partitions and fixtures	254	91	3.3	5.0	1.6	6.8	1.8
Miscellaneous furniture and fixtures	259	43	0.7	2.1	1.4	4.3	2.2
Pulp mills	261	13	-3.9	-4.4	-0.6	-4.6	-0.2
Paper mills	262	139	2.7	-0.1	-2.8	0.5	0.6
Paperboard mills	263	47	3.0	1.2	-1.7	3.0	1.7
Paperboard containers and boxes	265	218	1.1	1.6	0.5	3.8	2.2
Miscellaneous converted paper products	267	240	2.4	2.2	-0.2	3.5	1.3
Newspapers	271	442	-0.3	-0.9	-0.6	2.6	3.5
Periodicals	272	149	1.6	3.0	1.4	8.3	5.1
Books	273	126	0.9	1.5	0.6	4.8	3.2
Miscellaneous publishing	274	95	3.3	4.6	1.2	8.3	3.6
Commercial printing	275	560	1.5	1.7	0.2	3.6	1.9
Manifold business forms	276	43	-2.9	-4.7	-1.8	-0.9	4.0
Greeting cards	277	25	0.4	-0.1	-0.6	0.0	0.1
Blankbooks and bookbinding	278	60	2.4	0.8	-1.5	1.7	0.9
Printing trade services	279	47	1.9	-1.1	-2.9	-0.4	0.7
Industrial inorganic chemicals	281	72	2.8	-0.3	-3.0	0.5	0.8
Plastics materials and synthetics	282	154	4.1	2.5	-1.6	1.6	-0.9
Drugs	283	315	0.2	3.3	3.0	5.9	2.6
Soaps, cleaners, and toilet goods	284	155	1.9	1.5	-0.4	2.1	0.6
Paints and allied products	285	52	1.6	0.0	-1.5	3.1	3.1
Industrial organic chemicals	286	120	2.3	-0.3	-2.6	2.8	3.0
Agricultural chemicals	287	51	0.7	-0.4	-1.0	1.4	1.8
Miscellaneous chemical products	289	93	2.6	2.1	-0.5	3.2	1.1
Petroleum refining	291	85	5.1	1.4	-3.6	2.3	0.9
Asphalt paving and roofing materials	295	28	2.6	2.4	-0.1	2.1	-0.3
Miscellaneous petroleum and coal products	299	15	-1.3	0.8	2.1	2.6	1.9

See footnote and *Note* at end of table.

Table 4-2. Average Annual Percent Change in Output per Hour and Related Series: Manufacturing Industries, 1990–2000—Continued

Industry	SIC Code	2000 Employment (thousands)	Output per hour	Output	Employee hours	Total compensation	Unit labor costs
Tires and inner tubes	301	79	3.5	3.2	-0.3	3.2	0.0
Hose and belting and gaskets and packing	305	74	1.8	3.9	2.0	5.0	1.1
Fabricated rubber products, n.e.c.	306	108	2.9	3.3	0.4	3.8	0.5
Miscellaneous plastics products, n.e.c.	308	744	3.2	5.1	1.8	5.5	0.4
Footwear, except rubber	314	28	3.8	-5.4	-8.8	-4.8	0.6
Flat glass	321	16	5.2	4.0	-1.1	0.7	-3.2
Glass and glassware, pressed or blown	322	67	2.6	0.6	-2.0	0.9	0.3
Products of purchased glass	323	66	4.0	5.2	1.2	5.5	0.3
Cement, hydraulic	324	18	2.0	2.4	0.4	3.4	1.0
Structural clay products	325	34	1.3	0.5	-0.8	1.6	1.1
Pottery and related products	326	38	2.1	2.5	0.4	2.7	0.2
Concrete, gypsum, and plaster products	327	248	0.3	2.5	2.2	5.1	2.5
Miscellaneous nonmetallic mineral products	229	72	2.0	1.3	-0.6	2.7	1.4
Blast furnace and basic steel products	331	225	3.9	2.2	-1.5	0.9	-1.3
Iron and steel foundries	332	123	2.2	2.1	-0.1	2.4	0.3
Primary nonferrous metals	333	36	0.9	-1.4	-2.3	-0.9	0.5
Nonferrous rolling and drawing	335	176	2.4	2.9	0.4	3.1	0.2
Nonferrous foundries (castings)	336	94	2.2	4.0	1.7	4.0	0.0
Miscellaneous primary metal products	339	28	3.1	3.7	0.6	3.2	-0.5
Metal cans and shipping containers	341	36	3.1	0.2	-2.8	-1.3	-1.5
Cutlery, handtools, and hardware	342	121	2.6	2.0	-0.6	2.7	0.7
Plumbing and heating, except electric	343	60	2.6	2.8	0.2	4.3	1.5
Fabricated structural metal products	344	498	1.3	3.3	1.9	4.4	1.1
Metal forgings and stampings	346	255	3.1	4.9	1.7	3.6	-1.2
Metal services, n.e.c.	347	146	2.6	4.7	2.0	4.9	0.3
Ordnance and accessories, n.e.c.	348	38	1.2	-5.4	-6.5	-5.4	-0.1
Miscellaneous fabricated metal products	349	277	1.1	2.9	1.7	4.1	1.2
Engines and turbines	351	85	4.4	4.0	-0.4	1.6	-2.3
Farm and garden machinery	352	96	1.8	0.6	-1.2	2.4	1.8
Construction and related machinery	353	240	2.7	3.3	0.6	3.3	0.0
Metalworking machinery	354	330	2.5	2.4	-0.1	3.5	1.0
Special industry machinery	355	172	4.8	5.7	0.8	4.9	-0.7
General industrial machinery	356	251	1.6	1.7	0.2	3.2	1.4
Computer and office equipment	357	361	31.7	29.1	-2.0	0.7	-22.0
Refrigeration and service machinery	358	212	1.7	4.0	2.3	4.2	0.2
Industrial machinery, n.e.c.	359	373	2.8	4.6	1.7	4.8	0.2
Electric distribution equipment	361	85	3.9	2.6	-1.3	2.7	0.1
Electrical industrial apparatus	362	150	3.8	2.6	-1.2	2.7	0.0
Household appliances	363	116	4.4	3.6	-0.7	3.7	0.1
Electric lighting and wiring equipment	364	183	3.0	3.0	-0.1	2.8	-0.1
Communications equipment	366	290	13.7	14.7	0.8	6.3	-7.3
Electronic components and accessories	367	682	26.9	29.1	1.8	5.8	-18.1
Miscellaneous electrical equipment & supplies	369	146	5.6	4.2	-1.3	2.6	-1.5
Motor vehicles and equipment	371	1 013	2.2	4.8	2.6	4.8	-0.1
Aircraft and parts	372	465	2.9	-1.2	-4.0	-1.0	0.2
Ship and boat building and repairing	373	166	1.6	0.1	-1.5	0.7	0.6
Railroad equipment	374	36	4.5	5.4	0.8	4.3	-1.0
Motorcycles, bicycles, and parts	375	20	2.4	7.1	4.5	12.2	4.8
Guided missiles, space vehicles, parts	376	73	-0.3	-9.2	-8.9	-7.6	1.8
Search and navigation equipment	381	154	3.8	-2.5	-6.0	-2.2	0.2
Measuring and controlling devices	382	302	4.1	3.4	-0.6	2.9	-0.5
Medical instruments and supplies	384	288	3.6	5.3	1.6	5.7	0.4
Ophthalmic goods	385	33	7.5	5.5	-1.9	3.3	-2.0
Photographic equipment & supplies	386	70	4.6	1.1	-3.4	-1.1	-2.2
Jewelry, silverware, and plated ware	391	49	3.9	3.1	-0.8	2.7	-0.3
Musical instruments	393	17	0.8	3.7	2.9	6.7	2.9
Toys and sporting goods	394	104	2.7	2.7	0.1	3.7	0.9
Pens, pencils, office, and art supplies	395	31	0.6	-0.8	-1.3	1.4	2.2
Costume jewelry and notions	396	19	3.3	-2.8	-5.9	0.0	3.0
Miscellaneous manufactures	399	175	0.8	3.0	2.2	4.3	1.3

Note: n.e.c. = not elsewhere classified.

1. Employment figures are based primarily on the data from the BLS Current Employment Statistics (CES) program and the Current Population Survey (CPS).

Table 4-3. Average Annual Percent Change in Output per Hour and Related Series: Mining and Service Producing Industries, 1990–2000

Industry	SIC Code	2000 Employment (thousands) [1]	Average annual percent change, 1990–2000				
			Output per hour [2]	Output	Employee hours	Total compensation	Unit labor costs
MINING							
Copper ores	102	11	1.8	-1.1	-2.8	0.3	1.5
Gold and silver ores	104	12	7.0	1.5	-5.1	-0.2	-1.7
Coal mining	12	77	5.7	-0.7	-6.1	-3.8	-3.1
Bituminous coal and lignite mining	122	72	5.7	-0.7	-6.1	-3.5	-2.8
Oil and gas extraction	13	311	2.0	-0.7	-2.7	3.7	4.5
Crude petroleum and natural gas	131	125	3.9	-0.7	-4.5	2.6	3.4
Nonmetallic minerals, except fuels	14	114	0.2	0.6	0.5	3.7	3.0
Crushed and broken stone	142	45	0.0	1.4	1.4	4.7	3.3
TRANSPORTATION							
Railroad transportation	4011	194	5.1	2.7	-2.4	0.6	-2.0
Trucking, except local	4213	917	1.7	3.6	1.9	5.0	1.4
United States Postal Service	43	860	0.9	1.9	1.0	4.1	2.1
Air transportation	4512, 13, 22 (PTS)	740	1.8	4.4	2.6	5.2	0.8
COMMUNICATION AND UTILITIES							
Telephone communications	481	1 134	5.9	8.3	2.3	7.5	-0.8
Radio and television broadcasting	483	255	0.5	1.7	1.2	5.6	3.9
Cable and other pay television services	484	216	-0.6	5.5	6.1	12.1	6.2
Electric utilities	491, 3 (PT)	471	4.4	1.9	-2.4	2.6	0.7
Gas utilities	492, 3 (PT)	166	4.3	2.0	-2.2	3.1	1.1
RETAIL TRADE							
Building materials, hardware, garden supply, and mobile homes	52	1 050	3.7	5.9	2.2	6.0	0.0
Lumber and other building materials dealers	521	642	3.3	7.0	3.6	7.3	0.3
Paint, glass, and wallpaper stores	523	70	4.8	3.8	-0.9	2.6	-1.2
Hardware stores	525	178	2.4	1.9	-0.4	3.4	1.4
Retail nurseries, lawn and garden supply stores	526	112	6.2	6.7	0.4	3.9	-2.5
General merchandise stores	53	2 843	5.3	6.6	1.3	4.6	-1.9
Department stores	531	2 491	5.2	7.0	1.7	5.1	-1.8
Variety stores	533	160	7.9	6.6	-1.2	0.8	-5.5
Miscellaneous general merchandise stores	539	193	6.6	5.0	-1.5	1.5	-3.3
Food stores	54	3 639	-0.2	0.5	0.7	3.4	2.9
Grocery stores	541	3 179	-0.1	0.5	0.5	3.3	2.8
Meat and fish (seafood) markets	542	57	1.1	0.5	-0.5	1.1	0.6
Retail bakeries	546	214	-0.3	1.4	1.7	5.2	3.7
Automotive dealers and gasoline service stations	55	2 508	1.9	2.8	0.9	5.3	2.4
New and used car dealers	551	1 114	0.5	2.3	1.8	6.1	3.7
Auto and home supply stores	553	428	1.4	2.9	1.5	4.4	1.4
Gasoline service stations	554	671	3.0	1.9	-1.1	2.3	0.4
Apparel and accessory stores	56	1 243	5.5	4.9	-0.5	3.6	-1.2
Men's and boys' wear stores	561	86	3.6	1.0	-2.5	0.6	-0.4
Women's clothing stores	562	293	6.8	2.7	-3.8	0.6	-2.1
Family clothing stores	565	456	4.1	7.8	3.6	7.9	0.1
Shoe stores	566	204	4.0	2.3	-1.7	2.5	0.2
Furniture, home furnishings, and equipment store	57	1 239	7.0	9.3	2.2	6.6	-2.5
Furniture and homefurnishings stores	571	649	3.0	4.5	1.5	5.2	0.7
Household appliance stores	572	79	7.2	4.8	-2.2	0.1	-4.5
Radio, television, computer, and music stores	573	510	11.5	16.3	4.2	9.8	-5.6
Eating and drinking places	58	8 338	0.3	2.4	2.2	5.8	3.3
Miscellaneous merchandise stores	59	3 647	4.3	5.7	1.4	5.7	-0.1
Drug and proprietary stores	591	685	2.6	3.5	0.9	5.5	1.9
Liquor stores	592	139	1.9	0.6	-1.3	2.7	2.1
Used merchandise stores	593	209	7.7	11.9	3.9	7.5	-4.0
Miscellaneous shopping goods stores	594	1 254	3.4	5.1	1.7	5.3	0.2
Nonstore retailers	596	576	9.0	11.3	2.1	8.6	-2.4
Fuel dealers	598	98	3.3	1.5	-1.7	1.9	0.4
Retail stores, n.e.c.	599	686	3.9	5.5	1.5	4.9	-0.6

See footnotes at end of table.

Table 4-3. Average Annual Percent Change in Output per Hour and Related Series: Mining and Service Producing Industries, 1990–2000—_Continued_

Industry	SIC Code	2000 Employment (thousands) [1]	Average annual percent change, 1990–2000				
			Output per hour [2]	Output	Employee hours	Total compensation	Unit labor costs
WHOLESALE TRADE							
Wholesale durable goods	50	4 337	5.6	7.1	1.4	5.8	-1.2
Motor vehicles and automotive parts and supplies	501	540	3.3	4.6	1.2	4.5	-0.1
Furniture and home furnishings	502	187	1.2	3.0	1.7	5.5	2.5
Lumber and other construction materials	503	302	-1.7	0.6	2.4	5.9	5.3
Professional and commercial equipment and supplies	504	976	17.1	19.5	2.0	7.4	-10.1
Metals and minerals, except petroleum	505	165	-0.9	0.7	1.6	4.3	3.6
Electrical goods	506	599	9.2	11.0	1.7	7.3	-3.4
Hardware and plumbing and heating equipment and supplies	507	326	1.7	2.8	1.1	4.6	1.8
Machinery, equipment and supplies	508	871	2.4	3.0	0.5	4.1	1.1
Miscellaneous durable goods	509	372	3.9	4.9	0.9	4.5	-0.4
Wholesale nondurable goods	51	2 953	0.7	1.7	1.0	4.9	3.2
Paper and paper products	511	277	2.2	2.9	0.7	4.4	1.5
Drugs, drug proprietaries, and druggists' sundries	512	263	2.3	5.5	3.1	10.0	4.2
Apparel, piece goods, and notions	513	233	1.3	2.3	1.0	3.5	1.2
Groceries and related products	514	988	0.6	2.0	1.3	4.4	2.4
Farm-product raw materials	515	105	3.7	1.3	-2.4	2.0	0.7
Chemicals and allied products	516	168	-0.6	1.1	1.8	5.4	4.2
Petroleum and petroleum products	517	156	-0.1	-2.4	-2.3	2.0	4.5
Beer, wine, and distilled alcoholic beverages	518	165	0.1	1.2	1.1	4.2	3.0
Miscellaneous nondurable goods	519	598	0.3	1.4	1.1	5.1	3.6
FINANCE AND SERVICES							
Commercial banks	602	1 430	2.9	2.0	-0.9	5.5	3.5
Hotels and motels	701	1 874	1.7	3.3	1.6	5.7	2.3
Personal services	72	1 847	1.2	2.2	1.0	4.8	2.6
Laundry, cleaning, and garment services	721	518	1.9	1.8	-0.1	3.5	1.6
Photographic studios, portrait	722	86	1.3	3.5	2.1	4.8	1.2
Beauty shops	723	759	1.6	2.9	1.3	5.8	2.8
Barber shops	724	62	2.6	0.4	-2.1	0.3	-0.2
Funeral services and crematories	726	107	0.3	0.4	0.1	4.1	3.7
Automotive repair shops	753	917	1.8	3.0	1.2	4.7	1.7
Motion picture theaters	783	139	-0.5	1.7	2.2	3.8	2.1

1. Employment figures are based primarily on data from the BLS Current Employment Statistics (CES) program and the Current Population Survey (CPS). Other sources are the Association of American Railroads, the Department of Transportation, and the U.S. Postal Service.
2. Output per employee hour is measured in mining, transportation, communications, and SICs 531, 551, 602, and 783. Output per hour of all persons is used for all other trade and services industries. All persons include self-employed and unpaid family workers as well as employees. In SIC 4213 and 4512, 13, 22 (pts), output per employee hour is based on output per employee with the assumption of constant average weekly hours.

Table 4-4. Indexes of Multifactor Productivity and Related Measures, Selected Years, 1955–2000

(1996=100.)

Industry	1955	1960	1965	1970	1975	1980	1985	1986	1987	1988	1989
PRIVATE BUSINESS											
Productivity											
Output per hour of all persons	40.9	45.6	55.9	63.0	71.4	75.8	83.9	86.5	87.0	88.1	89.0
Output per unit of capital	115.5	112.0	123.3	113.1	104.1	103.3	99.5	99.0	99.2	100.4	101.0
Multifactor productivity	62.0	65.5	76.6	80.5	85.4	88.8	92.4	93.9	94.2	94.8	95.3
Output	24.9	27.5	35.6	42.0	48.5	59.4	71.0	73.6	76.3	79.6	82.4
Inputs											
Labor input	53.7	54.0	58.0	61.0	62.4	71.9	79.6	80.5	83.1	86.3	88.9
Capital services	21.6	24.6	28.9	37.1	46.6	57.6	71.3	74.4	76.9	79.2	81.6
Combined units of labor and capital inputs	40.2	42.1	46.5	52.2	56.8	66.9	76.8	78.4	81.0	83.9	86.4
Capital services per hour for all persons	35.4	40.7	45.3	55.7	68.6	73.4	84.3	87.4	87.7	87.7	88.1
PRIVATE NONFARM BUSINESS											
Productivity											
Output per hour of all persons	44.6	48.7	58.6	64.9	73.0	77.3	84.4	87.1	87.5	88.6	89.2
Output per unit of capital	126.4	121.9	133.1	120.5	109.1	107.6	101.4	100.7	100.5	101.7	102.0
Multifactor productivity	66.5	69.4	80.0	83.1	87.6	91.0	93.4	94.8	94.9	95.6	95.8
Output	24.4	27.2	35.5	41.9	48.4	59.6	70.8	73.5	76.2	79.7	82.4
Inputs											
Labor input	48.6	50.1	55.4	59.3	60.9	70.7	78.8	79.8	82.5	85.9	88.5
Capital services	19.3	22.3	26.6	34.8	44.3	55.4	69.8	73.0	75.8	78.3	80.8
Combined units of labor and capital inputs	36.7	39.2	44.3	50.5	55.2	65.5	75.8	77.6	80.3	83.4	86.0
Capital services per hour for all persons	35.3	39.9	44.0	53.8	66.9	71.8	83.3	86.5	87.1	87.1	87.5
MANUFACTURING											
Productivity											
Output per hour of all persons	34.4	37.1	43.0	48.1	56.9	62.1	73.0	76.1	78.4	79.9	80.0
Output per unit of capital	130.8	119.9	131.7	112.4	100.0	97.4	96.1	96.3	97.6	100.7	99.2
Multifactor productivity	66.7	68.1	77.5	79.1	78.8	81.2	89.0	90.5	93.3	95.0	93.3
Output	31.4	32.9	42.3	48.3	53.4	64.4	73.6	75.7	78.4	82.2	82.6
Inputs											
Hours at work of all persons	91.2	88.8	98.3	100.6	93.9	103.7	100.8	99.4	100.0	102.8	103.3
Capital services	24.0	27.5	32.1	43.0	53.4	66.2	76.5	78.6	80.3	81.6	83.3
Energy	39.5	48.0	62.6	79.8	82.0	86.3	80.9	81.5	86.6	90.1	90.3
Non-energy materials	32.0	32.5	35.2	38.2	52.4	63.6	72.5	74.2	71.4	72.7	75.8
Purchased business services	23.3	25.9	34.1	44.6	53.1	67.3	62.9	67.0	71.3	77.7	82.7
Combined units of all inputs	47.0	48.3	54.6	61.1	67.8	79.3	82.6	83.6	84.0	86.5	88.6

Table 4-4. Indexes of Multifactor Productivity and Related Measures, Selected Years, 1955–2000—*Continued*

(1996=100.)

Industry	1990	1991	1992	1993	1994	1995	1996	1997	1998	1999	2000
PRIVATE BUSINESS											
Productivity											
Output per hour of all persons	90.2	91.3	94.8	95.4	96.6	97.3	100.0	102.2	105.0	107.7	111.4
Output per unit of capital	99.7	96.5	98.0	98.7	100.4	99.8	100.0	100.3	99.2	98.0	96.8
Multifactor productivity	95.5	94.5	96.7	97.1	98.2	98.4	100.0	101.2	102.5	103.4	105.3
Output	83.6	82.6	85.7	88.5	92.8	95.8	100.0	105.2	110.5	115.7	121.0
Inputs											
Labor input	89.4	88.3	89.3	91.8	95.6	98.0	100.0	103.5	106.1	109.0	110.2
Capital services	83.8	85.7	87.5	89.7	92.5	96.0	100.0	104.9	111.4	118.0	125.0
Combined units of labor and capital inputs	87.5	87.4	88.7	91.1	94.6	97.3	100.0	104.0	107.8	111.9	114.9
Capital services per hour for all persons	90.4	94.6	96.8	96.6	96.2	97.5	100.0	101.9	105.8	109.9	115.1
PRIVATE NONFARM BUSINESS											
Productivity											
Output per hour of all persons	90.3	91.4	94.8	95.3	96.5	97.5	100.0	102.0	104.7	107.1	110.7
Output per unit of capital	100.4	97.0	98.2	99.0	100.4	100.0	100.0	100.0	98.9	97.5	96.1
Multifactor productivity	95.8	94.8	96.7	97.2	98.2	98.6	100.0	101.0	102.2	102.9	104.7
Output	83.5	82.5	85.5	88.4	92.6	95.8	100.0	105.1	110.5	115.6	120.9
Inputs											
Labor input	89.2	88.0	89.0	91.8	95.4	97.8	100.0	103.6	106.4	109.5	110.7
Capital services	83.2	85.1	87.0	89.4	92.2	95.8	100.0	105.1	111.7	118.5	125.8
Combined units of labor and capital inputs	87.2	87.0	88.4	91.0	94.3	97.2	100.0	104.1	108.1	112.4	115.4
Capital services per hour for all persons	89.9	94.3	96.5	96.3	96.1	97.6	100.0	101.9	105.8	109.8	115.3
MANUFACTURING											
Productivity											
Output per hour of all persons	82.3	84.2	88.6	90.3	93.0	96.6	100.0	104.2	109.3	114.9	119.5
Output per unit of capital	97.5	93.6	96.0	97.0	99.7	100.6	100.0	101.8	101.9	102.3	101.1
Multifactor productivity	93.1	92.2	93.8	94.8	97.4	99.2	100.0	103.3	105.4	108.1	110.1
Output	83.2	81.6	85.5	88.3	93.0	96.9	100.0	106.0	111.0	115.7	118.6
Inputs											
Hours at work of all persons	101.1	96.9	96.5	97.8	99.9	100.4	100.0	101.8	101.5	100.7	99.3
Capital services	85.3	87.2	89.1	91.1	93.2	96.4	100.0	104.1	108.9	113.1	117.3
Energy	93.2	93.4	93.3	96.7	99.9	102.1	100.0	98.5	105.0	101.8	104.6
Non-energy materials	78.3	79.2	84.6	87.1	90.0	93.0	100.0	102.0	110.0	114.9	115.9
Purchased business services	84.8	84.4	91.7	94.1	96.2	100.5	100.0	104.5	103.1	104.4	105.5
Combined units of all inputs	89.4	88.4	91.2	93.1	95.5	97.7	100.0	102.6	105.3	107.0	107.7

Table 4-5. Indexes of Multifactor Productivity and Related Measures, Manufacturing Industries, 1986–2000

(1996=100.)

Industry	1986	1987	1988	1989	1990	1991	1992	1993	1994	1995	1996	1997	1998	1999	2000
NONDURABLE GOODS															
Output per hour of all persons	82.0	83.6	84.9	84.5	86.5	88.3	92.0	92.5	94.3	97.1	100.0	103.9	106.5	108.4	112.4
Output per unit of capital	102.0	104.3	105.7	103.9	102.9	99.9	102.0	101.4	102.2	101.7	100.0	101.3	99.2	97.1	95.2
Multifactor productivity	99.4	101.0	102.2	99.9	99.0	98.2	98.7	99.0	100.1	100.7	100.0	102.1	102.0	103.1	103.1
Sector output	80.6	84.0	86.5	87.0	88.7	88.6	93.0	94.7	97.3	99.3	100.0	104.0	105.0	105.9	107.0
Hours of all persons at work	98.3	100.4	102.0	103.0	102.5	100.3	101.0	102.3	103.2	102.2	100.0	100.1	98.6	97.7	95.2
Capital services	79.1	80.5	81.9	83.7	86.2	88.7	91.1	93.4	95.2	97.6	100.0	102.7	105.8	109.0	112.4
Energy	77.7	81.0	83.5	85.4	89.7	90.7	92.7	96.6	98.8	102.1	100.0	97.0	101.7	99.7	102.1
Non-energy materials	76.2	77.8	77.6	79.7	82.7	83.4	89.6	90.5	93.8	95.0	100.0	102.4	105.4	103.8	105.7
Purchased business services	62.7	66.2	73.6	80.7	87.2	89.9	97.4	98.7	96.9	101.7	100.0	103.9	101.9	101.7	105.3
Combined units of all inputs	81.1	83.1	84.7	87.1	89.6	90.2	94.2	95.6	97.2	98.6	100.0	101.9	103.0	102.7	103.8
Food and Kindred Products															
Output per hour of all persons	89.0	89.5	91.9	89.4	90.2	93.3	98.2	98.4	98.8	100.9	100.0	102.2	106.2	104.2	105.2
Output per unit of capital	101.2	100.5	102.5	100.8	101.2	100.8	103.6	103.5	103.1	104.2	100.0	101.9	100.1	97.3	94.3
Multifactor productivity	102.4	102.9	106.5	102.3	101.0	101.9	101.4	102.7	100.5	104.5	100.0	101.2	100.6	103.1	102.9
Sector output	83.2	84.6	87.2	86.9	89.3	91.0	95.8	97.5	98.5	101.9	100.0	103.4	106.6	107.0	107.2
Hours of all persons at work	93.4	94.5	94.9	97.2	99.1	97.5	97.6	99.1	99.7	101.0	100.0	101.2	100.4	102.7	101.9
Capital services	82.2	84.2	85.1	86.3	88.3	90.2	92.5	94.2	95.5	97.7	100.0	101.5	106.6	110.0	113.6
Energy	81.7	84.5	87.1	88.0	88.4	91.3	93.4	96.1	100.1	104.8	100.0	101.9	109.9	104.4	109.1
Non-energy materials	79.1	80.6	78.9	81.9	85.6	86.1	92.9	92.6	97.4	95.6	100.0	102.7	108.1	103.5	103.7
Purchased business services	69.4	63.9	71.0	79.9	87.4	93.6	102.6	103.9	101.8	101.4	100.0	101.9	102.8	97.3	95.9
Combined units of all inputs	81.2	82.2	81.9	85.0	88.4	89.3	94.5	95.0	98.0	97.5	100.0	102.2	106.0	103.8	104.2
Textile Mill Products															
Output per hour of all persons	71.3	72.7	73.6	76.5	78.9	79.7	85.7	89.0	91.2	95.1	100.0	100.9	104.0	109.7	112.0
Output per unit of capital	88.5	95.0	94.7	96.5	93.7	93.2	100.4	104.1	105.1	101.8	100.0	98.9	94.1	90.5	87.5
Multifactor productivity	85.6	86.7	89.5	90.1	90.8	91.1	95.0	96.6	97.3	98.7	100.0	101.4	100.9	105.9	104.8
Sector output	80.4	86.6	86.4	88.3	86.2	85.8	93.0	97.7	101.5	100.5	100.0	100.7	99.6	97.1	95.4
Hours of all persons at work	112.8	119.1	117.4	115.5	109.2	107.6	108.5	109.8	111.4	105.7	100.0	99.8	95.7	88.5	85.2
Capital services	90.9	91.1	91.2	91.5	92.0	92.1	92.6	93.9	96.5	98.8	100.0	101.8	105.8	107.3	109.1
Energy	83.0	91.3	91.3	91.9	88.5	90.5	94.5	98.8	104.7	106.2	100.0	95.9	100.7	98.5	94.0
Non-energy materials	88.6	95.2	94.1	90.8	88.3	86.7	91.9	97.0	101.0	99.2	100.0	99.4	100.9	92.3	87.9
Purchased business services	57.7	63.4	71.0	80.5	81.0	86.5	97.4	101.0	105.0	103.6	100.0	95.8	88.5	78.6	71.6
Combined units of all inputs	94.0	99.8	96.6	98.1	95.0	94.2	97.9	101.1	104.3	101.9	100.0	99.3	98.6	91.7	88.0
Apparel and Related Products															
Output per hour of all persons	75.0	76.0	76.2	72.4	75.1	75.6	81.4	85.3	90.0	95.6	100.0	113.9	117.2	129.2	142.1
Output per unit of capital	103.3	106.0	102.6	99.5	97.8	98.1	102.6	101.5	102.9	99.5	100.0	108.1	96.9	95.4	91.0
Multifactor productivity	97.0	98.1	98.0	96.6	96.1	94.3	93.9	94.5	96.8	98.7	100.0	102.5	103.1	103.8	105.9
Sector output	91.0	93.5	92.3	87.8	87.0	86.3	93.5	96.3	100.8	101.6	100.0	107.2	103.1	104.3	102.4
Hours of all persons at work	121.3	123.0	121.1	121.2	115.8	114.1	114.8	112.9	112.1	106.3	100.0	94.1	88.0	80.7	72.1
Capital services	88.1	88.3	89.9	88.3	88.9	87.9	91.1	94.9	98.0	102.1	100.0	99.1	106.4	109.3	112.6
Energy	66.1	68.7	69.2	60.5	59.8	61.1	95.6	105.9	103.4	110.4	100.0	84.0	88.5	83.6	85.4
Non-energy materials	96.3	98.7	94.1	85.3	84.1	84.0	93.1	97.4	101.2	100.7	100.0	112.1	107.4	113.2	112.5
Purchased business services	33.0	31.9	40.2	48.0	59.3	71.7	93.3	97.1	100.6	102.8	100.0	107.4	98.5	99.1	93.4
Combined units of all inputs	93.8	95.3	94.1	90.9	90.5	91.5	99.5	101.9	104.2	102.9	100.0	104.5	100.0	100.5	96.7
Paper and Allied Products															
Output per hour of all persons	86.6	86.5	88.3	88.1	88.3	90.7	93.0	94.8	98.5	99.1	100.0	101.3	104.8	106.2	109.3
Output per unit of capital	105.1	105.7	107.5	105.0	101.1	98.4	100.2	101.3	104.8	103.3	100.0	100.3	98.9	99.2	97.1
Multifactor productivity	100.4	100.0	101.0	99.6	97.7	98.5	99.8	103.4	104.4	97.9	100.0	103.1	102.5	103.8	101.6
Sector output	82.4	84.6	87.8	89.1	89.6	90.2	94.1	96.3	100.6	100.4	100.0	102.3	103.6	105.4	103.8
Hours of all persons at work	95.2	97.8	99.4	101.1	101.4	99.6	101.2	101.6	102.2	101.3	100.0	101.0	98.9	99.3	95.0
Capital services	78.5	80.1	81.7	84.9	88.6	91.8	93.9	95.0	96.0	97.2	100.0	102.0	104.8	106.2	106.9
Energy	81.2	84.9	86.4	88.8	94.2	94.9	96.8	99.2	101.3	104.5	100.0	98.2	102.1	100.0	102.0
Non-energy materials	79.2	81.0	82.6	86.3	86.8	86.2	89.5	86.8	92.8	103.8	100.0	97.5	102.1	103.4	107.1
Purchased business services	63.8	70.0	80.5	90.3	90.5	91.1	95.7	90.8	94.3	113.6	100.0	96.3	96.0	93.1	95.8
Combined units of all inputs	82.1	84.6	86.9	90.4	91.7	91.6	94.3	93.2	96.4	102.6	100.0	99.2	101.1	101.6	102.2

Table 4-5. Indexes of Multifactor Productivity and Related Measures, Manufacturing Industries, 1986–2000—Continued

(1996=100.)

Industry	1986	1987	1988	1989	1990	1991	1992	1993	1994	1995	1996	1997	1998	1999	2000
Printing and Publishing															
Output per hour of all persons	104.3	106.6	101.5	99.5	98.0	96.9	100.4	98.4	97.1	97.2	100.0	101.8	102.2	104.0	105.5
Output per unit of capital	139.5	138.8	131.6	123.1	117.5	108.3	107.4	105.3	104.3	102.1	100.0	97.6	96.0	90.5	83.1
Multifactor productivity	112.9	112.8	110.8	109.5	106.8	104.4	105.6	101.8	102.4	100.6	100.0	99.9	100.1	101.3	101.7
Sector output	96.6	101.1	101.4	100.0	99.7	95.2	97.6	97.9	98.5	99.2	100.0	104.0	103.3	104.8	105.2
Hours of all persons at work	92.6	94.9	99.9	100.5	101.7	98.3	97.2	99.6	101.4	102.1	100.0	102.2	101.1	100.8	99.7
Capital services	69.2	72.8	77.0	81.3	84.8	88.0	90.9	93.0	94.4	97.2	100.0	106.5	107.7	115.8	126.5
Energy	73.4	85.7	91.6	91.9	95.9	94.9	95.8	98.8	97.9	98.9	100.0	94.4	94.0	92.8	91.8
Non-energy materials	88.5	92.7	90.0	86.6	88.8	86.9	88.6	95.2	91.4	93.8	100.0	103.8	102.6	99.7	95.9
Purchased business services	77.5	85.7	85.6	85.6	87.3	83.0	87.4	91.8	91.8	99.8	100.0	108.8	107.2	107.0	108.1
Combined units of all inputs	85.5	89.6	91.5	91.3	93.3	91.2	92.4	96.2	96.1	98.7	100.0	104.2	103.3	103.5	103.5
Chemicals and Allied Products															
Output per hour of all persons	78.3	85.0	86.4	86.1	87.5	87.5	89.0	89.2	94.9	97.9	100.0	107.1	106.5	108.0	113.1
Output per unit of capital	99.5	107.6	111.2	110.3	109.0	103.5	103.7	101.0	102.4	101.6	100.0	103.0	99.2	97.7	97.4
Multifactor productivity	97.3	103.4	102.5	100.3	100.7	97.8	97.4	96.9	100.3	99.7	100.0	103.4	102.1	102.7	102.3
Sector output	74.6	82.1	86.2	87.8	90.2	89.5	92.6	93.0	96.6	98.5	100.0	106.5	106.9	108.5	111.8
Hours of all persons at work	95.3	96.5	99.7	102.0	103.1	102.3	104.0	104.2	101.8	100.6	100.0	99.5	100.4	100.5	98.9
Capital services	75.0	76.3	77.5	79.6	82.8	86.5	89.3	92.0	94.3	96.9	100.0	103.4	107.7	111.1	114.8
Energy	73.6	79.3	82.9	85.4	90.4	90.1	90.9	95.4	97.4	99.4	100.0	92.2	95.1	96.4	97.3
Non-energy materials	72.9	75.8	81.5	84.7	84.9	87.0	91.7	90.9	91.9	96.4	100.0	106.5	106.8	110.0	120.5
Purchased business services	56.2	62.1	74.0	83.0	88.0	91.6	98.4	99.0	98.5	103.8	100.0	105.5	105.2	99.2	101.4
Combined units of all inputs	76.7	79.4	84.1	87.5	89.6	91.6	95.1	96.0	96.3	98.8	100.0	103.1	104.7	105.7	109.3
Petroleum Refining and Related Products															
Output per hour of all persons	76.6	79.4	83.4	84.1	83.8	83.4	85.7	91.1	92.2	97.0	100.0	105.4	107.9	112.4	119.2
Output per unit of capital	99.4	103.1	105.9	106.5	106.4	103.6	102.7	102.7	99.9	99.3	100.0	102.6	106.9	106.4	109.6
Multifactor productivity	98.7	98.7	99.4	99.2	98.6	98.7	99.5	100.3	99.8	99.9	100.0	101.0	102.4	102.4	103.8
Sector output	89.0	91.0	92.9	92.9	93.4	92.6	94.6	97.3	96.6	97.6	100.0	102.7	105.3	103.7	105.2
Hours of all persons at work	116.1	114.5	111.3	110.5	111.4	111.1	110.4	106.9	104.8	100.6	100.0	97.4	97.6	92.2	88.3
Capital services	89.6	88.2	87.7	87.3	87.8	89.4	92.1	94.8	96.7	98.4	100.0	100.0	98.6	97.5	96.0
Energy	102.8	90.3	90.3	94.0	106.5	104.7	100.5	103.5	99.8	103.9	100.0	100.5	108.9	99.3	106.9
Non-energy materials	90.1	92.7	94.6	94.4	94.4	93.2	95.0	97.8	97.8	97.0	100.0	102.5	104.9	103.3	104.3
Purchased business services	55.2	70.9	72.7	82.3	100.1	93.1	86.4	81.6	83.7	88.7	100.0	103.0	98.5	102.9	99.3
Combined units of all inputs	90.2	92.2	93.4	93.6	94.7	93.8	95.0	97.1	96.8	97.7	100.0	101.7	102.8	101.2	101.3
Rubber and Miscellaneous Plastics Products															
Output per hour of all persons	74.0	78.2	78.8	79.6	81.9	83.0	90.3	91.7	94.5	95.7	100.0	104.1	106.8	109.5	113.9
Output per unit of capital	93.8	99.4	100.6	99.5	97.5	92.1	100.6	103.1	106.7	102.6	100.0	99.4	95.6	93.3	90.3
Multifactor productivity	88.6	90.2	90.7	92.5	92.6	93.7	95.8	96.8	98.4	98.3	100.0	102.2	103.8	105.0	106.5
Sector output	62.1	67.5	70.1	71.9	73.4	71.9	81.2	86.7	94.3	96.4	100.0	106.1	109.7	114.0	117.2
Hours of all persons at work	83.9	86.3	89.0	90.4	89.7	86.6	89.9	94.6	99.8	100.7	100.0	101.9	102.7	104.1	102.9
Capital services	66.2	68.0	69.7	72.3	75.3	78.1	80.7	84.1	88.4	94.0	100.0	106.7	114.8	122.2	129.8
Energy	70.0	75.4	78.5	81.0	81.4	79.9	83.5	90.3	96.6	101.9	100.0	101.2	105.4	108.3	111.9
Non-energy materials	66.9	73.0	74.7	73.8	75.7	72.0	83.0	88.1	94.9	96.7	100.0	103.8	106.2	109.4	111.2
Purchased business services	47.3	54.2	60.5	63.9	68.2	69.0	82.7	87.3	95.4	100.5	100.0	106.7	102.9	104.1	104.9
Combined units of all inputs	70.1	74.9	77.3	77.8	79.3	76.7	84.8	89.6	95.8	98.1	100.0	103.7	105.7	108.6	110.0

Table 4-5. Indexes of Multifactor Productivity and Related Measures, Manufacturing Industries, 1986–2000—Continued

(1996=100.)

Industry	1986	1987	1988	1989	1990	1991	1992	1993	1994	1995	1996	1997	1998	1999	2000
DURABLE GOODS															
Output per hour of all persons	71.7	74.4	76.2	76.2	78.3	79.5	84.6	87.5	91.4	95.7	100.0	105.1	112.7	121.5	126.6
Output per unit of capital	91.8	92.5	96.4	95.0	92.6	87.7	90.9	93.5	98.2	99.9	100.0	102.3	104.0	106.1	105.2
Multifactor productivity	83.8	87.2	89.1	88.0	88.6	87.7	90.2	91.8	95.2	98.0	100.0	104.0	107.7	111.7	115.4
Sector output	71.8	74.2	78.8	78.9	78.4	75.1	79.0	82.8	89.3	94.9	100.0	108.2	116.6	124.7	129.3
Hours of all persons at work	100.1	99.7	103.4	103.5	100.2	94.5	93.3	94.7	97.7	99.1	100.0	102.9	103.5	102.7	102.1
Capital services	78.3	80.2	81.7	83.1	84.6	85.6	86.9	88.5	91.0	95.0	100.0	105.8	112.2	117.5	122.8
Energy	88.3	95.6	100.4	98.0	98.8	97.5	94.6	97.4	101.9	102.4	100.0	100.3	109.4	104.5	107.8
Non-energy materials	74.3	69.5	72.5	74.7	75.2	74.3	79.2	84.2	87.9	92.8	100.0	104.3	116.2	127.5	126.9
Purchased business services	71.4	76.5	81.9	84.8	82.3	78.9	86.0	89.5	95.4	99.2	100.0	105.2	104.3	107.2	105.7
Combined units of all inputs	85.7	85.1	88.5	89.7	88.5	85.6	87.5	90.3	93.8	96.8	100.0	104.0	108.3	111.7	112.0
Lumber and Wood Products															
Output per hour of all persons	106.4	107.9	105.4	102.5	103.8	106.0	106.2	100.0	99.4	99.6	100.0	98.6	99.6	101.8	101.5
Output per unit of capital	93.1	101.9	102.7	101.4	100.1	93.7	98.4	98.6	102.3	102.3	100.0	97.3	99.6	101.6	97.8
Multifactor productivity	105.8	110.6	111.6	110.8	111.6	111.3	110.5	101.7	101.2	102.5	100.0	98.6	98.5	99.1	98.6
Sector output	94.9	102.1	101.0	97.9	96.3	88.9	92.3	92.2	97.2	99.6	100.0	99.8	104.0	108.6	107.2
Hours of all persons at work	89.2	94.6	95.8	95.5	92.8	83.9	86.9	92.2	97.8	100.0	100.0	101.2	104.5	106.7	105.7
Capital services	101.9	100.3	98.4	96.5	96.1	94.9	93.7	93.5	95.0	97.4	100.0	102.6	104.4	106.9	109.7
Energy	77.9	88.1	92.9	90.9	92.0	92.0	85.4	94.9	100.6	98.5	100.0	99.1	101.2	103.8	104.0
Non-energy materials	92.9	94.4	89.2	83.8	80.9	73.6	78.9	86.0	93.6	94.5	100.0	100.2	107.7	114.4	114.3
Purchased business services	55.7	59.7	58.0	62.8	63.0	60.4	69.5	100.3	102.6	98.0	100.0	104.6	103.9	107.4	98.2
Combined units of all inputs	89.7	92.4	90.5	88.3	86.3	79.9	83.5	90.6	96.1	97.2	100.0	101.2	105.6	109.6	108.7
Furniture and Fixtures															
Output per hour of all persons	84.1	86.8	85.5	85.4	87.6	88.0	91.7	93.5	93.8	98.2	100.0	107.2	111.3	113.2	114.7
Output per unit of capital	102.9	104.6	101.0	99.9	96.7	90.5	97.0	99.7	100.4	101.2	100.0	107.0	108.9	108.4	105.5
Multifactor productivity	94.4	95.9	95.4	95.3	95.4	95.6	98.7	100.5	99.3	100.0	100.0	103.2	103.8	104.6	104.9
Sector output	82.5	87.2	87.1	87.7	86.4	80.9	87.4	92.0	95.0	98.7	100.0	110.9	119.0	123.9	127.2
Hours of all persons at work	98.1	100.5	101.9	102.7	98.6	91.9	95.3	98.4	101.3	100.5	100.0	103.5	106.9	109.4	110.9
Capital services	80.2	83.3	86.3	87.8	89.4	89.3	90.2	92.3	94.6	97.5	100.0	103.7	109.4	114.3	120.5
Energy	76.3	89.6	92.7	97.2	91.3	90.4	91.2	96.3	98.5	103.9	100.0	110.5	113.8	111.5	114.3
Non-energy materials	79.9	83.2	83.0	83.9	84.3	78.6	83.6	86.8	92.1	97.3	100.0	109.7	120.0	124.7	128.1
Purchased business services	103.0	111.9	108.5	106.2	101.6	90.4	93.5	95.3	97.8	101.3	100.0	112.3	118.0	120.0	121.4
Combined units of all inputs	87.4	91.0	91.3	92.0	90.6	84.6	88.6	91.6	95.7	98.7	100.0	107.5	114.7	118.4	121.3
Stone, Clay, and Glass															
Output per hour of all persons	89.0	91.2	90.2	89.9	92.1	91.0	95.7	95.8	96.1	97.3	100.0	103.9	108.5	108.7	108.2
Output per unit of capital	84.3	86.5	88.3	87.4	87.0	80.9	86.5	90.0	95.2	96.8	100.0	98.4	97.8	94.4	90.0
Multifactor productivity	93.0	94.6	94.7	95.8	96.6	94.5	98.9	97.5	99.4	99.9	100.0	103.9	103.2	103.4	102.8
Sector output	86.3	88.4	90.2	89.6	88.8	81.8	85.7	87.6	91.9	94.5	100.0	103.5	109.0	110.6	111.1
Hours of all persons at work	97.0	97.0	100.0	99.7	96.4	89.9	89.5	91.4	95.6	97.1	100.0	99.6	100.4	101.7	102.7
Capital services	102.4	102.2	102.2	102.5	102.0	101.0	99.1	97.2	96.5	97.6	100.0	105.2	111.4	117.2	123.5
Energy	100.4	102.6	104.5	101.7	101.6	97.0	99.6	100.6	98.7	104.3	100.0	101.7	112.2	107.3	109.7
Non-energy materials	86.3	86.6	87.5	84.3	83.4	78.2	78.5	84.4	87.3	89.6	100.0	97.2	108.1	109.2	108.5
Purchased business services	78.2	85.3	88.1	87.9	86.8	81.6	85.5	87.9	90.2	94.0	100.0	97.5	101.8	100.1	96.2
Combined units of all inputs	92.8	93.5	95.2	93.6	91.9	86.5	86.7	89.8	92.5	94.5	100.0	99.6	105.5	107.0	108.1
Primary Metal Industries															
Output per hour of all persons	81.2	85.1	87.7	85.2	85.3	86.0	91.4	95.2	96.0	97.7	100.0	100.8	106.3	105.8	104.3
Output per unit of capital	75.2	82.0	90.1	88.6	86.5	82.2	86.1	91.4	97.1	98.4	100.0	101.6	103.5	101.7	99.6
Multifactor productivity	98.0	97.0	96.0	94.5	96.3	96.7	99.9	103.1	101.8	99.0	100.0	100.4	103.5	104.8	103.8
Sector output	80.9	86.4	93.6	91.0	88.5	83.7	86.6	90.9	96.2	97.6	100.0	102.6	106.1	105.6	104.3
Hours of all persons at work	99.6	101.5	106.8	106.8	103.7	97.3	94.8	95.5	100.2	100.0	100.0	101.7	99.8	99.8	100.0
Capital services	107.5	105.3	103.9	102.8	102.3	101.8	100.6	99.5	99.0	99.2	100.0	101.0	102.5	103.8	104.8
Energy	95.5	98.9	111.5	103.2	105.2	107.0	99.7	99.0	110.2	99.9	100.0	94.6	110.8	102.2	105.5
Non-energy materials	69.3	78.3	88.0	86.6	80.7	75.7	78.1	80.6	88.1	96.9	100.0	103.5	103.9	102.6	101.6
Purchased business services	70.9	84.1	100.6	101.2	93.0	81.4	84.0	85.0	93.5	101.6	100.0	103.6	100.1	92.4	90.5
Combined units of all inputs	82.6	89.0	97.6	96.3	91.9	86.5	86.8	88.2	94.5	98.6	100.0	102.2	102.6	100.8	100.5

Table 4-5. Indexes of Multifactor Productivity and Related Measures, Manufacturing Industries, 1986–2000—*Continued*

(1996=100.)

Industry	1986	1987	1988	1989	1990	1991	1992	1993	1994	1995	1996	1997	1998	1999	2000
Fabricated Metal Products															
Output per hour of all persons	87.6	91.4	90.3	87.2	87.8	87.6	92.8	94.5	96.6	98.2	100.0	103.2	106.5	106.3	108.4
Output per unit of capital	95.5	95.5	98.4	95.7	92.6	87.4	91.9	94.6	100.0	100.2	100.0	103.5	103.5	101.3	101.8
Multifactor productivity	95.7	98.7	99.4	96.7	95.3	93.4	95.1	96.1	99.5	100.1	100.0	101.3	100.8	100.4	101.4
Sector output	83.4	85.1	87.7	85.3	83.4	79.1	83.7	86.9	93.5	96.8	100.0	106.4	110.7	111.5	114.8
Hours of all persons at work	95.1	93.1	97.1	97.9	95.0	90.3	90.2	92.0	96.8	98.6	100.0	103.1	104.0	104.9	105.9
Capital services	87.3	89.1	89.1	89.2	90.1	90.6	91.1	91.9	93.5	96.6	100.0	102.8	107.0	110.0	112.7
Energy	80.7	89.6	93.3	93.0	92.3	91.2	88.4	92.8	96.1	102.7	100.0	102.5	109.2	109.1	111.6
Non-energy materials	82.7	80.7	81.5	81.0	81.4	79.4	85.3	88.9	92.0	94.7	100.0	106.9	115.4	117.3	120.1
Purchased business services	80.3	85.2	90.0	90.7	88.1	83.2	89.6	91.0	94.8	99.2	100.0	107.0	109.3	105.1	107.1
Combined units of all inputs	87.1	86.2	88.3	88.2	87.5	84.7	87.9	90.5	94.0	96.7	100.0	105.0	109.8	111.1	113.2
Industrial and Commercial Machinery															
Output per hour of all persons	53.1	55.8	60.3	61.0	62.6	62.4	69.2	74.2	81.5	89.7	100.0	108.5	120.8	132.6	146.5
Output per unit of capital	73.6	75.1	82.1	81.0	79.2	73.4	77.3	81.8	88.4	95.2	100.0	104.4	105.6	102.1	100.9
Multifactor productivity	71.2	75.9	80.0	80.6	81.5	79.5	83.8	86.1	90.8	95.2	100.0	106.3	114.9	120.4	126.3
Sector output	50.4	52.3	59.2	60.5	60.8	57.6	62.4	68.5	77.8	89.1	100.0	113.1	126.3	132.9	143.7
Hours of all persons at work	94.9	93.7	98.1	99.3	97.1	92.4	90.2	92.2	95.5	99.3	100.0	104.2	104.6	100.2	98.1
Capital services	68.5	69.7	72.0	74.7	76.7	78.5	80.7	83.8	88.0	93.5	100.0	108.3	119.6	130.1	142.4
Energy	86.9	92.0	94.9	99.2	99.1	97.7	89.9	92.7	99.5	102.8	100.0	99.9	104.9	99.5	104.0
Non-energy materials	54.0	50.6	56.5	57.4	57.6	56.9	61.6	69.1	76.9	88.7	100.0	109.2	115.5	119.8	128.6
Purchased business services	74.1	75.2	80.5	80.6	76.2	70.7	74.0	79.8	88.9	95.7	100.0	100.4	96.7	91.8	91.4
Combined units of all inputs	70.8	68.9	74.0	75.1	74.6	72.5	74.5	79.6	85.6	93.6	100.0	106.4	109.9	110.3	113.8
Electrical and Electronic Equipment															
Output per hour of all persons	40.7	44.4	46.4	47.9	51.0	54.9	61.9	67.0	75.5	88.7	100.0	113.6	126.5	153.5	188.7
Output per unit of capital	66.0	66.0	68.3	67.8	66.9	66.7	71.8	76.2	84.6	94.2	100.0	105.4	110.0	122.7	144.7
Multifactor productivity	61.1	65.1	67.1	68.7	70.4	72.2	75.5	78.6	86.0	94.3	100.0	107.4	110.5	122.0	135.0
Sector output	42.6	45.3	48.3	49.3	50.1	50.7	56.0	61.5	71.7	86.4	100.0	115.1	129.2	152.5	191.0
Hours of all persons at work	104.6	102.0	104.1	102.7	98.2	92.5	90.4	91.7	94.9	97.4	100.0	101.3	102.1	99.4	101.2
Capital services	64.6	68.6	70.7	72.7	74.9	76.1	78.0	80.7	84.7	91.7	100.0	109.2	117.5	124.3	132.0
Energy	77.7	87.5	88.5	90.8	92.1	90.8	89.8	95.2	97.8	102.6	100.0	107.9	106.9	103.6	110.8
Non-energy materials	47.2	46.0	48.6	47.8	48.7	50.2	57.6	64.7	70.4	83.8	100.0	110.7	140.7	167.5	228.7
Purchased business services	58.8	62.2	64.5	63.6	60.9	58.0	66.9	70.6	82.0	95.0	100.0	111.9	112.2	128.7	147.2
Combined units of all inputs	69.7	69.5	72.0	71.7	71.2	70.3	74.1	78.2	83.3	91.6	100.0	107.2	117.0	124.9	141.4
Transportation Equipment															
Output per hour of all persons	75.9	78.0	78.8	78.7	80.5	80.3	87.8	92.9	97.8	98.0	100.0	106.4	114.7	123.9	119.1
Output per unit of capital	94.6	93.2	95.8	94.2	91.0	84.5	90.2	94.2	100.6	100.8	100.0	107.0	109.4	115.4	105.2
Multifactor productivity	102.2	103.6	102.8	100.0	98.9	97.7	97.7	100.1	101.6	101.4	100.0	102.2	104.9	106.6	105.1
Sector output	81.6	83.2	88.1	88.2	86.4	81.0	86.5	90.5	97.2	98.3	100.0	111.1	120.0	131.4	122.6
Hours of all persons at work	107.5	106.7	111.9	112.1	107.4	101.0	98.6	97.4	99.3	100.3	100.0	104.4	104.7	106.0	103.0
Capital services	86.2	89.3	92.0	93.6	95.0	95.9	95.9	96.1	96.6	97.5	100.0	103.8	109.7	113.9	116.6
Energy	78.1	100.8	97.3	95.2	95.7	92.6	95.9	101.2	101.7	104.9	100.0	103.9	107.8	105.4	110.1
Non-energy materials	67.1	66.8	72.0	74.3	75.0	70.4	79.6	83.8	91.6	94.0	100.0	112.1	121.7	135.8	126.6
Purchased business services	66.7	71.4	81.3	90.7	91.1	91.4	102.1	100.8	105.5	102.5	100.0	107.5	108.2	118.5	103.2
Combined units of all inputs	79.8	80.3	85.7	88.2	87.4	83.0	88.5	90.4	95.6	96.9	100.0	108.7	114.4	123.3	116.7
Instruments															
Output per hour of all persons	68.7	73.5	74.0	74.3	77.4	80.6	87.1	88.2	91.5	95.5	100.0	99.1	103.6	108.3	116.5
Output per unit of capital	116.6	125.5	126.1	117.0	111.9	106.3	104.5	100.8	99.0	99.1	100.0	96.7	94.9	91.6	92.6
Multifactor productivity	91.4	94.6	98.3	95.8	98.1	98.1	99.1	97.9	98.9	99.2	100.0	98.0	98.7	98.3	101.9
Sector output	79.9	84.9	88.2	87.8	89.1	89.3	92.7	92.5	92.5	94.9	100.0	102.1	105.8	108.5	115.7
Hours of all persons at work	116.3	115.5	119.3	118.1	115.2	110.7	106.4	104.9	101.1	99.3	100.0	103.0	102.1	100.2	99.3
Capital services	68.5	67.7	70.0	75.0	79.6	84.0	88.7	91.8	93.4	95.7	100.0	105.6	111.5	118.4	125.0
Energy	102.0	96.3	100.1	99.7	104.2	100.6	99.4	100.5	99.2	104.5	100.0	99.0	84.1	74.6	73.3
Non-energy materials	66.3	69.8	67.1	70.1	70.7	73.6	80.3	82.1	83.4	89.5	100.0	106.9	116.6	127.8	137.1
Purchased business services	82.3	89.6	89.4	94.8	92.6	92.8	99.9	104.5	103.7	104.3	100.0	99.1	94.8	94.7	95.9
Combined units of all inputs	87.4	89.7	89.7	91.6	90.9	91.0	93.6	94.5	93.5	95.6	100.0	104.2	107.1	110.4	113.6
Miscellaneous Manufacturing															
Output per hour of all persons	85.5	89.3	90.3	87.6	90.9	89.9	90.6	92.1	90.9	97.3	100.0	97.0	99.9	104.4	112.0
Output per unit of capital	89.9	91.8	96.9	93.5	93.7	91.1	92.3	95.7	96.0	98.2	100.0	100.2	99.3	99.3	101.3
Multifactor productivity	97.7	99.7	103.1	101.5	100.6	97.0	94.9	95.3	96.4	99.3	100.0	100.1	99.5	101.7	104.9
Sector output	79.6	83.4	88.8	86.9	87.6	84.5	87.6	92.5	94.2	96.8	100.0	102.1	103.9	106.5	111.4
Hours of all persons at work	93.2	93.4	98.3	99.2	96.4	94.0	96.7	100.4	103.6	99.5	100.0	105.3	104.0	102.0	99.5
Capital services	88.6	90.9	91.7	93.0	93.4	92.7	94.9	96.7	98.1	98.6	100.0	101.9	104.6	107.2	110.0
Energy	73.4	90.1	91.9	94.4	95.6	93.3	84.7	95.6	96.2	107.9	100.0	97.6	102.5	97.0	101.6
Non-energy materials	69.8	71.2	72.6	71.3	76.2	79.4	87.8	94.4	93.7	95.1	100.0	99.9	107.1	110.1	114.1
Purchased business services	83.2	92.1	95.3	91.1	90.3	86.0	92.6	97.6	95.4	97.9	100.0	100.5	97.2	92.8	95.2
Combined units of all inputs	81.5	83.7	86.1	85.6	87.0	87.1	92.3	97.0	97.7	97.5	100.0	102.0	104.4	104.8	106.2

PART FIVE

COMPENSATION OF EMPLOYEES

COMPENSATION OF EMPLOYEES

HIGHLIGHTS

This chapter covers three related topics: employment cost index for total compensation (ECI), covering wages and salaries and benefits; employee participation in various benefit plans; and occupational employment and wages derived from the Occupational Employment Statistics Survey (OES). All the surveys from which these data are derived are now components of the National Compensation Survey (NCS), which was more fully described in the previous edition of this handbook.

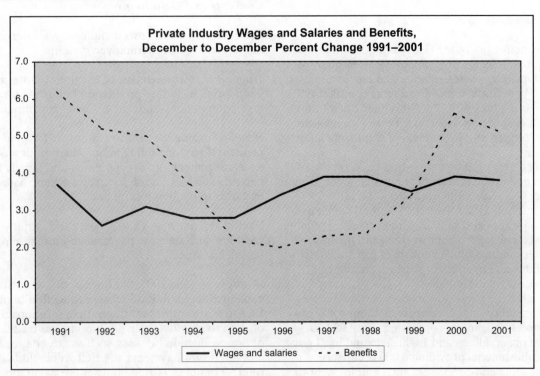

The slowdown in the increase in benefits in the private industry exceeded that of wages and salaries from 2000 to 2001, 5.6 percent to 5.1 percent v. 3.9 percent to 3.8 percent. However, the extent of the increase in benefits continued to exceed the increase in wages, a trend in the difference between the two that began in 2000. (Table 5-1 and 5-3)

OTHER HIGHLIGHTS:

- Fifteen of the 22 occupational groups covered by the OES increased the proportion of workers in the $43.75 per hour wage range in 2000. The largest increase was in management followed by computer and mathematical occupations. (Table 5-13 in the fifth and sixth editions)
- Legal occupations had the highest proportion in the over $43.75 wage range, 28.7 percent. (Table 5-13)
- Hospitals had the highest increase in wages in 2001, 5.9 percent compared with 3.8 percent for all private industry. Transportation and public utilities, aircraft manufacturing, and communications, among others, also exceeded the average increase in private industry. (Table 5-1)
- The largest major occupational groups in 2000 continued to be in office and administrative support, 17.7 percent, followed by sales and related occupations at 10.4 percent. The production sector declined from 9.9 percent to 9.6 percent reflecting the decline in manufacturing employment. (Table 5-15)
- In four of the lowest paid occupations, more than 50 percent of the workers earned less that $8.50 per hour. These are food preparation; building, grounds and maintenance workers; personal care and service; and farming. (Table 5-13)
- Physicians earned the highest mean hourly wages in 2000 with surgeons topping the list at $66.06. (Table 5-15)
- The percentage of participants required to contribute to family medical care benefits increased from 76 percent to 81 percent in small establishments but declined from 85 percent to 80 percent in larger establishments from 1999 to 2000. (Table 5-11)

NOTES AND DEFINITIONS

EMPLOYMENT COST INDEX

Note: The employment cost index is now part of the National Compensation Survey (NCS) which includes the Employment Benefits Survey and the Occupational Compensation Survey.

Collection and Coverage

The Employment Cost Index (ECI) is a quarterly measure of the rate of change in compensation per hour worked and includes wages, salaries, and employer costs of employee benefits. It uses a fixed market basket of labor—similar in concept to the Consumer Price Index's fixed market basket of goods and services—to measure change over time in employer costs of employing labor.

Statistical series on total compensation costs, on wages and salaries, and on benefit costs are available for private nonfarm workers excluding proprietors, the self-employed, and household workers. The total compensation costs and wages and salaries series are also available for state and local government workers and for the civilian nonfarm economy, which consists of private industry and state and local government workers combined. Federal workers are excluded.

The ECI probability sample consists of about 4,400 private nonfarm establishments providing about 23,000 occupational observations and 1,000 state and local government establishments providing 6,000 occupational observations selected to represent total employment in each sector. On average, each reporting unit provides wage and compensation information on five well-specified occupations. The occupations are defined narrowly enough so that all workers in the job carry out the same task at roughly the same level of skill. Data are collected each quarter for the pay period including the 12th day of March, June, September, and December.

From June 1986 to March 1995 fixed employment weights from the 1980 Census of Population were used each quarter to calculate the civilian and private indexes and the index for state and local governments. Employment counts for 1990 were introduced in March 1995. Prior to June 1986, the employment weights are from the 1970 Census of Population. These fixed weights, also used to derive all of the industry and occupation series indexes, ensure that changes in these indexes reflect only changes in compensation, not employment shifts among industries or occupations with different levels of wages and compensation. For the bargaining status, region, and metropolitan/nonmetropolitan area series, however, employment data by industry and occupation

are not available from the census. Instead, the 1980 employment weights are reallocated within these series each quarter based on the current sample. Therefore, these indexes are not strictly comparable to those for the aggregate, industry, and occupation series.

Concepts and Definitions

Total compensation costs include wages, salaries, and the employer's costs for employee benefits.

Wages and salaries consist of earnings before payroll deductions, including production bonuses, incentive earnings, commissions, and cost-of-living adjustments.

Benefits include the cost to employers for paid leave, supplemental pay (including nonproduction bonuses), insurance, retirement and savings plans, and legally required benefits (such as Social Security, workers' compensation, and unemployment insurance).

Excluded from wages and salaries and employee benefit costs are such items as payment-in-kind, free room and board, and tips.

Bonuses. In June 2000, the Bureau of Labor Statistics expanded the definition of nonproduction bonuses in the ECI to better represent the compensation packages offered to employees. In addition to the traditional types of nonproduction bonuses, such as attendance bonuses and lump sum payments, the ECI will include hiring and referral bonuses. Hiring bonuses are payments made by the employer to induce an individual to accept employment; referral bonuses are made by the employer to an employee for recommending an applicant who is hired by the establishment.

As part of its ongoing research program, the Bureau of Labor Statistics currently is conducting research on stock option plans. This research will be completed in stages. BLS has begun testing the incidence of stock option plans across all industries and occupations. The prevalence of these plans, based on test results and the potential impact on compensation costs, will determine the next stage of research. The results of the pilot incidence survey were published in October 2000.

Sources of Additional Information

Additional information on Employment Cost Index methodology and data is available in BLS Bulletin 2532, September 2000 and BLS news release 02-346. The quarterly publication, *Compensation and Working Conditions*, contains articles on the National Compensation Survey.

Table 5-1. Employment Cost Index, Private Industry Workers[1], Total Compensation and Wages and Salaries by Occupation and Industry, 1987–2001

(June 1989=100, not seasonally adjusted.)

Series and year	Total compensation					Wages and salaries				
	Indexes				Percent change for 12 months ended December	Indexes				Percent change for 12 months ended December
	March	June	September	December		March	June	September	December	
PRIVATE INDUSTRY WORKERS										
1987	91.0	91.6	92.5	93.1	3.3	92.0	92.6	93.5	94.1	3.3
1988	94.5	95.7	96.6	97.6	4.8	95.0	96.1	97.0	98.0	4.1
1989	98.8	100.0	101.2	102.3	4.8	99.0	100.0	101.2	102.0	4.1
1990	103.9	105.2	106.2	107.0	4.6	103.2	104.5	105.4	106.1	4.0
1991	108.5	109.8	111.0	111.7	4.4	107.3	108.4	109.3	110.0	3.7
1992	113.1	113.9	114.8	115.6	3.5	110.9	111.6	112.2	112.9	2.6
1993	117.1	118.0	119.1	119.8	3.6	113.9	114.6	115.7	116.4	3.1
1994	121.0	122.0	123.0	123.5	3.1	117.2	118.1	119.1	119.7	2.8
1995	124.5	125.4	126.2	126.7	2.6	120.6	121.5	122.4	123.1	2.8
1996	127.9	129.0	129.8	130.6	3.1	124.4	125.6	126.5	127.3	3.4
1997	131.7	132.8	133.9	135.1	3.4	128.6	129.7	131.0	132.3	3.9
1998	136.3	137.5	139.0	139.8	3.5	133.7	134.9	136.6	137.4	3.9
1999	140.4	142.0	143.3	144.6	3.4	138.1	139.7	141.0	142.2	3.5
2000	146.8	148.5	149.9	150.9	4.4	143.9	145.4	146.8	147.7	3.9
2001	153.0	154.5	155.9	157.2	4.2	149.4	150.9	152.1	153.3	3.8
Private industry workers, excluding sales occupations										
1987	91.0	91.7	92.7	93.4	3.5	92.1	92.7	93.8	94.5	3.6
1988	94.9	95.9	96.9	97.7	4.6	95.4	96.3	97.3	98.0	3.7
1989	99.0	100.0	101.2	102.1	4.5	99.1	100.0	101.1	101.9	4.0
1990	103.9	105.1	106.3	107.1	4.9	103.2	104.4	105.4	106.2	4.2
1991	108.6	109.8	111.1	112.0	4.6	107.4	108.4	109.4	110.2	3.8
1992	113.3	114.1	115.1	115.9	3.5	111.1	111.8	112.5	113.2	2.7
1993	117.5	118.5	119.5	120.2	3.7	114.2	115.0	115.9	116.6	3.0
1994	121.4	122.3	123.4	123.9	3.1	117.5	118.3	119.4	120.0	2.9
1995	125.0	125.7	126.5	127.1	2.6	121.0	121.8	122.6	123.4	2.8
1996	128.3	129.2	130.2	130.8	2.9	124.7	125.7	126.8	127.5	3.3
1997	131.9	133.0	134.1	135.2	3.4	128.6	129.9	131.2	132.4	3.8
1998	136.4	137.5	138.8	139.4	3.1	133.7	134.8	136.3	136.9	3.4
1999	140.5	141.9	143.2	144.5	3.7	138.2	139.6	140.8	142.0	3.7
2000	146.5	148.2	149.8	150.9	4.4	143.5	145.1	146.5	147.6	3.9
2001	153.0	154.4	156.0	157.2	4.2	149.5	150.8	152.2	153.3	3.9
WORKERS BY OCCUPATIONAL GROUP										
White-Collar Occupations										
1987	90.6	91.2	92.1	92.7	3.7	91.4	91.9	93.0	93.4	3.7
1988	93.9	95.1	96.2	97.3	5.0	94.4	95.6	96.7	97.8	4.7
1989	98.9	100.0	101.4	102.4	5.2	99.0	100.0	101.4	102.4	4.7
1990	104.1	105.5	106.7	107.4	4.9	103.6	104.9	106.0	106.6	4.1
1991	109.0	110.3	111.4	112.2	4.5	107.9	109.1	110.1	110.7	3.8
1992	113.4	114.2	115.1	115.9	3.3	111.7	112.3	112.9	113.7	2.7
1993	117.4	118.3	119.4	120.2	3.7	114.7	115.5	116.7	117.5	3.3
1994	121.5	122.5	123.5	124.1	3.2	118.3	119.3	120.2	120.8	2.8
1995	125.3	126.2	127.0	127.6	2.8	121.7	122.7	123.6	124.3	2.9
1996	129.0	130.0	131.1	131.7	3.2	125.8	127.0	128.0	128.7	3.5
1997	133.1	134.1	135.2	136.7	3.8	130.2	131.3	132.7	134.2	4.3
1998	138.1	139.4	141.1	142.0	3.9	135.7	137.0	139.0	139.9	4.2
1999	142.4	144.1	145.6	146.9	3.5	140.3	142.1	143.5	144.8	3.5
2000	149.3	151.1	152.6	153.6	4.6	146.6	148.3	149.7	150.6	4.0
2001	155.7	157.4	158.7	160.1	4.2	152.3	153.8	154.8	156.1	3.7
White-collar occupations, excluding sales occupations										
1987	90.6	91.3	92.5	93.2	4.3	91.4	92.0	93.4	94.0	4.3
1988	94.5	95.5	96.7	97.5	4.6	95.0	95.9	97.1	98.0	4.3
1989	99.0	100.0	101.3	102.2	4.8	99.2	100.0	101.2	102.1	4.2
1990	104.2	105.4	106.9	107.7	5.4	103.7	104.8	106.2	106.9	4.7
1991	109.2	110.4	111.8	112.7	4.6	108.2	109.2	110.5	111.3	4.1
1992	113.8	114.6	115.8	116.6	3.5	112.1	112.8	113.7	114.4	2.8
1993	118.3	119.2	120.2	121.0	3.8	115.7	116.4	117.4	118.2	3.3
1994	122.4	123.3	124.4	125.1	3.4	119.0	119.9	121.0	121.7	3.0
1995	126.3	127.0	127.8	128.6	2.8	122.8	123.4	124.3	125.2	2.9
1996	129.9	130.7	132.0	132.5	3.0	126.7	127.6	129.0	129.4	3.4
1997	133.7	134.8	135.9	137.4	3.7	130.8	132.0	133.4	134.8	4.2
1998	138.8	139.9	141.3	141.9	3.3	136.3	137.5	139.1	139.7	3.6
1999	143.0	144.5	146.0	147.3	3.8	141.0	142.5	143.9	145.2	3.9
2000	149.4	151.3	152.9	154.1	4.6	146.7	148.5	149.9	151.1	4.1
2001	156.5	158.1	159.6	160.9	4.4	153.0	154.4	155.7	156.9	3.8

See footnotes at end of table.

Table 5-1. Employment Cost Index, Private Industry Workers[1], Total Compensation and Wages and Salaries by Occupation and Industry, 1987–2001—*Continued*

(June 1989=100, not seasonally adjusted.)

Series and year	Total compensation					Wages and salaries				
	Indexes				Percent change for 12 months ended December	Indexes				Percent change for 12 months ended December
	March	June	September	December		March	June	September	December	
Professional specialty and technical occupations										
1987	90.3	90.8	92.1	92.9	4.0	91.0	91.5	92.8	93.8	4.6
1988	94.3	95.4	96.9	97.5	5.0	94.7	95.9	97.4	97.9	4.4
1989	99.0	100.0	101.8	102.9	5.5	99.3	100.0	101.6	102.5	4.7
1990	104.9	105.8	107.5	108.7	5.6	104.1	104.8	106.5	107.5	4.9
1991	110.1	111.1	112.8	113.9	4.8	108.6	109.5	111.1	112.0	4.2
1992	115.3	116.4	118.0	119.0	4.5	113.0	114.0	115.3	116.0	3.6
1993	120.4	121.3	122.2	122.9	3.3	117.1	117.9	118.9	119.5	3.0
1994	124.6	125.3	126.3	126.8	3.2	120.4	121.3	122.2	123.0	2.9
1995	127.7	128.4	129.3	129.9	2.4	123.7	124.4	125.3	126.1	2.5
1996	131.6	132.6	133.3	133.7	2.9	127.8	128.8	129.6	129.9	3.0
1997	134.6	135.9	136.7	137.8	3.1	131.0	132.4	133.7	134.8	3.8
1998	138.8	140.1	141.6	142.6	3.5	135.9	137.1	138.7	139.7	3.6
1999	142.9	144.1	145.2	146.7	2.9	140.7	141.8	142.6	144.1	3.1
2000	148.4	150.7	152.2	153.7	4.8	145.1	147.3	148.6	150.2	4.2
2001	156.3	157.5	159.2	160.3	4.3	152.1	153.2	154.8	155.9	3.8
Executive, administrative, and managerial occupations										
1987	91.6	92.2	93.5	93.9	4.4	92.1	92.6	94.1	94.5	4.3
1988	94.7	95.7	96.6	97.8	4.2	95.0	95.9	96.7	98.0	3.7
1989	99.1	100.0	100.9	101.5	3.8	99.3	100.0	100.8	101.5	3.6
1990	103.7	105.3	106.6	107.2	5.6	103.3	104.9	106.2	106.9	5.3
1991	108.9	110.3	111.5	112.3	4.8	108.2	109.4	110.6	111.4	4.2
1992	112.7	113.1	113.9	114.5	2.0	111.6	112.0	112.5	113.2	1.6
1993	116.5	117.2	118.1	118.9	3.8	114.7	115.3	116.2	117.0	3.4
1994	120.3	121.3	122.6	123.3	3.7	117.8	118.8	120.0	120.5	3.0
1995	124.9	125.4	126.2	126.9	2.9	121.9	122.5	123.4	124.4	3.2
1996	128.0	128.8	130.9	131.3	3.5	125.9	126.8	128.9	129.3	3.9
1997	133.0	133.9	135.2	137.4	4.6	131.0	132.1	133.6	135.8	5.0
1998	139.4	140.0	141.9	141.8	3.2	137.8	138.7	140.9	140.5	3.5
1999	143.7	145.8	147.7	149.1	5.1	141.9	144.3	146.4	147.6	5.1
2000	151.1	152.7	154.4	155.3	4.2	149.2	150.7	152.3	153.0	3.7
2001	157.3	159.4	160.2	161.8	4.2	154.7	156.5	157.2	158.6	3.7
Sales occupations										
1987	90.0	90.5	90.5	90.2	1.2	91.3	91.6	91.6	90.9	0.9
1988	91.4	93.6	94.1	96.3	6.8	91.9	94.3	94.8	96.9	6.6
1989	98.3	100.0	101.9	103.3	7.3	98.6	100.0	102.1	103.7	7.0
1990	103.6	105.6	105.9	106.0	2.6	103.3	105.3	105.4	105.2	1.4
1991	108.0	109.8	109.8	109.6	3.4	106.8	108.5	108.2	107.9	2.6
1992	111.6	112.2	111.8	112.6	2.7	109.7	110.1	109.7	110.7	2.6
1993	112.9	113.8	115.6	116.5	3.5	110.5	111.6	113.8	114.7	3.6
1994	117.2	118.8	119.2	119.6	2.7	114.8	116.2	116.5	116.7	1.7
1995	120.2	122.4	123.2	123.2	3.0	116.9	119.3	120.5	120.4	3.2
1996	124.8	126.9	126.7	128.1	4.0	122.0	124.4	123.9	125.9	4.6
1997	130.1	130.7	132.2	133.5	4.2	127.8	128.3	129.8	131.4	4.4
1998	135.3	137.3	140.4	142.6	6.8	133.1	135.2	138.8	141.3	7.5
1999	139.6	142.6	144.1	145.3	1.9	137.3	140.5	142.1	143.3	1.4
2000	148.9	150.3	151.2	151.4	4.2	146.7	147.9	149.0	148.7	3.8
2001	152.3	154.5	155.0	156.7	3.5	149.2	151.5	151.2	152.6	2.6
Administrative support occupations, including clerical occupations										
1987	90.0	90.8	91.8	92.6	4.0	91.1	91.9	93.0	93.7	4.1
1988	94.4	95.3	96.6	97.3	5.1	95.1	95.8	97.2	97.8	4.4
1989	98.9	100.0	101.2	102.3	5.1	99.1	100.0	101.1	102.2	4.5
1990	104.2	105.3	106.4	107.3	4.9	103.6	104.7	105.7	106.4	4.1
1991	108.6	109.9	111.0	111.9	4.3	107.6	108.6	109.6	110.4	3.8
1992	113.6	114.4	115.5	116.4	4.0	111.6	112.4	113.2	114.0	3.3
1993	118.1	119.2	120.3	121.2	4.1	115.2	116.1	117.1	118.0	3.5
1994	122.5	123.5	124.5	125.1	3.2	119.0	119.9	120.9	121.6	3.1
1995	126.5	127.3	128.1	129.0	3.1	122.9	123.5	124.3	125.3	3.0
1996	130.1	130.8	132.0	132.5	2.7	126.5	127.3	128.5	129.2	3.1
1997	133.7	134.7	135.9	137.0	3.4	130.6	131.7	132.9	133.9	3.6
1998	138.2	139.6	140.6	141.4	3.2	135.3	136.7	137.9	138.9	3.7
1999	142.6	143.7	145.0	146.2	3.4	140.4	141.4	142.7	143.8	3.5
2000	149.0	150.6	152.3	153.4	4.9	146.0	147.5	149.1	150.1	4.4
2001	156.1	157.7	159.5	160.8	4.8	152.3	153.6	155.3	156.5	4.3

See footnotes at end of table.

Table 5-1. Employment Cost Index, Private Industry Workers [1], Total Compensation and Wages and Salaries by Occupation and Industry, 1987–2001—*Continued*

(June 1989=100, not seasonally adjusted.)

Series and year	Total compensation					Wages and salaries				
	Indexes				Percent change for 12 months ended December	Indexes				Percent change for 12 months ended December
	March	June	September	December		March	June	September	December	
Blue-Collar Occupations										
1987	91.3	92.1	92.9	93.7	3.1	92.8	93.5	94.3	95.2	3.0
1988	95.4	96.4	97.1	97.9	4.5	95.9	96.8	97.4	98.2	3.2
1989	98.8	100.0	101.1	101.9	4.1	99.0	100.0	101.0	101.6	3.5
1990	103.5	104.7	105.6	106.4	4.4	102.7	103.8	104.6	105.2	3.5
1991	107.9	109.0	110.2	111.0	4.3	106.4	107.3	108.0	108.8	3.4
1992	112.5	113.4	114.3	115.0	3.6	109.7	110.4	111.1	111.6	2.6
1993	116.6	117.7	118.7	119.3	3.7	112.5	113.2	114.1	114.8	2.9
1994	120.3	121.2	122.3	122.6	2.8	115.6	116.5	117.5	118.0	2.8
1995	123.5	124.4	125.1	125.6	2.4	119.0	120.1	120.8	121.4	2.9
1996	126.6	127.6	128.1	129.0	2.7	122.5	123.7	124.3	125.1	3.0
1997	129.6	130.8	131.7	132.3	2.6	126.0	127.3	128.3	129.1	3.2
1998	133.1	134.3	135.2	135.9	2.7	130.2	131.3	132.4	133.2	3.2
1999	136.9	138.2	139.4	140.5	3.3	134.3	135.6	136.8	137.7	3.4
2000	142.6	144.1	145.5	146.4	4.2	139.1	140.5	141.9	142.8	3.7
2001	148.2	149.3	151.0	151.9	3.8	144.6	145.9	147.5	148.3	3.9
Precision production, craft, and repair occupations										
1987	92.0	92.7	93.7	94.4	3.1	92.8	93.5	94.5	95.1	2.8
1988	95.8	96.8	97.3	98.0	3.8	95.9	96.8	97.2	97.9	2.9
1989	98.7	100.0	101.2	102.0	4.1	98.8	100.0	101.0	101.6	3.8
1990	103.4	104.7	105.6	106.2	4.1	102.5	103.6	104.4	104.9	3.2
1991	108.0	109.2	110.5	111.0	4.5	106.3	107.0	107.8	108.4	3.3
1992	112.2	113.1	114.3	115.0	3.6	109.3	110.1	111.0	111.5	2.9
1993	116.6	117.6	118.7	118.9	3.4	112.4	113.2	114.2	114.7	2.9
1994	120.2	121.2	122.5	122.5	3.0	115.5	116.5	117.8	117.9	2.8
1995	123.4	124.4	125.4	125.7	2.6	118.8	119.9	121.0	121.4	3.0
1996	126.5	127.7	128.2	129.1	2.7	122.4	123.7	124.2	125.1	3.0
1997	129.6	130.9	131.7	131.9	2.2	125.8	127.4	128.2	128.7	2.9
1998	132.9	134.4	135.4	136.1	3.2	129.8	131.2	132.3	133.0	3.3
1999	137.2	138.4	139.6	140.6	3.3	134.3	135.6	136.7	137.5	3.4
2000	142.3	144.1	145.8	146.7	4.3	138.9	140.6	142.0	142.8	3.9
2001	148.7	149.7	151.8	152.5	4.0	144.6	145.7	147.7	148.4	3.9
Machine operators, assemblers, and inspectors										
1987	90.2	91.1	91.6	92.8	3.3	92.3	93.2	93.8	95.1	3.5
1988	94.7	95.8	96.5	97.6	5.2	95.6	96.5	97.1	98.1	3.2
1989	98.9	100.0	100.9	101.8	4.3	99.0	100.0	100.6	101.6	3.6
1990	103.7	105.0	105.9	106.9	5.0	103.0	104.2	104.9	105.8	4.1
1991	108.3	109.4	110.5	111.6	4.4	107.1	108.0	108.7	109.8	3.8
1992	113.9	114.6	115.0	115.8	3.8	110.9	111.6	111.7	112.4	2.4
1993	117.8	119.0	120.0	120.8	4.3	113.2	113.8	114.7	115.6	2.8
1994	121.3	122.2	122.9	123.4	2.2	116.2	117.2	118.0	118.8	2.8
1995	124.2	124.8	125.1	126.2	2.3	119.6	120.9	121.4	122.3	2.9
1996	127.1	128.1	128.7	129.5	2.6	123.4	124.5	125.4	126.4	3.4
1997	130.0	131.2	132.2	133.0	2.7	127.2	128.5	129.5	130.6	3.3
1998	133.6	134.7	135.7	136.8	2.9	131.6	132.7	133.8	134.9	3.3
1999	137.3	138.4	139.9	141.4	3.4	135.7	136.7	138.3	139.5	3.4
2000	144.0	145.0	146.0	146.8	3.8	140.7	141.6	142.9	143.7	3.0
2001	148.3	149.1	150.4	151.5	3.2	145.6	146.9	148.1	149.0	3.7
Transportation and material moving occupations										
1987	91.6	92.6	93.3	93.9	3.0	93.6	94.4	95.0	95.5	2.4
1988	95.3	97.0	97.9	98.2	4.6	96.1	97.4	98.4	98.6	3.2
1989	99.0	100.0	101.2	101.4	3.3	99.3	100.0	101.2	101.2	2.6
1990	103.1	104.3	104.9	105.5	4.0	102.0	103.1	103.6	104.1	2.9
1991	106.3	107.6	108.3	109.0	3.3	104.5	105.6	106.1	106.7	2.5
1992	110.4	111.4	112.5	113.0	3.7	107.4	108.3	109.3	109.7	2.8
1993	113.9	115.2	115.9	117.0	3.5	110.0	111.2	111.7	112.6	2.6
1994	118.5	119.1	120.3	120.6	3.1	113.5	114.0	115.2	115.6	2.7
1995	121.8	122.4	122.9	123.0	2.0	117.0	117.8	118.5	118.6	2.6
1996	123.9	124.7	124.9	125.2	1.8	120.0	120.6	121.0	121.1	2.1
1997	126.1	126.8	128.0	128.9	3.0	122.3	123.0	124.1	125.1	3.3
1998	129.3	129.9	130.7	130.7	1.4	125.9	126.4	127.6	127.8	2.2
1999	131.6	133.6	134.4	135.2	3.4	129.1	131.0	131.9	132.7	3.8
2000	137.5	138.6	139.9	141.1	4.4	134.1	135.2	136.5	137.6	3.7
2001	142.6	143.9	145.6	146.3	3.7	139.5	140.7	142.1	142.8	3.8

See footnotes at end of table.

Table 5-1. Employment Cost Index, Private Industry Workers[1], Total Compensation and Wages and Salaries by Occupation and Industry, 1987–2001—*Continued*

(June 1989=100, not seasonally adjusted.)

Series and year	Total compensation Indexes				Percent change for 12 months ended December	Wages and salaries Indexes				Percent change for 12 months ended December
	March	June	September	December		March	June	September	December	
Handlers, equipment cleaners, helpers, and laborers										
1987	91.3	91.7	92.5	93.5	2.7	92.6	93.2	94.0	95.0	3.0
1988	95.5	96.2	97.0	97.7	4.5	96.3	96.9	97.6	98.3	3.5
1989	98.8	100.0	101.3	102.2	4.6	99.1	100.0	101.1	102.0	3.8
1990	103.6	104.7	105.7	106.7	4.4	103.0	104.4	105.3	106.2	4.1
1991	108.1	109.3	110.4	111.4	4.4	107.3	108.5	109.2	109.9	3.5
1992	112.6	113.4	114.6	115.3	3.5	110.6	111.3	112.1	112.6	2.5
1993	116.8	117.6	118.4	119.1	3.3	113.6	114.3	114.9	115.7	2.8
1994	120.2	121.4	122.7	122.9	3.2	116.6	117.3	117.9	118.9	2.8
1995	124.1	125.3	125.9	126.8	3.2	120.1	121.2	121.5	122.6	3.1
1996	128.5	129.3	130.0	131.3	3.5	124.2	125.1	125.8	127.1	3.7
1997	132.8	133.4	134.2	135.8	3.4	128.4	129.3	130.2	131.8	3.7
1998	137.0	137.6	138.5	139.2	2.5	133.2	133.7	135.1	135.8	3.0
1999	141.0	142.3	143.2	144.4	3.7	137.3	138.3	139.4	140.4	3.4
2000	146.4	148.1	149.4	150.4	4.2	141.8	143.6	145.0	146.2	4.1
2001	152.2	153.4	154.9	156.5	4.1	148.0	149.8	151.0	152.4	4.2
Service Occupations										
1987	91.9	92.3	92.8	93.3	2.4	93.3	93.6	94.1	94.5	2.4
1988	94.6	95.6	97.1	98.2	5.3	95.5	96.4	97.7	98.7	4.4
1989	99.2	100.0	101.1	102.5	4.4	99.4	100.0	100.9	102.3	3.6
1990	103.9	104.9	105.7	107.3	4.7	103.1	104.2	104.9	106.4	4.0
1991	108.3	109.9	111.5	112.4	4.8	106.9	108.3	109.8	110.6	3.9
1992	113.5	114.2	115.4	115.9	3.1	111.2	111.6	112.5	112.9	2.1
1993	117.2	118.0	118.9	119.5	3.1	113.5	114.1	114.9	115.3	2.1
1994	120.6	121.0	121.8	122.9	2.8	116.3	116.8	117.6	118.8	3.0
1995	123.4	124.0	124.7	125.2	1.9	119.4	120.0	120.8	121.4	2.2
1996	125.8	126.5	127.4	128.9	3.0	122.2	123.0	124.1	125.7	3.5
1997	129.8	130.9	133.1	134.1	4.0	126.6	127.6	129.9	131.1	4.3
1998	135.3	136.0	137.3	138.0	2.9	132.1	133.0	134.4	135.3	3.2
1999	139.5	140.6	141.0	142.6	3.3	136.7	137.8	138.0	139.6	3.2
2000	143.9	145.4	146.6	148.1	3.9	141.0	142.5	143.5	144.9	3.8
2001	150.0	151.3	152.6	154.8	4.5	146.4	147.5	148.7	150.6	3.9
Production And Nonsupervisory Occupations										
1987	90.6	91.3	92.1	92.8	3.3	91.9	92.5	93.4	93.9	3.2
1988	94.3	95.5	96.6	97.5	5.1	94.8	96.0	97.0	97.9	4.3
1989	98.8	100.0	101.4	102.4	5.0	99.0	100.0	101.3	102.2	4.4
1990	103.8	105.1	106.0	106.9	4.4	103.2	104.3	105.2	105.9	3.6
1991	108.4	109.6	110.8	111.5	4.3	107.0	108.1	109.0	109.6	3.5
1992	113.0	113.8	114.8	115.5	3.6	110.6	111.3	112.0	112.6	2.7
1993	116.9	117.9	119.0	119.7	3.6	113.4	114.2	115.3	115.9	2.9
1994	120.7	121.6	122.6	123.1	2.8	116.6	117.5	118.5	119.1	2.8
1995	124.1	125.0	125.8	126.3	2.6	119.9	121.0	121.8	122.4	2.8
1996	127.5	128.6	129.2	130.0	2.9	123.7	124.9	125.6	126.5	3.3
1997	131.1	132.1	133.2	134.2	3.2	127.7	128.8	130.1	131.2	3.7
1998	135.3	136.6	138.0	139.0	3.6	132.3	133.6	135.2	136.4	4.0
1999	139.3	140.8	141.9	143.1	2.9	136.8	138.2	139.3	140.4	2.9
2000	145.3	146.9	148.4	149.5	4.5	142.1	143.7	145.0	146.0	4.0
2001	151.4	152.7	154.3	155.5	4.0	147.7	149.0	150.3	151.5	3.8
WORKERS BY INDUSTRY DIVISION										
Goods-Producing Industries [2]										
1987	91.5	92.1	92.9	93.8	3.1	92.8	93.4	94.3	95.2	3.1
1988	95.5	96.5	97.1	97.9	4.4	96.1	96.9	97.5	98.2	3.2
1989	98.9	100.0	101.1	102.1	4.3	99.1	100.0	101.0	102.0	3.9
1990	103.9	105.2	106.2	107.0	4.8	103.1	104.2	105.1	105.8	3.7
1991	108.5	109.8	111.0	111.9	4.6	107.0	108.0	108.7	109.7	3.7
1992	113.5	114.3	115.3	116.1	3.8	110.7	111.4	112.1	112.8	2.8
1993	118.0	119.1	119.9	120.6	3.9	113.8	114.5	115.3	116.1	2.9
1994	121.8	123.0	123.9	124.3	3.1	116.9	118.0	118.9	119.6	3.0
1995	125.3	125.9	126.5	127.3	2.4	120.4	121.4	122.1	122.9	2.8
1996	128.2	129.3	130.1	130.9	2.8	123.9	125.1	126.1	126.8	3.2
1997	131.4	132.7	133.6	134.1	2.4	127.5	128.9	129.9	130.6	3.0
1998	135.1	136.2	137.1	137.8	2.8	132.0	133.2	134.3	135.2	3.5
1999	138.9	139.9	141.1	142.5	3.4	136.3	137.3	138.5	139.7	3.3
2000	144.8	146.6	147.9	148.8	4.4	141.3	143.0	144.3	145.2	3.9
2001	150.7	152.1	153.1	154.4	3.8	147.0	148.6	149.5	150.5	3.7

See footnotes at end of table.

Table 5-1. Employment Cost Index, Private Industry Workers [1], Total Compensation and Wages and Salaries by Occupation and Industry, 1987–2001—*Continued*

(June 1989=100, not seasonally adjusted.)

Series and year	Total compensation					Wages and salaries				
	Indexes				Percent change for 12 months ended December	Indexes				Percent change for 12 months ended December
	March	June	September	December		March	June	September	December	
Goods-producing industries, excluding sales occupations										
1987	91.5	92.1	92.9	93.8	3.1	92.9	93.4	94.3	95.2	3.3
1988	95.4	96.5	97.1	97.9	4.4	95.9	96.9	97.4	98.2	3.2
1989	98.9	100.0	101.1	102.2	4.4	99.1	100.0	101.0	102.0	3.9
1990	103.9	105.1	106.1	107.0	4.7	103.0	104.2	105.0	105.7	3.6
1991	108.4	109.8	110.9	111.8	4.5	106.9	107.9	108.7	109.7	3.8
1992	113.4	114.1	115.2	115.9	3.7	110.5	111.2	112.0	112.6	2.6
1993	117.8	118.8	119.6	120.1	3.6	113.5	114.2	114.9	115.6	2.7
1994	121.4	122.5	123.5	124.0	3.2	116.4	117.4	118.4	119.1	3.0
1995	124.9	125.6	126.1	127.0	2.4	119.9	120.9	121.6	122.4	2.8
1996	128.0	129.0	129.8	130.5	2.8	123.5	124.6	125.7	126.3	3.2
1997	131.1	132.3	133.1	133.6	2.4	127.0	128.3	129.3	130.0	2.9
1998	134.5	135.6	136.5	137.2	2.7	131.3	132.5	133.6	134.4	3.4
1999	138.3	139.3	140.5	141.8	3.3	135.5	136.6	137.8	138.9	3.3
2000	144.2	145.9	147.2	148.2	4.5	140.5	142.1	143.4	144.6	4.1
2001	150.1	151.5	152.5	153.7	3.7	146.3	147.8	148.7	149.7	3.5
Goods-producing industries, white-collar occupations										
1987	. . .	92.3	93.1	94.0	. . .	. . .	92.9	94.0	94.9	. . .
1988	95.6	96.4	97.2	97.8	4.0	96.2	96.9	97.6	98.3	3.6
1989	99.0	100.0	101.2	101.9	4.2	99.2	100.0	101.0	101.9	3.7
1990	104.1	105.3	106.7	107.4	5.4	103.5	104.6	105.7	106.3	4.3
1991	108.8	110.1	111.2	112.3	4.6	107.4	108.5	109.5	110.4	3.9
1992	113.6	114.5	115.5	116.7	3.9	111.7	112.5	113.2	114.2	3.4
1993	118.6	119.6	120.5	121.1	3.8	115.4	116.4	117.3	118.2	3.5
1994	123.0	124.3	125.1	125.9	4.0	119.1	120.3	121.1	122.0	3.2
1995	127.2	127.6	128.1	129.0	2.5	123.0	123.8	124.4	125.3	2.7
1996	130.0	131.0	132.2	132.9	3.0	126.2	127.3	128.6	129.1	3.0
1997	133.5	134.8	135.6	136.2	2.5	130.0	131.4	132.3	132.9	2.9
1998	137.7	138.8	139.7	140.2	2.9	135.0	136.3	137.4	138.2	4.0
1999	141.7	142.7	143.9	145.5	3.7	139.4	140.5	141.7	143.0	3.5
2000	148.1	150.1	151.3	151.9	4.4	145.0	146.8	147.9	148.7	4.0
2001	154.5	156.5	156.8	158.1	4.1	150.5	152.3	152.6	153.6	3.3
Goods-producing industries, white-collar occupations, excluding sales occupations										
1987	. . .	92.2	93.0	93.9	. . .	. . .	92.9	93.9	94.8	. . .
1988	95.4	96.4	97.1	97.7	4.0	96.0	96.9	97.6	98.2	3.6
1989	99.0	100.0	101.2	102.0	4.4	99.2	100.0	101.0	102.0	3.9
1990	103.9	105.2	106.4	107.1	5.0	103.3	104.4	105.6	106.2	4.1
1991	108.5	110.0	111.1	112.2	4.8	107.2	108.5	109.5	110.5	4.0
1992	113.2	113.9	115.1	116.2	3.6	111.3	112.0	112.9	113.7	2.9
1993	118.1	119.0	119.7	119.9	3.2	114.9	115.6	116.4	116.8	2.7
1994	121.9	123.2	124.1	125.0	4.3	117.7	118.8	119.8	120.8	3.4
1995	126.2	126.7	127.2	128.2	2.6	121.8	122.5	123.2	124.2	2.8
1996	129.4	130.2	131.5	132.1	3.0	125.3	126.3	127.7	128.1	3.1
1997	132.6	133.8	134.5	135.0	2.2	128.9	130.0	130.9	131.6	2.7
1998	136.3	137.4	138.3	138.8	2.8	133.3	134.6	135.7	136.4	3.6
1999	140.4	141.3	142.5	143.9	3.7	137.8	138.8	140.1	141.3	3.6
2000	146.5	148.4	149.6	150.5	4.6	143.2	144.9	146.0	147.2	4.2
2001	153.0	155.0	155.3	156.5	4.0	148.9	150.5	150.8	151.7	3.1
Goods-producing industries, blue-collar occupations										
1987	. . .	92.1	92.8	93.8	. . .	. . .	93.6	94.4	95.3	. . .
1988	95.4	96.6	97.1	98.0	4.5	95.9	96.9	97.3	98.1	2.9
1989	98.9	100.0	101.1	102.3	4.4	99.0	100.0	101.0	101.9	3.9
1990	103.9	105.1	106.0	106.9	4.5	102.9	104.1	104.7	105.5	3.5
1991	108.4	109.7	110.8	111.6	4.4	106.8	107.6	108.3	109.2	3.5
1992	113.4	114.1	115.1	115.8	3.8	110.1	110.7	111.4	111.9	2.5
1993	117.6	118.7	119.6	120.2	3.8	112.8	113.4	114.1	114.9	2.7
1994	121.1	122.2	123.1	123.4	2.7	115.6	116.6	117.5	118.1	2.8
1995	124.1	124.9	125.5	126.3	2.4	118.8	119.9	120.7	121.4	2.8
1996	127.1	128.3	128.9	129.6	2.6	122.4	123.7	124.5	125.3	3.2
1997	130.2	131.4	132.4	132.8	2.5	126.0	127.3	128.4	129.2	3.1
1998	133.5	134.6	135.5	136.3	2.6	130.1	131.3	132.3	133.3	3.2
1999	137.1	138.3	139.4	140.7	3.2	134.3	135.4	136.6	137.6	3.2
2000	142.8	144.4	145.8	146.8	4.3	139.0	140.5	142.0	143.1	4.0
2001	148.2	149.3	150.8	151.9	3.5	144.7	146.1	147.4	148.4	3.7

See footnotes at end of table.

Table 5-1. Employment Cost Index, Private Industry Workers [1], Total Compensation and Wages and Salaries by Occupation and Industry, 1987–2001—*Continued*

(June 1989=100, not seasonally adjusted.)

Series and year	Total compensation					Wages and salaries				
	Indexes				Percent change for 12 months ended December	Indexes				Percent change for 12 months ended December
	March	June	September	December		March	June	September	December	
Construction										
1987	91.5	92.7	93.4	94.0	3.6	92.5	93.2	94.1	94.8	3.3
1988	95.2	96.4	97.2	98.0	4.3	95.7	97.0	97.7	98.3	3.7
1989	99.0	100.0	101.2	102.4	4.5	99.1	100.0	101.1	101.7	3.5
1990	103.1	104.3	105.2	105.6	3.1	102.0	102.9	103.5	103.7	2.0
1991	107.4	108.5	109.3	109.9	4.1	105.1	105.9	106.3	106.8	3.0
1992	110.6	111.7	113.1	113.8	3.5	107.2	107.9	108.7	108.9	2.0
1993	114.9	116.0	116.8	116.5	2.4	109.5	110.4	111.3	111.1	2.0
1994	118.6	120.2	121.4	120.8	3.7	112.2	113.6	114.6	114.7	3.2
1995	121.1	122.0	123.1	123.4	2.2	114.8	115.7	116.8	117.4	2.4
1996	124.3	125.3	125.9	126.4	2.4	118.3	119.6	120.4	120.8	2.9
1997	127.2	128.7	129.7	129.7	2.6	122.0	123.6	124.7	124.9	3.4
1998	130.6	132.7	133.4	134.3	3.5	126.0	128.1	128.5	129.3	3.5
1999	135.6	136.9	137.9	138.7	3.3	130.7	131.9	133.0	133.6	3.3
2000	140.8	143.2	145.1	146.7	5.8	136.0	138.0	139.4	140.7	5.3
2001	148.2	150.3	151.7	153.0	4.3	142.1	143.9	145.1	146.3	4.0
Manufacturing										
1987	91.1	91.6	92.5	93.4	3.0	92.7	93.3	94.2	95.2	3.4
1988	95.3	96.2	96.9	97.6	4.5	96.0	96.8	97.3	98.1	3.0
1989	98.9	100.0	101.1	102.0	4.5	99.0	100.0	100.9	101.9	3.9
1990	104.0	105.3	106.4	107.2	5.1	103.3	104.5	105.4	106.2	4.2
1991	108.6	110.0	111.2	112.2	4.7	107.4	108.4	109.3	110.3	3.9
1992	114.0	114.7	115.7	116.5	3.8	111.5	112.2	112.9	113.7	3.1
1993	118.6	119.7	120.6	121.3	4.1	114.7	115.5	116.3	117.3	3.2
1994	122.5	123.5	124.4	125.1	3.1	118.0	119.0	120.0	120.8	3.0
1995	126.2	126.9	127.3	128.3	2.6	121.9	122.9	123.5	124.3	2.9
1996	129.3	130.4	131.3	132.1	3.0	125.4	126.5	127.7	128.4	3.3
1997	132.6	133.8	134.6	135.3	2.4	129.1	130.3	131.3	132.2	3.0
1998	136.4	137.2	138.2	138.9	2.7	133.7	134.6	136.0	136.8	3.5
1999	139.9	140.9	142.1	143.6	3.4	137.9	139.0	140.2	141.5	3.4
2000	146.0	147.5	148.7	149.3	4.0	142.9	144.4	145.7	146.5	3.5
2001	151.3	152.6	153.3	154.6	3.5	148.5	150.0	150.7	151.7	3.5
Manufacturing, white-collar occupations										
1987	. . .	92.2	93.1	94.1	. . .	. . .	93.0	94.0	95.0	. . .
1988	95.7	96.4	97.1	97.7	3.8	96.2	96.9	97.5	98.2	3.4
1989	99.0	100.0	101.1	101.9	4.3	99.2	100.0	100.9	101.8	3.7
1990	104.1	105.3	106.8	107.4	5.4	103.7	104.7	105.9	106.4	4.5
1991	108.8	110.2	111.3	112.4	4.7	107.6	108.8	109.8	110.7	4.0
1992	113.6	114.6	115.5	116.6	3.7	111.9	112.9	113.6	114.6	3.5
1993	118.7	119.7	120.5	121.3	4.0	116.0	116.9	117.7	118.8	3.7
1994	122.7	123.9	124.9	126.0	3.9	119.5	120.6	121.7	122.7	3.3
1995	127.4	128.0	128.7	129.5	2.8	123.9	124.7	125.3	126.1	2.8
1996	130.5	131.6	132.8	133.6	3.2	127.1	128.2	129.6	130.1	3.2
1997	133.9	135.2	135.8	136.7	2.3	130.6	131.9	132.8	133.6	2.7
1998	138.2	139.1	140.1	140.5	2.8	135.6	136.8	138.3	139.0	4.0
1999	141.8	143.0	144.3	145.8	3.8	140.1	141.4	142.7	144.0	3.6
2000	148.2	150.2	151.4	151.5	3.9	145.8	147.7	148.7	149.2	3.6
2001	154.2	156.0	156.0	156.9	3.6	151.1	152.7	152.8	153.3	2.7
Manufacturing, white-collar occupations, excluding sales occupations										
1987	. . .	92.1	93.0	93.9	. . .	. . .	92.9	93.9	94.8	. . .
1988	95.5	96.3	97.1	97.7	4.0	96.0	96.8	97.4	98.0	3.4
1989	99.0	100.0	101.1	101.9	4.3	99.1	100.0	100.9	101.9	4.0
1990	104.0	105.1	106.4	107.0	5.0	103.4	104.4	105.6	106.2	4.2
1991	108.3	109.9	111.1	112.2	4.9	107.2	108.6	109.7	110.7	4.2
1992	113.0	113.8	115.0	115.9	3.3	111.4	112.2	113.0	114.0	3.0
1993	118.0	118.8	119.5	119.9	3.5	115.3	115.9	116.7	117.2	2.8
1994	121.3	122.5	123.6	124.9	4.2	118.0	119.1	120.2	121.4	3.6
1995	126.1	126.6	127.4	128.3	2.7	122.4	123.2	123.9	124.8	2.8
1996	129.5	130.5	131.8	132.5	3.3	126.0	127.0	128.4	128.9	3.3
1997	132.8	133.8	134.5	135.3	2.1	129.3	130.5	131.3	132.2	2.6
1998	136.5	137.3	138.3	138.7	2.5	133.8	135.0	136.3	137.1	3.7
1999	140.1	141.3	142.5	143.8	3.7	138.3	139.6	140.8	142.0	3.6
2000	146.2	148.2	149.3	149.7	4.1	143.7	145.6	146.6	147.5	3.9
2001	152.2	154.0	153.8	154.7	3.3	149.1	150.5	150.5	151.0	2.4

See footnotes at end of table.

Table 5-1. Employment Cost Index, Private Industry Workers[1], Total Compensation and Wages and Salaries by Occupation and Industry, 1987–2001—*Continued*

(June 1989=100, not seasonally adjusted.)

Series and year	Total compensation — Indexes				Percent change for 12 months ended December	Wages and salaries — Indexes				Percent change for 12 months ended December
	March	June	September	December		March	June	September	December	
Manufacturing, blue-collar occupations										
1987	...	91.3	92.0	93.1	...	...	93.5	94.4	95.4	...
1988	95.1	96.1	96.7	97.6	4.8	96.0	96.8	97.2	98.1	2.8
1989	98.8	100.0	101.1	102.1	4.6	98.9	100.0	100.9	102.0	4.0
1990	104.0	105.2	106.2	107.2	5.0	103.1	104.4	105.1	106.1	4.0
1991	108.5	109.8	111.1	112.0	4.5	107.3	108.2	109.0	110.0	3.7
1992	114.2	114.8	115.7	116.4	3.9	111.1	111.7	112.4	113.1	2.8
1993	118.5	119.6	120.5	121.3	4.2	113.9	114.5	115.2	116.2	2.7
1994	122.3	123.2	124.0	124.5	2.6	116.9	117.8	118.7	119.5	2.8
1995	125.3	126.0	126.3	127.5	2.4	120.4	121.6	122.2	123.1	3.0
1996	128.4	129.5	130.2	131.1	2.8	124.2	125.4	126.3	127.3	3.4
1997	131.7	132.8	133.7	134.3	2.4	128.0	129.2	130.2	131.2	3.1
1998	135.0	135.9	136.8	137.7	2.5	132.3	133.1	134.3	135.3	3.1
1999	138.5	139.4	140.5	142.1	3.2	136.3	137.2	138.4	139.7	3.3
2000	144.4	145.6	146.7	147.8	4.0	140.8	142.0	143.4	144.6	3.5
2001	149.1	150.0	151.3	152.7	3.3	146.4	147.8	149.1	150.3	3.9
Manufacturing, durable goods										
1987	91.3	92.0	92.6	93.5	2.6	93.0	93.7	94.5	95.5	3.1
1988	95.6	96.5	97.0	97.7	4.5	96.2	96.9	97.4	98.0	2.6
1989	99.0	100.0	101.1	102.2	4.6	99.0	100.0	100.7	101.9	4.0
1990	104.0	105.1	106.3	107.2	4.9	103.2	104.3	105.3	106.1	4.1
1991	108.5	109.9	111.2	112.1	4.6	107.3	108.3	109.2	110.2	3.9
1992	114.1	114.8	115.8	116.7	4.1	111.2	111.8	112.7	113.4	2.9
1993	119.0	120.0	121.0	121.9	4.5	114.4	115.1	115.9	117.2	3.4
1994	122.9	123.8	125.1	125.8	3.2	117.8	118.7	119.8	120.8	3.1
1995	127.0	127.7	128.2	129.0	2.5	121.9	122.9	123.6	124.3	2.9
1996	129.7	131.2	131.9	132.6	2.8	125.1	126.5	127.7	128.4	3.3
1997	133.0	134.1	135.0	135.7	2.3	129.0	130.1	131.2	131.9	2.7
1998	136.5	137.4	138.5	139.2	2.6	133.4	134.5	135.9	136.9	3.8
1999	139.9	141.0	142.3	144.0	3.4	137.9	139.1	140.4	141.8	3.6
2000	146.5	148.3	149.4	150.1	4.2	143.0	144.7	146.1	147.3	3.9
2001	151.8	153.1	154.0	155.3	3.5	149.0	150.5	151.5	152.6	3.6
Aircraft manufacturing (SIC 3721)										
1988	...	...	...	98.8	...	...	...	...	98.8	...
1989	99.2	100.0	101.0	103.6	4.9	99.4	100.0	100.6	102.2	3.4
1990	105.4	107.0	108.5	108.6	4.8	103.2	104.9	105.7	107.0	4.7
1991	110.2	111.8	113.1	114.8	5.7	108.4	109.8	110.9	112.6	5.2
1992	116.9	119.0	120.1	122.9	7.1	113.6	115.2	116.0	117.2	4.1
1993	124.1	124.5	126.7	125.2	1.9	117.9	118.8	120.5	121.6	3.8
1994	126.2	127.1	128.7	129.2	3.2	122.4	123.3	124.0	124.8	2.6
1995	130.6	131.0	131.5	133.8	3.6	125.7	126.5	127.4	128.1	2.6
1996	136.9	138.2	138.2	137.4	2.7	129.0	130.3	130.6	130.9	2.2
1997	137.3	138.4	137.8	136.9	0.4	132.0	133.5	133.3	134.0	2.4
1998	137.2	138.9	139.3	140.6	2.7	135.1	136.9	137.2	138.3	3.2
1999	140.5	142.4	143.7	146.9	4.5	139.4	141.5	142.7	143.6	3.8
2000	151.2	154.3	156.0	155.3	5.7	146.3	148.6	150.0	151.6	5.6
2001	159.8	160.4	160.3	163.4	5.2	154.3	155.1	156.6	158.3	4.4
Aircraft manufacturing (SIC 3721), white-collar occupations										
1988	...	...	...	98.8	...	...	...	...	98.7	...
1989	99.1	100.0	100.8	102.8	4.0	99.3	100.0	100.4	101.5	2.8
1990	104.6	105.9	107.2	106.8	3.9	102.3	103.8	104.2	105.0	3.4
1991	108.1	109.7	110.5	112.0	4.9	106.0	107.4	107.9	108.9	3.7
1992	114.2	116.3	117.0	119.0	6.3	110.0	111.6	112.2	113.1	3.9
1993	120.5	121.2	123.2	121.8	2.4	113.9	115.2	116.7	117.3	3.7
1994	122.7	123.8	125.3	125.3	2.9	118.1	119.1	119.8	120.2	2.5
1995	126.7	127.2	127.8	129.0	3.0	121.0	121.6	122.7	123.2	2.5
1996	132.4	133.9	133.8	133.7	3.6	124.1	125.9	126.1	126.5	2.7
1997	133.5	134.9	134.6	134.3	0.4	127.8	129.6	129.3	129.8	2.6
1998	134.7	137.1	137.4	137.4	2.3	131.2	133.7	133.9	134.5	3.6
1999	137.3	139.5	139.8	141.7	3.1	135.5	138.0	138.3	139.1	3.4
2000	146.6	150.7	151.8	151.2	6.7	142.1	145.2	146.0	146.2	5.1
2001	157.3	157.3	156.3	159.0	5.2	149.8	150.1	150.9	152.2	4.1

See footnotes at end of table.

Table 5-1. Employment Cost Index, Private Industry Workers[1], Total Compensation and Wages and Salaries by Occupation and Industry, 1987–2001—*Continued*

(June 1989=100, not seasonally adjusted.)

Series and year	Total compensation					Wages and salaries				
	Indexes				Percent change for 12 months ended December	Indexes				Percent change for 12 months ended December
	March	June	September	December		March	June	September	December	
Aircraft manufacturing (SIC 3721), blue-collar occupations										
1988	...	...	...	98.9	...	...	...	...	98.9	...
1989	99.5	100.0	101.4	104.7	5.9	99.6	100.0	100.9	103.3	4.4
1990	106.6	108.6	110.1	110.9	5.9	104.6	106.7	107.8	110.0	6.5
1991	113.2	114.7	116.7	118.8	7.1	112.0	113.5	115.4	118.0	7.3
1992	120.8	122.8	124.2	128.2	7.9	119.0	120.5	121.5	123.3	4.5
1993	129.2	129.2	131.5	129.8	1.2	123.9	124.1	126.1	127.9	3.7
1994	130.9	131.5	133.2	134.2	3.4	128.7	129.4	130.2	131.7	3.0
1995	135.7	136.1	136.3	140.5	4.7	132.7	133.6	134.1	135.1	2.6
1996	143.3	144.1	144.4	142.3	1.3	136.1	136.4	137.0	137.1	1.5
1997	142.3	142.8	141.8	139.6	-1.9	137.7	138.8	138.4	139.6	1.8
1998	139.6	140.1	140.8	144.4	3.4	140.1	140.5	141.0	143.2	2.6
1999	144.3	145.7	149.0	154.4	6.9	144.5	145.5	148.9	149.9	4.7
2000	157.8	158.5	161.4	160.4	3.9	151.8	152.1	155.1	159.3	6.3
2001	161.9	163.6	165.3	169.1	5.4	160.3	162.1	164.9	167.4	5.1
Manufacturing, nondurable goods										
1987	90.7	91.2	92.3	93.4	3.8	92.2	92.5	93.8	94.7	3.7
1988	94.8	95.6	96.5	97.5	4.4	95.8	96.5	97.2	98.2	3.7
1989	98.8	100.0	101.2	101.9	4.5	99.0	100.0	101.1	101.8	3.7
1990	104.1	105.5	106.6	107.4	5.4	103.6	104.8	105.7	106.3	4.4
1991	108.8	110.1	111.2	112.3	4.6	107.6	108.6	109.4	110.6	4.0
1992	113.8	114.7	115.4	116.3	3.6	111.8	112.8	113.2	114.3	3.3
1993	117.9	119.0	119.7	120.3	3.4	115.5	116.3	116.9	117.5	2.8
1994	121.7	122.8	123.2	123.8	2.9	118.3	119.5	120.3	120.8	2.8
1995	124.7	125.4	125.7	127.0	2.6	121.9	122.9	123.3	124.4	3.0
1996	128.3	128.9	130.0	131.0	3.1	125.8	126.5	127.6	128.5	3.3
1997	131.7	133.0	133.7	134.5	2.7	129.3	130.6	131.4	132.6	3.2
1998	135.9	136.7	137.6	138.2	2.8	134.2	134.9	136.0	136.8	3.2
1999	139.6	140.4	141.5	142.8	3.3	138.0	138.7	139.7	140.9	3.0
2000	144.9	146.0	147.5	147.7	3.4	142.7	143.9	145.0	145.4	3.2
2001	150.4	151.6	152.0	153.2	3.7	147.5	149.0	149.3	150.2	3.3
Service-Producing Industries [3]										
1987	90.5	91.2	92.1	92.6	3.7	91.5	92.1	93.1	93.4	3.4
1988	93.8	95.1	96.2	97.3	5.1	94.3	95.5	96.7	97.8	4.7
1989	98.8	100.0	101.3	102.3	5.1	99.1	100.0	101.4	102.2	4.5
1990	103.8	105.2	106.2	107.0	4.6	103.3	104.6	105.7	106.3	4.0
1991	108.5	109.8	111.0	111.6	4.3	107.5	108.7	109.7	110.2	3.7
1992	112.8	113.6	114.4	115.2	3.2	111.1	111.7	112.3	113.0	2.5
1993	116.4	117.3	118.5	119.3	3.6	113.9	114.7	115.9	116.6	3.2
1994	120.4	121.2	122.3	122.8	2.9	117.3	118.2	119.2	119.7	2.7
1995	123.9	124.9	125.8	126.2	2.8	120.7	121.6	122.6	123.2	2.9
1996	127.6	128.6	129.5	130.2	3.2	124.7	125.8	126.7	127.5	3.5
1997	131.6	132.5	133.8	135.3	3.9	129.0	130.1	131.5	133.1	4.4
1998	136.7	137.8	139.6	140.5	3.8	134.4	135.6	137.6	138.4	4.0
1999	140.9	142.8	144.1	145.3	3.4	138.9	140.8	142.1	143.3	3.5
2000	147.4	149.1	150.6	151.7	4.4	145.0	146.5	147.9	148.9	3.9
2001	153.8	155.3	156.9	158.2	4.3	150.5	151.9	153.2	154.5	3.8
Service-producing industries, excluding sales occupations										
1987	90.6	91.4	92.5	93.1	4.0	91.5	92.2	93.5	94.0	4.0
1988	94.3	95.4	96.7	97.5	4.7	94.9	95.8	97.1	98.0	4.3
1989	98.9	100.0	101.2	102.1	4.7	99.2	100.0	101.2	101.8	3.9
1990	103.9	105.1	106.4	107.3	5.1	103.4	104.5	105.8	106.6	4.7
1991	108.7	109.9	111.3	112.1	4.5	107.7	108.7	110.0	110.7	3.8
1992	113.2	114.0	115.1	115.9	3.4	111.5	112.2	113.0	113.7	2.7
1993	117.3	118.3	119.3	120.2	3.7	114.8	115.6	116.6	117.4	3.3
1994	121.4	122.1	123.3	123.8	3.0	118.3	119.0	120.2	120.7	2.8
1995	125.0	125.8	126.6	127.2	2.7	121.8	122.5	123.4	124.2	2.9
1996	128.4	129.2	130.3	130.9	2.9	125.6	126.5	127.6	128.3	3.3
1997	132.2	133.3	134.5	136.1	4.0	129.7	130.9	132.3	133.9	4.4
1998	137.4	138.5	140.0	140.6	3.3	135.2	136.2	137.9	138.5	3.4
1999	141.7	143.3	144.6	145.9	3.8	139.8	141.4	142.6	143.8	3.8
2000	147.7	149.4	151.1	152.2	4.3	145.3	146.9	148.3	149.4	3.9
2001	154.6	156.0	157.8	159.0	4.5	151.3	152.6	154.2	155.5	4.1

See footnotes at end of table.

Table 5-1. Employment Cost Index, Private Industry Workers [1], Total Compensation and Wages and Salaries by Occupation and Industry, 1987–2001—*Continued*

(June 1989=100, not seasonally adjusted.)

Series and year	Total compensation					Wages and salaries				
	Indexes				Percent change for 12 months ended December	Indexes				Percent change for 12 months ended December
	March	June	September	December		March	June	September	December	
Service-producing industries, white-collar occupations										
1987	...	90.7	91.8	92.1	...	...	91.6	92.6	92.9	...
1988	93.4	94.7	95.9	97.2	5.5	93.7	95.1	96.3	97.5	5.0
1989	98.8	100.0	101.4	102.6	5.6	99.0	100.0	101.5	102.5	5.1
1990	104.2	105.5	106.7	107.4	4.7	103.6	105.0	106.1	106.8	4.2
1991	109.1	110.4	111.5	112.1	4.4	108.1	109.3	110.3	110.7	3.7
1992	113.4	114.1	114.9	115.7	3.2	111.7	112.2	112.8	113.6	2.6
1993	116.9	117.8	119.0	119.8	3.5	114.5	115.2	116.5	117.3	3.3
1994	121.0	121.9	122.9	123.4	3.0	118.0	118.9	119.9	120.4	2.6
1995	124.6	125.6	126.5	127.1	3.0	121.3	122.3	123.2	124.0	3.0
1996	128.5	129.6	130.6	131.1	3.1	125.6	126.8	127.8	128.5	3.6
1997	132.7	133.7	134.9	136.6	4.2	130.1	131.2	132.6	134.3	4.5
1998	138.0	139.3	141.2	142.2	4.1	135.7	137.0	139.2	140.1	4.3
1999	142.3	144.3	145.8	147.0	3.4	140.3	142.3	143.8	145.0	3.5
2000	149.3	151.0	152.6	153.7	4.6	146.9	148.5	150.0	150.9	4.1
2001	155.8	157.4	159.0	160.3	4.3	152.5	154.0	155.2	156.5	3.7
Service-producing industries, white-collar occupations, excluding sales occupations										
1987	...	90.9	92.3	92.9	...	...	91.7	93.1	93.7	...
1988	94.1	95.1	96.6	97.5	5.0	94.5	95.5	96.9	97.9	4.5
1989	99.0	100.0	101.4	102.3	4.9	99.2	100.0	101.3	102.1	4.3
1990	104.4	105.6	107.1	108.0	5.6	103.8	105.0	106.4	107.2	5.0
1991	109.5	110.6	112.1	113.0	4.6	108.5	109.5	110.9	111.6	4.1
1992	114.1	114.9	116.1	116.8	3.4	112.4	113.1	114.0	114.7	2.8
1993	118.4	119.3	120.4	121.4	3.9	116.0	116.8	117.8	118.7	3.5
1994	122.7	123.4	124.6	125.1	3.0	119.6	120.4	121.5	122.1	2.9
1995	126.4	127.1	128.0	128.7	2.9	123.2	123.8	124.7	125.6	2.9
1996	130.0	130.9	132.2	132.6	3.0	127.2	128.1	129.5	129.9	3.4
1997	134.0	135.1	136.3	138.1	4.1	131.5	132.7	134.2	135.9	4.6
1998	139.5	140.6	142.2	142.8	3.4	137.3	138.4	140.2	140.7	3.5
1999	143.8	145.5	147.0	148.3	3.9	142.0	143.7	145.1	146.4	4.1
2000	150.3	152.1	153.9	155.1	4.6	147.8	149.6	151.2	152.3	4.0
2001	157.5	159.1	160.9	162.2	4.6	154.3	155.6	157.2	158.6	4.1
Service-producing industries, blue-collar occupations										
1987	...	92.2	93.0	93.8	...	...	93.2	94.1	94.8	...
1988	95.2	96.2	97.1	97.5	3.9	95.9	96.7	97.5	98.0	3.4
1989	98.7	100.0	101.1	101.1	3.7	99.0	100.0	100.9	100.9	3.0
1990	102.6	103.9	104.8	105.4	4.3	102.1	103.3	104.2	104.7	3.8
1991	106.6	107.6	108.7	109.4	3.8	105.6	106.5	107.3	107.8	3.0
1992	110.4	111.6	112.4	113.2	3.5	108.7	109.7	110.3	111.0	3.0
1993	114.3	115.5	116.6	117.2	3.5	111.9	112.9	114.1	114.6	3.2
1994	118.4	119.1	120.6	120.7	3.0	115.5	116.2	117.5	117.6	2.6
1995	122.1	123.1	123.9	124.0	2.7	119.2	120.3	121.1	121.4	3.2
1996	125.2	126.0	126.4	127.3	2.7	122.7	123.5	123.8	124.8	2.8
1997	128.2	129.2	130.0	130.9	2.8	126.0	127.2	127.9	128.9	3.3
1998	132.1	133.2	134.3	134.8	3.0	130.2	131.1	132.4	132.9	3.1
1999	136.2	137.8	139.1	139.8	3.7	134.4	135.9	137.0	137.8	3.7
2000	141.8	143.1	144.5	145.3	3.9	139.1	140.3	141.6	142.2	3.2
2001	147.7	148.7	150.9	151.4	4.2	144.3	145.3	147.5	148.1	4.1
Service-producing industries, service occupations										
1987	...	92.4	92.9	93.4	...	...	93.6	94.1	94.4	...
1988	94.6	95.6	97.1	98.4	5.4	95.3	96.3	97.7	98.8	4.7
1989	99.3	100.0	101.1	102.5	4.2	99.4	100.0	100.8	102.3	3.5
1990	103.9	105.0	105.8	107.4	4.8	103.2	104.3	105.0	106.5	4.1
1991	108.4	109.9	111.6	112.5	4.7	107.0	108.4	110.0	110.7	3.9
1992	113.4	114.1	115.2	115.7	2.8	111.3	111.7	112.6	112.9	2.0
1993	116.8	117.7	118.6	119.1	2.9	113.5	114.1	114.9	115.2	2.0
1994	120.2	120.7	121.3	122.5	2.9	116.3	116.7	117.3	118.7	3.0
1995	123.0	123.6	124.2	124.8	1.9	119.3	119.8	120.7	121.3	2.2
1996	125.3	126.1	127.1	128.6	3.0	122.0	122.8	124.0	125.6	3.5
1997	129.5	130.6	132.7	133.9	4.1	126.5	127.5	129.8	131.0	4.3
1998	135.0	135.8	137.0	137.8	2.9	132.1	133.0	134.2	135.2	3.2
1999	139.3	140.5	140.8	142.4	3.3	136.7	137.8	138.0	139.6	3.3
2000	143.6	145.1	146.3	147.9	3.9	141.1	142.5	143.5	144.8	3.7
2001	149.6	150.8	152.2	154.2	4.3	146.1	147.2	148.4	150.2	3.7

See footnotes at end of table.

Table 5-1. Employment Cost Index, Private Industry Workers [1], Total Compensation and Wages and Salaries by Occupation and Industry, 1987–2001—*Continued*

(June 1989=100, not seasonally adjusted.)

Series and year	Total compensation					Wages and salaries				
	Indexes				Percent change for 12 months ended December	Indexes				Percent change for 12 months ended December
	March	June	September	December		March	June	September	December	
Transportation and public utilities										
1987	92.9	93.9	94.4	94.8	3.0	94.7	95.6	96.1	96.2	2.1
1988	95.8	96.8	97.5	97.5	2.8	97.0	97.9	98.7	98.6	2.5
1989	98.7	100.0	100.7	101.2	3.8	99.5	100.0	100.7	101.2	2.6
1990	103.0	103.3	104.2	105.1	3.9	102.6	103.2	104.1	104.6	3.4
1991	106.0	107.7	109.0	109.7	4.4	105.4	106.6	107.7	108.4	3.6
1992	111.1	111.9	112.9	113.5	3.5	109.7	110.6	111.2	111.8	3.1
1993	114.8	116.0	116.8	117.5	3.5	112.9	114.0	114.7	115.4	3.2
1994	119.2	119.8	121.4	122.1	3.9	116.4	117.2	118.9	119.6	3.6
1995	124.0	124.7	126.0	126.6	3.7	121.2	122.0	122.9	123.7	3.4
1996	127.9	128.4	129.3	130.4	3.0	124.6	125.0	125.9	127.0	2.7
1997	131.3	131.7	132.9	134.2	2.9	128.2	128.8	130.1	131.3	3.4
1998	135.8	137.1	138.5	139.3	3.8	132.1	132.8	134.3	135.1	2.9
1999	139.7	140.9	141.8	142.3	2.2	135.4	136.8	137.5	137.9	2.1
2000	143.9	145.7	147.4	148.3	4.2	138.5	140.0	141.3	142.3	3.2
2001	150.5	152.4	153.5	155.5	4.9	143.7	145.7	146.7	149.2	4.8
Transportation										
1987	92.4	93.7	93.8	94.0	2.7	94.9	96.1	96.5	96.3	1.7
1988	95.3	96.9	97.6	97.3	3.5	97.1	98.2	99.0	98.7	2.5
1989	98.8	100.0	100.5	100.8	3.6	99.4	100.0	100.6	100.7	2.0
1990	102.8	103.0	103.8	104.6	3.8	102.3	102.3	103.3	103.5	2.8
1991	105.2	106.8	107.8	108.6	3.8	104.3	105.5	106.6	107.0	3.4
1992	109.9	110.5	111.7	111.8	2.9	108.3	109.2	109.8	109.9	2.7
1993	112.8	114.1	114.8	115.7	3.5	110.8	112.0	112.6	113.4	3.2
1994	117.1	117.7	119.7	120.3	4.0	114.2	114.8	116.7	117.5	3.6
1995	122.3	123.0	124.7	125.1	4.0	119.0	119.8	121.0	121.6	3.5
1996	126.9	127.7	128.2	129.2	3.3	122.9	123.2	123.8	124.7	2.5
1997	130.6	130.9	132.1	133.4	3.3	126.5	126.9	128.5	129.5	3.8
1998	134.0	134.9	136.7	137.3	2.9	130.1	130.4	132.4	132.9	2.6
1999	136.8	138.1	138.7	139.5	1.6	132.3	133.7	134.4	134.9	1.5
2000	140.4	141.8	142.8	143.9	3.2	134.9	136.2	137.4	138.6	2.7
2001	145.4	146.9	148.2	151.1	5.0	139.8	141.6	142.6	145.7	5.1
Public utilities										
1987	93.5	94.3	95.2	95.7	3.2	94.4	95.1	95.7	96.2	2.6
1988	96.4	96.7	97.3	97.7	2.1	97.0	97.6	98.3	98.7	2.6
1989	98.8	100.0	101.0	101.7	4.1	99.5	100.0	101.1	101.8	3.1
1990	103.2	103.8	104.8	105.7	3.9	103.0	104.1	105.0	106.0	4.1
1991	107.0	108.8	110.4	111.2	5.2	106.9	108.0	109.0	110.0	3.8
1992	112.6	113.7	114.4	115.6	4.0	111.4	112.4	113.0	114.1	3.7
1993	117.4	118.3	119.2	119.9	3.7	115.4	116.4	117.2	117.9	3.3
1994	121.7	122.6	123.6	124.4	3.8	119.1	120.1	121.4	122.3	3.7
1995	126.1	126.8	127.5	128.5	3.3	123.9	124.5	125.2	126.1	3.1
1996	128.9	129.1	130.4	131.7	2.5	126.5	127.1	128.4	129.8	2.9
1997	132.0	132.5	133.7	135.1	2.6	130.1	130.9	132.0	133.5	2.9
1998	137.9	139.7	140.7	141.9	5.0	134.5	135.7	136.5	137.8	3.2
1999	143.4	144.6	145.7	146.1	3.0	139.2	140.6	141.5	141.8	2.9
2000	148.6	150.9	153.5	154.1	5.5	143.2	144.9	146.4	147.1	3.7
2001	157.3	159.8	160.7	161.5	4.8	148.7	151.0	152.0	153.6	4.4
Communications										
1987	. . .	. . .	95.6	96.3	. . .	. . .	. . .	96.4	97.1	. . .
1988	96.7	96.9	97.5	97.5	1.2	97.6	98.1	98.9	99.0	2.0
1989	98.5	100.0	101.0	101.6	4.2	99.9	100.0	101.1	101.8	2.8
1990	103.1	103.1	104.2	105.2	3.5	103.1	104.1	105.0	106.1	4.2
1991	106.0	108.0	109.9	110.7	5.2	106.5	107.6	108.5	109.6	3.3
1992	111.8	112.7	113.4	114.7	3.6	110.8	111.7	112.2	113.5	3.6
1993	116.5	117.5	118.5	119.2	3.9	114.7	115.6	116.5	117.1	3.2
1994	121.0	122.1	122.9	124.0	4.0	118.4	119.5	121.0	122.1	4.3
1995	126.3	126.6	127.4	128.3	3.5	124.3	124.6	125.3	126.2	3.4
1996	128.0	127.5	129.1	131.1	2.2	126.1	126.5	128.2	130.3	3.2
1997	130.2	130.5	131.8	134.0	2.2	129.8	130.6	131.8	134.0	2.8
1998	136.6	139.2	140.5	141.7	5.7	134.4	135.8	136.7	138.0	3.0
1999	143.3	144.9	146.1	146.0	3.0	139.4	141.1	141.9	142.2	3.0
2000	148.4	150.9	153.9	154.7	6.0	143.4	145.0	146.7	147.4	3.7
2001	158.3	161.1	162.8	163.4	5.6	149.2	151.8	153.3	155.2	5.3

See footnotes at end of table.

Table 5-1. Employment Cost Index, Private Industry Workers [1], Total Compensation and Wages and Salaries by Occupation and Industry, 1987–2001—Continued

(June 1989=100, not seasonally adjusted.)

Series and year	Total compensation					Wages and salaries				
	Indexes				Percent change for 12 months ended December	Indexes				Percent change for 12 months ended December
	March	June	September	December		March	June	September	December	
Electric, gas, and sanitary services										
1987	...	...	...	95.0	...	...	...	...	94.9	...
1988	96.0	96.7	97.1	98.0	3.2	96.1	96.9	97.3	98.2	3.5
1989	99.2	100.0	101.0	101.7	3.8	99.0	100.0	101.0	101.7	3.6
1990	103.2	104.6	105.5	106.2	4.4	103.0	104.2	105.0	105.7	3.9
1991	108.3	109.8	111.0	111.7	5.2	107.3	108.6	109.5	110.5	4.5
1992	113.7	115.0	115.9	116.7	4.5	112.2	113.3	114.2	114.8	3.9
1993	118.6	119.4	120.2	120.8	3.5	116.3	117.4	118.2	118.8	3.5
1994	122.7	123.2	124.4	124.8	3.3	119.9	120.9	121.9	122.4	3.0
1995	125.9	127.0	127.7	128.7	3.1	123.4	124.4	125.2	125.9	2.9
1996	130.1	131.1	132.0	132.4	2.9	127.0	127.7	128.5	129.0	2.5
1997	134.2	134.9	136.0	136.4	3.0	130.4	131.2	132.2	132.9	3.0
1998	139.6	140.3	141.0	142.1	4.2	134.7	135.6	136.3	137.4	3.4
1999	143.4	144.2	145.1	146.1	2.8	138.9	140.0	140.9	141.3	2.8
2000	148.9	151.0	152.9	153.4	5.0	143.0	144.7	145.9	146.6	3.8
2001	156.0	158.1	158.1	159.1	3.7	148.1	149.9	150.4	151.7	3.5
Wholesale and retail trade										
1987	90.7	92.1	92.6	92.8	3.1	91.4	92.9	93.4	93.4	3.0
1988	94.0	95.8	96.8	97.6	5.2	94.3	96.2	97.2	97.9	4.8
1989	98.9	100.0	101.6	102.6	5.1	99.1	100.0	101.6	102.7	4.9
1990	103.5	105.0	105.6	106.2	3.5	103.3	104.6	105.1	105.6	2.8
1991	107.4	109.2	110.3	110.7	4.2	106.6	108.4	109.4	109.6	3.8
1992	111.4	112.5	113.0	113.7	2.7	109.9	111.2	111.5	112.3	2.5
1993	114.7	115.9	116.4	117.1	3.0	113.0	114.2	114.7	115.4	2.8
1994	117.6	119.4	120.5	120.6	3.0	115.5	117.4	118.3	118.4	2.6
1995	121.7	122.8	123.8	124.2	3.0	119.4	120.6	121.6	122.3	3.3
1996	125.5	126.4	127.5	128.6	3.5	123.9	124.8	125.8	127.0	3.8
1997	130.1	131.2	132.4	132.9	3.3	128.5	129.7	130.9	131.6	3.6
1998	134.7	135.8	137.6	138.2	4.0	133.3	134.6	136.6	137.0	4.1
1999	138.9	141.1	142.2	143.5	3.8	137.7	139.6	140.7	142.0	3.6
2000	145.6	147.3	148.3	149.4	4.1	143.8	145.5	146.4	147.4	3.8
2001	151.0	152.6	153.7	155.5	4.1	148.4	150.1	150.6	152.1	3.2
Wholesale and retail trade, excluding sales occupations										
1987	91.5	92.6	93.3	93.8	3.4	92.2	93.2	94.1	94.5	3.4
1988	94.9	96.2	97.3	98.2	4.7	95.3	96.6	97.5	98.4	4.1
1989	99.2	100.0	101.3	102.0	3.9	99.4	100.0	101.1	101.9	3.6
1990	103.0	104.5	105.4	106.1	4.0	102.6	104.2	104.9	105.5	3.5
1991	107.7	109.1	110.1	110.8	4.4	106.8	108.3	109.2	109.6	3.9
1992	111.5	112.7	113.5	114.1	3.0	110.1	111.4	112.1	112.6	2.7
1993	115.4	116.2	117.0	118.0	3.4	113.6	114.4	115.2	116.1	3.1
1994	118.6	119.8	120.9	120.9	2.5	116.5	117.8	118.7	118.8	2.3
1995	122.4	123.1	124.1	125.0	3.4	120.2	120.9	121.9	123.2	3.7
1996	125.9	126.4	128.0	129.0	3.2	124.4	124.9	126.5	127.7	3.7
1997	130.4	131.9	133.0	134.0	3.9	129.3	131.1	132.2	133.2	4.3
1998	135.5	136.3	138.1	138.8	3.6	134.7	135.6	137.6	138.2	3.8
1999	139.9	141.9	142.8	144.3	4.0	139.5	141.1	141.8	143.3	3.7
2000	146.4	148.1	149.6	150.6	4.4	145.2	146.8	148.2	149.0	4.0
2001	152.6	153.9	155.4	157.1	4.3	150.7	151.9	153.1	154.6	3.8
Wholesale trade										
1987	89.7	91.1	91.6	92.2	3.9	90.5	92.1	92.5	93.0	4.1
1988	93.0	94.7	95.6	96.1	4.2	93.3	95.1	96.1	96.4	3.7
1989	98.5	100.0	102.6	104.5	8.7	99.0	100.0	102.8	105.2	9.1
1990	104.8	105.4	105.8	106.5	1.9	104.6	105.2	105.5	106.2	1.0
1991	107.8	109.6	110.7	111.1	4.3	107.3	109.2	110.4	110.3	3.9
1992	112.5	113.5	113.2	114.4	3.0	111.4	112.5	111.9	113.5	2.9
1993	115.3	116.4	116.6	117.8	3.0	113.9	115.1	115.1	116.4	2.6
1994	117.9	119.7	120.6	121.5	3.1	116.2	118.3	118.9	119.9	3.0
1995	123.2	124.8	126.1	127.0	4.5	120.9	122.7	123.9	125.5	4.7
1996	127.5	129.3	129.9	130.9	3.1	126.1	128.0	128.5	129.6	3.3
1997	132.9	133.8	134.6	135.1	3.2	131.4	132.2	133.0	133.6	3.1
1998	137.7	138.6	140.8	142.8	5.7	136.2	137.1	139.3	141.3	5.8
1999	142.7	144.6	146.3	148.5	4.0	140.7	142.3	144.3	146.5	3.7
2000	150.0	151.8	152.1	154.4	4.0	147.4	149.4	149.6	151.6	3.5
2001	155.1	157.8	158.6	159.5	3.3	151.6	154.5	154.1	154.8	2.1

See footnotes at end of table.

Table 5-1. Employment Cost Index, Private Industry Workers [1], Total Compensation and Wages and Salaries by Occupation and Industry, 1987–2001—*Continued*

(June 1989=100, not seasonally adjusted.)

Series and year	Total compensation					Wages and salaries				
	Indexes				Percent change for 12 months ended December	Indexes				Percent change for 12 months ended December
	March	June	September	December		March	June	September	December	
Wholesale trade, excluding sales occupations										
1987	91.7	92.3	93.4	94.1	3.6	92.7	93.3	94.4	95.2	3.7
1988	95.2	96.2	97.2	97.7	3.8	95.7	96.7	97.7	98.3	3.3
1989	98.9	100.0	101.8	102.6	5.0	99.2	100.0	101.7	102.5	4.3
1990	103.7	105.0	105.4	106.2	3.5	103.2	104.7	105.2	105.9	3.3
1991	108.2	109.6	110.3	111.2	4.7	107.9	109.2	109.8	110.5	4.3
1992	112.5	113.5	114.1	114.9	3.3	111.5	112.7	113.3	114.1	3.3
1993	116.0	116.8	117.6	118.7	3.3	114.7	115.5	116.3	117.5	3.0
1994	119.3	120.3	121.3	122.0	2.8	117.8	118.8	119.6	120.2	2.3
1995	124.4	125.1	126.2	127.1	4.2	122.2	122.9	123.7	125.7	4.6
1996	127.4	128.7	130.0	130.9	3.0	126.3	127.6	128.9	129.8	3.3
1997	132.6	133.7	134.5	135.4	3.4	131.8	132.8	133.9	135.0	4.0
1998	137.0	138.2	140.0	141.2	4.3	136.5	137.8	139.6	140.8	4.3
1999	142.4	144.0	145.8	147.4	4.4	141.9	143.0	144.8	146.4	4.0
2000	149.6	151.1	152.7	154.9	5.1	147.9	149.7	151.3	153.2	4.6
2001	156.9	158.5	160.0	160.6	3.7	154.9	156.5	157.4	157.9	3.1
Retail trade										
1987	91.3	92.5	93.0	93.0	2.4	91.9	93.3	93.8	93.7	2.6
1988	94.5	96.3	97.3	98.4	5.8	94.8	96.6	97.7	98.5	5.1
1989	99.1	100.0	101.1	101.6	3.3	99.1	100.0	101.0	101.6	3.1
1990	103.0	104.8	105.5	106.0	4.3	102.7	104.4	105.0	105.3	3.6
1991	107.3	109.0	110.1	110.5	4.2	106.2	108.0	109.0	109.2	3.7
1992	110.8	112.1	112.9	113.4	2.6	109.3	110.6	111.3	111.8	2.4
1993	114.5	115.6	116.2	116.8	3.0	112.6	113.8	114.5	115.0	2.9
1994	117.5	119.2	120.4	120.1	2.8	115.2	117.0	118.0	117.8	2.4
1995	120.9	121.8	122.6	122.7	2.2	118.7	119.6	120.5	120.6	2.4
1996	124.5	124.8	126.2	127.4	3.8	122.8	123.1	124.4	125.8	4.3
1997	128.5	129.7	131.1	131.7	3.4	127.1	128.5	129.9	130.6	3.8
1998	133.1	134.4	135.9	135.6	3.0	131.9	133.3	135.2	134.8	3.2
1999	136.8	139.1	140.0	140.7	3.8	136.2	138.3	138.9	139.6	3.6
2000	143.2	144.8	146.2	146.6	4.2	142.1	143.5	144.8	145.2	4.0
2001	148.7	149.7	150.9	153.2	4.5	146.9	147.8	148.8	150.7	3.8
General merchandise stores										
1988	. . .	97.2	98.5	99.6	. . .	. . .	95.6	97.0	98.2	. . .
1989	100.5	100.0	100.4	101.5	1.9	99.2	100.0	100.3	101.4	3.3
1990	102.6	105.7	105.9	106.9	5.3	102.4	105.2	105.6	106.5	5.0
1991	108.3	110.1	111.2	111.1	3.9	107.8	110.0	110.9	110.6	3.8
1992	111.7	112.9	113.3	113.3	2.0	111.1	111.7	111.7	111.8	1.1
1993	114.1	114.7	115.5	116.3	2.6	112.4	113.4	114.5	115.0	2.9
1994	115.3	118.0	118.7	119.3	2.6	114.0	116.4	116.5	117.5	2.2
1995	120.1	120.7	121.0	121.7	2.0	117.9	118.6	119.0	120.1	2.2
1996	122.4	123.6	124.6	126.3	3.8	121.0	121.7	122.6	124.7	3.8
1997	126.4	127.7	128.6	130.0	2.9	125.0	126.2	126.7	128.4	3.0
1998	131.2	133.0	133.2	134.0	3.1	129.4	131.5	132.2	133.0	3.6
1999	135.0	135.6	137.2	138.3	3.2	133.7	134.3	135.6	136.7	2.8
2000	139.7	141.0	142.2	144.4	4.4	137.8	138.5	139.7	142.2	4.0
2001	147.3	149.4	149.7	150.9	4.5	143.8	145.5	145.7	146.5	3.0
Food stores										
1987	. . .	. . .	94.5	95.5	. . .	. . .	. . .	95.8	96.7	. . .
1988	96.3	96.8	97.1	98.2	2.8	97.3	97.8	98.2	99.0	2.4
1989	99.8	100.0	100.8	101.7	3.6	100.0	100.0	100.4	101.7	2.7
1990	103.2	104.6	105.7	106.4	4.6	102.8	104.3	105.1	105.8	4.0
1991	107.5	109.3	110.3	111.7	5.0	106.9	108.7	109.4	110.4	4.3
1992	112.6	113.6	114.2	115.1	3.0	110.9	112.3	112.9	113.7	3.0
1993	115.9	117.2	117.1	118.3	2.8	114.6	115.4	114.9	115.9	1.9
1994	119.6	120.6	120.3	120.0	1.4	117.0	117.8	117.4	117.3	1.2
1995	120.8	120.7	121.8	122.4	2.0	117.8	117.6	118.6	119.1	1.5
1996	123.6	124.4	127.0	128.4	4.9	120.5	121.2	123.1	124.7	4.7
1997	128.2	128.2	129.8	129.4	0.8	124.8	124.7	126.7	127.0	1.8
1998	131.3	132.9	133.7	132.7	2.6	129.0	130.5	131.7	130.5	2.8
1999	134.3	135.7	137.0	138.1	4.1	131.8	132.8	133.9	134.9	3.4
2000	140.1	142.5	143.4	144.5	4.6	136.7	139.5	140.2	141.6	5.0
2001	146.1	148.2	149.7	151.7	5.0	143.3	144.5	145.7	146.7	3.6

See footnotes at end of table.

Table 5-1. Employment Cost Index, Private Industry Workers [1], Total Compensation and Wages and Salaries by Occupation and Industry, 1987–2001—*Continued*

(June 1989=100, not seasonally adjusted.)

Series and year	Total compensation				Percent change for 12 months ended December	Wages and salaries				Percent change for 12 months ended December
	Indexes					Indexes				
	March	June	September	December		March	June	September	December	
Finance, insurance, and real estate										
1987	90.9	90.0	90.2	90.4	2.0	91.9	90.6	90.8	90.6	1.2
1988	91.5	92.8	92.9	96.2	6.4	91.5	92.9	92.9	96.3	6.3
1989	98.3	100.0	100.4	101.4	5.4	98.3	100.0	100.6	101.3	5.2
1990	102.6	104.4	105.4	105.5	4.0	101.8	103.5	104.9	104.8	3.5
1991	108.3	109.5	109.7	110.0	4.3	107.0	108.1	108.0	108.4	3.4
1992	111.7	110.8	111.1	111.3	1.2	109.5	108.2	108.2	108.3	0.1
1993	112.6	113.1	115.7	116.4	4.6	109.3	109.3	112.3	112.9	4.2
1994	117.7	117.7	118.5	118.9	2.1	113.7	113.2	113.8	114.2	1.2
1995	120.2	121.8	122.7	123.1	3.5	115.0	117.0	118.0	118.4	3.7
1996	124.5	126.3	126.7	126.0	2.4	119.8	121.9	122.2	122.2	3.2
1997	128.6	129.4	130.5	134.5	6.7	124.5	125.3	126.4	130.6	6.9
1998	136.7	138.4	141.0	142.5	5.9	132.6	134.8	138.1	139.8	7.0
1999	141.5	145.8	147.6	148.3	4.1	137.2	142.4	144.5	145.2	3.9
2000	152.0	153.1	155.2	155.7	5.0	148.7	149.5	151.7	151.7	4.5
2001	157.9	159.5	160.9	161.3	3.6	153.9	154.6	155.8	156.0	2.8
Finance, insurance and real estate, excluding sales occupations										
1987	90.8	91.1	92.0	92.6	4.2	91.3	91.5	92.5	92.9	3.7
1988	93.8	94.6	95.4	97.1	4.9	93.8	94.5	95.3	97.1	4.5
1989	98.5	100.0	100.1	101.0	4.0	98.4	100.0	100.2	100.9	3.9
1990	103.5	104.7	106.3	106.7	5.6	103.0	103.9	105.8	106.1	5.2
1991	108.6	109.5	110.6	111.4	4.4	107.6	108.4	109.5	110.4	4.1
1992	112.5	112.2	112.5	113.0	1.4	110.6	109.9	109.9	110.2	0.2
1993	114.9	116.4	117.5	118.2	4.6	112.0	113.1	114.0	114.6	4.0
1994	119.7	120.3	121.5	121.8	3.0	115.5	116.0	117.2	117.4	2.4
1995	123.7	124.6	125.4	125.7	3.2	119.3	120.2	121.1	121.3	3.3
1996	127.5	128.5	129.7	129.2	2.8	123.4	124.5	126.0	125.3	3.3
1997	131.5	132.4	133.5	137.6	6.5	127.2	128.1	129.3	133.6	6.6
1998	140.2	141.3	143.2	143.3	4.1	135.9	137.5	139.7	139.6	4.5
1999	145.6	148.8	151.0	151.6	5.8	141.0	144.8	147.5	148.0	6.0
2000	154.2	155.5	157.4	158.4	4.5	150.2	151.5	153.3	154.1	4.1
2001	161.2	163.1	164.7	165.0	4.2	156.6	157.6	159.1	159.1	3.2
Banking, savings and loan, and other credit agencies										
1987	89.8	90.7	91.4	92.3	5.5	89.8	90.9	91.7	92.4	5.4
1988	95.3	96.0	97.0	97.8	6.0	95.2	96.0	97.0	97.8	5.8
1989	98.8	100.0	100.6	100.7	3.0	98.8	100.0	101.1	100.9	3.2
1990	102.1	104.1	104.4	105.8	5.1	101.6	103.6	103.9	105.4	4.5
1991	107.4	107.0	107.5	107.4	1.5	106.6	105.9	106.4	106.3	0.9
1992	110.2	110.0	111.0	111.4	3.7	108.2	107.7	108.6	109.0	2.5
1993	114.6	116.0	116.9	117.8	5.7	112.1	112.9	113.7	114.5	5.0
1994	118.7	119.4	120.8	120.5	2.3	114.7	115.0	116.5	116.2	1.5
1995	123.5	124.1	124.8	124.4	3.2	119.2	119.7	120.4	120.1	3.4
1996	126.9	128.2	130.3	128.0	2.9	122.7	124.2	126.8	123.8	3.1
1997	130.6	131.6	133.1	140.6	9.8	125.9	126.8	128.9	138.3	11.7
1998	143.3	145.3	148.4	146.7	4.3	140.9	143.2	147.0	144.4	4.4
1999	148.8	155.4	159.3	159.8	8.9	146.1	154.5	159.2	159.6	10.5
2000	162.7	164.2	165.8	166.5	4.2	162.0	163.3	165.0	165.7	3.8
2001	170.8	172.7	175.4	174.3	4.7	169.4	170.8	173.2	171.7	3.6
Insurance										
1987	...	89.6	90.3	91.9	...	...	90.0	90.8	92.4	...
1988	92.6	95.0	95.8	97.0	5.5	93.1	95.4	96.2	97.4	5.4
1989	98.3	100.0	99.9	101.0	4.1	98.5	100.0	99.6	100.8	3.5
1990	103.2	105.2	106.5	106.0	5.0	102.3	104.1	105.8	105.1	4.3
1991	107.4	109.5	109.5	110.7	4.4	105.7	107.8	107.5	108.6	3.3
1992	113.2	114.7	114.9	115.2	4.1	111.2	112.7	112.7	112.7	3.8
1993	114.3	116.1	117.4	119.7	3.9	111.2	112.9	113.9	116.6	3.5
1994	119.9	120.5	121.5	122.3	2.2	116.0	116.8	117.7	118.6	1.7
1995	123.5	124.6	124.9	125.9	2.9	119.8	120.8	121.1	122.2	3.0
1996	127.6	128.2	129.3	129.6	2.9	123.6	124.1	125.4	126.0	3.1
1997	131.9	132.1	133.1	134.8	4.0	127.9	128.0	128.7	130.2	3.3
1998	137.4	138.9	141.9	141.7	5.1	133.1	134.8	138.7	138.5	6.4
1999	141.7	144.0	144.5	145.8	2.9	137.4	139.8	140.2	141.5	2.2
2000	149.9	151.3	154.8	155.2	6.4	145.5	146.6	150.7	150.8	6.6
2001	157.6	159.3	159.9	161.3	3.9	152.4	153.3	153.6	155.0	2.8

See footnotes at end of table.

Table 5-1. Employment Cost Index, Private Industry Workers[1], Total Compensation and Wages and Salaries by Occupation and Industry, 1987–2001—*Continued*

(June 1989=100, not seasonally adjusted.)

Series and year	Total compensation					Wages and salaries				
	Indexes				Percent change for 12 months ended December	Indexes				Percent change for 12 months ended December
	March	June	September	December		March	June	September	December	
Insurance, excluding sales occupations										
1987	. . .	90.9	91.9	92.3	. . .	. . .	91.6	92.6	93.0	. . .
1988	93.8	95.3	96.5	97.3	5.4	94.4	95.8	97.0	97.6	4.9
1989	98.6	100.0	101.0	101.8	4.6	98.5	100.0	100.9	101.5	4.0
1990	104.5	106.1	106.8	107.6	5.7	103.8	105.2	105.9	106.5	4.9
1991	108.7	110.3	111.4	112.5	4.6	107.1	108.7	109.4	110.5	3.8
1992	113.9	115.7	116.1	117.2	4.2	111.7	113.4	113.8	114.9	4.0
1993	118.6	120.6	121.8	122.7	4.7	115.8	117.6	118.3	119.2	3.7
1994	124.4	125.0	126.0	126.5	3.1	120.6	121.4	122.3	122.7	2.9
1995	127.6	129.0	129.6	130.2	2.9	123.8	125.2	125.7	126.3	2.9
1996	132.1	132.7	133.4	133.5	2.5	128.0	128.6	129.3	129.7	2.7
1997	136.0	136.6	137.4	138.6	3.8	131.6	132.2	132.9	133.7	3.1
1998	140.0	140.9	141.6	142.5	2.8	134.7	135.7	136.6	137.9	3.1
1999	144.5	145.4	146.2	147.0	3.2	139.1	139.9	140.9	141.6	2.7
2000	149.4	150.5	152.2	153.1	4.1	143.2	144.1	145.7	146.5	3.5
2001	155.6	157.6	158.0	159.4	4.1	148.3	149.6	149.8	151.2	3.2
Service industries										
1987	89.0	89.5	91.3	92.2	5.1	89.9	90.5	92.5	93.2	5.4
1988	93.6	94.5	96.4	97.5	5.7	94.2	94.9	96.9	97.8	4.9
1989	99.0	100.0	101.8	102.9	5.5	99.1	100.0	101.6	102.5	4.8
1990	105.0	106.5	108.1	109.3	6.2	104.2	105.7	107.1	108.3	5.7
1991	110.8	111.5	113.1	114.0	4.3	109.5	110.0	111.5	112.2	3.6
1992	115.3	116.4	117.8	118.9	4.3	113.2	114.0	115.2	116.1	3.5
1993	120.1	120.9	122.3	123.1	3.5	117.0	117.6	118.9	119.6	3.0
1994	124.4	124.9	125.9	126.6	2.8	120.8	121.3	122.2	123.0	2.8
1995	127.5	128.2	128.9	129.4	2.2	123.9	124.4	125.3	126.0	2.4
1996	130.7	131.7	132.7	133.4	3.1	127.6	128.7	129.7	130.5	3.6
1997	134.6	135.7	137.0	138.5	3.8	131.8	133.0	134.7	136.2	4.4
1998	139.3	140.3	141.8	142.7	3.0	137.2	138.3	140.0	140.8	3.4
1999	143.5	144.6	146.1	147.6	3.4	142.2	143.2	144.5	146.0	3.7
2000	149.4	151.2	152.9	154.1	4.4	147.4	149.1	150.6	151.8	4.0
2001	156.5	157.8	160.0	161.0	4.5	153.8	155.0	157.1	158.2	4.2
Business services										
1987	88.5	89.5	91.7	92.5	6.1	89.1	90.2	92.8	93.5	6.7
1988	93.8	94.9	96.2	97.2	5.1	94.3	95.1	96.5	97.4	4.2
1989	98.1	100.0	100.7	101.3	4.2	98.4	100.0	100.9	101.2	3.9
1990	103.6	105.3	106.3	107.4	6.0	103.0	105.1	105.7	107.4	6.1
1991	110.3	110.4	110.0	111.1	3.4	109.6	109.5	108.9	110.0	2.4
1992	112.5	113.6	115.2	115.9	4.3	111.0	111.7	113.3	113.9	3.5
1993	116.5	117.4	118.1	118.6	2.3	114.2	114.6	115.3	115.7	1.6
1994	121.3	122.1	122.4	123.0	3.7	118.8	119.4	119.9	120.4	4.1
1995	124.5	125.3	125.7	126.3	2.7	122.1	122.9	123.6	124.3	3.2
1996	128.9	129.2	130.2	131.8	4.4	126.9	127.7	128.5	130.1	4.7
1997	133.3	134.2	136.3	138.6	5.2	131.4	132.4	134.9	137.3	5.5
1998	139.5	140.7	143.5	145.9	5.3	137.6	139.2	141.8	144.1	5.0
1999	147.5	148.7	150.7	151.9	4.1	145.4	146.3	148.5	149.8	4.0
2000	154.2	156.3	157.5	158.4	4.3	152.0	154.1	155.3	156.0	4.1
2001	160.5	163.0	165.2	166.2	4.9	158.2	160.8	162.8	163.7	4.9
Health services										
1987	88.8	89.4	90.4	91.5	4.3	89.2	89.8	91.1	92.1	4.7
1988	92.6	94.1	95.6	97.0	6.0	92.7	94.4	96.0	97.3	5.6
1989	98.9	100.0	101.9	103.7	6.9	99.1	100.0	101.9	103.5	6.4
1990	105.8	107.1	109.0	110.8	6.8	105.3	106.3	108.1	109.7	6.0
1991	112.6	113.5	115.3	116.5	5.1	111.1	111.9	113.5	114.6	4.5
1992	117.9	118.9	120.6	121.8	4.5	115.6	116.3	117.9	118.9	3.8
1993	123.0	124.0	125.0	126.0	3.4	119.8	120.7	121.7	122.6	3.1
1994	126.7	127.1	127.9	128.7	2.1	123.1	123.5	124.3	125.4	2.3
1995	129.7	130.3	131.3	132.2	2.7	126.2	126.7	127.5	128.4	2.4
1996	132.6	133.5	134.2	134.5	1.7	129.3	130.1	130.8	131.4	2.3
1997	135.5	135.9	137.0	138.1	2.7	132.5	133.2	134.3	135.4	3.0
1998	138.2	138.7	139.0	139.0	0.7	136.2	136.5	137.5	137.4	1.5
1999	140.5	141.4	142.6	144.2	3.7	138.7	139.6	140.6	142.2	3.5
2000	145.8	147.5	149.0	150.6	4.4	143.5	145.3	146.6	148.1	4.1
2001	152.7	154.7	156.8	158.4	5.2	149.8	151.8	153.6	155.4	4.9

See footnotes at end of table.

Table 5-1. Employment Cost Index, Private Industry Workers[1], Total Compensation and Wages and Salaries by Occupation and Industry, 1987–2001—*Continued*

(June 1989=100, not seasonally adjusted.)

Series and year	Total compensation					Wages and salaries				
	Indexes				Percent change for 12 months ended December	Indexes				Percent change for 12 months ended December
	March	June	September	December		March	June	September	December	
Hospitals										
1987	87.8	88.3	89.9	91.0	4.8	88.2	88.8	90.4	91.5	5.1
1988	92.2	93.6	95.2	96.6	6.2	92.5	94.0	95.6	96.9	5.9
1989	98.8	100.0	101.9	103.5	7.1	98.9	100.0	101.9	103.3	6.6
1990	105.4	106.6	108.9	110.7	7.0	105.0	106.0	108.2	109.8	6.3
1991	112.2	113.2	114.9	116.1	4.9	110.8	111.6	113.2	114.4	4.2
1992	117.7	118.5	120.2	121.6	4.7	115.4	115.9	117.3	118.3	3.4
1993	122.7	123.4	124.5	125.6	3.3	119.3	119.9	121.0	122.0	3.1
1994	126.7	127.1	127.7	128.6	2.4	122.8	123.3	123.9	124.8	2.3
1995	128.9	129.7	130.3	131.3	2.1	125.4	125.9	126.6	127.7	2.3
1996	132.2	132.8	133.4	133.7	1.8	128.5	129.1	129.7	130.3	2.0
1997	134.0	134.4	135.4	136.5	2.1	130.7	131.2	132.2	133.2	2.2
1998	136.7	138.2	139.1	139.9	2.5	133.6	134.7	135.8	136.5	2.5
1999	141.2	142.1	143.0	144.6	3.4	137.6	138.3	139.3	140.9	3.2
2000	145.8	147.5	149.2	151.1	4.5	141.8	143.3	144.9	146.8	4.2
2001	153.5	155.9	158.4	160.3	6.1	148.5	151.0	153.3	155.4	5.9
Nursing homes										
1993	...	...	...	...	3.9	...	...	...	...	3.7
1994	...	...	...	...	3.3	...	...	...	...	3.6
1995	...	...	...	...	3.4	...	...	...	...	3.3
1996	...	...	...	...	2.6	...	...	...	...	2.8
1997	...	...	...	...	2.6	...	...	...	...	3.1
1998	...	...	...	...	3.2	...	...	...	...	3.7
1999	...	...	...	...	4.2	...	...	...	...	4.4
2000	...	...	...	...	6.1	...	...	...	...	5.8
2001	...	...	...	...	5.1	...	...	...	...	5.1
Educational services										
1988	...	...	...	98.3	...	...	...	...	98.8	...
1989	99.1	100.0	103.9	104.2	6.0	99.1	100.0	103.7	103.9	5.2
1990	105.4	105.9	110.2	111.4	6.9	104.7	105.0	109.2	110.2	6.1
1991	111.9	111.5	114.9	115.7	3.9	110.3	109.7	113.0	113.7	3.2
1992	115.8	116.3	119.3	120.0	3.7	113.4	113.6	116.5	117.1	3.0
1993	120.5	120.6	123.8	124.1	3.4	117.5	117.4	120.7	120.9	3.2
1994	124.5	125.4	128.2	128.4	3.5	121.2	122.2	124.9	125.1	3.5
1995	128.8	130.3	133.2	133.7	4.1	125.6	125.9	128.6	129.4	3.4
1996	134.4	134.8	137.5	138.0	3.2	130.1	130.4	133.3	133.8	3.4
1997	138.5	138.8	141.6	142.6	3.3	134.5	134.8	137.8	138.4	3.4
1998	143.4	143.9	147.0	147.7	3.6	139.1	139.6	142.8	143.5	3.7
1999	148.3	148.7	152.2	153.0	3.6	143.9	144.2	147.5	148.2	3.3
2000	154.0	154.9	158.8	159.9	4.5	148.9	149.6	153.4	154.3	4.1
2001	162.3	162.6	166.4	167.6	4.8	155.4	156.1	159.6	160.6	4.1
Colleges and universities										
1988	...	...	...	98.2	...	...	...	...	98.7	...
1989	99.0	100.0	103.3	103.8	5.7	99.1	100.0	103.3	103.7	5.1
1990	105.2	105.7	109.8	110.6	6.6	104.4	104.8	108.7	109.3	5.4
1991	111.3	112.0	115.5	116.3	5.2	109.6	110.2	113.7	114.2	4.5
1992	116.8	117.4	120.3	120.8	3.9	114.2	114.5	117.3	117.6	3.0
1993	121.5	121.5	125.0	125.3	3.7	118.0	117.7	121.3	121.6	3.4
1994	125.7	126.0	128.5	128.8	2.8	122.0	122.2	124.5	124.9	2.7
1995	129.3	131.3	134.6	135.2	5.0	125.5	125.9	129.0	130.1	4.2
1996	135.9	136.2	138.6	139.1	2.9	130.6	130.9	133.4	133.8	2.8
1997	139.5	139.9	142.5	143.7	3.3	134.6	135.0	137.8	138.7	3.7
1998	144.3	144.8	147.8	148.5	3.3	139.1	139.7	142.8	143.6	3.5
1999	149.2	149.6	152.6	153.3	3.2	144.1	144.4	147.2	147.9	3.0
2000	154.6	155.5	158.6	159.2	3.8	148.9	149.4	152.5	152.9	3.4
2001	162.2	162.6	166.2	167.5	5.2	154.1	155.0	158.4	159.6	4.4

See footnotes at end of table.

Table 5-1. Employment Cost Index, Private Industry Workers [1], Total Compensation and Wages and Salaries by Occupation and Industry, 1987–2001—*Continued*

(June 1989=100, not seasonally adjusted.)

Series and year	Total compensation					Wages and salaries				
	Indexes				Percent change for 12 months ended December	Indexes				Percent change for 12 months ended December
	March	June	September	December		March	June	September	December	
Nonmanufacturing Industries										
1987	90.9	91.5	92.4	92.9	3.6	91.7	92.3	93.3	93.7	3.4
1988	94.1	95.4	96.5	97.5	5.0	94.5	95.8	96.9	97.8	4.4
1989	98.8	100.0	101.3	102.3	4.9	99.1	100.0	101.4	102.2	4.5
1990	103.8	105.1	106.2	106.9	4.5	103.2	104.5	105.4	106.1	3.8
1991	108.5	109.7	110.9	111.5	4.3	107.3	108.4	109.3	109.8	3.5
1992	112.7	113.5	114.4	115.1	3.2	110.7	111.3	111.9	112.6	2.6
1993	116.3	117.2	118.4	119.0	3.4	113.4	114.2	115.4	116.0	3.0
1994	120.3	121.2	122.3	122.6	3.0	116.8	117.7	118.7	119.1	2.7
1995	123.7	124.6	125.5	125.9	2.7	120.0	120.9	121.9	122.5	2.9
1996	127.2	128.2	129.1	129.8	3.1	123.9	125.1	125.9	126.8	3.5
1997	131.1	132.1	133.3	134.7	3.8	128.2	129.3	130.7	132.1	4.2
1998	136.0	137.2	138.9	139.7	3.7	133.4	134.7	136.5	137.4	4.0
1999	140.3	142.0	143.4	144.5	3.4	137.9	139.7	141.0	142.1	3.4
2000	146.7	148.4	150.0	151.1	4.6	143.9	145.5	146.9	147.9	4.1
2001	153.1	154.7	156.3	157.6	4.3	149.5	150.9	152.2	153.5	3.8
Nonmanufacturing, white-collar occupations										
1987	...	90.8	91.8	92.2	...	...	91.7	92.7	93.0	...
1988	93.4	94.8	95.9	97.2	5.4	93.8	95.2	96.4	97.6	4.9
1989	98.8	100.0	101.4	102.6	5.6	99.1	100.0	101.5	102.5	5.0
1990	104.1	105.5	106.7	107.4	4.7	103.6	105.0	106.1	106.7	4.1
1991	109.1	110.4	111.5	112.1	4.4	108.0	109.2	110.2	110.6	3.7
1992	113.4	114.1	114.9	115.7	3.2	111.6	112.1	112.8	113.5	2.6
1993	117.0	117.9	119.0	119.9	3.6	114.4	115.2	116.4	117.2	3.3
1994	121.1	122.1	123.1	123.5	3.0	117.9	118.9	119.7	120.2	2.6
1995	124.7	125.6	126.5	127.0	2.8	121.1	122.1	123.1	123.8	3.0
1996	128.5	129.5	130.5	131.1	3.2	125.4	126.6	127.6	128.3	3.6
1997	132.7	133.6	134.9	136.5	4.1	129.9	131.0	132.4	134.1	4.5
1998	137.9	139.2	141.1	142.0	4.0	135.5	136.8	138.9	139.8	4.3
1999	142.3	144.1	145.6	146.9	3.5	140.1	142.0	143.5	144.7	3.5
2000	149.2	151.0	152.6	153.7	4.6	146.5	148.2	149.6	150.6	4.1
2001	155.8	157.5	159.0	160.5	4.4	152.3	153.8	155.0	156.4	3.9
Nonmanufacturing, white-collar occupations, excluding sales occupations										
1987	...	91.0	92.3	92.9	...	...	91.7	93.1	93.7	...
1988	94.1	95.3	96.6	97.5	5.0	94.5	95.6	97.0	97.9	4.5
1989	99.0	100.0	101.4	102.3	4.9	99.2	100.0	101.3	102.0	4.2
1990	104.3	105.6	107.0	108.0	5.6	103.8	105.0	106.3	107.2	5.1
1991	109.5	110.6	112.1	112.9	4.5	108.5	109.4	110.7	111.5	4.0
1992	114.1	114.9	116.0	116.9	3.5	112.3	113.0	113.9	114.6	2.8
1993	118.5	119.4	120.4	121.4	3.8	115.8	116.6	117.6	118.5	3.4
1994	122.8	123.6	124.7	125.1	3.0	119.4	120.2	121.3	121.8	2.8
1995	126.4	127.1	128.0	128.6	2.8	122.9	123.5	124.4	125.4	3.0
1996	130.0	130.8	132.1	132.5	3.0	126.9	127.8	129.2	129.6	3.3
1997	134.0	135.1	136.2	137.9	4.1	131.2	132.4	133.8	135.5	4.6
1998	139.3	140.5	142.0	142.7	3.5	136.9	138.1	139.8	140.3	3.5
1999	143.7	145.3	146.8	148.1	3.8	141.6	143.2	144.6	145.9	4.0
2000	150.2	152.0	153.8	155.1	4.7	147.4	149.1	150.7	151.9	4.1
2001	157.5	159.1	160.9	162.3	4.6	153.9	155.3	156.9	158.3	4.2

See footnotes at end of table.

Table 5-1. Employment Cost Index, Private Industry Workers [1], Total Compensation and Wages and Salaries by Occupation and Industry, 1987–2001—*Continued*

(June 1989=100, not seasonally adjusted.)

Series and year	Total compensation					Wages and salaries				
	Indexes				Percent change for 12 months ended December	Indexes				Percent change for 12 months ended December
	March	June	September	December		March	June	September	December	
Nonmanufacturing, blue-collar occupations										
1987	...	92.9	93.7	94.5	...	...	93.5	94.3	95.0	...
1988	95.7	96.8	97.6	98.1	3.8	95.9	96.9	97.7	98.1	3.3
1989	98.8	100.0	101.1	101.7	3.7	99.0	100.0	101.0	101.3	3.3
1990	102.9	104.1	105.0	105.6	3.8	102.2	103.2	104.0	104.3	3.0
1991	107.2	108.2	109.2	109.8	4.0	105.5	106.3	107.1	107.5	3.1
1992	110.7	111.8	112.8	113.4	3.3	108.2	109.1	109.7	110.2	2.5
1993	114.6	115.6	116.6	117.1	3.3	111.1	111.9	113.0	113.4	2.9
1994	118.2	119.1	120.5	120.5	2.9	114.2	115.1	116.4	116.4	2.6
1995	121.5	122.5	123.5	123.7	2.7	117.5	118.5	119.4	119.8	2.9
1996	124.6	125.6	125.9	126.7	2.4	120.9	122.0	122.4	123.1	2.8
1997	127.5	128.6	129.4	130.1	2.7	124.1	125.5	126.4	127.1	3.2
1998	131.0	132.4	133.4	134.0	3.0	128.2	129.5	130.5	131.1	3.1
1999	135.2	136.8	138.0	138.7	3.5	132.4	134.0	135.1	135.8	3.6
2000	140.6	142.3	143.9	144.8	4.4	137.4	138.9	140.3	140.9	3.8
2001	146.9	148.1	150.2	150.6	4.0	142.8	143.9	145.8	146.4	3.9
Nonmanufacturing, service occupations										
1987	...	92.4	92.8	93.3	...	...	93.6	94.1	94.4	...
1988	94.6	95.6	97.1	98.3	5.4	95.4	96.3	97.7	98.8	4.7
1989	99.2	100.0	101.0	102.4	4.2	99.4	100.0	100.8	102.3	3.5
1990	103.9	105.0	105.8	107.4	4.9	103.2	104.3	105.0	106.5	4.1
1991	108.4	109.9	111.7	112.5	4.7	107.1	108.4	110.0	110.7	3.9
1992	113.4	114.1	115.2	115.7	2.8	111.3	111.7	112.6	112.9	2.0
1993	116.8	117.7	118.6	119.1	2.9	113.4	114.1	114.8	115.1	1.9
1994	120.2	120.7	121.3	122.4	2.8	116.3	116.7	117.3	118.6	3.0
1995	123.0	123.5	124.2	124.7	1.9	119.2	119.8	120.6	121.2	2.2
1996	125.3	126.0	127.0	128.6	3.1	122.0	122.7	123.9	125.5	3.5
1997	129.4	130.5	132.7	133.8	4.0	126.4	127.4	129.7	130.9	4.3
1998	134.9	135.7	136.9	137.7	2.9	132.0	132.9	134.1	135.1	3.2
1999	139.2	140.4	140.7	142.3	3.3	136.5	137.7	137.9	139.5	3.3
2000	143.5	145.1	146.3	147.8	3.9	140.9	142.4	143.4	144.7	3.7
2001	149.5	150.7	152.1	154.1	4.3	146.0	147.1	148.2	150.1	3.7

1. Excludes farm and household workers.
2. Includes mining, construction, and manufacturing.
3. Includes transportation, communication, and public utilities; wholesale and retail trade; finance, insurance, and real estate; and service industries.

Table 5-2. Employment Cost Index, State and Local Government Workers, Total Compensation and Wages and Salaries by Occupation and Industry, 1987–2001

(June 1989=100, not seasonally adjusted.)

Series and year	Total compensation					Wages and salaries				
	Indexes				Percent change for 12 months ended December	Indexes				Percent change for 12 months ended December
	March	June	September	December		March	June	September	December	
STATE AND LOCAL GOVERNMENT WORKERS, TOTAL										
1987	89.8	90.0	92.1	93.0	4.5	91.0	91.2	93.3	94.1	4.2
1988	94.2	94.5	97.1	98.2	5.6	95.0	95.2	97.7	98.7	4.9
1989	99.4	100.0	103.3	104.3	6.2	99.5	100.0	103.1	103.9	5.3
1990	105.8	106.5	109.4	110.4	5.8	105.1	105.7	108.6	109.4	5.3
1991	111.8	112.0	113.9	114.4	3.6	110.6	110.9	112.8	113.2	3.5
1992	115.2	115.7	117.9	118.6	3.7	113.8	114.2	115.9	116.6	3.0
1993	119.3	119.6	121.4	121.9	2.8	117.2	117.4	119.3	119.7	2.7
1994	122.6	123.1	125.0	125.6	3.0	120.4	120.7	122.8	123.4	3.1
1995	126.4	126.9	128.7	129.3	2.9	124.3	124.6	126.6	127.3	3.2
1996	129.9	130.2	131.9	132.7	2.6	127.8	128.1	130.1	130.9	2.8
1997	133.2	133.3	135.0	135.7	2.3	131.4	131.5	133.6	134.4	2.7
1998	136.5	136.9	139.0	139.8	3.0	135.1	135.4	137.6	138.5	3.1
1999	140.5	141.0	143.1	144.6	3.4	139.0	139.6	142.2	143.5	3.6
2000	145.5	145.9	147.8	148.9	3.0	144.3	144.7	147.2	148.3	3.3
2001	150.3	151.2	154.3	155.2	4.2	149.3	150.1	153.0	153.7	3.6
WORKERS, BY OCCUPATIONAL GROUP										
White-Collar Occupations										
1987	89.4	89.6	91.9	92.8	4.6	90.7	90.8	93.1	94.1	4.6
1988	94.0	94.3	97.0	98.3	5.9	94.8	95.0	97.6	98.8	5.0
1989	99.5	100.0	103.6	104.6	6.4	99.6	100.0	103.4	104.2	5.5
1990	106.1	106.7	109.9	110.9	6.0	105.5	106.0	109.2	109.9	5.5
1991	112.2	112.3	114.2	114.6	3.3	111.0	111.2	113.1	113.5	3.3
1992	115.4	115.8	118.1	118.9	3.8	114.0	114.3	116.2	116.9	3.0
1993	119.5	119.6	121.5	121.9	2.5	117.5	117.6	119.6	119.9	2.6
1994	122.6	122.9	124.9	125.5	3.0	120.6	120.9	122.9	123.6	3.1
1995	126.2	126.6	128.6	129.1	2.9	124.4	124.6	126.8	127.4	3.1
1996	129.6	129.9	131.8	132.5	2.6	127.9	128.2	130.3	131.1	2.9
1997	132.9	133.0	134.8	135.5	2.3	131.4	131.5	133.7	134.5	2.6
1998	136.1	136.2	138.4	139.3	2.8	135.0	135.2	137.6	138.5	3.0
1999	139.8	140.2	142.6	144.0	3.4	138.9	139.3	142.1	143.4	3.5
2000	144.9	145.3	147.3	148.3	3.0	144.1	144.5	147.1	148.0	3.2
2001	149.5	150.4	153.7	154.4	4.1	149.0	149.8	152.7	153.3	3.6
Professional specialty and technical occupations										
1989	...	100.0	103.8	104.7	...	...	100.0	103.7	104.4	...
1990	106.4	107.0	110.3	111.2	6.2	105.8	106.3	109.8	110.6	5.9
1991	112.3	112.4	114.5	115.0	3.4	111.5	111.7	113.8	114.2	3.3
1992	115.5	116.0	118.5	119.2	3.7	114.5	114.8	117.0	117.6	3.0
1993	119.6	119.7	121.7	122.0	2.3	118.1	118.2	120.4	120.7	2.6
1994	122.5	122.7	125.0	125.5	2.9	121.1	121.3	123.6	124.2	2.9
1995	126.0	126.3	128.4	128.8	2.6	124.8	125.0	127.4	128.0	3.1
1996	129.1	129.5	131.6	132.3	2.7	128.3	128.6	131.1	131.7	2.9
1997	132.5	132.5	134.6	135.1	2.1	131.9	132.0	134.4	135.1	2.6
1998	135.6	135.6	137.7	138.5	2.5	135.5	135.6	137.9	138.7	2.7
1999	138.8	139.3	142.0	143.2	3.4	138.9	139.4	142.5	143.6	3.5
2000	144.1	144.5	146.6	147.4	2.9	144.3	144.7	147.4	148.2	3.2
2001	148.4	149.2	152.8	153.2	3.9	149.1	149.8	153.0	153.4	3.5
Executive, administrative, and managerial occupations										
1989	...	100.0	103.1	104.1	...	...	100.0	102.8	103.7	...
1990	105.7	106.4	109.3	110.1	5.8	104.9	105.7	108.4	108.9	5.0
1991	112.2	112.0	113.3	113.7	3.3	110.6	110.7	112.0	112.3	3.1
1992	115.0	115.2	116.8	117.8	3.6	113.3	113.5	114.7	115.5	2.8
1993	119.0	119.2	121.0	121.6	3.2	116.5	116.6	118.2	118.8	2.9
1994	122.8	123.4	124.7	125.3	3.0	119.8	120.3	121.6	122.4	3.0
1995	126.9	127.4	129.1	129.9	3.7	124.1	124.3	126.0	126.9	3.7
1996	130.7	131.0	132.0	132.9	2.3	127.7	128.0	129.3	130.2	2.6
1997	134.1	134.4	135.6	136.4	2.6	131.3	131.7	133.1	134.1	3.0
1998	137.5	137.9	140.4	141.6	3.8	135.1	135.6	138.0	139.3	3.9
1999	142.6	142.8	144.5	146.1	3.2	140.1	140.5	142.7	144.3	3.6
2000	147.0	147.2	149.2	150.7	3.1	144.9	145.1	147.3	148.8	3.1
2001	152.4	153.7	156.4	157.6	4.6	150.1	151.5	153.9	155.1	4.2

See footnote at end of table.

Table 5-2. Employment Cost Index, State and Local Government Workers, Total Compensation and Wages and Salaries by Occupation and Industry, 1987–2001—*Continued*

(June 1989=100, not seasonally adjusted.)

Series and year	Total compensation					Wages and salaries				
	Indexes				Percent change for 12 months ended December	Indexes				Percent change for 12 months ended December
	March	June	September	December		March	June	September	December	
Administrative support occupations, including clerical occupations										
1989	...	100.0	102.9	103.9	...	...	100.0	102.4	103.0	...
1990	105.4	106.0	108.7	110.2	6.1	104.4	104.8	107.2	107.9	4.8
1991	111.8	111.7	113.5	114.0	3.4	109.4	109.7	111.4	111.8	3.6
1992	115.4	115.7	117.5	118.5	3.9	112.7	112.9	114.1	114.9	2.8
1993	119.2	119.6	121.0	121.6	2.6	115.4	115.9	117.2	117.8	2.5
1994	122.7	123.3	124.9	125.6	3.3	118.9	119.4	120.9	121.7	3.3
1995	126.3	126.9	128.4	129.1	2.8	122.5	122.9	124.4	125.1	2.8
1996	130.0	130.4	131.8	133.0	3.0	125.8	126.1	127.7	129.0	3.1
1997	133.3	133.5	135.3	136.1	2.3	129.2	129.5	131.4	132.3	2.6
1998	136.9	137.2	139.5	140.3	3.1	133.0	133.3	135.4	136.5	3.2
1999	141.4	141.3	143.0	145.0	3.4	137.4	137.5	139.6	141.7	3.8
2000	145.9	146.5	148.3	149.4	3.0	142.4	143.0	145.0	146.2	3.2
2001	150.7	151.6	154.2	155.6	4.1	147.0	147.6	149.8	150.9	3.2
Blue-Collar Occupations										
1987	92.0	92.4	93.7	94.3	3.4	92.8	93.3	94.7	95.1	3.4
1988	95.4	95.4	97.0	97.5	3.4	96.1	96.1	97.8	98.2	3.3
1989	99.3	100.0	102.1	103.7	6.4	99.5	100.0	101.9	103.3	5.2
1990	105.5	106.3	108.2	108.7	4.8	104.3	105.3	107.2	107.7	4.3
1991	110.4	110.9	112.4	112.9	3.9	109.1	110.0	111.1	111.6	3.6
1992	114.2	115.3	116.9	117.8	4.3	112.5	113.7	115.0	115.6	3.6
1993	118.3	118.7	120.5	121.4	3.1	116.2	116.5	118.4	119.0	2.9
1994	122.3	122.7	124.2	124.7	2.7	119.7	120.1	121.8	122.5	2.9
1995	125.4	126.3	127.2	128.0	2.6	123.1	123.8	124.8	125.7	2.6
1996	129.0	129.5	130.3	131.2	2.5	126.6	127.0	127.9	128.8	2.5
1997	132.1	132.3	133.3	134.2	2.3	129.6	129.8	131.2	132.3	2.7
1998	135.0	135.2	136.8	137.8	2.7	133.1	133.5	135.1	136.0	2.8
1999	138.8	139.5	140.9	142.5	3.4	136.9	137.6	139.4	140.7	3.5
2000	143.7	144.2	145.9	147.2	3.3	141.5	142.1	143.9	145.1	3.1
2001	148.6	149.0	151.5	153.2	4.1	146.0	146.5	149.1	150.8	3.9
Service Occupations										
1987	90.2	90.7	92.2	92.9	4.3	91.7	92.1	93.5	93.9	3.6
1988	94.4	95.1	97.9	98.2	5.7	95.1	95.9	98.4	98.7	5.1
1989	99.2	100.0	102.8	103.6	5.5	99.3	100.0	102.4	102.9	4.3
1990	104.8	105.3	108.1	109.2	5.4	103.9	104.2	106.7	107.6	4.6
1991	111.0	111.3	113.4	114.0	4.4	109.3	110.1	112.0	112.7	4.7
1992	115.0	115.6	117.4	118.0	3.5	113.2	113.7	114.9	115.5	2.5
1993	119.1	119.7	121.4	122.1	3.5	116.3	117.1	118.3	118.9	2.9
1994	123.1	123.9	126.0	126.6	3.7	119.7	120.4	122.7	123.3	3.7
1995	127.6	128.8	130.1	131.0	3.5	124.6	125.2	126.6	127.3	3.2
1996	131.9	132.3	133.6	134.5	2.7	128.1	128.6	130.1	131.0	2.9
1997	135.6	135.6	137.0	137.8	2.5	132.4	132.4	134.2	135.2	3.2
1998	139.4	141.0	143.0	143.4	4.1	136.5	137.2	139.2	140.0	3.6
1999	144.3	145.3	146.7	148.6	3.6	141.1	142.1	144.1	145.7	4.1
2000	149.5	149.7	151.5	152.9	2.9	146.4	146.6	149.6	151.2	3.8
2001	155.3	156.5	159.0	160.5	5.0	152.8	153.7	156.1	157.4	4.1
WORKERS, BY INDUSTRY DIVISION										
Service Industries										
1987	89.0	89.2	91.7	92.5	4.4	90.3	90.5	93.0	93.8	4.2
1988	93.8	94.0	97.0	98.5	6.5	94.6	94.9	97.7	98.9	5.4
1989	99.5	100.0	103.8	104.7	6.3	99.6	100.0	103.6	104.3	5.5
1990	106.1	106.8	110.2	111.3	6.3	105.5	106.0	109.5	110.3	5.8
1991	112.4	112.6	114.8	115.3	3.6	111.3	111.5	113.7	114.1	3.4
1992	115.8	116.2	118.8	119.6	3.7	114.4	114.7	116.9	117.5	3.0
1993	120.0	120.2	122.2	122.6	2.5	118.1	118.2	120.3	120.6	2.6
1994	123.1	123.4	125.6	126.1	2.9	121.1	121.3	123.6	124.2	3.0
1995	126.7	127.1	129.2	129.6	2.8	124.9	125.1	127.6	128.2	3.2
1996	130.0	130.3	132.4	133.1	2.7	128.6	128.9	131.2	131.9	2.9
1997	133.2	133.3	135.4	136.0	2.2	132.1	132.2	134.7	135.3	2.6
1998	136.5	136.6	139.0	139.7	2.7	135.7	135.9	138.4	139.2	2.9
1999	140.0	140.5	143.2	144.5	3.4	139.5	139.9	142.9	144.0	3.4
2000	145.2	145.5	148.0	148.9	3.0	144.6	144.9	147.9	148.7	3.3
2001	149.9	150.6	154.4	154.9	4.0	149.5	150.2	153.7	154.2	3.7

See footnote at end of table.

Table 5-2. Employment Cost Index, State and Local Government Workers, Total Compensation and Wages and Salaries by Occupation and Industry, 1987–2001—Continued

(June 1989=100, not seasonally adjusted.)

Series and year	Total compensation					Wages and salaries				
	Indexes				Percent change for 12 months ended December	Indexes				Percent change for 12 months ended December
	March	June	September	December		March	June	September	December	
Service industries, excluding schools										
1987	89.8	90.3	91.4	92.2	3.7	91.5	92.0	93.2	93.9	3.6
1988	94.7	94.8	96.5	97.8	6.1	95.4	95.5	97.3	98.2	4.6
1989	99.1	100.0	102.5	103.2	5.5	99.1	100.0	102.5	103.0	4.9
1990	105.4	106.4	108.8	110.2	6.8	105.4	106.4	108.8	109.6	6.4
1991	112.2	111.7	113.7	114.4	3.8	111.4	111.4	113.5	114.2	4.2
1992	115.1	115.6	117.5	118.6	3.7	114.8	115.2	116.4	117.4	2.8
1993	119.6	120.0	121.4	121.9	2.8	118.4	118.7	120.1	120.4	2.6
1994	122.8	123.3	124.9	125.6	3.0	121.3	121.9	123.2	124.0	3.0
1995	126.4	127.7	128.9	129.4	3.0	125.0	125.5	126.9	127.4	2.7
1996	130.3	130.8	131.9	132.0	2.0	128.2	128.7	130.1	130.5	2.4
1997	132.5	132.9	134.4	135.3	2.5	131.2	131.6	133.3	134.4	3.0
1998	136.1	136.2	138.7	138.8	2.6	135.4	135.5	137.8	138.2	2.8
1999	139.6	140.3	142.6	143.8	3.6	139.0	139.6	142.1	143.2	3.6
2000	145.2	145.8	147.6	148.8	3.5	144.3	144.8	146.7	147.9	3.3
2001	150.1	151.9	154.5	156.1	4.9	149.1	150.7	153.2	154.9	4.7
Health services										
1987	89.5	90.1	92.0	93.0	4.7	89.9	90.5	92.3	93.2	4.4
1988	94.0	94.4	96.5	97.3	4.6	93.8	94.4	96.7	97.7	4.8
1989	98.8	100.0	103.1	104.2	7.1	98.9	100.0	102.7	103.7	6.1
1990	106.2	106.9	109.9	111.1	6.6	105.5	106.1	108.9	109.7	5.8
1991	112.6	112.2	113.9	114.9	3.4	111.1	111.7	113.0	114.0	3.9
1992	115.9	116.8	118.6	119.4	3.9	114.9	115.7	116.7	117.4	3.0
1993	120.2	120.7	122.2	123.1	3.1	118.1	118.8	120.4	121.0	3.1
1994	124.2	125.2	127.2	127.7	3.7	121.9	122.9	124.7	125.3	3.6
1995	128.4	129.8	131.0	131.6	3.1	126.0	126.6	127.9	128.6	2.6
1996	132.5	133.1	134.0	134.1	1.9	129.3	129.9	131.1	131.4	2.2
1997	134.5	134.9	136.0	137.2	2.3	132.1	132.6	133.9	135.3	3.0
1998	137.9	138.0	140.3	140.7	2.6	136.3	136.5	138.7	139.2	2.9
1999	141.2	142.0	144.2	145.8	3.6	139.7	140.4	142.8	144.2	3.6
2000	147.3	147.9	150.0	151.6	4.0	145.3	145.7	147.7	149.3	3.5
2001	152.1	154.4	157.1	158.6	4.6	149.9	151.9	154.2	155.8	4.4
Hospitals										
1988	94.0	94.8	97.0	97.6	. . .	94.0	94.8	97.0	97.9	. . .
1989	98.6	100.0	103.2	104.5	7.1	98.7	100.0	102.9	103.8	6.0
1990	106.0	107.0	109.8	111.4	6.6	105.0	105.9	108.6	109.8	5.8
1991	112.2	112.1	114.1	115.2	3.4	110.7	111.3	112.9	114.1	3.9
1992	115.9	116.7	118.6	119.4	3.6	114.5	115.2	116.5	117.1	2.6
1993	120.0	120.4	122.0	123.3	3.3	117.6	118.2	119.9	120.7	3.1
1994	123.7	124.5	127.0	127.7	3.6	121.2	122.0	124.2	125.1	3.6
1995	128.4	129.9	131.1	131.7	3.1	125.8	126.3	127.6	128.4	2.6
1996	132.6	133.2	134.2	134.3	2.0	129.1	129.7	130.9	131.3	2.3
1997	134.8	135.2	136.3	137.6	2.5	131.9	132.4	133.7	135.2	3.0
1998	138.4	138.4	140.7	141.2	2.6	136.3	136.5	138.6	139.1	2.9
1999	141.7	142.7	144.8	146.3	3.6	139.7	140.6	142.8	144.1	3.6
2000	147.9	148.4	150.7	152.0	3.9	145.3	145.6	147.7	149.2	3.5
2001	152.2	154.7	157.4	159.1	4.7	149.5	151.8	154.2	155.7	4.4
Educational services										
1989	99.5	100.0	104.1	104.9	. . .	99.6	100.0	103.8	104.5	. . .
1990	106.2	106.8	110.3	111.4	6.2	105.5	106.0	109.7	110.5	5.7
1991	112.4	112.6	114.9	115.3	3.5	111.3	111.5	113.8	114.1	3.3
1992	115.7	116.1	118.9	119.7	3.8	114.3	114.6	116.9	117.6	3.1
1993	120.0	120.1	122.3	122.7	2.5	118.0	118.1	120.3	120.6	2.6
1994	122.9	123.1	125.5	126.0	2.7	120.9	121.1	123.6	124.2	3.0
1995	126.5	126.8	129.0	129.4	2.7	124.8	124.9	127.7	128.3	3.3
1996	129.7	130.0	132.3	133.0	2.8	128.5	128.8	131.3	132.0	2.9
1997	133.1	133.2	135.4	135.9	2.2	132.1	132.2	134.8	135.3	2.5
1998	136.3	136.5	138.8	139.6	2.7	135.7	135.8	138.4	139.3	3.0
1999	139.9	140.3	143.1	144.4	3.4	139.5	139.8	142.9	144.0	3.4
2000	145.0	145.2	147.9	148.7	3.0	144.5	144.8	148.0	148.7	3.3
2001	149.6	150.1	154.1	154.5	3.9	149.5	150.0	153.6	154.0	3.6

See footnote at end of table.

Table 5-2. Employment Cost Index, State and Local Government Workers, Total Compensation and Wages and Salaries by Occupation and Industry, 1987–2001—*Continued*

(June 1989=100, not seasonally adjusted.)

Series and year	Total compensation					Wages and salaries				
	Indexes				Percent change for 12 months ended December	Indexes				Percent change for 12 months ended December
	March	June	September	December		March	June	September	December	
Schools										
1987	88.7	88.9	91.8	92.7	4.9	90.0	90.0	92.9	93.9	4.7
1988	93.4	93.7	97.2	98.7	6.5	94.4	94.6	97.7	99.1	5.5
1989	99.6	100.0	104.4	105.3	6.7	99.7	100.0	104.0	104.7	5.7
1990	106.4	106.9	110.6	111.6	6.0	105.5	105.9	109.7	110.5	5.5
1991	112.5	112.9	115.2	115.6	3.6	111.2	111.5	113.7	114.0	3.2
1992	116.0	116.4	119.2	119.9	3.7	114.3	114.6	117.0	117.5	3.1
1993	120.2	120.3	122.5	122.9	2.5	117.9	118.0	120.3	120.7	2.7
1994	123.2	123.4	125.9	126.3	2.8	121.0	121.2	123.8	124.3	3.0
1995	126.8	127.1	129.4	129.8	2.8	125.0	125.1	127.8	128.4	3.3
1996	130.0	130.3	132.6	133.4	2.8	128.7	128.9	131.4	132.2	3.0
1997	133.4	133.5	135.7	136.2	2.1	132.2	132.3	134.9	135.5	2.5
1998	136.6	136.7	139.1	139.9	2.7	135.8	136.0	138.5	139.5	3.0
1999	140.2	140.6	143.5	144.7	3.4	139.6	140.0	143.1	144.2	3.4
2000	145.3	145.5	148.2	149.0	3.0	144.7	144.9	148.1	148.9	3.3
2001	149.9	150.5	154.4	154.8	3.9	149.7	150.2	153.8	154.1	3.5
Elementary and secondary schools										
1987	88.6	88.7	92.1	92.9	5.0	89.7	89.8	93.1	93.9	4.7
1988	93.5	93.8	97.4	99.1	6.7	94.3	94.5	97.8	99.3	5.8
1989	99.6	100.0	104.6	105.5	6.5	99.7	100.0	104.2	104.9	5.6
1990	106.5	107.1	111.1	112.1	6.3	105.5	105.9	110.1	110.9	5.7
1991	112.9	113.0	115.7	116.2	3.7	111.6	111.7	114.3	114.7	3.4
1992	116.6	117.1	119.9	120.7	3.9	114.9	115.3	117.9	118.5	3.3
1993	120.7	120.8	123.0	123.6	2.4	118.7	118.8	121.1	121.6	2.6
1994	123.7	123.8	126.3	126.5	2.3	121.7	121.8	124.5	124.9	2.7
1995	127.1	127.4	129.8	130.1	2.8	125.5	125.8	128.7	129.2	3.4
1996	130.2	130.5	132.6	133.1	2.3	129.3	129.5	132.0	132.4	2.5
1997	133.1	133.3	135.5	135.8	2.0	132.4	132.6	135.3	135.7	2.5
1998	136.1	136.2	138.8	139.3	2.6	136.0	136.1	138.7	139.3	2.7
1999	139.6	140.0	142.9	144.1	3.4	139.5	139.9	143.1	144.1	3.4
2000	144.5	144.7	147.3	148.1	2.8	144.5	144.6	147.9	148.5	3.1
2001	148.5	149.0	152.8	153.1	3.4	149.0	149.5	152.8	153.1	3.1
Colleges and universities										
1989	99.6	100.0	103.4	104.7	...	99.6	100.0	102.9	104.1	...
1990	106.1	106.3	109.2	110.2	5.3	105.6	105.9	108.4	109.2	4.9
1991	111.3	112.5	113.4	113.5	3.0	110.2	111.0	112.0	112.0	2.6
1992	114.0	114.1	116.9	117.2	3.3	112.3	112.3	114.1	114.3	2.1
1993	118.4	118.5	120.8	120.7	3.0	115.5	115.6	117.8	117.7	3.0
1994	121.5	122.0	124.5	125.5	4.0	118.6	119.2	121.5	122.5	4.1
1995	126.0	126.1	128.0	128.7	2.5	123.2	122.9	125.0	125.9	2.8
1996	129.4	129.9	132.5	134.0	4.1	126.8	127.1	129.8	131.2	4.2
1997	134.3	134.1	136.3	137.2	2.4	131.5	131.4	133.6	134.6	2.6
1998	137.9	138.1	140.1	141.5	3.1	135.2	135.5	137.7	139.6	3.7
1999	141.7	142.1	144.8	146.5	3.5	139.6	139.8	142.6	144.4	3.4
2000	147.4	147.6	150.5	151.7	3.5	144.9	145.6	148.3	149.5	3.5
2001	153.7	154.3	159.0	159.6	5.2	151.4	151.8	156.5	156.7	4.8
Public Administration [1]										
1987	91.3	91.6	92.7	93.8	4.6	92.6	92.9	93.9	94.7	4.1
1988	95.2	95.8	97.5	97.8	4.3	95.8	96.4	98.1	98.4	3.9
1989	99.2	100.0	102.5	103.2	5.5	99.4	100.0	102.1	102.8	4.5
1990	105.1	105.5	107.8	108.7	5.3	104.3	104.6	106.5	107.3	4.4
1991	110.8	110.9	112.2	112.6	3.6	109.1	109.5	110.6	110.9	3.4
1992	114.0	114.6	115.8	116.3	3.3	111.9	112.4	113.1	113.6	2.4
1993	117.6	118.0	119.3	120.0	3.2	114.4	114.9	115.9	116.6	2.6
1994	121.5	122.2	123.7	124.2	3.5	117.9	118.5	119.9	120.6	3.4
1995	125.4	126.1	127.4	128.3	3.3	121.9	122.3	123.2	124.1	2.9
1996	129.2	129.6	130.7	131.8	2.7	124.9	125.3	126.6	127.7	2.9
1997	133.0	133.0	134.1	135.1	2.5	128.9	129.0	130.3	131.4	2.9
1998	136.4	137.4	138.9	139.9	3.6	132.7	133.2	134.8	135.9	3.4
1999	140.8	141.5	142.4	144.4	3.2	136.9	137.8	139.5	141.5	4.1
2000	145.7	146.1	146.9	148.3	2.7	142.5	142.9	144.6	146.1	3.3
2001	150.6	151.9	153.8	155.2	4.7	147.6	148.7	150.3	151.6	3.8

1. Includes executive, legislative, judicial, administrative, and regulatory activities of state and local governments, SICs 91 through 96.

Table 5-3. Employment Cost Index, Benefits, by Occupation, Industry, and Bargaining Status, 1987–2001

(June 1989=100, not seasonally adjusted.)

Series and year	Indexes				Percent change for 12 months ended December
	March	June	September	December	
CIVILIAN WORKERS [1]					
1987	88.0	88.6	89.6	90.5	3.7
1988	93.2	94.3	95.7	96.8	7.0
1989	98.6	100.0	101.9	103.2	6.6
1990	105.9	107.2	108.9	110.1	6.7
1991	112.2	113.6	115.4	116.3	5.6
1992	118.6	119.6	121.4	122.5	5.3
1993	125.0	126.2	127.4	128.1	4.6
1994	130.1	131.0	132.3	132.5	3.4
1995	133.8	134.5	135.2	135.5	2.3
1996	136.2	136.9	137.7	138.2	2.0
1997	138.9	139.6	140.3	141.1	2.1
1998	142.0	143.0	144.0	144.7	2.6
1999	145.3	146.6	147.9	149.5	3.3
2000	152.6	154.3	155.8	156.9	4.9
2001	159.7	161.3	163.7	165.1	5.2
PRIVATE INDUSTRY [2]					
1987	88.2	89.0	89.6	90.5	3.4
1988	93.4	94.7	95.7	96.7	6.9
1989	98.4	100.0	101.4	102.6	6.1
1990	105.5	106.9	108.3	109.4	6.6
1991	111.6	113.5	115.2	116.2	6.2
1992	118.6	119.7	121.2	122.2	5.2
1993	125.2	126.7	127.7	128.3	5.0
1994	130.7	131.7	132.8	133.0	3.7
1995	134.5	135.1	135.6	135.9	2.2
1996	136.6	137.4	138.1	138.6	2.0
1997	139.4	140.1	140.8	141.8	2.3
1998	142.6	143.7	144.5	145.2	2.4
1999	145.8	147.3	148.6	150.2	3.4
2000	153.8	155.7	157.5	158.6	5.6
2001	161.5	163.2	165.2	166.7	5.1
White-collar occupations					
1987	88.2	88.9	89.7	90.5	3.7
1988	92.8	94.0	95.0	96.2	6.3
1989	98.3	100.0	101.4	102.6	6.7
1990	105.6	107.1	108.6	109.7	6.9
1991	112.1	113.8	115.3	116.4	6.1
1992	118.4	119.4	121.0	122.0	4.8
1993	124.7	125.9	126.8	127.6	4.6
1994	130.5	131.6	132.8	133.3	4.5
1995	135.2	136.0	136.6	136.7	2.6
1996	137.7	138.4	139.5	139.7	2.2
1997	140.8	141.5	142.0	143.4	2.6
1998	144.7	145.6	146.6	147.4	2.8
1999	147.9	149.4	151.0	152.5	3.5
2000	156.3	158.5	160.4	161.5	5.9
2001	165.2	167.4	169.5	171.2	6.0
Blue-collar occupations					
1987	88.2	89.1	89.8	90.7	3.4
1988	94.2	95.7	96.5	97.4	7.4
1989	98.6	100.0	101.4	102.6	5.3
1990	105.2	106.6	107.9	109.0	6.2
1991	111.0	112.8	114.9	115.7	6.1
1992	118.7	119.7	121.2	122.2	5.6
1993	125.5	127.3	128.4	128.9	5.5
1994	130.5	131.5	132.7	132.5	2.8
1995	133.3	133.6	134.1	134.7	1.7
1996	135.2	136.1	136.2	137.0	1.7
1997	137.2	138.0	138.8	139.0	1.5
1998	139.1	140.4	141.0	141.6	1.9
1999	142.2	143.6	144.8	146.2	3.2
2000	150.0	151.6	153.1	154.1	5.4
2001	155.7	156.2	158.3	159.2	3.3

See footnotes at end of table.

Table 5-3. Employment Cost Index, Benefits, by Occupation, Industry, and Bargaining Status, 1987–2001—*Continued*

(June 1989=100, not seasonally adjusted.)

Series and year	Indexes				Percent change for 12 months ended December
	March	June	September	December	
Service occupations					
1987	88.2	88.4	88.7	89.7	2.4
1988	92.1	93.4	95.1	96.8	7.9
1989	98.7	100.0	101.6	103.0	6.4
1990	106.0	107.0	108.1	109.9	6.7
1991	112.3	114.5	116.5	117.8	7.2
1992	120.0	121.6	123.7	124.6	5.8
1993	127.7	129.3	130.5	131.5	5.5
1994	132.9	133.1	134.2	134.7	2.4
1995	135.0	135.6	135.7	136.0	1.0
1996	135.7	136.3	136.2	137.4	1.0
1997	138.3	139.6	141.4	142.0	3.3
1998	143.3	143.7	144.7	144.8	2.0
1999	146.3	147.6	148.4	149.9	3.5
2000	150.8	152.7	154.4	156.4	4.3
2001	159.5	161.1	163.2	166.0	6.1
Goods-Producing Industries [3]					
1987	88.7	89.4	90.0	90.9	2.9
1988	94.4	95.7	96.5	97.3	7.0
1989	98.7	100.0	101.5	102.6	5.4
1990	105.7	107.2	108.7	109.9	7.1
1991	111.9	113.9	115.8	116.7	6.2
1992	119.7	120.6	122.3	123.4	5.7
1993	127.3	129.0	130.0	130.3	5.6
1994	132.7	133.9	134.8	134.8	3.5
1995	135.9	135.9	136.2	137.1	1.7
1996	137.7	138.6	138.8	139.7	1.9
1997	139.9	140.9	141.5	141.5	1.3
1998	141.5	142.5	143.0	143.2	1.2
1999	144.3	145.2	146.3	148.2	3.4
2000	152.3	154.2	155.7	156.2	5.4
2001	158.5	159.6	160.8	162.6	4.1
Manufacturing					
1987	87.5	88.2	88.8	89.8	2.6
1988	93.7	94.9	95.8	96.6	7.6
1989	98.8	100.0	101.6	102.3	5.9
1990	105.5	106.9	108.4	109.5	7.0
1991	111.2	113.3	115.3	116.1	6.0
1992	119.3	120.1	121.5	122.6	5.6
1993	126.8	128.6	129.7	130.0	6.0
1994	132.0	133.0	133.9	134.3	3.3
1995	135.4	135.2	135.5	136.7	1.8
1996	137.5	138.5	138.8	139.8	2.3
1997	139.9	141.0	141.4	141.7	1.4
1998	141.7	142.4	142.6	142.7	0.7
1999	143.6	144.5	145.7	147.8	3.4
2000	152.3	153.9	154.9	154.8	4.7
2001	157.1	157.9	158.5	160.4	3.6
Aircraft manufacturing (SIC 3721)					
1988	. . .	. . .	. . .	99.0	. . .
1989	99.1	100.0	102.0	106.5	7.6
1990	110.1	111.4	114.5	111.9	5.1
1991	114.2	116.0	117.7	119.7	7.0
1992	124.1	127.3	128.9	135.1	12.9
1993	137.6	137.0	140.1	133.1	-1.5
1994	134.4	135.3	138.7	138.4	4.0
1995	141.0	140.8	140.5	146.1	5.6
1996	154.2	155.4	154.8	151.6	3.8
1997	148.6	148.8	147.6	143.0	-5.7
1998	141.7	143.1	143.8	145.3	1.6
1999	142.6	144.3	145.6	153.9	5.9
2000	161.9	166.6	168.7	163.1	6.0
2001	171.4	171.7	168.2	174.4	6.9

See footnotes at end of table.

Table 5-3. Employment Cost Index, Benefits, by Occupation, Industry, and Bargaining Status, 1987–2001—*Continued*

(June 1989=100, not seasonally adjusted.)

Series and year	Indexes				Percent change for 12 months ended December
	March	June	September	December	
Aircraft manufacturing (SIC 3721), white-collar occupations					
1988	. . .	. . .	. . .	99.1	. . .
1989	98.9	100.0	101.7	105.7	6.7
1990	109.9	110.9	114.3	111.2	5.2
1991	113.1	115.1	116.4	119.2	7.2
1992	124.0	127.5	128.4	133.0	11.6
1993	136.2	135.4	138.7	132.5	-0.4
1994	133.5	134.7	138.0	137.3	3.6
1995	140.1	140.2	139.9	142.5	3.8
1996	152.0	152.9	152.1	150.9	5.9
1997	146.8	147.3	146.8	144.8	-4.0
1998	142.9	145.0	145.5	143.9	-0.6
1999	141.3	142.7	142.9	147.6	2.6
2000	156.8	163.6	165.4	162.8	10.3
2001	175.0	174.2	168.9	175.0	7.5
Aircraft manufacturing (SIC 3721), blue-collar occupations					
1988	. . .	. . .	. . .	98.8	. . .
1989	99.2	100.0	102.3	107.4	8.7
1990	110.5	112.2	114.6	112.8	5.0
1991	115.5	117.1	119.3	120.4	6.7
1992	124.2	127.2	129.5	137.7	14.4
1993	139.3	139.0	141.9	133.5	-3.1
1994	135.0	135.6	139.0	139.2	4.3
1995	141.6	140.9	140.6	150.8	8.3
1996	156.7	158.4	158.4	152.2	0.9
1997	150.9	150.4	148.2	139.6	-8.3
1998	139.0	139.5	140.7	146.6	5.0
1999	144.2	146.3	149.5	163.0	11.2
2000	169.2	170.5	173.3	162.7	-0.2
2001	165.0	166.7	166.1	172.4	6.0
Service-Producing Industries [4]					
1987	87.8	88.6	89.4	90.2	3.9
1988	92.5	93.8	94.9	96.1	6.5
1989	98.2	100.0	101.4	102.6	6.8
1990	105.3	106.6	107.9	109.0	6.2
1991	111.4	113.0	114.6	115.7	6.1
1992	117.7	118.8	120.4	121.2	4.8
1993	123.4	124.6	125.7	126.7	4.5
1994	128.9	129.7	131.2	131.5	3.8
1995	133.2	134.1	134.8	134.7	2.4
1996	135.5	136.2	137.2	137.4	2.0
1997	138.5	139.2	139.8	141.4	2.9
1998	142.7	143.8	144.9	145.7	3.0
1999	146.1	147.9	149.4	150.7	3.4
2000	154.0	156.0	157.9	159.4	5.8
2001	162.6	164.6	167.1	168.4	5.6
Nonmanufacturing Industries					
1987	88.7	89.5	90.3	91.0	4.0
1988	93.2	94.5	95.5	96.8	6.4
1989	98.2	100.0	101.4	102.8	6.2
1990	105.4	106.9	108.2	109.3	6.3
1991	111.9	113.5	115.1	116.2	6.3
1992	118.2	119.4	121.0	122.0	5.0
1993	124.2	125.5	126.5	127.4	4.4
1994	129.9	130.8	132.2	132.3	3.8
1995	133.9	134.7	135.4	135.3	2.3
1996	136.0	136.7	137.5	137.9	1.9
1997	138.9	139.5	140.2	141.5	2.6
1998	142.7	143.9	145.0	145.8	3.0
1999	146.3	148.0	149.4	150.7	3.4
2000	154.0	156.1	158.1	159.7	6.0
2001	162.9	164.9	167.4	168.8	5.7

See footnotes at end of table.

Table 5-3. Employment Cost Index, Benefits, by Occupation, Industry, and Bargaining Status, 1987–2001—Continued

(June 1989=100, not seasonally adjusted.)

Series and year	Indexes				Percent change for 12 months ended December
	March	June	September	December	
Union Workers					
1987	89.0	89.7	90.2	91.1	3.2
1988	94.9	96.1	96.9	97.5	7.0
1989	98.6	100.0	101.3	102.1	4.7
1990	104.6	105.6	106.7	108.2	6.0
1991	110.1	112.1	113.9	115.2	6.5
1992	119.2	120.0	121.7	122.5	6.3
1993	126.6	128.5	129.7	130.6	6.6
1994	131.9	132.9	133.3	133.7	2.4
1995	134.8	135.5	136.6	138.0	3.2
1996	139.1	140.0	139.9	140.7	2.0
1997	140.2	140.9	142.2	142.0	0.9
1998	142.1	143.8	145.0	145.5	2.5
1999	145.8	146.9	148.3	149.7	2.8
2000	153.7	155.5	157.4	157.5	5.2
2001	158.5	160.1	161.9	163.4	3.7
Nonunion Workers					
1987	88.0	88.7	89.5	90.3	3.7
1988	92.6	94.0	95.1	96.3	6.6
1989	98.4	100.0	101.5	102.9	6.9
1990	105.8	107.4	108.9	109.9	6.8
1991	112.3	114.0	115.7	116.6	6.1
1992	118.4	119.5	121.0	122.1	4.7
1993	124.6	125.9	126.9	127.4	4.3
1994	130.1	131.1	132.6	132.7	4.2
1995	134.2	134.8	135.2	135.1	1.8
1996	135.8	136.5	137.4	137.8	2.0
1997	138.9	139.7	140.2	141.5	2.7
1998	142.5	143.4	144.2	144.9	2.4
1999	145.6	147.1	148.5	150.0	3.5
2000	153.6	155.5	157.3	158.6	5.7
2001	162.0	163.7	165.8	167.2	5.4
STATE AND LOCAL GOVERNMENT					
1989	. . .	100.0	103.9	105.3	. . .
1990	107.5	108.3	111.3	112.7	7.0
1991	114.6	114.4	116.4	117.1	3.9
1992	118.5	119.3	122.3	123.4	5.4
1993	124.2	124.5	126.2	127.0	2.9
1994	127.9	128.5	130.3	130.5	2.8
1995	131.1	132.2	133.6	133.9	2.6
1996	134.7	135.1	136.1	136.8	2.2
1997	137.4	137.4	138.2	138.6	1.3
1998	139.7	140.3	142.1	142.7	3.0
1999	143.6	144.0	145.0	146.7	2.8
2000	148.2	148.5	149.0	150.2	2.4
2001	152.3	153.5	157.3	158.4	5.5

1. Includes private industry and state and local government workers and excludes farm, household, and federal government workers.
2. Excludes farm and household workers.
3. Includes mining, construction, and manufacturing.
4. Includes transportation, communication, and public utilities; wholesale and retail trade; finance, insurance, and real estate; and service industries.

Table 5-4. Employment Cost Index, Private Industry Workers[1], Total Compensation and Wages and Salaries by Bargaining Status, Industry, Region[2], and Area Size, 1987–2001

(June 1989=100, not seasonally adjusted.)

Series and year	Total compensation					Wages and salaries				
	Indexes				Percent change for 12 months ended December	Indexes				Percent change for 12 months ended December
	March	June	September	December		March	June	September	December	
UNION WORKERS, TOTAL										
1987	92.5	93.0	93.6	94.5	2.7	94.3	94.8	95.3	96.4	2.7
1988	96.1	97.0	97.7	98.2	3.9	96.8	97.5	98.2	98.5	2.2
1989	99.0	100.0	100.9	101.8	3.7	99.2	100.0	100.6	101.6	3.1
1990	103.3	104.1	105.1	106.2	4.3	102.6	103.3	104.2	105.1	3.4
1991	107.5	108.8	110.1	111.1	4.6	106.2	107.1	108.0	108.9	3.6
1992	113.1	114.0	115.2	115.9	4.3	109.8	110.8	111.7	112.3	3.1
1993	117.8	119.1	120.0	120.9	4.3	113.1	113.9	114.8	115.7	3.0
1994	121.9	123.0	123.8	124.2	2.7	116.5	117.6	118.6	119.1	2.9
1995	125.1	125.8	126.8	127.7	2.8	119.8	120.6	121.5	122.2	2.6
1996	128.5	129.7	130.1	130.8	2.4	122.8	124.2	124.8	125.4	2.6
1997	131.0	131.8	133.2	133.5	2.1	126.0	126.9	128.3	128.9	2.8
1998	134.0	135.3	136.8	137.5	3.0	129.6	130.7	132.4	133.1	3.3
1999	138.0	139.0	140.2	141.2	2.7	133.6	134.7	135.7	136.5	2.6
2000	143.0	144.4	146.1	146.9	4.0	137.2	138.5	140.0	141.2	3.4
2001	147.9	149.5	151.0	153.1	4.2	142.1	143.7	145.1	147.4	4.4
Union workers, blue-collar occupations										
1987	...	92.7	93.2	94.2	...	...	94.5	95.0	96.2	...
1988	96.1	97.0	97.6	98.3	4.4	96.5	97.2	97.8	98.4	2.3
1989	98.9	100.0	100.9	101.7	3.5	99.1	100.0	100.7	101.5	3.2
1990	103.0	104.1	104.8	105.9	4.1	102.2	103.2	103.8	104.8	3.3
1991	107.4	108.6	109.7	110.7	4.5	105.8	106.7	107.3	108.2	3.2
1992	112.9	113.8	114.8	115.5	4.3	109.1	109.9	110.8	111.3	2.9
1993	117.4	118.7	119.7	120.6	4.4	112.0	112.8	113.7	114.5	2.9
1994	121.2	122.4	123.1	123.4	2.3	115.1	116.2	117.3	117.6	2.7
1995	124.0	124.8	125.7	126.3	2.4	118.2	119.1	120.0	120.3	2.3
1996	126.8	128.0	128.3	128.9	2.1	120.9	122.0	122.8	123.4	2.6
1997	128.9	129.9	131.2	131.6	2.1	123.6	124.7	126.0	126.7	2.7
1998	131.8	133.3	134.6	135.3	2.8	127.2	128.5	129.9	130.6	3.1
1999	135.6	136.7	137.8	138.9	2.7	131.2	132.5	133.6	134.5	3.0
2000	141.1	142.5	144.3	145.0	4.4	135.2	136.5	138.2	139.2	3.5
2001	145.9	147.2	148.7	150.0	3.4	140.3	141.8	143.3	144.7	4.0
Union workers, goods-producing industries [3]										
1987	91.8	92.3	92.9	94.2	3.0	93.7	94.3	94.8	96.3	2.9
1988	96.2	97.1	97.7	98.4	4.5	96.5	97.2	97.8	98.4	2.2
1989	98.9	100.0	100.9	101.9	3.6	99.0	100.0	100.6	101.6	3.3
1990	103.3	104.5	105.1	106.3	4.3	102.3	103.5	104.0	105.0	3.3
1991	107.9	109.2	110.3	111.3	4.7	106.2	107.1	107.7	108.7	3.5
1992	114.0	114.6	115.7	116.4	4.6	109.6	110.2	111.1	111.7	2.8
1993	118.7	120.0	121.0	121.9	4.7	112.2	113.0	113.8	114.8	2.8
1994	122.5	123.8	124.4	124.7	2.3	115.4	116.7	117.5	117.9	2.7
1995	125.2	125.9	126.7	127.5	2.2	118.4	119.3	120.2	120.6	2.3
1996	127.9	129.0	129.2	129.8	1.8	121.3	122.5	123.2	123.6	2.5
1997	130.0	131.2	132.3	132.5	2.1	124.1	125.4	126.6	127.1	2.8
1998	132.7	134.3	135.6	136.5	3.0	127.9	129.4	131.0	131.7	3.6
1999	136.8	138.2	139.2	140.8	3.2	132.3	133.8	134.9	136.1	3.3
2000	143.3	144.8	146.8	147.3	4.6	137.2	138.4	140.2	141.3	3.8
2001	147.9	149.3	150.6	151.8	3.1	142.4	144.2	145.3	146.3	3.5
Union workers, service-producing industries [4]										
1987	93.4	94.0	94.4	95.0	2.5	95.2	95.5	96.0	96.5	2.0
1988	95.9	96.9	97.6	97.9	3.1	97.1	97.8	98.8	98.8	2.4
1989	99.1	100.0	100.8	101.7	3.9	99.6	100.0	100.7	101.7	2.9
1990	103.2	103.6	104.9	106.0	4.2	102.9	103.1	104.4	105.2	3.4
1991	107.1	108.3	109.8	110.9	4.6	106.1	107.0	108.4	109.2	3.8
1992	111.9	113.2	114.6	115.2	3.9	110.1	111.5	112.5	113.1	3.6
1993	116.7	117.7	118.6	119.6	3.8	114.2	115.1	116.0	116.8	3.3
1994	121.0	121.8	122.9	123.6	3.3	118.0	118.7	120.1	120.6	3.3
1995	124.8	125.6	126.8	127.9	3.5	121.6	122.3	123.2	124.2	3.0
1996	129.0	130.3	131.0	131.7	3.0	124.8	126.2	126.8	127.6	2.7
1997	131.9	132.4	134.0	134.5	2.1	128.2	128.8	130.4	131.2	2.8
1998	135.3	136.2	138.0	138.5	3.0	131.8	132.2	134.1	134.8	2.7
1999	139.2	139.7	141.0	141.4	2.1	135.4	135.8	136.8	137.2	1.8
2000	142.5	143.9	145.2	146.4	3.5	137.6	138.9	140.1	141.5	3.1
2001	147.6	149.5	151.2	154.2	5.3	142.2	143.7	145.4	148.9	5.2

See footnotes at end of table.

Table 5-4. Employment Cost Index, Private Industry Workers[1], Total Compensation and Wages and Salaries by Bargaining Status, Industry, Region[2], and Area Size, 1987–2001—*Continued*

(June 1989=100, not seasonally adjusted.)

Series and year	Total compensation					Wages and salaries				
	Indexes				Percent change for 12 months ended December	Indexes				Percent change for 12 months ended December
	March	June	September	December		March	June	September	December	
Union workers, manufacturing industries										
1987	90.6	91.1	91.6	93.1	2.9	93.5	93.9	94.5	96.2	3.0
1988	95.5	96.4	97.0	97.8	5.0	96.4	97.0	97.5	98.3	2.2
1989	99.0	100.0	100.8	102.0	4.3	99.0	100.0	100.5	101.7	3.5
1990	103.6	104.7	105.3	106.6	4.5	102.6	103.8	104.3	105.5	3.7
1991	108.1	109.5	110.6	111.7	4.8	106.7	107.5	108.3	109.4	3.7
1992	114.8	115.2	116.1	116.9	4.7	110.4	110.9	111.7	112.5	2.8
1993	119.8	121.1	121.9	123.0	5.2	113.2	113.9	114.6	115.9	3.0
1994	123.6	124.8	125.3	125.8	2.3	116.6	117.8	118.5	119.2	2.8
1995	126.3	126.6	127.1	128.1	1.8	119.8	120.5	121.3	122.0	2.3
1996	128.8	129.8	129.8	130.6	2.0	122.9	123.9	124.5	125.2	2.6
1997	130.8	131.7	133.0	133.3	2.1	125.6	126.5	127.8	128.6	2.7
1998	133.6	134.6	136.0	136.9	2.7	129.6	130.4	132.2	133.0	3.4
1999	137.0	138.1	139.1	141.0	3.0	133.6	134.7	135.8	137.5	3.4
2000	144.5	145.4	147.1	147.4	4.5	138.8	139.7	141.4	142.6	3.7
2001	147.9	148.8	149.9	151.4	2.7	143.9	145.5	146.7	148.0	3.8
Union workers, manufacturing, blue-collar occupations										
1987	...	90.9	91.5	93.0	...	...	93.8	94.4	96.2	...
1988	95.5	96.4	96.9	97.8	5.2	96.4	97.0	97.5	98.3	2.2
1989	99.0	100.0	100.9	101.9	4.2	99.0	100.0	100.6	101.8	3.6
1990	103.5	104.6	105.1	106.5	4.5	102.6	103.8	104.2	105.4	3.5
1991	108.1	109.4	110.6	111.6	4.8	106.6	107.5	108.2	109.3	3.7
1992	114.7	115.1	116.0	116.8	4.7	110.3	110.8	111.6	112.4	2.8
1993	119.6	121.0	121.8	122.9	5.2	113.1	113.8	114.4	115.7	2.9
1994	123.5	124.6	125.1	125.6	2.2	116.4	117.6	118.3	118.9	2.8
1995	126.1	126.4	126.8	127.8	1.8	119.5	120.2	121.0	121.6	2.3
1996	128.3	129.4	129.5	130.1	1.8	122.4	123.5	124.2	125.0	2.8
1997	130.5	131.4	132.6	133.0	2.2	125.4	126.2	127.6	128.4	2.7
1998	133.1	134.2	135.5	136.4	2.6	129.0	130.0	131.4	132.4	3.1
1999	136.5	137.5	138.5	140.4	2.9	133.0	134.1	135.1	136.8	3.3
2000	143.9	144.8	146.5	147.0	4.7	137.8	138.7	140.4	141.7	3.6
2001	147.3	148.1	149.4	150.9	2.7	143.0	144.3	145.8	147.0	3.7
Union workers, nonmanufacturing industries										
1987	94.0	94.7	95.2	95.8	2.7	95.1	95.5	96.0	96.5	2.1
1988	96.6	97.5	98.3	98.5	2.8	97.0	97.9	98.8	98.8	2.4
1989	98.9	100.0	100.8	101.6	3.1	99.4	100.0	100.7	101.5	2.7
1990	103.0	103.7	104.9	105.9	4.2	102.5	103.0	104.1	104.8	3.3
1991	107.1	108.3	109.7	110.6	4.4	105.8	106.7	107.9	108.6	3.6
1992	111.8	113.1	114.5	115.1	4.1	109.4	110.7	111.7	112.2	3.3
1993	116.3	117.4	118.5	119.3	3.6	113.0	113.9	114.9	115.5	2.9
1994	120.5	121.5	122.6	123.0	3.1	116.4	117.3	118.6	119.0	3.0
1995	124.0	125.0	126.2	127.1	3.3	119.9	120.6	121.6	122.3	2.8
1996	128.0	129.2	129.9	130.4	2.6	122.8	124.3	124.9	125.5	2.6
1997	130.6	131.5	132.9	133.2	2.1	126.1	127.1	128.6	129.1	2.9
1998	133.9	135.3	136.9	137.4	3.2	129.6	130.8	132.4	133.1	3.1
1999	138.1	139.2	140.3	140.8	2.5	133.7	134.6	135.6	135.9	2.1
2000	141.7	143.4	145.0	146.2	3.8	136.4	137.8	139.2	140.4	3.3
2001	147.3	149.4	151.1	153.5	5.0	141.1	142.7	144.3	147.1	4.8
NONUNION WORKERS, TOTAL										
1987	90.5	91.1	92.1	92.7	3.7	91.3	92.0	93.0	93.5	3.7
1988	94.0	95.3	96.3	97.4	5.1	94.5	95.6	96.6	97.7	4.5
1989	98.8	100.0	101.4	102.4	5.1	99.0	100.0	101.3	102.1	4.5
1990	104.1	105.5	106.6	107.3	4.8	103.4	104.8	105.8	106.4	4.2
1991	108.8	110.1	111.2	111.9	4.3	107.6	108.7	109.7	110.3	3.7
1992	113.1	113.8	114.7	115.5	3.2	111.2	111.8	112.4	113.1	2.5
1993	116.8	117.7	118.8	119.5	3.5	114.1	114.8	115.9	116.6	3.1
1994	120.7	121.7	122.7	123.2	3.1	117.4	118.3	119.2	119.8	2.7
1995	124.3	125.2	126.0	126.5	2.7	120.8	121.8	122.6	123.3	2.9
1996	127.7	128.7	129.7	130.4	3.1	124.8	125.9	126.9	127.7	3.6
1997	131.8	132.8	133.9	135.3	3.8	129.1	130.3	131.6	133.0	4.2
1998	136.7	137.8	139.3	140.1	3.5	134.5	135.7	137.4	138.3	4.0
1999	140.8	142.5	143.8	145.2	3.6	139.0	140.7	142.0	143.3	3.6
2000	147.4	149.1	150.6	151.6	4.4	145.1	146.7	148.1	149.0	4.0
2001	153.8	155.3	156.7	157.8	4.1	150.8	152.2	153.4	154.4	3.6

See footnotes at end of table.

Table 5-4. Employment Cost Index, Private Industry Workers [1], Total Compensation and Wages and Salaries by Bargaining Status, Industry, Region [2], and Area Size, 1987–2001—*Continued*

(June 1989=100, not seasonally adjusted.)

Series and year	Total compensation					Wages and salaries				
	Indexes				Percent change for 12 months ended December	Indexes				Percent change for 12 months ended December
	March	June	September	December		March	June	September	December	
Nonunion workers, blue-collar occupations										
1987	...	91.6	92.6	93.3	...	...	92.6	93.7	94.2	...
1988	94.6	96.0	96.6	97.5	4.5	95.3	96.4	97.0	97.8	3.8
1989	98.7	100.0	101.3	102.1	4.7	98.8	100.0	101.2	101.7	4.0
1990	103.9	105.3	106.3	106.8	4.6	103.0	104.3	105.1	105.5	3.7
1991	108.3	109.4	110.6	111.2	4.1	106.8	107.7	108.5	109.2	3.5
1992	112.2	113.0	113.9	114.6	3.1	110.1	110.8	111.3	111.9	2.5
1993	115.9	116.9	117.8	118.2	3.1	112.8	113.6	114.4	115.0	2.8
1994	119.6	120.4	121.7	121.9	3.1	115.9	116.7	117.7	118.3	2.9
1995	123.0	123.9	124.5	125.1	2.6	119.5	120.7	121.4	122.1	3.2
1996	126.3	127.3	127.8	128.9	3.0	123.6	124.7	125.2	126.3	3.4
1997	129.9	131.2	131.8	132.6	2.9	127.5	128.9	129.7	130.6	3.4
1998	133.8	134.7	135.5	136.3	2.8	132.0	132.9	134.0	134.8	3.2
1999	137.6	139.0	140.3	141.4	3.7	136.2	137.5	138.7	139.7	3.6
2000	143.4	144.9	146.1	147.2	4.1	141.4	142.9	144.1	144.9	3.7
2001	149.4	150.3	152.2	152.9	3.9	147.1	148.2	150.0	150.5	3.9
Nonunion workers, goods-producing industries [3]										
1987	91.3	92.0	92.9	93.6	3.1	92.3	92.9	94.0	94.7	3.4
1988	95.1	96.2	96.9	97.7	4.4	95.8	96.8	97.3	98.1	3.6
1989	98.9	100.0	101.3	102.3	4.7	99.1	100.0	101.1	102.1	4.1
1990	104.2	105.5	106.7	107.4	5.0	103.5	104.5	105.5	106.1	3.9
1991	108.8	110.1	111.3	112.2	4.5	107.3	108.3	109.2	110.1	3.8
1992	113.3	114.1	115.1	116.0	3.4	111.2	111.9	112.6	113.3	2.9
1993	117.7	118.6	119.4	119.9	3.4	114.4	115.2	116.0	116.7	3.0
1994	121.5	122.6	123.6	124.1	3.5	117.6	118.6	119.5	120.3	3.1
1995	125.2	125.9	126.4	127.2	2.5	121.3	122.2	122.9	123.8	2.9
1996	128.3	129.4	130.4	131.3	3.2	124.9	126.1	127.3	128.0	3.4
1997	132.0	133.2	134.0	134.7	2.6	128.9	130.2	131.2	132.0	3.1
1998	135.9	136.9	137.7	138.3	2.7	133.6	134.7	135.7	136.5	3.4
1999	139.7	140.5	141.8	143.1	3.5	137.8	138.8	140.0	141.1	3.4
2000	145.4	147.2	148.4	149.3	4.3	142.9	144.7	145.8	146.8	4.0
2001	151.6	153.1	154.0	155.3	4.0	148.8	150.3	151.1	152.1	3.6
Nonunion workers, service-producing industries [4]										
1987	89.9	90.6	91.6	92.1	4.0	90.8	91.4	92.5	92.9	3.8
1988	93.4	94.7	95.9	97.2	5.5	93.8	95.1	96.3	97.6	5.1
1989	98.7	100.0	101.5	102.4	5.3	98.9	100.0	101.4	102.2	4.7
1990	103.9	105.5	106.5	107.2	4.7	103.4	104.9	105.9	106.5	4.2
1991	108.8	110.1	111.2	111.8	4.3	107.8	108.9	109.9	110.4	3.7
1992	113.0	113.7	114.4	115.2	3.0	111.2	111.7	112.3	113.0	2.4
1993	116.3	117.2	118.4	119.2	3.5	113.8	114.6	115.9	116.6	3.2
1994	120.3	121.1	122.2	122.7	2.9	117.2	118.1	119.0	119.5	2.5
1995	123.8	124.8	125.6	126.0	2.7	120.5	121.5	122.4	123.0	2.9
1996	127.3	128.3	129.2	129.9	3.1	124.6	125.7	126.6	127.5	3.7
1997	131.5	132.5	133.7	135.3	4.2	129.1	130.2	131.6	133.2	4.5
1998	136.7	138.0	139.7	140.6	3.9	134.6	135.9	137.9	138.8	4.2
1999	141.1	143.0	144.4	145.7	3.6	139.3	141.3	142.6	143.9	3.7
2000	148.0	149.6	151.2	152.3	4.5	145.8	147.3	148.7	149.6	4.0
2001	154.4	155.9	157.5	158.6	4.1	151.4	152.7	154.1	155.1	3.7
Nonunion workers, manufacturing industries										
1987	91.3	92.0	93.0	93.6	3.2	92.4	93.0	94.1	94.7	3.4
1988	95.2	96.1	96.8	97.6	4.3	95.8	96.7	97.2	98.0	3.5
1989	98.8	100.0	101.2	102.1	4.6	98.9	100.0	101.0	102.0	4.1
1990	104.2	105.5	106.9	107.6	5.4	103.6	104.8	105.9	106.5	4.4
1991	108.8	110.2	111.5	112.4	4.5	107.7	108.8	109.7	110.7	3.9
1992	113.6	114.5	115.5	116.4	3.6	111.9	112.7	113.4	114.2	3.2
1993	118.1	119.0	120.0	120.6	3.6	115.4	116.1	117.0	117.9	3.2
1994	122.0	122.9	124.0	124.8	3.5	118.6	119.5	120.5	121.5	3.1
1995	126.1	126.9	127.3	128.3	2.8	122.7	123.8	124.3	125.2	3.0
1996	129.3	130.5	131.7	132.5	3.3	126.3	127.5	128.8	129.6	3.5
1997	133.1	134.4	135.1	135.9	2.6	130.3	131.7	132.6	133.5	3.0
1998	137.2	138.0	138.9	139.4	2.6	135.1	136.2	137.3	138.2	3.5
1999	140.7	141.7	143.0	144.4	3.5	139.4	140.5	141.7	142.9	3.4
2000	146.5	148.2	149.2	149.9	3.8	144.4	146.1	147.2	148.0	3.6
2001	152.4	153.7	154.4	155.5	3.7	150.1	151.6	152.2	153.1	3.4

See footnotes at end of table.

Table 5-4. Employment Cost Index, Private Industry Workers[1], Total Compensation and Wages and Salaries by Bargaining Status, Industry, Region[2], and Area Size, 1987–2001—*Continued*

(June 1989=100, not seasonally adjusted.)

Series and year	Total compensation					Wages and salaries				
	Indexes				Percent change for 12 months ended December	Indexes				Percent change for 12 months ended December
	March	June	September	December		March	June	September	December	
Nonunion workers, manufacturing, blue-collar occupations										
1987	...	91.8	92.8	93.2	...	...	93.1	94.2	94.4	...
1988	94.6	95.7	96.4	97.4	4.5	95.4	96.3	96.8	97.8	3.6
1989	98.7	100.0	101.4	102.4	5.1	98.7	100.0	101.2	102.2	4.5
1990	104.4	105.9	107.2	107.9	5.4	103.6	105.0	106.0	106.7	4.4
1991	109.0	110.3	111.7	112.5	4.3	107.9	108.8	109.7	110.7	3.7
1992	113.8	114.6	115.5	116.2	3.3	111.9	112.5	113.1	113.7	2.7
1993	117.5	118.4	119.4	119.9	3.2	114.6	115.2	116.0	116.7	2.6
1994	121.2	121.9	123.0	123.5	3.0	117.5	118.1	119.1	120.0	2.8
1995	124.5	125.5	125.7	127.0	2.8	121.2	122.6	123.1	124.2	3.5
1996	128.1	129.3	130.3	131.4	3.5	125.4	126.7	127.8	128.8	3.7
1997	132.2	133.5	134.2	134.8	2.6	129.8	131.2	132.0	133.0	3.3
1998	136.0	136.7	137.4	138.3	2.6	134.4	135.1	136.2	137.2	3.2
1999	139.5	140.2	141.6	142.9	3.3	138.5	139.2	140.5	141.6	3.2
2000	144.4	145.8	146.7	148.0	3.6	142.8	144.2	145.4	146.6	3.5
2001	149.9	150.8	152.1	153.5	3.7	148.7	150.1	151.3	152.6	4.1
Nonunion workers, nonmanufacturing industries										
1987	90.1	90.7	91.8	92.2	3.7	90.9	91.6	92.7	93.0	3.7
1988	93.5	94.9	96.0	97.3	5.5	94.0	95.3	96.4	97.7	5.1
1989	98.8	100.0	101.4	102.4	5.2	99.0	100.0	101.4	102.3	4.7
1990	104.0	105.4	106.5	107.2	4.7	103.3	104.8	105.7	106.3	3.9
1991	108.8	110.1	111.2	111.7	4.2	107.6	108.7	109.6	110.1	3.6
1992	112.9	113.5	114.3	115.1	3.0	110.9	111.4	112.0	112.7	2.4
1993	116.3	117.2	118.3	119.0	3.4	113.5	114.3	115.5	116.1	3.0
1994	120.2	121.1	122.2	122.5	2.9	116.9	117.8	118.7	119.1	2.6
1995	123.6	124.5	125.3	125.7	2.6	120.0	121.0	121.9	122.6	2.9
1996	127.0	128.0	128.9	129.6	3.1	124.2	125.2	126.1	127.0	3.6
1997	131.1	132.2	133.4	134.9	4.1	128.5	129.7	131.1	132.6	4.4
1998	136.3	137.5	139.1	140.0	3.8	134.0	135.3	137.1	138.0	4.1
1999	140.6	142.4	143.8	145.1	3.6	138.6	140.5	141.8	143.0	3.6
2000	147.4	149.1	150.7	151.8	4.6	145.0	146.6	148.0	148.9	4.1
2001	153.9	155.4	157.0	158.2	4.2	150.7	152.0	153.3	154.4	3.7
WORKERS BY REGION										
Northeast										
1987	88.4	89.1	90.2	91.3	5.1	89.1	89.9	91.0	91.9	4.9
1988	92.4	93.8	95.0	96.7	5.9	92.7	94.0	95.1	96.9	5.4
1989	98.7	100.0	101.8	102.9	6.4	98.7	100.0	101.8	102.9	6.2
1990	104.4	105.3	106.5	107.6	4.6	104.0	104.8	105.9	106.9	3.9
1991	109.4	110.6	111.7	112.5	4.6	108.3	109.4	110.3	110.9	3.7
1992	113.9	114.5	115.5	116.4	3.5	111.7	112.2	113.0	113.7	2.5
1993	117.8	119.1	120.2	120.7	3.7	114.6	115.7	116.8	117.3	3.2
1994	121.6	122.8	124.0	124.3	3.0	117.8	118.8	120.0	120.2	2.5
1995	125.6	126.6	127.4	127.8	2.8	121.3	122.1	123.1	123.6	2.8
1996	128.9	129.7	130.6	131.1	2.6	124.9	126.0	127.0	127.7	3.3
1997	132.2	133.1	134.0	135.0	3.0	128.8	129.8	130.7	131.6	3.1
1998	136.0	137.0	138.7	139.5	3.3	132.6	133.8	135.4	136.4	3.6
1999	140.5	141.5	143.2	144.3	3.4	137.1	138.2	139.9	140.9	3.3
2000	146.3	147.6	149.3	150.3	4.2	142.3	143.7	145.3	146.0	3.6
2001	151.6	153.7	155.2	156.3	4.0	147.3	149.2	150.6	151.7	3.9
South										
1987	91.7	92.4	93.1	94.0	3.1	92.9	93.6	94.4	95.0	2.8
1988	95.1	96.7	97.4	98.1	4.4	95.7	97.2	97.9	98.4	3.6
1989	99.0	100.0	101.2	102.2	4.2	99.2	100.0	101.2	102.1	3.8
1990	104.0	105.7	106.3	106.9	4.6	103.5	105.2	105.7	106.1	3.9
1991	108.4	109.8	110.7	111.2	4.0	107.4	108.5	109.2	109.6	3.3
1992	112.5	113.3	114.1	114.8	3.2	110.8	111.5	112.0	112.7	2.8
1993	116.2	117.0	118.1	118.8	3.5	113.6	114.3	115.3	116.0	2.9
1994	120.0	120.8	121.8	122.5	3.1	116.6	117.4	118.5	119.1	2.7
1995	123.7	124.3	125.2	125.6	2.5	120.0	120.8	121.8	122.4	2.8
1996	127.0	127.8	128.8	129.7	3.3	124.1	125.1	126.0	127.0	3.8
1997	130.8	131.5	132.5	134.6	3.8	128.5	129.4	130.6	133.0	4.7
1998	135.5	136.4	137.6	138.1	2.6	134.0	134.9	136.5	136.7	2.8
1999	139.1	140.7	141.8	143.0	3.5	137.9	139.4	140.2	141.5	3.5
2000	145.0	146.7	147.6	148.6	3.9	143.0	144.6	145.3	146.3	3.4
2001	151.1	152.3	153.5	154.6	4.0	148.3	149.3	150.2	151.2	3.3
Midwest										
1987	91.6	92.4	93.1	93.5	2.9	93.1	93.9	94.7	94.9	2.9
1988	95.4	96.2	97.0	97.9	4.7	95.9	96.5	97.4	98.2	3.5
1989	98.9	100.0	101.0	101.9	4.1	99.1	100.0	100.8	101.6	3.5
1990	103.5	104.8	106.3	107.1	5.1	102.6	103.7	105.1	105.8	4.1

See footnotes at end of table.

Table 5-4. Employment Cost Index, Private Industry Workers[1], Total Compensation and Wages and Salaries by Bargaining Status, Industry, Region[2], and Area Size, 1987–2001—*Continued*

(June 1989=100, not seasonally adjusted.)

Series and year	Total compensation					Wages and salaries				
	Indexes				Percent change for 12 months ended December	Indexes				Percent change for 12 months ended December
	March	June	September	December		March	June	September	December	
1991	108.5	109.7	111.2	112.2	4.8	106.9	107.7	108.9	109.9	3.9
1992	113.8	114.6	115.3	116.1	3.5	110.7	111.3	111.8	112.5	2.4
1993	117.9	119.3	120.1	121.2	4.4	113.5	114.6	115.2	116.5	3.6
1994	122.8	123.6	124.6	125.0	3.1	117.5	118.3	119.5	120.1	3.1
1995	125.8	126.9	127.7	128.3	2.6	120.9	122.2	123.0	123.6	2.9
1996	129.5	130.7	131.3	132.1	3.0	125.1	126.2	126.9	127.7	3.3
1997	133.3	134.7	136.2	136.9	3.6	129.0	130.4	132.2	133.0	4.2
1998	138.3	139.6	140.9	141.4	3.3	134.7	136.0	137.5	138.0	3.8
1999	141.7	143.6	145.0	146.3	3.5	138.9	141.0	142.4	143.6	4.1
2000	148.9	150.7	152.2	153.3	4.8	145.3	147.1	148.6	149.6	4.2
2001	154.8	156.0	157.4	158.6	3.5	150.9	152.3	153.6	154.7	3.4
West										
1987	92.5	92.6	93.7	94.1	2.7	93.2	93.2	94.6	94.9	2.6
1988	95.4	96.3	97.0	97.7	3.8	95.9	96.7	97.7	98.2	3.5
1989	98.8	100.0	101.0	101.8	4.2	99.1	100.0	100.8	101.4	3.3
1990	103.3	104.5	105.6	106.3	4.4	102.5	104.0	104.8	105.4	3.9
1991	107.5	108.9	110.0	110.9	4.3	106.4	107.6	108.6	109.4	3.8
1992	111.9	112.9	114.1	114.9	3.6	110.2	111.1	112.2	112.8	3.1
1993	116.2	116.4	117.8	118.1	2.8	113.6	113.7	115.3	115.7	2.6
1994	119.4	120.5	121.3	121.7	3.0	116.6	117.9	118.1	119.0	2.9
1995	122.6	123.4	123.9	125.0	2.7	119.9	120.9	121.4	122.7	3.1
1996	125.9	127.3	128.3	128.9	3.1	123.3	124.8	125.8	126.5	3.1
1997	130.3	131.4	132.5	133.4	3.5	127.7	128.9	130.2	131.2	3.7
1998	135.2	136.6	138.5	140.0	4.9	132.9	134.5	136.7	138.4	5.5
1999	140.3	142.1	143.3	144.7	3.4	138.2	140.2	141.3	142.6	3.0
2000	147.0	148.8	150.8	151.8	4.9	144.7	146.3	148.2	149.2	4.6
2001	154.3	156.0	157.6	159.4	5.0	151.3	152.9	154.3	156.0	4.6
WORKERS BY AREA SIZE										
Metropolitan areas										
1987	90.6	91.2	92.1	92.7	3.3	91.8	92.3	93.2	93.9	3.4
1988	94.2	95.3	96.3	97.4	5.1	94.7	95.7	96.7	97.8	4.2
1989	98.8	100.0	101.4	102.2	4.9	99.0	100.0	101.3	102.1	4.4
1990	103.9	105.1	106.3	107.1	4.8	103.3	104.4	105.4	106.1	3.9
1991	108.5	109.8	111.0	111.8	4.4	107.3	108.4	109.3	110.1	3.8
1992	113.1	113.9	114.8	115.6	3.4	110.9	111.6	112.3	112.9	2.5
1993	117.1	118.1	119.1	119.8	3.6	113.9	114.7	115.8	116.5	3.2
1994	120.9	121.9	122.9	123.4	3.0	117.2	118.1	119.1	119.7	2.7
1995	124.5	125.4	126.2	126.8	2.8	120.6	121.6	122.4	123.2	2.9
1996	128.0	129.1	130.0	130.6	3.0	124.6	125.8	126.7	127.4	3.4
1997	131.7	132.8	133.9	135.1	3.4	128.7	129.9	131.1	132.3	3.8
1998	136.4	137.5	139.1	139.8	3.5	133.8	135.1	136.9	137.7	4.1
1999	140.4	142.0	143.3	144.7	3.5	138.3	139.9	141.2	142.5	3.5
2000	146.9	148.6	150.1	151.0	4.4	144.1	145.7	147.1	148.0	3.9
2001	153.1	154.6	156.0	157.4	4.2	149.8	151.2	152.4	153.7	3.9
Other areas										
1987	93.3	94.1	94.9	95.4	3.1	93.6	94.5	95.5	96.0	3.3
1988	96.6	98.0	98.5	98.9	3.7	96.8	98.4	98.7	98.9	3.0
1989	99.4	100.0	100.8	102.0	3.1	99.6	100.0	100.7	101.9	3.0
1990	103.6	105.2	106.0	106.8	4.7	103.0	104.6	105.3	106.0	4.0
1991	108.4	109.9	110.7	111.2	4.1	107.2	108.4	109.0	109.4	3.2
1992	113.1	113.7	114.8	115.6	4.0	110.7	111.2	112.0	112.8	3.1
1993	117.0	117.8	118.7	119.7	3.5	113.5	114.4	115.0	115.8	2.7
1994	121.3	122.5	123.2	123.5	3.2	117.0	118.1	118.6	119.0	2.8
1995	124.8	125.3	126.1	126.5	2.4	120.5	121.3	122.1	122.4	2.9
1996	127.2	128.0	128.7	130.2	2.9	123.4	124.2	125.0	126.5	3.3
1997	131.4	132.4	133.8	135.3	3.9	127.7	128.8	130.4	132.0	4.3
1998	135.9	137.1	138.2	139.4	3.0	132.5	133.4	134.7	136.0	3.0
1999	140.5	141.8	143.1	143.6	3.0	137.1	138.4	139.8	140.2	3.1
2000	146.0	147.7	148.8	150.3	4.7	142.2	143.7	144.7	146.0	4.1
2001	152.1	153.7	154.8	155.6	3.5	147.4	148.8	149.7	150.5	3.1

1. Excludes farm and household workers.
2. The regional coverage is as follows: Northeast: Connecticut, Maine, Massachusetts, New Hampshire, New Jersey, New York, Pennsylvania, Rhode Island, and Vermont; South: Alabama, Arkansas, Delaware, District of Columbia, Florida, Georgia, Kentucky, Louisiana, Maryland, Mississippi, North Carolina, Oklahoma, South Carolina, Tennessee, Texas, Virginia, and West Virginia; Midwest: Illinois, Indiana, Iowa, Kansas, Michigan, Minnesota, Missouri, Nebraska, North Dakota, Ohio, South Dakota, and Wisconsin; and West: Alaska, Arizona, California, Colorado, Hawaii, Idaho, Montana, Nevada, New Mexico, Oregon, Utah, Washington, and Wyoming.
3. Includes mining, construction, and manufacturing.
4. Includes transportation, communication, and public utilities; wholesale and retail trade; finance, insurance, and real estate; and service industries.

Table 5-5. Employer Compensation Costs per Hour Worked and Percent of Total Compensation, Private Industry, by Major Industry Group, March 2002

(Dollars, percent of total cost.)

Compensation component	All workers in private industry		Goods-producing industries [1]		Service-producing industries [2]		Manufacturing industries		Nonmanufacturing industries	
	Cost	Percent	Cost	Percent	Cost	Percent	Cost	Percent	Cost	Percent
TOTAL COMPENSATION	$21.71	100.0	$25.44	100.0	$20.66	100.0	$25.20	100.0	$21.06	100.0
WAGES AND SALARIES	15.80	72.8	17.47	68.7	15.33	74.2	17.19	68.2	15.55	73.8
TOTAL BENEFITS	5.90	27.2	7.96	31.3	5.33	25.8	8.01	31.8	5.51	26.2
Paid Leave	1.44	6.6	1.66	6.5	1.37	6.6	1.91	7.6	1.35	6.4
Vacation pay	0.72	3.3	0.86	3.4	0.68	3.3	0.97	3.8	0.67	3.2
Holiday pay	0.49	2.3	0.60	2.4	0.46	2.2	0.70	2.8	0.45	2.1
Sick leave	0.17	0.8	0.12	0.5	0.18	0.9	0.14	0.6	0.17	0.8
Other leave pay	0.06	0.3	0.08	0.3	0.06	0.3	0.10	0.4	0.05	0.2
Supplemental Pay	0.62	2.9	1.11	4.4	0.48	2.3	1.13	4.5	0.52	2.5
Premium pay [3]	0.24	1.1	0.54	2.1	0.16	0.8	0.56	2.2	0.18	0.9
Shift pay	0.06	0.3	0.08	0.3	0.05	0.2	0.11	0.4	0.05	0.2
Nonproduction bonuses	0.32	1.5	0.49	1.9	0.27	1.3	0.46	1.8	0.29	1.4
Insurance	1.40	6.4	2.01	7.9	1.22	5.9	2.11	8.4	1.27	6.0
Life insurance	0.04	0.2	0.06	0.2	0.04	0.2	0.06	0.2	0.04	0.2
Health insurance	1.29	5.9	1.84	7.2	1.13	5.5	1.92	7.6	1.17	5.6
Short-term disability [4]	0.04	0.2	0.08	0.3	0.03	0.1	0.08	0.3	0.03	0.1
Long-term disability	0.03	0.1	0.03	0.1	0.03	0.1	0.04	0.2	0.03	0.1
Retirement And Savings	0.63	2.9	0.88	3.5	0.56	2.7	0.74	2.9	0.61	2.9
Defined benefit plans	0.23	1.1	0.42	1.7	0.17	0.8	0.30	1.2	0.21	1.0
Defined contribution plans	0.40	1.8	0.46	1.8	0.39	1.9	0.44	1.7	0.40	1.9
Legally Required Benefits	1.80	8.3	2.25	8.8	1.67	8.1	2.05	8.1	1.75	8.3
Social security [5]	1.32	6.1	1.49	5.9	1.27	6.1	1.48	5.9	1.29	6.1
OASDI	1.06	4.9	1.20	4.7	1.02	4.9	1.19	4.7	1.03	4.9
Medicare	0.26	1.2	0.29	1.1	0.25	1.2	0.29	1.2	0.25	1.2
Federal unemployment insurance	0.03	0.1	0.03	0.1	0.03	0.1	0.03	0.1	0.03	0.1
State unemployment insurance	0.10	0.5	0.12	0.5	0.09	0.4	0.11	0.4	0.09	0.4
Workers' compensation	0.35	1.6	0.61	2.4	0.28	1.4	0.43	1.7	0.34	1.6
Other Benefits [6]	0.03	0.1	0.05	0.2	0.02	0.1	0.07	0.3	0.02	0.1

Note: The sum of individual items may not equal totals due to rounding.

1. Includes mining, construction, and manufacturing.
2. Includes transportation, communication, and public utilities; wholesale and retail trade; finance, insurance, and real estate; and service industries.
3. Includes premium pay for work in addition to the regular work schedule (such as overtime, weekends, and holidays).
4. Short-term disability (previously called sickness and accident insurance) includes all insured, self-insured, and state-mandated plans that provide benefits for each disability, including unfunded plans.
5. The total employer's cost for Social Security consists of an OASDI portion and a Medicare portion. OASDI is the acronym for Old-Age, Survivors, and Disability Insurance.
6. Includes severance pay and supplemental unemployment benefits.

Table 5-6. Employer Compensation Costs per Hour Worked and Percent of Total Compensation, Private Industry, by Region and Bargaining Status, March 2002

(Dollars, percent of total cost.)

Compensation component	Northeast		South		Midwest		West		Union		Nonunion	
	Cost	Percent	Cost	Percent	Cost	Percent	Cost	Percent	Cost	Percent	Cost	Percent
TOTAL COMPENSATION	$25.00	100.00	$19.49	100.00	$21.25	100.00	$22.68	100.00	$29.42	100.00	$20.79	100.00
WAGES AND SALARIES	17.97	71.9	14.34	73.6	15.29	72.0	16.68	73.5	19.33	65.7	15.38	74.0
TOTAL BENEFITS	7.04	28.2	5.14	26.4	5.96	28.0	5.99	26.4	10.09	34.3	5.41	26.0
Paid Leave	1.83	7.3	1.24	6.4	1.35	6.4	1.48	6.5	2.08	7.1	1.36	6.5
Vacation	0.92	3.7	0.62	3.2	0.68	3.2	0.74	3.3	1.08	3.7	0.68	3.3
Holiday	0.62	2.5	0.42	2.2	0.47	2.2	0.51	2.2	0.68	2.3	0.47	2.3
Sick	0.22	0.9	0.14	0.7	0.14	0.7	0.19	0.8	0.23	0.8	0.16	0.8
Other	0.08	0.3	0.05	0.3	0.07	0.3	0.05	0.2	0.10	0.3	0.06	0.3
Supplemental Pay	0.77	3.1	0.50	2.6	0.73	3.4	0.52	2.3	1.08	3.7	0.56	2.7
Premium Pay[1]	0.22	0.9	0.22	1.1	0.30	1.4	0.23	1.0	0.66	2.2	0.19	0.9
Shift differentials	0.06	0.2	0.04	0.2	0.08	0.4	0.05	0.2	0.16	0.5	0.04	0.2
Nonproduction bonuses	0.49	2.0	0.24	1.2	0.35	1.6	0.24	1.1	0.26	0.9	0.33	1.6
Insurance	1.62	6.5	1.25	6.4	1.47	6.9	1.35	6.0	2.76	9.4	1.23	5.9
Life insurance	0.05	0.2	0.04	0.2	0.04	0.2	0.04	0.2	0.07	0.2	0.04	0.2
Health insurance	1.48	5.9	1.14	5.8	1.35	6.4	1.26	5.6	2.57	8.7	1.13	5.4
Short-term disability	0.06	0.2	0.04	0.2	0.05	0.2	0.03	0.1	0.08	0.3	0.04	0.2
Long-term disability	0.03	0.1	0.03	0.2	0.03	0.1	0.03	0.1	0.05	0.2	0.03	0.1
Retirement And Savings	0.80	3.2	0.52	2.7	0.63	3.0	0.65	2.9	1.64	5.6	0.51	2.5
Defined benefit	0.27	1.1	0.17	0.9	0.28	1.3	0.22	1.0	1.16	3.9	0.12	0.6
Defined contribution	0.53	2.1	0.35	1.8	0.35	1.6	0.43	1.9	0.48	1.6	0.39	1.9
Legally Required Benefits	1.98	7.9	1.61	8.3	1.75	8.2	1.97	8.7	2.46	8.4	1.72	8.3
Social security[2]	1.47	5.9	1.20	6.2	1.29	6.1	1.39	6.1	1.65	5.6	1.28	6.2
OASDI	1.17	4.7	0.97	5.0	1.04	4.9	1.12	4.9	1.33	4.5	1.03	5.0
Medicare	0.30	1.2	0.23	1.2	0.25	1.2	0.27	1.2	0.32	1.1	0.25	1.2
Federal unemployment insurance	0.03	0.1	0.03	0.2	0.03	0.1	0.03	0.1	0.03	0.1	0.03	0.1
State unemployment insurance	0.14	0.6	0.06	0.3	0.09	0.4	0.12	0.5	0.13	0.4	0.09	0.4
Workers' compensation	0.34	1.4	0.31	1.6	0.34	1.6	0.43	1.9	0.65	2.2	0.32	1.5
Other Benefits[3]	0.04	0.2	0.02	0.1	0.03	0.1	0.02	0.1	0.07	0.2	0.02	0.1

Note: The sum of individual items may not equal totals due to rounding.

1. Includes premium pay for work in addition to the regular work schedule (such as overtime, weekends, and holidays.)
2. The total employer's cost for Social Security is comprised of an OASDI portion and a Medicare portion. OASDI is the acronym for Old-Age, Survivors, and Disability Insurance.
3. Includes severance pay and supplemental unemployment benefits.

Table 5-7. Employer Compensation Costs per Hour Worked and Percent of Total Compensation, State and Local Government, by Selected Characteristics, March 2002

(Dollars, percent of total cost.)

Compensation component	All workers		White-collar occupations [1]		Service occupations [1]		Service industries [1]	
	Cost	Percent	Cost	Percent	Cost	Percent	Cost	Percent
TOTAL COMPENSATION	$31.29	100.0	$34.78	100.0	$23.50	100.0	$32.80	100.0
WAGES AND SALARIES	22.14	70.8	25.21	72.5	15.31	65.1	23.92	72.9
TOTAL BENEFITS	9.15	29.2	9.57	27.5	8.19	34.9	8.88	27.1
Paid Leave	2.43	7.8	2.53	7.3	2.20	9.4	2.23	6.8
Vacation pay	0.84	2.7	0.78	2.2	0.94	4.0	0.62	1.9
Holiday pay	0.80	2.6	0.84	2.4	0.70	3.0	0.75	2.3
Sick leave	0.61	1.9	0.70	2.0	0.40	1.7	0.66	2.0
Other leave pay	0.19	0.6	0.21	0.6	0.15	0.6	0.20	0.6
Supplemental Pay	0.26	0.8	0.15	0.4	0.56	2.4	0.17	0.5
Premium pay [2]	0.13	0.4	0.04	0.1	0.29	1.2	0.06	0.2
Shift pay	0.06	0.2	0.04	0.1	0.13	0.6	0.05	0.2
Nonproduction bonuses	0.08	0.3	0.07	0.2	0.14	0.6	0.06	0.2
Insurance	2.82	9.0	2.98	8.6	2.33	9.9	2.82	8.6
Life insurance	0.06	0.2	0.06	0.2	0.04	0.2	0.05	0.2
Health insurance	2.69	8.6	2.86	8.2	2.20	9.4	2.71	8.3
Short-term disability [3]	0.03	0.1	0.02	0.1	0.07	0.3	0.02	0.1
Long-term disability	0.03	0.1	0.04	0.1	0.02	0.1	0.04	0.1
Retirement And Savings	1.74	5.6	1.87	5.4	1.54	6.6	1.73	5.3
Defined benefit plans	1.51	4.8	1.61	4.6	1.44	6.1	1.51	4.6
Defined contribution plans	0.23	0.7	0.26	0.7	0.10	0.4	0.22	0.7
Legally Required Benefits	1.84	5.9	1.96	5.6	1.50	6.4	1.86	5.7
Social security [4]	1.46	4.7	1.66	4.8	0.96	4.1	1.57	4.8
OASDI	1.13	3.6	1.28	3.7	0.73	3.1	1.21	3.7
Medicare	0.33	1.1	0.38	1.1	0.23	1.0	0.35	1.1
State unemployment insurance	0.04	0.1	0.04	0.1	0.04	0.2	0.03	0.1
Workers' compensation	0.34	1.1	0.27	0.8	0.50	2.1	0.25	0.8
Other Benefits [7]	0.06	0.2	0.07	0.2	0.06	0.3	0.07	0.2

Note: The sum of individual items may not equal totals due to rounding.

1. In state and local governments there are two major occupational groups: White-collar occupational groups, largely professional occupations, including teachers; and service occupations, including police and firefighters; and one major industry group, services. The service industries, which include health and educational services, employ a large part of the state and local government workforce.
2. Includes premium pay for work in addition to the regular work schedule (such as overtime, weekends, and holidays).
3. Short-term disability (previously called sickness and accident insurance) includes all insured, self-insured, and state-mandated plans that provide benefits for each disability, including unfunded plans.
4. The total employer's cost for Social Security consists of an OASDI portion and a Medicare portion. OASDI is the acronym for Old-Age, Survivors, and Disability Insurance.
5. Cost per hour worked is $0.01 or less.
6. Less than 0.05 percent.
7. Includes severance pay and supplemental unemployment benefits.

Table 5-8. Employer Compensation Costs per Hour Worked and Percent of Total Compensation, Private Industry, by Occupational and Industry Group, March 2002

(Dollars, percent of total compensation.)

Series	Total compensation	Wages and salaries	Cost per hour worked by year						
			Total	Paid leave	Supplemental pay	Insurance	Retirement and savings	Legally required benefits	Other benefits[1]
State and local government workers	$31.29	$22.14	$9.15	$2.43	$0.26	$2.82	$1.74	$1.84	$0.06
Occupational Group									
White-collar occupations	34.78	25.21	9.57	2.53	0.15	2.98	1.87	1.96	0.07
Professional specialty and technical	40.51	30.18	10.33	2.48	0.16	3.14	2.23	2.22	0.09
Professional specialty	41.82	31.29	10.53	2.49	0.14	3.23	2.31	2.27	0.09
Teachers	44.39	33.69	10.70	2.34	0.07	3.31	2.53	2.33	0.11
Technical	26.59	18.35	8.24	2.40	0.43	2.21	1.41	1.75	0.04
Executive, administrative, and managerial	39.42	27.57	11.85	4.03	0.17	3.21	2.16	2.25	0.04
Administrative support, including clerical	20.14	13.41	6.73	1.82	0.12	2.54	0.96	1.25	0.04
Blue-collar occupations	24.59	16.20	8.38	2.29	0.39	2.70	1.26	1.71	0.04
Service occupations	23.50	15.31	8.19	2.20	0.56	2.33	1.54	1.50	0.06
Industry Group									
Services	32.80	23.92	8.88	2.23	0.17	2.82	1.73	1.86	0.07
Health services	26.03	17.48	8.55	2.60	0.70	2.26	1.14	1.81	0.04
Hospitals	26.73	18.02	8.70	2.68	0.68	2.24	1.19	1.88	0.04
Educational services	34.17	25.23	8.94	2.15	0.10	2.90	1.84	1.87	0.07
Elementary and secondary education	33.29	24.73	8.55	1.89	0.08	3.04	1.69	1.76	0.10
Higher education	36.86	26.99	9.87	2.77	0.16	2.60	2.23	2.10	(2)
Public administration	28.61	19.02	9.59	2.83	0.42	2.76	1.78	1.75	0.06
Percent of Total Compensation									
State and local government workers	100.00	70.80	29.20	7.80	0.80	9.00	5.60	5.90	0.20
Occupational Group									
White-collar occupations	100.00	72.50	27.50	7.30	0.40	8.60	5.40	5.60	0.20
Professional specialty and technical	100.00	74.50	25.50	6.10	0.40	7.80	5.50	5.50	0.20
Professional specialty	100.00	74.80	25.20	6.00	0.30	7.70	5.50	5.40	0.20
Teachers	100.00	75.90	24.10	5.30	0.20	7.50	5.70	5.20	0.20
Technical	100.00	69.00	31.00	9.00	1.60	8.30	5.30	6.60	0.20
Executive, administrative, and managerial	100.00	69.90	30.10	10.20	0.40	8.10	5.50	5.70	0.10
Administrative support, including clerical	100.00	66.60	33.40	9.00	0.60	12.60	4.80	6.20	0.20
Blue-collar occupations	100.00	65.90	34.10	9.30	1.60	11.00	5.10	7.00	0.20
Service occupations	100.00	65.10	34.90	9.40	2.40	9.90	6.60	6.40	0.30
Industry Group									
Services	100.00	72.90	27.10	6.80	0.50	8.60	5.30	5.70	0.20
Health services	100.00	67.20	32.80	10.00	2.70	8.70	4.40	7.00	0.20
Hospitals	100.00	67.40	32.50	10.00	2.50	8.40	4.50	7.00	0.10
Educational services	100.00	73.80	26.20	6.30	0.30	8.50	5.40	5.50	0.20
Elementary and secondary education	100.00	74.30	25.70	5.70	0.20	9.10	5.10	5.30	0.30
Higher education	100.00	73.20	26.80	7.50	0.40	7.10	6.00	5.70	(3)
Public administration	100.00	66.50	33.50	9.90	1.50	9.60	6.20	6.10	0.20

Note: The sum of individual items may not equal totals due to rounding.

1. Includes severance pay and supplemental unemployment benefits.
2. Cost per hour worked is $0.01 or less.
3. Less than .05 percent.

NOTES AND DEFINITIONS

EMPLOYEE BENEFITS SURVEY

Note: The Employee Benefits Survey is now part of the National Compensation Survey (NCS) which also includes the Employment Cost Index and the Occupational Compensation Survey.

The statistics in this chapter represent a transitional step in the integration of data on employee benefits into the NCS. The tables contain data on all workers in private industry for 1999 and 2000. Prior to 1999, surveys of different sectors of the economy were conducted in alternating years; medium and large private establishments were studied during odd years, and small private establishments during even years. Since those surveys have been replaced by the new survey the tables previously presented in this handbook have been discontinued. In the future, the data for all private workers will be collected and published annually.

Definition of survey terms

Incidence refers to different methods of computing the number or percentage of employees that receive a benefit plan or specific benefit feature. Access to a benefit is determined on an occupational basis within an establishment; either all employees or no employees in an occupation in an establishment have the benefit available to them. The benefits published in Table 5–10 refer to employee access.

Participation refers to the proportion of employees covered by a benefit. There will be cases where employees with access to a plan will not participate. For example, some employees may decline to participate in a health insurance plan if there is an employee cost involved. The benefits published in Table 5–9 refer to employee participation. For a listing of selected benefit definitions, see *Glossary of Compensation Terms*, U.S Department of Labor, Bureau of Labor Statistics, August 1998, Report 923.

Survey Scope

The 2000 NCS benefits incidence survey obtained data from 1,436 private industry establishments, representing over 107 million workers; of this number, nearly 86 million were full-time workers and the remainder—nearly 22 million—were part-time workers. The NCS uses the establishment's definition of full- and part-time status. For purposes of this survey, an establishment is an economic unit that produces goods or services, a central administrative office, or an auxiliary unit providing support services to a company. For private industries, the establishment is usually at a single physical location.

Sources of Additional information

For a listing of selected benefit definitions, see *Glossary of Compensation Terms*, BLS. August 1998, Report 923. Additional data and further information on methodology and sampling are available in BLS news release USDL 02-389 (July 2002). The NCS was described in an article in the fifth edition of this handbook.

Table 5-9. Percent of Workers Participating in Selected Benefits, by Worker and Establishment Characteristics, Private Industry, 1999–2000

(Percent.)

Benefit program	Total	Worker characteristic[3]						Establishment characteristic				
		Professional, technical, and related employees	Clerical and sales employees	Blue–collar and service employees	Full–time	Part–time	Union	Nonunion	Goods–producing	Service–producing	1–99 workers	100 workers or more
1999[1]												
All	48	69	45	42	56	21	79	44	61	44	34	64
Retirement Benefits												
Defined benefit	21	29	17	21	25	9	70	16	36	17	8	37
Defined contribution	36	56	34	28	42	14	39	35	43	34	27	46
Health Care Benefits												
Medical care	53	68	51	48	64	14	73	51	69	48	46	61
Dental care	32	49	30	27	39	10	52	30	39	30	23	43
Vision care	18	30	14	15	22	6	39	15	21	17	12	25
Survivor Benefits												
Life insurance	56	76	54	48	68	15	78	53	69	51	43	70
Accidental death and dismemberment	43	61	38	37	52	11	65	40	55	39	30	57
Survivor income benefits	3	5	2	3	4	1	8	2	4	3	1	5
Disability Benefits												
Short-term disability	36	49	33	32	43	15	66	33	49	32	25	49
Long-term disability	25	48	26	15	32	4	27	25	29	24	17	36
2000[2]												
All	48	66	50	39	55	18	83	44	57	45	33	65
Retirement Benefits												
Defined benefit	19	27	18	17	22	6	69	14	...	18	8	33
Defined contribution	36	53	40	27	42	12	38	36	44	33	27	46
Health Care Benefits												
Medical care	52	64	50	47	61	13	75	49	...	48	43	61
Dental care	29	42	30	24	35	6	53	27	33	28	19	41
Vision care	17	24	17	15	21	4	41	15	20	17	10	26
Survivor Benefits												
Life insurance	54	76	52	47	65	11	82	51	69	50	37	75
Accidental death and dismemberment	41	58	39	36	50	8	66	39	58	36	24	62
Survivor income benefits	2	3	2	2	2	1	6	2	3	2	2	3
Disability Benefits												
Short-term disability	34	50	32	28	39	12	69	30	45	30	22	47
Long-term disability	26	51	27	14	31	4	28	25	31	24	13	40

1. The survey covers all 50 states. Collection was conducted between March 1999 and April 2000. The average reference period was September 1999.
2. The survey covers all 50 states and the District of Columbia. Collection was conducted between February and December 2000. The average reference period was July 2000.
3. Employees are classified as working either a full-time or part-time schedule based on the definition used by each establishment. Union workers are those whose wages are determined through collective bargaining.

Table 5-10. Percent of Workers with Access to Selected Benefits, by Worker and Establishment Characteristics, Private Industry, 1999–2000

(Percent.)

Benefit program	Total[3]	Worker characteristic[4]						Establishment characteristic				
		Professional, technical, and related employees	Clerical and sales employees	Blue–collar and service employees	Full–time	Part–time	Union	Nonunion	Goods–producing	Service–producing	1–99 workers	100 workers or more
1999[1]												
Paid Vacations	79	88	80	75	90	43	86	78	84	77	73	86
Paid Holidays	75	89	77	69	87	36	82	75	84	73	70	82
Employer Assistance for Child Care												
Total	6	12	5	4	6	6	5	6	2	7	3	10
Employer provided funds	4	7	3	3	4	4	4	4	2	4	2	6
On-site child care	3	6	2	2	3	3	1	3	1	3	1	4
Off-site child care	2	3	1	1	2	1	1	2	1	2	(5)	3
Adoption assistance	6	11	6	3	6	2	7	5	7	5	1	11
Long-Term Care Insurance	6	11	7	3	7	4	3	6	5	6	2	10
Flexible Work Place	3	7	3	1	4	1	2	3	3	3	2	4
Non–Wage Cash Payments												
Nonproduction bonuses	42	48	42	39	46	28	29	43	47	40	46	37
Supplemental unemployment benefits	2	1	1	3	2	(5)	10	1	5	1	1	3
Severance pay	22	36	24	14	26	8	28	21	25	21	13	31
Subsidized Commuting	4	9	4	3	5	3	7	4	4	5	3	6
Education Assistance												
Work related	41	63	39	34	47	21	46	41	46	40	29	55
Non-work related	10	14	10	9	12	6	15	10	14	9	5	17
Travel Accident Insurance	20	35	22	12	22	11	17	20	21	19	10	31
Health Benefit Programs												
Wellness programs	17	29	15	13	19	11	24	16	19	16	6	30
Fitness centers	9	18	8	6	10	5	7	9	8	9	4	15
2000[2]												
Paid Vacations	80	88	80	77	91	39	93	79	89	78	73	89
Paid Holidays	77	85	80	73	87	39	89	76	89	74	70	86
Employer Assistance for Child Care												
Total	4	11	5	2	5	3	8	4	2	5	1	9
Employer provided funds	2	4	3	1	2	1	6	2	1	2	(5)	4
On-site child care	2	6	1	1	2	1	2	2	(5)	3	(5)	4
Off-site child care	1	3	2	(5)	1	1	(5)	1	(5)	1	(5)	2
Adoption assistance	5	12	5	2	6	2	5	5	6	4	1	9
Long-Term Care Insurance	7	14	7	4	8	2	15	6	5	8	5	10
Flexible Work Place	5	12	4	1	5	2	3	5	4	5	2	7
Non–Wage Cash Payments												
Nonproduction bonuses	48	52	48	46	51	36	38	49	51	47	49	46
Supplemental unemployment benefits	1	1	1	1	1	(5)	8	(5)	4	(5)	(5)	2
Severance pay	20	35	24	12	23	10	31	19	21	20	11	32
Subsidized Commuting	3	6	3	2	3	1	2	3	1	4	2	5
Education Assistance												
Work related	38	62	37	28	44	15	57	36	45	36	26	52
Non-work related	9	19	8	6	11	3	18	8	14	8	3	17
Travel Accident Insurance	15	30	15	9	17	9	23	14	19	14	5	28
Health Benefit Programs												
Wellness programs	18	35	17	11	21	7	38	16	19	17	6	31
Fitness centers	9	19	10	4	10	5	11	9	10	9	4	16

1. The survey covers all 50 states. Collection was conducted between March 1999 and April 2000. The average reference period was September 1999.
2. The survey covers all 50 states and the District of Columbia. Collection was conducted between February and December 2000. The average reference period was July 2000.
3. The total may be less than the sum of individual items because some employees were receiving more than one type of employer assistance for child care.
4. Employees are classified as working either a full-time or part-time schedule based on the definition used by each establishment. Union workers are those whose wages are determined through collective bargaining.
5. Less than 0.5 percent.

Table 5-11. Medical Care Benefits: Percent of Participants Required to Contribute and Average Employee Contribution, Private Industry, 1999–2000

(Percent, dollars.)

Benefit program	Total	Worker characteristic[4]						Establishment characteristic				
		Profes-sional, technical, and related employees	Clerical and sales employees	Blue–collar and service employees	Union	Non–Union	Full–time	Part–time	Goods–producing	Service–producing	1–99 workers	100 workers or more
1999[1]												
Single Coverage												
Employee contributions not required	33	31	29	37	52	30	34	22	39	30	42	25
Employee contributions required	67	69	71	63	48	70	66	78	61	70	58	75
Average flat monthly contribution in dollars[3]	$48.30	45.34	47.70	50.67	48.65	48.27	47.81	57.49	42.08	50.92	52.52	45.16
Family Coverage												
Employee contributions not required	19	16	15	24	46	14	19	15	25	17	24	15
Employee contributions required	81	84	85	76	54	86	81	85	75	83	76	85
Average flat monthly contribution in dollars[3]	$169.84	163.31	174.18	171.12	129.08	173.77	168.68	192.65	149.73	178.94	191.93	150.74
2000[2]												
Single Coverage												
Employee contributions not required	32	25	28	38	...	27	31	...	36	30	34	30
Employee contributions required	68	75	72	62	...	73	69	...	64	70	66	70
Average flat monthly contribution in dollars[3]	$54.40	54.32	54.14	54.63	...	55.63	53.93	...	57.59	53.34	60.12	49.56
Family Coverage												
Employee contributions not required	19	15	16	23	...	13	19	...	25	17	19	20
Employee contributions required	81	85	84	77	...	87	81	...	75	83	81	80
Average flat monthly contribution in dollars[3]	$179.75	183.51	187.07	172.69	...	185.79	180.16	...	189.76	176.41	182.32	177.47

1. The survey covers all 50 states. Collection was conducted between March 1999 and April 2000. The average reference period was September 1999.
2. The survey covers all 50 states and the District of Columbia. Collection was conducted between February and December 2000. The average reference period was July 2000.
3. The average is presented for all covered workers and excludes workers without the plan provision. Averages are for plans stating a flat monthly cost.
4. Employees are classified as working either a full-time or part-time schedule based on the definition used by each establishment. Union workers are those whose wages are determined through collective bargaining.

NOTES AND DEFINITIONS

OCCUPATIONAL EMPLOYMENT AND WAGES

Note: The Occupational Employment Statistics (OES) Survey is now part of the National Compensation Survey (NCS).

Collection and Coverage

The OES survey is an annual mail survey measuring occupational employment and wage rates for wage and salary workers in nonfarm establishments, by industry. The OES is a Federal-State cooperative program between BLS and State Employment Security Agencies (SESAs). BLS funds the survey and provides the procedures and technical support, while SESAs collect the data.

The OES survey samples and contacts approximately 400,000 establishments each year and, over 3 years, contacts approximately 1.2 million establishments. The reference period for each year's survey is the fourth quarter of that year. While estimates can be made from a single year or 2 years of data, the OES survey has been designed to produce estimates using the full 3 years of sample. The full sample allows the production of estimates at fine levels of geographical, industrial, and occupational detail. Estimates from the 2000 survey, however, are based only on 2 years of data because of the conversion to the Standard Occupational Classification (SOC) system in 1999.

In 1999, the OES survey began using the Office of Management and Budget's occupational classification system—the Standard Occupational Classification System (SOC). The SOC system is the first OMB-required occupational classification system for Federal agencies. The OES survey categorizes workers in one of about 770 detailed occupations. Together, these detailed occupations comprise 22 major occupational groups. The SOC is described in an article in the third edition of this handbook.

Concepts and Definitions

Employment is the estimate of total wage and salary employment in an occupation across the industries in which it was reported. The OES survey form sent to an establishment contains between 50 and 225 SOC occupations selected on the basis of the industry classification and size class of the sampled establishments. To reduce paperwork and respondent burden, no survey form contains every SOC occupation. Thus, data for specific occupations are collected primarily from establishments within industries that are the predominant employers of labor in these occupations. Each survey form is structured, however, to allow a respondent to provide information for each detailed occupation employed at the establishment; that is, unlisted occupations can be added to the survey form.

Wages for the OES survey are straight-time, gross pay, exclusive of premium pay. Base rate, cost-of-living allowances, guaranteed pay, hazardous-duty pay, incentive pay including commissions and production bonuses, tips, and on-call pay are included. Excluded are back pay, jury duty pay, overtime pay, severance pay, shift differentials, nonproduction bonuses, employer cost of supplementary benefits, and tuition reimbursements. Employers report the number of employees in an occupation per each wage range.

Mean wage is the estimated total wages for an occupation divided by its weighted survey employment. With the exception of the upper open-ended wage interval, interval L ($70.00 an hour and over in 2000), a mean wage value is calculated for each wage interval based on occupational wage data collected by the BLS Office of Compensation and Working Conditions. The mean wage value for the upper open-ended wage interval is its lower bound (Winsorized mean). These interval mean wage values are then attributed to all workers reported in the interval. For each occupation, total weighted wages in each interval are summed across all intervals and divided by the occupation's weighted survey employment. The median wage is the wage at the midpoint of the distribution of wages.

An *establishment* is defined as an economic unit that processes goods or provides services, such as a factory, mine or store. The establishment is generally at a single physical location and is engaged primarily in one type of economic activity. The OES survey currently uses the Standard Industrial Classification (SIC) system to classify all establishments.

Sources of Additional Information

For additional data including area data see BLS news release UDL 01-415, BLS Bulletin 2549 and articles in *Compensation and Working Conditions*.

Table 5-12. Employment and Wages by Major Occupational Group, New Series, 2000

(Number, percent, dollars.)

Occupational group	Occupations		Employment		Mean hourly wage
	Number	Percent	Number	Percent	
Total	770	100.0	129 738 980	100.0	
Management	30	3.9	7 782 680	6.0	$32.78
Business and financial operations	28	3.6	4 619 270	3.6	23.30
Computer and mathematical	16	2.1	2 932 810	2.3	27.91
Architecture and engineering	35	4.5	2 575 620	2.0	25.99
Life, physical, and social science	39	5.1	1 038 670	0.8	22.97
Community and social services	14	1.8	1 469 000	1.1	15.82
Legal	9	1.2	890 910	0.7	33.14
Education, training, and library	58	7.5	7 450 860	5.7	18.22
Arts, design, entertainment, sports, and media ...	37	4.8	1 513 420	1.2	18.58
Healthcare practitioner and technical	46	6.0	6 041 210	4.7	23.07
Healthcare support	15	1.9	3 039 430	2.3	10.11
Protective service	20	2.6	3 009 070	2.3	14.80
Food preparation and serving related	16	2.1	9 955 060	7.7	7.72
Building and grounds cleaning and maintenance ...	9	1.2	4 318 070	3.3	9.41
Personal care and service	33	4.3	2 700 510	2.1	9.86
Sales and related	21	2.7	13 506 880	10.4	13.46
Office and administrative support	56	7.3	22 936 140	17.7	12.64
Farming, fishing, and forestry	13	1.7	460 700	0.4	9.07
Construction and extraction	58	7.5	6 187 360	4.8	16.56
Installation, maintenance, and repair	53	6.9	5 318 490	4.1	16.23
Production	112	14.5	12 400 080	9.6	12.72
Transportation and material moving	52	6.8	9 592 740	7.4	12.32

Note: The OES Survey estimates for 2000 are based on responses from establishments collected for 1999 and 2000, the first 2 years of SOC—based data collected in this 3 year survey. Employment estimates for 1999 were based on establishment responses for 1999 only and therefore are not directly comparable with previous years' data. See "Notes and Definitions" for information on revised SOC.

Table 5-13. Distribution of Occupations and Employment by Occupational Division, Old Series, 1997–1998

(Number, percent.)

Occupational division	Occupations		Employment	
	Number	Percent	Number	Percent
1997				
Total	777	100.0	121 592 210	100.0
Managerial	20	2.6	8 192 170	6.7
Professional	214	27.5	25 594 320	21.0
Sales	22	2.8	14 319 050	11.8
Clerical	77	9.9	21 251 910	17.5
Service	64	8.2	19 610 730	16.1
Agricultural	20	2.6	1 515 370	1.2
Production	360	46.3	31 108 660	25.6
1998				
Total	777	100.0	124 704 630	100.0
Managerial	20	2.6	8 320 910	6.7
Professional	214	27.5	26 427 600	21.2
Sales	22	2.8	14 814 380	11.9
Clerical	77	9.9	21 665 320	17.4
Service	64	8.2	19 942 840	16.0
Agricultural	20	2.6	1 566 630	1.3
Production	360	46.3	31 966 950	25.6

Note: See "Notes and Definitions" for information on revised Standard Occupational Classification System (SOC).

Table 5-14. Distribution of Employment by Wage Range and Occupational Group, New Series, 2000

(Percentage distribution.)

Occupational group	Total	Wage range								
		Under $8.50	$8.50 to $10.74	$10.75 to $13.49	$13.50 to 16.99	$17.00 to 21.49	$21.50 to 27.24	$27.25 to $34.49	$34.50 to $43.74	$43.75 and over
Management	100.0	1.8	2.4	4.7	8.4	12.0	15.6	16.5	15.3	23.5
Business and financial operations	100.0	2.5	3.4	8.3	16.5	21.3	20.7	14.4	7.6	5.4
Computer and mathematical	100.0	1.0	2.1	4.4	9.2	15.1	20.9	21.3	16.1	9.9
Architecture and engineering	100.0	1.1	2.5	5.7	11.0	17.0	22.3	20.4	13.3	6.7
Life, physical, and social science	100.0	3.7	5.2	9.5	16.0	18.9	18.8	13.7	8.0	6.3
Community and social services	100.0	9.9	13.6	20.0	21.0	17.6	11.5	4.5	1.3	0.5
Legal	100.0	1.9	3.4	7.0	12.0	13.3	12.2	10.9	10.6	28.7
Education, training, and library	100.0	14.6	9.1	10.7	16.7	18.6	15.3	9.0	3.9	2.3
Arts, design, entertainment, sports, and media	100.0	16.2	11.4	12.7	15.0	14.6	12.6	8.3	4.9	4.3
Healthcare practitioner and technical	100.0	4.2	6.4	10.2	16.0	21.6	18.9	9.9	4.6	8.3
Healthcare support	100.0	36.1	30.2	19.2	10.2	3.2	0.7	0.2	...	...
Protective service	100.0	24.7	15.1	13.5	13.5	14.0	11.2	5.7	1.8	0.5
Food preparation and serving related	100.0	75.2	13.8	6.5	2.9	1.1	0.3	0.1	...	...
Building and grounds cleaning and maintenance	100.0	52.4	21.6	13.3	7.8	3.4	1.1	0.3	0.1	...
Personal care and service	100.0	56.9	18.2	9.3	6.6	4.3	2.4	1.1	0.7	0.5
Sales and related	100.0	44.1	14.4	10.4	9.1	7.4	5.4	3.7	2.4	3.0
Office and administrative support	100.0	20.2	22.4	22.7	17.4	11.6	3.9	1.2	0.4	0.1
Farming, fishing, and forestry	100.0	63.4	14.5	9.2	6.9	3.7	1.5	0.6	0.2	...
Construction and extraction	100.0	9.5	14.1	17.5	18.7	17.1	13.7	7.1	1.8	0.6
Installation, maintenance, and repair	100.0	9.8	12.8	16.6	20.3	20.2	14.0	4.8	1.1	0.4
Production	100.0	24.3	21.7	19.7	15.4	9.9	6.6	1.9	0.5	0.1
Transportation and material moving	100.0	31.8	20.0	16.9	13.8	9.9	4.8	1.4	0.5	0.9

Note: The OES Survey estimates for 2000 are based on responses from establishments collected for 1999 and 2000, the first 2 years of SOC—based data collected in this 3 year survey.
　　Employment estimates for 1999 were based on establishment responses for 1999 only and therefore are not directly comparable with previous years' data.
　　See "Notes and Definitions" for information on revised SOC.

Table 5-15. Distribution of Mean Wage of Occupations by Occupational Division, Old Series, 1997–1998

(Percentage distribution.)

Occupational division	Total	Wage range								
		Under $8.50	$8.50 to $9.99	$10.00 to $11.24	$11.25 to $13.24	$13.25 to $15.74	$15.75 to $19.24	$19.25 to $24.24	$24.25 to $43.24	$43.25 to $60.00
1997										
Managerial	100.0	...	...	...	5.0	15.0	5.0	30.0	45.0	...
Professional	100.0	0.5	3.7	3.7	6.5	9.8	23.4	17.8	33.6	0.9
Sales	100.0	13.6	13.6	9.1	9.1	4.5	22.7	13.6	13.6	...
Clerical	100.0	7.8	24.7	19.5	33.8	7.8	5.2	1.3	...	...
Service	100.0	46.9	14.1	7.8	6.3	9.4	7.8	6.3	1.6	...
Agricultural	100.0	30.0	10.0	20.0	35.0	5.0	...	...	...	...
Production	100.0	5.8	11.7	16.1	21.9	21.1	16.7	6.1	0.6	...
1998										
Managerial	100.0	...	...	...	...	20.0	5.0	15.0	60.0	...
Professional	100.0	0.5	2.8	4.2	4.7	10.3	18.7	31.3	26.6	0.9
Sales	100.0	13.6	13.6	4.5	13.6	...	18.2	18.2	18.2	...
Clerical	100.0	5.2	19.5	15.6	44.2	7.8	5.2	2.6	...	...
Service	100.0	43.8	12.5	10.9	9.4	7.8	4.7	9.4	1.6	...
Agricultural	100.0	30.0	5.0	15.0	40.0	10.0	...	...	...	...
Production	100.0	4.7	8.9	15.0	23.3	23.6	16.9	6.9	0.6	...

Note: See "Notes and Definitions" for information on revised Standard Occupational Classification System (SOC).

Table 5-16. Employment and Wages by Occupation, 2000

(Number of persons, dollars.)

Occupational division and occupation	Employment	Mean hourly wages	Mean annual wages[1]	Median hourly wages
MANAGEMENT OCCUPATIONS				
Chief executives	519 890	50.30	104 630	54.72
General and operations managers	2 221 590	33.76	70 220	29.41
Legislators	52 750	13.29	27 650	6.78
Advertising and promotions managers	93 420	29.93	62 260	25.66
Marketing managers	202 100	36.23	75 360	34.25
Sales managers	344 180	35.69	74 230	32.94
Public relations managers	68 000	29.54	61 430	26.22
Administrative services managers	344 440	25.31	52 650	22.63
Computer and information systems managers	283 480	38.58	80 250	37.90
Financial managers	622 890	34.89	72 570	32.22
Human resources managers	224 970	30.49	63 420	28.36
Industrial production managers	205 370	31.55	65 620	29.64
Purchasing managers	126 030	27.64	57 500	25.50
Transportation, storage, and distribution managers	116 680	27.98	58 200	26.07
Farm, ranch, and other agricultural managers	5 370	21.07	43 820	18.46
Construction managers	229 200	30.43	63 290	28.00
Education administrators, preschool and child care center/program	49 460	17.47	36 330	14.62
Education administrators, elementary and secondary school	196 390	(2)	68 940	(2)
Education administrators, postsecondary	92 280	31.14	64 770	28.60
Engineering managers	242 280	41.08	85 450	40.42
Food service managers	282 290	16.51	34 350	15.25
Funeral directors	26 110	23.40	48 680	19.76
Gaming managers	3 720	27.99	58 220	25.66
Lodging managers	31 890	16.73	34 800	14.79
Medical and health services managers	230 410	29.63	61 640	27.10
Natural sciences managers	38 870	37.91	78 850	36.48
Postmasters and mail superintendents	26 850	22.24	46 260	21.28
Property, real estate, and community association managers	145 340	20.74	43 130	17.32
Social and community service managers	93 460	20.46	42 550	18.81
BUSINESS AND FINANCIAL OPERATIONS OCCUPATIONS				
Agents and business managers of artists, performers, and athletes	6 600	30.81	64 080	27.42
Purchasing agents and buyers, farm products	17 910	21.49	44 690	18.06
Wholesale and retail buyers, except farm products	137 040	20.48	42 590	17.89
Purchasing agents, except wholesale, retail, and farm products	228 940	21.23	44 160	19.89
Claims adjusters, examiners, and investigators	189 700	21.15	44 000	19.75
Insurance appraisers, auto damage	12 320	19.49	40 540	19.23
Compliance officers, except agriculture, construction, health and safety, and transportation	126 840	21.22	44 140	19.67
Cost estimators	196 420	23.59	49 070	22.02
Emergency management specialists	10 730	20.73	43 120	18.85
Employment, recruitment, and placement specialists	188 060	20.67	43 000	17.54
Compensation, benefits, and job analysis specialists	84 040	21.37	44 450	20.03
Training and development specialists	197 610	20.95	43 580	19.63
Management analysts	357 610	29.01	60 350	26.46
Meeting and convention planners	32 000	18.49	38 450	17.09
Accountants and auditors	863 320	23.12	48 090	20.91
Appraisers and assessors of real estate	53 560	20.05	41 700	18.41
Budget analysts	63 160	24.56	51 080	23.25
Credit analysts	63 420	21.87	45 490	19.32
Financial analysts	159 490	28.73	59 760	25.20
Personal financial advisors	77 420	32.42	67 430	26.60
Insurance underwriters	96 070	22.83	47 490	20.74
Financial examiners	23 560	28.12	58 480	25.51
Loan counselors	25 500	17.73	36 870	15.46
Loan officers	203 530	22.96	47 760	19.92
Tax examiners, collectors, and revenue agents	67 720	20.47	42 580	19.32
Tax preparers	65 280	14.77	30 720	12.30
COMPUTER AND MATHEMATICAL OPERATIONS OCCUPATIONS				
Computer and information scientists, research	25 800	35.30	73 430	33.94
Computer programmers	530 730	29.31	60 970	27.69
Computer software engineers, applications	374 640	33.80	70 300	32.53
Computer software engineers, systems software	264 610	34.08	70 890	33.43
Computer support specialists	522 570	19.08	39 680	17.53
Computer systems analysts	463 300	29.43	61 210	28.53
Database administrators	108 000	26.83	55 810	24.99
Network and computer systems administrators	234 040	25.81	53 690	24.65
Network systems and data communications analysts	119 220	27.83	57 890	26.20
Actuaries	12 890	34.84	72 470	32.02

See footnotes at end of table.

Table 5-16. Employment and Wages by Occupation, 2000—*Continued*

(Number of persons, dollars.)

Occupational division and occupation	Employment	Mean hourly wages	Mean annual wages[1]	Median hourly wages
Mathematicians	3 140	32.58	67 770	33.00
Operations research analysts	59 820	27.74	57 700	25.69
Statisticians	17 520	26.26	54 630	25.00
Mathematical technicians	1 540	20.10	41 800	16.73
ARCHITECTURE AND ENGINEERING OCCUPATIONS				
Architects, except landscape and naval	74 390	26.93	56 020	25.24
Landscape architects	17 130	23.61	49 120	20.93
Cartographers and photogrammetrists	7 360	19.98	41 560	18.95
Surveyors	52 750	18.78	39 060	17.64
Aerospace engineers	71 550	33.19	69 040	32.66
Agricultural engineers	2 170	28.29	58 840	26.85
Biomedical engineers	6 600	29.36	61 060	27.63
Chemical engineers	31 530	32.29	67 160	31.71
Civil engineers	207 080	28.07	58 380	26.80
Computer hardware engineers	63 680	33.70	70 100	32.36
Electrical engineers	162 400	31.89	66 320	31.21
Electronics engineers, except computer	123 690	31.97	66 490	31.17
Environmental engineers	48 270	28.70	59 710	27.78
Health and safety engineers, except mining safety engineers and inspectors	42 800	27.08	56 340	26.26
Industrial engineers	171 810	28.80	59 900	28.16
Marine engineers and naval architects	4 680	29.57	61 500	29.27
Materials engineers	24 430	29.05	60 420	28.41
Mechanical engineers	207 300	29.26	60 860	28.23
Mining and geological engineers, including mining safety engineers	6 690	30.96	64 390	29.24
Nuclear engineers	12 610	37.87	78 770	38.15
Petroleum engineers	10 250	38.42	79 910	37.94
Architectural and civil drafters	92 610	17.84	37 100	16.93
Electrical and electronics drafters	38 470	19.43	40 420	18.37
Mechanical drafters	69 620	19.39	40 330	18.19
Aerospace engineering and operations technicians	19 850	24.00	49 920	23.37
Civil engineering technicians	89 200	17.84	37 110	17.30
Electrical and electronic engineering technicians	244 570	19.81	41 210	19.24
Electro-mechanical technicians	40 770	18.57	38 630	17.38
Environmental engineering technicians	17 530	17.55	36 500	16.35
Industrial engineering technicians	65 220	21.31	44 330	19.67
Mechanical engineering technicians	58 490	19.93	41 460	19.03
Surveying and mapping technicians	51 640	14.61	30 380	13.48
LIFE, PHYSICAL, AND SOCIAL SCIENCE OCCUPATIONS				
Agricultural and food scientists	21 050	26.29	54 680	25.08
Biochemists and biophysicists	13 440	28.40	59 070	26.07
Microbiologists	15 880	25.50	53 040	23.51
Zoologists and wildlife biologists	11 710	21.94	45 630	21.15
Conservation scientists	12 980	22.99	47 820	22.67
Foresters	9 890	21.62	44 970	20.98
Epidemiologists	2 480	24.82	51 630	23.27
Medical scientists, except epidemiologists	35 570	30.49	63 430	27.79
Astronomers	910	35.37	73 580	35.82
Physicists	8 990	39.90	82 990	40.06
Atmospheric and space scientists	7 290	28.01	58 270	28.13
Chemists	82 320	26.10	54 280	24.07
Materials scientists	8 660	30.28	62 980	29.14
Environmental scientists and specialists, including health	54 860	23.12	48 090	21.24
Geoscientists, except hydrologists and geographers	21 810	30.01	62 420	27.04
Hydrologists	7 240	27.64	57 490	26.64
Economists	13 680	33.56	69 800	31.17
Market research analysts	99 030	27.21	56 600	24.61
Survey researchers	25 210	16.44	34 180	12.60
Clinical, counseling, and school psychologists	103 120	24.28	50 510	23.23
Industrial-organizational psychologists	1 280	33.22	69 090	32.15
Sociologists	1 360	24.16	50 250	21.96
Urban and regional planners	28 850	23.36	48 590	22.36
Anthropologists and archeologists	4 140	18.87	39 250	17.33
Geographers	660	23.48	48 840	22.45
Historians	1 880	20.25	42 120	19.16
Political scientists	4 250	37.92	78 870	38.96
Agricultural and food science technicians	15 260	14.34	29 820	13.02
Biological technicians	41 660	15.85	32 970	15.16
Chemical technicians	74 240	17.83	37 080	17.05

See footnotes at end of table.

Table 5-16. Employment and Wages by Occupation, 2000—*Continued*

(Number of persons, dollars.)

Occupational division and occupation	Employment	Mean hourly wages	Mean annual wages[1]	Median hourly wages
Geological and petroleum technicians	11 120	19.11	39 760	17.55
Nuclear technicians	4 110	29.79	61 970	28.44
Environmental science and protection technicians, including health	24 630	17.23	35 830	16.26
Forensic science technicians	6 150	18.95	39 410	18.04
Forest and conservation technicians	15 510	15.01	31 210	14.22
COMMUNITY AND SOCIAL SERVICE OCCUPATIONS				
Substance abuse and behavioral disorder counselors	56 080	14.47	30 100	13.71
Educational, vocational, and school counselors	188 000	21.08	43 850	20.24
Marriage and family therapists	19 420	17.66	36 730	16.66
Mental health counselors	65 780	14.61	30 390	13.25
Rehabilitation counselors	104 850	13.06	27 170	11.75
Child, family, and school social workers	266 570	16.12	33 530	15.13
Medical and public health social workers	103 390	17.50	36 400	16.73
Mental health and substance abuse social workers	79 740	15.50	32 240	14.50
Health educators	43 670	17.61	36 640	16.28
Probation officers and correctional treatment specialists	80 500	19.35	40 240	18.34
Social and human service assistants	260 910	11.46	23 840	10.74
Clergy	30 980	16.23	33 760	15.27
Directors, religious activities and education	13 610	14.38	29 900	12.98
LEGAL OCCUPATIONS				
Lawyers	489 530	43.90	91 320	42.44
Administrative law judges, adjudicators, and hearing officers	12 560	31.32	65 150	29.44
Arbitrators, mediators, and conciliators	4 850	24.68	51 330	20.70
Judges, magistrate judges, and magistrates	25 190	37.85	78 720	41.71
Paralegals and legal assistants	179 330	18.65	38 790	17.00
Court reporters	15 810	20.06	41 730	19.07
Law clerks	29 190	15.17	31 550	13.71
Title examiners, abstractors, and searchers	40 000	16.32	33 940	14.40
EDUCATION, TRAINING, AND LIBRARY OCCUPATIONS				
Business teachers, postsecondary	61 860	(2)	58 160	(2)
Computer science teachers, postsecondary	27 770	(2)	51 260	(2)
Mathematical science teachers, postsecondary	37 660	(2)	51 410	(2)
Architecture teachers, postsecondary	4 620	(2)	52 680	(2)
Engineering teachers, postsecondary	26 940	(2)	67 540	(2)
Agricultural sciences teachers, postsecondary	10 720	(2)	62 540	(2)
Biological science teachers, postsecondary	36 910	(2)	61 460	(2)
Forestry and conservation science teachers, postsecondary	1 980	(2)	60 950	(2)
Atmospheric, earth, marine, and space sciences teachers, postsecondary	8 000	(2)	60 080	(2)
Chemistry teachers, postsecondary	16 020	(2)	56 550	(2)
Environmental science teachers, postsecondary	3 530	(2)	58 180	(2)
Physics teachers, postsecondary	11 880	(2)	62 740	(2)
Anthropology and archeology teachers, postsecondary	4 400	(2)	58 620	(2)
Area, ethnic, and cultural studies teachers, postsecondary	4 070	(2)	56 990	(2)
Economics teachers, postsecondary	11 530	(2)	63 860	(2)
Geography teachers, postsecondary	3 570	(2)	56 670	(2)
Political science teachers, postsecondary	10 820	(2)	56 920	(2)
Psychology teachers, postsecondary	24 000	(2)	55 170	(2)
Sociology teachers, postsecondary	13 760	(2)	50 890	(2)
Health specialties teachers, postsecondary	78 680	(2)	67 140	(2)
Nursing instructors and teachers, postsecondary	35 870	(2)	49 130	(2)
Education teachers, postsecondary	41 180	(2)	48 310	(2)
Library science teachers, postsecondary	4 160	(2)	52 140	(2)
Criminal justice and law enforcement teachers, postsecondary	8 480	(2)	44 760	(2)
Law teachers, postsecondary	9 500	(2)	75 530	(2)
Social work teachers, postsecondary	6 570	(2)	50 970	(2)
Art, drama, and music teachers, postsecondary	55 160	(2)	49 170	(2)
Communications teachers, postsecondary	18 450	(2)	48 900	(2)
English language and literature teachers, postsecondary	50 560	(2)	47 790	(2)
Foreign language and literature teachers, postsecondary	18 380	(2)	48 150	(2)
History teachers, postsecondary	16 630	(2)	52 280	(2)
Philosophy and religion teachers, postsecondary	14 000	(2)	50 070	(2)
Graduate teaching assistants	129 270	(2)	24 170	(2)
Home economics teachers, postsecondary	4 380	(2)	50 350	(2)
Recreation and fitness studies teachers, postsecondary	14 050	(2)	43 810	(2)
Vocational education teachers, postsecondary	115 080	19.61	40 790	18.35
Preschool teachers, except special education	357 220	9.66	20 100	8.56
Kindergarten teachers, except special education	155 530	(2)	40 230	(2)
Elementary school teachers, except special education	1 409 140	(2)	41 980	(2)
Middle school teachers, except special and vocational education	561 200	(2)	41 890	(2)

See footnotes at end of table.

Table 5-16. Employment and Wages by Occupation, 2000—*Continued*

(Number of persons, dollars.)

Occupational division and occupation	Employment	Mean hourly wages	Mean annual wages[1]	Median hourly wages
Vocational education teachers, middle school	19 010	(2)	40 810	(2)
Secondary school teachers, except special and vocational education	933 800	(2)	43 030	(2)
Vocational education teachers, secondary school	103 200	(2)	43 240	(2)
Special education teachers, preschool, kindergarten, and elementary school	208 970	(2)	43 700	(2)
Special education teachers, middle school	87 790	(2)	41 730	(2)
Special education teachers, secondary school	116 760	(2)	44 100	(2)
Adult literacy, remedial education, and GED teachers and instructors	53 250	17.45	36 300	16.12
Self-enrichment education teachers	125 960	14.94	31 070	13.44
Archivists, curators, and museum technicians	18 100	17.88	37 190	15.90
Librarians	139 460	20.54	42 730	20.05
Library technicians	100 690	11.65	24 230	11.14
Audio-visual collections specialists	8 740	17.11	35 590	16.00
Farm and home management advisors	10 290	18.45	38 370	17.45
Instructional coordinators	77 100	22.27	46 320	21.27
Teacher assistants	1 159 110	(2)	18 770	(2)
ART, DESIGN, ENTERTAINMENT, SPORTS, AND MEDIA OCCUPATIONS				
Art directors	20 560	30.30	63 020	27.35
Fine artists, including painters, sculptors, and illustrators	11 930	17.20	35 770	15.00
Multi-media artists and animators	31 120	21.47	44 650	19.77
Commercial and industrial designers	33 910	24.55	51 060	23.45
Fashion designers	10 460	27.04	56 240	23.33
Floral designers	71 280	9.29	19 330	8.83
Graphic designers	133 630	18.25	37 970	16.62
Interior designers	30 680	19.55	40 670	17.57
Merchandise displayers and window trimmers	51 240	11.19	23 280	10.06
Set and exhibit designers	8 470	16.26	33 810	15.11
Actors	63 500	(2)	41 570	(2)
Producers and directors	46 750	(2)	48 740	(2)
Athletes and sports competitors	9 920	(2)	62 960	(2)
Coaches and scouts	68 220	(2)	33 470	(2)
Umpires, referees, and other sports officials	7 820	(2)	23 280	(2)
Dancers	20 900	13.44	27 950	10.80
Choreographers	10 860	15.42	32 080	12.99
Music directors and composers	6 660	(2)	36 900	(2)
Musicians and singers	52 180	(2)	44 520	(2)
Announcers	49 770	13.13	27 320	9.52
News analysts, reporters and correspondents	65 930	18.04	37 510	14.00
Public relations specialists	128 570	21.01	43 700	19.03
Editors	104 210	21.32	44 350	18.93
Technical writers	50 700	24.07	50 060	22.98
Writers and authors	41 410	22.81	47 440	20.32
Interpreters and translators	16 780	16.13	33 550	14.95
Audio and video equipment technicians	34 110	17.72	36 860	14.57
Broadcast technicians	33 560	15.89	33 060	12.96
Radio operators	3 060	15.89	33 050	14.07
Sound engineering technicians	10 380	25.56	53 170	18.98
Photographers	65 360	13.18	27 420	10.72
Camera operators, television, video, and motion picture	20 970	16.28	33 860	13.40
Film and video editors	10 990	19.81	41 200	16.42
HEALTHCARE PRACTITIONERS AND TECHNICAL OCCUPATIONS				
Chiropractors	16 740	35.96	74 790	32.23
Dentists	90 090	54.24	112 820	62.04
Dietitians and nutritionists	43 030	18.76	39 020	18.48
Optometrists	23 880	40.86	84 980	39.84
Pharmacists	212 660	33.39	69 440	34.11
Anesthesiologists	24 350	62.35	129 680	(3)
Family and general practitioners	132 620	51.82	107 780	54.89
Internists, general	50 450	59.22	123 180	68.46
Obstetricians and gynecologists	18 240	64.16	133 450	(3)
Pediatricians, general	25 580	56.26	117 020	60.56
Psychiatrists	21 280	51.95	108 060	57.04
Surgeons	48 770	66.06	137 400	(3)
Physician assistants	55 490	29.17	60 680	29.76
Podiatrists	7 870	48.59	101 070	51.71
Registered nurses	2 189 670	22.31	46 410	21.56
Audiologists	11 530	22.92	47 670	21.56
Occupational therapists	75 150	24.10	50 140	23.77
Physical therapists	120 410	27.62	57 450	26.35
Radiation therapists	13 100	25.59	53 230	22.82
Recreational therapists	26 940	14.23	29 590	13.77

See footnotes at end of table.

Table 5-16. Employment and Wages by Occupation, 2000—*Continued*

(Number of persons, dollars.)

Occupational division and occupation	Employment	Mean hourly wages	Mean annual wages[1]	Median hourly wages
Respiratory therapists	82 670	18.37	38 220	18.11
Speech-language pathologists	82 850	23.31	48 480	22.42
Veterinarians	40 270	32.99	68 620	29.28
Medical and clinical laboratory technologists	144 530	19.84	41 260	19.48
Medical and clinical laboratory technicians	146 060	13.93	28 970	13.24
Dental hygienists	148 460	24.99	51 980	24.68
Cardiovascular technologists and technicians	40 080	16.81	34 960	16.03
Diagnostic medical sonographers	31 760	22.03	45 820	21.55
Nuclear medicine technologists	18 030	21.56	44 850	21.22
Radiologic technologists and technicians	172 080	17.93	37 290	17.31
Emergency medical technicians and paramedics	165 530	11.89	24 740	10.80
Dietetic technicians	28 010	10.98	22 830	10.26
Pharmacy technicians	190 940	10.38	21 600	9.93
Psychiatric technicians	53 350	12.53	26 060	11.74
Respiratory therapy technicians	28 230	16.46	34 230	15.80
Surgical technologists	68 590	14.26	29 660	13.95
Veterinary technologists and technicians	50 370	10.93	22 730	10.41
Licensed practical and licensed vocational nurses	679 470	14.65	30 470	14.15
Medical records and health information technicians	143 870	11.74	24 430	10.94
Opticians, dispensing	66 580	12.67	26 360	11.75
Orthotists and prosthetists	4 750	24.32	50 590	21.99
Occupational health and safety specialists and technicians	32 390	21.34	44 380	20.55
Athletic trainers	13 820	(2)	33 650	(2)

HEALTHCARE SUPPORT OCCUPATIONS

Home health aides	561 120	8.71	18 110	8.23
Nursing aides, orderlies, and attendants	1 273 460	9.18	19 100	8.89
Psychiatric aides	57 680	10.79	22 440	10.45
Occupational therapist assistants	15 910	16.76	34 860	16.51
Occupational therapist aides	8 890	11.21	23 330	9.96
Physical therapist assistants	44 120	16.52	34 370	16.29
Physical therapist aides	34 620	10.06	20 930	9.46
Massage therapists	24 620	15.51	32 270	13.07
Dental assistants	250 870	12.86	26 740	12.49
Medical assistants	330 830	11.46	23 840	11.06
Medical equipment preparers	32 760	10.68	22 200	10.16
Medical transcriptionists	97 330	12.37	25 720	12.15
Pharmacy aides	59 890	9.10	18 930	8.52
Veterinary assistants and laboratory animal caretakers	55 210	8.55	17 790	8.00

PROTECTIVE SERVICE OCCUPATIONS

First-line supervisors, managers of correctional officers	29 380	21.33	44 370	20.14
First-line supervisors/managers of police and detectives	113 740	27.84	57 900	27.50
First-line supervisors/managers of fire fighting and prevention workers	59 500	25.47	52 990	24.99
Fire fighters	251 060	16.95	35 260	16.43
Fire inspectors and investigators	11 900	20.58	42 800	20.01
Forest fire inspectors and prevention specialists	1 040	15.82	32 910	15.45
Bailiffs	14 000	15.85	32 960	14.99
Correctional officers and jailers	405 360	15.71	32 680	14.99
Detectives and criminal investigators	87 090	23.96	49 830	23.50
Fish and game wardens	7 730	21.14	43 970	19.20
Parking enforcement workers	8 040	12.67	26 360	12.37
Police and sheriff's patrol officers	571 210	19.52	40 590	19.13
Transit and railroad police	5 760	19.98	41 560	19.41
Animal control workers	8 060	11.76	24 450	11.06
Private detectives and investigators	28 700	14.74	30 650	12.86
Gaming surveillance officers and gaming investigators	11 550	10.82	22 510	10.20
Security guards	1 104 400	9.36	19 470	8.45
Crossing guards	72 830	9.19	19 110	8.37

FOOD PREPARATION AND SERVING RELATED OCCUPATIONS

Chefs and head cooks	122 860	13.73	28 550	12.07
First-line supervisors/managers of food preparation and serving workers	624 180	11.83	24 600	10.91
Cooks, fast food	527 500	6.78	14 100	6.53
Cooks, institution and cafeteria	414 100	8.68	18 060	8.22
Cooks, restaurant	642 060	9.08	18 880	8.72
Cooks, short order	192 030	7.92	16 480	7.55
Food preparation workers	847 810	7.78	16 180	7.38
Bartenders	379 990	7.77	16 150	6.86
Combined food preparation and serving workers, including fast food	2 159 940	6.84	14 240	6.52
Counter Attendants, Cafeteria, Food Concession, and Coffee Shop	445 480	7.23	15 030	6.72

See footnotes at end of table.

Table 5-16. Employment and Wages by Occupation, 2000—*Continued*

(Number of persons, dollars.)

Occupational division and occupation	Employment	Mean hourly wages	Mean annual wages[1]	Median hourly wages
Waiters and waitresses	2 008 760	7.09	14 750	6.42
Food servers, nonrestaurant	199 600	7.77	16 170	7.07
Dining room and cafeteria attendants and bartender helpers	435 500	6.95	14 460	6.53
Dishwashers	505 500	7.00	14 560	6.69
Hosts and hostesses, restaurant, lounge, and coffee shop	312 390	7.32	15 230	6.95
BUILDING AND GROUNDS CLEANING AND MAINTENANCE OCCUPATIONS				
First-line supervisors, managers of housekeeping and janitorial workers	203 840	13.38	27 830	12.38
First-line supervisors/managers of landscaping, lawn service, and groundskeeping workers	95 760	16.21	33 720	14.70
Janitors and cleaners, except maids and housekeeping cleaners	2 083 330	9.17	19 080	8.26
Maids and housekeeping cleaners	948 230	7.78	16 190	7.41
Pest control workers	50 840	11.55	24 020	10.65
Landscaping and groundskeeping workers	754 340	9.63	20 030	8.80
Pesticide handlers, sprayers, and applicators, vegetation	22 200	11.74	24 410	11.11
Tree trimmers and pruners	44 570	12.30	25 590	11.41
PERSONAL CARE AND SERVICE OCCUPATIONS				
Gaming supervisors	28 480	18.35	38 170	18.22
Slot key persons	12 950	11.34	23 580	10.39
First-line supervisors/managers of personal service workers	88 940	14.59	30 350	13.06
Animal trainers	6 400	12.62	26 260	10.54
Nonfarm animal caretakers	86 840	8.46	17 600	7.67
Gaming dealers	84 310	7.48	15 550	6.41
Gaming and sports book writers and runners	11 680	8.79	18 290	8.22
Motion picture projectionists	8 590	8.82	18 350	7.08
Ushers, lobby attendants, and ticket takers	100 060	7.88	16 380	6.61
Amusement and recreation attendants	197 790	7.44	15 480	6.72
Costume attendants	4 290	11.92	24 790	10.71
Locker room, coatroom, and dressing room attendants	19 880	8.08	16 810	7.62
Embalmers	7 090	16.81	34 970	15.80
Funeral attendants	27 660	8.80	18 310	8.14
Barbers	13 290	9.78	20 340	8.53
Hairdressers, hairstylists, and cosmetologists	327 140	9.96	20 710	8.49
Makeup artists, theatrical and performance	900	15.65	32 550	12.33
Manicurists and pedicurists	28 230	8.13	16 920	7.42
Shampooers	13 140	6.97	14 490	6.58
Skin care specialists	13 420	11.26	23 420	9.65
Baggage porters and bellhops	55 450	9.78	20 350	7.80
Concierges	17 960	10.78	22 420	9.72
Tour guides and escorts	30 480	9.59	19 940	8.50
Travel guides	5 200	14.90	30 990	12.12
Flight attendants	126 380	(2)	45 220	(2)
Transportation attendants, except flight attendants and baggage porters	23 550	9.46	19 680	8.48
Child care workers	398 090	7.86	16 350	7.43
Personal and home care aides	371 280	7.67	15 960	7.50
Fitness trainers and aerobics instructors	157 230	13.82	28 750	10.96
Recreation workers	245 720	9.32	19 380	8.24
Residential advisors	42 630	10.38	21 600	9.65
SALES AND RELATED OCCUPATIONS				
First-line supervisors, managers of retail sales workers	1 269 870	15.47	32 170	13.23
First-line supervisors/managers of non-retail sales workers	322 560	27.33	56 850	23.54
Cashiers	3 338 840	7.56	15 730	6.95
Gaming change persons and booth cashiers	38 770	9.06	18 850	8.79
Counter and rental clerks	420 510	8.98	18 670	7.87
Parts salespersons	255 300	12.12	25 210	10.85
Retail salespersons	3 964 680	9.74	20 260	8.02
Advertising sales agents	151 140	21.62	44 960	17.24
Insurance sales agents	240 830	23.13	48 100	18.63
Securities, commodities, and financial services sales agents	269 310	33.85	70 410	26.96
Travel agents	124 030	12.79	26 600	12.09
Sales representatives, wholesale and manufacturing, technical and scientific products	373 630	28.19	58 630	25.30
Sales representatives, wholesale and manufacturing, except technical and scientific products	1 379 860	22.49	46 770	19.40
Demonstrators and product promoters	102 650	11.76	24 460	9.51
Models	3 590	11.05	22 990	9.17
Real estate brokers	31 120	28.89	60 080	22.93
Real estate sales agents	108 880	18.25	37 950	13.29
Sales engineers	88 240	29.54	61 450	27.17
Telemarketers	461 890	10.32	21 460	9.06
Door-to-door sales workers, news and street vendors, and related workers	33 830	14.05	29 220	11.56

See footnotes at end of table.

Table 5-16. Employment and Wages by Occupation, 2000—*Continued*

(Number of persons, dollars.)

Occupational division and occupation	Employment	Mean hourly wages	Mean annual wages[1]	Median hourly wages
OFFICE AND ADMINISTRATIVE SUPPORT OCCUPATIONS				
First-line supervisors, managers of office and administrative support workers	1 394 640	18.95	39 410	17.51
Switchboard operators, including answering service	243 100	10.05	20 900	9.71
Telephone operators	52 150	13.32	27 710	13.46
Bill and account collectors	387 870	12.82	26 670	12.17
Billing and posting clerks and machine operators	492 040	12.25	25 480	11.81
Bookkeeping, accounting, and auditing clerks	1 663 530	12.96	26 950	12.34
Gaming cage workers	21 070	10.40	21 620	9.99
Payroll and timekeeping clerks	191 310	13.57	28 220	13.07
Procurement clerks	75 960	13.64	28 380	13.33
Tellers	492 950	9.40	19 540	9.21
Brokerage clerks	80 150	16.19	33 680	14.93
Correspondence clerks	38 560	12.09	25 150	11.61
Court, municipal, and license clerks	97 630	13.36	27 780	12.57
Credit authorizers, checkers, and clerks	82 980	12.70	26 420	11.81
Customer service representatives	1 907 890	12.75	26 530	11.83
Eligibility interviewers, government programs	106 570	14.54	30 230	13.65
File clerks	264 720	9.49	19 730	8.99
Hotel, motel, and resort desk clerks	175 150	8.22	17 100	7.87
Interviewers, except eligibility and loan	156 340	10.75	22 360	10.02
Library assistants, clerical	95 100	9.32	19 380	8.65
Loan interviewers and clerks	140 040	13.40	27 870	12.70
New accounts clerks	88 390	11.71	24 370	11.10
Order clerks	351 580	12.08	25 130	11.35
Human resources assistants, except payroll and timekeeping	172 070	14.13	29 400	13.63
Receptionists and information clerks	1 054 300	9.99	20 780	9.63
Reservation and transportation ticket agents and travel clerks	199 700	12.57	26 140	10.87
Cargo and freight agents	64 320	14.63	30 440	13.73
Couriers and messengers	130 210	9.63	20 030	8.96
Police, fire, and ambulance dispatchers	82 050	12.83	26 680	12.38
Dispatchers, except police, fire, and ambulance	167 180	14.62	30 410	13.66
Meter readers, utilities	48 950	14.02	29 150	13.32
Postal service clerks	80 730	18.31	38 080	18.75
Postal service mail carriers	354 980	17.71	36 830	18.47
Postal service mail sorters, processors, and processing machine operators	231 770	14.81	30 810	15.42
Production, planning, and expediting clerks	330 120	15.64	32 520	14.71
Shipping, receiving, and traffic clerks	864 530	11.22	23 340	10.52
Stock clerks and order fillers	1 771 780	9.93	20 650	8.75
Weighers, measurers, checkers, and samplers, recordkeeping	79 480	12.62	26 250	11.36
Executive secretaries and administrative assistants	1 369 960	15.63	32 520	14.95
Legal secretaries	270 670	17.00	35 370	16.70
Medical secretaries	283 150	11.76	24 460	11.26
Secretaries, except legal, medical, and executive	1 698 080	11.98	24 910	11.47
Computer operators	186 460	14.15	29 430	13.30
Data entry keyers	458 720	10.66	22 170	10.24
Word processors and typists	257 020	12.22	25 420	11.88
Desktop publishers	35 460	15.72	32 700	14.71
Insurance claims and policy processing clerks	266 650	14.72	30 620	13.47
Mail clerks and mail machine operators, except postal service	182 460	9.96	20 710	9.54
Office clerks, general	2 674 710	10.72	22 290	10.16
Office machine operators, except computer	86 380	10.77	22 400	10.00
Proofreaders and copy markers	27 800	11.89	24 730	10.76
Statistical assistants	22 050	14.22	29 570	13.40
FARMING, FISHING, AND FORESTRY OCCUPATIONS				
First-line supervisors, managers of farming, fishing, and forestry workers	21 350	16.72	34 780	15.43
Farm labor contractors	8 290	8.95	18 620	6.82
Agricultural inspectors	12 210	14.72	30 620	13.75
Animal breeders	1 680	12.11	25 200	10.28
Graders and sorters, agricultural products	56 210	8.00	16 640	7.11
Agricultural equipment operators	23 230	8.66	18 020	7.68
Farmworkers and laborers, crop, nursery, and greenhouse	215 150	7.21	15 000	6.64
Farmworkers, farm and ranch animals	36 270	8.18	17 010	7.61
Forest and conservation workers	9 990	10.45	21 730	8.97
Fallers	9 910	14.59	30 350	12.33
Logging equipment operators	34 180	12.47	25 930	12.07
Log graders and scalers	5 470	13.81	28 730	13.07

See footnotes at end of table.

Table 5-16. Employment and Wages by Occupation, 2000—*Continued*

(Number of persons, dollars.)

Occupational division and occupation	Employment	Mean hourly wages	Mean annual wages[1]	Median hourly wages
CONSTRUCTION AND EXTRACTION OCCUPATIONS				
First-line supervisors, managers of construction trades, and extraction workers	502 010	22.95	47 740	21.53
Boilermakers	25 280	18.26	37 980	17.80
Brickmasons and blockmasons	108 590	19.78	41 140	19.37
Stonemasons	10 100	15.57	32 380	14.98
Carpenters	858 890	16.88	35 100	15.69
Carpet installers	38 010	15.88	33 030	14.46
Floor layers, except carpet, wood, and hard tiles	12 300	15.90	33 070	14.81
Floor sanders and finishers	7 610	14.95	31 100	13.17
Tile and marble setters	27 870	17.58	36 580	16.49
Cement masons and concrete finishers	169 550	14.92	31 020	13.50
Terrazzo workers and finishers	4 510	15.76	32 790	15.06
Construction laborers	821 210	12.95	26 940	11.15
Paving, surfacing, and tamping equipment operators	56 330	14.47	30 090	12.88
Pile-driver operators	4 320	19.99	41 570	19.85
Operating engineers and other construction equipment operators	333 200	17.39	36 170	15.99
Drywall and ceiling tile installers	118 280	17.11	35 580	15.80
Tapers	35 440	18.60	38 680	17.81
Electricians	640 260	20.29	42 210	19.29
Glaziers	46 160	15.56	32 360	14.32
Insulation workers	54 710	14.86	30 910	13.05
Painters, construction, and maintenance	261 040	14.24	29 610	13.10
Paperhangers	10 690	15.62	32 490	15.33
Pipelayers	59 560	14.53	30 220	13.20
Plumbers, pipefitters, and steamfitters	437 140	19.31	40 170	18.19
Plasterers and stucco masons	45 150	16.91	35 170	16.00
Reinforcing iron and rebar workers	27 010	18.17	37 800	16.78
Roofers	114 410	15.22	31 670	13.95
Sheet metal workers	218 020	16.85	35 050	15.31
Structural iron and steel workers	81 710	18.82	39 140	17.92
Helpers-brickmasons, blockmasons, stonemasons, and tile and marble setters	58 090	12.39	25 780	10.95
Helpers-carpenters	99 170	10.37	21 570	9.91
Helpers-electricians	112 820	10.93	22 740	10.27
Helpers-painters, paperhangers, plasterers, and stucco masons	26 910	10.28	21 380	9.28
Helpers-pipelayers, plumbers, pipefitters, and steamfitters	85 320	10.79	22 450	10.21
Helpers-roofers	24 160	9.77	20 320	9.35
Construction and building inspectors	68 690	19.10	39 730	18.63
Elevator installers and repairers	25 100	22.23	46 240	22.78
Fence erectors	18 370	12.02	25 010	10.53
Hazardous materials removal workers	34 070	15.21	31 630	13.71
Highway maintenance workers	145 790	13.21	27 480	12.82
Rail-track laying and maintenance equipment operators	9 940	14.84	30 870	14.93
Septic tank servicers and sewer pipe cleaners	15 040	13.91	28 930	13.02
Segmental pavers	2 680	13.48	28 050	12.46
Derrick operators, oil and gas	15 540	13.42	27 910	12.41
Rotary drill operators, oil and gas	15 500	15.99	33 270	14.83
Service unit operators, oil, gas, and mining	11 020	13.34	27 750	12.12
Earth drillers, except oil and gas	19 860	15.39	32 010	14.68
Explosives workers, ordnance handling experts, and blasters	4 680	16.15	33 590	15.84
Continuous mining machine operators	9 480	16.05	33 380	15.64
Mine cutting and channeling machine operators	(4)	16.68	34 690	16.65
Rock splitters, quarry	2 600	13.10	27 250	12.43
Roof bolters, mining	3 460	17.19	35 760	17.21
Roustabouts, oil and gas	38 590	10.88	22 640	9.83
Helpers-extraction workers	30 760	11.72	24 380	10.99
INSTALLATION, MAINTENANCE, AND REPAIR OCCUPATIONS				
First-line supervisors/managers of mechanics, installers, and repairers	421 740	22.39	46 560	21.27
Computer, automated teller, and office machine workers	142 390	15.80	32 860	15.08
Radio mechanics	7 110	16.73	34 800	15.86
Telecommunications equipment installers and repairers, except line installers	192 470	20.44	42 520	21.17
Avionics technicians	15 360	20.00	41 600	19.86
Electric motor, power tool, and related repairers	36 620	16.38	34 070	15.80
Electrical and electronics installers and repairers, transportation equipment	15 930	17.16	35 690	16.93
Electrical and electronics repairers, commercial and industrial equipment	81 760	17.88	37 190	17.75
Electrical and electronics repairers, powerhouse, substation, and relay	19 300	22.35	46 490	23.34
Electronic equipment installers and repairers, motor vehicles	12 480	12.71	26 440	12.06
Electronic home entertainment equipment installers and repairers	29 550	13.55	28 190	12.72

See footnotes at end of table.

Table 5-16. Employment and Wages by Occupation, 2000—*Continued*

(Number of persons, dollars.)

Occupational division and occupation	Employment	Mean hourly wages	Mean annual wages[1]	Median hourly wages
Security and fire alarm systems installers	38 810	15.92	33 100	14.66
Aircraft mechanics and service technicians	135 730	19.49	40 550	19.50
Automotive body and related repairers	168 170	16.21	33 710	15.00
Automotive glass installers and repairers	21 240	13.03	27 090	12.46
Automotive service technicians and mechanics	692 570	14.80	30 780	13.70
Bus and truck mechanics and diesel engine specialists	258 800	15.97	33 210	15.55
Farm equipment mechanics	37 010	12.83	26 690	12.38
Mobile heavy equipment mechanics, except engines	118 300	16.73	34 790	16.32
Rail car repairers	10 620	15.85	32 960	16.19
Motorboat mechanics	19 040	13.49	28 060	12.82
Motorcycle mechanics	11 720	12.90	26 820	12.07
Outdoor power equipment and other small engine mechanics	25 760	11.86	24 670	11.43
Bicycle repairers	7 940	9.04	18 810	8.67
Recreational vehicle service technicians	12 200	12.79	26 610	12.20
Tire repairers and changers	88 530	9.66	20 100	9.02
Mechanical door repairers	10 460	14.41	29 980	13.77
Control and valve installers and repairers, except mechanical door	34 910	19.66	40 890	19.87
Heating, air conditioning, and refrigeration mechanics and installers	197 930	16.43	34 180	15.76
Home appliance repairers	33 910	14.80	30 790	13.87
Industrial machinery mechanics	192 180	18.02	37 490	17.30
Maintenance and repair workers, general	1 216 250	14.14	29 420	13.39
Maintenance workers, machinery	107 500	15.47	32 170	14.89
Millwrights	75 940	19.42	40 400	19.33
Refractory materials repairers, except brickmasons	3 640	16.64	34 620	16.82
Electrical power-line installers and repairers	96 200	21.39	44 490	22.01
Telecommunications line installers and repairers	168 480	18.29	38 050	18.32
Camera and photographic equipment repairers	5 080	14.53	30 230	13.94
Medical equipment repairers	22 020	18.02	37 470	16.99
Musical instrument repairers and tuners	5 620	17.26	35 900	15.10
Watch repairers	4 000	13.12	27 290	12.08
Coin, vending, and amusement machine servicers and repairers	35 480	12.74	26 510	12.33
Commercial divers	2 920	21.13	43 940	15.47
Fabric menders, except garment	2 390	12.75	26 530	10.85
Locksmiths and safe repairers	13 150	14.29	29 720	13.22
Manufactured building and mobile home installers	13 410	11.06	23 010	10.43
Riggers	14 640	15.90	33 060	15.42
Signal and track switch repairers	5 540	18.94	39 400	19.25
Helpers-installation, maintenance, and repair workers	146 870	10.88	22 620	9.98
PRODUCTION OCCUPATIONS				
First-line supervisors/managers of production and operating workers	769 540	20.68	43 020	19.39
Aircraft structures, surfaces, rigging, and systems assemblers	32 680	18.34	38 150	19.64
Coil winders, tapers, and finishers	53 050	10.55	21 940	9.77
Electrical and electronic equipment assemblers	367 150	11.03	22 950	10.31
Electromechanical equipment assemblers	72 550	11.81	24 560	11.16
Engine and other machine assemblers	66 090	14.09	29 320	13.47
Structural metal fabricators and fitters	101 490	13.70	28 490	13.11
Fiberglass laminators and fabricators	46 700	11.75	24 430	10.82
Team assemblers	1 306 430	11.29	23 490	10.32
Timing device assemblers, adjusters, and calibrators	11 020	11.66	24 250	10.78
Bakers	156 100	10.12	21 050	9.48
Butchers and meat cutters	134 250	12.35	25 690	11.60
Meat, poultry, and fish cutters and trimmers	148 100	8.51	17 710	8.06
Slaughterers and meat packers	118 900	9.29	19 330	9.33
Food and tobacco roasting, baking, and drying machine operators and tenders	19 140	12.10	25 170	10.91
Food batchmakers	67 320	10.71	22 280	10.09
Food cooking machine operators and tenders	36 020	10.49	21 830	9.92
Computer-controlled machine tool operators, metal and plastic	162 360	13.84	28 780	13.17
Numerical tool and process control programmers	22 460	18.12	37 690	17.70
Extruding and drawing machine setters, operators, and tenders, metal and plastic	114 210	12.03	25 030	11.66
Forging machine setters, operators, and tenders, metal and plastic	53 950	13.30	27 660	12.11
Rolling machine setters, operators, and tenders, metal and plastic	49 710	13.39	27 850	12.85
Cutting, punching, and press machine setters, operators, and tenders, metal and plastic	351 050	11.67	24 280	11.03
Drilling and boring machine tool setters, operators, and tenders, metal and plastic	71 490	12.97	26 990	12.25
Grinding, lapping, polishing, and buffing machine tool setters, operators, and tenders, metal and plastic	124 080	12.42	25 820	11.71
Lathe and turning machine tool setters, operators, and tenders, metal and plastic	84 020	14.27	29 680	13.77

See footnotes at end of table.

Table 5-16. Employment and Wages by Occupation, 2000—*Continued*

(Number of persons, dollars.)

Occupational division and occupation	Employment	Mean hourly wages	Mean annual wages[1]	Median hourly wages
Milling and planing machine setters, operators, and tenders, metal and plastic	35 610	14.00	29 130	13.25
Machinists	420 320	15.20	31 610	14.78
Metal-refining furnace operators and tenders	19 770	14.12	29 370	13.47
Pourers and casters, metal	15 660	13.38	27 840	12.67
Model makers, metal and plastic	10 540	17.10	35 570	16.07
Patternmakers, metal and plastic	8 290	15.88	33 040	14.83
Foundry mold and coremakers	34 130	12.45	25 900	11.88
Molding, coremaking, and casting machine setters, operators, and tenders, metal and plastic	158 280	11.36	23 630	10.40
Multiple machine tool setters, operators, and tenders, metal and plastic	109 950	14.11	29 350	12.96
Tool and die makers	131 080	20.07	41 740	19.76
Welders, cutters, solderers, and brazers	413 720	13.98	29 080	13.13
Welding, soldering, and brazing machine setters, operators, and tenders	69 670	14.30	29 730	13.09
Heat treating equipment setters, operators, and tenders, metal and plastic	35 840	13.47	28 020	12.64
Lay-out workers, metal and plastic	16 770	15.22	31 650	14.27
Plating and coating machine setters, operators, and tenders, metal and plastic	54 760	11.82	24 580	11.23
Tool Grinders, filers, and sharpeners	28 360	14.22	29 580	13.22
Bindery workers	102 020	11.14	23 180	10.05
Bookbinders	9 080	12.89	26 810	11.42
Job printers	50 070	14.37	29 880	13.61
Prepress technicians and workers	104 920	15.31	31 840	14.57
Printing machine operators	214 880	14.47	30 090	13.57
Laundry and dry-cleaning workers	216 630	7.99	16 630	7.59
Pressers, textile, garment, and related materials	100 190	8.14	16 940	7.77
Sewing machine operators	362 010	8.39	17 450	7.80
Shoe and leather workers and repairers	12 210	9.07	18 860	8.32
Shoe machine operators and tenders	8 070	9.17	19 060	8.89
Sewers, hand	24 240	9.09	18 900	8.09
Tailors, dressmakers, and custom sewers	32 840	11.20	23 300	10.14
Textile bleaching and dyeing machine operators and tenders	38 350	9.49	19 750	9.42
Textile cutting machine setters, operators, and tenders	39 730	9.74	20 260	9.23
Textile knitting and weaving machine setters, operators, and tenders	69 110	10.45	21 730	10.32
Textile winding, twisting, and drawing out machine setters, operators, and tenders	82 320	10.12	21 040	9.89
Extruding and forming machine setters, operators, and tenders, synthetic and glass fibers	36 350	12.68	26 380	12.66
Fabric and apparel patternmakers	14 890	14.32	29 790	11.57
Upholsterers	42 410	12.30	25 580	11.42
Cabinetmakers and bench carpenters	132 630	11.60	24 140	10.83
Furniture finishers	36 870	10.95	22 770	10.34
Model makers, wood	4 900	13.31	27 680	11.70
Patternmakers, wood	5 420	14.50	30 160	13.59
Sawing machine setters, operators, and tenders, wood	54 330	10.71	22 290	10.23
Woodworking machine setters, operators, and tenders, except sawing	99 410	10.44	21 710	10.00
Nuclear power reactor operators	2 550	28.41	59 100	27.51
Power distributors and dispatchers	15 050	23.65	49 190	23.35
Power plant operators	34 720	21.79	45 330	22.16
Stationary engineers and boiler operators	56 330	19.94	41 470	19.43
Water and liquid waste treatment plant and system operators	87 760	15.60	32 450	15.09
Chemical plant and system operators	62 450	19.31	40 160	19.59
Gas plant operators	12 890	21.47	44 660	21.50
Petroleum pump system operators, refinery operators, and gaugers	31 230	21.15	43 980	21.72
Chemical equipment operators and tenders	60 380	17.46	36 310	17.21
Separating, filtering, clarifying, precipitating, and still machine setters, operators, and tenders	36 110	13.77	28 650	13.09
Crushing, grinding, and polishing machine setters, operators, and tenders	45 010	12.60	26 200	11.99
Grinding and polishing workers, hand	48 610	11.53	23 990	10.48
Mixing and blending machine setters, operators, and tenders	111 480	13.05	27 150	12.58
Cutters and trimmers, hand	34 340	11.07	23 030	9.78
Cutting and slicing machine setters, operators, and tenders	82 450	11.98	24 920	11.48
Extruding, forming, pressing, and compacting machine setters, operators, and tenders	76 370	12.57	26 150	11.94
Furnace, kiln, oven, drier, and kettle operators and tenders	31 800	13.60	28 300	13.13
Inspectors, testers, sorters, samplers, and weighers	571 220	13.47	28 010	12.22
Jewelers and precious stone and metal workers	31 030	13.91	28 930	12.66
Dental laboratory technicians	40 580	14.04	29 200	12.94
Medical appliance technicians	11 480	13.44	27 950	11.97
Ophthalmic laboratory technicians	36 980	10.45	21 740	9.88
Packaging and filling machine operators and tenders	370 080	10.43	21 700	9.45
Coating, painting, and spraying machine setters, operators, and tenders	103 650	12.09	25 140	11.37
Painters, transportation equipment	43 270	15.82	32 910	14.64
Painting, coating, and decorating workers	33 940	10.48	21 810	9.55
Photographic process workers	26 650	10.65	22 140	9.44
Photographic processing machine operators	51 950	9.39	19 540	8.39
Semiconductor processors	67 000	13.06	27 170	12.23

See footnotes at end of table.

Table 5-16. Employment and Wages by Occupation, 2000—*Continued*

(Number of persons, dollars.)

Occupational division and occupation	Employment	Mean hourly wages	Mean annual wages[1]	Median hourly wages
Cementing and gluing machine operators and tenders	34 220	11.14	23 170	10.49
Cleaning, washing, and metal pickling equipment operators and tenders	18 440	11.10	23 100	10.17
Cooling and freezing equipment operators and tenders	7 410	10.58	22 010	9.70
Etchers and engravers	11 060	11.42	23 740	10.12
Molders, shapers, and casters, except metal and plastic	40 260	11.83	24 620	11.24
Paper goods machine setters, operators, and tenders	121 300	13.32	27 700	12.75
Tire builders	15 790	16.30	33 910	17.56
Helpers-production workers	533 720	9.30	19 350	8.66
TRANSPORTATION AND MATERIAL MOVING OCCUPATIONS				
Aircraft cargo handling supervisors	9 960	19.57	40 710	18.19
First-line supervisors/managers of helpers, laborers, and material movers, hand	146 790	17.75	36 910	16.73
First-line supervisors/managers of transportation and material-moving machine and vehicle operators	186 710	20.73	43 120	19.37
Airline pilots, copilots, and flight engineers	94 820	(2)	99 770	(2)
Commercial pilots	18 040	(2)	51 370	(2)
Air traffic controllers	23 350	38.20	79 460	39.67
Airfield operations specialists	4 580	17.31	36 000	15.42
Ambulance drivers and attendants, except emergency medical technicians	15 700	9.46	19 680	8.57
Bus drivers, transit and intercity	175 470	13.10	27 250	12.36
Bus drivers, school	457 050	10.31	21 430	10.05
Driver, sales workers	373 660	11.08	23 060	9.79
Truck drivers, heavy and tractor-trailer	1 577 070	15.78	32 810	15.25
Truck drivers, light or delivery services	1 033 220	11.84	24 620	10.74
Taxi drivers and chauffeurs	130 200	9.10	18 920	8.19
Locomotive engineers	29 390	21.20	44 090	21.26
Locomotive firers	1 040	20.93	43 540	23.02
Rail yard engineers, dinkey operators, and hostlers	4 020	19.22	39 980	17.69
Railroad brake, signal, and switch operators	16 830	20.16	41 930	18.82
Railroad conductors and yardmasters	40 380	20.11	41 840	18.86
Subway and streetcar operators	(4)	19.74	41 060	20.10
Sailors and marine oilers	30 090	13.94	29 000	13.52
Captains, mates, and pilots of water vessels	21 080	23.30	48 450	22.84
Motorboat operators	3 540	14.61	30 400	13.83
Ship engineers	7 370	23.12	48 100	22.85
Bridge and lock tenders	4 790	14.60	30 370	15.59
Parking lot attendants	116 930	7.69	15 990	7.15
Service station attendants	106 010	7.87	16 370	7.35
Traffic technicians	4 590	16.19	33 670	14.82
Transportation inspectors	26 520	21.25	44 200	21.68
Conveyor operators and tenders	62 250	11.50	23 920	10.70
Crane and tower operators	55 770	16.99	35 340	15.89
Dredge operators	3 100	14.32	29 790	13.38
Excavating and loading machine and dragline operators	70 080	16.10	33 480	14.94
Loading machine operators, underground mining	2 680	14.22	29 570	13.87
Hoist and winch operators	9 280	16.02	33 320	14.40
Industrial truck and tractor operators	615 390	12.54	26 090	11.74
Cleaners of vehicles and equipment	301 330	8.36	17 380	7.55
Laborers and freight, stock, and material movers, hand	2 120 640	9.84	20 460	9.04
Machine feeders and offbearers	213 950	10.43	21 690	9.69
Packers and packagers, hand	1 020 640	8.19	17 030	7.53
Gas compressor and gas pumping station operators	6 510	20.05	41 700	20.32
Pump operators, except wellhead pumpers	13 730	18.00	37 440	17.16
Wellhead pumpers	9 790	16.04	33 360	16.35
Refuse and recyclable material collectors	118 910	12.51	26 020	11.83
Shuttle car operators	3 060	17.30	35 980	17.97
Tank car, truck, and ship loaders	17 480	15.62	32 490	13.78

1. Annual wages have been calculated by multiplying the hourly mean wage by a "year-round, full-time" hours figure of 2,080 hours; for those occupations where there is not an hourly mean wage published, the annual wage has been directly calculated from the reported survey data.
2. Hourly wage rates for occupations where workers typically work fewer than 2,080 hours per year are not available.
3. Represents a wage above $70.01 per hour.
4. Data not released due to high relative standard error.

PART SIX

PRICES AND LIVING CONDITIONS

PRICES AND LIVING CONDITIONS

HIGHLIGHTS

This chapter covers one of the most important aspects of the state of the economy, the movement of prices. Three price indexes are covered: prices received by producers (PPI), prices paid by consumers (CPI) and prices involved in foreign trade, export and import price indexes.

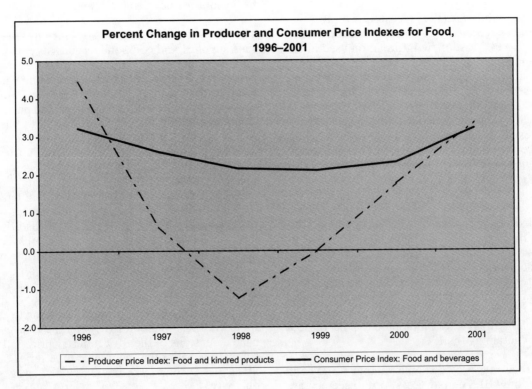

Percent Change in Producer and Consumer Price Indexes for Food, 1996–2001

- - Producer price Index: Food and kindred products —— Consumer Price Index: Food and beverages

Prices for food in the CPI accelerated in 2001, after years of relative stability. In the PPI, the increases began in 1999 and have continued throughout 2001.

OTHER HIGHLIGHTS:

- The movement of prices for energy in the CPI was mixed from 2000 to 2001. Motor fuel prices declined 3.6 percent, but piped gas and electricity increased 11.3 percent. (Table 6-8)
- The PPI for finished goods increased 2.0 percent, while the CPI for all items increased 2.8 percent in 2001. The PPI does not include shelter, which in the CPI increased 3.7 percent. (Tables 6-1 and 6-8)
- Medical care prices continued to rise rapidly in the CPI, 4.6 percent in 2001. Medical care services rose somewhat faster than medical care commodities, 4.8 percent v. 4 percent. Hospital care prices rose 6.6 percent. Prices in the health services industries in the PPI rose 3.2 percent, but drug industry prices rose only 2.2 percent. (Table 6-8 and 6-3)
- Prices of imports declined 9.1 percent from December 2000 to December 2001. The biggest decline was for fuels, both gasoline and natural and manufactured gas, which declined about 57.5 percent. (Table 6-13)

NOTES AND DEFINITIONS

PRODUCER PRICE INDEX

Coverage

The *Producer Price Index* (PPI) measures average changes in prices received by domestic producers of goods and services. Most of the information used in calculating the indexes is obtained through the systematic sampling of nearly every industry in the manufacturing and mining sectors of the economy. The PPI program also includes data from other sectors—agriculture, fishing, forestry, services, and gas and electricity. Because producer price indexes are designed to measure only the change in prices received for the output of domestic industries, *imports are not included*. The sample currently contains about 80,000 price quotations per month.

Producer price indexes are based on selling prices reported by establishments of all sizes selected by probability sampling, with the probability of selection proportionate to size. Individual items and transaction terms from these firms are also chosen by probability proportionate to size. BLS strongly encourages cooperating companies to supply actual transaction prices at the time of shipment to minimize the use of list prices. Prices are normally reported monthly by mail questionnaire for the Tuesday of the week containing the 13th.

Price data are always provided on a voluntary and confidential basis; only BLS employees, sworn to secrecy, are allowed access to individual company price reports. The Bureau publishes price indexes instead of unit dollar prices. All producer price indexes are routinely subject to revision once, 4 months after original publication, to reflect the availability of late reports and corrections by respondents.

There are three primary systems of indexes within the PPI program: (1) stage-of-processing indexes; (2) indexes for the net output of industries and their products; and (3) commodity indexes. The commodity-based *stage-of-processing* structure organizes products by class of buyer and degree of fabrication. The entire output of various industries is sampled to derive price indexes for the net output of industries and their products. The commodity structure organizes products by similarity of end-use or material composition.

Within the commodity stage-of-processing system, finished goods are commodities that will not undergo further processing and are ready for sale to the final demand user, either an individual consumer or a business firm. Consumer foods include unprocessed foods, such as eggs and fresh vegetables, as well as processed foods, such as bakery products and meats. Other finished consumer goods include durable goods, such as automobiles,

household furniture, and appliances; and nondurable goods, such as apparel and home heating oil. Capital equipment includes producer durable goods, such as heavy motor trucks, tractors, and machine tools.

The stage-of-processing category for intermediate materials, supplies, and components consists partly of commodities that have been processed but require further processing. Examples of such semi-finished goods include flour, cotton, yarn, steel mill products, and lumber. The intermediate goods category also encompasses physically complete nondurable goods purchased by business firms as inputs for their operations. Examples include diesel fuel, belts and belting, paper boxes, and fertilizers.

Crude materials for further processing are products entering the market for the first time that have not been manufactured or fabricated and that are not sold directly to consumers. Crude foodstuffs and feedstuffs include items such as grains and livestock. Examples of crude nonfood materials include raw cotton, crude petroleum, coal, hides and skins, and iron and steel scrap.

Producer price indexes for the net output of industries and their products are grouped according to the Standard Industrial Classification (SIC) and the Census product code extensions of the SIC. Industry price indexes are compatible with other economic time series organized by SIC codes, such as data on employment, wages, and productivity.

Net output values of shipments are used as weights for industry indexes. Net output values refer to the value of shipments from establishments in one industry shipped to establishments classified in another industry. However, *weights for commodity price indexes* are based on gross shipment values, including shipment values between establishments within the same industry. As a result, commodity aggregate indexes, such as the *all commodities index*, are affected by the multiple counting of price change at successive stages of processing, which can lead to exaggerated or misleading signals about inflation. Stage-of-processing indexes partially correct this defect, but industry indexes consistently correct this weakness at all levels of aggregation. Therefore, industry and stage-of-processing indexes are more appropriate than commodity aggregate indexes for economic analysis of general price trends.

Weights for most traditional commodity groupings of the PPI, as well as all indexes calculated from traditional commodity groupings (such as stage-of-processing indexes), currently reflect 1992 values of shipments as reported in the *Census of Manufactures* and other sources. Major industry group indexes, which are based on the SIC system, are currently calculated using 1992 net output weights. BLS is in the process of updating weights to take effect in 2002. The source data will be the most recent data from the Census of Manufactures and the Bureau of Economic Analysis. The new North American Industry Classification System (NAICS) is scheduled to be introduced in the PPI in 2004.

Sources of Additional Information

Additional information is published monthly by the BLS in the *Producer Price Index Detailed Report*. For information on the underlying concepts and methodology of the Producer Price Index, see chapter 14, "Producer Prices," in BLS *Handbook of Methods* (April 1997), Bulletin 2490.

Table 6-1. Producer Price Indexes by Stage of Processing, 1947–2001

(1982=100.)

Year	Crude materials for further processing				Intermediate materials, supplies, and components						Finished goods		
	Total	Food-stuffs and feedstuffs	Nonfood materials, except fuel, including crude petroleum	Fuel, excluding crude petroleum	Total	Materials and components for construction	Compo-nents for manufac-turing	Pro-cessed fuels and lubricants	Contain-ers	Supplies	Total	Consum-er goods	Capital equip-ment
1947	31.7	45.1	24.0	7.5	23.3	22.5	21.3	14.4	23.4	28.5	26.4	28.6	19.8
1948	34.7	48.8	26.7	8.9	25.2	24.9	23.0	16.4	24.4	29.8	28.5	30.8	21.6
1949	30.1	40.5	24.3	8.8	24.2	24.9	23.4	14.9	24.5	28.0	27.7	29.4	22.7
1950	32.7	43.4	27.8	8.8	25.3	26.2	24.3	15.2	25.2	29.0	28.2	29.9	23.2
1951	37.6	50.2	32.0	9.0	28.4	28.7	27.6	15.9	29.6	32.6	30.8	32.7	25.5
1952	34.5	47.3	27.8	9.0	27.5	28.5	27.6	15.7	28.0	32.6	30.6	32.3	25.9
1953	31.9	42.3	26.6	9.3	27.7	29.0	28.1	15.8	28.0	31.0	30.3	31.7	26.3
1954	31.6	42.3	26.1	8.9	27.9	29.1	28.3	15.8	28.5	31.7	30.4	31.7	26.7
1955	30.4	38.4	27.5	8.9	28.4	30.3	29.5	15.8	28.9	31.2	30.5	31.5	27.4
1956	30.6	37.6	28.6	9.5	29.6	31.8	32.2	16.3	31.0	32.0	31.3	32.0	29.5
1957	31.2	39.2	28.2	10.1	30.3	32.0	33.5	17.2	32.4	32.3	32.5	32.9	31.3
1958	31.9	41.6	27.1	10.2	30.4	32.0	33.8	16.2	33.2	33.1	33.2	33.6	32.1
1959	31.1	38.8	28.1	10.4	30.8	32.9	34.2	16.2	33.0	33.5	33.1	33.3	32.7
1960	30.4	38.4	26.9	10.5	30.8	32.7	34.0	16.6	33.4	33.3	33.4	33.6	32.8
1961	30.2	37.9	27.2	10.5	30.6	32.2	33.7	16.8	33.2	33.7	33.4	33.6	32.9
1962	30.5	38.6	27.1	10.4	30.6	32.1	33.4	16.7	33.6	34.5	33.5	33.7	33.0
1963	29.9	37.5	26.7	10.5	30.7	32.2	33.4	16.6	33.2	35.0	33.4	33.5	33.1
1964	29.6	36.6	27.2	10.5	30.8	32.5	33.7	16.2	32.9	34.7	33.5	33.6	33.4
1965	31.1	39.2	27.7	10.6	31.2	32.8	34.2	16.5	33.5	35.0	34.1	34.2	33.8
1966	33.1	42.7	28.3	10.9	32.0	33.6	35.4	16.8	34.5	36.5	35.2	35.4	34.6
1967	31.3	40.3	26.5	11.3	32.2	34.0	36.5	16.9	35.0	36.8	35.6	35.6	35.8
1968	31.8	40.9	27.1	11.5	33.0	35.7	37.3	16.5	35.9	37.1	36.6	36.5	37.0
1969	33.9	44.1	28.4	12.0	34.1	37.7	38.5	16.6	37.2	37.8	38.0	37.9	38.3
1970	35.2	45.2	29.1	13.8	35.4	38.3	40.6	17.7	39.0	39.7	39.3	39.1	40.1
1971	36.0	46.1	29.4	15.7	36.8	40.8	41.9	19.5	40.8	40.8	40.5	40.2	41.7
1972	39.9	51.5	32.3	16.8	38.2	43.0	42.9	20.1	42.7	42.5	41.8	41.5	42.8
1973	54.5	72.6	42.9	18.6	42.4	46.5	44.3	22.2	45.2	51.7	45.6	46.0	44.2
1974	61.4	76.4	54.5	24.8	52.5	55.0	51.1	33.6	53.3	56.8	52.6	53.1	50.5
1975	61.6	77.4	50.0	30.6	58.0	60.1	57.8	39.4	60.0	61.8	58.2	58.2	58.2
1976	63.4	76.8	54.9	34.5	60.9	64.1	60.8	42.3	63.1	65.8	60.8	60.4	62.1
1977	65.5	77.5	56.3	42.0	64.9	69.3	64.5	47.7	65.9	69.3	64.7	64.3	66.1
1978	73.4	87.3	61.9	48.2	69.5	76.5	69.2	49.9	71.0	72.9	69.8	69.4	71.3
1979	85.9	100.0	75.5	57.3	78.4	84.2	75.8	61.6	79.4	80.2	77.6	77.5	77.5
1980	95.3	104.6	91.8	69.4	90.3	91.3	84.6	85.0	89.1	89.9	88.0	88.6	85.8
1981	103.0	103.9	109.8	84.8	98.6	97.9	94.7	100.6	96.7	96.9	96.1	96.6	94.6
1982	100.0	100.0	100.0	100.0	100.0	100.0	100.0	100.0	100.0	100.0	100.0	100.0	100.0
1983	101.3	101.8	98.8	105.1	100.6	102.8	102.4	95.4	100.4	101.8	101.6	101.3	102.8
1984	103.5	104.7	101.0	105.1	103.1	105.6	105.0	95.7	105.9	104.1	103.7	103.3	105.2
1985	95.8	94.8	94.3	102.7	102.7	107.3	106.4	92.8	109.0	104.4	104.7	103.8	107.5
1986	87.7	93.2	76.0	92.2	99.1	108.1	107.5	72.7	110.3	105.6	103.2	101.4	109.7
1987	93.7	96.2	88.5	84.1	101.5	109.8	108.8	73.3	114.5	107.7	105.4	103.6	111.7
1988	96.0	106.1	85.9	82.1	107.1	116.1	112.3	71.2	120.1	113.7	108.0	106.2	114.3
1989	103.1	111.2	95.8	85.3	112.0	121.3	116.4	76.4	125.4	118.1	113.6	112.1	118.8
1990	108.9	113.1	107.3	84.8	114.5	122.9	119.0	85.9	127.7	119.4	119.2	118.2	122.9
1991	101.2	105.5	97.5	82.9	114.4	124.5	121.0	85.3	128.1	121.4	121.7	120.5	126.7
1992	100.4	105.1	94.2	84.0	114.7	126.5	122.0	84.5	127.7	122.7	123.2	121.7	129.1
1993	102.4	108.4	94.1	87.1	116.2	132.0	123.0	84.7	126.4	125.0	124.7	123.0	131.4
1994	101.8	106.5	97.0	82.4	118.5	136.6	124.3	83.1	129.7	127.0	125.5	123.3	134.1
1995	102.7	105.8	105.8	72.1	124.9	142.1	126.5	84.2	148.8	132.1	127.9	125.6	136.7
1996	113.8	121.5	105.7	92.6	125.7	143.6	126.9	90.0	141.1	135.9	131.3	129.5	138.3
1997	111.1	112.2	103.5	101.3	125.6	146.5	126.4	89.3	136.0	135.9	131.8	130.2	138.2
1998	96.8	103.9	84.5	86.7	123.0	146.8	125.9	81.1	140.8	134.8	130.7	128.9	137.6
1999	98.2	98.7	91.1	91.2	123.2	148.9	125.7	84.6	142.5	134.2	133.0	132.0	137.6
2000	120.6	100.2	118.0	136.9	129.2	150.7	126.2	102.0	151.6	136.9	138.0	138.2	138.8
2001	121.0	106.1	101.5	151.4	129.7	150.6	126.4	104.5	153.1	138.7	140.7	141.5	139.7

Table 6-2. Producer Price Indexes by Commodity Groups, 1913–2001

(1982=100.)

Year	All commodities	Farm products	Processed foods and feeds	Industrial commodities													
				Total	Textile products and apparel	Hides, leather, and related products	Fuels and related products and power	Chemicals and related products	Rubber and plastics products	Lumber and wood products	Pulp, paper, and allied products	Metals and metal products	Machinery and equipment	Furniture and household durables	Nonmetallic mineral products	Transportation equipment	Miscellaneous products
1913	12.0	18.0	...	11.9	...	...	...	...	...	...	...	...	...	...	...	...	...
1914	11.8	17.9	...	11.3	...	...	...	...	...	...	...	...	...	...	...	...	...
1915	12.0	18.0	...	11.6	...	...	...	...	...	...	...	...	...	...	...	...	...
1916	14.7	21.3	...	15.0	...	...	...	...	...	...	...	...	...	...	...	...	...
1917	20.2	32.6	...	19.5	...	...	...	...	...	...	...	...	...	...	...	...	...
1918	22.6	37.4	...	21.1	...	...	...	...	...	...	...	...	...	...	...	...	...
1919	23.9	39.8	...	22.0	...	...	...	...	...	...	...	...	...	...	...	...	...
1920	26.6	38.0	...	27.4	...	...	...	...	...	...	...	...	...	...	...	...	...
1921	16.8	22.3	...	17.8	...	...	...	...	...	...	...	...	...	...	...	...	...
1922	16.7	23.7	...	17.4	...	...	...	...	...	...	...	...	...	...	...	...	...
1923	17.3	24.9	...	17.8	...	...	...	...	...	...	...	...	...	...	...	...	...
1924	16.9	25.2	...	17.0	...	...	...	...	...	...	...	...	...	...	...	...	...
1925	17.8	27.7	...	17.5	...	...	...	...	...	...	...	...	...	...	...	...	...
1926	17.2	25.3	...	17.0	...	17.1	10.3	...	47.1	9.3	...	13.7	...	28.6	16.4	...	...
1927	16.5	25.1	...	16.0	...	18.4	9.1	...	35.7	8.8	...	12.9	...	27.9	15.7	...	...
1928	16.7	26.7	...	15.8	...	20.7	8.7	...	28.3	8.5	...	12.9	...	27.2	16.2	...	...
1929	16.4	26.4	...	15.6	...	18.6	8.6	...	24.6	8.8	...	13.3	...	27.0	16.0	...	...
1930	14.9	22.4	...	14.5	...	17.1	8.1	...	21.5	8.0	...	12.0	...	26.5	15.9	...	...
1931	12.6	16.4	...	12.8	...	14.7	7.0	...	18.3	6.5	...	10.8	...	24.4	14.9	...	...
1932	11.2	12.2	...	11.9	...	12.5	7.3	...	15.9	5.6	...	9.9	...	21.5	13.9	...	...
1933	11.4	13.0	...	12.1	...	13.8	6.9	16.2	16.7	6.7	...	10.2	...	21.6	14.7	...	...
1934	12.9	16.5	...	13.3	...	14.8	7.6	17.0	19.5	7.8	...	11.2	...	23.4	15.7	...	...
1935	13.8	19.8	...	13.3	...	15.3	7.6	17.7	19.6	7.5	...	11.2	...	23.2	15.7	...	...
1936	13.9	20.4	...	13.5	...	16.3	7.9	17.8	21.1	7.9	...	11.4	...	23.6	15.8	...	...
1937	14.9	21.8	...	14.5	...	17.9	8.0	18.6	24.9	9.3	...	13.1	...	26.1	16.1	...	...
1938	13.5	17.3	...	13.9	...	15.8	7.9	17.7	24.4	8.5	...	12.6	...	25.5	15.6	...	...
1939	13.3	16.5	...	13.9	...	16.3	7.5	17.6	25.4	8.7	...	12.5	14.8	25.4	15.3	...	...
1940	13.5	17.1	...	14.1	...	17.2	7.4	17.9	23.7	9.6	...	12.5	14.9	26.0	15.3	...	...
1941	15.1	20.8	...	15.1	...	18.4	7.9	19.5	25.5	11.5	...	12.8	15.1	27.6	15.7	...	...
1942	17.0	26.7	...	16.2	...	20.1	8.1	21.7	29.7	12.5	...	13.0	15.4	29.9	16.3	...	...
1943	17.8	30.9	...	16.5	...	20.1	8.3	21.9	30.5	13.2	...	12.9	15.2	29.7	16.4	...	...
1944	17.9	31.2	...	16.7	...	19.9	8.6	22.2	30.1	14.3	...	12.9	15.1	30.5	16.7	...	...
1945	18.2	32.4	...	17.0	...	20.1	8.7	22.3	29.2	14.5	...	13.1	15.1	30.5	17.4	...	...
1946	20.8	37.5	...	18.6	...	23.3	9.3	24.1	29.3	16.6	...	14.7	15.1	30.5	17.4	...	...
1947	25.6	45.1	33.0	22.7	50.6	31.7	11.1	32.1	29.2	25.8	...	14.7	16.6	32.4	18.5	...	26.6
1948	27.7	48.5	35.3	24.6	52.8	32.1	13.1	32.8	30.2	29.5	25.1	18.2	19.3	37.2	20.7	...	27.7
1949	26.3	41.9	32.1	24.1	48.3	30.4	12.4	30.0	29.2	27.3	26.2	20.7	20.9	39.4	22.4	...	28.2
1950	27.3	44.0	33.2	25.0	50.2	32.9	12.6	30.4	35.6	31.4	25.7	22.0	22.6	40.9	23.5	...	28.6
1951	30.4	51.2	36.9	27.6	56.0	37.7	13.0	34.8	43.7	34.1	30.5	24.5	25.3	44.4	25.0	...	30.3
1952	29.6	48.4	36.4	26.9	50.5	30.5	13.0	33.0	39.6	33.2	29.7	24.5	25.3	43.5	25.0	...	30.2
1953	29.2	43.8	34.8	27.2	49.3	31.0	13.4	33.4	36.9	33.1	29.6	25.3	25.9	44.4	26.0	...	31.0
1954	29.3	43.2	35.4	27.2	48.2	29.5	13.2	33.8	37.5	32.5	29.6	25.5	26.3	44.9	26.6	...	31.3
1955	29.3	40.5	33.8	27.8	48.2	29.4	13.2	33.7	42.4	34.1	30.4	27.2	27.2	45.1	27.3	...	31.3
1956	30.3	40.0	33.8	29.1	48.2	31.2	13.6	33.9	43.0	34.6	30.4	29.6	29.3	46.3	28.5	...	31.7
1957	31.2	41.1	34.8	29.9	48.3	31.2	14.3	34.6	42.8	32.8	33.0	30.2	31.4	47.5	29.6	...	32.6
1958	31.6	42.9	36.5	30.0	47.4	31.6	13.7	34.9	42.8	32.5	33.4	30.0	32.1	47.9	29.9	...	33.3
1959	31.7	40.2	35.6	30.5	48.1	35.9	13.7	34.8	42.6	34.7	33.7	30.6	32.8	48.0	30.3	...	33.4

Table 6-2. Producer Price Indexes by Commodity Groups, 1913–2001—*Continued*

(1982=100.)

Year	All com-modities	Farm prod-ucts	Proces-sed foods and feeds	Industrial commodities													
				Total	Textile prod-ucts and apparel	Hides, leather, and related prod-ucts	Fuels and related prod-ucts and power	Chemi-cals and related prod-ucts	Rubber and plastics prod-ucts	Lumber and wood prod-ucts	Pulp, paper, and allied prod-ucts	Metals and metal prod-ucts	Machin-ery and equip-ment	Furni-ture and house-hold dura-bles	Nonme-tallic mineral prod-ucts	Trans-porta-tion equip-ment	Miscel-laneous prod-ucts
1960	31.7	40.1	35.6	30.5	48.6	34.6	13.9	34.8	42.7	33.5	34.0	30.6	33.0	47.8	30.4	...	33.6
1961	31.6	39.7	36.2	30.4	47.8	34.9	14.0	34.5	41.1	32.0	33.0	30.5	33.0	47.5	30.5	...	33.7
1962	31.7	40.4	36.5	30.4	48.2	35.3	14.0	33.9	39.9	32.2	33.4	30.2	33.0	47.2	30.5	...	33.9
1963	31.6	39.6	36.8	30.3	48.2	34.3	13.9	33.5	40.1	32.8	33.1	30.3	33.1	46.9	30.3	...	34.2
1964	31.6	39.0	36.7	30.5	48.5	34.4	13.5	33.6	39.6	33.5	33.0	31.1	33.3	47.1	30.4	...	34.4
1965	32.3	40.7	38.0	30.9	48.8	35.9	13.8	33.9	39.7	33.7	33.3	32.0	33.7	46.8	30.4	...	34.7
1966	33.3	43.7	40.2	31.5	48.9	39.4	14.1	34.0	40.5	35.2	34.2	32.8	34.7	47.4	30.7	...	35.3
1967	33.4	41.3	39.8	32.0	48.9	38.1	14.4	34.2	41.4	35.1	34.6	33.2	35.9	48.3	31.2	...	36.2
1968	34.2	42.3	40.6	32.8	50.7	39.3	14.3	34.1	42.8	39.8	35.0	34.0	37.0	49.7	32.4	40.4	37.0
1969	35.6	45.0	42.7	33.9	51.8	41.5	14.6	34.2	43.6	44.0	36.0	36.0	38.2	50.7	33.6		38.1
1970	36.9	45.8	44.6	35.2	52.4	42.0	15.3	35.0	44.9	39.9	37.5	38.7	40.0	51.9	35.3	41.9	39.8
1971	38.1	46.6	45.5	36.5	53.3	43.4	16.6	35.6	45.2	44.7	38.1	39.4	41.4	53.1	38.2	44.2	40.8
1972	39.8	51.6	48.0	37.8	55.5	50.0	17.1	35.6	45.3	50.7	39.3	40.9	42.3	53.8	39.4	45.5	41.5
1973	45.0	72.7	58.9	40.3	60.5	54.5	19.4	37.6	46.6	62.2	42.3	44.0	43.7	55.7	40.7	46.1	43.3
1974	53.5	77.4	68.0	49.2	68.0	55.2	30.1	50.2	56.4	64.5	52.5	57.0	50.0	61.8	47.8	50.3	48.1
1975	58.4	77.0	72.6	54.9	67.4	56.5	35.4	62.0	62.2	62.1	59.0	61.5	57.9	67.5	54.4	56.7	53.4
1976	61.1	78.8	70.8	58.4	72.4	63.9	38.3	64.0	66.0	72.2	62.1	65.0	61.3	70.3	58.2	60.5	55.6
1977	64.9	79.4	74.0	62.5	75.3	68.3	43.6	65.9	69.4	83.0	64.6	69.3	65.2	73.2	62.6	64.6	59.4
1978	69.9	87.7	80.6	67.0	78.1	76.1	46.5	68.0	72.4	96.9	67.7	75.3	70.3	77.5	69.6	69.5	66.7
1979	78.7	99.6	88.5	75.7	82.5	96.1	58.9	76.0	80.5	105.5	75.9	86.0	76.7	82.8	77.6	75.3	75.5
1980	89.8	102.9	95.9	88.0	89.7	94.7	82.8	89.0	90.1	101.5	86.3	95.0	86.0	90.7	88.4	82.9	93.6
1981	98.0	105.2	98.9	97.4	97.6	99.3	100.2	98.4	96.4	102.8	94.8	99.6	94.4	95.9	96.7	94.3	96.1
1982	100.0	100.0	100.0	100.0	100.0	100.0	100.0	100.0	100.0	100.0	100.0	100.0	100.0	100.0	100.0	100.0	100.0
1983	101.3	102.4	101.8	101.1	100.3	103.2	95.9	100.3	100.8	107.9	103.3	101.8	102.7	103.4	101.6	102.8	104.8
1984	103.7	105.5	105.4	103.3	102.7	109.0	94.8	102.9	102.3	108.0	110.3	104.8	105.1	105.7	105.4	105.2	107.0
1985	103.2	95.1	103.5	103.7	102.9	108.9	91.4	103.7	101.9	106.6	113.3	104.4	107.2	107.1	108.6	107.9	109.4
1986	100.2	92.9	105.4	100.0	103.2	113.0	69.8	102.6	101.9	107.2	116.1	103.2	108.8	108.2	110.0	110.5	111.6
1987	102.8	95.5	107.9	102.6	105.1	120.4	70.2	106.4	103.0	112.8	121.8	107.1	110.4	109.9	110.0	112.5	114.9
1988	106.9	104.9	112.7	106.3	109.2	131.4	66.7	116.3	109.3	118.9	130.4	118.7	113.2	113.1	111.2	114.3	120.2
1989	112.2	110.9	117.8	111.6	112.3	136.3	72.9	123.0	112.6	126.7	137.8	124.1	117.4	116.9	112.6	117.7	126.5
1990	116.3	112.2	121.9	115.8	115.0	141.7	82.3	123.6	113.6	129.7	141.2	122.9	120.7	119.2	114.7	121.5	134.2
1991	116.5	105.7	121.9	116.5	116.3	138.9	81.2	125.6	115.1	132.1	142.9	120.2	123.0	121.2	117.2	126.4	140.8
1992	117.2	103.6	122.1	117.4	117.8	140.4	80.4	125.9	115.1	146.6	145.2	119.2	123.4	122.2	117.3	130.4	145.3
1993	118.9	107.1	124.0	119.0	118.0	143.7	80.0	128.2	116.0	174.0	147.3	119.2	124.0	123.7	120.0	133.7	145.4
1994	120.4	106.3	125.5	120.7	118.3	148.5	77.8	132.1	117.6	180.0	152.5	124.8	125.1	126.1	124.2	137.2	141.9
1995	124.7	107.4	127.0	125.5	120.8	153.7	78.0	142.5	124.3	178.1	172.2	134.5	126.6	128.2	129.0	139.7	145.4
1996	127.7	122.4	133.3	127.3	122.4	150.5	85.8	142.1	123.8	176.1	168.7	131.0	126.5	130.4	131.0	141.7	147.7
1997	127.6	112.9	134.0	127.7	122.6	154.2	86.1	143.6	123.2	183.8	167.9	131.8	125.9	130.8	133.2	141.6	150.9
1998	124.4	104.6	131.6	124.8	122.9	148.0	75.3	143.9	122.6	179.1	171.7	127.8	124.9	131.3	135.4	141.2	156.0
1999	125.5	98.4	131.1	126.5	121.1	146.0	80.5	144.2	122.5	183.6	174.1	124.6	124.3	131.7	138.9	141.8	166.6
2000	132.7	99.5	133.1	134.8	121.4	151.5	103.5	151.0	125.5	178.2	183.7	128.1	124.0	132.6	142.5	143.8	170.8
2001	134.2	103.8	137.3	135.7	121.3	158.4	105.3	151.8	127.2	174.4	184.8	125.4	123.7	133.2	144.3	145.2	181.3

Table 6-3. Producer Price Indexes for the Net Output of Selected Industries, 1988–2001

(December 1984=100, unless otherwise indicated.)

Industry	1988	1989	1990	1991	1992	1993	1994	1995	1996	1997	1998	1999	2000	2001
MINING INDUSTRIES														
Metal mining	100.7	100.3	93.4	82.2	76.6	69.7	81.4	101.4	92.1	85.8	73.2	70.3	73.8	70.8
Iron ores	80.9	81.5	82.2	82.7	82.8	82.1	82.1	91.0	95.7	95.3	94.5	94.0	93.9	95.2
Copper ores (06/88=100)	...	129.5	112.8	99.5	96.6	79.1	106.9	157.1	117.0	110.4	76.8	71.3	88.7	81.7
Lead and zinc ores (12/85=100)	...	...	...	...	...	82.2	93.5	103.1	109.4	138.6	107.0	111.8	118.8	89.2
Gold and silver ores	96.1	82.9	81.2	71.3	68.0	69.1	75.9	77.1	78.6	67.9	61.1	58.2	57.0	55.2
Metal mining services (12/85=100)	102.5	107.2	108.6	108.7	108.8	111.2	111.3	111.4	112.5	116.7	122.0	120.2	109.0	117.6
Miscellaneous metal ores (12/85=100)	87.9	57.9	58.0	49.2	33.9	32.6	32.9	33.6	31.9	29.9	27.6	25.9	26.4	24.7
Coal mining (12/85=100)	94.6	94.3	96.5	96.3	94.0	93.3	93.2	91.6	91.4	92.2	89.5	87.3	84.8	91.3
Bituminous coal and lignite (12/93=100)	...	...	...	...	...	...	...	...	...	...	...	...	...	9.0
Anthracite mining (12/93=100)	...	...	...	...	...	...	99.4	98.2	98.1	98.3	99.0	98.1	97.2	99.5
Coal mining services (06/91=100)	...	...	...	...	96.1	98.0	97.6	98.3	101.6	100.6	100.6	100.2	100.8	108.8
Oil and gas extraction (12/85=100)	68.5	75.7	82.7	77.9	76.5	76.2	71.1	66.6	84.8	87.5	68.3	78.5	126.8	127.5
Crude petroleum, natural gas, and natural gas liquids (06/96=100)	...	...	...	...	...	...	...	...	115.6	86.1	102.6	174.3	172.6	
Oil and gas field services (12/85=100)	90.9	91.2	95.7	99.1	95.5	100.6	103.8	107.1	108.8	120.7	125.5	116.2	122.6	144.3
Mining and quarrying of non-metallic minerals, except fuels	108.0	111.2	113.7	116.3	117.5	118.8	120.5	123.8	127.1	128.8	132.2	134.0	137.0	141.0
Dimension stone (06/85=100)	108.3	110.5	113.4	116.7	118.2	120.3	123.4	126.4	132.2	138.1	142.2	145.9	153.4	156.9
Crushed and broken stone, including riprap	111.8	113.6	115.7	118.7	120.6	123.4	126.3	130.7	133.2	135.4	138.8	142.1	147.3	152.2
Sand and gravel	113.0	115.5	119.6	123.1	125.3	129.1	134.0	137.6	141.6	145.4	152.1	157.4	163.1	168.9
Clay, ceramic, and refractory minerals	105.1	108.3	109.8	110.9	111.3	112.8	113.1	115.3	116.6	117.5	117.5	116.2	117.0	122.4
Chemical and fertilizer mineral mining	99.6	104.7	106.7	108.5	108.3	104.3	102.1	104.2	108.6	107.6	110.1	108.0	106.8	107.1
Non-metallic minerals (except fuels) services (06/85=100)	103.0	102.9	102.7	98.5	98.1	98.0	96.1	100.0	103.4	104.7	104.7	106.5	107.2	109.3
Miscellaneous nonmetallic minerals, except fuels	112.8	115.1	117.9	122.9	126.9	131.1	132.3	136.0	139.8	143.2	146.6	148.0	148.8	153.6
MANUFACTURING INDUSTRIES														
Food and kindred products	107.1	112.2	116.2	116.5	116.9	118.7	120.1	121.7	127.1	127.9	126.3	126.3	128.5	132.8
Meat products	103.9	110.0	118.1	114.8	110.0	113.6	110.7	109.3	114.6	116.1	109.2	108.9	115.0	120.3
Dairy products	100.1	108.0	113.5	111.0	113.7	114.1	115.6	115.8	125.0	123.9	133.1	133.8	129.9	141.2
Canned and preserved fruits and vegetables	108.9	114.5	119.5	119.5	121.5	121.2	123.7	125.5	129.7	129.9	130.1	131.7	132.1	133.3
Grain mill products	111.3	116.4	114.5	115.9	119.1	120.5	124.9	125.9	139.9	133.0	122.5	117.3	117.5	121.3
Bakery products	115.2	123.5	128.7	133.7	139.1	142.7	145.3	149.6	154.4	158.2	160.0	162.0	166.0	171.8
Sugar and confectionery products	106.0	110.2	112.5	117.4	117.0	118.7	120.4	123.3	127.7	129.3	128.8	129.4	127.5	129.3
Fats and oils	109.4	104.6	98.8	93.3	93.1	100.4	105.0	103.0	111.1	113.9	102.1	86.9	85.1	84.1
Beverages	105.8	109.0	112.0	116.4	117.9	118.5	118.8	123.1	125.5	126.3	127.2	129.8	134.4	138.6
Miscellaneous food preparations and kindred products	110.2	114.2	116.7	118.4	117.7	118.3	125.4	131.1	128.5	135.1	135.3	136.1	138.7	137.9
Tobacco manufactures	141.8	161.4	183.2	207.5	230.2	218.0	187.8	193.2	199.1	210.8	243.1	325.7	345.8	386.1
Cigarettes (12/82=100)	150.8	173.1	197.6	225.0	250.5	235.2	198.9	204.3	210.5	223.3	260.4	356.7	379.3	425.8
Cigars (12/82=100)	121.2	130.5	141.4	150.0	159.1	166.4	172.9	186.5	201.8	228.5	242.7	259.6	268.8	279.1
Chewing and smoking tobacco and snuff (12/82=100)	145.5	154.1	166.2	182.3	199.2	214.2	229.5	243.6	253.8	265.3	282.1	303.1	318.1	332.5
Tobacco stemming and redrying (06/84=100)	97.7	98.9	103.9	107.6	107.5	108.7	109.4	112.2	109.7	106.5	104.2	104.7	109.0	112.3
Textile mill products	106.8	109.3	111.6	112.5	113.6	113.6	113.6	116.5	118.2	118.8	118.6	116.3	116.7	116.9
Cotton broadwoven fabric (12/80=100)	107.6	107.2	109.3	109.6	112.8	112.2	113.5	118.6	119.1	118.5	117.4	114.2	110.6	111.7
Synthetic fiber and silk broadwoven fabric (06/81=100)	110.1	112.3	115.6	115.2	115.9	114.6	109.9	112.4	113.0	115.0	114.8	108.6	108.6	108.9
Wool weaving and finishing (06/85=100)	109.8	119.4	118.5	116.3	114.7	113.8	113.3	113.5	114.2	115.0	115.3	113.2	114.6	117.1
Narrow fabric mills (06/84=100)	103.1	108.1	111.7	113.2	114.6	115.6	116.8	119.7	121.2	122.7	123.8	124.3	125.3	126.2
Knitting mills	105.5	107.4	109.9	110.9	112.8	113.3	113.0	115.7	116.6	117.0	116.6	114.0	113.9	113.7
Dyeing and finishing textiles, except wool fabrics and knit goods	111.6	114.8	117.0	119.9	122.6	125.1	125.5	127.8	129.0	129.2	130.2	131.4	132.2	131.5
Floor covering mills	105.8	107.6	108.9	109.7	109.4	108.7	110.0	111.6	114.1	115.7	116.3	115.4	117.8	118.9
Yarn and thread mills	104.9	106.4	109.7	110.7	110.9	107.0	107.4	112.1	113.6	114.1	112.1	106.9	105.5	103.0
Miscellaneous textile goods	106.6	112.4	115.0	117.0	116.3	116.5	118.1	122.9	126.4	125.6	124.9	123.4	124.1	125.2
Apparel and other finished products made from fabrics and similar materials	107.2	110.2	113.3	116.0	118.0	119.2	119.7	120.6	122.3	123.4	124.8	125.3	125.7	125.8
Men's and boys' suits and coats (12/80=100)	131.6	140.3	145.7	149.2	151.8	151.9	154.0	155.8	158.1	160.2	166.8	168.5	168.2	166.3
Men's, youths and boys furnishings, work clothing and allied garments	106.9	110.1	113.0	116.2	119.7	121.9	122.7	124.0	125.5	125.7	126.1	126.0	125.6	124.9
Women's, misses, and juniors' outerwear	107.7	110.8	114.0	116.7	117.5	117.8	117.0	120.2	116.1	116.8	117.7	118.3	118.4	117.8
Women's, misses', children's, and infants' under-garments	107.3	109.4	111.2	112.9	115.3	116.8	118.3	118.9	119.3	120.1	121.0	122.1	123.3	123.0
Hats, caps, and millinery (06/85=100)	104.9	109.8	115.1	118.2	122.9	126.0	129.5	130.8	132.7	135.0	136.4	138.6	141.0	143.7
Girls', children's, and infants' outerwear	103.4	106.3	110.7	113.1	114.6	115.8	115.4	118.1	118.9	118.9	118.6	119.5	120.7	120.3
Fur goods (12/83=100)	115.9	104.9	98.7	100.5	102.6	101.4	107.5	103.8	119.4	127.3	128.5	134.4	141.5	148.4
Miscellaneous apparel and accessories (06/85=100)	106.9	110.8	115.2	117.6	119.3	120.6	120.8	123.2	125.7	128.0	130.4	131.0	131.3	132.6
Miscellaneous fabricated textile products	105.6	107.9	110.8	113.4	115.1	116.6	117.7	119.6	124.2	126.4	128.8	128.7	129.5	131.1
Lumber and wood products, except furniture	109.2	115.3	117.0	119.4	129.7	148.3	154.4	154.1	153.5	158.9	157.0	161.8	158.1	156.2
Logging camps and logging contractors (12/81=100)	112.8	128.0	135.6	135.0	151.3	186.4	192.6	194.3	185.7	191.2	188.1	182.7	177.5	167.5
Sawmills and planing mills	110.2	114.6	113.7	115.3	131.3	161.8	165.2	154.8	155.7	166.9	157.2	162.2	153.9	147.6
Millwork, veneer, plywood, and structural wood members	107.5	114.1	115.4	118.3	128.4	142.8	148.7	150.5	148.3	151.7	151.8	158.6	155.1	156.0
Wood containers (06/85=100)	103.8	109.7	113.9	115.8	123.5	141.7	147.5	148.6	147.7	151.5	155.5	156.0	156.6	157.1
Wood buildings and mobile homes	107.9	112.1	115.5	118.9	121.5	129.5	139.8	147.8	151.5	155.0	157.5	162.1	165.7	169.1
Miscellaneous wood products	108.6	113.3	114.9	118.0	123.4	132.8	140.9	144.9	145.1	145.9	147.6	152.8	149.6	145.7
Furniture and fixtures	111.4	115.6	119.1	121.6	122.9	125.4	129.7	133.3	136.2	138.2	139.7	141.3	143.3	145.1
Household furniture	110.1	114.0	117.2	119.9	121.6	124.8	128.7	132.2	134.7	136.4	138.4	140.3	142.5	144.4
Office furniture	115.0	119.0	123.4	125.8	125.3	127.3	132.9	137.5	140.7	142.5	142.3	143.0	144.5	146.4
Public building and related furniture	111.9	115.9	118.4	119.4	120.9	123.5	128.4	130.0	133.7	135.9	136.0	136.9	138.6	139.1
Partitions, shelving, lockers, and office and store fixtures	113.7	117.5	120.9	123.1	124.7	126.9	131.9	135.3	138.0	140.7	142.0	143.5	145.6	147.2
Miscellaneous furniture and fixtures	109.5	116.3	120.6	123.4	125.5	125.6	127.3	130.4	133.3	134.8	137.4	139.0	141.7	145.5

Table 6-3. Producer Price Indexes for the Net Output of Selected Industries, 1988–2001—*Continued*

(December 1984=100, unless otherwise indicated.)

Industry	1988	1989	1990	1991	1992	1993	1994	1995	1996	1997	1998	1999	2000	2001
Paper and allied products	113.7	120.8	121.9	121.1	121.2	120.2	123.7	146.7	138.6	133.5	136.2	136.4	145.8	146.2
Pulp mills (12/82=100)	141.7	161.3	153.8	121.8	118.5	105.8	116.5	182.4	135.5	131.0	125.1	122.7	143.4	122.9
Paper mill products except building paper (06/81=100)	127.4	134.6	134.0	131.0	126.6	126.6	128.6	164.8	152.2	143.2	144.5	139.7	148.8	150.5
Paperboard mills (12/82=100)	141.6	149.9	146.0	140.7	142.6	138.3	152.6	203.1	169.7	158.2	165.1	166.9	192.2	187.3
Paperboard containers and boxes	111.7	117.2	117.7	116.6	118.5	118.0	123.7	148.5	140.4	132.9	141.1	144.1	157.1	158.9
Converted paper and paperboard products, except containers and boxes (06/93=100)	...	...	...	...	...	...	100.7	110.1	109.5	108.7	108.2	108.2	111.7	112.4
Printing, publishing, and allied industries	118.2	124.7	130.5	136.4	140.8	145.6	149.7	159.0	165.6	169.1	174.0	177.6	182.9	188.7
Newspaper publishing (12/79=100)	193.9	206.9	220.4	235.7	248.7	259.5	269.5	286.7	306.9	317.7	328.7	339.3	351.3	367.9
Periodical publishing (12/79=100)	183.8	194.0	205.7	217.8	227.9	233.3	239.1	246.3	253.1	263.2	276.9	284.9	292.6	305.9
Books	117.7	125.3	132.3	138.7	143.7	147.8	153.4	162.3	169.4	174.0	178.9	184.7	190.2	195.6
Miscellaneous publishing (06/84=100)	123.1	128.2	133.8	142.0	148.3	154.6	160.6	167.1	174.5	181.1	187.7	194.5	201.3	210.0
Commercial printing	110.7	115.7	118.7	120.8	121.9	124.9	126.3	133.4	136.6	137.2	140.0	140.3	142.8	144.9
Manifold business forms (12/83=100)	120.3	124.9	124.6	123.9	121.0	128.6	134.0	163.9	168.4	165.8	167.0	170.5	185.8	193.1
Greeting cards (12/85=100)	108.4	114.4	120.3	125.3	131.3	139.4	145.7	156.5	162.7	164.9	169.2	174.3	177.7	180.6
Blankbooks, looseleaf binders, and bookbinding and related work (06/85=100)	111.9	119.6	124.8	132.3	135.4	139.0	142.9	150.1	155.6	158.7	159.6	159.8	163.0	164.7
Service industries for the printing trade (06/85=100)	106.1	108.4	109.3	110.7	112.3	113.5	114.1	115.2	116.1	116.4	117.2	117.7	119.0	116.7
Chemicals and allied products	113.0	119.6	121.0	124.4	125.8	127.2	130.0	143.4	145.8	147.1	148.7	149.7	156.7	158.4
Industrial inorganic chemicals	104.0	115.1	116.6	117.5	116.5	115.0	115.4	126.3	135.0	134.5	132.7	127.8	132.0	139.6
Plastic materials and synthetic resins, rubber, and non-glass fibers	114.7	118.0	114.9	113.2	110.0	110.6	113.8	127.8	123.1	124.4	115.9	115.4	128.0	126.2
Drugs	128.1	137.9	146.7	156.2	165.7	172.4	174.8	178.7	181.2	184.8	203.1	210.1	215.7	220.5
Soap, detergents, and cleaning preparations, perfumes, cosmetics and other toilet preparations	109.6	114.1	115.8	118.1	120.6	122.8	123.0	125.0	126.6	127.3	128.7	130.3	132.5	134.2
Paints and allied products (06/83=100)	111.7	119.5	125.0	130.3	132.3	133.5	136.0	143.1	147.6	152.3	155.1	157.6	160.7	164.1
Industrial organic chemicals	114.2	122.3	120.2	123.3	123.1	122.7	125.9	158.1	164.0	163.9	160.1	161.4	177.3	173.5
Agricultural chemicals	106.9	109.4	108.2	111.9	110.0	109.7	119.6	129.7	133.4	131.9	128.5	123.2	124.9	132.0
Miscellaneous chemical products	106.8	114.2	117.4	122.1	123.7	127.2	131.2	137.1	138.5	140.3	141.7	141.5	143.0	146.0
Petroleum refining and related products	67.7	75.7	91.4	83.1	80.3	77.6	74.8	77.2	87.4	85.6	66.3	76.8	112.8	105.3
Petroleum refining (06/85=100)	65.4	73.6	90.1	80.9	78.3	75.2	72.2	74.5	85.3	83.1	62.3	73.6	111.6	103.1
Paving and roofing materials	94.1	93.5	94.3	96.1	94.0	95.0	94.9	98.1	99.4	102.2	102.0	102.8	113.5	116.9
Miscellaneous products of petroleum and coal	104.3	114.4	123.6	131.1	128.4	129.9	130.6	136.3	140.9	142.0	142.5	142.1	150.3	159.3
Rubber and miscellaneous plastics products	106.7	110.2	111.3	113.7	114.2	115.4	117.1	123.3	123.1	122.8	122.1	122.2	124.6	125.9
Tires and inner tubes (06/81=100)	99.5	102.9	103.0	105.0	106.0	106.2	106.4	108.5	105.2	103.4	102.0	100.4	100.4	101.5
Rubber and plastics footwear (12/80=100)	114.6	120.2	121.5	122.0	122.8	124.1	125.5	126.9	128.3	127.1	128.0	129.1	131.2	126.8
Gaskets, packing, and sealing devices and rubber and plastics hose and belting (06/95=100)	...	...	...	...	...	...	...	102.7	104.4	105.5	106.0	107.1	109.4
Fabricated rubber products, n.e.c. (12/88=100)	...	102.4	105.0	107.5	108.6	110.3	111.9	115.6	118.3	119.8	120.2	119.9	120.5	121.3
Miscellaneous plastics products (06/93=100)	...	...	...	...	...	...	101.9	108.3	108.0	107.6	106.8	107.1	109.8	111.0
Leather and leather products	113.4	118.0	122.6	124.8	127.0	129.0	130.6	134.1	134.7	137.1	137.1	136.5	137.9	141.3
Leather tanning and finishing (06/81=100)	158.7	161.6	168.0	158.9	156.1	160.9	171.9	183.9	172.4	176.9	171.6	168.8	174.6	191.7
Boot and shoe cut stock and findings	114.6	116.7	119.6	122.3	123.3	124.4	125.0	129.6	132.4	133.3	133.8	133.8	135.2	139.5
Footwear, except rubber	112.1	117.5	122.2	125.2	128.1	130.3	131.6	135.3	137.5	139.5	140.5	139.3	139.7	140.6
Leather gloves and mittens (06/85=100)	108.1	112.0	117.6	118.6	120.1	120.7	125.8	131.5	137.4	138.7	140.8	141.3	141.3	142.1
Luggage	104.1	109.0	113.4	116.2	118.8	119.9	120.3	120.3	121.1	123.2	124.7	126.5	127.6	127.2
Handbags and other personal leather goods	111.6	114.2	118.1	121.3	122.4	123.5	121.5	122.8	122.8	123.5	124.1	124.6	124.7	127.3
Leather goods, n.e.c. (06/85=100)	113.5	117.7	122.1	123.7	123.4	125.1	127.2	131.7	135.6	140.6	141.0	142.5	144.5	145.6
Stone, clay, glass, and concrete products	105.8	107.9	110.0	112.3	112.8	115.4	119.6	124.3	125.8	127.4	129.3	132.6	134.7	136.0
Flat glass (12/80=100)	115.1	112.8	109.2	105.4	104.9	106.1	113.0	116.6	108.9	104.1	99.5	95.9	97.3	97.7
Glass and glassware, pressed or blown	107.6	110.5	113.8	117.4	118.4	119.7	121.8	125.0	125.0	123.2	121.8	121.0	122.6	126.2
Products of purchased glass (06/83=100)	113.4	116.7	117.6	118.8	120.4	122.1	123.7	126.8	126.3	127.1	127.5	128.4	131.6	133.7
Hydraulic cement (06/82=100)	101.2	101.1	102.7	105.8	105.4	110.0	118.7	127.2	132.9	138.1	144.2	149.1	148.6	148.7
Structural clay products	109.6	111.8	114.2	115.6	117.1	119.7	121.9	124.4	126.1	127.5	129.0	131.4	135.1	140.4
Pottery and related products	109.2	113.1	117.0	119.6	120.6	122.7	125.2	129.3	130.0	131.8	133.5	138.1	139.7	150.2
Concrete, gypsum, and plaster products	103.3	104.4	106.1	108.0	108.6	111.7	117.7	123.5	126.5	130.5	134.5	140.0	143.1	142.1
Cut stone and stone products	116.2	120.1	122.7	128.0	129.3	130.7	131.7	134.0	135.8	138.4	141.7	143.3	144.8	147.9
Abrasives, asbestos, and miscellaneous nonmetallic mineral products	105.7	109.1	111.5	114.2	113.3	116.0	119.2	123.6	125.6	126.2	127.4	131.3	130.9	132.0
Primary metal industries	113.0	118.8	116.5	113.1	111.7	111.4	117.0	128.2	123.7	124.7	120.9	115.8	119.8	116.1
Blast furnaces, steel works, and rolling and finishing mills	105.1	108.5	106.5	104.5	102.4	104.3	109.1	114.9	111.3	112.0	110.0	102.3	104.4	98.4
Iron and steel foundries	104.9	108.3	111.5	113.2	114.6	115.8	118.3	124.0	127.6	129.2	129.7	130.4	132.1	132.7
Primary smelting and refining of nonferrous metals (12/80=100)	127.2	134.6	123.4	103.6	98.4	90.3	106.7	134.2	115.5	115.5	98.5	93.6	103.0	96.6
Secondary nonferrous metals (06/80=100)	100.6	101.4	97.0	84.7	81.8	77.2	90.2	102.1	94.0	94.5	85.9	84.8	88.4	85.9
Rolling, drawing and extruding of nonferrous metals	127.8	138.4	132.7	127.5	126.2	122.8	129.4	151.0	143.0	144.8	137.8	133.7	142.8	139.8
Nonferrous foundries (castings)	112.0	119.5	121.1	120.9	121.7	122.7	125.7	132.8	131.4	133.8	132.7	131.6	133.5	134.1
Miscellaneous primary metal products (06/85=100)	112.2	116.1	115.9	116.1	116.3	115.9	119.0	124.4	126.2	126.7	126.1	126.0	126.5	134.9
Fabricated metal products, except machinery and transportation equipment	107.4	112.6	115.1	116.6	117.2	118.2	120.3	124.8	126.2	127.6	128.7	129.1	130.3	131.0
Metal cans and shipping containers	101.5	103.8	105.9	107.2	106.3	103.1	101.7	109.4	103.9	102.7	102.3	100.7	101.0	100.8
Cutlery, hand tools, and general hardware	106.1	111.7	116.5	120.7	123.2	125.7	127.9	131.3	133.8	135.2	136.5	137.8	139.9	142.4
Heating equipment, except electric and warm air; and plumbing fixtures	114.7	121.7	127.2	131.7	135.3	138.0	140.8	147.6	153.2	156.2	157.7	159.6	162.0	161.8
Fabricated structural metal products	110.7	116.3	117.9	118.1	117.7	118.8	122.6	129.6	131.8	134.0	136.1	137.1	138.5	138.2
Screw machine products, and bolts, nuts, screws, rivets, and washers	104.7	109.9	113.3	114.9	115.4	116.3	117.6	120.0	121.6	122.6	122.7	121.8	122.9	122.8
Metal forgings and stampings	102.4	107.1	109.4	109.5	109.7	109.8	110.5	111.9	112.9	113.9	114.0	112.9	113.2	113.2
Coating, engraving, and allied services	110.7	116.0	117.9	119.3	120.1	121.8	123.5	125.8	127.2	128.4	129.2	132.0	132.7	136.0
Ordnance and accessories, except vehicles and guided missiles (06/85=100)	108.2	111.2	112.6	116.4	120.2	124.3	125.5	127.6	129.5	129.2	130.5	133.3	135.1	137.9
Miscellaneous fabricated metal products	110.8	117.2	120.5	122.9	124.1	125.8	128.7	133.4	135.6	137.9	139.5	140.3	141.9	143.8

Table 6-3. Producer Price Indexes for the Net Output of Selected Industries, 1988–2001—*Continued*

(December 1984=100, unless otherwise indicated.)

Industry	1988	1989	1990	1991	1992	1993	1994	1995	1996	1997	1998	1999	2000	2001
Machinery, except electrical	106.4	110.7	113.9	116.4	116.7	116.8	117.5	119.0	119.2	118.5	117.7	117.3	117.5	118.0
Engines and turbines	105.0	109.8	116.5	121.4	123.8	125.8	128.3	130.8	132.3	133.6	133.9	135.7	136.6	137.7
Farm and garden machinery and equipment	102.9	107.6	111.1	114.3	116.9	118.7	120.9	123.4	126.1	127.4	128.1	129.1	130.1	131.8
Construction, mining, and materials handling machinery and equipment	105.9	109.8	113.5	117.5	120.1	122.9	125.0	128.1	131.4	133.7	136.0	138.0	139.4	141.1
Metalworking machinery and equipment	...	111.5	116.1	120.3	122.8	125.4	128.4	...	135.4	138.4	141.2	142.2	143.9	145.1
Special industry machinery, except metalworking machinery	112.6	117.5	121.6	125.6	128.4	132.1	134.2	137.3	140.5	143.0	145.4	147.2	148.7	149.9
General industrial machinery and equipment	...	...	119.6	124.3	127.4	130.6	133.4	137.8	141.7	144.7	146.9	149.3	151.7	154.3
Office, computing, and accounting machines	...	...	...	...	...	...	...	70.5	63.4	55.9	48.8	44.0	41.3	39.0
Refrigeration and service industry machinery	107.8	112.4	116.0	117.6	119.4	120.9	122.3	125.3	127.9	129.6	131.5	132.2	132.0	132.5
Miscellaneous machinery, except electrical	104.6	109.3	112.3	113.4	113.9	116.1	118.8	121.9	123.6	125.5	127.0	127.7	129.6	131.8
Electrical and electronic machinery, equipment, and supplies	104.6	107.1	108.9	110.1	110.8	112.0	112.7	113.3	113.2	111.6	110.4	109.5	108.3	107.0
Electric transmission and distribution equipment	105.8	113.2	118.7	122.0	122.8	123.4	125.8	129.5	130.5	131.3	133.6	135.9	138.5	140.4
Electrical industrial apparatus	108.5	113.5	117.5	120.7	122.9	125.7	127.1	130.1	132.7	134.9	136.6	137.2	137.8	139.5
Household appliances	100.4	102.9	105.2	106.0	106.8	108.1	108.7	108.8	109.7	108.3	107.5	107.2	106.2	104.6
Electric lighting and wiring equipment	108.3	113.4	116.3	118.6	119.8	122.1	123.2	126.6	128.1	129.4	129.4	128.7	128.4	128.1
Radio and television receiving equipment, except communication types	97.5	96.9	94.5	95.2	94.2	92.6	92.4	91.5	91.4	89.5	88.9	87.1	85.4	83.6
Communication equipment (12/85=100)	103.9	105.8	107.5	108.5	109.7	111.7	113.3	113.9	115.0	115.7	115.0	113.0	110.4	108.6
Electronic components and accessories	104.0	105.1	104.9	104.9	104.6	105.3	104.8	102.5	99.3	95.1	91.9	90.1	88.8	86.4
Miscellaneous electrical machinery, equipment, and supplies	105.4	107.8	109.8	110.6	110.9	110.4	110.7	111.9	112.8	113.0	112.4	112.5	112.4	113.0
Transportation equipment	107.8	112.1	115.6	119.8	123.0	126.3	130.1	132.2	134.2	134.1	133.6	134.5	136.8	137.9
Motor vehicles and motor vehicle equipment	107.7	110.7	113.0	117.4	120.5	123.8	127.5	129.1	130.4	129.0	127.7	128.3	129.2	128.5
Aircraft and parts (06/85=100)	105.5	112.1	117.7	122.3	126.6	130.1	134.0	137.3	140.8	142.7	143.4	144.8	149.9	154.7
Ship and boat building and repairing	111.0	116.0	120.1	122.7	125.7	129.9	133.0	135.0	138.2	142.0	144.1	145.6	149.0	152.6
Railroad equipment (06/84=100)	103.7	110.0	114.2	117.3	118.7	119.8	122.6	127.6	129.7	127.4	127.6	128.2	128.6	128.3
Motorcycles, bicycles, and parts	104.3	107.8	109.9	111.8	114.4	116.9	119.0	122.2	123.4	123.3	124.2	125.5	127.8	128.0
Miscellaneous transportation equipment	106.2	110.4	112.5	114.1	115.2	117.1	118.1	120.3	121.9	123.0	124.2	125.0	128.3	129.7
Measuring and controlling instruments; photographic, medical, optical goods; watches, clocks	107.0	110.8	114.6	116.8	118.7	120.8	122.1	124.0	125.1	125.6	126.0	125.7	126.2	127.3
Engineering and scientific instruments (12/85=100)	108.1	112.7	116.9	120.5	121.4	123.0	124.6	127.4	128.3	130.0	132.5	132.5	132.0	131.6
Measuring and controlling instruments	107.9	111.7	116.3	120.1	123.3	126.1	127.9	129.9	131.5	133.5	134.4	134.8	136.6	138.8
Surgical, medical, and dental instruments and supplies	111.5	115.9	120.7	124.1	127.9	131.9	133.4	134.1	134.9	134.4	135.0	135.6	136.7	138.3
Opthalmic goods (12/83=100)	112.1	115.1	117.0	117.6	121.0	123.4	124.9	126.4	124.7	124.3	123.7	123.5	123.3	123.3
Photographic equipment and supplies (12/83=100)	105.3	109.3	112.2	111.9	112.1	112.1	111.7	113.8	114.9	113.5	109.7	106.7	106.2	107.4
Watches, clocks and watchcases (06/83=100)	105.3	108.2	110.5	113.6	114.7	115.9	116.6	118.9	119.2	118.3	118.4	119.4	120.8	122.1
Miscellaneous manufacturing industries (12/85=100)	107.5	111.8	114.9	117.5	119.6	121.5	123.3	125.9	127.8	129.0	129.7	130.3	130.9	132.4
Jewelry, silverware, and plated ware (12/85=100)	112.5	115.3	119.3	121.0	121.6	123.5	124.7	126.3	128.0	128.0	127.1	126.4	127.1	128.0
Musical instruments (06/85=100)	110.4	115.7	119.5	123.7	128.3	134.4	140.2	147.5	152.9	157.1	161.1	163.6	166.6	170.1
Toys and amusement, sporting, and athletic goods (12/85=100)	105.9	110.6	113.0	115.3	117.3	117.9	119.2	120.7	122.2	123.7	124.2	123.8	123.0	123.5
Pens, pencils, and other office and artists' materials (12/85=100)	106.3	110.4	114.3	118.0	120.8	121.4	123.2	127.4	130.2	129.8	130.9	132.0	132.0	131.4
Costume jewelry, costume novelties, buttons, and miscellaneous notions (12/85=100)	103.1	107.7	111.0	113.8	116.0	117.1	117.9	119.1	120.7	122.4	122.2	123.5	124.8	126.1
Miscellaneous manufacturing industries (12/85=100)	106.9	111.4	114.4	117.3	119.6	122.8	125.1	128.5	130.3	131.6	132.9	134.5	136.1	138.5
SERVICE INDUSTRIES														
Railroad transportation (12/96=100)	...	...	...	...	...	...	...	...	...	100.5	101.7	101.3	102.6	104.5
Motor freight transportation and warehousing (06/93=100)	...	...	...	...	...	...	101.9	104.5	106.3	108.9	111.6	114.8	119.4	123.1
Trucking and courier services, except air (06/93=100)	...	...	...	...	...	...	101.9	104.5	106.4	109.1	111.9	115.0	119.7	123.5
Public warehousing and storage (06/93=100)	...	...	...	...	...	...	101.3	103.0	103.6	104.6	106.0	109.0	111.2	114.2
United States Postal Service (06/89=100)	96.6	100.0	100.0	117.9	119.8	119.8	119.8	132.2	132.3	132.3	132.3	135.3	135.2	143.4
Water transportation (12/92=100)	...	...	...	...	...	99.7	100.0	103.0	103.7	104.2	105.6	113.0	122.6	129.8
Deep sea foreign transportation of freight (12/96=100)	...	...	...	...	...	...	...	...	...	99.0	102.0	116.4	134.7	148.3
Deep sea domestic transportation of freight (12/96=100)	...	...	...	...	...	...	...	...	...	99.9	97.2	99.8	104.2	107.7
Freight transportation, Great Lakes-St Lawrence Seaway (12/96=100)	...	...	...	...	...	...	...	...	...	101.3	102.2	102.3	102.2	102.9
Water transportation of freight, n.e.c. (12/96=100)	...	...	...	...	...	...	...	...	...	99.5	100.3	104.3	110.3	115.5
Transportation by air (12/92=100)	...	...	...	...	...	105.6	108.5	113.7	121.1	125.3	124.5	130.8	147.7	157.2
Air transportation, scheduled and air courier services (12/89=100)	...	...	110.2	121.2	114.2	125.4	129.1	135.9	145.5	150.8	149.3	157.3	180.1	193.0
Air transportation, nonscheduled (12/96=100)	...	...	...	...	...	...	...	...	...	97.8	99.2	102.2	107.3	112.7
Airports, flying fields, and airport terminal services (12/96=100)	...	...	...	...	...	...	...	...	...	102.5	105.2	108.6	114.2	117.5
Pipelines, except natural gas (12/86=100)	94.8	94.4	95.8	96.1	96.4	96.6	102.6	110.8	104.6	98.8	99.2	98.3	102.3	110.3
Arrangement of transportation of freight and cargo (12/96=100)	...	...	...	...	...	...	...	...	...	99.4	97.7	97.3	98.3	98.2
Telephone communications (06/99=100)	...	...	...	...	...	...	...	...	...	...	...	...	96.4	93.6
Cable and other pay television services (12/96=100)	...	...	...	...	...	...	...	...	...	103.3	107.3	110.9	115.4	119.5
Food stores (12/99=100)	...	...	...	...	...	...	...	...	...	...	...	...	103.8	109.6
Grocery stores (12/99=100)	...	...	...	...	...	...	...	...	...	...	...	...	104.2	109.9
Meat and fish (seafood) markets (12/99=100)	...	...	...	...	...	...	...	...	...	...	...	...	99.5	104.7
Fruit and vegetable markets (12/99=100)	...	...	...	...	...	...	...	...	...	...	...	...	98.9	98.5
Candy, nut, and confectionery stores (12/99=100)	...	...	...	...	...	...	...	...	...	...	...	...	102.8	107.3
Retail bakeries (12/99=100)	...	...	...	...	...	...	...	...	...	...	...	...	99.3	103.8
Miscellaneous food stores (12/99=100)	...	...	...	...	...	...	...	...	...	...	...	...	102.3	123.5
New car dealers (12/99=100)	...	...	...	...	...	...	...	...	...	...	...	...	99.7	103.1
Life insurance carriers (12/98=100)	...	...	...	...	...	...	...	...	...	...	...	100.4	99.2	100.1
Property and casualty insurance 12/98=100)	...	...	...	...	...	...	...	...	...	...	...	100.7	101.9	104.3
Real estate agents and managers (12/96=100)	...	...	...	...	...	...	...	...	...	101.3	103.0	104.9	108.3	112.0
Hotels and motels (12/96=100)	...	...	...	...	...	...	...	...	...	104.2	108.1	112.7	116.2	121.3
Personnel supply services (12/96=100)	...	...	...	...	...	...	...	...	...	101.0	103.2	105.2	107.3	108.2
Health services (12/94=100)	...	...	...	...	...	...	...	102.4	104.6	106.1	107.7	109.9	112.8	116.4
Offices and clinics of doctors of medicine (12/96=100)	...	...	...	...	...	...	...	...	...	101.0	103.2	105.5	107.3	110.4
Hospitals (12/92=100)	...	...	...	...	...	102.5	106.2	110.0	112.6	113.6	114.4	116.4	119.4	123.0
Home health care services (12/96=100)	...	...	...	...	...	...	...	...	...	103.3	106.2	107.1	111.1	114.0
Legal services (12/96=100)	...	...	...	...	...	...	...	...	...	102.5	106.1	108.7	112.5	117.9
Engineering, architectural, and surveying services (12/96=100)	...	...	...	...	...	...	...	...	...	102.2	105.1	108.5	111.8	115.9
Accounting, auditing, and bookkeeping services (12/96=100)	...	...	...	...	...	...	...	...	...	101.5	103.9	107.5	110.8	112.9

NOTES AND DEFINITIONS

CONSUMER PRICE INDEX

Coverage

The *Consumer Price Index* (CPI) measures the average change in prices of goods and services that urban consumers purchase for day-to-day living. The weights used in calculating the index, which remain fixed for relatively long periods, are based on actual expenditures reported in the Consumer Expenditure Surveys. The quantities and qualities of the sample items in the "market basket" remain essentially the same between consecutive pricing periods, so that the index measures only the effect of price change on the cost of living. The index does not measure changes in the total amount families spend for living. Geographic area indexes measure price changes over time in individual areas, not relative differences in prices or living costs between areas.

Periodic Updating

The index for the years 1913–35 used a study of 1917–19 spending by households of wage earners and clerical workers as the basis for its weights. Since then, there have been six updatings, bringing the "market basket" of goods and services up to date, revising the weights, and improving the sampling methods. In the past 20 years, several major changes have been introduced into the CPI.

The 1978 revision of the CPI updated the CPI for Urban Wage Earners and Clerical Workers (CPI-W), and introduced a new index for All Urban Consumers (CPI-U), which includes salaried workers, the self-employed, the retired, and the unemployed, as well as wage earners and clerical workers. The CPI-W now represents the spending patterns of 32 percent of the population, the CPI-U, 87 percent. For years before 1978, changes in the CPI-U are based on changes in the CPI-W. The 1978 revision also instituted sampling for all levels of the index down to the selection of items within each retail outlet.

Starting with the index for January 1983, BLS changed the way the CPI-U measures homeowners' costs; the CPI-W made the same change starting in January 1985. The change converted the homeownership component from an asset approach, which included both the investment and consumption aspects of homeownership, to a flow-of-services approach, that measures only the cost of shelter services consumed by homeowners. The new approach uses a rental equivalence method to calculate homeowner shelter costs by estimating the implicit rent owners would have to pay to rent the homes they live in. The old method calculated homeowner costs as home purchase, mortgage interest costs, property taxes, property insurance, and maintenance and repair.

The 1987 major revision of both the CPI-U and the CPI-W introduced weights based upon data from the 1982, 1983, and 1984 Consumer Expenditure Surveys. The 1998 CPI revision, which went into effect with the index for January 1998, uses expenditure data from the 1993–95 Consumer Expenditure Surveys and population data from the 1990 Decennial Census.

Current Methodology

The CPI selected 87 pricing areas, comprising 38 different index areas, from around the United States. BLS resamples the outlets and items in its sample on a 5-year rotating basis. Before rotating the sample, the Bureau of the Census conducts a Point of Purchase Survey for BLS. This survey determines location of the retail outlets where consumers buy goods and services in various categories; it also determines how much they spend on each category in each reported outlet. BLS then draws outlet samples from the Point-of-Purchase Survey information. BLS field agents visit the selected retail outlets and sample within the item categories using checklists, which exhaustively define these categories of goods and services. The original selection of the specific items to be priced in a specific retail store is generally done by a data collector using the checklist in systematic stages that take into account in each stage sales information provided by the respondent. Outlets may be located outside of their pricing area to represent out-of-town purchases.

After the initial selection, the same item (or a close substitute) is priced from period to period so that, as far as possible, differences in reported prices are measures of price change only. All taxes directly associated with the purchase or continued use of the items priced are included in the indexes. Foods, fuels, rents, and a few other items are priced monthly in all areas. Prices of most other commodities and services are obtained monthly in the three largest areas and every other month in the remaining areas, half in the odd months and half in the even months. Between scheduled survey dates, prices are held at the level of their last pricing. BLS agents also collect data for a sample of rental units drawn from the Decennial Census of Population and Housing. This sample is heavily augmented with renter-occupied housing units in areas where there are many owner-occupied units. This survey is the basis for the Rent and Owners' equivalent rent components of the CPI.

BLS calculates basic indexes (elementary aggregates) for the 211 item strata in each of the 38 index areas. Basic indexes are combined with weights based on the 1993–95 Consumer Expenditure Surveys and the Census of Population.

BLS publishes CPI indexes for a variety of commodities and services, by region, by size of city, for cross-classifications of regions and population size classes, and for 26 metropolitan areas.

The purchasing power of the consumer dollar for any given date is calculated as the reciprocal of the index for that date, expressed in dollars, with the dollar's value in 1982–84 equal to $1.00. It shows changes in the value of the dollar resulting from changes in prices of consumer goods and services. The purchasing power of the dollar with reference to other bases can be calculated by dividing the index for the desired base date by the index for the current date and expressing the result in dollars.

The relative importance figures are percentage distributions of the cost or value weights used in the index calculation. The cost weights represent average expenditures for specific classes of goods and services by consumers. However, in the subsequent pricing periods, the value weights and the corresponding relative importance figures change as prices change differentially; i.e., the relative importance increases for an item or group having a greater than average price increase and decreases for one having a less than average price increase. Historically, the weights in the CPI have been updated about every 10 years. Beginning in 2002, the CPI will update its expenditure weights every 2 years, to keep the weights more up-to-date with consumer spending patterns.

Since the CPI traditionally measured price changes for a fixed market basket of goods and services, it was criticized as overstating inflation in that it did not account for the fact that consumers can substitute (buy more or less) as relative prices change. In 1999, the CPI began using a geometric mean formula to average the prices within most CPI item categories. This formula assumes a modest degree of substitution within CPI item categories as relative prices change.

In 2002, BLS created an additional price index using a "superlative" formula, to address consumer substitution across CPI item categories. BLS began publishing this index, called the Chained Consumer Price Index for All Urban Consumers effective with release of July data in August 2002. Designated the C-CPI-U, the index will supplement, not replace the existing indexes already produced by the BLS: the CPI for All Urban Consumers (CPI-U) and the CPI for Urban Wage Earners and Clerical Workers (CPI-W).

Sources of Additional Information

The CCPI is described in BLS new release 02-480. A press release dated April 1998, "Planned Change In The Consumer Price Index Formula", describes the geometric mean methodology.

The December 1996 issue of the *Monthly Labor Review* was devoted to a description and discussion of issues related to the 1998 CPI Revision. Further changes in methodology are described in BLS press releases. A detailed description of the CPI before 1978 is contained in *The Consumer Price Index: History and Techniques*, BLS Bulletin 1517 (1966). For further information see *The Consumer Price Index: Concepts and Content Over the Years*, BLS Report 517 (1977). *The Consumer Price Index Detailed Report* is published monthly and contains occasional articles.

Table 6-4. Consumer Price Indexes, All Urban Consumers (CPI-U): U.S. City Average, Major Groups, 1967–2001

(1982–1984=100, unless otherwise indicated.)

Year	All items	Food and beverages	Housing	Apparel	Transportation	Medical care	Recreation [1]	Education and communication [1]	Other goods and services
1967	33.4	35.0	30.8	51.0	33.3	28.2	...	...	35.1
1968	34.8	36.2	32.0	53.7	34.3	29.9	...	...	36.9
1969	36.7	38.1	34.0	56.8	35.7	31.9	...	...	38.7
1970	38.8	40.1	36.4	59.2	37.5	34.0	...	...	40.9
1971	40.5	41.4	38.0	61.1	39.5	36.1	...	...	42.9
1972	41.8	43.1	39.4	62.3	39.9	37.3	...	...	44.7
1973	44.4	48.8	41.2	64.6	41.2	38.8	...	...	46.4
1974	49.3	55.5	45.8	69.4	45.8	42.4	...	...	49.8
1975	53.8	60.2	50.7	72.5	50.1	47.5	...	...	53.9
1976	56.9	62.1	53.8	75.2	55.1	52.0	...	...	57.0
1977	60.6	65.8	57.4	78.6	59.0	57.0	...	...	60.4
1978	65.2	72.2	62.4	81.4	61.7	61.8	...	...	64.3
1979	72.6	79.9	70.1	84.9	70.5	67.5	...	...	68.9
1980	82.4	86.7	81.1	90.9	83.1	74.9	...	...	75.2
1981	90.9	93.5	90.4	95.3	93.2	82.9	...	...	82.6
1982	96.5	97.3	96.9	97.8	97.0	92.5	...	...	91.1
1983	99.6	99.5	99.5	100.2	99.3	100.6	...	...	101.1
1984	103.9	103.2	103.6	102.1	103.7	106.8	...	...	107.9
1985	107.6	105.6	107.7	105.0	106.4	113.5	...	...	114.5
1986	109.6	109.1	110.9	105.9	102.3	122.0	...	...	121.4
1987	113.6	113.5	114.2	110.6	105.4	130.1	...	...	128.5
1988	118.3	118.2	118.5	115.4	108.7	138.6	...	...	137.0
1989	124.0	124.9	123.0	118.6	114.1	149.3	...	...	147.7
1990	130.7	132.1	128.5	124.1	120.5	162.8	...	...	159.0
1991	136.2	136.8	133.6	128.7	123.8	177.0	...	...	171.6
1992	140.3	138.7	137.5	131.9	126.5	190.1	...	...	183.3
1993	144.5	141.6	141.2	133.7	130.4	201.4	90.7	85.5	192.9
1994	148.2	144.9	144.8	133.4	134.3	211.0	92.7	88.8	198.5
1995	152.4	148.9	148.5	132.0	139.1	220.5	94.5	92.2	206.9
1996	156.9	153.7	152.8	131.7	143.0	228.2	97.4	95.3	215.4
1997	160.5	157.7	156.8	132.9	144.3	234.6	99.6	98.4	224.8
1998	163.0	161.1	160.4	133.0	141.6	242.1	101.1	100.3	237.7
1999	166.6	164.6	163.9	131.3	144.4	250.6	102.0	101.2	258.3
2000	172.2	168.4	169.6	129.6	153.3	260.8	103.3	102.5	271.1
2001	177.1	173.6	176.4	127.3	154.3	272.8	104.9	105.2	282.6

1. December 1997=100.

Table 6-5. Consumer Price Indexes, All Urban Consumers (CPI-U): U.S. City Average, Commodity, Service, and Special Groups, 1967–2001

(1982–1984=100, unless otherwise indicated.)

Year	All items	All items less food	All items less shelter	All items less medical care	All items less energy	All items less food and energy	Commodities	Commodities less food and beverages	Energy commodities	Commodities less food and energy	Nondurables
1967	33.4	33.4	35.2	33.7	34.4	34.7	36.8	38.3	23.9	41.3	35.7
1968	34.8	34.9	36.7	35.1	35.9	36.3	38.1	39.7	24.4	42.9	37.1
1969	36.7	36.8	38.4	37.0	38.0	38.4	39.9	41.4	25.2	44.7	38.9
1970	38.8	39.0	40.3	39.2	40.3	40.8	41.7	43.1	25.6	46.7	40.8
1971	40.5	40.8	42.0	40.8	42.0	42.7	43.2	44.7	26.1	48.5	42.1
1972	41.8	42.0	43.3	42.1	43.4	44.0	44.5	45.8	26.4	49.7	43.5
1973	44.4	43.7	46.2	44.8	46.1	45.6	47.8	47.3	29.1	51.1	47.5
1974	49.3	48.0	51.4	49.8	50.6	49.4	53.5	52.4	40.4	55.0	54.0
1975	53.8	52.5	56.0	54.3	55.1	53.9	58.2	57.3	43.4	60.1	58.3
1976	56.9	56.0	59.3	57.2	58.2	57.4	60.7	60.2	45.4	63.2	60.5
1977	60.6	59.6	63.1	60.8	61.9	61.0	64.2	63.6	48.7	66.5	64.0
1978	65.2	63.9	67.4	65.4	66.7	65.5	68.8	67.3	51.0	70.5	68.6
1979	72.6	71.2	74.2	72.9	73.4	71.9	76.6	75.2	68.7	76.4	77.2
1980	82.4	81.5	82.9	82.8	81.9	80.8	86.0	85.7	95.2	83.5	87.6
1981	90.9	90.4	91.0	91.4	90.1	89.2	93.2	93.1	107.6	90.0	95.2
1982	96.5	96.3	96.2	96.8	96.1	95.8	97.0	96.9	102.9	95.3	97.8
1983	99.6	99.7	99.8	99.6	99.6	99.6	99.8	100.0	99.0	100.2	99.7
1984	103.9	104.0	103.9	103.7	104.3	104.6	103.2	103.1	98.1	104.4	102.5
1985	107.6	108.0	107.0	107.2	108.4	109.1	105.4	105.2	98.2	107.1	104.8
1986	109.6	109.8	108.0	108.8	112.6	113.5	104.4	101.4	77.2	108.6	103.5
1987	113.6	113.6	111.6	112.6	117.2	118.2	107.7	104.0	80.2	111.8	107.5
1988	118.3	118.3	115.9	117.0	122.3	123.4	111.5	107.3	80.8	115.8	111.8
1989	124.0	123.7	121.6	122.4	128.1	129.0	116.7	111.6	87.9	119.6	118.2
1990	130.7	130.3	128.2	128.8	134.7	135.5	122.8	117.0	101.2	123.6	126.0
1991	136.2	136.1	133.5	133.8	140.9	142.1	126.6	120.4	99.1	128.8	130.3
1992	140.3	140.8	137.3	137.5	145.4	147.3	129.1	123.2	98.3	132.5	132.8
1993	144.5	145.1	141.4	141.2	150.0	152.2	131.5	125.3	97.3	135.2	135.1
1994	148.2	149.0	144.8	144.7	154.1	156.5	133.8	126.9	97.6	137.1	136.8
1995	152.4	153.1	148.6	148.6	158.7	161.2	136.4	128.9	98.8	139.3	139.3
1996	156.9	157.5	152.8	152.8	163.1	165.6	139.9	131.5	105.7	141.3	143.5
1997	160.5	161.1	155.9	156.3	167.1	169.5	141.8	132.2	105.7	142.3	146.4
1998	163.0	163.4	157.2	158.6	170.9	173.4	141.9	130.5	92.1	143.2	146.9
1999	166.6	167.0	160.2	162.0	174.4	177.0	144.4	132.5	100.0	144.1	151.2
2000	172.2	173.0	165.7	167.3	178.6	181.3	149.2	137.7	129.5	144.9	158.2
2001	177.1	177.8	169.7	171.9	183.5	186.1	150.7	137.2	125.2	145.3	160.6

See footnotes at end of table.

Table 6-5. Consumer Price Indexes, All Urban Consumers (CPI-U): U.S. City Average, Commodity, Service, and Special Groups, 1967–2001—*Continued*

(1982–1984=100, unless otherwise indicated.)

Year	Nondurables less food	Nondurables less food and apparel	Services Total[1]	Rent of Shelter[2]	Gas (piped) and electricity	Transportation services	Medical care services	Other services	Services less medical care	Energy	Services less energy
1967	37.6	32.6	28.8	...	23.7	32.6	26.0	36.0	29.3	23.8	29.3
1968	39.1	33.7	30.3	...	23.9	33.9	27.9	38.1	30.8	24.2	30.9
1969	40.9	34.9	32.4	...	24.3	36.3	30.2	40.0	32.9	24.8	33.2
1970	42.5	36.3	35.0	...	25.4	40.2	32.3	42.2	35.6	25.5	36.0
1971	44.0	37.6	37.0	...	27.1	43.4	34.7	44.4	37.5	26.5	38.0
1972	45.0	38.6	38.4	...	28.5	44.4	35.9	45.6	38.9	27.2	39.4
1973	46.9	40.3	40.1	...	29.9	44.7	37.5	47.7	40.6	29.4	41.1
1974	52.9	46.9	43.8	...	34.5	46.3	41.4	51.3	44.3	38.1	44.8
1975	57.0	51.5	48.0	...	40.1	49.8	46.6	55.1	48.3	42.1	48.8
1976	59.5	54.1	52.0	...	44.7	56.9	51.3	58.4	52.2	45.1	52.7
1977	62.5	57.2	56.0	...	50.5	61.5	56.4	62.1	55.9	49.4	56.5
1978	65.5	60.4	60.8	...	55.0	64.4	61.2	66.4	60.7	52.5	61.3
1979	74.6	71.2	67.5	...	61.0	69.5	67.2	71.9	67.5	65.7	68.2
1980	88.4	87.1	77.9	...	71.4	79.2	74.8	78.7	78.2	86.0	78.5
1981	96.7	96.8	88.1	...	81.9	88.6	82.8	86.1	88.7	97.7	88.7
1982	98.3	98.2	96.0	...	93.2	96.1	92.6	93.5	96.4	99.2	96.3
1983	100.0	100.0	99.4	102.7	101.5	99.1	100.7	100.0	99.2	99.9	99.2
1984	101.7	101.8	104.6	107.7	105.4	104.8	106.7	106.5	104.4	100.9	104.5
1985	104.1	104.1	109.9	113.9	107.1	110.0	113.2	113.0	109.6	101.6	110.2
1986	98.5	96.9	115.4	120.2	105.7	116.3	121.9	119.4	114.6	88.2	116.5
1987	101.8	100.3	120.2	125.9	103.8	121.9	130.0	125.7	119.1	88.6	122.0
1988	105.8	104.0	125.7	132.0	104.6	128.0	138.3	132.6	124.3	89.3	127.9
1989	111.7	111.3	131.9	138.0	107.5	135.6	148.9	140.9	130.1	94.3	134.4
1990	119.9	120.9	139.2	145.5	109.3	144.2	162.7	150.2	136.8	102.1	142.3
1991	124.5	125.7	146.3	152.1	112.6	151.2	177.1	159.8	143.3	102.5	149.8
1992	127.6	128.9	152.0	157.3	114.8	155.7	190.5	168.5	148.4	103.0	155.9
1993	129.3	130.7	157.9	162.0	118.5	162.9	202.9	177.0	153.6	104.2	161.9
1994	129.7	131.6	163.1	167.0	119.2	168.6	213.4	185.4	158.4	104.6	167.6
1995	130.9	134.1	168.7	172.4	119.2	175.9	224.2	193.3	163.5	105.2	173.7
1996	134.5	139.5	174.1	178.0	122.1	180.5	232.4	201.4	168.7	110.1	179.4
1997	136.3	141.8	179.4	183.4	125.1	185.0	239.1	209.6	173.9	111.5	185.0
1998	134.6	139.2	184.2	189.6	121.2	187.9	246.8	216.9	178.4	102.9	190.6
1999	139.4	147.5	188.8	195.0	120.9	190.7	255.1	223.1	182.7	106.6	195.7
2000	149.1	162.9	195.3	201.3	128.0	196.1	266.0	229.9	188.9	124.6	202.1
2001	149.1	164.1	203.4	208.9	142.4	201.9	278.8	238.0	196.6	129.3	209.6

1. Includes tenants and household insurance, water, sewer, trash, and household operations services, not shown separately.
2. December 1982=100.

Table 6-6. Consumer Price Indexes, All Urban Consumers (CPI-U): U.S. City Average, Selected Groups, and Purchasing Power of the Consumer Dollar, 1913–2001

(1982–1984=100, unless otherwise indicated.)

Year	All items	Food	Rent of primary residence	Owners' equivalent of primary residence [1]	Apparel	Purchasing power of the consumer dollar [2]
1913	9.9	10.0	21.0	...	14.9	10.077
1914	10.0	10.2	21.0	...	15.0	9.942
1915	10.1	10.0	21.1	...	15.3	9.843
1916	10.9	11.3	21.3	...	16.8	9.152
1917	12.8	14.5	21.2	...	20.2	7.793
1918	15.1	16.7	21.5	...	27.3	6.635
1919	17.3	18.6	23.3	...	36.2	5.779
1920	20.0	21.0	27.4	...	43.1	4.989
1921	17.9	15.9	31.5	...	33.2	5.585
1922	16.8	14.9	32.4	...	27.0	5.962
1923	17.1	15.4	33.2	...	27.1	5.857
1924	17.1	15.2	34.4	...	26.8	5.845
1925	17.5	16.5	34.6	...	26.3	5.701
1926	17.7	17.0	34.2	...	25.9	5.647
1927	17.4	16.4	33.7	...	25.3	5.755
1928	17.1	16.3	32.9	...	25.0	5.833
1929	17.1	16.5	32.1	...	24.7	5.833
1930	16.7	15.6	31.2	...	24.2	5.986
1931	15.2	12.9	29.6	...	22.0	6.563
1932	13.7	10.7	26.5	...	19.5	7.317
1933	13.0	10.4	22.9	...	18.8	7.712
1934	13.4	11.6	21.4	...	20.6	7.464
1935	13.7	12.4	21.4	...	20.8	7.281
1936	13.9	12.6	21.9	...	21.0	7.213
1937	14.4	13.1	22.9	...	22.0	6.961
1938	14.1	12.1	23.7	...	21.9	7.093
1939	13.9	11.8	23.7	...	21.6	7.195
1940	14.0	12.0	23.7	...	21.8	7.126
1941	14.7	13.1	24.2	...	22.8	6.788
1942	16.3	15.4	24.7	...	26.7	6.132
1943	17.3	17.1	24.7	...	27.8	5.779
1944	17.6	16.9	24.8	...	29.8	5.680
1945	18.0	17.3	24.8	...	31.4	5.552
1946	19.5	19.8	25.0	...	34.4	5.115
1947	22.3	24.1	25.8	...	39.9	4.474
1948	24.1	26.1	27.5	...	42.5	4.151
1949	23.8	25.0	28.7	...	40.8	4.193
1950	24.1	25.4	29.7	...	40.3	4.151
1951	26.0	28.2	30.9	...	43.9	3.846
1952	26.5	28.7	32.2	...	43.5	3.765
1953	26.7	28.3	33.9	...	43.1	3.735
1954	26.9	28.2	35.1	...	43.1	3.717
1955	26.8	27.8	35.6	...	42.9	3.732
1956	27.2	28.0	36.3	...	43.7	3.678
1957	28.1	28.9	37.0	...	44.5	3.549
1958	28.9	30.2	37.6	...	44.6	3.457
1959	29.1	29.7	38.2	...	45.0	3.427

See footnotes at end of table.

Table 6-6. Consumer Price Indexes, All Urban Consumers (CPI-U): U.S. City Average, Selected Groups, and Purchasing Power of the Consumer Dollar, 1913–2001—*Continued*

(1982–1984=100, unless otherwise indicated.)

Year	All items	Food	Rent of primary residence	Owners' equivalent of primary residence [1]	Apparel	Purchasing power of the consumer dollar [2]
1960	29.6	30.0	38.7	. . .	45.7	3.373
1961	29.9	30.4	39.2	. . .	46.1	3.340
1962	30.2	30.6	39.7	. . .	46.3	3.304
1963	30.6	31.1	40.1	. . .	46.9	3.265
1964	31.0	31.5	40.5	. . .	47.3	3.220
1965	31.5	32.2	40.9	. . .	47.8	3.166
1966	32.4	33.8	41.5	. . .	49.0	3.080
1967	33.4	34.1	42.2	. . .	51.0	2.993
1968	34.8	35.3	43.3	. . .	53.7	2.873
1969	36.7	37.1	44.7	. . .	56.8	2.726
1970	38.8	39.2	46.5	. . .	59.2	2.574
1971	40.5	40.4	48.7	. . .	61.1	2.466
1972	41.8	42.1	50.4	. . .	62.3	2.391
1973	44.4	48.2	52.5	. . .	64.6	2.251
1974	49.3	55.1	55.2	. . .	69.4	2.029
1975	53.8	59.8	58.0	. . .	72.5	1.859
1976	56.9	61.6	61.1	. . .	75.2	1.757
1977	60.6	65.5	64.8	. . .	78.6	1.649
1978	65.2	72.0	69.3	. . .	81.4	1.532
1979	72.6	79.9	74.3	. . .	84.9	1.380
1980	82.4	86.8	80.9	. . .	90.9	1.215
1981	90.9	93.6	87.9	. . .	95.3	1.098
1982	96.5	97.4	94.6	. . .	97.8	1.035
1983	99.6	99.4	100.1	102.5	100.2	1.003
1984	103.9	103.2	105.3	107.3	102.1	0.961
1985	107.6	105.6	111.8	113.2	105.0	0.928
1986	109.6	109.0	118.3	119.4	105.9	0.913
1987	113.6	113.5	123.1	124.8	110.6	0.880
1988	118.3	118.2	127.8	131.1	115.4	0.846
1989	124.0	125.1	132.8	137.4	118.6	0.807
1990	130.7	132.4	138.4	144.8	124.1	0.766
1991	136.2	136.3	143.3	150.4	128.7	0.734
1992	140.3	137.9	146.9	155.5	131.9	0.713
1993	144.5	140.9	150.3	160.5	133.7	0.692
1994	148.2	144.3	154.0	165.8	133.4	0.675
1995	152.4	148.4	157.8	171.3	132.0	0.656
1996	156.9	153.3	162.0	176.8	131.7	0.638
1997	160.5	157.3	166.7	181.9	132.9	0.623
1998	163.0	160.7	172.1	187.8	133.0	0.614
1999	166.6	164.1	177.5	192.9	131.3	0.600
2000	172.2	167.8	183.9	198.7	129.6	0.581
2001	177.1	173.1	192.1	206.3	127.3	0.565

1. December 1982=100.
2. Purchasing power in 1982–1984= $1.00.

Table 6-7. Consumer Price Indexes, Urban Wage Earners and Clerical Workers (CPI-W): U.S. City Average, Major Groups, 1913–2001

(1982–1984=100, unless otherwise indicated.)

Year	All items	Food and beverages	Housing	Apparel	Transportation	Medical care	Recreation [1]	Education and communication [1]	Other goods and services
1913	10.0	...	...	15.0	...	...	...	...	...
1914	10.1	...	...	15.1	...	...	...	...	...
1915	10.2	...	...	15.4	...	...	...	...	...
1916	11.0	...	...	16.9	...	...	...	...	...
1917	12.9	...	...	20.3	...	...	...	...	...
1918	15.1	...	...	27.5	...	...	...	...	...
1919	17.4	...	...	36.4	...	...	...	...	...
1920	20.1	...	...	43.3	...	...	...	...	...
1921	18.0	...	...	33.4	...	...	...	...	...
1922	16.9	...	...	27.2	...	...	...	...	...
1923	17.2	...	...	27.2	...	...	...	...	...
1924	17.2	...	...	26.9	...	...	...	...	...
1925	17.6	...	...	26.4	...	...	...	...	...
1926	17.8	...	...	26.0	...	...	...	...	...
1927	17.5	...	...	25.5	...	...	...	...	...
1928	17.2	...	...	25.1	...	...	...	...	...
1929	17.2	...	...	24.8	...	...	...	...	...
1930	16.8	...	...	24.3	...	...	...	...	...
1931	15.3	...	...	22.1	...	...	...	...	...
1932	13.7	...	...	19.6	...	...	...	...	...
1933	13.0	...	...	18.9	...	...	...	...	...
1934	13.5	...	...	20.7	...	...	...	...	...
1935	13.8	...	...	20.9	14.1	10.2	...	...	...
1936	13.9	...	...	21.1	14.2	10.3	...	...	...
1937	14.4	...	...	22.1	14.5	10.4	...	...	...
1938	14.2	...	...	22.0	14.6	10.4	...	...	...
1939	14.0	...	...	21.7	14.2	10.4	...	...	...
1940	14.1	...	...	21.9	14.1	10.4	...	...	...
1941	14.8	...	...	23.0	14.6	10.5	...	...	...
1942	16.4	...	...	26.8	15.9	10.8	...	...	...
1943	17.4	...	...	28.0	15.8	11.3	...	...	...
1944	17.7	...	...	30.0	15.8	11.6	...	...	...
1945	18.1	...	...	31.5	15.8	11.9	...	...	...
1946	19.6	...	...	34.6	16.6	12.6	...	...	...
1947	22.5	...	...	40.1	18.4	13.6	...	...	...
1948	24.2	...	...	42.7	20.4	14.5	...	...	...
1949	24.0	...	...	41.0	22.0	14.9	...	...	...
1950	24.2	...	...	40.5	22.6	15.2	...	...	...
1951	26.1	...	...	44.1	24.0	15.9	...	...	...
1952	26.7	...	...	43.7	25.6	16.8	...	...	...
1953	26.9	...	...	43.3	26.3	17.4	...	...	...
1954	27.0	...	...	43.3	25.9	17.9	...	...	...

See footnotes at end of table.

Table 6-7. Consumer Price Indexes, Urban Wage Earners and Clerical Workers (CPI-W): U.S. City Average, Major Groups, 1913–2001—*Continued*

(1982–1984=100, unless otherwise indicated.)

Year	All items	Food and beverages	Housing	Apparel	Transportation	Medical care	Recreation [1]	Education and communi-cation [1]	Other goods and services
1955	26.9	...	...	43.1	25.6	18.3	...	...	...
1956	27.3	...	...	44.0	26.1	19.0	...	...	...
1957	28.3	...	...	44.7	27.6	19.8	...	...	...
1958	29.1	...	...	44.8	28.4	20.7	...	...	...
1959	29.3	...	...	45.2	29.6	21.6	...	...	...
1960	29.8	...	...	45.9	29.6	22.4	...	...	...
1961	30.1	...	...	46.3	30.0	23.0	...	...	...
1962	30.4	...	...	46.6	30.6	23.6	...	...	...
1963	30.8	...	...	47.1	30.8	24.2	...	...	...
1964	31.2	...	...	47.5	31.2	24.7	...	...	...
1965	31.7	...	...	48.0	31.7	25.3	...	...	...
1966	32.6	...	...	49.2	32.2	26.4	...	...	...
1967	33.6	35.0	31.1	51.2	33.1	28.3	...	...	35.4
1968	35.0	36.2	32.3	54.0	34.1	30.0	...	...	37.2
1969	36.9	38.0	34.3	57.1	35.5	32.1	...	...	39.1
1970	39.0	40.1	36.7	59.5	37.3	34.1	...	...	41.3
1971	40.7	41.3	38.3	61.4	39.2	36.3	...	...	43.3
1972	42.1	43.1	39.8	62.7	39.7	37.5	...	...	45.1
1973	44.7	48.8	41.5	65.0	41.0	39.0	...	...	46.9
1974	49.6	55.5	46.2	69.8	45.5	42.6	...	...	50.2
1975	54.1	60.2	51.1	72.9	49.8	47.7	...	...	54.4
1976	57.2	62.0	54.2	75.6	54.7	52.3	...	...	57.6
1977	60.9	65.7	57.9	79.0	58.6	57.3	...	...	60.9
1978	65.6	72.1	62.9	81.7	61.5	62.1	...	...	64.8
1979	73.1	79.9	70.7	85.2	70.4	68.0	...	...	69.4
1980	82.9	86.9	81.7	90.9	82.9	75.6	...	...	75.6
1981	91.4	93.6	91.1	95.6	93.0	83.5	...	...	82.5
1982	96.9	97.3	97.7	97.8	97.0	92.5	...	...	90.9
1983	99.8	99.5	100.0	100.2	99.2	100.5	...	...	101.3
1984	103.3	103.2	102.2	102.0	103.8	106.9	...	...	107.9
1985	106.9	105.5	106.6	105.0	106.4	113.6	...	...	114.2
1986	108.6	108.9	109.7	105.8	101.7	122.0	...	...	120.9
1987	112.5	113.3	112.8	110.4	105.1	130.2	...	...	127.8
1988	117.0	117.9	116.8	114.9	108.3	139.0	...	...	136.5
1989	122.6	124.6	121.2	117.9	113.9	149.6	...	...	147.4
1990	129.0	131.8	126.4	123.1	120.1	162.7	...	...	158.9
1991	134.3	136.5	131.2	127.4	123.1	176.5	...	...	171.7
1992	138.2	138.3	135.0	130.7	125.8	189.6	...	...	183.3
1993	142.1	141.2	138.5	132.4	129.4	200.9	91.2	86.0	192.2
1994	145.6	144.4	142.0	132.2	133.4	210.4	93.0	89.1	196.4
1995	149.8	148.3	145.4	130.9	138.8	219.8	94.7	92.3	204.2
1996	154.1	153.2	149.6	130.9	142.8	227.6	97.5	95.4	212.2
1997	157.6	157.2	153.4	132.1	143.6	234.0	99.7	98.5	221.6
1998	159.7	160.4	156.7	131.6	140.5	241.4	100.9	100.4	236.1
1999	163.2	163.8	160.0	130.1	143.4	249.7	101.3	101.5	261.9
2000	168.9	167.7	165.4	128.3	152.8	259.9	102.4	102.7	276.5
2001	173.5	173.0	172.1	126.1	153.6	271.8	103.6	105.3	289.5

1. December 1997=100.

Table 6-8. Consumer Price Indexes, All Urban Consumers (CPI-U): U.S. City Average, by Expenditure Category, 1987–2001

(1982–1984=100, unless otherwise indicated.)

Expenditure category	1987	1988	1989	1990	1991	1992[2]	1993[1]	1994[1]	1995	1996	1997	1998	1999	2000	2001
ALL ITEMS	113.6	118.3	124.0	130.7	136.2	140.3	144.5	148.2	152.4	156.9	160.5	163.0	166.6	172.2	177.1
Food And Beverages	113.5	118.2	124.9	132.1	136.8	138.7	141.6	144.9	148.9	153.7	157.7	161.1	164.6	168.4	173.6
Food	113.5	118.2	125.1	132.4	136.3	137.9	140.9	144.3	148.4	153.3	157.3	160.7	164.1	167.8	173.1
Food at home	111.9	116.6	124.2	132.3	135.8	136.8	140.1	144.1	148.8	154.3	158.1	161.1	164.2	167.9	173.4
Cereals and bakery products	114.8	122.1	132.4	140.0	145.8	151.5	156.6	163.0	167.5	174.0	177.6	181.1	185.0	188.3	193.8
Meats, poultry, fish, and eggs	110.5	114.3	121.3	130.0	132.6	130.9	135.5	137.2	138.8	144.8	148.5	147.3	147.9	154.5	161.3
Dairy and related products	105.9	108.4	115.6	126.5	125.1	128.5	129.4	131.7	132.8	142.1	145.5	150.8	159.6	160.7	167.1
Fruits and vegetables	119.1	128.1	138.0	149.0	155.8	155.4	159.0	165.0	177.7	183.9	187.5	198.2	203.1	204.6	212.2
Nonalcoholic beverages and beverage materials	107.5	107.5	111.3	113.5	114.1	114.3	114.6	123.2	131.7	128.6	133.4	133.0	134.3	137.8	139.2
Other food at home	110.5	113.1	119.1	123.4	127.3	128.8	130.5	135.6	140.8	142.9	147.3	150.8	153.5	155.6	159.6
Sugar and sweets	111.0	114.0	119.4	124.7	129.3	133.1	133.4	135.2	137.5	143.7	147.8	150.2	152.3	154.0	155.7
Fats and oils	108.1	113.1	121.2	126.3	131.7	129.8	130.0	133.5	137.3	140.5	141.7	146.9	148.3	147.4	155.7
Other foods	113.8	118.0	125.5	131.2	137.1	140.1	143.7	147.5	151.1	156.2	161.2	165.5	168.9	172.2	176.0
Other miscellaneous foods[1]	...	...	...	...	...	...	...	...	...	...	...	102.6	104.9	107.5	108.9
Food away from home	117.0	121.8	127.4	133.4	137.9	140.7	143.2	145.7	149.0	152.7	157.0	161.1	165.1	169.0	173.9
Other food away from home[1]	...	...	...	...	...	...	...	...	...	...	...	101.6	105.2	109.0	113.4
Alcoholic beverages	114.1	118.6	123.5	129.3	142.8	147.3	149.6	151.5	153.9	158.5	162.8	165.7	169.7	174.7	179.3
Housing	114.2	118.5	123.0	128.5	133.6	137.5	141.2	144.8	148.5	152.8	156.8	160.4	163.9	169.6	176.4
Shelter	121.3	127.1	132.8	140.0	146.3	151.2	155.7	160.5	165.7	171.0	176.3	182.1	187.3	193.4	200.6
Rent of primary residence	123.1	127.8	132.8	138.4	143.3	146.9	150.3	154.0	157.8	162.0	166.7	172.1	177.5	183.9	192.1
Lodging away from home[1]	...	...	...	...	...	...	...	...	...	...	...	109.0	112.3	117.5	118.6
Owners' equivalent rent of primary residence[2]	124.8	131.1	137.4	144.8	150.4	155.5	160.5	165.8	171.3	176.8	181.9	187.8	192.9	198.7	206.3
Tenants' and household insurance[1]	...	...	...	...	...	...	...	...	...	...	...	99.8	101.3	103.7	106.2
Fuels and utilities	103.0	104.4	107.8	111.6	115.3	117.8	121.3	122.8	123.7	127.5	130.8	128.5	128.8	137.9	150.2
Fuels	97.3	98.0	100.9	104.5	106.7	108.1	111.2	111.7	111.5	115.2	117.9	113.7	113.5	122.8	135.4
Fuel oil and other household fuels	77.9	78.1	81.7	99.3	94.6	90.7	90.3	88.8	88.1	99.2	99.8	90.0	91.4	129.7	129.3
Gas (piped) and electricity	103.8	104.6	107.5	109.3	112.6	114.8	118.5	119.2	119.2	122.1	125.1	121.2	120.9	128.0	142.4
Water and sewer and trash collection services[1]	...	...	...	...	...	...	...	...	...	...	...	101.6	104.0	106.5	109.6
Household furnishings and operation	107.1	109.4	111.2	113.3	116.0	118.0	119.3	121.0	123.0	124.7	125.4	126.6	126.7	128.2	129.1
Household operations[1]	...	...	...	...	...	...	...	...	...	...	...	101.5	104.5	110.5	115.6
Apparel	110.6	115.4	118.6	124.1	128.7	131.9	133.7	133.4	132.0	131.7	132.9	133.0	131.3	129.6	127.3
Men's and boys' apparel	109.1	113.4	117.0	120.4	124.2	126.5	127.5	126.4	126.2	127.7	130.1	131.8	131.1	129.7	125.7
Women's and girls' apparel	110.4	114.9	116.4	122.6	127.6	130.4	132.6	130.9	126.9	124.7	126.1	126.0	123.3	121.5	119.3
Infants' and toddlers' apparel	112.1	116.4	119.1	125.8	128.9	129.3	127.1	128.1	127.2	129.7	129.0	126.1	129.0	130.6	129.2
Footwear	105.1	109.9	114.4	117.4	120.9	125.0	125.9	126.0	125.4	126.6	127.6	128.0	125.7	123.8	123.0
Transportation	105.4	108.7	114.1	120.5	123.8	126.5	130.4	134.3	139.1	143.0	144.3	141.6	144.4	153.3	154.3
Private transportation	104.2	107.6	112.9	118.8	121.9	124.6	127.5	131.4	136.3	140.0	141.0	137.9	140.5	149.1	150.0
New and used motor vehicles[1]	...	...	...	...	...	...	91.8	95.5	99.4	101.0	100.5	100.1	100.1	100.8	101.3
New vehicles	114.4	116.5	119.2	121.4	126.0	129.2	132.7	137.6	141.0	143.7	144.3	143.4	142.9	142.8	142.1
Used cars and trucks	113.1	118.0	120.4	117.6	118.1	123.2	133.9	141.7	156.5	157.0	151.1	150.6	152.0	155.8	158.7
Motor fuel	80.2	80.9	88.5	101.2	99.4	99.0	98.0	98.5	100.0	106.3	106.2	92.2	100.7	129.3	124.7
Gasoline (all types)	80.1	80.8	88.5	101.0	99.2	99.0	97.7	98.2	99.8	105.9	105.8	91.6	100.1	128.6	124.0
Motor vehicle parts and equipment	96.1	97.9	100.2	100.9	102.2	103.1	101.6	101.4	102.1	102.2	101.9	101.1	100.5	101.5	104.8
Motor vehicle maintenance and repair	114.8	119.7	124.9	130.1	136.0	141.3	145.9	150.2	154.0	158.4	162.7	167.1	171.9	177.3	183.5
Public transportation	121.1	123.3	129.5	142.6	148.9	151.4	167.0	172.0	175.9	181.9	186.7	190.3	197.7	209.6	210.6
Medical Care	130.1	138.6	149.3	162.8	177.0	190.1	201.4	211.0	220.5	228.2	234.6	242.1	250.6	260.8	272.8
Medical care commodities	131.0	139.9	150.8	163.4	176.8	188.1	195.0	200.7	204.5	210.4	215.3	221.8	230.7	238.1	247.6
Medical care services	130.0	138.3	148.9	162.7	177.1	190.5	202.9	213.4	224.2	232.4	239.1	246.8	255.1	266.0	278.8
Professional services	128.8	137.5	146.4	156.1	165.7	175.8	184.7	192.5	201.0	208.3	215.4	222.2	229.2	237.7	246.5
Hospital and related services	131.6	143.9	160.5	178.0	196.1	214.0	231.9	245.6	257.8	269.5	278.4	287.5	299.5	317.3	338.3
Recreation[1]	...	...	...	...	...	...	90.7	92.7	94.5	97.4	99.6	101.1	102.0	103.3	104.9
Video and audio[1]	...	...	...	...	...	...	96.5	95.4	95.1	96.6	99.4	101.1	100.7	101.0	101.5
Education And Communication[1]	...	...	...	...	...	...	85.5	88.8	92.2	95.3	98.4	100.3	101.2	102.5	105.2
Education[1]	...	...	...	...	...	...	78.4	83.3	88.0	92.7	97.3	100.1	107.0	112.5	118.5
Educational books and supplies	138.1	148.1	158.0	171.3	180.3	190.3	197.6	205.5	214.4	226.9	238.4	250.8	261.7	279.9	295.9
Tuition, other school fees, and child care	140.0	151.0	162.7	175.7	191.4	208.5	225.3	239.8	253.8	267.1	280.4	294.2	308.4	324.0	341.1
Communication[1]	...	...	...	...	...	...	96.7	97.6	98.8	99.6	100.3	98.7	96.0	93.6	93.3
Information and information processing[1]	...	...	...	...	...	...	97.7	98.6	98.7	99.5	100.4	98.5	95.5	92.8	92.3
Telephone services[1]	...	...	...	...	...	...	...	...	...	...	...	100.7	100.1	98.5	99.3
Information and information processing other than telephone services[3]	...	...	96.3	93.5	88.6	83.7	78.8	72.0	63.8	57.2	50.1	39.9	30.5	25.9	21.3
Personal computers and peripheral equipment[1]	...	...	...	...	...	...	...	...	...	...	...	78.2	53.5	41.1	29.5
Other Goods And Services	128.5	137.0	147.7	159.0	171.6	183.3	192.9	198.5	206.9	215.4	224.8	237.7	258.3	271.1	282.6
Tobacco and smoking products	133.6	145.8	164.4	181.5	202.7	219.8	228.4	220.0	225.7	232.8	243.7	274.8	355.8	394.9	425.2
Personal care	115.1	119.4	125.0	130.4	134.9	138.3	141.5	144.6	147.1	150.1	152.7	156.7	161.1	165.6	170.5
Personal care products	113.9	118.1	123.2	128.2	132.8	136.5	139.0	141.5	143.1	144.3	144.2	148.3	151.8	153.7	155.1
Personal care services	116.2	120.7	126.8	132.8	137.0	140.0	144.0	147.9	151.5	156.6	162.4	166.0	171.4	178.1	184.3
Miscellaneous personal services	133.8	140.3	148.1	158.4	168.8	177.5	186.1	195.9	205.9	215.6	226.1	234.7	243.0	252.3	263.1

1. December 1997=100.
2. December 1982=100.
3. December 1988=100.

Table 6-9. Relative Importance of Components in the Consumer Price Index, U.S. City Average, New Series, December 1997–December 2001

(Percent of all items.)

Index and year	All items	Food and beverages	Housing	Apparel	Transportation	Medical care	Recreation	Education and communication	Other goods and services
All URBAN CONSUMERS (CPI-U)									
December 1997	100.0	16.3	39.6	4.9	17.6	5.6	6.1	5.5	4.3
December 1998	100.0	16.4	39.8	4.8	17.0	5.7	6.1	5.5	4.6
December 1999	100.0	16.3	39.6	4.7	17.5	5.8	6.0	5.4	4.7
December 2000	100.0	16.2	40.0	4.4	17.6	5.8	5.9	5.3	4.8
December 2001 (1993-1995 Weights)	100.0	16.4	40.5	4.2	16.6	6.0	5.9	5.4	4.9
December 2001 (1999-2000 Weights)	100.0	15.7	40.9	4.4	17.1	5.8	6.0	5.8	4.3
URBAN WAGE EARNERS AND WORKERS (CPI-W)									
December 1997	100.0	17.9	36.5	5.3	19.8	4.6	6.0	5.4	4.5
December 1998	100.0	18.0	36.7	5.2	19.2	4.7	5.9	5.4	5.0
December 1999	100.0	17.9	36.5	5.0	19.7	4.7	5.8	5.3	5.1
December 2000	100.0	17.8	36.8	4.8	19.9	4.7	5.7	5.2	5.2
December 2001 (1993-1995 Weights)	100.0	18.0	37.3	4.6	18.8	4.9	5.7	5.3	5.4
December 2001 (1999-2000 Weights)	100.0	17.2	38.1	4.8	19.4	4.6	5.6	5.6	4.5

Table 6-10. Relative Importance of Components in the Consumer Price Index, U.S. City Average, Old Series, December 1997 and Dates of Major Weight Revisions

(Percent of all items.)

Index and year	All items	Food and beverages	Housing	Apparel and upkeep	Transportation	Medical care	Entertainment	Other goods and services
ALL URBAN CONSUMERS (CPI-U)								
December 1977	100.0	18.8	43.9	5.8	18.0	5.0	4.1	4.4
December 1982	100.0	20.1	37.7	5.2	21.8	6.0	4.2	5.0
December 1995	100.0	17.3	41.3	5.3	17.0	7.4	4.4	7.1
December 1997	100.0	17.5	41.5	5.3	16.6	7.4	4.3	7.4
URBAN WAGE EARNERS AND CLERICAL WORKERS (CPI-W)								
1935-1939	100.0	35.4	33.7	11.0	8.1	4.1	2.8	4.9
December 1952	100.0	32.2	33.5	9.4	11.3	4.8	4.0	4.8
December 1963	100.0	25.2	34.9	10.6	14.0	5.7	3.9	5.7
December 1977	100.0	20.5	40.7	5.8	20.2	4.5	3.9	4.4
December 1984	100.0	21.3	34.9	5.0	24.1	5.6	3.9	5.2
December 1995	100.0	19.3	38.9	5.5	19.0	6.3	4.0	7.0
December 1997	100.0	19.4	39.0	5.3	18.6	6.3	4.0	7.3

Table 6-11. Consumer Price Indexes, All Urban Consumers, All Items, Selected Areas, Selected Years, 1960–2001

(1982–1984=100, unless otherwise indicated.)

Area	1960	1965	1970	1975	1980	1981	1982	1983	1984	1985	1986	1987	1988	1989	1990	1991	1992	1993	1994	1995	1996	1997	1998	1999	2000	2001
NORTHEAST																										
New York-Northern New Jersey-Long Island	30.2	32.6	41.2	57.6	82.1	90.1	95.3	99.8	104.8	108.7	112.3	118.0	123.7	130.6	138.5	144.8	150.0	154.5	158.2	162.2	166.9	170.8	173.6	177.0	182.5	187.1
Philadelphia-Wilmington-Atlantic City	30.6	32.8	40.8	56.8	83.6	92.1	96.6	99.4	104.1	108.8	111.5	116.8	122.4	128.3	135.8	142.2	146.6	150.2	154.6	158.7	162.8	166.5	168.2	171.9	176.5	181.3
Boston-Brockton-Nashua	29.8	32.5	40.2	55.8	82.6	91.8	95.5	99.8	104.7	109.4	112.2	117.1	124.2	131.3	138.9	145.0	148.6	152.9	154.9	158.6	163.3	167.9	171.7	176.0	183.6	191.5
Pittsburgh	29.7	31.4	38.1	52.4	81.0	89.3	94.4	101.1	104.5	106.9	108.2	111.4	114.9	120.1	126.2	131.3	136.0	139.9	144.6	149.2	153.2	157.0	159.2	162.5	168.0	172.5
NORTH CENTRAL																										
Chicago-Gary-Kenosha	30.4	31.7	38.9	52.8	82.2	90.0	96.2	100.0	103.8	107.7	110.0	114.5	119.0	125.0	131.7	137.0	141.1	145.4	148.6	153.3	157.4	161.7	165.0	168.4	173.8	178.3
Detroit-Ann Arbor-Flint	29.7	31.2	39.5	53.9	85.3	93.2	97.0	99.8	103.2	106.8	108.3	111.7	116.1	122.3	128.6	133.1	135.9	139.6	144.0	148.6	152.5	156.3	159.8	163.9	169.8	174.4
St. Louis	29.5	31.7	38.8	52.6	82.5	90.1	96.6	100.1	103.3	107.1	108.6	112.2	115.7	121.8	128.1	132.1	134.7	137.5	141.3	145.2	149.6	152.9	154.5	157.6	163.1	167.3
Cleveland-Akron	28.3	29.6	37.2	50.2	78.9	87.2	94.0	101.2	104.8	107.8	109.4	112.7	116.7	122.7	129.0	134.2	136.8	140.3	144.4	147.9	152.0	156.1	159.8	162.5	168.0	172.9
Minneapolis-St. Paul	28.3	30.1	37.4	51.2	78.9	88.6	97.4	99.5	103.1	107.0	108.4	111.6	117.2	122.0	127.0	130.4	135.0	139.2	143.6	147.0	151.9	155.4	158.3	163.3	170.1	176.5
Milwaukee-Racine	29.2	31.0	37.5	50.8	81.4	90.7	95.9	100.2	103.8	107.0	107.4	111.5	115.9	120.8	126.2	132.2	137.1	142.1	147.0	151.0	154.7	157.7	160.3	163.7	168.6	171.7
Cincinnati-Hamilton	29.1	30.5	37.4	51.8	82.1	87.9	94.9	100.8	104.3	106.6	107.6	111.9	116.1	120.9	126.5	131.4	134.1	137.8	142.4	146.2	149.6	152.1	155.1	159.2	164.8	167.9
Kansas City	29.3	32.2	39.0	53.2	83.6	90.5	95.0	100.5	104.5	107.7	108.7	113.1	117.4	121.6	126.0	131.2	134.3	138.1	141.3	145.3	151.6	155.8	157.8	160.1	166.6	172.2
SOUTH																										
Baltimore	29.8	31.6	39.1	55.2	83.7	91.5	95.6	99.9	104.5	108.2	110.9	114.2	119.3	124.5	130.8	136.4	140.1	143.1	146.9	150.7	154.2	...	...	...	...	...
Washington	29.7	31.9	39.8	54.7	82.9	90.5	95.5	99.8	104.6	109.0	112.2	116.2	121.0	128.0	135.6	141.2	144.7	149.3	152.2	155.3	159.6	...	...	...	...	...
Washington-Baltimore [1]	...	...	...	...	...	...	...	...	...	...	...	...	...	...	...	...	...	...	...	...	...	100.8	102.1	104.2	107.6	110.4
Dallas-Fort Worth	...	29.9	37.6	50.4	81.5	90.8	96.0	99.7	104.3	108.2	109.9	112.9	116.1	119.5	125.1	130.8	133.9	137.3	141.2	144.9	148.8	151.4	153.6	158.0	164.7	170.4
Houston-Galveston-Brazoria	27.8	29.6	36.4	51.4	82.7	91.0	97.3	100.0	102.7	104.9	103.9	106.5	109.5	114.1	120.6	125.1	129.1	133.4	137.9	139.8	142.7	145.4	146.8	148.7	154.2	158.8
Atlanta	29.6	31.2	38.6	53.6	80.3	90.2	96.0	99.9	104.1	108.9	112.2	116.5	120.4	126.1	131.7	135.9	138.5	143.4	146.7	150.9	156.0	158.9	161.2	164.8	170.6	176.2
Miami-Fort Lauderdale	...	...	...	...	81.1	90.5	96.7	99.9	103.5	106.5	107.9	111.8	116.8	121.5	128.0	132.3	134.5	139.1	143.6	148.9	153.7	158.4	160.5	162.4	167.8	173.0
Tampa-St. Petersburg-Clearwater [2]	...	...	...	...	...	...	...	...	...	...	...	100.0	103.7	107.2	111.7	116.4	119.2	124.0	126.5	129.7	131.6	134.0	137.5	140.6	145.7	148.8
New Orleans [2]	...	...	...	...	...	...	...	...	...	...	...	100.0	102.7	107.2	111.5	116.0	120.2	124.7	129.0	133.4	138.4	143.0	...	...	...	...
WEST																										
Los Angeles-Riverside-Orange County	30.0	32.4	38.7	53.3	83.7	91.9	97.3	99.1	103.6	108.4	111.9	116.7	122.1	128.3	135.9	141.4	146.5	150.3	152.3	154.6	157.5	160.0	162.3	166.1	171.6	177.3
San Francisco-Oakland-San Jose	28.6	30.8	37.7	51.8	80.4	90.8	97.6	98.4	104.0	108.4	111.6	115.4	120.5	126.4	132.1	137.9	142.5	146.3	148.7	151.6	155.1	160.4	165.5	172.5	179.2	189.9
Seattle-Tacoma-Bremerton	28.8	31.0	37.4	51.1	82.7	91.8	97.7	99.3	103.0	105.6	106.7	109.2	112.8	118.1	126.8	134.1	139.0	142.9	147.8	152.3	157.5	163.0	167.7	172.8	182.8	185.7
San Diego	...	28.2	34.1	47.6	79.4	90.1	96.2	99.0	104.8	110.4	113.5	117.5	123.4	130.6	138.4	143.4	147.4	150.6	154.5	156.8	160.9	163.7	166.9	172.6	182.8	191.2
Portland-Salem	29.8	32.3	38.7	53.5	87.2	95.0	98.0	99.1	102.8	106.7	108.2	110.9	114.7	120.4	127.4	133.9	139.8	144.7	148.9	153.2	158.6	164.0	167.1	172.6	178.0	184.2
Honolulu	...	34.4	41.5	56.3	83.0	91.7	97.2	99.3	103.5	106.8	109.4	114.9	121.7	128.7	138.1	143.0	148.0	155.1	160.1	164.5	168.1	170.7	171.9	171.5	173.3	178.4
Anchorage	...	35.3	41.1	57.1	85.5	92.4	97.4	99.2	103.3	105.8	107.8	108.2	108.6	111.7	118.6	124.0	128.2	132.2	135.0	138.9	142.7	144.8	146.9	148.4	150.9	155.2
Denver-Boulder-Greeley	...	28.8	34.5	48.4	78.4	87.2	95.1	100.5	104.3	107.1	107.9	110.8	113.7	115.8	120.9	125.6	130.3	135.8	141.8	147.9	153.1	158.1	161.9	166.6	173.2	181.3

1. November 1996=100.
2. 1987=100.

NOTES AND DEFINITIONS

EXPORT AND IMPORT PRICE INDEXES

Note: The index base has been changed to 2000.

Collection and Coverage

United States export and import price indexes cover transactions in nonmilitary goods between the United States and the rest of the world. The export price indexes provide a measure of price change for U.S. products sold to other countries, and the import price indexes provide a measure of price change for goods purchased from other countries by U.S. residents.

Prices used in constructing the indexes are initially collected through personal visits by BLS field representatives; thereafter, the prices generally are collected each month by mail questionnaire or telephone. To the extent possible, products are priced at the U.S. border for exports and at both the foreign border and the U.S. border for imports. For a given product, however, only one price basis series is used in constructing the index. For most products, prices refer to transactions completed during the first week of the month. Indexes published here are based on the Standard Industrial Trade Classification System (SITC), a United Nations product classification system. The SITC is especially useful for international comparisons. These indexes are also published by End Use Category as well as the Harmonized System nomenclature.

Prices are collected according to the specification method. The specifications for each product include detailed descriptions of the physical and functional characteristics of the product. The terms of transaction include information on the number of units bought or sold, discount, credit terms, packaging, class of buyer or seller, etc. When there are changes in either the specifications or terms of transaction of a product, the dollar value of each change is deleted from the total price change in order to obtain the "pure price change." Once this value is determined, a linking procedure is employed which allows for continued re-pricing of the item.

At the elementary level, the price changes for individual items within a given Company/Classification Group cell are generally averaged together using equal weights in order to produce an index at the cell level. These cells are then averaged together using the relative importance of a given company's trade in the product area, in order to produce an index at the Classification Group level. These Classification Group indexes are then averaged together using weights derived from these company weights in order to produce the lowest level publication strata. Successively higher levels of publication strata are then averaged together using their relative importance based on 1995 U.S. trade values.

A limited number of import price indexes based on locality of origin indexes are also produced. BLS also publishes indexes for selected categories of internationally traded services calculated on an international basis.

Sources of Additional Information

Concepts and methodology are described in the BLS *Handbook of Methods,* BLS Bulletin 2490, April 1997, chapter 15, and in monthly press releases.

Table 6-12. U.S. Export Price Indexes for Selected Categories of Goods, by Standard International Trade Classification, 1987–2001

(2000=100.)

Categories	Relative import-ance [1]	1987 March	1987 June	1987 September	1988 December	1988 March	1988 June	1988 September	1989 December	1989 March	1989 June	1989 September
ALL COMMODITIES	100.00	84.3	86.0	86.6	88.3	89.8	92.2	94.1	93.8	95.2	95.2	94.4
Food And Live Animals	5.61	82.1	84.6	81.6	89.0	89.6	97.3	111.8	107.6	110.7	108.7	103.9
Meat and meat preparations	0.88	75.6	79.7	78.1	76.8	80.8	86.2	90.1	85.7	87.4	84.3	78.5
Fish, crustaceans, aquatic invertebrates, and preparations thereof	0.39	80.1	86.0	89.6	94.7	96.3	99.2	120.3	119.0	115.6	108.7	93.8
Cereals and cereal preparations	1.80	84.8	88.2	84.2	96.1	99.1	108.3	134.7	126.7	134.6	132.2	126.0
Vegetables, fruit and nuts, fresh or dried	1.09	93.3	90.9	81.8	81.3	78.9	84.4	88.9	89.2	88.0	91.9	92.1
Feeding stuff for animals (not including unmilled cereals)	0.60	98.3	104.0	103.4	122.1	113.1	132.8	135.3	131.9	129.5	121.1	117.3
Miscellaneous edible products and preparations	0.41	85.3	85.7	85.5	85.5	87.2	87.6	89.7	89.4	91.2	92.0	91.8
Beverages And Tobacco	0.91	70.0	71.6	71.9	73.0	74.8	75.4	76.4	76.2	79.9	80.2	82.1
Tobacco and tobacco manufactures	0.70	69.7	71.4	71.8	72.8	74.7	75.3	76.2	76.0	80.0	80.2	82.2
Crude Materials, Inedible, Except Fuels	3.83	74.4	80.7	83.6	88.2	91.6	98.6	99.2	95.7	100.5	100.7	98.0
Oil seeds and oleaginous fruits	0.86	95.0	106.9	100.0	115.2	121.6	150.4	162.7	142.7	146.5	136.5	117.3
Cork and wood	0.53	47.5	49.6	60.5	62.3	64.1	63.9	64.0	63.4	67.1	72.8	75.8
Textile fibers and their waste	0.41	92.8	106.8	110.7	106.0	102.1	104.4	95.7	98.4	101.3	109.7	111.4
Metalliferous ores and metal scrap	0.57	73.4	79.5	87.2	93.5	97.9	108.4	107.6	111.7	121.4	116.7	111.7
Mineral Fuels, Lubricants, And Related Materials	1.78	61.6	62.8	64.1	62.6	60.1	62.3	60.3	60.2	62.0	65.2	66.7
Coal, coke, and briquettes	0.36	104.0	99.0	102.2	100.8	101.8	103.3	104.3	104.9	105.2	105.9	107.4
Petroleum, petroleum products, and related materials	1.26	...	...	...	52.9	48.0	51.4	47.2	46.7	50.0	55.8	57.5
Chemicals And Related Products, n.e.s.	10.78	78.0	83.6	84.3	88.4	92.4	95.3	97.9	98.3	98.3	95.5	92.2
Organic chemicals	2.42	80.7	93.7	91.9	97.8	106.9	114.5	121.3	119.4	118.4	114.8	106.1
Inorganic chemicals	0.72	...	...	...	...	...	...	...	...	...	...	...
Dyeing, tanning, and coloring materials	0.56	...	...	...	...	...	...	...	...	...	...	...
Medicinal and pharmaceutical products	1.80	84.2	84.6	85.2	87.9	91.2	88.6	88.4	89.7	90.9	90.8	91.2
Essential oils, polishing, and cleansing preparations	0.73	72.7	72.9	74.0	74.7	76.7	78.3	82.9	84.4	86.4	86.0	84.4
Fertilizers	0.33	...	...	...	...	...	...	...	...	...	...	...
Plastics in primary forms	1.74	...	...	...	...	...	...	...	...	...	...	...
Plastics in nonprimary forms	0.81	...	...	...	...	...	...	...	...	...	...	...
Chemical materials and products, n.e.s.	1.67	74.1	74.2	73.8	74.7	76.3	77.3	79.1	80.1	82.4	83.2	83.3
Manufactured Goods Classified Chiefly By Material	9.70	75.1	76.1	77.8	78.5	80.7	83.0	84.4	85.1	86.5	86.9	86.6
Rubber manufactures, n.e.s.	0.77	72.6	72.9	73.9	74.1	74.9	77.4	77.9	78.5	80.4	80.4	80.7
Paper, paperboard, and articles of paper pulp, paper or paperboard	0.54	...	...	...	...	...	...	...	...	...	...	...
Textile yarn, fabrics, and made-up articles, n.e.s.	1.50	79.6	79.9	80.2	81.1	82.1	83.1	83.7	86.0	87.8	88.9	89.2
Nonmetallic mineral manufactures, n.e.s.	1.45	72.2	73.5	74.6	75.3	76.7	77.2	78.2	79.0	81.4	82.8	83.8
Iron and steel	0.89	...	...	...	...	...	...	...	...	...	...	...
Nonferrous metals	0.95	70.0	74.2	80.8	81.6	88.0	94.2	97.9	98.4	99.6	95.7	92.2
Manufactures of metals, n.e.s.	2.31	70.3	70.2	70.9	71.7	72.4	74.6	76.1	76.8	78.0	78.9	79.3
Machinery And Transport Equipment	54.26	90.4	90.6	90.8	91.1	91.8	92.5	93.3	94.1	94.9	95.3	96.0
Power generating machinery and equipment	4.75	68.6	68.1	68.8	69.1	70.2	71.1	71.2	71.8	73.4	74.0	75.1
Machinery specialized for particular industries	4.51	73.1	73.1	73.5	73.8	74.6	75.7	76.5	77.4	78.4	79.5	80.3
Metalworking machinery	0.90	71.7	72.3	73.1	73.3	74.1	75.1	75.2	77.5	78.4	79.5	79.8
General industrial machinery, equipment, and parts, n.e.s.	4.86	72.7	72.9	73.0	73.5	74.4	75.4	76.3	77.0	78.6	79.1	79.7
Computer equipment and office machines	7.12	196.1	196.3	195.4	195.1	195.6	195.4	197.8	196.9	195.7	193.7	193.6
Telecommunications and sound recording and reproducing apparatus and equipment	4.36	89.1	88.8	88.7	89.2	89.9	91.5	91.1	92.0	93.4	94.1	95.1
Electrical machinery and equipment	14.14	106.7	107.0	107.4	106.8	108.0	108.4	110.4	110.8	111.2	111.6	112.1
Road vehicles	8.25	82.4	82.7	82.9	83.6	83.5	83.8	84.2	85.4	85.7	86.2	86.9
Miscellaneous Manufactured Articles	11.94	81.3	81.8	81.9	82.0	83.1	84.0	84.6	85.9	86.6	87.7	88.3
Furniture and parts thereof	0.72	81.7	82.4	82.4	84.2	85.1	85.3	85.5	87.4	87.5	89.8	89.8
Articles of apparel and clothing accessories	1.15	...	...	...	...	...	...	...	...	...	...	...
Professional, scientific, and controlling instruments, and apparatus, n.e.s.	4.48	68.5	69.3	69.8	70.3	72.2	73.0	73.9	74.8	75.8	77.6	78.5
Photographic apparatus, equipment and supplies, and optical goods, n.e.s.	1.16	99.5	99.2	95.9	94.8	94.5	96.9	96.3	96.7	95.4	96.1	96.3
Miscellaneous manufactured articles, n.e.s.	0.45	91.6	91.3	92.2	92.1	91.8	92.7	92.7	94.7	96.0	95.8	96.1

See footnote and *Note* at end of table.

Table 6-12. U.S. Export Price Indexes for Selected Categories of Goods, by Standard International Trade Classification, 1987–2001—*Continued*

(2000=100.)

Categories	1990 March	1990 June	1990 September	1990 December	1991 March	1991 June	1991 September	1991 December	1992 March	1992 June	1992 September	1992 December
ALL COMMODITIES	94.8	95.1	95.8	96.3	96.4	96.1	95.6	95.7	96.2	96.5	96.6	96.3
Food And Live Animals	101.1	102.4	96.2	93.3	96.4	99.0	98.0	100.3	104.3	101.0	98.8	98.2
Meat and meat preparations	82.8	81.4	81.8	84.7	85.0	84.2	85.3	82.8	86.6	87.7	86.4	88.2
Fish, crustaceans, aquatic invertebrates, and preparations thereof	89.9	86.8	88.8	87.2	86.7	83.5	77.6	83.2	90.0	86.5	84.5	80.0
Cereals and cereal preparations	122.1	126.5	112.4	104.7	107.9	112.7	112.7	119.6	127.4	122.0	115.3	114.2
Vegetables, fruit and nuts, fresh or dried	92.6	93.2	90.2	89.5	104.0	111.0	103.4	95.6	97.0	91.4	92.0	94.1
Feeding stuff for animals (not including unmilled cereals)	102.3	99.5	101.0	104.9	105.6	101.9	107.2	108.0	103.9	104.1	107.0	105.8
Miscellaneous edible products and preparations	93.4	94.0	93.8	95.0	93.9	94.5	93.8	94.0	93.4	94.2	94.9	95.1
Beverages And Tobacco	83.4	84.9	85.6	88.0	89.9	90.4	90.9	92.6	93.1	93.8	94.7	95.5
Tobacco and tobacco manufactures	83.4	85.0	85.7	87.9	89.9	90.3	90.7	92.4	92.9	93.7	94.5	95.4
Crude Materials, Inedible, Except Fuels	96.4	96.7	97.1	94.7	94.6	91.8	88.2	86.2	87.6	89.9	90.4	90.0
Oil seeds and oleaginous fruits	115.2	116.1	123.5	123.3	124.1	118.7	116.8	111.8	113.8	117.6	110.1	110.2
Cork and wood	77.1	76.5	74.2	71.9	73.2	73.4	74.3	74.2	78.9	82.5	89.8	93.7
Textile fibers and their waste	111.2	118.2	116.0	115.3	120.3	123.2	112.5	102.6	97.9	99.1	94.7	94.1
Metalliferous ores and metal scrap	102.8	105.9	111.9	103.5	102.2	94.5	92.3	87.2	91.0	90.2	91.0	87.0
Mineral Fuels, Lubricants, And Related Materials	68.9	67.2	78.3	80.7	69.1	66.3	66.3	67.0	61.3	63.8	64.7	63.6
Coal, coke, and briquettes	108.0	109.5	110.0	110.0	109.7	107.9	108.0	108.0	106.8	106.0	105.2	105.9
Petroleum, petroleum products, and related materials	60.1	57.5	77.2	79.2	59.3	54.9	54.9	56.1	47.4	52.9	54.6	52.2
Chemicals And Related Products, n.e.s.	90.4	90.4	93.3	97.1	96.1	92.5	91.0	90.3	90.2	90.4	90.1	89.0
Organic chemicals	97.4	93.9	99.5	105.1	100.7	93.6	88.6	88.6	88.5	90.5	91.9	89.7
Inorganic chemicals	0.0	...	...	...	...	...	...	...	...	...	...	87.9
Dyeing, tanning, and coloring materials	0.0	...	...	...	...	...	...	...	...	...	...	...
Medicinal and pharmaceutical products	91.4	91.7	92.0	92.5	92.2	92.4	94.0	94.0	95.1	95.7	95.6	95.8
Essential oils, polishing, and cleansing preparations	86.2	87.4	87.6	87.9	88.1	88.2	88.8	88.5	90.0	90.5	89.6	89.5
Fertilizers	...	...	...	...	...	...	...	...	...	...	...	78.8
Plastics in primary forms	...	...	...	...	...	...	...	...	...	...	...	92.9
Plastics in nonprimary forms	...	...	...	...	...	...	...	...	...	...	...	...
Chemical materials and products, n.e.s.	85.8	86.4	88.0	90.0	91.7	90.5	89.6	89.5	90.1	90.1	90.5	90.6
Manufactured Goods Classified Chiefly By Material	86.7	86.8	87.2	87.1	87.3	87.0	86.7	86.7	87.2	87.5	87.8	87.7
Rubber manufactures, n.e.s.	81.3	81.4	82.2	84.2	85.7	86.4	86.6	87.0	86.8	86.9	87.5	87.7
Paper, paperboard, and articles of paper pulp, paper or paperboard	...	...	...	...	...	...	...	...	...	...	...	100.1
Textile yarn, fabrics, and made-up articles, n.e.s.	91.7	91.2	91.2	92.1	94.1	95.3	94.8	95.1	96.5	96.7	97.0	97.3
Nonmetallic mineral manufactures, n.e.s.	86.3	85.8	85.8	86.6	87.2	87.2	87.2	88.0	88.2	89.2	89.3	89.4
Iron and steel	0.0	...	...	...	...	...	...	...	...	...	...	...
Nonferrous metals	86.1	87.1	89.2	85.0	81.0	76.5	76.0	73.9	75.4	76.3	76.4	73.9
Manufactures of metals, n.e.s.	80.9	81.2	81.3	82.0	83.1	83.5	83.7	84.0	84.2	84.2	84.8	85.6
Machinery And Transport Equipment	97.4	97.9	98.3	98.8	100.3	101.0	101.4	101.7	102.1	102.4	102.6	102.6
Power generating machinery and equipment	76.3	77.0	77.2	77.8	79.8	80.7	81.4	81.8	82.9	84.5	84.4	84.6
Machinery specialized for particular industries	82.6	82.7	83.4	84.5	85.3	86.1	86.2	86.6	87.3	88.0	88.4	89.0
Metalworking machinery	81.1	82.1	82.2	84.2	85.9	87.7	87.9	88.3	89.4	89.9	89.9	89.8
General industrial machinery, equipment, and parts, n.e.s.	81.8	82.5	83.0	83.4	85.3	85.8	86.4	86.4	87.6	87.8	88.1	88.6
Computer equipment and office machines	193.4	193.2	192.9	190.5	190.9	189.4	187.2	185.0	183.8	182.2	180.9	176.9
Telecommunications and sound recording and reproducing apparatus and equipment	95.5	97.3	97.8	98.3	100.7	103.4	104.9	105.8	104.5	105.3	105.7	105.8
Electrical machinery and equipment	113.1	112.7	112.4	112.7	112.8	113.4	115.5	116.3	117.6	116.8	117.4	117.2
Road vehicles	88.2	88.7	89.1	90.1	90.9	91.2	91.4	92.1	92.2	92.6	92.8	93.2
Miscellaneous Manufactured Articles	89.7	90.5	91.8	93.2	94.4	95.1	95.4	95.9	96.6	97.0	97.2	97.3
Furniture and parts thereof	92.3	93.6	93.4	95.2	96.9	97.6	97.7	97.5	98.4	98.2	97.8	98.1
Articles of apparel and clothing accessories	0.0	...	...	...	...	...	...	...	...	...	...	...
Professional, scientific and controlling instruments, and apparatus, n.e.s.	80.5	81.9	83.8	85.6	86.6	87.8	88.0	88.8	89.7	90.1	90.0	90.1
Photographic apparatus, equipment and supplies, and optical goods, n.e.s.	95.0	94.6	96.0	98.4	98.8	98.6	98.4	99.4	99.3	98.2	99.1	99.7
Miscellaneous manufactured articles, n.e.s.	97.6	98.1	98.7	99.4	101.1	101.2	101.9	101.7	102.1	103.0	103.6	103.3

See footnote and *Note* at end of table.

Table 6-12. U.S. Export Price Indexes for Selected Categories of Goods, by Standard International Trade Classification, 1987–2001—*Continued*

(2000=100.)

Categories	1993				1994				1995			
	March	June	September	December	March	June	September	December	March	June	September	December
ALL COMMODITIES	96.6	96.9	96.9	97.3	98.2	98.5	99.1	101.1	103.0	104.5	104.4	104.4
Food And Live Animals	97.7	96.1	100.4	105.9	106.7	102.0	100.6	104.9	106.3	112.1	121.6	126.5
Meat and meat preparations	89.8	92.2	88.4	88.5	91.3	88.7	89.0	90.1	92.9	95.7	99.4	101.4
Fish, crustaceans, aquatic invertebrates, and preparations thereof	81.5	85.1	79.8	77.8	83.1	86.5	93.4	97.8	106.8	107.1	105.6	96.3
Cereals and cereal preparations	112.7	105.8	111.8	129.4	130.4	118.5	111.9	121.0	120.1	133.2	149.6	167.9
Vegetables, fruit and nuts, fresh or dried	94.7	94.1	107.8	104.5	102.5	100.1	100.1	103.5	106.8	107.2	122.7	111.2
Feeding stuff for animals (not including unmilled cereals)	101.9	102.7	109.6	112.0	108.8	108.2	105.9	101.0	99.1	104.9	107.1	122.4
Miscellaneous edible products and preparations	93.9	94.4	94.0	90.6	91.9	92.0	93.1	93.1	92.9	94.8	94.0	95.3
Beverages And Tobacco	96.4	96.7	97.5	96.5	96.9	97.0	96.8	96.9	97.9	98.2	98.7	98.5
Tobacco and tobacco manufactures	96.3	96.4	97.2	96.1	96.6	96.7	96.4	96.5	97.5	98.1	98.6	98.3
Crude Materials, Inedible, Except Fuels	93.4	95.8	94.3	95.0	100.7	104.0	104.8	112.4	122.6	125.4	119.0	116.0
Oil seeds and oleaginous fruits	114.4	117.0	130.0	133.9	134.2	134.9	115.0	109.8	112.0	115.6	123.1	136.0
Cork and wood	110.0	121.0	111.4	110.0	114.7	112.0	111.8	113.6	117.9	117.5	111.4	112.0
Textile fibers and their waste	97.8	96.1	93.3	95.6	113.3	120.9	117.3	127.3	152.6	154.3	141.2	142.2
Metalliferous ores and metal scrap	87.8	89.0	89.0	90.3	96.0	96.7	106.2	123.5	132.4	132.2	125.0	116.4
Mineral Fuels, Lubricants, And Related Materials	64.5	64.9	63.2	60.4	61.8	64.5	64.6	65.9	65.6	68.5	67.5	68.5
Coal, coke, and briquettes	104.1	102.7	102.7	102.9	104.2	102.7	102.1	102.9	103.6	106.4	107.7	107.8
Petroleum, petroleum products, and related materials	53.5	55.3	52.6	48.2	50.1	55.0	55.6	56.7	56.1	59.6	57.4	59.2
Chemicals And Related Products, n.e.s.	89.1	89.2	88.5	88.6	89.5	91.9	96.4	101.3	107.1	108.4	104.3	102.1
Organic chemicals	89.2	89.5	87.8	86.7	87.7	91.8	97.9	107.4	117.0	122.8	112.6	105.8
Inorganic chemicals	86.0	85.1	82.5	82.5	79.7	82.8	88.2	90.4	102.4	100.9	101.7	102.2
Dyeing, tanning, and coloring materials	0.0	...	...	98.2	100.0	97.8	98.8	98.9	100.3	100.8	101.4	101.0
Medicinal and pharmaceutical products	97.2	98.3	98.7	99.5	100.0	99.6	99.2	98.7	99.5	100.4	100.5	99.9
Essential oils, polishing, and cleansing preparations	90.6	90.5	91.0	91.6	92.9	95.3	95.8	95.5	96.4	96.4	96.8	97.7
Fertilizers	...	...	...	...	...	...	...	...	...	...	...	...
Plastics in primary forms	78.7	80.5	79.9	79.2	80.1	83.9	95.8	105.6	111.8	110.6	99.7	94.4
Plastics in nonprimary forms	92.6	90.0	90.7	90.6	91.3	92.5	94.2	97.4	99.0	101.8	102.0	101.3
Chemical materials and products, n.e.s.	91.9	92.5	92.6	92.6	94.7	95.2	95.4	97.1	99.2	100.7	101.4	101.3
Manufactured Goods Classified Chiefly By Material	88.4	87.6	88.1	87.6	89.5	90.8	92.6	96.4	99.0	100.6	100.6	99.4
Rubber manufactures, n.e.s.	88.7	89.3	89.6	89.5	89.7	89.9	90.7	90.9	95.3	95.7	97.1	98.3
Paper, paperboard, and articles of paper pulp, paper or paperboard	99.3	97.5	97.5	98.5	97.6	96.3	96.0	99.8	97.4	104.2	102.4	101.7
Textile yarn, fabrics, and made-up articles, n.e.s.	97.3	97.8	97.8	97.0	97.7	97.7	97.0	97.2	99.0	102.8	102.6	103.7
Nonmetallic mineral manufactures, n.e.s.	89.6	90.8	91.9	91.2	92.1	92.4	92.7	93.5	94.1	94.3	94.4	95.2
Iron and steel	...	...	...	93.4	95.3	96.4	97.2	99.0	101.7	104.0	104.0	104.7
Nonferrous metals	74.3	70.6	72.3	68.6	76.3	80.3	85.7	96.7	100.1	98.2	98.9	93.7
Manufactures of metals, n.e.s.	86.1	85.5	86.2	86.8	87.5	87.3	87.7	89.4	91.6	92.3	92.7	93.2
Machinery And Transport Equipment	102.3	102.5	102.2	102.4	102.4	102.1	101.7	101.7	102.2	102.8	103.0	103.2
Power generating machinery and equipment	85.2	85.3	85.7	86.2	86.8	86.9	87.6	88.4	88.3	88.5	88.7	90.3
Machinery specialized for particular industries	89.6	90.0	90.5	91.0	91.1	91.5	91.6	91.6	93.0	94.0	94.8	95.2
Metalworking machinery	91.3	91.4	91.2	91.3	91.1	91.2	90.5	91.1	92.0	92.3	92.8	92.8
General industrial machinery, equipment, and parts, n.e.s.	89.2	89.6	90.1	90.6	90.9	91.0	91.3	91.3	92.4	92.0	93.1	92.9
Computer equipment and office machines	171.0	168.9	165.3	162.9	158.9	156.0	151.8	150.4	148.1	147.5	144.7	142.9
Telecommunications and sound recording and reproducing apparatus and equipment	105.0	106.4	105.7	105.6	104.6	104.4	103.8	103.4	103.4	103.8	103.2	102.4
Electrical machinery and equipment	116.1	116.7	115.9	116.6	116.8	116.3	114.8	114.4	115.2	117.2	117.5	116.8
Road vehicles	93.6	93.7	93.7	94.0	94.5	94.7	94.9	95.5	96.0	96.1	96.2	97.1
Miscellaneous Manufactured Articles	97.5	97.6	97.6	97.6	97.5	97.8	98.1	98.1	98.3	98.6	98.6	98.8
Furniture and parts thereof	95.9	94.3	94.2	94.4	94.6	94.9	95.4	94.1	94.0	94.7	94.8	95.1
Articles of apparel and clothing accessories	...	...	...	102.4	102.5	103.3	103.2	103.6	103.4	102.5	104.4	102.6
Professional, scientific and controlling instruments, and apparatus, n.e.s.	90.8	91.3	92.0	91.9	92.4	92.6	93.3	93.4	93.9	94.3	94.4	94.5
Photographic apparatus, equipment and supplies, and optical goods, n.e.s.	98.8	101.0	101.2	101.4	101.8	102.0	103.4	102.8	103.3	103.5	102.3	102.1
Miscellaneous manufactured articles, n.e.s.	102.8	102.5	101.7	101.5	100.6	100.9	100.6	100.7	100.9	101.0	100.9	101.9

See footnote and *Note* at end of table.

Table 6-12. U.S. Export Price Indexes for Selected Categories of Goods, by Standard International Trade Classification, 1987–2001—*Continued*

(2000=100.)

Categories	1996 March	1996 June	1996 September	1996 December	1997 March	1997 June	1997 September	1997 December	1998 March	1998 June	1998 September	1998 December
ALL COMMODITIES	104.6	105.4	103.9	103.2	103.6	103.2	102.9	102.0	100.7	99.9	98.5	98.5
Food And Live Animals	131.8	140.4	123.4	117.3	119.0	113.3	114.4	111.3	106.4	104.6	99.8	103.0
Meat and meat preparations	94.0	97.4	94.4	93.7	92.4	91.3	91.3	90.7	88.3	93.7	92.3	86.2
Fish, crustaceans, aquatic invertebrates, and preparations thereof	91.2	92.8	96.9	100.5	92.5	88.5	102.9	96.6	86.0	83.8	99.5	99.3
Cereals and cereal preparations	183.0	203.3	152.6	140.4	146.4	128.9	132.7	131.9	126.3	115.4	98.0	110.2
Vegetables, fruit and nuts, fresh or dried	114.9	117.8	119.0	112.6	112.8	113.3	108.8	102.6	102.3	109.8	110.6	111.1
Feeding stuff for animals (not including unmilled cereals)	129.5	130.7	135.5	128.0	133.7	135.7	128.9	121.1	107.8	101.3	94.4	98.4
Miscellaneous edible products and preparations	96.0	96.6	96.2	97.1	96.7	96.9	98.3	98.2	98.1	98.3	99.5	100.0
Beverages And Tobacco	98.7	98.8	98.8	98.7	98.4	99.1	99.3	98.8	98.4	98.2	98.0	99.0
Tobacco and tobacco manufactures	98.5	98.6	98.6	98.5	98.1	98.9	99.1	98.4	98.2	97.8	97.5	98.4
Crude Materials, Inedible, Except Fuels	109.6	108.7	109.3	106.8	112.2	112.4	110.3	105.6	101.4	98.7	93.8	91.8
Oil seeds and oleaginous fruits	143.0	152.0	157.6	137.5	159.3	161.1	143.8	139.4	129.7	122.8	109.8	114.4
Cork and wood	113.0	109.0	110.9	112.3	110.5	107.3	104.7	98.6	96.8	94.5	94.7	93.7
Textile fibers and their waste	133.4	131.6	125.1	120.5	122.9	120.3	121.2	115.5	112.5	114.4	110.2	101.9
Metalliferous ores and metal scrap	114.8	113.4	108.6	108.7	113.8	116.4	119.8	106.5	101.2	97.2	88.4	86.1
Mineral Fuels, Lubricants, And Related Materials	71.8	73.3	75.6	78.4	74.8	74.5	75.1	75.8	71.3	69.3	62.8	63.0
Coal, coke, and briquettes	108.9	109.5	107.7	108.0	108.5	108.2	108.1	107.5	107.2	106.2	105.5	105.5
Petroleum, petroleum products, and related materials	64.1	65.4	69.6	73.9	68.7	68.7	70.1	68.5	63.6	61.4	52.3	53.0
Chemicals And Related Products, n.e.s.	102.5	102.6	101.8	101.5	102.3	102.0	100.9	100.3	99.0	97.9	97.0	96.2
Organic chemicals	103.9	100.9	97.6	97.6	99.0	97.6	96.2	96.0	91.2	88.7	86.4	85.3
Inorganic chemicals	105.6	106.1	103.3	103.5	100.9	101.1	100.3	100.9	103.7	105.2	104.9	105.1
Dyeing, tanning, and coloring materials	101.2	101.3	101.3	102.7	102.9	102.5	103.2	103.2	102.6	101.2	100.1	100.6
Medicinal and pharmaceutical products	101.9	101.6	101.7	101.7	100.8	101.4	101.0	100.7	100.2	101.4	101.5	100.4
Essential oils, polishing, and cleansing preparations	96.8	97.6	98.5	98.3	99.0	99.7	100.4	98.7	98.4	98.2	99.4	98.5
Fertilizers [2]	...	...	...	133.3	128.2	128.1	126.6	125.6	122.7	128.0	130.5	127.8
Plastics in primary forms	96.4	100.7	101.3	99.0	103.1	102.4	98.8	98.2	96.7	93.7	92.4	90.2
Plastics in nonprimary forms	101.5	100.8	98.9	98.3	99.6	100.0	99.8	99.6	100.6	98.7	98.1	96.3
Chemical materials and products, n.e.s.	101.5	102.6	103.5	103.8	104.2	104.6	104.2	102.6	101.2	101.2	100.6	101.8
Manufactured Goods Classified Chiefly By Material	98.5	97.7	97.0	96.8	97.4	98.1	98.5	98.4	98.2	97.7	96.7	96.3
Rubber manufactures, n.e.s.	98.0	98.6	98.5	98.7	98.5	99.0	97.7	97.9	97.9	97.7	98.2	101.6
Paper, paperboard, and articles of paper pulp, paper or paperboard	99.1	97.9	97.9	94.4	96.5	96.1	97.6	96.7	96.8	96.0	93.7	93.8
Textile yarn, fabrics, and made-up articles, n.e.s.	104.8	105.5	104.8	104.1	103.4	105.0	105.0	104.8	105.3	104.9	103.0	102.7
Nonmetallic mineral manufactures, n.e.s.	96.1	95.4	96.3	97.9	98.0	98.3	100.0	100.9	100.8	100.6	100.7	101.1
Iron and steel	104.7	106.0	104.8	104.8	106.7	106.0	106.2	106.3	103.9	103.7	102.9	100.0
Nonferrous metals	91.6	91.9	87.3	86.9	90.3	92.0	91.8	89.6	89.8	86.7	84.1	82.6
Manufactures of metals, n.e.s.	94.4	93.6	93.6	93.7	95.1	96.3	96.2	96.3	96.8	98.6	98.4	98.1
Machinery And Transport Equipment	103.3	103.6	103.3	103.2	103.3	103.3	102.9	102.5	102.0	101.4	100.9	100.9
Power generating machinery and equipment	91.9	92.9	92.8	93.1	94.0	94.4	94.5	94.6	95.1	95.3	95.2	96.6
Machinery specialized for particular industries	95.9	96.5	97.0	96.8	97.6	98.0	98.3	98.7	98.8	99.0	99.2	98.9
Metalworking machinery	93.7	94.4	94.6	94.5	96.7	96.3	96.4	97.5	99.5	100.0	100.1	100.5
General industrial machinery, equipment, and parts, n.e.s.	94.0	94.8	95.0	95.4	96.3	97.3	97.3	97.5	97.9	98.1	98.4	98.5
Computer equipment and office machines	139.7	137.2	132.3	128.7	126.9	123.9	122.5	119.5	116.9	112.0	109.4	108.9
Telecommunications and sound recording and reproducing apparatus and equipment	104.6	104.6	103.7	104.2	103.4	103.0	102.6	102.1	102.0	102.1	101.6	100.9
Electrical machinery and equipment	116.2	115.3	113.9	113.5	112.5	112.3	110.7	109.9	108.3	107.2	106.1	105.4
Road vehicles	97.1	97.2	97.2	97.6	98.0	98.0	97.9	98.2	98.0	98.1	98.2	98.3
Miscellaneous Manufactured Articles	99.4	99.4	99.5	99.9	100.2	100.3	100.4	100.4	100.0	99.4	99.2	99.2
Furniture and parts thereof	96.7	96.0	96.4	96.4	97.0	97.9	97.9	98.1	98.7	98.4	98.5	98.5
Articles of apparel and clothing accessories	103.0	103.8	104.2	104.4	105.0	104.9	107.1	107.2	107.4	107.4	106.2	104.4
Professional, scientific and controlling instruments, and apparatus, n.e.s.	95.4	95.8	96.1	96.7	97.8	97.5	97.4	97.6	97.7	97.8	97.8	98.1
Photographic apparatus, equipment and supplies, and optical goods, n.e.s.	102.2	101.4	101.7	102.2	101.4	102.0	101.6	101.0	98.4	96.5	95.2	97.3
Miscellaneous manufactured articles, n.e.s.	102.0	101.9	101.7	101.9	101.4	101.8	101.6	101.5	100.6	99.3	99.5	99.3

See footnote and *Note* at end of table.

Table 6-12. U.S. Export Price Indexes for Selected Categories of Goods, by Standard International Trade Classification, 1987–2001—*Continued*

(2000=100.)

Categories	1999				2000				2001			
	March	June	September	December	March	June	September	December	March	June	September	December
ALL COMMODITIES	97.9	98.2	98.5	99.0	100.0	100.1	100.4	100.1	100.0	99.4	99.0	97.6
Food And Live Animals	101.1	102.6	99.6	98.5	99.9	100.6	98.8	102.1	102.5	101.1	103.3	101.2
Meat and meat preparations	86.2	87.6	93.4	96.7	95.3	104.8	100.8	101.5	102.6	106.1	107.8	97.8
Fish, crustaceans, aquatic invertebrates, and preparations thereof	109.8	123.0	100.8	102.6	98.9	100.6	100.1	98.4	99.0	90.8	90.4	88.6
Cereals and cereal preparations	105.9	106.0	101.5	95.7	103.9	100.0	94.7	105.8	107.9	102.6	106.4	107.2
Vegetables, fruit and nuts, fresh or dried	105.8	109.9	105.1	101.7	98.8	97.9	102.5	99.1	97.9	98.6	100.8	100.6
Feeding stuff for animals (not including unmilled cereals)	96.8	92.5	93.6	97.4	98.2	100.4	99.2	104.6	100.7	101.1	103.6	102.4
Miscellaneous edible products and preparations	100.0	100.1	100.6	100.7	99.8	100.0	100.0	100.2	100.1	100.1	100.1	100.1
Beverages And Tobacco	99.5	99.4	99.8	100.1	100.2	100.0	99.9	99.8	98.9	98.4	98.4	98.3
Tobacco and tobacco manufactures	99.3	99.2	99.7	100.1	100.1	99.9	99.9	99.9	98.9	98.2	98.2	98.1
Crude Materials, Inedible, Except Fuels	89.1	90.2	93.5	94.9	100.2	101.6	100.7	99.4	96.0	92.6	89.5	87.1
Oil seeds and oleaginous fruits	93.7	94.8	101.7	95.2	102.9	103.3	100.3	101.8	94.5	95.6	99.0	90.9
Cork and wood	93.8	94.4	95.4	97.9	100.4	99.8	100.1	98.9	96.1	92.8	90.2	88.0
Textile fibers and their waste	100.7	99.1	92.9	90.2	99.1	100.5	104.3	105.7	97.6	90.9	87.7	84.0
Metalliferous ores and metal scrap	88.6	89.7	93.3	99.5	102.6	99.2	99.9	94.8	92.0	91.0	85.1	81.9
Mineral Fuels, Lubricants, And Related Materials	62.5	68.5	77.5	85.0	102.2	97.4	111.7	105.8	102.4	103.2	103.3	82.4
Coal, coke, and briquettes	105.4	104.3	103.6	103.5	101.9	99.5	98.8	98.7	99.3	106.9	108.8	108.8
Petroleum, petroleum products, and related materials	52.3	61.9	74.0	80.6	103.1	96.8	117.0	105.6	99.2	101.8	103.6	74.6
Chemicals And Related Products, n.e.s.	95.7	96.4	97.6	98.9	99.7	100.9	99.8	98.3	98.7	96.2	93.8	92.8
Organic chemicals	84.7	86.4	90.6	96.3	98.8	102.1	99.6	96.0	95.9	90.6	84.9	83.9
Inorganic chemicals	104.7	102.7	100.4	99.7	99.6	101.2	99.8	101.4	104.1	103.3	103.2	102.8
Dyeing, tanning, and coloring materials	101.9	101.6	101.5	100.5	99.8	100.0	99.9	99.9	99.6	98.3	97.7	96.3
Medicinal and pharmaceutical products	100.3	100.4	99.6	100.1	100.0	99.5	100.0	100.0	99.2	99.5	101.1	100.9
Essential oils, polishing, and cleansing preparations	98.3	98.7	98.9	100.1	99.8	99.6	100.1	100.0	100.2	99.7	99.1	98.8
Fertilizers	125.2	119.4	113.2	97.8	96.5	96.1	105.3	102.0	105.3	94.9	91.8	94.0
Plastics in primary forms	89.0	93.2	97.2	100.2	100.8	103.4	97.8	94.9	97.8	93.9	88.6	86.5
Plastics in nonprimary forms	97.3	98.1	98.4	98.9	101.0	100.2	100.2	99.2	97.6	97.4	97.2	95.8
Chemical materials and products, n.e.s.	101.1	100.3	99.9	99.7	100.3	99.7	99.8	100.5	99.1	99.1	99.0	97.6
Manufactured Goods Classified Chiefly By Material	96.3	96.7	97.3	98.1	99.6	100.2	100.9	100.3	100.2	99.5	98.2	96.7
Rubber manufactures, n.e.s.	102.4	101.2	102.5	104.0	99.4	100.1	100.4	99.5	100.4	99.8	101.0	100.9
Paper, paperboard, and articles of paper pulp, paper or paperboard	93.6	95.6	96.0	98.5	99.7	99.0	100.8	100.7	102.2	100.7	101.3	100.2
Textile yarn, fabrics, and made-up articles, n.e.s.	101.3	100.8	100.3	100.3	100.0	100.2	100.1	98.4	98.8	98.5	98.8	97.5
Nonmetallic mineral manufactures, n.e.s.	100.3	100.2	99.9	99.7	100.1	100.4	100.0	99.5	99.8	100.8	101.1	102.1
Iron and steel	98.7	97.5	97.6	97.7	99.9	101.2	100.0	99.5	96.8	97.8	98.3	95.7
Nonferrous metals	82.7	83.7	86.6	90.9	100.3	98.5	103.4	103.3	104.9	98.0	90.2	83.1
Manufactures of metals, n.e.s.	99.8	100.2	99.0	98.8	98.6	100.9	101.5	101.1	100.9	101.5	101.8	101.7
Machinery And Transport Equipment	100.6	100.3	99.9	99.9	99.9	100.0	100.1	100.1	100.6	100.3	100.0	99.6
Power generating machinery and equipment	97.4	97.6	98.0	98.8	99.5	99.7	100.0	101.2	102.0	102.3	103.0	103.9
Machinery specialized for particular industries	99.4	99.8	99.5	98.4	99.8	100.2	100.0	100.3	100.5	100.3	99.5	100.5
Metalworking machinery	100.6	100.4	100.4	100.1	100.1	99.3	100.1	99.8	101.1	101.0	101.2	100.7
General industrial machinery, equipment, and parts, n.e.s.	99.1	99.2	99.5	99.8	99.9	100.1	100.0	100.3	101.0	101.3	101.9	101.7
Computer equipment and office machines	106.9	104.8	102.8	102.7	100.5	99.9	99.3	99.0	97.8	95.9	94.8	92.9
Telecommunications and sound recording and reproducing apparatus and equipment	100.9	100.2	100.2	100.0	99.9	100.3	100.1	99.6	99.8	99.8	98.5	97.7
Electrical machinery and equipment	104.0	103.1	102.0	100.9	100.5	99.8	99.9	99.3	99.2	98.3	97.6	95.9
Road vehicles	98.4	98.6	98.6	99.3	100.1	100.0	100.2	100.1	100.2	100.2	100.2	100.3
Miscellaneous Manufactured Articles	99.6	99.6	99.8	99.9	99.6	99.7	100.2	100.2	100.0	100.1	100.4	100.4
Furniture and parts thereof	98.5	99.0	99.7	99.5	99.4	100.1	99.8	101.1	101.0	101.0	101.8	101.6
Articles of apparel and clothing accessories	104.7	103.8	103.9	103.7	100.1	99.8	99.0	99.5	96.9	96.6	98.1	98.2
Professional, scientific and controlling instruments, and apparatus, n.e.s.	99.0	99.2	99.4	99.3	99.6	99.7	100.4	100.4	100.8	100.9	100.9	100.9
Photographic apparatus, equipment and supplies, and optical goods, n.e.s.	97.9	97.2	98.6	100.3	97.9	98.0	101.6	101.3	99.1	98.2	98.7	97.6
Miscellaneous manufactured articles, n.e.s.	99.2	99.5	99.4	99.5	99.7	99.9	100.0	99.9	100.3	100.5	100.6	101.0

Note: n.e.s. = not elsewhere specified.

1. Percent of total, based on 2000 trade values.

Table 6-13. U.S. Import Price Indexes for Selected Categories of Goods, by Standard International Trade Classification, 1987–2001

(2000=100.)

Categories	Relative import-ance¹	1987				1988				1989			
		March	June	September	December	March	June	September	December	March	June	September	December
ALL COMMODITIES	100.00	80.8	83.6	84.3	85.5	86.5	88.8	87.6	89.3	91.3	91.5	90.4	91.6
Food And Live Animals	3.17	86.6	89.2	89.8	92.6	93.9	93.8	92.8	94.1	94.0	91.7	87.4	89.1
Meat and meat preparations	0.36	91.1	93.7	99.2	98.4	96.7	92.8	96.5	94.2	96.5	95.1	107.6	116.3
Fish, crustaceans, aquatic invertebrates, and preparations thereof	0.74	68.4	70.8	73.3	73.6	74.4	72.6	70.7	71.2	71.3	68.9	68.3	68.6
Vegetables, fruit and nuts, fresh or dried	0.86	70.4	76.1	76.0	80.2	79.7	83.1	84.2	88.2	85.3	85.1	82.3	88.5
Coffee, tea, cocoa, spices, and manufactures thereof	0.37	143.0	138.3	135.4	144.0	150.0	148.5	139.0	144.0	145.1	135.7	99.3	91.2
Beverages And Tobacco	0.85	64.6	67.6	67.2	68.0	69.5	69.7	69.1	69.6	70.1	70.3	72.3	73.4
Beverages	0.75	68.3	69.6	69.9	70.8	72.3	73.0	72.4	73.0	73.5	73.5	74.8	75.6
Crude Materials, Inedible, Except Fuels	1.93	78.9	79.7	82.6	83.7	88.7	94.5	92.9	98.2	100.3	99.0	94.1	93.3
Cork and wood	0.75	65.8	63.8	68.0	63.1	65.1	64.6	63.5	62.5	65.0	65.1	65.8	64.7
Woodpulp and recovered paper	0.25	80.8	84.0	84.9	89.7	96.1	102.1	107.9	111.1	117.5	120.9	120.9	120.6
Metalliferous ores and metal scrap	0.31	71.2	72.3	74.6	80.0	87.7	97.3	99.9	119.2	118.6	123.2	106.4	102.5
Crude animal and vegetable materials, n.e.s.	0.24	...	...	...	...	...	...	...	...	...	...	...	...
Mineral Fuels, Lubricants, And Related Materials	10.98	57.9	63.7	63.8	57.7	52.0	54.5	49.6	48.4	57.4	63.0	59.1	63.6
Petroleum, petroleum products, and related materials	9.91	57.8	63.8	64.5	58.1	51.8	54.5	49.4	48.1	57.7	63.8	59.6	64.1
Gas, natural and manufactured	1.00	...	...	...	...	...	...	...	53.2	54.6	54.3	53.6	58.4
Chemicals And Related Products, n.e.s.	6.52	81.3	83.0	83.7	87.3	90.5	92.3	94.5	96.9	97.9	95.5	93.3	94.2
Organic chemicals	2.55	83.1	86.3	84.9	89.1	91.5	92.8	96.3	99.6	101.7	98.6	95.4	97.5
Inorganic chemicals	0.55	102.3	101.5	101.5	101.9	104.0	104.3	105.1	108.7	105.3	97.9	96.9	97.3
Dyeing, tanning, and coloring materials	0.23	...	...	...	...	...	...	...	...	...	...	...	...
Medicinal and pharmaceutical products	1.32	63.5	65.3	65.7	66.8	71.6	74.2	76.9	77.4	81.9	81.2	78.9	79.2
Essential oils, polishing, and cleansing preps	0.32	81.1	81.2	82.2	84.8	86.7	87.0	87.9	90.0	89.8	89.8	87.7	93.2
Plastics in primary forms	0.55	...	...	...	...	...	...	...	...	...	...	...	...
Plastics in nonprimary forms	0.38	...	...	...	...	...	...	...	...	...	...	...	...
Chemical materials and products, n.e.s.	0.48	74.4	76.1	78.0	80.7	89.7	96.1	99.3	101.2	100.1	98.1	97.2	97.6
Manufactured Goods Classified Chiefly By Material	11.19	73.5	76.2	78.7	81.1	84.2	89.5	89.5	91.4	92.9	92.1	91.6	90.7
Rubber manufactures, n.e.s.	0.66	93.2	93.5	92.2	93.5	94.7	96.2	97.5	99.3	99.8	100.3	101.6	101.9
Cork and wood manufactures other than furniture	0.62	70.6	74.4	76.7	76.7	80.1	82.7	81.4	80.2	81.9	83.6	84.2	84.1
Paper and paperboard, cut to size	1.26	77.2	77.2	81.2	82.7	86.3	87.2	88.0	88.3	88.8	89.0	88.2	87.5
Textile yarn, fabrics, made-up articles, n.e.s., and related products	1.33	80.2	81.2	83.2	86.1	87.2	87.6	86.5	87.5	87.5	88.7	88.4	89.2
Nonmetallic mineral manufactures, n.e.s.	2.24	67.1	70.5	72.6	74.2	76.4	79.3	77.7	78.9	82.1	83.2	84.4	85.2
Iron and steel	1.52	80.1	83.1	85.3	88.9	93.6	99.2	101.3	102.0	103.4	104.2	104.3	102.1
Nonferrous metals	1.51	60.2	66.0	71.0	73.9	77.9	93.8	93.3	99.3	101.5	93.1	88.5	84.6
Manufactures of metals, n.e.s.	1.93	78.1	78.6	79.9	82.2	84.4	88.5	88.9	91.2	92.3	92.5	92.9	93.3
Machinery And Transport Equipment	47.70	91.0	92.9	92.9	95.3	97.1	98.7	98.2	100.6	100.8	100.1	99.9	100.9
Power generating machinery and equipment	3.01	...	...	...	...	...	...	...	...	...	...	...	...
Machinery specialized for particular industries	2.01	71.5	74.6	73.6	77.9	80.5	82.1	78.8	82.6	81.7	79.9	79.9	81.3
Metalworking machinery	0.70	74.2	75.2	76.5	79.6	82.1	83.6	82.0	84.6	83.9	81.9	84.5	84.6
General industrial machinery, equipment, and machine parts, n.e.s.	3.08	73.2	74.9	74.5	78.4	80.4	82.3	80.0	82.6	82.9	81.9	82.3	83.3
Computer equipment and office machines	7.22	188.8	195.6	197.0	203.0	202.7	205.1	203.7	203.7	205.2	204.7	201.1	202.2
Telecommunications and sound recording and reproducing apparatus and equipment	5.92	120.0	119.7	119.7	121.7	122.5	123.5	123.7	125.4	125.5	125.6	124.9	123.6
Electrical machinery and equipment	9.48	97.9	100.9	100.3	103.0	106.5	108.2	109.7	112.6	113.7	112.9	112.1	112.4
Road vehicles	14.52	75.1	76.3	76.4	77.6	79.5	80.9	80.6	82.9	82.7	82.1	82.0	83.6
Miscellaneous Manufactured Articles	17.22	82.2	84.5	85.0	87.4	89.1	90.2	89.1	90.8	90.9	90.8	91.3	92.3
Prefabricated buildings; plumbing, heat and lighting fixtures, n.e.s.	0.45	80.8	84.7	84.2	87.7	89.3	91.9	90.1	92.1	94.1	95.3	96.4	98.9
Furniture and parts thereof	1.68	84.3	84.7	85.5	86.3	88.9	90.1	90.3	92.7	91.3	91.1	93.3	93.2
Travel goods, handbags, and similar containers	0.40	75.7	76.2	77.3	80.8	83.7	85.6	86.3	85.7	85.5	86.7	88.4	88.9
Articles of apparel and clothing accessories	5.75	83.6	85.8	88.0	88.3	90.9	90.3	91.7	92.1	93.1	94.2	95.0	95.6
Footwear	1.32	80.5	84.0	83.5	87.2	87.9	90.9	89.7	90.5	89.2	89.7	90.3	91.8
Professional, scientific and controlling instruments, and apparatus, n.e.s.	1.94	80.4	83.2	81.3	84.9	85.8	87.3	83.2	86.9	86.4	83.6	83.4	84.0
Photographic apparatus, equipment and supplies, and optical goods, n.e.s.	1.28	88.1	89.8	87.0	90.7	92.1	92.1	89.4	93.1	92.8	91.2	90.0	91.7
Miscellaneous manufactured articles, n.e.s.	4.41	80.4	83.2	84.0	87.4	88.7	90.7	88.0	90.2	90.5	90.2	90.6	91.9

See footnote and *Note* at end of table.

Table 6-13. U.S. Import Price Indexes for Selected Categories of Goods, by Standard International Trade Classification, 1987–2001—*Continued*

(2000=100.)

Categories	1990				1991				1992			
	March	June	September	December	March	June	September	December	March	June	September	December
ALL COMMODITIES	92.4	90.8	96.5	98.4	95.0	93.4	93.3	94.3	93.9	94.8	95.9	94.4
Food And Live Animals	91.9	92.1	93.9	95.7	95.7	95.6	94.6	95.6	97.4	91.4	92.1	93.2
Meat and meat preparations	113.1	118.4	121.7	120.5	120.9	125.0	119.5	115.9	114.8	112.3	111.5	109.5
Fish, crustaceans, aquatic invertebrates, and preparations thereof	70.7	70.9	74.5	77.1	79.7	78.9	78.2	78.3	79.1	79.1	80.3	78.3
Vegetables, fruit and nuts, fresh or dried	90.7	87.0	83.1	90.6	88.3	91.4	91.9	95.6	107.7	89.9	89.6	91.7
Coffee, tea, cocoa, spices, and manufactures thereof	103.7	105.4	110.6	104.5	104.7	98.8	98.2	98.5	90.0	82.0	81.6	96.1
Beverages And Tobacco	74.7	76.5	77.6	79.6	84.2	85.4	85.3	86.3	87.1	87.5	88.3	87.2
Beverages	77.3	78.9	80.0	81.5	86.6	87.6	87.2	88.2	89.0	89.4	90.5	89.1
Crude Materials, Inedible, Except Fuels	91.3	90.4	88.0	85.0	84.4	85.0	81.8	81.5	84.6	85.0	86.3	85.9
Cork and wood	66.0	66.7	66.2	61.6	62.9	70.1	66.6	68.0	75.3	76.1	77.1	79.1
Woodpulp and recovered paper	118.9	116.6	112.5	105.6	97.1	89.8	80.7	78.6	81.2	84.4	88.2	83.9
Metalliferous ores and metal scrap	97.5	93.2	90.2	89.1	89.1	86.6	86.8	86.2	86.0	84.3	85.4	83.7
Mineral Fuels, Lubricants, And Related Materials	64.3	54.7	87.3	93.0	65.8	62.3	63.6	63.3	56.8	64.9	65.3	60.0
Petroleum, petroleum products, and related materials	64.6	54.8	89.8	95.1	66.3	63.0	64.5	63.9	57.4	66.0	66.2	60.2
Gas, natural and manufactured	63.7	54.9	57.7	69.2	61.5	54.1	53.4	57.8	49.7	51.4	55.4	58.1
Chemicals And Related Products, n.e.s.	94.3	93.7	94.9	97.6	97.4	95.8	95.4	95.6	96.2	96.8	97.5	97.1
Organic chemicals	98.7	98.1	100.0	104.7	101.8	98.6	96.1	97.1	97.0	96.8	96.5	94.4
Inorganic chemicals	95.4	95.8	97.0	100.7	101.5	100.2	98.1	94.9	95.5	94.1	93.7	99.0
Dyeing, tanning, and coloring materials	...	...	...	...	...	...	...	...	...	...	...	105.6
Medicinal and pharmaceutical products	80.5	80.6	81.5	83.6	83.2	81.7	83.2	86.4	87.3	87.6	90.1	89.8
Essential oils, polishing, and cleansing preps	90.5	91.6	92.1	94.6	93.4	93.2	96.0	95.2	97.5	98.6	98.8	98.8
Plastics in primary forms	...	...	...	...	...	...	...	...	...	...	...	96.8
Plastics in nonprimary forms	...	...	...	...	...	...	...	...	...	...	...	109.9
Chemical materials and products, n.e.s.	97.2	92.9	91.6	90.2	89.6	88.1	88.3	90.1	94.0	97.1	101.0	100.1
Manufactured Goods Classified Chiefly By Material	90.5	91.3	93.2	92.3	92.7	91.1	90.3	90.6	91.0	91.3	92.0	90.4
Rubber manufactures, n.e.s.	102.9	103.3	103.3	104.6	104.3	104.1	103.7	104.8	105.7	105.6	107.0	106.8
Cork and wood manufactures other than furniture	84.7	86.4	87.8	85.3	84.1	84.8	85.9	86.3	90.0	93.0	95.1	92.4
Paper and paperboard, cut to size	86.5	89.3	89.8	90.2	92.2	89.9	88.2	87.8	85.1	83.7	84.3	84.3
Textile yarn, fabrics, made-up articles, n.e.s., and related products	90.6	91.4	93.4	94.8	96.3	95.4	96.8	98.4	98.9	98.1	100.9	99.3
Nonmetallic mineral manufactures, n.e.s.	87.7	88.9	89.4	90.3	91.9	92.1	92.2	93.0	93.3	94.0	94.9	94.6
Iron and steel	100.4	98.2	97.1	98.4	98.1	97.8	96.9	97.2	96.6	96.1	94.8	94.8
Nonferrous metals	80.9	84.2	92.6	83.6	82.1	75.9	72.9	70.8	73.7	75.6	75.6	70.0
Manufactures of metals, n.e.s.	94.6	93.9	95.2	96.0	96.8	96.1	95.5	96.9	97.6	97.8	99.6	97.9
Machinery And Transport Equipment	101.6	100.8	101.8	104.2	105.4	103.7	103.8	105.4	105.6	105.6	106.9	106.1
Machinery specialized for particular industries	86.3	87.1	90.4	94.1	95.6	91.0	90.7	93.4	94.2	94.3	99.0	95.4
Metalworking machinery	86.9	87.8	89.2	92.1	92.8	89.6	89.6	92.1	92.3	92.5	94.8	93.7
General industrial machinery, equipment, and machine parts, n.e.s.	86.5	87.6	90.9	93.6	94.5	91.0	91.1	93.7	94.0	94.0	96.8	95.0
Computer equipment and office machines	200.8	198.5	196.8	199.2	197.3	193.4	191.2	191.7	192.2	190.2	190.9	189.0
Telecommunications and sound recording and reproducing apparatus and equipment	122.5	120.9	119.3	120.1	118.7	118.0	117.3	117.8	117.4	117.3	117.3	117.6
Electrical machinery and equipment	113.1	111.3	112.7	114.0	115.5	113.4	112.8	114.5	114.3	115.1	116.3	114.6
Road vehicles	83.2	82.0	82.9	85.4	87.1	86.3	86.8	88.1	88.2	88.0	88.6	88.8
Miscellaneous Manufactured Articles	94.5	94.7	96.2	97.5	97.7	96.3	96.5	98.0	99.1	99.3	101.0	99.9
Prefabricated buildings; plumbing, heat and lighting fixtures, n.e.s.	102.7	102.0	104.2	105.6	101.9	101.6	101.4	102.8	103.8	105.2	106.8	105.5
Furniture and parts thereof	95.1	96.0	97.2	99.1	99.6	98.0	98.4	99.0	99.8	100.1	102.6	100.7
Travel goods, handbags, and similar containers	89.7	89.8	88.8	90.6	90.7	91.1	91.0	91.8	92.9	96.2	96.6	94.5
Articles of apparel and clothing accessories	95.7	96.5	96.4	95.5	95.5	94.8	95.4	95.9	96.9	97.7	97.5	97.9
Footwear	95.2	96.5	98.2	100.0	100.2	98.4	98.1	98.8	99.4	100.0	101.5	98.7
Professional, scientific and controlling instruments, and apparatus, n.e.s.	87.7	89.1	92.0	96.9	98.0	93.4	93.0	95.6	95.7	95.4	101.2	98.4
Photographic apparatus, equipment and supplies, and optical goods, n.e.s.	93.7	94.0	97.0	98.8	99.1	96.0	96.3	98.6	99.3	98.6	102.1	100.5
Miscellaneous manufactured articles, n.e.s.	95.6	94.3	96.6	98.6	98.5	98.0	98.3	100.8	102.6	102.0	104.1	103.1

See footnote and *Note* at end of table.

Table 6-13. U.S. Import Price Indexes for Selected Categories of Goods, by Standard International Trade Classification, 1987–2001—*Continued*

(2000=100.)

Categories	1993				1994				1995			
	March	June	September	December	March	June	September	December	March	June	September	December
ALL COMMODITIES	94.7	95.0	94.5	93.5	94.0	96.3	97.2	98.4	99.9	101.4	100.8	101.0
Food And Live Animals	91.2	94.4	95.6	95.3	96.3	101.8	110.9	110.8	112.6	108.6	106.7	104.7
Meat and meat preparations	113.4	117.6	115.9	111.3	114.3	107.8	108.8	108.5	104.9	100.8	97.3	99.6
Fish, crustaceans, aquatic invertebrates, and preparations thereof	78.9	79.1	79.9	83.6	85.5	88.9	90.6	93.8	93.6	92.5	89.2	86.5
Vegetables, fruit and nuts, fresh or dried	85.4	96.6	93.6	89.3	88.0	90.1	88.0	99.0	100.5	97.6	101.0	106.4
Coffee, tea, cocoa, spices, and manufactures thereof	89.8	86.1	104.2	107.8	109.3	145.4	214.4	182.7	194.8	176.3	165.7	141.9
Beverages And Tobacco	86.8	86.8	86.2	86.9	86.6	87.3	87.5	87.5	88.2	88.6	89.4	90.6
Beverages	89.1	89.6	89.0	89.3	89.2	89.6	90.1	90.2	91.0	91.2	91.7	92.0
Crude Materials, Inedible, Except Fuels	92.2	84.5	85.9	90.7	93.4	94.7	96.2	101.6	107.6	109.5	113.6	111.0
Cork and wood	105.9	84.9	92.4	110.9	108.7	104.1	101.3	97.4	93.4	85.3	94.7	88.5
Woodpulp and recovered paper	74.3	72.2	68.5	66.2	69.8	79.5	90.8	102.9	118.8	131.6	134.8	138.4
Metalliferous ores and metal scrap	82.8	81.7	80.6	77.0	83.5	82.9	85.4	90.0	98.6	98.4	101.5	100.2
Mineral Fuels, Lubricants, And Related Materials	61.5	59.8	55.0	47.7	48.2	57.1	55.0	56.4	59.2	61.9	57.6	59.2
Petroleum, petroleum products, and related materials	62.1	60.3	55.0	47.0	47.7	57.6	55.2	56.7	60.1	63.0	58.5	60.2
Gas, natural and manufactured	54.9	55.4	56.3	57.7	55.6	51.4	53.6	54.2	48.8	49.3	47.1	49.1
Chemicals And Related Products, n.e.s.	97.1	97.8	97.1	96.4	96.3	97.6	100.5	103.5	105.4	106.8	106.6	106.4
Organic chemicals	94.0	94.6	94.3	92.8	92.6	95.2	100.0	104.5	102.5	100.6	101.0	100.3
Inorganic chemicals	99.1	97.9	97.7	97.5	96.9	97.9	99.9	104.6	110.0	111.1	110.9	110.2
Dyeing, tanning, and coloring materials	104.8	106.7	105.6	105.5	106.7	107.2	108.2	108.7	112.3	114.7	114.7	115.9
Medicinal and pharmaceutical products	91.0	95.9	94.4	95.1	95.8	95.9	97.6	98.3	99.2	104.4	104.1	105.6
Essential oils, polishing, and cleansing preps	100.9	102.2	100.2	101.4	99.6	99.9	101.9	104.6	107.7	113.8	114.7	115.5
Plastics in primary forms	97.7	95.8	96.5	96.5	97.6	97.9	98.4	99.6	103.4	106.1	105.1	107.9
Plastics in nonprimary forms	109.0	109.3	108.5	107.1	104.7	108.0	112.9	117.7	126.9	129.6	124.5	117.4
Chemical materials and products, n.e.s.	98.7	98.0	96.1	94.5	95.4	94.5	97.8	96.4	96.5	98.7	101.6	104.2
Manufactured Goods Classified Chiefly By Material	90.8	91.2	90.7	89.8	91.2	92.8	94.6	97.7	100.2	102.7	105.0	104.3
Rubber manufactures, n.e.s.	107.6	107.5	106.8	106.9	105.2	106.0	105.0	105.9	106.4	108.7	110.0	110.4
Cork and wood manufactures other than furniture	100.5	103.8	104.8	103.9	106.1	108.8	101.7	99.4	101.4	102.7	100.1	100.9
Paper and paperboard, cut to size	85.6	86.0	84.9	83.8	83.6	85.1	88.4	93.6	101.8	111.3	120.5	121.6
Textile yarn, fabrics, made-up articles, n.e.s., and related products	99.4	100.0	98.9	98.2	98.8	100.8	101.8	102.0	103.2	106.3	106.4	106.1
Nonmetallic mineral manufactures, n.e.s.	95.1	96.2	96.0	96.2	96.1	96.7	97.8	98.4	98.7	99.2	99.6	99.9
Iron and steel	95.1	96.7	96.6	96.4	97.3	97.6	99.7	101.6	104.0	106.9	110.7	108.1
Nonferrous metals	68.3	65.4	64.8	61.7	68.5	72.7	77.6	88.0	90.3	88.5	90.5	87.2
Manufactures of metals, n.e.s.	98.1	99.2	99.0	98.7	98.6	99.3	100.7	101.0	102.9	105.1	105.2	105.9
Machinery And Transport Equipment	106.1	107.2	107.7	108.4	108.6	109.1	109.7	110.3	110.8	112.4	112.1	112.0
Machinery specialized for particular industries	94.9	96.2	95.8	96.0	96.9	98.1	99.8	100.6	102.0	104.7	103.8	105.6
Metalworking machinery	93.5	95.9	96.4	96.9	97.1	98.0	100.3	101.4	103.1	108.9	108.3	108.9
General industrial machinery, equipment, and machine parts, n.e.s.	94.4	95.9	95.9	96.7	97.2	97.7	98.9	100.0	101.3	104.5	104.7	105.5
Computer equipment and office machines	186.2	182.8	180.1	178.0	175.5	173.2	171.1	168.5	167.0	167.2	165.9	163.4
Telecommunications and sound recording and reproducing apparatus and equipment	117.3	118.3	119.5	118.5	117.5	117.6	117.7	118.0	117.8	119.1	119.0	118.0
Electrical machinery and equipment	115.2	117.2	119.4	118.9	119.1	119.6	120.2	120.1	120.5	122.9	120.7	119.7
Road vehicles	89.1	90.4	90.9	92.9	93.3	94.0	94.7	96.0	96.6	97.3	97.9	98.2
Miscellaneous Manufactured Articles	99.7	100.7	100.7	100.5	100.6	100.9	101.3	101.5	102.2	103.2	103.1	103.7
Prefabricated buildings; plumbing, heat and lighting fixtures, n.e.s.	104.4	105.7	105.9	105.6	104.9	103.2	104.4	103.3	107.2	107.4	108.3	109.7
Furniture and parts thereof	100.2	100.8	100.2	99.7	100.2	100.6	100.9	101.2	101.7	103.1	102.9	103.5
Travel goods, handbags and similar containers	94.8	95.5	95.8	94.9	94.8	94.5	95.7	96.0	96.4	98.5	100.5	99.3
Articles of apparel and clothing accessories	97.5	98.1	98.2	97.8	97.7	98.1	97.9	98.2	98.8	99.0	99.0	99.5
Footwear	98.0	98.7	97.8	97.6	97.1	97.7	98.4	98.5	98.5	99.3	99.6	100.1
Professional, scientific and controlling instruments, and apparatus, n.e.s.	98.9	101.0	100.2	100.9	102.0	103.3	104.2	105.1	105.1	107.2	107.5	107.1
Photographic apparatus, equipment and supplies, and optical goods, n.e.s.	100.5	102.5	103.5	104.2	104.0	104.6	106.2	106.0	106.4	110.6	109.9	109.9
Miscellaneous manufactured articles, n.e.s.	103.1	104.2	104.4	104.3	104.4	104.4	104.7	104.8	106.1	106.5	106.1	107.2

See footnote and *Note* at end of table.

Table 6-13. U.S. Import Price Indexes for Selected Categories of Goods, by Standard International Trade Classification, 1987–2001—Continued

(2000=100.)

Categories	1996 March	June	September	December	1997 March	June	September	December	1998 March	June	September	December
ALL COMMODITIES	101.6	100.7	101.8	102.5	100.0	98.8	98.4	97.2	94.1	93.1	92.2	91.0
Food And Live Animals	103.2	102.7	104.8	102.6	110.4	112.5	109.8	108.0	106.1	106.3	103.5	103.2
Meat and meat preparations	93.7	92.0	102.6	100.7	105.3	103.6	105.7	106.0	103.0	100.0	98.9	93.4
Fish, crustaceans, aquatic invertebrates, and preparations thereof	86.8	88.8	88.3	89.4	90.7	94.3	95.2	96.1	97.4	99.6	94.4	91.2
Vegetables, fruit and nuts, fresh or dried	102.4	98.8	107.1	102.4	111.8	102.2	104.0	103.1	96.2	104.0	107.3	111.2
Coffee, tea, cocoa, spices and manufactures thereof	144.3	143.7	135.8	129.0	169.7	203.7	172.1	158.5	161.8	141.3	133.1	129.2
Beverages And Tobacco	91.2	92.1	93.2	93.4	95.0	95.5	95.8	96.5	97.0	97.4	97.5	97.6
Beverages	92.1	92.5	93.5	93.9	94.3	94.9	95.2	96.1	96.6	97.0	97.1	97.3
Crude Materials, Inedible, Except Fuels	105.8	103.4	106.4	105.6	108.5	106.8	106.0	102.6	99.9	96.2	94.0	92.2
Cork and wood	91.3	104.5	115.9	110.9	116.2	112.7	111.5	104.1	101.8	93.1	98.7	98.4
Woodpulp and recovered paper	100.2	79.2	84.9	84.4	82.7	83.9	86.9	87.6	81.8	84.2	77.5	73.7
Metalliferous ores and metal scrap	100.3	100.1	95.9	96.0	101.4	104.1	102.9	100.7	98.8	97.0	91.5	91.3
Crude animal and vegetable materials, n.e.s.	...	...	...	94.2	99.1	91.7	97.1	100.8	103.7	106.6	99.2	93.6
Mineral Fuels, Lubricants, And Related Materials	66.3	65.1	72.6	79.8	67.1	61.6	63.0	60.8	47.3	45.7	45.6	38.0
Petroleum, petroleum products, and related materials	67.4	66.3	74.3	80.0	67.6	62.2	63.0	59.8	45.5	43.9	44.2	35.1
Gas, natural and manufactured	54.7	52.7	56.3	76.7	61.3	55.1	60.2	65.0	55.9	54.5	51.8	53.9
Chemicals And Related Products, n.e.s.	106.5	104.9	105.1	105.1	103.7	102.3	102.1	101.1	99.2	99.3	97.4	96.7
Organic chemicals	100.7	99.9	100.4	100.9	101.3	97.3	98.5	96.7	93.5	93.6	92.7	91.1
Inorganic chemicals	111.5	109.2	109.9	113.3	111.0	108.4	109.0	106.4	103.7	107.0	102.8	99.5
Dyeing, tanning, and coloring materials	117.6	116.4	116.9	114.4	110.5	111.5	107.1	110.5	108.1	108.1	108.1	110.0
Medicinal and pharmaceutical products	103.9	102.7	104.4	102.0	98.9	99.3	98.7	99.8	98.8	98.3	97.5	98.7
Essential oils, polishing, and cleansing preps	116.8	112.8	112.8	112.6	110.5	109.2	109.1	109.7	106.2	106.7	105.6	107.1
Plastics in primary forms	108.2	102.6	98.8	100.3	96.7	96.7	97.8	97.1	99.6	99.2	96.8	96.4
Plastics in nonprimary forms	110.8	108.6	108.1	108.2	107.4	110.6	108.5	103.3	101.7	98.7	92.4	92.0
Chemical materials and products, n.e.s.	107.4	107.1	107.5	105.3	104.1	103.0	102.7	102.6	101.2	100.9	100.1	99.0
Manufactured Goods Classified Chiefly By Material	103.3	102.0	99.8	98.2	98.7	99.5	99.6	98.7	97.3	96.7	95.4	94.3
Rubber manufactures, n.e.s.	108.7	108.8	108.2	107.0	105.7	106.0	103.2	103.7	102.8	103.1	102.4	102.5
Cork and wood manufactures other than furniture	101.4	104.4	103.7	101.7	102.2	102.0	102.4	102.1	95.7	95.6	98.6	98.0
Paper and paperboard, cut to size	118.9	112.7	104.0	96.3	95.0	97.7	99.2	98.9	98.2	97.8	97.2	96.2
Textile yarn, fabrics, made-up articles, n.e.s., and related products	105.9	105.4	105.5	105.8	105.8	105.8	105.2	104.5	103.1	102.3	101.8	101.4
Nonmetallic mineral manufactures, n.e.s.	100.9	100.8	101.6	102.3	102.5	101.9	101.4	101.0	100.0	99.9	99.4	100.0
Iron and steel	105.7	104.8	104.8	104.1	103.2	103.3	103.3	103.3	101.9	99.7	96.7	93.5
Nonferrous metals	85.4	84.2	77.8	76.0	81.8	85.4	87.1	82.7	81.9	81.6	77.5	74.5
Manufactures of metals, n.e.s.	106.0	105.0	105.8	105.7	104.0	103.6	102.6	103.1	101.8	101.0	101.0	101.1
Machinery And Transport Equipment	111.2	110.1	110.2	109.6	107.8	106.9	105.9	105.0	103.8	102.6	101.6	102.0
Power generating machinery and equipment	...	...	...	100.2	99.7	99.4	99.0	99.2	100.1	98.1	97.4	98.1
Machinery specialized for particular industries	106.3	104.7	104.9	105.1	103.2	102.8	102.0	102.6	101.6	101.1	100.2	102.0
Metalworking machinery	108.3	108.1	108.4	108.0	104.4	104.9	103.8	105.3	104.1	103.4	103.0	104.2
General industrial machinery, equipment, and machine parts, n.e.s.	104.9	104.4	105.2	104.6	102.2	102.1	101.0	101.0	100.3	100.3	100.3	102.1
Computer equipment and office machines	158.5	152.8	149.7	146.9	140.6	135.3	130.2	128.0	121.5	117.2	114.5	111.1
Telecommunications and sound recording and reproducing apparatus and equipment	116.5	115.3	114.3	113.5	111.9	110.6	109.8	108.7	107.5	105.9	105.3	104.6
Electrical machinery and equipment	118.0	115.6	114.8	112.1	110.9	109.1	107.9	104.7	103.4	102.2	100.6	101.8
Road vehicles	97.9	97.8	98.3	98.1	98.1	98.1	98.6	98.8	98.8	98.4	98.1	98.8
Miscellaneous Manufactured Articles	103.7	103.5	103.5	103.2	102.9	103.0	102.7	102.5	102.0	101.4	101.0	101.0
Prefabricated buildings; plumbing, heat and lighting fixtures, n.e.s.	108.6	106.5	108.7	106.2	102.7	103.0	101.9	103.1	103.5	102.7	102.2	100.9
Furniture and parts thereof	103.2	103.3	103.3	104.3	104.9	105.4	104.9	105.6	105.4	102.6	102.6	102.8
Travel goods, handbags, and similar containers	99.6	99.6	99.6	99.2	99.9	99.7	99.5	98.9	98.0	99.6	98.7	99.5
Articles of apparel and clothing accessories	99.9	100.4	100.1	99.9	100.6	101.5	101.7	101.7	101.5	101.5	101.7	100.9
Footwear	100.7	100.6	100.3	100.2	100.3	100.3	100.0	100.5	100.0	100.0	100.2	100.1
Professional, scientific and controlling instruments, and apparatus, n.e.s.	107.4	105.9	107.0	106.5	103.9	103.6	103.4	102.8	101.4	101.3	100.8	101.4
Photographic apparatus, equipment and supplies, and optical goods, n.e.s.	108.4	106.3	106.7	105.7	104.0	103.0	102.1	101.6	100.1	99.3	98.3	99.4
Miscellaneous manufactured articles, n.e.s.	107.1	107.2	107.2	106.5	105.9	105.6	104.7	104.2	103.5	102.2	101.1	101.4

See footnote and *Note* at end of table.

Table 6-13. U.S. Import Price Indexes for Selected Categories of Goods, by Standard International Trade Classification, 1987–2001—Continued

(2000=100.)

Categories	1999 March	June	September	December	2000 March	June	September	December	2001 March	June	September	December
ALL COMMODITIES	91.5	92.9	95.8	97.4	99.9	100.2	101.6	100.5	98.3	97.6	95.9	91.4
Food And Live Animals	101.1	101.2	99.3	102.7	101.0	99.0	99.0	100.2	100.9	96.0	95.1	94.8
Meat and meat preparations	95.7	96.1	101.2	100.1	100.9	100.8	100.7	99.1	102.2	106.2	113.5	109.8
Fish, crustaceans, aquatic invertebrates, and preparations thereof	94.0	94.9	93.9	97.2	98.3	99.3	102.5	99.3	93.0	90.0	86.3	82.9
Vegetables, fruit and nuts, fresh or dried	102.3	103.7	102.2	104.2	101.8	96.2	98.4	105.1	110.1	97.6	98.5	99.3
Coffee, tea, cocoa, spices and manufactures thereof	122.1	119.4	105.7	121.4	105.0	102.3	93.9	87.4	88.7	85.8	80.1	78.5
Beverages And Tobacco	98.1	98.1	99.7	99.5	99.2	100.4	100.9	100.5	100.4	101.7	102.0	103.0
Beverages	97.6	97.9	99.6	99.3	99.1	100.5	101.0	100.9	100.8	102.4	102.4	103.1
Crude Materials, Inedible, Except Fuels	94.7	99.1	100.5	101.1	103.5	99.4	97.5	97.0	94.5	102.8	96.6	89.9
Cork and wood	104.2	112.5	112.0	109.3	109.2	101.3	91.8	93.6	89.8	122.1	112.2	91.7
Woodpulp and recovered paper	73.5	77.3	84.1	86.9	92.3	102.0	104.5	106.3	102.5	87.1	77.3	77.7
Metalliferous ores and metal scrap	88.5	90.4	92.8	97.4	102.3	99.1	100.0	97.3	96.6	93.9	92.8	91.2
Crude animal and vegetable materials, n.e.s.	103.1	95.8	104.7	105.5	105.5	87.4	97.0	91.5	92.0	92.9	83.8	96.0
Mineral Fuels, Lubricants, And Related Materials	43.1	54.6	74.5	83.2	97.4	101.3	111.3	106.1	90.8	90.4	85.8	61.2
Petroleum, petroleum products, and related materials	41.9	54.6	75.1	84.5	99.5	102.2	112.1	97.9	86.5	89.3	86.8	59.8
Gas, natural and manufactured	47.5	51.8	69.2	73.1	83.1	95.2	106.2	161.6	119.1	97.4	77.8	68.6
Chemicals And Related Products, n.e.s.	96.4	96.2	96.9	97.6	98.5	99.8	101.2	100.7	102.4	100.5	98.3	97.4
Organic chemicals	91.7	91.6	93.2	94.3	95.9	100.4	102.5	102.1	101.5	102.1	99.3	96.1
Inorganic chemicals	97.0	94.9	94.8	96.3	97.2	100.1	101.2	103.0	107.2	100.1	98.1	97.6
Dyeing, tanning, and coloring materials	107.4	104.7	102.8	102.3	100.7	98.1	100.1	99.1	101.4	98.1	96.3	97.1
Medicinal and pharmaceutical products	99.7	99.1	100.0	100.3	100.3	99.8	99.7	98.6	97.5	96.7	97.0	97.0
Essential oils, polishing, and cleansing preps	105.3	104.1	103.9	101.6	101.0	100.8	100.0	96.2	99.7	98.4	99.7	100.1
Plastics in primary forms	97.1	98.8	99.1	99.2	99.2	99.6	100.6	101.2	101.1	102.1	99.7	99.8
Plastics in nonprimary forms	91.3	94.4	97.2	99.5	100.3	100.8	100.8	98.0	105.3	102.4	99.3	100.9
Chemical materials and products, n.e.s.	97.4	97.0	97.6	99.1	100.2	99.2	100.7	100.1	101.4	99.9	99.0	98.0
Manufactured Goods Classified Chiefly By Material	94.5	94.6	95.2	96.6	100.8	100.4	100.6	100.0	100.0	98.0	94.8	92.0
Rubber manufactures, n.e.s.	102.6	102.4	103.1	102.5	100.2	99.7	99.6	99.7	99.7	99.0	98.7	97.9
Cork and wood manufactures other than furniture	103.5	107.7	106.8	102.8	106.3	99.2	95.8	94.1	92.0	96.2	90.4	88.3
Paper and paperboard, cut to size	95.8	93.6	93.5	96.3	97.3	99.6	102.1	103.0	103.6	102.7	99.3	96.2
Textile yarn, fabrics, made-up articles, n.e.s., and related products	100.6	99.7	99.9	99.8	100.7	99.7	99.8	99.5	99.1	98.8	98.1	97.1
Nonmetallic mineral manufactures, n.e.s.	100.6	100.2	100.4	100.5	100.1	99.8	100.1	99.5	99.9	99.4	99.3	97.4
Iron and steel	91.2	92.0	92.5	95.5	100.4	103.9	100.7	97.9	95.5	93.5	94.0	92.5
Nonferrous metals	77.1	78.8	81.8	85.9	103.4	99.4	102.7	102.7	104.6	95.3	82.2	73.8
Manufactures of metals, n.e.s.	100.3	100.6	100.2	100.3	100.6	100.1	99.8	99.4	99.3	100.1	99.3	99.0
Machinery And Transport Equipment	101.6	100.9	100.5	100.3	100.2	100.1	99.8	99.4	99.2	98.5	98.0	97.7
Power generating machinery and equipment	98.8	98.5	98.6	99.3	99.5	100.4	99.9	100.1	99.2	98.8	98.6	98.5
Machinery specialized for particular industries	101.8	101.1	101.1	101.3	100.7	99.5	99.3	98.7	99.7	99.1	99.1	98.7
Metalworking machinery	102.6	100.9	100.6	101.5	100.2	98.8	100.3	99.8	100.6	99.4	100.1	99.7
General industrial machinery, equipment, and machine parts, n.e.s.	102.1	101.3	101.1	100.7	100.7	99.9	99.7	99.0	99.3	98.2	98.0	97.8
Computer equipment and office machines	107.3	105.1	102.7	102.7	101.6	99.9	99.5	97.8	95.7	93.6	90.0	88.8
Telecommunications and sound recording and reproducing apparatus and equipment	104.8	103.8	103.2	101.4	100.6	100.2	99.6	99.0	98.1	97.2	96.8	96.3
Electrical machinery and equipment	101.3	100.1	99.8	99.3	99.4	100.7	99.9	99.4	99.9	98.8	98.6	97.8
Road vehicles	99.2	99.6	99.5	99.6	99.9	100.1	99.9	100.1	100.1	99.8	100.0	100.3
Miscellaneous Manufactured Articles	101.1	100.5	100.7	100.7	100.3	99.7	99.7	99.7	100.2	99.8	99.6	99.1
Prefabricated buildings; plumbing, heat and lighting fixtures, n.e.s.	99.9	99.5	97.6	99.4	100.9	99.2	99.5	99.2	98.8	99.2	98.3	98.4
Furniture and parts thereof	102.6	101.1	100.8	100.1	100.5	99.6	100.3	99.7	99.8	98.5	98.9	98.9
Travel goods, handbags, and similar containers	99.2	100.3	100.9	100.1	100.5	99.8	99.9	99.8	100.1	99.0	99.3	98.7
Articles of apparel and clothing accessories	101.1	100.6	101.1	100.8	100.4	99.6	99.7	99.9	101.1	100.6	100.1	100.2
Footwear	100.4	100.0	100.1	100.1	100.0	99.6	100.2	99.8	100.8	100.1	100.4	100.3
Professional, scientific and controlling instruments, and apparatus, n.e.s.	101.0	100.4	100.8	101.3	100.1	99.8	99.8	99.2	99.1	98.7	98.5	98.5
Photographic apparatus, equipment and supplies, and optical goods, n.e.s.	100.1	99.6	99.7	100.9	100.1	99.9	99.7	98.9	99.7	98.5	98.2	98.4
Miscellaneous manufactured articles, n.e.s.	101.5	100.9	100.9	100.8	100.3	99.8	99.5	99.7	99.7	99.7	99.6	97.8

Note: n.e.s. = not elsewhere specified.

1. Percent of total, based on 2000 trade values.

Table 6-14. U.S. Import Price Indexes for Selected Categories of Goods, by Locality of Origin, 1991–2001

(2000=100.)

Category and year	Percent of U.S. imports 2000	Months			
		March	June	September	December
DEVELOPED COUNTRIES	100.0	...	...	...	...
1991	...	89.6	87.9	87.9	88.9
1992	...	89.2	89.6	90.9	90.1
1993	...	90.5	91.4	91.5	91.7
1994	...	92.3	93.4	94.8	96.1
1995	...	97.4	99.8	100.0	100.0
1996	...	99.7	98.8	99.3	99.4
1997	...	97.4	96.5	96.4	96.1
1998	...	94.6	94.0	93.3	93.8
1999	...	94.1	94.8	96.4	97.5
2000	...	99.5	100.1	100.9	101.4
2001	...	100.2	99.0	96.5	95.4
Manufactured Goods	90.0	...	...	...	...
1991	...	91.6	90.1	90.1	91.3
1992	...	91.8	91.7	93.0	92.4
1993	...	92.8	93.8	94.1	94.6
1994	...	95.1	95.9	97.4	98.8
1995	...	100.0	102.6	102.9	102.9
1996	...	102.1	101.1	101.4	100.7
1997	...	99.5	98.9	98.8	98.6
1998	...	97.8	97.5	96.7	97.3
1999	...	97.6	97.7	98.1	98.9
2000	...	100.2	99.9	100.2	99.8
2001	...	99.9	99.2	97.6	96.0
Nonmanufactured Goods	9.3	...	...	...	...
1991	...	64.2	62.2	62.3	62.7
1992	...	62.0	63.8	64.6	63.7
1993	...	64.5	63.8	61.8	58.7
1994	...	58.2	64.3	64.3	64.1
1995	...	66.3	67.6	65.2	66.0
1996	...	71.6	72.3	76.0	84.3
1997	...	73.3	68.9	69.4	68.5
1998	...	59.3	56.8	57.2	55.7
1999	...	56.9	65.1	78.7	83.2
2000	...	92.7	102.2	107.5	118.2
2001	...	103.9	97.2	85.2	89.3
DEVELOPING COUNTRIES	100.0	...	...	...	...
1991	...	94.1	93.5	93.8	93.6
1992	...	92.2	94.7	95.0	94.4
1993	...	94.2	93.5	92.3	89.6
1994	...	90.1	94.2	95.0	95.7
1995	...	97.5	98.7	97.4	97.6
1996	...	99.8	99.0	101.3	102.7
1997	...	100.6	99.4	98.7	96.6
1998	...	92.4	90.7	89.5	86.8
1999	...	87.7	90.3	94.5	96.9
2000	...	99.8	100.4	102.5	99.5
2001	...	97.0	96.6	95.0	96.0
Manufactured Goods	77.2	...	...	...	...
1991	...	105.2	105.1	104.9	105.2
1992	...	105.5	105.7	105.7	105.4
1993	...	104.6	104.5	104.2	103.7
1994	...	104.2	105.1	105.8	106.5
1995	...	107.3	108.8	108.6	108.4
1996	...	108.9	108.4	107.9	108.6
1997	...	108.4	107.8	107.0	105.3
1998	...	103.5	102.2	100.6	99.6
1999	...	98.8	98.9	99.0	99.3
2000	...	99.8	99.7	100.3	100.2
2001	...	99.6	98.8	97.9	96.0

Table 6-14. U.S. Import Price Indexes for Selected Categories of Goods, by Locality of Origin, 1991–2001—*Continued*

(2000=100.)

Category and year	Percent of U.S. imports 2000	Months			
		March	June	September	December
Nonmanufactured Goods	22.7	...	...	...	...
1991	...	64.8	63.8	64.6	63.8
1992	...	61.0	65.5	66.0	63.7
1993	...	64.9	62.8	59.1	51.9
1994	...	52.0	63.8	64.8	65.5
1995	...	69.5	70.3	66.1	67.3
1996	...	73.7	72.1	80.9	84.5
1997	...	75.8	72.6	72.2	68.8
1998	...	57.1	54.9	54.5	46.8
1999	...	53.0	63.6	80.3	89.2
2000	...	99.9	102.4	109.2	97.4
2001	...	88.9	89.7	86.1	95.9
CANADA	100.0	...	...	...	...
1991	...	87.2	87.3	86.9	87.2
1992	...	86.5	87.4	87.5	86.3
1993	...	86.5	85.9	85.2	85.1
1994	...	85.5	87.2	88.1	90.2
1995	...	92.1	93.8	94.8	94.7
1996	...	94.3	93.5	93.8	95.1
1997	...	93.2	92.6	93.2	92.0
1998	...	90.1	89.7	89.3	88.7
1999	...	88.8	90.6	93.5	94.7
2000	...	97.2	99.8	102.4	105.6
2001	...	102.6	101.8	97.0	96.1
Manufactured Goods	80.6	...	...	...	...
1991	...	93.2	93.1	93.0	93.6
1992	...	92.9	92.5	92.4	91.4
1993	...	91.6	90.8	90.4	90.9
1994	...	91.4	92.3	93.6	95.9
1995	...	98.0	99.4	100.7	100.5
1996	...	99.0	98.0	97.7	97.4
1997	...	98.0	98.0	98.3	97.3
1998	...	96.7	96.6	96.3	95.5
1999	...	95.5	96.1	96.9	97.7
2000	...	98.8	98.9	101.3	101.8
2001	...	101.6	102.8	99.9	98.1
Nonmanufactured Goods	19.1	...	...	...	...
1991	...	59.2	59.5	58.9	58.6
1992	...	58.1	60.7	61.2	60.0
1993	...	60.6	60.3	58.1	55.3
1994	...	54.7	61.1	60.1	60.3
1995	...	61.7	64.4	63.9	64.8
1996	...	70.3	70.7	74.4	84.3
1997	...	69.9	66.6	68.1	66.4
1998	...	58.4	56.6	56.5	56.3
1999	...	56.5	64.2	76.8	79.9
2000	...	89.3	103.6	107.6	124.4
2001	...	108.1	97.9	83.1	86.8
EUROPEAN UNION	100.0	...	...	...	...
1991	...	95.2	91.6	91.7	94.0
1992	...	94.2	94.9	97.7	93.1
1993	...	92.2	92.9	92.0	91.8
1994	...	91.9	93.1	94.9	96.2
1995	...	97.7	99.5	99.7	100.4
1996	...	101.3	101.0	101.7	101.9
1997	...	100.5	100.0	99.1	100.1
1998	...	98.9	98.8	98.7	99.4
1999	...	98.8	99.1	99.9	100.3
2000	...	100.8	100.1	100.0	98.9
2001	...	99.0	98.8	98.2	98.4

Table 6-14. U.S. Import Price Indexes for Selected Categories of Goods, by Locality of Origin, 1991–2001—*Continued*

(2000=100.)

Category and year	Percent of U.S. imports 2000	Months			
		March	June	September	December
Manufactured Goods	96.9	...	...	...	...
1991	...	94.8	92.1	92.0	94.4
1992	...	95.1	95.7	98.9	93.9
1993	...	93.0	93.8	93.0	92.8
1994	...	92.9	93.9	95.8	97.1
1995	...	98.6	100.4	100.9	101.5
1996	...	102.3	101.8	102.4	102.3
1997	...	101.0	100.8	100.1	101.0
1998	...	100.4	100.6	100.5	101.5
1999	...	100.9	100.6	100.8	100.8
2000	...	100.8	99.9	99.6	98.6
2001	...	99.2	98.8	98.7	98.4
Nonmanufactured Goods	2.8	...	...	...	...
1991	...	76.8	71.8	72.4	73.8
1992	...	73.0	73.9	74.9	74.1
1993	...	74.8	72.7	70.3	67.6
1994	...	67.6	73.5	71.9	72.0
1995	...	72.8	74.5	71.2	73.0
1996	...	78.8	80.6	85.7	91.7
1997	...	89.3	82.2	76.5	78.4
1998	...	65.6	58.7	58.8	53.4
1999	...	53.6	66.6	81.3	88.7
2000	...	100.4	102.9	107.9	106.2
2001	...	96.0	99.5	89.1	99.5
LATIN AMERICA	100.0	...	...	...	...
1997	...	...	...	...	89.0
1998	...	84.3	83.9	83.0	80.4
1999	...	81.7	85.3	90.7	94.2
2000	...	98.9	100.9	103.5	99.5
2001	...	99.5	98.9	97.2	100.0
Manufactured Goods	72.9	...	...	...	...
1997	...	...	...	...	97.2
1998	...	94.8	95.0	93.8	93.5
1999	...	92.0	93.6	94.6	96.0
2000	...	98.3	99.6	101.6	102.3
2001	...	104.2	103.5	102.5	101.4
Nonmanufactured Goods	26.9	...	...	...	...
1997	...	...	...	...	70.8
1998	...	60.8	59.7	59.4	51.9
1999	...	59.3	67.2	82.1	90.2
2000	...	100.2	103.5	107.8	93.6
2001	...	89.3	89.0	86.0	97.0
JAPAN	100.0	...	...	...	...
1991	...	94.5	93.4	93.9	95.2
1992	...	95.8	95.5	96.4	97.7
1993	...	98.5	100.9	103.5	104.4
1994	...	105.2	105.8	107.0	108.0
1995	...	108.6	112.5	112.0	111.0
1996	...	110.1	108.4	107.8	106.5
1997	...	104.6	103.2	102.7	101.0
1998	...	99.8	98.2	96.8	98.0
1999	...	98.2	98.2	98.6	99.6
2000	...	99.6	100.0	99.9	99.9
2001	...	99.4	98.6	97.8	97.0
ASIAN NEWLY INDUSTRIALIZED COUNTRIES	100.0	...	...	...	...
1991	...	120.4	120.3	120.4	121.0
1992	...	121.5	121.8	121.9	121.8
1993	...	121.5	121.2	121.2	120.8
1994	...	120.7	120.4	120.2	120.2
1995	...	120.9	121.3	121.5	120.8
1996	...	120.6	119.6	118.1	117.3
1997	...	116.6	115.3	113.8	111.3
1998	...	108.7	105.2	103.0	102.0
1999	...	101.3	100.8	100.7	100.8
2000	...	100.6	99.9	100.0	99.3
2001	...	97.3	96.4	95.2	93.8

Table 6-15. U.S. Import and Export Price Indexes and Percent Changes for Selected Categories of Services, December 2000–December 2001

(2000=100.)

Category	Trade (millions of dollars)	Index		Percent change				
				Annual	Quarterly			
		September 2001	December 2001	December 2000 to December 2001	December 2000 to March 2001	March 2001 to June 2001	June 2001 to September 2001	September 2001 to December 2001
IMPORTS								
Air Freight	4 168	95.9	95.6	-3.4	-0.1	-2.9	-0.1	-0.3
Atlantic	1 519	98.0	97.5	-0.7	3.6	-4.1	0.5	-0.5
Pacific	2 412	93.8	93.5	-5.6	-2.4	-2.4	-0.5	-0.3
Air Passenger Fares	18 253	116.4	105.7	6.9	2.2	11.6	3.2	-9.2
Atlantic	11 998	124.5	96.5	1.9	2.1	23.1	4.6	-22.5
Europe	11 250	126.6	95.9	1.4	2.1	24.7	5.1	-24.2
Pacific	3 407	104.1	112.2	12.3	-2.2	4.8	1.7	7.8
Asia	2 626	102.5	113.3	12.7	-5.6	12.3	-3.8	10.5
Latin American/Caribbean	1 916	115.5	117.0	12.1	6.1	1.4	2.8	1.3
EXPORTS								
Air Freight	2 836	98.6	97.9	-1.5	0.3	-1.3	0.2	-0.7
Air Passenger Fares	20 319	102.5	98.4	0.7	1.9	0.8	2.1	-4.0
Atlantic	5 546	112.2	105.1	7.8	6.1	3.6	4.8	-6.3
Europe	5 394	112.2	106.0	9.1	6.3	3.6	4.9	-5.5
Pacific	9 563	96.9	90.7	-6.0	-0.5	-0.6	1.6	-6.4
Asia	6 581	96.6	89.7	-6.5	-0.1	-0.6	1.5	-7.1
Japan	5 473	95.1	86.4	-9.3	-0.2	-1.8	1.8	-9.1
Latin American/Caribbean	3 474	110.0	119.5	14.9	6.3	0.6	-1.1	8.6

PART SEVEN

CONSUMER EXPENDITURES

CONSUMER EXPENDITURES

HIGHLIGHTS

The principal objective of the Consumer Expenditure Survey is to collect information on the buying habits of American households. The unique aspect of the survey is that the expenditures can be shown for the different demographic characteristics of the population such as income, age, family size, regions, etc. These data are used in a variety of research projects by government, business, and academic analysts. Another very important use of the survey is to provide expenditure weights for the periodic revisions of the Consumer Price Index.

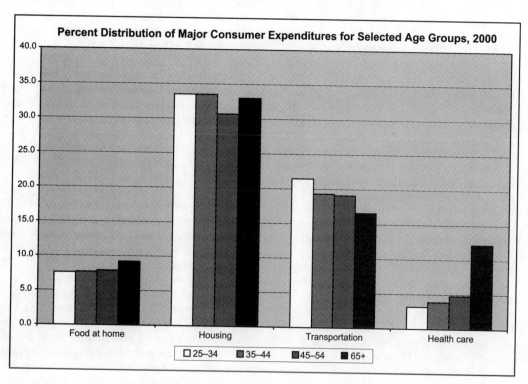

There is a stark difference in the distribution of expenditures among age groups, especially for health care. The lower share for transportation in the older age group is accounted for by lower vehicle ownership and lower gasoline consumption.

OTHER HIGHLIGHTS:

- Payments for pensions and social security are close to 10 percent of total expenditures for the 25-64 years working age group and around 3 percent for the over 65 group in 2000. (Table 7-3)
- The highest share of housing to total expenditures was in the Northeast region, closely followed by the West. Housing includes shelter and utilities. (Table 7-8)
- The highest quintile (20 percent) income group accounted for 38 percent of aggregate expenditures for all groups. The top 40 percent accounted for 60 percent of aggregate expenditures. (Table 7-2)
- In 2000, the share of transportation in total annual expenditures in rural areas was higher than in urban areas, 23.5 percent and 19 percent respectively. The health care share in rural areas was also higher, 7.3 percent to 5.2 percent. This is most likely due to the fact that the average age is higher in rural areas. (Table 7-7)
- The comparison of expenditure shares between single men and single women is influenced by the fact that income is higher for single men and the average age for single women is higher. The health share for single women is almost twice that for single men, 7.7 percent compared with 4.5 percent. The share for transportation is one third higher for single men than for single women. (Tables 7-16 and 7-17)

NOTES AND DEFINITIONS

Purpose, Collection, and Coverage

The buying habits of American consumers change over time as a result of changes in relative prices, real income, family size and composition, and other determinants of people's tastes and preferences. The introduction into the marketplace of new products and the emergence of new concepts in retailing also influence consumer buying habits. As the only national survey that can relate family expenditures to demographic characteristics, data from the Consumer Expenditure Survey (CEX) are of great importance to researchers. The survey data are also used to revise the Consumer Price Index market baskets and item samples.

The Bureau of Labor Statistics historically conducted surveys of consumer expenditures at intervals of approximately 10 years. The last such survey was conducted in 1972–73. In late 1979, in a significant departure from previous surveys, BLS initiated a survey to be conducted on a continuous basis, with rotating panels of respondents. The regular flow of data that results from this design substantially enhances the usefulness of the survey by providing more timely information on consumption patterns of different kinds of consumer units.

The current CEX is similar to its 1972–73 predecessor in that it consists of two separate components, each with its own questionnaire and sample: (1) an interview panel survey in which each consumer unit in the sample is visited by an interviewer every 3 months over a 12-month period, and (2) a diary, or record-keeping, survey, completed by other consumer units for two consecutive 1-week periods. The Bureau of the Census, under contract to BLS, collects the data for both components of the survey. Beginning in 1999, the sample was increased from 5,000 to 7,500 households.

The Interview survey is designed to collect data on the types of expenditures that respondents can be expected to recall for a period of 3 months or longer. These include relatively large expenditures—such as those for property, travel, automobiles, and major appliances—and expenditures that occur on a regular basis—such as rent, utilities, insurance premiums, and clothing. The interview also obtains "global estimates" of food expenditures both for food at home and food away from home. For food-at-home expenditures, respondents are asked to estimate the usual weekly expenditure at the grocery store, and how much of the expenditure was for nonfood items. Nonfood items are then subtracted from the total expenditure. Convenience and specialty stores are also included in the food-at-home estimates. The Interview survey collects approximately 95 percent of total expenditures. Excluded from the interview survey are nonprescription drugs, household supplies, and personal care products.

The Diary survey is designed to collect expenditures on frequently purchased items that are more difficult to recall over longer periods of time. Respondents keep detailed records of expenses for food and beverages at home and meals in eating-places away from home. Expenditures for tobacco, drugs—including nonprescription drugs—and personal care supplies and services are also collected in the diary.

Participants in both surveys record dollar amounts for goods and services purchased during the reporting period whether or not payment is made at the time of purchase. Excluded from both surveys are business-related expenditures as well as expenditures for which the family is reimbursed. At the initial interview for each survey, information is collected on demographic and family characteristics.

The tables present integrated data from the Diary and Interview surveys, providing a complete accounting of consumer expenditures and income, which neither survey component alone is designed to do. Data on some expenditure items are collected only in either the Diary or Interview survey. For example, the Diary does not collect data for expenditures on overnight travel, or information on reimbursements, as the Interview does. Examples of expenditures for which any reimbursements (e.g., from insurance) are netted out include those for medical care; auto repair; and construction, repairs, alterations, and maintenance of property.

For items unique to one or the other survey, the choice of which survey to use as the source of data is obvious. However, there is considerable overlap in coverage between the surveys. Because of this, integrating the data presents the problem of determining the appropriate survey component. When data are available from both survey sources, the more reliable of the two is selected as determined by statistical methods. As a result, some items are selected from the Interview survey and others from the Diary survey.

Data Included in this Book

The data in this edition are for the calendar year 2000 for a single characteristic or for an average of 1999 and 2000 for the tables cross-classified by two characteristics. Income values from the survey are derived from "complete income reporters" only. Complete income reporters are defined as consumer units that provide values for at least one of the major sources of their income: wages and salaries; self-employment income; retirement income; dividends and interest; and welfare benefits. Some consumer units are defined as complete income reporters even though they may not have provided a full accounting of all income from all sources.

Consumer units are classified by quintiles of income before taxes; age of reference person; size of consumer unit; region; composition of consumer unit; number of earners in consumer unit; housing tenure; race; type of area (urban or rural); and occupation.

Concepts and Definitions

A *consumer unit* comprises either (1) all members of a particular household who are related by blood, marriage, adoption, or other legal arrangements; (2) a person living alone or sharing a household with others or living as a roomer in a private home or lodging house or in permanent living quarters in a hotel or motel, but who is financially independent; or (3) two or more persons living together who pool their income to make joint expenditure decisions. Financial independence is determined by the three major expense categories: housing, food, and other living expenses. To be considered financially independent, at least two of the three major expense categories have to be provided by the respondent. The terms "family," "household," and "consumer unit" are used interchangeably in descriptions of the CEX.

The "*householder*" or "*reference person*" is the first member of the consumer unit mentioned by the respondent as owner or renter of the premises at the time of the initial interview.

Expenditures are averages for consumer units with the specified characteristics, regardless of whether a particular unit incurred an expense for that specific item or service during the record-keeping period. An individual consumer unit may have spent substantially more or substantially less than the average. The less frequently an item or service is purchased, the greater the difference between the average for all consumer units and the average of those purchasing. Income, age of family members, taste, personal preferences, and geographic location are among the factors that influence expenditures and should be considered when relating averages to individual circumstances.

Expenditures reported are the direct out-of-pocket expenditures of consumer units. Indirect expenditures may be significant for some expenditure categories, for example, utilities. Rental contracts may include some or all utilities, and renters with such contracts would record little or no direct expense for utilities. Therefore, caution should be exercised in making comparisons of expenditures for utilities by consumers of various income classes and types of housing.

Earner is a consumer unit member who reported having worked at least 1 week during the 12 months prior to the interview date.

Sources of Additional Information

A 2-year report, published biennially by the BLS, includes analytical articles, tables of integrated Diary and Interview survey data, a glossary, a description of survey methods, and a survey source of data for the integrated tables. Also see BLS news release 01-480 and Report 958.

Table 7-1. Consumer Expenditures, Averages by Income Before Taxes, 2000

Item	All consumer units	Complete reporting of income, total	Less than $5,000	$5,000 to $9,999	$10,000 to $14,999	$15,000 to $19,999	$20,000 to $29,999	$30,000 to $39,999	$40,000 to $49,999	$50,000 to $69,999	$70,000 and over
NUMBER OF CONSUMER UNITS (THOUSANDS)	109 367	81 454	3 627	7 183	8 037	6 677	12 039	9 477	7 653	11 337	15 424
CONSUMER UNIT CHARACTERISTICS											
Average Income Before Taxes[1]	$44 649	$44 649	$1 980	$7 638	$12 316	$17 319	$24 527	$34 422	$44 201	$58 561	$112 586
Age Of Reference Person	48.2	48.1	42.0	54.6	55.0	53.3	49.2	46.3	44.7	44.3	45.2
Average Number In Consumer Unit											
Persons	2.5	2.5	1.8	1.7	2.0	2.2	2.4	2.5	2.6	2.9	3.2
Children under 18	0.7	0.7	0.4	0.4	0.5	0.5	0.6	0.7	0.7	0.8	0.9
Persons 65 and over	0.3	0.3	0.2	0.5	0.5	0.6	0.4	0.3	0.2	0.1	0.1
Earners	1.4	1.4	0.9	0.5	0.7	0.9	1.2	1.4	1.5	1.8	2.1
Vehicles	1.9	1.9	1.0	0.9	1.2	1.4	1.7	1.9	2.2	2.5	2.9
PERCENT HOMEOWNER	66	65	33	42	51	58	58	63	67	79	88
With mortgage	39	39	12	7	14	20	27	38	47	60	72
Without mortgage	27	26	20	35	37	38	31	25	20	19	16
AVERAGE ANNUAL EXPENDITURES	$38 045	$40 238	$17 946	$15 703	$21 199	$24 331	$29 852	$35 609	$42 323	$49 245	$75 964
Food	5 158	5 435	2 627	2 462	2 984	3 743	4 507	5 118	6 228	6 557	8 665
Food at home	3 021	3 154	1 603	1 723	2 108	2 556	2 921	2 995	3 552	3 605	4 483
Cereals and bakery products	453	474	214	260	312	383	449	460	510	542	679
Meats, poultry, fish, and eggs	795	817	437	451	581	695	800	803	938	898	1 095
Dairy products	325	339	152	189	234	273	305	338	376	401	472
Fruits and vegetables	521	544	268	324	372	455	519	508	595	580	785
Other food at home	927	980	532	499	609	750	848	886	1 133	1 185	1 451
Food away from home	2 137	2 280	1 024	738	876	1 187	1 586	2 122	2 676	2 952	4 182
Alcoholic Beverages	372	423	231	168	227	187	301	373	393	549	788
Housing	12 319	12 527	6 670	5 559	7 576	7 995	9 372	11 115	12 872	14 914	22 932
Shelter	7 114	7 134	4 035	3 150	4 219	4 492	5 209	6 562	7 371	8 379	13 202
Owned dwellings	4 602	4 599	1 561	1 060	1 849	2 096	2 466	3 735	4 466	6 121	10 619
Rented dwellings	2 034	2 062	1 931	1 952	2 225	2 187	2 475	2 530	2 567	1 742	1 381
Other lodging	478	473	543	137	145	209	268	297	337	516	1 203
Utilities, fuels, and public services	2 489	2 487	1 468	1 559	1 881	2 084	2 224	2 444	2 596	2 873	3 543
Household operations	684	708	319	189	349	390	433	412	569	844	1 729
Housekeeping supplies	482	546	198	213	318	351	416	469	564	685	953
Household furnishings and equipment	1 549	1 652	650	448	809	677	1 089	1 228	1 772	2 132	3 504
Apparel And Services	1 856	2 004	899	852	816	1 174	1 391	1 686	1 986	2 359	4 004
Transportation	7 417	7 568	2 993	2 594	4 365	4 639	5 745	7 303	8 715	9 656	13 366
Vehicle purchases (net outlay)	3 418	3 466	953	1 175	2 265	2 120	2 545	3 380	4 261	4 408	6 015
Gasoline and motor oil	1 291	1 316	738	526	742	934	1 088	1 340	1 484	1 729	2 059
Other vehicle expenses	2 281	2 345	1 046	730	1 136	1 348	1 812	2 223	2 605	3 029	4 313
Public transportation	427	441	256	163	222	237	300	360	366	489	978
Health Care	2 066	2 120	982	1 382	1 912	1 981	2 018	1 977	2 173	2 320	2 882
Health insurance	983	985	503	658	879	928	977	953	1 031	1 083	1 259
Medical services	568	583	241	304	425	420	474	529	605	679	984
Drugs	416	447	206	358	530	550	480	411	433	423	467
Medical supplies	99	105	32	62	78	82	88	83	104	134	172
Entertainment	1 863	1 958	989	649	995	911	1 399	1 658	1 982	2 507	3 912
Personal Care Products And Services	564	595	321	298	346	413	479	522	652	718	993
Reading	146	156	64	72	81	93	127	138	151	191	294
Education	632	636	822	387	220	296	303	437	446	704	1 489
Tobacco Products And Smoking Supplies	319	333	239	270	278	277	358	357	411	384	329
Miscellaneous	776	832	355	402	423	573	692	804	1 006	1 068	1 328
Cash Contributions	1 192	1 344	423	274	375	985	1 251	1 125	1 003	1 269	3 151
Personal Insurance And Pensions	3 365	4 308	330	334	602	1 063	1 908	3 000	4 303	6 051	11 830
Life and other personal insurance	399	415	156	107	199	241	311	354	338	500	901
Pensions and Social Security	2 966	3 893	174	227	403	822	1 597	2 645	3 965	5 551	10 929

1. Components of income and taxes are derived from "complete income reporters" only.

Table 7-2. Consumer Expenditures, Averages by Quintiles of Income Before Taxes, 2000

Item	All consumer units	Complete reporting of income, total	Lowest 20 percent	Second 20 percent	Third 20 percent	Fourth 20 percent	Highest 20 percent	Incomplete reporting of income
NUMBER OF CONSUMER UNITS (THOUSANDS)	109 367	81 454	16 268	16 292	16 290	16 283	16 321	27 912
CONSUMER UNIT CHARACTERISTICS								
Average Income Before Taxes[1]	$44 649	$44 649	$7 683	$19 071	$32 910	$53 295	$110 118	(1)
Age Of Reference Person	48.2	48.1	51.9	51.7	47.0	44.4	45.3	48.4
Average Number In Consumer Unit								
Persons	2.5	2.5	1.8	2.3	2.5	2.8	3.2	2.6
Children under 18	0.7	0.7	0.4	0.6	0.7	0.8	0.9	0.7
Persons 65 and over	0.3	0.3	0.4	0.5	0.3	0.2	0.1	0.3
Earners	1.4	1.4	0.7	1.0	1.4	1.7	2.1	1.4
Vehicles	1.9	1.9	1.0	1.5	1.9	2.4	2.9	1.9
PERCENT HOMEOWNER	66	65	43	57	62	75	88	68
With mortgage	39	39	10	21	36	55	72	38
Without mortgage	27	26	32	36	25	19	16	30
AVERAGE ANNUAL EXPENDITURES	$38 045	$40 238	$17 940	$26 550	$34 716	$46 794	$75 102	$32 063
Food	5 158	5 435	2 673	4 178	5 183	6 452	8 679	4 517
Food at home	3 021	3 154	1 826	2 765	3 081	3 590	4 507	2 711
Cereals and bakery products	453	474	270	417	470	530	683	405
Meats, poultry, fish, and eggs	795	817	492	755	832	905	1 101	745
Dairy products	325	339	197	290	344	393	474	291
Fruits and vegetables	521	544	326	498	514	590	790	468
Other food at home	927	980	541	805	921	1 172	1 459	802
Food away from home	2 137	2 280	848	1 413	2 102	2 862	4 173	1 805
Alcoholic Beverages	372	423	206	248	366	513	780	254
Housing	12 319	12 527	6 509	8 482	10 857	14 152	22 611	11 789
Shelter	7 114	7 134	3 735	4 721	6 263	7 933	13 004	7 056
Owned dwellings	4 602	4 599	1 466	2 150	3 451	5 454	10 459	4 613
Rented dwellings	2 034	2 062	2 035	2 354	2 525	2 034	1 364	1 952
Other lodging	478	473	234	217	288	445	1 181	491
Utilities, fuels, and public services	2 489	2 487	1 632	2 113	2 400	2 766	3 522	2 494
Household operations	684	708	270	402	425	757	1 685	617
Housekeeping supplies	482	546	249	388	476	664	951	336
Household furnishings and equipment	1 549	1 652	622	858	1 293	2 032	3 450	1 285
Apparel And Services	1 856	2 004	844	1 301	1 615	2 265	3 989	1 505
Transportation	7 417	7 568	3 212	5 043	7 028	9 223	13 315	6 985
Vehicle purchases (net outlay)	3 418	3 466	1 443	2 302	3 241	4 317	6 018	3 280
Gasoline and motor oil	1 291	1 316	631	965	1 297	1 631	2 053	1 219
Other vehicle expenses	2 281	2 345	925	1 523	2 147	2 837	4 286	2 101
Public transportation	427	441	212	253	344	438	959	385
Health Care	2 066	2 120	1 470	1 988	1 964	2 312	2 864	1 919
Health insurance	983	985	690	945	943	1 090	1 254	977
Medical services	568	583	339	424	524	659	968	524
Drugs	416	447	381	534	412	438	470	339
Medical supplies	99	105	60	85	85	125	172	80
Entertainment	1 863	1 958	837	1 147	1 609	2 324	3 866	1 603
Personal Care Products And Services	564	595	318	442	534	699	983	491
Reading	146	156	73	105	136	175	291	118
Education	632	636	430	290	393	600	1 462	626
Tobacco Products And Smoking Supplies	319	333	257	317	366	390	336	276
Miscellaneous	776	832	365	595	833	1 047	1 318	619
Cash Contributions	1 192	1 344	332	1 163	953	1 217	3 050	750
Personal Insurance And Pensions	3 365	4 308	413	1 251	2 878	5 425	11 557	612
Life and other personal insurance	399	415	144	246	351	452	880	351
Pensions and Social Security	2 966	3 893	269	1 005	2 527	4 973	10 677	261

1. Components of income and taxes are derived from "complete income reporters" only.

Table 7-3. Consumer Expenditures, Averages by Age of Reference Person, 2000

Item	All consumer units	Under 25 years	25 to 34 years	35 to 44 years	45 to 54 years	55 to 64 years	65 years and over
NUMBER OF CONSUMER UNITS (THOUSANDS)	109 367	8 306	18 887	23 983	21 874	14 161	22 155
CONSUMER UNIT CHARACTERISTCS							
Average Income Before Taxes[1]	$44 649	$19 744	$45 498	$56 500	$58 889	$48 108	$25 220
Age Of Reference Person	48.2	21.3	29.8	39.5	49.4	59.1	75.0
Average Number In Consumer Unit							
Persons	2.5	1.9	2.9	3.3	2.7	2.1	1.7
Children under 18	0.7	0.4	1.1	1.3	0.6	0.2	0.1
Persons 65 and over	0.3	(2)	(2)	(2)	(2)	0.1	1.3
Earners	1.4	1.3	1.5	1.7	1.8	1.4	0.4
Vehicles	1.9	1.1	1.8	2.2	2.4	2.2	1.5
PERCENT HOMEOWNER	66	12	46	69	75	81	80
With mortgage	39	7	39	56	53	40	16
Without mortgage	27	5	7	13	22	41	63
AVERAGE ANNUAL EXPENDITURES	$38 045	$22 543	$38 945	$45 149	$46 160	$39 340	$26 533
Food	5 158	3 213	5 260	6 092	6 295	5 168	3 652
Food at home	3 021	1 643	2 951	3 484	3 657	3 071	2 448
Cereals and bakery products	453	238	429	531	560	441	376
Meats, poultry, fish, and eggs	795	437	770	918	970	832	626
Dairy products	325	175	317	383	377	321	275
Fruits and vegetables	521	253	488	552	626	558	495
Other food at home	927	541	946	1 101	1 124	918	676
Food away from home	2 137	1 569	2 309	2 607	2 638	2 097	1 205
Alcoholic Beverages	372	392	431	420	417	371	211
Housing	12 319	7 109	13 050	15 111	14 179	12 362	8 759
Shelter	7 114	4 574	7 905	8 930	8 297	6 587	4 597
Owned dwellings	4 602	634	4 142	6 433	5 964	4 780	3 043
Rented dwellings	2 034	3 618	3 514	2 067	1 614	1 123	1 140
Other lodging	478	322	248	430	719	685	413
Utilities, fuels, and public services	2 489	1 248	2 341	2 810	2 857	2 756	2 198
Household operations	684	226	871	896	583	542	661
Housekeeping supplies	482	194	437	570	532	585	421
Household furnishings and equipment	1 549	867	1 495	1 906	1 911	1 891	882
Apparel And Services	1 856	1 420	2 059	2 323	2 371	1 694	925
Transportation	7 417	5 189	8 357	8 702	8 827	7 842	4 397
Vehicle purchases (net outlay)	3 418	2 628	4 139	3 996	3 863	3 623	1 904
Gasoline and motor oil	1 291	947	1 341	1 577	1 592	1 349	735
Other vehicle expenses	2 281	1 397	2 482	2 677	2 868	2 375	1 374
Public transportation	427	216	395	451	505	495	385
Health Care	2 066	504	1 256	1 774	2 200	2 508	3 247
Health insurance	983	211	640	850	976	1 132	1 619
Medical services	568	178	367	555	699	721	672
Drugs	416	81	181	284	407	538	822
Medical supplies	99	34	69	85	118	117	133
Entertainment	1 863	1 091	1 876	2 464	2 231	1 955	1 069
Personal Care Products And Services	564	345	576	644	682	569	426
Reading	146	57	118	151	178	179	148
Education	632	1 257	585	615	1 146	380	108
Tobacco Products And Smoking Supplies	319	237	310	427	376	349	163
Miscellaneous	776	322	804	852	927	824	661
Cash Contributions	1 192	189	648	1 003	1 537	1 301	1 828
Personal Insurance And Pensions	3 365	1 216	3 614	4 570	4 795	3 838	939
Life and other personal insurance	399	54	242	412	549	587	378
Pensions and Social Security	2 966	1 162	3 373	4 158	4 246	3 252	561

1. Components of income and taxes are derived from "complete income reporters" only.
2. Value less than 0.05.

Table 7-4. Consumer Expenditures, Averages by Size of Consumer Unit, 2000

Item	All consumer units	One person	Two or more persons	Two persons	Three persons	Four persons	Five or more persons
NUMBER OF CONSUMER UNITS (THOUSANDS)	109 367	32 323	77 044	33 312	16 840	15 836	11 056
CONSUMER UNIT CHARACTERISTICS							
Average Income Before Taxes[1]	$44 649	$24 977	$53 314	$47 121	$54 600	$63 959	$54 746
Age Of Reference Person	48.2	51.9	46.6	53.0	43.4	40.8	40.7
Average Number In Consumer Unit							
Persons	2.5	1.0	3.1	2.0	3.0	4.0	5.6
Children under 18	0.7	...	0.9	0.1	0.8	1.6	2.8
Persons 65 and over	0.3	0.3	0.3	0.5	0.2	0.1	0.1
Earners	1.4	0.6	1.7	1.2	1.8	2.0	2.3
Vehicles	1.9	1.0	2.3	2.1	2.3	2.5	2.5
PERCENT HOMEOWNER	66	50	72	74	68	74	70
With mortgage	39	20	47	37	47	60	56
Without mortgage	27	31	25	37	20	14	14
AVERAGE ANNUAL EXPENDITURES	$38 045	$23 059	$44 251	$38 627	$45 156	$52 032	$49 100
Food	5 158	2 825	6 088	5 104	6 093	7 122	7 833
Food at home	3 021	1 477	3 634	2 894	3 687	4 247	5 111
Cereals and bakery products	453	221	546	421	550	647	805
Meats, poultry, fish, and eggs	795	352	971	774	1 007	1 109	1 366
Dairy products	325	162	389	306	395	449	566
Fruits and vegetables	521	279	617	522	611	695	826
Other food at home	927	462	1 111	872	1 124	1 346	1 549
Food away from home	2 137	1 348	2 454	2 210	2 407	2 875	2 722
Alcoholic Beverages	372	325	390	429	411	329	318
Housing	12 319	8 189	14 040	12 096	14 193	16 921	15 585
Shelter	7 114	5 054	7 979	6 936	8 023	9 510	8 862
Owned dwellings	4 602	2 332	5 555	4 535	5 338	7 351	6 385
Rented dwellings	2 034	2 435	1 866	1 765	2 160	1 665	2 009
Other lodging	478	287	558	636	525	494	467
Utilities, fuels, and public services	2 489	1 628	2 850	2 545	2 839	3 156	3 348
Household operations	684	387	809	501	921	1 308	846
Housekeeping supplies	482	224	585	515	553	663	755
Household furnishings and equipment	1 549	895	1 818	1 600	1 857	2 283	1 775
Apparel And Services	1 856	1 028	2 191	1 679	2 259	2 729	2 946
Transportation	7 417	3 732	8 963	7 529	9 721	10 711	9 629
Vehicle purchases (net outlay)	3 418	1 456	4 241	3 397	4 805	5 282	4 435
Gasoline and motor oil	1 291	682	1 547	1 307	1 572	1 813	1 850
Other vehicle expenses	2 281	1 272	2 704	2 324	2 879	3 146	2 955
Public transportation	427	322	471	501	465	469	389
Health Care	2 066	1 488	2 307	2 596	2 080	2 143	2 018
Health insurance	983	657	1 119	1 241	1 031	1 062	970
Medical services	568	418	631	663	575	651	588
Drugs	416	351	443	560	377	325	359
Medical supplies	99	62	114	132	97	104	101
Entertainment	1 863	1 026	2 212	1 821	2 192	2 797	2 598
Personal Care Products And Services	564	338	656	575	693	736	738
Reading	146	113	160	173	145	168	134
Education	632	407	726	476	841	952	986
Tobacco Products And Smoking Supplies	319	203	367	318	399	389	436
Miscellaneous	776	561	866	855	794	990	831
Cash Contributions	1 192	1 047	1 254	1 497	1 144	1 116	887
Personal Insurance And Pensions	3 365	1 778	4 031	3 480	4 191	4 930	4 160
Life and other personal insurance	399	155	501	484	480	560	499
Pensions and Social Security	2 966	1 623	3 530	2 996	3 711	4 370	3 661

1. Components of income and taxes are derived from "complete income reporters" only.

Table 7-5. Consumer Expenditures, Averages by Composition of Consumer Unit, 2000

Item	All consumer units	Husband and wife consumer units						Other husband and wife consumer units	One parent, at least one child under 18 years	Single person and other consumer units
		Total	Husband and wife only	Husband and wife with children						
				Total	Oldest child under 6 years	Oldest child 6 to 17 years	Oldest child 18 years or over			
NUMBER OF CONSUMER UNITS (THOUSANDS)	109 367	56 287	22 805	28 777	5 291	15 396	8 090	4 705	6 132	46 948
CONSUMER UNIT CHARACTERISTICS										
Average Income Before Taxes[1]	$44 649	$60 588	$53 232	$66 913	$62 928	$69 472	$64 725	$56 796	$25 095	$28 969
Age Of Reference Person	48.2	48.2	56.7	41.5	32.2	39.6	51.2	47.9	36.6	49.6
Average Number In Consumer Unit										
Persons	2.5	3.2	2.0	3.9	3.5	4.1	3.8	4.9	2.9	1.6
Children under 18	0.7	0.9	...	1.6	1.5	2.1	0.6	1.5	1.8	0.2
Persons 65 and over	0.3	0.3	0.6	0.1	(2)	(2)	0.2	0.5	(2)	0.3
Earners	1.4	1.7	1.2	2.0	1.7	1.9	2.6	2.4	1.0	1.0
Vehicles	1.9	2.6	2.4	2.7	2.2	2.6	3.2	2.8	1.1	1.3
PERCENT HOMEOWNER	66	81	85	79	68	79	87	78	37	51
With mortgage	39	53	41	63	62	66	59	54	28	23
Without mortgage	27	28	44	16	6	13	28	24	9	28
AVERAGE ANNUAL EXPENDITURES	$38 045	$48 619	$42 196	$53 586	$50 756	$54 170	$54 550	$49 646	$28 923	$26 524
Food	5 158	6 575	5 575	7 251	5 817	7 508	7 858	7 506	4 255	3 557
Food at home	3 021	3 892	3 155	4 357	3 659	4 458	4 724	4 815	2 647	2 010
Cereals and bakery products	453	590	456	680	542	702	749	723	388	295
Meats, poultry, fish, and eggs	795	1 018	846	1 113	819	1 155	1 271	1 333	754	529
Dairy products	325	420	335	481	415	497	505	474	279	214
Fruits and vegetables	521	665	578	710	619	717	771	839	408	361
Other food at home	927	1 199	940	1 373	1 265	1 388	1 428	1 446	818	610
Food away from home	2 137	2 683	2 420	2 894	2 158	3 050	3 134	2 692	1 608	1 547
Alcoholic Beverages	372	420	461	396	375	365	477	362	187	338
Housing	12 319	15 204	12 832	17 132	18 702	17 433	15 537	14 891	10 732	9 062
Shelter	7 114	8 536	7 153	9 693	10 398	10 035	8 581	8 155	6 331	5 512
Owned dwellings	4 602	6 505	5 234	7 587	7 864	7 937	6 743	6 050	2 797	2 556
Rented dwellings	2 034	1 355	1 121	1 502	2 162	1 543	993	1 590	3 315	2 681
Other lodging	478	675	798	604	372	556	845	516	219	275
Utilities, fuels, and public services	2 489	3 006	2 689	3 180	2 804	3 193	3 401	3 485	2 335	1 889
Household operations	684	911	533	1 221	2 380	1 183	534	850	786	399
Housekeeping supplies	482	647	573	703	618	724	730	669	368	297
Household furnishings and equipment	1 549	2 103	1 884	2 336	2 502	2 297	2 291	1 732	912	965
Apparel And Services	1 856	2 312	1 725	2 749	2 590	2 838	2 698	2 552	1 921	1 294
Transportation	7 417	9 910	8 309	11 088	10 745	10 644	12 158	10 470	5 017	4 742
Vehicle purchases (net outlay)	3 418	4 709	3 824	5 365	5 594	5 102	5 716	4 989	2 338	2 011
Gasoline and motor oil	1 291	1 697	1 411	1 879	1 594	1 866	2 092	1 966	894	857
Other vehicle expenses	2 281	2 984	2 493	3 352	3 150	3 192	3 793	3 112	1 518	1 539
Public transportation	427	520	581	491	407	485	558	403	267	335
Health Care	2 066	2 640	3 044	2 306	1 897	2 251	2 681	2 727	1 014	1 514
Health insurance	983	1 288	1 479	1 131	1 025	1 078	1 303	1 318	453	686
Medical services	568	717	738	698	548	731	732	733	363	416
Drugs	416	504	671	361	241	327	509	572	145	347
Medical supplies	99	132	157	116	84	115	138	104	54	65
Entertainment	1 863	2 454	1 968	2 864	2 191	3 250	2 586	2 304	1 433	1 211
Personal Care Products And Services	564	700	611	769	649	774	845	723	569	397
Reading	146	182	197	176	174	174	181	141	76	114
Education	632	811	447	1 126	420	1 032	1 769	651	395	448
Tobacco Products And Smoking Supplies	319	343	286	358	275	336	455	533	299	292
Miscellaneous	776	908	878	893	687	960	909	1 140	784	616
Cash Contributions	1 192	1 512	1 915	1 220	848	1 270	1 370	1 339	407	912
Personal Insurance And Pensions	3 365	4 648	3 949	5 257	5 388	5 334	5 027	4 308	1 834	2 027
Life and other personal insurance	399	608	613	601	482	590	702	629	150	179
Pensions and Social Security	2 966	4 039	3 335	4 656	4 906	4 744	4 325	3 679	1 683	1 848

1. Components of income and taxes are derived from "complete income reporters" only.
2. Value less than 0.05.

Table 7-6. Consumer Expenditures, Averages by Number of Earners, 2000

Item	All consumer units	Single consumers		Consumer units of two or more persons			
		No earner	One earner	No earner	One earner	Two earners	Three or more earners
NUMBER OF CONSUMER UNITS (THOUSANDS)	109 367	12 527	19 796	9 430	20 782	36 285	10 546
CONSUMER UNIT CHARACTERISTICS							
Average Income Before Taxes[1]	$44 649	$13 847	$31 246	$22 208	$42 133	$62 951	$68 931
Age Of Reference Person	48.2	68.8	41.2	65.4	46.4	42.1	45.7
Average Number In Consumer Unit							
Persons	2.5	1.0	1.0	2.3	3.0	3.1	4.4
Children under 18	0.7	...	...	0.3	1.1	1.0	1.2
Persons 65 and over	0.3	0.7	0.1	1.3	0.3	0.1	0.1
Earners	1.4	...	1.0	...	1.0	2.0	3.3
Vehicles	1.9	0.8	1.2	1.7	1.9	2.4	3.2
PERCENT HOMEOWNER	66	62	43	77	65	73	79
With mortgage	39	9	27	18	38	56	58
Without mortgage	27	53	16	60	27	17	21
AVERAGE ANNUAL EXPENDITURES	$38 045	$17 273	$26 657	$27 644	$37 924	$48 923	$55 810
Food	5 158	2 184	3 201	4 340	5 328	6 430	8 151
Food at home	3 021	1 507	1 460	2 956	3 379	3 640	4 825
Cereals and bakery products	453	237	211	444	514	541	731
Meats, poultry, fish, and eggs	795	366	344	790	907	965	1 311
Dairy products	325	170	158	328	365	392	490
Fruits and vegetables	521	305	265	571	579	601	801
Other food at home	927	429	482	823	1 015	1 141	1 493
Food away from home	2 137	678	1 741	1 385	1 949	2 790	3 326
Alcoholic Beverages	372	173	415	242	274	458	535
Housing	12 319	6 835	9 041	8 981	12 840	15 570	15 691
Shelter	7 114	3 793	5 851	4 495	7 344	9 007	8 808
Owned dwellings	4 602	1 895	2 609	2 876	4 732	6 436	6 540
Rented dwellings	2 034	1 705	2 897	1 140	2 121	1 981	1 617
Other lodging	478	194	345	478	491	590	651
Utilities, fuels, and public services	2 489	1 621	1 633	2 369	2 702	2 899	3 402
Household operations	684	607	249	438	702	1 030	588
Housekeeping supplies	482	220	227	495	534	609	691
Household furnishings and equipment	1 549	593	1 082	1 184	1 558	2 025	2 201
Apparel And Services	1 856	612	1 275	952	1 922	2 456	2 981
Transportation	7 417	2 178	4 715	4 980	7 148	9 948	12 716
Vehicle purchases (net outlay)	3 418	806	1 868	2 240	3 291	4 727	6 234
Gasoline and motor oil	1 291	403	859	880	1 292	1 680	2 187
Other vehicle expenses	2 281	731	1 614	1 488	2 178	3 015	3 764
Public transportation	427	238	374	372	388	526	531
Health Care	2 066	2 172	1 056	3 413	2 136	2 129	2 273
Health insurance	983	1 009	435	1 652	1 041	1 029	1 108
Medical services	568	508	361	696	585	637	641
Drugs	416	578	209	902	417	353	399
Medical supplies	99	77	52	164	93	110	125
Entertainment	1 863	663	1 253	1 145	1 958	2 498	2 697
Personal Care Products And Services	564	277	375	478	572	700	837
Reading	146	96	124	141	139	176	168
Education	632	163	561	121	640	755	1 337
Tobacco Products And Smoking Supplies	319	166	226	228	335	383	503
Miscellaneous	776	409	656	611	741	963	1 005
Cash Contributions	1 192	1 189	956	1 606	1 096	1 225	1 347
Personal Insurance And Pensions	3 365	156	2 803	406	2 795	5 233	5 571
Life and other personal insurance	399	135	167	380	488	502	632
Pensions and Social Security	2 966	[2]21	2 636	[2]26	2 307	4 732	4 939

1. Components of income and taxes are derived from "complete income reporters" only.
2. Data are likely to have large sampling errors.

Table 7-7. Consumer Expenditures, Averages by Housing Tenure, Type of Area, Race and Hispanic Origin of Reference Person, 2000

Item	All consumer units	Housing tenure		Type of area		Race of consumer unit		Hispanic origin of consumer unit	
		Homeowner	Renter	Urban	Rural	White and Other	Black	Hispanic	Non-hispanic
NUMBER OF CONSUMER UNITS (THOUSANDS)	109 367	71 834	37 532	95 627	13 740	96 137	13 230	9 473	99 894
CONSUMER UNIT CHARACTERISTICS									
Average Income Before Taxes[1]	$44 649	$53 447	$28 448	$45 877	$35 941	$46 260	$32 657	$34 891	$45 669
Age Of Reference Person	48.2	52.3	40.3	47.8	51.0	48.5	45.4	42.8	48.7
Average Number In Consumer Unit									
Persons	2.5	2.6	2.3	2.5	2.5	2.5	2.7	3.4	2.4
Children under 18	0.7	0.7	0.7	0.7	0.6	0.6	0.9	1.2	0.6
Persons 65 and over	0.3	0.4	0.2	0.3	0.4	0.3	0.2	0.2	0.3
Earners	1.4	1.4	1.2	1.4	1.3	1.4	1.3	1.6	1.3
Vehicles	1.9	2.3	1.2	1.9	2.4	2.0	1.3	1.6	2.0
PERCENT HOMEOWNER	66	100	...	63	83	68	46	47	68
With mortgage	39	59	...	39	38	40	29	29	40
Without mortgage	27	41	...	24	45	28	17	18	28
AVERAGE ANNUAL EXPENDITURES	$38 045	$43 603	$27 406	$38 942	$31 831	$39 406	$28 152	$32 735	$38 549
Food	5 158	5 698	4 124	5 254	4 500	5 304	4 095	5 362	5 139
Food at home	3 021	3 326	2 436	3 054	2 797	3 066	2 691	3 496	2 977
Cereals and bakery products	453	503	358	459	418	462	393	491	450
Meats, poultry, fish, and eggs	795	856	679	804	734	780	909	1 036	773
Dairy products	325	364	250	326	316	336	245	359	321
Fruits and vegetables	521	569	428	534	431	530	454	670	507
Other food at home	927	1 034	722	931	898	959	691	940	926
Food away from home	2 137	2 371	1 688	2 200	1 703	2 238	1 404	1 865	2 162
Alcoholic Beverages	372	393	331	390	247	394	211	285	380
Housing	12 319	13 874	9 341	12 828	8 775	12 651	9 906	10 850	12 458
Shelter	7 114	7 627	6 133	7 521	4 282	7 312	5 678	6 437	7 178
Owned dwellings	4 602	6 976	59	4 790	3 294	4 877	2 607	2 949	4 759
Rented dwellings	2 034	47	5 836	2 226	701	1 923	2 843	3 307	1 913
Other lodging	478	603	238	505	287	512	227	181	506
Utilities, fuels, and public services	2 489	2 917	1 669	2 494	2 453	2 478	2 571	2 170	2 519
Household operations	684	852	364	722	424	714	468	465	705
Housekeeping supplies	482	579	297	488	443	507	303	474	483
Household furnishings and equipment	1 549	1 899	878	1 603	1 173	1 640	887	1 303	1 572
Apparel And Services	1 856	2 052	1 482	1 931	1 343	1 878	1 695	2 076	1 836
Transportation	7 417	8 530	5 289	7 410	7 467	7 721	5 214	6 719	7 484
Vehicle purchases (net outlay)	3 418	3 916	2 465	3 370	3 751	3 574	2 285	3 146	3 444
Gasoline and motor oil	1 291	1 475	939	1 260	1 507	1 337	956	1 244	1 296
Other vehicle expenses	2 281	2 653	1 570	2 323	1 992	2 361	1 705	1 945	2 313
Public transportation	427	485	314	457	216	448	268	385	431
Health Care	2 066	2 561	1 117	2 028	2 328	2 198	1 107	1 243	2 144
Health insurance	983	1 227	516	958	1 152	1 030	639	600	1 019
Medical services	568	702	311	570	550	620	191	364	587
Drugs	416	512	233	399	537	441	235	211	436
Medical supplies	99	120	57	100	89	107	41	69	102
Entertainment	1 863	2 229	1 163	1 872	1 802	1 980	1 014	1 186	1 928
Personal Care Products And Services	564	628	441	584	426	555	627	564	564
Reading	146	173	95	153	101	157	72	59	155
Education	632	645	607	679	302	666	383	363	657
Tobacco Products And Smoking Supplies	319	311	334	310	378	329	243	173	332
Miscellaneous	776	917	505	786	704	804	572	602	792
Cash Contributions	1 192	1 505	593	1 249	802	1 260	700	645	1 244
Personal Insurance And Pensions	3 365	4 087	1 983	3 467	2 655	3 510	2 313	2 608	3 437
Life and other personal insurance	399	527	153	403	371	404	358	189	419
Pensions and Social Security	2 966	3 560	1 830	3 064	2 284	3 105	1 955	2 420	3 018

1. Components of income and taxes are derived from "complete income reporters" only.

Table 7-8. Consumer Expenditures, Averages by Region of Residence, 2000

Item	All consumer units	Northeast	Midwest	South	West
NUMBER OF CONSUMER UNITS (THOUSANDS)	109 367	20 994	25 717	38 245	24 410
CONSUMER UNIT CHARACTERISTICS					
Average Income Before Taxes[1]	$44 649	$47 439	$44 377	$41 984	$46 670
Age Of Reference Person	48.2	49.5	48.4	48.3	46.6
Average Number In Consumer Unit					
Persons	2.5	2.5	2.5	2.5	2.6
Children under 18	0.7	0.6	0.7	0.7	0.7
Persons 65 and over	0.3	0.3	0.3	0.3	0.3
Earners	1.4	1.3	1.4	1.3	1.4
Vehicles	1.9	1.6	2.2	1.9	2.0
PERCENT HOMEOWNER	66	62	70	68	60
With mortgage	39	35	41	38	40
Without mortgage	27	27	29	30	20
AVERAGE ANNUAL EXPENDITURES	$38 045	$38 902	$39 213	$34 707	$41 328
Food	5 158	5 377	5 255	4 724	5 554
Food at home	3 021	3 202	2 933	2 823	3 269
Cereals and bakery products	453	491	444	422	480
Meats, poultry, fish, and eggs	795	883	721	779	821
Dairy products	325	354	330	286	356
Fruits and vegetables	521	579	482	470	592
Other food at home	927	895	957	867	1 021
Food away from home	2 137	2 175	2 322	1 901	2 285
Alcoholic Beverages	372	390	388	304	449
Housing	12 319	13 505	11 961	10 855	13 972
Shelter	7 114	8 222	6 633	5 839	8 667
Owned dwellings	4 602	5 229	4 599	3 803	5 320
Rented dwellings	2 034	2 434	1 531	1 643	2 832
Other lodging	478	559	503	393	515
Utilities, fuels, and public services	2 489	2 570	2 513	2 596	2 226
Household operations	684	643	670	645	796
Housekeeping supplies	482	530	514	440	472
Household furnishings and equipment	1 549	1 540	1 631	1 334	1 811
Apparel And Services	1 856	2 115	1 917	1 617	1 945
Transportation	7 417	6 664	7 841	7 211	7 943
Vehicle purchases (net outlay)	3 418	2 719	3 759	3 566	3 430
Gasoline and motor oil	1 291	1 094	1 352	1 290	1 400
Other vehicle expenses	2 281	2 251	2 327	2 073	2 586
Public transportation	427	600	403	283	527
Health Care	2 066	1 862	2 172	2 147	2 001
Health insurance	983	908	1 047	1 063	853
Medical services	568	504	575	533	669
Drugs	416	349	439	470	368
Medical supplies	99	101	111	82	111
Entertainment	1 863	1 915	2 040	1 617	2 021
Personal Care Products And Services	564	578	544	550	594
Reading	146	172	164	114	158
Education	632	823	667	477	674
Tobacco Products And Smoking Supplies	319	326	360	334	245
Miscellaneous	776	738	798	729	859
Cash Contributions	1 192	1 064	1 615	953	1 233
Personal Insurance And Pensions	3 365	3 371	3 490	3 077	3 679
Life and other personal insurance	399	423	429	407	333
Pensions and Social Security	2 966	2 948	3 061	2 670	3 346

1. Components of income and taxes are derived from "complete income reporters" only.

Table 7-9. Consumer Expenditures, Averages by Occupation of Reference Person, 2000

Item	All consumer units	Self-employed workers	Wage and salary earners						Retired	All other, including not reporting
			Total wage and salary earners	Managers and Professionals	Technical sales and clerical workers	Service workers	Construction workers and mechanics	Operators fabricators and laborers		
NUMBER OF CONSUMER UNITS (THOUSANDS)	109 367	5 736	72 083	25 361	20 832	9 925	5 089	10 876	19 499	12 048
CONSUMER UNIT CHARACTERISTICS										
Average Income Before Taxes[1]	$44 649	$58 847	$51 905	$73 811	$43 489	$31 940	$45 903	$37 547	$22 306	$27 663
Age Of Reference Person	48.2	50.5	41.5	43.1	39.8	41.0	41.2	41.7	72.9	46.7
Average Number In Consumer Unit										
Persons	2.5	2.5	2.7	2.6	2.6	2.7	3.0	2.9	1.7	2.7
Children under 18	0.7	0.6	0.8	0.8	0.8	0.8	0.9	0.9	0.1	0.8
Persons 65 and over	0.3	0.3	0.1	0.1	0.1	0.1	0.1	0.1	1.2	0.2
Earners	1.4	1.7	1.8	1.7	1.7	1.7	1.9	1.8	0.2	0.7
Vehicles	1.9	2.3	2.1	2.2	1.9	1.7	2.5	2.2	1.5	1.5
PERCENT HOMEOWNER	66	80	63	73	57	49	69	59	81	53
With mortgage	39	46	46	58	42	30	51	39	17	27
Without mortgage	27	34	17	15	15	19	18	20	64	25
AVERAGE ANNUAL EXPENDITURES	$38 045	$48 986	$41 875	$54 185	$37 354	$30 279	$40 598	$32 948	$25 938	$29 329
Food	5 158	6 131	5 562	6 487	5 102	4 789	5 402	5 028	3 686	4 567
Food at home	3 021	3 424	3 127	3 397	2 866	2 908	3 157	3 148	2 453	3 078
Cereals and bakery products	453	512	465	511	428	430	449	463	374	479
Meats, poultry, fish, and eggs	795	862	824	826	757	801	939	906	636	839
Dairy products	325	369	332	364	310	303	337	321	277	333
Fruits and vegetables	521	642	519	592	465	472	471	511	487	527
Other food at home	927	1 039	986	1 103	906	902	961	948	680	900
Food away from home	2 137	2 707	2 434	3 090	2 235	1 881	2 245	1 881	1 233	1 489
Alcoholic Beverages	372	430	428	572	377	292	468	300	226	229
Housing	12 319	15 223	13 418	17 877	12 026	9 791	11 597	9 818	8 663	10 266
Shelter	7 114	8 551	7 936	10 603	7 126	5 843	6 988	5 621	4 413	5 886
Owned dwellings	4 602	6 233	5 138	7 627	4 147	3 035	4 772	3 320	2 937	3 319
Rented dwellings	2 034	1 510	2 293	2 139	2 587	2 577	1 843	2 041	1 098	2 250
Other lodging	478	808	505	837	392	230	373	260	379	318
Utilities, fuels, and public services	2 489	3 000	2 564	2 934	2 445	2 176	2 580	2 278	2 179	2 297
Household operations	684	950	727	1 172	618	355	477	350	574	482
Housekeeping supplies	482	584	499	642	443	370	355	447	436	403
Household furnishings and equipment	1 549	2 138	1 692	2 525	1 394	1 049	1 196	1 123	1 060	1 197
Apparel And Services	1 856	1 999	2 137	2 742	1 919	1 618	2 122	1 626	926	1 566
Transportation	7 417	8 729	8 497	10 073	7 782	6 245	10 330	7 387	4 399	5 215
Vehicle purchases (net outlay)	3 418	3 901	3 985	4 497	3 686	2 864	5 769	3 552	1 866	2 310
Gasoline and motor oil	1 291	1 569	1 457	1 586	1 355	1 170	1 747	1 478	761	1 026
Other vehicle expenses	2 281	2 711	2 600	3 259	2 369	1 924	2 541	2 147	1 404	1 588
Public transportation	427	548	455	731	372	287	273	210	368	290
Health Care	2 066	3 020	1 737	2 199	1 562	1 321	1 598	1 442	3 172	1 788
Health insurance	983	1 529	819	1 002	744	632	795	720	1 580	733
Medical services	568	822	528	729	459	361	470	373	668	522
Drugs	416	547	298	344	277	261	259	285	793	454
Medical supplies	99	123	92	124	83	67	75	63	130	78
Entertainment	1 863	2 424	2 105	2 826	1 835	1 356	2 010	1 664	1 105	1 372
Personal Care Products And Services	564	626	616	751	585	547	499	481	427	433
Reading	146	193	152	234	134	84	100	83	142	97
Education	632	598	773	1 152	755	416	473	387	123	628
Tobacco Products And Smoking Supplies	319	325	344	231	341	396	515	489	179	387
Miscellaneous	776	1 343	806	959	742	644	916	668	609	597
Cash Contributions	1 192	2 079	1 074	1 775	796	484	674	697	1 681	688
Personal Insurance And Pensions	3 365	5 867	4 226	6 307	3 399	2 295	3 895	2 876	600	1 497
Life and other personal insurance	399	683	408	606	324	258	336	275	338	308
Pensions and Social Security	2 966	5 184	3 819	5 701	3 075	2 037	3 560	2 601	262	1 189

1. Components of income and taxes are derived from "complete income reporters" only.

Table 7-10. Consumer Expenditures, Averages for Age Groups by Income Before Taxes, 1999–2000: Reference Person Under Age 25

Item	Complete reporting of income							
	Complete reporting of income, total	Less than $5,000	$5,000 to $9,999	$10,000 to $14,999	$15,000 to $19,999	$20,000 to $29,999	$30,000 to $39,999	$40,000 and over
NUMBER OF CONSUMER UNITS (THOUSANDS)	6 192	1 302	1 115	909	675	929	587	674
CONSUMER UNIT CHARACTERISTICS								
Average Income Before Taxes[1]	$19 018	$2 753	$7 077	$12 138	$17 065	$23 894	$34 222	$61 471
Age Of Reference Person	21.4	20.3	21.0	21.5	21.5	22.1	22.1	22.6
Average Number In Consumer Unit								
Persons	1.8	1.3	1.4	1.6	2.0	2.1	2.5	2.8
Children under 18	0.4	0.1	0.3	0.4	0.4	0.5	0.6	0.6
Earners	1.3	1.0	1.0	1.1	1.4	1.5	1.7	2.1
Vehicles	1.2	0.6	0.7	1.0	1.2	1.4	1.9	2.2
PERCENT HOMEOWNER	12	4	6	6	9	12	22	36
With mortgage	7	(4)	1	1	4	8	19	31
Without mortgage	4	4	6	4	5	4	3	4
AVERAGE ANNUAL EXPENDITURES	$23 146	$11 954	$14 865	$18 820	$21 656	$28 009	$33 285	$48 220
Food	3 303	1 856	2 200	2 833	3 347	3 797	4 262	5 902
Food at home	1 689	853	1 131	1 505	1 959	1 814	2 051	3 143
Cereals and bakery products	247	129	153	241	287	251	287	480
Meats, poultry, fish, and eggs	431	173	283	396	464	472	481	898
Dairy products	184	91	123	153	234	193	257	324
Fruits and vegetables	261	135	168	226	281	293	310	500
Other food at home	566	324	403	489	694	605	717	940
Food away from home	1 614	1 003	1 069	1 328	1 388	1 983	2 211	2 760
Alcoholic Beverages	421	281	327	257	444	512	565	674
Housing	6 931	3 670	4 652	5 717	7 046	8 511	9 484	13 862
Shelter	4 369	2 478	3 083	3 629	4 630	5 239	6 030	8 237
Owned dwellings	589	144	118	120	293	516	1 134	2 782
Rented dwellings	3 500	1 721	2 721	3 327	4 104	4 605	4 728	5 258
Other lodging	280	613	244	182	233	118	168	198
Utilities, fuels, and public services	1 200	526	883	1 137	1 228	1 490	1 712	2 237
Household operations	218	79	73	183	194	353	321	519
Housekeeping supplies	221	99	118	141	226	283	259	493
Household furnishings and equipment	924	487	496	628	769	1 146	1 162	2 376
Apparel And Services	1 363	655	1 062	1 126	1 038	2 043	1 554	2 372
Transportation	5 375	2 173	2 562	4 650	4 858	6 756	8 761	12 840
Vehicle purchases (net outlay)	2 887	1 070	1 053	2 778	2 385	3 708	4 534	7 519
Gasoline and motor oil	850	472	595	722	908	1 003	1 353	1 465
Other vehicle expenses	1 424	462	737	943	1 425	1 848	2 639	3 415
Public transportation	214	169	178	207	140	196	234	442
Health Care	573	170	231	403	439	934	1 035	1 356
Health insurance	238	56	68	168	208	331	511	629
Medical services	200	55	75	98	125	451	312	457
Drugs	95	43	61	116	81	106	141	166
Medical supplies	39	[5]15	26	20	[5]25	46	70	104
Entertainment	1 164	697	877	1 049	973	1 216	1 767	2 247
Personal Care Products And Services	360	226	254	243	324	465	555	601
Reading	67	38	63	58	75	70	100	103
Education	1 294	1 643	1 641	1 019	1 028	810	1 082	1 526
Tobacco Products And Smoking Supplies	242	116	143	266	250	334	377	361
Miscellaneous	344	106	271	207	445	446	428	794
Cash Contributions	223	147	153	160	167	222	258	603
Personal Insurance And Pensions	1 486	177	429	832	1 223	1 893	3 057	4 979
Life and other personal insurance	54	[5]7	[5]21	[5]23	34	75	134	162
Pensions and Social Security	1 432	171	408	808	1 188	1 818	2 923	4 817

1. Components of income and taxes are derived from "complete income reporters" only.
2. Value less than 0.05.
3. No data reported.
4. Value less than 0.5.
5. Data are likely to have large sampling errors.

Table 7-11. Consumer Expenditures, Averages for Age Groups by Income Before Taxes, 1999–2000: Reference Person Age 25–34

Item	Complete reporting of income, total	Less than $5,000	$5,000 to $9,999	$10,000 to $14,999	$15,000 to $19,999	$20,000 to $29,999	$30,000 to $39,999	$40,000 to $49,999	$50,000 to $69,999	$70,000 and over
NUMBER OF CONSUMER UNITS (THOUSANDS)	14 708	503	726	1 158	1 132	2 348	2 065	1 741	2 535	2 500
CONSUMER UNIT CHARACTERISTICS										
Average Income Before Taxes[1]	$43 966	$1 790	$7 594	$12 434	$17 113	$24 701	$34 330	$44 114	$58 061	$101 455
Age Of Reference Person	29.8	29.4	29.4	29.2	29.5	29.5	29.7	29.8	29.9	30.6
Average Number In Consumer Unit										
Persons	2.9	2.8	2.5	2.9	2.7	2.8	2.8	2.8	3.0	3.0
Children under 18	1.1	1.4	1.3	1.4	1.2	1.2	1.0	1.0	1.1	1.0
Persons 65 and over	(2)	(2)	(2)	(2)	(2)	(2)	(2)	(2)	(2)	(2)
Earners	1.5	1.0	0.8	1.2	1.2	1.4	1.5	1.6	1.8	1.9
Vehicles	1.8	1.0	0.8	1.2	1.3	1.5	1.8	2.0	2.3	2.4
PERCENT HOMEOWNER	45	20	19	22	24	35	43	47	60	73
With mortgage	39	12	5	13	17	26	36	43	56	69
Without mortgage	7	8	13	9	8	9	7	4	5	4
AVERAGE ANNUAL EXPENDITURES	$40 001	$21 292	$17 133	$22 527	$24 693	$28 765	$34 615	$41 641	$48 023	$70 199
Food	5 485	3 355	3 603	3 583	4 052	4 673	5 004	5 780	6 192	7 762
Food at home	3 020	2 010	2 296	2 517	2 642	2 887	2 638	3 110	3 407	3 671
Cereals and bakery products	444	260	330	342	378	431	387	480	506	537
Meats, poultry, fish, and eggs	782	605	567	733	768	780	720	745	834	905
Dairy products	333	234	287	259	233	306	302	354	396	396
Fruits and vegetables	490	397	413	422	455	459	411	463	527	639
Other food at home	971	514	700	762	808	911	818	1 068	1 145	1 193
Food away from home	2 466	1 345	1 307	1 066	1 410	1 786	2 365	2 670	2 785	4 091
Alcoholic Beverages	448	284	247	282	292	324	374	364	485	832
Housing	13 084	7 644	5 977	8 031	7 849	9 439	11 478	13 396	15 591	22 794
Shelter	7 822	4 953	3 379	4 735	4 742	5 583	7 005	8 184	9 118	13 730
Owned dwellings	4 048	1 185	473	1 099	930	1 734	2 977	3 912	5 572	10 052
Rented dwellings	3 525	3 527	2 838	3 538	3 722	3 729	3 871	4 095	3 280	3 004
Other lodging	249	[3]241	[3]68	98	90	121	157	177	266	674
Utilities, fuels, and public services	2 295	1 561	1 497	1 793	1 894	1 997	2 199	2 323	2 635	3 087
Household operations	867	336	309	421	407	422	488	708	1 145	2 110
Housekeeping supplies	501	211	470	265	224	323	387	598	653	789
Household furnishings and equipment	1 599	585	321	818	583	1 115	1 398	1 583	2 041	3 078
Apparel And Services	2 217	1 786	1 154	1 477	1 305	1 727	2 146	1 971	2 398	3 663
Transportation	7 982	4 626	2 826	4 724	5 518	5 641	7 096	8 703	9 152	14 014
Vehicle purchases (net outlay)	3 919	2 488	[3]1 302	2 521	2 978	2 582	3 381	4 401	4 077	7 243
Gasoline and motor oil	1 229	613	511	851	929	1 049	1 165	1 275	1 548	1 738
Other vehicle expenses	2 445	1 292	866	1 189	1 415	1 770	2 225	2 643	3 092	4 193
Public transportation	390	232	148	163	196	240	325	383	434	840
Health Care	1 265	443	387	827	810	1 068	1 128	1 431	1 734	1 789
Health insurance	635	204	155	380	437	543	612	723	860	885
Medical services	372	157	101	254	193	343	292	427	515	537
Drugs	185	63	98	140	144	139	169	203	243	247
Medical supplies	73	[3]18	[3]32	52	36	44	55	77	116	120
Entertainment	1 959	761	854	1 173	1 045	1 344	1 504	2 106	2 536	3 528
Personal Care Products And Services	578	373	329	366	431	423	492	673	699	861
Reading	126	51	37	63	58	93	107	126	165	234
Education	544	871	604	249	631	421	318	658	518	802
Tobacco Products And Smoking Supplies	309	266	259	301	275	328	333	326	330	282
Miscellaneous	834	306	379	308	490	682	907	950	1 112	1 198
Cash Contributions	746	[3]240	[3]61	241	518	374	552	613	910	1 822
Personal Insurance And Pensions	4 423	285	416	902	1 419	2 227	3 177	4 544	6 199	10 618
Life and other personal insurance	239	131	75	86	85	155	151	196	366	503
Pensions and Social Security	4 183	154	341	817	1 334	2 072	3 026	4 348	5 833	10 115

1. Components of income and taxes are derived from "complete income reporters" only.
2. Value less than 0.05.
3. Data are likely to have large sampling errors.

Table 7-12. Consumer Expenditures, Averages for Age Groups by Income Before Taxes, 1999–2000: Reference Person Age 35–44

Item	Complete reporting of income, total				Complete reporting of income				
		Less than $5,000	$5,000 to $9,999	$10,000 to $14,999	$15,000 to $19,999	$20,000 to $29,999	$30,000 to $39,999	$40,000 to $49,999	$50,000 to $69,999	$70,000 and over
NUMBER OF CONSUMER UNITS (THOUSANDS)	18 103	504	821	880	1 023	2 320	2 256	2 048	3 398	4 853
CONSUMER UNIT CHARACTERISTICS										
Average Income Before Taxes[1]	$55 026	$765	$7 654	$12 488	$17 494	$24 570	$34 365	$44 233	$58 794	$110 392
Age Of Reference Person	39.5	39.1	39.5	39.6	39.2	39.3	39.5	39.2	39.5	39.9
Average Number In Consumer Unit										
Persons	3.2	2.6	2.5	2.9	3.0	3.1	3.0	3.0	3.3	3.6
Children under 18	1.3	1.1	0.9	1.3	1.2	1.3	1.2	1.2	1.3	1.5
Persons 65 and over	(2)	(2)	(2)	(2)	(2)	(2)	(2)	(2)	(2)	(2)
Earners	1.7	1.2	0.9	1.1	1.4	1.5	1.7	1.7	1.9	2.1
Vehicles	2.2	1.4	1.0	1.2	1.5	1.8	2.1	2.3	2.5	2.8
PERCENT HOMEOWNER	67	42	28	39	40	51	61	67	80	89
With mortgage	56	27	13	21	26	36	47	57	71	80
Without mortgage	12	15	16	18	14	16	14	10	9	9
AVERAGE ANNUAL EXPENDITURES	$46 786	$24 376	$17 769	$20 886	$25 344	$29 178	$36 118	$42 259	$50 386	$75 911
Food	6 443	4 543	3 715	3 474	4 754	4 408	5 378	6 653	6 985	8 959
Food at home	3 666	3 187	2 745	2 380	3 167	2 802	3 155	3 794	3 989	4 580
Cereals and bakery products	573	476	439	387	474	427	499	548	653	721
Meats, poultry, fish, and eggs	930	1 039	865	674	882	817	824	983	1 007	1 023
Dairy products	418	322	284	267	334	306	371	413	486	525
Fruits and vegetables	583	534	430	344	518	457	519	617	575	749
Other food at home	1 161	817	727	708	958	796	941	1 231	1 269	1 562
Food away from home	2 777	1 355	969	1 094	1 587	1 606	2 223	2 859	2 996	4 378
Alcoholic Beverages	458	414	138	152	157	254	287	474	517	769
Housing	14 836	8 725	6 814	7 764	8 742	9 591	11 061	12 765	15 257	24 213
Shelter	8 701	5 256	3 963	4 701	5 112	5 629	6 606	7 646	8 912	14 081
Owned dwellings	6 212	2 506	1 039	1 797	2 122	2 657	3 833	4 933	6 864	12 024
Rented dwellings	2 093	2 472	2 821	2 841	2 891	2 841	2 613	2 453	1 635	1 195
Other lodging	396	[3]277	104	63	99	131	160	260	413	863
Utilities, fuels, and public services	2 700	1 978	1 784	1 984	2 090	2 254	2 412	2 553	2 853	3 490
Household operations	899	282	270	198	340	278	443	540	873	1 994
Housekeeping supplies	655	370	261	302	385	389	515	547	805	999
Household furnishings and equipment	1 882	839	535	580	816	1 041	1 086	1 479	1 814	3 648
Apparel And Services	2 394	1 811	1 102	1 064	1 846	1 523	1 808	2 124	2 439	3 776
Transportation	8 671	3 596	2 584	4 004	4 504	6 084	7 788	8 529	9 472	13 096
Vehicle purchases (net outlay)	4 057	[3]888	953	2 026	2 039	2 990	3 815	4 203	4 393	6 032
Gasoline and motor oil	1 459	946	672	748	983	1 130	1 378	1 526	1 650	1 906
Other vehicle expenses	2 727	1 516	809	1 001	1 341	1 755	2 294	2 521	3 035	4 319
Public transportation	427	246	150	229	141	209	301	278	394	838
Health Care	1 757	933	670	902	843	1 256	1 480	1 687	2 099	2 532
Health insurance	803	429	240	352	389	611	698	844	940	1 135
Medical services	555	318	225	226	218	380	464	469	649	860
Drugs	297	157	182	208	211	207	260	288	379	372
Medical supplies	102	[3]28	[3]22	116	25	57	58	86	130	165
Entertainment	2 564	1 304	822	897	1 037	1 265	1 738	2 038	3 081	4 473
Personal Care Products And Services	670	455	320	313	406	442	545	666	706	1 012
Reading	165	87	47	57	54	104	114	129	191	287
Education	602	296	174	258	141	317	398	443	622	1 148
Tobacco Products And Smoking Supplies	424	475	563	468	504	436	432	479	443	324
Miscellaneous	982	620	264	542	649	670	917	1 056	1 024	1 410
Cash Contributions	1 040	622	136	194	361	381	784	518	1 130	2 125
Personal Insurance And Pensions	5 780	495	420	796	1 347	2 448	3 387	4 697	6 420	11 787
Life and other personal insurance	422	272	84	94	183	201	299	287	468	791
Pensions and Social Security	5 358	224	336	702	1 164	2 247	3 088	4 411	5 952	10 996

1. Components of income and taxes are derived from "complete income reporters" only.
2. Value less than 0.05.
3. Data are likely to have large sampling errors.

Table 7-13. Consumer Expenditures, Averages for Age Groups by Income Before Taxes, 1999–2000: Reference Person Age 45–54

Item	Complete reporting of income, total	Complete reporting of income								
		Less than $5,000	$5,000 to $9,999	$10,000 to $14,999	$15,000 to $19,999	$20,000 to $29,999	$30,000 to $39,999	$40,000 to $49,999	$50,000 to $69,999	$70,000 and over
NUMBER OF CONSUMER UNITS (THOUSANDS)	15 628	444	723	824	786	1 636	1 917	1 661	2 806	4 830
CONSUMER UNIT CHARACTERISTICS										
Average Income Before Taxes[1]	$59 351	$-1 294	$7 662	$12 240	$17 157	$24 683	$34 388	$44 262	$58 467	$114 932
Age Of Reference Person	49.3	49.7	49.7	49.2	49.1	49.2	49.4	49.3	49.2	49.2
Average Number In Consumer Unit										
Persons	2.7	2.2	2.1	2.3	2.4	2.5	2.3	2.5	2.9	3.1
Children under 18	0.6	0.6	0.5	0.5	0.6	0.6	0.5	0.5	0.6	0.7
Persons 65 and over	(2)	(2)	(2)	0.1	0.1	(2)	(2)	(2)	(2)	(2)
Earners	1.8	0.9	0.8	1.1	1.3	1.4	1.6	1.7	2.1	2.3
Vehicles	2.4	1.3	1.1	1.6	1.5	1.9	2.2	2.3	2.7	3.2
PERCENT HOMEOWNER	75	43	36	47	52	61	68	74	86	93
With mortgage	54	24	13	24	23	36	48	58	63	76
Without mortgage	20	19	23	22	29	25	21	16	23	17
AVERAGE ANNUAL EXPENDITURES	$49 411	$21 475	$18 708	$22 487	$23 740	$30 706	$36 874	$42 819	$49 327	$78 928
Food	6 440	3 095	3 345	3 676	3 389	4 755	5 134	6 023	6 715	9 236
Food at home	3 718	2 127	2 437	2 516	2 404	3 268	3 183	3 673	3 756	4 814
Cereals and bakery products	568	272	402	357	361	478	464	547	566	765
Meats, poultry, fish, and eggs	956	555	723	686	666	941	831	978	918	1 180
Dairy products	391	231	268	256	256	340	344	376	383	513
Fruits and vegetables	632	338	409	441	422	554	539	625	619	827
Other food at home	1 171	732	635	775	697	955	1 005	1 148	1 269	1 530
Food away from home	2 722	968	909	1 160	985	1 487	1 951	2 351	2 959	4 421
Alcoholic Beverages	412	230	128	293	151	252	349	291	352	689
Housing	14 662	8 535	6 898	7 793	8 072	9 687	11 691	13 124	14 044	22 380
Shelter	8 513	5 112	3 986	4 365	4 548	5 594	6 915	7 711	7 813	13 162
Owned dwellings	6 117	2 490	1 610	1 759	1 706	2 977	4 409	5 211	6 122	10 637
Rented dwellings	1 658	2 378	2 261	2 464	2 640	2 424	2 239	2 095	1 114	880
Other lodging	738	244	115	142	202	193	266	406	576	1 645
Utilities, fuels, and public services	2 826	1 943	1 733	2 051	2 132	2 275	2 491	2 710	2 990	3 580
Household operations	613	248	187	286	143	302	284	508	501	1 179
Housekeeping supplies	633	297	283	358	226	484	588	575	690	888
Household furnishings and equipment	2 078	936	710	733	1 024	1 032	1 413	1 619	2 050	3 571
Apparel And Services	2 391	545	1 012	1 109	1 234	1 848	1 943	1 845	2 146	3 849
Transportation	9 090	3 820	2 826	4 401	4 751	6 070	7 223	8 668	9 814	13 505
Vehicle purchases (net outlay)	4 082	[3]1 289	[3]1 251	1 959	2 110	2 797	3 328	4 124	4 574	5 879
Gasoline and motor oil	1 489	820	549	950	876	1 103	1 278	1 424	1 687	2 004
Other vehicle expenses	3 044	1 576	870	1 304	1 592	1 925	2 333	2 846	3 173	4 689
Public transportation	476	135	156	187	173	245	283	274	380	932
Health Care	2 231	1 412	966	1 383	1 220	1 505	1 831	2 250	2 337	3 143
Health insurance	947	530	475	508	536	642	790	1 061	1 064	1 255
Medical services	741	479	207	321	255	399	548	702	685	1 234
Drugs	422	349	259	492	386	372	411	396	434	471
Medical supplies	121	[3]54	[3]25	62	44	93	82	92	154	182
Entertainment	2 378	1 114	679	1 110	823	1 277	1 855	1 702	2 631	3 891
Personal Care Products And Services	688	295	496	337	371	596	508	621	662	996
Reading	203	81	68	64	78	111	145	170	207	343
Education	1 083	565	215	225	188	398	560	441	974	2 276
Tobacco Products And Smoking Supplies	403	400	407	469	458	453	394	423	404	362
Miscellaneous	1 130	288	903	368	632	643	804	1 018	1 088	1 799
Cash Contributions	1 670	[3]636	312	180	759	630	855	1 036	1 267	3 498
Personal Insurance And Pensions	6 631	460	454	1 080	1 614	2 481	3 582	5 206	6 686	12 962
Life and other personal insurance	594	196	144	292	216	259	326	399	515	1 144
Pensions and Social Security	6 037	264	310	788	1 398	2 222	3 255	4 806	6 171	11 817

1. Components of income and taxes are derived from "complete income reporters" only.
2. Value less than 0.05.
3. Data are likely to have large sampling errors.

Table 7-14. Consumer Expenditures, Averages for Age Groups by Income Before Taxes, 1999–2000: Reference Person Age 55–64

Item	Complete reporting of income, total	Less than $5,000	$5,000 to $9,999	$10,000 to $14,999	$15,000 to $19,999	$20,000 to $29,999	$30,000 to $39,999	$40,000 to $49,999	$50,000 to $69,999	$70,000 and over
				Complete reporting of income						
NUMBER OF CONSUMER UNITS (THOUSANDS)	9 959	435	875	899	727	1 488	1 078	961	1 330	2 166
CONSUMER UNIT CHARACTERISTICS										
Average Income Before Taxes[1]	$48 764	$1 830	$7 509	$12 392	$17 275	$24 593	$34 323	$44 477	$59 096	$119 876
Age Of Reference Person	59.2	59.4	60.2	59.8	59.6	59.7	59.0	59.2	58.8	58.4
Average Number In Consumer Unit										
Persons	2.1	1.8	1.7	2.0	2.0	2.0	2.1	2.1	2.3	2.5
Children under 18	0.2	0.2	0.2	0.2	0.2	0.2	0.2	0.2	0.2	0.2
Persons 65 and over	0.1	0.1	0.1	0.1	0.1	0.1	0.1	0.1	0.1	0.1
Earners	1.3	0.8	0.5	0.7	1.0	1.1	1.4	1.5	1.7	2.0
Vehicles	2.2	1.4	1.2	1.7	1.8	2.1	2.1	2.4	2.7	3.0
PERCENT HOMEOWNER	80	55	55	65	76	80	86	81	89	93
With mortgage	41	19	14	18	29	36	44	40	56	64
Without mortgage	39	36	41	47	46	44	42	42	33	29
AVERAGE ANNUAL EXPENDITURES	$42 213	$23 262	$17 103	$22 367	$22 913	$30 028	$35 630	$40 540	$49 559	$78 593
Food	5 355	3 101	2 400	3 163	3 453	4 741	4 833	5 844	6 267	8 387
Food at home	3 151	2 140	1 699	2 235	2 320	3 230	2 987	3 612	3 457	4 221
Cereals and bakery products	453	308	266	316	349	476	461	498	490	582
Meats, poultry, fish, and eggs	822	533	468	625	642	859	794	984	806	1 087
Dairy products	332	181	173	242	232	318	331	386	370	451
Fruits and vegetables	579	417	291	392	387	502	502	649	665	832
Other food at home	965	700	501	660	709	1 001	898	1 095	1 125	1 269
Food away from home	2 204	962	701	928	1 133	1 511	1 846	2 232	2 810	4 166
Alcoholic Beverages	375	149	101	218	144	264	227	264	651	698
Housing	12 689	9 376	6 130	7 715	7 849	9 451	11 189	11 890	15 063	21 495
Shelter	6 826	4 941	3 300	4 235	4 096	4 740	6 332	6 029	7 685	12 125
Owned dwellings	4 877	2 631	1 604	1 998	2 585	3 244	4 918	4 078	5 756	9 529
Rented dwellings	1 216	2 079	1 456	1 965	1 303	1 113	1 006	1 530	963	799
Other lodging	733	231	239	273	208	383	408	421	965	1 798
Utilities, fuels, and public services	2 669	2 089	1 749	2 060	2 282	2 329	2 598	2 715	2 859	3 670
Household operations	540	664	155	187	308	386	356	379	467	1 212
Housekeeping supplies	658	343	305	352	481	574	585	581	741	1 134
Household furnishings and equipment	1 997	1 339	620	881	683	1 423	1 319	2 185	3 311	3 352
Apparel And Services	1 874	794	679	640	992	1 175	1 575	1 449	2 101	4 093
Transportation	7 635	3 747	3 368	4 444	4 086	5 311	6 995	8 036	9 057	13 507
Vehicle purchases (net outlay)	3 412	[2]1 393	[2]1 546	2 172	[2]1 255	2 070	3 223	3 828	3 809	6 396
Gasoline and motor oil	1 256	861	601	739	1 026	1 053	1 287	1 296	1 573	1 803
Other vehicle expenses	2 421	1 279	975	1 317	1 619	1 935	2 117	2 501	2 971	4 063
Public transportation	546	214	246	216	186	252	368	412	704	1 244
Health Care	2 572	1 854	1 506	1 799	2 062	2 477	2 519	2 630	2 998	3 434
Health insurance	1 094	890	542	695	922	1 140	1 122	1 199	1 310	1 356
Medical services	783	553	632	448	527	626	744	683	926	1 200
Drugs	552	333	274	557	537	591	524	563	584	662
Medical supplies	143	[2]77	58	99	75	120	129	185	178	216
Entertainment	2 288	1 616	796	1 561	963	1 929	1 720	2 109	2 311	4 342
Personal Care Products And Services	597	380	269	391	407	537	566	554	697	938
Reading	201	94	103	87	106	147	181	193	238	369
Education	425	[2]271	[2]97	264	107	130	157	243	368	1 206
Tobacco Products And Smoking Supplies	362	401	303	336	290	354	378	461	398	345
Miscellaneous	959	568	534	392	415	867	939	925	1 179	1 579
Cash Contributions	1 811	[2]293	383	598	684	634	1 005	1 500	1 910	4 863
Personal Insurance And Pensions	5 068	617	434	757	1 353	2 010	3 346	4 443	6 320	13 338
Life and other personal insurance	622	242	137	371	315	405	567	505	781	1 233
Pensions and Social Security	4 446	375	296	387	1 038	1 605	2 779	3 938	5 539	12 105

1. Components of income and taxes are derived from "complete income reporters" only.
2. Data are likely to have large sampling errors.

Table 7-15. Consumer Expenditures, Averages for Age Groups by Income Before Taxes, 1999–2000: Reference Person Age 65 and Over

Item	Complete reporting of income, total	Complete reporting of income								
		Less than $5,000	$5,000 to $9,999	$10,000 to $14,999	$15,000 to $19,999	$20,000 to $29,999	$30,000 to $39,999	$40,000 to $49,999	$50,000 to $69,999	$70,000 and over
NUMBER OF CONSUMER UNITS (THOUSANDS)	16 983	579	3 125	3 668	2 494	3 077	1 561	807	839	833
CONSUMER UNIT CHARACTERISTICS										
Average Income Before Taxes[1]	$25 903	$2 924	$7 867	$12 306	$17 462	$24 325	$34 602	$44 512	$58 529	$133 355
Age Of Reference Person	74.8	75.2	76.9	76.3	74.6	74.0	73.2	72.3	71.7	71.7
Average Number In Consumer Unit										
Persons	1.7	1.4	1.3	1.4	1.7	1.9	2.0	1.9	2.1	2.4
Children under 18	0.1	(2)	0.0	(2)	0.1	0.1	0.1	(2)	0.1	0.2
Persons 65 and over	1.3	1.2	1.1	1.2	1.4	1.5	1.5	1.5	1.5	1.5
Earners	0.4	0.3	0.2	0.2	0.3	0.4	0.7	0.7	1.1	1.3
Vehicles	1.5	0.9	0.8	1.2	1.5	1.8	2.0	2.4	2.5	2.8
PERCENT HOMEOWNER	79	63	63	76	83	87	86	91	92	93
With mortgage	16	14	7	13	18	18	19	20	27	38
Without mortgage	63	49	56	62	66	69	68	72	66	55
AVERAGE ANNUAL EXPENDITURES	$27 925	$17 244	$13 277	$19 407	$25 283	$29 721	$34 193	$41 539	$51 569	$79 921
Food	3 715	2 574	1 995	2 522	3 554	4 117	5 244	5 755	6 391	7 722
Food at home	2 427	1 780	1 550	1 857	2 453	2 696	3 304	3 442	3 703	3 834
Cereals and bakery products	376	274	261	289	387	423	530	490	558	521
Meats, poultry, fish, and eggs	605	490	394	475	622	642	826	760	929	990
Dairy products	273	192	160	218	281	304	367	393	426	431
Fruits and vegetables	488	320	309	371	481	563	656	737	706	784
Other food at home	684	505	425	504	682	763	926	1 061	1 085	1 110
Food away from home	1 288	794	445	665	1 102	1 422	1 939	2 312	2 688	3 888
Alcoholic Beverages	216	105	39	162	141	217	306	388	578	661
Housing	9 067	6 538	5 219	7 200	8 499	9 347	9 854	12 194	13 948	24 472
Shelter	4 614	3 668	2 811	3 805	4 336	4 799	5 114	6 160	6 652	11 257
Owned dwellings	3 034	1 789	1 393	2 356	2 839	3 346	3 389	4 106	5 205	8 592
Rented dwellings	1 151	1 527	1 326	1 285	1 208	955	1 035	1 257	597	864
Other lodging	429	352	92	164	289	497	691	797	850	1 801
Utilities, fuels, and public services	2 192	1 698	1 598	1 921	2 131	2 398	2 482	2 717	2 960	3 544
Household operations	756	497	229	400	630	574	413	994	1 389	5 197
Housekeeping supplies	454	271	205	322	416	530	541	681	859	1 070
Household furnishings and equipment	1 052	403	375	752	986	1 046	1 305	1 642	2 088	3 403
Apparel And Services	1 105	615	453	622	1 182	915	1 298	1 655	1 910	4 681
Transportation	4 559	2 105	1 855	3 452	4 270	4 816	5 653	8 253	8 667	11 449
Vehicle purchases (net outlay)	1 977	[3]511	849	1 655	1 933	1 841	2 061	4 251	3 341	5 545
Gasoline and motor oil	696	481	317	501	637	820	969	1 124	1 255	1 362
Other vehicle expenses	1 475	829	546	1 096	1 324	1 701	2 142	2 255	3 105	3 080
Public transportation	410	284	143	200	377	454	481	623	966	1 461
Health Care	3 259	2 190	2 004	2 691	3 532	3 710	3 981	3 982	4 592	5 336
Health insurance	1 629	980	1 105	1 387	1 619	1 863	2 060	2 025	2 091	2 624
Medical services	664	643	264	466	752	699	915	763	1 360	1 390
Drugs	809	457	544	711	992	979	809	877	923	1 111
Medical supplies	158	110	91	128	170	168	197	317	217	211
Entertainment	1 184	800	431	732	964	1 316	1 559	1 861	2 294	3 907
Personal Care Products And Services	453	316	250	357	421	504	570	652	754	914
Reading	167	91	78	124	149	196	217	256	288	391
Education	121	[3]136	27	51	41	92	181	94	450	705
Tobacco Products And Smoking Supplies	166	109	143	146	157	180	148	224	230	264
Miscellaneous	753	625	286	447	652	761	766	1 018	1 117	3 573
Cash Contributions	2 014	547	328	655	1 304	2 754	2 910	3 178	5 920	7 984
Personal Insurance And Pensions	1 145	494	169	244	414	797	1 506	2 031	4 429	7 863
Life and other personal insurance	388	261	149	204	277	477	634	573	760	1 184
Pensions and Social Security	757	233	20	41	137	320	873	1 459	3 670	6 678

1. Components of income and taxes are derived from "complete income reporters" only.
2. Value less than 0.05.
3. Data are likely to have large sampling errors.

Table 7-16. Consumer Expenditures, Averages for Single Men by Income Before Taxes, 1999–2000

Item	All single men	Complete reporting of income, total	Less than $5,000	$5,000 to $9,999	$10,000 to $14,999	$15,000 to $19,999	$20,000 to $29,999	$30,000 to $39,999	$40,000 and over
		Complete reporting of income							
NUMBER OF CONSUMER UNITS (THOUSANDS)	13 667	10 641	980	1 516	1 516	946	1 705	1 378	2 599
CONSUMER UNIT CHARACTERISTICS									
Average Income Before Taxes[1]	$29 267	$29 267	$1 784	$7 493	$12 126	$17 049	$24 453	$33 922	$67 472
Age Of Reference Person	45.1	45.2	33.2	48.5	51.4	46.3	46.0	43.8	43.8
Average Number In Consumer Unit									
Persons	1.0	1.0	1.0	1.0	1.0	1.0	1.0	1.0	1.0
Children under 18	...	...	...	...	...	...	...	...	...
Persons 65 and over	0.2	0.2	0.1	0.3	0.4	0.3	0.2	0.1	0.1
Earners	0.7	0.8	0.8	0.5	0.5	0.7	0.8	0.9	0.9
Vehicles	1.3	1.3	0.8	0.8	1.2	1.1	1.5	1.6	1.7
PERCENT HOMEOWNER	43	43	19	28	43	36	45	51	57
With mortgage	21	21	4	4	9	11	21	33	42
Without mortgage	23	22	15	25	34	25	24	18	15
AVERAGE ANNUAL EXPENDITURES	$24 760	$26 327	$13 298	$13 034	$17 757	$18 472	$23 992	$29 510	$46 515
Food	3 110	3 299	1 956	1 923	2 395	2 750	3 182	3 817	5 027
Food at home	1 386	1 485	891	1 061	1 463	1 436	1 604	1 527	1 841
Cereals and bakery products	202	216	127	153	215	230	218	223	268
Meats, poultry, fish, and eggs	346	369	191	276	382	332	419	394	441
Dairy products	147	158	94	122	169	147	172	159	189
Fruits and vegetables	238	253	118	185	240	249	291	258	318
Other food at home	452	488	360	325	457	478	503	493	625
Food away from home	1 724	1 814	1 065	862	932	1 314	1 578	2 290	3 185
Alcoholic Beverages	493	548	361	297	379	389	517	509	945
Housing	8 210	8 370	4 844	4 527	5 996	6 298	7 922	8 709	14 162
Shelter	5 401	5 424	3 237	3 033	3 793	3 987	4 956	5 813	9 221
Owned dwellings	2 281	2 261	617	750	1 311	1 195	1 878	2 614	4 770
Rented dwellings	2 738	2 749	1 953	2 103	2 334	2 699	2 895	2 961	3 477
Other lodging	382	414	667	180	149	94	183	238	973
Utilities, fuels, and public services	1 491	1 520	824	1 015	1 381	1 353	1 579	1 698	2 087
Household operations	283	300	170	92	236	165	308	157	629
Housekeeping supplies	178	203	89	99	134	154	266	168	332
Household furnishings and equipment	857	922	525	288	451	639	812	874	1 893
Apparel And Services	836	904	369	587	487	496	971	1 111	1 526
Transportation	4 571	4 648	2 233	2 183	3 925	3 396	4 735	6 227	6 976
Vehicle purchases (net outlay)	2 000	1 985	[2]789	[2]781	2 097	1 359	2 100	3 024	2 676
Gasoline and motor oil	796	821	596	491	638	735	822	1 046	1 115
Other vehicle expenses	1 482	1 545	633	771	1 018	1 170	1 555	1 836	2 621
Public transportation	292	297	215	140	172	133	257	320	564
Health Care	1 121	1 210	362	972	1 487	1 057	1 294	1 065	1 587
Health insurance	488	514	149	425	625	480	562	458	649
Medical services	374	418	129	288	452	294	457	380	622
Drugs	211	228	67	221	345	259	230	193	228
Medical supplies	48	51	[2]16	37	65	23	44	34	88
Entertainment	1 244	1 328	764	646	956	760	1 253	1 509	2 313
Personal Care Products And Services	226	234	144	149	159	225	222	272	346
Reading	108	117	46	73	88	84	126	113	194
Education	502	519	1 411	673	416	420	377	195	453
Tobacco Products And Smoking Supplies	271	279	231	275	295	297	307	338	233
Miscellaneous	636	673	204	182	230	379	547	1 080	1 364
Cash Contributions	1 151	1 319	163	137	343	803	610	1 498	3 572
Personal Insurance And Pensions	2 282	2 879	210	408	604	1 119	1 930	3 066	7 818
Life and other personal insurance	166	182	34	73	91	168	173	159	375
Pensions and Social Security	2 117	2 697	175	336	512	950	1 757	2 907	7 442

1. Components of income and taxes are derived from "complete income reporters" only.
2. Data are likely to have large sampling errors.

Table 7-17. Consumer Expenditures, Averages for Single Women by Income Before Taxes, 1999–2000

Item	All single women	Complete reporting of income						
		Complete reporting of income, total	Less than $5,000	$5,000 to $9,999	$10,000 to $14,999	$15,000 to $19,999	$20,000 to $29,999	$30,000 to $39,999	$40,000 and over
NUMBER OF CONSUMER UNITS (THOUSANDS)	18 270	13 988	1 232	3 206	2 709	1 561	2 025	1 305	1 951
CONSUMER UNIT CHARACTERISTICS									
Average Income Before Taxes[1]	$21 948	$21 948	$2 617	$7 625	$12 088	$17 286	$24 296	$34 115	$64 547
Age Of Reference Person	56.4	56.2	42.9	63.1	66.2	58.0	52.4	47.6	47.9
Average Number In Consumer Unit									
Persons	1.0	1.0	1.0	1.0	1.0	1.0	1.0	1.0	1.0
Children under 18	...	...	...	...	...	...	...	...	...
Persons 65 and over	0.4	0.4	0.2	0.6	0.7	0.5	0.3	0.2	0.1
Earners	0.5	0.6	0.6	0.3	0.3	0.6	0.8	0.9	0.9
Vehicles	0.9	0.9	0.6	0.6	0.9	0.9	1.1	1.1	1.1
PERCENT HOMEOWNER	55	54	25	48	62	62	55	55	65
With mortgage	18	18	7	5	10	19	20	32	47
Without mortgage	37	36	17	43	52	43	35	24	18
AVERAGE ANNUAL EXPENDITURES	$21 269	$22 657	$12 514	$12 567	$17 588	$22 174	$24 314	$29 852	$47 172
Food	2 475	2 555	1 816	1 859	2 241	2 571	2 783	3 332	4 026
Food at home	1 525	1 566	1 048	1 336	1 580	1 711	1 650	1 619	2 066
Cereals and bakery products	237	245	160	223	256	254	240	244	316
Meats, poultry, fish, and eggs	346	343	242	325	364	400	314	304	420
Dairy products	168	171	104	147	174	196	192	166	219
Fruits and vegetables	298	309	205	262	323	324	344	305	394
Other food at home	476	498	336	379	463	537	560	599	717
Food away from home	951	989	768	523	661	860	1 134	1 713	1 960
Alcoholic Beverages	157	166	150	69	132	120	166	322	336
Housing	8 190	8 440	4 577	4 939	6 946	8 452	9 099	11 071	16 377
Shelter	4 870	4 949	2 863	2 768	3 859	4 723	5 287	7 285	9 631
Owned dwellings	2 349	2 396	686	986	1 895	2 434	2 367	3 584	5 694
Rented dwellings	2 279	2 296	1 895	1 658	1 845	2 124	2 676	3 319	3 281
Other lodging	242	257	282	124	119	165	245	382	656
Utilities, fuels, and public services	1 664	1 694	980	1 357	1 635	1 823	1 866	1 870	2 382
Household operations	536	573	204	228	432	768	376	266	1 826
Housekeeping supplies	274	299	137	182	273	362	413	375	456
Household furnishings and equipment	847	925	393	405	748	776	1 156	1 275	2 082
Apparel And Services	1 108	1 243	717	569	630	1 241	1 293	1 765	3 357
Transportation	2 935	3 087	1 621	1 487	2 620	2 839	3 796	4 912	5 547
Vehicle purchases (net outlay)	1 093	1 155	[2]585	547	1 200	[2]903	1 250	2 107	1 918
Gasoline and motor oil	495	506	349	298	404	505	657	721	789
Other vehicle expenses	1 065	1 130	535	497	830	1 150	1 547	1 648	2 180
Public transportation	282	296	152	145	187	280	342	435	659
Health Care	1 632	1 701	848	1 466	2 209	2 031	1 630	1 369	1 954
Health insurance	747	756	351	745	1 030	878	716	587	708
Medical services	389	412	284	199	453	546	383	423	700
Drugs	416	444	185	438	621	506	448	286	421
Medical supplies	81	89	29	83	105	100	82	73	125
Entertainment	884	941	779	473	682	922	1 082	1 203	1 898
Personal Care Products And Services	417	452	277	281	391	435	512	653	767
Reading	126	134	56	72	117	131	160	204	241
Education	348	354	959	355	130	212	199	348	565
Tobacco Products And Smoking Supplies	140	139	103	116	126	164	202	136	133
Miscellaneous	593	651	218	365	386	526	705	774	1 727
Cash Contributions	940	1 107	210	302	650	1 615	779	666	3 858
Personal Insurance And Pensions	1 323	1 686	184	214	328	915	1 908	3 099	6 386
Life and other personal insurance	128	137	57	103	113	139	184	150	222
Pensions and Social Security	1 195	1 549	127	111	215	777	1 724	2 949	6 164

1. Components of income and taxes are derived from "complete income reporters" only.
2. Data are likely to have large sampling errors.

Table 7-18. Consumer Expenditures, Averages by Selected Metropolitan Statistical Areas, 1999–2000: Northeast Region

Item	Complete reporting of income				
	All consumer units in the Northeast	New York	Philadelphia	Boston	Pittsburgh
NUMBER OF CONSUMER UNITS (THOUSANDS)	20 987	7 483	2 074	2 512	1 010
CONSUMER UNIT CHARACTERISTICS					
Average Income Before Taxes[1]	$47 876	$57 063	$49 932	$49 557	$41 371
Age Of Reference Person	49.4	49.1	50.6	48.4	52.3
Average Number In Consumer Unit					
Persons	2.5	2.6	2.6	2.4	2.3
Children under 18	0.6	0.7	0.6	0.6	0.5
Persons 65 and over	0.3	0.3	0.3	0.3	0.4
Earners	1.3	1.4	1.4	1.4	1.2
Vehicles	1.6	1.4	1.7	1.5	1.7
PERCENT HOMEOWNER	63	54	75	61	73
AVERAGE ANNUAL EXPENDITURES	$38 763	$46 277	$39 666	$37 727	$35 526
Food	5 429	6 416	5 408	4 924	5 032
Food at home	3 144	3 611	3 062	2 596	2 682
Cereals and bakery products	489	555	464	400	444
Meats, poultry, fish, and eggs	857	1 049	855	702	702
Dairy products	357	392	347	298	323
Fruits and vegetables	572	695	571	506	433
Other food at home	869	920	824	689	780
Food away from home	2 285	2 805	2 346	2 328	2 350
Alcoholic Beverages	379	422	360	457	356
Housing	13 431	16 838	14 235	13 362	10 451
Shelter	8 239	10 962	8 455	8 633	5 293
Owned dwellings	5 271	6 634	6 107	5 455	3 420
Rented dwellings	2 429	3 697	1 688	2 636	1 421
Other lodging	539	630	660	543	452
Utilities, fuels, and public services	2 512	2 687	2 864	2 362	2 490
Household operations	650	915	616	667	383
Housekeeping supplies	516	544	533	384	675
Household furnishings and equipment	1 513	1 731	1 767	1 315	1 610
Apparel And Services	1 998	2 832	1 826	1 805	1 995
Transportation	6 565	7 003	6 872	6 587	6 359
Vehicle purchases (net outlay)	2 713	2 607	2 879	2 808	2 505
Gasoline and motor oil	1 000	982	931	965	1 026
Other vehicle expenses	2 283	2 513	2 576	2 214	2 465
Public transportation	569	900	487	599	363
Health Care	1 833	1 960	1 779	1 740	2 073
Entertainment	1 915	2 229	1 667	1 939	1 840
Personal Care Products And Services	569	712	597	522	562
Reading	184	214	167	202	159
Education	881	1 119	1 135	1 031	495
Tobacco Products And Smoking Supplies	322	325	306	319	388
Miscellaneous	782	902	854	598	935
Cash Contributions	1 082	1 299	1 146	854	1 458
Personal Insurance And Pensions	3 396	4 006	3 313	3 388	3 424
Life and other personal insurance	413	526	459	387	463
Pensions and Social Security	2 983	3 480	2 853	3 002	2 962

1. Components of income and taxes are derived from "complete income reporters" only.

Table 7-19. Consumer Expenditures, Averages by Selected Metropolitan Statistical Areas, 1999–2000: South Region

Item	All consumer units in the South	Complete reporting of income						
		Washington, D.C.	Baltimore	Atlanta	Miami	Tampa	Dallas-Fort Worth	Houston
NUMBER OF CONSUMER UNITS (THOUSANDS)	38 030	1 890	1 007	1 734	1 504	1 125	1 966	1 733
CONSUMER UNIT CHARACTERISTICS								
Average Income Before Taxes[1]	$41 196	$69 331	$50 813	$53 936	$46 034	$45 116	$56 046	$54 733
Age Of Reference Person	48.0	47.1	48.7	45.4	49.6	49.0	44.5	46.7
Average Number In Consumer Unit								
Persons	2.5	2.5	2.7	2.6	2.7	2.5	2.5	2.9
Children under 18	0.7	0.6	0.8	0.7	0.7	0.6	0.7	0.9
Persons 65 and over	0.3	0.3	0.3	0.2	0.4	0.3	0.2	0.3
Earners	1.3	1.5	1.3	1.4	1.4	1.3	1.5	1.5
Vehicles	1.9	1.8	1.7	1.9	1.6	1.8	2.0	2.0
PERCENT HOMEOWNER	68	66	70	71	64	71	58	61
AVERAGE ANNUAL EXPENDITURES	$34 102	$47 894	$41 725	$37 624	$39 773	$35 404	$46 600	$46 299
Food	4 670	5 705	5 531	4 689	5 560	4 589	6 865	6 080
Food at home	2 776	3 013	3 175	2 629	3 425	2 628	3 888	3 174
Cereals and bakery products	419	472	478	387	501	370	539	473
Meats, poultry, fish, and eggs	759	705	869	779	1 089	727	1 084	813
Dairy products	288	303	328	265	384	264	376	336
Fruits and vegetables	460	609	537	433	610	510	658	559
Other food at home	850	925	963	766	841	757	1 231	992
Food away from home	1 894	2 692	2 356	2 060	2 134	1 961	2 977	2 906
Alcoholic Beverages	280	470	334	322	427	326	326	609
Housing	10 598	16 978	13 779	13 663	14 535	11 258	14 339	13 870
Shelter	5 691	10 698	8 323	8 254	8 787	6 281	8 087	7 337
Owned dwellings	3 673	6 779	6 133	5 722	5 817	4 042	4 873	4 397
Rented dwellings	1 644	2 918	1 558	2 143	2 654	1 761	2 855	2 446
Other lodging	374	1 001	632	390	315	478	359	494
Utilities, fuels, and public services	2 521	2 639	2 483	3 055	2 768	2 576	3 041	2 929
Household operations	601	969	610	803	1 009	714	962	1 005
Housekeeping supplies	449	516	699	364	454	436	559	597
Household furnishings and equipment	1 337	2 157	1 664	1 188	1 516	1 250	1 690	2 002
Apparel And Services	1 617	2 059	1 894	1 873	1 950	1 101	2 429	2 376
Transportation	7 038	7 813	7 185	7 056	7 463	7 752	8 948	9 722
Vehicle purchases (net outlay)	3 516	3 222	3 214	3 194	3 023	4 130	4 441	4 813
Gasoline and motor oil	1 180	1 195	1 172	1 128	1 250	1 102	1 469	1 442
Other vehicle expenses	2 058	2 526	2 285	2 426	2 756	2 140	2 624	2 988
Public transportation	284	871	513	309	433	379	415	478
Health Care	2 052	2 222	1 843	1 910	1 746	2 388	1 963	2 195
Entertainment	1 604	2 535	2 013	1 551	1 483	1 568	2 180	2 225
Personal Care Products And Services	538	677	632	579	676	432	639	858
Reading	115	242	135	140	73	102	164	131
Education	465	724	798	342	505	427	617	460
Tobacco Products And Smoking Supplies	318	216	324	241	203	359	276	307
Miscellaneous	753	931	2 000	812	804	598	652	1 001
Cash Contributions	1 042	1 707	1 084	1 164	1 035	1 209	1 868	1 442
Personal Insurance And Pensions	3 012	5 614	4 173	3 281	3 314	3 294	5 333	5 023
Life and other personal insurance	409	716	444	423	308	643	475	459
Pensions and Social Security	2 603	4 898	3 730	2 858	3 006	2 651	4 858	4 564

1. Components of income and taxes are derived from "complete income reporters" only.

Table 7-20. Consumer Expenditures, Averages by Selected Metropolitan Statistical Areas, 1999–2000: Midwest Region

Item	Complete reporting of income								
	All consumer units in the Midwest	Chicago	Detroit	Milwaukee	Minneapolis-St.Paul	Cleveland	Cincinnati	St. Louis	Kansas City
NUMBER OF CONSUMER UNITS (THOUSANDS)	25 741	2 979	2 065	699	1 331	1 180	895	1 006	776
CONSUMER UNIT CHARACTERISTICS									
Average Income Before Taxes[1]	$43 171	$51 332	$49 041	$43 161	$60 574	$48 578	$45 737	$45 251	$51 298
Age Of Reference Person	48.4	48.0	48.3	49.7	46.5	50.8	45.8	48.7	45.6
Average Number In Consumer Unit									
Persons	2.5	2.7	2.7	2.6	2.4	2.4	2.3	2.5	2.5
Children under 18	0.7	0.8	0.9	0.7	0.6	0.6	0.6	0.7	0.7
Persons 65 and over	0.3	0.3	0.3	0.3	0.2	0.3	0.2	0.3	0.2
Earners	1.4	1.4	1.3	1.4	1.5	1.3	1.4	1.4	1.4
Vehicles	2.1	1.7	2.0	2.1	2.5	2.0	1.9	1.8	2.1
PERCENT HOMEOWNER	69	65	72	60	67	73	63	74	69
AVERAGE ANNUAL EXPENDITURES	$37 848	$43 437	$41 360	$38 877	$49 893	$38 834	$39 772	$38 935	$37 647
Food	5 059	5 452	6 040	4 627	5 794	5 274	5 492	5 619	5 302
Food at home	2 836	2 936	3 295	2 716	3 133	3 107	2 813	3 338	3 030
Cereals and bakery products	436	443	516	414	464	462	412	514	449
Meats, poultry, fish, and eggs	688	770	869	632	653	796	642	972	771
Dairy products	318	307	326	289	384	326	341	328	349
Fruits and vegetables	460	494	562	470	550	549	432	526	544
Other food at home	934	922	1 022	911	1 083	973	987	997	917
Food away from home	2 223	2 516	2 745	1 911	2 661	2 167	2 678	2 281	2 272
Alcoholic Beverages	355	422	428	518	663	315	369	324	274
Housing	11 744	15 322	13 845	13 313	15 637	12 567	12 749	11 557	11 513
Shelter	6 562	9 396	7 704	8 332	9 285	7 156	7 410	6 411	6 606
Owned dwellings	4 525	6 330	5 608	5 378	6 425	5 247	4 620	4 627	4 603
Rented dwellings	1 565	2 239	1 618	2 541	2 121	1 435	2 292	1 412	1 683
Other lodging	472	827	478	414	739	474	497	373	320
Utilities, fuels, and public services	2 457	2 796	2 637	2 271	2 414	2 584	2 411	2 668	2 645
Household operations	629	762	697	686	1 041	463	796	795	549
Housekeeping supplies	528	535	651	491	670	570	587	388	454
Household furnishings and equipment	1 569	1 833	2 157	1 533	2 226	1 795	1 545	1 294	1 259
Apparel And Services	1 772	2 095	2 498	1 862	2 266	1 815	1 802	1 944	1 722
Transportation	7 389	7 418	7 635	7 017	8 303	8 277	7 911	7 950	7 889
Vehicle purchases (net outlay)	3 570	3 374	2 871	3 369	3 312	4 253	3 872	4 345	3 824
Gasoline and motor oil	1 195	1 120	1 268	1 129	1 348	1 073	1 117	1 105	1 341
Other vehicle expenses	2 248	2 193	3 093	2 081	2 906	2 506	2 601	2 038	2 403
Public transportation	376	731	403	438	736	445	320	462	321
Health Care	2 130	2 033	1 638	2 283	2 334	1 770	1 882	2 133	1 931
Entertainment	2 070	2 054	2 071	1 927	2 959	1 861	1 961	1 877	1 864
Personal Care Products And Services	531	644	638	562	656	584	519	535	524
Reading	165	157	173	187	267	172	165	127	144
Education	617	1 022	602	726	634	535	681	687	562
Tobacco Products And Smoking Supplies	353	289	463	427	384	332	378	241	339
Miscellaneous	826	757	972	905	1 185	1 203	909	870	743
Cash Contributions	1 383	2 414	1 236	1 347	1 509	953	1 616	1 472	968
Personal Insurance And Pensions	3 454	3 358	3 122	3 176	7 302	3 176	3 339	3 599	3 873
Life and other personal insurance	403	354	376	364	491	357	398	429	449
Pensions and Social Security	3 051	3 003	2 746	2 812	6 811	2 818	2 940	3 170	3 424

1. Components of income and taxes are derived from "complete income reporters" only.

Table 7-21. Consumer Expenditures, Averages by Selected Metropolitan Statistical Areas, 1999–2000: West Region

Item	All consumer units in the West	Los Angeles	San Francisco	San Diego	Portland	Seattle	Honolulu	Anchorage	Phoenix	Denver
	Complete reporting of income									
NUMBER OF CONSUMER UNITS (THOUSANDS)	24 158	5 377	2 757	878	1 044	1 430	294	101	1 223	1 106
CONSUMER UNIT CHARACTERISTICS										
Average Income Before Taxes[1]	$47 086	$52 776	$64 818	$52 898	$49 035	$51 292	$51 906	$54 506	$47 492	$55 168
Age Of Reference Person	46.6	47.1	47.6	47.5	47.3	48.5	52.6	43.9	47.2	44.4
Average Number In Consumer Unit										
Persons	2.6	2.8	2.5	2.6	2.5	2.4	2.7	2.6	2.5	2.5
Children under 18	0.7	0.8	0.6	0.7	0.7	0.6	0.6	0.8	0.7	0.7
Persons 65 and over	0.3	0.3	0.3	0.3	0.2	0.3	0.4	0.2	0.3	0.2
Earners	1.4	1.5	1.4	1.4	1.4	1.4	1.5	1.5	1.3	1.5
Vehicles	2.0	1.9	1.8	2.0	2.2	2.3	1.6	2.5	1.8	2.3
PERCENT HOMEOWNER	60	52	60	55	64	64	56	60	64	64
AVERAGE ANNUAL EXPENDITURES	$41 933	$44 748	$55 040	$47 338	$44 331	$43 602	$41 972	$53 028	$41 991	$46 002
Food	5 508	5 490	7 442	5 243	5 655	6 543	5 771	6 964	5 486	5 676
Food at home	3 257	3 187	4 355	2 725	3 362	3 839	3 278	4 466	2 895	3 279
Cereals and bakery products	482	455	681	422	527	573	485	604	453	489
Meats, poultry, fish, and eggs	807	870	1 106	650	750	902	828	1 044	628	808
Dairy products	355	342	420	286	378	409	308	466	348	347
Fruits and vegetables	588	604	800	496	568	741	649	794	520	561
Other food at home	1 025	917	1 349	871	1 139	1 213	1 009	1 557	946	1 073
Food away from home	2 250	2 303	3 086	2 518	2 293	2 703	2 493	2 498	2 591	2 397
Alcoholic Beverages	407	337	781	406	519	427	409	591	467	621
Housing	14 086	16 550	19 682	17 011	14 654	14 644	14 084	17 504	13 123	15 773
Shelter	8 746	10 293	12 963	10 996	9 095	9 489	9 717	10 720	7 793	10 110
Owned dwellings	5 393	5 958	8 266	6 423	6 100	5 781	5 704	6 360	4 974	5 910
Rented dwellings	2 788	3 828	3 963	4 102	2 359	2 896	3 404	3 264	2 341	2 916
Other lodging	565	507	734	471	636	812	610	1 096	478	1 284
Utilities, fuels, and public services	2 202	2 290	2 226	2 104	2 344	2 225	2 113	2 485	2 599	2 311
Household operations	864	1 429	1 477	1 013	812	660	630	900	577	794
Housekeeping supplies	492	481	595	479	451	636	497	738	538	473
Household furnishings and equipment	1 781	2 056	2 421	2 419	1 953	1 634	1 127	2 661	1 616	2 084
Apparel And Services	2 021	2 450	3 137	2 020	1 517	1 917	1 974	2 490	1 979	2 178
Transportation	7 873	7 701	9 726	9 982	7 800	7 401	5 775	9 812	8 858	8 340
Vehicle purchases (net outlay)	3 462	2 933	4 409	5 323	3 304	2 766	1 553	4 276	4 223	3 257
Gasoline and motor oil	1 291	1 383	1 424	1 349	1 248	1 300	1 071	1 334	1 118	1 196
Other vehicle expenses	2 605	2 924	2 992	2 684	2 658	2 657	2 101	3 172	2 965	3 141
Public transportation	515	461	900	625	590	679	1 050	1 030	552	746
Health Care	1 982	1 833	2 030	1 927	1 984	2 514	2 211	2 530	2 168	2 045
Entertainment	2 181	1 962	2 290	2 888	2 718	2 301	1 997	3 392	2 042	2 548
Personal Care Products And Services	582	674	692	669	485	579	702	710	627	599
Reading	173	148	230	210	215	209	182	274	181	193
Education	701	695	967	575	824	609	906	701	562	617
Tobacco Products And Smoking Supplies	239	204	222	249	239	366	230	468	261	324
Miscellaneous	957	1 220	1 023	768	832	930	978	1 297	883	1 075
Cash Contributions	1 297	1 447	904	810	2 265	1 061	1 926	1 837	1 584	1 103
Personal Insurance And Pensions	3 927	4 038	5 915	4 580	4 623	4 100	4 826	4 459	3 770	4 909
Life and other personal insurance	356	370	354	545	378	421	655	496	364	524
Pensions and Social Security	3 571	3 668	5 561	4 035	4 245	3 679	4 171	3 963	3 406	4 385

1. Components of income and taxes are derived from "complete income reporters" only.

PART EIGHT

OCCUPATIONAL SAFETY AND HEALTH

OCCUPATIONAL SAFETY AND HEALTH

HIGHLIGHTS

This chapter includes data on work-related illnesses and fatal work injuries based on the Annual Survey of Occupational Injuries and Illnesses and the Census of Fatal Occupations. Data are classified by industry and selected worker characteristics. A new table shows fatal work injuries connected with the tragedy of September 11.

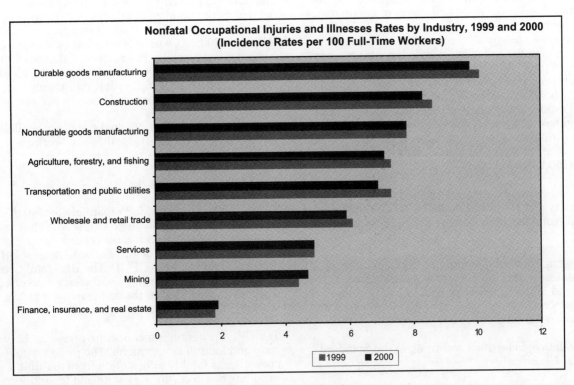

Nonfatal Occupational Injuries and Illnesses Rates by Industry, 1999 and 2000
(Incidence Rates per 100 Full-Time Workers)

The rank of the major industries continues in 2000. Declines in incidence were registered by most of the industries, but mining showed a significant increase. Durable goods manufacturing continued to have the highest incidence.

OTHER HIGHLIGHTS:

- The industry with the largest number of fatal injuries resulting from September 11 was finance, insurance, and real estate. Over 50 percent of those were in the security and commodity broker industry. (Table 8-6)
- Of the occupations affected in the service sector, fire fighting had the largest number of fatalities. (Table 8-6) Excluding September 11, the overall fatality level in 2001 was down slightly from 2000. (Table 8-4 in the fifth and sixth editions)
- Truck drivers continue to incur more workplace fatalities than any other individual occupation. (Table 8-5)
- While women accounted for 8 percent of fatal injuries in 2001, they accounted for 33 percent of non-fatal injuries in 2000. (Table 8-2 and 8-4).
- The largest number of non-fatal occupational injuries and illnesses was in manufacturing. (Table 8-1)

NOTES AND DEFINITIONS

Collection and Coverage

The Annual Survey of Occupational Injuries and Illnesses is designed to collect data on injuries and illnesses based on records that employers maintain under the Occupational Safety and Health Act of 1970. The survey sample selected by BLS consists of approximately 250,000 units in the following private industry groups: agriculture, forestry, and fishing; oil and gas extraction; construction; manufacturing; transportation and public utilities; wholesale and retail trade; finance, insurance, and real estate; and services (except private households). Excluded from the survey are self-employed individuals; farmers with fewer than 11 employees; employers regulated by other federal safety and health laws; and federal, state, and local government agencies.

Mining and railroad data are furnished to BLS by the Mine Safety and Health Administration and the Federal Railroad Administration and are included in the tabulations.

Federal grants covering a portion of the operating cost permit states to develop estimates of occupational injuries and illnesses and to provide the data from which BLS produces national results and provides technical assistance to the state agencies.

Industry data are classified according to the Standard Industrial Classification.

Concepts and Definitions

Nonfatal Occupational Injuries and Illnesses

Recordable occupational injuries and illnesses are: (1) nonfatal occupational illnesses; or (2) nonfatal occupational injuries that involve one or more of the following: loss of consciousness, restriction of work or motion, transfer to another job, or medical treatment (other than first aid). The annual survey measures only nonfatal injuries and illnesses. To better address fatalities, BLS implemented the Census of Fatal Occupational Injuries (see below).

Occupational injury is any injury—such as a cut, fracture, sprain, amputation, and so forth—that results from a work accident or from exposure involving a single incident in the work environment.

Occupational illness is an abnormal condition or disorder, other than one resulting from an occupational injury, caused by exposure to environmental factors associated with employment. It includes acute and chronic illness or disease that may be caused by inhalation, absorption, ingestion, or direct contact. Long-term latent illnesses can be difficult to relate to the workplace and are believed to be understated in this survey.

Lost workday cases are cases that involve days away from work, days of restricted work activity, or both.

The data are presented in the form of incidence rates, defined as the number of injuries and illnesses or cases of lost workdays per 100 full-time employees. The formula is (N/EH) x 200,000, where N=number of injuries and illnesses or lost workday cases, EH=total hours worked by all employees during the calendar year, and 200,000 represents the base for 100 full-time equivalent workers (working 40 hours per week, 50 weeks per year).

Comparable data for individual states are available from the BLS Office of Safety, Health, and Working Conditions.

Fatal Occupational Injuries

Data for 2001 are provided separately for fatalities resulting from the September 11 terrorist attacks. Beginning in 1992, BLS has collected a comprehensive count of work-related deaths in the Census of Fatal Occupational Injuries (CFOI). The BLS fatality census covers not only private wage and salary workers, but also workers on small farms, the self-employed and family workers, and public sector workers.

The CFOI program is a cooperative venture between the state and federal governments. The program collects and cross checks fatality information from multiple sources, including death certificates, state and federal workers' compensation reports, Occupational Safety and Health Administration and Mine Safety and Health Administration records, medical examiner and autopsy reports, media accounts, state motor vehicle fatality records, and follow-up questionnaires to employers.

Fatality counts from the BLS Census are combined with annual average employment from the Current Population Survey to produce a fatal work injury rate.

For a fatality to be included in the CFOI, the decedent must have been employed at the time of the event and present at the site of the incident as a job requirement. Because of the latency period of many occupational illnesses and the resulting difficulty associated with linking illnesses to work, it is difficult to compile a complete count of all fatal illnesses in a given year. Thus, information on illness related deaths are excluded from the basic fatality count.

Sources of Additional Information

For more extensive definitions and description of collection methods see BLS news release USDL 01-472 for illnesses, USDL 02-541 for fatalities, occasional articles in *Compensation, and Working Conditions*, and BLS Report 954.

Table 8-1. Nonfatal Occupational Injuries and Illnesses Incidence Rates by Industry and Case Types, 1992–2000

(Incidence rates per 100 full-time workers.)

Industry and type of case	1992	1993	1994	1995	1996	1997	1998	1999	2000
PRIVATE INDUSTRY [1], [2]									
Total cases	8.9	8.5	8.4	8.1	7.4	7.1	6.7	6.3	6.1
Lost workday cases	3.9	3.8	3.8	3.6	3.4	3.3	3.1	3.0	3.0
Agriculture, Forestry, And Fishing [2]									
Total cases	11.6	11.2	10.0	9.7	8.7	8.4	7.9	7.3	7.1
Lost workday cases	5.4	5.0	4.7	4.3	3.9	4.1	3.9	3.4	3.6
Mining [3]									
Total cases	7.3	6.8	6.3	6.2	5.4	5.9	4.9	4.4	4.7
Lost workday cases	4.1	3.9	3.9	3.9	3.2	3.7	2.9	2.7	3.0
Construction									
Total cases	13.1	12.2	11.8	10.6	9.9	9.5	8.8	8.6	8.3
Lost workday cases	5.8	5.5	5.5	4.9	4.5	4.4	4.0	4.2	4.1
General building contractors									
Total cases	12.2	11.5	10.9	9.8	9.0	8.5	8.4	8.0	7.8
Lost workday cases	5.4	5.1	5.1	4.4	4.0	3.7	3.9	3.7	3.9
Heavy construction, except building									
Total cases	12.1	11.1	10.2	9.9	9.0	8.7	8.2	7.8	7.6
Lost workday cases	5.4	5.1	5.0	4.8	4.3	4.3	4.1	3.8	3.7
Special trade contractors									
Total cases	13.8	12.8	12.5	11.1	10.4	10.0	9.1	8.9	8.6
Lost workday cases	6.1	5.8	5.8	5.0	4.8	4.7	4.1	4.4	4.3
Manufacturing									
Total cases	12.5	12.1	12.2	11.6	10.6	10.3	9.7	9.2	9.0
Lost workday cases	5.4	5.3	5.5	5.3	4.9	4.8	4.7	4.6	4.5
Durable goods									
Total cases	13.4	13.1	13.5	12.8	11.6	11.3	10.7	10.1	9.8
Lost workday cases	5.5	5.4	5.7	5.6	5.1	5.1	5.0	4.8	4.7
Lumber and wood products									
Total cases	16.3	15.9	15.7	14.9	14.2	13.5	13.2	13.0	12.1
Lost workday cases	7.6	7.6	7.7	7.0	6.8	6.5	6.8	6.7	6.1
Furniture and fixtures									
Total cases	14.8	14.6	15.0	13.9	12.2	12.0	11.4	11.5	11.2
Lost workday cases	6.6	6.5	7.0	6.4	5.4	5.8	5.7	5.9	5.9
Stone, clay, and glass products									
Total cases	13.6	13.8	13.2	12.3	12.4	11.8	11.8	10.7	10.4
Lost workday cases	6.1	6.3	6.5	5.7	6.0	5.7	6.0	5.4	5.5
Primary metal industries									
Total cases	17.5	17.0	16.8	16.5	15.0	15.0	14.0	12.9	12.6
Lost workday cases	7.1	7.3	7.2	7.2	6.8	7.2	7.0	6.3	6.3
Fabricated metal products									
Total cases	16.8	16.2	16.4	15.8	14.4	14.2	13.9	12.6	11.9
Lost workday cases	6.6	6.7	6.7	6.9	6.2	6.4	6.5	6.0	5.5
Industrial machinery and equipment									
Total cases	11.1	11.1	11.6	11.2	9.9	10.0	9.5	8.5	8.2
Lost workday cases	4.2	4.2	4.4	4.4	4.0	4.1	4.0	3.7	3.6
Electronic and other electric equipment									
Total cases	8.4	8.3	8.3	7.6	6.8	6.6	5.9	5.7	5.7
Lost workday cases	3.6	3.5	3.6	3.3	3.1	3.1	2.8	2.8	2.9
Transportation equipment									
Total cases	18.7	18.5	19.6	18.6	16.3	15.4	14.6	13.7	13.7
Lost workday cases	7.1	7.1	7.8	7.9	7.0	6.6	6.6	6.4	6.3
Instruments and related products									
Total cases	5.9	5.6	5.9	5.3	5.1	4.8	4.0	4.0	4.5
Lost workday cases	2.7	2.5	2.7	2.4	2.3	2.3	1.9	1.8	2.2
Miscellaneous manufacturing industries									
Total cases	10.7	10.0	9.9	9.1	9.5	8.9	8.1	8.4	7.2
Lost workday cases	5.0	4.6	4.5	4.3	4.4	4.2	3.9	4.0	3.6

See footnotes at end of table.

Table 8-1. Nonfatal Occupational Injuries and Illnesses Incidence Rates by Industry and Case Types, 1992–2000—Continued

(Incidence rates per 100 full-time workers.)

Industry and type of case	1992	1993	1994	1995	1996	1997	1998	1999	2000
Nondurable goods									
Total cases	11.3	10.7	10.5	9.9	9.2	8.8	8.2	7.8	7.8
Lost workday cases	5.3	5.0	5.1	4.9	4.6	4.4	4.3	4.2	4.2
Food and kindred products									
Total cases	18.8	17.6	17.1	16.3	15.0	14.5	13.6	12.7	12.4
Lost workday cases	9.5	8.9	9.2	8.7	8.0	8.0	7.5	7.3	7.3
Tobacco products									
Total cases	6.0	5.8	5.3	5.6	6.7	5.9	6.4	5.5	6.2
Lost workday cases	2.4	2.3	2.4	2.6	2.8	2.7	3.1	2.2	3.1
Textile mill products									
Total cases	9.9	9.7	8.7	8.2	7.8	6.7	6.7	6.4	6.0
Lost workday cases	4.2	4.1	4.0	4.1	3.6	3.1	3.4	3.2	3.2
Apparel and other textile products									
Total cases	9.5	9.0	8.9	8.2	7.4	7.0	6.2	5.8	6.1
Lost workday cases	4.0	3.8	3.9	3.6	3.3	3.1	2.6	2.8	3.0
Paper and allied products									
Total cases	11.0	9.9	9.6	8.5	7.9	7.3	7.1	7.0	6.5
Lost workday cases	5.0	4.6	4.5	4.2	3.8	3.7	3.7	3.7	3.4
Printing and publishing									
Total cases	7.3	6.9	6.7	6.4	6.0	5.7	5.4	5.0	5.1
Lost workday cases	3.2	3.1	3.0	3.0	2.8	2.7	2.8	2.6	2.6
Chemicals and allied products									
Total cases	6.0	5.9	5.7	5.5	4.8	4.8	4.2	4.4	4.2
Lost workday cases	2.8	2.7	2.8	2.7	2.4	2.3	2.1	2.3	2.2
Petroleum and coal products									
Total cases	5.9	5.2	4.7	4.8	4.6	4.3	3.9	4.1	3.7
Lost workday cases	2.8	2.5	2.3	2.4	2.5	2.2	1.8	1.8	1.9
Rubber and miscellaneous plastics products									
Total cases	14.5	13.9	14.0	12.9	12.3	11.9	11.2	10.1	10.7
Lost workday cases	6.8	6.5	6.7	6.5	6.3	5.8	5.8	5.5	5.8
Leather and leather products									
Total cases	12.1	12.1	12.0	11.4	10.7	10.6	9.8	10.3	9.0
Lost workday cases	5.4	5.5	5.3	4.8	4.5	4.3	4.5	5.0	4.3
Transportation And Public Utilities [3]									
Total cases	9.1	9.5	9.3	9.1	[4]8.7	[4]8	7.3	7.3	6.9
Lost workday cases	5.1	5.4	5.5	5.2	[4]5.1	[4]4.8	4.3	4.4	4.3
Wholesale And Retail Trade									
Total cases	8.4	8.1	7.9	7.5	6.8	6.7	6.5	6.1	5.9
Lost workday cases	3.5	3.4	3.4	3.2	2.9	3.0	2.8	2.7	2.7
Wholesale trade									
Total cases	7.6	7.8	7.7	7.5	6.6	6.5	6.5	6.3	5.8
Lost workday cases	3.6	3.7	3.8	3.6	3.4	3.2	3.3	3.3	3.1
Retail trade									
Total cases	8.7	8.2	7.9	7.5	6.9	6.8	6.5	6.1	5.9
Lost workday cases	3.4	3.3	3.3	3.0	2.8	2.9	2.7	2.5	2.5
Finance, Insurance, And Real Estate									
Total cases	2.9	2.9	2.7	2.6	2.4	2.2	1.9	1.8	1.9
Lost workday cases	1.2	1.2	1.1	1.0	0.9	0.9	0.7	0.8	0.8
Services									
Total cases	7.1	6.7	6.5	6.4	6.0	5.6	5.2	4.9	4.9
Lost workday cases	3.0	2.8	2.8	2.8	2.6	2.5	2.4	2.2	2.2

Note: Because of rounding, components may not add to totals.

1. Totals include data for industries not shown separately.
2. Exclude farms with fewer than 11 employees.
3. Data conforming to OSHA definitions for mining operators in coal, metal, and nonmetal mining and for employers in railroad transportation are provided to BLS by the Mine Safety and Health Administration, U.S. Department of Labor; and the Federal Railroad Administration, U.S. Department of Transportation. Independent mining contractors are excluded from the coal, metal, and nonmetal mining industries.
4. Estimates for 1996 and 1997 for this division may have had more variability than those for prior years.

Table 8-2. Number of Nonfatal Occupational Injuries and Illnesses Involving Days Away from Work[1] by Selected Worker Characteristics and Industry Division, Private Industry, 2000

(Numbers in thousands.)

Characteristic	Total cases	Goods producing				Service producing				
		Agriculture, forestry, and fishing[2]	Mining[3]	Construction	Manufacturing	Transportation and public utilities[3]	Wholesale trade	Retail trade	Finance, insurance, and real estate	Services
TOTAL CASES	1 664.0	37.3	14.1	194.4	376.6	207.0	125.6	281.3	39.5	388.3
Sex										
Men	1 097.1	29.7	13.8	189.9	281.0	160.9	106.4	153.1	18.9	143.4
Women	555.7	7.5	0.2	4.4	95.0	40.0	19.0	124.8	20.5	244.3
Age[4]										
14 to 15 years	0.6	(5)	...	...	(5)	...	...	0.3	(5)	0.1
16 to 19 years	54.1	1.9	0.4	4.9	7.8	3.6	2.6	23.3	0.6	9.2
20 to 24 years	186.3	6.4	1.6	24.4	37.8	18.2	15.6	42.2	3.7	36.3
25 to 34 years	430.9	11.4	3.5	57.5	97.0	54.1	34.9	67.9	8.7	96.0
35 to 44 years	481.3	8.3	3.5	60.6	114.3	66.1	37.7	69.2	10.6	110.9
45 to 54 years	325.8	5.9	3.5	31.7	78.0	44.0	22.8	45.4	9.3	85.2
55 to 64 years	142.5	2.5	1.3	10.8	34.9	17.4	9.5	22.8	5.4	38.1
65 and over	25.3	0.5	0.1	1.3	3.9	2.3	1.4	7.3	0.9	7.7
Occupation										
Managerial and professional specialty	99.1	0.8	0.3	2.5	5.6	3.5	5.2	10.8	4.9	65.5
Technical, sales, and administrative support	254.7	1.8	0.2	2.8	20.8	29.7	18.9	96.1	16.7	67.5
Service	278.1	0.8	(5)	0.4	6.7	12.8	1.9	70.4	9.3	175.8
Farming, forestry, and fishing	41.5	28.8	...	0.3	2.2	0.4	1.3	1.2	2.4	5.0
Precision production, craft, and repair	299.0	1.3	7.6	119.3	65.7	28.1	16.2	29.4	3.8	27.5
Operators, fabricators, and laborers	684.4	3.6	5.6	68.4	273.5	131.9	81.6	72.7	2.3	44.9
Length Of Service With Employer										
Less than 3 months	215.6	9.0	2.6	37.6	42.2	14.7	16.1	43.5	3.6	46.4
3 to 11 months	308.6	8.4	2.9	40.4	61.5	26.1	26.4	62.0	6.9	74.0
1 to 5 years	524.8	11.2	3.8	62.9	112.6	57.5	40.3	90.9	13.7	131.7
More than 5 years	404.8	6.5	3.9	36.6	119.1	58.2	30.4	51.6	10.4	88.1
Not reported	210.2	2.2	0.8	16.9	41.1	50.6	12.4	33.2	4.9	48.0
Race Or Ethnic Origin										
White, non-Hispanic	827.5	15.8	4.9	119.1	200.3	76.4	68.5	142.6	18.9	180.9
Black, non-Hispanic	139.3	1.3	0.1	9.1	30.7	16.5	10.1	21.2	3.3	46.8
Hispanic	186.0	14.8	1.3	26.6	45.5	12.3	15.1	27.6	4.6	38.3
Asian or Pacific Islander	25.9	0.4	...	1.4	6.3	1.8	2.3	4.5	0.7	8.5
American Indian or Alaskan Native	7.0	0.1	(5)	1.1	1.5	0.5	0.4	1.1	0.3	2.0
Not reported	478.4	4.9	7.7	37.2	92.2	99.6	29.1	84.4	11.7	111.7

Note: Because of rounding and nonclassifiable responses, components may not add to totals.

1. Days-away-from-work cases include those which result in days away from work with or without restricted work activity.
2. Exclude farms with fewer than 11 employees.
3. Data conforming to OSHA definitions for mining operators in coal, metal, and nonmetal mining and for employers in railroad transportation are provided to BLS by the Mine Safety and Health Administration, U.S. Department of Labor; and the Federal Railroad Administration, U.S. Department of Transportation. Independent mining contractors are excluded from the coal, metal, and nonmetal mining industries.
4. Information is not shown separately for injured workers under age 14; they accounted for fewer than 50 cases.
5. Value less than 50 cases.

Table 8-3. Number and Percent Distribution of Nonfatal Occupational Injuries and Illnesses Involving Days Away from Work[1] by Selected Occupation and Number of Days Away from Work, Private Industry, 2000

(Numbers, percent, days.)

Occupation	Total cases[2]	Total percent of cases	Percent of days-away-from-work-cases involving:							Median days away from work
			1 day	2 days	3 to 5 days	6 to 10 days	11 to 20 days	21 to 30 days	31 days and over	
TOTAL CASES	1 664.0	100.0	16.1	12.9	19.9	12.7	11.2	6.2	21.0	6
Truckdrivers	136.1	100.0	11.9	10.4	19.3	12.3	11.7	7.2	27.2	9
Laborers, nonconstruction	87.0	100.0	17.6	12.9	21.4	13.3	11.3	5.9	17.7	5
Nursing aides, orderlies	74.2	100.0	16.2	13.9	22.8	13.7	11.7	5.5	16.1	5
Construction laborers	45.4	100.0	12.7	12.5	19.4	11.7	11.4	7.3	25.0	8
Janitors and cleaners	40.7	100.0	16.6	10.8	19.9	13.5	11.5	6.1	21.7	6
Assemblers	38.9	100.0	17.5	11.8	19.2	11.9	11.9	7.9	19.8	6
Carpenters	38.3	100.0	15.8	11.9	14.6	12.6	13.1	7.5	24.5	8
Cooks	27.8	100.0	16.7	16.6	21.7	15.0	8.9	5.1	16.0	5
Cashiers	26.9	100.0	13.0	10.9	21.7	11.5	10.5	4.7	27.7	7
Registered nurses	24.5	100.0	19.3	16.0	22.5	11.8	10.7	5.3	14.4	4
Sales workers, other commodities	24.1	100.0	17.4	18.4	20.2	12.2	8.7	6.6	16.4	5
Supervisors and proprietors	24.1	100.0	12.6	14.9	18.6	14.1	12.4	7.1	20.2	7
Stock handlers and baggers	23.8	100.0	17.3	15.1	23.8	12.5	8.6	6.2	16.5	5
Welders and cutters	21.9	100.0	21.5	13.2	16.7	10.1	10.7	5.4	22.3	5
Maids and housemen	21.7	100.0	15.0	14.6	21.4	14.0	12.0	5.4	17.6	5
Miscellaneous food preparation	19.4	100.0	17.2	15.3	21.4	16.7	7.6	5.5	16.4	5
Shipping and receiving clerks	17.8	100.0	19.2	16.1	20.5	11.9	11.1	4.4	16.8	5
Electricians	16.8	100.0	12.8	10.8	16.3	14.2	12.9	8.2	24.9	9
Groundskeeps and gardeners, except farm ...	16.0	100.0	16.1	17.1	17.9	14.9	10.2	8.5	15.4	5
Mechanics, automobile	15.9	100.0	15.0	13.8	21.5	11.5	9.4	6.9	21.8	5
Farm workers	14.0	100.0	15.4	8.7	18.9	16.0	8.5	7.2	25.3	7
Driver-sales workers	13.9	100.0	13.2	12.4	21.1	12.2	11.2	5.7	24.3	7
Kitchen workers	13.1	100.0	24.6	14.6	22.1	10.0	7.5	2.9	18.3	4
Industrial truck operators	12.8	100.0	18.1	11.3	19.8	11.0	10.1	5.4	24.4	6
Plumbers, pipefitters, and steamfitters	12.2	100.0	14.9	10.8	16.9	12.3	14.4	6.2	24.4	8
Repairers, industrial machinery	12.1	100.0	14.9	14.4	14.6	13.3	12.2	7.4	23.2	7
Licensed practical nurses	10.8	100.0	19.6	14.9	23.5	6.3	13.2	5.5	17.1	4
Mechanics, bus, truck, stationary engine	10.8	100.0	18.7	15.5	16.1	10.0	14.1	4.3	21.3	5
Guards and police, except public	10.6	100.0	14.4	14.5	21.0	14.6	11.6	6.9	16.9	6
Stock and inventory clerks	10.4	100.0	16.6	14.9	21.8	13.7	10.1	5.2	17.7	5
Supervisors, production workers	10.2	100.0	21.3	10.1	19.6	11.6	12.6	7.0	17.8	5
Waiters and waitresses	10.0	100.0	13.7	15.6	23.6	16.0	7.6	5.3	18.1	5
Health aides, except nursing	10.0	100.0	16.4	17.5	24.1	15.9	8.8	5.4	11.9	4
Packaging, filling machine operators	9.7	100.0	17.8	13.8	16.5	15.4	9.4	6.9	20.1	6
Attendants, public transportation	9.0	100.0	6.7	8.3	23.0	17.6	16.3	7.1	21.0	8
Heating, air conditioning, and refrigeration mechanics	8.3	100.0	16.0	13.0	18.5	15.3	13.3	2.6	21.3	6
Painters	8.1	100.0	11.8	7.3	19.4	23.5	5.8	4.5	27.7	6
Butchers and meat cutters	7.6	100.0	14.6	13.4	21.7	14.3	8.6	9.1	18.2	6
Bus drivers	7.6	100.0	11.3	7.7	20.0	13.9	11.5	6.2	29.4	9
Hand packers and packagers	7.3	100.0	25.1	15.1	15.8	11.1	12.9	3.9	16.0	4
General office clerks	7.2	100.0	11.2	11.6	20.7	15.9	11.5	3.8	25.3	7

Note: Because of rounding and nonclassifiable responses, percentages may not add to 100.

1. Days-away-from-work cases include those which result in days away from work with or without restricted work activity.
2. Exclude farms with fewer than 11 employees.

Table 8-4. Fatal Occupational Injuries and Employment by Selected Worker Characteristics, 2001

Characteristics	Fatalities		Employment [1] (thousands)		Most frequent event [2] (percent of total)
	Number	Percent	Number	Percent	
Total, including fatalities from September 11	8 786	. . .	. . .	. . .	. . .
Total, excluding fatalities from September 11	5 900	100	136 252	100	Highway (24%)
Employee Status					
Wage and salary workers	4 770	81	126 298	93	Highway (26%)
Self-employed [3]	1 130	19	9 954	7	Homicides (15%)
Sex And Age					
Men	5 429	92	73 087	54	Highway (23%)
Women	471	8	63 164	46	Highway (29%)
Both sexes, by age [4]					
Under 16 years	20	. . .	. . .	. . .	Nonhighway (25%)
16 to 17 years	33	1	2 576	2	Highway (30%)
18 to 19 years	122	2	4 432	3	Highway (25%)
20 to 24 years	440	7	13 682	10	Highway (24%)
25 to 34 years	1 140	19	30 091	22	Highway (27%)
35 to 44 years	1 474	25	36 474	27	Highway (23%)
45 to 54 years	1 363	23	30 627	22	Highway (23%)
55 to 64 years	773	13	14 135	10	Highway (24%)
65 and over	529	9	4 175	3	Highway (20%) Falls (20%)
Race					
White	4 168	71	99 963	73	Highway (25%)
Black	563	10	14 815	11	Highway (28%)
Asian	172	3	. . .	. . .	Homicides (41%)
American Indian or Alaskan Native	48	1	. . .	. . .	Highway (23%)
Other races or not reported	43	1	. . .	. . .	Homicides (30%)
Hispanic Origin					
Hispanic [5]	891	15	14 815	11	Highway (19%)

Note: Totals may include subcategories not shown separately. Percentages may not add to totals because of rounding. (. . .) indicate less than 0.5 percent or data that are not available or that do not meet publication criteria.

1. Employment is an annual average of employed civilians 16 years of age and older, plus resident armed forces, from the Current Population Survey, 2000.
2. "Highway" includes deaths to vehicle occupants resulting from traffic incidents that occur on the public roadway, shoulder, or surrounding area. It excludes incidents occurring entirely off the roadway, such as in parking lots and on farms. Incidents involving trains and deaths to pedestrians or other nonpassengers are excluded from both categories.
3. Includes paid and unpaid family workers and may include owners of incorporated businesses or members of partnerships.
4. There were 6 fatalities for which age was not reported.
5. The categories 'White' and 'Black' do not include 'Hispanic or Latino' persons. Persons identified as Hispanic may be of any race.

Table 8-5. Fatal Occupational Injuries by Occupation and Major Event or Exposure, 2001

Occupation [1]	Fatalities		Major event or exposure [2] (percent)			
	Number	Percent	Highway [3]	Homicide	Struck by object	Fall to lower level
Total, including fatalities from September 11	8 786	...	...	...	...	...
Total, excluding fatalities from September 11	5 900	100	24	11	9	12
Managerial And Professional Specialty	637	11	23	19	5	8
Executive, administrative and managerial	378	6	20	24	5	10
Professional specialty	259	4	27	11	5	7
Technical, Sales, and Administrative Support	641	11	25	32	3	4
Technicians and related support occupations	154	3	20	3	...	3
Airplane pilots and navigators	87	1	...	...	...	...
Sales occupations	388	7	23	47	2	3
Supervisors and proprietors, sales occupations	191	3	18	53	3	3
Sales workers, retail and personal services	148	3	17	51	...	4
Cashiers	55	1	...	82	...	...
Administrative support occupations including clerical	99	2	39	16	8	7
Service Occupations	511	9	19	33	3	6
Protective service occupations	287	5	24	35	4	3
Firefighting and fire prevention occupations, including supervisors	50	1	22	...	...	...
Police and detectives including supervisors	159	3	34	39	...	...
Guards, including supervisors	78	1	...	49	9	...
Farming, Forestry, And Fishing	805	14	13	1	18	7
Farming operators and managers	321	5	12	...	17	4
Farmers except horticultural	305	5	11	...	16	4
Managers, farms, except horticultural	11	0	...	...	...	...
Other agricultural and related occupations	327	6	19	...	9	13
Farm workers including supervisors	170	3	22	...	6	6
Forestry and logging occupations	95	2	...	...	63	6
Fishers, hunters and trappers	62	1	...	...	...	...
Fishers including vessel captains and officers	62	1	...	...	...	...
Precision Production, Craft, And Repair	1 140	19	11	3	11	29
Mechanics and repairers	287	5	15	4	20	11
Construction trades	666	11	8	2	5	42
Carpenters and apprentices	112	2	6	...	4	62
Electricians and apprentices	109	2	8	...	...	16
Roofers	78	1	...	...	...	72
Structural metal workers	45	1	...	...	...	87
Operators, Fabricators, And Laborers	2 043	35	37	5	10	10
Machine operators, assemblers, and inspectors	208	4	5	2	15	12
Transportation and material moving occupations	1 185	20	55	6	8	3
Motor vehicle operators	966	16	65	7	5	3
Truck drivers	799	14	68	2	6	3
Taxicab drivers and chauffeurs	62	1	40	55	...	...
Material moving equipment operators	183	3	11	...	20	8
Handlers, equipment cleaners, helpers, and laborers	650	11	14	3	14	20
Construction laborers	349	6	13	...	13	26
Laborers, except construction	167	3	14	4	14	14
Military [4]	110	1	15	...	6	...

Note: Totals for major categories may include subcategories not shown separately. Percentages may not add to totals because of rounding. There were 40 fatalities for which there was insufficient information to determine an occupation classification. (. . .) indicate less than 0.5 percent or data that are not available or that do not meet publication criteria.

1. Based on the 1990 Occupational Classification System developed by the Bureau of the Census.
2. The figure shown is the percent of the total fatalities for that occupational group.
3. "Highway" includes deaths to vehicle occupants resulting from traffic incidents that occur on the public roadway, shoulder, or surrounding area. It excludes incidents occurring entirely off the roadway, such as in parking lots and on farms; incidents involving trains; and deaths to pedestrians or other nonpassengers.
4. Resident armed forces.

Table 8-6. Fatal Occupational Injuries from Events on September 11, 2001, by Industry and Occupation

(Number, percent.)

Characteristics	Total		Office building		Passenger airliner		Rescue efforts	
	Number	Percent	Number	Percent	Number	Percent	Number	Percent
Total	2 886	100	2 323	100	151	100	412	100
Industry								
Private industry	2 264	78	2 119	91	141	93	...	...
Construction	58	2	57	2	...	...	...	...
General building contractors	12	(1)	11	(1)	...	...	...	...
Heavy construction, except building ...	13	(1)	13	1	...	...	...	...
Special trade contractors	32	1	32	1	...	...	...	...
Transportation and public utilities	78	3	35	2	42	28	...	...
Transportation by air	37	1	...	...	36	24	...	...
Wholesale trade	27	1	18	1	9	6	...	...
Retail trade	118	4	108	5	10	7	...	...
Eating and drinking places	103	4	103	4	...	...	...	...
Finance, insurance, and real estate	1 715	59	1 708	74	7	5	...	...
Depository institutions	192	7	192	8	...	...	...	...
Security and commodity brokers	973	34	971	42	...	...	...	...
Insurance carriers	202	7	202	9	...	...	...	...
Insurance agents, brokers, and service	330	11	329	14	...	...	...	...
Real estate	13	(1)	12	1	...	...	...	...
Holding and other investment offices ...	5	(1)	...	...	3	2	...	...
Services	230	8	168	7	59	39	3	1
Business services	141	5	120	5	21	14	...	...
Government [2]	622	22	204	9	10	7	408	99
Federal government (including resident armed forces)	124	4	116	5	7	5	...	...
National security	118	4	114	5	4	3	...	...
State government	49	2	43	2	3	2	3	1
Local government	449	16	45	2	...	...	404	98
Police protection	25	1	...	...	...	...	23	6
Fire protection	344	12	...	...	...	...	343	83
Administration of economic programs	79	3	41	2	...	...	38	9
Occupation								
Managerial and professional specialty	1 271	44	1 157	50	104	69	10	2
Executive, administrative, and managerial	1 072	37	993	43	70	46	9	2
Professional specialty	199	7	164	7	34	23	...	...
Technical, sales, and administrative support	930	32	905	39	19	13	6	1
Technicians and related support occupations	92	3	78	3	8	5	6	1
Health technologists and technicians	8	(1)	...	...	...	...	6	1
Airplane pilots and navigators	8	(1)	...	...	8	5	...	...
Sales occupations	565	20	557	24	8	5	...	...
Service occupations	549	19	128	6	25	17	396	96
Protective service occupations	433	15	37	2	...	...	396	96
Firefighting, including supervisors	336	12	...	...	...	...	335	81
Police and detectives, including supervisors	64	2	3	(1)	...	...	61	15
Guards, including supervisors	33	1	33	1	...	...	...	...
Food preparation and service occupations	64	2	64	3	...	...	...	...
Cleaning and building services	25	1	25	1	...	...	...	...
Personal service occupations	27	1	...	...	25	17	...	...
Transportation attendants	25	1	...	...	25	17	...	...
Precision production, craft, and repair	61	2	60	3	...	...	...	...
Mechanics and repairers	20	1	20	1	...	...	...	...
Construction trades	39	1	38	2	...	...	...	...
Operators, fabricators, and laborers	14	(1)	12	1	...	...	...	...
Military occupations	54	2	54	2	...	...	...	...

Note: These totals include work–related fatalities only. They may differ from totals published by other organizations primarily due to the differences in how work relationship, industry, and occupation are categorized. Totals for major categories may include subcategories not shown separately. Percentages may not add to totals because of rounding. Dashes indicate no data reported or data that do not meet the publication criteria.

1. Less than 0.5 percent.
2. Includes fatalities to workers employed by governmental organizations regardless of industry.

PART NINE

LABOR MANAGEMENT RELATIONS

LABOR MANAGEMENT RELATIONS

HIGHLIGHTS

This chapter is concerned with historical trends in union membership and earnings and in work stoppages.

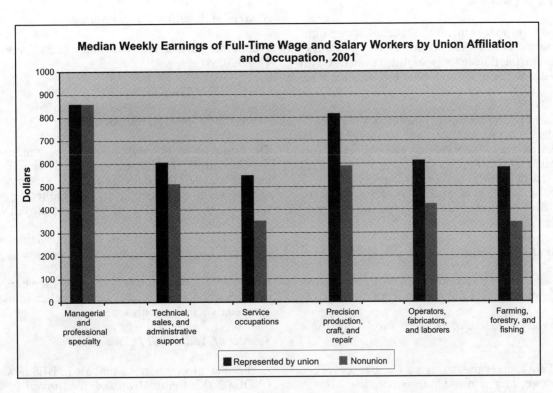

In all major occupational groups, median weekly earnings of those represented by unions are higher than for non-union members. However, the difference varies from a .1 percent increase in managerial and professional occupations to a 69 percent increase in farming. However, only 2 percent of wage and salary workers in agriculture are represented by a union.

OTHER HIGHLIGHTS:

- Among industries, union membership is highest among government workers, 37.4 percent. It is lowest among agricultural wage and salary workers. (Table 9-3)
- Weekly earning of union members exceeds those of non-union members by 24.9 percent. However, there has been a narrowing of the difference over time. (Table 9-4)
- Men had a somewhat higher rate of union membership, 15.1 percent of total employed compared with 11.7 percent for women. However, the number of men union members continues to decline while the number of women union members increased slightly between 2000 and 2001. (Table 9-2).
- For men and women, the 45-64 age group have the highest rates of union membership. (Table 9-2)
- Both Black men and women have a higher rate of union membership than White men and women. (Table 9-2)

NOTES AND DEFINITIONS

WORK STOPPAGES

Collection and Coverage

Data on work stoppages measure the number and duration of major strikes or lockouts (involving 1,000 workers or more) occurring during the year, the number of workers involved, and the amount of time lost because of stoppage.

Data are largely from newspaper accounts and cover only establishments directly involved in a stoppage. They do not measure the indirect or secondary effect of stoppages on other establishments whose employees are idle owing to material shortages or lack of service.
The current series is not comparable with the one terminated in 1981, which covered strikes involving six workers or more.

Concepts and Definitions

Stoppages are strikes and lockouts involving 1,000 workers or more and lasting a full shift or longer.

Workers involved are workers directly involved in the stoppage.

Number of days idle is the aggregate number of workdays lost by workers involved in the stoppages.

Days of idleness as a percent of estimated working time is aggregate workdays lost as a percent of the aggregate number of standard workdays in the period multiplied by total employment (excluding forestry, fisheries, and private household workers) in the period.

Sources of Additional Information

Additional information is available in BLS news release USDL 01-41.

UNION MEMBERSHIP

Collection, Coverage, and Definitions

The estimates of union membership are obtained from the Current Population Survey (CPS). The union membership and earnings data are tabulated from one-quarter of the CPS monthly sample and are limited to wage and salary workers. Excluded are all self-employed workers.

Union members are members of a labor union or an employee association similar to a union.

Represented by unions refers to union members as well as workers who have no union affiliation but whose jobs are covered by a union contract.

Sources of Additional Information

Additional information is available in BLS news release USDL 02-153, *Union Membership (Annual)*.

Table 9-1. Work Stoppages Involving 1,000 Workers or More, 1947–2001

Year	Stoppages beginning in the year [1]		Days idle during the year [1]	
	Number	Workers involved (thousands)	Number (thousands)	Percent of estimated total working time [2]
1947	270	1 629	25 720	...
1948	245	1 435	26 127	0.22
1949	262	2 537	43 420	0.38
1950	424	1 698	30 390	0.26
1951	415	1 462	15 070	0.12
1952	470	2 746	48 820	0.38
1953	437	1 623	18 130	0.14
1954	265	1 075	16 630	0.13
1955	363	2 055	21 180	0.16
1956	287	1 370	26 840	0.20
1957	279	887	10 340	0.07
1958	332	1 587	17 900	0.13
1959	245	1 381	60 850	0.43
1960	222	896	13 260	0.09
1961	195	1 031	10 140	0.07
1962	211	793	11 760	0.08
1963	181	512	10 020	0.07
1964	246	1 183	16 220	0.11
1965	268	999	15 140	0.10
1966	321	1 300	16 000	0.10
1967	381	2 192	31 320	0.18
1968	392	1 855	35 367	0.20
1969	412	1 576	29 397	0.16
1970	381	2 468	52 761	0.29
1971	298	2 516	35 538	0.19
1972	250	975	16 764	0.09
1973	317	1 400	16 260	0.08
1974	424	1 796	31 809	0.16
1975	235	965	17 563	0.09
1976	231	1 519	23 962	0.12
1977	298	1 212	21 258	0.10
1978	219	1 006	23 774	0.11
1979	235	1 021	20 409	0.09
1980	187	795	20 844	0.09
1981	145	729	16 908	0.07
1982	96	656	9 061	0.04
1983	81	909	17 461	0.08
1984	62	376	8 499	0.04
1985	54	324	7 079	0.03
1986	69	533	11 861	0.05
1987	46	174	4 481	0.02
1988	40	118	4 381	0.02
1989	51	452	16 996	0.07
1990	44	185	5 926	0.02
1991	40	392	4 584	0.02
1992	35	364	3 989	0.01
1993	35	182	3 981	0.01
1994	45	322	5 020	0.02
1995	31	192	5 771	0.02
1996	37	273	4 889	0.02
1997	29	339	4 497	0.01
1998	34	387	5 116	0.02
1999	17	73	1 996	0.01
2000	39	394	20 419	0.06
2001	29	99	1 151	(3)

1. The number of stoppages and workers relate to stoppages that began in the year. Days of idleness include all stoppages in effect. Workers are counted more than once if they are involved in more than one stoppage during the year.
2. Working time is for all employees, except those in private households, forestry, and fisheries.
3. Less than .005 percent.

Table 9-2. Union Affiliation of Employed Wage and Salary Workers by Selected Characteristics, 1996–2001

(Numbers in thousands, percent.)

Characteristics	1996 Total em-ployed	1996 Members of unions[1] Total	1996 Members of unions[1] Percent em-ployed	1996 Represented by unions[2] Total	1996 Represented by unions[2] Percent em-ployed	1997 Total em-ployed	1997 Members of unions[1] Total	1997 Members of unions[1] Percent em-ployed	1997 Represented by unions[2] Total	1997 Represented by unions[2] Percent em-ployed	1998 Total em-ployed	1998 Members of unions[1] Total	1998 Members of unions[1] Percent em-ployed	1998 Represented by unions[2] Total	1998 Represented by unions[2] Percent em-ployed
SEX AND AGE															
TOTAL, 16 YEARS AND OVER	111 960	16 269	14.5	18158.0	16.2	114 533	16 110	14.1	17923.0	15.6	116 730	16 211	13.9	17918.0	15.4
16 to 24 years	18 106	991	5.5	1146.00	6.3	18 571	968	5.2	1140.00	6.1	19 164	1 014	5.3	1151.00	6.0
25 years and over	93 854	15 278	16.3	17012.0	18.1	95 962	15 142	15.8	16783.0	17.5	97 566	15 198	15.6	16767.0	17.2
25 to 34 years	29 564	3 536	12.0	3994.00	13.5	29 408	3 434	11.7	3870.00	13.2	29 121	3 332	11.4	3711.00	12.7
35 to 44 years	30 619	5 132	16.8	5716.00	18.7	31 461	4 987	15.9	5571.00	17.7	31 865	5 013	15.7	5511.00	17.3
45 to 54 years	21 641	4 626	21.4	5106.00	23.6	22 714	4 645	20.5	5092.00	22.4	23 579	4 737	20.1	5220.00	22.1
55 to 64 years	9 527	1 795	18.8	1984.00	20.8	9 871	1 894	19.2	2045.00	20.7	2 574	1 923	18.4	2110.00	20.2
65 years and over	2 503	189	7.5	211.00	8.4	2 509	182	7.3	205.00	8.2	2 574	193	7.5	214.00	8.3
Men, 16 Years And Over	58 473	9 859	16.9	10761.0	18.4	59 825	9 763	16.3	10619.0	17.7	60 973	9 850	16.2	10638.0	17.4
16 to 24 years	9 392	627	6.7	709.00	7.5	9 666	612	6.3	691.00	7.1	9 927	637	6.4	719.00	7.2
25 years and over	49 080	9 232	18.8	10052.0	20.5	50 159	9 150	18.2	9928.00	19.8	51 046	9 213	18.0	9919.00	19.4
25 to 34 years	15 930	2 205	13.8	2434.00	15.3	15 832	2 132	13.5	2359.00	14.9	15 656	2 112	13.5	2301.00	14.7
35 to 44 years	15 921	3 100	19.5	3368.00	21.2	16 430	3 068	18.7	3346.00	20.4	16 768	3 055	18.2	3264.00	19.5
45 to 54 years	10 936	2 739	25.0	2960.00	27.1	11 471	2 718	23.7	2908.00	25.4	15 097	2 771	23.3	2982.00	25.1
55 to 64 years	4 978	1 079	21.7	1166.00	23.4	5 101	1 130	22.1	1198.00	23.5	5 404	1 177	21.8	1265.00	23.4
65 years and over	1 315	109	8.3	124.00	9.5	1 324	103	7.8	118.00	8.9	1 343	98	7.3	108.00	8.0
Women, 16 Years And Over	53 488	6 410	12.0	7397.00	13.8	54 708	6 347	11.6	7304.00	13.4	55 757	6 362	11.4	7280.00	13.1
16 to 24 years	8 714	364	4.2	437.00	5.0	8 906	355	4.0	449.00	5.0	9 237	377	4.1	432.00	4.7
25 years and over	44 773	6 046	13.5	6960.00	15.5	45 802	5 992	13.1	6855.00	15.0	46 520	5 985	12.9	6848.00	14.7
25 to 34 years	13 634	1 331	9.8	1560.00	11.4	13 575	1 302	9.6	1512.00	11.1	13 464	1 219	9.1	1410.00	10.5
35 to 44 years	14 698	2 032	13.8	2349.00	16.0	15 030	1 919	12.8	2225.00	14.8	15 097	1 958	13.0	2248.00	14.9
45 to 54 years	10 705	1 887	17.6	2146.00	20.0	11 242	1 927	17.1	2184.00	19.4	11 705	1 967	16.8	2238.00	19.1
55 to 64 years	4 549	716	15.7	818.00	18.0	4 770	764	16.0	847.00	17.8	5 023	746	14.9	845.00	16.8
65 years and over	1 187	80	6.7	87.00	7.3	1 184	80	6.7	87.00	7.3	1 231	95	7.7	106.00	8.6
RACE, HISPANIC ORIGIN, AND SEX															
White, 16 Years And Over	94 306	13 232	14.0	14761.0	15.7	96 104	13 088	13.6	14538.0	15.1	97 531	13 118	13.5	14460.0	14.8
Men	49 961	8 216	16.4	8961.00	17.9	50 941	8 171	16.0	8859.00	17.4	51 700	8 166	15.8	8788.00	17.0
Women	44 345	5 016	11.3	5800.00	13.1	45 163	4 917	10.9	5679.00	12.6	45 831	4 952	10.8	5673.00	12.4
Black,16 Years And Over	12 909	2 441	18.9	2733.00	21.2	13 346	2 394	17.9	2688.00	20.1	13 894	2 460	17.7	2739.00	19.7
Men	6 031	1 303	21.6	1428.00	23.7	6 201	1 251	20.2	1379.00	22.2	6 452	1 337	20.7	1458.00	22.6
Women	6 878	1 138	16.5	1305.00	19.0	7 145	1 143	16.0	1309.00	18.3	7 443	1 123	15.1	1282.00	17.2
Hispanic, 16 Years And Over	10 800	1 394	12.9	1573.00	14.6	11 881	1 407	11.8	1602.00	13.5	12 374	1 471	11.9	1634.00	13.2
Men	6 455	881	13.7	971.00	15.0	7 153	904	12.6	1023.00	14.3	7 360	937	12.7	1017.00	13.8
Women	4 345	513	11.8	602.00	13.9	4 728	503	10.6	579.00	12.2	5 015	534	10.6	617.00	12.3
FULL- OR PART-TIME STATUS [3]															
Full-Time Workers	90 918	14 762	16.2	16429.0	18.1	93 578	14 619	15.6	16227.0	17.3	95 595	14 825	15.5	16323.0	17.1
Part-Time Workers	20 810	1 477	7.1	1697.00	8.2	20 710	1 449	7.0	1653.00	8.0	20 862	1 354	6.5	1559.00	7.5

See footnotes and *Note* at end of table.

Table 9-2. Union Affiliation of Employed Wage and Salary Workers by Selected Characteristics, 1996–2001—Continued

(Numbers in thousands, percent.)

Characteristics	1999 Total employed	Members of unions[1] Total	Members Percent employed	Represented by unions[2] Total	Repr. Percent employed	2000 Total employed	Members of unions[1] Total	Members Percent employed	Represented by unions[2] Total	Repr. Percent employed	2001 Total employed	Members of unions[1] Total	Members Percent employed	Represented by unions[2] Total	Repr. Percent employed
SEX AND AGE															
TOTAL, 16 YEARS AND OVER	118 963	16 477	13.9	18182.0	15.3	120 786	16 258	13.5	17944.0	14.9	120 760	16 275	13.5	17875.0	14.8
16 to 24 years	19 606	1 110	5.7	1239.00	6.3	20 166	1 010	5.0	1152.00	5.7	19 819	1 034	5.2	1188.00	6.0
25 years and over	99 358	15 367	15.5	16943.0	17.1	100 620	15 248	15.2	16792.0	16.7	100 941	15 241	15.1	16688.0	16.5
25 to 34 years	28 657	3 415	11.9	3785.00	13.2	28 406	3 369	11.9	3720.00	13.1	27 710	3 180	11.5	3539.00	12.8
35 to 44 years	32 438	4 918	15.2	5428.00	16.7	32 470	4 822	14.9	5293.00	16.3	32 124	4 807	15.0	5242.00	16.3
45 to 54 years	24 665	4 881	19.8	5377.00	21.8	25 651	4 815	18.8	5305.00	20.7	26 503	5 015	18.9	5455.00	20.6
55 to 64 years	10 880	1 932	17.8	2107.00	19.4	11 204	1 998	17.8	2193.00	19.6	11 609	1 997	17.2	2185.00	18.8
65 years and over	2 718	221	8.1	247.00	9.1	2 889	243	8.4	281.00	9.7	2 995	242	8.1	267.00	8.9
Men, 16 Years And Over	61 914	9 949	16.1	10758.0	17.4	62 853	9 578	15.2	10355.0	16.5	62 727	9 502	15.1	10268.0	16.4
16 to 24 years	10 116	716	7.1	781.00	7.7	10 440	618	5.9	697.00	6.7	10 165	617	6.1	705.00	6.9
25 years and over	51 797	9 232	17.8	9977.00	19.3	52 412	8 960	17.1	9657.00	18.4	52 562	8 885	16.9	9562.00	18.2
25 to 34 years	15 330	2 142	14.0	2325.00	15.2	15 197	2 030	13.4	2207.00	14.5	14 856	1 913	12.9	2082.00	14.0
35 to 44 years	17 020	2 993	17.6	3241.00	19.0	17 028	2 871	16.9	3077.00	18.1	16 832	2 881	17.1	3075.00	18.3
45 to 54 years	12 395	2 800	22.6	3026.00	24.4	12 898	2 739	21.2	2956.00	22.9	13 359	2 808	21.0	3018.00	22.6
55 to 64 years	5 622	1 186	21.1	1267.00	22.5	5 770	1 191	20.6	1268.00	22.0	5 935	1 152	19.4	1241.00	20.9
65 years and over	1 431	111	7.7	118.00	8.2	1 519	129	8.5	148.00	9.8	1 580	132	8.4	147.00	9.3
Women, 16 Years And Over	57 050	6 528	11.4	7425.00	13.0	57 933	6 680	11.5	7590.00	13.1	58 033	6 773	11.7	7608.00	13.1
16 to 24 years	9 489	393	4.1	458.00	4.8	9 726	392	4.0	455.00	4.7	9 654	417	4.3	483.00	5.0
25 years and over	47 560	6 135	12.9	6966.00	14.6	48 207	6 288	13.0	7135.00	14.8	48 379	6 356	13.1	7125.00	14.7
25 to 34 years	13 327	1 273	9.6	1460.00	11.0	13 209	1 340	10.1	1513.00	11.5	12 855	1 267	9.9	1457.00	11.3
35 to 44 years	15 418	1 924	12.5	2187.00	14.2	15 441	1 951	12.6	2215.00	14.3	15 292	1 927	12.6	2167.00	14.2
45 to 54 years	12 270	2 081	17.0	2351.00	19.2	12 752	2 077	16.3	2348.00	18.4	13 145	2 208	16.8	2437.00	18.5
55 to 64 years	5 258	746	14.2	839.00	16.0	5 434	807	14.9	925.00	17.0	5 673	846	14.9	944.00	16.6
65 years and over	1 287	110	8.5	129.00	10.0	1 370	114	8.3	133.00	9.7	1 415	109	7.7	120.00	8.5
RACE, HISPANIC ORIGIN, AND SEX															
White, 16 Years And Over	99 147	13 349	13.5	14668.0	14.8	100 455	13 094	13.0	14453.0	14.4	100 384	13 125	13.1	14400.0	14.3
Men	52 492	8 246	15.7	8896.00	16.9	53 105	7 911	14.9	8541.00	16.1	52 970	7 849	14.8	8474.00	16.0
Women	46 655	5 103	10.9	5771.00	12.4	47 350	5 183	10.9	5912.00	12.5	47 414	5 276	11.1	5926.00	12.5
Black, 16 Years And Over	14 346	2 463	17.2	2757.00	19.2	14 544	2 489	17.1	2744.00	18.9	14 515	2 465	17.0	2705.00	18.6
Men	6 585	1 348	20.5	1464.00	22.2	6 701	1 282	19.1	1388.00	20.7	6 660	1 256	18.9	1357.00	20.4
Women	7 760	1 116	14.4	1293.00	16.7	7 843	1 208	15.4	1356.00	17.3	7 855	1 209	15.4	1347.00	17.2
Hispanic, 16 Years And Over	12 810	1 525	11.9	1684.00	13.1	13 609	1 554	11.4	1740.00	12.8	13 782	1 559	11.3	1729.00	12.5
Men	7 457	966	13.0	1052.00	14.1	7 884	972	12.3	1063.00	13.5	7 950	935	11.8	1024.00	12.9
Women	5 353	559	10.4	632.00	11.8	5 725	582	10.2	677.00	11.8	5 832	624	10.7	705.00	12.1
FULL- OR PART-TIME STATUS[3]															
Full-Time Workers	97 626	14 974	15.3	16501.0	16.9	99 917	14 822	14.8	16306.0	16.3	99 599	14 809	14.9	16218.0	16.3
Part-Time Workers	21 065	1 459	6.9	1634.00	7.8	20 619	1 395	6.8	1593.00	7.7	20 926	1 437	6.9	1625.00	7.8

Note: Data refer to the sole or principal job of full- and part-time workers. Excluded are all self-employed workers regardless of whether or not their businesses are incorporated. Detail for the above race and Hispanic-origin groups will not sum to totals because data for the Other races group are not presented and Hispanics are included in both the White and Black population groups. Beginning in January 2000, data reflect new composite estimation procedures and revised population controls used in the household survey.

1. Data refer to members of a labor union or an employee association similar to a union.
2. Data refer to members of a labor union or an employee association similar to a union as well as workers who report no union affiliation but whose jobs are covered by a union or an employee association contract.
3. The distinction between full- and part-time workers is based on hours usually worked. Data will not sum to totals because full- or part-time status on the principal job is not identifiable for a small number of multiple jobholders.

Table 9-3. Union Affiliation of Wage and Salary Workers by Occupation and Industry, 1999–2001

(Thousands of persons, percent.)

Characteristics	1999					2000					2001				
	Total employed	Members of unions [1]		Represented by unions [2]		Total employed	Members of unions [1]		Represented by unions [2]		Total employed	Members of unions [1]		Represented by unions [2]	
		Total	Percent of employed	Total	Percent of employed		Total	Percent of employed	Total	Percent of employed		Total	Percent of employed	Total	Percent of employed
OCCUPATION															
Managerial And Professional Specialty	34 693	4 594	13.2	5 352	15.4	35 378	4 536	12.8	5 277	14.9	36 276	4 654	12.8	5 355	14.8
Executive, administrative, and managerial	16 000	903	5.6	1 138	7.1	16 434	875	5.3	1 075	6.5	16 916	949	5.6	1 133	6.7
Professional specialty	18 693	3 691	19.7	4 215	22.5	18 944	3 661	19.3	4 202	22.2	19 360	3 705	19.1	4 222	21.8
Technical, Sales, And Administrative Support	35 514	3 191	9.0	3 609	10.2	36 124	3 119	8.6	3 521	9.7	35 953	3 193	8.9	3 587	10.0
Technicians and related support	4 188	461	11.0	523	12.5	4 279	431	10.1	500	11.7	4 393	474	10.8	533	12.1
Sales occupations	13 451	549	4.1	613	4.6	13 677	481	3.5	533	3.9	13 639	481	3.5	545	4.0
Administrative support, including clerical	17 874	2 182	12.2	2 474	13.8	18 167	2 207	12.1	2 487	13.7	17 921	2 239	12.5	2 509	14.0
Service Occupations	16 829	2 151	12.8	2 336	13.9	16 953	2 234	13.2	2 441	14.4	17 156	2 274	13.3	2 464	14.4
Protective service	2 427	927	38.2	991	40.8	2 384	938	39.4	1 003	42.1	2 460	935	38.0	998	40.6
Service, except protective service	14 403	1 224	8.5	1 346	9.3	14 569	1 295	8.9	1 438	9.9	14 695	1 339	9.1	1 466	10.0
Precision Production, Craft, And Repair	12 474	2 800	22.4	2 929	23.5	12 716	2 783	21.9	2 910	22.9	12 635	2 716	21.5	2 839	22.5
Operators, Fabricators, And Laborers	17 514	3 627	20.7	3 830	21.9	17 642	3 498	19.8	3 687	20.9	16 888	3 353	19.9	3 534	20.9
Machine operators, assemblers, and inspectors	7 255	1 490	20.5	1 572	21.7	7 043	1 366	19.4	1 442	20.5	6 502	1 317	20.3	1 383	21.3
Transportation and material moving occupations	5 041	1 148	22.8	1 216	24.1	5 182	1 195	23.1	1 260	24.3	5 153	1 202	23.3	1 276	24.8
Handlers, equipment cleaners, helpers, and laborers	5 218	989	18.9	1 042	20.0	5 417	938	17.3	984	18.2	5 233	834	15.9	875	16.7
Farming, Forestry, And Fishing	1 940	113	5.8	125	6.4	1 974	89	4.5	109	5.5	1 853	85	4.6	96	5.2
INDUSTRY															
Agriculture Wage And Salary Workers	1 721	43	2.5	48	2.8	1 821	38	2.1	45	2.5	1 667	27	1.6	33	2.0
Private Nonagricultural Wage And Salary Workers	98 304	9 376	9.5	10 168	10.3	99 989	9 110	9.1	9 924	9.9	99 938	9 086	9.1	9 838	9.8
Mining	531	57	10.6	60	11.4	499	54	10.9	57	11.4	531	65	12.3	69	12.9
Construction	6 230	1 187	19.1	1 224	19.6	6 666	1 220	18.3	1 268	19.0	6 881	1 264	18.4	1 305	19.0
Manufacturing	19 323	3 024	15.6	3 209	16.6	19 167	2 832	14.8	2 999	15.6	18 149	2 657	14.6	2 807	15.5
Durable goods	11 824	1 941	16.4	2 063	17.5	11 688	1 791	15.3	1 894	16.2	11 059	1 666	15.1	1 757	15.9
Nondurable goods	7 499	1 083	14.4	1 146	15.3	7 480	1 041	13.9	1 105	14.8	7 091	990	14.0	1 050	14.8
Transportation and public utilities	7 317	1 865	25.5	1 956	26.7	7 508	1 805	24.0	1 920	25.6	7 422	1 743	23.5	1 834	24.7
Transportation	4 450	1 136	25.5	1 186	26.7	4 573	1 135	24.8	1 203	26.3	4 441	1 069	24.1	1 126	25.4
Communications and public utilities	2 866	729	25.4	770	26.9	2 935	670	22.8	717	24.4	2 981	674	22.6	708	23.7
Wholesale and retail trade	24 671	1 278	5.2	1 406	5.7	25 133	1 194	4.7	1 315	5.2	25 045	1 174	4.7	1 284	5.1
Wholesale trade	4 573	248	5.4	281	6.1	4 766	243	5.1	265	5.6	4 540	249	5.5	268	5.9
Retail trade	20 098	1 030	5.1	1 126	5.6	20 366	951	4.7	1 049	5.2	20 505	926	4.5	1 016	5.0
Finance, insurance, and real estate	7 588	156	2.1	191	2.5	7 488	121	1.6	156	2.1	7 648	158	2.1	211	2.8
Services	32 645	1 809	5.5	2 121	6.5	33 528	1 884	5.6	2 208	6.6	34 261	2 026	5.9	2 328	6.8
Government Workers	18 938	7 058	37.3	7 966	42.1	18 976	7 110	37.5	7 976	42.0	19 155	7 162	37.4	8 004	41.8
Federal	3 264	1 047	32.1	1 275	39.0	3 233	1 033	32.0	1 186	36.7	3 284	1 037	31.6	1 201	36.6
State	5 233	1 527	29.2	1 781	34.0	5 464	1 641	30.0	1 867	34.2	5 677	1 732	30.5	1 957	34.5
Local	10 440	4 484	42.9	4 911	47.0	10 278	4 436	43.2	4 923	47.9	10 195	4 393	43.1	4 847	47.5

Note: Data refer to the sole or principal job of full- and part-time workers. Excluded are all self-employed workers regardless of whether or not their businesses are incorporated. Beginning in January 2000, data reflect revised population controls used in the household survey.

1. Data refer to members of a labor union or an employee association similar to a union.
2. Data refer to members of a labor union or an employee association similar to a union as well as workers who report no union affiliation but whose jobs are covered by a union or an employee association contract.

Table 9-4. Median Weekly Earnings of Full-Time Wage and Salary Workers by Union Affiliation, Occupation, and Industry, 1996–2001

(Dollars.)

Characteristics	1996				1997				1998			
	Total	Members of unions[1]	Represented by unions[2]	Non-union	Total	Members of unions[1]	Represented by unions[2]	Non-union	Total	Members of unions[1]	Represented by unions[2]	Non-union
TOTAL, 16 YEARS AND OVER	$490	$615	$610	$462	$503	$640	$632	$478	$523	$659	$653	$499
OCCUPATION												
Managerial And Professional Specialty	718	758.0	749	708	738	776	766	731	759	789	774	756
Executive, administrative, and managerial	699	742.0	745	694	725	757	752	721	755	801	789	753
Professional specialty	730	762.0	750	721	750	782	769	742	763	787	772	759
Technical, Sales, And Administrative Support	441	532.0	524	427	456	550	541	441	477	575	569	463
Technicians and related support	573	664.0	661	554	582	677	675	566	599	708	688	590
Sales occupations	474	451.0	459	475	482	467	469	483	502	496	492	502
Administrative support, including clerical	405	524.0	516	389	419	545	534	404	438	563	558	418
Service Occupations	305	490.0	484	282	313	516	505	293	327	557	542	305
Protective service	538	693.0	686	413	550	724	713	418	598	736	732	450
Service, except protective service	283	379.0	379	271	293	398	393	283	305	403	402	295
Precision Production, Craft, And Repair	540	703.0	698	494	548	724	718	501	572	753	747	514
Operators, Fabricators, And Laborers	391	528.0	522	353	401	572	561	365	415	585	580	381
Machine operators, assemblers, and inspectors	380	512.0	508	345	390	533	524	356	406	559	556	375
Transportation and material moving occupations	476	610.0	601	425	498	658	642	451	510	655	644	468
Handlers, equipment cleaners, helpers and laborers	330	481.0	477	308	329	509	506	310	351	514	514	326
Farming, Forestry, And Fishing	294	439.0	423	288	295	505	475	290	302	471	462	299
INDUSTRY												
Agricultural Wage And Salary Workers	306	(3)	(3)	305	306	(3)	(3)	305	315	(3)	(3)	314
Private Nonagricultural Wage And Salary Workers	475	584.0	579	458	490	610	603	476	509	626	620	496
Mining	693	698.0	699	690	680	717	717	668	684	733	723	673
Construction	504	748.0	742	464	518	771	760	484	534	790	783	496
Manufacturing	507	560.0	558	494	517	595	592	503	551	606	603	532
Durable goods	533	588.0	587	517	548	619	616	523	581	629	625	566
Nondurable goods	466	510.0	507	453	484	536	529	470	507	565	562	495
Transportation and public utilities	596	680.0	676	555	617	718	714	580	624	731	724	586
Transportation	527	656.0	649	491	573	702	697	513	570	704	695	519
Communications and public utilities	693	707.0	705	684	709	746	743	690	727	763	760	699
Wholesale and retail trade	380	450.0	444	375	391	457	451	387	410	480	476	405
Wholesale trade	503	566.0	551	500	525	545	536	524	562	611	604	557
Retail trade	343	408.0	408	338	352	419	415	347	373	442	439	369
Finance, insurance, and real estate	521	534.0	533	520	546	487	501	548	577	545	554	578
Services	456	501.0	498	451	475	517	512	470	498	540	548	494
Government Workers	592	657.0	651	518	605	681	671	530	620	694	688	558
Federal	672	677.0	679	663	684	689	687	678	694	690	693	696
State	557	610.0	605	514	584	628	621	540	596	646	638	563
Local	580	671.0	661	473	592	697	682	479	612	712	702	501

See footnotes and *Note* at end of table.

Table 9-4. Median Weekly Earnings of Full-Time Wage and Salary Workers by Union Affiliation, Occupation, and Industry, 1996–2001—Continued

(Dollars.)

Characteristics	1999				2000				2001			
	Total	Members of unions[1]	Represented by unions[2]	Non-union	Total	Members of unions[1]	Represented by unions[2]	Non-union	Total	Members of unions[1]	Represented by unions[2]	Non-union
TOTAL, 16 YEARS AND OVER	$549	$672	$667	$516	$576	$696	$691	$542	$597	$718	$712	$575
OCCUPATION												
Managerial And Professional Specialty	797	826	819	792	836	840	834	836	859	865	860	859
Executive, administrative, and managerial	792	823	829	789	840	834	854	839	867	869	880	865
Professional specialty	800	826	817	794	832	841	829	832	854	864	855	853
Technical, Sales, And Administrative Support	488	583	580	477	506	598	590	497	521	613	606	513
Technicians and related support	618	714	711	608	648	748	741	635	673	731	738	662
Sales occupations	523	513	519	523	550	526	522	552	574	559	556	575
Administrative support, including clerical	447	574	564	429	469	588	579	453	486	597	588	472
Service Occupations	336	536	529	314	355	554	542	327	377	556	550	352
Protective service	592	737	728	477	623	786	771	502	629	809	797	518
Service, except protective service	311	412	409	303	324	423	419	316	345	426	424	333
Precision Production, Craft, And Repair	594	755	747	546	613	784	778	570	629	822	817	590
Operators, Fabricators, And Laborers	429	591	584	398	446	605	602	411	467	620	613	425
Machine operators, assemblers, and inspectors	423	572	566	394	436	575	572	408	457	587	582	421
Transportation and material moving occupations	513	668	657	478	540	694	690	502	573	724	715	521
Handlers, equipment cleaners, helpers and laborers	363	507	499	340	378	555	551	355	389	530	523	369
Farming, Forestry, And Fishing	331	512	514	322	334	516	506	325	354	587	582	345
INDUSTRY												
Agricultural Wage And Salary Workers	340	(3)	(3)	337	347	(3)	(3)	344	371	(3)	(3)	370
Private Nonagricultural Wage And Salary Workers	525	634	628	513	555	664	657	537	583	685	677	572
Mining	734	710	731	735	768	746	748	774	795	816	816	789
Construction	552	778	772	509	584	814	810	529	609	864	854	569
Manufacturing	576	614	611	561	595	630	628	587	613	645	641	607
Durable goods	594	628	625	584	618	662	659	610	634	675	669	625
Nondurable goods	529	584	579	518	553	594	594	537	583	607	606	577
Transportation and public utilities	651	748	742	613	679	768	762	639	705	796	792	669
Transportation	596	727	718	551	615	744	741	582	644	781	776	609
Communications and public utilities	751	773	770	738	776	808	798	766	794	816	813	782
Wholesale and retail trade	421	499	492	418	444	518	514	439	468	540	528	464
Wholesale trade	573	584	570	573	595	607	608	593	624	654	660	621
Retail trade	391	472	463	387	403	495	490	399	421	497	488	418
Finance, insurance, and real estate	598	582	587	599	620	596	593	621	655	584	600	658
Services	517	554	563	515	543	567	574	540	580	599	597	579
Government Workers	641	714	709	585	665	730	726	609	684	753	749	620
Federal	729	721	723	737	745	736	738	755	772	762	767	777
State	615	683	677	578	633	685	681	606	649	718	712	610
Local	623	726	720	525	650	746	738	562	667	764	756	580

Note: Data refer to the sole or principal job of full-time workers. Excluded are all self-employed workers regardless of whether or not their businesses are incorporated. Beginning in January 2000, data reflect new composite estimation procedures and revised population controls used in the household survey.

1. Data refer to members of a labor union or an employee association similar to a union.
2. Data refer to members of a labor union or an employee association similar to a union as well as workers who report no union affiliation but whose jobs are covered by a union or an employee association contract.
3. Data not shown where base is less than 50,000 workers.

Table 9-5. Wage and Salary Employees Who Were Union or Employee Association Members, 1977–2001

Year	Wage and Salary employees who were union or employee association members (thousands)	Total wage and salary employment (thousands)	Union or association members as a percent of wage and salary employment
1977	19 335	81 334	23.8
1978	19 548	84 968	230.0
1979	20 986	87 117	24.1
1980	20 095	87 480	230.0
1981	...	...	...
1982	...	...	...
1983 [1]	17 717	88 290	20.1
1984	17 340	92 194	18.8
1985	16 996	94 521	180.0
1986	16 975	96 903	17.5
1987	16 913	99 303	170.0
1988	17 002	101 407	16.8
1989	16 980	103 480	16.4
1990	16 740	103 905	16.1
1991	16 568	102 786	16.1
1992	16 390	103 688	15.8
1993	16 598	105 087	15.8
1994 [2]	16 748	107 989	15.5
1995	16 360	110 038	14.9
1996	16 269	111 960	14.5
1997	16 110	114 533	14.1
1998	16 211	116 730	13.9
1999	16 477	118 963	13.9
2000	16 258	120 786	13.5
2001	16 275	120 760	13.5

1. Annual average data beginning in 1983 are not directly comparable with the May data for 1977–1980.
2. Data beginning in 1994 are not strictly comparable with data for 1993 and earlier years because of the introduction of a major redesign of the Current Population Survey questionnaire and collection methodology and the introduction of 1990 census-based population controls.

Table 9-6. Union Affiliation of Employed Wage and Salary Workers by State, 2000–2001

(Numbers in thousands, percent.)

State	2000					2001				
	Total employed	Members of unions [1]		Represented by unions [2]		Total employed	Members of unions [1]		Represented by unions [2]	
		Total	Percent of employed	Total	Percent of employed		Total	Percent of employed	Total	Percent of employed
U.S. TOTAL	120 786	16 258	14	17 944	15	120 760	16 275	14	17 875	15
Alabama	1 878	181	10	198	10	1 834	174	10	195	11
Alaska	259	57	22	64	25	267	59	22	66	25
Arizona	2 015	130	6	148	7	2 058	121	6	134	6
Arkansas	1 052	61	6	71	7	1 026	64	6	79	8
California	14 359	2 295	16	2 546	18	14 557	2 395	16	2 617	18
Colorado	1 923	173	9	193	10	1 931	168	9	196	10
Connecticut	1 508	246	16	262	17	1 497	237	16	250	17
Delaware	353	47	13	52	15	371	45	12	50	13
District of Columbia	244	36	15	40	16	242	41	17	50	21
Florida	6 399	434	7	554	9	6 473	422	6	550	8
Georgia	3 632	228	6	267	7	3 613	259	7	298	8
Hawaii	497	124	25	129	26	513	123	24	133	26
Idaho	533	41	8	48	9	554	42	8	48	9
Illinois	5 639	1 046	19	1 101	20	5 466	999	18	1 060	19
Indiana	2 687	418	16	461	17	2 696	385	14	413	15
Iowa	1 333	182	14	215	16	1 351	173	13	205	15
Kansas	1 200	109	9	135	11	1 179	110	9	136	12
Kentucky	1 729	208	12	235	14	1 678	192	11	209	12
Louisiana	1 711	122	7	155	9	1 750	135	8	176	10
Maine	556	78	14	92	17	559	72	13	81	14
Maryland	2 423	353	15	406	17	2 450	346	14	414	17
Massachusetts	2 841	406	14	445	16	2 840	420	15	451	16
Michigan	4 513	938	21	985	22	4 452	968	22	1 006	23
Minnesota	2 307	419	18	434	19	2 337	411	18	427	18
Mississippi	1 120	68	6	104	9	1 104	62	6	99	9
Missouri	2 567	338	13	365	14	2 543	362	14	390	15
Montana	369	51	14	58	16	365	48	13	55	15
Nebraska	775	65	8	89	12	770	60	8	84	11
Nevada	881	151	17	165	19	881	150	17	161	18
New Hampshire	576	60	10	67	12	593	60	10	67	11
New Jersey	3 668	762	21	801	22	3 637	712	20	759	21
New Mexico	692	56	8	70	10	702	56	8	67	10
New York	7 683	1 958	26	2 036	26	7 575	2 024	27	2 098	28
North Carolina	3 404	124	4	148	4	3 388	125	4	146	4
North Dakota	272	18	6	21	8	284	21	8	24	9
Ohio	5 071	879	17	955	19	5 075	899	18	967	19
Oklahoma	1 384	94	7	108	8	1 385	117	8	130	9
Oregon	1 457	234	16	251	17	1 444	228	16	245	17
Pennsylvania	5 149	870	17	926	18	5 228	888	17	956	18
Rhode Island	438	80	18	83	19	434	78	18	80	18
South Carolina	1 740	70	4	89	5	1 642	75	4	91	6
South Dakota	329	18	6	22	7	328	19	6	24	8
Tennessee	2 387	212	9	239	10	2 395	182	8	207	9
Texas	8 755	505	6	645	7	8 855	497	6	593	7
Utah	945	69	7	85	9	945	64	7	73	8
Vermont	274	28	10	34	12	276	30	11	34	12
Virginia	3 199	179	6	227	7	3 255	163	5	209	6
Washington	2 593	471	18	516	20	2 475	462	19	496	20
West Virginia	718	103	14	111	16	732	106	15	116	16
Wisconsin	2 533	446	18	473	19	2 533	411	16	436	17
Wyoming	216	18	8	22	10	220	20	9	24	11

Note: Data refer to the sole or principal job of full- and part-time workers. Excluded are all self-employed workers regardless of whether or not their businesses are incorporated.

1. Data refer to members of a labor union or an employee association similar to a union.
2. Data refer to members of a labor union or an employee association similar to a union as well as workers who report no union affiliation but whose jobs are covered by a union or an employee association contract.

PART TEN

FOREIGN LABOR AND PRICE STATISTICS

FOREIGN LABOR AND PRICE STATISTICS

HIGHLIGHTS

This chapter compares several summary statistics of labor force status, manufacturing productivity and consumer prices from the U.S. with other countries. Different concepts and methodologies make comparison difficult and BLS makes such adjustments as it can to reconcile some of the data. There are lags in receipt of the data from other countries, so comparisons here are based on the latest available data.

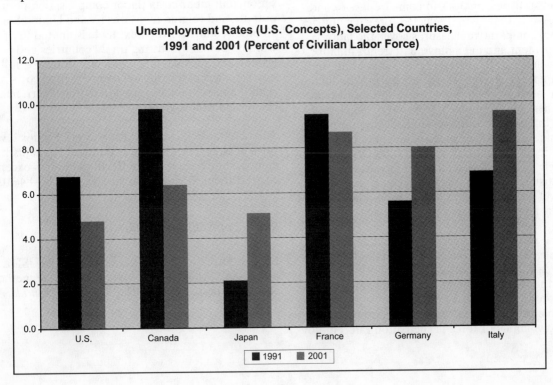

In spite of the increase in the U.S. unemployment rate in 2001, the United States has the lowest unemployment rate among major reporting countries. (Table 10-1)

OTHER HIGHLIGHTS:

- All reporting countries showed small increases in employment in 2001 except for the United States and Japan. This reverses the long-term trend in the relationship between the United States and other countries. (Table 10-1)
- Output per hour in manufacturing increased in all countries between 2000 and 2001 except Japan and Canada. Taiwan had the largest increase. Even though output declined substantially in Taiwan, hours declined even more, resulting in a 6 percent increase in output per hour. (Table 10-2)
- In the United States, manufacturing hours declined slightly more than output, resulting in a 1.9 percent increase in output per hour. (Table 10-2)
- Unit labor costs (U.S. currency basis) declined in almost all countries in 2001 but the largest decline was in Korea, 7.8 percent compared with only .3 percent decline in the United States. (Table 10-2)
- Inflation in most of the 16 countries compared remained relatively low. In only two countries did the Consumer Price Index increase more that 4 percent. (Table 10-5)

NOTES AND DEFINITIONS

Collection and Coverage

From its inception, BLS has conducted a program of research and statistical analysis to compare labor conditions in the United States and selected foreign countries. The principal comparative measures cover the labor force, employment and unemployment; trends in labor productivity and unit labor costs in manufacturing; and hourly compensation costs for manufacturing production workers. All of the measures are based upon statistical data and other source materials from (a) the statistical agencies of the foreign countries studied; (b) international and supranational bodies such as the United Nations, the International Labour Office (ILO), the Organization for Economic Cooperation and Development (OECD), and the Statistical Office of the European Communities (EUROSTAT), which attempt to obtain comparable country data; and (c) other secondary sources.

International statistical comparisons should be used cautiously because statistical concepts and methods in each country are fashioned primarily to meet domestic rather than international needs. Wherever possible, the Bureau adjusts the data to improve comparability.

The first table provides the Bureau's comparative measures of the civilian labor force participation rate, employment, and unemployment approximating U.S. concepts. The second table provides trend indexes of manufacturing labor productivity (output per hour), hourly compensation, unit labor costs (labor compensation per unit of output), and related measures for the United States and 13 other countries. The next table is limited to production workers in manufacturing for 29 countries and 6 country groups, and shows hourly compensation costs in U.S. dollars. Changes in unadjusted compensation costs reflect both the movements of costs in national currencies and changes in exchange rates.

The final tables provide consumer price index levels and rates of change for selected countries. No adjustments for comparability are made in the total indexes except to convert them to a uniform base year (1982–84=100).

Sources of Additional Information

More information is in BLS news releases USDL 02-543 and 02-549. An extensive description of the methodology can be found in the BLS *Handbook of Methods*, April 1997.

Table 10-1. Employment Status of the Working-Age Population, Approximating U.S. Concepts, 10 Countries, 1965–2001

(Numbers in thousands, percent.)

Year and category	United States	Canada[1]	Australia	Japan	France	Germany[2]	Italy	Nether-lands	Sweden	United Kingdom
CIVILIAN LABOR FORCE PARTICIPATION RATE										
1965	58.9	56.5	59.9	64.4	57.4	58.7	51.4	...	64.1	62.4
1966	59.2	57.3	60.6	64.6	57.3	58.2	50.0	...	64.2	62.3
1967	59.6	57.6	61.2	64.8	57.4	57.0	50.2	...	63.3	62.0
1968	59.6	57.6	61.2	64.9	57.1	56.9	49.7	...	63.8	61.6
1969	60.1	57.9	61.4	64.6	57.3	57.0	49.3	...	63.8	61.4
1970	60.4	57.8	62.1	64.5	57.5	56.9	49.0	...	64.0	61.1
1971	60.2	58.1	62.2	64.3	57.4	56.5	48.7	...	64.2	60.4
1972	[3]60.4	58.6	62.3	63.8	57.2	56.2	47.7	...	64.1	60.8
1973	[3]60.8	59.7	62.6	64.0	57.3	56.3	47.6	53.4	64.1	62.4
1974	61.2	60.5	63.0	63.1	57.4	55.7	47.7	53.5	64.8	62.2
1975	61.2	61.1	63.2	62.4	57.2	55.0	47.7	54.5	65.9	62.6
1976	61.6	[3]62.5	62.7	62.4	57.5	54.6	48.0	54.1	66.0	62.7
1977	62.3	62.8	62.7	62.5	57.8	54.4	48.2	54.2	65.9	62.7
1978	[3]63.2	63.6	61.9	62.8	57.7	54.4	47.8	54.0	66.1	62.8
1979	63.7	64.4	61.6	62.7	57.8	54.5	48.0	54.2	66.6	62.5
1980	63.8	64.9	62.1	62.6	57.5	54.7	48.2	55.4	66.9	62.5
1981	63.9	65.6	61.9	62.6	57.5	54.7	48.3	56.7	66.8	62.3
1982	64.0	64.8	61.7	62.7	57.5	54.6	47.7	56.6	66.8	61.9
1983	64.0	65.1	61.4	63.1	57.2	[3]54.3	47.5	[3]55.7	66.7	61.6
1984	64.4	65.4	61.5	62.7	57.2	54.4	47.3	55.7	66.6	62.3
1985	64.8	65.9	61.6	62.3	56.8	54.7	47.2	55.5	66.9	62.4
1986	[3]65.3	66.3	62.8	62.1	56.7	54.9	[3]47.8	56.0	67.0	62.5
1987	65.6	66.7	[3]62.9	61.9	56.5	55.0	47.6	56.3	[3]66.4	62.9
1988	65.9	67.0	63.3	61.9	56.2	55.1	47.4	[3]54.3	66.9	63.5
1989	66.5	67.4	64.1	62.2	56.1	55.2	47.3	54.8	67.3	64.0
1990	[3]66.5	67.3	64.7	62.6	55.9	55.3	47.2	56.1	67.4	64.1
1991	66.2	66.7	64.2	63.2	56.0	[3]58.8	[3]47.7	56.5	67.0	63.7
1992	66.4	65.9	63.9	63.4	[3]55.9	58.2	47.5	57.8	65.7	63.1
1993	66.3	65.5	63.5	63.3	55.8	[3]57.7	47.9	58.6	64.5	62.8
1994	[3]66.6	65.2	63.9	63.1	55.8	57.4	47.3	59.0	63.7	62.7
1995	66.6	64.9	64.6	62.9	55.6	57.1	47.1	59.2	64.1	62.7
1996	66.8	64.7	64.6	63.0	55.8	57.1	47.1	59.8	64.0	62.8
1997	[3]67.1	65.0	64.3	63.2	55.7	57.3	47.2	60.8	63.3	62.9
1998	[3]67.1	65.4	64.3	62.8	56.1	57.7	47.6	61.7	62.8	62.9
1999	[3]67.1	65.8	64.2	62.4	56.4	57.6	47.8	62.8	62.8	63.2
2000	[3]67.2	65.9	64.7	62.0	56.4	57.5	48.1	63.5	[4]63.8	63.3
2001	66.9	66.0	[4]64.7	[4]61.6	...	...	...	...	[4]64.2	...
UNEMPLOYMENT RATE										
1965	4.5	3.6	1.3	1.2	1.6	0.3	3.5	...	1.2	2.1
1966	3.8	3.4	1.6	1.4	1.6	0.3	3.7	...	1.6	2.3
1967	3.8	3.8	1.9	1.3	2.1	1.3	3.4	...	2.1	3.3
1968	3.6	4.5	1.8	1.2	2.7	1.1	3.5	...	2.2	3.2
1969	3.5	4.4	1.8	1.1	2.3	0.6	3.5	...	1.9	3.1
1970	4.9	5.7	1.6	1.2	2.5	0.5	3.2	...	1.5	3.1
1971	5.9	6.2	1.9	1.3	2.8	0.6	3.3	...	2.6	3.9
1972	[3]5.6	6.2	2.6	1.4	2.9	0.7	3.8	...	2.7	4.2
1973	[3]4.9	5.5	2.3	1.3	2.8	0.7	3.7	3.1	2.5	3.2
1974	5.6	5.3	2.7	1.4	2.9	1.6	3.1	3.6	2.0	3.1
1975	8.5	6.9	4.9	1.9	4.2	3.4	3.4	5.1	1.6	4.6
1976	7.7	[3]6.8	4.8	2.0	4.6	3.4	3.9	5.4	1.6	5.9
1977	7.1	7.8	5.6	2.0	5.2	3.4	4.1	4.9	1.8	6.4
1978	[3]6.1	8.1	6.3	2.3	5.4	3.3	4.1	5.1	2.2	6.3
1979	5.8	7.3	6.3	2.1	6.1	2.9	4.4	5.1	2.1	5.4
1980	7.1	7.3	6.1	2.0	6.5	2.8	4.4	6.0	2.0	7.0
1981	7.6	7.3	5.8	2.2	7.6	4.0	4.9	8.9	2.5	10.5
1982	9.7	10.6	7.2	2.4	8.3	5.6	5.4	10.2	3.1	11.3
1983	9.6	11.5	10.0	2.7	8.6	[3]6.9	5.9	[3]11.4	3.5	11.8
1984	7.5	10.9	9.0	2.8	10.0	7.1	5.9	11.5	3.1	11.7
1985	7.2	10.2	8.3	2.6	10.5	7.2	6.0	9.6	2.8	11.2
1986	[3]7.0	9.2	8.1	2.8	10.6	6.6	[3]7.5	10.0	2.6	11.2
1987	6.2	8.4	[3]7.9	2.9	10.8	6.3	7.9	10.0	[3]2.2	10.3
1988	5.5	7.3	7.0	2.5	10.3	6.3	7.9	[3]7.6	1.9	8.6
1989	5.3	7.1	6.0	2.3	9.6	5.7	7.8	7.0	1.6	7.2
1990	[3]5.6	7.7	6.7	2.1	9.1	5.0	7.0	6.2	1.8	6.9
1991	6.8	9.8	9.3	2.1	9.5	[3]5.6	[3]6.9	5.9	3.1	8.8
1992	7.5	10.6	10.5	2.2	[3]10.4	6.7	7.3	5.6	5.6	10.1
1993	6.9	10.8	10.6	2.5	11.8	8.0	[3]10.2	6.6	9.3	10.5
1994	[3]6.1	9.5	9.4	2.9	12.3	8.5	11.2	7.2	9.6	9.6
1995	5.6	8.6	8.2	3.2	11.8	8.2	11.8	6.9	9.1	8.7
1996	5.4	8.8	8.2	3.4	12.5	9.0	11.7	6.4	9.9	8.1
1997	[3]4.9	8.4	8.3	3.4	12.4	9.9	11.9	5.3	10.1	7.0
1998	[3]4.5	7.7	7.7	4.1	11.8	9.3	12.0	4.0	8.4	6.3
1999	[3]4.2	7.0	7.0	4.7	11.2	8.6	11.5	3.4	7.1	6.0
2000	[3]4.0	6.1	6.3	4.8	9.4	8.1	10.7	3.0	5.8	5.5
2001	4.8	6.4	6.7	[4]5.1	[4]8.7	[4]8.0	[4]9.6	...	[4]5.0	...

See footnotes at end of table.

Table 10-1. Employment Status of the Working-Age Population, Approximating U.S. Concepts, 10 Countries, 1965–2001—Continued

(Numbers in thousands, percent.)

Year and category	United States	Canada[1]	Australia	Japan	France	Germany[2]	Italy	Nether-lands	Sweden	United Kingdom
EMPLOYED										
1965	71 088	6 944	4 628	46 210	19 340	26 290	19 210	...	3 700	24 700
1966	72 895	7 242	4 785	47 200	19 530	26 220	18 890	...	3 736	24 760
1967	74 372	7 451	4 928	48 180	19 650	25 390	19 130	...	3 693	24 470
1968	75 920	7 593	5 046	49 100	19 640	25 400	19 080	...	3 737	24 470
1969	77 902	7 832	5 188	49 570	19 990	25 790	18 940	...	3 778	24 390
1970	78 678	7 919	5 388	50 140	20 270	26 100	19 080	...	3 850	24 330
1971	79 367	8 104	5 517	50 480	20 420	26 220	19 020	...	3 854	23 970
1972	[3]82 153	8 344	5 601	50 590	20 540	26 280	18 710	...	3 856	24 120
1973	[3]85 064	8 761	5 765	51 910	20 840	26 590	18 870	5 050	3 873	24 610
1974	86 794	9 125	5 891	51 710	21 030	26 240	19 280	5 100	3 956	24 680
1975	85 846	9 284	5 866	51 530	20 860	25 540	19 400	5 070	4 056	24 560
1976	88 752	9 680	5 946	52 020	21 030	25 400	19 500	5 100	4 082	24 360
1977	92 017	9 822	6 000	52 720	21 220	25 430	19 670	5 210	4 093	24 400
1978	[3]96 048	10 115	6 038	53 370	21 320	25 650	19 720	5 260	4 109	24 610
1979	98 824	10 550	6 111	54 040	21 390	26 080	19 930	5 350	4 174	24 940
1980	99 303	10 857	6 284	54 600	21 440	26 490	20 200	5 520	4 226	24 670
1981	100 397	11 184	6 416	55 060	21 330	26 450	20 280	5 550	4 219	23 800
1982	99 526	10 850	6 415	55 620	21 390	26 150	20 250	5 520	4 213	23 560
1983	100 834	10 940	6 300	56 550	21 380	[3]25 770	20 320	[3]5 420	4 218	23 560
1984	105 005	11 209	6 494	56 870	21 200	25 830	20 390	5 490	4 249	23 930
1985	107 150	11 516	6 697	57 260	21 150	26 010	20 490	5 650	4 293	24 290
1986	[3]109 597	11 866	6 974	57 740	21 240	26 380	[3]20 610	5 740	4 326	24 470
1987	112 440	12 209	[3]7 142	58 320	21 320	26 590	20 590	5 850	[3]4 340	25 010
1988	114 968	12 591	7 413	59 310	21 520	26 800	20 870	[3]5 840	4 410	25 850
1989	117 342	12 866	7 734	60 500	21 850	27 200	20 770	5 990	4 480	26 510
1990	[3]118 793	12 961	7 877	61 710	22 080	27 950	21 080	6 230	4 513	26 740
1991	117 718	12 747	7 698	62 920	22 120	[3]36 870	[3]21 360	6 350	4 447	26 090
1992	118 492	12 672	7 660	63 620	22 020	36 390	21 230	6 560	4 265	25 530
1993	120 259	12 770	7 699	63 810	21 740	35 990	[3]20 270	6 630	4 028	25 450
1994	[3]123 060	13 027	7 942	63 860	21 720	35 760	19 940	6 670	3 992	25 720
1995	124 900	13 271	8 256	63 890	21 910	35 780	19 820	6 760	4 056	26 070
1996	126 708	13 380	8 364	64 200	21 960	35 640	19 920	6 900	4 019	26 380
1997	[3]129 558	13 705	8 444	64 900	22 090	35 510	19 990	7 130	3 973	26 880
1998	[3]131 463	14 068	8 618	64 450	22 510	36 060	20 210	7 380	4 034	27 210
1999	[3]133 488	14 456	8 808	63 920	22 940	36 360	20 460	7 640	4 117	27 530
2000	[3]135 208	14 827	9 068	63 790	23 530	36 540	20 840	7 810	4 229	27 830
2001	135 073	14 997	9 157	[4]63 470	...	...	[4]21 280	...	[4]4 309	...
UNEMPLOYED										
1965	3 366	263	61	570	310	70	690	...	44	540
1966	2 875	251	76	650	320	70	730	...	59	570
1967	2 975	296	94	630	420	340	670	...	80	830
1968	2 817	358	94	590	550	290	700	...	80	810
1969	2 832	362	96	570	480	170	680	...	73	770
1970	4 093	476	91	590	530	140	640	...	59	770
1971	5 016	535	107	640	580	160	640	...	101	980
1972	[3]4 882	553	150	730	610	190	740	...	107	1 070
1973	[3]4 365	515	136	680	590	190	720	160	98	820
1974	5 156	514	162	730	630	420	620	190	80	790
1975	7 929	690	302	1 000	910	890	690	270	67	1 180
1976	7 406	[3]711	298	1 080	1 020	890	790	290	66	1 540
1977	6 991	829	358	1 100	1 160	900	840	270	75	1 660
1978	6 202	890	405	1 240	1 220	870	850	280	94	1 650
1979	6 137	827	408	1 170	1 390	780	920	290	88	1 420
1980	7 637	849	409	1 140	1 490	770	920	350	86	1 850
1981	8 273	883	394	1 260	1 760	1 090	1 040	540	108	2 790
1982	10 678	1 289	495	1 360	1 930	1 560	1 160	630	137	3 000
1983	10 717	1 428	697	1 560	2 020	[3]1 900	1 270	[3]700	151	3 140
1984	8 539	1 370	641	1 610	2 360	1 970	1 280	710	136	3 180
1985	8 312	1 309	603	1 560	2 470	2 010	[3]1 310	600	125	3 060
1986	[3]8 237	1 209	613	1 670	2 520	1 860	[3]1 680	640	117	3 080
1987	7 425	1 122	[3]612	1 730	2 570	1 800	1 760	650	[3]97	2 860
1988	6 701	998	558	1 550	2 460	1 810	1 790	[3]480	84	2 420
1989	6 528	982	490	1 420	2 320	1 640	1 760	450	72	2 070
1990	[3]7 047	1 082	563	1 340	2 200	[3]1 460	1 590	410	84	1 990
1991	8 628	1 388	788	1 360	2 330	[3]2 200	[3]1 580	400	144	2 520
1992	9 613	1 505	897	1 420	[3]2 550	2 620	1 680	390	255	2 880
1993	8 940	1 539	914	1 660	2 900	3 110	[3]2 300	470	415	2 980
1994	[3]7 996	1 373	829	1 920	3 060	3 320	2 510	520	426	2 720
1995	7 404	1 246	739	2 100	2 920	3 200	2 640	500	404	2 490
1996	7 236	1 289	751	2 250	3 130	3 510	2 650	470	440	2 340
1997	[3]6 739	1 252	760	2 300	3 120	3 910	2 690	400	445	2 030
1998	[3]6 210	1 169	721	2 790	3 020	3 690	2 750	310	368	1 830
1999	[3]5 880	1 080	658	3 170	2 890	3 440	2 670	270	313	1 770
2000	[3]5 655	962	611	3 200	2 450	3 210	2 500	240	260	1 620
2001	6 742	1 031	661	[4]3 400	...	...	2 270	...	[4]228	...

1. There is a break in the published series as of 1966, resulting from sampling changes and a raising of the lower age limit from 14 to 15. The effect was to lower the as-published unemployment rate by about 0.4 percentage point.
2. Unified Germany for 1991 onward. Prior to 1991, data relate to the former West Germany.
3. Break in series.
4. Preliminary.

Table 10-2. Indexes of Manufacturing Productivity and Related Measures, 14 Countries, 1970 and 1986–2001

(1992=100.)

Item and year	United States	Canada	Japan	Korea	Taiwan	Belgium	Den-mark	France	Germany[1]	Italy	Nether-lands	Norway	Sweden	United King-dom
OUTPUT PER HOUR [2]														
1970	...	54.9	37.5	...	...	32.9	52.7	43.1	52.0	44.3	37.9	58.8	52.2	43.2
1986	86.0	87.6	76.1	58.9	66.6	87.8	91.2	80.6	89.6	87.9	90.2	89.8	87.5	73.9
1987	92.9	87.8	80.2	63.2	72.8	88.9	90.7	82.1	88.1	89.3	91.0	94.2	89.2	78.1
1988	96.9	89.6	83.9	68.7	76.4	92.0	94.1	87.7	91.5	93.9	93.1	93.1	90.5	82.6
1989	95.7	92.5	88.5	73.2	83.1	96.9	99.7	92.2	94.6	95.5	96.9	95.5	93.2	86.2
1990	96.9	93.4	94.4	81.3	88.9	96.8	99.1	93.8	99.0	95.8	98.5	97.6	94.6	89.2
1991	97.9	95.3	99.0	91.4	96.6	99.1	99.4	97.0	98.3	95.9	99.6	98.2	95.5	93.8
1992	100.0	100.0	100.0	100.0	100.0	100.0	100.0	100.0	100.0	100.0	100.0	100.0	100.0	100.0
1993	102.1	105.8	101.7	108.1	102.9	102.5	100.8	100.6	101.8	101.4	101.6	99.6	107.3	103.9
1994	107.3	110.8	103.3	118.0	106.7	108.4	...	108.2	109.5	104.9	113.2	99.6	119.4	107.1
1995	113.8	112.4	111.0	129.2	115.1	113.2	...	113.9	112.2	108.0	118.2	100.7	121.9	104.9
1996	117.0	109.7	116.1	142.5	123.1	117.0	...	114.6	113.9	108.1	120.2	102.5	124.5	103.8
1997	121.3	113.5	121.0	163.3	129.2	127.0	...	121.9	119.4	109.9	122.3	102.0	132.3	105.2
1998	126.5	113.1	121.2	182.9	135.8	129.2	...	127.7	120.3	110.0	125.0	99.9	139.5	107.0
1999	135.3	116.0	126.9	202.3	143.1	129.5	...	132.7	120.4	109.9	128.5	103.6	149.7	111.6
2000	142.9	118.4	134.1	218.4	150.6	133.4	...	142.5	127.9	113.0	133.8	104.5	158.0	118.0
2001	145.6	116.1	128.1	225.5	159.6	134.1	...	146.3	129.2	115.0	...	105.3	160.4	119.8
OUTPUT														
1970	...	58.9	39.2	7.0	12.7	57.6	68.0	64.1	70.9	48.1	59.1	90.6	80.7	90.2
1986	88.6	96.8	75.5	57.9	74.7	89.1	103.6	87.3	89.7	86.4	87.6	108.9	104.0	90.2
1987	96.4	100.7	79.0	68.5	84.3	88.8	99.4	87.2	88.0	89.0	88.8	111.5	106.6	94.5
1988	103.2	108.5	85.3	76.7	87.7	93.3	100.9	92.2	90.9	95.0	92.1	106.1	109.8	101.4
1989	102.4	111.3	90.9	79.4	90.8	99.1	104.4	97.2	94.0	98.3	96.6	102.1	110.9	105.5
1990	101.6	106.0	97.1	86.7	90.0	101.0	102.8	99.1	99.1	99.4	99.9	100.9	110.1	105.4
1991	98.3	99.0	102.0	95.0	96.1	100.7	101.5	99.8	102.3	99.3	100.4	100.0	104.1	100.0
1992	100.0	100.0	100.0	100.0	100.0	100.0	100.0	100.0	100.0	100.0	100.0	100.0	100.0	100.0
1993	103.5	105.9	96.3	105.4	102.4	97.0	95.6	95.7	92.4	96.5	98.4	101.7	101.9	101.4
1994	111.1	114.1	94.9	116.8	108.5	101.4	105.6	100.3	95.1	102.4	104.6	104.6	117.1	106.1
1995	118.4	119.6	98.9	129.9	114.9	104.2	111.6	104.9	95.2	107.2	108.1	107.3	128.4	107.8
1996	121.3	119.6	103.0	138.7	120.3	106.6	106.7	104.6	92.5	105.4	108.7	110.3	131.1	108.5
1997	127.9	127.7	106.5	147.8	128.3	113.8	115.2	109.7	95.7	108.8	111.5	114.2	138.0	109.9
1998	133.1	132.8	100.2	136.8	132.6	116.4	115.7	115.0	97.2	110.7	114.8	113.7	147.6	110.8
1999	141.2	141.0	101.9	165.6	141.5	118.0	115.1	118.7	95.8	110.5	118.1	113.6	157.8	111.1
2000	147.0	148.8	107.6	191.9	151.8	122.2	122.9	124.1	101.7	113.9	123.7	110.2	168.7	113.3
2001	141.3	143.9	99.1	195.2	142.6	121.7	126.7	126.3	101.8	114.6	...	108.9	167.4	110.7
TOTAL HOURS														
1970	104.4	107.1	104.4	...	...	174.7	129.0	148.5	136.3	108.5	156.1	153.9	154.7	208.8
1986	103.0	110.5	99.2	98.3	112.2	101.5	113.7	108.3	100.1	98.3	97.2	121.2	118.9	122.0
1987	103.8	114.7	98.5	108.3	115.8	100.0	109.6	106.3	99.9	99.7	97.6	118.3	119.5	121.0
1988	106.6	121.2	101.7	111.6	114.8	101.5	107.2	105.1	99.3	101.2	98.9	114.0	121.4	122.8
1989	107.1	120.2	102.7	108.5	109.2	102.3	104.7	105.5	99.3	103.0	99.7	106.8	119.0	122.4
1990	104.8	113.5	102.9	106.6	101.3	104.3	103.7	105.6	100.1	103.7	101.4	103.4	116.4	118.1
1991	100.4	103.9	103.1	103.9	99.5	101.5	102.1	102.9	104.1	103.6	100.9	100.8	109.0	106.6
1992	100.0	100.0	100.0	100.0	100.0	100.0	100.0	100.0	100.0	100.0	100.0	100.0	100.0	100.0
1993	101.4	100.1	94.7	97.5	99.6	94.7	94.8	95.1	90.8	95.2	96.8	102.1	94.9	97.6
1994	103.6	103.0	91.9	98.9	101.6	93.6	...	92.7	86.8	97.6	92.4	105.0	98.1	99.1
1995	104.0	106.4	89.1	100.6	99.8	92.0	...	92.1	84.9	99.3	91.5	106.6	105.3	102.7
1996	103.6	109.0	88.7	97.3	97.7	91.1	...	91.3	81.2	97.5	90.4	107.6	105.3	104.6
1997	105.4	112.4	88.0	90.5	99.3	89.6	...	90.0	80.1	99.0	91.1	112.0	104.3	104.5
1998	105.2	117.5	82.7	74.8	97.7	90.1	...	90.0	80.7	100.6	91.8	113.7	105.8	103.6
1999	104.4	121.5	80.3	81.9	98.9	91.1	...	89.4	79.6	100.5	92.0	109.6	105.4	99.6
2000	102.8	125.6	80.2	87.9	100.8	91.7	...	87.1	79.5	100.7	92.5	105.4	106.8	96.0
2001	97.1	123.9	77.4	86.5	89.4	90.7	...	86.3	78.8	99.7	...	103.4	104.3	92.4
COMPENSATION PER HOUR NATIONAL CURRENCY BASIS [2,3]														
1970	23.7	17.1	16.4	...	...	13.7	13.3	10.4	20.7	5.3	20.2	11.8	10.7	6.1
1986	78.5	73.0	76.0	35.2	55.7	77.3	73.2	76.1	72.8	65.9	85.1	69.1	63.4	57.6
1987	80.7	74.7	77.8	40.3	60.9	79.7	80.1	78.9	76.0	69.4	87.9	78.4	67.6	64.3
1988	84.0	77.5	79.1	50.0	65.6	81.1	82.9	81.9	79.1	74.6	87.8	83.3	71.8	68.7
1989	86.6	82.6	84.0	57.6	74.3	85.9	87.7	86.3	83.2	80.9	88.6	87.2	79.4	73.8
1990	90.8	88.3	90.5	68.5	85.3	90.1	92.7	90.9	89.4	87.6	90.9	92.3	87.8	82.9
1991	95.6	95.0	96.4	86.1	93.5	97.3	95.9	96.4	91.5	94.2	95.3	97.5	95.5	93.8
1992	100.0	100.0	100.0	100.0	100.0	100.0	100.0	100.0	100.0	100.0	100.0	100.0	100.0	100.0
1993	102.7	102.0	102.8	114.0	106.0	104.8	104.6	102.6	106.4	105.7	103.8	101.5	97.4	104.6
1994	105.6	103.7	104.9	129.5	111.1	106.1	...	106.0	111.7	106.8	108.2	104.4	100.0	106.7
1995	107.9	106.0	108.3	158.1	120.3	109.2	...	110.0	117.5	111.3	110.7	109.2	106.5	107.9
1996	109.4	107.0	109.2	184.1	128.2	110.9	...	112.1	122.3	119.0	113.0	113.6	114.4	109.5
1997	111.5	109.3	112.9	197.7	132.3	114.9	...	112.0	124.7	123.0	115.8	118.7	119.4	113.9
1998	117.4	110.5	115.8	214.8	140.2	116.6	...	112.6	126.5	122.2	120.6	125.7	124.4	120.5
1999	122.1	112.3	115.2	211.1	144.0	118.3	...	116.3	129.3	124.6	124.0	133.0	129.3	129.6
2000	131.1	113.9	114.5	221.1	146.2	121.1	...	120.8	133.5	127.8	131.0	140.0	131.8	135.2
2001	133.1	117.8	115.0	240.2	162.7	125.9	...	126.6	137.7	132.6	...	147.6	137.2	140.4

See footnotes at end of table.

Table 10-2. Indexes of Manufacturing Productivity and Related Measures, 14 Countries, 1970 and 1986–2001—*Continued*

(1992=100.)

Item and year	United States	Canada	Japan	Korea	Taiwan	Belgium	Den-mark	France	Ger-many [1]	Italy	Nether-lands	Norway	Sweden	United King-dom
COMPENSATION PER HOUR U.S. CURRENCY BASIS [2][3]														
1970	23.7	19.8	5.8	...	...	8.9	10.7	9.9	8.9	10.3	9.8	10.3	12.0	8.3
1986	78.5	63.5	57.2	31.2	37.0	55.6	54.6	58.1	52.4	54.4	61.1	58.0	51.8	47.9
1987	80.7	68.1	68.2	38.3	48.3	68.6	70.6	69.5	66.0	66.0	76.3	72.3	62.1	59.7
1988	84.0	76.2	78.2	53.5	57.7	70.9	74.3	72.8	70.4	70.6	78.0	79.3	68.2	69.3
1989	86.6	84.3	77.1	67.0	70.8	70.1	72.3	71.6	69.1	72.7	73.4	78.4	71.6	68.4
1990	90.8	91.5	79.1	75.6	79.7	86.6	90.4	88.3	86.4	90.1	87.7	91.7	86.4	83.7
1991	95.6	100.1	90.8	91.7	87.9	91.5	90.5	90.4	86.0	93.5	89.5	93.3	91.9	93.9
1992	100.0	100.0	100.0	100.0	100.0	100.0	100.0	100.0	100.0	100.0	100.0	100.0	100.0	100.0
1993	102.7	95.5	117.3	111.0	100.9	97.4	97.4	95.8	100.4	82.8	98.2	88.8	72.8	89.0
1994	105.6	91.7	130.1	126.0	105.6	102.1	...	101.1	107.6	81.7	104.6	91.9	75.5	92.5
1995	107.9	93.3	146.2	160.5	114.2	119.1	...	116.8	128.2	84.2	121.4	107.1	86.9	96.4
1996	109.4	94.8	127.2	179.4	117.4	115.1	...	116.0	127.0	95.0	117.9	109.3	99.3	96.7
1997	111.5	95.3	118.3	163.7	115.6	103.1	...	101.5	112.2	88.9	104.3	104.1	91.0	105.6
1998	117.4	90.0	112.0	120.4	105.1	103.2	...	101.0	112.3	86.7	106.9	103.4	91.1	113.1
1999	122.1	91.4	128.4	139.2	112.1	100.5	...	100.0	110.0	84.5	105.4	105.9	91.0	118.7
2000	131.1	92.6	134.7	153.4	117.7	89.1	...	90.0	98.4	75.1	96.5	98.7	83.7	116.0
2001	133.1	91.9	119.9	145.9	121.0	89.8	...	91.5	98.4	75.6	...	102.0	77.3	114.5
UNIT LABOR COSTS NATIONAL CURRENCY BASIS [2][3]														
1970	...	31.1	43.8	...	23.8	41.7	25.2	24.0	39.8	11.9	53.3	20.1	20.6	14.1
1986	91.2	83.3	99.9	59.8	83.5	88.0	80.3	94.3	81.2	74.9	94.4	76.9	72.4	77.9
1987	86.9	85.1	97.0	63.8	83.7	89.7	88.3	96.2	86.3	77.8	96.6	83.2	75.8	82.4
1988	86.7	86.6	94.3	72.8	85.9	88.1	88.1	93.4	86.5	79.4	94.2	89.5	79.4	83.2
1989	90.5	89.3	94.9	78.7	89.5	88.7	88.0	93.6	87.9	84.8	91.4	91.3	85.1	85.6
1990	93.7	94.6	95.9	84.2	95.9	93.0	93.5	96.9	90.3	91.5	92.3	94.6	92.9	92.9
1991	97.6	99.6	97.4	94.1	96.8	98.1	96.5	99.3	93.1	98.2	95.6	99.2	100.0	100.1
1992	100.0	100.0	100.0	100.0	100.0	100.0	100.0	100.0	100.0	100.0	100.0	100.0	100.0	100.0
1993	100.6	96.4	101.1	105.4	103.0	102.3	103.7	101.9	104.5	104.3	102.1	101.9	90.8	100.7
1994	98.5	93.6	101.5	109.8	104.1	97.9	96.2	97.9	102.0	101.9	95.6	104.8	83.8	99.7
1995	94.8	94.3	97.6	122.4	104.5	96.4	96.4	96.6	104.7	103.0	93.7	108.4	87.4	102.9
1996	93.5	97.5	94.0	129.1	104.1	94.7	103.7	97.8	107.4	110.0	94.0	110.8	91.9	105.5
1997	91.9	96.2	93.3	121.0	102.3	90.5	99.7	91.9	104.4	111.9	94.7	116.4	90.2	108.2
1998	92.8	97.7	95.5	117.4	103.2	90.2	102.9	88.2	105.2	111.1	96.5	125.7	89.2	112.7
1999	90.2	96.8	90.8	104.4	100.7	91.4	105.4	87.7	107.4	113.4	96.6	128.4	86.3	116.2
2000	91.7	96.1	85.4	101.2	97.1	90.8	101.8	84.8	104.4	113.1	97.9	134.0	83.4	114.5
2001	91.4	101.5	89.8	106.5	102.0	93.9	101.7	86.5	106.6	115.4	...	140.1	85.5	117.2
UNIT LABOR COSTS U.S. CURRENCY BASIS [2][3]														
1970	...	36.0	15.5	...	14.9	27.0	20.2	23.0	17.1	23.3	25.9	17.5	23.1	19.1
1986	91.2	72.4	75.2	53.0	55.6	63.4	59.9	72.1	58.5	61.9	67.8	64.6	59.2	64.8
1987	86.9	77.6	85.0	60.6	66.3	77.2	77.8	84.7	74.9	73.9	83.8	76.7	69.6	76.5
1988	86.7	85.0	93.2	77.8	75.5	77.0	78.9	82.9	76.9	75.2	83.8	85.2	75.4	83.9
1989	90.5	91.1	87.1	91.6	85.2	72.3	72.5	77.7	73.0	76.1	75.8	82.1	76.8	79.4
1990	93.7	98.0	83.8	93.0	89.7	89.5	91.2	94.1	87.3	94.1	89.1	94.0	91.3	93.9
1991	97.6	105.1	91.7	100.3	91.1	92.3	91.0	93.1	87.5	97.5	89.9	95.0	96.3	100.1
1992	100.0	100.0	100.0	100.0	100.0	100.0	100.0	100.0	100.0	100.0	100.0	100.0	100.0	100.0
1993	100.6	90.3	115.4	102.7	98.1	95.1	96.5	95.2	98.7	81.6	96.6	89.2	67.8	85.6
1994	98.5	82.8	125.9	106.8	99.0	94.2	91.4	93.4	98.2	77.9	92.4	92.3	63.2	86.4
1995	94.8	83.0	131.7	124.3	99.2	105.2	104.0	102.5	114.2	77.9	102.7	106.4	71.3	91.9
1996	93.5	86.4	109.6	125.9	95.4	98.4	108.0	101.2	111.5	87.9	98.1	106.6	79.8	93.2
1997	91.9	84.0	97.7	100.2	89.5	81.2	91.0	83.3	94.0	80.9	85.3	102.1	68.8	100.4
1998	92.8	79.6	92.4	65.8	77.4	79.9	92.7	79.1	93.3	78.8	85.5	103.5	65.3	105.7
1999	90.2	78.8	101.2	68.8	78.3	77.6	91.0	75.4	91.4	76.9	82.1	102.2	60.8	106.4
2000	91.7	78.2	100.4	70.2	78.1	66.8	75.9	63.2	76.9	66.4	72.1	94.5	53.0	98.3
2001	91.4	79.2	93.6	64.7	75.8	67.0	73.7	62.5	76.2	65.7	...	96.8	48.2	95.5
EXCHANGE RATE [4]														
1970	100.0	115.8	35.4	252.7	62.9	64.7	80.5	95.7	42.8	196.5	48.6	86.9	112.3	135.6
1986	100.0	87.0	75.3	88.7	66.5	72.0	74.6	76.4	72.0	82.6	71.8	84.0	81.7	83.1
1987	100.0	91.1	87.7	95.0	79.2	86.1	88.2	88.0	86.9	95.0	86.8	92.2	91.8	92.8
1988	100.0	98.2	98.9	106.8	87.9	87.4	89.6	88.8	88.9	94.6	88.9	95.2	94.9	100.8
1989	100.0	102.1	91.8	116.4	95.3	81.6	82.5	83.0	83.0	89.8	82.9	89.9	90.2	92.7
1990	100.0	103.6	87.4	110.4	93.5	96.2	97.5	97.2	96.6	102.8	96.6	99.4	98.4	101.0
1991	100.0	105.5	94.2	106.5	94.0	94.0	94.3	93.7	94.0	99.3	93.9	95.7	96.3	100.1
1992	100.0	100.0	100.0	100.0	100.0	100.0	100.0	100.0	100.0	100.0	100.0	100.0	100.0	100.0
1993	100.0	93.7	114.1	97.4	95.2	93.0	93.1	93.4	94.4	78.3	94.6	87.5	74.7	85.0
1994	100.0	88.4	124.1	97.2	95.1	96.2	95.0	95.4	96.3	76.5	96.7	88.1	75.5	86.7
1995	100.0	88.1	134.9	101.5	95.0	109.1	107.8	106.2	109.1	75.6	109.6	98.1	81.6	89.4
1996	100.0	88.6	116.5	97.5	91.6	103.8	104.1	103.5	103.8	79.9	104.3	96.2	86.8	88.4
1997	100.0	87.3	104.7	82.8	87.4	89.8	91.3	90.7	90.0	72.3	90.1	87.7	76.2	92.7
1998	100.0	81.5	96.5	56.0	75.0	88.5	90.1	89.7	88.8	70.9	88.7	82.3	73.3	93.8
1999	100.0	81.3	111.5	65.9	77.8	84.9	86.4	86.0	85.1	67.8	85.0	79.6	70.4	91.6
2000	100.0	81.4	117.6	69.4	80.5	73.6	74.6	74.5	73.7	58.7	73.7	70.5	63.5	85.8
2001	100.0	78.0	104.3	60.7	74.4	71.3	72.5	72.2	71.5	57.0	71.4	69.1	56.3	81.5

1. Unified Germany for 1991 onward. Prior to 1991, data relate to the former West Germany.
2. The data relate to employees (wage and salary earners) in Belgium, Denmark, and Italy, and to all employed persons (employees and self-employed workers) in the other countries.
3. Compensation adjusted to include changes in employment taxes that are not compensation to employees, but are labor costs to employers.
4. Index of value of foreign currency relative to the U.S. dollar.

Table 10-3. Hourly Compensation Costs in U.S. Dollars for Production Workers in Manufacturing, 29 Countries and Selected Areas, Selected Years, 1975–2001

Country or area	1975	1980	1985	1990	1995	1998	1999	2000	2001
United States	6.36	9.87	13.01	14.91	17.19	18.64	19.11	19.72	20.32
Canada	5.96	8.67	10.95	15.95	16.10	15.60	15.61	16.05	15.64
Mexico	1.47	2.21	1.59	1.58	1.65	1.64	1.83	2.08	2.34
Australia	5.62	8.47	8.21	13.24	15.56	15.22	15.99	14.47	13.15
Hong Kong SAR [1]	0.76	1.51	1.73	3.23	4.91	5.57	5.54	5.63	5.96
Israel	2.25	3.79	4.06	8.55	10.54	12.02	11.91	12.86	13.53
Japan	3.00	5.52	6.34	12.80	23.82	18.29	20.89	22.00	19.59
Korea	0.32	0.96	1.23	3.71	7.29	5.67	7.35	8.48	8.09
New Zealand	3.15	5.22	4.38	8.17	9.91	9.01	9.14	8.13	7.74
Singapore	0.84	1.49	2.47	3.78	7.33	7.72	7.13	7.42	7.77
Sri Lanka	0.28	0.22	0.28	0.35	0.48	0.47	0.46	0.48	. . .
Taiwan	0.38	1.02	1.49	3.90	5.85	5.18	5.51	5.85	5.70
Austria	4.51	8.88	7.58	17.75	25.32	22.21	21.85	19.46	19.40
Belgium	6.41	13.11	8.97	19.17	27.62	24.31	23.92	21.59	21.04
Denmark	6.28	10.83	8.13	18.04	24.98	23.90	24.11	21.49	21.98
Finland	4.66	8.33	8.25	21.25	24.32	21.89	21.55	19.45	19.94
France	4.52	8.94	7.52	15.49	19.35	17.49	17.19	15.66	15.88
Germany, Former West	6.29	12.21	9.50	21.81	31.60	27.45	26.78	24.01	23.84
Germany, Unified	. . .	. . .	. . .	. . .	30.27	26.28	25.66	22.99	22.86
Greece	1.69	3.73	3.66	6.76	9.06	8.75	. . .	. . .	. . .
Ireland	3.05	6.03	5.99	11.81	13.78	13.58	13.61	12.50	13.28
Italy	4.67	8.15	7.63	17.45	16.22	16.35	15.88	14.01	13.76
Luxembourg	6.26	11.54	7.49	16.04	23.45	19.84	19.79	17.70	17.37
Netherlands	6.58	12.06	8.75	18.06	24.12	21.40	21.29	19.07	19.29
Norway	6.77	11.59	10.37	21.47	24.38	24.07	24.45	22.44	23.13
Portugal	1.58	2.06	1.53	3.77	5.37	5.48	5.35	4.75	. . .
Spain	2.53	5.89	4.66	11.38	12.80	12.06	12.03	10.78	10.88
Sweden	7.18	12.51	9.66	20.93	21.44	22.02	21.61	20.14	18.35
Switzerland	6.09	11.09	9.66	20.86	29.30	24.38	23.56	21.24	21.84
United Kingdom	3.37	7.56	6.27	12.70	13.78	16.75	17.04	16.45	16.14
TRADE-WEIGHTED MEASURES [2,3]									
All 28 foreign economies	. . .	. . .	. . .	. . .	. . .	13.83	14.20	14.08	13.61
OECD [4]	4.18	7.08	7.21	12.85	16.36	14.81	15.28	15.10	14.56
OECD less Mexico, Korea [5]	4.96	8.45	8.72	15.71	19.93	18.07	18.52	18.18	17.47
Europe	5.03	9.80	7.92	17.19	21.84	20.53	20.26	18.47	18.38
Asian NIEs [6]	0.51	1.17	1.64	3.72	6.50	5.93	6.45	7.00	6.95

1. Hong Kong Special Administration Region of China.
2. The trade weights used to compute the average compensation cost measures for selected country or economic groups are relative importances derived from the sum of the U.S. imports of manufactured products for consumption (customs value) and the U.S. exports of domestic manufactured products (free alongside ship value) in 1992 for each country or area and each economic group.
3. Data for Germany relate to the former West Germany only.
4. Organization for Economic Cooperation and Development.
5. Mexico joined the OECD in 1994; Korea joined in 1996.
6. The Asian NIEs consists of the four newly industrializing economies of Hong Kong, Korea, Singapore, and Taiwan.

Table 10-4. Consumer Price Indexes, 16 Countries, 1950 and 1955–2001

(1982–1984=100.)

Year	Consumer price index [1]															
	United States [2]	Canada [3]	Japan	Austra-lia [4]	Austria	Bel-gium [5]	Den-mark [6]	France [7]	Ger-many [8]	Italy	Nether-lands	Norway [9]	Spain	Sweden	Switzer-land [10]	United Kingdom
1950	24.1	21.6	14.8	12.6	...	24.0	12.3	11.1	...	...	...	13.6	5.5	13.4	33.2	9.8
1955	26.8	24.4	20.2	18.9	...	26.8	15.0	14.5	...	10.9	...	18.4	6.3	17.5	36.0	12.9
1956	27.2	24.8	20.3	20.1	...	27.4	15.8	14.8	...	11.2	...	19.1	6.7	18.4	36.5	13.5
1957	28.1	25.6	20.9	20.6	...	28.2	16.1	15.3	...	11.4	...	19.6	7.4	19.2	37.3	14.0
1958	28.9	26.3	20.8	20.9	31.6	28.6	16.3	17.6	...	11.7	...	20.6	8.4	20.0	37.9	14.4
1959	29.1	26.6	21.1	21.3	32.0	29.0	16.5	18.7	...	11.7	...	21.0	9.0	20.2	37.7	14.5
1960	29.6	26.9	21.8	22.1	32.6	29.1	16.7	19.4	...	11.9	...	21.1	9.1	21.0	38.2	14.6
1961	29.9	27.1	23.0	22.6	33.8	29.3	17.4	20.0	...	12.2	...	21.6	9.2	21.5	38.9	15.1
1962	30.2	27.4	24.6	22.6	35.3	29.8	18.8	21.0	43.1	12.7	...	22.8	9.7	22.5	40.6	15.8
1963	30.6	27.9	26.4	22.7	36.2	30.4	19.8	22.0	44.4	13.7	...	23.4	10.6	23.2	42.0	16.1
1964	31.0	28.4	27.4	23.2	37.6	31.7	20.5	22.7	45.4	14.5	...	24.7	11.3	23.9	43.3	16.6
1965	31.5	29.1	29.5	24.1	39.5	32.9	21.8	23.3	46.9	15.2	...	25.7	12.8	25.1	44.8	17.4
1966	32.4	30.2	31.0	24.9	40.3	34.3	23.3	23.9	48.6	15.5	...	26.6	13.6	26.8	46.9	18.1
1967	33.4	31.3	32.3	25.7	41.9	35.3	25.0	24.6	49.4	16.1	...	27.8	14.5	27.9	48.8	18.5
1968	34.8	32.5	34.0	26.3	43.1	36.3	27.0	25.7	50.2	16.3	...	28.7	15.2	28.4	50.0	19.4
1969	36.7	34.0	35.8	27.1	44.4	37.6	27.9	27.3	51.1	16.7	40.6	29.6	15.5	29.2	51.3	20.5
1970	38.8	35.1	38.5	28.2	46.4	39.1	29.8	28.8	52.8	17.5	42.1	32.8	16.4	31.3	53.1	21.8
1971	40.5	36.2	40.9	29.9	48.5	40.8	31.5	30.3	55.6	18.4	45.3	34.8	17.7	33.6	56.6	23.8
1972	41.8	37.9	42.9	31.6	51.6	43.0	33.6	32.2	58.7	19.4	48.9	37.3	19.2	35.6	60.4	25.5
1973	44.4	40.7	47.9	34.6	55.5	46.0	36.7	34.6	62.8	21.6	52.9	40.1	21.4	38.0	65.7	27.9
1974	49.3	45.2	59.1	39.9	60.8	51.9	42.3	39.3	67.2	25.7	58.1	43.8	24.8	41.7	72.1	32.3
1975	53.8	50.1	66.0	45.9	65.9	58.5	46.4	43.9	71.2	30.0	63.8	49.0	29.0	45.8	76.9	40.1
1976	56.9	53.8	72.2	52.1	70.8	63.8	50.5	48.2	74.2	35.1	69.6	54.5	34.1	50.5	78.2	46.8
1977	60.6	58.1	78.1	58.5	74.6	68.4	56.1	52.7	77.0	41.0	74.1	58.3	42.4	56.3	79.2	54.2
1978	65.2	63.3	81.4	63.1	77.3	71.4	61.8	57.5	79.0	46.0	77.2	63.1	50.8	61.9	80.1	58.7
1979	72.6	69.1	84.4	68.8	80.2	74.6	67.7	63.6	82.3	52.8	80.5	66.1	58.8	66.4	83.0	66.6
1980	82.4	76.1	90.9	75.8	85.3	79.6	76.1	72.3	86.7	64.0	86.1	73.3	67.9	75.5	86.3	78.5
1981	90.9	85.6	95.4	83.2	91.1	85.6	85.0	82.0	92.2	75.4	91.9	83.3	77.8	84.6	91.9	87.9
1982	96.5	94.9	98.0	92.4	96.0	93.1	93.6	91.6	97.1	87.8	97.2	92.7	89.0	91.9	97.1	95.4
1983	99.6	100.4	99.8	101.8	99.2	100.3	100.0	100.5	100.3	100.7	99.8	100.5	99.9	100.0	100.0	99.8
1984	103.9	104.7	102.1	105.8	104.8	106.6	106.4	107.9	102.7	111.5	103.0	106.8	111.1	108.1	102.9	104.8
1985	107.6	108.9	104.2	112.9	108.2	111.8	111.4	114.2	104.8	121.8	105.3	112.9	120.9	116.0	106.4	111.1
1986	109.6	113.4	104.8	123.2	110.0	113.3	115.4	117.2	104.7	129.0	105.6	121.0	131.5	121.0	107.2	114.9
1987	113.6	118.4	104.9	133.7	111.6	115.0	120.0	120.9	104.9	135.1	105.1	131.6	138.5	126.1	108.8	119.7
1988	118.3	123.2	105.7	142.9	113.8	116.4	125.5	124.2	106.3	141.9	106.1	140.4	145.1	133.4	110.8	125.6
1989	124.0	129.3	108.1	154.1	116.6	120.0	131.5	128.6	109.2	150.8	107.1	146.8	155.0	142.0	114.3	135.4
1990	130.7	135.5	111.4	165.3	120.5	124.1	135.0	133.0	112.1	160.5	109.9	152.8	165.4	156.7	120.5	148.2
1991	136.2	143.1	115.1	170.7	124.4	128.1	138.2	137.2	100.0	170.6	113.3	158.0	175.2	171.5	127.5	156.9
1992	140.3	145.3	117.0	172.4	129.5	131.2	141.1	140.6	105.1	179.4	116.9	161.7	185.6	175.6	132.7	162.7
1993	144.5	147.9	118.5	175.5	134.1	134.8	142.9	143.5	109.8	187.5	120.0	165.4	194.1	183.9	137.0	165.3
1994	148.2	148.2	119.3	178.8	138.2	138.0	145.8	145.9	112.8	195.0	123.3	167.7	203.3	187.8	138.3	169.3
1995	152.4	151.4	119.2	187.1	141.3	140.1	148.8	148.4	114.7	205.1	125.7	171.8	212.8	192.4	140.8	175.2
1996	156.9	153.8	119.3	192.0	143.9	142.9	151.9	151.3	116.3	213.4	128.2	174.0	220.3	193.5	141.9	179.4
1997	160.5	156.2	121.5	192.5	145.8	145.3	155.3	153.2	118.5	217.7	131.0	178.5	224.8	194.8	142.5	185.1
1998	163.0	157.7	122.2	194.1	147.1	146.7	158.2	154.3	119.7	222.0	133.6	182.5	228.8	194.2	142.7	191.4
1999	166.6	160.5	121.8	197.0	147.9	148.3	162.0	155.0	120.3	225.7	136.5	186.7	234.2	195.1	143.8	194.3
2000	172.2	164.8	121.0	205.8	151.4	152.1	166.8	157.7	122.6	231.4	140.0	192.5	242.1	196.9	146.0	200.1
2001	177.1	169.0	120.1	214.8	155.5	155.8	170.8	160.3	125.7	237.8	146.3	198.4	250.8	201.6	147.4	203.6

1. The indexes are calculated by rebasing the official indexes of each country to the official U.S. base year. Because of the rebasing to 1982-84, the indexes may differ from official indexes published by national statistical agencies.
2. Urban worker households prior to 1978.
3. All households from January 1995, all urban households from September 1978 to December 1994, and middle-income urban households prior to September 1978. In February 1994, excise and duty taxes on cigarettes were reduced by the federal government and three provinces.
4. Urban worker households prior to September 1998.
5. Excluding rent and several other services prior to 1976.
6. Excluding rent prior to 1964.
7. Paris only prior to 1962. Urban worker households prior to 1991.
8. Unified Germany from 1991 onward. Prior to 1991, data relate to the former West Germany.
9. Urban worker households prior to 1960.
10. Urban worker households prior to May 1993.

Table 10-5. Consumer Price Indexes, 16 Countries, Percent Change from Previous Year, 1956–2001

Year	Percent change in consumer price index [1]															
	United States [2]	Canada [3]	Japan	Australia	Austria	Belgium [5]	Denmark [6]	France [7]	Germany [8]	Italy	Netherlands	Norway [9]	Spain	Sweden	Switzerland [10]	United Kingdom
1956	1.5	1.5	0.4	6.3	...	2.9	5.3	1.9	...	3.4	...	3.7	5.9	5.0	1.5	4.9
1957	3.3	3.2	3.1	2.7	...	3.1	2.2	3.5	...	1.3	...	2.7	10.8	4.3	1.9	3.7
1958	2.8	2.6	-0.5	1.1	...	1.3	0.7	15.1	...	2.8	...	4.8	13.4	4.4	1.8	3.0
1959	0.7	1.1	1.1	1.9	...	1.2	1.8	6.1	...	-0.4	...	2.2	7.3	0.8	-0.7	0.6
1960	1.7	1.2	3.7	4.0	...	0.3	1.2	3.6	...	2.3	...	0.3	1.2	4.1	1.4	1.0
1961	1.0	0.9	5.3	2.6	3.6	1.0	4.2	3.3	...	2.1	...	2.6	1.1	2.1	1.9	3.4
1962	1.0	1.2	6.8	-0.3	4.4	1.4	7.5	4.8	...	4.7	...	5.3	5.7	4.8	4.3	4.3
1963	1.3	1.8	7.6	0.5	2.7	2.1	5.3	4.8	2.9	7.5	...	2.5	8.8	2.9	3.4	2.0
1964	1.3	1.8	3.8	2.4	3.8	4.2	3.6	3.4	2.4	5.9	...	5.7	7.0	3.4	3.1	3.3
1965	1.6	2.4	7.6	4.0	5.0	4.1	6.5	2.5	3.1	4.6	...	4.3	13.2	5.0	3.4	4.8
1966	2.9	3.7	5.1	3.0	2.2	4.2	6.7	2.7	3.7	2.3	...	3.2	6.2	6.4	4.7	3.9
1967	3.1	3.5	4.0	3.2	4.0	2.9	7.5	2.7	1.7	3.7	...	4.4	6.4	4.2	4.0	2.5
1968	4.2	4.1	5.3	2.7	2.8	2.8	8.0	4.5	1.5	1.4	...	3.5	4.9	1.9	2.4	4.7
1969	5.5	4.5	5.2	2.9	3.1	3.7	3.5	6.4	1.9	2.7	...	3.1	2.2	2.7	2.5	5.4
1970	5.7	3.3	7.7	3.9	4.4	3.9	6.5	5.2	3.4	4.9	3.7	10.6	5.7	7.0	3.6	6.4
1971	4.4	2.9	6.3	6.1	4.7	4.3	5.8	5.5	5.3	4.8	7.6	6.2	8.2	7.4	6.6	9.4
1972	3.2	4.8	4.9	5.9	6.3	5.5	6.6	6.2	5.5	5.7	8.0	7.2	8.3	6.0	6.7	7.1
1973	6.2	7.5	11.7	9.5	7.6	7.0	9.3	7.3	6.9	10.8	8.1	7.5	11.5	6.8	8.7	9.2
1974	11.0	10.9	23.2	15.1	9.5	12.7	15.2	13.7	7.0	19.1	9.8	9.4	15.7	9.9	9.8	16.0
1975	9.1	10.8	11.7	15.1	8.4	12.8	9.6	11.8	6.0	17.0	9.9	11.7	17.0	9.8	6.7	24.2
1976	5.8	7.5	9.4	13.5	7.3	9.2	9.0	9.6	4.3	16.8	9.0	9.1	17.6	10.3	1.7	16.5
1977	6.5	8.0	8.1	12.3	5.5	7.1	11.1	9.4	3.7	17.0	6.4	9.1	24.5	11.4	1.3	15.8
1978	7.6	9.0	4.2	7.9	3.6	4.4	10.1	9.1	2.7	12.1	4.2	8.1	19.8	10.0	1.1	8.3
1979	11.3	9.1	3.7	9.1	3.7	4.5	9.6	10.8	4.1	14.8	4.3	4.8	15.7	7.2	3.6	13.4
1980	13.5	10.1	7.7	10.2	6.4	6.6	12.3	13.6	5.4	21.2	7.0	10.9	15.5	13.7	4.0	18.0
1981	10.3	12.5	4.9	9.7	6.8	7.6	11.7	13.4	6.3	17.8	6.7	13.6	14.6	12.1	6.5	11.9
1982	6.2	10.8	2.8	11.2	5.4	8.7	10.1	11.8	5.3	16.5	5.7	11.3	14.5	8.6	5.6	8.6
1983	3.2	5.8	1.9	10.1	3.3	7.7	6.9	9.6	3.3	14.7	2.7	8.4	12.2	8.9	2.9	4.6
1984	4.3	4.4	2.3	4.0	5.6	6.3	6.3	7.4	2.4	10.8	3.2	6.2	11.3	8.1	3.0	5.0
1985	3.6	4.0	2.0	6.7	3.2	4.9	4.7	5.8	2.1	9.2	2.3	5.7	8.8	7.3	3.4	6.1
1986	1.9	4.1	0.6	9.1	1.7	1.3	3.6	2.7	-0.1	5.9	0.2	7.2	8.8	4.3	0.7	3.4
1987	3.6	4.4	0.1	8.5	1.4	1.6	4.0	3.1	0.2	4.7	-0.4	8.7	5.3	4.2	1.5	4.2
1988	4.1	4.1	0.7	6.9	2.0	1.2	4.6	2.7	1.3	5.0	0.9	6.7	4.8	5.8	1.8	4.9
1989	4.8	5.0	2.3	7.9	2.5	3.1	4.8	3.6	2.8	6.3	1.0	4.6	6.8	6.5	3.2	7.8
1990	5.4	4.8	3.1	7.3	3.3	3.5	2.6	3.4	2.7	6.5	2.6	4.1	6.7	10.4	5.4	9.5
1991	4.2	5.6	3.3	3.2	3.3	3.2	2.4	3.2	3.7	6.3	3.1	3.4	6.0	9.4	5.8	5.9
1992	3.0	1.5	1.6	1.0	4.1	2.4	2.1	2.4	5.1	5.2	3.2	2.3	5.9	2.4	4.0	3.7
1993	3.0	1.8	1.3	1.8	3.6	2.8	1.2	2.1	4.5	4.5	2.6	2.3	4.6	4.7	3.3	1.6
1994	2.6	0.2	0.7	1.9	3.0	2.4	2.0	1.7	2.7	4.0	2.7	1.4	4.8	2.1	0.9	2.4
1995	2.8	2.1	-0.1	4.6	2.2	1.5	2.1	1.7	1.7	5.2	2.0	2.4	4.6	2.5	1.8	3.5
1996	3.0	1.6	0.1	2.6	1.9	2.1	2.1	2.0	1.4	4.0	2.0	1.3	3.6	0.5	0.8	2.4
1997	2.3	1.6	1.8	0.3	1.3	1.6	2.2	1.2	1.9	2.0	2.2	2.6	2.0	0.7	0.5	3.1
1998	1.6	0.9	0.6	0.9	0.9	1.0	1.9	0.7	1.0	2.0	2.0	2.3	1.8	-0.3	0.1	3.4
1999	2.2	1.7	-0.3	1.5	0.6	1.1	2.5	0.5	0.6	1.7	2.2	2.3	2.3	0.5	0.8	1.5
2000	3.4	2.7	-0.7	4.5	2.3	2.5	3.0	1.7	1.9	2.5	2.6	3.1	3.4	0.9	1.5	3.0
2001	2.8	2.6	-0.7	4.4	2.7	2.5	2.4	1.7	2.5	2.7	4.5	3.0	3.6	2.4	1.0	1.8

1. The figures may differ from official percent changes published by national statistical agencies due to rounding. In the case of Sweden, the official percent changes are not calculated from the published index.
2. Urban worker households prior to 1978.
3. All households from January 1995, all urban households from September 1978 to December 1994, and middle-income urban households prior to September 1978. In February 1994, excise and duty taxes on cigarettes were reduced by the federal government and three provinces. In 1994, the consumer price index excluding tobacco increased 1.5 percent.
4. Urban worker households prior to September 1998.
5. Excluding rent and several other services prior to 1976.
6. Excluding rent prior to 1964.
7. Paris only prior to 1962. Urban worker households prior to 1991.
8. Unified Germany for 1992 onward. Prior to 1992, data relate to the former West Germany.
9. Urban worker households prior to 1960.
10. Urban worker households prior to May 1993.

INDEX

INDEX